10,000

GARDEN QUESTIONS

Answered By 20 Experts

10,000 garden

questions

ANSWERED BY 20 EXPERTS
NEW, REVISED EDITION

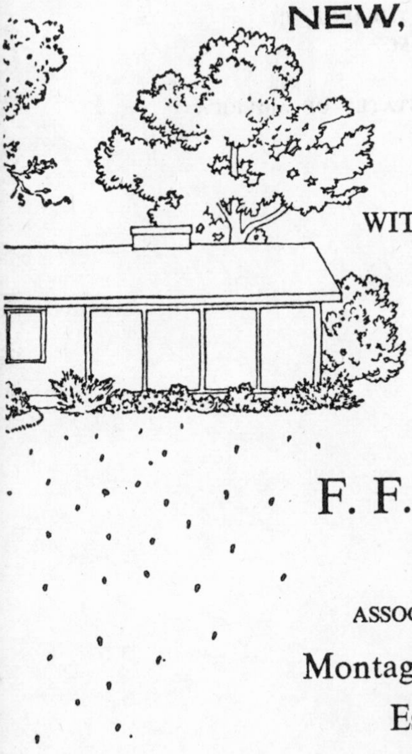

WITH OVER 400 ILLUSTRATIONS
AND TEMPERATURE AND
PLANTING MAPS

F. F. Rockwell
EDITOR

ASSOCIATE EDITORS

Montague Free, T. H. Everett
Esther C. Grayson

AN AMERICAN GARDEN GUILD BOOK

Published by

DOUBLEDAY & COMPANY, INC., Garden City, New York

The Editors of
10,000 Garden Questions Answered

THE HORTICULTURAL authorities who have planned and guided the preparation of *10,000 Garden Questions Answered* are well known to the American gardening public. Their combined experience covers pretty much the entire range of gardening activities. In the preparation of this book they have had, in addition to their own broad backgrounds of knowledge upon which to draw, the services of a score of specialists in certain lines.

F. F. ROCKWELL, editor in chief of the American Garden Guild Book Club, and senior editor of *Flower Grower—The Home Garden Magazine,* has long been familiar to this country's amateur gardeners through more than a score of books and his lectures, articles and natural-color photographs. At GrayRock, the country home of the Rockwells, extensive experiments and tests are carried on. Mr. Rockwell is a past president of the Men's Garden Clubs of America, and the 1955 recipient of its gold medal for horticultural achievement.

MONTAGUE FREE, for more than twenty-five years was horticulturist of the great Brooklyn Botanic Garden and is now senior editor and staff horticulturist of *Flower Grower—The Home Garden Magazine* and editor of the American Garden Guild Book Club. He is the author of many garden books and nationally known as an authority on all phases of gardening and a leading figure among garden writers.

T. H. EVERETT, well known lecturer and author of many books, has long been horticulturist of the New York Botanical Garden, a post which has brought him exceptionally broad contacts with the problems of amateur gardeners. His organization and direction of the Garden's courses in practical horticulture have been highlights in his career.

R. C. ALLEN, Ph.D., formerly secretary of the American Rose Society and on the staff of the Department of Floriculture and Ornamental Horticulture at Cornell University, and now Director of Kingswood Center, is a well known specialist in flowering plants, especially roses and delphiniums.

R. S. LEMMON, formerly published *Real Gardening,* and is one of the country's most widely and favorably known garden editors and lecturers. He has specialized in the field of native plants and wildflowers, and was one of the organizers of the American Rock Garden Society.

P. J. McKENNA, was for many years assistant horticulturist of the world-famous New York Botanical Garden, and later chairman of horticulture for the Federated Garden Clubs of New York State, Inc. He lectured on and taught many horticultural subjects and was a president of the Men's Garden Club of New York.

W. E. THWING, is well known for his work with wildflowers, and his natural-color motion pictures of wild plants have won him wide recognition in the field of photography.

ALEX LAURIE, Ph.D., formerly professor of floriculture at Ohio State University is internationally famous as an authority on the soil and its fertility, plant feeding, and related subjects which have to do with the practical phases of plant growth.

C. H. CONNORS, Ph.D., heads the Department of Ornamental Horticulture at Rutgers University, besides being ornamental horticulturist of the New Jersey Agricultural Experiment Station; an all-round authority of long and varied experience.

DONALD WYMAN, Ph.D., is horticulturist of the world-renowned Arnold Arboretum of Harvard University where he has earned a national reputation in the field of trees, shrubs and other woody plants.

T. A. WESTON, was the author of the famous newspaper column *One Man's Garden,* and one of America's leading authorities on growing all types of bulbs, corms and tubers; and on the principles and practices of most other phases of flower gardening.

CYNTHIA WESTCOTT, D.Sc., best known to many gardening readers as "The Plant Doctor", is a foremost authority on the prevention and control of plant insect pests and diseases. Of her many successful books *The Gardeners' Bug Book* and the *Plant Disease Handbook* are the most outstanding. She is always in close personal contact with the actual practice of what she preaches.

ESTHER C. GRAYSON (Mrs. F. F. Rockwell), is known to gardeners the country over as an expert on flower arrangement, house plants and the growing and use of herbs. Of equal importance is her wide knowledge and experience in the growing of vegetables and garden flowers.

HELEN VAN PELT WILSON, author of numerous garden books and a favorite writer on many phases of home gardening, is especially conversant with plants for the house and herbaceous perennials.

HELEN S. HULL, ex-president of the National Council of State Garden Clubs, Inc., and author of *Wild Flowers for Your Garden,* operates large gardens of her own and knows every plant in them.

LOUIS PYENSON, Ph.D., Professor and Chairman of the Biology Division of the State of New York Agricultural and Technical Institute at Farmingdale, Long Island, N.Y., is the author of books on pest controls, and a well known writer, lecturer and photographer in this field.

O. WESLEY DAVIDSON, Ph.D., is Professor and Research Specialist in Ornamental Horticulture at Rutgers University and the New Jersey Agricultural Experiment Station.

GEORGE L. SLATE, M.S., Professor of Pomology, Cornell University, New York State Agricultural Experiment Station, Geneva, N.Y., is a noted authority on lilies and fruits. He is editor of the Lily Year Book of the North American Lily Society, and his best-known book, *Lilies for American Gardens,* is recognized as a leading work in its field.

Other well-known authorities who have assisted in answering questions are:

MILTON CARLETON, Ph.D., Director of Research of the Vaughan Seed Company in Chicago, is known to gardeners throughout the country as a writer and speaker on horticultural subjects. **FRANCIS C. COULTER**, formerly an executive of one of the country's largest seed concerns, has written many articles and several books which are erudite as well as informative. **ALEX CUMMING**, who was widely known as a specialist in the breeding of fine chrysanthemums and author of a successful book on these popular plants, long headed a New England nursery which has served the gardening public for many years. **HENRY E. DOWNER** has practiced and taught horticulture in this country for a quarter century. He is horticulturist and superintendent of grounds at Vassar College.

KATHLEEN N. MARRIAGE is a widely known authority on rock gardening and the native flora of the Western highlands. **JOHN MELADY** is a noted specialist on lawns and all that goes into their establishment and maintenance. **H. DEWEY MOHR,** a specialist on dahlias, has developed many outstanding new varieties.

H. STUART ORTLOFF, landscape architect and co-author with H. B. Raymore of several excellent books and numerous articles on garden design, planting and maintenance, combines the artistic and practical angles of his profession with unusual success. To him "Will it work?" is really the acid test. **HILDEGARD SCHNEIDER,** head gardener at The Cloisters in New York, is an all-round plantswoman of long experience. **P. J. VAN MELLE** had a particular flair for native plants and rock gardening, and an accurate knowledge of plant histories and types. **THOMAS A. WILLIAMS** was known to hundreds of thousands of radio fans as "The Old Dirt Dobber" on his nationally heard C.B.S. program. **PROFESSOR PAUL WORK,** of the Department of Vegetable Crops, New York State Agricultural Experiment Station, "knows his onions" literally as well as figuratively. **DR. J. H. CLARK,** associate pomologist of the New Jersey State Agricultural Experiment Station, had a prominent part in the extensive fruit-testing and experiment program at that institution.

Other specialists and gardeners who have contributed valuable experience and knowledge to the preparation of this volume are: John H. Beale, George A. Buchanan, George E. Burkhardt, L. C. Chadwick, Dr. A. S. Colby, Charles F. Doney, Professor E. V. Hardenburg, D. C. Kiplinger, Stuart Longmuir, Harriet K. Morse, George D. Oberle, E. L. Reber, Roy P. Rogers, Kenneth D. Smith, Nancy Ruzicka Smith, John V. Watkins, Robert E. Weidner, Natalie Gomez and John Wingert.

Artists who have prepared illustrations are: George L. Hollrock, Pauline W. Kreutzfeldt, Helen Reddy, Carl Sigman, William Ward, Eva Melady, Tabea Hofmann, H. B. Raymore, Natalie Harlan Davis, Frederick Rockwell, Esther C. Grayson, Katharine Burton, Laurence Blair and Russell J. Walrath, who did the temperature and frost maps, adapted from data by the U. S. Department of Agriculture.

Contents

PAGE

Introduction to the New, Revised Edition   XI
What Is *Your Question?*   XV

SECTION

    I   Soils and Fertilizers   1
   II   Landscaping   87
  III   Ornamental Plants and Their Culture   205
        Trees and Shrubs   279
        Bulbs, Tubers, and Corms   411
        Roses   477
        Perennials   523
        Annuals and Biennials   593
   IV   Lawns and Turf Areas   631
        Temperature Zone Map of the United States   687
    V   The Home Vegetable Garden   691
   VI   Home Grown Fruits   833
  VII   House Plants   929
 VIII   Plant Troubles and Their Control   1043
   IX   Regional Garden Problems   1221
    X   Miscellaneous: *Sources for Further Information*   1309
        Bibliography   1309
        Agricultural Experiment Stations   1318
        Horticultural and Special Plant Societies   1319
        Garden Centers   1321
        Frost Maps—Maps of the United States Showing Average Last Killing Frosts in Spring and First Killing Frosts in Autumn.   1325

Index   1331

Introduction
To the New, Revised Edition

IT IS of course gratifying to the publishers and editors when any work, after a dozen years, is still sufficiently in demand to justify the expense and work involved in getting out a revised edition. For more than a decade now *10,000 Garden Questions Answered* has been, for hundreds of thousands of home gardeners, the family bible of garden information. This new edition, redesigned and reset, brings it completely up to date, making it even more helpful than in the past.

The preparation of 10,000 Garden Questions Answered was originally undertaken in response to numerous requests from readers of *The Home Garden Magazine*. It seemed worth while to present, in some organized and permanent form, the wealth of information which the answers to these questions convey.

Our purpose was to make this data available to the reader in a form that would enable him to refer to it quickly, and find readily, all the information on any particular subject. The most practical method of obtaining this objective, it seemed to us—after carefully studying several plans which suggested themselves—was to arrange this widely diversified mass of material in ten general categories that would cover the whole field. In the present edition these sections or divisions are:

I   Soils and Fertilizers
II   Landscaping
III   Ornamental Plants and Their Culture
    Trees and Shrubs
    Bulbs, Tubers, and Corms
    Roses
    Perennials
    Annuals and Biennials
IV   Lawns and Turf Areas
V   The Home Vegetable Garden
VI   Home Grown Fruits
VII   House Plants
VIII   Plant Troubles and Their Control
IX   Regional Garden Problems

X Miscellaneous: *Sources for Further Information*
Bibliography
Agricultural Experiment Stations
Horticultural and Special Plant Societies
Garden Centers
Frost Maps (4 pages)

THE "INTRODUCTIONS"

For each of these sections an introduction which gives general information on the subject covered has been prepared. The introductions are *based upon the questions most generally asked* concerning the subject discussed. In other words, these questions, instead of being answered individually, have been answered in a composite reply that presents the general principles involved and provides a background for the more specific questions which follow.

This treatment has two distinct advantages. In the first place, it enables the reader to get much more from the answers to the individual questions; in the second, it has saved a great amount of space. Actually, the *answers* to more than 13,000 questions are contained in the present volume.

The advantages of having questions answered by experts widely experienced in many lines are obvious. Too often such answers are compiled from outdated reference books. The answers in this volume are by persons who are actually *doing* the things they write about. Many of them are recognized internationally as authorities in their respective fields. At the same time, with few exceptions, their daily work brings them into direct contact with the problems of amateur gardeners the country over.

AN ADVANCE WORD TO CRITICS

With some fifty different persons contributing information of one sort or another, it is inevitable that many differences of opinion have arisen. In so far as possible, the recommendations and suggestions made on any specific subject have been brought into harmony by correspondence or discussion. There are cases where this has not been possible. The result is honest differences of opinion such as would be forthcoming on almost any garden question that might be asked of any group of experts—differences similar to those that would be found in every field of human endeavor, in any science or art, and horticulture partakes of both.

Unfortunately, too, we have in this country no generally recognized single authority in the realm of plant nomenclature. An attempt in this direction has been made in the publication of *Standardized Plant Names*. Botanists in general have been unwilling to follow all the recommendations of the hard-working committee which for many years unselfishly struggled with this perplexing problem. Excellent as has been the intention of this committee, many of its recommendations—particularly in abolishing, changing, and creating new common or English names—have not seemed acceptable even to the non-botanist. Nevertheless, those authorities who will not recognize *Standardized Plant Names* as the last word cannot agree among themselves on any other single authority. Thus this entire subject still remains in a chaotic state.

Even the least-informed beginner can imagine, with this condition existing, and with half a hundred contributors, each with his or her own ideas on the subject, what a problem we have faced in regard to nomenclature. In general, *Standardized Plant Names* has been followed; but in many instances—where it seemed that following its recommendations could only make "confusion worse confounded"— it has not.

The result, we realize, will leave the door wide open to the critics. However, our primary concern has been for the amateur reader; and where he can get the *meaning* of a question or an answer, we are content to let the scientists and botanists wrangle with us—and with each other—as to names, spelling, precedents, and authorities.

The botanically minded critic, too, will find some gall for his ink when it comes to botanical terms. For the most part the questions have been left in the dirt gardener's terminology in which they were written, and often the answers are in kind. Where the questioner has asked about how to plant a dahlia "tuber," for instance, it has not been deemed necessary to instruct him that he should have said "root" (or, more accurately, "bulbous root"). A too-strict adherence to botanical terminology often tends to confuse the beginner rather than to enlighten him, and this volume is primarily for beginners.

I wish to take this opportunity, also, to express my appreciation for the co-operation we have had from the group of contributors who have made possible this volume, and especially to the assistant editors, Montague Free, T. H. Everett, and Esther C. Grayson for the untiring effort they have put into the work of handling the thousands of details involved in its preparation.

Our aim has been to present the amateur gardener with *practical* information in readily available form, concerning his own personal problems. To the extent that this has been accomplished, we will have succeeded in making the kind of book we set out to create.

F.F.R.

What Is YOUR Question?

(Suggestions as to how to use this book most effectively)

To GET from these pages the information you wish, most completely and in the shortest time, read carefully the following paragraphs. They explain, first, how this book is put together; and, second, the definite steps to take in finding the answer to a specific problem, or to one so general in character that it might not be possible to locate it through the Index.

ORGANIZATION PLAN

As you know, there are ten main divisions or sections, covering Soils and Fertilizers, Ornamental Plants and Their Culture, Lawn and Turf Areas, Landscaping, Home Vegetable Gardening, Home Grown Fruits, House Plants, Plant Troubles and Their Control, Regional Problems, and Miscellaneous Lists of Agricultural Experiment Stations, Flower, Fruit and Tree Societies, Garden Centers, and Books and Bulletins on Special Subjects.

Each of these sections is organized along the following lines:

1. A general introduction, giving basic information about the subject concerned. (The introduction for Soils and Fertilizers, for instance, describes the function of the soil in connection with plant growth, different types of soil, soil acidity, the various nutrients essential to plant growth, the part which humus plays in the soil, and so on.)

2. Following the introduction, the questions, in most sections, are arranged in the following order:

What to Grow	Winter Protection
Soils	Propagation
Fertilizers	Varieties
Planting and Transplanting	Specific Plants
Culture	(In Alphabetical Order)

USE OF INDEX

In most instances any specific question can be located through the use of the Index.

1. Formulate your question in your own mind as definitely as possible. (It will be helpful to write it down on paper.)
2. Pick out the KEY WORD in the question. (For instance, it might be "How should I train *tomatoes?*" "How can I *graft* a good variety of apple on a wild tree?" or "What is a good *perennial* to grow in the *shade?*"
3. Then look up the key word ("tomato," "graft," "perennial" or "shade") in the Index. Under this item, in the Index, you will probably find several references. One of these (example: "tomato, staking") may indicate exactly what you are looking for, and you can then turn at once to the specific question you have in mind.

MORE GENERAL QUESTIONS

The question in your mind may, however, be of such a nature that you do not know what to look for in the Index to locate it. Suppose, for example, that you have seen somewhere, growing high on a wall, a vine-like plant with hydrangea-like flowers, and you would like to know what it is. A search through the section on "Vines—Perennial" would quickly reveal that it is the Climbing Hydrangea (*Hydrangea petiolaris*).

It is recommended that, in looking up questions on any general subject—such as fertilizers, lawns, vegetables, fruits—*the introduction be read in full first.* Here you will find in text form the answers to many questions, some of which may not reappear in the questions and answers. Familiarity with the introduction will also help materially in augmenting the information to be gained from the answers to specific questions.

In the answers to some questions the reader is referred to his State Experiment Station. A list of these stations is given on page 1318, and a list of Garden Centers is given on page 1321. Frost maps (showing dates of last killing frost in spring, and first in fall) are on pages 1326 to 1329.

The list of books and bulletins (page 1309) will guide the reader to full and detailed information on many different garden subjects.

10,000

GARDEN QUESTIONS

Answered By 20 Experts

SECTION I

Soils and Fertilizers

INTRODUCTION

AND O. WESLEY DAVIDSON

THE SOIL in which we garden is a product of physical, chemical, and biological forces acting on mineral materials and organic residues. It is teeming with life—up to 3 percent of the weight of a good composted soil is that of the microorganisms present in it—supported by the plant and animal residues. This biological activity makes possible some of the most important processes in our soil:

(1) It makes nutrients available by decomposing complex or insoluble substances containing them.

(2) It produces nutrients by reaction with air.

(3) It produces substances that improve the structure of soils and thus increases the amounts of oxygen available to plant roots.

(4) It transforms some organic materials into substances that bind nutrients to the soil in such a manner that they are available to plant roots but resistant to being washed out.

(5) It produces antibiotic substances that control or limit the development of disease organisms.

Your garden soil, therefore, is not a mass of "dirt" (i.e. "matter out of place," or "filthy substance"). Rather, it is an amazingly complex medium in which processes of inestimable value to society occur. Our care of a soil may drastically influence not only its supply of nutrients to plant roots, but also its very structure and its microbial activity.

Soil Types

Soils vary in texture (size of the individual particles of which they are made up), in structure (the arrangement of the particles), in organic matter content, in water-holding capacity, in heat retention, and in the supply of plant nutrients they contain. According to their texture, soils are classed as sand, silt, and clay.

Loam is an intermediate between any two of these. Thus we have sandy loam, silt loam, or clay loam. The best structure is "crumb," which means granular. This is dependent upon the presence of humus, without which granular structure is hard to obtain. It tends to hold small particles together. Freezing and thawing, cultivation, and the action of roots also help to produce granular structure.

Humus is a dark-brown substance resulting from the decomposition of plant or animal residues. Soil organisms are needed in this process of decomposition. Humus is an important component of soils. It modifies the soil color, texture, structure, water-holding capacity, and air-holding capacity. Likewise, it serves as a source of energy for the minute organisms. In speaking of humus and its action it should be remembered that humus is not synonymous with *undecomposed* organic matter. Organic matter such as manure, straw, or green manure (crops grown to be turned into the soil), becomes humus *only when it has reached an advanced stage of decomposition.*

Other Soil Factors

Soil Aeration. Air is important in the soil. It circulates through the space around the soil particles, making it possible for roots to grow. Furthermore, air is necessary for the existence of certain important soil organisms. It is known that carbon dioxide is given off in the decomposition of organic matter. An accumulation of this gas is injurious to the roots; consequently its removal from the soil by entrance of fresh air is desirable. Poorly granulated soils and wet soils lack aeration. Additions of organic matter help, together with the incorporation of fine sand or fine cinders. In general, *most plants grow best when the soil is well aerated.* Many of our troubles come from lack of appreciation of this fact.

During the past 10 years a number of soil conditioning agents have been developed. Some of these have been offered for sale to gardeners. The function of these materials has been to improve the structure of the soil by cementing clay and silt particles into larger units called aggregates or granules. The spaces between the aggregates are much larger than those between the unaggregated clay and silt particles. Such spaces, in fact, are large enough to permit rapid exchange of carbon dioxide and oxygen in the soil, thereby improving root growth. The aggregated particles, moreover, are relatively resistant to erosion.

Synthetic conditioning agents function in the same manner as do the cementing by-products of microorganisms that decompose organic matter in soils. Although some of the synthetic agents are capable of developing somewhat more stable aggregates than are formed by soil microbes, the differences, nevertheless, have been greatly exaggerated in advertising claims. In many good garden soils aggregation is already adequate, and synthetic conditioning agents fail to improve crop growth, even though they may give the soil a better "feel."

These synthetic conditioners are most effective on silty and clayey soils, especially when the latter are low in organic matter.

Soil Water. The water in the soil most essential to plant growth is capillary water—the water which surrounds and clings to the soil particles. The amount of this water in the soil depends on the size of the particles and upon their structure. The smaller the particles, as in clay, the greater the water content. Sands, because of their relatively large-sized particles, have comparatively low moisture-holding capacity. Clays, on the other hand, comprising extremely small particles, have high moisture-holding capacity. Organic matter tends to improve the moisture-holding capacity of the sands and the drainage and aeration of the clays.

Heavy rains and forcible application of water cause greater losses of water into drainage channels. Hence, in practice, even when heavy watering is required, it should be applied so gradually that it will not run off the surface.

Control of Moisture. Water loss from the soil may be reduced by good tillage, mulching, and additions of organic matter and fertilizers.

Good tillage means plowing or spading at the proper time and to a suitable depth. In regions where fall and winter rainfall is light, fall spading is preferred. The resulting loose surface absorbs any available moisture instead of allowing it to run off. Heavy soils should be spaded deeper than sandy soils unless the latter are well supplied with humus.

The texture of the soil should be considered at the time of spading. If heavy soils are spaded when wet, clods will form. Sandy soils may be worked when relatively wet. Cultivation is also part of tillage. Its chief function is to keep down weeds which draw moisture and nutrients from the soil; its secondary function is to reduce evaporation from the soil by breaking the crust. In heavy soils this secondary function may be advantageous; in sandy soils it may do more harm than good by causing the top to dry out more quickly, without sufficient capillarity to bring up the stored moisture from below.

Mulching is a method of covering the surface of the soil with some organic or inert material which prevents evaporation and yet admits air. Manures, peats, straw, hay, alfalfa or clover chaff, cottonseed hulls, ground corncobs, leaves, mulch paper, may all be used for the mulching purposes.

The gradual decomposition of organic mulches adds humus to soils, improving both the structure of the soil and its capacity to retain added nutrients. The latter effect is one of the most important functions of organic matter in soils. It protects nutrients from loss by leaching.

Soil and Plant Nutrients

Soil Composition. The soil forms a comparatively thin layer over the earth's surface. Its chief constituent is mineral matter; but organic matter, bacteria, soil, air, and water are also essential constituents. The plant derives most of its essential elements from this mineral matter. These elements form only a small percentage of the composition of the plant tissues, and their importance varies. Phosphorus and potassium are two important elements derived from mineral matter that are lacking in the average soil, or exist in forms that are made available too slowly to meet the needs of most cultivated crops. Other essential elements derived from mineral matter are calcium, magnesium, sulfur, iron, manganese, boron, zinc, copper, molybdenum, chlorine, and perhaps sodium.

Nitrogen is one of the most essential elements and is almost universally limited. In nature, nitrogen is added to the soil by means of decaying organic matter and by bacteria found in nodules on the roots of many plants, chiefly the legumes. A small but appreciable amount of nitrogen is added to soils as ammonia carried down with rainfall.

Carbon, hydrogen, and oxygen (which in different combinations form carbohydrates and water) make up the bulk of the plant. These elements are derived from the air and from the soil moisture. Because of the universal presence of each they are not considered as problems to the gardener, although water is often deficient and carbon dioxide may not be present in sufficient quantity for optimum growth.

The Functions and Sources of the Nutrient Elements

Nitrogen forms a part of *all* proteins. Protein makes up the bulk of the protoplasm which is the living matter. Nitrogen is an essential constituent of chlorophyll (the green colored bodies in the leaves and stems of plants). Chlorophyll is essential for the manufacture of sugars. Nitrogen is also a constituent of amino acids, alkaloids, and aromatic compounds within the plant. Nitrogen stimulates the vegetative growth, and size of foliage, and color in flowers.

> *Because of the importance of nitrogen in plant growth it is essential to have an available supply. Since nature cannot provide nitrogen in sufficient quantities, other sources are essential; namely, commercial fertilizers and manures. Nitrate of soda, sulfate of ammonia, dried blood, cottonseed meal, and the various manures are some of the materials used for supplying extra nitrogen when it is needed in greater amounts than the soil seems able to provide.*

Phosphorus is an essential constituent of the proteins. It occurs abundantly in the nucleus and, to a less extent, in the cytoplasm (body cells). It is also essential to cell division. Phosphorus is associated with reproduction: seeds are rich in phosphorus. It is helpful in root development and in balancing nitrogen. Excessive amounts of phosphorus, however, make iron and zinc unavailable, and cause chlorosis —the yellowing of foliage—and stunting of growth.

The phosphorus problem is a nationwide one. Most soils are naturally low in this element and most of the phosphorus present is in the form of tricalcium phosphate—a form that is only slightly available to most garden crops.

> *To enrich the soil with phosphorus, a commercial fertilizer is applied. Superphosphate (20 per cent phosphorus) or treble phosphate (45 per cent phosphorus) are the most effective materials for building up available phosphorus. Bone meal carries about 23 per cent phosphorus, but in less available form.*

Potassium is an element required by plants in relatively large amounts, even though it does not become a part of the cell walls nor any solid portion of a plant. This element functions in association with enzymes, the organic "catalysts" which regulate the digestion and translocation of foods and of some nutrients. Potassium plays an important role in the activity of lateral meristems which are associated with growth in diameter, such as the thickening of beets, potatoes, and dahlia tubers. Potassium also plays an important part in adapting plants to withstand low temperatures.

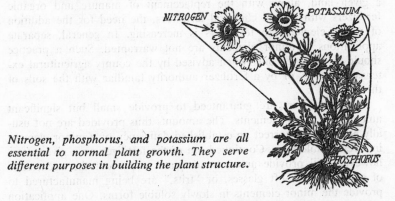

Nitrogen, phosphorus, and potassium are all essential to normal plant growth. They serve different purposes in building the plant structure.

Most soils are deficient in potassium in an available form. Many soils with an apparent potassium deficiency contain as high as 50,000 lbs. per acre, but it exists in chemical combinations, forming compounds which cannot be used by the plant. A heavy soil well supplied with organic matter usually has enough available potassium for plant use. *A soil deficient in organic matter is usually deficient in potassium.*

The organic matter favors beneficial bacterial action, and organic acids render the combined potassium available.

> *Potassium may be added to the soil in the form of potassium chloride or potassium sulfate (muriate or sulfate of potash), or in hardwood ashes and manures.*

Calcium and magnesium are both found in most limestones, and in many fertilizers. Calcium is required by plants for the development of cell walls of all new tissues. It is also essential for the utilization of nitrates in some plants. Magnesium is necessary for the formation of chlorophyll and for the functioning of a number of plant enzymes.

Sulfur is a common constituent of most, but not all, commercial fertilizers. It is also a constituent of some amino acids, proteins, and hormones in plants.

Minor, or trace, elements (iron, manganese, boron, zinc, copper, and molybdenum) have been given considerable attention lately by agricultural research workers and by fertilizer manufacturers. These elements all play very important roles in the growth and development of plants. The fact that each of them is required by the plant in minute quantities has relegated them to the category of "minor elements."

Many years ago, the relatively unrefined fertilizers of the time contained most of these minor elements, and in significant amounts. Manures and various organic fertilizers show traces, or even appreciable amounts, of the minor elements.

In contrast, most of the modern inorganic fertilizer materials are free of minor elements. As a consequence of the continued tillage of a given land, along with the replacement of manure and organic fertilizers with refined chemical fertilizers, the need for the addition of minor elements to fertilizers is increasing. In general, separate applications of minor elements are not warranted. Such a practice should be followed only when advised by the county agricultural extension service, or by a fertilizer authority familiar with the soils of the area.

Some fertilizers are guaranteed to provide small but significant amounts of minor elements. The amounts thus provided are not usually adequate to correct an established deficiency of a minor element in a reasonable time. Continued use of the fertilizer on a given area, however, will provide amounts adequate to prevent the occurrence of a deficiency. Soft glasses, or "frits," are being manufactured to provide the minor elements in slowly soluble forms. One application will furnish enough of these nutrients to see a crop through two or more seasons.

Manures

Barnyard manure has, until recently, been the mainstay in maintaining soil fertility. This type of fertilizer has its advantages in that in addition to supplying some plant nutrients, humus and desirable bacteria are also added. These improve the physical condition of the soil, increase the moisture-holding capacity, provide better aeration, and render unavailable nutrient elements more available.

As far as the *actual value of the chemical nutrients* is concerned, manure is expensive. Some nitrogen and potassium are returned to the soil by adding manure. The quantity of potassium is small; the amount of phosphorus is so little that manure is valueless as a phosphorus fertilizer. The nitrogen content varies greatly with the type of manure and the way it is handled. If this manure is properly cared for while accumulating, so as to prevent leaching and burning, considerable nitrogen as well as potassium can be returned to the soil through its application. But the average manure is handled in such a way that little nitrogen and potassium is retained.

Synthetic Manure. Due to the growing scarcity of manure, the practice of making synthetic manure has increased. Such manure, or, more accurately, compost, made from straw, leaves, weeds, and other garden refuse, is equal in value to manure. The compost pile

Into the compost heap may go anything that will decay. Soil and peatmoss are added to garden refuse. Lime and chemicals hasten decomposition, enrich the compost.

should be 4 to 6 ft. high. The straw or leaves are arranged in 6-inch layers and the reagent (fertilizer) scattered over the surface of each layer. The top of the compost pile should be flat to retain the water. Fermentation starts immediately and within 3 or 4 months, under favorable conditions, decomposition is sufficiently complete for much of the material to be utilized in place of manure. (Portions not entirely decomposed can be used to start a new heap.) The following formula has been worked out for an inexpensive and effective reagent for use in making the compost:

Sulfate of ammonia	60 lbs.
Superphosphate	30 lbs.
Potassium chloride	25 lbs.
Ground limestone	50 lbs.

These materials, when mixed with 1 ton of dry straw, will make 2 or 3 tons of artificial manure. If the heap is made in the spring, with sufficient water applied during the season, good manure may be had by early fall.

Green manures are crops grown for the purpose of being plowed or dug into the soil. Cowpeas, buckwheat, soybeans, oats, rye, clovers, and alfalfa have long been used for this purpose, and are valuable in maintaining the humus content of the soil, preventing excessive leaching of soluble nutrients, increasing bacterial content, aeration, and drainage, and in making certain elements more available. Legumes add nitrogen to the soil. The use of green manures has become more popular with the increasing scarcity of barnyard manure.

Commercial Fertilizers

It has required long experience for the gardener to place his faith in maintaining the fertility of his soil through the use of commercial fertilizers. Many gardeners are still not convinced that commercial fertilizers are all that their advocates claim them to be. This is only to be expected. The confidence in any new thing is not gained until after it has passed the period of experimentation. The value of commercial fertilizers has been definitely proven, and when they are used as recommended, there is little danger of damage. It must be remembered that this type of fertilizer is in an extremely concentrated form and that there is always danger of overdosage, *especially if the humus content of the soil is not maintained.*

Commercial fertilizers may be obtained in a "complete" form, or as fertilizers containing one or more of the individual elements. A complete fertilizer contains nitrogen, phosphorus, and potassium, mixed in various proportions, such as 4–12–4, 5–10–5, or 8–8–8. The first figure represents the percentage of nitrogen, the second of phosphorus, and the third of potassium. Some of the commercial fertilizers offered for sale in certain areas may contain magnesium, as well as some or all of the minor elements. Dealers in fertilizers and garden supplies usually stock the fertilizers recommended for their particular areas.

Soil Acidity

The degree of acidity in the soil is another factor which influences the growth of plants. Practically all the vegetables, and the great majority of ornamental plants, grow well in a slightly acid soil. With some plants, however, a soil too acid or too alkaline will seriously retard growth, or may even prove fatal.

The symbol pH is a means of expressing the acidity or alkalinity of the soil. In technical terms it stands for the hydrogen-ion con-

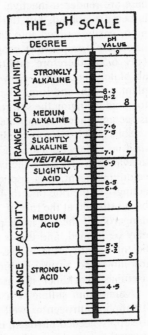

THE pH SCALE

The degree of acidity or alkalinity of the soil is indicated by the pH scale, which ranges from 1 to 10, with 7 as the neutral point. Practically all vegetables, and the great majority of other plants, thrive in neutral to moderately acid soil, with a pH of 6 to 7.

centration. This is measured by means of a potentiometer; or, more commonly, by special synthetic dyes, used as indicators. The colors of the dyes change with the increase or decrease of the hydrogen-ion concentration, and the symbold pH is used as the indicator. The pH scale is graded from 1, which is extremely acid, to 10, which is extremely alkaline. The gradations between 1 and 10 are not exactly uniform, however. The neutral point is, accordingly, 7. The majority of garden plants do best at a pH of 6.0 to 6.5, or slightly acid. Plants requiring acid conditions (such as rhododendrons, azalea, and laurel) generally do best in a soil with a pH of 5.0 to 5.5.

Acid soils are usually common in humid sections. This condition arises through the lack of certain active bases, and, when excessive, is detrimental to many plants in three main ways—(1) unfavorable hydrogen-ion concentration; (2) presence of substances harmful to plant growth, as active aluminum, iron, and manganese; (3) improper nutrition from the lack of calcium.

The most common method of rectifying a soil that is too acid is by the application of lime. Other bases could be used, but lime has its advantages in that it is cheap; it is an essential element; it is easily handled; an excess is not detrimental; and it is an agent which aids in maintaining other nutrients in available form. When lime is applied, it neutralizes the free acids; and the toxic aluminum, iron, and manganese are rendered inactive. Lime is usually applied when the seedbed is being prepared, but during the dry season in the fall the lime is more easily worked into the soil and will be more beneficial to the next year's crop. Most crops do best in soils which are slightly acid (pH 6.5); therefore additions of lime should be made only when absolutely necessary. However, calcium is an important element in plant growth, and it may be lacking in the soil. In such cases, in order to avoid changing the soil reaction (acidity) gypsum (calcium sulfate) is recommended at the rate of 2 to 4 lbs. to 100 sq. ft.

Soils which are too alkaline (above pH 7) usually have to be acidified, as otherwise many of the elements of plant growth may become unavailable. To be effective over a long period sulfur is the best acidifying agent. It is applied—in the fall, preferably, since it is slow acting—at the rate of 2 to 4 lbs. per 100 sq. ft. Aluminum sulfate may be substituted at the rate of 1 lb. per 100 sq. ft. It is quick acting, but is dangerous if the soil lacks phosphorus. In such a case free aluminum may be formed, and this is injurious. If phosphorus is present in sufficient quantity, the excess aluminum combines with it to form an insoluble and harmless aluminum phosphate. Iron sulfate likewise is useful as an acidifier; it is used at the same rate as aluminum sulfate.

Ammonium sulfate is a particularly useful acidifying agent, since it supplies nitrogen as well as acidity. When used in proper amounts to supply needed nitrogen, each pound of ammonium sulfate develops more than enough acidity to neutralize a pound of limestone. Pound for pound, ammonium sulfate develops more than twice as much acid in a soil as does iron sulfate or aluminum sulfate.

Building Up the Fertility of Home Grounds

To summarize the procedures involved, it is best, first of all, to have your soil tested by your State Experiment Station for its acidity and the available elements present. The next step is to be sure that proper drainage exists. After that, to be on the safe side, organic matter, preferably in the form of a 2-in. layer of manure or compost, should be spaded into the soil in the fall. The soil is best left rough and uneven over winter, as this increases the pulverizing action of alternate freezing and thawing. If needed, lime may also be added at the same time. It is well to add phosphorus, too, in the form of super-phosphate, to make sure that this material is worked down into the soil deep enough to do the most good. Further additions of complete fertilizers should be made in the spring and during the growing season.

Peatmoss is rapidly taking the place of manure in suburban garden-ing, because animal manure is not readily available. Peatmoss can be incorporated into a garden soil at any time, since it does not need to be composted. It has very high capacity to retain fertilizer nutrients and to prevent their loss by leaching but, at the same time, it keeps them available to the plant. In acid soils the addition of a cup of pul-verized limestone to each bushel of peatmoss, before the latter is mixed with the soil, helps prevent a further increase in acidity and so may lead to maximum plant growth. In soils that are neutral or alkaline, no limestone need be added with peatmoss.

TYPES OF SOIL

What are the different kinds of soil? How are they prepared for planting? *Sandy soil:* contains less than 20 per cent clay and silt; water lost quickly; fertilizer elements leach quickly; contains too much air; absorbs too much heat. Add as much organic matter as possible. *Clay soil:* contains very fine particles; holds too much water; lacks air; sticky after rain; "puddles"—i.e., runs together in thick mud. Add organic matter and fine cinders or sand. *Loam:* intermediate, between sand and clay, and the most satisfactory for general use.

How do you recognize the value of natural soil? How do you improve it? The nutritional value of soil is hard to determine by casual inspection. A test must be made to determine it. However, dark soils usually have organic matter. To determine good structure use a trowel: loams when lifted will fall apart in small crumbs; sandy soils break up into individual particles; clay soils can be broken apart only by force, and then into clods.

Are there special kinds of soil for different plants? Root crops require friable, light soils for best development. Crops with fine roots do better in coarse open soil, while coarse-rooted plants grow better in more dense soils composed of finer particles.

SANDY SOIL

We have a sandy lot and wish to enjoy good results. Should we put black topsoil on? Yes. Extremely sandy soil needs loam.

What depth of topsoil should we use on sandy ground? Add 3 ins. loam and spade to a depth of 6 ins.

What kind of fertilizer is best for sandy soil? Use a complete fertilizer, such as a 5–10–5, and manure or peatmoss. Fertilizer is best applied frequently, in small amounts.

To build up sandy soil, I have used straw as a mulch and spaded in manure and peatmoss. Still I cannot get many plants to grow. Why? Add loam, plus more manure and peat, and fertilizers in small amounts frequently.

Our soil is very sandy. Results are poor. Can chicken manure be used for improvement? Yes. Apply poultry manure at the rate of 10 to 20 pounds per 100 sq. ft. Use dried, pulverized poultry manure according to the recommendations on the package. To balance the fertilizer value of this, add a pound of 0–14–14 fertilizer per 100 sq. ft. Results will be greatly improved if peatmoss is used at the rate of 5 or 6 bushels per 100 sq. ft.

How can I fertilize a very sandy soil that has little top soil? Incorporate one or more green-manure crops. Add a commercial fertilizer suitable for the crop to be grown.

Can fallen leaves be used to improve a gravelly soil, and how? Yes. Let them decompose first.

I have a very sandy soil that is very rocky. What should I do with it? At present soil seems dead; plants grow, but soon die. Remove surface rocks. Add soil and manure and work in. Add a complete fertilizer several times each year.

How do you loosen a sandy loam that packs? Add manure, peatmoss, or leafmold, and incorporate in the top 6 ins. of soil.

I have a steep gravel bank which I have terraced and planted, but which still looks barren. It is hot, dry, and steep. What will encourage plants to grow? Dig holes in the bank; fill with compost of soil and manure. Gradually the plants set out in this fashion will cover the bank.

How can light sandy soil with gravel base be made productive for LAWN and for FLOWER and VEGETABLE garden? By heavy applications of organic matter—manure, etc.

What plants and GRASS do you recommend where the soil is essentially sandy, and where plants such as wild Mountain Laurel, huckleberry, sumach, etc., flourish extremely well? Have soil tested yearly and apply correct amount of lime. Then plants will grow. Kentucky Blue Grass is most satisfactory.

How can I improve the soil for CACTI? (West Virginia.) The requirements of cacti are simple. Well-drained, sandy soil with little if any fertilizer added. Hot, dry, infertile conditions are best.

What shall be added to soil in FLOWER bed that packs after rain and forms hard crust on top? Soil is of sandy nature. Add 3 ins. of manure, peatmoss, or leafmold, and spade to a depth of 6 ins.

My front yard is mostly sand. What FLOWERS would be best to plant? Portulaca, California poppy, annual phlox, calliopsis, cockscomb, morningglory, anthemis, milkweed, aster, babiesbreath, liatris, yucca. To remedy situation, add manure and fertilizer.

Our soil is sandy. How can we grow good ROSES? Add manure or peatmoss. Keep soil fertilized and water heavily when necessary.

Our soil (on river front) is solid sand. Would surfacing it with black dirt be sufficient for planting FRUIT TREES? No. A very large hole should be dug for each tree, and filled with good soil in which to plant.

What would you suggest for a HOME GARDEN at the seashore where there is a lot of sand? Additions of animal manure will help, although it would be better to mix some loam with the sand. Also dig under green cover crops.

I have a piece of very sandy land and wish to grow excellent CORN. Can it be done? Yes, manure heavily; also apply a complete fertilizer several times during growing season.

Our soil is all gravel. How can I adjust this for growing VEGETABLES? Add mixture of loam and manure to a depth of 3 ins. and spade to a depth of 6 ins.

What is the best way of keeping land in shape for VEGETABLES? The soil is light and sandy but well drained. Spade in manure every fall. Keep well fertilized and properly cultivated.

Our soil is very sandy and is acid. What can we do so we can grow a VEGETABLE garden? Increase the organic content of the soil by incorporating green-manure crops, farm manures, or other non-acid materials such as leaves, straw, plant refuse, or non-acid peat. Apply lime as needed to modify the acidity.

Our Long Island soil is very sandy; my VEGETABLES are never much of a success. Is this because of the soil? No matter how much topsoil we put on, it sinks in. Add loam and plenty of manure. A 3-in. layer should be spaded to a depth of 6 ins. Any vegetable can be grown if well watered and fertilized.

Our soil is sandy; fertilizer seems to cause worms in the underground VEGETABLES. Is this due to the soil? The soil is infested with wireworms. Apply 2 pounds of a 5 per cent chlordane dust per 1,000 sq. ft. of soil surface in Eastern States. In Western States, apply 2 pounds of a 10 per cent DDT dust per 1,000 sq. ft. about 6 weeks before planting. In both cases dusts should be worked thoroughly into the upper 6 or 8 inches of soil.

My ground is sandy. What is the best VEGETABLE to plant? Any vegetable will grow in sandy soil if fertilized frequently. Apply fertilizer high in phosphorus and potash.

For sandy soil plant material see also Sandy Environment, Section III.

CLAY SOIL

What makes clay so sticky? Clay is composed of very minute particles which have a large surface to absorb water. High water content causes the stickiness.

Should clay soil be worked when wet? No; never. It puddles and makes a poor environment for roots. Digging too soon in spring may make it practically useless for the season.

How much wood ashes is it safe to use on heavy clay soil? At least 10 lbs. per 100 sq. ft.

My garden plot is heavy clay soil and produces well, but it is hard to work up. Would well-rotted manure and wood ashes be of benefit? Yes. Fine cinders would also be beneficial.

Should coal ashes be sifted before using them on clay soil? In general, no. Large cinders or lumps should be broken or removed.

How coarse should the coal ashes be for use on clay soil? One fourth in. or finer.

What proportion of sifted coal ashes should be mixed with clay to make it good for flowers? A 2-in. layer of sifted ashes spaded in will be safe.

Are sifted coal ashes in clay soil better than sand? Yes; they are of more help in opening it up and admitting air.

Does it make any difference what kind of sand is mixed with clay soil to lighten it? To what depth should the sand be spread on before spading in? Yes. Coarse or ungraded sands, containing a large proportion of $\frac{1}{16}$- to $\frac{1}{8}$-inch particles, will bring about the greatest improvement when added to a clay soil. Incorporate a 2-inch layer of such sand.

What shall I do to keep ground loosened? It gets sticky and lumpy. I mixed in sand and ashes but they did not help. Probably too little sand was used. Manure and/or peatmoss should improve such a soil.

My ground gets hard and dry on the surface, so that it is difficult for the young shoots to break through. It is soft enough beneath the surface. What can I do? Incorporate sand, and, if possible, well-rotted manure, in the upper surface.

My garden soil is mostly clay. I dug under quite a few leaves in an effort to add humus to the soil. Will leaves tend to make the soil acid? Usually not; but it would be advisable, in any case, to test the soil for acidity, which see.

Is chemical fertilizer harmful to clay soil? No. Often necessary to furnish mineral elements so plants will grow.

What can be added to a clay soil to increase root growth? It is slightly acid, and in partial shade. If wet, soil must be drained by use of tile. Add manure or peatmoss. Slight acidity is all right for vegetables and for most ornamental plants. (See Acidity, this section.)

What kind of fertilizer is best for inert clay soil? Incorporation of organic matter and lime will probably benefit such a soil. The fertilizer to apply will depend upon the crop to be grown.

How may I improve a heavy, extremely wet clay soil? Pine trees thrive on it. The physical condition of an extremely wet clay soil can be improved by using 4 in. agricultural drain tile (see Drainage) and the incorporation of liberal amounts of screened cinders or sand. Add ground limestone, as necessary, to lower the acidity.

Will adding ashes and dry leaves to thin clay soil bring it to the consistency of loam? Yes, if you add enough, and wait long enough. Apply manure, peatmoss, or both, to hasten the process.

The soil in the garden is very clayey and needs conditioning. How can I do that with all the SHRUBBERY and perennials in? Remove perennials after hard frost and spade in 3 ins. of manure and 2–3 ins. of coarse sand. Replant perennials at once.

What are the best materials to mix with a heavy soil of BLUE CLAY? Peatmoss, manure, and fine cinders.

What crops would help to break up soil of blue clay? Shallow-rooted ones, such as rye and oats.

Is lime helpful to soil of blue clay? Have soil tested to determine if lime is needed; usually it is helpful. (See Lime, this section.)

How does GRAY CLAY differ from red clay? Depends on kinds of minerals the clay is composed of and amount of air present when clay was formed. Red clay usually contains iron.

Is gray clay fertile? Yes, but probably would be better for plants if it is fertilized.

What can be done with gray clay soil to make it produce? Add humus first, then apply fertilizers as crop growth may indicate the need for them.

Is it best to grow a green-manure crop in gray clay soil over winter, or dig it up in the fall and leave it so? Fertilize soil, grow a winter cover crop, and plow under in spring.

What will darken light-colored (gray) clay soil? How many years will it take to make such soil black in color? Organic matter—manure, etc. It would require several years of constant applications, but it is not at all necessary to make the soil black in order to have it productive.

Is PIPE-CLAY soil acid? Clay soils vary in their degree of acidity. To determine the reaction of the particular soil in mind, test it or send a sample to your State Agricultural College. (See Acidity, this section.)

I have a patch of heavy RED CLAY soil to condition. Is there an easy way to do it? I've used peatmoss, sand, leafmold, and well-rotted manure. Use more of the same. Sorry; no easy way.

My tract of land has heavy, tough red clay base, with only light topsoil covering. What is best treatment? Grow cover crops of soybeans plowed under before beans are ripe. Follow with crop of rye to be plowed under the following spring.

Will peatmoss make a red clay soil heavier? No. It loosens it up and makes it easier to handle.

What green-manure crop is best for ROCKY CLAY soil, and when should it be sown? Grow soybeans planted in spring, and plow under before beans are ripe. Follow with rye or oats, to be plowed under the following spring.

I have a rocky clay soil that has never been used except to grow grass. Should it be exposed to the winter, or put to cover crop? For a small area, remove surface rocks, add 3 ins. of manure or peatmoss with some sand or ashes, and plow under. Do not disk or harrow until spring.

What does a WHITE CLAY soil need, when it becomes baked hard after a rain? In the early spring it is loose and mellow. Needs organic matter in the form of peatmoss, manure, or leafmold. Apply a 3-in. layer and spade in.

How can a very heavy YELLOW CLAY soil around the foundation of a house be improved so that plants will grow in it? Incorporate 2 ins. of coal ashes screened through ¼-in. mesh, and 2 ins. of manure, straw, or peat, preferably in the fall.

What is the best way to prepare heavy clay for FRUIT TREES? Drainage must be good for fruit trees in heavy soils. Spade or plow under a liberal quantity of manure. Sod spaded under is likewise good.

The soil of my garden consists mostly of clay. Would it be suitable for planting trees such as apples, pears, and cherries? Yes, if well drained.

How can I prepare clay soil in full sun for growing LILIES? All varieties will grow in moderately heavy soil. Add 3 ins. of manure and spade to a depth of 6 ins. Soil must be well drained for satisfactory results with lilies.

What ornamental PLANTS will grow in clay soil? If well prepared—organic matter added, well drained, fertilized—clay soils will grow almost all plants.

What SHRUBS, FLOWERS, and TREES grow best in red clay soil? If soil is well drained, most shrubs and trees will grow. For flowers, add manure or peatmoss along with fine cinders or ashes.

We have clay ground and must prepare it inexpensively. What

VEGETABLES will be successful? Spade in a 3-in. layer of manure. Any vegetable will grow. However, root crops will do better in lighter soils.

Is it practical to begin a VEGETABLE garden on a rocky clay soil of poor color and texture? Probably not, unless no other soil is available. Remove surface rocks and add large quantities of manure or peatmoss each year. Fertilizer will be needed.

SOIL PROBLEMS

What kind of soil is most adaptable for general gardening? Any well-conditioned soil which would grow a crop of corn.

Is there any way to change the condition of a poor soil? Unless the soil condition is extremely unfavorable, it can be improved to the extent that it will produce good crops.

I am planning my first garden. How do I go about preparing the land for it? Manure it (600 lbs. per 1,000 sq. ft.); or 5 bales peatmoss (50 bushels) per 1,000 sq. ft.; fertilizer it (5–10–5), 30 lbs. per 1,000 sq. ft.; lime it (if test shows need). (See also Handling of Soil.)

Is it advisable to apply lime and commercial fertilizer through the winter on the snows for early melting and absorption? Lime and commercial fertilizers, for some crops, can be applied in the fall, but in most cases they are more economically applied in the spring. Nothing is to be gained by making the applications in winter.

Can soil for a garden be improved during the winter? Spade manure or straw in in the fall. Allow to lie in the rough over winter.

Are wood ashes as good or better than coal ashes for the garden? Under what conditions should each be used? Wood ashes and coal ashes serve two distinct purposes—the former adds potash, the latter improves mechanical condition of soil.

If annuals are cut off at the ground in fall, instead of being pulled out, will the soil benefit by decomposition of the roots? Yes.

In clearing off my vegetable plot, I burned the old tomato vines. Does this in any way injure the soil for next year's crop? No. It really should be of benefit.

What can I do to improve tough, gummy black virgin soil? I have added sand. Not enough added. Apply a 3-in. layer of manure or peatmoss. Fertilizer will also help.

What is best treatment for a soil that does not produce root crops? It probably is too heavy; lighten with manure and cinders. It may lack phosphorus and potassium, which may be added in the form of superphosphate and potassium chloride. (See Introduction.)

Our soil is a heavy black gumbo and bakes badly. Should I use manure, sand, sawdust, or peatmoss?   For long-lasting improvement, incorporate 2 to 3 inches of peatmoss, a mixture of half peatmoss and half coarse sawdust, plus 2 inches of coarse sand many of whose particles are $\frac{1}{16}$- to $\frac{1}{8}$-inch in diameter.

How can I make a hard-packed, black alkali soil friable and productive? (Nevada.)   Sulfur must be added to neutralize the alkali. If not, soil must be drained by use of tile. Add manure or peatmoss to loosen soil.

DEPLETED SOIL

What is the quickest way to bring an old used garden spot back into quick production?   Spade in manure in the fall. In the spring, apply superphosphate, hoe, rake, and plant. Add complete fertilizer just before planting, and again during summer.

I have been raising flowers on the same ground for some time. What can I use to keep it in shape?   Incorporate organic matter such as leaves, well-rotted manure, or peatmoss in the soil between the plants. Apply a 4–12–4 fertilizer as needed.

Can bulbs and annuals be planted every year in the same soil without using fertilizer, except manure once a year?   No. It would be better to use the manure when preparing the soil, and then apply a complete fertilizer to bulbs just as flower buds begin to form; and to annuals during the season of most active growth.

I have planted flowers in the same spot for the last 15 years, using only a commercial fertilizer. My flowers do not have as large blossoms as they used to, but bloom very well. Should I add anything more, or do as I am doing?   Unless the soil is very rich, it would be beneficial to add manure or leafmold, or some other form of humus.

ERODED SOIL

What causes erosion?   Erosion—the washing away of soil on slopes by the runoff of surface water—results when the soil is left more or less bare and is so handled that it lacks humus to absorb mosture.

Please tell me how to handle a lot that is very sandy and slopes. The water washes the soil off as fast as it is replaced. I had thought of making about 3 different elevations (terraces). Is this too many for a garden about 50 ft. deep?   If the slope is not too steep, the trouble may be overcome by increasing the organic content of the soil through the use of green manures, farm manure, or peatmoss. On steep slopes handle the situation by strip-working the lot, or by terracing. Two terraces should be sufficient on a 50-ft. lot unless the grade is very steep.

How do you keep sharp slopes from opening and washing out?
Avoid cultivation near and in these areas. If practical, plant black
locust trees (small) to hold soil. If possible, grade off sharp slopes.

**What suggestions do you have for hillside soil that is mostly de-
composed granite?** Prepare small pockets or local areas of good
soil by using manure or peatmoss, and use plants which root as they
spread.

**How can one improve clay soil on a hillside to make it good gar-
den soil?** Add manure, spade under, and plant ground covers (ornamental) to hold soil in place. If wanted for vegetables, arrange
the slope in terraces.

**I have a 10-ft. hill, about 30 ft. from the house, where I am going
to build a rock garden. What can I do to prevent the sand from
washing down?** Use plants that spread and root: sedum, ajuga,
Ranunculus acris, some creeping phlox (*P. subulata*), pachysandra,
ivy, myrtle, arabis, ceratostigma, etc.

FOR FLOWERS

What type of soil is best for a mixed flower border? A sandy
loam, slightly acid (pH 6.5) in reaction, with manure worked in.

**My annuals and perennials grow tall and spindly. Could this be
due to overfertilization, lack of sun, or lack of some fertilizer element?
The garden site receives sunlight half the day.** The spindling growth
of annuals and perennials may be due to lack of sunlight, improper
fertilization, or other factors; or to any combination of them. Give
as much sunlight as possible; improve the drainage and aeration of
the soil; increase the phosphorus and potash in relation to nitrogen
in the fertilizer used. A 2–10–10 fertilizer may be best in this case
for a few years.

**Why do plants grow thin and scraggly? What is lacking in soils
that produce such growth?** Lack of balanced nutrition. Usually an
addition of complete fertilizer (4–12–4 or 5–10–5) will help. Drainage should be good. Calcium (lime or gypsum) may be needed to
make good roots. Test your soil.

**My flowers grow very poorly, and usually die before long. What
causes this?** The chances are your soil lacks fertility, moisture-
holding capacity, and aeration. Additions of humus and fertilizers
should correct these handicaps.

**How can you keep soil sweet and in good condition in the grimy
atmosphere of New York City?** Adequate drainage should be provided. A periodic soil test will determine the amount of lime necessary
to maintain the correct soil reaction.

Do soil conditions cause double cosmos to be single? Doubling
of flowers is a hereditary tendency. Soil conditions rarely have any

effect. Improper selection of seed is the usual cause. Many flowers never come 100 per cent double from seed.

Are angleworms harmful or beneficial in the garden? I find in a short time they eat up all humus in the soil the same as they do when they get into flower pots. Angleworms are not harmful in outdoor soils, unless present in very unusual numbers. In the greenhouse or in pot plants they are a nuisance. If too numerous, apply 5 lbs. of arsenate of lead to 1,000 sq. ft. and water in.

LAKE-SHORE SOIL

Would a garden plot laid out on the edge of a lake be satisfactory? And how would one get it in condition? Yes. Add manure at rate of 600 lbs. per 1,000 sq. ft. Humus content is likely to be low.

NEGLECTED SOIL

Why is soil that has lain idle for years so deficient in plant food? When grass, weeds, leaves, etc., are continually decaying on it, wouldn't natural compost be made? The weeds which grow on poor soils may not require the same proportions of elements for growth as cultivated plants. When these weeds die down, they fail to change these proportions. Besides, insufficient aeration, due to lack of turning the land, may cause trouble.

How can I restore the fertility of an old garden? Soil is sand, with a clay subsoil. I've tried manure, lime, and commercial fertilizer. The predominance of sand seems the difficulty. Try heavy applications of humus—manure, straw, alfalfa, hay, or the use of green manure. (See Index.)

Last year was the first time my garden was plowed in 30 years. I think I need lime, as the ground showed green moss. How much should I use? The best way to tell lime need is to test soil. Green moss is not an indication of acidity. More likely drainage is poor, or nutrients are lacking.

I had a ½-acre vegetable garden last year; plot had been uncultivated for 15 years. Applied a ton of lime after plowing and 2 truckloads of manure direct to plants. Seeded the plot to rye and Perennial Rye Grass last fall, and it looks all right. What, if anything, would you suggest adding this season before and after plowing? Apply 40 to 50 lbs. of 20% superphosphate per 1,000 sq. ft.

I recently bought a 171-acre farm which has not been worked for about 9 years. How can I determine what to plant? Have your soil tested. Insure proper drainage. Consult your county agent.

Have just bought a 3-acre place which has not been worked for 4 years, but annual crop of hay has been cut. Can I bring this into cultivation in a year? Yes. Plow in the fall. Fertilize heavily in the spring.

The plot I expect to use as a vegetable garden is a vacant lot infested with weeds. Will turning the weeds under with a plow be sufficient preparation of the soil? The plowing under of weeds will add humus to the soil. However, it may be too acid or alkaline: test for this. It may be poorly drained. It may need fertilization.

Our back yard is full of wild grass and weeds. Will soil be suitable for anything after condition is changed? If the soil is heavily contaminated with weed seeds, the best practice would be to let it lie fallow (unplanted) for 1 year before planting the desired crops. The chances are good that the soil can be modified to produce the common vegetables and garden flowers satisfactorily.

If the soil produces a vigorous crop of weeds, is it a sign that it will grow desirable things well? Usually, yes. If the desired crops are adapted to the soil type supporting the weed growth, they should do well.

What is the best way to handle soil which has been allowed to grow with bracken and creeping berry vines and has lain idle for years? Mow or cut off and remove all undesired plants. (They may be put into compost heap.) Remove undesired woody material such as limbs and small trees. Plow or dig and leave in rough condition through winter. In spring, redig, fertilize heavily, and plant.

POOR SOIL

How can subsoil fill be converted so that vegetables can be grown? Takes too long—not worth doing unless topsoil is hauled to a depth of 6 to 8 ins.

How can I build up soil that is mostly cinders? In the upper 8 to 10 ins. incorporate manure and haul in soil. The final proportion of cinders should be not more than ¼ of the total volume in top 6 ins.

My garden plot is mostly brown dirt and not too fertile. How can I make it fertile? Apply manure and a complete fertilizer.

My soil is very poor. How can I improve it? Add 3 ins. manure or peatmoss; spade to a depth of 6 ins. Before raking add 4–12–4 or 5–10–5 fertilizer at 4 lbs. per 100 sq. ft.

What garden truck will grow on soil that has just been dug out for a basement 8 ft. deep and is left 3 ft. deep on garden plot? Would you lime and fertilize soil? Only the top 6 ins. of that soil may be expected to be good. If the topsoil was not separated from subsoil, additions of manure and fertilizers would be needed; but even under such a treatment, not much should be expected the first year.

Are flowers or vegetables likely to grow in soil from which the top 18 ins. has been removed? Usually not. By manuring the subsoil and planting green-manure crops, the soil may be made fairly good after 2 or 3 years.

How much topsoil do you advise using over fill in order to grow flowers and vegetables? At least 6 ins.; preferably more.

I am planning to make a garden where the sod is rather heavy. How can I destroy this? Plow or spade in the fall or spring. Apply complete fertilizer before spading to hasten decomposition. Sod land makes the finest of soils.

I have a brand-new home; the builder put in very little loam, and the soil itself is very poor. How can I improve it? Without adding topsoil, the process of improvement will be very slow. Heavy additions of manure would have to be substituted. This should be worked in in the fall or spring. Soil should be tested for acidity and proper corrections made. Fertilizers should be added, and green-manure crops planted—rye in the fall (2 to 3 lbs. per 1,000 sq. ft.), followed by soybeans next spring (after plowing rye under). After plowing the soybeans under, soil should be in fair shape.

I used topsoil from the farm to enrich my soil, but results were poor. How can I determine what is wrong? Drainage may be poor. May need fertilizer. Add 4–12–4 or 5–10–5 at 4 lbs. per 100 sq. ft. Consult your local county agricultural agent.

What is the quickest, cheapest, and best way to rebuild "stripped" land, where loam was scraped off? By use of manure, fertilizers, and green-manure crops.

Will it be necessary to add extra fertilizer to the topsoil we have just put on? Add a fertilizer high in phosphorus and potash.

STONY SOIL

To produce a good crop of the common vegetables, what fertilizer is best for shale ground that has not been farmed for several years? Any complete fertilizer, such as 4–12–4 or 5–10–5, applied at 4 lbs. per 100 sq. ft., twice or three times a year.

Do stones continually work to the surface? If so, why? Yes, small ones do. Alternate freezing and thawing in winter, digging and cultivation, and also wetting and drying in spring, summer, and fall, bring stones to surface.

What shall I do for stony land? I continually rake stones off, but more appear. There is no remedy other than to keep on removing surface rocks.

WET SOIL

Will you explain the terms "well-drained soil" and "waterlogged soil"? A well-drained soil is one in which surplus water runs off quickly and which dries out readily after a rain or watering. A waterlogged soil is the opposite and contains too much water and little air.

Can a low, wet area be used for general gardening? Only if it can be drained.

What vegetables will stand a wet, soggy soil best? Beets seem to like wet sour spots, but carrots won't even come up in these spots. Beets usually do not do well in poorly drained soil. This is true of practically all vegetables. Cabbage will suffer as little as any vegetable in such a soil.

Our soil is in the shade and has too much moisture. What can we do for it? Improve the drainage by the installation of 3- or 4-in. agricultural tile, 12 to 15 ins. deep, with lines 12 to 15 ft. apart, and incorporate liberal amounts of organic matter.

What can be done to eliminate excess water at the foot of a terraced hill? The water always stands in the garden at the foot of the hill. Provide a shallow grass-covered or stone-paved ditch to carry off the excess water, or install a tile drain.

The earth in back of my home is wet and mossy. Is there anything I can do about fertilizing it for a garden? At present nothing will grow. Soil must be drained by use of agricultural tile. Apply 4–12–4 or 5–10–5 fertilizer at 4 lbs. per 100 sq. ft.

My garden is on a slope and the lower end is wet, with heavy soil. Is there any simple way to drain this ground and loosen the soil? Incorporate sand or cinders. If this does not rectify the situation, tile drain.

My garden plot is low and level, the soil moist and heavy in the spring. Will leaves and grass cuttings help, or should I use sand? Soil should be drained by use of tile. The addition of humus will help the soil but will not correct poor drainage.

How much lime should be used to correct soil in wet condition? Lime is not a corrective for wet soils. Add lime only if the soil is too acid for crops to be grown. Improve drainage first.

A sewer pipe backed up last fall and overflowed in a small plot where vegetables were planted. What can I do to purify the ground? Dig it up, and leave in rough, open condition. In a very short time the ground will "purify" itself.

Will waste water from a sand-washing plant damage land where it settles? (Texas.) Since sand-washing plants differ greatly in their practices, this is a difficult question to answer. Have the soil tested for acidity, nitrogen, phosphorus, potash, soluble salts, and organic matter. Consult your county agent.

MOSSY SOIL

The soil turns green in one of my perennial garden beds. What is the best way to remedy this condition? As it is probably caused by poor drainage and lack of aeration, improve the drainage by one of the methods previously suggested.

What kind of fertilizer should be used when the soil is heavy and

has a green top coating? Plowing under a green-manure crop will add humus and improve the aeration of heavy soils. The best kind of fertilizer to use under such conditions will depend upon the requirements of the crop to be grown. In general, a 4–12–4 fertilizer will be satisfactory. Addition of lime may be beneficial.

What is the cause, and what the remedy, for soil that has a green mosslike formation over the top? Moss grows on moist soil and often indicates poor drainage. Install tile drains, or incorporate 40 to 50 lbs. agricultural gypsum per 1,000 sq. ft. every 3 to 5 years.

Does green moss growing on the soil in the borders indicate an acid condition of the ground? No. It usually indicates poor drainage or lack of fertility. If it is a green scum (algae), excess nitrogen (especially if from organic sources) and poor aeration may be responsible.

How can I overcome excessive moss on slope? Usual reasons for the excessive growth of moss are poor underdrainage and infertile soil. Rake out as much moss as possible, apply a ½-in. layer of dehydrated manure, and maintain fertility by applying fertilizer rich in nitrogen (10–5–5) in spring and fall.

What is the best type of fertilizer for soil which has not had previous nourishment and which contains a large percentage of clay? Although sunny it tends to become mossy. Tile drain the garden plot; incorporate farm manures or green manures; add commercial fertilizer suitable to the crop to be grown.

Will you tell us what to do for garden soil that packs and turns greenish, even after fertilizer and manure have been added? Too much algae present due, probably, to poor aeration and excess nitrogen. Addition of manure may make it worse. Digging in rotted straw should be helpful.

I have a strip of soil a few feet wide where everything dies that is planted. Why? Maybe due to packing of soil by constant walking. Try aerating by adding screened cinders or fine sand. The trouble may also be caused by the application of some toxic weed killer.

WOODLAND AND SHADED SOIL

What is the quickest, cheapest, and best way to convert a former wood lot into usable land? Remove stumps by hand, tractor, or dynamite, then plow and disk.

Does a garden of vegetables and flowers do well in soil which has just been cleared of hickory, oak, and wild cherry trees? There is a great deal of leafmold in the soil. It will do better in subsequent years, when aeration changes the structure of the soil. When well rotted, leafmold is a good soil conditioner.

Is acid woodland soil in any way beneficial as fertilizer? Woodland soil is not a fertilizer but may serve as a soil conditioner. It may be used as a satisfactory mulch, containing a high percentage of organic matter, and later worked into the soil.

In red virgin soil under and near CEDAR would oak leafmold and chicken fertilizer, mixed with sand, produce good vegetables? Only if the trees do not shade the garden spot.

What can I do with soil surrounded by FIR trees to make it suitable for flowers? Deep spading and incorporation of a 2-in. layer of finely screened cinders should help.

What attention must be given soil from which OAK trees have been cleared? Through the years many layers of oak leaves have rotted and naturally form a part of this soil. Such a soil may be somewhat acid. It should be tested and, if necessary, lime applied.

What is the best treatment of soil under PINE trees for the growth of roses and old-fashioned annuals? If the shade is dense, despite soil preparation neither will grow.

A WILLOW tree shades my yard; the roots mat the soil for yards around. Is there any way to make flowers grow beneath it? Not satisfactorily.

My soil receives sun from noon on. The few things which grow taste like wood (tomatoes, strawberries, etc.). Why? Soil tested poor, but 5–10–5 was added, plus sheep manure. Not enough sun. No fertilizer can substitute for sunlight.

How should I treat the ground where no sun ever shines? The ground packs. Outside of ferns and shade-loving plants, nothing should be grown under such conditions. The packing of the ground may be reduced by working in leafmold or peatmoss.

How can damp, cold, shady soil be fertilized to substitute for sunshine? There is no substitute for sunshine. Additions of nitrogen are helpful if trees take all the nourishment. Flowering plants and vegetables should not be planted in such localities.

What is deficient in soil when plants run to slender stems instead of branching? May not have enough sun. Add a fertilizer low in nitrogen (2–10–10 or 0–12–12), 5 lbs. per 100 sq. ft.

HANDLING OF SOIL

(See also General Culture, Section III.)

PLOWING; DIGGING

When should soil be plowed? Any time of year when not so wet as to roll in large clods, or so dry as to be a powdery dust.

Does it harm soil to work it while wet? Yes, especially if the soil is heavy. Plowing compacts such soils, and clods and unbreakable lumps will result.

What is the result of turning soil while it is wet? Heavy soils will puddle and bake and will be difficult to work into a friable state.

What makes soil break up into large, hard lumps after it is plowed? The structure is bad—too clayey. Add manure and cinders, or sand. Do not plow or dig while soil is wet.

Is it better to plow gardens in the fall or spring? Fall plowing is better, especially when there is sod to be turned under. It reduces erosion, exposes heavy soils to frost, kills exposed insects, brings about decay of organic matter, and makes for earlier planting. In the South, however, where little or no freezing occurs, fall plowing is apt to cause leaching.

Why is it best to plow in the fall? If done early enough, the organic matter decays partially before planting in the spring; the action of freezing and thawing improves the soil structure; some insect pests are killed when exposed; earlier planting (in spring) is made possible.

We had land plowed which has not been cultivated for about 40 years. What is the best time to put lime and fertilizer on soil? Plow early in the fall. Add lime at 2 lbs. or more per 100 sq. ft. (as test indicates) and a complete fertilizer at the same rate (or preferably a week or two later) and cultivate in. In the spring, hoe, apply fertilizer, rake, and seed.

I have a field that hasn't been plowed for years. I would like to have a vegetable garden. Is it best to plow in fall? Fall plowing is best in such cases.

How can soil be best prepared to yield plentifully when it has not been used for over 15 years? Plow in the fall; keep rough during winter; add fertilizers in spring. (See preceding question.)

Last year I made a new garden by filling in about 10 to 18 ins. deep with loam. What should be done with this ground to put in proper shape for this year's home garden? Manure and plow, preferably in the fall.

We plan to make a garden on a city lot infested with poison ivy, wild honeysuckle, and blackberry vines. Can you make any suggestions as to how we can rid soil of these? Will the roots from these vines ruin such root crops as potatoes? Should be plowed, disked, and harrowed in spring. Plant vegetables and remove, by frequent hand hoeing, shoots of weeds that appear. Roots of the vines will decompose and not injure vegetables.

Should ground be tilled or loosened up each year before planting, or only a little hole dug to put in bulbs or seeds? Always plow or spade soil before planting each crop.

Is it necessary to turn over the soil in a truck garden both in the fall and in the spring? Plowing or digging in the fall and disking or cultivating deeply in the spring are the common practices.

Is it undesirable to leave soil barren after plowing, or after crops have been harvested? It should either be kept cultivated, or mulched. If there is time (before the plot will be needed for future use) grow a green-manure crop.

Does burning weeds on vacant lots in any way harm the soil for growing vegetables? The lots have lain idle for a great many years. No. A certain amount of minerals is added and weed seeds are killed. Where there is a choice in the fall, between burning or plowing, it is better to plow.

Should I burn off the garden in the fall, or should stalks be plowed under? If your old stalks are disease free, it is better to plow under than burn. Diseased material should be burned.

In plowing cleared ground that had a growth of wild berries and brush, what should the procedure be? If necessary, tile for drainage (which see), plow, disk, and harrow to prepare land for crop.

How can I loosen up hardpan soil on 40-acre field? Use a subsoil plow.

How do you prepare soil in the fall for spring flower beds? Spade in a 2-in. layer of manure (600 lbs. per 1,000 sq. ft.). Apply bone meal or superphosphate (30 lbs. per 1,000 sq. ft.). After spading, leave ground surface rough.

Will you please define spading and trenching? See Section V.

After spading in fall, how does one proceed in spring? If manure is dug in at time of spring spading, can lime also be used? How? When spading in the fall, leave soil rough. In the spring, cultivate or hoe if the soil packed then rake and plant. Lime may be used either in spring or fall, but use it only after the soil is tested. Don't guess.

CULTIVATING

What is meant by the term "in good tilth"? Soil which has suitable crumbly structure, sufficient humus, and is well drained. To secure good tilth, use manure; tile if necessary.

Soil is ready to be dug when a handful, firmly compressed, crumbles apart readily. If it remains in a sticky mass, with moisture on the surface, it is still too wet.

How can I determine when to begin to work the soil in early spring? A soil is in good mechanical condition for working when after being compacted in your hand it gradually crumbles when the pressure is released. If the form is retained, it's too wet.

How fine should soil be prepared for planting? For seedbeds fine enough so that few lumps remain, else seed covering will be difficult. For large plants, coarse soil is better than fine.

How can I know that my soil is right for growing vegetables and flowers? If the structure is crumbly, the soil is dark; if manure and a complete fertilizer are added, good crops will grow. To make sure, have a soil test made.

The double-edged Dutch or scuffle hoe, used with a back-and-forth sliding motion, is one of the garden's most useful tools.

Is it possible to grow a vegetable garden in soil which had been treated a year ago with arsenate of lead? Yes, unless the application was extremely heavy. Five to 10 lbs. of arsenate of lead to 1,000 sq. ft. will do no harm. Higher amounts may.

Is cultivating—stirring the soil—necessary except to control weeds and grass in such crops as corn and potatoes? Yes, cultivation aids in holding moisture in the soil and in admitting air. (See Introduction.)

Are the rotating types of hand garden cultivators efficient? When the soil is in good condition and weeds are under control, the rotating type of cultivator will maintain that condition better than any other. This tool is useless in the preparation of a seedbed or the fitting of the soil and is very inefficient in lumpy, cloddy, or strong land.

What is the best way to tell if soil is in condition to cultivate? Put a *clean trowel* or spade into your soil. If, when you pull the tool out of the soil, many particles cling to the clean surface, the soil is too wet to be cultivated.

FALLOWING

What is meant by "fallow"? Fallow means plowing the land and allowing it to stand idle with no crop. May be plowed more than once a season.

What is the purpose of fallowing? For the control of weeds by plowing them under. Soil standing idle 1 year stores moisture for next year's crop. For this reason, it is used mostly in arid regions.

DRAINAGE

How can I properly drain a garden that stays wet too long? If the situation cannot be corrected by incorporation of 3 to 4 ins. of

Wet soils are improved by laying tiles to increase drainage—a very simple operation.

sand or cinders, install 3- or 4-in. agricultural drain tile. Set the tile 15 to 18 ins. deep, with the lines 15 to 18 ft. apart. Carry the lines to an open ditch or storm sewer.

What is best way to drain off a 1-acre garden that is too wet? Would some kind of furrow arrangement be sufficient? Would it be better tiled, or drained to storm-water sewer? Installation of tile drains would be the more satisfactory and in the end more economical on such a large plot.

We have so much subsoil water that in winter our ground in spots is continually water-soaked. What can I do to counteract this in spring? Tile drain the lot. (See previous questions.)

How can we provide drainage economically at low end of lot? Water forms in pool during heavy rains. If the situation cannot be corrected by slight modification of the grade, or shallow ditching, install 3- to 4-in. agricultural drain tile.

Our lot is wide, but slopes. At this spot (at the end of the lot) we have "soggy" soil for days after a rain. Is there anything we can do about it? Tile drain the lower end of the lot. Carry the tile to an open ditch or storm sewer if possible. Drain into sump holes if the water cannot be carried off.

I plan a combination vegetable garden and orchard on a very poor site. Since drainage would be expensive to install, would you advise against the project? If drainage is the only drawback, the project should be entirely practical.

COAL ASHES

Will coal ashes help to break up a heavy clay soil? Yes. (See also Clay Soil, this section.)

Can hard-coal stoker cinders be plowed into heavy soil to lighten it without bad effect? Yes; but if any clinkers are present sift them to get fine ashes for use. Clinkers may be used for drainage deep under topsoil.

Are sifted coal ashes good for the flower garden? Sifted coal ashes help, but the particles must be fine; otherwise they do more harm than good.

Will too much coal ashes harm a flower border? We have been covering beds as we take ashes from grate. It is well to let ashes lie out and be washed by rain and weathered for several weeks before use.

Soil in home vegetable garden packs hard when dry. Would coal ashes benefit this condition? Yes, use 1 in. incorporated into top 6 ins. of soil. Screen through a ¼-in. mesh before applying.

What are the benefits from the fine siftings of coal ashes applied to a vegetable garden and mixed with the soil? The mechanical condition is improved, more air is admitted, bacteria work more efficiently, and roots grow faster.

Are sifted coal ashes of any help to a lawn? Doubtful value if applied to surface. If incorporated in lower portion of soil, they would help drainage.

Can coal ashes be used in the garden at the same time bone meal is worked into the soil? Yes, they can be used at the same time, but they should be fine enough to lighten soil.

Do coal ashes affect manures? No. When added to heavy soils a combination of well-rotted manure and screened ashes greatly helps the mechanical condition.

Are coal ashes of any use as a chemical fertilizer? Coal ashes have very little, if any, fertilizer value. They do improve the mechanical condition of most soils.

Do coal ashes help prevent cutworms? To a degree. If a 1-in. layer is placed about bases of plants, cutworms will have difficulty in attacking them.

A couple of years ago I noticed that an acquaintance had dumped his winter's coke ashes in a low spot in back of his yard. In spring he smoothed them out and set his tomato plants there, and they bore a heavy crop of fruit. Is there any plant food in coke ashes that is good for tomatoes? Or was that just an accident that the plants did so well in the ashes? The coke ashes improved the soil aeration, and thus helped produce better growth.

What would you suggest as the best way to reclaim a back yard that has been filled with coal ashes 8 to 10 ins. deep? Topsoil is worth its weight in gold, and hard to get. The dirt near by is acid woodland soil. Remove at least half the ashes and fork in the balance. Then add half-and-half mixture of your woodland soil and *good* topsoil. Apply lime, as needed, to decrease excessive acidity.

Are briquette ashes good for entire garden? I burn briquettes in the fireplace. Yes; for mechanical betterment of the soil, improving its texture.

Will ashes from fireplace, in which some cannel coal has been used, be harmful in garden use? No; but it is better not to use them fresh from the grate.

Can the fine white ash of cannel coal be used to lighten a heavy soil? Yes. (See previous question.)

I understand cannel-coal ashes are strong in phosphorus and potash. Are they suitable to be added to the flowers and vegetable garden? As mechanical aids mostly; they have but little nutrient value.

SOIL ACIDITY

pH

What is the meaning of the symbol pH? See Introduction.

I have several books on flower growing, but none gives the types of soils (acid or alkaline) in which all plants thrive best. Can you give

me this information? No *complete* list has ever been worked out. Of the vast number of plants grown, comparatively few show marked preferences for decidedly acid or alkaline soils. The vast majority exhibit a wide tolerance. (See following questions.)

What plants grow well on acid soils of fair to good fertility (pH 5 to 5.5)?

Arbutus	Ferns	Raspberry
Azalea	Fir	Red Top
Beans	Hemlock	Rhubarb
Bent Grasses	Huckleberry	Rhododendron
Birch, White	Hydrangea (Blue)	Rye
Blackberry	Lily	Serradella
Blueberry	Millet	Soybean
Brussels Sprouts	Oak, Scrub	Spruce
Buckwheat	Oak, Red	Squash
Carrot	Oats	Strawberry
Cabbage	Orchard Grass	Sweet Potato
Cedar, White	Orchid	Tobacco
Cineraria	Parsley	Tomato
Clover, Crimson	Pea	Turnip
Cowpea	Peanut	Vetch, Hairy
Corn	Pepper	Violet
Cranberry	Pine	Watermelon
Cucumber	Plantain	Wintergreen
Cyclamen	Potato	Wheat
Dewberry	Pumpkin	Zinnia
Endive	Radish	

What plants grow better on slightly acid or neutral soils (pH 5.6 to 6.5)?

Beans	Oats	Soybean
Blackberry	Orchard Grass	Squash
Buckwheat	Parsley	Strawberry
Carrot	Pea	Sweet Potato
Cabbage	Pepper	Tobacco
Clover, Crimson	Pumpkin	Tomato
Corn	Radish	Turnip
Cowpea	Red Top	Wintergreen
Cucumber	Rhubarb	Wheat
Endive	Rye	

What plants do not grow well on strongly acid soils, but prefer slightly acid or slightly alkaline soils (pH 6.5 to 7)?

Alfalfa	Aster	Babiesbreath
Apple	Aurora Flower	Barley
Asparagus	Avens	Balsam

Beets
Beggar Weed
Berseem
Blue Grass
Bokhara
Broccoli
Brome Grass
Camomile
Candytuft
Carnation
Cauliflower
Celery
Chard
Cherry
Chicory
Chrysanthemum
Clover, Alsike
Clover, Hungarian
Clover, Japanese
Clover, Mammoth
Clover, Red
Clover, White
Clover, Yellow
Collards
Columbine
Cosmos
Cotton
Currant
Dahlia
Eggplant
Elm, American
Everlasting Pea

Fescue, Sheep's
Fescue, Tall
Flax
Foxglove
Foxtail
Gladiolus
Gooseberry
Grape
Helianthus
Hemp
Horseradish
Hops
Hydrangea (Pink)
Iris
Kale
Kohlrabi
Lady's Finger
Larkspur
Leek
Lentil
Lettuce
Linden, American
Lobelia
Lupine
Mangel Wurzels
Maple
Marigold
Meadow Grass
Meadow Oat
Mignonette
Muskmelon
Nasturtium

Oak, White
Onion
Pansy
Parsnip
Peach
Pear
Peppermint
Petunia
Phlox
Plum
Poppy
Quince, Orange
Rape
Salsify
Sorghum
Spearmint
Speltz
Spinach
Stock
Sunflower
Sweet Alyssum
Sweetpea
Sweet Vernal
Sweetwilliam
Timothy
Vetch
Walnut
Watercress
Willow
Wisteria
Witchazel
Woodbine

ACID

What makes the soil acid? Soil acidity is common in many regions where rainfall is sufficient to leach large proportions of calcium and magnesium out of the soil. The loss of these salts results in a preponderance of acid-forming ions in the soil.

Soils also become acid due to the use of acid-forming fertilizers, such as sulfate of ammonia and ammonium phosphates. The following table shows the relative acidifying or alkalinizing power of various fertilizing, liming, or acidifying materials, rated in terms of commercial limestone (calcium carbonate) as 1.0:

Material	Acidifying	Alkalinizing
Dolomitic Limestone	– –	1.1
Hydrated Lime (Calcite)	– –	1.4
Hydrated Lime (Dolomitic)	– –	1.7
Sodium Nitrate	– –	0.3
Calcium Nitrate	– –	0.2
Potassium Nitrate	– –	0.2
Ammonium Nitrate	0.6	– –
Ammonium Sulfate	1.1	– –
Monoammonium Phosphate	0.6	– –
Diammonium Phosphate	1.1	– –
Urea	0.8	– –
Sulfur	3.1	– –
Ferrous Sulfate	0.4	– –
Aluminum Sulfate	0.5	– –

What is the chemistry involved in the gradual acidification of soils: when lying fallow? When becoming part of the forest floor? In humid regions removal of calcium and magnesium may cause a high concentration of hydrogen ions which results in acidity. This is more apt to happen on the forest floor, because of a greater amount of organic matter and thus greater generation of carbon dioxide.

Where can soil be sent to have its acidity determined? To your State Agricultural Experiment Station, college or university. (See list of Stations, page 1318).

What simple means can be used to detect acid soil? The litmus-paper test is probably the simplest means of detecting soil acidity. A Soil-tex test (with a testing kit made for the purpose) is easily made and more valuable and reliable.

Is moss an indication of acidity? Moss may result as often from a poorly drained condition of the soil, or from heavy shade, as it does from an acid condition.

Testing the soil for acidity is a simple job which any amateur can do with a test kit. Testing for nutrients is more complicated.

Are toadstools an indication of soil acidity? No, they are not.

What will an acid soil produce? Notable among the plants that do best in an acid soil are those of the Ericaceae family, which includes such plants as azalea, rhododendron, leucothoe, pieris, mountain laurel, and others. (See previous question under pH.)

How can an acid soil be neutralized? An acid soil can be neutralized by adding ground limestone. The amount required can be determined by a soil analysis. (See Introduction.)

What is "sour" soil? A "sour" soil is a term sometimes used to denote the condition that develops in a poorly drained soil. More often, as the term is used, it is synonymous with an acid soil.

How can sour soil be sweetened? If by "sour" soil is meant an acid soil, it can be sweetened by adding agricultural ground limestone or other forms of lime.

What can I do to counteract sour soil in seed boxes? The "sour" soil condition in seed flats can be prevented or corrected by providing sufficient drainage. Separate the boards on the bottom of the flat ¼ in., or bore a few holes in the bottom. Raise the flats on bricks or wood strips. "Sourness," in these cases, generally does not mean acidity.

How can a sour soil be treated to produce? If the "sour" soil condition is being caused by poor drainage, it can be corrected by improving drainage. If the sour soil is an acid soil, with a reaction so low that it will not produce satisfactory crops, the condition can be corrected by adding ground limestone.

How may I improve a dry, acid, heavy clay soil? Incorporate a liberal amount of peatmoss, but first mix 10 to 15 pounds of pulverized limestone with each bale of peat before the latter is worked into the soil. Apply additional limestone to the soil if needed.

I am making a vegetable garden on a piece of lawn; the soil is very acid. Will it be worth trying? Since most vegetables will do well on a slightly acid soil, this very acid soil could be changed without undue expense to grow vegetables.

How should I treat a very acid soil in order to grow vegetables? Apply agricultural ground limestone, preferably in the fall, before planting in the spring. Make a second application if necessary. Most vegetables prefer soil that is slightly acid, so there is danger in using too much lime.

What type of fertilizer is used in planting vegetables in acid soil? If the soil is too acid to produce the vegetable crop in mind, apply lime. In addition apply a fertilizer best suited to the particular crop. A 2–10–10 is recommended for most root crops; a 4–12–4 for others.

Is acidity favorable or unfavorable to crabgrass? A highly acid soil is unfavorable to crabgrass. It is difficult to maintain a sufficiently high degree of acidity to discourage crabgrass on the average lawn.

My soil is neutral. Is there any chemical I can add to the soil to make it acid? I wish to try acorns from red oaks, and other things. Finely ground sulfur or aluminum sulfate can be used to make the soil more acid. Red oaks, however, will do well on a neutral soil.

Can the soil in a garden in a limestone country be made permanently acid? No. An acid soil made under such conditions can be maintained only by periodic treatment.

What use is sulfur for soil? How do you use it? Sulfur is used to increase the acidity of the soil. One to 2 lbs. to 100 sq. ft. are needed to lower the soil each ½ pH.

What materials should be used in maintaining an acid-soil garden in a limestone country? Acid peatmoss or oak leafmold, flowers of sulfur and aluminum sulfate.

How should acidifying materials be handled in the development and maintenance of an acid-soil garden in a limestone country? Make provision for perfect drainage of the area. Incorporate a liberal application of peatmoss. Add flowers of sulfur in the quantity, and as often, as soil tests (made at least once a year) indicate that it is necessary.

What are the best kinds of leaves for producing an acid condition in the soil? Leafmold from oak leaves has long been considered the ideal acidifying material for plants requiring an acid soil, such as rhododendrons, azaleas, and laurel. Recent experiments, however, indicate that this assumption is incorrect. Oak-leaf compost increased the pH temporarily, but after 45 days the pH value was higher (*less acid*) than before the application. However, there is no doubt that oak leafmold is beneficial to the growth of the acid-loving plants.

Will you please tell me how to prepare a soil mixture using oak leafmold for growing blueberries? Dig a hole 3 to 4 ft. wide for each plant; incorporate 3 ins. of leafmold in the bottom; mix the soil for filling with ⅓ its bulk of leafmold, and pack tightly around the roots. Keep the surface over the roots mulched heavily with the oak leafmold, or with sawdust.

ALKALINITY

What is the best method for soil reconstruction? Our soil is of a lime structure (moderately alkaline). Our water is hard and slightly chlorinated. Well-rotted manure at the rate of 1 lb. to a sq. ft. and 2½ lbs. of superphosphate for each 100 sq. ft. This should be thoroughly mixed with the soil. Sow green-manure crops in the fall. Use an acid commercial fertilizer for plants.

What is the best way to counteract highly alkaline soil? Sulfur or aluminum sulfate is used for the purpose. A soil with pH 8 (alkaline) will require 4 lbs. of sulfur to 100 sq. ft. to make it slightly acid (pH 6), or 10 lbs. of aluminum sulfate for the same area. Aluminum sulfate acts much more quickly than sulfur, but in acid soils may do damage unless phosphates are present in sufficient quantity. See question "what makes the soil acid."

Would like to know what grows best in alkaline soil. What will counteract too much alkali? Very few plants do well in strongly alkaline soil. Use sulfur or aluminum sulfate for acidification.

What plants like slightly alkaline soil? See question under pH.

Our soil and water are alkaline. How can I keep a small bed for fringed gentians acid? An acid-soil condition may be maintained by the periodic application of flowers of sulfur or aluminum sulfate.

We have alkaline soil. I succeed with most flowers but not with gladiolus. The bulbs rot. What is the reason? (Washington.) Gladiolus plants do better in slightly acid soil—acidify it with sulfur and use acid-forming fertilizer.

Our soil has considerable alkali in it. For that reason I have hesitated about trying to raise ladyslippers. What can I do to grow these? Leafmold acidified with sulfur will produce satisfactory growth. Acid peatmoss mixed with leafmold will also do.

What will improve an alkaline soil for growing garden peas (early spring)? The use of sulfur of aluminum sulfate will reduce alkalinity.

What vegetables will grow in alkali ground? No vegetables grow well in highly alkaline soil. The most tolerant of alkalinity are asparagus, beet, lima bean, cauliflower, muskmelon, parsnip, and spinach. (See question under pH.)

Can any chemical be used to correct alkali in soil? My soil is heavy and moist. The best methods of control for such conditions consist of (1) providing a soil mulch to retard evaporation, and (2) applications of gypsum if the soil needs calcium; or sulfur, if it need to be acidified.

I have had much difficulty in growing flowers and plants, as many turn yellow. (Soil has been diagnosed by county agent as highly alkaline.) Why? Poor drainage may cause accumulation of alkaline salts. Apply iron sulfate at 1 to 2 lbs. per 100 sq. ft. More than 1 application may be necessary.

What can one add to alkali water to make it suitable for irrigation on a small garden plot? (Kansas.) Water may be acidified by sulfuric, phosphoric acid, or other acids. This should be done, however, only on the advice of your Agricultural Experiment Station.

LIME

What are the functions of lime in soil improvement? Lime furnishes calcium which is needed for root development, strengthening of cell walls, and for formation of protoplasm and proteins; counteracts acidity; hastens decomposition of organic matter; aids in development of nitrogen-fixing bacteria; reduces toxicity of certain compounds.

What type of lime should be used in the garden? Agricultural lime is the slowest but the most lasting. Several weeks may pass before its effect on soil is noticed. Hydrated and burned lime are much quicker in action, but tend to destroy humus. One hundred lbs. of ground limestone is equivalent in action to 74 lbs. of hydrated lime, or 56 lbs. of burned lime. The amounts to use will vary with the acidity of the soil. Usually 2 lbs. of agricultural limestone per 100 sq. ft. is sufficient, unless soils are extremely acid.

What is raw ground limestone? Raw ground limestone is calcium carbonate, and is the material most commonly used for counteracting acidity.

What is agricultural lime? Raw ground limestone.

What is hydrated lime? Hydrated or slaked lime is formed from burned or quicklime (calcium oxide) and water. Hydrated and burned or quicklime are quicker acting than ground limestone (calcium carbonate).

What is "slaked" lime? This is the same as hydrated lime.

What is quicklime? This is another term used for burned lime (calcium oxide). This form of lime should *not* be used in the garden, as it destroys humus, and is toxic when in contact with roots.

Is lime the only material with which to sweeten an acid soil? Some form of lime is usually used to correct soil acidity. The most commonly used forms are ground limestone, dolomitic limestone, and hydrated lime. Other materials that may be used are calcium cyanamide and wood ashes.

Can dry lime, left over from plastering a room, be used in any way as a fertilizer? It may be used to alkalize acid soil, but is apt to be too coarse and lumpy. If lime is needed, apply it in the fall.

Would lime, such as I can purchase at the hardware store, be good for acid soil? Yes. Use a pulverized limestone for this purpose.

Can marl be used in the place of lime, with the same, or as good, results? Marl (a natural deposit of calcium-bearing clay) is coarse, and its effect is very gradual and slow. Ordinarily, lime is both less expensive and much more satisfactory.

What is "overliming" injury? Too much calcium (lime) in the soil causes the soil to become alkaline. Some elements as boron, manganese, zinc, etc., are not soluble in an alkaline solution, and because they are needed in small amounts by plants, poor growth develops. Usually the growth is chlorotic (yellow). Overliming can be corrected by applying sulfur to the soil at 1 lb. per 100 sq. ft. More than one application may be necessary to bring about the desired acidity.

When and under what conditions should lime be added to the soil? Only when the soil is too acid for plants, and when calcium is low.

When, and when not, should lime be used around flowers and shrubs? Use lime only if the soil is so acid as to require correction. Use lime if calcium is lacking and the soil is acid. Use gypsum (calcium sulfate) when calcium is lacking and the soil is alkaline.

What is gypsum? A mineral composed of calcium sulfate which contains 2 molecules of water. Used in horticulture to add needed calcium to the soil when it is not necessary to decrease acidity. It is also used to improve the physical condition of soils and, under some conditions, to improve drainage and soil aeration.

Is lime needed to improve a gravelly soil? Have soil tested; it may not need it.

How can lime benefit clay soil, if the soil is originally composed of disintegrated limestone? As stated by some authorities, benefit is obtained by cementing finer particles into larger ones. The flocculation (cementing of particles) of clay soils as a result of liming has been questioned.

When lightening clay soil with coal ashes, should pH be corrected by addition of lime? In any case low pH (acid) can be corrected by additions of lime.

Should a garden be treated with lime in the fall or spring? If ground limestone is used, it is best applied in the fall, but may be applied in spring. Hydrated lime should be mixed in the spring.

How much lime should be used (for one application)? Two lbs. per 100 sq. ft.

Is it necessary to put lime on the garden every year? Lime should be used only on acid soils. If needed, apply agricultural lime in the fall; hydrated lime in the spring. Usually 2 lbs. per 100 sq. ft. is sufficient.

Can lime be strewn over the ground in winter with the snow? Yes, although it is better to apply early in the fall.

When rotted manure is put on garden in spring, will a coat of ground limestone affect the manure in any way? Not if pulverized limestone is used.

Why is it harmful to put Vigoro and lime into the soil at the same time? What chemical reaction takes place? If lime is allowed to come into contact with superphosphate of fertilizer, the solubility, and hence the availability, of the latter may be reduced, especially in a non-acid or slightly acid soil. In soils that are acid, there is no objection to the application of fertilizer and lime at the same time, providing they are well incorporated into the soil.

When leaves are spaded in, in the fall, should lime be used in the spring?   Most leaves do not produce an acid reaction, so that liming is not necessary unless your soil is naturally acid.

What crops need lime in the soil, and which do better without it? *Legumes* do better in neutral or slightly alkaline soils, hence lime additions are often necessary. *Acid-tolerant plants* like azaleas, rhododendrons, etc., need no lime although they need calcium. (See questions under pH.) For most plants lime should be applied only when the soil is very acid, since they do best in *slightly* acid soil (6. to 6.5 pH.).

Instead of sand, I put very fine limestone on my soil, which has a preponderance of gumbo. It has made soil nice to work with. Will this small amount be apt to affect garden annuals and perennials? I have also added a great deal of barnyard fertilizer.   Small amounts of lime can do no harm. The change in the soil structure was probably due to the manure rather than to the lime.

In foundation planting, if cedars (which require acid soil) are used I assume it is possible that lime coming loose from building and washing into soil may have disastrous effect on such acid-loving plants as azaleas and rhododendrons. Is this so?   There is rarely much lime in the soil from this source. However, any chunks of plaster should be removed. If soil seems alkaline, apply flowers of sulfur at 2 to 4 lbs. per 100 sq. ft. Sulfur is an acidifying agent.

Should I sprinkle my lawn with lime in the fall?   If soil needs lime, it will be most effective when applied in the fall. In acid soil areas, periodic applications of limestone are recommended.

Will lime put on lawn on which oak and dogwood trees are growing injuriously affect such trees?   Not unless excessive amounts are used. Have the soil tested and apply limestone only when needed.

My soil is covered with white-pine needles from adjacent trees. Should this make additional liming or other treatment advisable? Pine needles produce acidity, hence constant use of lime may be required to counteract this condition.

Sewage sludge is very acid from aluminum sulfate. Is lime the proper neutralizer, or does it leave the valuable plant and soil bacteria elements in a non-desirable form?   Sewage sludge does not necessarily contain aluminum sulfate. If it does, lime is a good corrective; or superphosphate may be used.

When vegetable soil is too acid, as ascertained by laboratory test, how much lime should be applied to overcome a state of hyperacidity? The amount of lime required will vary with the degree of acidity and with the texture of the soil. In general, the following amounts will be required, per 1,000 sq. ft., to raise the soil from pH 5.5 to 6.5:

	Sandy Loams	Loams	Clay Loams
Pulverized Limestone	40 lbs.	85 lbs.	125 lbs.
Hydrated Lime	25 lbs.	60 lbs.	90 lbs.

I am planning to plant a small vegetable plot. Can one add too much lime? Lime should not be added, unless a test shows it is needed. Decidedly it can be overdone.

SOIL TESTING

What is the best method of determining the treatment a given soil requires? Test your soil; or have it tested. Your county agent or State Agricultural or Experiment Station will do this for you.

What is the approximate cost of having soil analyzed? It varies. A few states make no charge, but most charge $0.75 to $1.00.

What is the difference between soil analysis and a soil test? A *complete soil analysis* includes the total elements—those available to plants, and the reserve held in the soil in unavailable forms. A *microchemical soil test* gives an approximation of *available* elements only.

Does the test, or the analysis, give more information? The test is more practical than the complete analysis. It is valuable as indicator of needs, but does not tell the exact amounts to apply. However, an experienced soil tester is able to indicate what to apply, and how much.

Are the chemistry sets on the market practical? Many of the soil-testing kits are satisfactory and practical if intelligently used.

Are there any tests available for amateurs to make which will determine soil acidity and alkalinity without sending samples away? Yes, there are several outfits on the market which are simple to use. Write your Agricultural Experiment Station for information covering them.

Could you please tell me how to make an inexpensive soil-test kit? It would be safer, and probably cheaper, to buy a soil-testing kit.

Can I learn the true nature of the soil from a test? Yes. A good soil-testing kit will give acidity, nitrates, phosphates, potassium, calcium, etc.

Where can soil tests be made? What fee charged? What size sample desired? Your Agricultural Experiment Station will test your soil—usually for a small fee. Send ½ pint of soil, taken from at least 10 places. Sample the soil to a depth of at least 6 inches in each of the

10 places. Mix the various samples together in a bucket and send about ½ pint of this composite soil in a tight container.

How can I obtain information on soil analysis without the necessity of taking a course in chemistry?   Write to your Agricultural Experiment Station for information on soil testing. Several stations have published bulletins on this subject.

After testing, how can I know what to add to soil, in what quantities, and when?   Without experience in testing, one cannot tell from a soil test just what kinds of quantities of fertilizers to use. Send your sample to your Agricultural Experiment Station. All fertilizers contain analysis on each bag.

Which soil should I send for analysis? Soil screened last fall and stored in cellar, or fresh soil as soon as frost is out of it?   Send stored soil, or else wait until outdoor soil warms up, before taking sample.

How can we determine what vegetable or fruit a soil is best suited to produce?   The best procedure is to consult your local county agricultural agent.

Should untilled soil be analyzed to determine its fertility?   Yes.

Should I have my soil tested to determine its acidity?   If plants grown do well, it is not necessary. It is desirable to have periodic tests of soils which are used to grow plants that require specific soil reactions, such as rhododendrons and azaleas.

If the ground is poor, how can one tell what is lacking in the soil?   By having a soil sample analyzed.

Can soil condition be determined by what is found growing on it, such as wild blueberries and sour-grass? Can soil with fine shell stone be good?   Yes. For example, blueberries indicate acid soil; dandelions alkaline soil. Too much lime from shells may be detrimental to some plants.

PLANT NUTRIENTS

ELEMENTS OF PLANT NUTRITION

What are the various elements of plant nutrition; and their uses?
The 3 most important essential elements for plant growth, and their effect on plant growth, are as follows: *Nitrogen:* this element enters into the structure of protoplasm, chlorophyll, and various plant foods; it is needed for both the vegetative and reproductive stages of growth; its use is usually manifested by an increase in vegetative growth. *Phosphorus:* it is essential to cell division and for the formation of nucleoproteins; it aids root development; hastens maturity, or stiffens tissues; and stimulates flower and seed production. *Potash:* this element is necessary for the manufacture and translocation of starches

and sugar; it is a general conditioner, overcoming succulence and brittleness, hastening maturity and seed production, and aiding in root development.

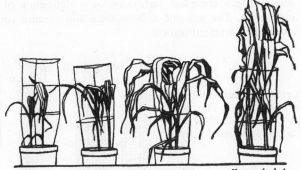

Nitrogen, phosphorus, and potassium are all needed for normal plant growth. Of the four pots of corn above, the first (left) lacked nitrogen; the second, phosphorus; the third, potassium. The one on the right was supplied with all three.

NITROGEN

How can I recognize nitrogen deficiency? The whole plant is dwarfed and the older leaves turn from green to yellow, and then to brown, and remain attached to the plant. Stalks are slender, and few new stalks develop.

How can nitrogen deficiency be corrected? Apply ammonium sulfate at ¾ lb. or sodium nitrate at 1 lb. per 100 sq. ft. A complete fertilizer (as 4–12–4, or 5–10–5) will correct the deficiency of nitrogen as well as supply phosphorus and potash.

What is lacking in my garden soil, since the carrots I raise, though of good size, are almost tasteless and colorless? Nitrogen is lacking; a complete fertilizer (4–12–4, or 5–10–5) at 4 lbs. per 100 sq. ft. will correct this.

What causes yellowing of foliage? It may be due to poor drainage, or to lack of nitrogen.

What shall I do for soil that grows annuals and perennials too large and weedy, but weak-stemmed? Probably too much nitrogen in the soil and not enough phosphorus and potassium. Use a 0–10–10 fertilizer, or something similar, 2 lbs. per 100 sq. ft.

All foliage and few flowers is my trouble. What is wrong? Too much nitrogen and probably not enough phosphorus and potash; add both in the form of a 0–10–10 fertilizer (or similar) at rate of 2 lbs. per 100 sq. ft.

What causes an excess of nitrogen in the soil? Have added 10 lbs. of

bone meal in a 35-sq.-ft. bed for annuals, and some Bovung (100 lbs.) for spring. Excess nitrogen, or the symptoms of excess nitrogen, may be brought about through the excessive use of nitrogenous fertilizers, high-nitrogen complete fertilizers, or a deficiency of phosphorus and potash. The amount of bone meal and manure you have applied constitutes overfertilization.

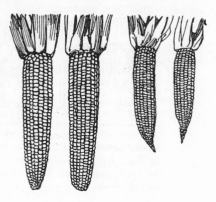

Potash is especially important for fruit and grain crops. The two ears of corn at the right show the result of potash (potassium) deficiency.

PHOSPHORUS

How can I recognize phosphorus deficiency? The whole plant is dwarfed, but the foliage is a dark, dull green; leaf stem (petiole) often turns purple. Areas between veins on leaf sometimes turn purple, and leaf margins often turn yellow. Loss of lower foliage follows.

How can phosphorus deficiency be corrected? Apply treble superphosphate or superphosphate, at 5 lbs. per 100 sq. ft. Bone meal is too slow acting to be of immediate benefit.

POTASH

How can I recognize potash (potassium) deficiency? Lower foliage begins to turn yellow at leaf margin; leaf often mottled yellow and green in between veins; margins of leaves turn brown and foliage drops from plant; plant generally stunted.

How can potash (potassium) deficiency be corrected? Apply muriate of potash or sulfate of potash, 1 lb. per 100 sq. ft.

What fertilizer should I use to encourage fruits and vegetable roots? Plants grow all to tops. Withhold nitrogen and increase the proportion of phosphorus and potash in the mixture. Use a 2–10–10 fertilizer for a few years, adding additional nitrogen only where, and as, needed.

Some soils tend to develop barren vines. What is lacking? This is usually the result of too little phosphorus and potash.

What does soil lack that produces an abundant crop of any vegetable above ground, but no root vegetables such as potatoes, beets, turnips, or salsify? Phosphorus and potassium are probably deficient in this soil. (See previous questions.)

My garden is made of filled earth and has a large amount of street sweepings in it, high in leafmold. All root crops fail; beans and corn are only crops that succeed. Why? Have soil tested; lack of phosphorus and potassium may cause the trouble.

TRACE ELEMENTS

What are "trace" elements? Elements (present in most soils) which are needed in very small amounts, for plant nutrition. Some of these are present in such small quantities that they are known as trace elements (see discussion page 6).

What are the principal trace elements? Boron, chlorine, copper, iron, manganese, zinc, and molybdenum.

Is boron a necessary ingredient in all types of soils? A small amount of boron is essential for plant growth, and to prevent various physiological disorders. It is present in most soils in sufficient quantity. It is most apt to be deficient in soils low in organic matter.

How should boron be used in the soil? Boron is commonly applied in the form of borax, at the rate of 10 to 15 lbs. *per acre*. This is only 4 to 5 ozs. per 1,000 sq. ft.

How can I be sure that my soil will have enough sodium for good growth of beets? Use ½ to 1 lb. nitrate of soda, or ½ lb. table salt, per 100 sq. ft.

My garden soil turns a red color on top when dry; why? The red color probably is due to a surface growth of red algae. These minute plants do no harm and are often found on moist soils. They go unnoticed until the soil surface dries and their red color is then apparent by contrast.

Are iron or steel filings beneficial in darkening colors of perennials, especially roses and lilacs? No. Iron sulfate (copperas) is beneficial where iron in soil is low; chiefly useful in greening foliage, not darkening flower color.

Do the nutrients in dolomite and basic slag leach from the soil? Magnesium from dolomite and phosphorus from basic slag move very slowly in the soil, so there is little loss from leaching.

HUMUS

What is humus? For practical purposes, humus may be defined as the resultant brown or dark-brown substance that develops following the breakdown of organic materials by various soil organisms.

How does one recognize the different types of humus, such as peat, leafmold, muck, etc?   *Peat:* soft, brown, spongy, semigranular material; domestic peats, unless kiln dried, contain more water than the imported type. *Muck:* black, represents further state of decay than peat—not so useful. *Bacterized Peat:* supposedly treated; usually no better than muck. *Leafmold:* brownish-black material with some undecomposed leaves and twigs present; useful soil conditioner. *Wood soil:* usually leafmold, but further decomposed; useless without additions of fertilizer.

In what forms is humus available to the average amateur home gardener?   See previous question. Manure, straw, peatmoss, kitchen waste, hay—all these must decompose before becoming humus. The compost pile (which see) is probably the best of all sources of humus for the home garden.

What is the function of humus in the soil?   Among the important functions of humus are to effect granulation of the soil, thereby improving drainage and soil aeration; to increase its water-holding capacity; to increase the bacterial activity; to increase the percentage of such essential elements as nitrogen and sulfur; and to help in transforming essential elements from non-available to available forms.

Is humus important to soil fertility?   Yes; by increasing moisture absorption and the activity of several of the essential elements, especially nitrogen.

How is humus incorporated into the soil?   By spading or plowing.

Is spring or fall the best time to add humus to soil?   In the fall preferably, but it may be added at any time.

Our soil is rich but hard to work. What is the best source of humus?   Manure, peatmoss, or a compost heap.

What method do you recommend to maintain humus and bacteria in soils?   Keep soils aerated by the addition of manures. Use green-manure crops (which see) wherever possible.

What is to be done when humus keeps the earth too moist?   Incorporate sand or cinders.

What would you recommend to keep a very rich black soil from caking? It forms a hard crust about an inch deep.   Add humus—manure, peat, alfalfa hay. Incorporate fine cinders in the top 6 ins.

What causes soil to become very hard?   Lack of organic matter.

A bog was dug up to make a lake; stuff removed looks like excellent humus. How can this material be converted to garden use?   The material should make an excellent mulch, or to mix with soil. Unless soil on which this is used is very acid, the acidity of the humus will have no detrimental effect. If the material is lumpy, place in small piles to dry; pulverize before applying.

Do commercial fertilizers supply humus? The application of organic fertilizers such as soybean and cottonseed meals supplies a very small amount of humus. The inorganic fertilizers do not supply humus.

PEATMOSS

What is the difference in value between peatmoss and peat? Between domestic and imported peat? Peatmoss is moss (usually sphagnum) in an advanced state of disintegration; peat is a product of some kind of vegetation (not necessarily moss) largely decomposed. Domestic peat is usually of sedge origin, although we have some sphagnum peat in this country. Imported peat is usually sphagnum peat.

What is peatmoss good for? Is manure good to mix with it? Peatmoss makes an excellent mulch. It adds acidity to soils, holds moisture, adds organic matter. When it breaks down, it adds nitrogen. Peat and manure make an excellent combination.

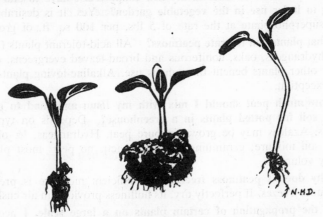

Humus in the soil absorbs and holds moisture, encouraging fibrous root growth. Center seedling above was grown in a half-soil, half-peatmoss mixture; the others in plain soil.

Does peat have any value as a fertilizer? Yes. Domestic sedge peat contains up to 3 per cent nitrogen, which becomes available slowly. Sphagnum peat ("peatmoss") contains less than 1 per cent nitrogen. It is slower in availability than the sedge peat.

Is peatmoss good for flower gardens in general? Yes. When dug into the soil, it helps retain moisture, and in other ways increases productiveness.

When is the best time to use peatmoss—spring or autumn? Apply the peat as a mulch in the fall, and work into the soil in the spring.

Is it true that peatmoss worked into the soil will make a heavy soil lighter and will cause a light soil to hold more moisture? Yes. In this respect its action is similar to that of manure.

As a winter protection is peatmoss considered as good as straw or leaves? This depends upon what is to be mulched. It mats down too much for some plants, such as delphiniums, foxgloves, campanulas, etc. For roses and most shrubs, and especially for rhododendrons and azaleas, it is excellent. The cost is much higher than for leaves, straw, or similar materials.

What is the best way to use peatmoss in flower gardens and on old lawns? In flower gardens apply as a mulch, and later work it into the bed. A thin covering on lawns is beneficial in the fall.

Is putting peatmoss around flowers in the fall harmful? My chrysanthemums seem to be dying. Not if applied only 1 to 2 ins. deep, unless continuous rains make such an application undesirable. Peat holds moisture.

I use peatmoss as litter in my hen coop. Will I have to add anything to it for use in the vegetable garden? Yes. It is desirable to add superphosphate at the rate of 5 lbs. per 100 sq. ft. of ground.

What plants can tolerate peatmoss? All acid-tolerant plants (azaleas, hydrangeas, oaks, coniferous and broad-leaved evergreens, etc.). Most other plants benefit through its use. Alkaline-loving plants are the exception.

How much peat should I mix with my loam and sand to get a good soil for potted plants in a greenhouse? Depends on type of plants. Azaleas may be grown in pure peat. Hydrangeas, ½ of the total soil mixture; geraniums, no peat; cacti, no peat; most plants, ¼ by volume.

Why doesn't peatmoss freeze? If sufficient moisture is present, peatmoss freezes. If perfectly dry, its fluffiness provides an air cushion.

In the propagation of certain plants on a large scale, I need to have about ¼ of my soil mixture consist of peatmoss. Is there any suitable substitute that could be found in the South Carolina low country? Shredded sugar cane, shredded redwood bark, or decomposed pine needles.

What is the best substitute for peatmoss? Sedge peat, bagasse (sugar cane pulp), leafmold, pine needles, shredded redwood bark, ground barks of most trees, and sawdust used in smaller amounts than peat.

MANURES

What does a ton of manure mean in terms of yards? A ton of manure is approximately a cubic yard, and will cover about 2,000 sq. ft., 2 ins. thick. However, the weight per yard varies greatly with the moisture content.

When purchasing manure, should it be bought dry, damp, or wet? If it is in good shape, the drier the better; otherwise you are paying for water.

How is it possible to store well-rotted manure without losing valuable properties by leaching? Keep under cover, on a concrete

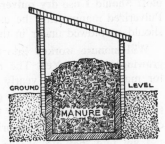

Manure keeps best under cover. A concrete or brick-lined pit, with protecting board roof, will prevent loss of valuable nutrients which manure heap rots down for garden use.

floor. Add superphosphate to it, and keep moist. If no cover is available, stack in piles 4 ft. deep with perpendicular sides. To secure even decomposition, turn the manure pile 2 or 3 times during year.

Where and how should manure be stored to rot? Preferably in a pit of concrete, or on a concrete floor, with a roof over it. Keep moist to prevent firing. Turn every 2 or 3 months.

If there is a roof over a manure pit, will the fresh manure heat up and perhaps cause a fire from spontaneous combustion? I am told the manure is better if roofed over. A roof over a manure pit is desirable. The manure will not burn if kept moist. If there is any sign of its heating badly, turn it "inside out." (It will not start a fire, though the manure itself may "burn out.")

How long should manure be rotted before use? Depends entirely upon the temperature and other conditions. Usually 6 months.

Are pine shavings harmful when mixed in manure? No; but they should be thoroughly decomposed.

I have cow, horse, sheep, and chicken manure. Could you tell me the best way to use them, on vegetables, shrubs, and flowers? Mix the cow and horse manure, allow to decay, and use in the spring. If fresh, plow under in the fall. The sheep and poultry manure (which see) may better be handled separately, because of their high nitrogen content.

Should garden soil be fertilized with barnyard manure every year? Yes, if the manure is available.

How much manure should be spread over the garden each year? A coating about 2 ins. thick.

How is manure applied to the unplanted garden? Apply at the rate of 600 lbs. per 1,000 sq. ft. and plow or dig under in the fall.

Should fresh or half-rotted manure be dug into the ground in the fall, or should the ground be dug first and then the fresh or half-rotted manure spread on the ground for the winter and dug under in the spring? Spread over the surface and spade it under in the fall.

Is the middle of March a good time to put manure on a vegetable plot? Should I use dry pulverized (Bovung) or fresh stable manure? Pulverized manure may be used in the spring. Fresh stable manure should be plowed under in the fall.

Will manure worked into the ground this fall help beyond one growing season? Yes. The residual effect of manure may remain for many seasons. A yearly application is advisable nevertheless.

What is the best fertilizer to put over a vegetable garden during the winter, for turning under in the spring? Manure. Withhold the commercial fertilizers until spring.

I am told that old garden soils are often deficient in minerals, resulting in the same lack of minerals in vegetables grown in same. Does barnyard manure supply minerals? Not in sufficient amounts. A complete fertilizer should be used in addition to the manure.

I made a new garden, size 50 × 12. As fertilizer I used about 10 bu. of chicken manure and 16 bu. of mushroom manure. Do you think this is enough fertilizer for this plot? Yes; in fact, you have overfertilized. You have applied considerably more nitrogen and potash but less phosphorus than would be incorporated if a 4–12–4 fertilizer was applied.

Is manure necessary for FLOWER gardens if a complete fertilizer is added to the soil several times a year? Yes. Manure has other properties besides fertilizer value. If manure is not available, add humus or green manure (which see) yearly.

I fertilize my GARDEN with Vigoro, and continually add humus in form of oak leaves, vegetable tops, and peelings. Is manure also necessary? Weeds are so much worse when I use manure, but I want to keep the soil built up. If you maintain the humus content without manure, its application is unnecessary.

Can barnyard manure be put on young GRASS in the fall without injury? Do not use manure on lawns, except when preparing soil for seeding, or unless it is dried and pulverized.

Should barnyard fertilizer be used in ROSE beds? Yes. Use when making the beds originally, and as a mulch each winter. The mulch is worked into the ground in the spring.

Should manure, used to fertilize single PLANTS or BULBS, be placed in the holes where they are to be planted? In such cases use well-rotted manure only. Place in the hole, cover with 2 ins. of soil, then plant.

CAT AND DOG MANURE

Are cat and dog manure helpful to soil, or the opposite? They have some fertilizing value, but are best when composted with other materials.

I expect to have a dog kennel soon. Could I use dog manure for fertilizing a flower garden? Yes. (See previous question.)

CHICKEN MANURE

Is chicken manure harmful to plants? No. On the contrary, it is very beneficial, as it is high in available nitrogen. It should be used sparingly.

How can chicken droppings be used as fertilizer? Allow to dry for a few weeks, under cover, and thus lose some of the quick-acting ammonium. Mixed with peat or litter, chicken manure is safe to use; but apply in small quantities.

Will you tell me how to use chicken fertilizer? How to determine when it is old? Mix with soil or peat, half and half. When odor of ammonium is dissipated, *unmixed* chicken manure is safe to use in small quantities.

In using chicken manure for fertilizer, how is it applied? Ten to 20 lbs. of dried or well-rotted chicken manure per 100 sq. ft. if broadcast just before, or at time of, planting. Or a half trowelful or so, mixed in the planting hole, for setting out individual plants.

When can one use chicken manure most effectively for results in gardening? See previous question. If at all fresh, apply to the soil several weeks before planting.

Can you please give me a formula for a well-balanced fertilizer, using poultry manure to supply nitrogen? It is difficult, mechanically, to mix animal manures with chemical fertilizers. Better apply separately. The following may be used: to 100 sq. ft. apply 15 lbs. poultry manure, 3 lbs. superphosphate, ½ lb. potassium chloride.

Have 15 hens and clean the dropping-board every day, then spread superphosphate over dropping-board. Is it proper to save the manure in iron barrel? Yes, saving in a container will reduce leaching. Keep dry.

Is it necessary to use commercial fertilizer if I use manure from 200 chickens? Yes. You would have to add superphosphate and potash, unless very large amounts of manure were used, in which case there would be an excess of nitrogen.

I am collecting quite a bit of chicken manure, mixed with sawdust,

and keeping it piled throughout the winter. **What way can I get the best use of it for my lawn and garden? What value has it?** This should make an excellent fertilizer for the garden, but not for the lawn—the sawdust would be objectionable. Apply in the spring or fall at the rate of 5 to 10 lbs. per 100 sq. ft.

Is it good practice to use poultry manure and goat manure, mixed with wood shavings, as litter? There is no objection to the use of wood shavings for litter. They decay slowly, and because of that are not so satisfactory for soil improvement as other forms of litter mixed with manures.

Is a mixture of chicken manure and peatmoss all right to topdress a lawn in winter? (New Jersey.) Yes, very satisfactory; but it would be better not to apply until March.

Can chicken manure be mixed with wood ashes? Do not use together if manure is fresh. Otherwise, the combination is good.

What proportion of chicken manure should be mixed with wood ashes? Mix ashes and chicken manure at 3-to-1 ratio.

How can leaves and poultry manure be prepared for fertilizer in the flower garden? Layer of leaves 12 ins. deep; layer of poultry manure 1 in. deep; sprinkling of complete fertilizer; water well. Repeat until heap is 4 ft. high; water frequently. In 3 months turn "inside out."

Is compost containing chicken manure too strong for most plants? Not if it is well decomposed.

Is chicken manure containing approximately 30 per cent screened sand, 50 per cent ground sugar cane, and 20 per cent droppings suitable for young APPLE trees (not in bearing) on a sandy loam? Yes, excellent.

Would hen manure used on CORN and TOMATOES force them into bearing early, and then cause them to die? The high nitrogen of poultry manure would produce heavy vegetative growth at first, which would affect the corn and would make tomatoes late in setting fruit. It should not hasten death of the plants.

Is chicken manure a good fertilizer for the FLOWER garden? If so, if a year old is it still O.K. to use? It is safer when a year old than when fresh. Very satisfactory for the flower garden. Use at rate of 10 to 20 lbs. per 100 sq. ft.

Can poultry manure be used to good effect on GARDEN ground, especially where potatoes are to be grown? Poultry manure cannot be applied so heavily as barnyard manure. It would be too costly, and would contain too much nitrogen. For potatoes, on a small scale, it would probably be best to apply as a side dressing, when plants are a few inches high, at rate of 8 to 10 lbs. per 100 ft. of row.

I am using old chicken manure on ROSEBUSHES. Can you tell me how much of it to put on each bush? If it is well rotted, 1 to 2 shovelfuls per plant.

Can poultry compost be used on anything other than ROSES and PANSIES? Yes, in small quantities it may be used on any crop. It is especially good for leaf crops, such as lettuce or cabbage.

What can I do for my garden soil that has had too much chicken droppings put on it for several years? Now nothing grows. Apply lime at 5 lbs. per 100 sq. ft. and then water heavily several times. Then spade and add superphosphate at 5 lbs. per 100 sq. ft.

COW MANURE

What is the best all-purpose manure for the garden? Well-rotted cow manure.

Is horse manure or cow manure better for gardens? Fresh horse manure contains more ammonium than cow manure and is apt to "burn out" more readily. Well-rotted cow manure is usually not so badly leached and burned as horse manure. So in general cow manure is preferred. If both are available, the horse manure could be used for earliest spring crops.

Which is the best dressing for flowers, hen manure or cow manure? Cow manure is safer; hen manure is richer, especially in nitrogen.

How can you test cow manure for strength? There is no simple test for this purpose. Manure that has become well decomposed under cover will contain the most nutrients per ton—it has become concentrated. When stored outside and leached by rains, it will lose much of its nutrient value.

How should cow manure be treated to be applied to a garden? Keep under cover and on cement floor to prevent leaching. Do not allow to dry out. It makes better fertilizer when well rotted.

Is cow or horse manure preferred to commercial fertilizers? If so, why? Manures are not balanced fertilizers. Usually additions of phosphates are needed with manures. One ton of manure contains 10 lbs. nitrogen, 5 lbs. phosphate, 10 lbs. potassium. These become available slowly. A complete commercial fertilizer is more quickly available, and 110 lbs. of it would give as much nutrition as a ton of manure. However, manure is valuable because of organic matter, water-holding capacity, addition of bacteria and other organisms to soil, help in changing unavailable materials to available, earlier warming of soil in spring. Thus best results are had when both manure and fertilizers are employed.

Should I use cow manure and oak leaves for my entire garden? Yes; this will prove a good general fertilizer for most plants. It would, however, be still better if supplemented by chemicals. (See previous question.)

On what, and when, should cow manure be used? On almost any plants. Dig under in the fall. Use as a mulch in the fall. Use as a mulch during summer if you don't mind appearance.

Is it better to leave cattle manure on the ground all winter, or should it be turned under and the ground plowed or spaded up again the following spring? Plow the manure under in the fall. Disk or hoe the ground in spring.

If I plow under fresh cow manure in the spring and then plant, is there any danger of crops burning? No, but for a period there will be stoppage of growth. This is due to the fact that while manure is decomposing the bacteria causing this action deplete the soil of nitrogen at the expense of the plants. This can be offset, however, by applying a side dressing of nitrate of soda, chicken manure, or some other quick-acting, high-nitrogen fertilizer.

When fresh cow manure is put on the land, is there any material to add to it so it will rot faster? Use lime on it.

Will cow manure be helpful to EVERGREENS? Yes. Apply when well rotted only. The best time is fall, so that the manure will serve a double purpose—mulch and nutrition. Can be worked into the soil in the spring.

Is cow manure (if well rotted) safe to put around RHODODEN-DRONS? Yes, but if worked into the soil, sulfur or aluminum sulfate may have to be added.

Is cow manure suitable for SHRUBS and LAWNS? For trees and shrubs, yes. For lawns, no. It is likely to infest the lawns with weeds.

Is it advisable to spread rotted manure over a planted TULIP bed, or over a perennial bed after frost? It is better not to use manure on a tulip bed. For mulching purposes, well-rotted manure is too costly and is apt to pack. If used, 4 ins. in depth is needed. Straw or corn fodder will answer the mulching purpose better.

DRIED MANURE

I planted a small vegetable garden of about 2,000 sq. ft. I plan to enrich soil with a compost and Bovung (dried rotted cow manure) this year. How much should be used? At least 100 lbs. of dried cow manure should be used to 1,000 sq. ft. If you can afford it, triple the amount.

I am no longer able to get barnyard fertilizer for my garden plot. Is there a commercial fertilizer that I can procure? "Commercial" (dried and ground) cow manure and sheep manure are available. Incorporate green manures, and, in addition, apply a 4–12–4 fertilizer.

Under what conditions can dried manure be used in place of rotted manure? Only when well-rotted stable manure cannot be obtained.

GOAT MANURE

Can a garden have too much goat manure? Goat manure is reasonably strong in nitrogen. It should be used in about the same way as described for sheep manure.

Should goat manure and straw be put on frozen ground, or put in compost heap until spring? Better in compost heap, if mixed with other materials, otherwise, it would be better to spread the manure and straw on the ground. If left in a pile, some leaching will take place, and not on the spot where wanted.

GUANO

What is guano? Guano is old seafowl, turtle, seal, or bat manure. It is now difficult to obtain, and seldom used in this country. Large deposits of seafowl guano are found in such localities as the Peruvian Islands. Bat guano is found to some extent in bat caverns of the southern United States.

HORSE MANURE

Got fresh horse manure but find it difficult to keep it from burning. Can leaves be mixed with it? When horse manure is "burned," it loses most of its nitrogen, but it is still good as a soil conditioner. Mixing peat or leaves or chopped straw with horse manure and keeping it wet will reduce burning.

Will wood shavings harm horse manure? No. Apply to soil in the fall.

Is horse stable manure harmful to roses and delphiniums? No.

LIQUID MANURE

Is there any fertilizer that can be used as a liquid for the small home garden? Soak fresh animal manure in water, and use the liquid. (See Section VII.) Five teaspoons of a regular 5–10–5, 5–10–10, 7–7–7, or similar grade of complete fertilizer per gallon of water will make a satisfactory liquid fertilizer. Such fertilizers are about 75 per cent soluble. Do not use premium grades of fertilizers containing much organic materials. Apply 1 gal. to 5 sq. ft.

How can you make liquid fertilizer, using chemical ingredients which are cheap to buy? A liquid fertilizer containing 1 teaspoonful each of saltpeter (potassium nitrate), superphosphate (monocalcium phosphate), and Epsom salts (magnesium sulfate) is satisfactory.

PIGEON MANURE

Will it be feasible and practical to scatter pigeon droppings on soil in the fall, which will be sown to lawn in the spring?   Yes.

What is the value of pigeon manure as a fertilizer, mixed with hard coal ashes?   Any animal manure may be used to advantage, particularly when at least partially decomposed. Mixed with fine cinders, soil condition is improved. Pigeon manure is as good as chicken manure.

PIG MANURE

Is pig manure as good as any other manure? What would be best to use it for in growing vegetables?   In nutrient content, pig manure does not differ essentially from cow manure, except that it is higher in potash. It is, however, more difficult to handle, and to break down into a crumbly condition.

Should pig manure be mixed with something else?   Mix with straw or hay.

When is pig manure best applied?   Apply in the fall.

Will pig manure that has been stored under cover all winter be good for flowers in the spring, or will it burn them?   Use pig manure only after it has rotted down.

RABBIT MANURE

What value has rabbit manure in a vegetable garden? How should it be used?   It is valuable for its high nitrogen content. Mix with peatmoss or straw, and allow to lie exposed for several weeks before applying to soil. 5 to 10 lbs. per 100 sq. ft. is enough.

Is rabbit manure too strong for use on a vegetable garden?   If fresh and applied in the spring, it may do damage unless used as a very light covering. If applied in the fall, rabbit manure is one of our strongest animal manures. When well rotted, especially if mixed with peatmoss, it can be used freely and safely.

SHEEP MANURE

How does sheep manure, as a fertilizer, compare with cow manure or horse manure?   Sheep manure contains about twice as much nitrogen, and 1½ times as much phosphate and potassium as cow manure.

One hundred lbs. of pulverized sheep manure is equivalent in fertilizer value to what quantity of rotted cow dressing?   From the standpoint of nitrogen content it would take 500 lbs. of dried cow manure to equal 100 lbs. of sheep manure, but the bulkiness of the cow manure makes it a more desirable soil conditioner.

Is sheep litter good to fertilize holly trees with? If allowed to decompose, yes.

GREEN MANURES

GREEN-MANURE CROPS

What is a green-manure crop? A cover crop? The term "green-manure crop" refers to any crop that may be turned into the soil in an undecomposed, green-tissue stage. In contrast, a cover crop refers to a more or less permanent crop used for the purpose of preventing erosion.

How are green-manure crops planted? For small areas, seeds of the green-manure crops can be broadcast. For large areas a drill is used. Seeds should not be covered too deeply—approximately twice their diameter is sufficient.

What are several good summer green-manure crops? The crops most commonly used for summer green manure are alfalfa, cowpeas, Crimson Clover, Red Clover, Sweet Clover, crotalaria, lespedeza, soybeans, and Sudangrass.

Legumes—such as clover, vetch, and soybeans—increase the soil's nitrogen supply.

What green-manure crop can be left on the ground over winter, to be turned under in spring? The most common winter green-manure crops are rye, Perennial Rye Grass, and oats.

What quantity of seed should be sown, per 1,000 sq. ft., of green-manure crops? Alfalfa, ½ lb.; cowpeas, 2½ to 3 lbs.; Crimson Clover and Red Clover, ½ lb.; Sweet Clover, ½ to ¾ lb.; crotalaria, ½ to ¾ lb.; lespedeza, ½ lb.; soybeans, 2–3 lbs.; Sudangrass, ½ to ¾ lb.; rye, 2 to 3 lbs.; rye grass, 1 to 2 lbs.; buckwheat, 1½ lbs. These are approximate amounts. For thick and quick coverage, on small areas, they can be increased up to double these quantities.

I cannot obtain cow manure. What do you suggest as a substitute? Old, partly rotted straw, or alfalfa hay, together with a complete fertilizer, may be used as substitutes. Plow in early in the fall and add fertilizer at time of plowing. Or use a green-manure crop.

How tall should a green-manure crop be before it is turned under?
In general, it is best to turn under green crops when their succulence
is near the maximum, yet at a time when abundant tops have been
produced. This stage occurs when they are about, or a little beyond,
half mature.

Are clover and buckwheat good for soil?   Clover and buckwheat
are good green-manure crops, but soybeans and rye are better and
quicker. Sow soybeans in the spring and plow under in early fall.
Sow rye in September and plow under in the spring. Use 2 lbs. per
1,000 sq. ft.

**Where a green-manure crop is plowed under in fall, is it advisable
to follow with a winter crop?**   Yes, this is an advisable practice,
especially where there is possibility of soil erosion.

**What winter green-manure crops can be used following the turning
under of Red Clover?**   Rye, rye grass, or oats.

*Green manures, such as rye, are dug under
(while still in an immature state) to add
humus to the soil.*

**How soon after the summer green-manure crop is turned under
can the fall crop be sown?**   It is advisable to delay the sowing of the
second crop 2 weeks, if possible; but follow the specific planting
dates recommended for the winter crop used.

When should winter green-manure crops be sown?   Late August
or early September. Rye can be sown as late as first week of October.

**If soil is respaded in spring, following turning under of green
manure (clover) in fall, will the crop come to the top?**   If the green-
manure crop is turned under at the proper time, it will be sufficiently
decomposed by spring so that respading can be done.

When land is cleared, and winter rye sown, what should be done

in spring to prepare for vegetables? Plow the rye under in April. Apply 5–10–5 fertilizer at 3 to 4 lbs. per 100 sq. ft.

How can organics and nitrogen be supplied in city gardens without manure or chemical fertilizer? Peatmoss and dried manures may be used. Soybean meal and cottonseed meal will add nitrogen.

Should turf and large roots be removed from virgin soil or turned under to make humus? It is advisable to turn under as much organic matter as possible in preparing soil for planting. Turf and roots of annual and herbaceous plants should be turned under. Remove the large roots of woody plants.

Can a green-manure crop be planted which will raise the pH and sweeten the soil? No, green-manure crops in themselves exert very little influence on the degree of acidity of the soil.

When there is a shortage of animal fertilizer, what kind and proportion of other fertilizer are suggested for garden use? Incorporate green manures. Apply 4–12–4 or 2–10–10, 30 to 40 lbs. per 1,000 sq. ft. in the spring.

Do any plants, other than legumes and green-manure crops, supply any nutrients to soil? Any plant which is turned under supplies a certain amount of nutrients. The proportions vary with the type of plant.

RYE

Does planting rye in fall and plowing under in spring keep up fertility of the soil? The use of rye as a green-manure crop will do little toward increasing the nitrogen content of the soil; in fact, it may even decrease it temporarily. It does, however, add humus, and thus help to increase crop production.

Should green-manure crops such as rye be used every year? In gardens devoted to the production of vegetables or annual flowers, it is advisable to sow a winter green-manure crop each autumn.

At what stage should rye be turned under? When it is 18 to 24 ins. tall.

Should rye be completely covered when it is turned under? Yes, but the green-manure crop should be incorporated with the upper 8 to 12 ins. of soil instead of being plowed or dug under in a layer. If a few of the stems are not covered, it is all right.

LEGUMES

What is a legume? All leguminous plants belong to the Pea family, recognizable by the formation of their flowers. Peas, beans, and clovers are legumes. They all attract bacteria which collect nitrogen and store it on the roots. The small nodules on the roots, when they decay, add nitrogen to the soil.

What is the special advantage of using a leguminous green-manure crop?   The advantage of a legume (as compared to a non-legume) is that the nitrogen content of the soil will be increased by the root-nodule organisms. However, the legume crops take longer to grow. For a small garden, rye or Perennial Rye Grass is usually more practical.

Are inoculant powders for use on legumes really helpful?   Yes. These inoculant powders are listed under various trade names (such as Legume Aid, Nod-O-Gen, etc.) and are obtainable in local seed stores. They are used to assist in the development of nitrogen-fixing bacteria on the roots of leguminous plants. They are applied when seeds are planted. The mixtures vary with the crop to be planted, so the crop should always be mentioned when buying these products.

Is it advisable to try to grow ALFALFA for soil improvement in southern part of Maine?   Yes. But plant early (mid-August) to avoid heaving out and winter killing. Sow 12 to 15 lbs. per acre.

How is the land prepared for growing ALFALFA?   Same as for any other crop. It may be necessary to add lime.

When is it best to plant CRIMSON CLOVER and expect results from it in improving the soil for a garden?   Crimson Clover is usually seeded in July or August, or at least 6 weeks before normal date of the first killing frost in fall. It may be turned under the following spring or early summer.

Do you plow CRIMSON CLOVER under when it is in bloom? It is best to turn it under when in bloom, or shortly after this stage. It can, however, be turned under at any stage; but the less growth has been made, the less humus will be produced.

Are Austrian PEAS good to use as a green-manure crop?   Yes, they are a good winter crop. Use soybeans as a summer crop. Plow both under to add organic matter to the soil.

At what rate should SOYBEANS be sown for a green-manure crop?   Three lbs. per 1,000 sq. ft.

COMPOST

What is "compost"?   Compost is the term applied to organic matter—such as leaves, weeds, grass clippings, and the like—which has been sufficiently decayed to form a light, crumbly mold. In making compost in a compost heap, soil and manure are often mixed with the vegetable matter.

Should the average home gardener have a compost heap?   Yes, by all means.

COMPOST HEAPS

What materials are used in making a compost heap? Plant refuse: cornstalks, cabbage stems, dead foliage, and discarded vegetables; leaves, grass cuttings, garbage, soil, manure (in fact, any vegetable matter that will decay), plus lime and complete fertilizers. Weeds, even when seeding, may be used if the heap is to be remade at the end of each 3 months, turning it inside out so that every part of the heap is completely decomposed before use. A heap treated in this way is so well rotted that most seeds and insect eggs are destroyed.

How is a compost heap constructed? Heaps 4 ft. wide and 6 ft. long are a convenient size for the small place. Dig out this area to a depth of from 12 to 18 ins. and throw the soil to one side. The bottom layer should be cornstalks, cabbage stems, and other coarse material, tamped down. Over this lay 2 or 3 ins. of soil, and then 2 or 3 ins. of manure, if available. Peatmoss can be used if manure cannot be had. Sprinkle raw ground limestone over each layer at the rate of a pint to a wheelbarrowload of compost material. Add layers of leaves, cuttings, weeds, etc., with a layer of soil, manure, or peatmoss every 12 to 18 ins. Sprinkle soil layers with complete fertilizer containing at least 4 per cent nitrogen thickly enough to whiten the surface like a light snowfall. Keep sides even but sloping very gradually inward toward top. When all material has been placed in layers, soak thoroughly with hose and cover entirely with 3 ins. soil, well firmed down. The top is left saucer-shaped to receive and absorb rainfall. Do not let heap dry out at any time. At end of 3 months remake entire heap, turning inside out, if rapid decomposition is desired.

What length of time is required for a well-made compost heap to rot? Four months to a year, depending on its composition and whether or not ingredients have been added to hasten decay; usually about 9 months.

What is a good formula for making a compost pile rot quickly? I understand lime should not be used as it causes loss of nitrogen. Lime should be used. (For formula, see Introduction, this section.)

Do you advise the use of a chemical such as Adco for the compost heap? Adco is an inoculum used to hasten decomposition. It gives good results, but it is not a substitute for the rather large amounts of fertilizer also needed for the composting process. For instance, a 4–12–4 or 5–10–5 fertilizer (150 lbs.) and 50 lbs. of hydrated lime are sufficient for the decomposition of a one-ton pile of straw.

How often should a new compost heap be started? To maintain a constant supply of compost, a new heap should be started every 6 months.

How is rotted compost used in gardening? It should be sieved through a coarse (1-in.) screen and then diluted with 3 or 4 parts of garden soil. It can be worked into the garden by applying a 1½ in. layer and cultivating it into the upper 6 inches of soil. For a lawn dressing, apply the sieved compost without dilution with soil.

How should decomposed compost be removed from the heap? Cut sections down vertically with a spade, leaving straight, clean sides where it has been removed. Sift through a 1-in. sifter and save coarse siftings for a new compost heap.

GARBAGE

Are these any good for the compost heap: orange peels, banana peels, tea and coffee grounds, and green corn shucks? Yes, any vegetable refuse free of disease is all right. Even weeds with seeds are all right if properly fermented.

Can fresh table refuse and garbage be applied to the garden? I have been putting everything through a meat chopper and this makes a fine lot of refuse. The problem is how to apply it. Are orange skins of much fertilizing value? The materials mentioned, by themselves, do not constitute fertilizers, but when rotted in a compost pile they are valuable.

The refuse from my incinerator consists mostly of ashes and unburned garbage, such as grapefruit, orange peels, etc. Is this O.K. to bury in soil having a large clay content? Yes; but better to make a compost heap with 6-in. alternate layers of soil, garbage, grass cuttings, etc. It would take a year to make a good compost, but it's worth the trouble.

After apples have been crushed and squeezed for cider, would it be advisable to use the apple pomace in the compost pile? Yes, apple pomace is all right to add to compost; cover with soil.

What is the case for, and against, adding garbage to the compost heap? Garbage is a most desirable source of compost. Each layer of garbage must, however, be immediately covered with soil to prevent odors. If dogs run loose in your community, unsorted table garbage will attract them unless the heap is fenced in. Garbage also attracts rodents. Garbage can be placed in a pit, at a distance from house, each layer being sprinkled with a layer of soil and of raw ground limestone. When the contents of the pit are decomposed, it can be added in layers to a new compost heap when one is being built. In this way rodents are kept out of the compost heap and garbage is decomposed underground without odor.

GRASS CLIPPINGS

What good are grass cuttings? How fast do they decay? Clippings make satisfactory compost. If layered with soil in thin layers (4 ins. of soil and 2 ins. of clippings), or added to a mixed heap, a compost will be ready in less than a year.

Is it a real advantage, economical or otherwise, to accumulate grass clippings and convert them into "organic manure" by the use of chemicals such as Adco? Yes.

HICKORY HULLS

Do the hulls (not shells) from hickory nuts cause soil acidity? We have 3 hickory trees on a double lot and don't know whether to put the hulls into the compost pile or burn them? Hickory hulls may be composted satisfactorily with layers of soil.

LEAVES

Should the leaves for compost be rotted? It is best to have them at least partly rotted before placing them in compost heap. If not, it is likely to take a full year for them to decompose, unless manure or peatmoss is also used in the compost pile.

Are elm leaves good to use on the compost heap? Yes.

How do you make fertilizer out of maple leaves? Add to compost heap in the same way as other leaves.

LEAF COMPOSTS

Should anything be used with leaves for compost? Manure or peatmoss, lime, and complete fertilizers. (See page 61)

What can be added to accumulated leaves in the fall to hasten decomposition? Make a pile 4 ft. wide and any desired length. Each layer of leaves 12 ins. deep should be sprinkled with a complete commercial fertilizer (4–12–4) at the rate of 150 lbs. to each ton of leaves. Lime should be added at 50 lbs. to the ton.

Is soil put on the compost pile (made largely of leaves) to help decomposition? Yes.

Will this fall's leaves be fertilizer by next spring? Can anything be done to hurry the process? Not that soon. It will take about a year. Leaves saved from fall and composted in the spring may make good leafmold by fall.

Much has been said about the value of a compost of rotted leaves. I understand that some leaves, due to high acid content, have practically no value as manure. Which should be burned and which should be saved? The leaves of a few kinds of trees, notably oaks, form an acid leafmold. Leafmold from most trees, however, is only slightly, if at all, acid. This reference is to leaves of deciduous trees. Evergreens, however, will produce acid leafmold. The use of lime is an easy way to correct any such acidity.

Are the ashes from burned leaves and grass cuttings of any benefit, or of as much benefit, as those same leaves and cuttings if they were permitted to decay? No. If leaves and clippings are made into a compost, they serve a much better purpose than when burned.

MANURE

In rotting down the compost heap, would it be wise to add hen manure, or would there be a loss of plant food? Hen manure is satisfactory; but superphosphate, potassium chloride, and lime should likewise be added.

MUSHROOM COMPOST

Is it possible for me to get compost from a mushroom farm? How should such compost be used? Is it suitable for garden use? Yes, very satisfactory. Use as a mulch 2 ins. deep, or mix in the soil. Unless a mushroom farm is fairly near by, transportation costs of the material may be too high.

SPECIAL PROBLEMS

What can the home gardener make from refuse, etc., to take the place of 5–10–5 and nitrate of soda? Make a compost pile of straw, weeds, grass clippings, leaves, and other plant parts. (See Compost, Introduction, this section.)
(Or, as a substitute for the above, apply 150 lbs. of cyanamid to a ton of plant refuse.) Keep the pile moist and decomposition will be rapid.

All the refuse from our lawns and vegetables and flower gardens has gone into our compost pile. This includes corn and dahlia stalks, peonies, etc. The entire pile has been covered with clay subsoil (top-soil being scarce). A little fertilizer has been added and some leaves. It is our intention to use this pile, accumulated during summer and fall, by digging it into the vegetable gardens. Is this good practice? A better method would have been to make alternate layers of soil and refuse together, with a definite amount of commercial fertilizer and lime. The only thing to do now is to turn the pile several times, mixing all the ingredients together.

Is composted fertilizer, testing 2 per cent nitrogen, 2 per cent phosphoric acid, and 2 per cent potash, homemade from organic materials, as good as the $60 per ton stuff of the same test from chemical materials? $60 a ton for a 2-2-2 fertilizer is entirely too high. The organic fertilizer will do just as well as the one made of chemicals, but it will be much slower in action, though of longer lasting quality.

Will you give me an idea of the fertilizer value of compost, with inorganic chemicals added, as compared to that made of organic matter only? Organic fertilizers are less satisfactory to add to composts than inorganic, largely because of their slower action. Once decomposed, there should be little difference between the two. Inorganic fertilizers and lime are added to the compost heap both to hasten decomposition and to supply nutrients otherwise low or lacking.

In making a compost pile, is it more advisable to pile up on top of ground, or to dig pit and gradually fill in? Either method is satisfactory. In a pit, however, the pile is less likely to dry out, which is undesirable.

How do you keep a compost pile from smelling? Use lime and cover it with a layer of soil. A well-made heap is not likely to give off any objectionable odor.

What is a good substitute for city dwellers for the objectionable compost pile? A compost pile, when properly made, is not objectionable.

Does the compost lose any of its elements when kept in the house all winter and dried up? The mechanical structure of such soils is affected more than its nutritional value. If stored inside, keep moist.

Compost pits are sometimes thickly inhabited by very large, fat earthworms. Are these harmful, or should they be left in the decomposing material? Worms do no damage in the compost; in fact, they assist in the decomposition of vegetable matter. When compost is sifted for use, they will be eliminated.

PESTS AND DISEASES

In making a compost heap, how can we avoid carrying over diseases of previous year, as tomato and potato blight, etc.? Do not use diseased tops, vines, or fruits for composting, unless special care is taken in "turning" heap. (See next question.)

Some of the waste vegetable matter I put in my compost heap had a lot of aphids or similar insects on it. I put lime and superphosphate with the compost. Will the aphids be killed during the winter? The adults will probably die, but the eggs may carry over. At the time of making the compost the vegetable matter should have been sprayed with Black Leaf 40. However, if the heap is turned "inside out" every 3 months and if every part is thus thoroughly fermented, most insects and diseases will be destroyed.

Does it do any harm to put moldy fruit, vegetables, or mildewed shrubs and leaves into the compost? Any vegetable matter which is not infected with disease or infested with insects may be used safely for composting. Molds resulting from decay do no harm.

Explain the chemistry of the compost heap. Would the pests it might harbor outweigh the advantages for a small (50 × 100 ft.) garden? A compost heap is a mixture of soil, fertilizer, and organic matter. In decomposing, the combination does not always get rid of all diseases and pests. To save organic matter, a compost pile is worth having.

ORGANIC FERTILIZERS

What is organic fertilizer?   An organic fertilizer is one which is derived from organic materials—plant or animal substances. All are compounds of carbon. Some of these materials, such as cottonseed meal, bone meal, tankage, and castor pomace, may add small amounts of humus as well as nutrients to the soil. Others, such as urea or urea-form, may not add humus.

What is best for vegetable garden, stable manure or chemicals? Use both. They complement each other. Stable manure is organic but is not a balanced fertilizer, while a chemical fertilizer contains no organic matter to supply humus.

What fertilizers are best for loose soil?   Loose soil will be benefited by the incorporation of organic matter, to increase the humus. The use of commercial fertilizer does not depend upon the soil structure.

What causes soil to crack in dry weather?   Heavy soils will crack unless sufficient organic matter is present to prevent cohesion of the fine particles.

BONE MEAL

What types of bone meal are available, and for what purpose is each used?   Coarse, raw, ground bone releases phosphorus slowly into the soil. Fine bone flower is used for quicker fertilization. Raw bone meal contains 2 to 4 per cent nitrogen and 20 to 25 per cent phosphoric acid. It is less dangerous than quicker-acting fertilizers for such plants as daffodils, tulips, roses, etc., and is often used as a top-dressing in the greenhouse. It is applied at the rate of 30 to 60 lbs. per 1,000 sq. ft. Steamed bone meal contains 1.65 to 2.50 per cent nitrogen and 20 to 30 per cent phosphoric acid, and is more quickly available as fertilizer material than raw bone meal.

When should bone meal be applied for best results?   Early in the spring, when the soil is prepared. Work it into the upper 3 to 5 ins. of the soil.

Is bone meal a good fertilizer for all plants?   No. Bone meal is a safe fertilizer to use, but it contains no potash. Based on amount of essential ingredients contained, it is more expensive than some chemical fertilizers. However, gardeners use it for many purposes.

Does bone meal act as a complete fertilizer on grass and garden? Bone meal is *not* a complete fertilizer, since it does not contain potash, only a small amount of nitrogen, and considerable phosphorus.

Would bone meal mixed with a small amount of soil, kept in cellar

during winter, and moistened occasionally, work faster when used in the spring than new bone meal? Its activity will be hastened to some extent, but not sufficiently to make the practice worth while.

Will bone meal ever turn soil acid? Bone meal exerts little effect on the soil reaction. If there is any change, it is to make the soil more alkaline.

What percentage of nitrogen is there in ground bone meal? Raw bone meal contains 2 to 4 per cent nitrogen and 22 to 25 per cent phosphoric acid. Steamed bone meal contains 1 to 2 per cent nitrogen and 22 to 30 per cent phosphoric acid.

Will the use of bone meal as a fertilizer harm plants that like acid soil, such as hydrangeas, wildflowers, etc.? No; bone meal exerts little influence on soil reaction.

What is a good application of bone meal? Three to 5 lbs. per 100 sq. ft.

What would the analysis be of 100 lbs. of bone meal? Approximately 3–22–0.

Are the effects of bone meal spread over a greater period in the soil than phosphate? The phosphorus in bone meal penetrates the soil *very* slowly and becomes available very slowly.

Is bone meal good for pot plants? If soils are not too acid and deficient in phosphorus, bone meal is a satisfactory fertilizer for pot plants.

COTTONSEED MEAL

What nutrients does cottonseed meal contain? Cottonseed meal contains approximately 7 per cent nitrogen, 2.5 per cent phosphoric acid, and 1.5 per cent potash.

How long does it take for cottonseed meal to mix with soil? Part of the nitrogen and other essential elements of cottonseed meal are readily available; the remainder becomes available more slowly.

On what plants can cottonseed meal be used, and in combination with what other fertilizer? It may be used on nearly all plants as it contains about 7 per cent nitrogen, which becomes available slowly; also 3 per cent phosphorus, and 2 per cent potash. It can be used with superphosphate.

DRIED BLOOD

Is blood meal a fertilizer? Dried blood is a complete but unbalanced fertilizer containing approximately 12 per cent nitrogen, 1 per cent phosphoric acid, and .75 per cent potash.

LEAFMOLD

In using leafmold as a fertilizer should it be used liberally or spar-

ingly? Leafmold is not a very high-grade fertilizer. It is a good conditioner, and as such can be used liberally—a covering 4 ins. deep is all right.

What effect do pine needles have on soil? They acidify it, and help improve condition.

When should fallen leaves be used? After decomposition; apply to soil at any time of the year.

Last fall I spaded my garden a foot deep and on the bottom I put a heavy layer of maple leaves. This was covered over with a foot of earth. Was this worth while? It would be better to spade leaves into the soil in the fall; or let them decay first and add to soil later.

How do hard maple tree leaves affect the soil if left where they fall over winter? It is better to compost them. Little value if left on top of soil.

Do large quantities of mixed leaves (elm, maple, oak, beech) make good fertilizer when rotted? They make a good soil conditioner but are of comparatively little fertilizer value; not nearly so effective as manures unless a heavy dosage of fertilizer is added in rotting them.

Is it true that the leaves of Silver Leaf and other poplars, spaded into the soil, are toxic or poison to the growth of flowers? No.

Will oak leaves make the ground sour? No. When decomposed, they make an excellent soil conditioner. Used in quantity, they will make the ground acid but only temporarily. They are frequently employed for this purpose.

SLUDGE

The dried and pulverized sludge from sewage-disposal plants is used as a fertilizer not only for lawns and flowers but vegetables as well. Therefore, would not the liquid and sludge from septic tanks, after it has passed from the first compartment and just before it passes into the third or final compartment, be a good fertilizer? How would it compare with the liquid manure used by farmers? Such sludge should be satisfactory as a fertilizer. It should compare favorably with liquid manure.

The local sewage disposal sells sewage settlings at 55¢ per 100 lbs. Nothing has been added to this. How does this compare in value with barnyard manure and with other commercial fertilizers, for use on lawn and garden? (I have sandy soil.) If sewage sludge can be obtained for 55¢ per 100 lbs. it should be a fairly good buy. It contains nearly twice the essential nutrients found in average manure. Be sure the sludge contains no toxic substances. Sewage sludge at 55¢ per 100 lbs. is expensive when compared with commercial fertilizer, such as 4–12–4.

What is the value of sludge from sanitary district beds? At what rate

should it be applied for flower or vegetable gardens? Recent reports from the Ohio Agricultural Experiment Station indicate that the analysis of sewage sludge from 10 different cities varied as follows: nitrogen, 0.88 to 2.98 per cent; phosphoric acid, 0.42 to 2.10 per cent; potash, 0.05 to 1.6 per cent. The report further showed that the nitrogen in sewage sludge was not more than 10 to 15 per cent as effective as the nitrogen in nitrate of soda.

TANKAGE

What is tankage? Tankage is a by-product of slaughterhouses, which contains such refuse as lungs, intestines, bones, etc. These are processed, dried, and ground to produce a material used in stock feeds and for fertilizer.

What is the value of tankage? It contains about 4 to 10 per cent nitrogen and 7 to 14 phosphoric acid. It is lacking in potash content.

How is tankage applied? About 4 lbs. per 100 sq. ft.; usually as a top- or side-dressing to growing plants, hoed or cultivated into the soil. It is often employed in place of nitrate of soda, which is quicker acting. It must be kept *perfectly dry* in storage, or it will quickly decay.

WOOD ASHES

Are wood or leaf ashes good for the garden? Yes. They contain potash and lime.

How do wood ashes affect manures? Wood ashes containing lime have a tendency to hasten the decomposition of manure.

Where can I use wood ashes and chicken manure to the best advantage? Do *not* use together, if chicken manure is fresh. Otherwise the combination is good. Mix ashes and chicken manure at 3 to 1 ratio.

Is it unwise to use wood ashes and horse manure at the same time? Yes. Horse manure, unless well rotted, contains quickly given off ammonium. Wood ashes are apt to hasten the process and "burning" of plants may result.

What lilies may have wood ashes? What is the best way to apply wood ashes to roses? Since the majority of lilies do better in somewhat acid soils, wood ashes should not be used. Apply wood ashes to roses in the spring; about ½ to 1 lb. around each plant.

What is the best way to use wood ashes in acid soil? Wood ashes tend to reduce acidity because of lime content. Apply to the soil in fall or spring; 4 to 6 lbs. per 100 sq. ft.

What plants and trees benefit by an application of wood ashes? Almost all plants. Those that need potash—fruit trees, vegetable root crops, hydrangeas, carnations, roses, peonies, etc.—are especially benefited.

How can we use to the best advantage, on vegetables, flowers, shrubs, and trees, our accumulation of wood ashes? Work into the soil after growth starts in the spring.

Will the action of wood ashes and cinders destroy alkali on irrigated land? (Washington.) Neither wood ashes nor cinders would have any effect. If the soil is alkaline, sulphur is needed.

Every year I burn a considerable amount of brush. Are the ashes good fertilizer? Wood ashes are especially good for their potash content.

Do oak wood ashes have any value as fertilizer for flowers or vegetables? Yes. They contain potash, and are always safe to use.

If I put wood ashes from our fireplace on the vegetable and flower beds, will the oil from the coal ashes mixed with them harm the plants? No; not unless you use fresh coal ashes.

Is there any value in wood coke from bonfires if applied to garden in fall? Applied in fall, it would be partly wasted. Better to save it under cover and apply in the spring.

Should I spread the wood ashes from my fireplace around as they are available during the winter; or must I store and use during the growing season? Store your ashes under cover to prevent leaching of potash. Leached wood ashes contain little potash, though still of some value.

Are the ashes of burned leaves, twigs, and winter-killed dry stalks of vegetation of any material value if burned on the garden plot? Yes; but the ashes would have more value if stored under cover and scattered in the spring.

OTHER MATERIALS

Is CRAB MEAL a good fertilizer? Fresh crab contains 2 to 3 per cent nitrogen and 2 to 3 per cent phosphoric acid. Its immediate efficiency is relatively low. Mixed fertilizer made with dried and ground king crab may contain 9 to 12 per cent nitrogen.

Can CRAB MEAL be used on most garden plants with benefit? Yes. Its cost will govern the extent of its use.

Is CHARCOAL good to add to soil to help plants? Yes, it adds a small amount of phosphorus and considerable potash and lime. These materials, however, as found in charcoal, become available very slowly.

Are rotted CRANBERRIES good as a fertilizer? They would add a small amount of organic matter, but very small quantities of the essential elements for plant growth.

What effect is caused on soil by a daily application of COFFEE GROUNDS?   Coffee grounds may be considered as a soil conditioner if applied in sufficient quantities. Little value would accrue from the daily application of grounds from the family table.

Would water from old COFFEE GROUNDS keep soil acid, or would it kill the plants?   The incorporation of coffee grounds with the soil will result in little change in soil reaction. Excessive amounts may be toxic.

Some people say that COFFEE GROUNDS, SOAP WATER, etc., are beneficial to soil and growth of vegetation. Is this so?   Coffee grounds help in making the mechanical condition of the soil better if sufficient quantities are applied. Soapy water is not beneficial, and sometimes injurious if large amounts are poured in one spot, particularly where soap contains naphtha.

Are COFFEE GROUNDS and TEA LEAVES good for the soil?   Coffee grounds, tea leaves, and any other vegetable refuse, when rotted, serve an excellent use as humus. Do not apply to house plants. They are unsightly and do not serve any purpose.

What fertiilzer value is there in EGGSHELLS?   Eggshells contain a considerable quantity of calcium, and a very small amount of nitrogen. Crush or grind them.

What about burying FISH TRIMMINGS deep in the earth?   Fish remains make an excellent fertilizer. Bury them just deep enough to avoid objectionable odors.

I'm burying all my GARBAGE around the plants. Do you think this will be sufficient fertilizer?   No; garbage at its best is a very low-grade fertilizer; it is excellent to add humus, but should be supplemented by a complete fertilizer.

Can LEATHER DUST be used as a garden fertilizer?   Leather dust contains some nitrogen, but it decomposes *very* slowly, so that quick results should not be expected.

Is SAWDUST good to put on a garden?   It can be used to lighten soil and as a mulch. Use lightly.

I have some very fine SAWDUST, of white pine. What would be its effect if worked into soil in which vegetables or flowers are planted?   It should help lighten your soil if it's heavy. Do not use thicker than 1 in.

How does one prepare kelp and other common SEAWEEDS (which wash up on beaches along Long Island Sound) for fertilizer?   If conditions are such that it can be done, the kelp can be handled as a green manure or plowed or spaded under. Otherwise, it can be composted and applied at an opportune time.

What value is SEA KELP as a fertilizer?   Sea kelp is high in potash, will compare favorably with farm manure in nitrogen, but is low in phosphorus.

Where can I buy SEA KELP in Iowa for fertilizer? Most of the sea kelp is processed for fertilizer on the West coast. In its natural state it is too bulky to be shipped any distance.

Can SEA KELP be used immediately, or must it be stored? Sea kelp is used fresh as a green manure by farmers and gardeners near the seashore. For shipping, it is dried, then burned to an ash. In this state it can be used at once, or stored. The ash contains about 30 per cent potash.

Are other SEAWEEDS as valuable as a fertilizer as sea kelp? Seaweeds vary considerably in nutritive value. They are worth using if readily available.

Will you please tell me if SEAWEED is any good to use as a fertilizer. If so, how can I use it for best results, as I live on the seashore? I can get all the seaweed I need. Seaweed is a good fertilizer. For one who can get the material fresh it is best used as a green manure spread on the land and turned under.

What soil-conditioning property has chimney SOOT? When is it applied? Soot possesses very little or no soil-conditioning value. It does contain about .5 per cent nitrogen.

Is SOOT taken from an oil burner any use whatever in a garden? Soot contains some nitrogen and may be applied to the soil as a side dressing.

INORGANIC FERTILIZERS

What is inorganic fertilizer? An inorganic fertilizer is one derived from mineral or chemical substances, such as phosphate rock, potash salts, nitrate salts (nitrate of soda).

What is a chemical fertilizer? A chemical fertilizer is one derived from chemically processed or manufactured materials, rather than from natural organic substances. The term is somewhat misleading in that organic fertilizers also may be treated with chemicals to increase their rate of availability. Many fertilizers contain both types of materials.

Are chemicals injurious to future plant growth? Not if they are used correctly. They do not, however, add humus to the soil.

Why don't we use stone dust as a natural fertilizer, which it really is? Pulverized granite (granite meal) is used as a source of potash in some areas. It contains about 5 to 10 per cent potash, along with a wide assortment of other elements. It is applied at rates of ½ to 2 tons per acre, and lasts for a long time. On acid soils pulverized phosphate rock is usually a satisfactory source of phosphate when used liberally. Some rocks are nearly devoid of fertilizer elements.

When preparing the soil in the spring for a garden of either flowers or vegetables, is it necessary to apply a chemical for better results? Usually additions of chemical fertilizers decidedly help production.

What is the fertilizer value of calcium carbonate? Calcium carbonate in itself is of no value as a fertilizer, since it is insoluable in water. It must be converted into the bicarbonate form, or some other soluble calcium salt, before calcium becomes available to the plant. It may also beneficially modify the structure of the soil.

NITRATE OF SODA

For what purpose is nitrate of soda used? Nitrate of soda furnishes a readily available source of nitrogen. Nitrogen stimulates the vegetative growth of the plant and is also essential for the reproductive phases.

What can we use in place of nitrate of soda? Ammonium sulfate, ammo-phos, cottonseed, soybean meal, or tankage.

SULFATE OF AMMONIA

What is sulfate of ammonia used for? This is used as a source of nitrogen. It contains about 20 per cent nitrogen.

When should sulfate of ammonia be used? How much? This is a good fertilizer to use when nitrogen is required. Apply about 5 to 10 lbs. per 1,000 sq. ft.

Is ammonium sulfate best spread on ground when soil is being dug, or later, and raked in? Ammonium sulfate is best applied after the soil is spaded and raked into the upper 2 to 4 ins. of the surface soil.

UREA

What is urea? Urea is a water-soluble organic compound containing 45 to 46 per cent nitrogen. In soil urea almost immediately decomposes to ammonium nitrogen and carbon dioxide.

Does urea leave an acid residue? Yes, but only a slight amount of acidity is left—about a third as much as would be left from a similar amount of nitrogen from sulfate of ammonia.

Can urea be used for foliar fertilization? Yes, but be sure to obtain a grade of urea suitable for that purpose. Urea for foliar fertilization is readily available in many areas. Unlike fertilizer urea, that intended for foliar application should contain less than 0.25 per cent biuret. A safe rate of application is usually 5 to 8 pounds per 100 gallons of water.

SUPERPHOSPHATE

Is there any way to add phosphorus to soil without using com-

mercial fertilizer? Yes, in the form of pulverized phosphate rock, bone meal, or basic slag.

Are the effects of superphosphate somewhat similar to those of bone meal? Yes, the effects are similar. Bone meal contains a low percentage of nitrogen not found in superphosphate. The phosphorus in bone meal, however, becomes available much more slowly.

How should one use agricultural lime and acid phosphate? They should not be mixed. If so, the phosphates are made unavailable.

Is there any advantage in applying superphosphate to perennial border or rock gardens? Many soils are deficient in phosphorus. If perennials or rock plants are planted in such a soil, they will be benefited by applications of superphosphate.

How should phosphate be used? I have some and do not know how to apply it to flowers. Phosphate is best applied when the flower beds are first prepared, by working it into the upper 4 to 6 ins. of soil. If plants are already in the bed, apply the phosphate between the plants and work it into the soil as deep as possible (down 6 to 8 ins.) without disturbing or injuring the roots. Apply 30 to 40 lbs. per 1,000 sq. ft.

When and how often should superphosphate be applied to perennials and rock plants? In addition to the use of superphosphate at the time the beds are prepared, yearly applications of phosphorus are advisable, especially in soils tending to be deficient in this element, by an application of a complete fertilizer in the spring.

Will superphosphate take the place of commercial fertilizer when mixed with manure? Farm manures fortified with superphosphate will make a good general garden fertilizer. Additional nitrogen may be needed for some crops.

MURIATE OF POTASH

What is the best time and method to apply muriate of potash to a vegetable garden? If the amount of potash applied in the complete fertilizer recommended for vegetable gardens is not sufficient, apply an additional quantity (1 lb. per 100 sq. ft.) and incorporate it in the surface 2 to 3 ins.

How often should muriate of potash be applied? Usually one application a year is sufficient. Soil tests will show if additional quantities are needed.

My soil is deficient in phosphorus and potash. What shall I apply to correct this condition? Apply commercial fertilizers such as 2–10–10 or 0–10–10; or superphosphate and muriate of potash.

COMPLETE COMMERCIAL FERTILIZERS

What are the principles of fertilization? Stated briefly, fertilization is practiced to supply the necessary essental elements to secure a normal growth of the plant.

What is commercial fertilizer? The term "commercial fertilizer" applies to any carrier of essential nutrient elements, that is sold (by itself or mixed with other such carriers) commercially.

How can an amateur tell what formulas—such as 10–6–4 and 8–5–3—mean? Formulas such as 10–6–4, 8–5–3, etc., are used to express the percentages of the major ingredients in fertilizers; namely, nitrogen, phosphorus, and potash. A 10–6–4 fertilizer denotes 10 per cent nitrogen, 6 per cent phosphorus, and 4 per cent potash.

Do commercial fertilizers aid or destroy existing bacteria and humus in the soil? Commercial fertilizers aid the beneficial bacteria of the soil. At the same time they may hasten the decomposition of humus.

Does commercial fertilizer burn the minerals out of the ground? No; it adds essential minerals to the soil.

Will commercial fertilizer restore a worn-out soil? Commercial fertilizers will furnish the necessary essential elements and can restore the soil in this respect. To restore humus and to improve the physical condition of the soil, incorporate farm or green manures. (See Introduction.)

What are some substitutes for fertilizer? There are no substitutes for fertilizer. Manure is used for its organic value, but there is little fertilizer value in manure, unless applied in very heavy quantities (at least 20 tons per acre).

Is there a fertilizer generally good as an all-plant fertilizer, for shrubs, perennials, vegetables, rhododendrons, trees, and grass lawns? There is no one fertilizer that would be considered best for all these groups of plants. A 4–12–4 or 5–10–5 comes as near being a general-purpose fertilizer as we have. Recommended for shrubs, 4–12–4 and 10–6–4; for perennials, 4–12–4 and 2–10–10; for vegetables, 4–12–4 and 2–10–10; for azaleas and rhododendrons 4–12–4 with at least 25 per cent of the nitrogen of an organic source such as soybean meal; for lawns, 10–6–4 or 11–48–0.

How can one tell just what kind of fertilizer is best to use? Soil tests will give a partial answer; the habit of growth of the plant is also a determining factor. Ornamental plants normally showing vigorous top growth respond best to a low-nitrogen fertilizer, and vice versa. Fleshy-rooted plants respond best to a fertilizer similar to a 2–10–10.

Can one add certain chemicals to the soil of the garden vegetable patch, in order to get bigger and better crop yields? A 2–10–10 is advocated for root crops. Use a 4–12–4 for other vegetables. Side dressings of a nitrogen fertilizer may be advisable for the leafy vegetables.

How long does it take for organic or inorganic fertilizers to become available to plants? Inorganic nitrogenous fertilizers are readily available. The insoluble organic nitrogenous fertilizers are slowly available. Phosphorus from superphosphate penetrates the soil slowly, but is readily available in the monocalcium form. Potash is readily available.

How can minerals be supplied to old garden soils? By using a 4–12–4 or 5–10–5 fertilizer, applied at 4 lbs. per 100 sq. ft.

What is the best fertilizer for a new vegetable garden? In general, a 4–12–4 or 5–10–5 fertilizer. For root or tuber crops a 2–10–10 is satisfactory.

What fertilizers should be added to the soil to make vegetables yield bountifully? See previous question. For leafy vegetables, follow the spring application with a side dressing of ammonium sulfate when the tops are half grown.

What is the best fertilizer to use in spring? In general, a 4–12–4 or a 5–10–5 fertilizer. For root or tuber crops, a 2–10–10 is usually satisfactory.

What is the best fertilizer to use in midsummer? For leafy crops, ammonium sulfate or nitrate of soda. For other common vegetables, a 4–12–4, if needed.

Is it possible to mix one's own fertilizer for a successful home garden? To make your own fertilizer, several separate ingredients are needed. It is usually much more satisfactory to buy a ready-mixed fertilizer.

What is the best and simplest method of making chemical fertilizers for the vegetable garden? Generally, it does not pay for the average gardener to mix his own fertilizer. Buy it already mixed. If it is advisable to mix your own fertilizer, use the following ingredients to make 100 lbs. of 4–12–4 fertilizer: 20 lbs. ammonium sulfate, 60 lbs. superphosphate, 8 lbs. muriate of potash, 12 lbs. sand.

Are there garden fertilizers that are good, and more reasonable in price than the highly advertised brands? In general the regular 4–12–4, 5–10–5, and 7–7–7 farm fertilizers are the least expensive. They are good fertilizers.

Is a commercial fertilizer, such as Agrico, enough to use for the garden? Or should something be used in the fall and left through the winter? Agrico is a complete fertilizer and should be sufficient in itself. Additional nitrogen may be required for some crops; if so, it should be applied in the spring or when its need is obvious. Green manures are needed in addition.

I have on hand a 100-lb. bag of Agrico lawn fertilizer; also 100-lb. bag of bone meal. Can these be used? In what proportions? Rather than attempt to mix these fertilizers, use the Agrico fertilizer for the lawn and most flower and vegetable crops. Use the bone meal for plants with fleshy and tuberous roots.

Have been using a fertilizer called Emseco. Is this a good product? The Thomas W. Emerson Co. of Boston puts out a number of trade-name "Emseco" fertilizers. Some of these are 4–8–4, 5–8–7, and 7–7–7; not all of these are garden fertilizers. A 4–8–4 should be the most satisfactory for general garden fertilization.

What is the chemical analysis of the trade fertilizer called Loma? A 5–10–4.

Is Sacco 4–12–4 considered a fertilizer? Yes, it is the trade name of a commercial fertilizer.

What is the phosphorous, nitrogen, and potash content of Vigoro? Vigoro contains 5 per cent nitrogen, 10 per cent phosphorus, and 5 per cent potash, plus small amounts of trace elements.

Is commercial 5–10–5 fertilizer comparable to fertilizers like Vigoro, Armour's garden and lawn fertilizer, and Scott's turf builder? Trade-name fertilizers such as Vigoro and others are usually somewhat better than commercial grades of similar analysis, due to the use of better materials, better mixing, and sometimes the addition of trace elements. The standard formula fertilizers, however, are used with success by commercial growers.

Does the continuous use of Vigoro leave a deposit on the soil which eventually ruins the soil? No, Vigoro may be used continuously without detrimental effects.

What are the relative merits of cottonseed meal, 5–7–5 commercial fertilizer, nitrate of soda, bone meal, Vigoro, rotted oak and woods dirt, as fertilizer for fruit trees, dogwood, holly, grapes, and flowers? Vigoro or a 5–7–5 commercial fertilizer would be generally satisfactory as a fertilizer for these plants. Cottonseed meal contains about 7.5 per cent nitrogen, 2.5 per cent phosphoric acid, and 1.5 per cent potash. It is not a balanced fertilizer but is a good source of organic nitrogen. Nitrate of soda is a good inorganic nitrogen fertilizer. Bone meal is a source of phosphorus and also contains a small amount of nitrogen. Rotted oak or woods dirt has little value as a fertilizer but does act as a soil corrective.

What garden fertilizer such as Vigoro, hydrated lime, nitrate of soda, etc., can be kept several seasons? Which should be used the season it is bought? Practically all garden fertilizers can be kept for several years *if* they are kept dry. Some, such as ammonium sulfate, cake on standing and should be crushed before applying.

Are fertilizers in tablet form recommended? Plant tablets have long been used and they are effective and easily applied, especially to house plants.

What plant tablets are best?   There are several kinds on the market that are effective. Avoid the ones that have extravagant claims made about them. No plant tablets will work "miracles." Vitamin B_1 usually has little or no effect.

What commercial fertilizers are reliable for garden use?   A 4–12–4, or 5–10–5. Other complete fertilizers, and also carriers of nitrogen, phosphorus, and potash. (See Introduction.)

What quantity of commercial fertilizer is the minimum essential for a vegetable garden 80 × 30?   Fifty lbs. of a 4–12–4.

I have a plot 20 × 20 ft., just covered with 6 ins. of sandy loam. What kind of fertilizer could I use to make good soil for raising FLOWERS of various kinds?   Incorporate 12 to 16 lbs. of a 4–12–4 fertilizer in the upper 3 to 5 ins. of the soil.

What formula, in a commercial-type fertilizer, gives best results for growth of ANNUALS, PERENNIALS, and SHRUBS in a mixed border?   Use a 4–12–4 or 5–10–5 fertilizer applied at the rate of 3 to 4 lbs. per 100 sq. ft.

What type of fertilizer should be used on PLANTS IN WINTER to have blooms and good color in foliage?   Poor results in winter are often due to lack of light or presence of illuminating gas. A 4–12–4 or 5–10–5 are good fertilizers; they should be used sparingly, when light conditions are unfavorable.

What commercial fertilizers are suitable for FRUIT TREES?   Complete fertilizers; also ammonium sulfate, cyanamide, nitrate of soda, superphosphate, muriate of potash, and several others.

What kind of fertilizer can one obtain to take the place of horse manure for ROSES and VEGETABLES?   Where horse manure or other animal manures are not available, other types of organic matter, plus commercial fertilizer, can be substituted. For roses use peat-moss, plus a 4–12–4 fertilizer as needed. For vegetable gardens, incorporate green manures, and add a 4–12–4 or a 2–10–10 fertilizer as required.

APPLYING FERTILIZERS

When should one fertilize the garden—fall or spring?   For lawns, permanent plantings of shrubs, evergreens, and flowers, fertilizers may be applied in the fall or spring with equal success. It is best to apply fertilizers to annual crops at, or just previous to, planting time.

Is it better to place fertilizer on the garden in the fall and turn it over in the spring? Or turn the soil first, and then apply the fertilizer?   Commercial fertilizers for the most part are best applied after spading or plowing, a week or 10 days before planting, and raked into the upper 2 to 3 ins. of the soil. Superphosphate may be spaded in in either fall or spring.

Should I plant first, and then fertilize? Or vice versa?   Fertilizer can be applied and worked into the soil just before planting, or at planting time. One or more subsequent applications may be necessary during the growing season. (See Side Dressing.)

For a new garden, do I have to fertilize the ground before I plant? Usually it is necessary to fertilize. A soil analysis will indicate what is needed.

At what time of the year should fertilizer be applied to the garden? If manure is used, apply it in the fall, unless it is very well rotted. If well rotted, or if commercial fertilizer is used, apply in spring when preparing ground for planting.

Are better blooms obtained when fertilizer is used at time of setting out plants, or at time buds form?   For best results apply the fertilizer at the time the plants are set. Make a subsequent application at or previous to bud formation. (See Side Dressing.)

Do you advocate putting fertilizer in the rows under the seed; or between the rows?   Recent experiments show that it is best to apply the fertilizer 2 to 3 ins. to the side and 1 to 2 ins. below the seed, rather than to place it in the row beneath the seed.

My soil is very rich but no fertilizer added since last fall. Is it necessary to apply any when ground is so good?   No. Except to make sure the soil is maintained in that condition.

What is the best fertilizer to use for soil that has been cleared of trees and in which it is desired to make a vegetable garden?   A 4–12–4, unless a soil analysis shows otherwise.

How do you fertilize plants that remain in the same spot in the garden?   Apply the fertilizer between the plants and hoe it into the upper few inches of soil without disturbing or injuring the roots of the plants. If soil is dry, water thoroughly.

How often during the season should the flower garden be fertilized? When?   Once or twice a season. Apply fertilizer in the spring as growth starts, and again in midsummer if growth is not satisfactory.

What kind of fertilizer is best for peat soil which is turning acid? Peat soils usually becomes *less* acid as they are cultivated. A soil test would be advisable. If soil is acid, use a non-acid fertilizer. (See Introduction.)

Is it good practice to use a commercial fertilizer on acid-loving plants?   Yes, if it is needed. A 4–12–4 fertilizer with ¼ to ⅓ of the nitrogen furnished by an organic source is satisfactory.

We are plowing a field that has never been productive. What is the

best fertilizer? The productivity of this soil may not be due to a lack of essential elements for growth. Be sure the drainage and the organic matter content of the soil are satisfactory. The best fertilizer to use will depend upon the crops to be grown. Consult your county agricultural agent.

Am draining cedar swamp for garden. Soil is black swamp muck, highly nitrogenous, about 2 ft. thick; white sand subsoil. What fertilizer should be used? The fertilizer to apply will depend upon the nutrient test of the soil and the crops to be grown. In general a 2–10–10 should be satisfactory.

How much water should be applied to garden after fertilizing? Soil is sandy and both commercial and fresh manures are used. Water garden when needed as indicated by tendency of plants to wilt. (See Watering.) Make several applications during the year of a 4–12–4 or 5–10–5 fertilizer at 4 lbs. per 100 sq. ft.

MISCELLANEOUS

SOIL STERILIZATION

What are the different ways to sterilize soil for seeds? Steam, very hot water, and chemicals, such as tear gas (chloropicrin), methyl bromide and vapam.

How does the gardener sterilize soil with steam? Make a soil pile 12 ins. deep. Place 4 ins. agricultural tile 2 ft. apart in center of pile and running full length. Plug tile at one end. Insert steam pipe or hose in the other end. Cover entire pile with building paper or canvas. Inject steam for 2 hrs.; remove cloth; allow to cool. Remove tile, and continue the process. Steam sterilization makes structure better. Its effects are entirely beneficial. This is usually impractical for a gardener to do. Small quantities of soil for pot plants may be sterilized in a pressure cooker, without closing the steam valve.

What is an easy and efficient method of sterilizing soil for growing seedlings in small greenhouse where steam is not used? Boiling hot water should be poured over the soil and, in addition, the seeds should be dusted with Cuprocide, Spergon, Terrachlor (PCNB) or similar compounds.

What is Larvacide? It is a gas which is packaged in bottles or cylinders as a liquid (chloropicrin, or tear gas) and is applied to the soil with a special applicator. The soil should be 60° F. or warmer, and medium moist. Three c.c. of liquid (a small teaspoonful) is injected about 3 to 6 ins. deep, spaced 10 ins. each way. A heavy watering is applied immediately. Follow with two other applications on successive days. The treatment controls soil diseases, insects, and weeds.

How are small quantities of soil sterilized with Larvacide? (1) In boxes: Have soil moist and loose; make holes 4 ins. deep and 10 ins. apart; insert 1 medicine dropper full of Larvacide. Cover with soil and immediately lay several thicknesses of newspapers over the surface. Keep tight and wet for 3 days. Then uncover; loosen up the soil. After a week, planting can be safely done. The same process may be employed in outdoor beds, but the temperature of the soil should be 60° F. or higher. Watering the soil 3 days in succession will take the place of wet newspapers. (2) In bins: Allow ¾ lb. Larvacide for each cubic yard. Make a layer of soil 6 ins. deep; pour ⅓ of the Larvacide over it; cover with 6 ins. of soil; add another third of the Larvacide and cover again. The final third may be poured into holes in the top layer and the whole wet down and covered with wet newspapers. This material is tear gas, so do not breathe it. It will make the eyes smart badly.

When is manure added to soil to be sterilized? Apply manure *before* sterilization to avoid infection later. Commercial fertilizers may be added before or after. Generally, superphosphate and bone meal are best added before—others after, as needed.

How do you sterilize soil with formaldehyde? Where steam is not available, formaldehyde may be used. Use commercial formalin— 1 gal. to 50 gals. of water. One gal. of the solution is used to 1 sq. ft. of soil 6 ins. deep. Pour solution on, cover for 24 hours, then uncover and permit to dry for 2 weeks before using.

How do you sterilize soil for potted plants? Use steam, hot water, or chemicals. A pressure cooker may be used satisfactorily.

An easy way to sterilize soil or compost for starting seeds; place in flat and drench thoroughly with boiling water.

How is sand, used as a rooting medium, best sterilized? If small quantities are wanted, place sand in shallow flat or box, and pour boiling water through it.

How do you sterilize soil in a perennial bed? This cannot be done satisfactorily unless chemicals are used—formaldehyde, chloropicrin, or mercuric compounds. Beds must be free of plants before chemicals are applied.

PLANT STIMULANTS

How is Vitamin B₁ used in garden?   Don't waste your time with Vitamin B_1; it has proved a failure under most conditions.

What plants do not need to be fertilized with Vitamin B₁?   No plants need to be fertilized with Vitamin B_1. Under normal conditions, plants make B_1 in their leaves; soil bacteria make it; all types of organic matter have some. The plants have a normal supply without being fed pills containing it.

Can Vitamin B₁ be used on all growing plants regardless of their soil requirements?   Almost all plants make enough B_1 in their leaves for their own use. Any B_1 added is superfluous. Fertilizer is much more important.

When my lawn shrubs and evergreens need watering I slip 5 or 6 B₁ tablets into the hose. The results seem to be good. Do you consider this a good practice? Should the B₁ be applied to the foliage, or only to the soil?   Results are due to water only. Almost all plants make enough B_1 in their leaves for their own use; if soil contains no humus, B_1 additions may be helpful.

What is gibberellic acid? How does it affect plants?   Gibberellic acid is a growth-stimulating substance produced by a fungus that attacks rice plants and causes them to grow rapidly for some time before the fungus finally injures too much of the tissue. When applied to some plants, a 10 part per million solution of gibberellic acid in water will stimulate a marked increase in rate of growth—especially in the length of stems and petioles. This stimulated growth is sometimes attractive and sometimes not. Gibberellic acid often hastens flower maturity and, in some instances, it increases flower size. Dwarf varieties of a given species usually respond most markedly to gibberellic acid. Standard sorts respond less, and giants are generally unresponsive. One of the interesting and perhaps most valuable properties of gibberellic acid is that of overcoming the dormancy effect in some plants and seeds.

What is colchicine, and how is it used?   An alkaloid from colchicum is used by plant breeders in attempts to change inherited characteristics of plants by doubling the chromosomes.

Where can I acquire colchicine?   From drugstore or local chemical supply house. It is a very poisonous substance; must be used with caution. Comes in paste or solution, which is applied to top buds of shoots of plants. Of some use to plant breeders, not to average gardener.

Are there any recent new developments in chemical gardening or use of hormones and vitamins for plants?   See gibberellic acid discussion.

Perhaps one of the most interesting developments in chemical gardening is the use of plastic forms of nitrogen and glass forms of potash and minor elements. (These are called frits.) Urea-formaldehyde plastic may be manufactured with 38 per cent of nitrogen, one quarter of which is readily available, whereas the remainder is slowly released over a period of 2 to 5 months, depending on soil temperatures. An application of 2½ to 4 pounds of urea-form (urea-formaldehyde), worked into 100 sq. ft. of soil will usually furnish enough nitrogen to supply most crops through the summer months.

Potassium can be used to make a glass that dissolves rapidly enough, when ground to a coarse powder, to supply liberal amounts of potash to growing crops for 4 to 12 months despite the leaching effect of rain. One such potassium glass available on the West coast is known as Dura-K.

Minor elements are also furnished in slowly available, long-lasting sources in various glasses or frits. See discussion on page 6.

I desire information concerning "hormones." Hormones (more properly called root-inducing substances) are useful for reducing the time required for some cuttings to root. Most all of them are dusts in which the cutting is dipped. Some are sprayed on developing fruits to prevent drop. Some are sprayed on flowers and thus produce fruits without pollination (tomatoes, holly, etc.). Some are used to increase keeping quality of fruits and vegetables in storage.

Is there anything to the theory of enrichment of the soil with chemicals to include all those needed by the body? Yes. Plant and animal nutrition studies conducted by the various agricultural experiment stations show that an animal that obtains all its food and water from a given area will make a normal or an abnormal growth response, according to the adequacy of the composition of the plants and water fed to it. We should consider ourselves fortunate perhaps, that modern transportation facilities make it possible for Americans to have a daily diet of foods not only from various parts of our large country, but from other countries also.

SOIL DETRIMENTS

Have soapsuds or soapy water from washing clothes any value as fertilizer? The amount of material added in washing water will have very little effect on the nutrient content of the soil. Grease tends to clog the soil, and is objectionable. Naphtha is detrimental.

Is baking powder (double-action) of any use as fertilizer? If so, how is it used? Under the usual soil conditions it has no fertilizer value, and it might even be detrimental.

Is castor oil good for soil around plants? No.

Is cod-liver oil a good plant food for flowers?   No. Use a 4–12–4 or 5–10–5 fertilizer.

Do castor beans and sumac sap the soil much?   Yes, the very luxuriant foliage depletes soils of nitrogen in particular.

SOILLESS CULTURE

What is water culture?   Growth of plants in a watertight container filled with a weak solution of fertilizer salts.

What is sand culture?   Growth of plants in a container of sand through which a weak fertilizer solution either drips continually, or is poured on at intervals.

What house plants can be grown in sand culture?   With care, almost any house plants.

What is gravel culture?   Growth of plants in a watertight container filled with some inert medium, preferably slightly acid, which is flooded, manually or mechanically, from below with a weak fertilizer solution.

What flowering crops may be grown in gravel culture if a greenhouse is available?   Any crop which can be grown in soil. Roses, carnations, chrysanthemums, snapdragons, calendula, annuals, orchids, are all successfully grown.

What vegetable crops may be grown by an amateur in gravel or water culture?   It is not practical to attempt to grow vegetables unless a greenhouse is available. Tomatoes, lettuce, cucumbers, radishes, spinach, kale, etc., can be grown.

What type of soilless culture is best suited for the home?   Sand culture; it requires less equipment than gravel culture, and is more foolproof than water culture.

What type soilless culture is best suited for commercial use?   Gravel culture. Less troublesome than water culture; requires less labor than sand culture.

Will chemical gardening (soilless culture) succeed commercially?   Probably not. Good soil has many advantages over soilless culture, not the least of which is the former's adaptation to the use of large-scale equipment. When people realize that good soil is clean and very responsive to proper enrichment with all necessary nutrient elements, soilless culture will become a by-gone fad, except where it is used as a valuable research method.

Has the experiment with tank farming contributed much to general practices and knowledge in general gardening?   Tank farming (which is water culture) has not contributed much; but gravel and sand culture have been very helpful in the study of general garden problems, particularly from the standpoint of plant nutrition. However, much has been learned about the needs of minor elements from studies in water culture.

In chemical gardening, which containers are best? Under any conditions for commercial use, concrete is best. In the home, wood can be used.

What chemicals are the best to buy for a water chemical garden, especially tomatoes? I have been told Vigoro is all that is needed to put in the water; is that correct? Vigoro will not be satisfactory for water culture. Obtain the following chemicals from your druggist and use the formula herewith: (The numerals indicate ounces.)

Monobasic potassium phosphate	0.5
Potassium nitrate	2.0
Calcium nitrate	3.0
Magnesium sulfate	1.5
Iron sulfate	1 tsp.
Water	25 gals.

What is a "nutrient solution," for soilless gardens? It is composed of fertilizer elements completely soluble in water. Obtain chemicals from your druggist and use the following formula for water, sand, or gravel cultures:

Potassium nitrate	1.0 oz.
Monocalcium phosphate	0.5 "
Magnesium sulfate	0.75 "
Water	5 gals.
Iron sulfate	1 tsp.

SECTION II

Landscaping

INTRODUCTION

BY DONALD WYMAN

FEW OWNERS of small places can have all the landscaping done at
one time. Usually it is extended over several years, a tree or two
being added one season; a group of shrubs the next; a perennial
border later; and so on.

But if a well-conceived plan—no matter how rough a one—is
made in advance, many mistakes are avoided, and the result finally
attained is lasting and more pleasing. This will save much time and
money later on. Trees and shrubs are permanent fixtures, and should
be given their place in the landscape plan only after careful thought
and study.

Usefulness and beauty should be considered in that order. Think
for a moment of the new house on a bare lot, with no planting
whatsoever. Of course it looks bare, if not actually ugly. Trees, shrubs,
and flowers, placed in the right situations, will make the house blend
into the land, and at the same time fulfill many other desirable
purposes. The trees will give shade in the summer and, if properly
placed, help keep the building cool. Evergreens will help in the
screening of objectionable views and aid in keeping the building
warmer in the winter by shielding it from high winds.

Shrubs can be used for beauty and also for the necessary function
of screening and hedgemaking, protecting the property from unwanted
trespassers. Vines can be added for softening the harsh lines of buildings and to help beautify hard wall surfaces. Annuals, perennials, and
bulbs can be planted for beauty and usefulness as well.

The reasons for placing trees, shrubs, and flower borders in definite
areas, and in definite relation to each other, should be thought out
in advance of planting. It is expensive and very time-consuming to
"try" a tree for a year or two in a certain situation and then, later
on, move it to another. If a specimen tree is wanted, and the Siberian
Elm is selected, it is most disheartening to have this tree split from

top to bottom by heavy winds or by snow and ice after it has been thriving for a number of years. It would have been far better to take more time at the beginning, when the plan for the landscaping was being made, to select a sturdy tree rather than a fast-growing but weak-wooded one.

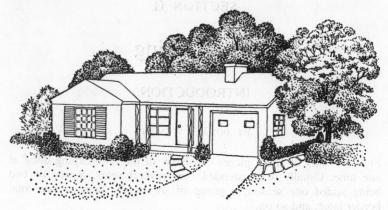

The ideal around-the-house planting provides over-head shade and "ties the house to the ground" without obscuring walls or obstructing windows.

With the great exodus of city dwellers to the country, many families have come to live on small properties in the open, but know little about growing plants. As a result there is an increase of interest in gardening and horticulture. Classes are being formed in many communities, more and more are joining horticultural organizations, more horticultural books are being read, and many commercial nurseries are enjoying some of their best sales' periods.

A very important factor calling for an interest in low-growing plants is the popularity of the picture window. The use of such plants has many advantages. One of these is that the owner may enjoy, to a much fuller extent, all plantings in his garden. The most inexperienced gardener who has a picture window must realize that he will benefit by so arranging his plantings that the garden view from his particular window is as interesting and beautiful as he can possibly make it at all times of the year.

With gardens being forced into smaller and smaller lots, many accessories are being used to make them more interesting and to eliminate as much labor as possible. For instance, there are several types of stripping and metal edgings which are being recommended for edging garden beds and lawn areas to prevent lawn grasses from encroaching on walks or flowers. These certainly make for trim looking beds.

Various types of modern lawn furniture are appearing. Some of it is made of redwood or other substantial material, but some is constructed of light aluminum—in fact so light that the smallest breeze often carries these new chairs over the hill and into the shrubs! Stepping stones are of course still in vogue, but the chain saw has made it comparatively easy and inexpensive to cut thin cross sections off large logs. These are now becoming available as long-lasting stepping "stones" in garden walks, and their use is proving most effective and naturalistic.

Garden labor is being made to look disagreeable by the appearance of all the mechanized garden machinery to mow the lawn, dig the soil, saw the trees, prune off the branches and clip the hedges. After all, a certain amount of muscular work is good for most of us, and there is no better way to obtain just the right amount at the ideal time, than in the garden. Hence, the active gardener might well shun many of these new extras and plan to spend a small amount of his time working at the age-old garden chores. It will do him good physically, and certainly he will become better acquainted with his plants.

Plastics are finding a very important place in the garden in the form of hoses, tools and especially the polythene film. A black type is now being made that is being placed on the ground to smother weeds and to prevent overly rapid water evaporation from the soil. The transparent type of polythene has many uses, for wrapping all kinds of flowers and plants, either for shipping abroad or for delivery to a neighbor down the street. Polythene bags are made for collecting cut flowers and cut branches and for keeping them turgid a day or so.

Also, this same film is being used as a means of winter protection for certain shrubs that might otherwise winter-kill or be burned from excessive winter winds. Plants are not completely enclosed with the film, for if this were done, temperatures might be raised greatly on sunny days, thus resulting in burning of the foliage. However, it is used as a windbreak or shield (with the top open) about plants to protect them from high winter winds and resulting windburn.

Polythene is being used on an increasingly large scale as the covering for small greenhouses, for it is much less expensive than glass; many commercial growers are using it for plant forcing houses. One of its many good properties seems to be its ability to retain heat in any enclosure about which it is securely and tightly fastened.

The selection of the right kind of plant material for the right place does take time, but pays in the end. In making the plan, the trees should be located first, then the evergreens, then the flower borders, shrubs, and vines—in about that order. A typical plan of this sort is shown on page 90. In order to make such a plan intelligently, the gardener must have some knowledge of the different groups of plants, how they can be used, and the types of material available in each. In the following pages these groups are discussed.

Trees

Trees should be considered first because they are the largest and usually the most costly items on the home grounds, and because they require the most time to grow to the desired size. It may take years

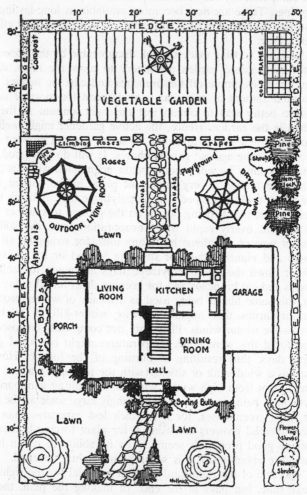

Typical landscape planting plan for a small place, showing the general layout of the entire plot. Detail plans for the different areas can be worked out later.

for a tree to become sufficiently large to give the effect we expect from it. First and foremost, the tree gives shade, either to the house or to the terrace in the garden. It can be planted to obscure some objectionable view, or to aid in giving privacy to the garden. Plenty of room should be given for its full development at maturity (some grow a hundred feet tall, others only twenty-five feet)—a fact not always realized at the time of planting. When trees are well placed they can be beautiful as well as useful.

Sturdy trees should always be selected for permanence, for although many weak-wooded trees do make a good showing in a short time, they are easily broken by wind, snow, and ice. They should never be given a place on the small property unless this fact is well understood. If planted for quick results, it is well to plan to remove or replace them at some future date.

If a tree is to be located where the branches may interfere with service wires, as is frequently necessary, select a tree, such as the wide-arching elm or the wide-spreading oak, for open spaces in the branching of these trees freely permit a pathway for wires, whereas the close-branching habit of a Norway Maple is such that branches must be cut from it to permit a pathway for the wires. Trees should be given plenty of good soil in which to grow. They should not be planted too near flower or vegetable gardens, where their roots undoubtedly will take much nourishment away from the smaller plants.

Small trees, such as the dogwoods, crabapples, and magnolias, are primarily planted for their beauty but can be useful for screening purposes also. Large trees, such as maples, oaks, and lindens, are primarily shade trees but can be counted upon for brilliant autumn color. In planting dig the hole comfortably larger than the roots of the young tree, remembering always that it is far better to put a fifty-cent tree in a two-dollar hole than a two-dollar tree in a fifty-cent hole.

The average house is becoming smaller and the property on which it is situated is becoming smaller. Both these factors are bringing about a change in the type of plants that are being grown on the home grounds. With the size of the average home reduced frequently to one story, there is no need for the continued planting of large 50 to 75 foot shade trees on small properties. Rather there is an increasing interest in trees that mature at about 35 feet, or even less, in height. Many of the once little known maples and crabapples are becoming very popular for this purpose, as well as other trees in this lower class. Because of the wide-spread troubles from the Dutch elm disease, elms are being planted in diminishing numbers. Oaks are still popular but even these are being avoided on the smaller properties. Small trees for small properties seems to be very much the mode at present.

There are many ornamental trees that seldom grow more than 25 to 30 ft. tall. This is well to remember, for frequently there is a place for a small ornamental tree—a crabapple, magnolia, or Oriental cherry, for instance—where a mighty oak or stately elm would dwarf everything else in the planting.

Evergreens

These very useful trees, shrubs, and ground covers are used because of their winter appearance, keeping some of Nature's green foliage color the year 'round. Because of their dense habit of growth, they are especially valued as screening and windbreak plants, and the smaller ones as foundation plants next to the house. They require little attention when soil and climate are to their liking, and are available in a wide assortment of sizes and varieties.

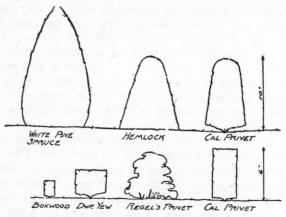

In selecting shrubs and evergreens, for hedges especially, it is important to consider habit of growth and ultimate height.

Some of the evergreens—hemlocks, pines, and spruces—are big trees. Many others are small trees, bushes, or even low, creeping ground covers. As a group they are more difficult to grow than deciduous plants, so they should be selected with care. Before purchasing an evergreen one should ascertain the soil and climatic requirements of the particular kind desired. In the hot, dry, windswept areas of the Midwest only a very few evergreens survive. They need much more moisture in the summer than conditions prevalent in those areas permit.

In the eastern part of the country there is a wide selection from which to choose. Not only many species and varieties of the narrow-leaved, cone-bearing evergreens do well, but also the many bright-flowering, shrubby rhododendrons and evergreen azaleas. These are truly worth while even though they need especially prepared acid soil in which to grow. It should be remembered that some are decidedly hardier than others, and in areas where high winter winds and very low temperatures prevail only the most rugged types should be selected, for many of the more tender types may be injured by adverse weather conditions and show it by the browning of their foliage. High and dry winds in early spring are especially hard on all evergreens.

Shrubs

Shrubs ranging in height from 1 to 20 ft. make up the bulk of the permanent planting after the trees and the evergreens have been properly placed. They are the plants that do the real bordering or hedging, or those which supply the flowers and fruits to make the grounds colorful. Three very important questions should be asked about every shrub used on the small home grounds, namely:

1. *Are the flowers and fruits ornamental?*
2. *When do they appear, and how long are they effective?*
3. *What is the autumn color of the foliage; and is the plant of interest in the winter?*

Some plants, such as the viburnums and the dogwoods, are colorful in flower and fruit and in their autumn hues, and may even have some interest in the winter. Their color can be enjoyed, during three different seasons, for a total of 6 to 8 weeks at least. On the other hand, there are other plants, such as the lilacs, mockoranges, and weigelas, which are colorful only for a 2-week period when they are in flower, and have no interesting fruits or autumn color. When only a small amount of space is available, it is of the utmost importance to select shrubs which are colorful for several seasons, and so are of interest for a much longer time. Hence it pays well to find out the seasons of interest for the different shrubs, and to select the ones that have interest for several periods each year.

With smaller houses and gardens, we are becoming more anxious to use smaller shrubs too. The tall growing lilac and the once popular, vigorous growing, *Euonymus europaea,* are giving over in popularity to lower growing shrubs not over three to four feet in height. Nurserymen are continually looking for even smaller types of new plants for foundation plantings about the house. Some gardeners are going to the extreme trouble of growing espaliered fruit trees on walls and fences, as well as becoming interested in the ancient Japanese art of Bonsai, in an effort to grow more plants in a smaller space.

The ultimate size of the shrubs is very important; the taller ones should be used for backgrounds and screening purposes, while the smaller ones can be used as specimens in the foreground. Locating single-specimen plants is very difficult, even for the trained landscape architect. The most common mistake is to plant a specimen in the dead center of some lawn area. Usually this is absolutely wrong, for open lawn areas lend beauty and increase the apparent size of any property. So it is desirable to place specimens off center or at the side of lawn areas, leaving as long and clear a sweep of unobstructed lawn as possible.

Dense-growing shrubs, such as the barberries, privets, most of the shrub roses, yews, etc., are used as hedges. In fact, almost any shrub can be clipped enough to make it usable as a hedge plant, but the denser-growing types prove best and easiest to trim. Since there are more than one hundred kinds of plants that make good hedges, it is advisable to define clearly at first the exact reasons why a hedge is needed, then to select the plant material that most closely fills the bill. In this way you will be assured of a serviceable hedge, while at the same time you can select some material out of the ordinary which will lend considerable interest to the general appearance of the place. In placing a hedge, never put it on the exact center of a property line, for some future disgruntled neighbor would have the full right to dig up the half on his property. Prune hedges so that they are wider at the bottom than at the top, thus insuring sturdy branches from the ground up.

Vines

Vines are used either for beauty or for screening purposes, or both. They can be divided into two large groups, those that climb by clinging to a wall or support by means of small rootlike holdfasts (as the English Ivy), and those that climb by twining, like the bittersweets and honeysuckles. Never plant a clinging vine on a wooden house, for it will have to be removed every time the house is painted (and usually cannot be replaced), and the small holdfasts will injure the wood, aiding in its decay. Such vines are for stone and brick walls and tree trunks.

Twining vines can be used on wooden houses provided they have a trellis of some sort, or merely a single wire on which to twine. These supports may be made removable, at least at the top, so that the vine can be taken down and put up again at will, without seriously injuring the vine itself. The supports should be held 4 to 6 ins. away from the wooden boards. Or vines such as bittersweet, honeysuckle, and the Fiveleaf Akebia can be trained to twine around rainspouts. An established vigorous twiner will grow 2 stories high in 2 or 3 years, so that if twining on a rainspout it would not be a serious handicap to cut the vine to the ground when painting and repairs are necessary. Wisteria is frequently used, but often it proves too vigorous for the small home.

Clematis vines, like the Sweetautumn Clematis and the Jackman Clematis, and grapes, really belong to the twining group, for they climb by means of tendrils or modified tendrils. Some of the large-

flowered clematis are difficult to grow, requiring just the right kind
of limestone soil. Many annual vines, too, are available, some of which
make a remarkable growth in one season. For a permanent screen,
however, the perennial vines are best; but for flowers, it is difficult to
surpass some of the annuals.

Basic Principles

In this section of the book, information has been included concerning the basic principles of landscaping for the small home and about
special types of gardens.

Needless to say, these particular topics cannot be fully covered in
question-and-answer form; but the number of questions received indicates a very widespread interest in them. Readers who seek further
information are urged to procure, or to obtain from libraries, the
books referred to in the following pages.

A careful study of the illustrations herewith will give the beginner
definite suggestions as to how to attain pleasing results with his plantings and to solve some of the simpler problems of construction in laying out his place.

LANDSCAPE DESIGN AND PLANTING

DESIGN

Why should home grounds be "designed"?   To get the most
efficient use out of them. Hit-or-miss planting never results in full
or efficient use of the land, and it is pictorially ineffective.

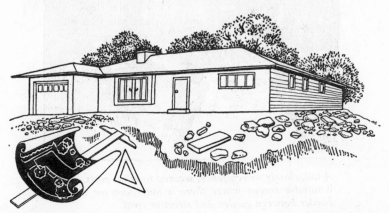

What relationship has planting design to garden design?   Garden
design has to be carried out largely in terms of planting. This is to
say that any plant used should be chosen because it has a definite

place *in the design,* rather than merely because we like its flowers or foliage.

Which is the more important, the artistic or the practical, in designing a small property? Neither; one supplements the other. Any garden, no matter how artistic its design may be, will be ineffective unless the layout is practical. If practical matters only are considered, however, the garden is unlikely to be an artistic success.

Is it necessary to make a plan of a garden? For any but the very simplest of gardens a plan will be found to be a great help in carrying out your intentions. Only by planning ahead of time can you be sure that desirable color combinations will actually be achieved. Changes and rearrangements are more easily made on paper than in the garden itself. A plan is also most useful in estimating quantities; if the planting is not to be done all at once, it is essential.

Why should a garden be "balanced"? Balance, whether symmetrical or irregular, gives a garden picture a feeling of stability and restfulness. A garden that lacks it will be less pleasing, although it may not be immediately apparent what the trouble is, particularly in a naturalistic composition.

What is the "garden axis" we read about? Why is it important? A garden axis is the center line of the composition. It is the basic line on which a design is built. Without it balance and symmetry, which give the garden a pleasing, restful appearance, are hard to develop.

A tall, closely woven fence, secured by stout posts, makes a suitable screen where there is not room for a shrub border between garden and street or road.

What is a "terminal feature"? This is a feature placed at the end of an axis in an oblong composition. It terminates the axis and turns one's attention back to the detail within the garden. A garden house, seat, pool, wall fountain, or group planting make suitable terminal features.

What is meant by the term "focal point"? A focal point is a point of highest interest in the development of the design, such as a pool, garden house, or a group of particularly striking plants. It serves as a center around which the design is built up.

In a square garden, where should the focal point be? In the center, usually. In a square design the important lines lead to or from the center.

What is a vista? A vista is a narrow view framed between masses of foliage. It tends to concentrate the observer's attention, rather than allowing it to spread over a wide panorama.

Must a flower garden be level? A geometrical garden need not be level, but the slope should be away from the principal point from which the garden is seen, rather than from side to side. A naturalistic garden should have, if possible, a natural grade, irregular rather than level or smoothly sloping.

How do you decide on the size of a garden? How large a garden can you take care of? Don't lay out more plantations than you can properly care for. A garden should be in scale with its surroundings, not too big for the house; nor so small as to seem insignificant. If the size of the property is limited, it is well to have the garden occupy the whole space instead of leaving a fringe of unusable space around it.

What is the rule for good proportion in the size of a garden? There is no hard-and-fast rule. Oblong areas are most effective when they are about one and a half times as long as they are wide; but the method of treating them and the surrounding foliage masses affect this considerably. Generally an oblong is better than a square; and an oval (on account of perspective) more effective than a circle.

How can you accent a planting? Is it necessary? Plantings made up of all one kind of plant, or of a few similar varieties, are likely to be monotonous and uninteresting. By using an occasional plant of a different sort an accent is created that makes the planting more interesting. For example, a pointed evergreen in a group of flowering shrubs.

FORMAL AND INFORMAL GARDENS

What is the difference between a formal and a naturalistic garden? Formal design uses straight lines and circular curves or arcs. Informal design uses long, free-flowing curves. Formality emphasizes *lines;* informality emphasizes *space*.

What is required in a formal garden?   A formal garden is essentially a composition in geometric lines—squares, oblongs, circles, or parts thereof. It need not be large, elaborate, or filled with architectural embellishment. Most gardens, on account of space limitations, are basically formal.

Which is the better suited to a small place, a formal or an informal garden?   Topography controls the type of design. On flat ground in proximity to buildings the rectangular (formal) type of design is easier to adapt. On rough land greater informality is desirable, particularly on slopes and in wooded areas.

PLANNING

What are the steps necessary to develop a small property?   Rough grading; staking out walks, drives, and garden area; plan for drainage, if necessary; installation of utilities (water, gas, sewage, etc.); preparation of planting areas; finish grading (top-soil); planting trees, shrubs, and perennials; making the lawn, are of importance in this order.

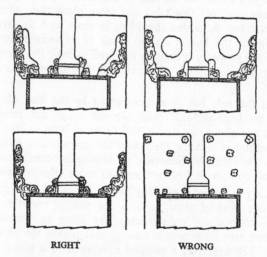

RIGHT   WRONG

Mistakes to avoid in planting. (Top) Leave lawn areas open, free from beds or borders in center of grass plots. (Below) Shrubs planted in polka-dot pattern, and better arrangement of massing them in borders.

Is there anything that can be done in advance of building on a lot that would improve the land or save time later on? The lot is 100 × 100 ft., with trees, bushes, weeds, etc.   Clear out undesirable wild growths and trees where they are too thick. Avoid destroying attractive native shrub masses in locations near the property lines where they may be valuable as part of future shrub borders. Plow and harrow the land. Get rid of roots and stones and plant a cover crop, such as winter rye, until you are ready to use the land.

We have a new home to garden completely, and very little money to put into it. What do you advise concerning first plantings in our garden, to take away the bare, new look? Shade trees come first. Then important screen and background plantings of shrubs, flowering trees, and evergreens. These are the framework of the landscape picture. Add details later.

I have just built a new home, with a large front yard, in a country town. What would be best to set out or plant? Shade trees are important. Plant a few in such a way that they will throw their shade where it is most needed, and where they will compose best with the mass of the house. Shrub borders along the side property lines will help frame the picture. Avoid too much planting against the house, also isolated flower beds.

How would you go about designing a town-house garden area about 18 × 25 ft.? It is shady half the day. In such a garden you will have to depend largely upon the pattern of the design and upon architectural accessories. The planting should be mostly specimen evergreens, vines, and spring bulbs. For the summer, a few annuals, either in pots or beds, will give color.

Can you suggest economical landscaping for a small temporary home? Maintain extreme simplicity. Use the minimum of planting next to the house and in the area facing the street. In the rear, if possible, have a compact vegetable garden bordered with annual and perennial flowers.

What sort of garden would you plant in a plot 60 × 30 ft.? An area of this sort is usually most effectively developed by having an open grass panel in the center, with herbaceous borders along the sides backed up by shrub borders, or hedges, and a strong terminal feature at the end. This last could be a pool or garden house backed up by a heavy planting.

How can one arrange flowers in the garden properly? They are best arranged in groups; the size of the groups to conform to the size of the border, 3 to 5 plants of medium and low kinds, 3 of tall kinds. Space the tall plants 18 to 24 ins. apart, and others 9 to 12 ins. apart. Keep the very tall ones to the rear, with an occasional tall group toward the center. Irregularity of outline, irregularity in size of groups, and the avoidance of straight lines are among some of the things to be observed in arranging plants in a border.

What is the best way to arrange plants in a flower bed or border?

Plants in a flower border should be arranged according to height. Keep the low ones near the front edge and the tallest ones at the back. Occasionally, for accent, a tall plant can be brought farther forward than it normally would be. Of course in beds with a path on *both* sides of it, the tall plants would be placed in the center.

In arranging the mixed flower border, tall-growing subjects (such as delphiniums, hollyhocks, and digitalis) are kept to the rear.

How wide should a flower border be?   To provide succession of bloom throughout the season a border 10 to 14 ft. wide is none too much. Narrower borders can be treated effectively for seasonal bloom, but there will be times when few if any flowers will be present. A width of 4 ft. is about the least that can be effectively planted.

How should I plan a perennial flower garden?   Consult one or two good books that carry plans of such gardens. Select a plan that can be fitted easily into your scheme, and of a size you can manage. Consult a table of perennials that gives height, season of bloom and color. Study the arrangement well the first year after planting. Then is the time to do the final replanting. (See other questions.)

Will you give suggestions for a practical mixed perennial and annual flower border?   Two plans can be followed when combining annuals with perennials. One is to leave spaces in the border where annuals can be sown or plants set out early. The other is to raise annual plants for filling in bare spots as they occur. The former plan requires less work since by using this plan one can sow annual seeds directly in place and not go to the trouble of setting out individual plants. Annuals generally are used to pick up the blooming period, which begins in July. In May, sow seeds of *Phlox drummondi*, alyssum, cosmos (early), marigold, zinnia, directly in the border. Obtain plants, or sow seeds in April, of lobelia, nicotiana, petunia, *Salvia farinacea*. Verbenas should be sown early in March. Annuals should, where possible, be planted near those perennials which do not bloom in summer.

I should like a mixed bed of irises, phlox, and chrysanthemums. How can I have blooms spring, summer, and fall? Is this possible? If so, how big a bed? How many plants, and how far apart should they be to make an effective planting? The size of the bed must depend upon how much time you have to devote to it. Time and labor are involved in maintaining a perennial planting. It takes a lot of each. (See questions about size.) Using irises, phlox, and chrysanthemums, so place them in the bed that at their particular season there is a good distribution of bloom. Don't use too much iris, or too large groups. Distribute in the same way a few varieties of the novae-angliae and novibelgi hardy asters for September bloom. Tie all these together with such perennials as *Achillea ptarmica,* anthemis, aquilegia, *Campanula persicifolia,* coreopsis, dictamnus, gypsophila. Plant in groups of 3, placing plants 15 ins. apart. Toward the edge use *Anemone japonica* varieties, dwarf asters (hardy), *Campanula carpatica, Dianthus deltoides* and *D. latifolius,* and geums. Plant in groups of 3, 6 to 12 ins. apart. For early spring, use tulips and narcissi interplanted in groups throughout the planting. Along the edge, plant arabis, aubrieta, *Alyssum saxatile* and *A. saxatile citrinum, Phlox subulata* varieties, and pansies. (See Chrysanthemums for other suggestions.)

Which perennial flowers are most satisfactory for a small garden? Any whose habit of growth and size of flower are not out of scale for a small area. A list of such are *Alyssum argenteum; Arabis albida;* aquilegia, various; dianthus, various; *Aster subcoeruleus* (Himalayan Daisy); bleedingheart; *Campanula carpatica* and *C. persicifolia;* lily-of-the-valley; *Delphinium chinense,* dwarf; candytuft; forget-me-not; chrysanthemum, dwarf; *Geum borisi;* Gypsophila Rosy Veil; heuchera, various; Hemerocallis Goldena; *Lychnis floscuculi; Nepeta mussini; Plumbago larpentae;* primula, various; pyrethrum; *Lilium tenuifolium, L. concolor,* and *L. flavum;* Iceland Poppy; peonies— *P. tenuifolia* and *P. latifolia, Phlox divaricata* and *P. decussata; Veronica incana* and *V. amethystina.*

How can I plan for a continuous succession of bloom from early spring until late fall? First by having a wide planting space, at least 10 or 12 ft. in width, and by so planning that you have a few plants for each season in each part of the border.

Is it all right to plant roses and flowers together? Hybrid tea roses do not do well with other plants, but the floribundas, polyanthas, and hybrid perpetuals can be so used.

Backed by peonies and climbing roses, we have a rectangular bed 15 × 18 ft. What do you advise for a front planting? Interplant Regal Lily and *L. speciosum* among peonies. Enrich soil, plant solid with phlox, such as Africa, Charles Curtis, Columbia, Mary

Louise, Pinkette, Salmon Beauty. Edge with cushion chrysanthemums. For early color you could interplant between the phlox with small groups of cottage tulips and an edging of pansies.

BACKGROUNDS

Should a small garden be enclosed? Yes. Any garden picture is more effective if the flowers can be seen against a background of shrubs, hedge, wall, or fence. Furthermore, views out of a garden tend to distract attention from the garden itself.

The charm of the half-hidden: an enclosing wall leads the imagination to beauty beyond.

Should flower borders and beds have a background? Isolated flower beds with no background are rarely effective. Borders in front of shrubs, hedges, or walls make better places for color compositions.

What makes the best background hedge for a flower garden? Evergreens are probably better than deciduous shrubs because they do not grow so fast or provide such serious root competition. They are also effective in winter. Arborvitae, cedar, hemlocks, or Japanese Yew are suitable. (See also Hedges—Section II.)

I should like to plant a hedge for a background around my garden and have flowers in front. Would the hedge roots interfere with the

flowers? Yes, unless the flowers were planted at least 3 or 4 ft. away from the hedge. To prevent root interference, dig a trench about 3 ft. down, between the hedge and the flower border, and put in a thin wall of concrete to discourage the hedge roots from occupying the border.

I have a square area, about 40 ft. on a side, that I can enclose with a hedge and shrubbery, and which I would like to use for a flower garden. What arrangement of beds would you suggest? In such a definitely circumscribed area a geometrical pattern is almost mandatory. But it can be either a pattern of beds, planted with low bedding plants, or an open-center pattern where taller flowers and some shrubs are used in wide borders around the sides.

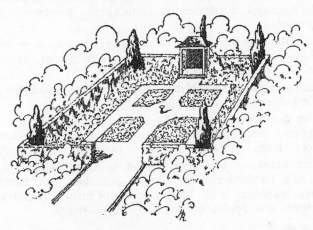

Typical enclosed formal garden of symmetrical design.

FLOWER BEDS

Our flower beds are best viewed from our porch. We use the porch more in July and August. What flowers should be used to give lots of color in these months? Among the perennials: phlox, hollyhock, gaillardia, daylily, coreopsis, heliopsis, rudbeckia, penstemon, stokesia, and plantainlily are all good. Satisfactory annuals are zinnia, marigold, cosmos, salvia, ageratum, calliopsis, calendula, celosia, and cornflower.

What are "bedding" plants; and how are they used? Bedding plants are low, compact annuals set out each year to form a definite pattern. They are most effective when used in a garden that is viewed from above.

Which type of plant makes the best edging for a flower bed?

Low, compact evergreens, such as boxwood or Dwarf Teucrium give the most finished effect. Low, compact perennials, such as dwarf asters, armeria, and heuchera, give a softer effect. Perennials that can be sheared after flowering, such as candytuft and dianthus, can be used.

TO ATTRACT BIRDS

Which flowers attract birds? Birds are attracted by the seed of the plants and then only seed-eating birds. Sunflowers, *Eryngium amethystinum,* rudbeckia, coreopsis, poke, lily-of-the-valley, wild and species roses, partridge-berry, wild strawberry, wintergreen.

Which flowers can I plant that are most attractive to hummingbirds? Aquilegia, delphinium, monarda, phlox, penstemon, physostegia, tritoma.

Which vines attract birds? Vines that produce seeds or berries: bearberry, bittersweet, cranberry, dewberry, the grapes, the honeysuckles. Virginia creeper, morningglories.

Which evergreens attract birds? Redcedar, fir, hemlock, the pines, yew, the junipers, arborvitae, hollies.

Which shrubs encourage birds? Most of the berried shrubs. Some are bayberry, benzoin, blackalder, blackberry, chokeberry, elderberry, hawthorn, holly, mulberry, shadbush, snowberry, the viburnums.

Which deciduous tree shall I plant to attract birds? Alders, White Ash, linden, beech, the birches, box elder, elm, hackberry, the oaks, hornbeam, larch, Black Locust, the maples, mountain-ash, wild cherry, crab apples, oriental cherries, hawthorns.

BORDERS

Will you list a few low plants for edging or the front of a border of perennials? Aethionema (Persian Stonecress); *Ajuga genevensis* (Geneva Bugle); *Alyssum citrinum; Arabis alpina* fl. pl. (Double Rockcress); *Artemisia abrotanum* (Southernwood); dianthus in variety; *Globularia trichosantha* (globedaisy); heuchera in variety; *Jasione perennis* (Shepherd's Scabiosa); *Nepeta mussini; Phlox divaricata* (Canada Blue Phlox); *Polemonium reptans* (Greek Valerian); *Scutellaria baicalensis* (Azure Skullcap); *Silene schafta* (Autumn Catchfly); *Armeria maritima* (thrift); *Stokesia laevis* (Stokes Aster); *Veronica incana* (Woolly Speedwell); viola in variety.

Please give explicit plans for an effective border, mostly of perennials. I have a border on either side of a concrete walk in my back yard, 72 ft. long and 4 ft. wide. I should like to follow a well-planned design that would look well and furnish cutting flowers. How close together can plants in a border be placed? Plan and design your border, including such reliable cut-flower selections as peonies, irises, delphiniums, Regal and Madonna Lilies, together with hardy chrysanthemums for fall cutting. Toward the front of the border you should include such reliable bulbs as tulips, Dutch irises, and narcissi. All of the things mentioned are almost necessary to any good perennial border, but there are many other excellent perennials listed in flower catalogues from which to choose. For constant cutting it will be necessary for you to add some of your favorite annuals each year. The best rule for determining the distance between plants is to visalize them at their blooming season and give them sufficient space so that they will not be crowded by their neighbors. (See also Planning, this section.)

What are good companion plants for tall-bearded irises in a narrow border along driveway? Lupine, pink, veronica, doronicum, *Phlox suffruticosa,* geum, and delphinium.

FOR COLOR

Should a garden have a "color scheme"? If so, how do you make one? Restricted color schemes for small gardens have been overdone. Color harmony is important, and plants should be so placed that interesting color combinations result and violent clashes do not occur. Sometimes it is wise to rule out certain "difficult" colors, such as red and purple.

How important is good foliage in a color scheme? Are the flowers only to be considered? Good foliage should be considered because it creates a background for the flowers. Use strong-foliaged plants near or among weak-foliaged ones, or those whose foliage disappears. Often the foliage itself (which may be gray-green, yellow-green, or bluish-green) plays an important part in the color scheme.

How can I plan lovely color combinations in my garden? Effective color combinations in the garden must be thoughtfully worked out on paper beforehand. Make lists of plants according to color, and also time of bloom. Then with a large-scale plan of the garden and a set of colored crayons indicate their proposed position on paper before you start to plant.

Can you suggest some other BLUE FLOWERS besides larkspur and cornflowers? Ageratum, lobelia, browallia, torenia, Swanriver-daisy (brachycome), linaria, nigella, morningglory, scabiosa, *Aconitum fischeri,* forget-me-nots, aquilegia, aster, companula, catananche, delphinium, clematis, echinops, mistflower, polemonium, *Salvia farinacea,* anchusa, cynoglossum, pulmonaria, ajuga. Bulbs: scilla, grapehyacinth, chionodoxa, hyacinth.

I plan to have a garden of primarily bright RED PLANTS. Can you name some? Zinnia, marigold, poppy, mallow, salvia, geranium, celosia, cardinalflower, nicotiana, hollyhock, penstemon, peony, beebalm, geum, Gaillardia Ruby, dahlia, rose, nasturtium, Heuchera Queen of Hearts, semperflorens begonia. Bulbs: tulip, tigridia, nerine.

Can you suggest some RED FLOWERS for a circular bed around my flagpole? I have planned to use dwarf blue ageratum with white sweet alyssum, but can find no bright red flower with dwarf and free-flowering habits. Try dwarf scarlet sage (salvia), dwarf red zinnia, cockscomb (celosia), red geranium, or verbena.

I have heard that gardens planted with only WHITE FLOWERS are effective. Are they? All-white gardens are often effective if one has room for background material such as evergreens and shrubs. They give a feeling of spaciousness and quiet. However, an all-white garden is likely to become tiresome unless one has space enough for other types of gardens and for borders of colorful plants.

What plants would you suggest for an all-white garden? Phlox, arabis, asters, chrysanthemum, larkspur, babysbreath, iberis, peony, platycodon, scabiosa, stokesia, yucca, veronica, alyssum, saponaria, petunia, poppy, nicotiana, sweetpea, morningglory, moonflower, arctotis. Bulbs: snowdrop, crocus, hyacinth, tulip, narcissus.

Will you suggest some bright YELLOW FLOWERS for the garden? Potentilla, thalictrum, oenothera, daylily, sunflower, zinnia, marigold, snapdragon, doronicum, chrysanthemum, dahlias, California Poppy, coreopsis, baptisia, *Alyssum saxatile,* anthemis, gaillardia, cosmos, celosia, calendula, nasturtium. Bulbs: snowdrop, crocus, daffodil, tulip, sternbergia.

FLOWERS FOR CUTTING

What are some desirable perennials for cut flowers, blooming in May and June, besides iris, etc.? *Doronicum caucasicum, Dicentra eximia, Dianthus plumarius* and varieties, *Delphinium belladonna, Alyssum saxatile citrinum, Saponaria ocymoides splendens, Pulmonaria saccharata, Phlox suffruticosa* and varieties, *Phlox divaricata,* Geum Fire Opal, *Anchusa myostidiflora,* Peony and Oriental Poppy.

Can you tell me how to have cut flowers as early as possible, and for as long a time as possible? Tall-bearded iris, Siberian iris, coreopsis, Delphinium Belladonna, *Eupatorium coelestinum,* gaillardia, geum, gypsophila, helenium, penstemon, physostegia, aster, chrysanthemum; spring bulbs.

Which flowers are best suited for show and cutting purposes? Tritoma, antirrhinum, aster, campanula, gaillardia, coreopsis, *Anemone japonica,* artemisia, chrysanthemum, and doronicum. Roses, delphinium, daffodil, tulip, peony, gladiolus, iris.

Which garden flowers are best for cutting, and last longest after

being cut? Aster, tritoma, chrysanthemum, helianthus, scabiosa, zinnia, aquilegia, *Stokesia lilacina, Verbena bonariensis,* celosia, and marigold.

Anticipating an August wedding, which white or pastel-colored flowers can we plant with which to decorate the church? White Shastadaisy, delphinium, chrysanthemum, phlox, aster, stock, scabiosa, gladiolus, and gypsophila.

FOR EDGING

What is a desirable perennial edging between lawn and border? Dwarf Teucrium (*T. chamaedrys*), *Iberis sempervirens* Little Gem, *Dianthus caesius.*

I have a formal garden with 100 tulips and phlox at end. Which flowers are best to plant for edging and gradual build-up in size to height of phlox? *Doronicum caucasicum, Phlox arendsi, Phlox divaricata, Dianthus plumarius, Anchusa myosotidiflora, Ajuga genevensis, Alyssum saxatile compactum, Anemone hupehensis, Anemone magellanica, Veronica spicata, Veronica incana,* dwarf asters, dwarf chrysanthemums.

Can you suggest some low edging plants with white flowers (not sweet alyssum) to plant where tulips have finished blooming? Dwarf petunia; annual phlox; dwarf verbena.

I want to lay out a colonial garden using beds in some design. What shall I edge the beds with? Dwarf box edging is typical. Dwarf teucrium and clipped English Ivy can be substituted.

PLANNING FOUNDATION PLANTINGS

(See also Foundation Material—Section III.)

What kind of shrubbery would you plant in front of a new house with a 30-ft. frontage? Use tall, upright-growing plants at the corners and low-growing, rounded masses between. Avoid too much planting. If the house foundation is low enough, leave some spaces bare to give the house the effect of standing solidly on the ground. Either deciduous or evergreen material is suitable.

We have large trees (oak, Gray Birch, maple, and ironwood). What should be planted near the house? The yard slopes toward the south and the house is new, so we are starting from scratch. Let the trees constitute the principal landscape feature. Use a minimum of planting near the house—vines on the foundation, a few shade-loving shrubs at the corners or either side of the entrance.

What is the best method of foundation planting for an "unbalanced" house—one with the door not in the center? An unbalanced composition for a foundation planting can be made extremely attractive. The fact that the door is not in the center will make it even more interesting. Naturally the doorway should be the point of interest, and your maximum height should begin on either side, tapering irregularly to the corners of the house where a specimen shrub or overgreen may go a little higher in order to break the sharp lines of the house corner. These corner accents should not be so tall as the main planting on either side of the doorway.

A symmetrical balanced entrance planting.

What is best for planting around a small house on a small acreage? Everyone has evergreens. Can't we have simplicity and still be different? Deciduous shrubs can be just as interesting throughout much of the year although it is the evergreens which lend interest in the winter. Why not use both deciduous shrubs with a few evergreens as a background?

I want to plant flowers along the base of our house. Will you suggest what kind of flowers to plant? Unless the house is an architectural jewel which should not be hidden, shrubs or vines, or both, as a background, with flowers planted in front of them, give a better effect than flowers which, alone, are apt to look too small and inadequate near a house foundation. Flowers to plant in front of shrubs by house: tulip, narcissus, crocus, *Scilla sibirica,* followed by dictamnus, polyantha roses, and *Phlox decussata.* Or use long drifts of one variety of annual, limited to one or two colors, such as Petunias Elks Pride and Snowdrift, or Heavenly Blue or Rosy Gem; or for a gay effect a good mixture of marigolds.

CAPE COD

How shall I landscape the front of our Cape Cod house? It was built about 1810 and during the 6½ years we have owned it every minute has been spent in restoring the old pine paneling within doors and developing the flower and vegetable gardens outside. There is the main house with front door in the center, an ell, and a long shed-garage combination. What treatment all along the front would you suggest? Planting for a Cape Cod house should be very simple. A suitable planting is shown in the accompanying sketch. Shade trees are important and should be carefully placed. A small dooryard enclosed by a low picket fence often adds to the charm if the house sets far enough back from the highway to permit its being used.

The Cape Cod type of home calls for a low foundation planting, in keeping with its architectural lines.

We have a small home, Cape Cod. Which shrubs can be planted that would not be too expensive or difficult to grow? Among the "sure-fire" shrubs are *Amorpha nana;* berberis, various (barberry); *Caragana aurantiaca; Cotoneaster horizontalis; Deutzia gracilis; Euonymus alatus; Genista tinctoria;* broom; *Hypericum patulum* and *H. frondosum* (St. Johnswort); Philadelphus Mt. Blanc and P. Norma; wild roses; lilac; spirea.

COLONIAL

What can be done with a narrow front lawn between an old-fashioned house with a high porch and the street—which is lined with large, old maples? Grass will probably not be very successful in such a place. Use *Vinca minor* or *Pachysandra terminalis* in place of it, and hide the porch foundation with a planting of laurel (*Kalmia latifolia*), rhododendron, or other shade-loving shrubs. Such a planting will require heavy applications of acid, humus-making fertilizer and frequent watering.

ENGLISH

Could you tell me what kind of foundation planting I could use for an English-type home? The English style, being informal, calls for informal planting. Avoid symmetrically balanced groups of planting, or too much planting. Accent the doorways, the corners, and leave the rest open. Vines are important to soften brickwork or stone.

FARMHOUSES

Do you suggest landscaping a plot around a farmhouse? A farm home needs planting, but it does not need the intensive landscape development that characterizes the average suburban home. Use a few well-placed clumps of hardy shrubs and small-flowering trees.

What native material can be collected in Maine that would be suitable for landscape use around a farmhouse? Hemlock, witchhazel, winterberry, birch, Sugar Maples, Red Maples, pines, larch, arborvitae, Virginia Rose, blueberries, and many other shrubs. Take a walk through the woods there and see for yourself.

FRENCH

What sort of foundation planting is appropriate to an informal French house? An informal house should have informal planting.

A small home calls for simplicity of design in landscaping.

Avoid rigid balance, and hold the planting down to the minimum. Use a few choice things rather than many ordinary plants. Clumps of broad-leaved evergreens are particularly effective.

MODERN

What plants should be used around a modern ranch-type house in front of a large rock outcrop? Make use of the natural rock by all means, planting rock plants and creeping junipers around it. Low yews, azaleas and pieris might be in the foundation planting with a dogwood and crabapples used as the trees.

RUSTIC

We have a cabin among trees and woodland. We would like to make the immediate grounds of the cottage look much nicer than they now are. How could we go about it? Underplant the area with various kinds of native ferns and woodland wildflowers.

FOR HEDGES

See page 391.

HILLSIDE PLANTING

How could a rather steep hillside, partly wooded, be planted to make it more attractive? Such a wooded hillside could be underplanted with native shrubs, evergreens, ferns, and woodland wildflowers. An interesting system of trails leading through the area would add to its interest.

SCREENS

How can I disguise my chicken house and yard so that they will not injure the appearance of my property? If the wire of the chicken run is strong enough, you might plant a vine such as honeysuckle on it. The house itself can be made less conspicuous by planting a group of pines and spruces around it. Or the whole thing can be hidden behind a dense hedge.

Would a mixture of plants with various colored leaves or blossoms be satisfactory in an informal screening for enclosing a yard? Usually a suitable boundary screen consists of one variety of shrub. Too varied a planting competes with the interest inside the garden instead of merely framing it. Variety in leaf, flower, and fruit may be inside the boundary screen or in foundation plantings of buildings.

What are some fast growing vines that would make good screens? Bower Actinidia, Dutchman's Pipe, Virginia Creeper, Kudzu Vine and grape species.

What type of shrubs make good informal screening for enclosing yard? Choice is determined by size of area to be enclosed and height of objects to be "screened out." Persian Lilac is excellent for areas of a quarter acre and larger. Smaller gardens may use *Rosa hugonis, Rosa rubrifolia,* Truehedge Columnberry, or privet, untrimmed.

SHRUBS

Should shrubs and small trees be used in a flower garden? Yes, an occasional compact-growing tree or shrub in the garden relieves the monotony of perennial and annual planting.

We plan to landscape a 3-acre tract. Will you name flowering shrubs that give a succession of bloom throughout the year? For spring: azalea, forsythia, lonicera, *Viburnum carlesi*. For summer: hydrangea, buddleia, roses, abelia, heather, rose-of-sharon. For fall: abelia, witch-hazel. For autumn color: Euonymus alatus, dogwoods, viburnums, Japanese barberry, sumacs and spice bush.

Can you suggest hardy shrubbery for a small country home? Standard varieties of deciduous shrubs, such as spirea, lilac, deutzia, philadelphus, and weigela, can always be relied upon to thrive with the minimum amount of care. Interest can be added to the planting by using some of the rarer varieties, such as *Philadelphus virginalis,* hybrid lilacs, and a few of the small-flowering trees, such as Tatarian honeysuckle, flowering crab, dogwood, and redbud.

FOR SHADE

See also Shady Environment—Section III.

There is no sun in my garden from September until May. What is the best way to treat a garden of this kind? Since the floral display in this garden will be effective only from late spring to early fall, make sure the garden background is interesting enough to make the garden attractive during the rest of the year. Use evergreen, berry-bearing shrubs and ones that have good, full color. Then for flowers select only those plants that bloom during the time when sunlight is available.

Will you suggest plants for a garden in an all-shade yard? Aconitum, ajuga, aquilegia, campanula, cimicifuga, dicentra, digitalis, ferns, hosta, hemerocallis, hesperis, lily-of-the-valley, thalictrum, tradescantia, trillium, valeriana, and viola are the principal shade-loving kinds of garden flowers. There are many varieties of most.

Which flowers are best for part shade? Perennials for part shade: *Achillea filipendulina,* aconite, cimicifuga, digitalis, *Anemone japonica, Lobelia cardinalis,* mertensia, hosta, helleborus, daylily, trollius, primrose, Virginia-cowslip, may-apple, Showy Ladyslipper.

Which perennial flowers, tall, medium, low, may I use in a garden shaded by oak trees? What soil improvements should be made to overcome acidity from oaks? Most perennial plants are not particular as to the acidity or alkalinity of soil. If there is overacidity from the leaves of your oak tree this may be corrected by an annual sprinkling of ground limestone worked shallowly into the topsoil. Your location should be ideal without treatment for all of your native wildflowers.

The low-growing group would include cypripediums, woods ferns, etc. (See Woodland Wildflowers.) For taller plants you have a wide choice from such things as holly, mountain laurel, azalea, blueberries, and rhododendron. The combination of these should be an attractive planting.

Please name a few plants that will grow in dense shade, around base of large tree. Must I put them in pots on account of roots of tree? Few plants will subsist on what's left in the soil after the roots of a large tree have filled the surface and used all available food. Try digging out pockets, filling them with good loam, and planting one of the following: *Viola canadensis, Mahonia repens, Vinca minor,* Kenilworth Ivy, pachysandra. Potted plants would be of only temporary value.

Which flower is the best to plant under a big maple tree where there are lots of roots and practically no sun? Altitude is 6,600 ft. Norway Maple (*Acer platanoides*) foliage is so dense that few plants can survive both shade and the fight for root space and food. Deep watering of all maples encourages the development of deeper rooting, thus freeing the surface from this strangling network. Ground covers that accept the challenge of most maples are *Vinca minor, Mahonia repens,* pachysandra, *Sedum stoloniferum.*

Which plants would grow well along a shady wall? *Euonymus radicans vegetus,* aquilegia, ladyslipper, hepatica, *Epimedium niveum, Plumbago larpentae,* dicentra, digitalis, sanguinaria, ferns, mertensia, anemone, primula, pulmonaria, aconitum, dodecatheon, thalictrum, *Anchusa myosotidiflora.* Trees which provide shade for plants in nature also supply abundant humus in the soil by their decayed leaves. Shade plants in the garden appreciate humus too.

SLOPES AND BANKS

See also Section III.

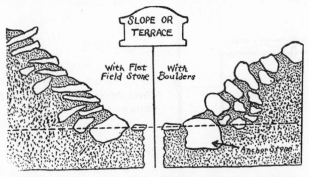

Method of placing stones to hold a slope or a terrace, without a wall.

Will you suggest some shrubs or trees for the sloping terrace in front of my house? Roses such as Max Graf and *Rosa wichuraiana, Jasminum nudiflorum,* lonicera, bearberry, or dwarf, spreading evergreens.

How should a sloping area (15 × 3 ft.) along a driveway be planted? Fence or wall would be unsuitable. The location is sunny. Such a place is best treated by planting the slope with some easy-to-take-care-of, low, trailing shrub or perennial. *Phlox subulata alba, Teucrium chamaedrys, Juniperus chinensis sargenti,* or *Euonymus fortunei vegetus* would be suitable.

How fast does the Memorial Rose grow? And how far apart should it be planted? This is one of the best shrubs for bank planting, rooting all along its stems which can grow 4′ a year. A new planting should have the plants spaced about 4′ apart.

SURFACE DRAINAGE

What is a dry well, and what is it used for? A dry well is a pit dug 5 or 6 ft. deep, filled with stones and gravel. A pipe or sewer leading either from the house or from a poorly drained area leads into this, and provides drainage for difficult situations.

What can be done to prevent rain water from draining off the highway onto a sloping property, causing erosion? A low bank along the highway should be constructed, and at the lowest point in the gutter so created a catch basin can be installed to gather the water and lead it, through a pipe, to a place where it will do no harm. Such a catch basin can be simply 2 18-in. sewer tiles, one on top of the other, with a grating fitted into the top and a 4-in. side outlet about 1 ft. below the top. If there is a great deal of water, it may have to be a brick, concrete, or stone basin.

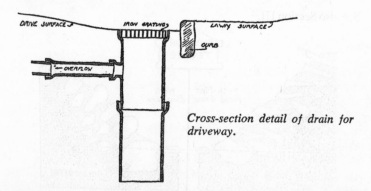

Cross-section detail of drain for driveway.

How can I construct a catch basin to take off surplus rain water from the drive? Two pieces of 18-in. sewer tile, set one on top of the other, and with an iron grating fitted into the top, make a good, cheap catch basin. Smaller tile are too difficult to clean; larger are seldom needed. If the amount of water to be taken care of is large, a 4-in. or 6-in. tile pipe can be taken from the top catch-basin tile (which can be obtained with a side outlet) and carried some distance away to a low point where the water will do no harm, or to the storm sewer.

TREES

Should trees be removed from gardens? Not necessarily. If the trees are fine old specimens, they should be left, and the garden designed around them using plants that will withstand shade; otherwise they should be taken out. Often trees form an important part of the garden's design.

Many American elms are being removed in our town because they have succumbed to the Dutch elm disease. What are some good large shade trees to use as substitutes? Maples, hackberry, yellow-wood, beech, ash, honey-locust, especially the "Moraine" and the yellow leaved "Sunburst" locusts, sweet gum, cucumber tree, Amur cork tree, Buttonball, Sargent cherry, various oaks, sophora, lindens and zelkova.

Can you suggest desirable evergreens and deciduous trees for use in landscaping a suburban home? See Section III.

GARDEN FEATURES AND ACCESSORIES

ARBORS

I want to buy an arbor for my garden on which to train roses. What type is best? White-painted wooden arbors are inexpensive and look well. Get one that is sturdy and well designed. Rustic arbors, made from cedar or redwood, are also suitable.

BIRD BATHS

What type of bird bath is good for the small garden? Any well-made concrete, marble, clay, wood, or stone bird baths that are available, as long as they are well designed and unobtrusive. Select a design which fits your garden plan. Homemade cement-and-field-stone bird baths are not usually desirable. For a small garden a height of 2½ ft. is about right. If the bath is detached from the pedestal, it will facilitate cleaning.

Are the bird baths which are set on the ground without a pedestal practical? Yes, they are very effective if well designed. Handmade ceramic or metal basins are interesting, or a hollowed stone may be used. They are usually placed in a sheltered spot surrounded by ivy or other ground cover, evergreens, or shrubs. It must be remembered, however, that this type bird bath can be used only where no cats are around to harm the birds when they use it.

How often should you clean bird baths?   As often as they look dirty or stained, which is usually 2 or 3 times a week at least in warm weather. It will help to have a special scrubbing brush for the bird bath for removing scum around the edges.

What can be used to remove algae from a bird bath?   Usually water or soapy water and a scrubbing brush are all that is necessary. Borax may be added, or a bleaching disinfectant. These, however, must be well rinsed off before filling the bath with water for the birds.

CURBINGS

Would you recommend brick or stone edging for a driveway or path?   For a driveway, brick edging is somewhat too fragile unless the bricks are set in a heavy foundation of concrete. Then they are likely to be ugly. Granite paving blocks (Belgian blocks) are better because they are heavy enough to stay put without cement. For pathways, brick is ideal. Small rounded stones are useless for either purpose.

What sort of edging should I use for a brick walk?   There are 3 standard sorts of edging: sawtooth, rowlock, and stretcher. For garden paths where there are no grass edges, sawtooth looks well, and it uses less brick than does rowlock. Against a lawn or grass edge rowlock is better because the mower can be run up on it and there is less hand clipping. Stretcher edging uses the least brick of all, but, since the bricks do not go down into the ground any farther than the bricks of the walk itself, it provides less stability for the walk.

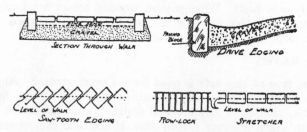

Types of edging for walks and drives.

What can I use to edge a driveway that will look well, but also make a strong, permanent edge?   Granite paving blocks are ideal for this. They are so heavy they will stay in place without concrete to hold them. Do not let them stick up above the lawn area. Set them on end, with the short dimension parallel to the line of the driveway.

Should flower beds be edged with stones, brick, or plants?   Stone edgings are a nuisance, since the grass around them has to be hand clipped. Brick edgings have the same fault but in connection with gravel paths give a prim, quaint effect. In most cases edgings of flowering plants are more suitable.

DOORWAYS

The doorway of my house is a reproduction of an old colonial door, with leaded side lights and fanlight. How should I plant this so as to enhance rather than detract from its beauty?   For an elaborate doorway, which is sufficiently interesting in itself, elaborate planting is unnecessary. Possibly the most effective thing would be to plant a big old lilac on either side of the door, train a light vine, possibly a large-flowered clematis, over the door itself, and leave it at that.

Suggestion for planting a colonial doorway.

Should planting either side of the front door always be alike on both sides?   Certainly not. If the house is in an informal or picturesque architectural style, the planting should also be informal and picturesque. Use a tall, dark plant on one side, with a few smaller things around its base, and on the other side use something lighter, more graceful and spreading. Don't use too many kinds of plants and too many sorts of foliage.

My colonial house seems to me to have a very plain doorway. How can I plant it to make it seem more important?   Where the doorway is formal, but very plain, interest must be created through the planting. Use identical groups on either side, but select the various plants carefully for form texture and foliage color. Evergreens give great dignity and are less likely to get too large in a short time. Tall masses to accent the lines of the doorway, with more spreading plants around them, usually make the most effective arrangement.

A nicely balanced, but not symmetrical, front-door planting.

DRIVEWAYS

What material do you recommend for the building of a driveway?
Many materials make satisfactory driveways, but much depends on
whether the drive is straight or curved, flat or sloping, in cold country
or warm. A good, cheap driveway for a level drive in the New York
area can be made of either cinders mixed with loam and sand or
bank-run gravel. Either can be finished with grits or bluestone screenings. If there are curves or grades, crushed stone with a tar binder is
practically mandatory.

**How would you build a driveway on a steep slope to prevent wash-
ing? What material should be used?**   For a short driveway on a steep
slope, granite paving blocks set in sand make an ideal material. They
are rough enough to give good traction in icy weather, they need no
maintenance, they are good-looking. For a long driveway, they may be
too uneven for comfortable riding, and concrete, heavily scored to
provide traction, may be better. But it is a hard, uncompromising-
looking material.

**I am building a driveway for my home. What sort of parking space
for visiting cars do you recommend, and where should it be located?**
Parking space for at least one guest car should be provided right at the
front door or the path leading to it, so arranged that the use of the
driveway by other cars is not prevented. (See next question.) Parking
for a larger number of cars should be located at a distance from the
front entrance of the house. It should be constructed of the same
material as the driveway.

**When guests come to the house and leave their cars before the
front door, it is impossible for anyone else to use the driveway from
the garage to the street. How can I avoid this situation?**   Construct
a pass court in front of the door wide enough so that a car can stand
at the door and another pass it on the outside. The court should be

about 30 ft. long and 16 ft. wide. Any interesting shape can be given it to make it a pleasing part of the landscape picture.

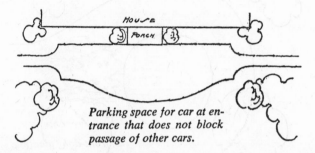

Parking space for car at entrance that does not block passage of other cars.

What is the most practical shape for a turn court at the garage on a small property? The so-called Y-turn takes up the least space and yet provides for easy turning, either for your own car coming out of the garage, or for other cars using the driveway. The radius of the curves in the accompanying sketch should be 15 ft. to 20 ft., and it is important that the space into which the cars back be at least 14 ft. wide.

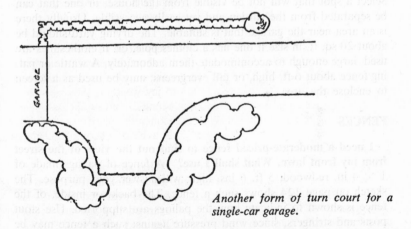

Another form of turn court for a single-car garage.

How large should a turn-around in front of the house be? The largest cars require a turning space about 60 ft. in diameter for making a complete turn without backing. An area of bluestone or gravel that large is often out of proportion to the house. It can be broken up with a grass island (but this should not have anything else planted in it). To make arrival at the house door easy, it is wise to distort the shape of the turn-around somewhat, making it more of an apple shape instead of a true circle.

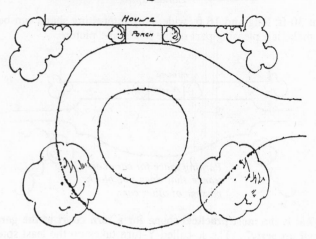

Turn-around for car.

DRYING YARD

How can one go about making a drying yard on the home grounds?
Select a spot that will not be visible from the house, or one that can
be separated from the garden and yet easily accessible. Usually there
is an area near the garage that is suitable. The drying yard should be
about 20 sq. ft. in size if one has a clothes pole, or, if clotheslines are
used, large enough to accommodate them adequately. A wattle or paling fence about 6 ft. high, or tall evergreens, may be used as a screen
to enclose the area.

FENCES

**I need a moderate-priced fence to shut out the view of the street
from my front lawn. What shall I use?**   A fence of palings made of
1 × 4 in. redwood, 5 ft. 6 ins. high, will answer your purpose. The
sketch on page 124 shows such a fence. The back, or inside, of the
fence is shown to indicate how the palings are supported. Use stout
posts and stringers, since wind pressure against such a fence may be
very great.

Is a wattle fence appropriate for the home garden?   A woven
wattle fence made of saplings or thin split logs is expensive, and
because of this is not recommended for the small garden unless there
is an objectionable view to be blocked or sturdy protection from
animals to be provided. Wattle fences are excellent for such purposes
as enclosing a drying yard, screening a highway, or to give privacy in
a courtyard, small flower or herb garden.

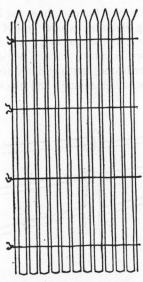

WOVEN-SAPLING FENCE

Where can I get a design for a picket fence?   The accompanying sketch shows a typical picket fence such as used to be seen often on village streets. Many modern picket fences are less substantially built, and hence tend to look flimsy. The effectiveness of such a fence depends largely on delicacy of detail, but it must also be, and look, strong.

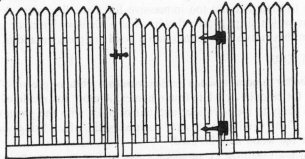

PICKET FENCE

Shall I use perennials or annuals (a) for trellis fence; and (b) for chimney? How fast growing?   (a) Ipomoea "Heavenly Blue"—annual, fast-growing; *Lathyrus latifolius*—perennial, fast-growing; *Clematis montana rubens*—perennial, strong grower. (b) *Euonymus fortunei vegetus*—perennial, fast-growing; *Ampelopsis lowi*—perennial, slow-growing; *Hedera helix baltica*—slow-growing, for north or northwest side only.

What sort of fence is best for use along the highway in front of a farm where something elaborate would be out of place? A simple post-and-rail fence, such as the one in the accompanying sketch, has proved very satisfactory. It can be painted white, or, if made of dead chestnut, cypress, or redwood, left unpainted to weather. If it has to be made proof against small animals and chickens, wire can be attached to the inside.

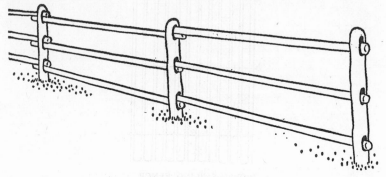

POST AND RAIL FENCE

*A post-and-rail fence is excellent support for
climbing roses or vines of moderate growth.*

FOUNTAINS

Do you recommend putting a fountain into a small home garden? Elaborate fountains throwing large streams of water are rather expensive to maintain and too impressive for a small garden. A small fountain which drips water slowly over a shallow basin or a wall fountain that runs a tiny stream into a bowl are pleasing and in scale.

FURNITURE

Is it better to paint wooden garden furniture white or green? White is good for colonial or white frame homes. Almost any shade of green paint is likely to look artificial and out of place with the green of the garden. Clear varnish, or a soft brownish stain which brings out the grain of the wood may be used.

Is garden furniture recommended for the small garden? Yes. It must be of good design, however, and suit the type of the house. It should be comfortable, light weight (or heavy enough to be placed permanently), resistant to weather, and preferably of a color which will become part of the garden scene.

What kinds of garden furniture are best? The rustic type, made of cedar or other water-resistant wood, if comfortable, usually blends well with any type garden. Being inconspicuous, it does not dominate the garden scene. White-painted wooden furniture is desirable in some gardens, especially if the house is also white. Metal furniture is comfortable, and good for outdoor living rooms or terraces. Stone benches and tables are suitable for the large garden. Cane or woven chairs may be used if not subjected to bad weather. Canvas chairs are comfortable and easy to move about, but also must be protected from rain.

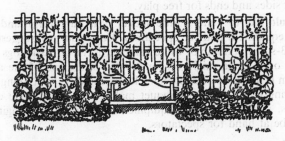

Garden seats should be placed where they will invite use—not stuck out in the middle of a lawn.

GARDEN HOUSES

What kind of garden house is most suitable for the small garden? A very simple house which fits the architecture of the house and the landscape plan of the garden. The English style, with a sloping tiled or thatched roof, is fitting for an English-type garden. Rustic styles are good in a natural setting, out of sight of the main house. Avoid fantastic or baroque styles.

GAME AREAS

How can I lay out a badminton court? Allow about 30 by 60 ft. of lawn space for a badminton court. (See also Lawns.)

I want to make part of my garden into an area for a bowling green and for horseshoe pitching. How much room is necessary? For a bowling green you should have a smooth grass area about 128 ft. sq. A gutter of sand 1½ ft. wide and about 6 ins. deep should surround this strip. For horseshoes, you will need an area 10 × 50 ft. The sand pit at either end should be 6 ft. sq., with a stout wooden or iron stake in the center.

How much room does a croquet lawn require? About 30 × 60 ft. A level, well-mowed area is essential for this game. (See Lawns.)

What games or equipment would be suitable for a children's game area? A wading pool, sandbox or sand pit, swings, seesaw, sliding board, ball court.

My children want a tennis court. What is the most practical type; and how should it be constructed? Clay courts are most satisfactory. See that the drainage of the area is good. Lay down tile lines across the area if necessary. Put in 6 ins. of good clay, tamped and rolled smooth. Let the whole court slope about 6 ins. from one end to the other, or 3 ins. from each end to a low point at the net line. Surface with an inch or less of fine sifted clay with a little sand mixed in.

What area is needed for a tennis court?   The playing space of a double court is 38 × 78 ft., but at least 66 × 138 ft. is needed to give room at sides and ends for free play.

I would like to build a little shelter near our playground area for storing equipment and for spectators. Have you any suggestion?   A simple 3-sided building of white clapboards, or of rustic logs or siding with an open front, might be constructed at the end of the area. The floor can be of stone or concrete. Closets could be built along one wall for storing tennis rackets, croquet mallets, etc. Allow one closet for sweaters, shoes, and other equipment. Comfortable lounging chairs should be at hand for spectators.

GATES

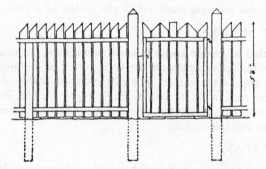

Gate for a picket fence.

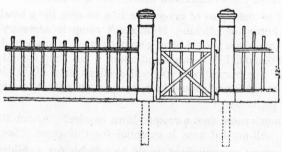

Gate for an open picket fence.

What kind of garden gate do you recommend?   Wrought iron or wood (either rustic or painted). A paling gate would look well with a fence of the same material.

What kind of gate is best to use with a clipped privet hedge?   A well-designed gate of stained, weathered, or painted wood, or wrought iron.

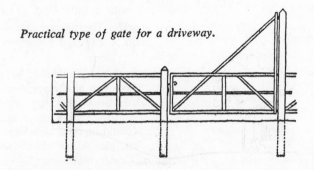

Practical type of gate for a driveway.

Do you recommend wire gates for gardens? Wire gates are not usually so decorative as wooden or iron gates. They are suitable for vegetable areas or dog runs.

To be correct, must the planting either side of a garden gate or entrance be the same? A symmetrically balanced arrangement is the usual thing, but it is often less interesting than an unsymmetrical treatment such as the one in the accompanying sketch. Here 3 elements

Example of a balanced (but not symmetrical) gateway planting.

—the vine on the wall, the urn filled with flowers, and the low, rounded shrub—have been balanced by the tall, dark evergreen on the other side. Such a treatment is easier to arrange when the position of the entrance, or conditions of shade, etc., make a symmetrical arrangement difficult. It is more lively and striking.

LAWNS

Should a garden have a lawn space in the middle? Not all gardens should be so designed, but there are many advantages to this type of layout. A grass panel serves as a foreground to the floral displays in the beds and as a space for chairs and tables. Such a garden is easier to maintain than one made up of many small beds.

Where the house is below the street level, water may be drained away by sloping grade down from both house and street to form slight depression at a low point.

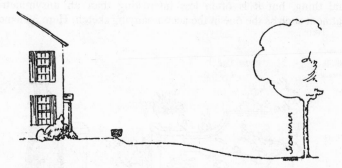

Grading: a flat terrace with a step, and curved slope to side-walk is more attractive than a uniform grade from door to street.

How would you grade a front lawn where the house is small and is several feet below the highway level? A gradual slope from the house up to the street is usually more pleasing than abrupt terraces. To prevent water draining toward the house, however, the grade should be carried down from the house slightly, to a low point from which the water can drain off to the sides before the slope up to the street begins. (See Section IV, Lawn and Turf Areas.)

PATHS

What materials are suitable for making paths? For an average flower garden, grass paths are usually best, for they present a green foreground for the garden picture. They need no maintenance other than what the lawn receives. Gravel or blue stone paths in the flower garden are likely to be a nuisance to take care of. Where a path must be dry, or at least passable in all sorts of weather, brick and flagstone are serviceable. Often it is possible to make a grass path more practical by laying a line of stepping-stones down its middle, or along either edge.

Should a path be laid out in a straight line or with a curve? Generally speaking, a path should be as direct as possible, because the purpose of it is to provide a passage between two points. However, a natural-looking path should follow the contour of the garden, curving around trees or shrubs that are in a direct line. Sharp curves are to be avoided, and all unnecessary turns. When a curve is to be made, it should have a long, gentle sweep. For very small paths, a straight line, with no curves at all, is advisable.

BRICK AND STONE

How should I construct a brick walk? Brick walks look best when laid in sand rather than cement mortar. Provide a gravel or cinder bed about 6 ins. thick, then put down a layer of fine sand, set the edge courses, and fill in the field brick in whatever pattern you wish. Fill the cracks between the bricks with fine sand, wash it well, and tamp thoroughly. In tamping, lay a heavy board on the walk and pound that rather than the bricks themselves. The walk will be smoother if you do this and you will break fewer bricks. (See curbings, this section.)

What pattern should be used in laying a brick walk? There are two standard patterns, basket and herringbone. Either may be varied

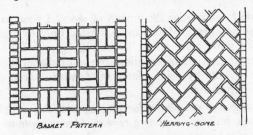

BASKET PATTERN   HERRING-BONE

Two "patterns" for laying bricks for a walk.

somewhat according to taste. The basket pattern is more economical, since there is no cutting of brick. The accompanying sketch shows basket pattern with a rowlock edge and herringbone with a sawtooth edge. In laying out the walk, set only one edge course first. Lay out a section of the field to see how the pattern is working out, then set the other edge. Do not decide on a predetermined width for the walk and then try to fit the pattern into it.

FLAGSTONE

The front of my garage is about 50 ft. from street, joined to house; driveway level on one side; 4-ft. slope on other; no walk to house as yet. Would you suggest shrubs, rock garden, stone wall with flagstone walk, or low flowers?   A stone wall with flagstone walk to the front door would make the most dignified treatment. The front yard is usually no place for a rock garden or flowers of any sort.

GRAVEL

I have been thinking of putting in a gravel path. Is it commonly used in the garden?   Gravel paths are often used. They are inclined to look a bit formal and cold, however, and they are not so comfortable to walk upon as grass or tanbark.

STEPPINGSTONES

What sort of stones are suitable for a path of steppingstones? Water-washed flat stones with rounded edges are the most effective. If these are unobtainable, other flat stones or random slates or flagstones can be used, which are thick enough to bear the weight of traffic.

Are sections of tree trunks practical and long lasting as stepping "stones"?   Yes, the chain saw has made it simple and inexpensive to cut flat cross sections of any sized tree trunk, 4–6″ thick. These can be treated with some wood preservative or used in their natural state as stepping stones in the garden and be expected to have a long life.

Is it possible to encourage the growth of moss? I want to put some between steppingstones.   Moss can be started only by transplanting sods of it from some place where it naturally grows. Find a variety that is growing under similar conditions of sun or shade. Probably you will get better results by using plants of *Arenaria verna caespitosa,* which can be purchased.

Will you suggest some plants for placing between steppingstones? Various thymes, sedums, *Veronica repens, Mazus reptans, Potentilla tridentata, Achillea tomentosa, Tunica saxifraga.*

TANBARK

Do you recommend a tanbark path?   Tanbark paths are expensive and do not adapt themselves to the small garden so well as several other types of path. They are suitable for woodland, rose, or rock gardens.

PATIOS

Which plants are suitable for a patio? In the northeast or north a patio might include a permanent planting of broad-leaved evergreens, an espaliered fruit tree (if there is a sunny wall), and a wisteria vine. Potted foliage plants (monstera, *Nephthytis afzelli,* dracaena, dieffenbachia, etc.) and potted geraniums, fuchsias, lantanas, begonias, and caladiums; crown-of-thorns and other succulents (such as crassulas) could be set out in warm weather. Patios in warm climates have a wider choice of plants, including such shrubs as oleanders, camellias, and gardenias; also bougainvillea and passiflora vines and other semitropical plant material.

I would like to have a patio garden. Would this be suitable with a colonial house? Patio gardens are usually made within a courtyard or similar enclosure. They are of Spanish origin and suited to this type of dwelling. However, if you have or can arrange a suitable protected terrace or courtyard adjacent to your colonial house, you might use flat stones or flagging to pave the area, put potted plants in white containers instead of Spanish pottery ones and, by using colonial ornaments and furniture, arrange a fitting outdoor living room which would serve the same purpose as a patio.

PERGOLAS

What is a pergola? A pergola is a passageway covered by an arbor which supports grapevines or large flowering vines. The structure is usually somewhat elaborate, with decorative columns and crosspieces. It is of Latin origin and is suitable to only a limited number of American gardens.

Is a pergola recommended for the small garden? A pergola can be useful in the small garden for supporting a grapevine over a path and provide a practical as well as ornamental accessory. It is sometimes effective to put a pergola over the path to the garage, thus softening the harsh effect of the building and providing a place for vines. Whenever it is used, the pergola should provide a passageway from one place to another.

POOLS

How should a small pool be constructed? The accompanying sketch shows a simple concrete pool and the necessary plumbing connections. For the successful growing of aquatics the deep part of the pool should be 1½ ft., and if it is to be used at all by birds, some part of it should be shallow enough for them. They do not like water more than 2 ins. deep.

How shall I go about building a small pool?   Excavate the ground about 6 ins. deeper on bottom and wider at the sides than you wish the pool to be. Insert drainage if pool is to be large enough to require it (see accompanying sketch); if it is very small, this will not be necessary. Fill hole with gravel layer, tamp down firm, or line with chicken wire. Pour cement, 1 part cement to 3 parts mixed sand and gravel. Add water enough so that mixture will spread evenly. Layer should be about 4 or 5 ins. thick. Next day finish with a coat of cement mortar, 1 part cement to 2 parts sand, applied with a trowel.

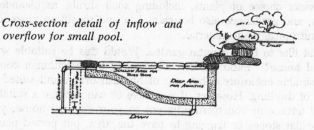

Cross-section detail of inflow and overflow for small pool.

How thick should the concrete walls of a garden pool be?   The thickness of the walls of a pool depends on its size. A large pool naturally has to have thicker walls. For the average small pool (6 ft. or so in diameter) walls 6 ins. thick are sufficient. Some reinforcement in the form of wire or steel rods should be used.

How soon after finishing the construction of a small pool can plants be put in?   Leave the pool filled with water for about 2 weeks, flushing occasionally, before planting or putting in fish.

Are Plastic Pools feasible? I do not want to go to the expense of putting in a concrete pool, but would like to have a small pool for a few years' trial.   Plastic pools are now available in small sizes and are quite inexpensive when compared with concrete pools. Various types are frequently advertised in the garden magazines. They can be easily installed by any gardener.

I want to paint my pool blue. What kind of paint shall I use?   There is a special paint available from seed or department stores for just this purpose.

I want to get some complete information on the construction of a small pool. Can you suggest some publication?   A book entitled "Garden Pools, Fountains, Recreation Areas" by R. H. Hawkins and C. H. Abbe, published by Van Nostrand of Princeton, N.J. contains excellent information on this subject.

What shape should a small pool be?   It depends on your location and general garden design. If your garden is informal, an informally shaped pool would be best. This should be basically circular or "egg-shaped" with gently curving, irregular contours. By using the garden hose to lay out the shape of the pool, good curves may be attained. Avoid sharp curves and too many irregularities. Simplicity is the keynote.

I want to build a small informal pool. About what size should I make it? A good-looking small pool might be about 25 sq. ft. in size.

I want to build a small formal pool with a fountain and statue at the back. What shape would be best for the pool? A round or oblong formal pool is always good. If your garden is very formal, you could have a rectangular pool.

Will gold fish live over winter in my pool? That depends on how deep and how large the pool is. Goldfish can live over in large pools that do not freeze solid in the winter, but will not live over winter in small pools that either freeze solid, or have only a few inches of water under the ice in winter. Under such conditions the fish actually smother to death.

STATUARY

I want to have some statuary in my garden. Can you suggest some types? In the small garden, care must be taken not to overdo use of statuary. One well-designed piece, not too large, used as a center of interest, is sufficient. A statue is usually placed at the end of a vista or in a niche formed of evergreens. It needs a background of green plant material to fit it into the garden picture. Avoid use of pottery figures of gnomes, ducks, etc., and other novelties.

A simple treatment of steps in a steep bank—English Ivy for year-round greenery.

STEPS

Of what shall I build my garden steps? Steps of stone with brick or flagstone treads harmonize well in many gardens. All-brick steps often look too harsh and formal. Field stone is all right if you can find enough flat ones. Concrete is much too unyielding.

Grass steps held in place by steel bands imbedded in the turf are beautiful but hard to make and to maintain. For very informal situations, sod, gravel, or tanbark steps held up by field-stone or log risers are most effective. Sometimes the steps themselves are made of squared sections of cypress or Black Locust logs.

SUNDIALS

Do you recommend using a sundial in the garden? A sundial is very effective in the right setting as the center of interest in a rose garden, or formal garden. It must, of course, be placed where the sun will hit it all day. The base can be planted with vines or low-blooming flowers. A sundial is usually placed at the axis where four paths meet, though a sunny position in a border or bed past which a path runs, is also good. Or it may occupy the center of a section of lawn.

TERRACES

How should I construct a flag terrace, and the steps down from it to the lawn? The flagstone, 2 ins. or so thick, can be laid on a bed of cinders or gravel covered with a thin layer of fine sand. No mortar is needed if the flags are heavy enough to stay in place. Slate cannot be used so easily. Brick can be substituted for flag. Steps should have treads with at least 1 in. overhang, and there should be a solid concrete foundation under them. Ramps, parapets, or wing walls should be substantial and have copings with the same overhang as the step treads. Steps and walls should be laid in cement mortar.

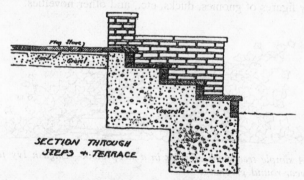

Cross-section detail for concrete and brick steps.

Which flowers will grow on a very windy terrace? Dwarf phlox, astilbe, dianthus, *Eupatorum coelestinum, Gypsophila repens,* hemerocallis, iberis, lavandula, *Anchusa myosotidiflora.*

Will you suggest a plant giving a long period of bloom for the

narrow border around my flagged lounging terrace? Lantana. Purchase young blossoming plants from a florist or seed store and plant 18 ins. apart. They will grow into sturdy shrubs by midsummer; not winter hardy. Try an edging of lobelia on the inside.

TOOL HOUSE

I want to fix up some space in my garage as a tool house and potting shed. How can I arrange this? Build a long bench, at convenient height for standing, to be used for potting plants, mixing sprays, etc. Under this have drawers or shelves for pots, labels, and baskets, and bins for fertilizers and mulching materials. Over the bench, racks may be built for holding vases, and strips of wood nailed close to the wall will be convenient holders for small tools such as trowels, dibbers, and hand cultivators. A space against one wall should be left for the wheelbarrow and lawn mower. Wooden racks for rakes, hoes, and other long-handled tools (which are hung handle down) can be made by nailing a strip of wood on the wall, about 6 ft. above the floor. Pairs of tenpenny nails protruding from this hold the tools. Or an overhead hanging shelf may be notched on both sides to accommodate tool handles. Heads of tools are placed above the shelf. The garden hose needs a special rack where it will not be damaged by sharp tools. A stout 2-ft. bracket jutting out from the wall will be convenient for this purpose.

Where and how can I provide a convenient storage place for my vegetable garden tools and equipment? A small addition to the garage, opening out into the vegetable garden, makes an ideal tool house. If the garden is fairly large and the garage not conveniently near, a small separate building, disguised as a garden house, will serve. On a sloping lot, enclosed space under a rear porch often makes a good place for this equipment.

TOOLS AND EQUIPMENT

What are the most essential tools for the gardener to have? Rake, hoe, shovel, spade, spading fork, trowel, lawn mower.

Will you name other desirable tools for the garden in addition to the main essentials? Onion hoe, hedge shears, grass shears, pruning shears, wheelbarrow, hose, hand cultivator, scuffle hoe, pruning saw, sharp knife, sickle, dibber, lawn roller, lawn sprinklers, cultivator and wheel hoe, manure fork, watering can, lawn weeder, lawn edger, bamboo or steel grass rake.

What is an onion hoe? An onion hoe has a very shallow blade which cultivates only the upper surface of the soil without cutting into the soil or "hacking." It is convenient for cultivating close to plant rows.

What is a scuffle or Dutch hoe?   A scuffle or Dutch hoe has a flat, sharp cutting blade which cultivates the upper part of the soil. It is efficient for making a dust mulch and for weeding.

What is a dibber?   A dibber is a small rounded piece of wood about 6 ins. in length and 1 to 2 ins. in diameter shaped to a rounded point, used for making holes in which to set plants or bulbs. Sometimes dibbers are made of metal or have the point cased in brass. They may be bought, but they are easily made at home from broken tool handles. The dibber should not have a sharp point. This causes a small air space in the bottom of the plant hole.

I want to buy a complete set of garden tools. Do you have any suggestions?   Never buy cheap tools; it doesn't pay. Buy good-quality tools from a reliable company. Avoid "novelties." Standard-type tools, suited to your needs, will usually give better results.

Should tools be cleaned after using?   Yes, decidedly. Wipe them off thoroughly, with a piece of burlap or an old rag each time after using. Rub occasionally with a cloth dipped in oil.

I want to store my tools through the winter. What shall I clean them with first?   Clean off all dirt and spots with an oily cloth.

Will plastic hose (set in the ground) last any appreciable time?   Yes; but plastic *pipe* is much better. This will last for years and makes it possible for gardeners to pipe water underground to all parts of the garden at very little cost. It is best to drain the hose or pipe in winter, but not absolutely essential since it will not crack or break when the water it contains freezes.

What accessories or equipment is necessary for gardening?   A line and reel, stakes, measuring rod (8 to 10 ft.), labels, basket, sprayers, dusters, tying material (twine and patent twisters), flowerpots, plant bands, bulb pans, seed sowers, flats, plant supports.

I have heard of "plant bands" but do not know what they are. Can you describe them?   Plant bands are used, in place of flowerpots, for potting young plants and seedlings. They are made of very thin wood, and are square, thus taking up less room than ordinary flowerpots and making them easy to fit into a flat for carrying. They will collapse when empty, so are easily stored. More important, they are deep enough to allow ample room for root development and are easily removed so that a large ball of earth may be left on the plant when transplanting.

Are there such things as pots that will disintegrate when set in the soil?   Yes, they are made of either heavy paper or a mixture of pressed manure or wood pulp and peat. Plants can be started in them in the greenhouse and then pot and all are planted out in the soil.

What are "canned plants"?   This probably refers to plants grown in tin cans or tubs so that they can be moved anytime during the spring, summer and fall. More and more small plants are being grown in this fashion throughout the entire country, making transplanting possible anytime during the growing season.

LABELS

What kind of labels do you suggest for seedling flats? Plain wooden labels, available in your local dime or seed store. Dip a corner of a clean rag in white paint and rub over the label. Then, while it is still wet, letter with an ordinary lead pencil.

What type label is best for greenhouse plants? Small border-type labels that fit down into the soil of the pot; or pointed wooden labels, in several lengths, like those recommended for flats.

What kind of label is best for the perennial border? Although border labels, similar to rock-garden labels, are sometimes recommended, they are inclined to heave during winter. Best results are usually obtained with wired labels fastened to garden stakes. These should be weather proof and copper-wired.

What type labels would you suggest for a rock garden? Four- or 5-in. weatherproof markers that are plunged into the soil and provide an oblong space for writing. One type has a blank space for marking which slides into a glassine pane; another need only be marked with a pencil on the outside and will remain legible.

I want to buy some labels for my rose garden. What kind would be best? Most permanent are of metal with the lettering pressed in. These are wired to the plant. If these are not available, get waterproof wired wooden ones, mark in waterproof ink, and wire to the plant.

TOPIARY WORK

What is topiary work? Pruning of hedges, shrubs, or trees in specific shapes, as of animals, houses, balls, spools, figures, or geometric forms. Used only in formal gardens and primarily associated with medieval landscape design. Practiced today more in Europe than in America. Boxwood and yew, and less frequently, privet, are employed for this purpose.

VIEWS

I have read that a garden should not "compete with a view." Why? How is it prevented? The intimate detail of a garden suffers by comparison with a wide view into the surrounding landscape. It is usually wiser to surround the garden with an enclosure to shut off outside views, but if these are worth-while, provision should be made to take advantage of them from some point outside the garden.

My house is surrounded by trees, but there is a fine view now ob-

scured by foliage. What should I do?   Do not hesitate to cut out trees to form a vista so that the view can be seen from some vantage point in the house or on the terrace. Often this can be achieved by removing lower branches rather than whole trees.

WALLS

Would a field-stone wall be satisfactory for fencing off a small garden?   In some localities it would be appropriate. A field-stone wall is suited to a country property rather than a city or suburban plot.

How should I construct a retaining wall, to be built of field stones? Since it may be called upon to withstand considerable pressure, a dry wall must have an adequate foundation, and the stones must be firmly bedded. The accompanying sketch shows that the foundation is as wide or wider than the wall and goes down below frost level. The face of the wall slopes back slightly, and all the stones are set with the long dimension horizontal. Use squarish rather than rounded stones, and use as large ones as you can get. Avoid "chinking" with small stones.

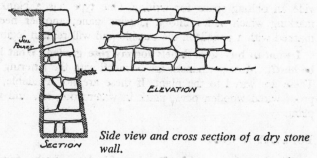

SOIL POCKET

ELEVATION

SECTION

Side view and cross section of a dry stone wall.

How do you make soil pockets in a dry wall?   As the wall is being laid up, leave gaps all the way through it, about 4 ins. in diameter. Be sure these openings slope downward toward the back of the wall to keep soil and plants from being washed out. See that the soil is continuous from the face of the wall to the soil back of the wall to permit moisture to penetrate to it constantly. Fill the holes thus made with rich soil. Be sure the stones above them make solid bridges over the holes.

WEATHER VANES

Should weather vanes be used on small properties?   The use of weather vanes has been overdone in some sections. They are best used in the country, on barns, tool sheds, or other outbuildings. For a small place, get a simple style, not too large, to be used on the garage or garden house.

SPECIAL TYPES OF GARDENS

HERB GARDENS

WHAT TO GROW

Which herbs are annuals and which perennials? I am confused which ones to expect to come up a second year. The annual herbs most widely used are anise, dill, summer savory, fennel, coriander, and borage. The perennial herbs include horse-radish, lemon balm, winter savory, pot marjoram, sage, horehound, mint, tarragon, and beebalm. Parsley and caraway are, technically, biennials, but are grown as annuals. All of these grow in full sun and like a well-drained garden soil. Sow annuals as early in spring as weather permits, either in rows or broadcast.

Which herbs are the best to plant—annuals or perennials? This depends entirely upon your needs and garden facilities. A reasonably good selection of herbs includes both annuals and perennials.

Will you list 6 annual herbs for the kitchen garden? Basil, borage, chervil, parsley (really biennial but treated as an annual), Summer Savory, and Sweet Marjoram.

Sweet Marjoram and Summer Savory—two of the most popular annual herbs.

Which 6 perennial herbs do you suggest for the kitchen herb garden? Chives, horse-radish, mint, sage, tarragon, and thyme.

Which herbs do you suggest for a fragrant herb garden? Bergamot, lavender, lemonverbena, rosemary, scented geraniums, southernwood, sweet wormwood, lovage, valerian, lemon balm, sweetcicely, thyme, and costmary.

What herbs may be grown successfully at home, and preserved for winter use? Try the mints (if there is a moist spot in the garden, and care is taken to prevent the plants from overrunning their space); also sage, thyme, parsley, caraway, dill, and anise.

What are the best combinations of herbs for tea (as a beverage)? For flavoring tea, try mints or lemonverbena. In combination, one authority suggests equal parts of elder flowers and peppermint; another, peppermint and lemonverbena. Sage and chamomile, each used alone, make tasty beverages. Never use a metal container.

How should I start a small herb garden of a half-dozen varieties of herbs? Plant informally in little groups, taller plants more or less in back.

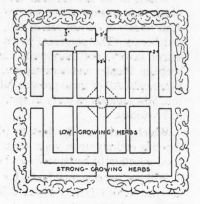

Design for a small formal herb garden.

Can you give some information on herbs—some to eat and some to smell? Good herbs for flavoring: basil (sweet) for salads, soups, and tomato sauces; chives for salads and pot cheese; dill for pickles; fennel to eat like celery, or cooked; sweet marjoram, seasoning for stuffings, etc.; mints for teas and sauces; rosemary for seasoning roasts and chicken; sage for dressing; savory (summer) for flavoring vegetables, particularly string beans; thyme, seasoning for foods and salads; tarragon, to flavor vinegar, and in salads. Herbs for scent: beebalm, lavender, lemonverbena, mints, and scented geraniums.

Which herbs grow successfully in the house? Basil, dittany of Crete, lemonverbena, parsley, rosemary, sweet marjoram, tarragon, and perhaps peppermint, if the room is cool and has plenty of light.

Which herbs do you suggest for an herbaceous border? Some of them grow too tall and scraggly. Lavender, calendula, marjoram, rosemary, rue, sage, thyme, hyssop, and the gray artemisias.

Which herbs are particularly attractive to bees? Thyme, lavender, germander, beebalm, lovage, hyssop, lemon balm, sweetcicely, borage, and marjoram.

Can you name some herbs suitable for low hedges? Hyssop, lavender, santolina, germander, southernwood, and rue. In fairly mild climates—rosemary.

Can you suggest herbs for a usable kitchen garden for the novice? Where can I get information as to their culture, preservation, and use? The following are particularly good for a beginner's garden: sage, tarragon, parsley, chives, shallots, basil, dill, rosemary, some of the thymes, and sweet marjoram. For further information write The Herb Society of America, 300 Massachusetts Ave., Boston, Massachusetts.

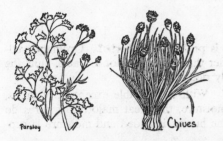

Two of the most useful culinary herbs—Parsley and Chives—often grown in the vegetable plot.

Which geraniums are particularly suited for planting (in summer) in an herb garden? These geraniums are botanically *Pelargonium*. The lemon-scented, peppermint-scented, apple-scented, and rose-scented are all good. (See Fragrant Gardens.)

Do any herbs endure shade? Many medicinal herbs grow well in shade, among them bloodroot, digitalis, ginseng, goldenseal, selfheal, and snakeroot.

Which herbs will tolerate part shade? Balm, bergamot, chervil, sweet fennel, tarragon, sweet woodruff, mints, angelica, sweetcicely, parsley, comfrey, and costmary.

Can you give me information on herbs suitable for an herb rock garden? The garden should be well drained and sunny; the soil on the lean side rather than overrich. Almost any of the lower-growing herbs can be used effectively, with a few taller ones for accents.

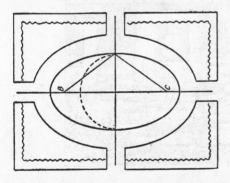

Method of laying out ellipses for a small herb garden. String is secured to stakes at B and C.

Of the varieties of herbs formerly imported, which ones can be grown in northern and central New York? Some of them are coriander, anise, fennel, dill, cumin, and sage.

What is ironweed? Several different plants have been shown me, but

I want to be sure, as I wish to use it in an old-time medical recipe. The ironweed of eastern United States is *Vernonia noveboracensis*. It usually grows in moist places, is 3 to 6 ft. high, and has open-branched cymes with many purple flowers. A full description is given in Gray's *Manual of Botany*.

SOIL

What general type of soil is preferred by herbs?   Ordinary well-drained garden soil, lean rather than rich, and not too acid, suits the majority. Mints prefer a fairly rich, moist soil.

Do herbs like sandy soils?   With the possible exception of mints, which require considerable moisture, the great majority of herbs do very well in sandy soil if some humus is added and moisture is supplied in very dry weather.

I understand that most herbs need dry soil conditions. Can you suggest some for a moist, but not waterlogged, place?   Angelica, bergamot, sweetcicely, sweetflag, yellow-stripe sweetflag, lovage, mints, parsley, English pennyroyal, snakeroot, valerian, and violets.

PLANTING

What is the best exposure for an herb garden?   A southeast exposure is ideal, but any location that gets full sunshine during the growing season will do. The soil and cultural practices, which include winter protection, are equally important.

A decorative herb garden at the kitchen door.

Must herbs be grown in an herb garden?   No. They will thrive anywhere where soil and exposure are right: in the vegetable garden, by the kitchen door, in a dry wall (certain kinds), and good-looking ones in the flower border.

CULTURE

What are the general cultural requirements for herbs? A rather poor, well-drained sweet soil, warmth, sunlight, and a free circulation of air. Space the plants adequately, according to kind. Keep weeds down and surface soil tilled. This is a generalization; a number of herbs require distinctly different conditions.

What is the most practical arrangement of annual and perennial herbs—to interplant them, or to keep them separate? Plant the perennial kinds together and the annual kinds together. The area devoted to annuals can then readily be prepared afresh each spring and the perennial area is disturbed only every few years, when replanting becomes necessary.

Is it necessary to make more than one sowing of the various annual herbs each season? Yes, if it is desired to pick them fresh throughout the summer. About 3 sowings of most are desirable, the last made in late June or early July.

Is watering important in the herb garden? A few herbs (as mints) need generous supplies of moisture, but the majority develop their fragrances and flavors best when they are subjected to rather dry conditions; therefore, apply water with discrimination. Newly transplanted herbs and young plants need more attention in this respect than established plantings.

Should herbs be fertilized during the summer? The majority of true herbs require no fertilization. Feeding induces rank growth but does not favor the production of the essential oils which give to them their flavor and fragrance.

Can any non-hardy herbs be over-wintered successfully in a cold frame? Thyme, lavender, sage, and other "hardy" herbs which are often susceptible to winter killing can be kept over winter in a cold frame. Really tender subjects, like rosemary, pineapple sage, scented geraniums, and lemonverbena, must be kept in a temperature safely above freezing.

HARVESTING, CURING, AND STORING

Should herbs be washed before drying, and what is the appropriate time needed for this? What is a safe insecticide to use on these plants? Washing is not needed unless foliage is mud spattered. Time needed for drying varies according to kind and environment. A rotenone or pyrethrum insecticide is recommended.

How shall I cure herbs properly so as to retain their flavor? Dry as quickly as possible in a warm, airy, well-ventilated place, *without exposure to sun.*

How does one cure herb leaves for drying? Pick them just before the plants begin to flower, any time in the day after the dew has disappeared. Tie in bundles, each of a dozen stems or so. Hang in an airy, warm, but not sunny place. When they are completely dry and crisp, strip off leaves and put in tight jars. The leaves may also be stripped fresh, right after cutting, and placed in shallow screen-bottomed trays until dry.

When should herb seeds be harvested? When they have matured, and before they fall naturally from the plants.

How should herb seeds be dried? Collect the heads or seed pods and spread them in a tray made of screening, or in a thin layer on a cloth in a warm, well-ventilated room. Turn them frequently. At the end of a week or so they will be dry enough for threshing.

What is the best method of storing dried herbs? In airtight containers.

How can seeds in quantity, such as caraway, be best separated from stems and chaff? Remove as much of the stems as possible. Rub the heads or pods between the palms of the hands. If possible, do this outdoors where a breeze will help carry away the chaff. A kitchen strainer or screen is useful in the final cleaning.

GENERAL

What are "simples"? Herbs that possess, or are supposed to possess, medicinal virtues.

What is the "Doctrine of Signatures"? An ancient belief that plants, by the shape or form of their parts, indicated to man their medicinal uses. The spotted leaves of the lungwort showed that this plant was a cure for diseases of the lungs; the "seal" on the roots of Solomonseal promised the virtue of sealing or closing broken bones and wounds; and so on.

Can you recommend a good book on herbs and herb culture? *Herbs, How to Grow Them,* by Helen N. Webster; *Herbs, Their Culture and Uses,* by R. E. Clarkson; *Gardening with Herbs for Flavor and Fragrance,* by H. M. Fox; and *Old Time Herbs for Northern Gardens,* by M. W. Kamm, are all excellent.

Am interested in medicinal herbs. Are there any books on same? *Try Growing Herbs,* by Helen M. Whitman, published by The Tool Shed Press, Bedford, New York; and *Medicinal Plants,* by Crooks and Sievers, published by the United States Department of Agriculture.

COMMERCIAL GROWING

Where can I obtain information on commercial herb growing? The following bulletins give information on this subject: *Circular 157,*

New York State Agricultural Experiment Station, Geneva, New York; *Circular 83*, Vermont State College of Agriculture, Rutland, Vermont; *Circular 104*, Michigan State College of Agriculture, East Lansing, Michigan; *Bulletin 461*, Indiana College of Agriculture, Purdue, Indiana; *Circular 149*, Connecticut Agricultural Experiment Station, New Haven, Connecticut; and *Extension Circular 64*, Minnesota Agricultural College, University Farm, Minnesota. Also *Miscellaneous Publication 77*, *Circular 581*, and *Farmers' Bulletins Nos. 1184* and *1555*, all obtainable from Office of Publications, United States Department of Agriculture, Washington, D.C.

HERB WHEELS

I would like to put plants around the spokes of an old wagon wheel that I have. How would you suggest doing this?   A wagon wheel or oxcart wheel can be made the central feature of a small, formal herb garden. Select a level, sunny spot in the garden with enriched, well-prepared soil. Place the hub down into the ground and put a few plants of each variety in between the spokes. A narrow path edged with thyme can surround the wheel. Low-growing, compact plants are better for a wheel-planting than tall, straggly ones.

What culinary herbs would be best in a "wheel garden"?   Thyme, chives, sage, parsley, mint, lemon balm, French tarragon, winter savory, sweet basil, sweet marjoram, chervil. Or the wheel can be planted exclusively with low-growing varieties of thyme.

Would you suggest some fragrant herbs that would look well planted in an oxcart wheel?   Lemonverbena, mint, southernwood, rosemary, Rose Geranium, santolina, sweetcicely. (See Herbs.)

I want to plant some small, bright-blooming flowers in a wagon wheel. What would you suggest?   Dwarf marigolds, zinnias, linaria, alyssum, lobelia, portulaca, ageratum, dwarf anchusas.

SPECIFIC HERBS

ANGELICA

How do you grow angelica and what is it used for?   Sow in fall as soon as seed is ripe, thin out seedlings, and transplant following spring. Soil should be moist and fairly rich. Light shade is beneficial. The seeds are slow to germinate. The plant is biennial under some conditions, so it is better to sow a few seeds each year to maintain a supply. The stems and leafstalks are used for salads and candied to decorate confections; the seeds for flavoring and for oil.

ANISE

Can you give some information on growing anise?   It is an annual, so it must be sown each year. The seeds should be fresh because old seed will not germinate. Sow when the soil has warmed a little (about beginning of May) in rows where the plants are to stand (anise does not transplant readily). Prepare the soil deeply and make it very fine. Sow in rows 15 ins. apart and thin the plants out to 9 ins. apart in the rows. Water in very dry weather.

BALM

Is balm difficult to grow? Is it a useful herb? Lemon balm or sweet balm (*Mellisa officinalis*) is a hardy perennial of easy culture. It can be grown from seeds sown in prepared soil in July or August; the seedlings are transplanted, when large enough, to their flowering quarters. Balm can also be propagated by division in spring. Any ordinary garden soil is satisfactory. The leaves of balm are used for seasoning, particularly liqueurs. They are also used for salads and for potpourris.

Sweet Basil

BASIL

Can you give me information on growing basil? When should I sow the seeds? Seeds are sown outdoors after settled warm weather has arrived; or they are started indoors in April and the seedlings transplanted outdoors later. Allow 12 ins. apart between plants. Basil yields abundantly. When cut, it repeatedly sends out new growth. Plants can be lifted in the fall and potted for winter use if desired.

BORAGE

Is borage annual or perennial? Can it be grown from seed? An annual, easily grown from seed in any good garden soil. Sow in spring when all danger of frost is past. The seedlings can be transplanted if care is exercised, but the plants are better if grown undisturbed. About 15 ins. should be allowed between plants.

CARAWAY

How is caraway grown? From seeds sown outdoors in late May in rows 2 ft. apart. The plants are thinned to about 9 ins. apart. The first year low-growing plants are formed; the second year seeds are produced; then the plants die. Seed is most abundantly produced if the soil is not too rich. Do not water much, as this tends to keep the stems soft and causes the blossoms to fall before setting seed. Dry, sunny weather favors this crop.

CHERVIL

How is chervil grown? From seeds sown in spring where the plants are to grow. Thin plants to stand 9 ins. apart. Light shade is beneficial. Chervil is an annual.

CHIVES

Can chives be grown from seeds or must I buy plants? They can be grown from seeds sown outdoors early in spring. Thin the little plants out to about ½ in. apart. They are hardy perennials, multiply rapidly, and need little attention. Divide every second year. They like a moderately moist soil.

CLARY

Clary dies out with me. Is it difficult to grow? Clary is a biennial and dies after flowering. Sow seeds in early spring; thin out to 6 ins. apart; as the plants develop pull out every other one. Those removed can be dried for use. The plants bloom and set seeds the second year. A rich soil is advantageous.

CORIANDER

Is it easy to grow coriander seed? Yes. Sow (thinly) in spring in well-drained, average soil and in sunny position. Thin out to stand 9 or 10 ins. apart. Plants and fresh seeds are unpleasantly scented, but ripe seeds become very fragrant as they dry.

COSTMARY

How is costmary grown? Propagate it from seeds or by root division. Plant in full sun or very light shade. Space plants about 3 ft. apart. Lift and replant every third year. A freely drained soil is needed.

Dill

DILL

How do you grow dill? Dill is a fast-growing annual that matures in about 70 days. Sow in early spring in well-prepared soil, in rows

2 ft. apart, where the plants are to stand. The plants grow about 3 ft. tall and make a good-sized bush. Thin out the seedlings to 3 or 4 ins. apart at first; later give a final thinning so that they stand a foot apart.

DITTANY OF CRETE

What is dittany of Crete and how is it grown in the herb garden? It is *Origanum dictamnus*. Increase it by seeds or cuttings. It is not hardy where winters are cold and must be wintered indoors in pots. A sandy soil, perfect drainage, and full sun are cultural desiderata.

FENNEL

Have you data on perennial fennel that grows 10 ft. tall? The common fennel (*Foeniculum vulgare*) has escaped to the wild down South and grows 8 ft. in height. In colder climates, fennel is less tall, rarely reaching 4 ft.

How is Florence fennel grown? As an annual. Seeds are sown in spring where the plants are to mature. The seedlings are thinned out to 6 ins. apart. The plants mature in about 60 days.

GINGER

Can ginger root be grown in New York State? Common ginger (*Zingiber officinale*) is a tropical plant adapted for culture only in warm climates. The wildginger (*Asarum canadense*) is a native of our own rich woodlands. It responds to cultivation if given a rich, rather moist soil.

DIGITALIS

Is the foxglove (digitalis) a perennial? No, a biennial, although occasionally a plant will persist for 3 years. Sow seeds each June. They like a well-drained soil that is deep and fairly moist.

Can digitalis (foxglove) be grown in partial shade? Yes, if you are growing it for its decorative effect; but when raised commercially for drug purposes it must be grown in full sun, as the valuable alkaloid does not develop satisfactorily in shade-grown plants.

HORSE-RADISH

See Section V.

HYSSOP

What are the cultural requirements of hyssop? Give this perennial full sun or light shade, and a warm, freely drained well-limed soil. Allow about a foot between plants. Trim plants back after flowering. Easily propagated by seeds, cuttings, or root division.

LAVENDER

What is the care and use of lavender? Grows well in any well-drained soil, not too acid, in a dry, sunny place. Protect in winter with evergreen boughs; but, even with protection, plants 3 years old or more have a way of dying back in winter. Cut dead branches back in spring after new growth near base is fairly strong. It is best propagated from cuttings of the season's growth taken in the late fall or early spring. The plants are grown for ornament and fragrance. The flowers are used in perfumes, aromatic vinegar, sachets, and are tied into bundles for use in linen closets, etc.

How can I make lavender plants bloom? They give much more prolific bloom, with better fragrance, if grown in a light, well-drained soil high in lime content. Rich or heavy soils encourage foliage growth rather than bloom.

When should lavender flowers be harvested? Just as soon as they are fully open.

Can sweet lavender grow and live over winter as far North as Boston? *Lavandula officinalis* should, if given good winter protection.

Do you have to protect thyme and lavender in winter, and how? The true lavender, *Lavandula officinalis,* is hardier than others of its kind. However, it prefers a sheltered spot. Both lavender and thyme die during the winter because of excessive moisture rather than of cold. Salt hay or evergreen boughs are good mulches. It is safer, if there is any question about the drainage, to winter both of these plants, in the North, in a cold frame.

How can I start lavender from seed? Seeds are rather slow to germinate, and the tiny plants grow slowly. Start seeds indoors in early spring, and set out the new plants after all danger of frost is past. Do not allow them to bloom the first year. Protect through first winter by placing them in a cold frame, if possible. A well-drained soil is essential to success.

Can I propagate lavender from cuttings? Take 2-in. shoots off the main stems and branches in late fall or early spring, each with a "heel" (or portion of older wood) attached to its base. Cut the heel clean. Remove lower leaves for about 1 in. from base. Insert in well-packed sand in a cool greenhouse, and keep the sand moist. Slight bottom heat will help rooting. While roots are not more than ½ in. long, put up in small pots in a mixture of ½ sand, ½ soil. Keep in cool greenhouse for winter if fall-made cuttings, or in a cold frame if spring made.

LEMONVERBENA

How is lemonverbena grown? Lemonverbena is a tender shrub which, in cold climates, must be taken in for the winter. Cut plants back in fall; water just enough to keep them from drying out. In February bring into the light, in a cool temperature. Repot and set out again in the garden when danger of frost is past.

When should cuttings of lemonverbena be made?   In fall, when the plants are trimmed back before being brought inside; or in spring, when new growth is made. Give same treatment as advised for cuttings of lavender.

LOVAGE

Is lovage suitable for a tiny herb garden?   Hardly. It is a perennial 6 or 7 ft. tall, and plants need to be spaced about a yard apart.

What soil and culture for the herb lovage that has flavor of celery?   Propagate by seeds sown in early fall, or by root division in spring. Provide a rich, moist soil in full sun or light shade.

MARJORAM

Can you winter over in the house a plant of marjoram dug up from the herb garden?   If you refer to sweet marjoram, this is the only way to keep it for another year. It is a tender perennial, sensitive to frost. Pot the plant in September, before there is any danger of frost, and let it get accustomed to its new quarters before bringing it indoors. Cuttings can be rooted in September, keeping the young plants indoors also. Pot marjoram is a hardy perennial.

In what soil and situation, and how far apart, should sweet marjoram plants be set?   Give light, well-drained, non-acid soil; full sun; space 9 or 10 ins. apart. This is a tender perennial that may be grown as an annual. Sow seed in spring. It is slow to germinate.

Are there any hardy perennial kinds of marjoram?   Yes. Pot marjoram, showy marjoram, and wild marjoram. Of these, pot marjoram is the best known for culinary purposes.

MINT

Would like a list of all mints that can be grown, and is there a sale for them and where?   The mints are very numerous. Write The Herb Society of America, 300 Massachusetts Ave., Boston, Massachusetts, with regard to these and to their marketability.

What is the culture of peppermint? How is oil extracted from it?   Grows best in deep, rich, humusy soil which is open and well drained. The runners are planted in spring, 2 to 3 ft. apart, in shallow trenches. Keep well cultivated and free from weeds. When in full bloom the plants are cut and cured like hay. The oil is extracted by distillation with steam. For information concerning commercial cultivation ask the Department of Agriculture, Washington, D.C.

Why can't I start a successful mint patch?   Mints are usually easy and very weedy. They like rich, humusy soil and plenty of moisture. Cultivate and weed them well. They should grow.

POTMARIGOLD

What is potmarigold? What is it used for? Is it hard to grow? *Calendula officinalis*—one of our most useful decorative annuals. As an herb, the flower heads are used for seasoning and coloring butter. It thrives best in cool weather. Sow outdoors in spring, or indoors in March for spring planting. Transplant 12 ins. apart. Sow again about July 1 for fall crop. The plants from this sowing will grow on into late fall and will survive light frost.

Rosemary

ROSEMARY

What is the best way to grow rosemary? Rosemary is a tender shrub, not hardy in the North; but it may be plunged outdoors in a sunny, sheltered spot during the summer, and carried over winter in a cool, light room. Pot in well-drained soil to which a sprinkling of lime has been added. Propagate by cuttings.

What is the best protection for rosemary in this location? (Illinois.) It is a tender shrub and must be brought in for the winter in cold climates. If there is not space for so large a plant, make a few cuttings, which will root readily in moist sand and be ready to set out in the spring.

RUE

Is rue hardy in Northern gardens? Could you give its culture? Rue is hardy to Long Island, N.Y. It will not winter over outdoors in very severe climates, so it is much safer to keep it indoors during winter. It is easily grown from seeds sown early in spring in rows 18 ins. apart. Thin seedlings to 8 ins. apart, and again remove every other one. Keep the soil well cultivated. The leaves can be used whenever they are large enough. Any ordinary garden soil is satisfactory.

SAGE

Which variety of sage is used for culinary use? *Salvia officinalis.*

I have been unsuccessful in growing sage. What are its needs? Sage enjoys best a sweet, well-drained, light sandy soil. Sow seeds in very early spring, or in August; or set out good-sized plants in early spring. Sage is not difficult. Give very little water; cultivate during the early part of the season. In spring give a light dressing of bone meal. Easily propagated by means of cuttings.

What are the methods of cultivating sage? See preceding question. Transplant to permanent position when seedlings are 3 to 4 ins. high. Plant in rows 2 ft. apart with 12 ins. between the plants in the row. Cut back established plants in spring to let new growth develop. Do not overwater.

Can sage planted from seed be used and dried first year it is planted? Yes. Don't strip the whole plant bare, however. Take only the largest leaves, or a branch here and there.

When is the best time to "pick" sage; and what is the best method of curing it? Harvest in late summer. Cut shoots before they bloom, tie into bundles, and hang up; or strip leaves and place loosely in shallow trays in a warm, airy place, not exposed to sun.

How does one gather sage? Shoots may be cut twice or three times during summer and early fall.

SAVORY

What kind of soil and culture does savory need? There are 2 kinds of savory: summer savory (annual) and winter savory (perennial). Both grow best in a rather poor but well-limed soil, in an exposed sunny site. The annual kind is considered better than the perennial. The seeds are very small and are best sown indoors in pots and barely covered. Watering is done by immersing the pot in water, as the seeds wash out easily. Seedlings are set out when all danger of frost is over. Set seedlings in rows, 8 ins. between plants, 15 ins. between rows. The perennial sort can be handled in the same way.

SWEETCICELY

What are the garden requirements for growing sweetcicely? Sow seed in early fall, in well-drained average soil, and in light shade. When plants are mature they should stand 18 to 20 ins. apart. It is a hardy perennial and may be increased by root division.

SWEETFLAG

I want to grow sweetflag in my herb garden. Does it need full sun?

Full sun is not necessary, but it must have moist soil. It is really a waterside plant. Propagated by division of rhizomes.

SWEET WOODRUFF

What conditions in the garden does sweet woodruff need? An open, rather moist soil, where drainage is good, and shade or partial shade. A fine perennial ground-cover plant in the right location.

TARRAGON

What soil for tarragon? Shade or sun? Almost any well-drained garden soil. Sun preferred, but will endure light shade.

Will you give me all information possible to grow tarragon? When to plant? Tarragon, a hardy perennial, needs a well-drained soil, moderately rich, with considerable lime. It does best in a lightly shaded location. This plant, since it seeds but little, is propagated by stem or root cuttings, or by division. Stem cuttings are taken any time during the summer, rooted in sand, and planted out. Root cuttings or divisions can be set out in early spring, 12 ins. apart. Do not use chemical fertilizer to force growth, as the quality of the leaves is affected by a too-rich diet.

THYME

I would like to grow thyme for seasoning. Will it stand our severe winters? (Western New York.) There are many varieties of the common thyme that may be used in the herb garden. The greatest menace to thymes during the winter is not so much cold as wetness. Wet crowns, caused by snow, will winter kill. One of the means of preventing this is to grow on rather poor soil, containing gravel or screened cinders. Do not feed in summer to force growth, and do not cut tops after September 1. A cold frame is an excellent place to keep thyme over the winter, where it will be dry. Otherwise, covering the plants with boxes to keep the snow off will help materially. Be certain their position is well drained to begin with. Seeds and plants are available from most houses listing herbs.

How can I grow common thyme? What soil? Shade? Sun? (Massachusetts.) It is best grown on a light, well-drained soil. If the soil is inclined to heaviness, work in screened cinders or gravel. Seeds can be sown in early spring outdoors, or earlier in pots indoors. Transplant seedlings 6 ins. apart. When growth is advanced, do not water much; omit fertilizer, as this tends to force soft growth that will winter kill. Do not cut foliage after September 1, as this depletes vitality. Winter protection is given by covering with light evergreen boughs, or by using brushwood with a light covering of marsh or salt hay. Lift and divide every 2 or 3 years. Grow in full sun.

Will you name several creeping thymes for planting in steps and paths? Mother-of-thyme (*Thymus serpyllum* and its variety *lanuginosus*); Caraway Thyme (*T. herba-barona*); British Thyme (*T. britannicus*).

WATERCRESS

How could I grow watercress for table use in my home garden that has no water? Watercress is a plant of running water, growing in the edge of clear, fresh streams. It may be grown, after a fashion, in a moist spot in the garden, and the plants will last for a time in such a location if it is shady, but they will not live through the winter unless covered with water. They become true perennials only when grown in running water. As an alternative, you can grow the garden cress, or peppergrass. This is an annual, and furnishes salad in 3 to 4 weeks. Sow seed thickly in shallow drills 12 ins. apart. Make 2 sowings, 2 weeks apart in spring, and 2 sowings in August.

POTPOURRIS

Would you please tell me where I may obtain information for formulas for making rose jars, potpourris, and sachets? A good book containing complete information on this subject is *Magic Gardens,* by Rosetta E. Clarkson, published by the Macmillan Company.

What leaves and petals can be used for making potpourri? Any leaves or petals that have a pleasing fragrance may be used. Some of the best are rose, lavender, lemonverbena, jasmine, marigold, stock, mignonette, heliotrope, violet, geranium, rosemary, lemon balm, mint, southernwood, santolina, pink, wallflower, thyme.

I want to make a potpourri of rose petals from my garden. How can I do this? Pick the rose petals (red holds its color best) when the flowers are in full bud but not completely blown. Spread them carefully on sheets of paper or strips of cheesecloth in a dry, airy room, away from the sun. Turn daily. Let them dry completely. This will take from a few days to a week. To each quart of petals add 1 oz. of orrisroot. Spices such as cloves, cinnamon, coriander, and mace may be added, if desired, ½ teaspoon of each. Keep in an airtight earthen jar.

What is "wet potpourri" and how is it made? Potpourri made by the wet method contains rose petals and the petals of any other fragrant flowers that are available. These are spread on cloths or papers to dry out partially. They are then packed in an earthenware jar with layers of table salt or coarse salt between. Add a layer of petals, then a sprinkling of salt, until the jar is filled. One oz. of orrisroot or violet powder is added, and, if desired, some cloves, allspice, and cinnamon. Put a weight on the petals and let them stand in the jar, covered, for several weeks before mixing. In addition to rose petals, lavender, lemonverbena leaves, and geranium leaves are the most commonly used ingredients.

What is a "fixative," and for what is it used in potpourris? A fixative is used to retain the natural scent of leaves or petals and aids in preserving them. Orrisroot, violet powder, ambergris, and gum storax are common fixatives.

In making a sweet jar of flower petals, what can be used to keep the natural color of such flowers as delphinium, pansy, aconitum, and other colorful blooms? If the flowers are carefully dried, out of direct sunlight, they partially retain their color naturally. Orrisroot also seems to have a color-fixing effect.

ROCK GARDENS

PLANNING

To build, or not to build, a rock garden is the question with us. Answerman, what counsel? Can you fit this kind of garden properly into your home landscape without the effect being unnatural? Is there a bank or slope that could be utilized in making the garden? Have you access to natural rock material that could be used? If the area is all level, is there a section where low, natural rock outcrops could be simulated? The extent of the garden will be determined by the time, labor, and money that can be spent on it. A rock garden is costly to build and costly to maintain. These are the facts that need to be considered in deciding to build—or not to build.

Outcropping ledges of rock make an ideal setting for a rock garden. Where such a site is not available, every effort should be made to simulate the same effect.

Will I have as much in a rock garden as in other kinds of gardens? The floral display will be concentrated between early spring and mid-June. From then on your enjoyment will come mostly from pleasing mats and mounds and spreading foliage effects; these are decidedly worth-while.

Can I have flowers in a rock garden all summer long? Yes, by introducing a variety of small annuals and summer- and autumn-flowering bulbs. The use of these may relieve monotony; but it may easily be overdone and spoil the illusion of a mountain garden, which has but one main, brilliant burst of blossom, in the spring.

How can I best fit a rock garden into my place? Use, if you have it, a somewhat steep slope, not overhung by foliage. A natural ledge of porous rock, of acceptable, weathered appearance, and provided with deep fissures, is ideal. Where such a ledge lies buried, it pays to expose and use it.

What exposure is best for a rock garden? For easy-to-grow, sun-loving plants, such as many sedums, pinks and rockcresses, any exposure but a north one. For gardens containing also more finicky, choicer plants, if along a building or a fence, an east exposure; otherwise, an open slope facing east or northeast. As between south and north slopes, choose the latter.

Is there a rock-garden organization? Yes, the American Rock Garden Society, Secretary, 238 Sheridan Avenue, Ho-Ho-Kus, New Jersey.

SOIL AND FERTILIZER

Should the rock-garden soil mixture be acid or alkaline? Some rock plants insist upon acid, some on alkaline soil. But most will do with an approximately neutral soil; it is, therefore, best to provide this kind of mixture throughout, and then to acidify or alkalize special areas for particular plants.

Do all rock-garden plants need a specially prepared soil? No. Many robust, easy-to-grow plants, such as most sedums, pinks, and rockcresses, will thrive in soil that would suit other garden plants. But in sharply drained places even these will be helped by an admixture of some peatmoss, to help retain moisture in summer.

What is a good average rock-garden mixture? Approximately 1 part each of good garden loam, fine leafmold, peatmoss, sand, and fine gravel (preferably ⅛-in. screen). The mixture should be gritty. It should let surface water penetrate promptly, but should be retentive enough to hold a reasonable supply of moisture.

What depth of prepared soil is desirable in a rock garden? About 1 ft. For gardens made above the surrounding grade, there should be, underneath, another foot of a coarse mixture of rubble and retentive ingredients, such as peatmoss or sphagnum moss, to act as a sponge.

In a rock garden is it necessary to provide the great depth of drainage that I read about in books? For gardens laid above the grade—no. In sunken gardens or in low-lying parts, unfailing provision must be made to prevent stagnant moisture below. In our dry summer climate we must think of drainage in reverse as well— of retaining some moisture below, which later will find its way back to the surface.

I have a rock garden at the side of my house and would like to rearrange it. Can you make any suggestions concerning soil preparation and enrichment? It should be deeply dug, and a liberal amount of peatmoss added. Also incorporate cinders, leafmold, well rotted manure, a little bone meal, and a little tankage.

What is the best fertilizer to use for rock-garden plants, and when should I put it on? The majority of rock-garden plants should not be heavily fed; rich feeding causes soft growth which invites disease and leaves the plants subject to winter killing. Mix in fine bone meal and leafmold with the soil when preparing it, and in early spring dress established plantings with a top-dressing containing bone meal mixed with soil and leafmold.

CONSTRUCTION

What type of rock is best for rock gardens? Any porous, weathered rock that will look natural in place. It is all the better if it is deep fissured. Use only one kind of rock throughout the garden.

What about tufa rock? No rock is more acceptable to a wide diversity of plants than a soft, porous grade of tufa. But because of its glaring, bony color in sunny places it is not an attractive-looking material. In shade, and moisture, it quickly accumulates mosses and then becomes very beautiful.

Are large rocks desirable, or will small ones do as well? Construction should simulate Nature. She works with massive rocks. Therefore, in gardens large or small use rocks as large as you can handle; or match smaller ones together in such manner that they will create an effect of large masses.

Can you give me a few pointers on the placing of rocks? Embed the rockwork deeply enough to create an effect of natural outcroppings. Leave no lower edges exposed to betray superficial placing. Have the several rock masses extend in parallel directions, and carry out this principle even with the lesser rocks. Match joints and stratifications carefully. Try to get the rhythm of natural ledges and outcroppings.

How shall I build a rockery in a corner of my level lawn? In the foreground of corner shrubbery create the effect of a smoothish, shelved outcropping with several broad, low shelves. Push this arrangement back far enough for the shrubs to mask the sheer drop behind.

How should I arrange a rock garden and pool in the center of a small lawn without natural elevation of rock? Create the effect of one large, flattish, or somewhat humped rock, broken, so as to provide two or more broad crevices for planting. Locate the pool, somewhat off-center, immediately against this rock effect.

Have you any suggestions for a little rock garden, of slight elevation, with shrubbery as a background? Place or simulate the effect of one large, flattish outcropping, with fissures or wide joints for planting. Place the pool immediately against this rock mass. Your idea of a background of shrubs is excellent.

PLANTING

When is the best time to plant rock gardens? If pot-grown plants are available and you can arrange to water and shade them carefully, planting may be done almost any time from spring to early autumn. Spring is a proper season everywhere. In moderately cold climates (as in lower New York State), September and October are also good months.

What rock-garden plants should one set out in early spring? (New Mexico.) Any of the sedums, pinks (dianthus), dwarf phlox, primroses, painted daisies, bellflowers, and saponarias as well as most any other rock plants.

I am planting a rock garden. What distance between the plants will be necessary? Much will depend upon the kind of plants you are using. If they are spreading kinds, such as cerastium, phlox, helianthemum, sedums, thyme, and dianthus, set the plants about 12 ins. apart. Plants that spread more slowly, such as primulas, sempervivums, saxifragas, candytufts, arenarias, aubrietas, douglasia, anemones, pulsatillas, and the dwarf achilleas, plant 6 to 8 ins. apart.

How deep should rock plants be set in the ground? Most form a spreading top that either roots as it spreads or grows directly from a central root system. The crown of the plant must not be covered. Dig a hole with a trowel; gather the loose tops in the hand; hold the plant at the side of the hole, the crown resting on the surface, the roots extending into the hole while held in position; firm the soil around the roots. When the hole is filled, the crown should be resting on the surface. A good watering will then help establish it.

The soil on the slopes in my rock garden keeps washing out, especially after planting. How can I prevent this? If a considerable stretch is exposed, set in a few good-sized rocks at irregular intervals and tilt them so that their upper surfaces slope downward into the hill. Into the surface 2 ins. incorporate screened cinders mixed with peat or leafmold. Set the plants in groups 9 to 12 ins. apart (depending on their size) and cover the spaces between the groups with peat or leafmold until the plants effect a covering.

CULTURE

What are the main items of upkeep in a rock garden? Weeding; thinning; repressing too-rampant growths; removal of old flower stalks; occasional division of robust plants; watering; winter covering.

For the choicer, high-mountain plants, maintain a gravel mulch about their base and top-dress with compost on steep slopes each spring.

When is the best time to trim and thin plants that begin to overrun a rockery? Cut back the running kinds any time during their growing period.

Will you please discuss spring work in the rock garden? Remove winter covering when all danger of frost is over. If there is danger of cold winds and some plants have started to grow, uncover gradually. Firm back into the soil any plants that have been loosened. Replant as may be necessary. Top-dress with a mixture of 3 parts good soil, 1 part old, rotted manure, leafmold, or peatmoss, and 1 part coarse sand or screened cinders, with a 6-in. potful of fine bone meal added to each wheelbarrowload. When top-dressing, work this down around the crowns of the plants and over the roots of spreading kinds by hand. If a dry spell occurs in spring, give a good watering.

WATERING

How should the rock garden be watered and how often? With a fine sprinkler, so as to avoid washing the soil off the roots. Frequency of watering depends upon type of soil, amount of slope, kind of plants, and whether they are established or are newly planted, amount of shade, exposure, and of course weather. If dry spells occur in spring and early autumn, watering should be done in a very thorough fashion; toward late summer, unless a very prolonged dry spell occurs, watering should be confined to such plants as primulas, globeflowers, and other moisture-lovers. Ripening and hardening of most rock plants are necessary if they are to winter over properly.

WINTER PROTECTION

What is the best winter cover? When applied and when removed? A single thickness of pine boughs or any narrow leaved evergreen that will hold its leaves all winter after being cut. It is more quickly applied and removed than salt hay. Apply after the surface has frozen solid. It is needed, not as a protection against frost, but against thawing of the soil. Remove when danger of very hard frost seems past. Just when is always something of a gamble.

Is salt hay a good winter cover? Yes, but it is not quickly removable in the spring. Use it lightly, lest you invite mice and kindred vermin.

WHAT TO GROW

Will you please name a dozen foolproof rock-garden plants, stating flower color and season? *Alyssum saxatile citrinum* (lemon-yellow; May), *Arabis albida* (double-flowered, white; April to May), *Arabis procurrens* (white, April to May), *Campanula carpatica* (blue; July),

Ceratostigma plumbaginoides (blue; September to October), *Dianthus plumarius* (white and varicolored; June), *Phlox subulata* varieties (white, rose, dark rose, pink; May), *Sedum sieboldi* (rose; September to October), *Sedum album* (white; June), *Sedum ellacombianum* (yellow; July), *Thymus serpyllum coccineum* (deep rose; July), and *T. s. album* (white; June to July).

Can you give a list of some of the best rock plants for spring flowers? *Alyssum saxatile, Anemone pulsatilla, Arabis albida* (double-flowered), *Aubrieta deltoides, Corydalis halleri, Crocus* species, *Epimedium niveum, Scilla sibirica* and *S. bifolia,* and *Tulipa kaufmanniana.*

What are the best plants for a rockery for early spring and midsummer bloom? For early spring: *Tulipa kaufmanniana, Crocus* species, snowdrops, *Scilla sibirica,* and grapehyacinths. Non-bulbous plants: *Arabis albida, Aubrieta deltoides, Viola odorata,* primulas, *Anemone pulsatilla, Armeria caespitosa, Alyssum saxatile* and *A. saxatile luteum,* drabas, epimediums, *Erysimum ruprestre,* and *Phlox subulata.* For midsummer bloom: *Dianthus plumarius, Campanula carpatica, Antirrhinum asarina, Bellium bellidioides, Campanula cochlearifolia, Carlina acaulis, Globularia cordifolia, Lotus corniculatus, Dianthus knappi, Linum alpinum, Linaria alpina, Nierembergia caerulea,* penstemons, *Rosa rouletti, Santolina viridis, Silene achafta,* and *Ceratostigma plumbaginoides.*

Will you list a few of the best rock plants to flower from about May 15 to early June? *Dianthus neglectus, D. plumarius, D. strictus, D. arenaria, Cymbalaria pallida, Dodecatheon* species, *Gentiana acalis, Saxifraga* (encrusted species), and *Veronica teucrium rupestris.*

Can you name 12 good perennials suitable for rock gardens, which bloom at different periods? *Phlox subulata* and varities (April to May), *Aubrieta deltoides* (May), *Alyssum saxatile* and its variety *luteum* (May), *Primula polyanthus* (May), *Dianthus plumaris* (June), *Campanula carpatica* (June), *Lotus corniculatus* (July), *Veronica spicata alba* (June to July), *Thymus serpyllum* and its varieties (July), *Calluna vulgaris* (August to September), *Ceratostigma plumbaginoides* (September to October).

Will you list late-flowering rock plants? *Ceratostigma plumbaginoides, Allium pulchellum, A. flavum,* antirrhinum asarina, *Calluna vulgaris* and its varieties, *Chrysogonum virgineanum,* Clochicums, autumn crocuses, *Silene achafta, Saxifraga cortusaefolia,* and *Sedum sieboldi.*

What are the fastest-growing plants and vines for a rock garden? *Cerastium tomentosum, Ajuga reptans, Thymus serpyllum* and its varieties, *Lamium maculatum, L. m. album, Phlox subulata* and its varieties, *Arabis albida,* sedums, *Saponaria ocymoides, Lotus corniculatus, Campanula carpatica,* and *Asperula odorata.*

Should I try to furnish my new rock garden quickly with fast-growing plants, or do it gradually, with smaller plants? By all means the latter. Most people come to regret their first impatience, and wind up by rooting out the rampant growers, and replacing them with choicer, small plants; they are so much more delightful.

Which flowers are best to plant in a small rock garden? Such things as the drabas, *Aubrieta deltoides, Gypsophila repens, Myosotis alpestris, Nierembergia rivularis, N. caerulea, Primula vulgaris, Armeria caespitosa, Veronica teucrium rupestris, Androsace sarmentosa, A. villosa,* and *Rosa rouletti.* Avoid the use of coarse creeping plants; they will overrun the garden.

Can you suggest some plants for a very steep rock garden? *Thymus serpyllum* and its varieties, *Cerastium tomentosum, Sedum spurium, S. hybridum, Phlox subulata,* sempervivums, *Lotus corniculatus, Ceratostigma plumbaginoides, Antirrhinum asarina, Muehlenbeckia axillaris,* and *Campanula carpatica.*

Which perennial plants can I use for a very exposed location in a rock garden? *Arabis albida, Anemone pulsatilla, Phlox subulata* varieties, *Veronica teucrium rupestris, Cerastium tomentosum, Dianthus deltoides, D. plumarius, Lamium maculatum, Aquilegia canadensis, A. vulgaris, Campanula carpatica,* and *Dicentra eximia.*

Can you suggest a few small, decorative plants to fill small crevices in rocks and tiny pockets? My garden is in full sun. *Draba aizodes, Globularia repens (G. nana), Sedum dasyphllum, Sedum acre minus, Sedum anglicum minus,* and sempervivums (the tiny kinds).

Which are some good plants for shady corners in my rock garden, for spring flower? *Anemone nemorosa* (several kinds), *Brunnera macrophylla, Chrysogonum virginianum, Epimedium niveum, Iris cristata, Phlox divaricata laphami, Phlox stolonifera, Pulmonaria saccharata,* and *Saxifraga umbrosa.*

Which perennials, not over 10 ins. in height, bloom between June 15 and September 15, and are suitable for a rock garden in shade? *Chrysogonum virginianum, Corydalis lutea, Mitchella repens, Myosotis scorpioides, Sedum ternatum, S. Nevi, Allium Moly, Saxifraga cortusaefolia, Arenaria montana, Gentiana asclepiadea, Cymbalaria muralis, Scilla sinensis,* and *Dicentra formosa alba.*

Which are some small summer-blooming plants for the shady rock garden? *Chrysogonum virginianum, Cotula squalida, Mitchella repens, Sedum ternatum,* and *S. Nevi.*

Which are the most hardy rock-garden plants that will grow in semi-shade? *Primula polyanthus, P. veris, P. vulgaris,* epimediums, aubretias, aquilegias, *Iris verna, Phlox divaricata laphami, Chrysogonum virginianum, Viola odorata, V. priceana, Vinca minor, Lysimachia nummularia, Sedum ternatum, Ceratostigma plumbaginoides, Asperula odorata,* trilliums, erythroniums, and dodecatheons.

Will you name rock plants that will grow and bloom in the shade of a large oak tree? *Phlox divaricata laphami, Dicentra eximia, Chrysogonum virginianum, Asperula odorata,* erythroniums, trilliums, *Gaultheria procumbens, Mitchella repens, Iris verna, Vinca minor, Lysimachia nummularia,* and *Primula veris.*

Can you name several plants which will grow between rocks of a patio in very sandy soil; preferably fast growers? *Arenaria verna caespitosa, Thymus serpyllum* and its varieties, *Sedum acre, Dianthus deltoides, Muehlenbeckia axillaris, Mazus reptans,* and *Ajuga reptans.* Keep the soil reasonably moist.

Which rock plants require acid soil? Rhododendrons, azaleas, Mountain Laurel, pieris, shinleaf, partridge-berry, *Cypripedium acaule,* erythroniums, galax, and shortia.

Will you name a dozen or so of the choicest and most unusual plants that I may hope to grow in my rock garden? *Androsace lanuginosa, Androsace sarmentosa, Armeria juniperifolia, Campanula cochlearifolia alba, Dianthus callizonus, D. neglectus, Saxifraga burseriana, S. irvingi,* and encrusted saxifragas.

Will all kinds of rock-garden plants grow successfully in a garden without rocks? Yes, although many of them look better against or between rocks.

ALPINES

What is the best site for alpines? A gentle slope facing northeast or northwest.

What soil is best for alpines? One that is not too rich. A neutral, porous soil, well drained, and with grit and cinders to lighten it, will be satisfactory for most alpine plants.

Need I know a lot about alpines to have a good rock garden? No. You may use, more or less exclusively, plants from high, intermediate, or low altitudes. A good rock garden need not be filled with "high-brow" plants. It should afford a happy glimpse of Nature's play with rocks and plants—be it in a mountain scree or on a roadside ledge.

Would you advise me, a beginner, to try an alpine garden? No. Most of the best rock gardens one sees are not alpine gardens, but bits of small-scale, intimate mountain or hillside scenery, with occasional patches of true alpine flora.

Why are alpine plants so difficult to grow? Because the conditions prevailing in lowland rock gardens are so utterly different from those at or above timber line: the heavy winter pack of snow, the short summer, pure, crisp air, and chilly baths of mountain mist. One must learn gradually to devise acceptable equivalents or approximations to these conditions.

Can you name a few alpine plants not too difficult for an amateur

to grow? The following high-mountain plants (not all strictly alpines) are suggested: *Armeria juniperifolia, Androsace lanuginosa, A. sarmentosa, Campanula cochlearifolia, Dianthus alpinus, D. callizonus, Douglasia vitaliana, Gentiana acaulis,* and saxifragas (encrusted and kabschia kinds).

What are the best alpine campanulas for the rock garden? Campanulas *allioni, alpina, cochlearifolia, elatines, fragilis, lasiocarpa, portenschlagiana, poscharskyana, pulla, raineri,* and *tomasiniana.*

What winter care should be given alpines? Cover lightly with evergreen boughs or salt hay after the ground is frozen—usually in December.

BULBS FOR ROCK GARDEN

How should chionodoxa (glory-of-the-snow) be used in the rock garden? Scatter the bulbs in groups of 2 dozen or more in various places among low ground covers. They may also be used effectively beneath shrubs that may form a background to the garden.

Will you give a list of crocuses suitable for the rock garden? Spring-flowering: crocuses *aureus, biflorus, chrysanthus* and its varieties, *imperati, susianus, tomasinianus.* For autumn: *cancellatus albus, longiflorus, pulchellus, speciosus* and its varieties, *zonatus.*

Can you suggest some good narcissi for the rock garden? The best kinds are the small ones, such as *Narcissus minimus, cyclamineus triandrus, t. albus* (angel's tears), *concolor, bulbocodium* (hooppetticoat daffodil), and *B. citrinus.* The sweet jonquils and campernelles can also be used, such as *Narcissus jonquilla, j. flore-pleno,* and *odorus.*

Can you tell me kinds of tulips to plant in a rock garden and what conditions they need? The best are the species tulips, also called "botanical" tulips. These need well-drained soil and sunshine. Plant them about 6 or 7 ins. deep. The following are among the best: *kaufmanniana, acuminata, clusiana* (Lady Tulip), *dasystemon, greigi, praecox, praestans, fosteriana* varieties, *sylvestris,* and *turkestanica.*

Which spring-flowering bulbs are suitable for the rock garden? Squills, glory-of-the-snow, snowdrops, spring-snowflakes, crocuses, grapehyacinths, miniature daffodils. And also dogtooth violets, fritillaries, calochortuses, brodiaeas, and *Iris reticulata.*

Which bulbs are suitable for a rock garden at the side and front of the house? *Crocus* species (for fall and spring), *Galanthus nivalis* (snowdrops), *Leucojum vernum* (snowflake), *Chionodoxa luciliae* (glory-of-the-snow), muscari (grapehyacinths), scillas (squills), narcissi species, colchicums, Tulips *kaufmanniana* and its hybrids, and *dasystemon.*

When are small spring-flowering bulbs planted in the rock garden?

In late August plant snowdrops, winter-aconites, autumn-flowering crocuses, and colchicums. Plant the small daffodils and crocuses in September and others, mentioned in previous replies, in October.

I wish to plant a number of small bulbs in my rock garden. Should I dig up the other plants before planting the bulbs? How deep must I plant the bulbs? Unless the soil needs improving it is not necessary to remove the plants. Use a bulb trowel (a tool with a narrow concave blade), push it into the soil through the mat of plants, pull the handle toward you, and then push the bulb into the soil and smooth the plants back again. Plant these small bulbs in groups and closely together. The depth at which they are set should be, roughly, 3 times the depth of the bulb.

EVERGREENS

Can you tell me some evergreens for a rock garden which will withstand severe winter exposure? *Taxus cuspidata, Juniperus communis, J. horizontalis, J. sabina tamariscifolia, Pinus mughus, Pieris floribunda,* and *Ilex glabra.*

Which are some small evergreens that may be used effectively in a rock garden? *Juniperus procumbens nana* (for a low, flat spread), *Juniperus squamata prostrata* (to drape over a rock), *Juniperus horizontalis* "Bar Harbor"; the dwarfest and most compact of Japanese yews and of hemlocks.

What soil does Daphne cneorum require? This is a much-debated question. Its success seems to depend mostly upon climate. It does better in the cold parts of New England (with a winter covering), than in warmer climates. Plant in a well-drained soil, away from the fiercest sun.

SHRUBS

Will you suggest some shrubs to use in a rock garden near the front of my house? Rhododendrons and azaleas are suitable. Mountain-laurel, *Daphne mezereum,* and *D. genkwa* would also look well against a taller evergreen background.

Will you name a few small shrubs that may look well in a small rock garden? *Spiraea decumbens, S. bullata, Cotoneaster microphylla, Berberis verruculosa, Ilex crenata helleri.* In part shade and an acid, humusy soil, *Rhododendron obtusum* and its varieties, and *R. racemosum* should be satisfactory.

Which shrubby plants would make a good background for our rock garden along the side of the garage? In east to northeast exposures: rhododendrons, azaleas, laurel, pieris, Japanese holly, and *Mahonia aquifolium.* In sunnier exposures: *Berberis koreana, B. vernae, Symphoricarpos chenaulti,* and perhaps an upright yew.

I have a natural spot for a rock garden about 25 ft. long by 5 ft. wide, on a slope exposed to north and west winds. Are there any shrubs sufficiently hardy to winter in such a location?   *Rhododendron mucronulatum, Daphne mezereum, Enkianthus campanulatus, Forsythia ovata, and Cercis chenensis* should do well.

SPECIFIC ROCK GARDEN PLANTS

What is the proper treatment of ALYSSUM SAXATILE which has grown "leggy"?   It is best to raise new plants from seed. This plant does not usually last much longer than 3 years. It is inclined to rot away during winter. If it survives, wait until new shoots appear near the base of the plant, then cut the leggy, long ones away.

Does AUBRIETA remain in bloom for a long period?   No. Its blooming season is short. However, it flowers in very early spring and is worthy of a place in the garden.

Are the plants called CINQUEFOILS suitable for the rock garden? Can you suggest a few?   Many cinquefoils (potentilla) are excellent, others are worthless weeds. *Potentilla nepalensis, tridentata,* and *verna* are worth trying. Give them full sun and well-drained, gritty soil.

How best to grow pinks in the rock garden?   Dianthuses do best in a well-drained, sunny position. Do not make the soil very rich and do not overwater them. They are good on gentle slopes, planted so that they can spread over the top of a rock, or in flat, well-drained pockets. Start with young, pot-grown plants if possible, and plant them out at about 9 ins. apart. Some kinds die after a time, so it is best to keep raising a few fresh plants each year.

What kinds of DIANTHUS do you suggest for a rock garden? *Dianthus deltoides* (Maiden-pink), *plumarius* (Grass-pink), *gratianopolitanus* (Cheddar-pink), and *neglectus* (Glacier-pink).

What can I do to make GENTIANA ANDREWSI grow?   It appreciates a moist, semi-shaded situation, preferably on the edge of a pond, and a deep, humusy soil. Top-dress in spring with peatmoss mixed with a little cow manure.

Which IRISES are suitable for the rock garden?   Irises *reticulata, gracilipes, arenaria, pumila* (in many varieties), *dichotoma, minuta, cristata, cristata alba, lacustris, tectorum,* and its variety *album.*

What conditions do PRIMULAS need in the rock garden?   A rich, moist soil and a shady or semi-shady situation. Some, like *Primula pulverulenta,* grow best in almost boggy conditions along the sides of streams. Practically all need plenty of moisture. If very moist conditions cannot be given, grow them in shade.

Will you suggest some primulas for the rock garden?   Primulas:

polyantha, veris (the cowslip), *farinosa, bulleyana, rosea, denticulata, frondosa,* and *japonica.*

What care should be given LEONTOPODIUMS that were raised from seeds? The edelweiss likes a well-drained, limy soil, full sun in spring, semi-shade in summer, and light protection in winter. Either evergreen boughs or salt hay should be used, as leaves pack too hard and keep the plant waterlogged, which may result in rotting. From seed they should bloom well the second year. Carry the plants over in a cold frame, in pots, the first year.

Will you name a few PENSTEMONS that would grow in my rock garden? Are they difficult to grow? *Penstemon glaber, heterophyllus, rupicola* and *unilateralis.* These are not difficult. They require gritty soil and do not like a position that becomes sodden in winter. They are not long-lived plants and in order to maintain them it is necessary to raise a few each year.

What soil is suitable for PHLOX subulata? Any light, well-drained garden soil.

Where does Phlox subulata grow wild? In the Eastern, Western, and Southern parts of the United States, on dry banks and in fields.

Do most of the Western species of phlox require scree conditions in the Eastern states? Yes, they seem to do better under either scree or moraine conditions in the East.

What are some good kinds of phlox for a rock garden, not tall ones? Some of the most suitable besides the various varieties of *Phlox subulata* are *Phlox amoena, divaricata* (and its variety *laphami*), *douglasi,* and *stolonifera.*

What is the best place in the rock garden for SAXIFRAGAS? What kind of soil? A partially shady situation facing east or west. Soil should be gritty, open, and well drained. Mix garden soil, leaf-mold, and stone chips, or screened cinders, in about equal proportion, and have a foot depth of this in which to plant. Limestone chips are beneficial for the encrusted saxifragas.

Which saxifragas are not too difficult to grow? Saxifragas: *aizoon, apiculata, cochlearis, decipiens* (a mossy type, requiring partial shade), *hosti, macnabiana,* and *moschata.*

How many species and varieties of rock-garden SEDUMS are there? Approximately 200. Perhaps not more than 50 distinct and useful kinds are available in nurseries.

Which are the best sedums? Sedums: *Album, anglicum, brevifolium, caeruleum* (annual), *dasyphyllum, ewersi, kamtschaticum, lydium, middendorffianum, nevi, oreganum, populifolium, pilosum, reflexum, rupestre, sempervivoides, sexangulare, sieboldi, spurium ternatum, stoloniferum, hybridum,* and the self-sowing biennial *nuttallianum.*

Can I get information regarding the culture of sedums? Most are easily propagated from cuttings taken in the fall or spring. They root best in sand, either in flats or in cold frames. When well rooted, transfer them into small pots or put them directly into their permanent places in the garden. The location should ordinarily be sunny, the soil sandy and well drained. Western-America sedums prefer a semi-shaded position.

Are the SUNROSES (helianthemums) hardy? Do they require much care? They are not very hardy; they thrive fairly well in the vicinity of New York but farther North they are doubtful subjects. They need no more care than ordinary rock-garden plants. Give them a well-drained soil in a sunny location. Protect them in winter with salt hay or evergreen boughs, and cut them back to within a few inches of their crowns in spring, to encourage fresh growth.

Do helianthemums survive the winter without protection? That all depends upon the winter, and upon where they are growing. In a sheltered spot they would probably come through. In an exposed position, cover them with evergreen boughs. They are not overhardy in lower New York State.

MORAINE GARDEN

Can you explain what a moraine garden is? How is it made? A moraine is constructed for the purpose of growing certain alpine plants from high altitudes. The garden contains little or no soil, the growing medium being mostly stone chips and shale. The important factor is water. The most complete moraines have cool water circulating below the growing medium so that the roots of the plants are in a cool, moist medium much as are alpines in their native haunts. A moraine can be built in a water-tight basin 2 ft. deep and of any length and breadth. A foot-thick layer of stones is laid in the bottom. The remaining space is filled with a mixture of 5 parts crushed stone (½ in.), 1 part sand, and 1 part leafmold. Water is supplied during the growing season through a pipe at the upper end and the surplus is drawn off by one at the other end 12 ins. below the surface. Sub-irrigation is sometimes dispensed with and the garden is then known as a "scree."

Will you give me a list of plants suitable for a moraine garden? Aethionema, androsace, *Arenaria montana, Dianthus sylvestris, Campanula speciosa, Silene acaulis,* and saxifragas (the encrusted kinds).

PATHS

What are the most suitable kinds of paths for the rock garden and how are they constructed? See Paths, this section.

PAVEMENT PLANTING

How are plants grown between the flags in a pavement? For the plants to succeed, the flags should be laid on sand overlying several inches of soil. Watering during hot, dry weather is very helpful.

How are plants arranged in a pavement planting?   Do not overdo the planting or it will look untidy. Use for the most part flat types of plants, with an occasional taller plant to relieve the monotony.

How are plants planted between flagstones?   Planting is first done as the flat stones are laid. When the spot for a plant is selected, the plant is set so that when the surface is leveled for the next flagstone, the top of the plant is resting at the correct level. The stone may have to be chipped to avoid crushing the plant.

Which plants are suitable for planting in a flagged walk?   Those that will withstand much walking are: *Festuca ovina glauca, Sagina subulata,* and *Tunica saxifraga.* Others to use are *Thymus serpyllum* varieties, *Mentha requieni* (both fragrant), *Alyssum montanum, Erinus alpinus, Veronica repens,* and *Lysimachia nummularia.*

POOLS

How do you construct a small pool for the rock garden?   See Pool Construction, this section.

I have a hillside rock garden with an uneven 6-ft.-diameter pool. Will you give me advice as to plants for inside the pool and for outside to hold up the dirt which seems to wash away with each rain? Plant *Nymphoides peltatum* inside the pool. *Caltha palustris* (marsh-marigold) along the edge, also *Primula rosea, Trollius europaeus,* and 2 or 3 *Lobelia cardinalis.* In between plant solid with *Myosotis scorpioides,* which will hold the soil.

A small informal pool not only adds interest to the landscaping but can provide congenial conditions for moisture-loving plants.

STEPS—PLANTING

I have some rough flagstone steps and wish to set some plants in

them. How should I arrange them? What kind should I use? The width of the steps will have to be considered in the arrangement. The primary purpose of steps is to link certain areas. Plants, if used, are for decoration. Don't overplant and avoid regularity. Low plants should be used mostly with an occasional bushy one interspersed. The sides can be more thickly planted than the centers. (For kinds, see Pavement Plantings.)

WALL GARDENS

What exposure for a wall garden? Eastern, except for shade-loving plants such as ramondia, haberlea, *Saxifraga sarmentosa,* English ivies, and certain ferns. For these a northern exposure.

What is the best type of rock for a wall garden? For an informal effect, any natural, porous rock with a good facing surface; squarish pieces, such as one might use for an ordinary dry wall, are best. A good wall garden can be made of bricks.

How does one make a wall garden? Much like a dry retaining wall, but the joints are packed with prepared soil and the stones are tilted backward to keep the soil from washing out and to direct the rain water toward the plant roots. To prevent squashing of roots, chink the horizontal joints with small pieces of stone. Place plants in position as the laying up proceeds, and firm the soil well at the back of the wall.

What special upkeep does a wall garden need? Upkeep is reduced by using suitably compact, small, rock-hugging plants. Remove all old flower stalks. Pull out weeds and excess seedlings. Prune and thin so as to maintain a balanced distribution of planting effect. On top of the wall, provide a watering trench or trough, and use it freely to prevent drying out in summer.

Wide terrace with planted dry wall.

How are plants planted in a wall? In a wall garden, building and planting are done at the same time. If the plants are located at the joints, the soil is packed in, the plant set, a little extra soil added, and then the stones are placed. Chips placed between the stones near the plants prevent them from sinking and squeezing the plants. If plant-ing has to be done after building, the job is more difficult. The roots must somehow be spread out in a narrow space, and the soil rammed in with a piece of stick. Don't plant fast-growing plants near slow-growing ones or the latter will be smothered.

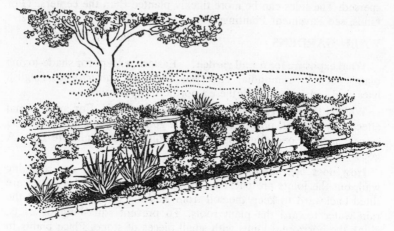

In planting a wall care must be taken to spot the plants with a natural-looking irregularity that avoids any studied pattern or design.

What summer upkeep is necessary for a rock wall?   Keep plants well watered and weeded. Spray if necessary.

Can you tell me what spring care should be given a rockery made in an old stone wall?   Trim dead pieces off plants; fill washed-out cracks with new soil. Push heaved-out plants into soil or take them out altogether and replant.

What winter cover for a wall garden?   Stick a row of pine boughs into the ground thickly enough to provide shade from the brightest sun of winter. Or place a row of two-by-fours, slanting against the wall, and over them stretch a burlap cover. The pine boughs will be better looking.

What winter care is necessary for a rock wall?   Cover with ever-green boughs when the ground is frozen. Take off during early April.

Which plants are particularly suitable for use in a rock wall?   All the sempervivums, Sedums: *hybridum, coccineum, nevi,* and *sieboldi,* Nepeta *hederacea,* Campanulas *carpatica: cochlearifolia,* and *rotundi-folia, Silene caroliniana,* Linarias: *pallida* and *aequitriloba, Phlox stolonifera, Achillea ageratifolia,* and *Mazus reptans.*

Are wall gardens easy to maintain?   They are at their best in moist climates (England) where there are not long drought periods. If left unwatered in long summer droughts many of the plants will die. They require more attention than other types of gardens, especially care in watering.

WATER GARDENS

(*See also Pool Construction*)

PLANTING

What background materials should I use for my small informal pool? Small evergreens, yew, arborvitae, cedar, hemlock, azalea, laurel, rhododendron, leucothoe, euonymus, cotoneaster, daphne.

Can you tell me some flowering shrubs I can put around my pool? Viburnum, forsythia, abelia, mockorange, lilac, deutzia, kolkwitzia, spirea, azalea, rhododendron, laurel, lonicera. Shrub roses would also be a good choice here.

I want a formal-looking clipped hedge around the sides of my formal pool, which is at the rear of my garden. What would you suggest? Yew, hemlock, barberry, box (for sheltered positions), privet.

Can I have a successful fish pond in a plot about 9 × 15 ft.? How could anything so small be landscaped? Why not pave the area with flagstones, leaving wide cracks between stones? These could be planted with rock plants. The pool would be the central feature.

Have you any planting suggestions for rim of a pool? Astilbe, cardinalflower, Japanese iris, loosestrife, marshmarigold, rosemallow, Siberian iris and moneywort.

I have a rocky ledge by my pool. What evergreen might be grown over it? Depending on size of ledge and pool, low growing bearberry (arctostaphylos), or one of the creeping junipers might be used. For larger pools, there is nothing quite as graceful as a dwarf weeping Canada hemlock planted with its branches hanging down over the rocks.

Which flowering plants can be grown in a pool other than waterlilies? Floatingheart (*Nymphoides peltatum*); true forget-me-not; waterhyacinth (*Eichornia*); waterpoppy (*Hydrocleis*); water-snowflake (*Nymphoides indicum*). The last 3 are not winter hardy.

What can be used to break the monotonous flatness of a lily pool? Tall-growing water plants, such as American and Hindu Lotus; calla;* cattails (if pool is large); flowering rush; yellow and blue flags; taro;* water plantain.

With what flowers shall I border informal pool 6 × 10 ft.? *Spiraea venusta* and *S. filipendula*, *Iris ochroleuca*, *Trollius ledebouri*, *Lythrum salicaria*, hemerocallis, *Liatris pycnostachya*, *Myosotis palustris semperflorens.*

*Not winter hardy

SPECIFIC WATER PLANTS

HINDU LOTUS

Which is the best way to keep sacred lotus through winter? If growing in a pond that is drained during the winter, cover the roots with a sufficient depth of leaves to prevent the frost penetrating to the tubers. When this plant is grown in water 2 or 3 ft. deep, usually no winter protection is necessary.

WATERHYACINTH

How can I grow waterhyacinth? Float in 6 ins. water above a box or tub containing 6 ins. or more of soil. Keep from drifting by confining within an anchored wooden hoop. Bring plants indoors before frost.

How do you winter waterhyacinths that have been in an outside pool? Bring them indoors before the leaves are injured by cold. Float them in a container of water which has 3 or 4 ins. of soil in the bottom. Keep in a sunny window in a temperature of 55° to 60° F.

WATERLILIES

What is proper soil for waterlilies? Heavy loam, composted for a year before use with cow manure in the proportion of 2 to 1. If this is out of the question, use rich soil from vegetable garden.

What shall I use to make waterlilies bloom better? Possibly your plants are starved. Divide and replant in the soil recommended above, adding a 5-in. potful of bone meal to each bushel of soil.

How can I make waterlilies blossom in a small artificial pond? See answer to preceding question. Perhaps, however, the failure of your plants is due to insufficient sunshine. Waterlilies need full sun all day for best results.

How large should containers be for waterlilies? Depends on the variety. Small-growing kinds can be grown in boxes 15 × 15 × 10 ins., while the tropical varieties can be grown to advantage in sizes up to 4 × 4 × 1 ft.

In a small concrete pool is it better to cover the bottom with soil or use separate boxes for waterlilies? The lilies are better off if the bottom is covered with soil, but it is easier to avoid muddying the water in the pool if the soil is confined in wooden boxes or similar containers.

How deep should the water be over waterlilies? Six ins. to 3 ft. Preferably 1 ft. for tropical varieties, 1 to 2 ft. for hardy varieties, provided this is enough to prevent roots from freezing in winter.

What is the most practical way of caring for a waterlily pool in the

winter? If the pool is small enough to be bridged by boards, do so and then cover with a sufficient thickness of straw or leaves to prevent the water from freezing. If the pool is drained and the lilies are growing in tubs, move the tubs together and cover around and over them with leaves held in place with wire netting or something similar.

Supposing the mud is not sufficiently deep to support the growth of waterlilies? Plant the lilies in rich soil in a shallow wicker or chip basket, or fruit crate with openings sufficiently wide to allow roots to emerge, then gently slide the planted container into the pond.

How often should waterlilies be divided? Whenever the container becomes so crowded that growth is poor—usually after 3 or 4 years.

Would colored pond lilies grow where wild white ones grow in a lake with muddy bottom? Yes.

Which waterlily can be grown in a pool fed from an underground stream? Water is cold the year around and is in dense shade. Waterlilies will not grow in such a location.

How can I plant HARDY WATERLILIES in a natural pond? If the pond has a rich mud bottom, merely tie a heavy sod or half brick to the tuber or rhizome and drop it in the pond where water is between 1 and 3 ft. deep.

When is the best time to plant hardy waterlilies? When ice has left the pond in the spring, but they may be planted successfully up until mid-June.

Should hardy waterlilies be left outside in the pool through the winter? (New York.) Yes, if they are growing in water so deep that there is no danger of the roots freezing—18 ins. should be enough in your locality.

How early can TROPICAL WATERLILIES be set out? (New York.) Not until all danger of frost is past and the water has become warm—about the second week in June in the vicinity of New York.

How are tropical waterlilies planted? Pot-grown plants are commonly used. A hole is scooped in the soil of the container deep enough to receive the ball of earth about the roots, then the roots are covered with soil, taking care not to bury the crown of the plant.

Can tropical waterlilies be kept through the winter as other bulbs are? It is difficult to carry over tropical waterlilies unless one has a sunny greenhouse. When it is possible to find small tubers around the crown of the old plant, these may be gathered in the fall, stored in sand, protected from mice, and started in an aquarium in a sunny window in April.

Can I carry my Dauben Nymphaea over the winter? Lilies of this type produce young plantlets on the leafstalks. If a greenhouse or sunny window is available, the plantlets can be gathered in the fall, planted in a watertight vessel about 12 ins. in diameter, filled to within

3 ins. of its rim with soil, the remainder of the container being filled with water.

Can tropical waterlilies be carried over the winter in this climate? (New York.) Not out of doors. See answer to 2 preceding questions. Usually it is better to obtain new plants from dealers each spring.

During the past 2 summers some sort of leaf miner has eaten the leaves (making marks like Chinese ideographs) of my waterlilies. Consequently the leaves soon die. What are they and how may I get rid of them without injuring the fish in the pond? The larvae of a midge— *Chirononus modestus.* Waterlily foliage is sensitive to insecticidal sprays, so it is best, whenever possible, to use mechanical means to get rid of pests; therefore pick off infested leaves as fast as they appear, and destroy by burning, which will ultimately eliminate the miner.

We have an old pond on our place but now it is almost one solid growth of waterlilies. How can these be eradicated? By spraying the waterlily foliage with a mixture of half 2,4-D and half 2,4,5-T in early August, applied at the rate of one gallon of concentrate (containing 2 lbs. of acid equivalent of 2,4-D and 2 lbs. of acid equivalent of 2,4,5-T) in 2 gallons of water. Or sodium arsenite has proved effective as a spray—15 lbs. of sodium arsenite in 100 gallons of water.

WILDFLOWER GARDENS

SOIL

What soil and fertilizer should be used for wildflower planting? Generally speaking, the soil should approximate that in which the plants grow naturally. Woodland plants thrive in rich leafmold. Many prefer slightly acid soil. No artificial fertilizer should be used; well-rotted compost is next best to natural leafmold.

What fertilizers are recommended for woodland wildflowers? None. Leafmold is enough.

Should the soil around wildflowers be cultivated? The weeds should be kept out, but the soil does not need cultivating.

PLANNING

What is the best location for a wildflower garden? This depends on the type of flowers to be grown. Some wildflowers grow naturally in woodlands, and others in a sunny meadow. Try to make the condition in your garden most like the one which the particular plants came from.

Should a wildflower garden be attemped in an ordinary backyard garden? If so, what type? No, not in general. However, an informal sort of garden may be made, using the more common types of either woodland flowers or meadow flowers.

What plants go well with mertensia, bloodroot, and Dutchman's-breeches to fill in when their foliage dies down in late spring? Use Christmasfern or evergreen woodfern with mertensia and bloodroot; use spleenworts and grapeferns among the Dutchman's-breeches. These ferns do not have crowding habits and are almost evergreen. Their colors are good with the flowers mentioned.

Which wildflowers and trees can be established in dry, sandy, stony soil? Trees for dry, stony soil in your location are the Redcedar (*Juniperus virginiana*) and the locust (*Robina pseudoacacia*). Many shrubs will grow, such as bayberry, barberry, scrub oak, raspberries and blackberries, sumacs, blueberries. The blackhaw may assume the stature of a tree. Flowers include many of the flowers of the open field—daisies, asters, blackeyedsusans, everlasting.

PROPAGATION

Is it best to grow wildflowers from seed, or to buy the plants? Choice plants may be started from seed. Plants of most varieties may be purchased.

Which wild native plants may be started from seed and how is this done? Practically all of the field flowers, such as asters, milkweeds, goldenrods. Also columbine, pale corydalis, climbing fumitory (vine), celandine poppy, bloodroot, early saxifrage, bishop's cap, foamflower, and painted cup. With more patience, try arbutus and fringed gentian. The seeds are best started in flats in a protected cold frame. Sow in early winter or spring, using a light, sandy, leafmoldy soil mixture.

What is a good all-around soil mixture in which to sow wildflower seeds? One half ordinary garden soil, ¼ leafmold, and ¼ coarse fresh-water sand, thoroughly mixed and worked through a ⅛-in. mesh sifter to remove all stones and lumps.

How long can wildflower seeds be kept before planting them? Much depends on what kind they are. Some, such as trillium, bloodroot, and others that are produced in a more or less pulpy berry or pod, should be sown immediately before they dry at all; many other harder and thinner kinds can be kept for 5 or 6 months. A good general rule is to sow as soon as the seed is ripe, regardless of the time of the year.

Which kinds of wildflower seeds can be sown in a cold frame late in the fall? Practically all of the perennial kinds, especially those which flower in midsummer or later. Keep the sash on the frame to protect from winter rains, and shade with slats or cheesecloth to prevent undue heating before spring.

I want to have thousands of beautiful kinds of wildflowers all over my meadow. Can't I get them by strewing handfuls of seed in all directions—a "wildflower mixture," you know, like I see advertised in the catalogues? Sorry—but you can't. Only the toughest and commonest, such as daisies and goldenrod, will catch hold and grow, so all you'll really have in a couple of years will be a bumper crop of weeds. Rather raise the kinds you want from seed sown in a place where they won't be overrun, and set the plants out in the meadow when they're big enough to hold their own.

What wildflowers self-sow so quickly as to become pests if planted in the garden?   Goldenrod, cattails, wild carrot, jewelweed, ironweed, blackeyedsusan, sunflower, asters, golden ragwort, mullein, daisy, and many others.

I am not a botanist but like to identify wildflowers. Can you give me one or two references to well-illustrated books that would help me identify wildflowers from illustrations?   Wild Flowers—Homer D. House; Macmillan Co. 1934. The Macmillan Wild Flower Book, C. J. Hylander & E. F. Johnston, Macmillan 1954.

COLLECTING

How can wildflowers be identified?   By a study of botany or by reference to a reliable illustrated book on the wildflowers growing in your locality.

Which wildflowers cannot be collected from the wild without breaking the conservation laws?   Nearly every state has its own list of native plants under conservation, so a complete list of all protected species is impossible. Some of the more important kinds are trilliums, trailing arbutus, Mountain Laurel, all native orchids, anemone, lilies, dodecatheon, Fringed Gentian, cardinalflower, Birdsfoot Violet, bluebells, wild pink.

Where can wildflowers be obtained?   There are special dealers in wildflowers throughout the country who carry all types of these plants.

How do you start a wildflower preserve?   Start a wildflower preserve by acquiring a spot that already has enough trees and flowers and beauty to suggest preserving. Gradually bring in groups of plants which you wish to include and see that they are planted in situations such as they seek in nature. This involves a good working knowledge of the soil and other conditions which the plants prefer and matching these conditions in the places you plant them.

May a flower preserve be joined with an arboretum?   It should be a splendid addition to an arboretum.

BOG

What conditions are necessary for a bog garden? Is it different from water gardening?   Generally a swampy piece of ground, not under water, but where at all times there is plenty of moisture and usually too soft to walk upon. In water gardens the plants are immersed or floating. In bog gardens, the plants grow free above the soil.

Which plants grow in wet marshland? Swamp milkweed, marsh-marigold, Joepyeweed, yellowflag, blueflag, cardinalflower, loosestrife, forget-me-not, sedges, marshmallow, water plantain, Yellow- and White-fringed Orchises, and many more.

Are tall-growing wildflowers, such as hibiscus, cardinalflower, and lobelia, suitable for the wild garden? Yes. They are best grown in the bog garden or in a moist border.

Which wildflowers are suitable for planting near a naturalistic pool in sun and shade? *Iris pseudacorus, Iris prismatica, Aruncus sylvestris, Vernonia noveboracensis, Anemone canadensis, Asclepias incarnata, Calla palustris, Caltha palustris, Chelone glabra, Gentiana andrewsi, Hypoxis hirsuta, Lilium superbum, Parnassia caroliniana.*

Which wildflowers do you suggest for the edge of a slow-moving, shaded stream? Cardinalflower, boneset, turtlehead, Great Lobelia, Fringed and Bottle Gentians, forget-me-not, monkeyflower, mertensia, blueflag (iris), marshmarigold, American globeflower. A little distance from the stream, but where they profit by some of the moisture, you can grow Yellow ladyslipper, trilliums, Yellow Adders-tongue, Fringed Polygala, Solomonseal, false Solomonseal, foamflower, Jack-in-the-pulpit, White Violet, windflower (anemonella).

MEADOW

Can you give me some pointers on planning and setting out a meadow wild garden? The meadow where wildflowers are to be grown should be open, sunny, and preferably fenced with either a rustic fence or rock wall. The soil for common meadow flowers should be dry, porous, and preferably a little sandy. Most meadow flowers are easily grown from seed and then transplanted. Weeds should be kept away from the plants so that they are not choked out. Room should be allowed for them to reseed themselves and form natural-looking patches.

What are the general cultural requirements for growing meadow wildflowers in the garden? The conditions should be as much like those of a meadow as possible: full sun, plenty of room for the plants, and undisturbed conditions. The soil should be porous and loamy except for moist meadow plants.

What sun-loving wildflowers are suitable for rural garden planting to give color and succession of bloom? *Phlox amoena,* April to May; *Iris cristata,* May; *Corydalis glauca,* May to June; *Epilobium angustifolium,* June to July; *Gillenia trifoliata,* June to August; *Campanula rotundifolia,* June to October; *Cassia marilandica,* July to August; *Asclepias tuberosa,* July to August; *Aster linariifolius,* September; *Aster ericoides,* September to October.

Which wild plants will grow well in a sunny meadow? Daisies, blackeyedsusans, the goldenrods, butterflyweed, phlox, Joepyeweed, hawkweed (devil's-paint-brush), yarrow, thistles, ironweed, lupine, Pearly and Sweet Everlastings, American Artichoke, tansy, chicory; New England, Smooth, and New York Asters, trumpet creeper and Bush Honeysuckle, Queen Anne's lace, wild sweetpea.

WOODLAND

How can a woodland wild garden be planned and arranged? A woodland garden made for wild plants should simulate natural wild conditions. There should be shade and semi-shade formed by such trees as grow in the woods. The soil for wood plants should be rich and leafmoldy and slightly damp. The plants are best placed in natural-looking clumps around the base of the trees. A few rocks may be used as focal points, and plants placed around them.

How does one go about starting a wildflower garden beginning with a piece of wild woodland in Vermont? It's just a small patch about ¼ acre. How do you get cardinalflowers started to grow in such a garden? Start your wild garden by gradually replacing and replanting under and around trees, along paths, etc. You will have greatest success with the plants that grow naturally in Vermont woods. Cardinalflower (*Lobelia cardinalis*) likes the stream sides, will grow in partial shade almost in the water, although it sometimes thrives when transplanted to garden soil with less moisture.

Will bloodroot, trillium, and columbine grow under pine trees? If not, what will grow there? The plants mentioned grow well under oak trees. They will grow under pine trees if the shade is not too great and the soil is loamy. Why not try partridge-berry for ground cover, also the club mosses? Plant Christmasfern and Shieldfern. Pipsissewa and shinleaf (*Pyrola elliptica*) will be dainty but difficult additions, as well as wintergreen (*Gaultheria procumbens*) and bunchberry (*Cornus canadensis*).

What are the best methods of growing wild plants under shady conditions? Try to create the conditions in which the plants grow naturally. The amount of shade, moisture, and kind of soil are all important. If under oak trees, you may plant most of the early spring flowers, such as bloodroots, Dutchman's-breeches, partridge-berry, hepatica, bishop's cap, violets, shinleaf, woodbetony, and many ferns and club mosses, such as Shieldfern, polypody, Christmasfern, spleenworts. The club mosses include ground cedar, runningpine, and staghorn. The last, however, are very difficult to transplant.

What are the general cultural requirements for wildflowers? Such as grow in the woods? A leafmoldy soil, semi-shade, and undisturbed conditions.

What mulching materials are suitable for woodland wild plants? Fallen leaves and evergreen boughs.

Do woodland wildflowers require a mulch? A mulch of leaves is helpful.

When woodland wildflowers have been transplanted from their natural habitat, should they be protected over winter? Yes, especially the first year to prevent heaving.

Do woodland wildflowers require any special care in planting? They need the same careful planting as all flowers. Put them in well-dug soil with enough room for the roots and do not crowd them. Tamp the soil firmly around them.

My property is a Gray Birch grove. Which wildflowers can I plant in among the birches? Under your Gray Birches you may grow speedwell (*Veronica officinalis*), violets, wild strawberries, Pearly Everlasting, pipsissewa, shinleaf, *Phlox divaricata*, Rue and Wood Anemones, mertensia. Ferns: Christmasfern, spleenwort, and polypody; the lycopodiums (club mosses.)

Can you suggest a group of native American wildflowers for planting in a wooded lot on home grounds? *Aralia nudicaule*, *Aralia racemosa*, trilliums, *Dicentra eximia*, *Gillenia trifoliata*, *Shortia galacifolia*, *Tiarella cordifolia*, *Actaea alba* and *A. rubra*.

Which wildflowers will grow in a beech grove? Springbeauty (claytonia), wild columbine, harebells, hepatica, violets, mertensia, *Phlox divaricata*, *Trillium grandiflorum*, Jack-in-the-pulpit, Red Baneberry, the anemones, Yellow Ladyslipper (if moist), Solomonseal, false Solomonseal, bloodroot. Ferns: Walking and the woods ferns.

Which wildflowers will grow in a woodland where there are hemlocks and oaks? A few are Pink Ladyslipper, Painted Trillium, Wood Lily (*L. philadelphicum*), arbutus, bellwort, *Iris verna*, wintergreen, Purple-fringed Orchis, Wood Anemone, partridge-berry, Wood Aster. Shrubs: rhododendron, wild azalea (Pinkster bloom), and laurel.

SPECIFIC WILDFLOWERS

ANEMONES

I have tried several times to transplant Rue Anemones (Anemonella thalictroides) from the woods, without success. What could be wrong? They should be dug with a large ball of soil right after flowering, before the leaves die down. Take enough of the soil in which they are found to establish them in their new location. Plant in light shade. They require light, moist soil and are indifferent to acidity. The Wood Anemone (*A. quinquefolia*) requires moderate acidity.

What are the soil conditions required by the Wood Anemone (A. quinquefolia)? Moist, open woodland. Likes the borders of streams.

Must have moderately acid soil. Dig with a large ball of soil just after flowering.

ARBUTUS

What is the correct name for trailing arbutus or mayflower? *Epigaea repens*.

How can I grow trailing arbutus? Best to get pot-grown plants from a nursery, since they more easily adapt themselves to changed soil conditions. Where arbutus grows in abundance in nature there is usually a sandy base to the soil, often ancient sandy river beds, or along the shore as on Long Island or the pine barrens of New Jersey. Soil should be light, strongly acid, and rich in organic matter, with good drainage.

BLUETS

I should like to have a large patch of bluets (or quakerlady or innocence, as they are called). How can this be done? They are best in a rather moist, acid soil, in full sun. If you get them from the wild, put them in a place as much like the one they were in as possible. They should reseed themselves and form a patch.

What kinds of bluets are there besides the common quakerlady? Only one, if you are thinking of kinds that are worth planting. This one is the Creeping Bluet (*Houstonia serpyllifolia*), from the southern Appalachians. It is a mat-forming, rather short-lived perennial that flowers profusely for about 3 weeks in May. It will usually self-sow freely.

Dogtooth Violet (left) and Bloodroot, two of our most charming native spring flowers.

BLOODROOT

How is bloodroot transplanted? Take care to get the whole root. Set it carefully in a well-dug soil in light shade, in August. Indifferent to soil acidity.

How may one germinate bloodroot seed? Collect the seed capsules just before they burst open. When seeds have ripened, they may be planted immediately in a prepared spot in the garden where they are to stay.

BUTTERFLYWEED

Is butterflyweed difficult to transplant from the field to the garden? *Asclepias tuberosa* is, as its scientific name implies, tuberous-rooted. In moving a mature specimen, a very large, thick ball of earth must be dug with it in order not to break the tubers. It can be transplanted in fall. Is one of the last things to appear above ground in spring.

Can I grow butterflyweed from seed? Yes. Sow in fall or spring—preferably the latter. Transplant seedlings to place where they are to grow when about 6 ins. tall, being careful not to break the very long taproots. Give full sun and well-drained soil.

CARDINALFLOWER (LOBELIA CARDINALIS)

Is cardinalflower suitable for wild plantings? Yes, if you have a moist, partly shaded situation. It is ideal for the edge of a stream or naturalistic pool.

How can cardinalflower be propagated? By late-fall or early-spring sowing of fresh seed; by dividing large plants; and by pinning down a strong stalk on wet sand in August and half covering it with more sand until young plants start where the leaves join the main stem.

COLUMBINE

I have heard that wild columbine (Aquilegia canadensis) grows much taller and fuller in good garden soil than in the wild. Is this true? Yes, but the improvement is limited to the stems and foliage; the flowers remain the same size. The result is a plant devoid of most of the grace and charm which make it so attractive in the wild. We recommend retaining its natural characteristics by giving it a rather poor, dryish soil.

What causes wild columbine to rot off at the crown when other things flourish around it? Columbine is used to thin, poor, neutral soil. Perhaps your soil is too moist, or the roots may be burned by too much fertilizer. Or it may have been attacked by columbine borer.

CREEPING JENNY (LYSIMACHIA NUMMULARIA)

Where can I plant creeping Jenny? In a low, damp, pasture-like location in the sun.

DUTCHMAN'S-BREECHES

What is the Latin name for Dutchman's-breeches? In what climate do they thrive? *Dicentra cucullaria*. The plant grows in thin woods and on rocky slopes, from New England south to North Carolina and west to South Dakota and Missouri. Prefers neutral soil.

FERNS

Which wild ferns can I plant in my woodland wildflower garden? Those which grow in your locality in wooded sections. Give them conditions as nearly as possible like those in which you find them. Among the best possibilities are Evergreen Woodfern, Christmasfern or Swordfern, Sensitivefern, Ostrichfern, Interruptedfern, Royalfern. (The last 3 need very moist situations.)

Why can't I grow Walkingfern successfully in my rocky woodland? I give it just the kind of place it likes, but the leaves turn yellowish and just barely stay alive. Sounds as if the soil is acid, as is likely to be the case in a region where the rock ledges and outcrops are granite. Walkingfern appears to be a lime-lover, so we suggest having your soil tested for acidity.

In what section of the United States does the Climbingfern, Lygodium palmatum, grow as native? The Climbingfern, *Lygodium palmatum,* strangely enough is a native of fields in which shrubs are abundant, often in old river beds. It is found sporadically along the East coast and abundantly in the pine barrens of New Jersey.

GENTIANS

Is there any way to start or plant blue gentians? Fringed Gentians need a very moist situation in sun. Turn the soil, sow absolutely fresh seed on the surface in autumn, press it in, and cover with tow cloth to prevent washing. Remove tow cloth in spring as soon as frost is out of ground. Or, if you prefer, buy pot-grown seedlings.

Is Bottle Gentian a biennial? And is it hard to grow? Bottle or Closed Gentian (*Gentiana andrewsi*) is definitely a hardy perennial. It is easy to grow in rather heavy, dampish soil that is kept cool in summer by the shade of other plants.

HEPATICAS

What sort of soil is preferred by hepaticas? Can they be placed in a wildflower garden? There are 2 native hepaticas: *H. acutiloba,* with pointed 3-lobed leaves, and *H. americana,* with rounded 3-lobed leaves. Common near Atlantic seaboard. Either can be planted in the home garden in shaded locations, near rocks, if soil is suitable. A neutral soil is preferred, though the last-named is considered more tolerant of acid.

IRIS

Which wild irises can be used in the garden? *Iris cristata,* which needs a protected, moist situation and is indifferent to soil acidity.

I. verna, wooded hills, very acid soil. *I. versicolor,* marshes, wet meadows, thickets; needs some sun. *I. prismatica,* marshes, swamps; full sun.

JACK-IN-THE-PULPIT

Can Jack-in-the-pulpits be grown in the wild garden? Yes. Give them a deeply prepared soil. If they are transplanted from the woods, take care to get all of the roots and tubers.

LYCOPODIUMS (CLUB MOSSES)

When is the best time to transplant such things as princesspine? Transplant runningpine and other lycopodiums early in the spring before new growth starts. All club mosses are difficult to establish if conditions are not very close to their native habitats. May be moved any time if the place is damp enough.

MARSHMARIGOLD

Is it difficult to transplant marshmarigolds? No, very easy. Dig or pull the plants gently from their position in marsh or stream. Do not let roots dry out. Replant promptly in similar situation in edge of stream or naturalistic pool.

How can I propagate marshmarigolds? The simplest way is to divide the clumps in spring, right after flowering. Merely wash the mud away from around the roots so you can see what you're doing, and separate the numerous small crowns (with their roots and leaves) with your fingers. Replant at once in bog garden or in edge of slow-moving stream or near outlet of naturalistic pool.

MERTENSIA

Is mertensia easy to grow in the garden? Yes. Though *Mertensia virginica* is found in very moist situations—chiefly along the edges of slow-moving streams—it is adaptable to partly shaded positions in the average garden.

How can I keep rabbits from eating up my mertensia plants? The only way we know of is to get rid of the rabbits, by fair means or foul. Mertensia seems to be a special favorite of theirs in some localities.

ORCHIDS

How can I get wild orchids without breaking the conservation laws? Purchase them from a wildflower specialist.

How many native American cypripediums (ladyslippers) are there? Which of these are suitable for use in the garden? There are about 10 native cypripediums, of which the following are the best for naturalistic gardening (none are suitable for gardens in the ordinary sense

—they need special soil and care): *Cypripedium acaule* (pink); *C. montanum* (white); *C. parviflorum* (yellow); *C. pubescens* (yellow); *C. reginae,* (white and rose); *C. candidum* (white).

Can ladyslippers be transplanted to a semi-wild garden successfully? When should transplanting be done?   Yellow ladyslippers, both *Cypripedium parviflorum* and the larger *C. pubescens* and the Showy Ladyslipper, *C. reginae,* are transplanted with less risk than most other types. Best done in late summer or fall, but may be accomplished in spring if a firm root-ball is taken to prevent injury or disturbance to the roots.

Which of our native cypripediums are perennial? How deep should roots be set?   All are perennial. Roots should be set so that the growing bud, formed in fall, is just under the surface. Use rich woods soil, the surface kept from drying out with a thin layer of oak leaves. Whenever you transplant these cypripediums, take as much as possible of the soil in which they have been growing.

Can you tell me what to do with a moccasin plant after it is through blooming?   If by moccasin plant you mean our native Pink Ladyslipper, *Cypripedium acaule,* and if it is planted in a suitable place, you need do nothing after it blooms. An oak-leaf mulch in fall is desirable.

Does Showy Ladyslipper (Cypripedium reginae) require a neutral soil? (Minnesota.)   It generally is found in the wild where the soil is boggy and acid but is said to tolerate neutral soil.

ORCHIS

Where will I find the Showy Orchis?   The Showy Orchis (*Orchis spectabilis*) and the Pink Ladyslipper (*Cypripedium acaule*) inhabit rich, moist woods from Maine to Georgia, especially oak woods and hemlock groves. The Showy Orchis, however, is said to be tolerant of nearly neutral soil if rich enough.

Where will the Purple-fringed Orchis grow?   In woods, swamps, and meadows, or locations in the garden which simulate such conditions.

Where can I plant the White-fringed Orchis in my wild garden?   If you have a bog garden, plant it there. Native to swamps and bogs.

Can I grow the Yellow-fringed Orchis in my garden?   Perhaps, if you have a strongly acid, continuously moist wild garden.

PARTRIDGE-BERRY

Can partridge-berry be grown in the wild garden?   Yes, especially if it is damp. It requires an acid, rich woods soil.

PHLOX DIVARICATA

How can I get Phlox divaricata and what are its uses?   It can be purchased from many nurseries, especially those which deal in wild plants. Its uses are innumerable. Plant in open shade of deciduous trees. It blends well with mertensia, trilliums, and other plants of the open woodland. Self-sows.

PITCHERPLANT

Can pitcherplant (Sarracenia purpurea) be grown in the wild garden? Yes. This is a good bog-garden subject.

SHOOTINGSTAR

Is shootingstar a good wild-garden subject? Yes. *Dodecatheon meadia* is a showy wildflower suitable for woodland planting in slightly acid or neutral soil.

SPRINGBEAUTY (CLAYTONIA)

What are the cultural requirements of springbeauty (Claytonia)? Damp, leafmoldy soil and full shade in summer.

TRILLIUM

Which trilliums are best for the wild garden? *Trillium grandiflorum* (Large-Flowering White Trillium); *T. nivale* (small white, earliest); *T. luteum* (yellow); *T. stylosum* (rose); *T. californicum* (sessile type in white or red).

Can trilliums be purchased? Yes, specialists in wild plants and some other nurseries list them.

How can trilliums best be propagated from seed? The best way to propagate trilliums is by division of old, large clumps. Absolutely fresh seed, sown before it has a chance to dry, may germinate the following spring, but growth is very slow and all conditions have to be just right.

VIOLETS

Are violets dug up from the woods suitable for planting in the wild garden? Yes. They are easily transplanted.

What sort of conditions does Birdsfoot Violet need? Give a dryish, well-drained, sandy, very acid soil in full sun.

WINTERGREENS

Will you please name and describe some native wintergreens? Spotted Wintergreen (*Chimaphila maculata*) with white-veined lanceolate evergreen leaves; showy white flowers. Pipsissewa (*Chimaphila umbellata*), rather like the above but with wedge-shaped unmarked evergreen leaves and smaller flowers, sometimes blush pink. Shinleaf (*Pyrola elliptica*), oval basal leaves, persistent but not evergreen; white flowers on 5- to 10-in. stalks, in racemes. Round-leaved American Wintergreen (*Pyrola americana*), leaves basal, rounded; showy blush-white flowers on tall stalks. Creeping Wintergreen (*Gaultheria procumbens*), evergreen, blunt, aromatic leaves; creeping subterranean stems; blush flowers in leaf axils; edible red berries; 2 to 6 ins. tall. Flowering Wintergreen or Fringed Polygala (*P. paucifolia*), evergreen leaves; rose-purple, fringed flowers, or, sometimes, white; low-growing, and spreading.

How is pipsissewa (Chimaphila umbellata) propagated? By cuttings of new growth taken the first half of July and rooted in sand in a seed flat.

GARDENS OF OTHER TYPES

CHILDREN'S GARDEN

How much space would you suggest giving a child in which to make his own garden? This depends on the size of the child and on how much space is available. A little tot should have a tiny space—4 or 5 ft. square. The area may be increased as he grows older.

What would be a good location to give a child for a garden? A spot that has full sun all day, where the ground is in good condition and easily workable. Children are easily discouraged if their garden does not produce, so do not select any unfit "leftover" area.

Which plants would be suitable for a child to grow in his own garden? Bright, easily grown annuals, which can be raised from seed: zinnias, marigolds, alyssum, scabiosa, and portulaca. These will give him an opportunity to learn how seeds are planted and what the plants look like as they come up. A few easy perennials might be given him to plant too. If a fence encloses his garden, morningglories can be used to cover it.

Will you list some easy vegetables that a child might grow from seed? Carrots, beets, leaf lettuce, beans, radishes, and New Zealand spinach.

I am very much interested in planning a garden that will interest my children. Just what arrangement would you suggest? I have in mind something to go along with their own yard and playhouse. Any garden for children should be scaled down to their size. They like intricate patterns and odd plants. Paths should be narrow, and all plants relatively small. Choose varieties that will stand the maximum amount of abuse. Leave plenty of play space.

CITY GARDENS

Will you give some hints on making a city garden? The keynote of the city garden is simplicity. Remember that you cannot grow all the flowering plants that thrive in the country. If you have shade, plant interesting shrubs that will tolerate shady conditions, and some ground covers, such as pachysandra and ivy. Get a few pieces of suitable furniture and arrange them attractively. Pots of bright flowers, or window boxes, may be set about in sunny places. Vines are good for most city gardens, as they afford protection as well as greenery. (See also City Conditions, Section III.)

ENGLISH GARDEN

How does one begin to plan an English country garden? Is there any set plan or style to follow? This subject is too large to cover in a few words. Better consult such books as *Gardens for Small Country Houses,* by Gertrude Jekyll and Lawrence Weaver; *English Flower Garden,* by W. Robinson.

FRAGRANT GARDENS

I would like some fragrant annuals in my garden. What do you suggest? Nicotiana, nasturtium, sweet alyssum, petunia, marigold, stock, heliotrope (tender shrub), mignonette, sweetpea.

Will you name some bulbs for a fragrant garden? *Crocus versicolor* and *C. biflorus; Scilla italica* and *S. campanulata; Fritillaria imperialis;* hyacinths; narcissi (jonquils and hybrids; poetaz; poeticus; tazetta); tulips: Ambrosia, Arethusa, Dido, De Wet, Leda, Early Yellow Rose; lily-of-the-valley; scented irises (rhizomes, not bulbs); Liliums: *auratum, candidum, longiflorum, regale, speciosum;* tuberose.

What are some fragrant hardy flowers? *Dianthus caesius* and varieties; *Dianthus caryophyllus* and varieties; scented bearded iris; lily-of-the-valley; *Viola odorata* and varieties; *Lavandula officinalis;* hemerocallis; buddleia; primula; clematis; sweetwilliam; monarda; phlox; peony; roses; Arabis Snowcap; salvia.

Which herbs shall I plant in a fragrant garden? See Herbs.

Which flowers shall I plant for night fragrance? Nicotiana; moonvine; petunia; *Pelargonium triste;* nightblooming waterlilies.

Will you tell me which geraniums to buy for fragrance? *Pelargonium tomentosum* (mint); *P. graveolens* (rose); *P. limoneum* (lemon); *P. odoratissimum* (nutmeg.)

What will give fragrance in the late garden? Chrysanthemums, clematis, wallflowers.

Which shrubs shall I plant for fragrance? Pink (winterbloom) and Swamp Azalea; *Jasminum nudiflorum* and *J. primulinum;* benzoin; magnolia; Flowering Almond; lilac; honeysuckle; daphne; roses; mockorange; strawberry-shrub; English Hawthorn; wisteria; witchhazel. Tender: lemonverbena; rosemary; heliotrope.

KNOT GARDENS

What is a knot garden? A garden of low-growing plants or hedges planted in a formal, intricate design. Common to medieval landscape design, when colored sand was often used to form the paths or sections which outlined the beds. Now used in parks, herb gardens, and formal gardens.

A "knot" design herb garden. The herbs used are: 1. Thyme or Roman Wormwood; 2. Sweet Violet or Santolina viridis; 3. Lavender cotton or dwarf Lavender; 4. Germander or Rosemary.

What plant materials can be used for a knot garden? Boxwood, artemisia, santolina, iresine; low-bedding flowers; herbs.

OUTDOOR LIVING ROOM

What is an "outdoor living room"? An area with comfortable tables and chairs set aside for lounging and loafing. It should be secluded, at least partially walled in by evergreens, shrubs, or other plant material. It is desirable to have the outdoor living room away from the house, but easily accessible. The ideal "room" gives a view of the garden through an arch in the hedge or by leaving one side unscreened. It is often placed in the shade of a large tree. Some people like to include equipment for barbecues and picnics in this area.

Invitation to leisure: at least one corner of the garden, no matter how small, should be arranged for outdoor living.

We are planning a simple rose garden in an outdoor living room

surrounded by poplar trees. Will you help us with the layout? The typical rose garden is formal in design. Square or circular areas divided into small beds by narrow paths, and provided with a central feature such as a sundial, make an effective arrangement. (See also Roses and previous question.)

ROOF GARDENS

What soil mixture should be used to fill the boxes on a roof garden? A good, friable loam is ideal. Avoid heavy clay or very sandy soil.

What kind of fertilizer should I use for the plants on my roof garden? Liquid manure, or a complete commercial fertilizer.

Should one use a mulch on the soil in roof-garden boxes? Yes; a mulch will help prevent sudden drying out of the soil from wind and sun on the roof. Peatmoss, rotted manure, or leafmold could be used.

Can one grow vegetables successfully on a roof? Yes, with full sun and good soil, a few can be grown. In boxes about 8 ins. deep grow lettuce, parsley, radishes, bush beans, endive, onions (from sets), New Zealand spinach, Swiss chard. Try stump-rooted carrots and beets. Tomatoes planted in deeper boxes, staked and sheltered so that they will not blow over, will probably thrive.

I would like to grow some herbs on my roof garden. Do you think they would be successful? Yes, they probably would. Herbs are a good choice for the shallow boxes usually used on a roof. Try thyme, chives, parsley, mint, sage, and basil. (See Herbs for soil and culture.)

Will you give a list of annual flowers for growing on a roof? Marigolds, zinnias, ageratum, petunias, calendulas, alyssum, lobelia, portulaca, celosia, iberis, forget-me-nots, salvia, coreopsis, aster, scabiosa.

I am planning to make the boxes for plants on my roof garden. Can you give me some suggestions? Your boxes should be made deep enough to hold 8 to 12 ins. of soil. They can be as wide as you like. Use cypress wood that will withstand water. Provide drainage holes in the bottom of each box so that the soil will not become sour. The inside of the boxes can be painted with asphaltum to protect the wood, and the outside with several coats of durable outdoor paint.

I want to grow some vines on my roof. How could I effectively support them? Make an arbor over part of the roof. This would not only be a good support for your vines, but would also supply shade and some shelter on the terrace. Otherwise, use a trellis against the side of the building, or put vine supports along the side of the building, on which to tie the vines.

What kind of furniture can I use for my roof garden? Any comfortable, well-designed furniture that will withstand the weather. Avoid types that must be taken in each time it rains. Metal chairs and tables are good, if kept well painted, and are heavy enough not to blow over; or stout wooden ones. If you care to be different, make your own furniture out of boxes and barrels, and paint with bright colors.

I want to make a roof garden that is good-looking but will not be expensive. Will you make some suggestions? Edge the railing or wall with window boxes painted dark green or any color which fits your scheme. Grow such plants as petunias, ageratum, geraniums, alyssum, marigolds, and calendulas. Some potted plants can be arranged about the roof. If you can get some large boxes or barrels, try a few shrubs, such as privet or forsythia, or trees, such as cedars or yews, for a background. Train vines against the wall or building. Ivy, honeysuckle, or morningglories would do well. Comfortable chairs and tables will be needed.

What can be done on a flat roof, approximately 10 × 10 ft., on the west side of an apartment? Can dirt be put on the roof to sufficient depth to raise anything successfully? Six to 8 ins. of soil will successfully grow many flowers or even a few vegetables. Check with engineer before putting this considerable weight on roof. Otherwise confine efforts to a few soil-filled boxes.

I have some large roof-garden boxes. How can I tell if the soil is sour? How can I fertilize the earth before we plant? If in doubt, have a soil test made. For most plants add lime every 2 years. Bone meal and dried cow manure are excellent fertilizers; or use any complete commercial fertilizer. Do not mix lime and fertilizer at one time. Add lime in fall or very early spring, and fertilizer at planting time.

SUNKEN GARDENS

I have a natural spot for making a sunken garden. How can I plan this? The sunken garden is viewed from above and the basic layout is very important because of this. An informal or untidy effect would spoil it. A formal garden, with a path running through the center, and a center of interest at the end, would probably work out well. If your garden is well drained, you might plan a formal rose garden; or an herb garden with thyme-planted steps and borders of fragrant plants around the four sides of the area in front of the walls. Leave the center in turf.

There is an old foundation on our property, where a house burned down. Would this make a good place for a sunken garden? Yes, it should be excellent. You may have to provide drainage, if water collects in the foundation. Build steps down into the garden of the same kind of stones as the foundation. Perennials of doubtful hardiness and shrubs, which need much protection from cold winds, can be incorporated in your planting plan.

WINDOW BOX GARDENS

What special problems are involved in window-box gardening? First provide appropriate boxes with holes in bottom for drainage. Put in 2 or 3 ins. of cinders or broken brick, and fill with rich, porous soil. Plant with appropriate material in spring. Regular attention to watering is of prime importance. Fertilize as often as necessary.

Can you give some pointers on making window boxes? Make box to fit window space, but if the length is in excess of 3 ft. make in two sections. For good results the box should be not less than 8 ins. deep and 10 ins. wide. Use cypress or white pine at least 1 in. thick. Bore ½-in. holes, 6 ins. apart, in bottom for drainage.

What is the best soil for window boxes? One that is rich, with plenty of humus to retain moisture. Use 2 parts loam, 1 part rotted manure or leafmold, with a 5-in. pot of bone meal mixed with each bushel.

Are wooden window boxes better than those made of concrete? They are inexpensive and less weighty to handle if they have to be moved occasionally. On the other hand, they are less permanent.

Are the metal "self-watering" boxes satisfactory? Yes; but don't place too much reliance on the "self-watering" feature.

Can an old hot-water tank (cylindrical) be used as a porch box? Yes. Have a tinsmith cut out a strip equal to ⅓ to ½ of the circumference for the entire length. Punch holes in the opposite side to drain off surplus water.

Is there any flowering plant suitable for window boxes which will hold up all summer and be colorful? Lantana. Get potted plants in May; usually then in flower, they will bloom until frost. They stand heat, drought, and city conditions, but are at their best when well watered and pruned occasionally to restrain lanky growth. Stand partial shade, but prefer full sun. Balcony petunias are also good.

The garden club in our town wants to promote a window box project in the hope of winning more plant growing enthusiasts. Can you refer me to a publication which covers this subject completely so our committee can be well informed? Yes, "Window-box Gardening" by Henry Teuscher, published by Macmillan, 1956, covers the subject thoroughly.

Which flowers grow in window boxes? Among the most satisfactory are begonias, geraniums, fuchsias, ageratum, petunias, dwarf marigolds, torenias, pansies, sweet alyssum, morningglory, vinca, sedum, balsam, portulaca, and lobelia.

Is there a blooming plant that will grow in window boxes under

awning? (West Virginia.) None that you can be sure of. Try *Begonia semperflorens* varieties, petunias, and *Lobelia erinus* varieties.

What would you suggest for flowers (not tuberous begonias) for window boxes that are very shaded? Would like plenty of color. You will probably have difficulty with any flowering plant if the shade is heavy and continuous. Fuchsias, *Begonia semperflorens,* torenias, and lobelias will stand as much shade as any.

What shall I plant in a window box, outdoors, on north side? (Washington.) Flowering plants: tuberous begonias, fuchsias, lobelias, torenias. Foliage plants: aucuba, boxwood, Japanese Holly, Dwarf Yew, arborvitae, privet, English Ivy, vinca, Kenilworth Ivy.

What could we plant in outdoor front-stoop window boxes which will survive New York City winter climate, such as evergreen, yew, dwarf pine, etc.? Among the most satisfactory plants are small yew, arborvitae, Japanese Holly, privet, and English Ivy. All suffer, however, when the soil is frozen solid. Make sure soil is well soaked in fall. *Sedum acre* and *S. spectabile* will survive year in, year out.

What can be put in a window box (southern exposure) during the winter months? (Virginia.) Small evergreens, boxwood, arborvitae, junipers, spruces, with English Ivy and trailing myrtle to droop over edge. This material cannot be expected to thrive permanently, however, because of poor environment.

Is it necessary to put ivy and myrtle grown in window boxes into the ground for the winter? If the soil about their roots freezes solid, they cannot take up water to replace that lost by leaves, and the plants die. Place boxes on ground, pack manure or straw well about them, and cover with burlap or light layer of straw.

How early can pansies be planted in outdoor window boxes? (North Carolina.) Pansies are much hardier than most people realize. The established plants can be put in the outdoor window box as soon as the severe portion of winter is passed. Plants grown indoors should be hardened off by gradually exposing them to cooler temperatures before setting them in the outdoor boxes. March 15, or even earlier, in your locality, might be about right.

Are hanging baskets practical? Yes, provided they are made right with plenty of moss on the outside of the soil and are never allowed to dry out.

MISCELLANEOUS

CACTI FOR OUTDOORS

What are the hardiest kinds of cacti? *Opuntia compressa* (*vulgaris*), *O. fragilis, Echinocereus viridiflorus,* and *Pediocactus simpsoni.*

Are there any varieties of cactus, other than opuntia, that can be left outside all winter in south Jersey? You might try *Echinocereus viridiflorus* and *Pediocactus simpsoni.*

Will cactus from the Arizona desert thrive in Oklahoma? Those native from north of Phoenix will possibly grow if given a thoroughly well-drained and sheltered position.

Can spineless cacti of the type that Luther Burbank developed be grown in a climate which is hot and dry in the summer and cold and wet in the winter? No. The spineless opuntias do not thrive where wet winters are experienced.

What are names of some cacti that will live out of doors in south central North Carolina? *Opuntia compressa* (*vulgaris*), *O. fragilis, O. rhodantha,* (*O. xanthostemma*), *O. polyacantha, O. imbricata, O. basilaris, O. ursina, Echinocereus viridiflorus, E. reichenbachi, E. baileyi,* and *Pediocactus simpsoni.*

GOURDS

WHAT TO GROW

Will you tell me which gourds to grow for curing—gourds to be used for winter decoration? White pear, bicolor pear, goose egg, ringed pear, spoon, miniatures, ladle, warty hardhead, snake, *lagenaria* in variety.

Which kinds of gourds are suitable for bird houses? The ordinary dipper gourds as well as others of the *lagenaria* genus.

How can I produce dipper-type gourds? Have heard it is necessary to tape the neck of the gourd. Dipper gourds are known to seedsmen under that name and culture is the same as for other gourds. Shaping of necks is not ordinarily necessary for dipper gourds, but if you want to modify their shape this could be done.

CULTURE

Is there any fertilizer that will cause gourd plants to grow more rapidly? The same provisions that are made for cucumbers and melons will work well with gourds. Use a 5–10–5 fertilizer or a combination of manure and a smaller amount of fertilizer, or stable manure and superphosphate. Stable manure alone is also satisfactory.

How do you raise gourds? Gourds are not particularly difficult to grow. They can be allowed to run on the ground but are better planted along a wire fence or provided with a trellis. General requirements are about the same as for cucumbers and melons—a moderately rich, well-fertilized soil with reasonable moisture supply. They thrive under a wide range of conditions, and most varieties of small gourds will mature in the Northern part of the country. Seed is sowed about 1 in. deep and plants are thinned to 2 or 3 ft. apart, according to varieties. Dusting may be necessary to control the striped cucumber beetle. In Northern climates plants may be started under glass as are cucumbers and muskmelons. Shallow cultivation should be practiced to control weeds.

What is the earliest date gourds can be planted? Gourds are planted at about the same time as cucumbers, 2 or 3 weeks after average date of last killing frost in the spring or at about the time tomatoes are set out. Gourds will not stand frost.

How do you start gourds from seed? Ornamental gourds are usually raised in pots from seed sown in April or May and transplanted out in June. Some find it advisable to sow gourd seeds directly in pots (in the greenhouse) made of pressed peat and dried manure. When set out in the ground these quickly disintegrate but save the roots from being disturbed in the transplanting operation. Seed may also be sown outdoors when danger of frost is past.

How can one take care of gourds after they are picked so that they will not decay? Gourds should be thoroughly matured on the vines before they are picked. They will not stand freezing if they are still succulent. If by necessity they are taken at the immature state, they should be handled with the utmost care and allowed to dry and cure indoors, but mold is likely to attack them. Some recommend washing gourds, but wiping with a soft cloth is probably better. Disinfectant solutions may be of some service, but not too much. To keep gourds in their natural state, waxing is one of the best methods, using ordinary floor wax and polishing lightly. Some use shellac, but this changes the color and appearance. Some also like to decorate and paint them in simple or fanciful fashion. Stems should be left on the gourds, removing them from vines by cutting. Maturity may be judged by feeling them, but it is not wise to test with the fingernail. They should be dry and the stem should be withered.

What is a good spray to combat the stem borer of gourds? It is best to grow the gourds on ground where curcubits have not been grown the previous year or where their refuse remains. Early summer squash may be used as a trap crop. When the borer is already at work in the vines, surgery is resorted to, cutting lengthwise of the vine with a thin knife to destroy the larvae, then the cut portion is covered with earth and little harm is done to the plant. Rotenone spray or dust applied 3 or 4 times may be effective in destroying the borers just after they are hatched.

Is there a gourd society in this country? Yes. The Gourd Society of America, Inc., Horticultural Hall, Boston, Massachusetts.

WEEDS

GENERAL

Can you keep weeds down; and how? By constantly attacking them while they are yet young, and above all by preventing them from seeding. On cultivated ground, use the cultivator and hoe, plus hand weeding; on lawns, hand weeding and good culture to encourage desirable grasses; on drives and paths, weed killers.

I have 6 acres, not worked for about 20 years, full of weeds. What is the best way to get rid of them? Is it best to plow in fall or spring? Maintain a bare fallow through one season. Plow in spring and harrow or plow shallowly at frequent intervals throughout summer, so the surface is never permitted to show any signs of green growth.

We intend fencing our lot (natural pickets) in spring. Adjoining are open fields. How can I keep down weeds at base of fence on the outside? If you are not planting too close to inside of fence, use regular weed killer. If the right one is selected, most of the broad leaved weeds will be killed and one can easily keep the grass mowed to prevent tall weeds from becoming established.

Would it be advisable to burn all dried-up flowers and weeds in our flower garden in early spring? (Due to illness, garden was not tended in fall.) Under the circumstances the burning treatment would be satisfactory. The seeds produced by the weeds are already dispersed, however, so burning will not materially reduce the season's weed crop.

Is there any method other than burning trash or dry brush on a seedbed, to kill weed seeds? Burning is not very satisfactory, for weed seeds will stand considerable heat. A good method is to keep the bed moist to encourage germination and then to hoe 2 or 3 times (allowing 10 days between each hoeing) to destroy seedlings. Sterilization with chloropicrin (which see) is also effective, but special equipment is needed.

How can I get rid of weeds before and during growth of parsley, besides weeding when small? Hand weeding in the rows and frequent hoeing between the rows are the best methods for annual weeds. If the ground is infested with perennial weeds, these should be dug out to the last root before the parsley is sown.

Is it possible to spray carrots to control the weeds? Yes, several so-called selective sprays are now being used by the vegetable growers for this very purpose. For latest information on these in your area, consult your Agricultural Extension Service.

In August I put turf-builder around a privet hedge. Six weeks later a broadleaf weed came in thick around hedges. Could it be the turf-

builder?   Turf-builder is a proprietary plant food that certainly does not contain weed seeds. It probably stimulated the growth of weeds present in the soil, thus proving its efficiency as a fertilizer.

Is there anything that will kill weeds, yet not destroy flowers or vegetables?   While certain selective sprays have limited uses in the control of weeds in grainfields and in lawns, no substance has been (or probably ever will be) found to meet the requirements you state. This is because many weeds are closely related botanically to favorite flowers and vegetables.

I have heard that "Sovosol", a dry cleaning fluid, is a weed killer. How can it be applied?   This is sprayed lightly at full strength on the young weeds in the garden. Care should be taken to hold the nozzle of the spray gun close to the weeds, so that the wind will not blow the spray to valued plants. This spray is particularly effective in controlling small seedlings of purslane in early summer.

What can be done to keep a cinder drive free from weeds?   Procure a commercial weed killer from a dealer in horticultural supplies, and use according to directions. Crankcase drainings, diluted with kerosene so that they can be sprayed over the drive, are alternatives.

What is the name of a compound to put in paths between flower beds to eliminate weeds?   Any good commercial weed killer will do this. Be careful not to let any of it get onto the flower beds, lawns, or other places where you desire vegetation to grow.

What is best to use in killing weeds in a brick drain?   Providing the drain does not carry water into a pond or stream used by fish or animals, any commercial weed killer should prove effective.

Is 2, 4–D dangerous to use?   No, providing normal caution is taken in pouring the material and in *thoroughly cleaning the sprayer* afterward. However, extreme precaution should be taken in applying it on a windy day since the wind may blow the material, which is highly volatile, to quite a distance where it can kill other vegetation.

How can I tell different kinds of weeds and grasses?   *Weeds,* by Walter Conrad Muenscher (Macmillan, 1955) and *Weeds of Lawn and Garden,* by John M. Fogg (Univ. of Penna. Press, 1945) are two excellent books on this subject.

SPECIFIC WEEDS

Am planting a garden over an old asparagus bed and have tried many ways to kill the asparagus, even to digging up the crowns, but the stuff persists. How may I rid myself of this nuisance?   Keep digging. Every time an asparagus stem appears dig out the root from which it arises.

How can one get rid of bindweed on lawn without killing roses,

trees, and shrubs by using poison? You probably cannot, especially if the weed is intertwined with the shrubbery. Digging out would be the only solution here.

How can I exterminate an extremely hardy vine resembling a morningglory, having white flowers and seemingly endless roots? Doubtless a bindweed, a pernicious weed with fleshy roots which descend several feet, every fragment of which will grow. Where it exists, either don't plant anything and constantly hoe, so that no leaves can build up a food store in the roots, or plant only low-growing crops which can be hoed frequently so that no vines can get started. Also it has been determined that the proper application of 2, 4–D while the weed is actively growing can kill it nearly 100%.

How can I get rid of Bermuda Grass? Where ground freezes, plow or fork shallowly in fall so roots are exposed to air through winter. Farther South rely upon forking out and frequent cultivation; or smother with crop of fall-sown rye, followed by crop of cowpeas or velvet beans. Chemical methods of eradication have not proved too successful.

What can I do for Bermuda Grass in flower borders? (Tennessee.) In your section, Bermuda Grass doubtless is a troublesome weed, but it is used to make lawns in the South. In the borders it must be kept down by frequent hoeing.

How can I clear land of blackberry vines? Spray vines twice during season, when foliage is present, with ammonium sulfamate; strength, 1 lb. to 5 gals. of water. The solution reaches the roots through the vines and kills them. Also, 2, 4, 5–T can be used as a spray since this has proved very effective in eliminating blackberries which are not killed by 2, 4–D alone. The best time to apply the first spray is when the leaves are almost fully developed.

Narrowleaf Plantain, a deep-rooted pest in lawns; watch for and dig up seedling plants. (Right) The Broadleaved Plantain.

Can you name a formula to kill buckthorn or plantain? At what time of year should it be used? Dig out by hand or mow down and burn before seeding stage is reached. Also spraying with 2, 4–D weed killers early in the summer affords good control.

Which is more effective in killing weeds 2, 4–D or a material under the trade designation of 2, 4, 5–T. The latter has proved more effective especially on difficult-to-kill plants like poison-ivy, sumac and blackberries.

We have some patches of Canada Thistle in our garden. Is digging them up the best remedy? Yes, if the work is well done. Any pieces of root left in the soil will grow, however, and digging should be followed by repeated hoeings.

We have a large hay field next to us with a few bad patches of Canada thistle. The seeds blow over into our garden. Can these patches be eliminated by spraying? Yes. Use sodium chlorate as a summer spray (1 lb. per gal.) and again in early September when regrowth has occurred. Sometimes 2, 4–D has also proved effective.

What is the best way to clean cattails and rushes from lake edge? The only practicable method is to dig them out completely. If surface of lake could be lowered for a considerable period, they may die out from lack of moisture.

What is the best method of fighting crab grass? Pull every seedling as soon as big enough to recognize, thus preventing seeding (crab grass is an annual). Fertilize lawn generously to stimulate desired grasses. (See also Lawn and Turf Areas.)

Crab grass: bane of the lawn maker.
For control see Lawn and Turf Areas
(page 638).

How can creeping Jenny be eradicated? Creeping Jenny is a name applied to a golden-flowered lysimachia as well as to the white-flowered wild morningglory. The former is controlled by hand forking and frequent surface cultivation. (For control of wild morningglory, see other answers.)

How can I fight the curse of a neighbor's dandelion seed blowing into my yard? Three procedures are possible: eliminate dandelions on neighbor's property; dig out young dandelions as fast as they appear in your yard; learn to tolerate dandelions. Probably best and easiest means of eradication is to spray both your neighbor's dandelions and yours with 2, 4–D or some specific chemical weed killer. Effective control is easily maintained this way.

What is the best method for controlling dandelions? Digging them out. Alternate methods are: cut the plants off well below surface and drip a few drops of sulphuric acid onto the cut root; spray with an iron sulfate solution (1 lb. to 1½ gals. water) every 10 days; or spray with 2, 4–D.

Dandelion: to control, cut tap root well below ground with an asparagus knife and prevent stray plants from seeding.

How can one effectively destroy dock weeds? Specimens of small size can be pulled out when soil is very wet. With larger plants, cut tops off an inch below ground surface, pierce root with a skewer, and pour a few drops of sulphuric acid (or a large teacupful of salt) on cut surface.

What can be done to get rid of "dodder," also called lovevine, gold-thread, strangleweed, Desire's-hair, and hellbind? Dodder is a parasitic annual. Cut down and burn all infected plants before the dodder has a chance to seed.

What method of controlling chickweed do you recommend to the home gardener? In flower and vegetable garden, surface cultivation; remove *at once* every plant, with its spreading root system, as it appears, *and destroy*. In lawns, fertilize to encourage growth of grasses. Use lime if soil is at all too acid. Another method is to dust lightly with sulfate of ammonia on a dewy morning, and water well the same evening. More than one application may be necessary. Also a mixture of TCA and 2, 4–D to which a wetting agent has been added has proved successful as a spray control.

Chickweed: one of the worst pests in gardens. Remove plants—getting all the roots—in early spring, and burn.

In absence of sulfate of ammonia, what would be a good substitute for control of chickweed? Spraying with 2, 4–D gives fairly good control. Dimet and Sodar are new and effective.

Will you suggest a remedy for much-branched, green, leafy weed

with tiny daisy flowers each having 5 white petals? I think it is called galinsoga. This is an introduction from tropical America. It is very sensitive to frost, but is an annual and so over-winters as seed. Hand pulling large plants *before seeds form* and cultivation to kill young ones are most practical remedies.

Is it possible to remove Johnsongrass or quackgrass from a vegetable garden so that it will not be back the next season? These are two distinct species. Both may be eliminated by forking out as much as possible by hand, taking pains to get every root, and then by repeatedly cultivating the surface throughout summer. Johnsongrass is particularly resistant, and vigorous methods must be used. Advances have been made recently in the use of 2,2 dichloroproprionic acid at proper strengths in the control of Johnsongrass. We suggest contacting one of the large weed-chemical manufacturing companies now for a trade name product of this material and its proper use.

Lambsquarters is common in my garden. How do you keep it down? This weed usually favors rich soils. It is controlled by cultivating and is easily hand pulled. When the plants are young, lambsquarters makes excellent greens.

We have a shrub called Mexican bamboo which is becoming a nuisance. How can it be eradicated? This is *Polygonum cuspidatum*. If you want other plants to grow in same place, dig it out as thoroughly as possible, then cut every shoot off that appears when not more than an inch high. Otherwise use commercial weed killers. Some of the chemical weed killers have given partial control of this pernicious pest but it must be sprayed several times at proper intervals before it can be killed out altogether.

I have a weed which grows very tall and multiplies rapidly, roots are red and run under the ground and sprout. What is the proper name and how can I kill it? Probably *Polygonum cuspidatum*. Only relief other than poisoning ground with weed killer is to dig out all roots (which go very deep) and keep surface hoed afterward to kill any sprouts that appear.

What will kill moonvine or wild morningglory? Dig out as much as possible, then keep the ground surface cultivated at frequent intervals so that no new shoot ever attains a height of more than 2 ins. before being cut off. Spraying with 2, 4–D and 2, 4, 5–T also gives good control if spray is applied to plants when they are actively growing.

How can a fairly large patch of nettle in a field be eliminated? By repeatedly mowing so that the plants are never permitted to get more than a few inches high. Also, by spraying the plants when young with a commercial weed killer.

Nutgrass is a troublesome weed in my garden. Can you suggest a

means of eliminating it? This is not really a grass but a sedge which is partial to wet places. Drainage, followed by a year's clean cultivation, is the only real remedy.

What can be done to destroy petunia seedlings? I would like to plant something else in the former petunia bed, but the petunias come up by the hundreds each year. Hand weeding and scuffle hoeing after the seedlings are up are the only practicable means. The hoeing will not only destroy the petunias but will also encourage the growth of whatever else you may plant in the bed.

Can you suggest any means of getting rid of plantain (both narrow- and broad-leaved) in quantity? Digging, even with a special tool, is slow and laborious. Plantains on lawns can be killed by using a pinch of salt in the center of each plant on a hot day. Two or 3 drops of sulphuric acid will also serve. There are compounds sold that will kill broad-leaved weeds in lawns when dusted on. (See Lawns.) Spraying with 2, 4–D also proves effective.

How can I get rid of poisonivy without spending a fortune? Syringe or spray the plants while green with fuel oil or crankcase oil thinned down with kerosene. Spray in late spring with sodium sulfamate or a mixture of 2, 4–D and 2, 4, 5–T, and again when new young leaves are formed in late summer. A final spray or two the following year should eradicate the bed, but it should be remembered that getting rid of poisonivy is no one-shot proposition.

How can I eliminate poisonivy? By the use, according to the maker's directions, of the Du Pont spray, ammonium sulfamate. By digging out the roots.

How may I get rid of poisonivy growing in a bed of lily-of-the-valley? Get someone immune to poisonivy to carefully dig up the bed. Transplant lily-of-the-valley to another location for 2 or 3 years. Meantime eliminate any ivy that appears on old site.

What is the poison-oak plant and how can it be destroyed? Poison-oak (*Toxicodendron quercifolium*) is similar to poisonivy (*T. radicans*), but has more oaklike leaves. Spray with ammonium sulfamate according to maker's directions.

Every summer my garden is invaded by purslane. What can I do? This is an annual that develops rapidly in warm weather and rich soil. Attack vigorously with hoe and cultivator while weeds are yet tiny. If plants get large, rake them up and burn or compost, otherwise they will root and grow again. To keep areas of very small seedlings under control without hoeing, one can spray with one of the dry cleaning fluids, one of which is termed "Sovosol".

Which is the most effective way of ridding ground of quackgrass? It grows in soil around shrubbery and cannot be exposed to anything that would harm these plants. In the spring work the whole area over with a spading fork and carefully remove all underground stems of the grass. Follow this throughout the summer by forking out every piece of the grass that appears before the leaves are an inch high.

How can I eradicate redroot (pigweed)? Practice clean cultivation. Mow plants down before they reach the seeding stage.

How do you get rid of sandburs? Practice clean cultivation. The plant is an annual and cannot reproduce if all plants are hoed or pulled out before they seed.

How can I destroy sheepssorrel and at the same time use the ground for vegetables and flowers? Sheepssorrel is a sure sign of poor, infertile, and, usually, acid soil. Apply fertilizer generously and test for lime needs. Nitrogenous fertilizers are especially helpful.

How can I eradicate sumac? The most satisfactory remedy is to grub out the roots. It has also been killed out by three consecutive cuttings, the first when the plant is actively growing in late spring, and the other two following shortly thereafter when regrowth has again started.

Is there any method of destroying sumac other than digging it out? Spraying young foliage with a mixture of 2, 4–D and 2, 4, 5–T when half mature in spring and a second time when regrowth is at about the same stage, has given good control.

I have an old trumpetvine root in the ground and want to plant a fruit tree instead. How can I kill the heavy root so it won't take the strength from the fruit tree? The only satisfactory procedure is to dig out the trumpetvine root and turn over and fertilize the soil before planting the fruit tree. Other than digging out root, the best way of killing the old root is to paint the stump with a concentrated solution of sodium sulfamate, or chip down the bark around the stump and insert small crystals of sodium sulfamate.

How can I get rid of white clover in my garden? White clover in lawns may be discouraged by maintaining the soil on the acid side. Liming encourages its growth. If troublesome in flower and vegetable garden, hoeing and hand weeding are recommended.

What is best method of getting rid of white snakeroot? Grub out the roots.

How is the best way to get rid of wild carrot? The plant is biennial and does not reproduce itself if it is cut down before it reaches the seeding stage.

Wild garlic is becoming troublesome. How shall I eliminate it? A most pernicious weed, once established. If area is not too large, hand digging, followed by destruction of every bulb, is best. Cultivate surface frequently. Spraying with 2, 4–D or a combination of 2, 4–D and 2, 4,

5–T has proved successful but best results are obtained when leaves are actually growing. Poor results occur when bulblets are dormant.

How can wild grapevines and poisonivy be killed out? These seem to cover every rock and bit of space on our farm. Goldenrod and milkweed mingle with these weeds. Both poison ivy and wild grapes are effectively killed when sprayed two or three times while still actively growing with a mixture (half and half) of 2, 4–D and 2, 4, 5–T. If this is delayed until late summer, a very poor killing results.

Can wild morningglory be exterminated around the trunk of fruit trees without killing or damaging the trees? Maintain a circle of bare ground around the tree and keep this clean of all growth by scuffle hoeing every few days throughout 2 successive growing seasons. As an alternative, cover infested area with heavy roofing paper for 2 seasons.

Poison Ivy (left); (right) Virginia-creeper, often mistaken for it.

How can I get rid of wiregrass? This name is applied to several distinct species of grasses, and also to a kind of rush. Several of these indicate soils low in fertility. Some are annuals, some perennials. Frequent cultivation and prevention of seeding are recommended treatments.

How can I kill a large and vigorously growing poplar tree on our property. I do not want to go to the expense of cutting it down at this time? Cut the bark from the trunk in strips about 6″ long in a circle around tree, place some crystals of sodium sulfamate between them and the trunk, tying the strips back in place and let nature take its course from there on.

I have a poplar tree, recently cut down but the roots keep sending up suckers. How can I kill this two and a half foot stump once and for all without having to dig it out? Make a groove or hollow in the stump and place a half cup-full of crystals of sodium sulfamate there which will gradually dissolve in rain water and be absorbed by wood.

Can I spray brush while it is dormant in the winter and still expect

a good kill? Yes, using a mixture of 2, 4–D and 2, 4, 5–T in kerosene and directed to the base of the plants so that the stems are thoroughly wet on all sides.

In reading a trade magazine I saw an advertisement of a power company spraying brush along the power lines to kill the growth. Can I use this same material on my property? Certainly, it is usually a mixture of 2, 4–D and 2, 4, 5–T mixed with water for use when plants are in leaf, and mixed with kerosene when plants are dormant. It is easily applied and very effective on many plants.

We have an old pasture covered in spots with hawthorns as much as 6″ in diameter. How can I best eliminate these plants without having to pull each one out with a tractor? Try spraying the lower base of the trees with a concentrated solution of 2, 4–D and 2, 4, 5–T in the winter while trees are dormant.

ODDS & ENDS

Will you explain the meanings of floriculture and horticulture? Horticulture covers the cultivation of all plants that may be grown in a garden. Floriculture is that branch of horticulture that deals with the growing of flowers—often used to denote the commercial culture of flowers outside and under glass.

What is meant by "deciduous" trees and shrubs? Those which shed their foliage in the autumn. Some, which retain their dry leaves, all or partly, through the winter, like beech and some oaks, are commonly included in "deciduous" trees.

Is it possible that a chain or a peg fastened to a tree at a certain distance from the ground will ever be further from the ground, no matter how old the tree? No, there will be no elevation of anything driven into a tree at a given point.

How much sunshine and air circulation do most blooming plants need? Some flowering plants are happiest in all the sunshine possible. Others appreciate shade during the hottest part of the day, and some are tolerant of a good deal of shade. All appreciate good air circulation but dislike drafts.

Will you tell me how to change the color of flowers? For instance, what would the procedure be if I wanted to raise a blue marigold? Colors in flowers result from inheritance. You cannot get a blue marigold. In some instances (hydrangea) chemicals like aluminum added to the soil change the color from pink to blue.

What is the usual procedure in the treatment of seed by X ray for the origination of new varieties? Both time of exposure and intensity of the rays seem to affect the results. Sometimes dormant seeds are irradiated and sometimes young flowers. Write to Research Laboratory, General Electric Co., Schenectady, New York.

We hear so much about "activated" phosphorous and its use in fertilizers, as well as the use of some of the by-products in the manufacture of atomic energy. Where can I write specific questions concerning how these materials can be used in growing plants?   Address all questions to the Brookhaven National Laboratories of the Atomic Energy Commission, Brookhaven, Long Island, New York.

What use are radio-active fertilizers in growing plants?   Chiefly of value as tracers, since their uptake and transfer from one part of the plant to another can be traced either on photographic film or by Geiger counters.

Will you state what effect, if any, the moon has on planting gardens? The moon has no effect on planting gardens.

What is the truth about planting in the signs of the zodiac?   There is no scientific basis for these superstitions.

SECTION III

Ornamental Plants and
Their Culture

INTRODUCTION

BY MONTAGUE FREE

MOST OF our leading garden plants have their origin in wildflowers. A few have been cultivated for so long that the original species is unknown or uncertain. They have been greatly changed by domestication, so that they are quite different from the wild prototypes. Hybridizing and selection have improved the form, size, color, and garden value.

Taken as a whole, the number of different kinds and varieties of garden flowers available to the home gardener is staggering. He can easily become bewildered by the great array of different types from which to choose. No one should attempt to grow all the varieties of the more important plants in the average home garden. It is wisest to select a few that are known to be especially adapted to the region.

Many flower lovers prefer to specialize in one or a few groups and become experts in growing roses, irises, dahlias, or chrysanthemums. There is much to recommend the practice, because the gardener comes to know his particular plants thoroughly. Those who are familiar with the interesting habits of their plants get the most fun from gardening. It is usually better to learn to grow one kind well, and to be thoroughly acquainted with its many varieties, than to dabble with all sorts of plants and know little about any of them. Most of the leading horticulturists of the country have been specialists to a certain degree, and have then in turn mastered the culture of many groups.

PLANTS AS GARDEN MATERIAL

The real gardener is interested not only in the plants themselves, but also in the garden pictures he can create with them. Floriculture is a combination of both science and art. Each complements the other. To be able to grow good flowers without the skill to use them artistically in and about the home furnishes only part of the enjoyment from them that is possible. Merely using plants and flowers for decorative purposes, without understanding their culture, is an empty form of art.

Joining a garden club or special flower society is to be recommended. Such organizations are dedicated to the improvement of horticulture or to promoting the culture and development of a particular flower. Besides furnishing helpful information through their meetings and publications, they give an opportunity to become acquainted with other gardening hobbyists. The friendships and sociability encouraged by horticultural organizations are by no means a minor factor in making the world a better place in which to live.

The gardener who knows something of plant structure, plant physiology (which deals with the functions of the various plant parts), and ecology (the relation of plants to their environment) finds such knowledge helpful in dealing with problems of plant culture. Furthermore, a smattering of general botany adds greatly to the pleasures and interest which come from gardening.

Structure of the Plant. All of us know that the function of the *roots* is to anchor the plant in place and to absorb water containing dissolved nutrients from the soil. The botanists can tell us, in addition, that roots of most plants, in order to remain healthy, require air. When we know this we appreciate more the importance of cultivation which, among other things, admits the air to the soil. We can also understand why some plants fail to thrive when set in poorly drained soil from which the air is driven by waterlogging. Knowing the need of roots for air we can see the importance of adequate underdrainage for plants growing in pots and the need to avoid overwatering which drives out air from the spaces between the particles of soil.

The information that water, with its dissolved minerals, is absorbed mainly near the root tips indicates to us that fertilizers should be applied to that area where the roots are actively growing, and not in close proximity to the stem or trunk, where there are few if any actively "feeding" roots.

Plant stems, in addition to supporting the leaves and flowers, provide a connecting link which distributes water (with the dissolved nutrients absorbed by the roots and the food materials manufactured in the leaves) between the roots and other parts of the plant. The internal structure of the stem has an important part to play in some aspects of plant culture. For example, in those plants which have two or more seed leaves the stem contains a layer of actively growing cells between the bark and wood: this is the *cambium layer*. It is essential for the gardener engaged in grafting or budding to be aware of this because the cambium layer of the understock must be brought into close contact with that of scion or bud to be grafted on it; otherwise union cannot take place.

The leaves are the factories of the plant where water, containing dissolved minerals absorbed from the soil, and carbon dioxide, taken in by the leaves, are combined to form complex food substances which are then transferred by the sap to other parts of the plant where they are needed. When we realize the importance of the work carried on by the leaves we can readily understand the necessity of keeping them healthy and why we should never remove too many of them. If the work of leaves were more widely understood, there would be fewer beginners expecting a harvest of edible roots from young beets from which all the leaves have been cut for use as "greens." The function of leaves is recognized in the oft-repeated advice to leave plenty of foliage when cutting such flowers as gladioli, peonies, or tulips, and thus avoid weakening the underground parts.

The flowers produce seeds and thus provide a means of reproduction. Commonly they are "perfect": that is, the male and the female elements are contained in a single flower—as in a rose, or a sweetpea. But sometimes they are "monoecious"—that is, with stamens and pistils in separate flowers on the same plant; for example, corn, squash, and oak. In some cases the male and female flowers are "dioecious" and are produced on separate plants, as in holly and willow. While, contrary to a widespread impression, it is never necessary to have plants of both sexes growing in proximity for flowers to be produced, fruits are possible on dioecious plants only when both sexes are growing fairly close together. Also many varieties of fruits, such as apple, pear, plum, and cherry, although their flowers are "perfect," require another variety of the same kind growing near by to provide cross-pollination, because their own pollen is incapable of securing a good "set" of fruit.

Environment Is Important

Often it is helpful to the gardener to know the kind of surroundings in which the plants thrive in the wild state. The study of such environment is known as plant ecology. Some plants are found always growing in the shade; others revel in hot, dry situations. They must, in most cases, be accorded similar conditions when we grow them in our gardens. Again, some plants are more perfectly at home in heavy clay soils, while some thrive in sand. There are those which have to be grown in water, and others which languish if their feet are too wet. Some plants demand a soil with an acid reaction; some prefer a soil which is abundantly supplied with lime; and others—many of them— seem almost indifferent to the chemical reaction of the soil. It is obvious that the right kind of soil and its proper preparation are among the most important factors in plant culture.

Some knowledge of the natural environment of plants is of great help to the gardener. Species that thrive in sheltered positions, for instance, cannot be expected to do well if fully exposed to storms and winds.

Other things also have to be considered, such as shelter and exposure to wind. Climate, of course, has a very important bearing. In some regions the extreme cold of winter prohibits us from growing some plants outdoors throughout the year, and to others the heat of summer may be inimical. Many plants are adapted to dry air; and in this group we find a large proportion which are successful as house plants. The polluted air of large cities is fatal to many plants, but there are some which can endure it; these, of course, are of special interest to those whose gardening has to be conducted in urban surroundings.

Competition for food, light, and air among themselves, and from other plants, is another environmental factor which affects growth. In order to secure room for adequate development it is necessary for us either to thin or transplant the seedlings which we raise; and it is also necessary to insure that they are not starved, smothered, or crowded by weeds.

Information bearing on these environmental factors can be obtained from observation, from books, and from the experience of friends. But sometimes if the gardener's special bent is the cultivation of rare and unusual plants, he may have to experiment for himself before he is able to discover a location and conditions in which his plants will thrive. A knowledge of the natural environment is always helpful, but there are isolated cases where plants seem to thrive better under garden conditions when their usual environment is changed. An example is our native cardinal flower, which grows naturally in wet places, usually in shade, but which, in our garden, we find does better in the rich soil of the perennial border where it gets sun for most of the day. The wise gardener first selects plants which are adapted to the environment of his garden. If he is ambitious to grow other kinds, he must change the environment to suit them if that is possible.

Propagation of Plants

Starting new plants is an absorbing garden operation which never loses its thrill. Even an old-timer like myself, who has been an active gardener for more than forty years, can still get a kick out of watching seeds germinate (though I no longer dig them up the day after planting to see if they have started to grow!), and from inserting cuttings with the expectation of getting roots on them.

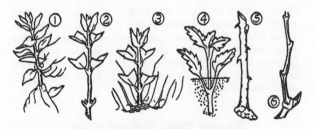

PROPAGATING PLANTS BY CUTTINGS

Many plants are readily propagated by means of cuttings —a trick which the amateur can readily master. Most commonly used for house plants, perennials, tender annuals, and some shrubs, are softwood cuttings. In (1) above such a cutting is being made; (2) shows it trimmed up, ready for (3) inserting in sand or sand and peat- moss, to root. (4) Cutting properly inserted in rooting medium. (5) Hardwood cutting of rose, showing callus formed at bottom. (6) "Mallet cutting" of grape.

Nature increases plants by means of seeds, spores, bulbils, tubers, rhizomes, runners, offsets, suckers, and stolons. The gardener uses all these methods and in addition makes cuttings of stems, leaves, and roots. He also increases his plants by division, by layering, and by budding and grafting.

During the past ten years or so several new methods, or variations of old ones, have come to the fore. Among them are: the use of constant mist, (see p. 246) and a plastic film, Polythene, sold under various trade names, as an aid in rooting cuttings and in propagation by means of air-layering. New rooting media have also come into the picture. These include: powdered glass, shredded styrofoam, perlite and mixtures of these.

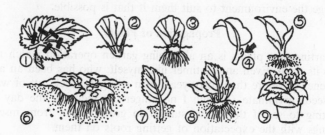

LEAF CUTTINGS

Some species of plants are readily propagated by leaf cuttings. (1) and (6) show begonia leaf cut across main ribs and laid flat on moist sand, with new plants starting from cuts; (2) and (3) show triangular leaf cutting of begonia; (4) and (5) leaf cutting with bud; and (7), (8), and (9) leaf cutting of African-violet, and young plant developed from it.

Keeping Plants Well and Happy

The Art of Transplanting. The gardener's job is not finished when he has started or purchased his young plants. They must be properly cared for in order to get best results from them. The seeds may be sown where they are to mature (after proper preparation of the soil, of course); and then they have to be thinned, the soil cultivated, and weeds kept down. Sometimes seeds are started either in seed pots indoors or in seedbeds out of doors. Then the seedlings have to be transplanted once or oftener before the plants are installed in their permanent location. Cuttings usually are started in a propagating frame, and their subsequent treatment involves transplanting. Transplanting is usually done to temporary nursery rows, or to pots, preliminary to their final shift to the garden. In some cases, however, the rooted cuttings can be transferred directly to the garden.

Transplanting is an important operation. It must be done at the right season for best results, and care must be taken to avoid undue injury to the root system. Usually trees and shrubs are transplanted when they are more or less dormant, provided the ground is unfrozen. Most of them can be moved either in spring or fall, but for best results some require spring transplanting. Frequent transplanting (every year or two), when the trees are young, produces roots that make possible transplanting, even when they are of large size, with little injury. Each transplanting inevitably shortens the wide-spreading roots, and this causes the remaining roots to branch freely. Thus the plant produces a compact mass of fibrous roots which enables it to be transplanted easily. For this reason plants obtained from a nursery (where regular transplanting is practiced) can be moved with much less loss than those which are dug from the wild.

Seedlings, and young plants in general, can be transplanted when they are actively growing because it is possible to move them with the root system almost intact. There are some exceptions among those plants which produce a deep taproot. Carrots and annual poppies, for example, cannot be transplanted with good results. Occasionally transplanting is done to promote fruitfulness, as with dwarf fruit trees, growing in rich ground, which are making excessive branch and leaf growth at the expense of flowers. The loss of roots brought about by transplanting often results in checking such vegetative growth and promoting the formation of flower buds.

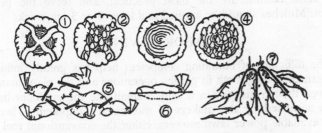

PROPAGATING BULBS, ROOTS, AND RHIZOMES

Hyacinth bulb (1) cut across bottom to induce formation of bulblets (2). Hyacinth bulb (3) scooped out at bottom, to produce bulblets (4). Old iris rhizome (5) cut into sections or divisions, and divisions planted (6). Dahlia root cut into sections, each containing an eye (7).

Benefits of Cultivation and Mulching. Cultivation is the term applied to the loosening of the surface soil. It aids in the aeration of the soil, enables rain to penetrate more easily, and, perhaps most important, it helps keep down weeds.

Cultivation is accomplished in many ways, and a variety of tools is involved. In pots or flats a pointed stick or an old dinner fork may be used. For cultivating soil in crowded areas there are various types of hand cultivators. In flower borders the scuffle hoe is the most useful tool, while in the vegetable garden either the scuffle hoe, draw hoe, or wheel hoe may be brought into action. In large areas, where the crops are grown in rows, either motor-driven or horse-drawn cultivators are used.

Cultivation after rains is usually recommended to prevent the formation of a surface crust and to kill weed seedlings; but cultivation must not be done until the moisture has had a chance to penetrate and the surface is beginning to get dry. Frequent cultivation is essential to cope adequately with weeds. It is much easier to kill them while they are still in the seedling stage. Furthermore, this prevents them from stealing the food and moisture which properly belong to the cultivated crops.

A mulch is sometimes applied in order to lessen or obviate the necessity for cultivation. Paper treated to make it somewhat waterproof has in some cases been successfully used. Some plants, however, do not respond to a paper mulch and under garden conditions there are several objections to it, such as its appearance, the difficulties of anchoring it to the ground, and of working among the plants without disturbing it.

Ordinarily mulches of organic materials, most of which can be incorporated with the soil at the end of the growing season to decay and form humus, are the most practical, and serve the purpose better. Mulches should be applied in a layer 2 or 3 ins. thick.

LABOR SAVING

The difficulty of obtaining competent help has greatly influenced modern gardening, both in garden operations and the plant materials.

Even though his garden is only a small one the gardener has not been neglected by the makers of motorized equipment. There are now available power lawn mowers, either the conventional reel kinds or the rotary types with all sorts of attachments ranging from snow removal to tillers.

Other labor-saving devices include metal strips which can be pushed into the ground to make a barrier between the lawn and flower border. This, to a large extent, eliminates the tedious job of trimming the whiskery grass by handshears. If even this short chore is hateful an electric trimmer can be bought which will enable him to do the job without that backbreaking effort that gets a man down.

Mulching the surface as a means of controlling weeds is another labor-saver. Among the organic materials that can be used for mulching are: buckwheat hulls, peatmoss, ground corn cobs, shredded sugar cane (bagasse) sold as chicken litter, salt-meadow hay, grass clippings, sawdust, wood chips, excelsior and pulped newspaper. Most of these serve a triple purpose—that of making it easier to control weeds; conserving soil moisture by checking evaporation; and adding organic matter. Naturally there are some drawbacks to the wide use of mulches. Among them are the possibility of an increase in the slug population and the temporary depletion of available nitrogen in the soil. Fortunately these drawbacks can be counteracted by putting out slug bait containing metaldehyde, and by keeping a close watch on the plants and applying quick-acting nitrogen in the form of nitrate of soda or sulfate of ammonia at the first sign of yellowing foliage.

As part of the endeavor to cut down on labor there is a diminution of interest in bedding plants which have to be started fresh every year; and a trend toward permanent plants, especially trees and shrubs, which once they are planted take care of themselves, to some extent at least. Among the newcomers in woody plants are Moraine locust, a form of Honey locust (*Gleditsia triacanthos,* var. *inermis*); a spineless variety; and a form of this, the Sunburst locust, in which the new leaves are yellow. Another new tree is a form of Schwedler maple, sold as Crimson King. This, although it does not quite live up to the colored pictures in the advertisements, is an advance over the dull summer color of Schwedleri. Among the comparatively new shrubs are the contorted hazel (*Corylus avellana contorta*), *Chaenomeles* (*Cydonia*) Spitfire, a columnar form; and a hybrid *Viburnum carlcephalum* (*V. Carlesi* x *V. Macrocephalum*).

Watering. Plant physiologists tell us that the plant nutrients in the soil can be absorbed by the roots only when they are in solution. The necessity for abundant moisture is therefore obvious. Cultivation and mulching both have a bearing on the conservation of moisture already in the soil. In recent years the value of cultivation has been questioned by some investigators regarding the moisture-holding value of a dust mulch, but most practical gardeners still accept it.

In addition to conserving the moisture already in the soil it is sometimes necessary to *supplement* the rainfall. This is accomplished by irrigation, or by watering with the aid of a hose or watering pot.

Simple method of applying water in a fine spray without wasting time "hose-holding."

The important thing to remember about watering is that light sprinklings, which penetrate the soil only an inch or so, are not desirable, because they encourage roots to come to the surface where they are exposed to too much heat from the sun and where they may be killed by cultivation, or by drought if for any reason the daily sprinkling is neglected. When watering is done, *it should be thorough,* so that the soil is wet, if possible, to a depth of 6 to 8 ins. Do not water again until the soil begins to get dry.

The same principle should be followed when watering potted plants. Sometimes it may be desirable to let the soil become so dry that the plant is almost wilting. The soil shrinks when drying, and this opens up pore spaces, permitting the entrance of air which, as we have already seen, is a necessity for the roots of most plants.

Pruning. In a reaction against the plant butchering which went under the name of pruning many gardeners have come to look on all cutting back of plants as a practice to be avoided. Actually, however, pruning is not altogether bad. By pruning it is possible to aid the

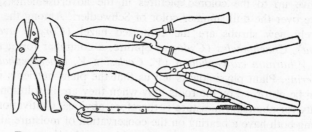

Types of pruning equipment. The pruning shears and pruning knife (left) are the most useful in the small garden.

rejuvenation of sickly plants and assist in the control of insect pests and fungous diseases. Pruning can be used to correct faulty habits of growth, to promote interesting branch formations, and to bring about earlier blossoming. In certain cases it is possible to develop larger flowers on longer stems by pruning to reduce the number of flowering shoots. The complete removal of dead and dying branches is an operation that can be safely performed at any time.

There are several principles which are helpful to the would-be pruner:

(1) Severe pruning *when the plant is dormant* stimulates the production of strong, leafy shoots; contrariwise, pruning *when the plant is actively growing* tends to check exuberant growth and helps bring about the formation of blossom buds.

(2) Trees and shrubs which *blossom early,* in the spring, ordinarily should be pruned immediately after they flower; while those which bloom in summer or autumn, on shoots of the current season's growth, can be pruned in the spring.

(3) In general, the aim of the pruner should be to maintain the natural habit of growth of the tree or shrub. Sometimes, however,

when plants of definite outline are required (as, for instance, privet hedges, or shrubs or small evergreens used as accent points in a formal garden), "shearing" or light surface pruning is practiced. This alters and controls the plant's habit of growth.

(4) Pruning, limited to *pinching out the tips* of the growing shoots, (called "pinching back") stimulates branching and develops a plant of compact habit. Chrysanthemums are commonly thus treated. The same principle is sometimes followed with woody plants, with the same purpose in view.

(5) In pruning, *no stubs should be left* which will die and decay. The cuts should be made close to the supporting branch or trunk, or just above a bud—preferably one which is pointed in the direction it is wished to have the bush or tree develop.

(6) Wounds more than an inch or so in diameter should always be painted with a protective covering to keep out moisture and spores of disease organisms.

In pruning shrubs with a natural, loose-growing or drooping habit—such as forsythias, deutzias, and weigelas—old stems are cut out clear to the ground if thinning seems necessary.

Pruning is a complex subject full of interest and worthy of the thoughtful study of all gardeners.

Winter Protection. Gardeners everywhere commonly grow plants which are not able to survive the winter without help. In some cases this requires that the plants should be dug up and stored in a frost-free place, such as a greenhouse, cellar, or cold frame. Often sufficient protection is afforded merely by placing a mulch of insulating material on the soil over the roots. Sometimes the tops have to be covered to protect them from the effects of drying winds and winter sunshine.

Plant Supports. Some of the most useful decorative plants have twining or climbing habits. To be effectively displayed, such plants usually have to be provided with supports. These may be walls, fences, pergolas, arches, trellises, or poles stuck in the ground.

There are other plants which are not climbers but which, under garden conditions, have weak stems likely to be toppled over as a result of heavy rains or strong winds. These can be held upright by staking and tying, or by pushing twigs in between and around the clump before the plants have attained their full height.

Plant Enemies. In addition to all these operations, plants have to be protected from the various insect pests and plant diseases to which they are subject. In keeping the garden free from pests, sanitation must be practiced, plus close observation to note any departure from the normal so that remedial measures (fully discussed in Section VIII) can be put into effect before much damage has been done.

There has been tremendous increase in growing plants in the home. This interest has been sparked by the furor attendant on the amazing success of the culture of Saintpaulia (African-violet). In part this is due to the discovery that many kinds of plants can be grown without any daylight at all, merely by the use of fluorescent lights combined with a sufficient number of the ordinary tungsten light bulbs to provide from 300 to 600 ft. candles. The result of this has been that many plants which formerly were believed to be unsuited for culture in the home can be grown without too much difficulty.

ENVIRONMENT

CITY CONDITIONS

PLANT MATERIAL

I have a small yard in the heart of the city. Will you suggest flowers for cutting that I can grow from May until October? Columbine, pinks, thalictrum, iris, zinnia, marigold, cosmos, petunia, nasturtium, eupatorium, phlox, calendula.

What are the best varieties of ANNUAL FLOWERS for a small, sunny city back-yard garden? Alyssum, China-aster, balsam, calliopsis, candytuft, celosia, cynoglossum, dianthus, four-o'clock, lobelia, dwarf marigold, annual phlox, portulaca, salvia, verbena, dwarf and medium zinnia.

Which annuals would you advise for a very small half-shaded city garden? Balsam, begonia, calliopsis, campanula, celosia, cleome, lobelia, nicotiana, petunia, torenia, vinca, viola.

Which annuals and potted plants stand shade in a city garden? Very few. Lobelia, nicotiana, and torenia thrive in partial shade. Begonia, fuchsia, and lantana are good. Potted plants include begonia, caladium, calla, fuchsia, Zanzibar Balsam.

How can I grow sweetpeas? (New York City.) As a rule, they do not succeed in or around New York. Sweetpeas should be planted either in late fall or *very* early spring (mid-March if possible) in full sun. They need cool weather to come to perfection. Soil is prepared 18 ins. deep, rotted manure being mixed in. Seeds are planted 2 ins. deep in a 4-in. trench. As plants grow, trench is filled in and supports are provided for vines to climb on—twiggy branches, chicken wire, or stakes.

Which are the best varieties of PERENNIAL flowers for a small city back-yard garden? Ajuga, *Alyssum saxatile, Anchusa myosotidiflora,* aquilegia, Artemisia Silver King, astilbe, hardy aster, campanula, chrysanthemum (hardy), coreopsis, daylily, *Dianthus barbatus,* bleedingheart (both tall and dwarf,) *Eupatorium coelestinum,* gaillardia, heuchera, hosta (plantainlily), tall bearded iris, lily-of-the-valley, mertensia, *Phlox divaricata,* platycodon, plumbago, sedum and sempervivum in variety, tradescantia, viola.

Are there any other BULBS which furnish bloom in a city garden besides narcissi and other early spring ones? Calla, caladium (colored leaves), tuberose for very late bloom, most lilies that are listed as easy of culture and tolerant of partial shade, gladiolus for sunny, well-drained situations, small-flowered dahlia.

How can we grow EVERGREEN trees successfully in New York City? Select only ones that are known to be smoke- and gas-resistant. Give them good soil, occasional fertilizer, plenty of water, and protect them from dogs. The trick is to select resistant species such as: Austrian pine, *Pinus nigra;* Japanese black pine, *P. Thunbergi;* and American holly. But don't be too disappointed if they fail. None will survive in closed-in shaded places, except, possibly, Japanese Yew.

Which evergreens are suitable for a shady city garden? *Broadleaf evergreens*—andromeda, azalea, *Ilex crenata,* kalmia, leucothoe, mahonia, rhododendron, wintercreeper, abelia, pyracantha (the last two semi-evergreen), and varieties of yew.

How shall I care for evergreens in the city? Soil should be prepared to a depth of 18 to 24 ins., incorporating well-rotted manure and leafmold. Transplant only in early fall or spring. Never allow roots to dry out, and wash foliage frequently with fine but strong spray from hose. Broadleaf evergreens require acid soil.

We don't want a paved area in our city garden, and it is too shady for a lawn. What GROUND COVERS are best (perennial preferred)? English Ivy, suitable for formal as well as informal gardens; and vinca (common periwinkle) which has blue flowers in the spring. A pleasing effect is achieved with ajuga, either green or bronze-leaved, which has blue flowers in spring, good foliage all season, and is very hardy.

How can I have a good LAWN in the city? Difficult unless garden gets at least 6 hours of direct sunshine. Soil should be rich and deep (at least 8 ins.) with good drainage. Prepare soil and sow a good grade of lawn seed (without bent grasses) in early September.

What can I plant in a shady CITY ROCK GARDEN? If you furnish proper soil, rich in leafmold, you can have an attractive planting of ferns, small-leaved ivies, and native woodland wildflowers, with small bulbs—such as chionodoxa, snowdrop, Siberian squill and crocus—for spring bloom.

Can ROSES be successfully grown in a city garden? Yes, providing there is abundant sunshine, deep, rich soil, and the garden is outside of congested metropolitan areas.

Can you suggest roses which succeed best in a city garden? Area is open and sunny. Excelsa, New Dawn, and Paul's Scarlet Climber are good climbers; Mme. Jules Bouche, President Macia, Radiance, Soeur Therese, and Talisman are good hybrid teas. Gruss an Teplitz is excellent, but needs much room.

What deciduous SHRUBS tolerate shade in a city garden? Aralia; calycanthus (sweetshrub); deutzia; *Euonymus alatus;* rose-of-Sharon; hydrangea; kerria; privet, clethra (sweetpepper bush); rhodotypos (jetbead); stephanandra; viburnum in variety.

Can you recommend any distinctive shrubs for a city garden? We don't want only privet and forsythia! If your soil is good, the following will succeed: *Abelia grandiflora; Acanthopanax sieboldianus; Berberis julianae; Euonymus alatus,* brilliant red foliage in fall; *Pyracantha coccinea lalandi* (firethorn)—transplant only when young, preferably potted; stephanandra; tamarix.

Which small ornamental and FLOWERING TREES can you recommend for a city garden? *Aralia spinosa* (devils-walking-stick); flowering crab, peach, plum, Japanese cherry; Flowering dogwood (only for more open situations and good, deep soil); hawthorn; honey locust; *Magnolia soulangeana;* Russian olive; umbrella catalpa; weeping mulberry.

Would a pink hawthorn or a mountain-ash grow in a city garden? Hawthorns do very well, but mountain-ash is completely intolerant of urban conditions.

What good-sized trees stand city life? We don't want ailanthus. Catalpa, ginkgo, London Plane, *Magnolia soulangeana,* Norway Maple, Paper Mulberry, Pin Oak, willow.

We cannot build new fences for our city garden and would like VINES which would cover the old ones within a year or so. What can you recommend? Fastest-growing and most tolerant perennial vines are fleeceflower (*Polygonum auberti*); Hall's Honeysuckle; kudzu-bean (dies to the ground in winter but grows rapidly every summer); Virginiacreeper for shade particularly. Hyacinth bean, or morning-glories, if annuals are preferred.

Which is the fastest-growing vine to cover an old brick wall in city? Either Virginiacreeper or Boston Ivy.

PROBLEMS

It is difficult to maintain humus supply in our city garden because

everything has to be carried through the house. Could I grow "green" manure? Yes. Plant winter rye seed in late September in bare places, and dig under in spring.

What locations and conditions in an average city home are suitable for starting seeds in flats? South or southeast window, with sunshine available for the major part of the day; fresh air without direct drafts or chilling; even temperature not exceeding 65° F. during daytime, 10° lower at night; humidity, provided by syringing, pans of water, or humidifiers; freedom from cooking or heating gas fumes.

How can we keep dogs away from plants? If the dogs belong to you, fence off a small exercise yard for them; it is an aid in training the dogs. If they do not, low wire fencing or special curved wire guards may be placed around shrubs or borders. Spraying individual plants with a solution of 40 per cent nicotine sulfate, 2 teaspoons to 1 gal. of water, is sometimes effective; as are proprietary preparations sold by garden supply dealers. Spraying must be renewed at intervals.

FOUNDATION MATERIAL (GENERAL)

What are some good, low-priced materials for foundation planting under adverse conditions? Coralberry, Five-leaved Aralia, Gray Dogwood, jetbead, physocarpus, privet.

Will you give suggestions as to medium-height foundation planting, without using evergreens? Bridalwreath, *Cotoneaster apiculata,* Five-leaved Aralia, Flowering Quince, Japanese Witchhazel, lilac, Persian Lilac, *Rosa rugosa, Deutzia gracilis, Viburnum dilatatum,* and *V. wrighti.*

Will you name several hardy foundation plantings which will not take up much width in the bed and will not look too dilapidated in winter? Low shrubs, in general, tend to spread horizontally. The following are narrow or compact. *Deciduous shrubs:* Anthony Waterer Spirea, *Berberis thunbergi erecta,* dwarf privet, *Physocarpus monogynus. Evergreens:* Redcedar varieties, Chinese Column Juniper (both narrow, tall-growing), Hatfield and Brown's Yews, Spiny Greek Juniper.

What is a good evergreen or deciduous shrub to use for foundation concealment—one that will not grow more than 2 or 3 ft. high and will not be too bushy? Most dwarf shrubs tend to be broader than tall. The following are slow-growing and can easily be kept at 3 ft. by careful pruning: *Berberis thunbergi erecta, Picea glauca conica; Taxus canadensis stricta,* and *Taxus media hatfieldi* (yews); *Thuja occidentalis rosenthali.*

What would be a good thing to plant between two windows to fill blank wall on south side of house in full sun? There is only 4 ft. from house to lot line and ground is sandy, from excavating cellar. Most plants die from heat. The house is Cape Cod style. *Juniperus chinensis columnaris,* or *Juniperus virginiana cannaerti.* Remove the poor soil, and replace with good, light, loamy soil enriched with about ⅕ part of leafmold.

Which shrubs and flowers would be best to plant along a house that has a high foundation? These shrubs average around 4 or 5 ft. in height: coralberry, *Cotoneaster apiculata,* Fragrant Sumac, Mapleleaf Viburnum, *Physocarpus intermedius,* hydrangea, Sweetpepper Bush; Vanhoutte Spirea. Some tall perennials are boltonia, delphinium, Michaelmas daisy (*Aster novibelgi*), rosemallow, *Helenium autumnale.*

What is a suitable planting on west side of house along foundation, space about 6 ft. from house to driveway? Deciduous materials: *Cotoneaster apiculata,* Flowering Quince, *Physocarpus monogynus,* rose-of-Sharon, Rugosa Rose, Slender Deutzia. Evergreen kinds: dwarf hemlock varieties, Spiny Greek Juniper, *Juniperus virginiana; Taxus cuspidata nana* (if kept pruned), also *Taxus media browni, hatfieldi,* or *hicksi* (yews).

Which is best evergreen for a corner? Want a tall one that is graceful and smooth and not too spreading, for yard is small. (D.C.) Arborvitae, Chinese Column Juniper, redcedar varieties.

What would be suitable foundation plantings for an old (1792) farmhouse in southern New Hampshire? The shrubs that grow naturally in the fields and woods of your area and which are in harmony with the general surroundings. Arborvitae; arrowwood; Canada Yew; chokeberry (*Aronia melanocarpa*); *Rosa humilis;* Flowering Raspberry; hemlock; highbush blueberry; Maple-leaf Viburnum; Mountain Laurel; pinkster-flower (wild azalea); Prostrate Juniper (*Juniperus communis depressa*); winterberry. Of exotic shrubs, lilacs would not be out of place, nor would *Chaenomeles lagenaria,* Japanese Quince or *C. japonica* (Dwarf Japanese Quince).

What can be done with 3 feet of space under eaves which does not get any natural moisture in summer? This space is always barren, and nothing seems to grow even though watered with the hose. Such a spot should be watered with unfailing regularity. Occasional neglect may be ruinous. Improve soil by working in leafmold or peatmoss. If this is done, try *Symphoricarpos chenaulti, Berberis thunbergi erecta* (Truehedge Columnberry), Spirea Anthony Waterer. These will grow about 3 to 4 ft. high.

How may one grow shrubbery about the house that has eaves projecting 3 feet, without excessive watering? A 6-in. layer of peatmoss at the base of roots and a generous amount of it mixed in planting soil would limit artificial watering.

Does close foundation planting (3 ft. away) affect walls of house in any way—possibly causing dampness on inside walls? Probably not. While the planting keeps sun and air from the walls, it also sheds rain and the roots absorb much water.

FOUNDATION MATERIAL FOR SHADE

FLOWERING

Which plants bloom in a location next to a garage wall where very little sun reaches the ground except in late afternoon? Balloonflower, bugbane, columbine, coralbells, meadowrue, monkshood, plantainlily, Showy Sedum (*Sedum spectabile*).

What would give me profusion of color, or at least greens, on a narrow strip (about 10 ins. wide) on driveway and against the house? Strip is on the north side and therefore sunless. Ferns, goutweed (*Aegopodium podagraria variegatum*), Japanese Spurge (*Pachysandra*), lily-of-the-valley, plantainlilies.

What are good perennials for the shady north side of the house? It is at the front, and there is a space approximately 3 × 14 ft. between the house and the walk around the house. Astilbe in variety, balloonflower, columbine, coralbells, daylily, *Eupatorium coelestinum*, plantainlily, *Anemone japonica*.

EVERGREENS

What can I plant in shade of building under oaks, on a sandy ridge? Nothing worth trying, unless you prepare the ground thoroughly, mixing in abundant humus, leafmold, and some very old manure. Having prepared an acid mixture of this sort, try rhododendrons and Mountain Laurel.

Can azaleas and rhododendrons be used in a foundation planting about the house? Yes, but special precautions must frequently be taken to keep the soil acid. The stucco or brick foundations contain cement, which is alkaline. Rain falling against this washes a certain amount of lime into the soil close to the house, frequently resulting in its gradually becoming alkaline.

Can I safely put in a foundation planting of evergreen trees where the outer branches of the street maples reach? Probably only the native yew would thrive; and at the point farthest from the maples, perhaps a hemlock or two. The Japanese Yew might survive, but would not thrive. Both the shade overhead and the roots below would trouble evergreen trees.

The planting north of my house looks spindly. Which evergreens can I use to replace it? In soil well prepared with leafmold and old manure try *Taxus canadensis* and its variety *stricta*. In the somewhat more sunny ends, hemlock, especially its dwarf varieties, and Japanese Yew. In an acid, humusy soil try *Rhododendron maximum.* At the more sunny ends: *Rhododendron carolinianum,* Mountain Laurel, and *Pieris floribunda.* All of these are evergreen shrubs.

Which plants for foundation plantings are best suited for northern New England? Especially for shady north side of house?   Evergreens would be best, especially the broad-leaved types, such as Mountain Laurel and Mountain Andromeda. Because of shade only a small amount of flowers could be expected from any plants. Yews would be useful.

SHRUBS

Can you advise if there is any flowering shrub which will grow in a totally shady place in the front of the house—north side? (New York.) Few, if any, shrubs will bloom satisfactorily in complete shade. *Rhododendron maximum,* Mountain Laurel, and jetbead (*Rhodotypos scandens*) are worth trying. One of the best shrubs for north exposures, totally shaded by the house (not over-hung by trees), is *Euonymus patens.*

What can be planted, to grow successfully, on the north side of the house? The ground is covered with fine green moss.   Prepare the ground deeply, mixing in a liberal supply of leafmold and old manure. Then you may safely try *Euonymus patens, Symphoricarpos orbiculatus, S. albus laevigatus,* honeysuckle (lonicera) various kinds. If you will prepare an acid soil, such a situation may do well for rhododendrons, Mountain Laurel, azalea, pieris.

Which shrubbery is best for foundation planting in a very shaded spot facing west?   Deciduous shrubs: *Symphoricarpos chenaulti, Rhodotypos scandens, Physocarpus monogynus, Lonicera morrowi.* Evergreen shrubs (for acid soil): *Rhododendron maximum, R. catawbiense, Pieris floribunda, P. japonica,* Mountain Laurel.

Which shrubs would best grow on north side of porch facing east, with a joining hallway next to it? Prefer something not to grow over 5 to 6 ft. high that would flower with some fragrance, as it will appear on front of house.   Chokeberry, mockorange, sweetpepper bush (*Clethra alnifolia*), *Viburnum carlesi,* Winter Honeysuckle.

Which inexpensive ground and foundation plants can be used to fill in north-side foundation?   Low to medium-height shrubs: *Viburnum patens, Mahonia aquifolium, Symphoricarpos orbiculatus.* Taller shrubs: *Lonicera tatarica, L. morrowi,* Regel Privet. Ground covers: *Pachysandra terminalis, Vinca minor.*

Which shrub can be used beside a house for sort of a hedge, to grow 5 ft. high? Not much sun hits spot, and not too good a soil.

I don't want barberries. Amur River Privet, Five-leaved Aralia, Gray Dogwood, Siberian Peatree.

GROUND COVERS

Is it harmful for ground ivy to grow over ground where flowers (perennials and annuals) grow? If the other plants are small, the ground ivy (*Nepeta hederacea*) may smother them.

What ground cover flowering plants are suitable for a steep bank with northeast exposure? *Ajuga reptans,* Japanese Honeysuckle, moneywort (*Lysimachia nummularia*), Vinca minor.

What can I use for ground cover between sidewalk and curb, on a 2-ft. bank, 3½ ft. wide, with some shade? *Vinca minor,* Bowles variety.

We have a small, steep terrace shaded by trees. It is next to impossible to grow grass on it. Last year I planted ivy (Hedera helix gracilis), which seemed to grow only fairly well. Was our selection wise? *Hedera helix gracilis* is a well-recommended plant for dry banks and will probably do much better when it has become established. Try giving it a mulch of leafmold or well-rotted cow manure this winter.

What is the best coverage to plant where there is full sun, on a hill? Grass and weeds make it hard to cut. Honeysuckles are good, so are trailing roses. Ask your local nurseryman to supply you with suitable kinds.

What is the most beautiful flowering ground cover for Regal Lilies in a perennial border? *Myosotis sylvatica* (forget-me-not) should please you.

Which evergreen euonymus vine would grow well as a ground cover? Purple-leaf Euonymus (*E. coloratus*).

What is a good ground cover to plant along house wall between two houses, space about 4 ft. wide running north and south, with steppingstone path in center? Strip gets rain but not dew. Would like something deep-rooted, short, and not viny. *Arenaria montana* (Mountain Sandwort), *Arenaria verna caespitosa* (Moss Sandwort). Both of these are very low, tufted-growing grass substitutes; they are the best plants available for planting between flagstones in a walk.

Which ground cover do you suggest to border a stream? Moneywort (*Lysimachia nummularia*) which is also known as Creeping Jenny or Creeping Charlie—(take your choice!), is an excellent semi-evergreen ground cover which might be used near the stream.

FOR BULB BEDS

What is a good ground cover for my tulips? Pansies may be used to advantage to flower with the tulips, also forget-me-nots, especially to underplant yellow tulips. To follow these, petunias would give a good display until frost.

Will it be harmful to bulbs left in the ground if they are over-planted with annuals for summer bloom? Not if the bulbs are planted at the proper depth and the soil is enriched annually. Any kind may be used—from alyssum to zinnia—that will conform to the situation.

Is it practical to plant seeds of annuals over spring bulbs, in the fall? Not if desirable mulch of manure is placed over beds. Wait until mulch has been removed in early spring.

What is the best way to start annuals for planting in a bulb bed? Those kinds which give best results from an early start, such as ageratum, petunia, snapdragon, torenia, and verbena, may be started under glass in March and set out between the bulbs in late May. Marigold and zinnia may be transplanted at this time; or they may be sown where they are to flower, especially if a late display is most desirable. These kinds are best sown in place: sweet alyssum, California Poppy, candytuft, coreopsis, *Gilia capitata,* nigella, portulaca.

I have a triangular bed of tulips in the front lawn. What fairly low-growing plants can I place between the tulips after the foliage dies down? The bed is partially shaded in the morning. For color and profusion of bloom nothing will outdo petunia for the purpose, particularly those of the bedding type. Other good dwarfs are ageratum, sweet alyssum, portulaca, verbena.

FOR SHADE

What can I do to get grass to grow under oak trees? If trees are low-headed and dense, remove lower branches and thin top to admit more light and air. Better, perhaps, use a shade-enduring ground cover, such as pachysandra, ivy, ajuga, or gill-over-the-ground.

Grass will not grow on a terrace which is quite shady. What is the best ground cover for such a location? The terrace is about a 45° slope. Japanese Pachysandra, English Ivy, Hall's Honeysuckle, *Ajuga reptans.*

We have just planted a flowering cherry tree in our back lawn. Will you tell us what to grow around the tree? Something that blooms early spring to late fall and spreads around to cover the earth under tree. Only annuals would give you flowers from summer into autumn; petunias, for instance. For a permanent ground cover, try the evergreen periwinkle or Japanese Spurge. The former has blue flowers in the spring; the latter no appreciable flower at all.

Which ground cover might be used under large elm trees? *Ajuga reptans,* Canada Yew, English Ivy, *Euonymus fortunei,* ferns, yellowroot, (*Xanthorhiza apiifolia*). Best of all, *Pachysandra terminalis,* the Japanese Spurge.

What would be a good ground cover under large plantings of 3-year-old lilacs? *Veronica rupestris, Plumbago larpentiae, Phlox divaricata,* and *P. stolonifera, Ajuga reptans;* but these or any others will likely pass out of the picture as the lilacs get older.

What will really grow under maple trees as a substitute for grass? *Pachysandra terminalis* is the court of last resort, especially under Norway Maples. If this will not grow, nothing will; you might as well save time and money and stop further experimentation. Maples cast dense shade and their roots are very near the surface.

Which ground cover shall I plant (other than sedums) in shade under maples? Most things I try grow leggy and floppy. See preceding answer. Manure and dig soil and try Japanese Spurge, moneywort, periwinkle, English Ivy, or *Ajuga reptans.*

Is there a low-growing or creeping plant that would form a carpet for a shady pine grove in southern Vermont? The pines are young and do not shed enough needles to cover the ground. Partridgeberry (propagated by seed), Mother of Thyme (easily propagated by division); blueberries—especially the smooth-leaf low-bush blueberry (propagated by seed); yellowroot (easily propagated by root division). As the pines increase in size they may be expected to kill everything beneath them.

How can I plant English Ivy from cuttings for low cover under tree? Suggest rooting the cuttings first in propagating frame, then prepare soil well with leafmold or rotted manure. Plant rooted cuttings 6 to 8 ins. apart in early spring and keep watered until established.

Is Japanese Spurge (pachysandra better than creeping myrtle for a ground cover in the shade? Yes.

What fertilizer or special care is needed to maintain healthy pachysandra plants? Pachysandra prefers partial shade. Dig soil 8 ins. to 1 ft. and incorporate manure before planting. If foliage of established plantation is not deep green, spread a ¼-in. layer of dehydrated cattle manure on the surface of the soil in the fall.

Does pachysandra grow better in acid or alkaline soil? It is reasonably tolerant. If the soil is quite acid, plant pachysandra; if alkaline, use English Ivy.

SANDY SOIL

Which annuals grow best in very light, sandy soil? Sweet Alyssum, *Lobularia maritima,* arctotis, calendula, California Poppy, castor bean, geranium, lantana (a tender shrub treated as annual), marigold, nasturtium, petunia, *Phlox drummondi,* portulaca, *Cleome spinosa,* statice, verbena, zinnia.

Which hardy flowers grow best in sandy loam soil? *Penstemon barbatus,* butterflyweed (*Asclepias tuberosa*); *Nepeta mussini,* false-indigo, *Anthemis tinctoria, Phlox subulata, Achillea ptarmica,* The Pearl.

Which perennials grow best in very light, sandy soil? Achillea; *Anchusa italica; Arabis albida; Arenaria montana;* armeria in var.; *Artemisia abrotanum* (old-man); *A. stelleriana* (old-woman); *Cerastium tomentosum; Dianthus deltoides;* globe-thistle; lupin; *Nepeta mussini;* Oriental Poppy; balloonflower; *Salvia azurea; Santolina incana;* sedums; yucca.

Which shrubs and trees are suitable for a sandy soil in a sunny location? With proper, ordinary care in planting and after care until established, the following commend themselves: Medium to tall shrubs—*Elaeagnus umbellata;* hydrangea (various); hypericum; *Hippophae rhamnoides* (seabuckthorn); *Lespedeza thunbergi;* bayberry; *Rosa rugosa; R. setigera; Robinia hispida* (rose-acacia); *Vitex agnuscastus;* tamarix. Tall-growing—Siberian Peatree; Russian Olive; Goldenrain Tree.

Which edging plants, preferably flowering kinds, will do well in dry, sandy soil? Several kinds of statice (armeria); *Sedum hybridum, S. ellacombianum,* and *S. spurium;* Silver Mound Artemisia (*A. schmidtiana nana*).

SEASHORE

Which ANNUALS are suitable for planting near the ocean? Sweet alyssum (*Lobularia maritima*); California Poppy; geranium; lantana (tender shrub treated as annual); petunia; *Phlox drummondi;* portulaca; nasturtium; *Cleome spinosa;* verbena. If sufficient depth of topsoil (6 to 8 ins.) is provided, and sufficient water in dry periods, practically all annuals that grow successfully inland, provided the low-growing types are selected.

Which PERENNIALS endure salt spray and high winds? Tall-growing kinds will require staking in windy places. Among perennials able to withstand salt spray and shore conditions are Carpathian Bellflower (*Campanula carpatica*); *Allium schoenoprasum;* daylily; echinops (several kinds); *Erigeron speciosus;* eryngium (several kinds); gaillardia; Bearded Iris; coralbells; statice; perennial flax; lythrum; New York and New England Asters; pinks; rudbeckia; sedums; *Silene maritima;* statice (armeria)—several kinds; veronica; *Yucca filamentosa.*

Are there any SHRUBS which will grow near the shore exposed

to salt-laden air?   Yes, but immature leaves are damaged by salt-laden fogs in spring and late spring. This applies to native shrubs also. The following are good: arrowwood, bayberry, beach plum, chokeberry, coralberry, groundselbush, highbush Blueberry, inkberry (*Ilex glabra*), Japanese Barberry, *Rosa rugosa* and *R. humilis,* and *R. lucida,* Russian Olive, seabuckthorn, shadbush, sumac, winterberry, and tamarisk in several varieties.

Which TREES are most suitable for seashore planting?   Birch; Black Jack Oak (*Quercus marilandica*), but does not transplant well; Chinese Elm does fairly well; hawthorn; pepperidge (*Nyssa sylvatica*), but does not transplant well; Red Maple; sassafras; White Poplar, White Willow; mulberry.

Which evergreen trees resist salt air?   American Holly, best broad-leaved evergreen; Austrian Pine; Japanese Black Pine—best; Redcedar especially good.

Which evergreens will grow best near salt water with danger of water occasionally reaching roots? (Massachusetts.)   No evergreen tree hardy in Massachusetts will *thrive* where salt water reaches the roots occasionally. Redcedar is best bet.

Will you suggest protective planting for sloping shore bank, about 18 ft., which is inclined to wash, due to wind, rain, high water? Chesapeake Bay area.   Toe of slope *must* first be stabilized with retaining wall of timber, boulders, or concrete. Abutting properties, if similarly subject to attack, should also receive attention. Study the vegetation of similar situations and plant that material closely on your own bank. Beachgrass, bearberry, elaeagnus, goldenrod, povertygrass, Sand Blackberry, sumac, Virginiacreeper, wild grape (Fox or Frost Grape), and wild roses are good, especially *Rosa rugosa.*

Which fertilizers are best for sandy seashore gardens?   Seashore soils usually are benefited by heavy applications of humus (rotted leaves, grass, or other vegetation) and old, well-rotted barnyard manure. This is largely to improve their physical condition. Moderate applications of commercial fertilizer will help build up the nutrient content of the soil. Applications should be small but frequent.

SLOPES; BANKS

I have a steep bank at the end of my lawn to the street. Can you advise the best plants to keep the soil from washing away?   Cover it with plants that make a dense mat, or tangle of growth: Japanese Barberry, Japanese Honeysuckle (especially in shade), *Juniperus horizontalis,* matrimonyvine, *Rosa wichuraiana,* yellowroot (especially in shade). If low-growing plants are desired, Japanese Spurge, or trailing myrtle.

What would you suggest to plant on a bank, across the front of our yard, about 4 ft. high off the highway and about 375 ft. long? Akebia, English Ivy, Japanese Honeysuckle, Japanese Spurge (if shaded), Memorial Rose (*R. wichuraiana*), *Vinca minor*.

What can I plant on a sunny south slope now covered with tufted grass? Coralberry, Five-leaved Aralia, Fragrant Sumac, Gray Dogwood, jetbead, Rose Acacia, Scotch Broom.

What can I plant on a dry, sunny slope (southern exposure, formal surroundings) on which it is impossible to grow any grass? Japanese Barberry, Box Barberry, Chenault Coralberry, Tibet Honeysuckle.

What can best be planted on a sandy slope that will cover well, look nice, and keep sand from blowing? *Arenaria montana, Cerastium tomentosum, Dianthus deltoides* and *D. plumarius* (Cottage Pink). Mix equal parts of seed of Domestic Rye Grass and Chewings's Fescue Grass, and add 1 part of the seed to 10 parts of soil by bulk, and broadcast this. If your home is near the seashore, dig up roots of wild perennials, mostly weeds and grasses, that are growing above high-water mark, divide them, and plant them on your property; surround the plants with a little soil when setting them.

What are good shrubs for south slope of a gravel hill, soil loose and sandy? Try barberry, Beach Plum, Scotch Broom.

What can be used for fast coverage of a steep bank, heavy clay soil? We now have barberries, but after 2 years they are not covering very quickly, and deep gorges are being cut in the bank. Suggest keeping barberries in but also plant clumps of Hall's Honeysuckle, or bittersweet. Fill gullies with brush to catch and hold soil. Mulch slope with manure, to check washing.

Which flowering plants can be planted on a sandy, rocky bank? *Phlox subulata, Gypsophila repens,* and columbines are suitable perennials; use a good half pailful of soil in each planting hole. Buy seed of single mixed portulaca, mix it with screened soil (1 part of seed to 10 parts of soil); broadcast the mixture, and look forward to a fine display in summer.

SHADE

WHAT TO PLANT

In a shaded location, which flowers will bloom in each month of the season? The month of bloom may vary with the degree of shade and the geographical location, but one can depend upon the following plants to flower in the broader seasonal divisions of spring, summer, and fall. *Spring:* barrenwort (epimedium); bleedingheart, *Ajuga reptans, Pulmonaria saccharata,* spring bulbs (chionodoxa, muscari, scilla, etc.), *Mertensia virginica. Summer:* daylily, foxglove, Fringed Bleedingheart (*Dicentra eximia*), monkshood, plantainlily. *Fall: Aconitum autumnale, Eupatorium coelestinum,* and *E. urticae-folium, Anemone japonica.*

Which low-growing flowering plants thrive best in shade? Epimedium in variety, *Ajuga genevensis* and *A. reptans, Dicentra eximia, Iris cristata,* lily-of-the-valley, *Pulmonaria saccharata, Lysimachia nummularia, Vinca minor,* plantainlily.

Which flowering plants will grow well in an area that receives only about 2 or 3 hours of strong sun daily? Iris, phlox, anemone, digitalis, coreopsis, *Primula japonica,* veronica, bleedingheart, primrose.

Due to many trees adjacent to the entire length of south side of yard, my garden stretch is damp and shady all day. What type of planting would you suggest? Arrowwood, *Monarda didyma,* Five-leaf Aralia, Cornelian Cherry (*Cornus mas*); Mountain Laurel, plantainlily, spicebush (*Lindera benzoin*).

What can I grow to cover a small space under a cluster of oak trees, on the type of rock-garden material? Unless utterly shaded: barrenwort (epimedium), Fringed Bleedingheart. If only lightly shaded: *Iris cristata* and *I. gracilipes.* Or little evergreen shrubs, in not-too-heavy shade, in acid, humus soil: *Rhododendron indicum balsaminaeflorum, R. carolinianum.*

Have had no success with shade-loving plants, put near trees. Have enriched the soil but trees take all moisture. Would a mulch be of use? I can use blue grass clippings, old flax straw, rotted or regular grain straw, but peat is not available. Nor is a garden hose available. If your trees are maples or elms, your problem is a difficult one. Try *Pachysandra terminalis,* Japanese Spurge, planting it in the spring while the ground is moist—after first spading and raking the ground—then apply a mulch as well. This plant will often succeed where nothing else will.

Which flowers grow the best in tubs on a terrace that is shaded very heavily from a tree that is in the center? You will have to bring into bloom elsewhere, and use for temporary effects on the shaded terrace, any flowering plant that lends itself to pot culture; such as hydrangea varieties, lantana, geraniums, calla, caladiums (for colored foliage).

I have a row of Lombardy Poplar trees. Can I plant flowers in front or back, or in between spaces? Yes, particularly on the sunny side: *Aquilegia canadensis, Iberis sempervirens, Digitalis purpurea,* Rose Paul's Scarlet Climber, *Anemone japonica.*

What could one plant in shade of a mulberry tree? If a mere ground cover is wanted, prepare the area, working in leafmold and some old manure, and plant either Japanese Spurge or periwinkle; the former 6 to 9 ins. apart each way, the latter 8 to 12 ins., depending upon size of plants. If shade is not very dense, the following shrubs may, with proper preparation, be used: symphoricarpos (any), *Clethra alnifolia,* Morrow Honeysuckle (about 7 ft. tall). In an acid, humus soil: *Azalea rosea* and *A. calendulaceum.*

ANNUALS AND PERENNIALS

Which annuals can I grow in a section that is in complete shade after the trees are in full leaf? Practically none. Try cornflower, flowering tobacco, and nasturtium.

Which annuals grow best in a shady location? In general annuals must have sunlight to grow satisfactorily. There are a few, however, which get along fairly well in the shade: *Begonia semperflorens, Torenia fournieri,* cornflower, flowering tobacco (nicotiana), *Myosotis arvensis, Impatiens balsamina, Lobelia erinus, Vinca rosea,* monkeyflower, nasturtium, pansy, Tuberous-rooted Begonias (which see).

West garden border of my house is shaded half the day; would you name 6 annuals that would bloom in it? *Begonia semperflorens, Torenia fournieri,* monkeyflower, calliopsis, cornflower, petunia.

Which are best annuals for partial shade and all-summer flowers? Balsam, flowering tobacco, lobelia, *Vinca rosea,* nasturtium, petunia.

Will begonias grow and bloom outdoors in a spot that is shaded all day, but not densely so? And how should soil be prepared for them? They get along very well in partial shade. Soil must be moist but well drained. Work into it generous quantities of leafmold, old rotted manure, or other humus material; also dressing of bone meal. (See also Tuberous-rooted Begonias.)

I have a semi-shady spot in my perennial border in which I have been able to grow only wild violets. Can you give me some suggestions? The ground in this spot is inclined to remain damp. Astilbe in variety, beebalm, bugbane, bugle (*Ajuga reptans*), buttercup, cardinalflower, ferns, Great Blue Lobelia, plantainlily in variety.

Which perennials can be grown in a dry, shady place? Bugle, *Aquilegia canadensis,* moneywort, Red Baneberry, White Snakeroot, *Aster ericoides.*

Which perennials should I plant on terraces in the shade of immense forest trees high up the hill? Balloonflower, bleedingheart, coralbells, daylily in variety, ferns, foxglove, *Anemone japonica.*

What can I plant in a damp place in the shade of a neighbor's garage? Hardy primulas are good for spring, along with lily-of-the-valley. Pachysandra and English Ivy are good ground covers. Foxglove, funkia, forget-me-not, ground ivy, and periwinkle. Tuberous-rooted begonias may be planted every spring if soil is well drained.

SHRUBS

Which shrubs will grow in a shaded place? Andromeda (*Pieris floribunda*);* arrowwood (*Viburnum dentatum*); Cornelian-cherry; Five-leaf Aralia; hemlock;* jetbead; Mountain Laurel;* *Rhododendron maximum;* spicebush (*Lindera benzoin*); Sweetpepper-bush (*Clethra alnifolia*); yellowroot (*Xanthorhiza simplicissima*); American Yew.

Which shrubs can be planted near front of house shaded by tall maple trees? If the soil is full of tree roots, very few plants will get along well; try Five-leaf Aralia.

What kind of shrubs will grow the best along the west side of the house in almost constant shade of large oak trees? If you will prepare a deep, humusy, acid soil, this would seem fine for rhododendrons, azaleas, Mountain Laurel, leucothoe, and pieris.

Will shrubs do well near evergreen trees? Near—yes; not *under* them. On the north and northeast sides, in properly prepared acid soil, even rhododendrons, laurels, and such might do well.

SUN

Which shrubs will thrive along the south side of a brick house in full sun? In deeply prepared, enriched, well-drained soil, kept sufficiently moist in summer, your choice is almost unlimited. Within the limits of permissible ultimate height and width, select from catalogues any good shrubs which require no special conditions or shade. Avoid rhododendron, azalea and, generally, evergreen shrubs.

Which shrub would suit an open, sunny, enclosed corner atop a retaining wall? Whatever you plant, prepare the soil 18 ins. deep with leafmold, old manure, and some peatmoss. See that the place does not dry out in summer. Usually, for a place like this, a shrub is best which will drape its branches somewhat over the wall. You might plant any of these: *Cotoneaster racemiflora, Lespedeza thunbergi, Rosa hugonis, Spreaea arguta* or *S. thunbergi, Forsythia suspensa* varieties.

What would you suggest as a fairly low, long-blooming flower for about 2-ft. space between brick house and sidewalk on south side of house? Harmony Marigolds would be excellent. Or dwarf zinnia, or the little blue *Torenia fournieri* (wishboneflower).

Can you suggest an edging for a 24-in.-wide border between house and driveway. South side of house. Germander, *Teucrium chamaedrys*. This may need some pruning which may be done in the spring by thrusting a spade in the soil alongside the row to check its lateral growth, using shears to trim the top growth.

*Evergreen

WET GROUND

Are there any flowers or flowering shrubs that like wet ground throughout the year? Perennials: cardinalflower, loosestrife (*Lythrum salicaria*), rosemallow. Shrubs: *Viburnum den tatum, Cephalanthus occidentalis, Aronia arbutifolia,* Swamp Azalea (*A. viscosum*).

The boundary line of my property is quite low and wet. I have put up a 5-ft. fence. Which vines would grow in such soil (clay)? Which shrubs or hedges could I plant there as a screen? *Vines:* porcelainvine (*Ampelopsis brevipedunculata*); Dutchmanspipe, bittersweet, Japanese Honeysuckle. *Screen: Clethra alnifolia, Viburnum cassinoides, Ilex verticillata, Lindera benzoin.*

Our lot is about 1 ft. lower than the lot next door. Consequently, after a rain water stands in this spot for some time. The space is 3 × 6 ft. I would like the names of low-growing shrubs that would not interfere with the grass. The spot receives sun all day long. Do you have any other suggestion as to what to plant on the spot? *Aronia arbutifolia,* Dwarf Willow (*Salix purpurea nana*), *Ilex glabra,* snowberry (*Symphoricarpos*), *Itea virginica.* Pruning may be necessary to keep them low.

What shall we plant on a space which is liable to be flooded during bad storms? Rosemallow, Japanese Iris, *Lythrum salicaria.*

How should sides of a stream be treated or built up to prevent caving in? The stream, which meanders for 210 ft., is about 1 ft. deep and 18 ins. wide; it is completely dried out in the dry season. Set some large rocks in the bank, at 10 to 15 ft. apart. Plants mentioned in preceding question should hold the bank once they are established.

Which annuals grow best in wet soil, in the shade? Jewelweed and monkeyflower.

Which perennials will thrive in wet soil? Beebalm, boneset; cardinalflower, *Iris pseudacorus;* Japanese Iris; Joepyeweed, *Lythrum salicaria,* marshmarigold, rosemallow, starwort (*Boltonia asteroides*).

What herbaceous planting is suitable for the sides of a small stream which becomes a full storm sewer after a rainfall? *Myosotis palustris semperflorens, Lysimachia nummularia, Iris pseudacorus, Lythrum salicaria.*

Which shrubs will thrive in wet soil? Buttonbush (*Cephalanthus occidentalis*), *Aronia arbutifolia* and *A. melanocarpa,* Highbush Blueberry, *Lindera benzoin,* Siberian Dogwood, *Clethra alnifolia,* sweetshrub (*Calycanthus floridus*), Swamp Azalea (*A. viscosa*), winterberry (*Ilex verticillata*).

Which trees will thrive in wet soil? American Elm, Pin Oak, Red Maple, Swamp White Oak, sycamore, Sour Gum (*Nyssa sylvatica*); Weeping Willow.

What kind of trees and shrubs shall we plant around a swimming pool? *Trees:* Red Maple; Sour Gum (*Nyssa sylvatica*)*;* Sweetgum (*Liquidambar styraciflua*); sycamore; Weeping Willow. *Shrubs: Cephalanthus occidentalis, Lindera benzoin, Clethra alnifolia.* Leaves and fruits falling in the water might be objectionable, if planting is too close to pool.

Which flowering plants will grow in a boglike spot? Japanese Iris, Siberian Iris, astilbe, flowering rush, marshmarigold, cardinalflower, *Primula japonica* and *P. pulverulenta*, trollius, *Myosotis palustris*, loosestrife.

ORNAMENTAL PLANTS AND THEIR CULTURE

(*For soils and fertilizers in general, see also Section I; for individual plants, see under Specific Plants, this section. For plant material for special decorative effects, see also Landscaping, Section II.*)

GENERAL CULTURE

CULTIVATION

What are the reasons for cultivating the surface soil? To kill weeds and maintain a loose surface that is readily penetrated by rain. It helps also in soil aeration in those cases where a crust forms on surface.

In cultivation, should the soil be left level or mounded around plants? Generally level cultivation is best, because it exposes less surface from which soil moisture can evaporate. When it is desirable to get rid of excess soil moisture, hilling or ridging is sometimes practiced. Corn and similar crops are mounded with soil to help them stay erect; potatoes to prevent "greening" of the tubers.

How soon after a rain should one hoe the soil? When it has dried to such an extent that it no longer sticks to the hoe in sufficient amount to impede the work.

Is it desirable to cultivate the surface every week? No. Cultivate according to circumstances rather than by the calendar. Hoe after rains to prevent the formation of a crust, and to kill weeds when the surface has dried somewhat. If no more rain falls, hoe only to kill weeds.

How deep should surface soil be cultivated? This depends on character of soil, time of year, and the root formation of the plants cultivated. Sometimes it may be desirable, in some soils, to cultivate deeply—3 to 4 ins.—early in season to dry the surface. Later shallow cultivation, 1 in. deep, is preferable to avoid injury to crop roots. Modern tendency is toward shallow cultivation.

My soil forms a crust after every rain. What shall I do? Cultivate with hoe or cultivating tool to break crust; or use a mulch of organic matter. (See Mulches.) Improve soil by adding bulky organic material—strawy manure, partly decayed leaves, sedge peat, peatmoss—annually until condition is cured.

Does a dust mulch really conserve soil water? Probably not in most soils, if the soil is stirred to a depth of more than 1 or 2 ins. Moisture in the loosened soil is quickly lost by evaporation and the dust mulch is likely to absorb all the water from light showers before it has a chance to reach the soil occupied by roots.

MULCHING

See also Winter Protection under Perennials, Evergreens, etc.

What is meant by mulching? The application of various materials —usually organic—to the soil surface to hold moisture in soil, to prevent weed growth, and, in some cases, to help keep the ground cool.

Essential small tools for the gardener—shovel, hoe, iron rake, trowel, and spading fork.

Should mulches be applied early in spring? Better wait until soil has warmed up. The chief reason for mulching is to conserve moisture in the soil during hot, dry weather.

Once a mulch has been put on, is it necessary to do anything further about it? Not much; just keep it loose. Peatmoss must be watched because it is likely to pack down after a heavy rain, forming a felted surface when dry which sheds water like a roof.

Mulches are put on to conserve water in the soil. Don't they also work in the opposite direction by absorbing rain which otherwise would reach crop roots? Yes, to some extent. Some mulch material, however—buckwheat hulls and cranberry tops, for example—allows easy penetration of water and does not absorb a great deal. Examination of soil after rain will show whether or not mulch is too thick.

What can I use to mulch my perennial border? I want something

not unsightly. Peatmoss, leafmold, buckwheat hulls, shredded sugar cane, pine needles, coconut-fiber refuse. Peatmoss and pine needles might make the soil too acid in some gardens, unless lime or extra nitrogen is used with them.

Of what value, if any, are grass cuttings for garden beds, and how should they be used? They are of use as a water-conserving mulch, and if incorporated with the soil after they are partly decayed they add to its humus content. They should be spread in a layer of 1 to 2 ins. thick.

Is a paper mulch practicable in a small garden? Scarcely. It is objectionable on the score of appearance, and because it is difficult to anchor it. Not all plants do well under a paper mulch.

What are the advantages in using mulch paper in the garden? It keeps moisture in soil; it eliminates cultivation; it keeps down weeds, but is difficult to keep in place, and will tear readily.

Is Polythene plastic film good material to use as a mulch? It can be used, but it is difficult to apply. One has to anchor it to prevent it from blowing away; and it is also essential to make provision for the ingress of water by punching holes in it. Except that it does not tear easily it has the same defects as mulching paper.

Can Polythene be used to mulch newly planted shrubs? Yes. In this case it can be used to advantage. Cut off a square of three or four feet, slit to a little beyond the center, put it in place and anchor it by covering each corner with soil. It is desirable to punch a few holes in the plastic film so that water can get in over the entire space.

My cottage is on a salt-water beach; is it beneficial or injurious to mulch with seaweed washed up in abundance on shores? Or could the presence of salt kill plants? Seaweed makes an excellent mulch. The amount of salt present should do no damage unless the seaweed is used in excess.

Since peatmoss is getting so high in price, would shredded sugar-cane fiber answer the purpose of peatmoss for mulching, especially around acid-loving plants such as azalea and rhododendron? Yes. It works very well.

What is your opinion of the use of coffee grounds? We can get a bushel a week, and we have a heavy clay soil. Coffee grounds make an excellent mulch, but should not be used too thickly, or air will be excluded. ½ in. deep is sufficient.

What plants would be benefited by mulching with pine needles? Pine needles are especially good for cone-bearing evergreens and acid-soil plants such as rhododendrons.

How about the use of well-rotted sawdust around plants, and on lawns, as a mulch? Sawdust makes a satisfactory mulch during the summer. Do not apply deeper than 1 in. unless it is mixed with sulfate of ammonia at the rate of 1 pound to 100 sq. feet.

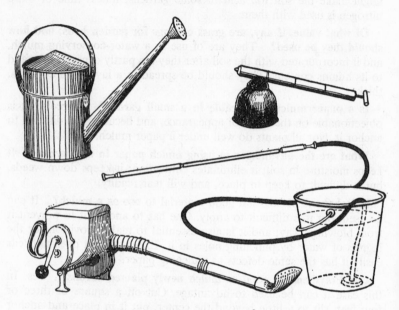

Types of sprayers and dusters for applying insecticides and liquid fertilizers. Watering can; small hand sprayer; crank duster for small garden; and "trombone" sprayer.

WATERING

How should one water flowers?   Water in at planting time if the soil is dry. When growth is active, and soil is really dry, water before the plants suffer. Mere surface sprinkling does no good. Give enough to wet the soil 6 ins. down. Cultivate the surface as soon as dry enough to work freely.

Are there any objections to spraying or watering plants in the evening?   Some authorities believe that if the foliage is wet when the temperature is falling, the plants are more susceptible to attacks by disease organisms. Under outdoor conditions this is probably not important, but in greenhouse or hotbed it is wise to spray or water early in the day.

Is it harmful to water plants when sun is shining on them?   Generally speaking, no. But, theoretically, it is better to water in early morning or in evening, so that water has a chance to penetrate the soil before much is lost by evaporation.

When watering newly set annuals, should water be applied to the

soil, or over all by sprinkling? If water is in limited supply, leave depression around each stem and fill with water. If ample, sprinkle whole bed, making sure water penetrates several inches.

I mulched my kitchen garden with wood chips and sawdust. The crops did not grow at all well. The foliage looked peaked and yellowish. I presume this was caused by acid soil as a result of the mulch. Is there anything I can do to counteract this? It is doubtful if this condition is caused by acid soil. More likely it is due to the depletion of nitrogen by the need for nitrates of the microorganisms which bring about the breakdown of the organic matter in the mulch. Apply sulfate of ammonia—1 pound to 100 square feet; or nitrate of soda at 1½ pounds. You should test the soil and, if it shows a reaction of less than pH 5.5, pulverised limestone should be applied—the amount is contingent upon the degree of acidity plus the character of the soil (more will be needed if it is a heavy clay). Your county agricultural agent should be consulted on this matter.

I have read somewhere that when undecayed organic materials are put in or on the soil that it is necessary to add chemical fertilizer to supply food for bacteria that cause its decay. How much and what kind? Chemical fertilizer is not absolutely necessary but it is usually more convenient to obtain. Nitrogen is the element that is most likely to be lacking; this can be provided by sulfate of ammonia at one pound to 100 square feet, or 1½ pounds of nitrate of soda. Phosphorus can be added by superphosphate at 5 pounds to the same area. Organic fertilizers such as poultry manure can be used at 5 pounds to 100 square feet, or sheep manure at the rate of about 10 pounds. It is important to watch the behavior of the plants and if they become yellow indicating nitrogen deficiency, use quick acting nitrogen such as nitrate of soda or sulfate of ammonia, either in liquid, or dry and watered in.

PRUNING

See also under Trees, Shrubs, Evergreens, etc.

Please give us otherwise "green-fingered" amateur gardeners the real low-down on what, to me, has always been mystifying and most vexing—the art of pruning. There simply must be some fundamentals that apply. Are there not some simple rules to follow? Read the section on pruning in the introduction to this division and the answers to the pruning questions. Then, if you are still in doubt about pruning, follow the advice which Mr. Punch gave to those about to marry—"Don't."

What is the difference between shearing and pruning? Shearing is a form of pruning in which all young shoots extending beyond a definite line are cut off. Pruning proper involves cutting individual shoots or branches with a view to improving the tree or shrub.

When is the best time to trim trees? If the purpose is to check growth, it is better to prune trees when they are actively growing. Ordinarily, however, trees are pruned when they are dormant, in the fall or late winter. This stimulates strong shoot growth.

What is meant by "dormant"? Plants are said to be dormant when they are not actively growing. In deciduous trees and shrubs it is a period between leaf fall and starting into growth the following year.

Is it all right to trim trees in the winter? Yes, provided the temperature is not too low. From the standpoint of comfort for the operator and the danger of breaking surrounding branches when they are brittle from frost, it is desirable not to prune when it is very cold. However, it is preferable to wait until late winter.

How can I avoid tearing the bark on the trunk when cutting off large limbs? Make the first cut from underneath the branch, cutting upward until the saw binds. Then cut from above, which results in the removal of the branch. The stub may now be cut off with safety by sustaining it with one hand while the few last cuts with the saw are being made.

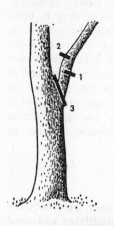

Proper way to cut off a large limb.
(1) – make an "under cut" near trunk;
(2) – saw off limb, leaving stub; (3) –
saw off stub as close to trunk as possible.

Is there any special rule to follow when making the cuts in pruning? Yes; branches should always be cut off close to, and parallel with, the branch from which they spring. When shoots are shortened, the cut should be made just above a growth bud, pointing in the direction you wish to have the tree develop.

Should a single or double leader be developed? Generally speaking, a single leader is preferable, especially for those trees which naturally grow with a single trunk. Some trees, and all shrubs, have a diffuse habit and cannot well be restricted to a single leader.

Does pruning help make a tree bushy? Yes, if it is limited to cutting off the tips of the leading shoots. It can be done during the growing season if the tree is too vigorous.

Is it better to use hedge shears or pruning shears when trimming trees into globes, squares, etc.? If the leaves are large, as in linden, cherrylaurel, etc., it is better to use pruning shears, because the use of hedge shears results in obviously marred leaves. In the case of small-leaved trees, hedge shears can be used.

What is used to paint over wounds made in pruning? Several coatings of shellac, renewed when necessary, are excellent. Or you could use tree-wound paint, obtainable from horticultural supply houses, asphaltum paint, or white lead and linseed oil in which a little lampblack has been mixed to make it less conspicuous.

Is pruning of any help in the case of trees infested with scale insects? Yes. Branches dying as a result of attack by scale insects should be cut off. This will tend to strengthen the rest of the tree. The cut-off branches should be destroyed by burning and measures taken to kill the insects remaining. (See Scale—Section VIII.)

Is pruning sometimes used as an aid in controlling plant disease? Yes; for example, canker on roses, and fire blight on trees and shrubs of the apple family. The affected limbs must be cut off well below the point of injury, and the tool used should be disinfected after every cut.

We have a young tree with the center broken off; will it grow into a tree or should we dispose of it? If there is a strong side shoot near the break, it could be trained to take the place of the broken leader. Tie a stout stake securely below the break, and let it project two or three ft. above it; then tie the side shoot to this.

How can I keep tree wounds from bleeding? Maples and birches, if pruned in spring, will bleed, but this is temporary. Another form of bleeding is caused by "slime flux," and this is often very difficult to control and may cause the bark to decay if it persists for a considerable time. Sometimes a short length of pipe is inserted to carry off the flux, or in the case of large wounds the wood is seared with a blowtorch. These practices, however, are not always effective.

What tools are necessary for pruning? For close work on trees, a narrow-bladed pruning saw is desirable. In some cases it is helpful to have one attached to a long pole to get at branches which otherwise would be difficult to reach. To cut branches ½ in. in diameter, or less, sharp pruning shears should be used, or a pruning knife. In pruning old, overgrown shrubs, long-handled "lopping" shears are useful.

DISBUDDING AND PINCHING

What is meant by disbudding? The removal of some flower buds while they are still small, so that those remaining will develop into flowers of larger size. Plants on which disbudding is commonly practiced include carnation, chrysanthemum, dahlia, peony, rose.

When are plants disbudded?   As soon as the buds to be removed are large enough to handle, usually about the size of a pea or bean.

How often should plants be pinched to force blooms? Should they be kept pinched as long as they bloom?   Pinching a plant delays blooming instead of forcing it, but results in a bigger, more stocky plant. Some plants, such as snapdragon, give good, bushy plants with only 1 pinching. Others, such as chrysanthemum, may be pinched 3 or 4 times until late July. A plant such as geranium, after the first pinching (soon after rooting), may be pinched just beyond each flower bud as it appears.

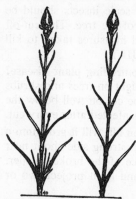

Disbudding—pinching out most of the buds in order to secure fewer but larger blooms—is often practiced with some plants, such as carnations, dahlias, chrysanthemums, and roses.

What plants should I pinch; and when?   These are a few examples: coleus, carnation, chrysanthemum, dahlia, fuchsia, heliotrope, iresine, salvia, and the garden geranium. One pinching, when the plants are a few inches high, may be sufficient, but in the case of coleus and chrysanthemum, pinching may be repeated more than once if extra-large plants are desired. Some woody plants are pinched back during the growing season to make them more compact.

What is meant by "terminal bud"?   The topmost bud on a shoot.

ROOT-PRUNING

What are the reasons for root-pruning?   To promote formation of fibrous roots, to induce blossoming, and to check excessive shoot and leaf growth.

How many roots should be cut off when root-pruning a tree or shrub to check growth or induce flowering?   Impossible to say definitely, for each specimen is a problem in itself. Sometimes cutting the taproot is all that is necessary, and sometimes one or more horizontally spreading roots also must be cut. Root-pruning is a hazardous practice not to be attempted by the beginning gardener.

What is the technique of root-pruning?   If the tree or shrub is a large one, dig a trench halfway around the tree (distance from trunk depends on size of tree) and sever all thonglike roots encountered. Do the other half the following year—if necessary. Sometimes one must undermine the tree to cut the taproot.

Can I, by root-pruning ahead of time, make it possible to move some shrubs with greater safety?   Yes. In the spring thrust a sharp spade into the ground to its full depth all around the shrub a few inches inside the digging circle. This will induce the formation of fibrous roots which will enable it to be easily moved the following fall or spring.

Is there any simple method of dwarfing plants?   It is helpful to start off with naturally dwarf varieties. Restrict the roots by growing the plants in comparatively small containers, or by root-pruning if in the open ground. Prune the top at frequent intervals during the growing season by shortening new growth. In the case of fruit trees (which see) the use of a dwarfing understock is indicated.

SUPPORTS

What is the best method of staking perennials and annuals?   The type of support varies with the subject. Those with only comparatively few slender stems (delphinium, for example), should have individual slender stakes to which the stems are loosely tied. Low, bushy plants can be supported by twigs stuck in the ground around them before they have completed their growth. For others, such as peonies, wood or metal hoops, on 3 or 4 legs placed over the plants, afford the best solution.

Many flowers require support, and many devices have been developed for this purpose. Detail drawing (upper right) shows proper method of securing plant stem to stake: string is first tied tight around stake; then ends are tied in a loose loop around stem.

Any pointers on staking plants?   Always maintain the natural habit of growth. Don't tie stems in a bundle and fasten to a broomstick. (See answer to preceding question.)

How can one obtain twiggy shoots for staking perennials? Save all suitable material from shrub pruning. Keep one or more privet bushes solely for this purpose—cutting off the twigs early in the fall so that they will dry up and not grow when stuck in ground. Gray birch twigs are ideal, if available.

I want to use espaliered trees to enclose a small flower garden. How can I support them? If in a continuous row, use galvanized wire stretched tightly on posts; or a wood fence with horizontal members. Isolated specimens are best supported on wooden trellises.

How are "espaliered" trees or shrubs supported on walls? Sometimes by fastening directly to the wall, but this is considered undesirable where exposed to full sun in regions having hot summers. They can be fastened to wires strung on brackets 6 ins. or more from wall, or on wood trellises, thus allowing circulation of air between plant and wall.

Staking an annual (cosmos). Tie is first made fast around stake and then looped loosely around stem of plant.

How can I attach trained shrubs directly to a wall? Use broad tape; or use cloth or leather (old gloves) cut into strips ½ in. wide, 3 to 6 ins. long, passed around branches and fastened to wall with stubby nails. Also special wall nails are obtainable from firms dealing in horticultural supplies.

I want to use vines for "accent points" in my flower garden. What is best for holding them up? Use redcedar posts, sunk 2 to 3 ft. in the ground, or a "tepee" support (see page 762).

What are the best supports for roses, vegetables (such as tomatoes, peas, pole beans, etc.), fruit trees in bearing, etc.? See Index for specific plants to be supported.

PLANT PROPAGATION

See also Cold Frames, Hotbeds, Greenhouse, and Propagation under Plant Groups.

What are the various methods of plant propagation? Seeds, spores, bulbils, cormels, tubers, rhizomes, runners, offsets, suckers, stolons, layers, division, cuttings, grafting.

SEEDS

What are the main factors in seed germination? Quality and freshness in seed. Correct temperature, even moisture supply, and sufficient air. Some seeds must never be allowed to become really dry (usually these are stratified in a moist medium); some must be sown as soon as they are ripe; some wait a year or more before germinating; and some require an "after-ripening" period at low temperatures.

How can germination be hastened in hard-shell seeds? Soak in warm water overnight, or longer, to soften shell; or nick hard shell of large seeds with a sharp knife. Sometimes seeds are treated with acids, but this is not recommended for beginners.

What is meant by "stratification" of seeds? It is the term applied to the practice of storing seeds over winter, or longer, in moist material such as sand or peatmoss. Seeds which lose their vitality if allowed to become dry (oak, chestnut, etc.), and "2-year seeds" (hawthorn, dogwood) are commonly so treated.

Should seeds be treated with a disinfectant before planting? Yes, if trouble has been experienced in the past with seed-borne diseases. (See Section VIII.)

BULBS; CORMS; TUBERS

What is the usual method of propagating bulbs? By digging them up when dormant and taking off small bulbs formed around the mother bulb. They should be planted separately, and grown on to flowering size.

Is there any way of inducing bulbs to form offsets for propagating purposes? Planting shallower than normal is supposed to be helpful. Commercial growers, in the case of hyacinths, either scoop out the base of the bulb, or cut into it in several directions to induce the formation of bulbils. Special after-treatment is necessary.

What are offsets? Shoots with short stems with a miniature plant at the end—sometimes applied to the small bulbs produced around the mother bulb. Typical offsets are produced by houseleeks. They may be taken off and used to start new plants.

How are plants propagated by tubers? By separating or cutting, and planting. Sometimes, as in the potato, the tuber may be cut into several pieces, each having an "eye," or growth bud.

Can the little gladiolus bulbs that form on the old ones be used? Yes. These are known as cormels (the large bulb is really a corm) and may be planted 1 in. deep in rows in the spring in much the same way that one would sow peas.

CUTTINGS—GENERAL

What is meant by softwood cuttings? These are made from shoots that are still actively growing, and are taken from hardy shrubs during May and early June. Nurserymen sometimes place suitable plants in greenhouses to force young growth for cuttings.

What is meant by half-ripe wood cuttings? Cuttings of half-ripe wood are taken when the shoots have finished growth but are not yet mature. July and August are suitable months.

What are hardwood cuttings? Hardwood cuttings are made from fully matured shoots, generally of the current year's growth. These are taken after there have been a few frosts, packed in moist sand or peatmoss, stored in a temperature of 35° to 40° F., and planted out the following spring.

How does one propagate softwood and hardwood plants? This depends entirely upon the plant under consideration. In most cases softwood plants may be increased by stem cuttings, and many of the hardwood plants may be increased in the same way; but there are innumerable exceptions in both groups.

What is the best and surest way to root cuttings for the average amateur? I have a cold room in cellar, no heat, facing east, with two small windows. Also have a dark closet behind the furnace where it is always warm. The dark closet behind the furnace is most unsuitable. Probably you could root most of the commoner shrubs and house plants in the cellar room if the cuttings were placed near the window. However, you would be more likely to succeed with a small cold frame or propagating box in a shady place in the garden.

How best can one propagate plants from cuttings without greenhouse or hotbed? Many shrubs, some trees, most of the plants used for summer bedding, herbaceous perennials, many rock garden plants, and several house plants can be propagated during the summer almost as readily in a cold frame as in a greenhouse or hotbed.

What is Polythene? Polythene or Polyethylene is the name given to a plastic film which has the properties of permitting the passage of gases and retaining water vapor.

How is Polythene used in plant propagation? It is used in the same way as glass. Among the advantages as compared with glass are: its light weight; it usually eliminates any need for additional watering. It is also used to enclose the moist sphagnum moss when air-layering is practiced.

How can I make a propagating frame? An ordinary cold frame is satisfactory; or you can use a box 10 to 12 ins. deep, covered tightly with a pane of glass. Make ½-in. drainage holes in bottom; cover with 1 in. of peat moss, and put in 4 ins. of some rooting medium (such as sand or sand and peatmoss) packed down firmly.

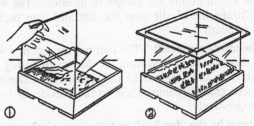

A miniature greenhouse for indoor use. Panes of glass, set around sides of a deep flat, are held in place by sand or compost in which cuttings are to be placed or seeds sown. A fifth pane of glass forms the "roof." By this simple arrangement moisture for the plants can be controlled.

A bulb pan or a flower pot, covered with an inverted glass jar, makes an excellent miniature propagating frame for the amateur gardener. In it cuttings can readily be rooted.

What are the essentials in using Polythene in rooting cuttings? Thoroughly soaking the rooting medium; and completely enclosing the cuttings. When only a few cuttings are to be rooted they are put in a flower pot which is then put in a Polythene bag and the open end is tightly closed. Or, on a slightly larger scale a shallow box (flat) can be used. In this case some kind of support is needed to keep the film from contact with the cuttings. It can be wire coat hangers or willow twigs. After the cuttings are inserted and have been thoroughly watered the whole is wrapped in plastic, taking care that no opening is left to permit the escape of moisture. The best way to do this is to drape the plastic over the flat and then tuck the sides and ends underneath it.

What is the after-treatment?   The cuttings are put in a well-lighted place where they can be shaded from the direct sun during the hottest part of the day. In six weeks or so they should be examined, and if they are rooted, gradually inure them to the outside air by loosening the cover progressively.

What is meant by the "fog box" or "constant mist" system of propagation?   This is a method whereby cuttings are rooted by keeping their leaves constantly moist by subjecting them to a fine mist-like spray.

I am interested in the possibilities, on a small scale, of rooting cuttings by constant mist. How does one go about it?   You will need a nozzle that will deliver about 1½ gallons of water per hour, and water pressure of 30 to 50 pounds. This should be sufficient to cover an area of about one square yard. The site should be in the open in full sun; if in a windy location a windbreak may be necessary which may be of plastic fastened to a wooden frame (about 4 by 3 feet). There must be free drainage, therefore the rooting medium should be coarse sand, and the pots or flats should be placed on a platform of galvanized hardware cloth raised an inch or two above the ground.

Is it necessary to keep the spray going all the time?   No, it is not—although no great harm will accrue if it is left on night and day. It is considered desirable however to have an intermittent mist. This may be accomplished by the installation of an electronic leaf which automatically shuts off the water when it is wet and turns it on when it is dry.

What are the advantages and the drawbacks of this method of rooting cuttings by constant mist?   *Pro.* It enables us to root larger cuttings than is possible by conventional means; and cuttings usually considered difficult often may be rooted with ease.

Con. on the other hand, while you may have a hundred percent rooting, there may be great mortality when they are transplanted. The operation was successful but the patient died! Doubtless means will be devised to overcome these defects.

Will you please tell me something about air-layering by using plastic film? This is a method that can be used successfully outdoors on a large number of different trees and shrubs. Here is the way of it. With a sharp knife cut a slit in a stem at the point where it is desired to have roots form. (Other ways of wounding the stem are to cut a small notch in the stem or to remove a cylinder of bark, about an inch long.) The wound is wrapped with a wad of moist sphagnum moss, which is tied in place with twine, preparatory to covering it with the plastic film which should be between 2 and 4 thousandths of an inch thick.

When is the best time to make the layer? This has not yet been definitely determined. Probably early spring.

Is it a foolproof method? It is not. Care must be taken to avoid getting the medium too wet. This involves squeezing out as much of the water as possible prior to applying the moss; also in putting on the wrap it is essential to ensure that no water gets in. Thus be careful to have the overlap on the underside; and see that the ties, both top and bottom, are made watertight by taping them spirally so that rain cannot seep in.

How does one know when to remove the layer? When roots are visible through the plastic. The removal of the layer is probably the most critical period. The layers, when they are rooted, should be treated for a time as though they were unrooted cuttings, by potting them, keeping them in a closed and shaded cold frame, and gradually hardening them off. (See page 261 for details.)

What is the best material in which to root cuttings? Sand is most commonly used, but recently a half-and-half mixture of peat and sand has become popular for almost all kinds of cuttings. Sifted coal ashes, sphagnum moss, decayed spruce or pine needles vermiculite and perlite are other materials used for special purposes.

Is there any special trick in inserting cuttings? Make individual holes with a pointed stick; or make a narrow trench by drawing a blunt knife or label through the rooting medium. It is important to be sure that the bases of the cuttings touch the rooting medium and that it is well firmed about them.

Is there any reason for cutting back leaves when inserting cuttings in wet sand? The reason for cutting back leaves is to prevent undue loss of moisture from the plant tissues by transpiration. Its value has been questioned by some propagators in recent years, and it is probably only necessary in the case of cuttings with very large leaves.

Why do professional growers use a powder when planting cutting in wet sand? Is this powder a talc, or some special powder? A root stimulant is used for the purpose of obtaining a higher percentage of rooting, to shorten the time required for the production of roots, and, in many instances, to obtain a bigger root system. Talc is sometimes the carrier with which small amounts of active chemical substances are mixed.

Which chemicals are used as stimulants for cuttings?   Many chemicals have been tried—indoleacetic acid, naphthaleneacetic acid, etc. —and others are under trial. Indolebutyric acid seems to be most generally used at present.

Why are acids used, and what kinds are used, to promote good cuttings?   Most cuttings root better in an acid than in a neutral or alkaline medium. Old-time propagators frequently added vinegar to water applied to cutting beds. (See answer to preceding question.)

Are chemical stimulants poured on sand used to root cuttings? Or are the cuttings kept in water?   The use of stimulants applied to the sand has not proved very satisfactory, and it is now customary to apply it to the base of the cuttings before they are inserted in the sand. The cuttings are not kept in water to form roots, but some of the substances used to induce rooting are made up in solution in which the base of the cuttings is allowed to stand for a given number of hours.

Can anyone use root-inducing chemicals?   As prepared for general use these can be very readily applied by anyone. The most popular are in powder form. The bases of the cuttings are merely dipped into this before being inserted in the rooting medium.

Is the use of commercial rooting preparations safer than the older methods?   Provided that the instructions of the manufacturer are strictly followed, the use of such preparations is quite as safe as the older methods, and in many cases a better root system is produced in a shorter time.

How do you treat cuttings started with the aid of chemical stimulants?   The treatment of cuttings after the application of the root-inducing stimulant is the same as for untreated cuttings.

What about the use of Vitamin B_1 and hormones in rooting plants?   Vitamin B_1 is probably present in sufficient quantities in any soil reasonably well supplied with humus, so that the addition of this substance is unnecessary (see also Section I), but in soils deficient in humus it may be of service. If by hormones you mean the substances now on the market for facilitating the rooting of cuttings, there is little room for doubt that they are a definite aid to propagation.

What is the general treatment of cuttings after they have been placed in a propagating frame?   Keep rooting medium moist and frame closed until roots have formed, then gradually increase ventilation to harden cuttings. Frame must be in a shady location, or shaded by a double thickness of cheesecloth on sash.

How can one know when a cutting has developed roots, and is

ready to be transplanted?   When it is judged that sufficient time has elapsed for roots to have developed, gently pull on 1 or 2 cuttings, and if they offer resistance it is a good indication that they have rooted. Most of the plants commonly rooted in summer produce a good root system in from 6 to 10 weeks. Many conifers, however, require as many months.

How are cuttings treated after rooting?   Those rooting early (July, August) are potted up, and the pots plunged in sand, peatmoss, or ashes in a cold frame, to be planted out the following spring. Late rooters may be left in the rooting medium. Both kinds should be protected by scattering salt hay, or similar litter, among them after first severe frost.

ROOT AND LEAF CUTTINGS

Can root cuttings be put in ordinary soil, or must sand be used? A sandy soil is desirable, as there is less probability of the root cuttings decaying, and a better root system is produced.

Rooted leaf cutting of sansevieria or snake-plant, with roots sufficiently developed for transplanting.

When are root cuttings usually made?   Usually late in autumn for hardy plants. They should be planted ½ to 1 in. deep in sandy soil, and kept in a cool greenhouse; or the flats may be stored in a cold but frost-free place.

Does it make any difference which end of a root cutting is inserted in soil?   Yes. In order to be certain that the right end will be uppermost, it is customary to make a straight cut across the upper end of the cutting and a sloping cut at the basal end. However, with thin cuttings (such as phlox), both ends are cut straight across and the cuttings are laid flat.

How many kinds of root cuttings are usually made? When true roots, as distinguished from underground stems, are being dealt with, there is only one type of root cutting. Such cuttings are usually from 1 to 3 ins. long, depending upon their thickness.

How are cuttings of fine, stringy roots made? Cut them into lengths of an inch or a little more and lay them flat in the container in which they are to grow.

Are root cuttings more sure than stem cuttings? This depends entirely upon the plant to be propagated. The roots of all plants do not produce buds, and in these cases it is useless to attempt to reproduce them by root cuttings. In those instances where past experience has shown that a plant will produce buds on severed root pieces, this method is generally a little less trouble than stem cuttings.

What type of plant is mostly propagated by root cuttings? Many plants can be raised from root cuttings. These include apple, pear, cherry, rose, blackberry, horse-radish, phlox, trumpetcreeper, daphne, locust, bouvardia, and many others. It must be understood, however, that if root cuttings are made of grafted or budded plants, it will be the understock that is propagated.

Are any indoor plants propagated by root cuttings? Not many of the more familiar house plants are propagated from root cuttings, but dracaena and bouvardia are sometimes increased in this way.

Will leaves make new plants if treated in the same way as stem cuttings? In some cases, yes. Among the plants commonly propagated in this way are African-violet, gloxinia, Rex Begonia, pick-a-back plant, and many succulents, such as the sedums.

Can all plants be propagated by leaf cuttings? No. Some will root—croton, for example—but never form a growth shoot. If, however, the leaf cuttings are taken with a growth bud and a sliver of the parent branch attached, they are successful in the case of most of the plants commonly increased by stem cuttings.

LAYERING

What is meant by layering? As generally understood, layering means bringing a shoot of the plant into contact with the earth with the object of having it form roots. Such shoots are slit with an upward cut, twisted, or girdled, either by having a ring of bark removed, or by encircling them with a tight wire, in order to induce the formation of roots at the injured part. This injured part must be covered with soil and kept moist.

How long before layers are ready to transplant? Many herbaceous plants will form roots in a few weeks. Shrubs layered in the spring will usually have a satisfactory root system by the end of the growing season. Some shrubs, such as rhododendrons and others that form roots slowly, require 2 years. After new roots form, the layers may be severed from the parent plant to become new plants on their own roots.

How many kinds of layering are there? Layering may be broadly divided into two classes: (a) layering in the ground, and (b) air layering. Class (a) may be divided into simple layering, serpentine layering, continuous layering, and mound layering. In all these ways it is necessary to bring the branches to ground level. Air layering

Some plants, such as the Strawberry-begonia or Strawberry-geranium (Saxifraga sarmentosa) multiply themselves by runners, which are easily rooted in pots while still attached to the parent plant.

(b) refers to rooting stems at points above the ground, by means of "layering pots" filled with soil; or by wrapping moist moss around the stem.

When is layering done? Spring is the best time, as in most cases a good root system will then be developed before winter. It may be done at any time, however, but in the colder parts of the country

New plants produced by layering. English Ivy (1) rooting at each joint or leaf node. (2) "Serpentine" layering, with stem covered at intervals, to induce rooting.

the roots may be torn off the layers due to winter heaving if plants are layered at a later period.

What is the best kind of wood for layering? If shrubs are to be layered, stout, 1-year-old shoots are preferred, as they form a root system much more readily than older wood.

How large should the layers be? Not so large as implied by the over-optimistic advertisements of dealers! If the layer is made in the spring it should, in general, be put at the base of the shoots made the preceding year; if it is a summer job shoots of the current season are preferred.

Is there a limit to the size of branch used in layering? For practical purposes, yes. The younger they are the more readily they may be expected to root. However, layering frequently takes place when large branches, many years old, come in contact with the ground, but it may take many years before they form a root system sufficiently large to support them independently.

SUCKERS; STOLONS; RUNNERS

How are plants propagated by SUCKERS? If the plant is not grafted and is a type that produces suckers (lilac, for instance), rooted suckers can be dug up, cut back, and planted to produce new plants.

What is a STOLON? A branch which grows downward and roots at the tip, where it comes into contact with the soil. When rooted, it may be detached from the parent, dug up, and planted, to lead an independent existence. Forsythia and matrimonyvine commonly produce stolons.

How are plants propagated by RUNNERS? Merely by digging up the runners when rooted. In special cases, to avoid root disturbance, small flower pots may be filled with earth and the developing runner fastened to the soil with a hairpin.

GRAFTING

What is meant by a "graft"? A graft is the union of parts of 2 plants in such a manner that they will grow together to form 1 plant. It consists of 2 parts: the *understock* and the *scion*. The union of these 2, by grafting, results in a new plant having the roots of one plant and the branches, leaves, flowers, and fruit of the plant from which the scion was taken.

What is double grafting? This refers to the practice of first grafting onto the understock a scion that will unite readily with it, and later grafting onto the first scion a second one of a kind that will unite with it but will not unite satisfactorily with the understock when grafted directly upon it.

Can any plant be grafted on any other plant? Only those plants that are closely related can be grafted.

What is a scion? A scion is one of the 2 parts necessary when making a graft, and consists of a short portion of stem of the plant that is to be duplicated. It usually contains 2 or more buds, and the base is cut in such manner that the cambium, a layer of actively growing tissue between bark and wood, or a part of it, will come in direct contact with the corresponding layer of the understock, which is cut to fit the scion.

What is meant by understock? The understock is the part that constitutes the root system of a grafted or budded plant. Seedlings, or pieces of root, or rooted cuttings, are generally used as understocks. It is the part to which the scion or bud is attached that is to become the new plant.

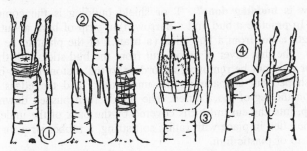

Grafting is an interesting operation which, with a little practice, the amateur can accomplish. Above are shown (1) bark grafting; (2) whip or tongue grafting; (3) bridge grafting; (4) cleft grafting. In each case the detail sketch shows how the scion (or bud wood) is cut.

When is grafting done? Grafting is usually practiced in spring, either in the open or in greenhouses, just as the understocks are beginning to break dormancy. The understocks should be beginning growth while the scions must still be dormant. For this reason the scions are buried in the ground or kept on ice until required for grafting. Summer grafting of some ornamental trees and shrubs is also practiced.

Why are plants grafted? To propagate horticultural varieties which do not "come true" from seed; to increase plants which are difficult to propagate by other vegetative means, such as cuttings or divisions; to modify growth of scion by use of dwarfing understocks, etc.; to hasten flowering; and to produce plants of special form as when "weeping" trees (mulberry, elm, etc.) are "worked" on a tall understock.

TYPES OF GRAFTING

How are ornamental trees grafted? In several ways, depending upon the plant being grafted. Splice, whip, veneer, and side graft are probably more commonly used than others, but saddle grafting and grafting by approach are other forms frequently employed.

What sort of roots are ornamental trees grafted on? Can any root be used? The kind or root that an ornamental tree is grafted on must be very closely related to it. Oaks cannot be grafted on elms, for example, nor beech on ash. Even in a group as large as the oaks, not all oaks can be grafted on just one kind of oak.

What is meant by BUDDING? Budding is a form of grafting by means of which a single bud and a portion of its surrounding bark are brought in contact with the cambium layer of a suitable understock.

How is budding done? T or shield budding is the commonest form. In practice a bud and a narrow, thin strip of bark about ¾ in. in length is cut from a bud stick (a branch of the plant to be propagated). The thin sliver of wood, cut from the bud stick with the bud, may or may not be removed, according to the custom of the budder. A T-shaped cut is made on the understock, and the edges of the bark on the leg of the T lifted. The bud is then pushed down, from the top, into the cut until it is covered by the bark of the understock. It is then tied in place with raffia, soft string, a rubber strip, or a narrow strip of plastic film.

What is a bud stick? A bud stick is a shoot, usually of the current year's growth, from which buds are cut for budding.

Why is budding practiced in preference to grafting? Because only 1 bud is required to produce a new plant, consequently a given amount of scion wood will furnish more buds than scions for grafting, as each scion would require about 4 buds. In the case of stone fruits, budding insures a better union than grafting. Also, since less time is consumed in budding than in grafting, it is preferred where suitable.

When is budding done? Budding is usually a summer operation, as it can be done only when the sap is running and the bark lifts easily from the wood. June, July, and August are the usual months.

How does grafting differ from budding? The principal differences are in the time of year when each is performed, and the amount of scion or budwood required. A graft consists of an understock and a scion; i.e., a short length of shoot containing 2 or more buds. In budding, an understock is also required, but in place of a scion a single bud is inserted on the understock.

Has the plant on which the bud is placed (understock) any influence on the budded portion? Very definitely in many cases. Weak-growing garden roses are much more vigorous when budded on a suitable understock than when on their own roots. Recently dwarf apple trees have attracted much attention. Such trees are dwarf because they have been budded or grafted on understocks that cause dwarfing.

What is BARK GRAFTING? The tree is prepared as for cleft grafting (which see) but the branches are not split. Instead, a slit is made in the bark, about 1½ ins. long, from the stub down. The scions are prepared by making a sloping cut at their bases, but a shoulder is cut at the top of the slope so that the lower part of the scion, which is to be pushed under the bark, is quite thin. Several scions may be placed on one stub, depending upon its size. On large stubs the scions may be secured with brads; on smaller ones they are tied in. All must be covered with grafting wax.

What is the purpose of BRIDGE GRAFTING? This form of grafting is confined to the repair of tree trunks (particularly fruit trees) which have been entirely or largely girdled by rodents. Its purpose is to maintain a connection between top and roots. Unless the girdled portion is bridged in this way the tree will shortly die.

How is bridge grafting done? Trim away ragged bark. Make longitudinal slits above and below wound and loosen bark. Cut scions (from the tree being operated on) of 1-year-old wood about 3 ins. longer than the wound. Bevel each end with cuts ½ to 1 in. long; bend scion in middle; insert under slit bark; fasten with small brads. Cover points of insertion with grafting wax. Scions should be placed every 2 ins. around the trunk.

What is CLEFT GRAFTING? Cleft grafting is one of the simpler forms, and involves the insertion of scions cut to a long wedge shape in a cleft of the understock. It is chiefly used in "making over" fruit trees and in grafting certain herbaceous plants.

What is the purpose of cleft grafting? The particular value of this form of grafting is in the conversion of unsuitable kinds of apples, pears, and sometimes such stone fruits as cherries and plums, to the production of fruit of better quality, or greater productiveness.

How is cleft grafting done? Cut back all branches to be grafted to leave a shapely tree; smooth over the cut faces; split each cut end with a grafting chisel. Cut scions with a wedge-shaped base about 1½ ins. long. Open cleft with end of chisel and insert scions, 2 in each cleft. See that the inner edges of bark on scions and stock are in contact. Tie in the scions on small branches; on the thicker ones this will be unnecessary. Cover scions and all parts of the cleft with grafting wax. If both scions unite, the weaker one may be cut off level with stump the following spring. At least one branch should be left to be grafted the second year, otherwise there will be an enormous growth of water sprouts.

When is cleft grafting carried out? In spring, as soon as the buds show the first indication of swelling. The scions must be completely dormant.

What is WHIP GRAFTING? The base of the scion is cut across with a downward, long, sloping cut, about 1¼ ins. long, then an upward cut ½ in. long is made on this face, commencing about ½ in. from the lower end of the first cut. The understock is cut in a similar way. Press the tongue of the scion into the cut in the understock until the one face covers the other. Tie together with raffia or soft string, and cover the union with grafting wax; or pack in moist material and treat the same as hardwood cuttings.

What is the procedure in whip grafting if the understock is much thicker than the scion? The first cut should be straight across. Then on one side of the understock, and near the top, cut off a strip of the same length and width as the cut face of the scion. Cut a tongue in it as previously described; tie; wax. Where scion and understock are not exactly of the same width it is most important that the inner edges of the bark of scion and understock *come in contact on one side* of the joint; otherwise they will not unite.

GLASS

COLD FRAMES

Should every garden have a cold frame? Not necessarily. Some gardens are too small for a standard-size frame. However, cold frames are a handy addition to the smallest gardens, even if there is space for only a 2 × 4 ft. frame.

How can I make a simple cold frame? Use a 12-in. plank for back, a 6-in. one for front. Make ends of one 6-in. plank and half a 6-in. plank cut diagonally lengthwise (to allow for slope from back to front) cleated together. Standard sash is 6 × 3 ft., so width of frame should be 6 ft. and the length made up of units of 3 ft. plus about 1¼ in. allowance between each sash to accommodate cross ties, usually 1 in. thick. Above specifications do not allow much headroom—a height of 9 to 12 ins. front and 15 to 18 ins. in back is preferable.

Can I make a cold frame in December? I have a large, dry cellar where I can thaw out the ground. It is possible to construct a cold frame of wood in December, and get the soil in place ready for spring planting.

I have been informed that plants will not do so well in a cold frame constructed with concrete walls instead of wood. Is this true? No, it is not true. In fact, concrete frames can be kept more sanitary.

How deep should the layer of cinders or coarse gravel be when preparing the soil in a cold frame? What should be the composition of the soil that is placed over the cinders; and how deep should it be? Cinders should be deep enough to allow for good drainage—usually 3 ins. or so. This would differ in various soils. In light, well-drained soil no gravel or cinders are used. Over this use about 6 ins. of a mixture of equal parts humus, garden soil, and sand.

How do you make a seedbed in a cold frame? If soil in frame is a sandy loam, spread a 2-in. layer of sifted leafmold and mix with the upper 6 ins. If soil is clayey, remove 6 to 8 ins. and replace with a screened mixture of sand, loam, and leafmold.

What should be added to the cold frame each year, and at which season should this addition be made? Well-rotted manure or leafmold shortly before plants are to be set.

CARE OF PLANTS

How do I go about starting plants in a cold frame? In March and April seeds of annuals and vegetables that can be transplanted may be sown, either in flats or directly in a bed of good, friable soil. Seeds of perennials may also be sown at this time. In June greenwood cuttings of some shrubs may be rooted in a few weeks if kept under rather close conditions and shaded from bright sun. In August seeds of pansy, forget-me-not, and English Daisy can be sown for early-spring bloom outdoors.

What is the best way to use cold frames (of which I have quite a few) to obtain maximum year-round efficiency? Seeds of perennials and biennials can be sown in cold frames in summer, and the seedlings transplanted and wintered over in same. A cold frame is also a convenient place in which to root greenwood cuttings of certain shrubs, inserting in sandy soil in June and July and keeping closed for a few weeks until rooted. A frame provides good conditions for seed flats of certain woody plants (as dogwood) over winter; also to winter stock plants of chrysanthemums and other perennials not reliably hardy. With the approach of spring sow certain annual flowers and vegetables for early planting outdoors. In April and May a frame is useful to harden off greenhouse-grown plants for a short time before planting out. Any vacant space in summer could be utilized for the growing of tomatoes, melons, and cucumbers.

Is it possible to get early blooms from bulbs and other spring plants in a cold frame? Pansies and forget-me-nots from August-sown seeds flower well in a cold frame in early spring. Good divisions of polyanthus primrose planted at the same time would also reward with nice flowers. The chaste flowers of Christmasrose open to perfection under cold-frame protection. Potted bulbs of narcissus, tulip, scilla, and snowdrop can be plunged in the frame in October to be brought out early in the year for flowering indoors if need be, or planted directly in the frame to flower in place. Leave the sash off until freezing weather threatens, and ventilate on all warm days during winter. In very severe weather it would help to have the frames banked outside with leaves, and the sash covered with mats or similar material.

Can violets be grown in cold frames for flowering in spring? Yes. Plant strong, field-grown plants in early September. Cover with sash for a few days to help them recover, keep moist but admit some air, and shade lightly from bright sun. When established, give all light possible and plenty of air until hard freezing weather. Put mats or some other covering over the sash on very cold nights, and ventilate on every warm day in winter.

Will you tell me how to operate cold frame with plants in pots and flats? Provide a bed of sifted ashes 4 to 6 ins. deep on which to stand plants during early spring. If to be kept in frame throughout the year, pots should be buried to their rims to conserve moisture in summer and help to prevent breakage from frost in winter. (See answers to preceding questions for general management.)

Why do I have such a hard time growing plants from seeds in cold frames, even though care and thought have been used? Plants grown in frames require more careful attention than when grown in the open. Correct soil, temperature, watering, *and especially* ventilation, all are of utmost importance. Attention to these should produce satisfactory results.

I have a cold frame. When the soil freezes do I fill it in with salt hay and close it for the winter; or do I have to give it ventilation on warm days? A light covering of salt hay put on plants when the soil freezes will give added protection. Ventilate on warm days. If the frame is vacant, a covering of hay or leaves will keep out some frost but is hardly necessary.

How would you manage a small cold frame containing little perennial seedlings and some very choice perennial slips for rooting during winter? See that the soil is moist before hard freezing. After this, lightly cover the plants with clean litter, such as salt hay or pine needles. Provide ventilation on warm days.

When plants are stored in a cold frame over winter, what protection should be provided? Cover with a mulch and then use a mat over the glass. Put a mulch around the outside of the frame.

Is commercial fertilizer good to put in a cold frame to give added heat? Commercial fertilizers are of no value in this respect. (See Hotbeds.)

HOTBEDS

What is the difference between a hotbed and a cold frame? A cold frame has no other heat than that provided by the sun. A hotbed is heated by fermenting material, electricity, steam, or hot water.

How can I make a medium-size, manure-heated hotbed to start early tomato plants? Assuming you have the frame complete, a pit should be made 2½ ft. below ground level and the same size as the frame. Then mix 2 parts fresh stable (horse) manure with 1 part unrotted leaves. Turn 2 or 3 times at about 4-day intervals, and moisten if dry. When well heated, place mixture in the pit in 6-in. layers, each one well packed, until there is a solid 2-ft. bed, or a little more. Finish off to ground level with 4 to 6 ins. of good, fine soil in which to grow the plants.

Is it necessary to line a hotbed pit? If soil holds together, and if only a temporary hotbed is required, no. Permanent hotbed pits are usually lined with concrete or boards.

I am planning to raise flower and vegetable plants for sale to gardeners. Which is the best way of heating my beds each 6 × 17 ft.? If this is a more or less permanent proposition, the installation of electric heating cable or of electric bulbs, arranged in series, would be the best if possible. A mixture of 2 parts fresh stable manure and 1 part leaves of the previous fall would be the best fermenting material. You can, however, raise good flower and vegetable plants for amateurs' gardens in just sun-heated frames.

I expect to start a hotbed March 1. Manure is available February 15 and March 15. How can I store the February manure so I can make use of it later? The manure you gather in February can be left piled, either indoors or out, for hotbed use in March.

When is the best time to start a hotbed in northern Vermont? Late March is soon enough. Put the sash on the frames before snowfall, so they do not have to be emptied of snow.

Does the depth of manure in a hotbed depend on climate? Yes, to some extent. Around New York City 2 ft. is the usual depth. Farther North 2 ft., 6 ins., is desirable; in the South 18 ins. or less is enough.

How much soil should be put over the manure in an outdoor hotbed? If seeds are to be sown directly in the bed, about 6 ins. of good, friable soil is sufficient. If to be sown in flats, then 1 in. or so of soil over the manure will do.

How does one know when a manure-heated hotbed is ready for sowing seeds? Stick a hotbed thermometer in the manure and close the frame. When the temperature *recedes* to 90° F. (it will go higher at first), it is safe to sow seeds.

Does the manure in a manure-heated hotbed have to be changed every year? Yes, it will not heat up a second time. Clear it out after the plants are removed and use it in the compost heap.

What can be used for hotbeds in place of horse manure besides electricity? Under certain conditions, such as where the frames are close to a greenhouse, it is possible to heat them with steam or hot water piped from the greenhouse system. Or a pipe may be run from the house heater if the frame adjoins the house.

Is there anything besides leaves suitable to mix with manure in the making of a hotbed? If obtainable, tanbark and spent hops give good results in prolonging the period of heat in a hotbed. Chopped cornstalks can also be used.

How, or in what way, are cornstalks used for a hot bed to take the place of manure for heating in the hotbed? Cut stalks into 1- or 2-in. lengths, wet thoroughly, pack in 2-in. layers to a total depth of 6 ins. in excess of depth when manure is used. Sprinkle each layer of 18 sq. ft. (area of standard hotbed sash) with ½ lb. cottonseed meal, ½ lb. ground limestone, and 3 oz. superphosphate. This increases heat and improves fertilizing value of cornstalks when rotted.

Can one raise hotbed plants without manure? In recent years electric heating cable or ordinary light bulbs, arranged in series, with thermostatic control, have often been used in place of manure for heating hotbeds. The installation is good for some years, and the disagreeable features of the old-time hotbed procedure have been eliminated. (See preceding queries and answers.)

When and how may a hotbed be prepared to supply a small garden in town? If obtainable, special electric heating cable is more convenient for city gardeners than fresh stable manure for providing heat in a hotbed. Where spring is slow in arrival, last half of March would be soon enough to start. If neither method is practical for you, sun heat alone would do for an early start in the frame, as compared to outdoor sowing.

Can glass substitutes be used successfully on hotbeds? Good plants have been grown beneath glass substitutes, but the sash must be in first-class condition, and may not be good for more than 1 or 2 seasons.

Is it necessary to ventilate hotbeds? Yes; every day except in severe weather. Tilt the sash on the side or end opposite to the direction from which the wind is blowing.

Are any special precautions necessary when watering seedlings in hotbed? Yes; because of humid air seedlings are specially vulnerable to attack by "damping-off" fungi. Water in morning, so that leaves dry more readily. Water only when soil begins to get dry.

Do hotbeds need any special protection during cold snaps? If started when freezing weather is still to be expected, the frames are usually banked with manure or coal ashes. When specially cold nights are anticipated, the sashes are covered with mats or boards as an additional protection.

How is it best to make a hotbed for seeds to be left outdoors all the year around if the seedlings should have to stay 2 or more years? In this case a cold frame will serve the purpose better than a hotbed. Depending on kinds, the seeds could be sown in the fall or spring, and the seedlings transplanted in the bed of the frame until ready to plant outside.

GREENHOUSE

HARDENING OFF

What is meant by "hardening off"?   The process whereby plants are gradually inured to change in environment.

Is it necessary to "harden off" plants before they are moved from greenhouse or hotbed to open ground?   Yes. A sudden change to more intense sunlight, lower humidity, and exposure to wind, is injurious to them.

How does one harden off plants which have to be moved from a greenhouse into the open?   By transferring them first to a cold frame, where they are gradually exposed to outdoor conditions by progressively increasing the amount of ventilation until, at the expiration of 10 days or so, the sash is entirely removed.

Potted plants which I place on my sunny terrace during summer have their leaves scorched when they're transferred from the greenhouse. Is there any way of overcoming this?   Ventilate greenhouse as freely as possible for a week before they are moved. Keep them in a partially shaded location outdoors for a week or so before putting them on the terrace.

EQUIPMENT

What essential equipment is needed in the small greenhouse?   Soil, leafmold, or peatmoss; sand; fertilizer; pots; flats; watering can; trowel; sprays and sprayer; labels; water.

WHAT TO GROW

I am building a small greenhouse. Will you give me information on early planting of vegetables and flowers to transplant for summer production?   Start about mid-February. Follow instructions given under annuals, vegetables, and propagation for details of planting. If house is to be heated, even though no higher than 45° F., chrysanthemums, azaleas, etc., and forced spring bulbs, could be used for fall and winter display.

I am building a 10 × 12 ft. home greenhouse. Can you give a few pointers as to what I can grow?   Assuming the minimum temperature is 55° F., the following could be raised from seeds: begonia, calceolaria, cineraria, cyclamen, primula. Obtain plants or bulbs from dealers of the following: acacia, azalea, camellia, Easter Lily, erica, gardenia, genista, gloxinia. Books on this subject include *The New Greenhouse Gardening* and *How to Grow Rare Greenhouse Plants,* both by Ernest Chabot, published by Barrows, and *Beneath the Greenhouse Roof,* by C. H. Potter, published by Criterion Books.

Which plants, besides geraniums, can be grown in a small home greenhouse maintained at 55° to 65° F., and also planted in borders during summer? Fuchsia, begonia, lantana, abutilon, acalypha, and heliotrope.

Which flowers are suitable for an amateur to grow in a small greenhouse for winter bloom? Among the easiest are calendula, stock, snapdragon, forget-me-not, daffodil, tulip, freesia, chrysanthemum, and buddleia. All of these grow in a night temperature of 45° to 50° F.

I have a glass-covered frame over the well which is outside of our home (east side); normally it is used to give light and air in basement. Will you advise which plants or vines might do well? Also what type of soil would produce best results? English Ivy; chrysanthemums could be dug up and potted when budded; also such annuals as carnation, petunia, and marigold not completely flowered out could be dug from garden to finish out the season. Begonia of the bedding type lifted and cut back would flower well in spring. Bulbs: daffodil, tulip, freesia, and amaryllis should do well. For summer, coleus. A good soil mixture would be 2 parts good loam, 1 part leafmold, ½ part sand; 5-in. potful bone meal to each bushel.

How can I start a small greenhouse, and which flowers are the most popular to sell? As this is a commercial venture you had better consult a book, such as *Commercial Floriculture,* by Fritz Bahr. Public taste varies in different locations. Your local florists are best fitted to inform you concerning most popular flowers.

Which plants, other than the little English Daisy and blue forget-me-not, would be suitable to raise in a small greenhouse for small corsages? What other flowers would you suggest? Ageratum, alyssum, babysbreath, candytuft, cornflower, lily-of-the-valley, linaria, lobelia, French Marigold, annual phlox, primrose, Sweetheart Roses, and verbena.

Which plants will grow most successfully in my small lean-to greenhouse (southwest exposure)? (There is no heat except what comes from cellar; it is cold nights, but warm during the day.) Chrysanthemums, Jerusalem-cherry, decorative peppers, hardy bulbs, herbs.

What can I grow in a practically unheated lean-to greenhouse? Strong specimens of various early-flowering hardy perennials could be dug in fall and potted or planted to flower well in advance of their season. Hardy bulbs; St. Brigid Anemone, Kurume Azalea, snap-dragon, calendula, stock, larkspur, clarkia, nigella, *Phlox drummondi,* and annual chrysanthemum should all do well. Early vegetables and choice rock-garden plants could also be grown.

Am unable to heat my greenhouse. What practical use can be made of it, if any? If span-roofed and fully exposed, perhaps best to wait until March, and then sow seeds of flowers and vegetables that can be transplanted for early start outdoors. If there are benches of soil, such plants as radish, beet, lettuce, and carrot could be sown and grown inside until big enough to use. During summer, chrysanthe-mums could be grown to finish before winter really started. Hardy, early-flowering plants dug and planted in fall would give earlier blooms than those left outdoors.

TEMPERATURES

What temperature should be maintained in a small greenhouse? Depends on what is grown. A minimum night temperature of 50° to 55° F. will suit a large variety of plants commonly grown.

At what temperature should a small greenhouse be kept to germi-nate various seeds, and at same time keep seedlings at right tempera-ture? For usual run of annuals and vegetables, night temperature of 50° to 55° F. with rise of 5 to 10° in daytime is about right. Seed pots or flats may be stood in propagating case, having slightly higher tem-perature until they germinate; or placed near heating pipes until seeds *start* to sprout.

Will you advise as to minimum night temperature acceptable for small greenhouse for winter growing of sweetpea, stock, snapdragon, calendula, and begonia? Fifty degrees. The sweetpea, stock, and calendula would do better at 45° F., the begonia at 55°F.

Is temperature of 65° to 70° F., maintained by hot-water heat, correct in a flower conservatory? Depends upon what is to be grown. For general-purpose house a night temperature of 50° to 55° F. (with a 5 to 10° rise in daytime) would be right.

We are keeping a coal furnace going in our one-wing greenhouse. How low can the temperature drop at night without harm to plants? Depends on what is being grown. Azalea, calceolaria, camellia, cine-raria, cyclamen, erica, genista, hydrangea, primula, violet, and many others can endure 45° without injury.

I have a greenhouse built alongside of my house at the basement windows. I use it for starting vegetable and flower seeds, and heat it with warm air from the basement through the windows. What tem-perature should I have in it? A night temperature of at least 45°, and better close to 55°, would be suitable. The day temperature would vary according to sun heat, but ventilation should be increased if it rises above 65°.

Is bottom heat more important than the temperature around the plants? It is under certain conditions of plant propagation, and for the growing of some plants under glass. For general culture it will not take the place of air temperature.

GENERAL CARE

What is proper soil mixture for flower seed sown in small greenhouse built off basement window? Want to avoid damping off. One part each loam and leafmold and 2 parts sand. A formaldehyde dust (used according to directions on container) may be mixed with the soil before sowing; or pots could be prepared and drenched with boiling water a day or two previous to sowing seed, to check damping off.

How is it possible to tell when soil in pots is dry? By sight, touch, and hearing. If soil looks dry, feels dry, and the pot "rings" when tapped with knuckle or stick, watering is necessary, provided the plant is in active growth.

How often should pot plants be watered? The correct answer is "when needed." The need varies with the kind of plant, its condition, and environment. When plants are in active growth, water when the soil appears to be getting dry; give enough to *wet the soil all through*.

What is the procedure in watering newly potted plants? Be sure the ball of soil is thoroughly moist at potting time. Water well immediately after potting, then wait until the soil is dry on surface. It is very easy to overwater newly potted plants. If they tend to wilt, syringing the foliage once or twice a day will be beneficial.

Is the amount of watering and damping down influenced by weather? Yes. On cloudy, moist days little is needed, especially if temperature is low. When it is sunny and dry, especially in winter when artificial heat is used, much more water must be applied to keep the air moist and plants from wilting.

Is there any way of cutting down on the need for frequently watering pot plants? Bury pots to their rims. Outdoors: in earth, ashes, sand, or peatmoss. Indoors: in cinders, pebbles, peatmoss, or sphagnum. If this is done, great care must be taken to avoid overwatering in damp, cloudy weather, and when plants are not actively growing.

How often should greenhouse plants be sprayed with water; and when? Tropical foliage plants can be sprayed every sunny day. This is an excellent prophylactic measure against insect pests. Generally plants in bloom should not be sprayed because of the danger of marring flowers. Spraying should be done in the morning, after plants have been watered.

How can humidity be controlled in a greenhouse? By careful attention to heating, ventilating, and wetting down of the paths and other interior surfaces, and the balancing of these factors to produce the desired result. A wet-bulb thermometer is useful to indicate the relative humidity.

Is it necessary to sprinkle frequently to keep air humid in greenhouse? Depends on what is grown. Cacti and succulents get along

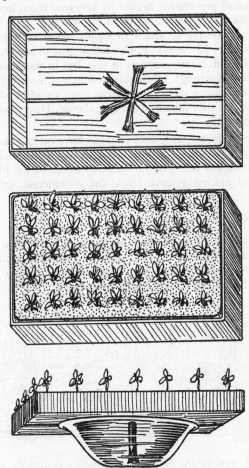

The "wick method" of keeping soil moist for seedlings or cuttings—especially useful where plants must be left to themselves for several days. Wick (made for this purpose) inserted through hole in bottom of flat is spread out in several directions; flat is then planted and placed over pan or pail, filled with water, which is drawn up by wick as soil needs it.

in dry air. Most cool-house plants—primroses, cyclamens, stocks, house plants, etc.—with moderate humidity, provided by sprinkling walks once or twice on dry, sunny days. Tropical plants from moist climates may require the sprinkling of walls, floors, and benches 3 or 4 times a day.

I have a small greenhouse heated by kerosene room heater, supplemented by thermostatically controlled electric heater. A large bucket of water is kept on top of heater to supply plenty of humidity. Temperature is kept at 55° to 60° F. Geranium growth is good, but leaves brown and fall off. Some progress in size, but in time the same thing happens. What is wrong? Probably insufficient humidity. Wet down floors once or twice a day. Fumes from your kerosene stove may be escaping into the atmosphere of the greenhouse. Have you a flue from stove to outdoors?

What direct effect, if any, does coal gas have on greenhouse plants? Am thinking of a small greenhouse heated by a small stove. Even minute quantities of coal gas will seriously injure or kill plants. If you have in mind placing a stove *inside* the greenhouse, drop this idea at once.

REPOTTING

When is the best time for repotting? For plants that are rapidly increasing in size, whenever the roots get crowded in the pots. For plants which have "settled down" and slowly increase in size, at the end of the resting season—usually midwinter or late winter.

A well-lighted bench corner assists materially in carrying on the various greenhouse operations.

When do plants need repotting? When pot is crowded with roots and available plant nutrients are exhausted. Also when, because of poor drainage, overwatering, or unsuitable soil, the roots are unhealthy.

How does one repot a plant? Prepare new pot by cleaning it and putting broken pots, small clinkers, or something similar in the bottom for drainage—from ½ in. to 2 ins., depending on size of pot, and the plant's need for quick drainage. Cover with ½ in. moss or fibrous loam. Remove plant from old pot by turning it upside down and tapping rim of pot on bench or table. Place in new pot at correct depth; fill around with new soil; tamp soil firmly with a potting stick—a small piece of lath will do. Surface soil should be a sufficient distance below rim for convenience in watering.

Would good soil brought from country and stored in boxes make good potting soil? Should box be kept inside or out of doors? Yes; but such soil may need modifying by addition of leafmold, sand, fertilizer, etc., according to needs of plants. Store inside only for convenience in use. Outside storage will do no harm.

REPOTTING A PLANT

Removing plant from pot. Rim of pot (1) is rapped sharply on edge of bench or table to remove root-ball; (2) root-ball is loosened up to remove some of old earth; (3) crock (drainage material) and more earth removed from bottom of root-ball. Plant is now ready for repotting.

Plant is placed in larger pot, partly filled with fresh soil, and (4) more soil filled in around it. Cross section of pot (5) with crock over drainage hole. Soil is tamped in firmly (6) around old root-ball.

VENTILATION

What about ventilation in a small greenhouse? Open ventilator daily, even if it is only a mere crack, for a short time. Avoid drafts by opening on the side opposite to that from which wind is blowing.

When air outside is warm and still, ventilate freely except when plants requiring high humidity are grown, when it is necessary to exercise discretion to maintain air moisture.

REST

How are plants "rested"? By lowering the temperature and reducing the supply of water to their roots. Northern plants become more or less dormant in winter; some (certain bulbs) in summer, as a means of tiding over summer drought. Certain tropical plants almost completely suspend activities during the dry season.

How can I tell when my greenhouse plants need rest? By close observation, and by reading up on the culture of specific plants. When a plant has grown actively for 6 to 9 months it may indicate its need for rest by yellowing and dropping leaves; example, the poinsettia.

For how long should plants be rested? Varies with the subject; amaryllis, October to February; poinsettia, January to May; tulips, May to November. These are approximate resting periods of some commonly grown examples.

INSECTS

I am growing vegetables under glass and have trouble with whitefly. What kind of fumigant is best to use? Have tried nicotine fumes. Surest control is hydrocyanic gas (a most deadly poison) generated by use of cyanogas. Use strictly in accordance with manufacturer's directions.

What is the best way to fumigate a small home greenhouse (8 × 12 ft.) with ground benches? Green aphids seem to have taken over. Fumigate with tobacco dust according to manufacturer's instructions. Be certain that fumes have no access to dwelling house.

SPECIFIC GREENHOUSE PLANTS

Are ABUTILONS easy to grow in a small greenhouse? Yes. Take cuttings from outdoor plants in September, or from greenhouse plants in February. Pot in ordinary soil. Pinch tips of shoots occasionally to induce bushiness. They like sunshine and temperature, about 50° F. at night. Can also be raised from seeds.

Can small plants of yellow-flowered "mimosa" (ACACIA) be grown in pots? Several kinds are well adapted for growing in pots in cool greenhouse (night temperature, 40° to 45° F.). Try *A. armata*, *A. pubescens*, *A. drummondi*, and *A. longifolia*.

What is the correct treatment for an acacia plant grown in a tub

in a greenhouse? Cut old flowering branches back to length of 6 ins. Retub or top-dress as necessary, using light, porous, peaty soil. Spray tops to encourage new growth. After danger of frost has passed place outdoors, with tub buried nearly to rim. Bring inside before freezing weather in fall. Keep cool. At all times give plenty of sun. Beware of dryness at root. Feed established plants during summer.

What is the proper way to winter an ALLSPICE tree? The all-spice tree (*Pimenta officinalis*) is not suited to outdoor growing where freezing temperatures occur. If the plant is in a tub, it could be wintered in a cool greenhouse or other suitable light place under cover, where the temperature range is between 40° and 50° F. Water only enough to keep the soil from getting bone dry.

How shall I plant and care for bulbs of AMARYLLIS (hippeastrum) in greenhouse? Pot bulbs firmly in porous loam enriched with dried cow manure and bone meal, using pots 4 ins. to 6 ins., according to size of bulbs. Leave top half of bulb out of soil. Keep nearly dry until roots form, then gradually increase water supply. Spray foliage with clear water on bright days. Temperature 60° to 65° F. at night, 70° to 75° F. by day. Give full sunlight until flowers appear, then light shade. (See also under Tender Bulbs.)

I would like to grow ANEMONES from seed for blooming in my greenhouse. How is it done? Sow in April or May. Transplant individually to 2½-in. pots. Grow in summer in cool, shaded cold frame or greenhouse (pots buried to rims in sand or ashes). Repot into 4-in. pots, or plant 6 ins. apart in benches, in September. Grow in cool temperature.

Will ANTHURIUMS thrive in a greenhouse where Cattleya Orchids grow well? Indeed they will. Both need humid atmosphere and a 60° F. temperature at night. Pot the anthuriums in a mixture of orchid peat, sphagnum, and charcoal. Keep moist at all times.

What greenhouse conditions best suit ANTIRRHINUMS (snapdragons)? Night temperature 45° to 50° F.; full sunshine; free air circulation; light but rich soil; 9 ins. to 1 ft. between plants in benches; or 4-in. to 6-in. pots; judicious feeding when in vigorous growth. Avoid wetting leaves. Pinch plants in early stages to encourage branching. Propagate by seeds or cuttings.

When should snapdragon seed be sown for fall flowering? For early-spring flowering (in greenhouse)? From middle to end of May for fall. Late August or early September for spring.

I saw the interesting and beautiful flowering vine, ARISTOLOCHIA ELEGANS growing at the Brooklyn Botanic Garden. I would like to grow it in my own greenhouse. Can you tell me how? Very easily. Sow seeds in light soil in spring and grow seedlings in sunny greenhouse where night temperature is 55° F. Prune plants back each spring, and top-dress or repot as necessary. Unlike some aristolochias this one is not evil-smelling.

Can you give me instructions for forcing spireas (ASTILBE) for Easter blooming in a greenhouse? Plant strong clumps in fall in pots just large enough to hold them; plunge in cold frame; bring indoors January or later; give plenty of water and grow in light position. They need from 10 to 14 weeks, in temperature 55° to 60° F., to bring them into bloom.

What treatment should be accorded greenhouse AZALEAS that are kept from year to year? After flowering, trim plants back lightly, repot if necessary (using an acid, peaty soil), and grow in temperature of about 60° F.; spray frequently to encourage new growth. Plunge outdoors, in sunny or partially shaded place, from June to September, then bring into cool house in light position. Never let plants suffer from lack of moisture in the soil.

I am greatly interested in BEGONIAS and, having acquired a small lean-to greenhouse, would like to grow a collection. What temperature, etc., should I maintain? Night, 55° F., rising 5 or 10° in daytime. Shade lightly during March, April, and September; more heavily from May to August. Ventilate to keep atmosphere buoyant rather than stagnant; damp down sufficiently to keep air fairly humid. Be sure to keep house clean at all times. (See also Begonia—Section VII.)

How can I grow BOUVARDIA? Propagat by stem or root cuttings in spring. Grow in sweet (slightly alkaline) soil that is well supplied with humus yet is porous. Give plenty of water during active growing periods. Plenty of sunlight is needed, and a greenhouse temperature of about 55° F. Keep plants pinched freely during early growth to make them bushy.

What soil does a BOUGAINVILLEA (grown under glass) require? If in a pot, a rich but porous soil is needed. If planted in a ground bed, a less rich soil is preferable. Good drainage is essential, and the soil should be coarse (not sifted) and loamy.

The florists' winter-blooming BUDDLEIA—how can I grow it in the greenhouse? There are 2 types—*asiatica* (white) and *farquhari* (light pink). Root cuttings in spring; pinch out tips of young growing plants to encourage bushiness; plunge pots outdoors in summer; use good, rich soil; feed when pot-bound. Bring into greenhouse before hard freeze, and keep cool; give plenty of sun and air. Never let them suffer from dryness.

I would like to have a succession of BULBS for my greenhouse. Which bulbs shall I buy, and how plant them? Paper-white Narcissi can be planted at 2-week intervals, from October 1 to January 1. Roman Hyacinths, at 3-week intervals, from September to December

1. Callalilies are constant bloomers. Plant amaryllis in November. Lachenalia planted in September will bloom for Christmas. Try veltheimia also. Plant tulips in November. (See also Tender Bulbs.)

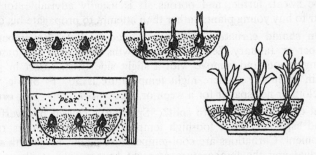

Tulips for indoor bloom: bulbs are planted with tips level with soil surface; stored in a cold frame, pit, or cool cellar for several weeks to form roots; brought indoors to cool temperature to start top growth; and then given higher temperature and abundant water to develop flowers.

Will you give instructions on raising CALCEOLARIA from seeds? Sow in shallow pans, well drained, using sand, leafmold, peat, and loam in equal parts, sifted through ¼-in. sieve. Firm soil, make level, sow seeds, and gently press them in with tamper. Moisten by standing pan in vessel of water for half-hour. Cover with pane of glass; shade with newspaper. When seeds germinate, tilt glass; remove entirely after few days. Keep cool.

What conditions are needed to grow calceolarias in the greenhouse? A well-drained soil that contains a liberal amount of humus, together with some cow manure and bone meal. Give free circulation of air; shade from strong sunshine; provide a cool, moist ash bed beneath the pots, uniform moisture, and a night temperature of 50° F.

How is it possible to force calceolarias into bloom early? I used to see them in full bloom at the Spring Flower Show in New York. By using electric light to provide supplemental illumination for about 5 hours each evening from November on.

I would like to grow some CALENDULAS for winter flowering in my greenhouse. Can you tell me how? Sow seed of good greenhouse strain in early August. Prick off seedlings into small pots, and later set out in benches (14 or 15 ins. apart), or pot into 5-in. pots. Use rich soil. Grow in full sun with night temperature of 45° to 50° F. Good air circulation is necessary.

Is it possible for me to grow CARNATIONS for winter bloom, along with other greenhouse plants? Yes, if the other kinds are chosen so that their needs are similar; however, carnations are usually at their best when grown in a house by themselves. They need full sunlight, free ventilation, and night temperature of 45° to 50° F. Soil must be sweet, fertile, and porous. It is usually advisable for the amateur to buy young plants rather than attempt to propagate his own.

When should carnation cuttings be made? Late November or December or January. Select strong growths from near the base of flowering shoots and remove with a slight side twist. Insert in sand bench in greenhouse where night temperature is 50° F. Shade with cheesecloth or newspaper for a week or two.

What causes carnations to split? Splitting is caused by overfeeding, and especially by a too-high temperature, which induces rapid development. Carnations are cool-temperature plants, so growth must be gradual and the temperature at night kept evenly at about 52° to 55° F.

What are important points for an amateur grower (with a small greenhouse) to bear in mind when growing indoor CHRYSANTHE-MUMS in pots? Secure healthy stock. Keep plants repotted as they grow (without permitting them to become potbound) until they are in their flowering pots. Feed after flower buds have set. Keep greenhouse cool (night temperature of 40° to 45° F.). Full sunshine is necessary.

What kind of soil is best for growing chrysanthemums in pots? A rich mixture containing plenty of mellow, fibrous loam, about a sixth part by bulk rotted cow manure, a good sprinkling of bone meal, a generous dash of wood ashes, and sufficient sharp sand to keep the whole porous. A sandier mixture, without manure or fertilizer, is preferred for the first potting of cuttings.

Can greenhouse chrysanthemums be planted in the vegetable garden in the summer and then be dug up in fall and transplanted to soil beds in greenhouse? Yes. Plant in fertile soil. Dig up carefully before severe frost (keeping as much soil on roots as possible), replant, and then water thoroughly. Shade from bright sunshine for a few days and lightly sprinkle foliage with water to prevent wilting.

Can large chrysanthemums be grown in a greenhouse, and at what temperature? List some names of large varieties. Cool (40° to 50° F.) greenhouse culture is best for large-flowered chrysanthemums. (See previous questions for culture.) Barbara Phillips, yellow; Henry Woolman, crimson; Louisa Pockett, white; Nagirroc, bronze; Vermont, pink, are good exhibition varieties.

How does one propagate greenhouse chrysanthemums? After blooming, old plants are cut back close to ground and stored in a light place (just above freezing). In January or February they are placed in temperature of about 45°, and young shoots, that soon appear, are made into cuttings when about 2 ins. long. These are inserted in sand propagating bench.

What culture is required for CINERARIAS? Sow seed June to September. Transplant to flats, later to small pots. Keep potted on as plants grow, using rich, porous soil containing fair amount of humus. Grow in full sunshine during winter weather, and stand pots on cool, moist bed of ashes. Keep moist; spray with water on sunny days. Grow cool (night temperature of 40° to 45° F.).

Do cinerarias need much feeding? They are heavy feeders; therefore provide rich soil, but do not use liquid fertilizers until they are well rooted in their flowering pots; then feed once or twice a week until flowers are open. Cease feeding when flowers open.

How is the fragrant, yellow-flowered genista handled in the greenhouse? Correctly named **CYTISUS** racemosus. After blooming, shear plants and repot, using sandy, peaty, fertile soil. Spray with clear water to encourage new growth, and grow in cool, sunny greenhouse. Plunge pots outdoors in sunny place through summer, and bring in again in fall. Night temperature of 40° to 45° F. Propagate by cuttings in spring.

Can bleedinghearts (DICENTRA spectabilis) be forced into bloom early in the small greenhouse? Yes. Plant strong roots in fall or winter in pots just large enough to hold them. Bury pots to rim in cold frame; about February bring into light greenhouse (temperature of 45° to 50° F.). Keep soil moist.

What soil and culture are required for EUCHARIS grandiflora (Amazon- or Eucharis-lily)? It needs tropical greenhouse conditions. Soil rich, medium, well drained. Must be partially dried off for a month or 6 weeks twice a year, to induce blooming. Feed generously with organic fertilizer when growing.

How can I grow the tender Maidenhair FERN in my little greenhouse? Adiantums are easily grown in a temperature of 60° to 65° F., if the atmosphere is kept humid. Pot in a sand-peat soil. Avoid wetting foliage, but keep soil evenly moist (except that plants may be rested by partially drying off for a couple of months in winter). Propagate by division in early spring.

Can I grow ferns in a conservatory? What is the best temperature? Ferns do well in a conservatory. Keep the temperature above 55° F., and the house shaded in summer. Adiantum, pteris, davallia, nephrolepis (in variety) are good kinds to start with.

When should I sow FORGET-ME-NOTS (myosotis) for blooming in greenhouse? Also hints on culture? Sow in May or June. Select variety recommended by seedsman for greenhouse culture. Transplant seedlings 3 ins. apart in flats. Later pot, or plant in benches. Grow in cool, airy conditions. Shade from strong sunshine. Keep soil always moist.

What causes GERANIUMS (pelargoniums) suddenly to turn yellow and then die? Gas in the air; poor drainage; overwatering; underwatering; or disease might cause this.

What is the best way to propagate geraniums that damp off or rot before rooting? Expose cuttings to sun for one day before setting in rooting medium. Water after planting, then keep on the dry side until roots are formed.

I have GERBERIAS that were raised from seed in my greenhouse; the potted plants are now nearly a year old, but have never bloomed. Why? Gerberias need rich, well-drained soil. Crowns should be just above soil level. Feed with liquid manure as blooming period approaches. Should be grown in cool house (night temperature of 50° F.).

Can you give me advice on how to raise and grow HYDRANGEA for blooming in greenhouse? Propagate by cuttings from February to May. Grow in light, well-drained loam in temperature of 50° and full sun. Pinch once or twice before June. Keep in cold frame, water freely, and spray foliage with water during summer. From September on keep drier, and just above freezing. Start into growth in temperature of 45° in January or February.

How is the LEOPARD-PLANT (Farfugium) grown? The correct name is *Ligularia kaempferi*. Ordinary greenhouse culture, or conditions that suit ferns or saintpaulia (temperature around 60° F.), shade, and high humidity; but avoid wetting the leaves much.

What is Russian Statice? Can I grow it in my little greenhouse? This is *LIMONIUM suworowi*. Sow seeds in September in sandy soil. Prick off seedlings into well-drained flats, and later pot singly into 4-in. pots. Grow in full sun, in temperature of 50° to 55° F. Be careful with watering and watch out for aphids.

I have a breadfruit plant, so called. Will you tell me more about this plant, and how to care for it? Probably it is *MEXICAN BREADFRUIT* (not related to real breadfruit) or ceriman— MONSTERA *deliciosa;* often sold as philodendron. Its fruits are edible. Prefers a warm, moist atmosphere, but will grow almost anywhere provided the temperature does not fall below 50°. When planted in good soil, it is a vigorous grower, climbing high on tree trunks by means of its stem roots. It succeeds well as a pot plant.

What treatment do Calanthe ORCHIDS require? Pot in spring in a mixture of fibrous loam, sand, and old cow manure, being sure drainage is perfect. Water with extreme care at first; more generously as roots take possession of soil. Shade spring and summer. Grow in warm temperature. Reduce water supply when foliage begins to die away in fall. After blooming, keep dormant pseudobulbs in warm, dry place until spring.

What kind of soil should I use for potting a Cattleya Orchid?
Soil (in the ordinary sense) is not used for epiphytic orchids such as cattleyas. Instead they are potted in osmunda fiber (the wiry-roots of osmunda fern). With a potting stick pack the fiber firmly between and around the roots. Recently, because of the difficulty of obtaining osmunda fiber, different materials have been tried as substitutes. Among the most promising are bark fragments or wood chips; the bark of fir and birch chips have proved to be satisfactory. One advantage of using bark or chips is that they make it much easier for the beginner to pot orchids.

Would an amateur be likely to have any chance of success in raising Dendrobium nobile from seed? No. The raising of orchids from seed calls for specialized skill and closely controlled environment.

I have some PALM tree seeds. Can you tell me how to plant these?
Plant in sandy, well-drained soil in 4-in. flowerpots (in flats, if quantity is large). Space seeds about 1 in. apart, and cover about ½ in. deep. Keep moist in temperature of about 70° F.

How are PANSIES grown for flowering during the winter in the greenhouse? Seeds are sown in July, and resulting plants are grown in cold frame until October, when they are planted in benches, or in pans of sweet, light, fertile soil. They are grown in a light, cool greenhouse, and flowers are picked promptly to prevent seed forming.

Which PRIMULA would you recommend for growing in a small home greenhouse (temperature of 45° to 50° minimum)? *Primula malacoides* (white, lavender, pink, red); *P. sinensis* (same color range); *P. stellata* (same color range); *P. kewensis, P. verticillata,* and *P. floribunda* (all yellow). It may be well to avoid *P. obconica* because it causes dermatitis in some people.

Will you give some pointers on growing greenhouse primulas?
Soil, medium loam with plenty of humus; grow in cool temperature; keep pots standing on layer of moist ashes; shade in summer-time; keep soil moist at all times, but not waterlogged; feed dilute manure water when final pots are filled with roots.

Can you tell me how to grow greenhouse RANUNCULUS from seeds? Treat exactly as greenhouse anemones (which see) from seed. Both like a porous soil that is well supplied with humus.

Can I force Crimson Rambler and other climbing ROSES into bloom early in my greenhouse? Obtain strong plants in November and set in pots just big enough to contain roots easily. Use medium-heavy, fertile soil. Bury pots to rim in deep cold frame. Bring inside, in January, to temperature at first 45°, later 55°. Spray with clear water to encourage growth. Water freely. No pruning necessary.

How should roses be pruned when they are potted, in fall, for spring forcing in the greenhouse? Tall-growing ramblers and climbers not at all, other than removal of any dead or broken growths. Dwarf polyanthas, hybrid teas, hybrid perpetuals, etc., cut back to within 9 or 10 ins. of base. Leave strong shoots longer than weak shoots.

Which varieties of roses are best for blooming in tiny greenhouse during early spring? Polyanthas, such as Ellen Poulsen, Gloria Mundi, Edith Cavell, and Orange Triumph; and miniature roses, such as Oakington Ruby, Pixie, Rouletti, and Tom Thumb.

Would it be practical for me to grow roses for cut flowers in a very small greenhouse in which I want to grow a good many other kinds of plants? Hardly. To grow cut-flower roses with even moderate success demands fair space and rather exacting conditions. Why not try a few plants in pots?

What makes the leaves turn yellow and fall off my miniature rose plant? Poor drainage in the pot; not enough light; too much water; too rich a soil; too high a temperature; red spider infestation, and black-spot disease—one or more of these may be responsible.

I would like to grow SALPIGLOSSIS in pots for spring blooming in the greenhouse. Is this possible? Quite practicable. Sow seeds in sandy soil in August; transplant seedlings; and later pot them individually. Beware of burying plants too low in soil. Water with care. Afford full sunlight and grow in temperature of 50° F. Fumigate with tobacco if aphids appear.

Would it be possible to grow a Bird-of-Paradise-flower (STRELITZIA) in a greenhouse built against my house? It should be. Healthy specimens need a large pot or tub, good drainage, medium-heavy soil, plenty of water, and feeding when pot-bound. They like abundant light and a night temperature of 50° to 55° F.

Can you tell me how to grow in winter the feathery STEVIA that is used for mixing with cut flowers? Propagate by cuttings taken from January to March. Keep plants potted on as one does chrysanthemums. Plunge pots outdoors from May to September, then bring into cool greenhouse (temperature of 45° to 50° F.). Water well at all times. Feed when pot-bound.

Are STOCKS good flowering plants for the home greenhouse? Yes. They can be grown either in pots or in benches. Sow seeds August to January, using rich, sweet soil. Finish in 4- to 6-in. pots. If planted in benches, set branching types 8 × 6 ins. apart; non-branching types closer. Grow in full sun and night temperature of 40° to 45° F.

Can you give instructions for growing SWEETPEAS in a greenhouse that has scarcely any artificial heat? Sow in October in sweet, moderately fertile soil, preferably in a ground bed. Rows should be 3 ft. apart. Thin plants to 6 ins. apart. Ventilate freely, and avoid encouraging too much growth until February. Provide strings or other means of support. Feed when flower buds form. They need full sunshine. They can also be grown in 10-in. pots (though not so well), using brushwood for support.

Trees and Shrubs

DECIDUOUS TREES AND THEIR CULTURE

WHAT TO GROW

How can I start an arboretum? Professor Sargent, first director of the world-famous Arnold Arboretum, used to say that in order to start an arboretum one should have a thousand acres of land and a million dollars' endowment. The best advice would be to consult some recognized arboretum authority to ascertain what can best be grown in the proposed locality, how much it will cost to plant and care for it, what future purpose will be best fulfilled by the arboretum, and how this can be accomplished most economically.

Which trees are undesirable on the home grounds because of their spreading, greedy roots? Maple, elm, and poplar.

Which food plants (shrubs or trees) can be used on a lawn of less than 1 acre, without detracting from the ornamental aspects? For beautiful blossom, any of the fruit trees. For added beauty of fruit, any of the showy-fruited apples and crabapples. If acid soil, blueberries for autumn color. For early-spring blossom and good jelly fruit, the flowering quinces. Hickories and black walnuts are very acceptable as ornamental trees.

Which tree would be a good companion for a magnolia in front of the house? If it is a Star Magnolia, the Arnold Crabapple might do well. If it is a Saucer Magnolia, a fringetree could be used.

Which trees can you plant close to the house to be sure their roots will not get into the drains? The kinds will depend upon soil and the amount of space you can sacrifice for shade. Avoid the following: elms, maples, willows, and poplars.

We live in the country. Our driveway is on the north side of the house and unprotected. Driveway is east and west. On which side of the drive should trees and shrubs be planted to avoid snowdrifts? On the side away from the house, providing the winds causing those drifts come from a northerly direction.

How near the house is it safe to permit an oak or elm to grow? An elm could grow nearer than an oak (say 10 ft.), for the elm has high, wide-spreading branches and would eventually top the house. The oak, on the other hand, would have wide-spreading branches nearer the ground and might have to be twice the distance from the house so that its branches would not interfere with the building.

Will maidenhair (ginkgo), and laburnum grow in the northeast? Yes.

DISTINCTIVE FOLIAGE

What tree can I get whose leaves have a silvery effect? Silky White Willow, 30 to 80 ft.; White Poplar, 30 to 70 ft.

We are going to buy a few more trees with handsome foliage. We already have a Hedge Maple and an American Beech. What else? English Oak, Black Oak, corktree, Fernleaf Beech, Honey Locust, especially the Moraine and/or the Sunburst varieties.

We do not like dense-leaved, heavy-looking trees, such as Norway maples. Prefer airy, delicate foliage. What do you suggest? Birch, poplar, Honey Locust, willow.

Are there any trees with distinctively tinted spring foliage? Not many. Here are a few: Katsura Tree (*Cercidiphyllum japonicum*); flowering cherries (*Prunus serrulata*); sourwood (*Oxydendrum arboreum*); some Japanese Maple varieties; Schwedler Maple, Purple Smoke-tree (*Cotinus coggygria var. purpureus*).

I should like to plant a few small trees with good autumn foliage. Will you name a few? *Cornus florida*, dogwood, and its varieties; *Cercidiphyllum japonicum*, Katsura Tree; *Crataegus phaenopyrum*, Washington Thorn; *Oxydendrum arboreum*, sourwood.

FAST GROWING

We would like to plant a good shade tree that would grow rapidly. Which of the following grows more rapidly: mountain-ash, Chinese Elm, Silver Maple, or Rock Maple? Chinese or Siberian Elm is the fastest, with the Silver Maple a close second.

Can you give me some idea of a fast-growing shade tree for about a 61 × 50 ft. back yard? The Siberian Elm, *Ulmus pumila*. However, it grows so fast that proper steps should be taken to prune it regularly and vigorously each year to keep it at the height you prefer.

Will you name some fast-growing trees for southern New England? Elms, especially the Siberian Elm, Red Maple, Silver Maple, pine, Red Oak, oriental cherries, and American ash.

Which tree of rapid growth is best to plant for shade about a new home? Goldenrain tree, Flowering Dogwood, Washington Thorn, apple if the house is small. Elms, Red Oak, and Sugar Maple.

What kind of shade tree should I plant that has a rapid growth, is well shaped, is comparatively clean during the summer, will not re-

quire spraying, and whose lower limbs, when mature, will not be less than 15 ft. from the ground?   Tuliptree (*Liriodendron tulipifera*) and Sweetgum (*Liquidambar styraciflua*) are favorites. Other good ones: sycamore, Scarlet Oak, and Pin Oak.

FLOWERING

Which small ornamental flowering trees would you recommend besides fruit trees and dogwoods?   Laburnum, silverbell, redbud, magnolia, goldenrain-tree, crabapple, flowering cherries.

What is a good tree to use on a small place: one which will not have too wide root spread?   Crabapple, magnolia, flowering cherry.

What type trees should be planted, on front of lot, for decorative purposes, where large trees are not desired because of their effect on the lawn? Are dogwoods, flowering cherries, etc., suitable?   Dogwoods and crabapples are both superior to flowering cherries for this purpose.

What kinds of trees can be planted in a pasture used by hogs (that they will not root out or eat)?   Hawthorn.

FRUITING—FOR BIRDS

Can you name a few small trees with decorative fruit?   *Cornus florida* (dogwood); *Crataegus phaenopyrum* (Washington Thorn), and *C. mollis* (Downy Hawthorn); *Sorbus aucuparia* (European Mountain-ash).

Which trees provide food for birds?   Cherries, mulberry, mountain-ash, hawthorn, small-fruited flowering crabapple, flowering dogwood, hollies, fringetree, buttonwood.

LAWN TREES

Which are the best deciduous trees for specimen lawn planting? Flowering cherry, weeping willow, Norway Maple, dogwood, American Elm, beech, and Moraine Locust. Among the fruits, apple is best, although crabapple is often used.

Will you name some lawn trees good for the windy southern New England coast?   Red Maple, Red Oak, poplar (especially White Poplar and Quaking Aspen), sassafras, White Willow, sourgum.

FOR SHADE

Can you suggest a shade tree nice for a back yard?   Canoe Birch; yellowwood.

What are the best deciduous trees to plant for shade on landscaped grounds?   Elm, maple, apple, red oak, European Birch, buttonball are good.

How does one identify the sex in shade trees?   The only certain way is to study the flower, when open. Those with flowers having both stamens and pistils are bisexual. Most trees, especially fruits, are of this type. Then there are trees like the hollies, willows, and mulberries which have only pistillate or fruiting flowers on one tree— these are the female or fruit-bearing trees. Staminate (male) flowers are produced on a separate tree. These latter are the male or non-fruiting trees.

CULTURE

SOIL

How should I prepare the ground for planting trees? Over a well-drained subsoil there should be, throughout the area, a foot of good topsoil. Beyond this, prepare individual planting holes for trees to a depth somewhat in excess of the depth of root balls or root systems. Remove any excavated soil of poor quality and improve the remainder with leafmold and some old manure.

Most trees and shrubs seem to grow poorly in my soil, which is very sandy. What can I do? Select kinds especially suited for light, very sandy soil. For any others work in, around their root spread, a liberal quantity of peatmoss, leafmold or humus and some old manure.

My soil, though well drained, is heavy, clayish. It bakes and cracks in summer. Will it do, generally, for trees and shrubs? You should lighten it by mixing into all planting areas, about a foot deep, a liberal quantity of fine cinders (not fine ashes). At the same time work in some humus matter (leafmold, peatmoss, rotted manure). In addition you might try a synthetic soil conditioner such as Krilium.

Few trees and shrubs succeed on my place, which adjoins a swampy tract. What can I do about this? The only cure for lack of drainage is to provide it. Either raise the level of your ground considerably, or limit your selection to those trees or shrubs which will accept the condition. Among these are aronia, *Azalea vaseyi,* blackalder, button-bush, gordonia, Pussy Willow, tupelo, Weeping Willow.

My soil is shallow, with hardpan beneath. Any special precautions when planting trees and shrubs? Before investing heavily in planting, break up the hardpan so that it will let water through. For the run of ordinary shrubs there should be a depth of about a foot of good soil; for trees, about 2 ft. Neglect of these things may greatly limit your success.

What will I plant in front of an apartment house, where the soil is "sour," of yellow clay, and the spot shady? Have tried several types of evergreens. An unpromising condition. In amply prepared pockets, try untrimmed privet, bush honeysuckle, or *Euonymus patens.* Or, in an elaborately prepared, acid, humusy bed, rhododendron and Mountain Laurel. If tree roots intrude, the prospects of success are poor.

What do I use to make soil acid? See Acidity—Section I. Three to 6-in. layer of oak leafmold, rotted pine needles, or acid peatmoss is one way of acidifying soil. Aluminum sulfate applied at varying rate (4 oz. to 12 oz. per sq. yd., depending upon the alkalinity of the soil and the degree of acidity required) is another, but generally less satisfactory, method. Flowers of sulfur can also be used making the initial application at the rate of 6 ounces per square yard.

Our soil is rich but moist and acid. What tree do you advise— something with good autumn color? Sweetgum (Liquidambar) would be a tree for you. The fall color is crimson. Red (Swamp) Maple, tupelo, pepperidge, or sour-gum (*Nyssa sylvatica*) are also appropriate.

TRANSPLANTING

Is fall preferable to spring for the planting of trees? Yes; with certain exceptions. Birch, redbud, magnolia, certain hawthorns, and all doubtfully hardy or notoriously finicky kinds are best set out in spring. Plant bare-rooted trees when the leaves drop. They will then continue to produce new root growth well into the winter, even under the frozen surface.

What is your opinion of winter planting? By this you probably mean moving in the depth of winter with a frozen ball of earth about the roots. This method is often used successfully by professional tree movers. For the average gardener, it should be avoided, because specialized equipment is needed to do the job successfully, except with very small specimens.

What is the advantage to be gained from a mass of fibrous roots? Ease of transplanting. Good nurserymen transplant their trees and shrubs regularly, thus inducing fibrous root growth. Or they root-prune their stock by dragging a U-shaped blade beneath the soil of the rows, thus severing wide-spreading and deep-penetrating roots.

Can all deciduous trees be moved with bare roots? Probably yes, if sufficient care is taken; but experience shows that some kinds— birch, dogwood, magnolia, oak, for example—are best transplanted with a ball of earth.

How large a tree can be transplanted? It depends upon the kind of tree. Fibrous-rooted, easily transplanted kinds, with trunk up to 1 ft. in diameter if proper machinery and equipment are available.

I have a shade tree 10 ft. high that I want to transplant. How do I dig it up? Dig a trench around it 18 ins. deep. If many thick roots are encountered, keep farther away from trunk. With a digging fork carefully pick away the soil from roots, moving it into trench. Sway top back and forth to loosen remaining roots, and transplant before they dry out.

When planting trees is it best to mound the dirt around them, or leave a pocket to hold moisture to soak down to the roots? Do not mound the soil. Have it flush with the grade when planting is completed. It will then probably settle a couple of inches below grade, which is proper. A slight, saucerlike depression is sometimes advisable to facilitate watering.

Is it necessary to cut back trees when they are transplanted? If so, how much? Not if they are balled and burlapped. If the roots are scant in relation to the top, reduce the lateral growths in the crown, leaving the leader unpruned. If roots and tops are balanced, pruning may not be necessary.

Is it desirable to wrap the stems of newly planted trees with burlap? How long does one keep the wrappings on the tree? It is excellent practice. The bare stem is the most vulnerable part of the transplanted tree. Keep the wrappings on as long as they can be tolerated. They will prevent sun cracks on the bark. Spraying with a liquid solution (Wiltpruf, Protex) is sometimes employed instead of wrapping.

Is it necessary to support the stem of a newly planted young tree? In wind-swept places, and where school children pass—yes. Before setting the tree, drive a stout stake into the center of the hole and snuggle the tree up to it. Fasten it by means of non-abrasive tape, crossed between stake and tree. Large trees are usually held firm by securing them with wires to 3 or 4 pegs driven in ground around tree several feet from it.

What should be done in the spring for fall-translated shade trees? Do what necessary pruning may have been deferred in the fall planting. Check over fastenings, and prevent chafing of the bark. Replenish the mulch if necessary.

How can I help my newly transplanted trees (large) to form a new and strong root system? If planted in proper soil, do not overfeed your trees, nor overwater. Keep a mulch at the base. Keep bandages on the stems. Prevent drying out of the soil.

When transplanting trees why do they shoot from the ground instead of the branches? When suckers appear at the base, and no growth develops in the top, there is trouble. It is probably due to root injury and failure to prune top.

Is it correct, in pruning newly fall-set shade trees of 5 to 8 ft. in height, to cut back the whip or leader 1/3 or more as most garden books recommend? Do not cut the leader back. When necessary, reduce competing growths so as to prevent the development of future crotches.

When planting trees in the fall of the year, when is the best time

to prune them? Practice varies. If roots and tops are well balanced, pruning (if any is needed) may be deferred till spring. If roots are scant and tops large, the top should be reduced; leave the leader untrimmed, but reduce side branches.

Should fall-planted trees be pruned? Not necessarily. If a tree has properly balanced roots and top, pruning, if any, may be deferred till spring. If the roots are scant or poor, tops should be reduced, retaining the leader and pruning laterals.

What is meant by "heeling in"? The *temporary* planting of trees or plants, close together, in a trench—with at least the roots covered, and properly watered. It serves to tide plants over an interval between their receipt and permanent planting. If so kept over winter, they should be laid in a little deeper (usually at an angle of 45°) and covered, over all, with a thick layer of straw, leaves, or other mulch.

We heeled in 150 tree seedlings in November, and the weather prevented us from planting them. Will they be ruined, or can they be planted in spring? It depends upon the kinds of trees and on the severity of the winter. It would have been much safer to have buried them, if deciduous, in a trench covered with a mulch of straw.

CARE

When shall tree food be given to shade trees? November and April are perhaps the best times to apply fertilizer, whichever month is most convenient to do the work.

How can I stimulate the growth of newly planted flowering trees? If the planting hole was well prepared no special stimulant should be needed until the trees are well established. However, it is good practice to put a mulch of manure on the soil over the roots in the fall.

How shall I feed an old tree which seems to be weakening? An old tree responds well to loosening the soil beneath and just beyond the spread of the branches. Do this in the fall, and put on a layer of 2 to 3 ins. of rotted manure. In spring incorporate this with the topsoil, in readiness for reseeding if need be. If this method is not possible, then make holes with a crowbar 2 ft. apart and 18 ins. deep. Distribute a complete fertilizer (such as a 10–6–4) in the holes and fill with fine soil. A fair application is 1 lb. for each inch of circumference of the trunk. Take measurement above ground-line bulge.

Three years ago I started a grove of various shade trees on a plot 100 × 250 ft. There are approximately 100 trees. I am keeping the place very clean of any weeds with a small power cultivator, thereby also loosening the soil for better penetration of rain. The trees seem to do well. But am I right in keeping the plot scrupulously clean? The longer you keep the plot cultivated the more vigorously you may expect the trees to grow, but as it is an ornamental plantation and the trees are now well established and growing to your satisfaction, you can sow it down to grass. This would slow down the rate of growth a little but otherwise would not be injurious.

What is the procedure to follow when watering trees? Give thorough soaking so that soil is moist to a depth of 2 ft. If necessary, loosen topsoil with spading fork to facilitate penetration of water. Or use a tool (obtainable from horticultural supply houses) designed to deliver water below surface by means of a hollow, pointed rod.

Why is it that after a spring and summer of heavy rainfall, the trees, including the oaks, this fall shed their leaves earlier than usual? This is one of the things about plants not always of easy explanation. Rainfall is not the only determining factor; temperature may be equally important, and a period of cold weather toward the end of the summer undoubtedly hastens leaf fall.

The grade has to be changed around my house, necessitating a "fill" averaging 2 ft. around a large oak tree. Will this harm the tree? It will probably kill it. (See following question.)

Can anything be done to help trees survive when grade over their roots has to be raised? Build a "well" of rocks around trunk, keeping it at least a foot away. Spread a 6-in. layer of coarse gravel on soil. Lay agricultural tiles in rows, radiating from well to outer spread of roots. Bring these to surface of the fill by means of tiles, set vertically, at end of each line. The purpose of all this is to admit air to soil in which roots are growing. Unless soil is exceptionally well drained it might be wise to install drain tiles, 2 ft. below original grade, to prevent roots from suffering from too much water.

How deep is it safe to raise the grade over roots of trees? Depends on the kind of tree and soil in which it is growing. Six inches probably would not harm surface rooters, such as elms and maples, especially if the soil and fill is porous. Willows and ash can endure even more fill than this. The statement has been made that trees can survive a fill of 8 to 10 ft. if protected by a dry well.

What can we do to stop a tree from bleeding? This depends upon the kind of tree and the cause of the bleeding. If it is merely bleeding due to pruning in spring such trees (for example, maples and birches) as should be pruned in summer, the bleeding soon stops. If it is due to "slime flux," it may be exceedingly difficult to control. (See Section VIII.)

What is used to treat a decayed hole in a tree? Is common cement used to fill hole after it has been cleaned out and treated? For sterilizing the cavity use copper sulfate, 1 lb. dissolved in 3 gallons of water; or bichloride of mercury, 1 oz. to 7½ gals. of water. (Both these substances are poisonous to animals and human beings.) Cement mortar or concrete is one of the materials used for filling.

Will the roots of trees affect a garden?   The roots of some trees are very objectionable. For instance, maples root right up to the surface of the ground, and elms are nearly as bad. Oaks and hickories are deep rooting and cause less interference with other plants. But the most serious objection to trees is to the amount of moisture they take out of the soil; and with it any soluble plant food in the vicinity.

How do you tell when a tree is bark bound?   Newer branches outgrow older portions. Bark seems tight and lifeless. To remedy the condition, scrape off the dead outer bark and scrub the trunk with soapy water. Some authorities suggest making a longitudinal slit through the bark with a sharp knife.

Does smoke from a smelter damage trees?   Yes. Trees growing near a smelter may be seriously injured or killed, particularly if growing in such a position that the smoke is constantly carried to them by the prevailing wind.

For what reason are the lower parts of trees whitewashed? Also when is proper time, spring or fall?   To prevent growth of moss and lichens, and to destroy insect eggs. But with the development of improved insecticides—which are much more efficient—it is little practiced nowadays. Early spring is probably the best time to apply it.

What is used to whitewash yard trees?   Lime and water. But why whitewash them? Its only value is for the destruction of lichens, as its use as an insecticide is now recognized as negligible.

How can I prevent seed formation on trees and shrubs?   By cutting off the dead flowers.

KILLING ROOTS

How can you kill tree roots growing in the sewers?   Dissolve 1 lb. or more copper sulfate crystals (poisonous) in hot water, and pour down a drain. If pipe is badly matted it must be cleared by plumber with roto-rooter machine. The copper-sulfate treatment will tend to prevent the return of tree roots; but the only sure remedy is to eliminate offending trees or install root-proof pipes.

Can you tell me a sure way of killing a large buttonball tree and stopping the roots from growing farther without cutting the tree down? I have girdled the tree, and filled holes bored into it with copper sulfate.   It should be unnecessary to do anything more to the tree; but to prevent shoots coming up from the stump, uncover the larger roots for some distance and peel the bark off them.

Is there any way to prevent elm tree feeder roots from spreading all over the lawn? I have heard that the United States Government recommends trenching the grass plot 12 × 36 ins. deep, and lining both sides and bottom of trench with tar paper. Will that work?   This will work for a time. It would be better to sink a concrete trench into the ground. The deeper it is, the less the opportunity for the roots to grow underneath it and up to the surface on the other side. It may be necessary to dig down beside such a barrier every 4 or 5 years and cut all the roots growing around it.

How can I prevent roots from shrubs in a neighbor's yard from taking over in a seeding bed of mine? They have become a very thick mat, stopping growth and preventing even digging tubers like dahlias. Dig a trench 2 ft. deep along boundary and install a barrier below soil surface. This may be a narrow concrete wall, sheet metal, or the asphalt-impregnated roofing material which comes in rolls.

How can one combat shrub roots where shrubs and flowers are in the same bed? Chop off roots annually in the spring with a spade or a lawn edger; or install barrier as described in previous question.

What season is best for ridding property of wild cherry trees and elderberry bushes; and what is the best method? If possible, grub them out by roots with mattock; or pull up with tractor in early fall and burn when snow is on the ground. If cutting down is the only practicable method for you, do so in summer and chop off sprouts as soon as they appear. This will starve roots.

How can I remove a wild cherry tree and not have some shoots appear later? This tree is on a lawn. Cut down tree, grub out stump and largest roots. Any suckers that appear will be cut off when lawn is mowed. The remaining roots will soon die if no foliage is allowed to grow to nourish them.

What can I use to kill out a large lilac bush; also a tree? Can be done by application of salt or commercial weed killers to soil; but as the tops and stumps will have to be removed in any case, to avoid unsightliness, it is best to cut them down and grub out largest roots.

I cut a hickory tree down to about 20 ft. from the ground. The tree is a foot in diameter. I would like to put a large birdhouse on the part that remains. What can I use to prevent the tree from sprouting from what remains and still have a strong pole for the birdhouse? Cut off a ring of bark at the base of the tree, or better still take all the bark off; the stump will then last longer.

What can you do when a neighbor to the south plants poplar trees and shuts off all sunlight along the entire lot line? Dig 3-ft. deep trench along lot line, cut off all roots encountered, install barrier of asphalt roofing material, and plant shade-loving material. Cut off branches projecting over your boundary.

How best can I kill a sycamore tree which is growing so fast that it shades our perennial garden? It is about 8 or 9 years old. Is there any chemical that can be used? If so, how? The safest way to kill the tree would be by cutting off a ring of bark about 6 ins. wide all the way around the trunk. Any chemical you might use on the roots would also kill any other plants near it. Why not take it out?

What is the best method to get rid of alder and alder roots so that we may greatly enlarge our vegetable garden? If there is much ground to clear, pulling them out with a tractor would be the cheapest. If there are only a few, then grub them out. Subsequent plowing would cut up the smaller roots.

How can old roots of large trees be removed from the ground when other trees are growing? If you attempt to take out the old roots there is sure to be some injury to the roots of the growing trees. The extent of the injury will depend upon how greatly the roots are intermixed. If the old roots must come out, dig them out with a grubbing ax. But it will do no harm to the growing trees if the old roots are left to decay.

Is there anything you can put on tree stumps to make them rot quicker? Drill holes in the stump with an auger, fill with saltpeter, or with sulfuric or nitric acid, then place stoppers in the hole. *Use with care,* as the acid will burn clothes or flesh when it comes in contact with them.

TREE AND SHRUB PROPAGATION

CUTTINGS AND SEEDS

How should I store oak and maple seeds over the winter? It is better to sow as soon as ripe. This is particularly necessary with some of the white oaks. Maple and some oak seeds may be kept until spring by mixing them with sand in a box (stratification) and covering them with 6 ins. of soil outdoors.

Can trees be started from cuttings? The percentage of rooting of many kinds is so small as to make this method impractical. (See Propagation, Cuttings, this section.)

What general procedure is followed in making cuttings of shrubs? Softwood cuttings are usually from 3 to 5 ins. long, whereas hardwood cuttings may be from 5 to 8 ins. long. Softwood cuttings must be rooted in a close, humid atmosphere such as that provided by a cold frame. Hardwood cuttings are taken in the late fall, after there have been a few frosts, stored in sand in a cool cellar (or buried in the earth) until early spring, when they are set in the open ground. (See also page 246, mist propagation.)

When making cuttings of shrubs and trees is the time of year, or the condition of the wood, the determining factor? Probably the condition of the wood is the more important, but as the most desirable condition occurs only at a particular time of year there is a rather narrow range during which the best results may be obtained.

SPECIFIC TREES

AILANTHUS

Of what special value is the ailanthus tree? It is useful in city back yards, where it grows rapidly and endures almost any soil conditions, smoke, and dust.

Why do some ailanthus trees give off a disagreeable odor when in flower? These are the male, or staminate, trees. The female, or pistillate, plants are inoffensive.

What is the ultimate height of the tree-of-heaven (ailanthus)? Sixty feet.

BIRCH

What is the difference between the Paper Birch and the Gray Birch? Paper Birch bark peels off in shreds; Gray Birch does not. Paper Birch has horizontal black marks on its bark; Gray Birch has triangular black patches. Gray Birch has softer wood, subject to fungous disease, and is comparatively short-lived (20 to 30 years), while Paper Birch survives more than twice that long.

Which species of birch has white bark and several stems that come from the ground? Gray Birch (*Betula populifolia*).

I bought some White Birch trees and when they came the bark was gray instead of white. Did they send the wrong trees? Probably not. When very young the bark is gray; turns white later.

Would a Weeping Birch make a good tree to plant in front of a house? No. This is a variety of the European Birch, all of which are susceptible to the pernicious bronze birch borer. The best birch is the Canoe or Paper Birch, native all over New England, and a splendid ornamental, very resistant to the bronze birch borer.

Are birch and sycamore trees suitable for shade on a small property? Birch trees would be better because they are considerably smaller. The sycamore takes a great deal of room. (See "What to Grow," this section.)

At what time of the year should Weeping White Birch trees be planted? (Missouri.) In the spring, if bare-rooted. In the case of large specimens, balled, burlapped, and platformed, autumn or winter should be safe in your climate.

When is proper time for transplanting birches? (New York.) In the spring, before growth starts. In the milder parts of the state, balled and burlapped trees may be moved almost throughout the winter.

Is it practical to plant White Birch in this locality (25 miles east of Pittsburgh, Pennsylvania)? Please give directions for type of soil, and any special care necessary to keep it healthy. Yes, it can be planted. All it needs is a good, well-drained soil, preferably on the sandy side. Susceptible to serious infestations of leaf miners which can be kept in check by spraying. (See Section VIII.)

Last spring we planted a 14-ft. Paper Birch tree (it was balled in burlap). It did not fully leaf out and was attacked by aphids for which we sprayed. The tree did not seem to do well. Is there anything we can do for it this spring to make it healthier? Birch trees do not transplant too readily, but if yours was properly balled it should survive. Try placing a mulch of old manure, peat, or leafmold over the surface of the soil occupied by the roots. Put this on in May, after the soil has had time to absorb some warmth.

What is the life span of birch trees? Can they be planted near fruit trees? Yes, the birch tree—especially the Paper or Canoe Birch (*Betula papyrifera*)—will live to be 50 to 75 years old or more. These trees do not send up suckers, nor do they harm fruit trees in any way.

Vandals have removed a cylinder of bark 6 or 8 ins. wide from my Canoe Birch. Will it harm the tree? Yes, if the inner bark has been removed. The leaves may start into growth because the sap passes up through the wood to the branches, but the roots will ultimately die of starvation because the food which nourishes them passes downward through the bark. If the injury is discovered early enough, it can sometimes be repaired by bridge grafting—which see.

If a young White Birch tree is pruned, do the branches need to be treated where pruned? It is unnecessary to paint wounds when they are less than ½ to 1 in. in diameter. Large wounds should be covered with tree paint or something similar to keep out moisture and spores of disease organisms.

Can White Birch be raised from cuttings? It is next to impossible to root White Birch from cuttings.

BLACKGUM

See Sourgum.

BUCKEYE

See Horsechestnut.

BUTTONBALL

See Sycamore.

CATALPA

What is the origin of the so-called umbrella tree? This is a dwarf form of catalpa (*C. bignonioides nana*), usually grafted or budded, at a height of 6 ft. or so, on straight, single-stemmed plants of *Catalpa bignonioides*.

I have 2 catalpa trees; bark is becoming loose and the part of one

top looks rather dead. Can I save these trees? Your description suggests root trouble, possibly due to poor drainage; or frost injury. Cut out all dead branches, and note whether the wood below the loose bark is also dead, for if it is you may have difficulty saving the trees. If the grade has been changed, this may have produced conditions unfavorable to the trees.

How do you prune an umbrella (catalpa) tree? It is the practice to cut it back annually if a formal effect is desired. Prune during the growing season; or in spring just before growth starts. It may, however, be left unpruned; then the head will present a more natural appearance and increase considerably in size over pruned specimens.

Should all the branches of the so-called umbrella tree be cut away in the fall? It is the usual practice to cut them in the fall, but this leaves an ugly stubby knob. If pruning has to be done, delay it until just before growth starts in the spring. (See preceding question.)

Is there any special way of trimming a catalpa tree if it has branched out too close to the ground? Mine is about 2 ft. from ground and the leaves are so heavy they smother the grass underneath. The lower branches may be cut off to raise the head of the tree. It should be done gradually, taking not more than 1 or 2 in any one year.

CHINESE ELM

How far apart and how close to the house should Chinese Elms be planted? How close to septic tank and drainage bed? Keep them some 25 ft. away from drains. If you have in mind a row of them, plant no closer than 25 ft. apart, and at least 20 ft. from the house. A single tree might be set closer to the house if for some reason that should seem desirable.

What is wrong when a Chinese Elm does not thrive? It is impossible to give a definite answer without more information. The soil may be at fault, but more probably you have not had it long enough for it to become established.

When and how should I prune a Chinese Elm, now about 10 ft. high, and very bushy, with lowest branch about 3 ft. from ground? Growing V-shape on top. If a high-headed tree is required, prune by removing 1 or 2 of the lowermost branches every year. This can be done in early spring before growth starts. It might be desirable to eliminate the "V," because of the danger of splitting, by removing the weaker of the 2 branches forming it.

How should I trim Chinese Elm trees for effective shade? Cutting back the tips of the main shoots will stimulate branching and thus make the head more compact to provide denser shade.

Will you give suggestions for pruning (not trimming) Chinese Elms

to globe shape and square shape?   When trees are trimmed to formal shape by shearing them, usually no further pruning is necessary.

I planted 2 Chinese Elms which have grown along entirely different lines. One grew very rapidly, with spreading, upright branches and sparse foliage. The other grew slower, with dense foliage, and has a tendency to droop, very similar to a weeping maple. Since I prefer the second, could you tell me whether there are 2 varieties, and the name of the second?   There are many variations in the Chinese (also called Siberian) Elms, unnamed as yet. Ask some nurseryman to propagate the one you like from cuttings.

CORKTREE (PHELLODENDRON)

What does a Chinese Corktree (phellodendron) look like?   It is a round-headed, wide-spreading tree. The leaves are compound, with 7 to 13 leaflets, aromatic and handsome.

ELM

What is the best time to put out American Elms?   Either in early spring or in autumn, after the leaves drop.

At what season should elm trees be trimmed?   During the growing season, if it is desired to check growth. Otherwise pruning may be done in the fall or late winter.

EUONYMUS

Can you tell me why euonymus does not have berries in the fall? It has white blossoms in the spring, and was supposed to have berries in the fall.   Euonymus species frequently perform in this fashion. They are probably alternate-bearing, like our fruit trees. It may also have been that weather conditions were such that when the pollen was ripe it was not distributed properly by wind or insects. Fertilize with a complete fertilizer containing ample amounts of available phosphorus and potash. This could be done in the very early spring.

GINKGO

For what special uses is the ginkgo suitable?   The ginkgo, or maidenhair, is quick growing, resistant to smoke and fumes, and therefore useful as a city tree. It is picturesque and erratic in its habit of growth and is remarkably insect and disease resistant. Autumn color is clear yellow.

Will you tell me something of the history of the ginkgo tree? How long has it been grown in this country?   The ginkgo, since ancient times, has grown about temples in China. It is sole survivor of a large group of plants with a long geological ancestry, perhaps unchanged for a million years. Is probably more ancient than any other tree except the Dawn Redwood, *Metasequoia glyptostroboides*. Introduced in this country in the early nineteenth century.

When and how shall I transplant 2 5-foot ginkgo trees, standing 4 ins. apart, with roots intertwined? In the spring, before growth starts. Try to untangle the roots. If you can do no better, save the roots of one intact and cut those of the other if necessary. Set as deeply as they stood. Water them well. Mulch the base, and prevent soil drying.

HONEY LOCUST

Is the Honey Locust good for the small place? I have recently seen one without thorns. The Thornless Honey Locust (*Gleditsia triacanthos inermis*) is a very desirable, lacy-leaved tree. It may, however, grow too tall for a small property. It is more slender than the common Honey Locust, which is undesirable under certain conditions because of the vicious thorns on trunk and branches and its habit of suckering freely.

HORNBEAM

What is the difference between the American and the European Hornbeam? The native tree reaches a height of about 30 ft. while the European one grows to 50 ft. and is more vigorous when young. The European is more treelike; the American tree is hardier North.

HORSECHESTNUT (BUCKEYE)

What is the difference (if any) between horsechestnut and a buckeye? Generally speaking, the horsechestnut has 5 to 7 leaflets in a cluster, while the buckeye has only 5. Also the horsechestnut attains greater height, and the fruits, flowers, and leaves are larger. We commonly think of *Aesculus hippocastanum* as "the" horsechestnut. This is a native of Europe. The members of the Aesculus genus native in America we commonly consider buckeyes.

Is the horsechestnut a good lawn tree? Yes, though rather untidy and, unless pruned to a high head, it is difficult to get grass to grow beneath it.

How long will it take for a 35-ft. horsechestnut tree to re-establish after transplanting? It is about 10 ins. in diameter at base. If successfully moved into a suitably moist, well-drained soil, it will probably take 2 years for the tree to resume approximately normal growth.

LARCH

We have a tree which looks like a pyramidal evergreen but loses its foliage in winter. What is it? A larch; probably the European Larch (*Larix decidua*).

Is the larch a desirable lawn tree?   Yes. The European Larch is best for lawns, while the American Larch (commonly known as tamarack and hackmatack) is best in low, moist places.

Would a larch tree make a good growth in rather heavy clay soil? (Ohio.)   Yes, it might grow well in a heavy clay soil, but it prefers a cool, rather moist atmosphere such as that of the lower mountainous regions of the northern and northeastern United States.

How and when should a larch be transplanted? (New Jersey.)   In fall or spring, with a ball of earth.

LIQUIDAMBAR (SWEETGUM)

In the late fall I purchased from an Ohio nursery a sweetgum or liquidambar tree 10 ft. high. It was then covered with bright red leaves, beautiful fall coloring. Here it has not shown any fall coloring, only a drab yellow; why? (Pennsylvania.)   It should have a western exposure and plenty of available nitrogen to make vigorous growth. Often it takes several years after transplanting to really "reach its stride." Soil conditions often affect coloring.

MAPLE

I would like to have a maple tree but haven't much room. What shall I select?   The Hedge Maple is comparatively small, its leaves are handsome, but it casts a rather heavy shade.

What kind of hard maple has reddish or purplish leaves all summer?   The Schwedler Maple has a reddish tinge to the foliage throughout the season. Crimson King is a new variety said to be an improvement on Schwedler.

What kind of maple is Acer negundo?   Commonly called Box Elder or Ash-leaved Maple; this is a large, rapid-growing tree which withstands cold, dryness, and strong winds.

Will you please tell me the common names of the following maples: Acer circinatum, A. macrophyllum, A. floridanum, and A. grandidentatum?   1. Vine maple; 2. Bigleaf Maple; 3. Florida Maple; 4. Bigtooth Maple.

In what kind of soil and location do HARD MAPLES thrive?   In any not utterly sandy soil of fair quality; not too acid and well drained.

I have a maple tree facing northwest, which gets a lot of wind. The branches are very short and high up. Can you advise how to get a fuller and shadier tree?   It is probable that on the windy side the branches will always be shortest, as it is so exposed. You might try feeding it with a good tree food, or mulching the ground under the branches with manure.

What is best time to transplant maple trees about 12 to 15 ft. high?

In the spring, before growth has started; or in the autumn, after leaves have dropped.

My maple grows very thick and casts too dense a shade. How can I overcome this? Thin out superfluous branches during the summer months. Do this in such a way that the tree has a pleasing branch pattern. In some instances you may find it necessary to cut branches up to 10 ft. long. Always make the cuts close to the parent branch.

How can the top 6 ins. of soil be kept clear of roots of a 30-year-old hard maple? This is a surface-rooting tree, and there is no means of preventing the roots coming to the surface without injuring the tree in the attempt.

How hardy is JAPANESE Red Maple? What sub-zero temperatures can it endure? Probably cannot live through consistently sub-zero winters.

What location and what kind of soil should the Japanese Maple have (the cut-leaved variety)? A well-drained, open situation and a light loam of fair quality, but not necessarily rich. Mulch the soil around newly planted trees.

Would you recommend covering with burlap my Japanese Red Maple tree? (New York.) If you do not mind the appearance, this is a good idea. Japanese maples are subject to winter injury. They may stand uninjured for a number of years, and then some abnormal winter condition will cause one side of the tree to die.

My Japanese Maple has unsightly, withered leaf edges. I am told that the soil isn't right. Is that so? Condition is probably caused by sunscorch during the period of soft spring growth, at which time the leaves are extremely sensitive. All you can do is provide some slight protection from the brightest sun in the spring.

How can one root cuttings of dwarf Japanese Maple? Take cuttings in June and place them in a shaded cold frame or glass-covered box. Unless you have had some experience with the propagation of plants you may not be very successful. Usually propagated by grafting.

What is the NORWAY Maple like? A large, massive, quick-growing tree with big, dark-green foliage. It creates a shade so dense, and its roots are so greedy, that practically nothing can be made to grow under it.

When is the best time to plant Norway Maple? As soon as the ground has dried off and warmed up so as to be thoroughly workable; *before* the trees start into growth.

When is the best time to cut large lower limbs on Norway Maples? Should cuts be painted? If so, with what? As soon as the leaves have fallen; or in summer. When the wound has dried, paint with shellac, tree-wound paint, or white lead and linseed oil.

Why does a RED MAPLE tree turn green in the summer? This is quite normal for some varieties.

When is the proper time of year to prune an ornamental Red Maple tree? In the spring. If it is a matter of promoting bushiness and checking growth, shoots may be shortened during the growing season.

I have a SILVER MAPLE tree on which the leaves dry up before fall. One other Silver Maple tree on the same place is all green. What may be the reason? Probably a difference in soil or moisture conditions. However, it may be due to a leaf blight.

I should like to transplant some SOFT MAPLES. How much should they be pruned? It would depend upon the relative proportions of roots and tops. If roots are scant and coarse, reduce the length of side branches, leaving the leader intact.

What causes the bark on a large soft maple tree to split and hang in tatters? Apparently the tree is otherwise healthy. It is natural for the bark on old soft maples to peel off; this need cause no alarm, provided the bark immediately below that which is peeling is in good condition.

When and how does one plant and care for SUGAR MAPLE trees? Where can they be bought? Sugar Maples may be purchased (by that name) from many nurseries. Plant in the spring, before growth has started; or in autumn after the leaves have dropped. They require no special care or coddling and will thrive in any well-drained soil of fair quality.

MOUNTAIN-ASH

What can be done to make mountain-ash produce more berries? Does it need a special soil? Mountain-ash or rowan-tree (*Sorbus aucuparia*) will grow well in any reasonably good garden soil. However, if your trees have reached the age where they may be expected to fruit heavily, and fail to do so, they may be in need of fertilizer.

Would the mountain-ash be hardy here where dogwood trees are not? (Northern Maine.) Yes.

How close to house can I plant a mountain-ash tree? I want its shade to fall on roof of sun parlor. As close as is consistent with comfort and convenience. As close, if you wish, as 5 or 10 ft. It would develop more perfectly if set at least 15 ft. away.

Is a mountain-ash 6 ft. high easily transplanted in the fall? (New Jersey.) In New Jersey—yes.

I have a 3-year-old mountain-ash. Would moving harm the tree; and could you advise as to the best time? Move it in the spring. Dig the entire root system. Have the hole large enough to accommodate it in a natural position. Water well, and place a mulch about the base.

Why doesn't my mountain-ash, age 5 years, bloom? If your tree is healthy, it should bloom within the next year or two. When the growth is very vigorous, blooming is sometimes delayed; but it is too early to worry about that on a 5-year-old tree.

What treatment will encourage bloom on young mountain-ash trees? As they get older they should flower more freely, but there is no treatment that will insure equally free flowering every year. Whatever the age of the tree, in some years it will flower more profusely than in others. Make sure the supplies of phosphates and potash in the soil are adequate.

Why does my mountain-ash have a tree full of blossoms but only about 10 clusters of red berries in the fall? The tree is 6 years old. Weather conditions at flowering time may have been too cold or too wet, so that only partial pollination took place.

My mountain-ash is weak. I fed it last spring with Treewiz. Bloomed with heavy crop of seeds, then became thin. When may I prune? Some branches are weak and broken. It is in an open northeast location. The production of a heavy crop of seeds is a severe drain upon the resources of a tree and may account for the appearance of thinness. Feed it at least after every heavy fruiting. Cut out the broken branches immediately. Any other pruning should be done in spring before growth starts. Have you looked for borers in the trunk? (See Section VIII.)

I planted a small mountain-ash tree this summer. The branches are long and growing more perpendicular than I like. Would pruning help? If so, when should it be done? Shorten the young shoots about ½ in late winter. During the growing season, if any shoots show excessive vigor, pinch out their tips.

I know that the berries of mountain-ash are bright orange, but what are the blooms like? Broad clusters of creamy white flowers in May.

OAK

Which are the fastest-growing oaks? Red Oak and Pin Oak.

How can I identify the different oaks? Black (*Quercus velutina*), bark very dark brown; inner bark orange; leaves to 10 ins. long, 7 to 9 ins. broad, toothed lobes, shining dark green above. White (*Q. alba*), very light bark; leaves to 9 ins. long; 5 to 9 rounded lobes. Red (*Q. rubra*), leaves to 9 ins. long; 7 to 11 pointed lobes, indented halfway to middle; pale beneath. Scarlet (*Q. coccinea*), leaves to 6 ins. long; 7 to 9 very deep, pointed lobes; bright green. Pin (*Q. palustris*), pyramidal form; lower branches drooping; leaves to 5 ins. long; 5 to 7 oblong, pointed lobes; bright green.

When is the best time to transplant oak trees? In the spring, before growth starts.

Why must a Pin Oak be transplanted in the spring only? Practice indicates that bare-rooted Pin Oaks are better planted in the spring only. Balled, burlapped, and platformed trees are often moved successfully in the fall or winter.

When and how should a small oak, grown from seed, be transplanted? In the spring, before growth commences. Dig out the whole root system. Have the hole wide enough to accommodate it; water the soil thoroughly; place a mulch at the base and see that the roots do not lack moisture at any time.

When is the proper time to transplant 5-year-old oaks; and how? In the spring, before growth starts. (See preceding question.)

In transplanting Red Oak trees is it wise to cut the tap root? When transplanting oak trees not previously transplanted, it is inevitable. Young trees may survive it, but old trees will resent it and are, therefore poor planting risks.

How should I feed a Pin Oak? Put a 3-in. mulch of manure over the root area, in fall or spring.

What does my soil need to make White Oak leaves turn red in the fall instead of just drying up? Also, my Pin Oak leaves turned brown with very little of the normal red. White Oak leaves seldom turn red—usually purplish—in the fall. Pin Oak leaves should turn a brilliant red some seasons when climatic conditions are just right. If your tree has a full western exposure, has plenty of nitrogenous fertilizer, and the weather is just right, it should turn the desired red. But the reasons vary considerably from year to year, some years resulting in "good" color and other years being decidedly "poor."

PEPPERIDGE

See Sourgum.

PLANE

See Sycamore.

POPLAR

During heavy, wet, unseasonable snow, when leaves were on trees, several Bolleana Poplars with trunks over 4 ins. in diameter broke off and had to be trimmed 'way down. What trimming shall I do on upright branches from low side branches? Paint wounds; leave upright branches to develop.

What time of year should Lombardy Poplars be topped? Ordinarily Lombardy Poplars are not planted in situations where it is necessary to cut off their tops. If it has to be done, they may be cut back at any time without injury. Cutting back during the growing season checks growth; during the dormant season it promotes strong, leafy shoots.

How can I choose new leaders for some Lombardy Poplars which lost their tops due to a severe wind and rain storm? Select the strongest shoot near to the top and center of the tree, to make new leader. Cut off the splintered stub just above the shoot. Make a slanting cut which will shed rain, and paint the wound.

SASSAFRAS

Is it easy to transplant sassafras trees from the wild? This interesting tree, with large, various-shaped leaves which turn brilliant yellow, rose, and scarlet, is not easily transplanted. Choose trees not more than 10 or 12 ft. high.

My yard has numerous sassafras trees growing. Do they have any ill effect on the soil? No. They are desirable trees, especially when they reach maturity. Picturesque in winter because of its gnarled branches; very wind resistant.

SOPHORA

What is the sophora tree like? What is its common name? *Sophora japonica* is called Japanese Pagoda-tree or Chinese Scholar-tree. It has a rounded top with leafage which suggests the locust and casts a light shade. In summer it has small, yellowish-white, pealike flowers in large panicles. Hardy as far north as Massachusetts. Though it may attain a height of 60 ft., it remains small for many years.

SOURGUM (NYSSA SYLVATICA)

I am told that a Sourgum, (also known as Blackgum, Tupelo, and Pepperidge) would be appropriate for a place with poor drainage. What is this tree like? In silhouette when young a little like Pin Oak. Slow-growing, moisture-loving, attaining a great height; very hardy; distinguished tree; noted for scarlet, crimson, and copper foliage in autumn; difficult to transplant.

SYCAMORE (PLANE, BUTTONBALL)

Sycamore, planetree, or buttonball tree—which is the correct name? All three common names are used for sycamore.

What is the best plane tree for city streets? London Plane (*Platanus acerifolia*).

What is the difference in appearance between the bark of the American Plane and that of the London Plane? When the bark is shed the trunk of the American is white; the London Plane is yellowish.

Are the plane trees, buttonballs and sycamores the same? Yes. Sycamore is primarily the term used in forestry.

What is the rate of growth of a plane tree? When young, averages about 2 or 3 ft. of growth in height each good growing season.

Does London Plane prefer spring or fall planting? What are best soil conditions?   Plant in early spring or in the fall. It will grow well in any good soil.

Does the plane tree shed its bark untidily?   Yes; but the white inner bark thus disclosed is definitely decorative.

Can a sycamore root about 3 in. in diameter growing out of slope be removed without harming tree?   If the tree is well provided with roots on the side away from the slope, cutting off the root should not hurt the tree. As soon as the cut surface is dry, cover it with tar or hot asphalt.

When is the best time to cut large lower limbs on sycamore?   This may be done in late winter or early spring before growth begins. It is not advisable to cut off more than 1 or 2 limbs at one time because of the danger of promoting excessive sappy growth.

TULIPTREE (LIRIODENDRON TULIPIFERA)

Which tree is it that grows tall and stately and has cream, green, and orange tulip-shaped flowers in June? In autumn the coloring is yellow.   Tuliptree (*Liriodendron tulipifera*). It does not flower, however, until it has attained good size—probably 10 years or more after planting.

Is it possible to grow tuliptrees in northern New York State?   Near Rochester and Buffalo—yes. In the upper Adirondacks—no.

How shall I prune a tuliptree that was transplanted this spring, having 3 or 4 new shoots at the base? The original tree died.   Before growth starts in the spring remove all shoots but the strongest. Avoid leaving any stubs which might decay.

TUPELO

See Sourgum.

WILLOW

What is a good willow (not weeping)?   White Willow (*Salix alba*).

When is the best time to move a willow tree?   In the spring, before growth starts.

Can a 4-year-old WEEPING WILLOW be moved from one side of lawn to the other side without injuring the roots?   It can be moved safely, but not without cutting some of the roots. This will not be serious. Willows move easily in moist soils.

How far should a Weeping Willow tree be planted from a sewer? Are their roots a particular menace to sewer pipes?   At least 25 ft. or 30 ft. away. Their roots are very likely to be troublesome.

Will the roots of willow trees damage concrete pits, septic tanks, or drilled wells? I am anxious to plant a pair near these things and have

been told that the roots damage underground constructions. The roots of willows will enter the tiniest crevices where they may obtain moisture, and unless all joints are screw joints or are filled with lead you may have considerable trouble in a few years.

Is a Weeping Willow tree self-pruning? I notice all the small limbs have dropped off; or is this caused by a disease? Many willows shed some of their twigs annually by the development of what the botanist calls "abscission layers." Probably this is what your tree has been doing. Not a disease.

SPECIFIC DECORATIVE FLOWERING TREES

CHERRY

Are there flowering cherry trees whose leaves unfold brown and then turn green? Yes. Among these are Sargent Cherry with single pink blossoms, and Kwanzan (*Prunus serrulata lannesiana*) with double pink ones.

Which flowering cherry trees have white and pale pink flowers? Try 2 beauties, Naden with semi-double fragrant blossoms in pink and white, and Shirotae with double white flowers.

I once saw a cherry tree blooming in autumn. What was it? It must have been Autumn Cherry (*Prunus subhirtella autumnalis*), pink, which blooms in spring and again sparingly in the fall.

What is the best way to propagate Nanking Cherry (Prunus tomentosa)? Either from seeds, which should be stored cool, 40° to 50° F., in moist sand over winter; or from cuttings taken in July and placed under a bell jar; or in a cold frame kept closed until roots are formed.

CRAB, FLOWERING

Can you recommend a few decorative crabapple trees? Arnold Crab (*Malus floribunda arnoldiana*), pink and white blossoms, yellow fruits; Carmine Crab (*M. atrosanguinea*), blossoms red-purple-pink, red fruits; Toringo Crab (*M. sieboldi*), pink to blush flowers, fruits orange-yellow; Sargent Crab (*M. sargenti*), white blossoms, dark red fruit.

I have a sunny space alongside my house about 10 ft. wide. Will you recommend a flowering tree that will not spread too much and will not grow over 20 ft. tall? Any one of 20 different kinds of crabapples.

Would you advise spring planting of flowering crab? Yes.

What is the best way to move flowering crabapple trees 3 ins. in diameter, about 8 ft. high? Balled, burlapped, and platformed—

preferably in the spring; but safe enough in the autumn, after the leaves have dropped.

Where should a BECHTEL CRAB TREE be planted? What kind of soil and drainage? How to prune, if at all? Plant in good soil with good drainage and plenty of sunlight. Needs little (if any) pruning —only the removal of diseased or broken limbs.

What is the care of Bechtel Crab trees? Need no special care except the application of a dormant oil spray every few years if scale is bad in your area, and elimination of cedar trees if cedar-apple rust is prevalent.

Why doesn't my Bechtel Flowering Crab bloom? It is 10 ft. tall and a nice tree. It will bloom—all crabapples do eventually. It is simply that in some soils it takes longer than others. Try applying super-phosphate, 6 oz. per sq. yd., and forking it into the soil under the tree in the fall or early spring.

I have planted a Bechtel's Crabapple, 3 ft. high. Does one prune it much the first year? Assuming that it was pruned at the time it was transplanted (by cutting it back about ⅓), further pruning is not likely to be necessary except for the removal of dead branches.

What care does the DOLGO CRAB tree need in winter? No more care is needed than would be given an apple tree. A mulch of manure spread around in the fall would be helpful.

Is there any way of preventing a flowering crabapple from increasing in size too rapidly, without loss of the flower display? Yes. Shorten young shoots each season, about ½ when they are ⅔ grown.

DOGWOODS

Does the Flowering Dogwood tree come in any color except white? Yes, there is pink or rose form listed as *Cornus florida rubra*.

What is the Japanese Flowering Dogwood like? Similar to our native flowering dogwood, but the flowers (bracts) are pointed instead of blunt. The Japanese species (*Cornus kousa*) blooms a few weeks later. The berries grow together in a head and seem, from afar, to resemble cherries.

Should soil for dogwood be acid or alkaline? It grows well in both, if not extreme. Slightly acid preferred.

What is the best fertilizer for dogwoods? How applied and when? Flowering Dogwood (*Cornus florida*) is usually planted in spring. In such cases mix a 10–6–4 with a good compost at the rate of 4-in. potful to a wheelbarrow of soil, and use this to fill about the ball of soil. Thereafter, if necessary, fall applications of 10–6–4. A 4-in. tree (diameter of trunk) will need 10 lbs. applied over the area covered by spread of branches and a little beyond.

I have been told that white Flowering Dogwood (Cornus florida)

would not bloom if planted in an unprotected place, but only if in a wooded place. Is this true? (Michigan.)   This may be true in the colder parts of Michigan, where the wooded areas give it winter protection and prevent its buds from winter killing from too severe cold. Farther south the dogwood will do well either in the open or in wooded areas.

When is the best time to move dogwood from the woods to a garden?   In the spring only—before growth starts.

Should the pink dogwoods be planted at a different time from the white kind? (Kentucky.)   Both white and pink dogwoods can be planted at the same time. Transplant with a ball of earth—not bare root, unless plants are very young.

Are dogwood trees, 3 to 4 ft., hardy in northern New York?   In Rochester and Buffalo—yes; but in the Adirondacks these trees are frequently subjected to such low temperatures that winter killing results.

How soon after transplanting wild dogwood do they bloom?   From 1 to 5 years, depending on the size and age of the plant and the growing conditions.

What would cause a white dogwood to show only 2 bracts to a flower, every flower, every season?   Winter injury—the outside bracts being killed or stunted by severe weather. Also there may be individuals in which this is characteristic. Such specimens should be replaced with normal plants.

What makes all the buds fall from my white dogwood in the spring? They set perfectly in the fall, but just drop off.   They are frequently killed by severe winters. This is especially true in New England.

Can dogwood be grown in this section? Our soil is alkaline. My tree had about 6 leaves on all summer. (Utah.)   Give it the best garden soil you have available. Mix acid leafmold with it. The chances are the summers are too hot and the winters too cold for Flowering Dogwood (*Cornus florida*) to amount to very much in many sections of Utah.

I have a white dogwood tree 5 or 6 years old. Appears to be very healthy, but does not blossom. What should be done?   Merely have patience; and try working superphosphate into the soil about the roots.

My pink dogwood has faded to a dirty white. Is there anything I can fertilize with and bring back to original lovely pink?   Possibly a heavy application of a nitrogenous fertilizer would help. It might be that the pink-flowering part has died and you now have the white-flowering understock left in its place, since pink dogwoods are usually grafted plants. If this is the case, and the understock only remains, it will never have pink flowers.

What is the treatment to insure blooming of red dogwood?   Every well-established Flowering Dogwood should bloom if the soil is normal. If it does not, a 3-ft. ditch 18 ins. deep could be dug around the tree several feet from the base. Superphosphate should be mixed with the soil as it is returned to the ditch. This treatment frequently results in aiding the flowering of dogwoods, and of wisterias.

A transplanted twin (2-stemmed) wild dogwood bloomed for the first time this year. When is the proper time to cut the shoot or twin which does not bloom?   Any time, preferably just after flowering. However, both branches will bloom eventually.

When is the best time to prune and transplant a dogwood tree? Ours has small flowers, and is getting too large. The branches have fallen over the ground and rooted themselves. Can I use these in any way?   Dogwoods can be pruned either in the spring or fall, but are most easily moved in the early spring. The branches that have rooted can be cut off and transplanted, and in this way should make separate plants.

When can native dogwood trees be trimmed?   Any time; preferably just after they are through blooming.

What winter protection should be provided for very young dogwood trees?   Mulching the roots with peatmoss or rotted manure would help the first year or two.

Is it true that there are 2 kinds of dogwood trees—male and female? No; dogwood flowers are "perfect," having both stamens and pistil in the same flower. They are borne in clusters and form the center of what commonly is considered the dogwood "flower." The large "petals" are really bracts or modified leaves surrounding the clusters of the tiny *true* flowers.

Is it difficult to grow dogwoods from seed? (North Carolina.)   No. Sow 1 in. deep in late fall; protect carefully from mice; and leave outdoors all winter to freeze. Germination will begin in spring, and may continue for a year. Transplant when 4 ins. high.

Will pink dogwood tree seedlings bloom true?   Probably not. They should be propagated either by grafts or budding to insure the young plants having the identical characteristics of the parents. These are termed asexual methods of propagation. Propagation by seed is the sexual method.

Can I propagate pink or red Flowering Dogwood from seeds? The seedlings are not likely to be red-flowered. The usual method is to graft scions of a colored form on seedling understocks of the common flowering dogwood. Layering is practicable if it is possible to bend the branches down to earth to root them. (See Propagation.)

RUSSIAN OLIVE (ELAEAGNUS)

See Shrubs.

FRINGETREE (CHIONANTHUS)

Is the Fringetree native? What is it like? Yes. This tree or large shrub bears loose, shredlike tassels of fragrant green-white flowers, in May or June, and has glossy tapering leaves. Male plant has larger flower trusses, but female has plumlike fruits in September.

GOLDRAINTREE (KOELREUTERIA)

Is there any tree I can get that has yellow flowers? Goldraintree and laburnum, which see.

I want to try an uncommon flowering tree. What do you advise? Please describe same. The Goldraintree (*Koelreuteria paniculata*) is a small, decorative tree with rounded top. Large panicles of small yellow flowers bloom in July or August. In September it has papery pods, and the foliage turns bright yellow.

Would a Goldraintree be appropriate on a small informal place? We like yellow blossoms. (Mid-New England.) Excellent, if given a sheltered location; otherwise branches may be killed back during severe winters. It likes full sun.

GORDONIA

What is the Franklinia alatamaha, also known as Gordonia alatamaha? A beautiful shrub or small tree originally from Georgia. Introduced to cultivation in 1790 by John Bartram, who discovered it on one of his plant-collecting trips to the South; it has since never been found in the wild. It has handsome, glossy, bright green leaves about 5 ins. long. In autumn its foliage turns orange-red and it bears cup-shaped, fragrant white flowers to 3 ins. across, with handsome golden anthers. A large specimen in Bartram's Garden near Philadelphia was long supposed to be the only living specimen. All other specimens in cultivation are believed to have been propagated from the Bartram tree, which is now dead.

Does the "lost tree" (gordonia) have any special requirements? Mine does not grow well. It prefers a moist but well-drained soil. Not reliably hardy inland far north of New York City.

Does the Franklin-tree (gordonia) require an acid or alkaline soil? There is a conflict of opinion on this point. Usually it is considered that an acid soil is preferred, but some have found that it responds to an application of lime.

Is Loblolly Bay (Gordonia lasianthus) hardy in Pennsylvania? Probably not. Native from Virginia to Florida. *Gordonia alatamaha* (see previous questions), if sheltered, may be hardy to Massachusetts.

HAWTHORN

What color are the flowers and berries of the hawthorns? To choose a few popular kinds—Washington Thorn and Cockspur Thorn have white flowers; English Hawthorn has several varieties, single and double, varying in color from white to scarlet. These all have red berries, the Washington Thorn bearing the most decorative ones.

What is a May Day Tree? Perhaps you mean the May-tree of England, which is a hawthorn, either *Crataegus oxyacantha* or *Crataegus monogyna*.

Do you need 2 trees to make hawthorn bloom? No.

I transplanted a hawthorn tree in November. Is it natural that the leaves should die in a few days? I cut back all the tips of the branches at the time of transplanting. If planted with bare roots (which would be hardly advisable), then any leaves left on the tree would promptly wither. But this would not be harmful so late in the season.

What is the reason why a very flourishing pink hawthorn tree starts to shed its leaves in early August and has new leaves and even blossoms in September? Can this condition be corrected? The fact that the hawthorn sheds its leaves in August suggests that the tree has been attacked by spider mites, or by a leaf blight. For the spider mites use diluted miscible oil as a dormant spray; for the blight, use Bordeaux mixture. See also Section VIII.

When should red hawthorn trained on a wall be pruned? It should be pruned, after flowering, by shortening new shoots as they are produced during the summer. The following spring, before growth begins, thin out some of the weakest shoots if they appear to be crowded.

How shall I prune my Paul's Double-Scarlet Hawthorn? If it is growing vigorously, and you wish to keep it within bounds, shorten the leading shoots in July. If growth is weak, cut out branches in late winter, having in mind the desirability of maintaining its interesting branch pattern.

LABURNUM

I saw in June a small tree that had flowers like wisteria, only yellow in color. What was it? Goldenchain Laburnum (*L. anagyroides*).

How hardy is the Laburnum vossi? This is now called *Laburnum waterei;* probably the hardiest of the laburnums. However, it is not reliably hardy much farther north than New York City.

Will you describe necessary soil, exposure, and give any other suggestions for culture of "Golden Tree," which I understand is a variety of laburnum? (Massachusetts.) These trees prefer a sandy soil, not too acid, which must be well drained. Protection from cold winds is also necessary.

Will you give some advice on the culture of Laburnum vossi? I have had difficulty growing this tree. This should not present any difficulties provided it is growing in a well-drained position. (See previous question.) Do aphids attack it? If so, spray with nicotine whenever they are present; otherwise they may completely ruin the new growth.

MAGNOLIA

How can I learn about every species of magnolia?   Would suggest *Magnolias,* by A. G. Millais, published in 1927 by Longmans, Green & Co., New York.

Are Magnolias fraseri, macrophylla, kobus, and soulangeana lennei hardy in Pennsylvania?   Yes. All these should be hardy in Pennsylvania except in the coldest areas.

Are the following varieties of magnolias good for southern New York: M. glauca (Sweet Bay), M. acuminata (Cucumbertree), and M. hypoleucea (Silver Magnolia)?   Yes.

Would any magnolia trees be hardy north of New York City? Would their leaves be evergreen?   Leaves would not be evergreen. The Cucumbertree, the Saucer Magnolia, and the Sweet Bay (or Swamp Magnolia) are hardy in Boston.

Will a magnolia tree grow around Woodridge, New York? Certainly. The Star Magnolia, the Cucumbertree (*Magnolia acuminata*), or any one of several varieties of the beautiful Saucer Magnolia should all do well.

Sweet or acid soil for magnolias?   Slightly acid, pH 6.5

When is the best time to transplant magnolias?   In the spring, even during, or immediately after, the flowering period. Move with as good a ball of fibrous roots as it is possible to obtain.

Should a small potted magnolia tree be kept growing in the house in sunny window for the winter, to be planted outdoors in the spring? Do not attempt to keep the magnolia growing through the winter, as it requires a rest at that time. Keep it in a cool cellar or garage, but do not allow the soil to become entirely dry. It may be planted in the garden in the spring.

When may I move magnolia trees from woods to garden, and what treatment should be given?   In the spring. The Cucumbertree (*Magnolia acuminata*) is not easily transplanted from the wild. Get as many of the fibrous root ends as possible. Have the hole wide enough to accommodate them. Mulch the soil over the roots. Wrap the trunk with burlap, and spray tops with Wilt-pruf *before digging.*

What are the "rules" for growing magnolias?   Magnolias require rich soil, therefore the addition of cow manure is advisable. While they require a moist soil for best results, it is equally important that it be well drained. For most, a position with full exposure to the sun is desirable.

Will you give the year-around treatment which would be best for the growth of Magnolia soulangeana in my locality? Particularly the establishment of young trees. (Pennsylvania.)   Once the plants begin to grow satisfactorily after they are planted in the garden they require little in the way of extra attention. A mulch over the roots, particularly a mulch of cow manure, will feed them and keep the roots cool in summer.

How can I get results with a magnolia in this district? (Pennsylvania.)   The Star Magnolia is the easiest to grow and is also the hardiest. If it is given a good soil and a dormant oil spray applied in case scale appears, it should do well. The many varieties of the Saucer Magnolia (*Magnolia soulangeana*) can also be grown with no particular attention other than the supplying of good soil.

Our Magnolia soulangeana, planted in October, had scant bloom and very few leaves the following spring and summer. Will it survive? We mulched with cow manure in fall. What else can be done?   Magnolias frequently make very little growth during the year after they are transplanted. Mulching is beneficial. For the first winter at least, protect from sun and wind with a screen of burlap, evergreen branches, or boards. It should make good growth after the first year.

What can I do to make a magnolia bloom? I have had the tree for 5 years and it is 7 ft. high and grows well, but has never bloomed. Our soil is sandy.   It is possible that you have a seedling of one of the tree magnolias, in which case it may be 3 or 4 or more years before the tree blooms. As the growth is satisfactory, do not worry.

I have a Magnolia soulangeana which was in bloom when I bought it from the nursery; it bloomed the next season but hasn't bloomed for two seasons. What should be done?   Magnolias resent moving and sometimes take a few years to become established after transplanting. If it is planted in good soil in a well-drained position it will soon resume its flowering. If you have any doubt about the quality of the soil, top-dress it with cow manure.

How do you cut back a Magnolia glauca (6 to 7 ft. tall) when transplanting?   If it was moved with a good ball of fibrous roots you need not cut it back; if moved bare-rooted with a good root system, and it must be pruned, reduce the main stems to about ⅔. If it appears to be making good growth, do not cut it.

My young magnolia produced many sucker shoots this summer. Should they be cut or left on?   If the shoots originate from below the ground line, they probably come from the understock on which the magnolia is grafted, and should be cut off. If, however, they come from *above* the ground line, they may be left, provided they are not too crowded.

How should I protect magnolias, planted in spring, during the

first winter? (Michigan.)   Sometimes it is advisable to wrap the trunks in burlap, especially for the first winter. If the plants are small, you might build a burlap screen about them for the winter and even partly fill it with leaves, which would aid in protecting the roots from too-severe winter cold.

Do young magnolia plants (4 to 5 years) need winter protection? The magnolias commonly grown should not need protection at that age unless your garden is so situated as to be exposed to northwest winds. If that is the case, erect a screen on that side of the plants.

Can you start a new magnolia from cuttings from an old tree? If so, how can it be done?   Some of the magnolias may be rooted, but they are very difficult. Sideshoots, about 5 ins. long, are generally the most successful. Cut very close to the branch, so that a little of the old wood is taken also. They must be kept in close, humid conditions until rooted. A cold frame or glass-covered box in a place out of the sun would be required. Magnolia stellata (and possibly others) can be easily rooted by the "mist" method. See page 246.

A branch was broken from my young magnolia bush. It has one bud on it. I placed it in a bottle of water and it started blooming. How can I grow roots on it?   You can't! (See answer to preceding question.)

Where and how should magnolia seeds be planted?   Soak in water until fleshy covering can be removed. Plant seeds ½ in. deep in soil of cold frame, or in cool place over winter. They will germinate the following spring.

PEACH, FLOWERING

When is the best time to transplant a flowering peach? (New Jersey.) In early fall or in spring.

PLUM

How and when shall I prune Purpleleaf Plum (Prunus pissardi)? Severe pruning of trees related to plums and the stone fruits generally is to be avoided. Unless there is some urgent reason to the contrary, pruning of *Prunus pissardi* should be restricted to shortening "wild" (too energetic) shoots during the growing season.

REDBUD (CERCIS)

Which other native tree would make a good companion to the white-flowered dogwood?   The redbud; it flowers simultaneously and likes a similar environment.

What does redbud look like?   In open places it has wide crown and grows 15 or more ft. high. In shaded and crowded quarters it will grow taller and slimmer. It has deep pink, pea-shaped flowers which grow in clusters along the stems. The leaves which follow are large and roundish.

Can redbud be successfully moved in fall?   Redbud is not one of the easiest shrubs to move, and spring is much safer than fall for the operation. Move it with a ball of earth, held by burlap, attached to the roots and, unless the soil-ball is very firm, do not attempt to remove the burlap when the plant is in its new position.

This is the second year for a redbud tree. Will it bloom this spring if I move it quite early?   Do not expect redbuds to flower much the first spring after transplanting. Do not transplant them unless necessary. They are not very good-natured about being moved.

Why does my redbud tree not bloom freely? Has grown nicely, but has very few blossoms.   Redbuds, dogwoods, and some other flowering trees often fail to produce flowers during periods of vigorous growth. Do not feed your tree with nitrogenous fertilizers.

SHADBLOW (AMELANCHIER)

What is a good small flowering tree for light woodland?   Serviceberry (*Amelanchier canadensis*); also called shadblow or shadbush. It has delicate white flowers in spring.

Does the serviceberry grow well near the salt water's edge?   Yes. Thicket serviceberry, *Amelanchier oblongifolia,* endures salt-laden winds.

SILVERBELL (HALESIA)

Is the silverbell a desirable small tree?   Yes. Its main attraction is in spring, when the dainty white flowers are produced.

Where would the silverbell be attractive?   On the edge of woodland in company with a ground cover of Mertensia, violets, and other woodland flowers.

SMOKETREE (COTINUS)

What gives the smoketree its name?   When the seed pods form in June they produce whorls of gray-lavender hairs. As they become full blown the bush seems enveloped in a whorl of smoke.

What would be the reason for my young smoketree not growing taller? I have had it 6 years and it is only the same height as when I bought it.   Either it is being recurrently killed by cold winters, or the soil is not to its liking. Would suggest fertilizing with well-rotted manure in the fall, *after* digging it up and examining the roots and transplanting it to some new situation which you know has fertile soil.

Why does my smoketree blossom but not set any seeds? The blossom stems wither and drop off. It is more than 20 years old.   The sexes are sometimes on separate individuals and this particular plant is probably the male or staminate type which never bears fruits.

I have a smoketree 6 years old and more than 10 ft. high. Why doesn't it bloom? It gets leaves, but no flower buds. You may have the native smoketree, which is sparing of its smoke! The European (*Cotinus coggygria*) is more floriferous.

My smoketree has leaves with beautiful autumn coloring, but no "smoke." The seed panicles do not produce the "smoke" effect until the shrub is fairly mature.

How should a smoketree be trimmed to tree form, instead of a bush? No attempt should be made to change common smoketree (*Cotinus coggygria*) to tree form—it naturally forms a bush. American Smoketree is occasionally seen as a tree. This form can be encouraged by the gradual removal of the lower branches, starting when the tree is young.

YELLOWWOOD (CLADRASTIS)

What tree is it that has white flowers resembling wisteria? It has a sweet perfume. I saw it at night and it was beautiful. It was probably yellowwood, *Cladrastis lutea*.

Will yellowwood resist high winds? No. The wood is inclined to be brittle.

DECIDUOUS SHRUBS AND THEIR CULTURE

WHAT TO GROW

Can you give me a list of uncommon, but worth-while, hardy shrubs? *Berberis mentorensis; Buddleia alternifolia; Cotoneaster divaricata; Euonymus alatus* and *E. europaeus; Jamesia americana; Kerria japonica; Rubus deliciosus* (thimbleberry); *Shepherdia argentea* (buffaloberry); *Symphoricarpus vulgaris* (snowberry); *Viburnum burkwoodi; V. carlcephalum.*

We cannot afford evergreen foundation planting for our little place. Could you suggest good shrubs, and a few with interesting winter habit? Flowers not essential. Regel Privet, Fiveleaf Aralia, shrub dogwoods with colored branches, Cork Bark or Winged Euonymus, European and Japanese Barberry.

What deciduous shrubs should we plant under our windows to harmonize with the evergreen shrubs which are already there? Azaleas in variety, Flowering Quince, *Abelia grandiflora*, cotoneaster, (various low-growing varieties) *Viburnum carlesi.*

Will you name a few pretty shrubs, beside lilacs and forsythia, that grow rather heavy and would make a "wall" for an out-of-door

room? Beautybush (*Kolkwitzia amabilis*); chokeberry (*Aronia melanocarpa elata*); Gray Dogwood (*Cornus paniculata*); honeysuckle (*Lonicera korolkowi*); *Viburnum dilatatum*.

Which shrubs will give us bloom in the garden from spring to fall? We have a narrow strip on one side of our house. *April*—forsythia; *May*—*Spiraea prunifolia* and Vanhoutte spirea, lilac; *June*—mockorange, beautybush (*Kolkwitzia*), lilac (continued); *July*—vitex, Snowhill Hydrangea, roses, buddleia; *August*—Peegee Hydrangea, roses, rose-of-Sharon; *September*—rose-of-Sharon and roses (continued), clematis.

Will you list some dwarf shrubs? *Juniperus horizontalis; Juniperus horizontalis plumosa; Mahonia* (*Berberis*) *repens; Euonymus radicans; Euonymus Fortunei minimus* (*kewensis*); *Daphne cneorum; Cotoneaster horizontalis* and *C. adpressa; Prunus nana,* Rose Max Graf.

Can you name some shrubs which can be used for training on walls? *Cotoneaster horizontalis;* English Hawthorn (*Crataegus oxyacantha*); firethorn (*Pyracantha coccinea*); Flowering Almond; *Forsythia suspensa;* goldenchain (*Laburnum anagyroides*); *Jasminum nudiflorum;* matrimonyvine (*Lycium halimifolium*); peach (*Prunus persica*).

Which bush can be planted near a window, as a screen which will stand much trimming? If by trimming you mean close shearing, privet will take it. As an irregular bush that will tolerate removal of some growths and still flower, try forsythia; but prune out old growths right after blooming.

BERRIES

In order to have a continuous succession of colorful berries along a driveway, which shrubs should be planted? The driveway has very little sun during the summer. To provide fruits throughout late summer and winter use the following: barberries, Cornelian Cherry, Red-stemmed Dogwood, Gray-stemmed Dogwood, Siebold's Viburnum, American Highbush Cranberry, and Linden-leaved Viburnum.

Can you name a few shrubs with outstandingly bright fruit? *Aronia arbutifolia brilliantissima; Berberis amurensis japonica, B. koreana, B. vernae,* and *B. vulgaris atropurpurea;* callicarpa species; *Cotoneaster zabeli miniata, C. dielsiana,* and *C. francheti; Euonymus europaeus; Ilex laevigata,* and *I. verticillata; Rosa rugosa; Symplocos paniculata; Viburnum dilatatum,* and *V. setigerum.*

Are there any shrubs with decorative fruit, other than the usual bright reds? Beautybush (bright lilac); Yellowberry Flowering Dogwood (yellow); Gray Dogwood (white, on red stalks); privet, several kinds (black); Sapphireberry (*Symplocos paniculata*) (clear blue);

Chenault Coralberry (*Symphoricarpos chenaulti*) (pinkish); *Viburnum cassinoides* (at first white then pinkish, later black).

What are some of the names of berried shrubs and their culture?
Barberry, viburnum, shrubby dogwood, and cotoneaster. For culture see Specific Plants.

BIRDS

Which shrubs, easily grown in part shade, will attract birds?
Buckthorn (*Rhamnus cathartica*); Fragrant Thimbleberry (*Rubus odoratus*) red (*R. strigosus*) and blackcap (*R. orientalis*) raspberries; Red-berried Elder (*Sambucus pubens*); viburnum species; shadblow (*Amelanchier canadensis*); chokeberry (*Aronia arbutifolia*); *Cornus alba, C. mas,* and *C. racemosa; Ilex glabra; Lonicera morrowi;* chokeberry (*Aronia arbutifolia*).

What shrubs should I plant to call birds to my garden? (Vermont.)
Bush honeysuckle, chokeberry, cotoneaster, honeysuckle, shadbush, spicebush, wild roses, and most other berry-bearing shrubs.

BLOOM

We would like succession of bloom in our shrub border. Our place is informal and we like native plants. Can you help us?   February and March—Vernal Witchhazel; April—spicebush, Cornelian Cherry, shadblow, redbud; May—Pinkshell Azalea, dogwood, rose-acacia, Red Chokeberry, rhododendron, viburnum—various; June—Silky Dogwood and Gray Dogwood, Mountain Laurel, Snow Azalea, rhododendron, Prairie Rose, Flowering Raspberry; July—Jersey Tea (*Ceanothus americanus*), Showy Cinquefoil, summersweet (*Clethra alnifolia*); August, September, and October—colored foliage and pods and berries; witchhazel (*Hamamelis virginiana*).

What shrubs can be planted to bloom from early spring until late fall?   To obtain a succession of bloom, one must plant several plants which bloom in sequence. *Hamamelis mollis* (earliest); *Abelia grandiflora,* 12 to 15 weeks; *Potentilla fruticosa,* 10 to 12 weeks; *Spiraea bumalda* Anthony Waterer, 8 to 10 weeks; forsythia in variety, 3 to 4 weeks; vitex, 8 to 10 weeks; *Hibiscus syriacus,* 8 to 10 weeks; azaleas; lilacs; rhododendrons; roses; hydrangeas; rose-of-Sharon; common witchhazel (latest). (See preceding question.)

Can you name some shrubs with fragrant flowers?   Honeysuckle (*Lonicera fragrantissima*); mockorange (*Philadelphus coronarius* and *P. virginalis*); *Viburnum carlesi;* clethra; common lilac; *Daphne cneorum;* sweetshrub.

We are planting a little old-fashioned summer cottage with old-time shrubs. Can you remind us of a few blooming from June to September?   June—rose-acacia, mockorange, sweet azalea, shrub roses, *Spiraea bumalda,* lilacs, hydrangea; July—sweetshrub, smoke-bush, hydrangea; August—summersweet, rose-of-Sharon.

Will you name 5 deciduous shrubs desirable for flowers, berries, and foliage color? *Aronia arbutifolia, Berberis koreana, Viburnum prunifolium, Vaccinium corymbosum, Chaenomeles lagenaria* (Japanese Quince).

FOLIAGE

Which shrubs have distinctive autumn color, other than the brilliant reds and orange shades? Here are a few: *Abelia grandiflora* (reddish-bronze); *Cotoneaster divaricata* (purplish); *Mahonia aquifolium* (chestnut and bronze tints); *Viburnum carlesi* (purplish-red); *V. tomentosum* (purplish).

Can you name some shrubs with outstandingly bright autumn foliage? *Berberis koreana, B. vernae, B. thunbergi pluriflora,* and *B. dictyophylla; Cotoneaster adpressa; Euonymus alatus* and *E. alatus compactus;* fothergilla; *Gordonia alatamaha; Itea virginica; Rhododendron arborescens, R. schlippenbachi,* and *R. obtusum kaempferi; Rhus aromatica; Stephanandra incisa; Vaccinium corymbosum; Xanthorhiza simplicissima.*

I am partial to shrubs with foliage of a fine, lacy quality. Can you mention a few? *Acer palmatum dissectum* varieties; *Abelia grandiflora; Berberis vernae; Cotoneaster dielsiana; Neillia sinensis; Rosa hugonis* and *R. eglanteria; Spiraea arguta, S. thunbergi; Symphoricarpos chenaulti;* tamarisk; Rosa *hugonis.*

Will you name a few shrubs with aromatic foliage? *Calycanthus floridus, Comptonia asplenifolia, Cotinus* species, *Elsholtzia stauntoni, Benzoin aestivale, Rhus aromatica, Rosa eglanteria, Rhododendron micranthum* and *R. racemosum.*

CULTURE—GENERAL

SOIL; FERTILIZER

How should I prepare the ground for planting shrubs? The subsoil must be well drained. Plow or disk in a layer of leafmold and old manure, thus providing a 1-ft. depth of good topsoil. Prepare planting holes to required depths. Remove the excavated soil that may be of very poor quality; improve the better part with leafmold or humus and old manure, for refilling holes. (See also Soil Preparation—Trees, this section.)

What is the best fertilizer to use to stimulate the growth of shrubs? In the planting of shrubs, use leafmold, peatmoss and old manure mixed into the soil. For established shrubs, a mulch of the same. In default of these ingredients, top-dress with a balanced commercial fertilizer.

What is the best commercial fertilizer to use around shrubs? A 10–6–4 if making weak, short growth; or a 0–12–4 if blooms are scant.

Are commercial pulverized manure and peatmoss as beneficial for shrubs as raw cow or horse manure for mulching? Just about, provided the soil is not made too acid thereby.

Which of these shrubs like a soil with lime? Barberry, Japanese Quince, mockorange, Irish Juniper, crapemyrtle, nandina, and roses? Any of them will grow in an alkaline soil. Roses seem to do best in a slightly acid soil, however.

PLANTING, TRANSPLANTING CARE

I want to plant a double row of mixed flowering shrubs between lawn and garden, using tall and medium varieties. How far apart should they be planted in order to avoid either a sparse or a crowded appearance? As you do not give the names of the shrubs you intend to use for your border, exact directions cannot be given. As a general rule 4 to 5 ft. should be sufficient distance between plants in the front row; about 6 to 8 ft. between those in the back row.

When is the best time to transplant flowering shrubs? Spring and fall are the most suitable seasons, but the transplanting of all shrubs which are recognized as difficult to move and all tender shrubs should be undertaken only in spring. In spring, transplant before the shrubs begin to leaf. In fall, as soon as the greater part of the leaves have fallen; but at this season planting must cease before the ground freezes.

In setting out roses, shrubs, and large perennial plants, the soil (unless wet) is made firm about the roots with the feet or a tamping stick.

PLANTING DETAIL

Can most flowering shrubs and berry bushes be set out in the fall and winter, instead of waiting until spring? Shrubs (with some exceptions) and berry bushes may be safely set out in the fall; but the work should be undertaken as early as possible, while there is still sufficient warmth in the soil, to develop new root growth. It is impossible to plant satisfactorily when the soil is largely composed of frozen lumps.

Could I transplant between December 15 and end of March the following: common lilac, French pussy willow, forsythia, deutzia,

syringa, snowball, hydrangea, and bridalwreath? Do the transplanting in late March rather than in December.

Is the fall the best time of year to plant trees and shrubs in a climate as cold as that of central Vermont? No; early spring is better.

How does one go about digging up shrubs for transplanting? If they are small, thrust a spade to its full depth in a continuous circle, at a sufficient distance from center to avoid undue root injury, and pry out. Roots are likely to extend at least as far as the spread of the branches.

Is it necessary to cut back shrubs when they are transplanted? If so, how much? Balled and burlapped specimens need not be pruned after planting. Vigorous young shrubs of quick-growing kinds are best pruned to about half the length of main stems. Older, bare-rooted shrubs, with poorish root systems and large tops, are best pruned back to from ⅔ to ½ their length.

What is the reason for cutting back shrubs when they are transplanted? It reduces the plant to a size more easily supported by a disturbed root system; it reduces the area exposed to the drying effect of wind and sun, and divides the vigor of the new growth over a smaller number of growing points. (See "Pruning.")

How low should fall-planted barberry, Spiraea Vanhouttei, and althea be pruned? With the barberry and spirea cut out, at about ground level, half of the strongest stems; reduce the remainder about half their length. If the althea is on a single stem, it must not be cut to the ground. Cut out some of the branches at a point where they fork, and shorten the remaining ones to ½ or ⅓ their length.

Why do shrubs bloom well some years and others very poorly? Last spring my forsythia and flowering crab had only a few blooms. For two reasons. Some winters are cold enough to kill the flower buds of plants such as forsythia. Then, too, many flowering and fruiting ornamentals, such as crabapples, bear alternately—that is, they have profuse flowers and fruits one year and but few the next year. There is little the homeowner can do to change this sequence.

PRUNING SHRUBS

See also General Pruning, this section.

Do all shrubs get pruned? How does one know which to prune? It is not necessary to prune all shrubs. Some are benefited by pruning —such as most varieties of roses and certain flowering shrubs whose branches become crowded and cluttered with worn-out wood which does not bloom freely. Generally speaking, if a shrub does not give satisfaction it is worth while to try the effect of pruning. Prune, in the main, *only* where necessary to keep materials within their allotted space, and to keep them at the highest pitch of effectiveness.

Is it better to prune flowering shrubs in spring or fall? Few, if any, should be pruned in the fall in Northern climates. Generally, shrubs which blossom on old wood (forsythia, for example) should be pruned in spring immediately *after* flowering. Those whose blossoms are produced on shoots of the current season may be pruned in the spring before growth starts.

Which shrubs should be pruned in the fall? (South Carolina.) Where severe winters are experienced it is desirable to defer pruning until the worst of the winter has passed. In your section fall pruning might be permissible for those shrubs which produce their blooms on young shoots of the current season. Examples are H.T. roses, P.G. hydrangea, rose-of-Sharon, and late-blooming tamarisks.

When is the best time to prune a hedge? Hedges are best pruned when their young shoots are nearing the completion of their growth. With many hedges, one trimming at this time is sufficient; with others a second trimming may be necessary in late summer. In order to keep a fast-growing privet hedge in shipshape condition, trimming has to be done several times in a season. (See Hedges.)

What is the reason back of the recommendation to avoid, during the dormant season, the pruning of shrubs which blossom on the old wood? Because such pruning results in loss of branches which would produce flowers the following spring. Sometimes exceptional circumstances make it desirable to sacrifice flowering wood to attain a definite purpose; as, for example, when old, scraggly lilacs are cut back to rejuvenate them, reduce their height, and make a more compact bush.

Why are some shrubs pruned back every spring to mere stubs? This is done in the case of some shrubs which, though pruned back short, will flower on the new growth made after pruning. It affords a method of keeping them within limited proportions, without sacrifice of blossom. It is often done with Hills of Snow Hydrangea, vitex, abelia, and Spirea Anthony Waterer.

Should you remove dead flowers from shrubs? Yes—if you want to increase the bloom of plants such as lilacs the next year. No—if you wish these plants to produce fruits.

Should shrubs, such as mockorange, Hills of Snow Hydrangea, rose-of-Sharon, weigela, roses, and beautybush, be pruned the first fall after spring planting? Shrubs usually require little if any pruning the first year after planting—certainly not in the fall. In the spring Hills of Snow Hydrangea and rose-of-Sharon may have the growth of the preceding year cut back ⅔.

When is the proper time for, and what is the correct method of, thinning out shrubs and bushes that have not been cared for properly for years? Should they be cut to the ground and allowed to grow up again? Indiscriminate cutting to the ground may upset the balance between root and top. Thinning out crowded branches can be done during the winter. Those shrubs which normally are pruned by shortening the shoots of the preceding year in the spring should be so treated. Any large, overgrown specimens may be cut back ⅓ to ½.

How many branches should be left when shrubs are espaliered against wall?   Average is about 1 ft. apart, but this is determined by the character of the shrub. Enough should be left so that the wall is well covered when the branches are clothed with leaves and shoots during the growing season.

WINTER PROTECTION

Are leaves good for mulching shrubs in the fall?   Yes, where a mulch is desirable. Oak leaves are especially valuable around rhododendrons, and should be left in place finally to rot down.

I have read that maple leaves are not the right kind to use for a winter covering. Is this true?   It all depends on what is being covered. They could be safely used as a mulch among shrubs. They are not so good as a cover for many perennials, as they tend to make a sodden mass with a smothering effect.

What is "salt" hay?   It is hay from salt marshes cut and dried the same as ordinary hay. It is used for covering plants in winter as protection. May be obtained from dealers in horticultural supplies or nurserymen in your vicinity.

Do shrubs have to be covered for the winter with peatmoss or salt hay after their first winter?   No.

When is the proper time to remove mulching around shrubs?   For the sake of appearance, when the spring cleanup is under way. If manure was used, leave all possible for the benefit of the shrubs. In the case of rhododendrons and related plants, a perpetual mulch is desirable.

PROPAGATION

Generally speaking, when should I take slips from hardy shrubs?   The majority root most readily during July and early August. Lilac and beautybush are two notable exceptions. The latter part of May, while the shoots are still growing, is the best time for lilac and mid-June for beautybush.

How are slips from hardy shrubs rooted?   By placing them under preserving jars, bell jars, or in a cold frame, in a shady place. Sand, or a sandy soil, forms the best rooting medium.

What procedure should be followed after slips taken from hardy shrubs have rooted? (Wisconsin.)   They may be potted up singly, or be planted in boxes. In the Northern states it is exceedingly risky to plant them in the open ground late in the fall. The pots or boxes should be stored in a cool place, such as a garage or cold cellar, where they will not be subjected to hard freezing. In the spring they may be planted in the open ground. (See also Propagation, Cuttings, this section.)

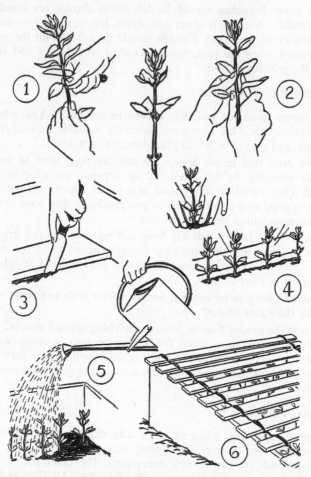

**SUMMER PROPAGATION WITH
SOFTWOOD CUTTINGS**

(1 and 2) Making the cutting or slip, and trimming it up, ready for planting. (3 and 4) Marking line with knife in rooting medium (sand), inserting cutting, and firming sand along row of cuttings. (5) Watering in the cuttings. (6) Shading frame from sunshine, with lath screen. Sometimes it is necessary to cover with glass sash also.

Are there any shrubs which can be increased by division? Yes. Some types of boxwood, hydrangea, rose, spirea, etc.

SPECIFIC SHRUBS

ABELIA

How would abelias harmonize with broad-leaved evergreens? Very well. They like peaty soil as the evergreens do, but not too much shade.

Are Abelia grandiflora and the crapemyrtle hardy in the Pittsburgh, Pennsylvania, area? *Abelia grandiflora* is hardy in Pittsburgh, but the crapemyrtle may not prove completely hardy. Certainly it should be tried only in the most protected areas.

How long is the blooming season of Abelia grandiflora? From June or July to late October, or even November.

ARALIA, FIVE-LEAF (ACANTHOPANAX)

A nurseryman recommends acanthopanax for planting in shade. Is it any good? Flowers and fruits negligible; beautiful 5-parted, lacy leaves; fast-growing, well shaped; will grow under trees or in any shaded place, or in full sun; drought resistant. Height about 5 ft.

ALMOND (PRUNUS TRILOBA)

How do you prune a Flowering Almond (Prunus triloba)? The flowers are produced on the shoots made the preceding year, therefore, as soon as the flowers fade, cut back flowering shoots to within 2 ins. of the point of origin.

Can I root cuttings of an almond? Yes. The cuttings must be taken in July and placed in a cold frame, or glass-covered box, in order to have the requisite moist, humid conditions to induce rooting.

AMORPHA

What is the Indigobush? Is it hardy in northern Ohio? Indigobush (*Amorpha fruticosa*) is somewhat weedy, with purplish flowers, in spikes, during June and July. Will grow in poor soil, and should be hardy in northern Ohio.

AZALEA

See Ericaceous Shrubs.

BARBERRY

What is Korean Barberry? A very decorative shrub growing 6 to 7 ft. high, erect when young and then spreading and arching. Thick, broad, wedge-shaped leaves turning orange-red in autumn. Small yellow flowers in spring, followed by scarlet berries in fall.

Is there a barberry suitable for a very low hedge? Yes. Box Barberry (*Berberis thunbergi minor*), very like a miniature of the well-known Japanese Barberry. There is also a variety called Truehedge Columnberry. It grows narrower and more erect. Good for its fine autumn color.

When shall I transplant barberry bush 3 years old? How far apart? When to prune? Barberry bushes of the kinds that lose their leaves every fall may be transplanted in spring or fall, while they are leafless. Evergreen kinds are better transplanted in spring. If they are to be planted in a shrub border where every plant is to be allowed enough room for normal development, the smaller kinds may be allowed 4 to 5 ft. and the taller ones 6 to 7 ft. at least. Pruning should be done immediately after transplanting.

When shall I prune barberry? Barberry ordinarily requires little if any pruning, except in those cases when a special shape is desired, as in hedges, or in a formal garden. Then the practice is to shear it when the new shoots have almost completed their growth in late spring.

I want to drastically prune my barberry. Should it be done in spring or fall? If it has to be cut back, do it in the spring. It may suffer from winter injury if done in the fall.

If Japanese Barberry bush is trimmed to the ground in December, is it possible to transplant same in the spring to another spot in garden? If any small part of the stems were left above ground, you may safely move it in the spring. If cut clear to the ground, then wait until new growth starts.

How can the Truehedge Columnberry Barberry be raised from seed? This plant is what botanists term a "clon." It will not reproduce itself from seed.

How can I best propagate Japanese Barberry? The simplest method is from seeds, which should be stored in a cool place in moist sand over winter, and sown very early in spring. Or they may be rooted from cuttings taken in July and kept in a closed cold frame until rooted.

BAYBERRY (MYRICA)

When is proper time to transplant bayberry bushes? (New Jersey.) Spring; or, in New Jersey, early autumn.

Wild bayberries were planted on the north side of house. Will these grow? Not a good situation. They prefer open situations, and will take only very light, partial shade.

What is proper cultivation of bayberry? Where may it be obtained?

It is by nature a shrub of open, sunny, sandy coastal tracts. Therefore, in cultivation, it should be kept out of shade. It is a poor-soil shrub. Plant it, balled and burlapped, in the spring, in non-alkaline soil. Few nurseries grow it. One may have to obtain it from dealers in native plants.

BEARBERRY (ARCTOSTAPHYLOS)

Is Bearberry (Arctostaphylos uva-ursi) a good ground cover to plant just back of a dry retaining wall? Yes, one of the best if there's plenty of sun and the soil is well drained and sandy. Be sure to get only pot-grown plants from a reliable nursery; wild plants are *very* difficult to transplant.

What conditions are necessary for growth of Bearberry? Full sun or light shade, well drained and aerated, very sandy soil, slightly acid.

BEAUTYBUSH (KOLKWITZIA)

I've heard about kolkwitzia. What is it like? Beautybush is top ranking. It suggests weigela, but is finer by far. Flowers are smaller, more abundant, and a pale pink with yellow throat, in early June. Slow-growing. Ultimate height to 9 ft.

Last year I planted a Beautybush. It has not bloomed and has thrown out only one new shoot. It gets morning sun and careful attention. Should it not have flowered? Next spring prune back the one shoot. It will probably branch out and begin to form a solid shrub. It might flower the following spring. The Beautybush often doesn't flower at an early age.

What kind of fertilizer should be used on a Beautybush to get it to bloom? No need for special fertilizer. This shrub often does not flower at an early age. Wait. It is worth waiting for.

Should a Beautybush (Kolkwitzia amabilis) be pruned? If so, when? If the bush is crowded, cut away the oldest flowering branches to the ground immediately the flowers have faded. Otherwise, little or no pruning required.

How can I start new plants from my Beautybush? Either from seeds, which take several years to reach flowering stage; or from cuttings. Cuttings must be of soft wood, i.e., taken from the tips of the shoots while they are still growing actively. If taken at a later stage, they will form a large callus but generally fail to form roots. Softwood cuttings can only be rooted in a shaded cold frame or glass-covered box.

BENZOIN

At approximately what age does Lindera benzoin (Spicebush) flower? Does it make a good screening shrub? How far apart should

it be planted for that effect? Is it thoroughly winter hardy in Connecticut? It begins to flower when 5 to 8 years old. In New England it grows to about 8 to 10 ft. tall. Makes a fair screen, with plants set 5 to 6 ft. apart. It is relatively pest free and requires no special attention, but is not completely hardy in the most severe winter.

BLUEBERRY

I want to grow blueberries for their ornamental foliage. Any special soil requirements? Make soil acid by mixing with it rotted oak leaves (which see), rotted pine needles, or peatmoss. Maintaining a 3-in. layer of oak leaves or peatmoss on soil over roots is a good plan to help keep soil moist.

BROOM (CYTISUS)

What is the scientific name of the shrub called "Scotch Broom"? It has yellow flowers similar to sweetpeas, with the seed borne in a pod like peas. Has it commercial possibilities? *Cytisus scoparius.* Probably no commercial possibilities except as an ornamental. Is used in a limited way for making brooms, in basketry, for thatching, etc.

What soil is best for Scotch Broom? It succeeds well in many places in poor, almost barren sand dunes, roadsides, and embankments. It prefers a light, sandy soil, non-alkaline. The admixture of a little peat will be helpful. Plant in well-drained, open places. Start with small plants—pot-grown, if you can get them.

BUTTERFLYBUSH (BUDDLEIA)

Which kinds of buddleia bloom in late summer? There are several, but the varieties of *Buddleia davidi,* with flowers ranging from mauve to deep purple, are the best.

Which buddleia is the most reliably hardy? *Buddleia alternifolia,* which has short, dense clusters of fragrant blue flowers in June.

Where would be the best place to plant buddleia? In a sunny place or shady place? Makes its best growth in full sun.

How should buddleias be planted? Buddleia, dug from a nursery, should be planted in spring. Probably the roots will have been roughly pruned when the plant is received, but before planting they should have any ragged ends cut clean. Plant an inch or two deeper than previously, and pack the soil carefully between the roots. Cut the stems back to 2 ins. from the point where growth started the previous spring. Give full sun.

Is it too late to cut branches from Buddleia in April? I understand they should be cut late in November. Spring is the correct time to prune buddleias. They should not be cut back in the fall because of the danger that a severe winter will injure them and necessitate still more pruning in the spring.

Is it advisable to debud the first spikes of buddleias? No particular advantage to be gained from this practice.

Should butterflybush be cut down every year in Pennsylvania? In your section the effects of winter are almost certain to make pruning necessary. Wait until the buds begin to grow in the spring, then cut the top down to vigorous shoots.

Is Buddleia alternifolia pruned in the same way as the butterflybush buddleias? No. Its flowers are produced on old wood; therefore pruning should be done immediately *after* flowering, merely thinning out crowded shoots and shaping up bush.

What care should be given buddleia (butterflybush or summerlilac) for winter protection? A mulch of littery material around the base is all that may be needed. It is advisable not to cut the tops back until spring.

Can butterflybushes be grown from slips? If so, how is it done? When are cuttings made? Yes. The cuttings, 4 to 5 ins. long, are made in July or August, from side shoots. Cut off the bottom pair of leaves, and make a clean cut through the stem, just below the joint from which the leaves were cut. Insert ⅓ of their length in sand, in a propagating case.

CARYOPTERIS

What is caryopteris like? The one commonly grown (*Caryopteris incana*) is a shrub bearing bluish flowers. It is not fully hardy in the North, where it is treated as a perennial herb.

How should one prune caryopteris, and when? Wait until the buds swell in spring and then cut back each branch to a strong-growing bud. If winter killed to ground, remove dead stalks in early spring.

CHASTETREE (VITEX)

Is chastetree really a tree? Mine is more like a shrub. It may develop into a small tree in a favorable climate. In the North its young branches often are killed by low temperatures, which make it assume a shrubby habit.

Does chastetree (Vitex macrophylla) require acid soil? It appears to reach its best development in a sandy peat. This would indicate a preference for a non-alkaline but not highly acid soil. It grows readily enough in average, light garden soils.

How and when is proper time to prune chastetree (Vitex macrophylla)? This blossoms on shoots of the current season and should be cut back in spring. Wait until growth begins (it is a late starter) and cut back the branches to strong-growing buds.

COTONEASTER

What are some of the best cotoneasters for border planting?
C. hupehensis, 6 ft. high; *C. salicifolia floccosa,* 10 ft.; *C. zabeli-miniata,* 6 to 8 ft.

We are looking for a cotoneaster which is lower growing than C. horizontalis. What do you suggest? *C. adpressa* grows only 9 to 12 ins. high; has glossy berries in fall like *C. horizontalis,* but it is hardier.

How can I grow the cotoneasters successfully? Give them a sunny position, in well-drained soil. *Protect young plants from rabbits* in rural districts.

CRAPEMYRTLE (LAGERSTROEMIA)

What kind of soil does crapemyrtle need? It has no special requirements, and will thrive in any ordinary garden soil.

What is the proper care of crapemyrtle as to fertilizer, trimming, watering, and winter protection, if needed? (Maryland.) Crapemyrtle has no special soil preferences. Fertilize by mulching with rotted manure in the fall, which will also help protect the roots against winter injury. If in an exposed location, cover the top with cornstalks. Shorten shoots of the preceding year ½ to ⅔ in the spring. Cut back flowering shoots when the blossoms have faded. Water only during droughty periods.

Why did my 8-year-old crapemyrtle fail to bloom the past summer? Two of them have always bloomed beautifully until last season. (Kentucky.) The chances are that they were injured by the very severe winter.

Can you advise why my crapemyrtle shrubs do not bloom? (Brooklyn, New York.) I have had these shrubs for 4 years and protect them each winter. They bloomed only the first year after planting. Winter injury and not enough heat during the growing season. They bloom freely about once in 10 years as far North as this. Grow in the warmest, sunniest situation; cut back in the spring to strong-growing shoots.

The crapemyrtle, an old bush, very tall and about 10 ft. from an oak, is thrifty as to foliage but no blooms. We have a stratum of clay soil but have put in many tons of topsoil and plenty of fertilizer. What is wrong? The proximity of the oak may be a factor in the failure of the crapemyrtle to bloom. Omit nitrogenous fertilizers and try the effect of an application of superphosphate to the soil over the roots, at the rate of 6 oz. per sq. yd. Maybe the soil is too acid.

Can a crapemyrtle be protected sufficiently to winter safely out of doors in a climate where the temperature falls to 10 to 15° below zero? No.

How shall I care for crapemyrtle, and do they need pruning? (California.) Not satisfactory in southern California. Pruning consists of cutting back the shoots, immediately after flowering, to encourage new growth and further flowering.

CYDONIA

See Quince.

DAPHNE

What is the name of the daphne which blooms very early? February Daphne (*D. mezereum*). It is valued for its early blooming, and lilac-purple fragrant flowers. Height may reach 3 ft.; stiff, erect; deciduous.

Why do the leaves of a Daphne mezereum turn yellow and drop off during the months of August and September? It is characteristic of this species to shed its leaves during drought in late summer.

DEUTZIA

Are there any low-growing deutzias? If so, when do they bloom? *Deutzia gracilis,* with white flowers in May; *Deutzia rosea* has pinkish flowers, otherwise resembles the preceding.

What are the advantages of the tall deutzias? Are they interesting in winter? Their flowers are showy; otherwise their foliage and their branch pattern are uninteresting.

When should I transplant deutzias? In spring or early fall.

When is the proper time to trim deutzias? They should be pruned by cutting out worn-out and crowded flowering shoots immediately the blossoms have faded.

DOGWOOD (CORNUS)

See also under Decorative Flowering Trees.

Which dogwood shrubs have colored twigs in winter? *Cornus alba* (Tartarian D.), bright red twigs; *Cornus stolonifera* (Red Osier D.), deep red; *Cornus stolonifera flaviramea* (Goldentwig B.), yellow; *Cornus paniculata* (Gray D.), gray; *Cornus sanguinea* (Bloodtwig D.), dark blood-red; *Cornus sanguinea viridissima* (Greentwig D.), green.

What color are the berries of the dogwood shrubs? Tartarian Dogwood, whitish; Silky Dogwood, pale blue; Bloodtwig Dogwood, black; Pagoda Dogwood, dark blue; Red Osier Dogwood, white or bluish; Gray Dogwood, white.

How are the shrubby dogwoods used to best advantage? In masses as woodland border, or as an informal hedgerow planting of mixed shrubs.

I have had a Cornus mas (Cornelian Cherry) for 3 years, but it has not grown. Can you prescribe? Takes a few years to become established. If you have given it good soil, fertilized it occasionally with well-rotted manure or a complete commercial fertilizer, and given it plenty of water, you have done the best you can for it.

ENKIANTHUS

What is Enkianthus campanulatus like? A graceful, upright shrub with an ultimate height of 12 to 15 ft., but slow-growing. In May and June it bears drooping clusters of yellowish bell-shaped flowers. Its chief value is in its foliage, glossy turning brilliant orange and scarlet.

What deciduous shrub with good autumn color can we put in among the evergreens at the east and west side of our house? *Enkianthus perulatus,* growing to 6 ft., would be a good choice because, like the broad-leaved evergreens, it prefers acid soil. Use *E. campanulatus* if a taller shrub is required.

EUONYMUS

I have seen a shrub which has curious corky flanged bark on its branches. Its leaves turn deep rose in the autumn. What is it? Winged Euonymus (*E. alatus*).

FORSYTHIA

What different kinds of forsythia are there? About 5 species; several varieties. Among the best are, urnlike in form *F. intermedia spectabilis;* and fountainlike (or drooping), *F. suspensa.*

There is such a difference in the number of flowers on forsythias that I wonder if it is due to soil or location; or if there is more than one kind of plant. (Arkansas.) There are several kinds of forsythia. *Forsythia intermedia spectabilis* is a very showy one.

What is the hardiest forsythia? A species called *F. ovata,* earliest to bloom; flowers, however, are less effective and more amber in color.

When is the best time to transplant forsythia? Does it require cultivation? This shrub may be safely transplanted in spring or fall, any time that it is leafless. Cultivation around newly transplanted shrubs for a period of 1 or 2 years is decidedly beneficial.

Our forsythia had a late fall bloom this year. Will that impair the spring bloom? Yes, for the flower buds are formed in the fall, and if some open then the bloom the following spring will be just so much reduced.

Why do forsythias bloom around the bottom of bushes only? Because in cold areas the flower buds—present all winter long—are killed by low temperatures except where they are protected by a blanket of snow.

I have forsythia on southwest corner of our house, about 6 years old; used to bloom in spring; now blooms in October and November. Why? The chances are the autumns have been unusually mild in this particular location.

Why doesn't my forsythia bloom? The buds seem to dry up. They have been killed by winter cold. Try *Forsythia ovata*. This is the most hardy of all the forsythias.

How and when should forsythia be pruned? Cut out some of the oldest branches annually, making the cut not far from the base of the bush. This can be done in February, and the cut branches brought indoors and placed in water to force them into bloom; or wait until the bush has flowered, and prune it immediately the flowers have faded.

How do you prune forsythia when grown too high? Cut it back to the required height immediately after flowering.

How can I keep forsythia bushes from getting so awfully straggling? Make them more compact by pinching out the tips of strong-growing shoots during late spring and early summer. Comparatively compact varieties, such as *F. viridissima* and *F. ovata,* are preferable if there is an objection to a straggling habit.

Can forsythia or goldenbells be pruned in fall as well as in spring? Usually the shrub gets very awkward after spring pruning. Forsythia produces its flowers on preceding year's growth, and any cutting back during the time it is dormant results in a diminution of the floral display in the spring. Try pinching out the tips of strong-growing shoots during the growing season.

When is proper time to trim Weeping Forsythia? The beauty of this variety is in its long, trailing growth. It should not be trimmed in the usual sense of cutting back the tips. Thinning out crowded branches is permissible in the spring immediately the flowers have faded.

HAZELNUT

Are there any garden forms of the European hazel nut that are grown for their beauty rather than the production of nuts? There are two outstanding ones. One is a variety of the filbert (*Corylus maxima purpurea*). The other is the European hazel (*Corylus avellana* var. *contorta*), which is interesting rather than beautiful. The leaves of *purpurea* are dark purple, especially in early spring; and in *contorta* the stems are twisted and curled in a way that makes it an excellent conversation piece.

HONEYSUCKLE (LONICERA)

Do the honeysuckles have berries?   Yes. Amur, Morrow, and Tatarian Honeysuckles have red berries. There are also yellow-fruited varieties of the two last named. Mistletoe Honeysuckle has white fruit.

Can you mention a few desirable honeysuckle bushes?   Fragrant Bush Honeysuckle—April, white; Morrow Bush Honeysuckle—May, cream-yellow; Blueleaf Bush Honeysuckle—May, pink; Amur Bush Honeysuckle—May, white; and Tatarian Bush Honeysuckle—May, rose and white.

How can I best propagate bush honeysuckle?   In order to have plants of uniform kind, it is best to root the plants from cuttings. Many of them root quite readily from hardwood cuttings, and this is the simplest way. Or they may be raised from cuttings taken in July and kept in a closed cold frame until rooted.

HYDRANGEA

Varieties

Will you tell me what is the real name of the hydrangea with pink or blue flowers?   Bigleaf Hydrangea (*Hydrangea macrophylla*). There are many varieties of this species, both with blue flowers and with pink flowers. Rosea is a popular variety with pink flowers.

What are some hydrangeas other than the usual Peegee and Snow Hill?   Try Panicle Hydrangea, the parent of Peegee, with flowers more opened out, not so "top-heavy"; Climbing Hydrangea (*H. petiolaris*), as vine or shrub; Oakleaf Hydrangea, with interesting foliage.

Culture

What exposure to sun should hydrangeas have?   The common species do best in full sun, although they will stand slight shade.

Do Oakleaf Hydrangeas need a shady or sunny location?   Shady.

What plant foods do hydrangeas need and when?   They require no special fertilizer treatment. The use of well-rotted manure or a mixed commercial fertilizer in the spring is satisfactory.

Can a hydrangea tree be transplanted in my state in the month of October or November? (New York.)   Yes.

Would transplanting a large hydrangea into another section of the garden cause injury to the plant?   No, not permanently, if properly done. Transplant in early spring.

When is the best time to move hydrangeas?   Either fall or early spring for very hardy types; spring in the case of "French" hydrangeas.

Should a potted hydrangea with a large beautiful blue flower which came from a hothouse be transplanted to the outdoors? (Kansas.) No, not in Kansas. It would not live over winter.

My mother gave us a 4-year-old hydrangea to transplant in our yard. Could you tell me what to do to make it bloom next year? Protect canes from winter injury by covering them in the fall with cornstalks or something similar. Do not cut back the canes in the spring any more than is necessary to remove injured tips.

Does Peegee Hydrangea require any special care? I don't seem to be able to grow them. One of easiest shrubs to grow. Needs no special care.

Why do the leaves on my pink hydrangeas appear yellow and mottled? The soil is too sweet or alkaline. Have it tested and add aluminum sulfate to reduce the pH value to 6.8 or lower.

What would cause a hydrangea to stop flowering after having bloomed beautifully for 3 seasons? Too much shade, poor soil, over-fertilization, improper pruning, and winter injury are some of the more important factors that affect the flowering of hydrangeas.

Why do my French hydrangeas bloom some years and not others? (New York.) Cold injury to the flower buds is the most common reason for failure to flower. The flower buds are formed in the fall, and if the winter is severe they may be killed even though the plant is not seriously injured.

Why has my hydrangea plant (French type) not bloomed for 15 years, even though it grows well and is kept pruned? (Massachusetts.) Undoubtedly the flower buds which form in the fall are killed during the winter. Give more winter protection by covering with leaves, held in place by chicken wire, etc. Pruning at the wrong time of year (each spring or fall) will prevent flowering by removing the flower buds. Prune immediately *after* blooming (late July).

After blooming should the old flowers be cut from hydrangeas? Not necessarily, unless they are unsightly.

Do hydrangeas bloom on old or new wood? Some common species, such as *Hydrangea paniculata grandiflora* and the Hills of Snow type, bloom on new wood, and may be pruned in the early spring. On a few other types, particularly the common greenhouse or French (*Hydrangea macrophylla,* formerly called *H. opuloides*) varieties, the buds originate near the tips of the canes formed the preceding year, and should be pruned *after* flowering, or not at all.

How near to the ground do you prune hydrangeas? This depends on the species. *Hydrangea arborescens* can be cut off at the ground each year. (See preceding answer.)

When is the proper time to cut back a blue hydrangea? This species (often called French hydrangea) should be pruned immediately after flowering. Pruning in the fall or in the early spring will reduce the number of flowers or prevent flowering.

What is the best way to prune a standard hydrangea?   Since round, uniform tops are desired, all branches should be cut back so that only 2 or 3 buds are left at the base of each old stem. Pruning should be done on this type (*Hydrangea paniculata grandiflora*) in the early spring.

How should Peegee Hydrangeas be pruned?   This is the strong-growing shrubby type which sometimes almost attains the dimensions of a small tree. It blossoms on shoots of the current season, and if large heads of bloom are desired, the shoots of the preceding year should be cut back to one bud in the spring.

When should the Oakleaf Hydrangea be pruned?   Immediately after flowering. This is another species, like the French type, in which the flower buds form in the fall. Since the buds are likely to be injured during severe winters, the plants should be protected.

I never get any blooms on my French hydrangeas. Is this because I cut them to the ground every spring?   Yes. Many varieties of French hydrangea fail to bloom if severely pruned in spring. Merely cut back the tips of canes injured by winter.

Why do my hydrangeas have so many leaves and so few flowers? Too much nitrogenous fertilizer and improper pruning may encourage the growth of foliage instead of flowers. In warm climates the common French hydrangeas may not set flower buds in the fall because of high temperatures.

Why do not the pink and blue hydrangeas flower for me outdoors? (Connecticut.)   Some bear flowers only on last summer's branches. These will not flower outdoors in your climate. Some flower on the current summer's growth; these should flower in your garden. The 2 types are not clearly distinguished in books and catalogues. Search out plants which bloom outdoors in your locality, in gardens or nurseries, and obtain stock of these.

What care should be given blue hydrangeas for the winter? (Eastern exposure.)   Wrap in burlap or straw, and mulch soil heavily with leaves.

Should hydrangeas be covered during winter in this section? (New York.)   The blue- and pink-flowering hydrangeas only need be protected in winter in this locality.

Can blue hydrangeas be propagated?   Yes, by cuttings. However, the flowers may appear as pink when grown under different soil conditions.

Color (How to Change)

What causes pink hydrangeas to turn blue?   Experiments have conclusively demonstrated that the presence of aluminum in the tissue of hydrangea flowers causes the blue coloration.

Can all kinds of hydrangeas be made to produce blue flowers? No. Only the pink varieties of the common greenhouse or French hydrangea (*Hydrangea macrophylla*) will turn blue.

Could the Oakleaf Hydrangeas and Climbing Hydrangeas be made to have pink or blue flowers?   No.

Will my hydrangeas be blue if I plant them in an acid soil?   Pink varieties of the common greenhouse or French hydrangea produce blue flowers when grown in acid soil (pH 5.5 or below). Soil acidity is an indirect factor in the production of blue flowers because of its relationship to the solubility of aluminum in the soil. The aluminum is soluble and can be absorbed by the plants when the soil is acid (pH 5.5 or below). In neutral or slightly alkaline soil the aluminum is insoluble.

What chemical will change the color of hydrangea flowers to blue? Aluminum sulfate is the most effective chemical, but common alum (potassium alum) will also bring about the blue color.

Can dry aluminum sulfate be mixed with the soil to produce blue flowers?   Dry aluminum sulfate may be used in the spring at the rate of 1 lb. for each square yard of ground area. It may be necessary to repeat the treatment for several years. Aluminum sulfate may also be mixed with the soil when it is prepared. The soil should be tested to determine its reaction (pH). If the soil is neutral, mix in thoroughly ½ lb. for each bushel.

How does one make hydrangeas growing in pots have blue flowers? Water 5 to 8 times, at weekly intervals, with a 2½ per cent solution of aluminum sulfate (1 lb. to 5 gals. water). Use 1 gal. to each plant.

If rusty nails are put in the soil will a hydrangea produce blue flowers?   Rusty nails or any other form of metallic iron has no effect upon flower color. Potassium alum (common alum), however, will induce blue coloration.

How can I make a blue-flowering hydrangea produce pink flowers? The soil should be made neutral or very slightly alkaline (pH 6.7 to 7.2) by the addition of lime. Too much lime will cause mottling of the leaves, as the result of a lack of iron. The required amount of lime should be deeply and thoroughly mixed with the soil. It is best to lift the plants in the fall, shake off as much soil as possible, and replant it in the especially prepared lime soil.

How can one prevent discoloring of hydrangea flowers?   Flowers of intermediate hues between pink and blue are produced when the soil reaction is between pH 6 and 6.5. If pure blue flowers are desired, add aluminum sulfate to make the soil more acid (pH 5.5). For pink flowers, add lime to bring the soil reaction to pH 6.8 to 7.0.

KERRIA

What is Kerria japonica? This shrub grows 4 to 8 ft. high and produces bright yellow flowers. Variety pleniflora is double and more vigorous. Both have green stems. It is a shrub of easy culture, and does well in part shade.

I have an old kerria shrub, but only 1 or 2 branches bloom. How can I treat or prune it? Winter injury or crowded branches may be responsible for its failure to bloom. Cut out weak shoots in spring and remove flowering branches as soon as the flowers have faded.

How can I best propagate Kerria japonica pleniflora? Either by means of cuttings in July, which must be kept in close, humid, shady conditions until rooted; or by hardwood cuttings, taken in late fall, buried in the soil over winter, and set in the garden in early spring.

LILAC (SYRINGA)

Types and Varieties

What are the best lilacs (French hybrids) in each color? A *few* of the "best" lilacs are: white—Edith Cavell (double) and Marie Finon; violet—Cavour and Marechal Lannes (double); blue—President Lincoln, Olivier de Serres (double); lilac—Marengo, President Fallieres (double); pink—Lucie Baltet, Macrostachya; magenta—Congo, Marceau; purple—Ludwig Spaeth, Mrs. W. E. Marshall.

Are there ever-blooming lilac bushes? No.

What are so-called "own-root" lilacs? Those lilacs so propagated that the roots and tops are from one continuous piece of plant, i.e., not grafted with two pieces grown together as one. Hence, they are not susceptible to the serious graft-blight disease. "Own-root" lilacs are the best kind to buy.

Would you consider a Syringa japonica (Japanese lilac) a good lawn specimen tree? How tall does it grow? Yes. It may grow 40 ft. high and more but usually is under 20 ft.

What is the difference between species lilacs and the other, or common, lilacs? Lilac species are the wild lilacs of the world found growing in uninhabited places. The "common lilacs" are usually considered either natural hybrids, which have appeared in gardens, or (more frequently) as the direct result of hybridizing efforts.

Why are French hybrid lilacs so called? Because hybridizers in France have had much to do with their production.

Culture

What kind of soil and nourishment are best for lilacs? Any fair, not too heavy, well-drained, alkaline garden soil. If needed, every other year apply a 3-in. mulch of cow manure, alternated with a dose of lime. Do not feed them unless the need is indicated, lest they grow too tall and must be cut back.

Please advise when to plant a lilac bush; spring or fall?   Either. Lilacs are among the easiest of plants to transplant and will grow under almost any conditions.

I planted lilac the last of November. Was it too late?   Probably; but if ground didn't freeze until late December this date for planting should have been satisfactory.

Can a large lilac bush be moved and continue blooming—that is, without waiting several more years?   Yes, if moved with a large ball of soil about the roots, and if the branches are pruned back ⅓ in the operation.

How long do lilacs have to be planted before blooming?   This depends on many things, such as soil, skill of transplanting in the soil, etc. Some plants, grown properly, will bloom profusely when only 4 ft. tall. Others may take years before they will start to bloom.

I transplanted a lilac bush. Should the leaves be stripped at the bottom in the spring or left alone?   Always prune off some of the branches when transplanting; approximately ⅓ of the total branches is a good average. Stripping off the leaves is not a good practice in this case.

What is the ultimate height of the French lilacs?   Depends on the variety; 10 to 25 ft.

Which lilacs, if any, will thrive with only forenoon sunshine?   All lilacs need sunshine. The less sunshine they have the fewer the flowers.

Will you give me information pertaining to the culture, pruning, and general care of own-root, French hybrid lilacs, for specimen bloom? I have a collection of young plants comprising 12 varieties.   The general care of these lilacs is no different from that of any others. For specimen blooms, cutting out a few of the weakest flowering shoots in winter is helpful. Read other questions and answers.

Why do the leaves on new lilac bushes turn brown?   Transplanting injury, lack of sufficient water, or too much fertilizer.

We have lilacs of different species, some more than 10 years old. The foliage always looks clean, but the plants never have any buds or flowers. Neighbors have flowers on their lilacs. Why not ours?   When lilacs fail to bloom, 4 things can be tried, since every lilac should bloom if grown properly: 1. Thin out some of the branches at the base of the plant. 2. Root-prune by digging a 2-ft. ditch around the plants. 3. When the soil is removed from the ditch mix with it a generous amount of superphosphate (about 8 oz. to every 3 ft. of ditch) and return the soil to the ditch. 4. Apply lime if soil is acid. One of these methods, or a combination of all, should force the plant to bloom. Some lilacs, like many other plants, are alternate-blooming, flowering profusely one year and sparsely or not at all the next. This, unfortunately, is to be expected.

Why do lilacs fail to bloom even though flower buds are formed? This may be due to severe drought in the late summer after the buds have been formed.

We have old-fashioned lilacs, large clumps 8 or 10 years old, that have only 5 or 6 blossoms each year. Can you suggest what is cause for not blooming freely? Probably too many young suckers at the base. Cut out most of these and you probably will be repaid with good blooms.

I have some Persian Lilacs, also French Lilacs, none of which seem to do well. What kind of soil and conditions do they require? They need a good alkaline soil with sufficient moisture throughout the summer. Try applying lime in spring and a 3-in. mulch of manure in fall to see if they help.

Pruning

How does one prune lilacs to keep them a decent height and still have blooms? Do not give all the pruning in one year, but over a period of several years. Do not allow them to become too dense, for this forces them to grow high. Allow each branch room to grow, and "top" it at the 6-ft. height.

Should lilacs be pruned? Yes, prune out most of the young suckers and all of the dead or diseased wood. Some of the older branches could be cut out also, to allow more light to reach the branches in the center of the plant. Prune just *after* blooming.

How much pruning should lilacs have? When is the time to to it? Just enough pruning to keep the center open, to cut out dead and diseased wood, keep down the suckers, and to remove the dead flower stalks. This may best be done immediately *after* they are through blooming.

My lilacs are 10 ft. tall. How can I bring them down to eye-level height? In 2 ways: 1. Cut them down to within 2 or 3 feet of the ground and so start entirely new plants. 2. If this is too drastic, do the same thing, but over a period of 3 years, hence thinning out only ⅓ of the branches each year and allowing for continuous bloom.

Will severe pruning force old-fashioned lilacs to give more bloom? Yes, it may; but do not expect flowers for a year or two.

What is the best way to cut back very old, tall, uncared-for lilac bushes? Cut them down nearly to the ground.

What is the best way to start growth again on lilac bushes—all the growth seems to be at the top, leaving the lower part very unsightly. Can it be done? Yes; cut back to within a foot of the ground, and start all over again.

What can be done, if anything, to prevent lilacs from suckering?
There is no preventive measure, but once started this suckering habit
should be stopped immediately merely by cutting out a majority of the
young suckers.

Should any suckers be allowed on French Hybrid Lilacs?   Yes, if
they have been propagated on their own roots. However, if they have
been grafted, the suckers from the understock may prove to be either
California Privet or some very different lilac. Therefore *all* should be
cut out of grafted plants.

**My French Hybrid Lilacs were propagated by cuttings and are grow-
ing on their "own roots." Can I allow suckers to grow?**   Yes—to
some extent. A few of these can be allowed to grow to replace the
older branches which are cut out or to allow the bush to increase in
size. Do not allow all to grow, however, as the bush will become too
dense, and flower formation will be decreased.

**Is it necessary, or better, for the bushes, to cut off dead flowers
from lilacs before they bloom again?**   Yes. Cut them off as soon as
they are finished blooming. This prevents seed formation and allows
more nourishment to go to the flower buds for the next year.

**What is the proper time and method of root-pruning lilacs to bring
them into bloom?**   Dig a 2-ft. trench in spring slightly within the outside limit of the branches, in this way cutting all roots encountered.

How can you stop lilacs from spreading into your neighbor's yard?
Sink a concrete barrier down in the soil, or continually dig and cut
roots on that side of the plant.

Propagation

How do you start new bushes from an old lilac bush?   The best
method is to raise a new stock from cuttings; or, if it is not a grafted
plant, rooted suckers may be dug up, tops cut back ½, and planted.

**I have a lilac bush "President Grevy"; one branch has flowers of a
different color, pale pink with a yellow center. How can I propagate
this sport? It is not from the rootstock, as it appears on a bush 10 ft.
high.**   Either by cuttings, or by grafting or budding it on California
Privet. This privet is not recommended as an understock, but in order
to work up a stock of the "sport" that has occurred on your lilac,
you would be justified in using it until you could obtain enough plants
on their own roots, i.e., from cuttings.

When should lilac cuttings be made?   While the shoots are still
growing, usually about the middle of May. Make cuttings 5 to 6 ins.
long; remove bottom leaves; make a clean cut through stem ¼ in.
below place where leaves were attached. However, lilacs are sometimes raised from hardwood cuttings (taken in early winter) which are
planted in boxes of sand and kept in cool but frostproof sheds until
spring, when rooting takes place.

How is lilac best rooted from cuttings? Outdoors, cold frame, or greenhouse?   Either in propagating cases in a greenhouse, or in a shaded cold frame. The cuttings are placed in sand and kept in a close, humid atmosphere until rooted. (See preceding question.)

How is Persian Lilac propagated?   Either from seeds sown in spring, or from cuttings in May. Also from suckers.

Will lilacs root from the buds on the stems if placed in sand?   It is possible that this method of propagation might be successful if cut off with a sliver of old wood, with leaf still attached.

Pests and Diseases

The leaves of my lilacs are a gray-green instead of true shade. What is the remedy?   The chances are they have mildew. This happens especially in the late summer or during a moist season. It is not serious and can be ignored. Dusting with powdered sulfur as soon as mildew appears is the remedy.

What is lilac "graft blight"?   This is a disease occurring on plants which have been grafted on California Privet understock. A plant which has this disease will look sickly, have yellowish leaves, and may die even in good growing weather. The only remedy is to dig up and destroy such a plant.

How can one eliminate chlorosis in lilacs?   This is not well understood. Chlorosis occurs even on healthy plants growing in normal soil during dry seasons. During the following year the same chlorotic plants may appear healthy. About all one can do is to see that they have some fertilizer and lime, and water thoroughly during dry spells.

MIMOSA

Will a mimosa tree survive a Michigan winter?   The hardiest mimosa—*Albizzia julibrissin rosea*—might be tried in southern Michigan. This proves fairly hardy in Boston, Massachusetts. The mimosa of the South will not be hardy.

Are you supposed to prune mimosa trees?   Yes, when they require it to make them shapely. Where they grow rapidly, they incline to be too flexible and "weak-backed" unless pruned.

MOCKORANGE (PHILADELPHUS)

Which are some of the best mockoranges?   *Philadelphus coronarius* (the old-fashioned syringa); also certain Lemoine hybrids as, for instance, Avalanche and Mont Blanc, with single flowers; Virginale, semi-double; Girandole and Boule d'Argent (double); and certain *cymosus* hybrids like Voie Lactee, Conquete, Banniere, Norma, and Rosace.

Will you give me a statement on the comparative merits (ease of

growth, hardiness, floriferousness, fragrance, shape, and height) of the following hybrid mockoranges: Banniere, nivalis, Norma, Pavillon Blanc, Pyramidale, and Voie Lactee?   These are all of approximately equal hardiness—not reliably hardy north of Philadelphia—but they are being grown as far North as Boston. They are all about 5 to 7 ft. tall; equally easy to grow; but vary in beauty and amount of flowers and fragrance. Using another hybrid, "Avalanche," as a basis for good flower and the old-fashioned fragrant *P. coronarius* as best for fragrance, and rating these both at 10 points, the varieties could be rated as follows: Banniere—flower, 5; fragrance, 4; *nivalis*—flower, 3; fragrance, 6; Norma—flower, 6; fragrance, 4; Pavillon Blanc—flower, 2; fragrance, 0; Pyramidale—flower, 3; fragrance, 0; Voie Lactee—flower, 2; fragrance, 2.

I once saw some mockoranges with large double flowers. What might they have been?   Virginal, or perhaps Argentine; beautiful but less hardy than some.

Why don't my mockoranges, planted last spring, bloom? They have so much brush in them.   They need a year or two in order to recuperate from the shock of transplanting. Thin out a few of the branches if they are too crowded.

Although pruned, why does Mockorange Virginal not bush out, but grow only lanky shoots at the top?   This variety is naturally gawky. It can be made a little more compact by pinching out the tips of lanky shoots when they are actively growing.

How should I trim an overgrown mockorange bush?   Thin it out during winter by cutting the oldest branches as near the ground line as possible. Shorten those remaining about ⅓, if it seems necessary. This drastic treatment will result in few, if any, flowers the following spring.

When and how is the best way to prune a mockorange shrub?   Immediately after flowering by cutting out the oldest and weakest shoots, making the cuts as near the ground line as possible.

PRIVET

See also Hedges, this section.

If a privet is not pruned, what kind of flowers does it have? And berries?   Cream-white flowers in small panicles somewhat like lilacs, but with a distressing odor in midsummer. Berries are black.

What is the name of a privet which forms a broad bush?   Regel Privet—*Ligustrum obtusifolium regelianum.*

What is the best time to prune Amur River Privet?   When grown as a bush, needs no pruning. As a hedge it should be sheared when the new growth is 6 to 8 ins. long. Repeat shearing in August.

QUINCE, FLOWERING (CHAENOMELES (CYDONIA) JAPONICA)

What colors are to be had in flowering quinces? When do they bloom? The following are some varieties of *Chaenomeles lagenaria:* Nivalis—white; Double Scarlet; Corallina—salmon-pink; Baltzi—rosy pink; Columbia—deep rose; Marcocarpa—red; Rubra Grandiflora—deep crimson. One known as Spitfire, a newcomer, is noteworthy because of its narrow form and upright growth. It can be used for accent or for hedges. Its flowers are deep crimson.

What kinds of flowering quince bushes are there? Are some varieties taller than others? The tall shrub *Chaenomeles* (also called *Cydonia lagenaria*) grows to about 6 ft. high. The dwarf species (*C. japonica*) is a broad, low shrub, growing to 3 ft. high. A still lower variety (*C. j. alpina*) spreads into a low patch seldom over 1½ ft. high.

I have a flowering quince (red) that does not bloom, although the plant is 6 years old. The sprout was taken from a beautiful bush which blooms each year. This plant has never bloomed and it's planted beside 2 other quinces that bloom each year. Why? It may well be that the original plant was a grafted plant and the understock was the common quince, which blooms only after reaching some size. Would suggest that you check the 2 in foliage. If they differ, discard yours. If they do not differ, check them again when the parent is in flower next spring.

The blossoms of my flowering quince are produced toward the center of the bush and are not well displayed. Can this be avoided? Yes. Prune the bush by shortening the new shoots as they are produced throughout the summer. This will cause the formation of flower spurs near the tips of the branches.

I have a shrub in my garden that I have been told is a variety of flowering quince. It has never bloomed and I was wondering what could be done to force it to bloom. Would pruning help? Summer pruning will help, as described in the preceding answer. The incorporation of superphosphate in the soil over the roots, at the rate of 6 oz. per sq. yd., may be helpful. Root-pruning (which see) should be resorted to if these measures fail.

How can I slip my flowering quince? The flowering quince may be treated in the same manner as flowering almond (which see).

Is the fruit of the so-called "burning bush," or Chaenomeles japonica, edible? It is very sour, but can be used in making jellies. Incidentally "burning bush" is a misnomer as an English name for this shrub. It is more correctly applied to the wahoo, or strawberry bush, *Euonymus americanus,* which see.

ROSE-ACACIA (ROBINIA)

What is a rose-acacia?   A hardy shrub native to the Allegheny Mountains. Grows to 12 ft. with dark, rich green foliage and racemes of rose-colored, pealike blossoms in late spring.

Where shall I plant a rose-acacia shrub?   In a spot protected from heavy winds, in light soil. Good for dry banks and as a screen. It suckers freely and, if neglectd, forms a dense thicket.

Do rose-acacia shrubs have to be grafted stock to bloom, or can they be taken from old plants?   No. If the old plants spread from year to year by suckers then it is a simple matter to dig up and re-plant some of the suckers, and so form new plants. However, rose-acacia is sometimes grafted high to form "standards," in which case any growth taken from the base would merely increase the under-stock, probably black locust.

ROSE-OF-SHARON (HIBISCUS SYRIACUS)

What colors does the rose-of-Sharon come in?   Double—white, pink; single—purple, red, blue, and white.

The most beautiful rose-of-Sharon I have seen has single lavender-blue flowers with carmine eye. What is its name?   Coelestis.

What is shrub-althea?   Same as rose-of-Sharon, *Hibiscus syriacus*.

What kind of soil does rose-of-Sharon thrive in? Mine was doing poorly. I put lime around it and it died.   It needs a deep soil which has plenty of water—even a tendency to be very moist occasionally. A complete fertilizer and water would possibly have saved your plant.

Can rose-of-Sharon shrubs or trees be transplanted in the fall? May be safely transplanted in fall except in places subjected to high, cold winds during the winter.

What is the correct care of rose-of-Sharon? (Maine.)   There are many places in Maine where the rose-of-Sharon simply will not grow because of winter cold. Where it will survive, cut back the last year's shoots to about 4 buds early in the spring. This heavy pruning usually results in heavy flower production—providing, of course, it has good soil.

What is the cause of my rose-of-Sharon buds falling off before they open?   Partly a varietal characteristic. Other factors might be insufficient phosphorus or potash in the soil; too little or too much soil moisture; or attack by aphids.

When and how should rose-of-Sharon (Hibiscus syriacus) be pruned?   Blossoms are produced on shoots of the current season, so the shoots of the preceding year can be cut back to within 1 bud of their point of origin in spring, with no loss of blooms. However, this heavy pruning makes an ungainly bush, and many good gardeners prefer to prune them lightly or let them go unpruned.

What are the best conditions for rose-of-Sharon? Can it be budded or grafted? Rose-of-Sharon (*Hibiscus syriacus*) will grow quite well in any reasonably good garden soil. It may be budded or grafted, but this trouble hardly seems justified, as most of the varieties root very readily from cuttings taken in the summer.

RUSSIAN OLIVE (ELAEAGNUS)

What shrub would give a distinct silvery effect? Russian Olive (*Elaeagnus angustifolia*), with narrow leaves, silvery on reverse side, a shrub to 20 ft. high; Silverberry (*E. commutata*)—bushy, to 12 ft., leaves silver on both sides, fast-growing; Cherry Elaeagnus (*E. multiflora*), leaves silvery beneath, grows 4 to 9 ft.

Does Elaeagnus have flowers or fruits? Flowers inconspicuous but strongly fragrant in *E. angustifolia,* Silverberry, and *E. umbellata.* Small, yellow-silvery berries on Silverberry; brown-red berries on *E. umbellata.*

In what manner and how severely should Russian Olive (Elaeagnus angustifolia) be pruned if 3 years old and about 15 ft. high? Usually needs no pruning when growing in poor, dry soil and a sunny location to which it is adapted. Yours evidently is in rich ground and should be pruned by shortening lanky growths about midsummer.

SNOWBERRY (SYMPHORICARPOS)

How and when should the snowberry bush, Symphoricarpos, be trimmed? If it is behaving itself by producing plenty of fruits on a shapely bush, leave it alone. If not, cut it down to the ground in late winter.

SPIREA (SPIRAEA)

I would like to know if I should snip the tips of bridalwreaths? If so, when? Do not snip off the tips, as this spoils the grace of the bush. Instead, cut out some of the shoots as soon as the blossoms have faded.

Is it possible to trim and drastically reduce bridalwreath (Spiraea prunifolia) in size? Yes; cut back all flowering shoots immediately the flowers have faded. Shorten those remaining, if necessary, to reduce to the height required.

How should Spirea Anthony Waterer be pruned? This is a late bloomer, producing its flowers on shoots of the current season; therefore, it may be cut back about ½ in the spring, just as growth begins.

We have a number of spirea plants on an old lot which are much too large and tall for our present building lot. How drastically can these shrubs be pruned? Spireas in general can withstand severe pruning. It may be done in late winter, but this results (in the case of early-blooming varieties) in no blooms the following season.

STEPHANANDRA

What is stephanandra?   A shrub with panicles of white or greenish flowers. *S. incisa* is drooping, with deeply lobed leaves; *S. tanakae* has larger leaves, shallowly lobed. These are hardy in the North with some winter protection.

How do you make cuttings of stephanandra? Most descriptions make it difficult to understand.   Cuttings of half-ripe wood root readily in July. From shoots of normal thickness cut off the terminal 4 to 5 ins. Remove 1 or 2 of the lowest leaves on the cutting so formed, and make a clean cut through the stem, just below the joint from which the lowest leaf was cut. The cutting is then ready for placing in moist sand in a shaded cold frame. Or make hardwood cuttings, 6 ins. long, in November, pack in moist sand in a cool place (or bury outdoors over winter), and plant in early spring.

SUMAC

Can Fragrant Sumac be closely trimmed, down to say 4 ins.? When?   Yes; in the spring before growth starts. But better leave it a little longer than 4 ins.

SWEETSHRUB (CALYCANTHUS)

What color are the flowers of sweetshrub (Calycanthus)? When does it bloom?   Reddish or purplish brown. Blooms in June and July.

Is calycanthus a difficult shrub? We planted one, pruned it, and gave it plenty of water, but it slowly died after having come out in full leaf.   Calycanthus should not present any great difficulty, though it is sometimes slow to start into vigorous growth after moving. The treatment you gave your plant appears to be correct. If you make another attempt, cut out at least half of the older stems at ground level, and reduce the remainder about half their length. Be careful not to give too much water.

A sweetshrub bush which formerly produced very fragrant flowers now continues to have lovely blooms which, however, have no scent. Is there anything that can be done?   No, unless you wish to try fertilizing it heavily with well-rotted manure or some complete commercial fertilizer. Sometimes increased vigor produced in this manner will make the flowers more fragrant.

STRAWBERRY-BUSH (EUONYMUS AMERICANUS)

Does the Strawberry-bush require pruning?   Strawberry-bush or Brook Euonymus (*Euonymus americanus*) ordinarily does not need pruning. Any "wild" shoots (those which in growth greatly outstrip the majority) may be shortened in late winter or during the growing season.

I have a Strawberry-bush I wish to move. Can I do it more successfully in the late fall or in the early spring? Early spring is preferred; but as you are moving it from one position to another in your own garden it should be quite safe to move it in the fall as soon as it has lost the greater part of its leaves.

TAMARISK

What does a tamarisk (tamarix) look like? Handsome, picturesque shrub with a plumy effect. Leaves resemble heather. Flowers pink to white. Some of the hardiest (to southern New England) are *T. parviflora*, *T. pentandra,* and *T. odessana*.

I have been told that the tamarisks can stand ocean spray and wind. Is that true? (Massachusetts.) Yes. It is one of the finest of all shrubs for shore planting, and thrives in sandy soil.

When and how is a tamarisk pruned? We have one which has 6 or 7 long branches which begin at the ground level and sprawl. Pruning depends on the group to which it belongs. Some bloom early on old wood, while others flower on wood of the current season. The first type should be cut back severely after flowering; the latter in the spring. In both cases the (approximately) 1-year-old shoots should be cut back ½ to ⅔.

VIBURNUM

Which viburnums do you recommend for autumn coloring and fruiting? Linden viburnum (*V. dilatatum*); witherod (*V. cassinoids*)*;* Wright, or Oriental (*V. wrighti*)*;* Mapleleaf (*V. acerifolium*); Blackhaw (*V. prunifolium*).

Which viburnums have the most effective flowers? Double-file Viburnum (*V. tomentosum*)*;* Japanese Snowball (*V. tomentosum sterile*). The former has flat flower heads which seem to lie along the horizontal branches.

Which viburnum would lend itself best to foundation planting? The sweet-scented and early blooming *V. carlesi;* or, *V. carcephalum* which has larger heads of bloom.

Which viburnum will stand the most shade for woodland planting? Mapleleaf Viburnum, also called Dockmackie (*V. acerifolium*).

Is there a low, compact viburnum? Yes; Dwarf Cranberry Bush (*V. opulus nanum*), to 2½ ft. high.

Does Viburnum carlesi prefer a neutral soil? It will grow well enough in any approximately neutral garden soil of good quality, and not likely to become parched.

Why is Viburnum carlesi so difficult to grow on its own roots, and Viburnum burkwoodi so easy when the plants are practically identical? This is one of Nature's many as-yet-unanswered questions. In fact,

V. carlesi is one of the parents of *V. burkwoodi*—which only makes the answer more difficult.

When and how should I prune Viburnum carlesi? Usually does not require any pruning. If the center of the bush becomes crowded, superfluous shoots may be thinned out immediately after flowering.

Why did my Viburnum dilatatum fail to produce berries? It may have been that a cool rainy spell predominated just when the pollen was ripe. This would have prevented insect activity and wind from disseminating the pollen at the proper time.

Can you suggest reasons why three Japanese Snowballs (Viburnum tomentosum sterile) I planted died? The European Snowball (V. opulus roseum) American Cranberrybush (V. trilobum) lived. Possibly killed by winter. The Japanese Snowball is not so hardy as the European.

When and how can I prune my snowball bush (viburnum) which has grown too high and too shaggy? You might take a chance on cutting it back immediately after flowering; or in early spring if you are prepared to sacrifice the season's crop of bloom; but often snowball bushes do not respond well to severe pruning.

I have a snowball bush 5 or 6 years old that has never bloomed. What is wrong with it? The flower buds have probably been killed by winter cold. May be lack of nutrients in soil.

WEIGELA

Is there a weigela with very showy blooms? Yes, variety Bristol Ruby, with red blossoms; or Eva Rathke or Vanicek both of which have a tendency to recurrent bloom from June to August.

What is the best way to treat a weigela bush that is very old and produces very few flowers? Thin out the bush by removing some of the oldest branches during the winter. Cut them as near as possible to the ground line. Annual pruning should consist of the removal of worn-out flowering branches as soon as the blossoms have faded.

WILLOW, PUSSY

Will a Pussy Willow do well in dry soil? Pussy Willow (*Salix discolor*) adapts itself to a dry soil but prefers a moist. In dry soil it may become quite susceptible to diseases, and it will grow more slowly and remain smaller.

Why does my Pussy Willow burst forth in December and not in spring? (Massachusetts.) Mild winter days frequently force pussy willows into premature growth, especially if the tree is growing in a protected spot.

When is best time to prune Pussy Willows? If it is desired to have the "pussies" develop on long, wandlike shoots, the tree should be pruned severely before growth starts by cutting back all of the shoots made the preceding year to 1 or 2 buds. Otherwise no pruning is necessary.

Is it best to let a Pussy Willow grow in a bush or tree form? How tall should it grow?   It is best to keep it in bush form by pruning out any central leader that may appear. The height depends upon conditions, varying from 10 to 20 ft.

How can I start Pussy Willows in ground? What time of year?   As soon as the frost is out of the ground in spring make cuttings 8 to 10 ins. long. Place ¾ of the cutting in the ground.

WINTERBERRY (ILEX VERTICILLATA)

I have seen a shrub in the wild which in fall has shining scarlet berries close to the stem after the leaves are gone. What is it?   Probably winterberry (*Ilex verticillata*).

Two good plants for autumn and winter color—American Holly and its relative, the native Winterberry. The latter is much hardier, but is not evergreen.

How can winterberry or blackalder be used?   In a shrub border, preferably in moist soil. It grows somewhat lank, so plant it in back of lower shrubs as, for instance, inkberry, an evergreen relative.

Does blackalder (winterberry) require wet feet or does it grow in spite of the water?   Winterberry is a shrub often found in the wild state in swampy ground. However, it grows quite successfully in any good garden soil, provided it is not too dry.

Will you tell me the best way to move, transplant, and grow the blackalder or winterberry holly?   Dig it carefully in the very early spring, with or without a ball of earth about the roots. Place in a good garden loam, slightly on the moist side if possible. Prune back ⅓. Water well.

WITCHHAZEL (HAMAMELIS)

Where would you plant a witchhazel?   In the woodland, or in the rear of a shrub border, or near a window of the house so the blossoms may be enjoyed from indoors at close range. They are not showy, but valued for their time of bloom.

What is the ultimate height of the witchhazel? The tallest witchhazel your answer man has seen was an old specimen of the native *H. virginiana,* some 40 ft. high. That is exceptional. Another native species, *H. vernalis,* usually remains less than 8 ft. high.

When do the witchhazels bloom? October or November—native witchhazel; February or March—Japanese, Chinese, and Vernal.

Will witchhazel grow in half shade? Is it worth growing? Witchhazels are eminently suited for planting as undershrubs in wooded places. Their unseasonal flowers are more interesting than spectacular. Showiest in flower is the Chinese (*H. mollis*). Where open woodland situations are to be planted, the witchhazels are well worth while.

EVERGREEN TREES AND THEIR CULTURE

WHAT TO GROW

What does coniferous mean? It means cone-bearing. Among the cone-bearing trees are firs, spruce, pines, Douglasfir, and hemlocks.

What are retinosporas? This is a term applied to juvenile or immature forms of false-cypress (*Chamaecyparis*) and arborvitae (*Thuja*).

What are the best evergreen trees for specimen lawn planting? (Northern New England.) Douglasfir, White Fir, hemlock, White and Red Pine; arborvitae, yew, and Hinoki Cypress if small trees are preferred.

I want to put some evergreens back of my White Birch trees. What would harmonize? Hemlock or Red Pine.

Would like a few dignified evergreen trees. What do you suggest that would in time become very large? Hemlock, White Pine, Red Pine, firs, and most spruces where climates are not too hot.

Will you recommend some medium-size, erect-growing evergreen trees? Arborvitae (*Thuja occidentalis*)*;* Redcedar (*Juniperus virginiana*); Chinese Juniper (*J. chinensis*); Upright Yew (*Taxus cuspidata* and *T. media* varieties).

Can you suggest some drooping evergreen trees to plant beside our garden pool? Weeping Hemlock, Weeping Norway Spruce, Weeping Douglasfir.

We are planting a wildflower sanctuary in our woodland. Which evergreens would be the best to introduce there? Hemlock, rhododendrons, Canada Yew.

What is the fastest-growing evergreen?   In the northern United States this is probably the hemlock, although the White Pine might run first when grown in good soil.

Are there any evergreen trees with berries?   Redcedars have blue-gray berries, and the yews sometimes have red berries, but they usually drop quickly.

What are some evergreens that can be grown for Christmas decorations?   Hollies, all kinds, both deciduous and evergreen; pine, spruce, fir, hemlock, arborvitae, juniper, yew, Mountain Andromeda, Japanese Andromeda, Mountain Laurel, rhododendron, etc. Spruce and hemlock quickly drop their needles when cut unless stood in water.

I wish to set out 50 or 75 evergreens for use later as cut Christmas trees. What kind of trees would you recommend for western Pennsylvania?   Douglasfir (*Pseudotsuga taxifolia*). Balsam Fir is best if it will grow in your section.

LOW-GROWING

What evergreens, 4 to 6 ft. high, are spreading in habit?   Common and Pfitzer Juniper, Japanese Yew, Sargent Weeping Hemlock.

Two types of small evergreens; the prostrate or spreading varieties are desirable for banks or terraces.

Which low evergreens could be used to edge our terrace in a sunny, dry location?   Pfitzer Juniper, plumy; Globe Redcedar, compact.

Which formal evergreen would be suitable for each side of our sunny front door?   *Picea glauca conica,* the Dwarf Alberta Spruce.

Is there a dwarf evergreen with red berries in winter?   Yes, dwarf forms of Japanese Yew.

Are there any evergreens which will remain low—not more than 2 ft.?   Mugho Pine; Spreading English Yew; Compact Japanese Yew; many dwarf junipers, such as Bar Harbor and tamarix; Maxwell Spruce, and other dwarf varieties. After several years it may be necessary to slow down rate of growth by summer pruning.

Are there low-growing conifers suitable for a rock garden?
Spreading English Yew, Dwarf Japanese Yew, Dwarf Hinoki Cypress,
Andorra Juniper, Bar Harbor Juniper; dwarf forms of Mugho Pine.

*For picturesque effects in the rock garden, or
in more or less formal plantings, such evergreens as Mugho Pine and the Oriental or
Chinese Arborvitae are selected.*

**Which evergreens would make suitable foundation planting for the
four sides of a large farmhouse? Are fruit-bearing bushes practical
for such use?**   Evergreens would be selected from the rhododendrons
(for shady areas), yews, arborvitaes, and junipers. Yes, fruit-bearing
shrubs, such as the blueberry, viburnum, and cotoneaster, would be
assets in such a planting.

*For foundation plantings low-growing evergreens
that stay low (such as Pfitzer Juniper and Dwarf
Alberta Spruce) are a wise choice.*

CULTURE

SOIL

What kind of soil is best for evergreens?   A soil suitable for most
kinds is a good loam, well drained, but somewhat retentive of
moisture. On such a soil, additional nourishment may be supplied for

yews, which like a rather rich diet. Junipers, pines, and Douglasfir should not require it. Most broad-leaved evergreens need an acid soil.

Can good results be expected from evergreen trees planted on land stripped of its topsoil?   Such land is not suited for the intensive cultivation of evergreen trees, but pockets may be prepared for occasional trees. In a clayish subsoil, prepare these pockets by mixing in cinders and humus matter; in sandy soil, work in plenty of humus.

Our soil is dry. Would pines and junipers be advisable?   Yes, most pines and junipers tolerate dry soil.

FEEDING

What is the best fertilizer for dwarf evergreens?   Some, including dwarf junipers and pines, will require none, unless the soil is very poor. Arborvitae, yews, and chamaecyparis like some fertilizer. The best way to apply nourishment to established plants is by applying a top-dressing of leafmold or peatmoss mixed with old manure before snow falls.

Do evergreens need a leaf-and-manure fertilizer?   In planting—depending upon the quality of the soil—mix more or less leafmold and old manure with the planting soil. For established evergreens in good soil, nothing more than a top-dressing of the same. Yews like a top-dressing of old manure.

Can evergreens be fed in the winter?   A rich mulch (2- to 3-in. layer of manure or leafmold) applied before snow falls, or during open weather in winter, is beneficial.

How often should bone meal be placed around evergreens?   Do not use bone meal. Use, rather, somewhat acid artificial fertilizers; or, still better, top-dressings of leafmold or peatmoss with some old manure. (See previous question.)

TRANSPLANTING

How are evergreens transplanted?   Very small specimens are moved with a ball of earth, held in place by burlap, attached to their roots. Large specimens should be moved with a platform beneath them, installed by someone with experience.

When is it best to transplant small evergreens in southern New York State; and how?   Either early September or early spring. Dig a hole twice as wide and twice as deep as the root system of the plant; have plenty of good soil available; be certain there is drainage at the bottom of the hole. Set in plant carefully—no deeper in soil than it formerly grew—untie burlap and remove it (if possible without the root ball collapsing, otherwise tuck it in between the side of the hole and the root ball) fill in soil, make firm, and water thoroughly. Leave a slight depression in soil about plant so that it will receive plenty of water until it becomes well established.

I would like to change several little evergreens to another location. When and how do I go about it? If plants are small, dig them in the spring with the best possible root-ball. Plant in a friable soil mixed with leafmold or old manure. Water thoroughly; mulch the base to prevent drying out. If larger trees, transplant either in spring or early autumn.

When is the best time of the year to plant little evergreens (seedlings)? In the spring, when the ground has dried and warmed so that it is friable; and before the evergreens have started growth.

When is the best time to transplant evergreens? For well-grown nursery grades, spring, before growth has started; or early autumn, from August 1 on. For plants that have not been transplanted recently, spring is best. Large trees, properly balled and platformed, may be moved in the spring, or as late into the autumn as the ground can be dug.

Evergreens planted with the burlap on do not grow for me, although I have raised beautiful evergreens. Should I remove burlap instead of slitting it? Unless it might break a weak root-ball, remove the burlap; at least open the knots, spread it out in the bottom of the hole, or cut it off close to the base of the ball.

How early in the spring can evergreens be transplanted? Wait till all frost is out of the ground and the soil has dried off and warmed up, so that it is thoroughly workable. Transplant evergreens before they have started into growth.

When does the fall planting season for evergreens begin? Generally, as soon as the early summer growth has become hardened. In the case of pines, spruces, and firs, this means as soon as the annual growth has been completed and has hardened and the terminal buds firmly "set." In dry seasons, one usually waits for a favorable moist spell of weather.

In New York, what are the best months for planting evergreens? And what months in spring and fall are the deadlines for planting? Plant preferably in early September (first choice); or March to April (second choice).

Which evergreens could be planted in December? In lower New York State large specimens of the hardy kinds, if properly balled and platformed. While December is late for smaller evergreens, one might take a chance on them, if they had solid, fibrous root-balls, and were handled carefully.

Is it O.K. to move evergreens in midwinter, so long as the ground is not frozen, but may freeze up any time after the planting? Safe enough for large trees, dug with solid fibrous root-balls, carefully planted, well watered, and mulched. Not advisable for small evergreens; unsafe for trees that have not been previously transplanted.

Why do I lose so many evergreens, purchased with solid-looking balls and tightly burlapped? Possibly because these good-looking trees had been dug and kept out of the ground for some time prior to your purchase. Freshly dug trees, promptly planted, stand a far better chance of succeeding than "pre-dug" stock.

I often find roots of dead evergreens packed hard in a dry ball, despite repeated soakings. How come? Root-balls dug in clayish soil, or puddled in clay, when planted in a lighter soil may easily become caked hard, so that water cannot penetrate them. Loosen the surface of hard-looking balls before planting.

Why do so many evergreen trees die after transplanting? There are many possible causes. Trees may not have had fibrous root systems; they may have been dug with inadequate root-balls, or planted at the wrong season; they may have perished from drought; or they may have been tender kinds.

Will oak sawdust, if it is put in the ground while transplanting evergreens, help them or do harm? On a soil deficient in humus, if no other humus-forming material is available, a little rotted hardwood sawdust may be helpful. But when possible use leafmold, woods earth, peatmoss, or old manure.

CARE

Our water supply comes from a deep well and is quite hard. We have planted many seedling evergreens. Will it be harmful to use well water on them; and will it injure the foliage should any get on it? Alkaline water is definitely harmful to all broad-leaved evergreens, and might injure some narrow-leaved ones, such as pines, hemlocks, spruce, fir, cypress. Foliage will be injured through damage done to the whole plant by introducing alkali into soil, not by contact of water with leaves.

Should one cultivate around evergreens? Cultivation at the base of established evergreens may disturb surface roots and do more harm than good. Keep the soil from caking, rather, by means of a mulch of leafmold or peatmoss, with perhaps a little old manure.

Should one at all times keep a mulch about the base of evergreen trees? Mulch all newly planted evergreens. While a mulch will be helpful to many established evergreens, not all kinds require it if planted in a suitable soil.

What is the reason that evergreens, such as Pyramidal Arborvitae or Scotch Pines, turn a rusty brown and lose their needles? This may represent only a normal shedding of old foliage. Drought and soil exhaustion may cause premature shedding. Virorous growth and proper sanitation tend to reduce it.

My arborvitae has a lot of brown leaves. I have dusted it with sulfur. **Can you give any advice? Prevent caking of the soil, and see that the roots do not lack water. Just before ground freezes, give a very thorough soaking. Keep a mulch of leafmold or peatmoss about base.

I have poor luck with Mugho Pine and Koster Blue Spruce. I lost two Mughos, and the spruce doesn't look well. What is wrong? Both kinds, unless transplanted frequently in the nursery, makes coarse roots, which mean great risk in transplanting. Most losses are due to this. Secure transplanted, fibrous-rooted plants. These will usually grow right along in any fair soil, if planted where they get sun.

Would the exhaust from autos, blowing into the evergreens, cause their death? Repeated and protracted exposure to these gases may cause the death of evergreens, especially hot exhaust gas on a cold winter day.

Should healthy evergreen trees turn yellowish? Color is not a natural condition. No. A yellowish discoloring may indicate any of several causes of trouble: poor drainage, overwatering, or a poor quality of soil.

In the planting about our house one corner plant died 6 months after planting. A reset did the same. The soil was examined, and no lime pocket was found, nor sign of insect trouble. All other plants are doing well. What may have been the trouble? Corner plants often suffer from a strong draft of air. This may be fatal to newly planted trees. A windscreen might prevent the trouble.

I have cedars and Pfitzer Junipers, planted about 2 years ago. They are not growing and look dry, although I have tried to treat them right. I hoe around them and water thoroughly. They are on west side of open porch (not very close to porch) and pretty far apart. What do they need? Examine them for spider mites. It these are found, spray promptly and repeatedly with malathion. The ground may be hard and poor. Cultivate and apply a mulch.

Do evergreen trees need shade or sun? Nearly all prefer an open situation. The native yew prefers shade. Balsam fir and hemlock prefer a situation open overhead, but some partial protection from the brightest winter sun from near-by tall trees.

When is the best time to apply a dormant oil spray to evergreens (in central Pennsylvania)? What should the temperature be? Early spring; but this kind of spray should always be used on evergreens most carefully, for if too strong, it will quickly burn the foliage and possibly kill the plant. It will remove "bloom" from types such as Blue Spruce. Temperature should be under 65° F.

How can I straighten spruce and other evergreens bent from snow-storms? Pull them back into position. Light trees may be held in place by stakes; larger ones by guy wires or ropes fastened to pegs in the ground, or to overhead points. After a snowstorm, go over your evergreens and shake off snow with a broom or the back of a rake.

PRUNING

When and how should an evergreen be trimmed to make it bushy instead of a tall tree? Different kinds may be trimmed at different times, but the season which will suit all is in late June or July period of soft spring growth. In upright growing kinds, trim both top and side branches so as to avoid a chopped-off effect.

What can one do to train evergreens to be bushy instead of tall and straggly? Trim them annually, from the start. And see that those which like a rich soil, such as yews and chamaecyparis, are kept suppled with a nourishing top-dressing.

Can evergreen trees, which have been allowed to grow too tall near the house, be trimmed back? It can be done with the kinds which will "break" readily from the old wood; but not with pines, firs, spruce, or Douglasfir. Trimming back, however, may leave large evergreens in an unsightly condition.

Can evergreen trees be kept low by cutting the tops? Yes; but a radical "topping" will spoil the appearance and natural beauty of most—especially pines, spruces, and firs, which will not "break" from the old wood, and will remain stunted.

Is it advisable to heavily prune small evergreens to control shape? With the exception of erect-growing pines, spruces, firs, and Douglas-fir (which are best left with a minimum of pruning), most young evergreens will be benefited by pruning uneven shoots that they will eventually make more solid and compact plants.

Does it harm a spruce or pine to cut branches from it for indoor purposes? It may not threaten the life of a large tree, but may easily spoil its appearance.

Can evergreens be trimmed in winter? Never prune them during freezing weather. Do not trim in winter any of those evergreens which make one annual shoot terminated by a prominent bud, like pine, spruce, fir, and Douglasfir. These should be trimmed in early summer. Young shoots of pine may be shortened before the needles develop.

WINTER PROTECTION

Will you outline winter care of untransplanted seedling evergreens, and of once- or twice-transplanted ones? For the seedlings and once-transplanted, a covering with dry leaves in late autumn; for the twice-transplanted, a mulch over the ground and light branches (not necessarily evergreen) laid over the rows or beds. Water the plants thoroughly just before winter hard freezing and previous to applying mulch.

How should pines and junipers be cared for during the winter?
If well established, no special winter protection is needed. In the case
of newly set plants a mulch of leaves or other littery material, applied
as the ground is about to freeze, might be helpful and would certainly
do no harm.

**How should I care for Douglasfir, Picea omorika, Austrian Pine,
and Mugho Pine in the winter? (New York.)** The evergreens mentioned are quite hardy in New York and need no special winter
protection.

**Is it true that I shouldn't mulch with oak leaves around my small
firs?** There is nothing harmful to firs in oak leaves; but in a planting
near the house, for instance, the leaves may be too loose to be the
best mulching material.

**What is proper procedure for protecting low evergreen shrubs and
trees in the winter (located at the seashore with only the house to
protect them)?** If the soil is dry, give a good watering before the
ground freezes, then put on a mulch of leaves or litter several inches
deep. Protection from wind is probably important, and this may be
afforded by sticking evergreen boughs in the ground around them. In
some cases it may be advisable to erect a temporary windbreak made
of boards or burlap.

**Will it be worth while to cover bases of evergreens with partly
decayed leaves now (January) after the ground has been covered with
snow for some time? The trees were planted in October.** If the
snow is likely to remain all winter, there is no need for a mulch at
this time; but if a midwinter thaw occurs, then it would be advisable
to spread leaves to curtail bad effect of alternate freezing and thawing.

Is there any way to prevent windburn on evergreen trees? The
injury referred to is probably the scorched appearance of foliage
sometimes noted in the spring, especially on firs. This is caused by
the sun in winter and can be prevented largely by placing trees so
that they will have some slight protection from the brightest sun in
winter.

**How shall I take care of evergreens in winter, when they can-
not be watered?** There is not much to be done in this case. In some
cases, such as small specimens in a foundation planting, or in a very
exposed position, evergreen boughs could be stuck in the ground
around them to give some protection from winter sun and wind. A
liquid latex preparation has been sprayed on with good results.

PROPAGATION: SEED AND CUTTINGS

Is it possible for an amateur to raise evergreens from seeds? Yes,
providing one has reasonable patience and is prepared to give careful
attention to the seeds and seedlings. (See following questions.)

How can I grow evergreens from seed? Sow fall-collected seed in spring in shallow boxes filled with light, well-drained soil. Cover, to about diameter of seed, with sifted soil. Place flats in cool, shaded cold frame and keep evenly moist. When watering, avoid disturbing surface soil. Transplant when large enough to handle.

How do you keep seeds of evergreens until planting time? Store in tins, jars, or tight paper bags that are nearly airtight, in a cool, dry place.

When should evergreen tree seed be planted; and how old should the seed be? Seed collected in fall should be sown in spring. Older seed, kept under proper conditions, will germinate, but vitality becomes progressively less with each passing year.

Can evergreens be propagated by using the clippings for cuttings? (Wisconsin.) Most of the yews, junipers, cypresses (chamaecyparis), arborvitaes, and some of the spruces may be propagated by means of clippings. These may be taken in late August, but as a rule many of them do not form roots before winter, therefore a greenhouse is desirable, particularly in your climate. If you have a greenhouse (night temperature 50° to 55° F.) you could also take cuttings in November and December.

What is best temperature to root pines and spruces from slips in hothouse beds? The percentage of pine cuttings that can be rooted is so small as to make this method almost valueless. Some of the spruces may be rooted, and for these a greenhouse with a night temperature of 50° to 55° F. is required.

Will you describe the simplest way to start cuttings of arborvitaes and junipers? Take the cuttings in the latter part of August, and set them out, about 1½ ins. apart, in boxes of sand. The boxes should not be more than 4 ins. deep, but any convenient size; the sand must be made firm before the cuttings are put in. Keep them in a cold frame until there is the possibility of the sand freezing, then place them in a cool, frostproof storage for the winter.

Should boxes filled with sharp sand and leafmold, containing cuttings of yew and boxwood, be placed in deep shade, or in semi-shade, for best results? The important thing is that the cuttings must not be directly exposed to the sun, except possibly very early in the morning or late in the evening. Beyond this give all the light possible.

SPECIFIC EVERGREENS

ARBORVITAE

See also Hedges.

Which arborvitae would be best in our Northern climate, to serve

as a boundary-line screen? Pyramidal Arborvitae, *Thuja occidentalis fastigiata*.

Would an arborvitae stand city conditions? Not very well but it will grow in the city if conditions are not too severe. Needs good moist soil and sunshine for at least half of the day.

Will Golden Arborvitae do as well in shade as in sun? No. All "colored" evergreens require full sun to bring out their peculiar coloring.

When is the best time to plant arborvitae? What soil? Plant in spring, before growth starts, or early fall, up to October 1; baby trees, only in the spring. Dig them, in spring or fall, with solid root-ball. Set as deeply as they formerly stood. Fill around the ball with friable soil enriched with humus, and water this down well. When settled, add more soil, flush with the grade. Mulch the base, and in dry weather administer occasional soakings.

How shall I care for an arborvitae foundation planting? Do not set plants in shaded areas; see that they do not lack for water; just before winter, give a thorough soaking; spray promptly and repeatedly in case of spider mites; keep the soil from caking. In a poorish soil, a mulch of leafmold or peatmoss, with a little old manure, will be helpful.

Why are arborvitaes so hard to grow? They are by nature lovers of open situations and moist soils. Their use in foundation plantings, therefore, is highly artificial and unnatural. (See previous questions.)

Can an arborvitae be pruned if the tree becomes too tall and thin? When is the proper pruning time? This can be done effectively in the case of quite young plants. Pruning and topping will do little good to old plants. Pruning should be done during the period of soft spring growth. To improve the denseness of old plants, apply a nutritious top-dressing of leafmold and old manure.

When and how is the best time to trim arborvitae? During the period of soft spring growth shear the outer surface slightly, trimming the extremities of the soft growths. Close shearing results in a dense, formal appearance; light shearing in a less formal appearance.

CEDAR

Could I grow a Cedar-of-Lebanon here? What is its botanical name? (Southern Pennsylvania.) *Cedrus libani* would probably grow for you, but it is not hardy much farther North, though a strain of the cedar-of-Lebanon, said to be fairly hardy, has been introduced by the Arnold Arboretum near Boston.

CRYPTOMERIA

What is the cryptomeria like? The Japanese Temple-cedar is a rapid-growing tree with tufted branches. It attains 125 ft. in Japan. It is not hardy much above Zone VI. In this country is handsome when young, but soon becomes scrawny.

CYPRESS

I have a tiny dwarf tree which has frondlike foliage and seems very tolerant and hardy, and looks very well in the rock garden. What is it? It is probably Dwarf Hinoki Cypress (*Chamaecyparis obtusa nana*).

FIR

What does the Nikko Fir look like? Large, broadly pyramidal tree with spreading upturned branches, and glossy dark-green leaves. Needles spread upward forming a V over the twig. Identify it by its grooved branchlets.

What is a good fir as a specimen tree? (New Hampshire.) White Fir (*Abies concolor*).

Which of the evergreens is very dark in color, of pyramidal form, tall, and with pendulous branches? This is probably the Douglasfir (*Pseudotsuga taxifolia*), one of the best.

Will you suggest some good fir trees? Douglasfir, White Fir, Nikko Fir, Nordmann Fir, Veitch Fir.

Can we grow fir trees in a dry, rather hot part of the East? Probably not; they require a cool, somewhat humid climate; but if you must try one, the White Fir would probably do best.

Can one grow a Balsam Fir in New Jersey? Perhaps; but it does best north of Connecticut; or in mountains south of Virginia.

Do fir trees grow well in a fairly sandy soil? How early in spring can they be planted? Yes, in a somewhat sandy soil, enriched with leaf-mold or other humus matter. Plant not too early in the spring. Wait till the ground has dried and warmed.

How can I grow Christmas trees in Massachusetts? In New England the "Christmas tree" is usually the Balsam Fir (*Abies balsamea*), which requires the cool, moist climate of the mountains. It has a difficult time in the warmer areas about Boston, and on Cape Cod. If the climate is right, young trees 6 to 18 ins. high can be set out in any field and be expected to begin to yield suitable Christmas trees in from 7 to 10 years. However, because of the time element involved, only marginal land should be used for this purpose.

Is it wise to buy a tubbed fir Christmas tree and then, on a mild day, after the holidays, plant it outdoors (the hole having been previously dug and filled with leaves)? From a viewpoint of gardening economy better buy proper kinds and grades of trees for ornamental use, in the proper seasons, and buy your Christmas trees cheaply, without balls. However, many living Christmas trees are successfully set out after the holidays.

How does one plant trees used indoors as Christmas trees? Prepare the planting hole in advance. Fill and heap it over with leaves. Have planting soil ready indoors. Keep the tree moist; remove it promptly, after use, to a cool place. Plant on a frost-free day, and water thoroughly. Apply a thick mulch, and place a burlap screen around it.

How can I prune a fir tree which is growing too tall and narrow? Does it need fertilizing? The soil is very poor. Many fir trees grow naturally tall and narrow. It is not practicable to prune back a fir tree after it has reached any great size. In poor soil, apply a nutritious mulch of leafmold and some old manure at the base.

Would four Douglasfir trees take all the nourishment from 4 lots 25 × 100 ft.? No, not at all. The shade, however, might make it difficult to grow most other plants.

HEMLOCK

We have an extremely shady garden. Would any evergreens do well for us? Hemlocks and yew only.

Which evergreen trees obtained in ordinary woods would be best to put around a home? I wish to stunt their growth. How is this done? Hemlocks would be best of all, for they can be kept at any height merely by trimming or clipping their new growth, once or twice a year, in the early summer and late summer or early fall.

What type of soil is best for young hemlocks? Do they require much water? A light loam, rich in humus. In an ordinary garden soil, up to 25 per cent of leafmold or other humus may be worked in; in a light, sandy soil twice this amount. Hemlocks should not be permitted to suffer for lack of water; but do not keep the soil drenched.

When is the best time to transplant hemlocks? (New York.) Either very early in the spring, before growth has started, or in early autumn, during favorable, moist weather, up to about October 15.

What conditions and methods are advocated for most successful transplanting of hemlocks from woods in same locality? The safest method is to root-prune the tree a year in advance of moving. When actually transplanting, the roots should all be carefully dug and *not allowed to dry out* while the plant is being moved from one place to the other.

Can a 25-ft. hemlock, once transplanted, regain new needles on branches now bare, due to moving of tree to different spot in garden? If the bare branches do not develop new leaves during the spring following transplanting, they never will. In that case, remove the dead branches.

What is the proper care of hemlock trees? They prefer a situation sheltered from strong winds and a soil very rich in humus. They revel in leafmold. Use lots of it when planting, and apply a leaf mulch about the base. Do not let them get dry, and, in dry autumns, soak the soil thoroughly just before winter. If set in a sun-scorched place, partial shade will be helpful in establishing seedling trees.

Why do hemlocks die back soon after planting? They should not. The trouble may be due to one or more of several causes: lack of a good, solid, fibrous root-ball when transplanted; improper planting; lack of humus in the soil; lack of water; or windy exposure.

How would you propagate hemlock from cuttings? Do they need heat? In July make cuttings 3 to 4 ins. long. Insert in a mixture of sand and peat, in boxes, in shaded cold frame. They root slowly, and if it is possible to carry over to the following year any not rooted in the fall, the percentage of rooting would be greater. For this a warm (50° to 55° F.) greenhouse is desirable.

JUNIPER

Which juniper would grow tall, compact, and narrow? Canaert Redcedar. Or one of the Chinese junipers, such as *J. chinensis columnaris,* would be good.

Are Irish Junipers of same family as Redcedar trees? Can they be safely planted near apple trees? Yes, they both belong to the genus *Juniperus.* They serve as alternate hosts for the cedar-apple rust, and should not be grown within several hundred yards of apple trees.

Will Irish Juniper do well in an east foundation planting? Mine don't look very good. Red spider might be the trouble, as they were not sprayed this year. A northeast exposure would be better. This juniper is subject to winter burn on the sunny side. Spider mites are often injurious; but the effect would spread over the entire tree, not merely on the sunny side.

How can I keep my Irish Juniper from turning brown each spring? Keep the brightest sun in winter from the foliage, either by locating the junipers in a northeast exposure, or by means of a burlap screen or other protection.

Are cedar and Redcedar the same thing? No. The word "cedar," when correctly used, applies to the genus *Cedrus*—a group of trees native in North Africa, and southwest Asia. These are quite different from our native "Redcedar" (*Juniperus virginiana*) of the eastern United States.

What is the best time of year to transplant Redcedar from a field? Cedars over 7 ft. high should be root-pruned in September and moved a year later, or in the spring thereafter. This will ensure a fibrous root system, so necessary to successful transplanting.

What can be done to improve the appearance of Redcedar trees planted in front of a house?   Examine them for the presence of spider mites. If these are present, spray promptly and repeatedly. Cultivate the surface lightly, without disturbing roots. Mulch with leafmold or peatmoss and a little old manure. See that there is no lack of moisture.

What time of year should I plant Spreading Juniper?   Spring, after the ground has become thoroughly workable, before growth has started; or early autumn. In lower New York State, up to about November 1. In dry autumns, take advantage of such wet spells as may come along.

What fertilizer do Spreading Junipers need?   Established, thriving plants, in soil of fair quality, need none. In poor soil, apply a top-dressing of leafmold or peatmoss mixed with some old manure. Avoid alkaline fertilizers.

What winter and summer care does an erect cedar or juniper, 2 to 3 ft. high, require? Is it possible to prevent dead branches at the base? Is this due to dogs?   Examine branches for spider mites. If found, spray promptly. See that the soil does not cake. Apply a mulch. Dogs may well be responsible for injury to lower branches.

When are junipers pruned; and how?   The principal annual pruning is done during the period of soft spring growth. If a formal appearance is desired, a second, lighter pruning may be given, about September 1, to upright-growing kinds like the Redcedar.

Can I cut about 27 ins. off the top of a Meyer Juniper without damaging the tree for summer growth? Our tree is too tall.   Yes, you may reduce the height by cutting back. It will produce new growth below the cut, which will eventually cover the stubbed effect.

Please tell me the right way to trim Savin Junipers. Can the long branches be trimmed back?   For proper development, Savin Junipers should be pruned rather heavily in their young stages. This will make them bushy. When old branches are pruned back, they may be slow in producing new growth and the effect may be unsightly.

After the top is broken off a Silver Juniper, Juniperus virginiana var. argentea will it ever be a nicely shaped tree?   It will readily develop a new leader of acceptable appearance within 2 or 3 years. The process may be helped by staking up the new leader and pruning back competing growths.

How long does it take for juniper berries to get ripe; and when is the time to pick them?   Some junipers will never have berries. Only the female (pistillate-flowering) trees bear fruit. The Rocky Mountain Redcedar (*Juniperus scopulorum*) and several other junipers take 2 years to mature their fruits. These could be picked in the late summer or early fall of the second year.

How do nurserymen increase junipers? I have done it by slicing a

branch and burying it until it roots, but there must be a quicker way. Either by cuttings or grafting. Cuttings are placed in the greenhouse in summer or early winter. Cuttings of some junipers will remain alive and in good condition for more than 2 years without rooting. Grafting is done early in the year.

Can I start Pfitzer's Juniper from cuttings? It is possible but this juniper does not root too readily. Make cuttings, about 5 ins. long, in latter half of August. (See Propagation, this section.)

PINE

Which is the more satisfactory, Red Pine or Austrian Pine? They are similar, but the former is less susceptible to insect pests than the latter.

We like pine trees, but our soil is moist. Would any of them do well? White Pine (*Pinus strobus*) and Pitch Pine (*P. rigida*) are occasionally found growing wild in swamps in New Jersey. In the South, Longleaf Pine (*P. palustris*) could be planted.

We were advised to buy pine trees for our garden near the windy seashore. Is Scotch Pine a good choice? Yes. Japanese Black Pine is most resistant however.

I would like to plant a pine tree which is not coarse in texture. What do you suggest? Use either White Pine or Japanese Red Pine.

How can I tell the principal pine trees apart? Many of them by the length of their "needles," and the number of each cluster (fascicle). White Pine—5 in a cluster, 5 ins. long (soft bluish); Austrian Pine—2 in a cluster, 6½ ins. long (stiff); Scotch Pine—2 in a cluster, 3 ins. long (twisted); Red Pine—2 in a cluster, 6 ins. long (glossy); Japanese Black Pine—2 in a cluster, 4½ ins. long (sharp-pointed).

What is the best fertilizer to keep a pine tree healthy and growing? Is bone meal O.K.? Bone meal when transplanting, but it is not a complete fertilizer, which may be applied later on. However, if the ground is of good quality and the tree healthy, no feeding will be required. At the slightest sign of soil exhaustion, apply a top-dressing of leafmold or peatmoss mixed with old manure.

Can pine trees be planted all year 'round? No. Not during the period of soft growth, from May to August.

I have some fine 4-year-old White Pine and Norway Pine. When is the best time to transplant them, and should they be in full sun or partial shade? (Wisconsin.) Transplant in spring, before growth starts. Mulch the surface. An open situation is best, but some temporary shading would be desirable.

When is the best time to transplant pine trees? (New York.) In the latitude of New York City fibrous-rooted trees may be transplanted either in the spring, or in the autumn, between August 1 and November 1. Pines not previously transplanted had better be planted in the spring only, with as good a ball as possible.

How should pine trees be transplanted?   Untransplanted trees over 6 ft. high should be root-pruned (which see) in September and moved a year later. Transplanted trees with fibrous root systems may be dug with a ball of roots, burlapped, in the spring or in early autumn. Water down the filling soil. Fill the hole flush with the grade. Mulch soil over roots.

Is it too late to transplant pine trees that were set out as seedlings, and are now about 10 ft. tall?   No. Root-prune (which see) them in September; move them a year later, or in the spring of the second year. They should then have developed sufficient fibrous roots to facilitate successful transplanting.

How old may pine trees be transplanted safely?   There's no age limit. The only limits are those set by available machinery for moving, and by obstructions in the path of travel.

Should grass be kept away from the ground around young pines? Yes.

When and how does one prune Mugho Pines?   When the candlelike spring growths have about reached their full length, but before the leaves have spread out, cut these "candles" back partly. When they are reduced to ¼ or ⅓ their length each year, a Mugho Pine will form a dense, cushionlike plant.

I have a matched pair of Mugho Pines. One is getting larger than the other. Is it possible to trim them back?   Yes. In the annual pruning of the candlelike spring growths, cut those on the larger plant a little farther back than those on the smaller plant. This ought, in a year or two, tend to even the two plants up. Do not prune into the old wood.

What can be done to save young pine trees badly browned by the heat from burning brush?   If the scorched branches produce new leaves in the spring following injury, no harm will have been done. If not, nothing can restore the damage; cut off the burned parts.

Will you please tell me what makes our pines so thin looking, and with brown edges?   Probably unsuitable environment, such as inadequate underdrainage, or too much shade.

Are pine trees started by seed or cuttings?   Pine trees are started from seeds sown in spring. Some varieties are grafted. Most species and varieties are exceedingly difficult to raise from cuttings.

Can pine trees be grown from seed?   Yes. Seed ripens September to November, the cones that produce the seed being 2 or 3 years old. Collect cones before seed has shed and place in shallow boxes in warm, dry place. (See answers to other inquiries.)

Is there any disease that pine trees catch from fruit trees? No, but the white-pine blister rust lives for part of its life on gooseberry and currant bushes. This is a very serious disease.

REDCEDAR

(See Juniper.)

SPRUCE

Which are some of the outstanding spruce trees? Oriental Spruce (*Picea orientalis*); Siberian Spruce (*P. omorika*); Colorado Spruce (*P. pungens*) (some varieties of this are bluish in tone).

What is the best fertilizer for Blue Spruce? An occasional top-dressing of leafmold or peatmoss with old manure mixed into it. When planting, mix leafmold and some old manure with the planting soil.

I have planted spruce trees in oyster shell. I was advised to use sulfate of ammonia and pine needles to make the soil acid. Was it wrong? Oyster shell is not suitable for evergreens. Add a large quantity of acid humus material, such as peatmoss, hemlock or pine-needle leafmold.

What type of soil is suitable for spruce trees? A good loam, enriched with humus. Untransplanted trees over 6 ft. high should be root-pruned in September and moved a year later. Trees previously transplanted should be dug with a good ball, either in spring or in early autumn. Water the soil after planting. Fill flush with the grade. Mulch.

Should ground be frozen to remove spruce and pine from woods to lawns? Not necessarily. The main thing is to secure an adequate, solid ball of fibrous roots and earth. Large trees are sometimes most conveniently moved with frozen balls.

How much space should be available in front of a home to plant a Blue Spruce? It should have an area 20 ft. or more in diameter in which to grow.

In a Blue Spruce, successfully transplanted last year, the old foliage has lost its bright color. Will it return? This happens often when in transplanting or transit a Blue Spruce is tied in tightly or crowded. The blue, waxy coat of the foliage rubs off and does not renew itself. Subsequent new growth will eventually cover up the dull inner foliage. The color rubs off most readily on the soft new growth.

I have had little success with Blue Spruces. Will you give information on their culture? Be sure to procure transplanted, fibrous-rooted plants. Plant in a well-drained, sunny place in any fair, loamy soil. Plant in the spring before growth starts, or shortly after August 1, during suitable damp weather. Water plentifully; mulch the base.

Keep the roots moist, but not too wet, and in dry autumns soak thoroughly just before winter.

What is the proper care for Norway Spruce and Blue Spruce seedlings, now 1½ ins. high? Assuming that they were planted in well-prepared planting beds, merely keep under lath shades, and maintain soil moisture with a light, fine surface mulch.

Can you prune and shape a Blue Spruce? If so, when is the proper time? Yes. Prune only during the period of soft spring growth. The shaping process may sometimes be aided by tying in misdirected branches and staking a crooked leader.

How shall I trim sides of Colorado Blue Spruce too wide for parking space? If this involves cutting into old wood, it will not be found practicable. Better move the whole tree back from the drive.

I have a Blue Spruce which is growing lopsided. How shall I trim it? If the leader is crooked, stake it. If any branches can be tied into place, do this before you use the pruning knife. If it is a matter of one or more protruding branches in an otherwise well-balanced plant, then reduce these branches as necessary.

How does one prune Blue Spruces to prevent them from growing too large? They are by nature tall-growing trees. They may be kept down artificially by means of annual prunings or shearings, during the period of soft growth in spring. This involves the snipping off of the extremities of the shoots.

Can spruce trees be kept trimmed to a small size? Yes, by means of annual prunings during the period of soft growth. This will result in plants of compact, formal appearance. Once so treated, plants will never again develop into normal, natural-looking specimens.

In 2 spruce trees that serve as windbreaks the lower branches are dying. How can I improve their appearance and discourage any great increase in height? Once the lower branches have died, nothing will bring them back to life, and no new growth will replace them. To prevent further loss of lower branches, remove all crowding near-by growths which may shut out light. Keep a mulch about the base; eventually cut off top shoots if necessary.

Can I get information about propagating Blue Spruce? Can they be increased by cuttings? They can be rooted from cuttings, but not very readily. Use shoots of one year's growth with a very small "heel" of old wood, inserted in January in a propagating case in a warm greenhouse.

How can Moerheim Blue Spruce be propagated? Usually propagated by grafting; cuttings taken in January may be rooted, but not readily, in a warm greenhouse.

How, when, and where should one plant seeds of Norway Spruce and Colorado Blue Spruce? Sow ¼ in. deep in a bed of fine soil, shaded by lath screens, until seeds have germinated; or in flats in cold frame in spring.

Will handling spruce and cedar Christmas trees, after they have been in the house, cause a bad case of poison on the hands and face? Such a difficulty is not common. Some individuals might be allergic to the resins in these trees, but cases of poisoning are rare.

YEW

Which yews grow in tree form? English Yew and the single-stem Japanese Yew; but they rarely attain great height in this country except in the Pacific Northwest.

Which yews make upright growth? Hatfield, Hicks, and Irish Yew (where winters are not severe); also Japanese Upright Yew.

Hemlock will not survive here but we have had best success with Japanese Yew. What else shall we plant? There are several varieties of yew, available from nurserymen, which differ in shape and height. These could be used.

Do dwarf yews prefer an acid soil? No, they will grow well in either acid or alkaline soils.

When is the best time to move yews? Either in spring, before growth starts, or in early September.

Should Dwarf Japanese Yew be fed? If so, what and when? Not necessarily. If their color is good, leave them alone. Dwarf Japanese Yews always grow slowly. Well-rotted manure makes a good fertilizer, when needed.

I have 2 Japanese Yews. One has retained its dark green, but the other has a slight yellow cast. Why? Frequently Japanese Yews are grown from seed. Then there are wide differences in the resulting plants. Height, shape, and color of foliage are all variables in such instances.

My Japanese Yew is dying. I have given it plenty of water and fertilizer, sprayed the foliage, all to no avail. What is the trouble with it; and how can I correct it? The roots of this plant are probably being attacked by the grubs of the strawberry root weevil. This is frequently controlled by the use of poison baits for the beetles, and pyrethrum sprays (soaked into the ground above the roots) to kill the grubs which are actually doing the damage by feeding on the roots.

I planted 2 yews 4 years ago. One seems to be dying. It has been this way for 2 seasons. Foliage is green but very thin. There are no grubs around roots. This is a condition frequently related with finding aphis on the roots. If this is not the case, the explanation could be in some peculiar soil condition. Would suggest digging the plant up, removing the soil about the roots, and transplanting in some other situation.

When is the best time to trim Japanese Yew? Just after growth has been completed, in late June or early July.

Should yew trees be trimmed in August, or are they prettier left untrimmed? Usually they are prettier untrimmed when grown as specimens, but some years a small amount of trimming (which really can be done any time) is necessary to keep certain branches from growing too much out of proportion to the rest of the plant.

Should low-spreading yews, in foundation plantings, be pruned? Not if they stay low and do not grow out of proportion to the other plants.

Should the branches of Taxus cuspidata capitata be tied for winter protection or supported in some way? The branches break easily. This might be done if they are growing in situations where snow and ice will accumulate on them, as under the eaves of the house.

How can I best propagate Japanese Yew for a hedge? Seedling yews would be the best for this purpose, as they grow upright. The seeds require stratification for a year before being sown, and grow slowly during their first few years. Probably better to buy small plants.

Is there any method for the home gardener to raise Japanese Yew? I have a yew hedge, but some have died and I need more to fill in. If you have a hotbed (either manure or electric), take cuttings in the early summer; insert in pure sand in the hotbed. Keep temperature of sand 80° to 90° F. Shade, keep moist, but not wet, and rooting should take place in 4 to 6 weeks. Then plant rooted cuttings in carefully prepared soil and mulch well over the first winter.

Can you advise how to grow the Taxus or Japanese Yew from seeds? Clean the fleshy pulp from the seed; stratify by placing alternate layers of moist peatmoss and seeds in a box; keep at a temperature of 30° to 40° F., and sow in the early spring. Some seeds may not germinate for a full year, so don't be discouraged if they all do not come up the first year.

How can I raise seedlings from berries on a Hicks Yew? This can be done (see preceding question), but Hicks Yew is a hybrid and seedlings of it will not all have the characteristic upright shape of the Hicks Yew. A better method would be to propagate by cuttings taken in early summer.

BROAD-LEAVED EVERGREENS

(See also Ericaceous Shrubs)

Which broad-leaved evergreens will grow best in New York City? *Ilex crenata* (Japanese Holly); *I. opaca,* (American Holly); Rhododendron hybrids; *Rhododendron obtusum amoenum.*

Which is a good informal evergreen, besides rhododendron and laurel. Either inkberry (*Ilex glabra*), or leucothoe.

Which broad-leaved evergreens can be planted beneath a bay window? Mountain Andromeda, evergreen azaleas, leucothoe. A few dwarfish rhododendrons, such as the Carolina Rhododendron.

Can you suggest a very low, dainty evergreen, suitable for planting near a front door? *Daphne cneorum* is low and spreading, with narrow little leaves, producing pink flowers in April, and often again in September.

What kinds of native shrubs, besides azaleas, need acid soil? Rhododendrons and all other broad-leaved evergreens; blueberries, huckleberries, and bayberries. As a general rule, provide acid soil conditions for all kinds that grow naturally in oak or evergreen woods.

SPECIFIC BROAD-LEAVED EVERGREENS

BOXWOOD

I have heard about Korean Box; what is it like? It does not grow more than 3 ft. high, resembles dwarf box, and is the hardiest of all the boxwoods.

Will box grow in woods soil, or should we use lime? Boxwood should grow well in woods soil, if not too acid. A reaction of pH 6 to 8 is considered best.

In making an English Box garden in a space 50 × 75 ft., what should spacing be? This depends on the height at which the box bushes will be kept. If a height of 3 to 4 ft. is desired, then plants could be spaced 18 ins. apart, for a hedge. Single specimens, if allowed to grow unclipped should be allowed a space at least 5 ft. in diameter.

What fertilizer should I use on boxwood? Well-rotted manure is best. Commercially prepared chemical fertilizers should be used with discretion, for fear of burning the foliage.

What is the best time of year to move large boxwoods? Commercial tree movers transplant them at any time of year. The amateur might best do it in early spring, or very early fall.

Would small boxwood plants, of which we have a number to be transplanted, do well along a cemented parkway about the building? How far apart should these be planted? When? These would grow satisfactorily if given good soil and sufficient room. They should be set 10 ins. apart if this is the dwarf variety, *Buxus sempervirens suffruticosa*. Transplant in early spring.

Should boxwood be covered for a time after transplanting? If the weather is very hot, shading with a burlap screen will help cut down the water loss. Also syringing the foliage during the evenings of hot days will aid young boxwoods in pulling through. Covering such young plants the first winter is a good practice.

What winter and summer care do boxwoods require?   A thick mulch of leaves or straw on soil for the winter; plenty of water during hot, dry summer weather.

Many of the leaves of my boxwood drop off in midsummer, and the plants become unsightly. What causes this?   Probably the box-wood leaf miner (which see), the most serious of boxwood pests. The tiny maggots tunnel within the leaves, causing irregular swellings or blisters in the leaf.

What material should I use to spray my boxwoods for boxwood leaf miner?   Timing is most important. Keep a close watch on the under-sides of the leaves during late April and early May and when the pupae are beginning to get active it is necessary to spray right away with DDT. A better way to determine the timing is to open some of the blisters and if the pupae have black heads it is time to spray. When the infestation is heavy one spraying is not sufficient; so, spray with lindane early in summer. Follow directions on the containers and observe all precautions.

When is the best time to trim boxwood?   Late June.

Can boxwood be trimmed close to the ground in order to thicken the growth at the base of the plant, where many of the limbs are very lanky?   In the case of old plants with very thick trunks and branches it is practically impossible to coax new growth from the base. In young plants, this may be feasible, but cutting heavy branches back severely should be avoided.

How shall I protect old, very large, and dense boxwood during winter?   Prune out any dead or diseased branches. Thoroughly water, if ground is dry. This is frequently necessary, for winter injury may result if they enter winter with dry roots. Cover with burlap supported on wood frames if injured by winter in previous years.

What makes some box turn reddish brown in winter? Is there any remedy?   Either too-low temperatures, or too much bright, warm sun while the ground is still frozen. The remedy is to protect the box-wood with a screen of wood, burlap, or pine boughs.

What makes boxwood winter kill?   Many complex physiological factors. The chief cause for winter killing is bright, warm sunshine in early spring, while the ground remains frozen. Another cause is low temperature.

Is the Truedwarf Box hardy in Boston?   It will survive with pro-tection, but is not reliably hardy there.

How can I root cuttings of boxwood?   Put them in boxes of sharp sand in July or August, and keep in a cold frame until there is danger of sand freezing. Then remove them to a frost-proof building. Keep the sand moist, but not wet, during the winter months.

Can you tell me how to root the slow-growing boxwood? (Georgia.)

Boxwood roots readily in a cool greenhouse if the cuttings are taken in November. However, in Georgia they could be rooted in a cold frame and kept there over winter if precautions are taken to prevent frost heaving the cuttings out of the sand.

DAPHNE

I have tried out Daphne cneorum five times and had no luck. I tried full sun; half shade; shade in sandy soil enriched with fertilizer; wet soil; dry soil; and also clay soil. Can you advise? There is a controversy as to whether this plant does best in alkaline or acid soil. As a matter of fact, it grows in *both* types of soil. What is more important is that the soil should be a sandy loam and well drained. Shade has little to do with it. Such successive failures as indicated above would point to the possibility that the acidity or alkalinity of the soil might be at fault, and the soil should be made nearer the neutral point.

Is it possible to transplant a daphne which has been in one place for 5 years? (Michigan.) If the daphne is growing satisfactorily in its present position it would be better not to attempt to move it. If it must be moved, transplant in spring, with a ball of earth attached to the roots.

What is the proper method of pruning Daphne cneorum? My plants sprawl all over the place. It is the nature of this species to be wide-spreading. Pinching out the tips of the growing shoots will help keep it more compact.

Can Daphne odora be pruned? Daphnes are inclined to resent severe pruning. You can keep them compact by pinching out the tips of the growing shoots.

Should a daphne plant receive special protection during the winter? Generally it seems desirable to protect *Daphne cneorum* from winter sun and wind, though some plants come through perfectly without, even when exposed to morning sun. A loosely arranged overcoat of pine branches is sufficient.

How can an amateur best propagate the dwarf daphne? The Rose Daphne can be rooted from cuttings, but with difficulty, by usual means. Under constant mist 100 percent rooting may be expected. Shoots may be layered in the usual way. Another method (mound layering) is to place sandy soil in among the shoots in the form of a mound, leaving only a few inches of the ends of the shoots protruding. At the end of the season the earth is drawn away and the rooted shoots are potted singly. The great objection to the latter method is that the resulting plants are rather spindly.

EUONYMUS

Which evergreen euonymus does not climb but remains a shrub?

E. japonicus, not reliably hardy north of Washington, D.C., and varieties of *E. radicans* (now called *E. fortunei*). One is the variety *carrierei.* Another is *E. r. vegetus,* but this will climb if near a wall.

HOLLY (ILEX)

What is the difference between Osmanthus aquifolium and holly? Osmanthus is often mistaken for holly because of the similarity of the foliage, but they are easily distinguished by the opposite leaves of osmanthus and the alternate leaves of holly. There is no close botanical relationship between the two.

What is the hardiest kind of holly? We have a "Christmas garden" and would like to add this to it. (Massachusetts.) The American Holly (*Ilex opaca*) might grow near the coast, or if protected; English Holly probably would not. *Ilex pedunculosa* and the native inkberry, *I. glabra,* are the hardiest, but they do not look like the Christmas holly.

Does the American Holly grow low or high? Both the American and English hollies are trees, growing eventually to 50 ft. or more in height.

What kind of soil does the American Holly prefer? A light, sandy soil, containing some decaying leafmold. Heavy clay soils should be avoided in planting hollies.

What fertilizer shall I use for American Holly? If it is growing well, do not apply any fertilizer. Well-rotted leafmold, worked well into the soil, is about the best material which can be applied. In the South, rotted manure can be applied in the late fall as a mulch, but is best used only sparingly on American Hollies in the North. Hollies prefer a light, sandy soil.

When is the best time to plant a holly tree? In early September; or early April, just as the new leaf buds begin to open.

When and how is it best to transplant holly, especially in a hedge? In areas where the climate is moist, either spring or very early fall. In the eastern United States very early spring is usually best. The plants should be dug carefully with a ball of earth about the roots. If planted as a hedge, space 2 ft. apart.

How can I most successfully transplant hollies? The safest way is to move them with a ball of earth about the roots. If they are to be dug up in the woods, sizable trees should be root-pruned (which see) a year in advance of transplanting.

Are there any real hollies that can be grown in Ohio? Of the evergreen hollies, the English cannot be grown satisfactorily in Ohio, but our native American Holly (*Ilex opaca*) is worthy of a trial in the warmer parts.

Is it possible to raise holly that is used for Christmas decorations

in Maine, or is that too far North? Maine is too far North. The northernmost limit for American Holly is Cape Cod. English Holly can be grown very little in the northeast except on Long Island and further south near the coast.

Can I get holly to grow in my garden? (Michigan.) It is doubtful if either the American or the English Holly will grow in Michigan except in extremely well-protected situations.

Is it true that in Ohio holly should be planted where the winter sun will not hit it? It is not the winter sun so much as the high, dry winds of late winter which injure holly trees. If these are prevalent, it will pay to protect the holly trees from such winds.

Where is the beautiful English Holly grown commercially? In the moist region of Oregon and Washington.

Have set out native American Hollies, using leafmold and dirt from the woods as a fill around the roots. How should I fertilize and care for them from now on? You have done the best possible. Keep the soil moist, sprinkle the tops in the evening of hot days throughout the first summer. If you have good soil, do not fertilize until one year after transplanting.

How shall I care for small holly trees? Water well, especially through the first summer after transplanting. Apply a mulch of well-rotted leafmold in the fall, and place a protective screening of burlap or pine boughs about them the first few winters.

Why do some English Holly trees have no berries? The male or pollen-bearing trees never have berries. Only the trees with the female or pistillate flowers will fruit.

I have a thriving grafted English Holly which sets good berry crop each year. When the berries are half formed, they all drop. Have tried less water, more water, and fertilizer—with no results. Why? This sounds very much as if the female flowers had not been properly fertilized with pollen. A male tree should be near by to make certain pollination occurs.

We have a female English Holly which flowers, but no berries set. Tried grafting male cuttings, but none took. Would you suggest trying budding instead? If so, what type of bud and when and where on the limbs should I do the budding? English Hollies can easily be budded. Use the shield bud, commonly used in propagating peaches. Insert buds in August or very early September. Be certain that only the pointed leaf buds found on the more vigorous shoots are used. Insert buds only on the current year's growth. (See Propagation.)

What is the matter with a holly tree that has stopped producing berries, even though male trees are present? Such incidents are difficult to explain. Some trees are alternate in their bearing habit, having a large crop of fruits one year and very few fruits the next.

Sometimes a cold, rainy season, just when the pollen is ripe, prevents its distribution by wind and insects.

A holly tree purchased 3 years ago, which then had berries, has failed to produce them since. The pH of the soil is 5.4, and there is a male tree within 70 ft. Why does it fail to bear? It may be recuperating from the shock of transplanting. Fertilize and water well. Berries will soon be formed if the near-by tree really is a male.

When and to what extent should holly trees be pruned? Pruning, especially of fruiting plants, might be done just before Christmas, by cutting short branches for decoration. Other pruning should be limited to taking out dead or diseased wood and crossed branches. Slight trimming, to make the tree dense and compact in habit, can be done during early spring, before growth starts.

How can one tell sex of a lone holly plant? I want to buy more but don't know sex needed. Observe the flowers, which are very small and inconspicuous, and appear in June. The pistillate or fruiting flowers have a well-developed pistil in the center, and undeveloped stamens. In the male flowers the pistil is small and undeveloped, and the stamens bear pollen.

Should you plant more than one Burford Holly for it to bear berries? No, the Chinese Holly (*Ilex cornuta*) (of which the Burford Holly is a variety) is unique among the hollies in this respect. The fruiting plants will bear fruits even though their flowers do not receive pollen from male plants.

How is English Holly propagated from cuttings? In a greenhouse, either in sand or a mixture of sand and peat. Use cuttings 4 to 5 ins. long taken in August or September. Shade with cheesecloth.

How is American Holly propagated from cuttings? Usually in a greenhouse, though it may be done in a cold frame. Cuttings should be 4 to 5 ins. long, of the current year's wood, taken in August or September.

INKBERRY

Does inkberry have attractive flowers? If not, why is it popular? While the inconspicuous flowers are small, it has attractive black berries and glossy leaves, somewhat like box. It is hardy and shade enduring.

MAGNOLIA

See also Flowering Trees.

Is Magnolia grandiflora hardy North? There is a large specimen growing in a sheltered spot in Brooklyn, New York, but it is not usually hardy north of Washington, D.C.

MAHONIA

Is Oregon Grapeholly the low-growing shrub with leaflets something like holly? This is *Mahonia aquifolium* (Oregongrape). The leaves vary in color from deep green to rich purple-red. If its environment is suitable and not too exposed, it has yellow flowers followed by little grapelike bunches of black berries. It prefers half shade.

Which is the hardiest kind of mahonia for use as a ground cover? *M. repens.*

What exposure suits the mahonia? A northeast exposure, where it gets enough winter sun to bring out the bronzy colors in the foliage, but not enough sun and wind to scorch the leaves.

Is mahonia (Oregongrape) hardy at sub-zero temperature? Yes, it will withstand temperatures of 5 to 10° below zero. Persistent temperatures any lower than this will probably cause injury.

How and when shall I trim mahonia, planted on north side of the house? Some of it grows upright, but part lies almost on ground. I thought there was only 1 kind of mahonia, but I seem to have 2 different kinds. There are several kinds, 2 of which are commonly grown in the East, one upright and shrubby—*Mahonia aquifolium,* and another which is really a ground cover—*Mahonia repens.* They can best be pruned in early spring before growth starts. *M. Bealei* and the closely related *M. japonica,* which are dubiously hardy on Long Island, N.Y., are excellent in the southern states.

PYRACANTHA

Are any of the pyracanthas hardy? Yes. *P. coccinea,* or firethorn, is fairly hardy in the middle states. Sometimes winter kills in the vicinity of New York City.

Would like to plant 2 pyracanthas, one either side of large living-room window, to grow against house. However, there are 3 small oak trees, about 9 to 12 ft. distant, on front lawn. Would their shade cause the pyracantha not to fruit, or to lack color? Planting where you suggest would not be advisable. For an abundance of berries full light is needed. Though the oaks may not be very big at present, it is probable that in a few years they would cast a shade too dense for the pyracanthas to fruit satisfactorily.

When is the best time to transplant Pyracantha coccinea lalandi? A difficult plant to move successfully, particularly if it has attained any size. Spring is the most suitable season, and it must be moved with a ball of earth. Do not attempt to remove the burlap when replanting. A more certain method is to enclose the ball of earth in a box when transplanting.

What can one do to make pyracantha bushes have more berries?
Keep in good health and growing vigorously. They frequently bear
good crops only in alternate years. A fertilizer rich in superphosphate,
combined with root-pruning if bush is growing vigorously, might
aid in increasing fruit production. Full sunshine, or at least uninter-
rupted light, is a requisite.

*Firethorn—most colorful of ber-
ried shrubs for winter.*

How should pyracanthas be treated when dead branches appear?
Pyracanthas are susceptible to fire blight, a serious disease of apples
and pears, their close relatives. When this appears, cut out the
branches immediately and burn them. The cut should be made
considerably below the injured part. (See Section VIII.)

**Last year my pyracantha was full of berries. This year it had none.
Why? How can I keep it from growing so tall?** Most berried shrubs
are alternate in their bearing, producing heavy crops one year and
light crops the next. Pyracantha can be restrained at any height by
pruning—preferably in summer.

How are pyracantha cuttings rooted? Take the cuttings in July
and place them in 3 to 4 ins. of sand in a fairly deep box. Cover the
box with a sheet of glass, and keep it in a position out of the sun but
with good light; or root them in a cold frame.

VIBURNUM, EVERGREEN

Is there a good evergreen viburnum? Yes, Leatherleaf Viburnum
(*V. rhytidophyllum*), with long, oval, leathery wrinkled leaves. Protect from too much winter sun. Not reliably hardy north of Philadelphia, Pennsylvania.

ERICACEOUS SHRUBS

What does "ericaceous" mean? This term is applied to the plant
family Ericaceae, consisting mainly of shrubs and small trees which
in general require a sandy, peaty acid soil. Among the Ericaceae are
the following: andromeda, arbutus, heather, enkianthus, wintergreen,
blueberry, Mountain Laurel, sandmyrtle, leucothoe, pieris, rhododendron (including azalea).

CULTURE

What fertilizer ingredients, in what formula, would you suggest for feeding ericaceous plants, and at the same time maintain acidity in the soil? Tankage or cottonseed meal applied at the rate of 5 lbs. per 100 sq. ft. is satisfactory for small plants. For large plants use 6–10–6 fertilizer in which cottonseed or soybean meal is used to supply ¼ to ½ of the nitrogen. Apply at the rate of 2 to 3 lbs. per 100 sq. ft. of bed area. If the soil is sufficiently acid, 7½ lbs. nitrate of soda, 10 lbs. superphosphate, 2½ lbs. sulfate of potash could be used to approximate the above formula. (See also Azalea and Rhododendron.)

What soil is best for Mountain Laurel? Moist, acid, bountifully supplied with humus. Grows well in rhododendron soils.

Do rhododendrons, Mountain Laurel, etc., require special soil? Yes. A well-drained subsoil beneath, 12 to 18 ins. of topsoil containing up to 50 per cent acid humus matter. A totally uncongenial soil should be removed bodily, and replaced with a suitable compost. For acid humus, use pine, spruce, hemlock, or oak leafmold; or peatmoss. Peatmoss, mixed with a little very old manure, makes a good soil for plants of this type.

Can I condition my alkaline soil for rhododendrons with aluminum sulfate? If your soil is rich in humus matter—yes, but flowers of sulfur is safer. Periodic applications may be required to maintain a properly acid condition. Do not expect success with aluminum sulfate in uncongenial soils poor in humus. Acidity is only one factor in preparing a soil suitable for plants of the heath family.

My soil is very acid, but rhododendrons do not grow well; why? The soil may be too acid, and poorly drained. Bring it up to pH 5.5 by adding pulverized dolomitic limestone. Dig out bed to a depth of 18 ins., put in 6 ins. cinders and return soil.

SPECIFIC ERICACEOUS SHRUBS

AZALEA

What to Grow

What types of azaleas would be hardy for this section of the country? The temperature often goes to 20° below, but not for any great length of time. (New York.) Many azaleas can be grown in northern New York and New England. Some are *calendulacea, nudiflora, rosea, vaseyi, arborescens, viscosa, schlippenbachi,* and *obtusa kaempferi.* Many of the Ghent hybrids are also worth a trial, and will grow and bloom even when temperatures drop as low as 20° below zero.

What are the best varieties of azaleas to plant in southern New York State? Practically any of the azaleas except the Kurume and the India varieties. Many of the colorful Ghent hybrids are hardy even as far North as central Maine.

How can I lengthen the period of bloom in azaleas? By selecting types which bloom successively. The following should insure 2 months of continuous flowers from April to early July: *Azalea mucronulata, A. vaseyi, A. nudiflora, A. calendulacea, A. arborescens,* and *A. viscosa.*

Are there any azaleas which will grow in swampy places? *Azalea viscosa* grows naturally in swampy ground. *A. vaseyi* is also satisfactory.

What can you combine with azaleas for summer and fall bloom? Soil is part clay. Have put oak-leaf mulch around azaleas, but nothing else seems to thrive. For a midsummer shrub, try *Clethra alnifolia.* For autumn flower, the low, matting, blue-flowered Ceratostigma. For both of these the clay soil should be lightened with sand and peat.

Soil and Fertilizer

What conditions are necessary for growth of Ghent azaleas? These deciduous azaleas need a fairly open situation and deep, well-drained acid soil, with ⅓ humus-forming materials—leafmold from oaks or evergreens, rotted hardwood sawdust, or peatmoss.

Where and in what soil should I plant Pinkshell Azalea? Light shade such as that given by thin woodland. Deep, moist soil, with plenty of humus.

How can I be certain a soil is acid? Send samples to your county agricultural agent or to State Agricultural Experiment Station for testing; or buy one of several soil-testing kits available for just this purpose. (See Acidity—Section I.)

Our soil is definitely alkaline, but I want to grow azaleas and rhododendrons. What should I do? The best way is to excavate the soil in the area for planting to an approximate depth of 2½ ft. Place in the excavation only acid soil rich in humus.

With a soil only slightly alkaline, how does one make it acid with a minimum amount of trouble? The *second* best way of acquiring an acid soil is to apply aluminum sulfate to the soil in question, at rates depending on the alkalinity, or pH. Following figures indicate reaction of soil at start, and amount of aluminum sulfate per sq. yd.: pH 5.5 to 6.0, ¼ lb.; pH 6.5 to 7.0, ½ lb.; pH 7.0 to 8.0, ¾ lb. This should be well watered in, and the soil again tested at the end of 2 weeks. If the soil has not reached the desired acidity, to a depth of 6 to 12 ins., apply sulfur at ⅙ of the rate given above.

How acid should soil be for azaleas and rhododendrons? For most of them, pH 5 to 6.

Should a soil in which azaleas and rhododendrons are growing be tested more than once a year? Only if the plants fail to grow well.

Do deciduous azaleas and evergreen azaleas need the same amount of soil acidity? Yes.

Will coffee and tea grounds sprinkled around azaleas help to acidify the soil? Would this practice be harmful? No, it would not acidify soil to any marked degree; but it would not be harmful.

What is the best time of year to feed azaleas? They can be fed either in early spring or fall.

We use cottonseed meal for fertilizer a great deal down here. Can this be used on azaleas? (South Carolina.) Yes. A mixture of 2 lbs. of cottonseed meal and 1 lb. of ammonium sulfate, used at the rate of 1 to 2 lbs. per 100 sq. ft., makes a very good acid fertilizer. (See also under Rhododendron.)

What type of soil does wild azalea (Azalea nudiflora) require? A normally moist, acid soil.

Transplanting

When is the best time to put out azaleas? (Georgia.) In your region, late summer and fall planting only are preferable. Most varieties of azaleas, however, can be transplanted in full bloom, if they are carefully dug, balled, and burlapped.

At what season of the year should wild azalea (wild honeysuckle) be transplanted? It can be transplanted either in the fall after its leaves have dropped or in the early spring, before new growth starts. Spring is the preferred season. Should be carefully dug to preserve all roots, with soil adhering to them. The roots should not be allowed to dry out while plant is being moved.

Why do I have trouble growing azaleas dug in the woods when those purchased from nurserymen do very well indeed? Most plants growing in the woods have considerably longer but fewer roots than if they were grown in the nursery, where they are periodically root-pruned. In digging azaleas in the woods usually much of the root system is cut off.

Culture

What summer and winter care do azaleas need? Water thoroughly during drought in summer. Mulch with oak leaves, pine needles, or peatmoss to maintain acidity and to protect roots in winter. Tender varieties should have evergreen boughs or burlap placed about them.

Is it possible to grow rhododendron and azalea successfully in Ohio? What are the soil requirements? Yes. Azaleas are easier to grow than the evergreen rhododendrons, but both can be grown from Maine to Florida, and west to the Mississippi River, *providing* they have acid soil, plenty of moisture, and not too severe winter temperatures.

What is the proper treatment for azaleas the year 'round? Our bushes are not blooming. (Minnesota.) Many azaleas, especially in the colder parts of the United States, have their flower buds killed by very low temperatures. Plant only the hardiest kinds in cold areas, such as the Pinkshell Azalea, Flame Azalea, Pinxterflower, and some of the Ghent hybrids.

How can I grow azaleas (which come from West Virginia) between lakes Ontario and Seneca, in soil that is not naturally acid? First make the soil acid. Practically anything which is hardy in the mountains of West Virginia will prove hardy in central New York.

I have 2 plants of Azalea rosea and 2 of Azalea nudiflora. They have been in for 3 years and both of the former have bloomed each year, but the latter never have. Why? What degree of temperature is the minimum under which the Azalea nudiflora will bloom? Both these azalea species need acid soil, and if grown in identical conditions the one should bloom if the other does. *Azalea nudiflora* will bloom even though temperatures fall considerably below zero.

Have a wild azalea. How can it be made to bloom? If collected in Massachusetts this is probably *Azalea nudiflora*. If given acid soil, plenty of water, and a mulch of pine needles, oak leaves, or peatmoss, it will undoubtedly bloom well in 2 years' time.

How do you pinch back azaleas? Merely pinch off end of growing twigs. This will force several side buds to grow, and will result in a bushier shrub.

How should azaleas be pruned? Cut out diseased or dying branches from the base of the plant. Often it is advisable to cut off a few twigs here and there to force out thick growth. Otherwise they need little pruning.

Should seed pods be pruned from azaleas? Cut off dead flowers before seed pods form, then more strength will go into flower-bud formation for the next year.

When should azaleas be sprayed? How often? Lace bug and red spider are the most serious pests of azaleas. (See Section VIII.)

Winter Protection

Do azaleas need winter protection in vicinity of New York? How is this best provided? Only the more tender evergreen sorts need the kind of protection provided by a burlap screen or pine boughs, so placed about the plant as to protect it from high winds and sun. All azaleas will do better if provided with a mulch of some acid material (oak leaves, pine needles, or peatmoss) about their roots in winter.

Should azaleas be covered completely for the winter? If by this is meant the complete covering of leaves, the answer is, No! But if a mere shading of the plant is meant, this proves very helpful when tender varieties are being grown.

Should young azaleas be covered for the winter if they are not sheltered by shrubs?   The evergreen varieties might well be covered, since these are the least hardy. Covering material should be light, allowing air circulation.

How can potted azaleas purchased at the florist and full of buds and flowers, be taken care of so as to bloom again?   Most of the florists' potted azaleas are Kurume azaleas, and are not hardy north of Philadelphia, Pennsylvania. They will grow out of doors the first summer but will be killed by winter cold. In the South, such plants can be planted out of doors in acid soil, protected the first winter, and usually come through in fine shape.

Should azaleas be kept in hothouses or a lath house during the winter months? (California.)   This really depends on the section of California and the kind of azalea. The more tender sorts should not be exposed to more than a few degrees of frost.

Should azaleas have a mulch about their roots? Why?   Yes. Because their roots grow best when the soil is cool and moist. In the winter a mulch protects the roots against extremely low temperatures.

Is it good to cover azaleas and rhododendrons with manure?   Not if it is fresh. Well-rotted manure can be used in moderation without injury to the plants.

When should a mulch be applied to azaleas?   It is well to put a mulch over the roots just before winter weather sets in. This, if not more than a few inches deep, may be left on until time to place new mulching material for the next winter.

What makes a good mulching material for azaleas and rhodo-dendrons?   Oak leaves, pine needles, and acid peatmoss. Upon decomposition all these are beneficial to the growth of this type of plant.

I have no oak leaves but plenty of maple leaves. Could I use these as a mulch?   It would be better to use peatmoss instead. Maple leaves tend to pack closely when wet, thus keeping air from the plant roots. When very tightly packed they frequently "cake" and have been known to kill azaleas for this reason. Also, maple leaves are alkaline when decomposed.

Propagation

Are azaleas propagated by seed?   Azaleas are propagated from cuttings, by grafting, and also from seeds, depending upon the kind and the purpose for which they are needed. Any of the wild forms, native or exotic, may be raised from seeds, as the seedlings will reproduce the characters of the parent. Hybrid forms and "sports" cannot be reproduced from seeds.

How can I start azalea from seed? Collect seed pods in late fall when they are ready to open. Keep dry, and in February shake seeds out on milled or ground sphagnum moss 1 inch deep on top of acid soil well firmed in pots. Keep moss moist, preferably by using a fine mist spray from time to time. In several months seedlings should be of right size to prick off and transplant.

Can azaleas be propagated by cuttings? It is exceedingly difficult to root cuttings of the native azaleas, but some of the more familiar garden forms, such as Snow, Hinodegiri, Torch, and Amoena, can be rooted with good success in July. The cuttings should be about 3 ins. long, taken (just after new growth is completed) from the tips of the shoots and placed in a rooting mixture of sand and peat in a cold frame.

Are azaleas propagated by grafting? The grafting of azaleas is almost entirely confined to some of the tender kinds, normally grown in greenhouses. Propagating cases in a warm greenhouse are needed, and the grafting has to be done very skillfully to be successful.

EVERGREEN

How can I grow the evergreen azaleas? They need much the same conditions as rhododendron, with which they are now included by botanists.

A group of Azalea Hinodegiri have become too large. Can they be clipped rather severely, after next bloom, without injury or serious loss of future bloom? Yes, they withstand heavy pruning.

Will you discuss winter protection for azaleas in this region? Mine fail to blossom in the spring; most of the leaves are brown and new growth is slow to start. During the summer they grow well. (Northern New York.) The evergreen types are not completely hardy in northern New York. If you build a screen of burlap or pine boughs, this may help to bring them through in better condition; but if the flower buds are killed, even with this protection, then the thing to do is to plant a hardier variety. *Azalea calendulacea, A. nudiflora,* and *A. viscosa* are among the hardiest of the deciduous azaleas.

Last June and July I made over 200 evergreen azalea cuttings of the current season's growth, 3 to 5 ins. long. I dipped half in Rootone and the other half in No. 1 Hormodin powder, placed them in a mixture of sand and peat, in a shady open cold frame, and kept bed moist, with temperature around 70° F. After 4 or 5 weeks the leaves would fall, leaving a dried, withered stem, minus roots. Where was my mistake? If by the term "open cold frame" you mean that you did not put the sash on the frame, then that was the mistake. Except for removing condensed moisture from the glass, the frame should be kept closed for 6 weeks, after which a *little* ventilation is desirable. Some of the tender greenhouse azaleas do not root readily from cuttings and, consequently, are grafted.

What evergreen azaleas are hardy in New Jersey? Amoena Azalea, magenta; Hinodegiri Azalea, strong rose color; and Rose Azalea, white.

HEATHER (CALLUNA)

I want to plant a little "sheet" of Scotch Heather. What kind of soil? Choose a well-drained situation. Prepare a cushion, fully a foot deep, made up of about ⅓ garden loam, ⅓ sand, and ⅓ highly acid leafmold. If the latter is not available, use peatmoss instead, and add a little very old manure.

Can heather be satisfactorily grown out of doors in the vicinity of New York? Scotch Heather grows quite well, in peat soil, along the Eastern seacoast. The plants usually kill back in about 3 years, and new plants should be used for replacement.

Should Scotch Heather be pruned? Early-blooming varieties should be cut back to the base of the flowering shoots as soon as the blossoms have faded. In sections where heather suffers from winter injury it should be cut back in spring just as growth is beginning.

MOUNTAIN LAUREL (KALMIA LATIFOLIA)

When does Mountain Laurel bloom, and what color are the blossoms? Will it stand shade? Deep pink buds and pink-white flower clusters, in June. Sun or shade.

Must Mountain Laurel have shade? Will grow in full sun if soil conditions are right, but seems to do best in partial shade. For soil and culture see rhododendron.

What are some uses for Mountain Laurel? Foundation planting; mass planting, in woodland: among azalea, rhododendron, leucothoe, ferns, hemlock.

When is the proper time to transplant the wild Mountain Laurel? In the early spring, before the buds have started growth.

Is Mountain Laurel hardy in Cleveland, Ohio, without any protective covering? Yes; but be certain the soil in which it is planted is acid.

In transplanting laurel from woods have been generally unsuccessful, even with utmost care exercised on basis of rules governing growth of this plant. Any specific reasons? Sounds like soil trouble. Perhaps by bringing in considerable leafmold and soil from woods you could succeed in growing it.

Will you give proper culture for Kalmia latifolia? Mine is 7 or 8 years old and has never bloomed, though it seems to be healthy.

If the plant is healthy, this shows it to be growing in good soil. You might try the effect of superphosphate (15 to 20 per cent) applied beneath the mulch, at the rate of 4 oz. per sq. yd. Perhaps the shade is too dense.

LEUCOTHOE

What is Leucothoe catesbaei? How is it used? An evergreen with arching stems clothed with handsome long racemes of white flowers and long, oval leathery leaves. Acid soil and partial shade. Good for woodland plantings, with rhododendron, laurel, and hemlock.

How can I grow leucothoe? Needs well-drained, acid soil containing ⅓ or more organic matter—acid leafmold or peatmoss. Partial shade preferable.

PIERIS

When do the "andromedas" bloom? What are the blossoms like? Mountain Andromeda (*Pieris floribunda*) has erect panicles of tiny cream-colored waxy bells in May. Japanese Andromeda (*Pieris japonica*), drooping panicles slightly longer than on the Mountain Andromeda, in April to May.

Would Japanese Andromeda be hardy in northern New England? No; but our native Mountain Andromeda probably would be.

What is the difference between our native Mountain Andromeda and the Japanese species? The native (*Pieris floribunda*), though hardier, is not so easily content nor is it as handsome of leaf and flower as *P. japonica*. The latter is better suited to formal plantings and the former to woodlands.

Which andromeda has leaves that turn reddish bronze in winter and new spring leaves with a rose-colored cast? Japanese Andromeda.

What soil is required by the andromedas? Moist, peaty or sandy soil. Part shade desirable.

Would Pieris japonica stand through the winter on Long Island, if planted on a north or west exposure, with a peatmoss mulch? Yes, if the winter winds are not too high. *P. floribunda* is more hardy, while *P. japonica* is easier to grow.

RHODODENDRON

What to Grow

Which types of rhododendron are the hardiest and the most satisfactory for growth in southern New England (as mass planting, not as specimen plants)? The Giant Rosebay (*Rhododendron maxi-*

mum) is the hardiest of all the rhododendrons. It is not so colorful as some of the hybrids, but it can be used for massing.

What are some of the best and hardiest rhododendron hybrids? Red—Atrosanguineum, H. W. Sargent; pink—Abraham Lincoln, Roseum Elegans; purple—Purpureum Elegans, Purpureum Grandiflorum; white—Album Elegans, Album Grandiflorum.

What color are the flowers of different native rhododendrons? Carolina Rhododendron, pink; Catawba Rhododendron, rosy-purple; Rosebay (*R. maximum*), pale pink.

How tall does the Carolina Rhododendron grow? Six ft. maximum height; usually less under cultivation.

Soil and Fertilizer

I would like to grow rhododendrons here. How can I make soil acid? (Illinois.) See under Azaleas for method of making soil acid. In Illinois, especially the northwestern part, the summers are very hot and dry and the winters very cold, which is extremely hard on rhododendrons. Precautions should be taken to give foliage and roots plenty of moisture in the summer; also to give winter protection, especially in exposed situations.

My soil is very dry, and some of my rhododendrons have died. What should I do? Mix decomposed vegetable matter (rotted manure, rotted oak or pine leaves and peatmoss) with the soil. Then apply a mulch of rotting oak leaves, pine needles, or peatmoss about the base of the plants. All these help to conserve moisture.

What is a good fertilizer for rhododendrons and azaleas? Mr. C. O. Dexter of Sandwich, Massachusetts, has recommended the following mixture, and it has worked very well indeed: 7 lbs. of Chilean nitrate of soda, 3 lbs. muriate of potash, 20 lbs. superphosphate; use 2 to 3 lbs. per 100 sq. ft.

What is the best formula for fertilizers for rhododendrons and azaleas, to help their color but not too much of a growth stimulant? The fertilizer mixture mentioned above is excellent for this purpose, for although it carries some nitrate, it contains high percentages of phosphates and potash, and these aid primarily in flower production.

What fertilizer should one give rhododendrons growing in a poor, sandy soil? Add decaying vegetable material, such as rotted manure, decaying oak leaves, pine needles, and peatmoss. Chemical fertilizers alone added to a poor, sandy soil would not be sufficient.

Is flowers of sulfur a desirable fertilizer for azaleas and rhododendrons? It acts as a fertilizer, for in making the soil more acid it releases certain materials which were not formerly available to the plant.

Planting and Culture

Will rhododendrons grow in full sun?   Yes; but partial shade is preferable.

Are there any particular requirements, as to sun or shade, for rhododendrons?   Rhododendrons bloom most profusely in the full sun; but if grown in partial shade they will bloom sufficiently well to be attractive. In deep shade most varieties bloom very little.

Do rhododendrons and azaleas need the same general growing conditions?   Yes, except that rhododendrons will grow better in shaded situations.

When should rhododendrons be planted?   Preferably in the early spring.

Where should rhododendrons be planted?   Where they get some shade and some direct sunlight. Also, they should be protected from high winter winds. Their roots should not be allowed to dry out at any time.

My place is exposed to wind from ocean. Will rhododendrons thrive?   No. In any case they need shelter from strong wind— especially in winter.

How old must rhododendrons be to bloom? Mine are 5 years old, growing well in prepared acid soil and partial shade, but do not bloom. Many rhododendrons bloom when they are about 5 years old. This particular plant may be growing too fast vegetatively. Root-pruning might be practiced by pushing a spade into the soil around the base of the plant, not too near the stem. Or you might try superphosphate (15 to 20 per cent), applied beneath the mulch, at the rate of 4 oz. per sq. yd.

Can you tell me why my rhododendron did not bloom although it has healthy foliage and growing conditions (acid) are favorable?   It may have been that the flower buds were killed by an unusually cold winter. Also, rhododendrons are like many other ornamentals in that they bloom profusely one year and very little the next. There is little that the amateur can do about this "alternate-bearing" habit.

How is Rhododendron maximum made to bloom better?   This species does best only in the shade. Ornamentally it is not so good as the earlier-flowering hybrids, because the flowers appear *after* the new growth has started, and this frequently hides the flowers. Plenty of moisture, acid soil, and an acid mulch are helpful aids.

Winter Protection

Would it be helpful or harmful to tie burlap sacks around the branches of my rhododendrons and to cover the buds, in winter?   It would be harmful. Air must circulate about these plants in the winter, and wrapping stems and branches would not permit this. It is far better to build a *screen* of burlap about them, slightly open at the base to permit free air circulation at all times, but also giving a screening and shading protection.

What is the best protection for rhododendrons exposed to strong winds? Burlap screens, or screens of evergreen boughs, so designed and placed as to give protection from winds, and some shade during winter months—especially February and March.

When should leafmold mulch be applied to rhododendrons? In fall.

Propagation

How are rhododendrons propagated? Can they be propagated by hardwood cuttings? The large-flowered garden kinds are usually grafted, but Carolina, Rosebay, and Catawba Rhododendrons are raised from seeds. Some of the hybrid kinds can be raised from cuttings taken in August, but with most of them the percentage of rooting is not very large.

Can I root leaf cuttings of Rhododendron? Dr. Henry T. Skinner has had good success in rooting leaf-bud cuttings. These were made in late July by cutting leaves with a sliver of wood together with a growth bud attached. These were treated with a root-inducing growth regulator and inserted in a mixture of 3 parts by bulk of quartz sand and 2 parts peatmoss. They were kept in a propagating frame in a greenhouse until they were rooted.

Can rhododendron cuttings be rooted by the constant mist method? Yes, it is well worth a trial.

What is the proper time for grafting rhododendrons? Rhododendrons are generally grafted, in heated greenhouse, during January and February. (See also Grafting, this section).

Can rhododendron grafting be done outdoors? While this is not altogether impossible, it is not a method to be recommended, as there would be too many failures for every union obtained.

What is the type of graft used on rhododendron? The veneer graft is most commonly used. The understock is not cut back at the time of grafting. A downward, slanting cut is made on the stem of the understock, about 1½ ins. long and about ⅓ of the way through the stem. A second cut into the stem (at the base of the first) removes the piece of bark and attached wood. The base of the scion is cut to correspond to the cuts on the understock.

Can any kind of root be used as an understock for grafting rhododendrons? No. It must be another rhododendron. The one most commonly used for understocks is *Rhododendron ponticum*. The tenderness of this species, however, makes it anything but satisfactory for the purpose in this country.

How should rhododendrons be separated? Rhododendrons as a rule should not be "separated" in the same sense that one thinks of separating perennials. They grow as individual plants, often in clumps. Any attempt to divide these clumps would probably prove disastrous.

Insects and Diseases

See Section VIII.

Is there any insect that destroys the leaves of rhododendrons? The lace bug is the most serious pest of rhododendron foliage. This is a small insect with lacelike wings appearing on the undersurface of the leaves. It appears in May and June, to be followed by a second infestation later in the summer.

When should rhododendrons be sprayed to control the lace bug? What material should be used? Spray as soon as the insects appear, usually in June. Several materials are available for control. Use nicotine-soap solution; or lindane, 1 tablespoonful of 25 percent to 1 gallon; or malathion emulsion at 1 teaspoonful per gallon. Spray forcibly on the *under* surfaces of the foliage, on a cloudy day when the temperature does not exceed 80° F. Spraying in full, hot sunshine will burn the foliage. (See Section VIII.)

SPECIFIC TENDER SHRUBS

ACACIA

Can we grow the yellow-blossom acacia trees one sees in California? (Connecticut.) No, they will not endure temperatures much below 20° F.

Where can I get plants of the acacia with small yellow blossoms? Can it be grown in the garden? (Missouri.) Many California nurseries can supply acacias. They are perennials (either trees or shrubs). They are not hardy where winter temperatures drop below 20° above zero.

BAY TREE (LAURUS)

How hardy is bay tree and when is the best time to trim to formal shape? It is not really hardy north of Philadelphia, Pennsylvania. Trim when the new shoots have almost completed their growth. A second trimming may be necessary if the first stimulates the production of new shoots.

CAMELLIA

See also Regional Section.

In a Southern garden I saw a shrub or plant that I became very much interested in. The owner called it Camellia japonica. It had a

double flower like a rose and as large. Please tell me where I can buy this shrub? (Pennsylvania.)   Camellias in many beautiful forms and colors can be obtained from Southern nurseries. *C. sasanqua* will be hardy with you in Pennsylvania.

Soil, Fertilizer, and Planting

At what pH do camellias grow best? Will they do better at 5.7 to 6.2 or from 6 to 7?   Camellias are less particular in this regard than gardenias and some other plants. They should thrive in either of the soils mentioned providing it is physically in good condition and is fertile.

What soil preparation is necessary for camellias? (California). Make the soil rich and friable to a depth of at least a foot, or, better still, 2 ft. Mix with it very generous amounts of leafmold, or peatmoss and very old rotted manure. Good compost may also be used.

What is the best fertilizer for camellias? When should it be applied? Old cow manure (or dehydrated manure or cottonseed meal, plus compost) applied as a mulch at the beginning of the growing season, followed, a few weeks later, by a light dressing of any complete fertilizer.

Are chemical plant foods good for camellia bushes?   They respond best to organic fertilizers of a comparatively mild character. Old rotted manure, cottonseed meal, and bone meal are all excellent.

What is the best way to start and grow camellias?   For outdoor culture, prepare ground so that it is rich and well drained but retentive of moisture. Select lightly shaded position. Obtain good plants from nursery of repute. If possible, visit gardens and nurseries where camellias are grown and familiarize yourself with their needs.

When is best time to move Camellia japonica?   During the dormant season, in winter or in early spring.

Culture

Can camellias be forced to bloom earlier? If so, how?   They can be encouraged to bloom early by planting them in sheltered locations; a more certain method is to grow them in pots, tubs, or planted out in ground beds in a cool, airy greenhouse.

What causes few blossoms rather than many on a well-fertilized camellia bush?   Possibly the plant is in too dense shade. Some protection from strong sunlight is helpful, but lack of sufficient light is harmful. Also overfertilization may result in too vigorous growth at expense of flower production.

What is it that eats holes in camellia leaves? Have never found anything on them, and no spray that I have used seems to do any good. Probably the Asiatic beetle or the black vine weevil. Before specific advice can be given, a surer diagnosis is desirable. Send specimens to your State Agricultural Experiment Station. Spraying with lead arsenate probably best control.

What causes my camellia leaves to fall off? Damage to roots due to careless transplanting; waterlogged soil; lack of sufficient water, particularly during growing season; or spray damage.

What causes the leaves of an apparently healthy camellia plant to turn brown just before coming into blossom? This may be due to very cold weather, disease, or extreme drought. Spray injury could also be responsible.

My camellia has rusty coat on buds, and they do not open in the spring. What should I do? (Texas.) You seemingly have a variety unsuited to outdoor conditions. There are some kinds that are satisfactory in greenhouses, but not outdoors. Replace plant with variety recommended by local nurseryman.

Will frequent sprinkling of camellias while in bud cause the buds to rot and drop off? I understand they should be sprinkled during hot weather. Spraying of the foliage during hot weather is beneficial. Make sure, however, that the ground also is kept moist to a good depth. Do not be deceived by merely wetting the surface.

Why do many full buds fall off my red camellias late in the season? They are planted on the east side of the house, with just the morning sun. Should they be moved? The commonest reason for bud-dropping is lack of sufficient moisture at the roots of the plant. This is particularly true of secondary buds that develop if a late frost has killed early growth. Certain diseases also cause bud-dropping.

Propagation

Can I increase my favorite camellia by layering? Yes. See Propagation. In June or July, nick a low branch with a knife, bend to the ground, hollow out a little trench, and lay the branch in this. Cover with sandy soil and use a brick or other heavy object to prevent motion. Be sure that the layer is kept constantly moist.

How and when can we start camellias from cuttings? July. Select firm, young growths, 3 or 4 ins. long; cut away lower leaves and cut stem horizontally below joint with sharp knife. Plant firmly in sand or sand and peatmoss. Keep lightly shaded, moist, and in humid atmosphere. Slight bottom heat helps rooting.

Diseases and Pests

See Section VIII.

What makes the buds on my Soeur Therese Camellia turn brown on edges of petals? This may be due to flower-blight disease. Send specimens to your Agricultural Experiment Station for examination.

What spray can I use to destroy the Asiatic beetle which is destroying my camellia plants? Spread lead arsenate (1 lb. to 100 sq. ft.) over surface of ground and wash it well into soil. Spray foliage with 5 lbs. lead arsenate and 4 lbs. wheat flour to 100 gals. of water. (See Section VIII.)

What is the scurfy white substance on the under side of my camellia leaves? This is tea scale, and must be controlled by carefully spraying with an oil-emulsion spray during late summer and fall. (See Section VIII.)

The leaves on one of my camellias have large, dark spots, and drop off the tree. What causes this? Possibly the black mold disease, which is often associated with another infection called spot disease. Spray with Bordeaux mixture, or dust with dusting sulfur.

GARDENIA

See also House Plants.

In growing gardenias, we are advised if the leaves turn yellow to use aluminum sulfate around them. How much shall I use and how often? Use at the rate of from 4 to 12 oz. to each 10 sq. ft., and frequently enough to keep the pH of the soil at 4.5. A soil test is necessary to determine this.

I know Capejasmine (gardenia) requires acid soil. I have fed copperas and aluminum sulfate, but still the leaves are yellow and smutty-looking, and no blooms. Can anything be done? Use more natural methods of acidifying the soil. Mix oak leafmold, rotted pine needles, or granulated peatmoss with the soil, 1 to 3. The smutty appearance is indicative of the presence of scale insects. Spray with a good contact spray to get rid of them. (See Section VIII.)

When is the best time to transplant a gardenia, crowded in its present location? At the very beginning of the growing season, when new shoots and leaves are observed to be starting.

May gardenia plants remain outside in garden all year 'round? (New York.) Even with protection gardenias are not hardy in New York. Virginia is about as far North as *Gardenia florida* can be successfully grown outdoors.

How can I make gardenias bloom in my yard? The Capejasmine or *Gardenia florida* needs a sheltered, sunny position, a moist (not waterlogged) acid soil, and protection from frost.

Is it necessary to protect small gardenia plants by building frame around them, and wrapping with sacks? They need protection of this kind if there is danger that they will encounter frost.

JASMINE

Which jasmines are hardy North? None reliably hardy though

Jasminum nudiflorum (a good wall shrub), blooming very early before leaves appear, can be grown in the vicinity of New York City if given a southern exposure with the protection of a sheltering wall. *J. humile,* an erect evergreen to 20 ft. with yellow flowers, and *J. officinale,* climbing, with white flowers, are grown near the seaboard in the Middle Atlantic states.

Can jasmine (the flowers of which are used for tea) be grown as far North as Cleveland, Ohio?   Not very well. In a protected spot it might live through the winter; normally one would expect it not to be hardy.

OLEANDER

How can I succeed with oleanders in my garden? (California.) They are easily grown out of doors in the South. Watch for scale. (See Section VIII.)

Will you tell me how to start slips of oleanders?   Cuttings taken in July and August root readily in sand if kept in close, humid surroundings such as a cold frame or glass-covered box. Or shoots may be kept in water until rooted, and then potted in soil.

POMEGRANATE

What soil is best for pomegranate?   A heavy, deep loam. Suited only to tropical and subtropical climates, or for the greenhouse.

When should a pomegranate (flowering) be pruned?   Shorten strong-growing shoots about ⅓ when they have almost attained their full length.

HEDGES AND WINDBREAKS

WHAT TO GROW

What would be the best kind of hedge to set out on the north side of a lot?   This depends on the height. For under 6 ft. a yew hedge would be good, but expensive. For over 6 ft. a hemlock or White Pine hedge. These are evergreens and so would give protection 365 days a year. Evergreen hedges cost more, but they are worth it for their winter protection.

Which flowering hedge would look well around a vegetable garden? It should be low so that it will not shade the vegetables. Spirea Anthony Waterer, with its flat-topped, deep red-rose flowers would give color to the area. Prune back after it has bloomed and more blossoms should follow.

Which flowering shrubs would make good hedge plants, even if unpruned?   Barberry, especially upright-growing types; *Abelia grandi-*

flora; Peatree or Peashrub (*Caragana*); Japanese Quince, especially the variety "Spitfire"; deutzia; hydrangea, bush honeysuckle, spirea, common lilac, many of the viburnums. Unpruned privet makes a good tall hedge or screen.

What are the beautiful hedges made of that one sees in England? Can they be grown here? (Maryland.) Many different species are used. Perhaps you have reference to the English Hawthorn and English Holly combination. This could be done here by substituting American Holly for the less-hardy English species.

What would be a good low deciduous hedge, not above 2 ft. high, to put around a sunken garden? One of the dwarf barberries (*Berberis thunbergi minor*); Slender Deutzia; the dwarf Cranberrybush Viburnum (*Viburnum opulus nanum*).

What would be good as a fairly high deciduous hedge for screening? Acanthopanax, Corkbark or Winged Euonymus, rose-of-Sharon, privet, buckthorn, Vanhoutte's Spirea, various lilacs.

Could you suggest some good deciduous trees which would screen our garage driveway from our out-of-door sitting room—something natural-looking for an informal place where there is plenty of room? (Massachusetts.) European Beech. It can be sheared.

What is the name of a hedge plant that would grow at least 6 ft. tall? I do not want privet or barberry. The one I have in mind has dark berries on it. The American Cranberrybush with red berries (*Viburnum trilobum*); or the Glossy Buckthorn with red and black berries (*Rhamnus frangula*).

What is the difference between buckthorn (Rhamnus cathartica) and Alder Buckthorn (R. frangula)? Which is better for a hedge? (Maine.) The former, because it is hardier than Alder Buckthorn. The latter, however, has pointed glossy leaves, while the former has dull rounded ones.

What is the best fast-growing hedge for screening (not privet)? (North Carolina.) Myrtle (*Myrtus communis*); Laurelcherry (*Prunus laurocerasus*); Portuguese Laurelcherry, (*Prunus lusitanica*).

Is a flower border or a shrub border better to screen a vegetable garden from view? Either kind of border would be proper; shrubs would be the more permanent. Why not plant a yew hedge, which would not take up more than 2½ to 3 ft. of width; or a single, informal row of *Spiraea Vanhouttei;* or bush fruits, such as blueberries or gooseberries?

What hedges are recommended for the lazy gardener who prefers not to have the work of clipping every week? Truehedge Columnberry; the Upright Privet (*Ligustrum lucidum erectum*); Truedwarf Box, Dwarf Winged Euonymus, the Dwarf Hedge Yew, and other similar plants are ideal for the lazy man's hedge. They need practically no clipping. At most this need be done but once a year.

What hedge would be best for city property—one that would need least attention?   One of the best would be the Five-leaved Aralia (*Acanthopanax sieboldianus*). Japanese Barberry hedges are also good under adverse conditions; and privet, of course—but this needs attention.

Can you suggest a neat, small, broad-leaved evergreen shrub to use at the edge of a terrace? (We want to have the plants untrimmed, but not more than a few feet high.)   English Ivy trained on a frame; Boxleaf Holly (*Ilex crenata nummularia*); Dwarf Box; *Euonymus vegetus*. Warty Barberry (Berberis verruculosa).

What is the rate of growth of a Canadian Hemlock hedge? Which low shrubs would go well in front of it?   A well-established young hemlock hedge in good soil will average at least 18 ins. a year. Such a hedge in itself is very beautiful, but if shrubs have to be placed in front of it, some low-growing types—coralberry (*Symphoricarpos*), Slender Deutzia, roses, Oriental quinces, and the like—might be used.

What kind of evergreen can I grow for a hedge, not more than 6 ft. high, that will keep a neat shape without shearing?   Hicks Yew will do this, although it will take quite a few years for it to grow 6 ft. high if small plants are purchased. Farther South the Irish Yew would be ideal.

What could be used for a low evergreen hedge (not box) for between vegetable garden and lawn?   A yew called *Taxus canadensis stricta*, or *Ilex crenata convexa* (commonly called the Convex-leaved Japanese Holly), would answer.

Would spruce trees make good hedges? (New Hampshire.)   Yes. Norway Spruce (*Picea excelsa*) either trimmed or untrimmed; also various forms of White Spruce (*P. glauca*).

Are there any evergreen barberries for hedge purposes?   Yes; Juliana Barberry, with black berries, grows to about 5 ft. *Berberis verruculosa,* with tiny holly-like leaves, growing about half as tall, is also suitable.

What hedge material would give a soft, blue-gray tone?   Pfitzer Juniper.

Can you give us advice on which evergreens to grow across the front of our place to form a hedge that people can neither see over nor through?   Either *Ilex crenata,* Redcedar, or American Arborvitae (all are evergreen).

Could we have an evergreen hedge, unclipped, which would have berries?   Yes, firethorn (pyracantha).

Which evergreen would make a handsome hedge that, without trimming, need never exceed 6 ft.—preferably less?   Dwarf Hinoki Cypress (*Chamaecyparis obtusa compacta*). Also, other dwarf forms of this evergreen.

Which trees, other than native hemlock, make a good hedge? Northern exposure, semi-clay soil. The hedge is wanted for beauty as well as to serve as a windbreaker. White Pine, Red Pine, redcedar, Serbian Spruce.

Which tall evergreen—not too expensive—would you suggest for use as a fence along boundary line? Hemlock or White Pine.

FERTILIZERS AND PLANTING

What is a good fertilizer for hedges? Any complete commercial fertilizer, or well-rotted manure. For instance, 5–10–5 might be applied at the rate of 5 to 10 lbs. per 100 ft. of hedge, depending on the size of the plants.

How shall I plan a hedge? Decide whether you want it low or high, thorny or flowering, evergreen or deciduous. Just why you want it. Then select the best plant material to fit the need.

How does one plant a hedge? Dig a trench 2 ft. wide, 1 to 2 ft. deep, close to property lines, but at a safe distance away from sidewalk or street, so hedge will have plenty of space to expand up to the size at which it is to be permanently maintained. Put well-rotted manure on bottom of trench, then some good soil, and tramp firm. Space plants 1 to 3 ft. apart (depending on size), filling in soil about their roots. Make firm, and water in well. Cut back severely if a deciduous shrub is being used.

How far apart (approximately) should 6- to 8-ft. shrubs be planted for screening purposes? It depends upon the kinds used and on how quickly you want a solid screen. For instance, rose-of-Sharon might be set 6 to 7 ft. apart and the Morrow Honeysuckle 8 to 10 ft.

When is the best time to move a hedge of flowering shrubs? Should they be cut back? We want to keep them as large as possible for a screen. They can be moved after leaves have fallen in the autumn; or in the early spring. In transplanting their tops should be cut back about ⅓ for best results.

TRIMMING AND TRAINING

What is the best way to prune hedges? Different sorts of plants used as hedges demand different treatments. Large plants like White Pine and spruce should be allowed to retain approximately their outline. Hemlock hedges should always be much wider at the bottom than at the top. Large privet hedges should also be somewhat wider at the bottom, although smaller ones may be trimmed with the sides vertical. Regels Privet and other shrubs of that sort should be allowed to grow as naturally as possible. Hedges of dwarf yew should be broader than they are high. Dwarf boxwood and other edging plants can be trimmed to a rectangular shape.

How should one prune a deciduous hedge the first year? Cut back to within 6 to 12 ins. of the ground at planting time. Lightly shear whenever new shoots reach a height of 10 to 12 ins. if a close, compact hedge is needed.

Should hedges be trimmed to any special shape?   Wider at bottom, preferably with a rounded top.

Do all hedge plants have to be trimmed several times in the season? No. Most evergreens can be kept tidy with one shearing. The same is true of such deciduous shrubs as althea, barberry, buckthorn, and spirea.

Should hedges be trimmed during the winter?   This can be done with no injury to deciduous hedges, if hardy.

How shall I cut a hedge to make it grow?   Cutting or pruning never makes a hedge "grow." It is good soil, fertilizer, and plenty of water offered the roots which really make the hedge grow.

I have heard that constant trimming devitalizes a hedge. Is this true?   Yes, to some extent. Privet, for example, sheared every 3 weeks is more likely to succumb to the effect of a severe winter than one sheared only 2 or 3 times during the growing season.

Are electric hedge shears satisfactory?   Yes; a good type will do the work in about ¼ the time required with hand shears.

Is it necessary to cultivate the soil along a hedge?   Yes. Primarily to keep out weeds, which might grow and choke lower branches of hedge.

SPECIFIC HEDGE PLANTS

How shall I plant an ARBORVITAE hedge? (Topsoil is rather poor and only 9 ins. deep.)   Dig a trench 2 ft. wide and 1½ ft. deep. Put topsoil on one side. Either remove 9 ins. of subsoil and replace with good soil; or take out 3 ins. and fork in 4 to 5 ins. of rotted manure or leaves and make firm by tramping. Return topsoil, and proceed with planting. The young trees should be set from 18 ins. to 3 ft. apart, according to their size.

When and how should an arborvitae hedge, about 18 ins. high, be trimmed?   Top it evenly, during the period of spring growth, to about 1 ft. high. Thereafter, if you want a solid hedge, permit it to gain each year not more than 6 ins., until the desired height has been reached. From then on keep it closely sheared.

What is the best treatment to produce a thriving BARBERRY hedge?   Give it good soil to grow in from the start. Fertilize with manure or commercial fertilizers once a year if needed. Keep watered during very dry spells. In trimming, keep the hedge slightly wider at the base than at the top.

When, and in what manner, should barberry and privet hedges be

trimmed? Always trim hedges so that they are wider at the base than the top, thus giving the lower branches plenty of exposure. Trimming might best be done when the young shoots are half grown, or nearly full grown, in late spring. However, trimming can be done without injury at practically any time.

What time of year is best for planting a BOXWOOD hedge? Either early spring or early fall.

To make CHINESE ELMS form a thick hedge, what procedure should be followed? Cut them back hard. Any plants up to 3 ins. in diameter at the base (and possibly larger) could be cut back to within 6 ins. of the ground. Then a trimming before active growth has stopped, and another a month later, will aid in forcing bushy growth.

I planted a hedge of TRUEHEDGE COLUMNBERRY, 18 to 24 ins. tall, last spring, cutting back half the growth, and trimming the new growth occasionally throughout the summer. Although no plants were lost they did not bush out enough from the base. What procedure shall I follow? How far should they be cut back next spring? These plants never will bush out at the base, for this is a columnar or up-right-growing variety. If the shoots at the base have their ends pinched off occasionally, this may help somewhat. It is only necessary to trim the tops once a year. If the plants are still too far apart to make a hedge, move them closer together.

What is the cause of scant foliage on lower part of a MONTEREY CYPRESS hedge? (California.) Not sufficient room at the base. Hedges should be *wider* at the base than the top; this gives the lower branches plenty of sunlight and exposure. When hedges are clipped perpendicularly, or narrower at the base than at the top, the lower branches can be expected to become sickly and die.

What is the best way to grow a thick EVERGREEN hedge and yet not stop its upward growth too much? Allow it to elongate up-ward a full year untrimmed, then merely trim off the terminal buds of the branches several times during the next season. If it thickens up well in that year, allow it to grow with little trimming the next, and so on.

Will a HEMLOCK hedge thrive in a northwestern exposure with-out protection from sweeping winds? Depends on the area. If in the middle states, or in the South, yes. If in the extreme northern parts of Minnesota, Illinois, Wisconsin, where winds are high and extremely cold, some "burning" might result in winter. If in Midwest, where winds are very hot and very dry in summer, the answer is, No!

In planting 18-in. hemlock bushes for a hedge, should spacing be 2 ft. or less? Best spacing would be 18 ins. apart.

When do you shear a hemlock hedge? Shorten new growth about the end of June.

When is best time to prune a LAUREL hedge?   This can be pruned any time; the best time (i.e., when one trimming would do the most good) is when the new shoots have nearly completed their growth for the current year. To avoid cutting leaves, use knife or pruning shears rather than hedge shears.

How about purple LILAC for a hedge?   It makes a splendid tall hedge, but you must remember that the more it is clipped the more flower buds are removed. Also, in many places it must be sprayed annually for bad infestations of lilac scale.

At what season should a PEASHRUB (caragana) hedge be trimmed for the first time?   At the time it is planted; not again until the very early spring of the next year.

How does one trim WHITE PINE into a compact hedge, solid from the ground up?   Trim during the period of soft growth, reducing the new, candlelike growth, but not pruning into old wood. Permit only a slight annual gain in height. Shape the hedge so that it tapers up from a wide base to a narrower, rounded top. Keep the base free from weeds.

PRIVET

How do I go about planting a privet hedge?   If soil is fairly good, no special preparation is necessary beyond removal of weeds and trash. An overrich soil may cause privet to grow embarrassingly fast. Stretch a line as a guide in planting. Starting at one end, dig a hole deep enough to set the plant 3 ins. deeper than it formerly grew. Dig hole for the next plant and use soil for covering roots of first plant; and so on to end of hedge, when the soil removed in making the first hole can be used for filling in around the last plant.

I want to plant a Waxleaf Privet hedge. Please tell me how tall this privet grows? How far apart to set plants? And if they need lime. (New Jersey.)   This privet, untrimmed, may grow to 30 ft. in height. For a hedge, space 18 to 36 ins. apart, and keep trimmed to height desired. Privets grow well in either acid or alkaline soil, but this species would be hardy only from southern New Jersey southward.

In the first warm spell can I broadcast some bone meal around my California Privet hedge so that it may get a quick start in spring? I planted the hedge last May.   You can, but the "early start" would be doubtful for bone meal is very slow in taking effect. You might better use a commercial fertilizer, or well-rotted manure.

How low should a privet hedge be cut when planted?   Shorten all branches at least ⅔.

What is the procedure in trimming a newly planted privet hedge, to make it bushy?   Shear it whenever the new shoots attain a length of about 1 ft., cutting them back ½.

What is the best thing to do with an old overgrown privet hedge? Cut it off 6 ins. above the ground, and in this way force it to start anew.

How often is it necessary to shear a privet hedge? About 3 times during the growing season, giving the last clipping early in September. It is better to shear every few weeks if a very trim hedge is required.

How and when should Ibolium Privet be trimmed to make thickest hedge, about 15 to 18 ins. high? Cut off to a few inches above the ground when it is planted, and then shear at the required height several times a year.

I was unable to trim and shape privet hedge last fall. Now it is unsightly. When is the earliest time to trim? A privet hedge can be trimmed any time of year except late summer, when a trimming might force new growth which would not mature by winter.

What makes privet hedge die from the roots? The common privet (*Ligustrum vulgare*) is subject to a serious blight which kills the plants and for which there is no known cure. Better use some other kind; they all do well in normal soils.

How can I start a hedge from cuttings without a cold frame? See Propagation. Privet can be raised from cuttings set in sandy soil in early spring. One or 2 years after the cuttings are set they may be transplanted to form the hedge. When planting the hedge set the plants about 3 ins. deeper than before, and as soon as the planting is finished cut all the shoots back to a few ins. above the soil to insure a dense base to the hedge.

When is the time to make cuttings of privet hedges? How do you go about doing it? Late spring or early summer is best. Take 6-in. cuttings of the new wood, and place them in sand in a hotbed, with some bottom heat if possible. Keep moist but not wet, shade, and they should be rooted in 4 weeks or less.

At what time of the year should a SPIREA hedge be trimmed? Just after it has flowered, then one gets the full benefit of the flowers.

How can you get a hedge of spireas 2½ ft. apart, to grow together at the bottom? Best plan would be to cut it down to the ground and thus force it to make bushy new growth. If it doesn't grow together then, reset the plants 18 ins. apart—as they should have been set in the first place.

I planted a hedge of 6- to 8-ft. NORWAY SPRUCES 3 ft. apart. How should I trim them so that they will stay thick and rich at their base? Top in the spring to 5½ or 6 ft. Thereafter, in the annual shearing, allow only little gain in height. Trim sides no more than necessary for an even appearance. Shape the hedge so that it tapers from a wide base to a narrow, rounded top.

Can TAMARISK be used for a hedge? It makes an excellent

informal hedge. If late-blooming species, cut back in spring. If a May or June flowering species, cut back when flowers have faded.

Can you tell me whether a GOLDEN WILLOW hedge would be suitable for a boundary around a farm building? (Iowa.)   If a tall, quick-growing hedge is required, the willow would be quite suitable.

What distance apart should JAPANESE YEW (2 to 3 ft.) be planted for a straight border-line hedge?   Eighteen inches is best, but if this costs too much 24 to 30 ins. would do. It would take the hedge a longer time to grow together in the second instance.

When is the best time to trim a yew hedge?   It can be trimmed almost any time. Trim "wild" shoots in spring; give main shearing at end of June.

Do you approve the use of ROSA MULTIFLORA as a hedge plant?   No! It grows much too large for use on small properties. A 3-year-old can be 8 ft. high and 12 ft. across.

WINDBREAKS

For how great a distance does a windbreak exert its influence? About twenty times its height.

Which trees are suitable for use as windbreaks?   If soil is sandy, Red Pine and the Riga variety of Scotch Pine. For sandy loam, White Pine, Douglasfir, spruce. For heavy soil, arborvitae, Balsam Fir, White Spruce.

We need a windbreak on the west line of our property. The spot is quite shaded. Would Scotch or Jack Pine thrive there?   No, not in shade. Use hemlock if height is needed; or Japanese Yew, upright form.

Which evergreens are best to use for windbreak? We get heavy windstorms from the southwest, and the garden is on a hill sloping to the south.   Red Pine.

What can I plant for a hedge and windbreak—something that will grow fast? There is a strong north wind all summer; space is ample. The Siberian Elm is one of the fastest-growing trees we have. Plant it thickly, about 5 ft. apart, if the hedge is to be over 20 ft. high; about 3 ft. apart if hedge is to be nearer 10 ft. high. It is one of our best trees for dry climatic conditions.

I haven't much room on my property but would like a windbreak on the north and west sides. Any suggestions?   Plant arborvitae; redcedar; upright form of Japanese Yew; or White Pine. Keep in bounds by annual pruning.

What would make a good windbreak for a garden that is exposed on all sides?   Closely set evergreens, such as cedar, hemlock, or arborvitae, are good. A 6-ft. paling fence or a storm fence might also help.

VINES AND THEIR CULTURE

How do different vines climb? By clinging rootlets, such as English Ivy, trumpetcreeper, euonymus; by adhesive disks, such as Boston Ivy; by coiling tendrils, as balloonvine, *Cobaea scandens,* sweetpea; by stems which twine, such as wisteria, bittersweet.

Is any special preparation needed before planting vines to grow on a house? Make sure there is sufficient depth (1½ ft.), and width (2 ft.) of good soil. All too often the planting area next to a foundation is filled with builder's rubbish.

WHAT TO GROW

See also Landscaping.

I have a partially shaded back yard in the city. Which flowering vines could be grown on the fence? Cinnamonvine (*Dioscorea batatas*); silverlace-vine (*Polygonum auberti*); wisteria. The last will bloom only if it can climb to where there is sun. All these vines need a trellis, or to be supported in some way.

Which flowering vines would look well growing over a stone wall? We would like to enjoy seeing the flowers from our porch, 100 ft. away. Perennial pea, wisteria, clematis, hyacinth bean, trumpetvine, rambler roses.

Which flowering vines will cling, without support, to the wall of our garage? Trumpetcreeper; Climbing Hydrangea; Boston Ivy.

Which vines shall I grow on our clapboard house, which will need painting occasionally? Do *not* use climbing vines, such as the ivies, Climbing Hydrangea, or trumpetcreeper; nor wisteria, which will thrust strong stems between the clapboards, sometimes destroying them. Honeysuckle, silverlace-vine, clematis, akebia, should do well. A trellis hinged at bottom will be advisable so you can lay it (with the vine) down at painting time.

Which hardy flowering vines will stand the winter in southwest corner of Massachusetts? Elevation 1800 ft. Bittersweet, trumpetcreeper, sweet-autumn clematis.

Which vines would you suggest for growing on stone walls, chimneys, and house walls? *Euonymus fortunei* (*radicans*); ivy (*Hedera*), small-leaved varieties; *Cotoneaster horizontalis*. The latter is not a vine but can be trained as such.

Which vines will grow and climb in oak shade? Virginiacreeper, wild grape, bittersweet.

Which are the best climbing vines for this area (S. E. New York)?

Clematis, bittersweet, Hall's Honeysuckle, silverlace or fleece-vine, and wisteria.

Which vines will thrive in water?   None, in the northern United States.

Is it in good taste to plant climbing roses and climbing honeysuckle to grow up the four wide pillars along stucco porch of a stucco bungalow? I plan to plant a few low evergreens and shrubs for foundation planting around the whole house.   Yes; but from the standpoint of good growth of the plants, it would be better to plant either roses or honeysuckle, not both.

What kind of a flowering vine or climber will grow every year to a height of 15 or 20 ft. on the north side of a house, where it would get the early morning and late-afternoon sun?   Sweet-autumn Clematis, silverlace- or fleece-vine. Also *Cobaea scandens,* an annual.

Which vine can be planted on top of a ledge where soil is very shallow and dry in ordinary years? Foliage is desired to keep dust from house.   Very few vines would do well under such circumstances, but bittersweet and Sweet-autumn Clematis might be tried. Virginiacreeper is another possibility.

Which flowering vines are satisfactory for use on the north side of a house, in shade during most of the day?   It is improbable that any flowering vine will thrive very well, but you might try trumpet honeysuckle, climbing hydrangea, or silverlace-vine. *Cobaea scandens,* annual, and mountainfringe (adlumia), a biennial, might do well.

What are some of the easiest-grown and most beautiful flowering perennial vines?   Wisteria, honeysuckles, trumpetcreepers, silverlace-vine, Sweet-autumn Clematis.

I have a terrace 13 × 14 ft.; no roof over it; sunny most of the day. I want to "grow a roof." What would you suggest? Something that will grow fast and give protection in summer, and at the same time something that will be decorative and useful as a more permanent screen. How about a grapevine? How long would it take to provide a screen, and how many should I plant? The soil is sandy.   Grapevines would serve well. Plant 4 on each of two opposite sides. It will take at least 3 to 4 years to cover this area. The kudzuvine might cover the areas in a shorter time—but it has no grapes!

Which perennial vines are good for screening purposes?   Kudzuvine, the fastest-growing vine; Dutchmanspipe, also fast-growing, with large, rounded leaves; turquoiseberry (*Ampelopsis brevipedunculata*); easy to grow, and with profuse foliage and berries. The first named however, behaves as a herbaceous perennial in the north.

Which vine gives quickest growth for trellis at window for shade? Kudzuvine grows the fastest (and the most!) of any of our "perennial" vines. Where it is not hardy, bittersweet, the Fiveleaf Akebia, or the Bower Actinidia, might be used. All these are rapid-growing vines and have smaller and more interesting leaves than the large, coarse-leaved gloryvine (*Vitis coignetiae*) which is about the fastest-growing of the grapes.

Which flowering vine would be pretty to cover top of cave, the end and sides of which will be planted as a rock garden?   Sweet-autumn Clematis, or rambler roses.

Is there an evergreen vine which will cling to a wall in shade? English Ivy (*Hedera helix*); Wintercreeper (*Euonymus fortunei radicans*).

Which evergreen vine do you recommend to hang down from the top of a driveway wall?   Wintercreeper (*Euonymus*), or English Ivy, where hardy.

What is the best creeping vine for walls of stucco?   *Euonymus fortunei* or one of its varieties is very good. Boston Ivy usually adheres well also.

Which ivy can I plant by the doorway that will hang down from the top in a place that is shaded most of the time?   Either Boston Ivy or English Ivy; the last being evergreen. Give both good soil in which to grow; keep moist during dry weather.

Is there some small-leaved vine which will cling to rocks? Would like something besides ivy and euonymus. (Delaware.)   Creeping Fig (*Ficus pumila*). Its small leaves lie flat. Not reliably hardy north of Baltimore, though it has been known to survive 80 miles north of New York City.

ANNUAL VINES

We have rented a summer cottage and would like to grow some annual vines to cover lattice. What would be appropriate, easy to grow, and have attractive flowers?   Morningglory, moonflower, scarlet runner bean, hyacinth bean (dolichos), *Cobaea scandens*.

Which vine can be grown over a poultry fence to provide shade, and for concealment? Have tried Heavenly Blue Morningglory, but chickens eat it. Is there any annual vine distasteful to poultry?   Try canarybird-vine, climbing nasturtiums, hyacinth bean, wild cucumber, Japanese hop (humulus), scarlet runner bean, and cardinal-climber. Mix seeds together, sow quite thickly along the bottom of your fence, on outside. Chickens may take some and leave enough of others to give you a show. If necessary, thin to stand about 1 ft. apart.

Can you suggest vines—annuals—which will grow in a place which has shade ¾ of the day?   Try cup-and-saucer-vine (*Cobaea scandens*), hyacinth bean, morningglory, and cardinal-climber.

Will you give the correct information of how to grow adlumia or

Alleghenyvine from seed? I have not been at all successful. Reproduce the conditions natural to this native plant of the northeast United States. Give it a cool, damp situation, as it would be in woodland, protected from sun and wind, with shrubs to climb on. It is a biennial.

What does the Scarlet Runner Bean look like? It resembles in leaf and habit the pole beans we grow in our vegetable gardens, but the blossoms are larger and scarlet in color. The pods and green beans are edible.

I saw a beautiful vine twining on strings to cover a cellar window wall. It had purple sweetpea-like flowers in late summer, and then broad, flat, red-purple beans. What was it? Hyacinth bean (dolichos) of easy culture.

Is the Cup-and-saucer-vine (Cobaea scandens) a satisfactory annual? Yes, if started indoors 6 weeks before ground warms up. Plant individual seeds in pots or plant bands. Set out at tomato-planting time. Grows to the top of a 3-story house in one season. Lovely foliage, tendrils; showy buds, flowers, and seed pods late summer and autumn. Foliage colors red-purple in light frosts. Grows on until hard freeze.

Is MOONFLOWER a good annual vine? Yes. Large leaves, beautiful, fragrant, night-blooming flowers late summer and autumn. Give it something to climb high on. Start indoors. (See Cup-and-saucer-vine.)

What is the proper procedure in propagating moonflowers? Sow seeds. Proceed as suggested for morningglories below or start seeds in individual pots indoors in early April.

Is there a variety of moonflower which climbs and has colored flowers? Moonflower is a twining night-bloomer with white flowers. There are also pink varieties. Twining day-bloomers are morningglories.

Which large-flowered MORNINGGLORIES are best? Heavenly Blue, Scarlett O'Hara—crimson; Pearly Gates—a white sport of Heavenly Blue. Start indoors in pots for early bloom in the North.

I would like some morningglories for a window box; not the large-flowered varieties. You want the Japanese type, which are to be had in white, crimson, purple, blue, and other colors. They grow 2 to 8 ft. high, while Heavenly Blue grows 10 to 20 ft. The dwarf morningglories grow only about a foot high.

Should I plant morningglories in the same place a second time? Theoretically it is wrong; but practically there is little objection. Dig the soil deeply, and work in decayed manure; if, after a few seasons, morningglories seem to be doing less well, sow instead hyacinth bean, *Cobaea scandens,* or tall nasturtiums.

Will you tell me how to make Heavenly Blue Morningglories grow?
Dig soil 1 ft. deep, mixing bone meal with it, ¼ lb. per sq. yd. Sow
seeds about ½ in. deep and 2 ins. apart, after soaking in water overnight. Thin out to 6 ins. from plant to plant. Make your sowings at
the base of a fence, trellis, or some similar support.

Do morningglories require a rich soil?　Soil of average quality is
good enough. If it is too high in nitrogen, you may have large plants
with small flowers; if you work in a balanced fertilizer, however, they
should have large flowers and remain in bloom for a longer period
each day.

**Had some Heavenly Blue Morningglories and watched for seed,
with no success. How are they propagated?**　They grow readily from
seeds which you purchase. It is possible that fertile seeds cannot be
collected in your part of the country. Seeds are produced in large
quantities for the trade in southern California.

**Is there any known way to keep morningglories open longer in the
morning?**　No.

**When picking morningglories, how do you keep them open in the
house in a container?**　Cut buds at sunset, selecting those ready to
open. Keep in water up to their necks in a cool cellar overnight. Clip
stems and place in position in morning. Moonflowers cut in late
afternoon will open in containers indoors.

How tall will climbing NASTURTIUMS grow? How do they cling?
To 6 ft. They climb by means of coiling leaf stalks.

SWEETPEA

See Annual Flowers.

PERENNIAL VINES

AKEBIA

**What do you recommend to mask an ugly leader pipe near our
front entrance?**　*Akebia quinata* deserves such a place where one
views it closely. It has dainty oval leaves, five to a group, and a
decorative manner of growth. It will festoon itself around any upright
support. At intervals along a leader pipe the vine will have to be
tied up. Sun or shade suits akebia.

**Is there any vine, except English Ivy, that remains green during the
winter, and that is suitable for covering the side of a frame building?**
The Fiveleaf Akebia (*Akebia quinata*) is worthy of a trial. It climbs
by twining and would have to be supplied with wire for support. It
is not completely evergreen, but leaves remain on the vine long into
the winter. Another evergreen vine, *Euonymus radicans,* would satisfy

these requirements but it is susceptible to serious infestations of scale, and so must be used with caution.

Does akebia have flowers?   Small rose-purple waxy flowers neither conspicuous nor numerous, but very interesting at close range.

AMPELOPSIS AND PARTHENOCISSUS

I have cement blocks about 4 ft. high on the 3 sides of my porch and would like to know what will grow up and cling to these blocks so they will not be conspicuous. It is on the north side, therefore not much sun.   Wintercreeper or St. Paul Virginiacreeper (*Parthenocissus quinquefolia hirsuta*).

What plant will cover a stone wall where the location is hot, dry southern exposure?   The ordinary ivy which flourishes on the north wall does not thrive here. Boston Ivy or St. Paul Virginiacreeper.

Which deciduous ivy is the best to cover a stone wall? What kind of soil? Should it be covered by a mulch for the winter?   The Boston Ivy, St. Paul Virginiacreeper, or even the Virginiacreeper could be used to cover a stone wall. These do not need any special soil, simply a good garden loam. No winter mulch is required.

How shall I order an "ivy" which has deeply cut leaves and berries which turn lilac to bright blue?   This is porcelainvine (*Ampelopsis brevipedunculata maximowiczi*).

Which deciduous ivy has the best autumn coloring?   Virginiacreeper (not a true ivy) has the most brilliant crimson foliage in autumn.

Where would Virginiacreeper grow?   In the woods, on the ground, up a tree, in the sun or shade, along a wall, on the sand dunes. Very hardy and very adaptable.

What kinds of deciduous clinging vines are there?   Among them are Virginiacreeper and its several smaller-leaved varieties. Then there is Boston Ivy and its small-leaved varieties, and trumpetcreeper.

BITTERSWEET

I have heard that the Oriental species of bittersweet is better than our native kind. Is that so?   It is more vigorous and has better foliage, but the fruits are about the same.

How would bittersweet look growing on a trellis by the front door?   As it is rather rampant, we doubt if you would like it there. Its chief charm is in its dark bare stems with their clinging berries in fall and winter.

If bittersweet seeds are planted, how long will it take before the vine produces berries? Does bittersweet prefer acid soil?   About 3 years. They grow well in either acid or alkaline soil.

At what time of year can bittersweet be planted?   Spring or fall.

Will bittersweet climb on a stone chimney? Not unless you provide a wire around which it can twine. It is a *twining* vine not a *clinging* one.

How can I make my small patch of bittersweet larger? Allow some of the shoots to touch the ground, cover portions of them with soil, and they will soon take root, especially if you cut part way through the vine on the under side of the portion to be covered with soil.

What causes blossoms to fall from stems at base of a bittersweet vine? Probably the male flower blossoms, which never have any fruits and fall off the plant after the pollen has been dispersed.

I have several bittersweet vines on trellises. The clusters which I gather in fall are usually small and imperfect. Is there anything I can do so that these vines will produce clusters such as I see in the florist shops in the fall? Be certain that 1 or 2 strong male or pollen-bearing plants are close by, preferably growing in with the fruiting vines. Another method is to note when they bloom in June, obtain cut branches of male flowers from some distant plant, put in bottle of water, and tie up in your fruiting vine. Leave there for 2 weeks and the pollen distributed by insects and winds will fertilize the pistillate or fruit-bearing flowers, insuring a good crop of fruits.

Should bittersweet be pruned while growing? Mine grows 4 or 5 ft. high and then starts long runners 7 or 8 ft. long and of course there is no trellis for them. Yes, it can be pruned while growing.

I have a bittersweet vine. When should the berries be picked for winter bouquets? Any time after heavy frosts.

I have read that only the female plants of bittersweet have berries. How can you sort the seedlings to discard male plants? They can't be sorted as seedlings. It is necessary to wait until they are old enough to bloom.

CLEMATIS

I am interested in clematis. Which species or variety is best in bloom, and easy to care for? *Clematis paniculata,* the Sweet-autumn Clematis, is one of the easiest of all to grow. The Jackman Clematis can be grown fairly easily if the soil is alkaline.

Which clematis is it that one sees in our woodland? Rock Clematis, *Clematis verticillaris,* blooming in May or June; or virginsbower, *C. virginiana,* with white flowers in August to September. Must climb into sunlight to bloom well.

Could you tell us the name of a clematis with rosy-pink flowers about 2 in. across? There are 4 petals and yellow stamens. Bloom in May. Pink Anemone Clematis (*C. montana rubens*).

Is there any clematis with red flowers that is easier to grow than the big-flowered hybrids? Scarlet Clematis (*C. texensis*) is a native of Texas. Grows to about 6 ft., with flowers about 1 in. long; blooms July to September.

Can you tell me a yellow clematis that would grow in Maine? I saw a beautiful small variety (on the ground) in Canada but could not find its name. *Clematis tangutica,* the Golden Clematis, is certainly worthy of a trial. It is the best of the yellow-flowered species, a native of China. Will need winter protection.

Culture

What is the best exposure for Jackman Clematis? (Illinois.) In Illinois as protected a situation as possible, but not complete shade. All clematis bloom better where the vines reach full sun, but they like shade at their bases.

What fertilizer does clematis need? Should one cultivate around it, or are the roots near the surface of the ground? Most clematis varieties require lime and a cool, moist soil, best supplied by a mulch of leafmold. Roots are very near the surface.

Is it always necessary to shade the roots and lower stem portions of clematis? This is necessary on most of the many large-flowered hybrids, but it is not necessary on our native clematis types nor on the Sweet-autumn Clematis.

What type of trellis is best for clematis? Chicken-wire netting supported in rigidly upright position on a light frame.

Will different varieties of clematis, planted very close, "cross," thus spoiling the species? No, this will not change the plants or flowers a particle. Seeds from the flowers might yield seedlings of mixed parentage.

How can I grow large-flowered clematis? They do well for 6 months or a year, and then die. Unfortunately many large-flowered clematis are susceptible to a rather serious disease which kills them during the summer months. No manure should be applied, nor should water be allowed to stand at the base of the plants. If the disease occurs, spray with wettable sulfur at once, and again in a week or ten days.

Pruning

How and when should one prune clematis? Those which bloom on old wood (such as *C. florida, montana,* and *patens*) need little or no pruning beyond the removal of dead or diseased wood. The *lanuginosa, jackmani,* and *viticella* types bloom on wood of the current season, and may be cut back in spring before growth begins.

A white clematis planted in the fall grew about 10 or 12 ft. the following summer, but did not flower. Should I have pinched it back

after it was 3 or 4 ft. high? No. Let it grow and gain nourishment; it will bloom the second or third year.

When and how should Clematis paniculata be pruned? In many places in New England this clematis will be killed to the ground by winter cold. In such places it should be pruned back, in early spring, to just above where the buds break. In situations where it does not kill to the ground, merely cutting out some of the older wood is all that is necessary.

Should clematis be pruned in fall or summer? I notice some cut them down to ground, but I have never cut mine and have lovely vines. What is the best preventive for aphis? If you have lovely vines, continue the same treatment. Cutting them down does not help. (See preceding questions.) Aphis can be controlled by spraying with nicotine sulfate.

Should a Clematis jackmani be trimmed or pruned in springtime? Yes; but only if the vine is cluttered up with a mass of unproductive shoots.

Propagation

Can you start clematis from cuttings? Clematis are rather difficult to propagate. This can be done either by cuttings or seeds. For the amateur, sowing the seed in the fall is the easier method. Many of our large-flowered hybrids must be propagated by cuttings, or by grafting.

Can clematis be grown from slips? Many varieties may be rooted from slips in the latter part of July. Cut young shoots into 6- to 8-in. lengths, making the basal cut between joints. Place them in a glass-covered box or cold frame, and keep out of direct sunlight until rooted. Most of the large-flowered named varieties are grafted.

DUTCHMANSPIPE

Which vine would make a good solid screen to hide the compost pile? Please describe Dutchmanspipe. Dutchmanspipe would be fine if grown on a series of vertical cords or slats. The big roundish leaves, 10 ins. in diameter, overlap each other. Flowers, nondescript in color, resemble a Dutchmanspipe.

EUONYMUS FORTUNEI; WINTERCREEPER, EVERGREEN BITTERSWEET

Which one of the wintercreeper vines has berries like bittersweet? The best of the berried varieties is the Bigleaf Wintercreeper (*E. fortunei vegetus*).

Our wintercreeper is especially noticed because of its leaves, which are variegated sometimes with white or pinkish tones. What variety could it be? Silver-edge Wintercreeper (*E. fortunei gracilis*).

Which euonymus vine has very tiny leaves? Baby Wintercreeper (*Euonymus fortunei minimus*).

Which is the hardiest of all evergreen vines that will cling to a stone wall? Wintercreeper (*Euonymus fortunei*) and its varieties.

Is Euonymus fortunei the new name for what we used to call Euonymus radicans? Yes. It is now *Euonymus fortunei radicans*. (Until the botanists decide to change it again!)

I have a euonymus which I thought would climb on a wall, but it remains a bush. What is the trouble? It must be the variety called Glossy Wintercreeper (*E. fortunei carrierei*) which is shrubby, non-climbing. There is another shrubby variety which remains so unless planted near a wall (*E. fortunei vegetus*), the Bigleaf Wintercreeper.

GRAPE

See Fruits—Section VI.

HONEYSUCKLE

Which honeysuckle has flowers that are yellowish on the inside and rose-purple outside? Everblooming Honeysuckle (*Lonicera heckrotti*).

Please describe the Scarlet Trumpet Honeysuckle (Lonicera sempervirens). I believe it used to grow in gardens long ago. Yes, it is long in cultivation. Orange-scarlet flowers with long tubes, yellow inside, produced from May to August.

What low-growing variety of honeysuckle would you recommend for a northern exposure, with semi-shade? Hall's Honeysuckle—but watch out; it is a pernicious weed if it gets out of bounds.

What low vine may one plant under the shade of a large maple tree, but unprotected from the wind; one which will grow with myrtle, where grass will not? You might try Hall's Honeysuckle, but it is very difficult to coax anything to grow under most maples.

Our honeysuckle vine (2 years old this past spring) had only one spray of bloom. Why? The foliage is beautiful and healthy-looking. It needs time to become well established before it will bloom properly.

My honeysuckle lost all leaves in midsummer, then bore leaves and blooms and seeds at one time. What should be done this year? Give it more water. This was probably due to unusually dry weather.

Does Japanese Honeysuckle eventually work its way into water drains? Should it be planted near them? Like the roots of most plants it probably will, but usually the roots won't do much damage in this respect.

How does one trim out honeysuckle which is very thick, and about 12 ft. high? If there is too much wood, it may be necessary to cut it off at the base and start all over again.

Will you tell me whether honeysuckle vine can be pruned, and at what time of the year? Prune it in the early spring when the buds are breaking. Unless the vine is to be restrained within a limited area, it is necessary to prune out only dead or diseased wood.

What is the proper way to prune a honeysuckle for profuse blooming? Mine is a cutting about 3 years old, with very few flowers. Is a trellis necessary? Don't prune; allow it to grow profusely on some support, and if good soil, plenty of water, and sunshine are available, it will soon bloom well.

HYDRANGEA

How tall does the Climbing Hydrangea grow? How does it climb? *Hydrangea petiolaris* can grow 50 ft. or more in time, but it is slow. It clings to a wall without support, sends out branches at right angles to the wall, and blooms in June.

What kind of flowers does the Climbing Hydrangea have? Flowers are white, in round, flat, open clusters, resembling some of the viburnum flowers.

IVY

How can one tell whether an ivy is a variety that will be hardy if placed outdoors? We want to plant some on a new cottage chimney. Try several. The hardiest evergreen variety is the Baltic Ivy (*Hedera helix baltica*). If this winter kills, no English Ivy will grow there.

What does Baltic Ivy look like? Its leaves are slightly smaller than those of the typical English Ivy, and the white veins are often more prominent.

Which evergreen vine can I plant on north side of brick house? English Ivy, if a tall-growing kind is required; otherwise, use winter-creeper, which is hardier.

Which vine is suitable for planting on west slope, to cover up ground and stay green all the year 'round—one that won't spread too much? Baltic Ivy.

SECTION III-B

Bulbs, Tubers, and Corms

INTRODUCTION

BY F. F. ROCKWELL

THE VARIOUS bulbs and other bulb-like plants—those which form tubers and corms instead of true bulbs—have more rapidly gained in popularity during the last decade or so than any other group of decorative plants. The reasons for this growing popularity are not far to seek, for many bulbs are much more rewarding for the time and room required for their culture, than are most other flowers. Moreover, a considerable number of them flower very early in spring and add brilliant color to the garden scene by the time most perennials and shrubs have begun to don their summer garments of green.

There are still many gardens, however, where one looks in vain for any sight of spring bulbs other than a few long out-dated daffodils and perhaps a planting of that ubiquitous, sensational tulip Red Emperor. The owners of such gardens are overlooking a wide range of easily grown plants which could provide them with beautiful and interesting flowers, very literally, from one end of the year to the other, for there are a number of bulbs and corms that may readily be flowered indoors. The most easily obtained and grown of these are commented on in the following pages. You can add to your store of garden pleasures by becoming acquainted with them.

HARDY BULBS, CORMS, TUBERS, ETC.

WHAT TO GROW

Which hardy bulbs may be used in permanent plantings? Among the most satisfactory are narcissi, grapehyacinths, squills, chionodoxas, snowdrops, crocuses, the hardier lilies, alliums, colchicums, and camassias. Tulips may give several years' bloom without being taken up, especially if planted deep (to ten inches).

Which bulbs can be left in the ground the year round? Alliums, brodieas, calochortus, camassias, chionodoxas, colchicums, crocuses, erythroniums, fritillarias, grapehyacinths, hyacinths, tulips, narcissi, irises, leucojum, ornithogalum, lilies, puschkinia, squills, shootingstars, snowdrops, snowflakes, sternbergia, and zephyranthes.

We have spring-flowering bulbs. Which hardy bulbs shall I plant for summer bloom? Hardy kinds: summer-hyacinth, hardy begonia (*B. evansiana*), lycoris, garden lilies, sternbergia, colchicum, fall-flowering crocuses, *Scilla chinensis,* zephyranthes and some of the flowering onions or alliums.

SOIL AND FERTILIZER

What kind of soil should I use for spring-flowering bulbs? A rather light, but fertile and well-drained, slightly acid soil is best. Avoid the use of fresh manure. Very old manure and bone meal are good fertilizers.

Bulbs do not multiply readily in the soil in my garden. Tulips do not last over 3 years. What element in the soil is lacking? Possibly your soil is not suitable, but this is not unusual for tulips. Heavy, clayey soils are not conducive to increase. Most bulbs prefer a loose, fertile soil that has been well worked to a depth of 10 or 12 ins.

Does well-rotted manure above, but not touching, the bulbs rot them? No. But it is much better to spade the manure under before planting, so that it is well below the bulbs, but not in direct contact with them.

PLANTING AND TRANSPLANTING

How deep should bulbs be planted? Is the general rule 4, 5, or 6 times the thickness of the bulb? No general rule can be applied to all bulbs. Some lilies should be planted 8 or 9 ins. deep, others 2 ins. deep; so the depth varies. If possible, obtain specific information for each kind before planting. If this is not available, a rough rule that can be followed in the case of the hardy spring-flowering bulbs is to cover them with soil equal in depth to 2 or 3 times the diameter of the bulb.

How late in the fall may bulbs be planted? Bulbs planted in December will grow and thrive, and instances are known of January-planted bulbs succeeding. But earlier planting is recommended.

Early-flowering bulbs arrived after sub-zero weather and snow. How can I take care of them over winter and when can I plant them? They are winter aconites, scillas, tulips, etc. Keep in cool, dry place and plant any time when ground thaws, up to January. An alternative would be to plant bulbs in pots or flats of soil and cover with 6-in. layer of sand or cinders outdoors. They cannot be kept over winter out of the soil.

Can spring-flowering bulbs (tulips, narcissi, etc.) be put in the

ground in January in Maryland with any success? Yes, if the bulbs have kept well in storage until this time; but it is much better to plant them earlier.

Can you plant bulbs in spring that call for planting in fall? Certain hardy, summer-flowering bulbs can be held in cold storage and planted in spring as, for instance, lilies; but fall planting is better. Spring-flowering bulbs must be planted in fall.

Bulbs held temporarily, awaiting planting, should be stored in a cool, dark place, away from artificial heat, and safe from rodents.

Can a person plant bulbs of all kinds in spring? Only summer- and fall-blooming kinds can be planted at that time.

Will bulbs planted in September bloom in the spring if they sprouted, and in some cases bloomed, in October and November? Surely bulbs that bloomed in October and November are fall bloomers rather than spring bloomers. They will retain this characteristic from year to year, and will not bloom in spring. Spring-blooming kinds that sprouted before planting will probably bloom in spring.

Will daffodils, scillas, and similar bulbs bloom after the first season, and multiply, if planted the first week of December? Yes. It would be better, however, to plant them somewhat earlier.

Can you take up crocus and jonquil bulbs, separate, and replant them as soon as the leaves die down? Or must you wait until fall? Yes. It is always best to transplant narcissi before mid-July.

Should bulbs be watered after planting? This is usually not necessary. Very little moisture is needed for their early root growth, but in case of a long, dry spell with no rain within a month after planting, a thorough watering is beneficial.

What is the best way to handle the small bulbs one finds growing on older bulbs? Plant them separately in specially prepared nursery beds where the soil is loose and fertile. Grow them on in these beds until they reach blooming size.

CULTURE

What can be done with spring-blooming bulbs which come through the ground in December, due to a warm spell? Probably planted too shallowly. Cover them carefully with a layer of sifted earth, sand, or cinders; mulch with leaves or other covering.

If true bulbs have their flower bud within them, do they need full sunshine in order to bloom? Yes, they need sunshine and moisture to bring the blooms to maturity.

Does it weaken the bulbs to cut flowers of hyacinths, tulips, and narcissi, being careful not to remove more than one third of the leaves? Any removal of foliage has a weakening effect.

Does it inhibit next year's bloom to pick flowers of the bulbous plants—daffodils, narcissi, etc.? No; not if most of the foliage is left. This is needed to manufacture food that feeds the bulb and produces the next year's bloom.

What can I do with the unsightly foliage of my spring-flowering bulbs after bloom is over? Removal of foliage before it has matured (turned yellow and wilted) is sure to prevent normal bloom the following year, as the maturing foliage provides nutrients for the flowers to come. Water in dry spells to keep foliage growing as long as possible. Overplant maturing bulb foliage with shallow-rooted annuals, such as petunias, which spread and cover the unsightly dying leaves.

Do spring-flowering bulbs need fertilizer after planting? An application of a complete plant food should be applied and gently raked into the surface each spring just after the first weeding. In light, sandy soil a second application in late spring after bloom is over is also advisable.

Do you advise the use of a summer mulch on bulb beds? Yes, by all means. A mulch of peatmoss, sawdust, pine needles, buckwheat hulls, shredded sugar cane or other similar material may be applied early in spring after weeding and fertilizing. If bed is later overplanted with annuals, the mulch remaining on the bed will help to control weeds and retain moisture through the summer heat.

What causes bulbs to disappear in the soil? Such hardy bulbs as jonquils, tulips, lilies, and irises are examples. Unsuitable soil or location; cutting the flowers without leaving sufficient foliage to make food to fatten up the bulbs; cutting of leaves before they wither naturally; and disease or the depredations of rodents.

How short a rest period should bulbs have after being taken up from the soil? This varies with the kind of bulb. Colchicums and lilies, for example, should be replanted with least possible delay, as also should narcissi. Tulips are stored out of ground for 3 months or more without harm.

PROTECTION

Should tulips, narcissi, and jonquils have mulch (leaves) over them

in fall? When should they be uncovered? Not necessary except in extremely cold sections (Zones 2 and 3, see map) unless you are in an area subject to frequent alternate freezing and thawing. Damage is then from "heaving" of roots and bulbs from soil. Under these conditions cover *after* the ground has frozen hard, with leaves, peatmoss, or salt hay. This keeps ground uniformly cool and prevents damage to roots by heaving. Uncover gradually when growth appears.

RODENTS

Have had much trouble losing lily and tulip bulbs in winter. Some rodent makes burrows 3 ins. below surface of ground. Have used wire baskets in planting, but to no avail. Also poison and traps. What can I do? You may have to encircle the whole bed with fine mesh wire netting, 12 inches wide, buried vertically, and extending 2 to 3 inches above ground surface. Do not *mulch* bed until ground is well frozen.

SPECIFIC HARDY BULBS

ALLIUM

Do flowering alliums possess that unpleasant onion odor? Ordinarily not, unless the stems or leaves are crushed or bruised. *Allium tuberosum* (sometimes sold as *A. odorum*) has violet-scented flowers.

Are there any flowering onions that are suitable for outdoor gardens? Many species of allium are excellent for planting in borders. Among the best are *tuberosum* (white), *moly* (yellow), *stellatum* (pink), *caeruleum* (blue), *flavum* (yellow), *senescens glaucum* (lavender), *pulchellum* (pink-lavender), and *schoenoprasum* (rose-purple).

What soil and treatment do Allium flavum and other summer-blooming onions require? A rather light, well-drained loam is best, although they will thrive in most soils, providing drainage is good. Full sunshine is preferred by most species. Divide and transplant whenever crowded: either fall or early spring. Most are very easy to grow.

ANEMONE

Will anemone tubers survive winter in New York (Long Island) if planted in fall? Will they bloom if planted in spring? If so, when should they be planted in the vicinity of New York? Rock-garden tuberous-rooted kinds (such as *apennina, blanda, ranunculoides, quinquefolia,* and *nemorosa*), are hardy and should be planted in fall. The florists' tuberous-rooted kinds are not hardy. You might try storing them in a cool place (40°) over winter, and planting them in the spring.

How should one plant tuberous anemones, such as nemorosa, ranunculoides, etc.? Plant in early fall in porous soil containing generous proportion of humus. Set tubers 2 or 3 ins. apart, and cover about 2 ins. deep. Light woodland shade is needed.

ARUM

I have a lily plant which produces a flower, dark purplish in color, almost black, on a stem 8 ins. tall, with leaves 5 × 3 ins. It seems to prefer the cold, for it survives our occasional frosts. It becomes dormant in summer. Could you please identify? Probably Black Calla (*Arum palaestinum*).

BELAMCANDA

Can you tell me something about a plant called Blackberry Lily? *Belamcanda chinensis,* a hardy iris relative from the Orient, is now naturalized in many parts of this country. Easily grown in sun or light shade, and propagated by seeds or division. Orange flowers, spotted with purple-brown, are followed by blackberry-like fruits. Blooms in the summer.

BRODIAEAS

What treatment do brodiaeas, such as grandiflora, capitata, and ixioides, need in the garden? Plant in fall in gritty soil in full sun. Set bulbs about 2 ins. apart and cover 3 or 4 ins. deep. Protect with light winter covering of salt hay or similar material.

Are brodiaeas good bulbs for Eastern gardens? Many are excellent, and they should be used more extensively. Among the most satisfactory are *bridgesi* (violet), *capitata* (lavender), *coccinea* (red and green), *douglasi* (lavender), *grandiflora* (purple), *ixioides* (yellow), *lactea* (white), and *laxa* (purple-blue).

Can you tell me the name of the floral firecracker plant? *Brodiaea coccinea,* one of the many fine species of this genus native to western America. The flowers bear a close resemblance to a gaily-colored bunch of firecrackers.

CALOCHORTUS

Can calochortus (or Mariposa Tulips) be successfully grown in the Middle Atlantic states? Yes, but they are not very easy to keep from year to year. Plant at twice their own depth, late in fall, in bed of specially prepared, very gritty soil. Protect lightly through winter. Water freely when growing, but keep bed as dry as possible in late summer and fall. They need sunshine.

CAMASSIA

Will you tell me something of camassias and their care? They thrive in any good garden soil that is not too dry; prefer full sun or light shade; bloom in May (flowers blue or white), then die down. Plant in early fall, so that bulbs are 4 ins. below surface and 7 or 8 ins. apart. Do not transplant as long as they bloom well.

Are camassias good garden flowers? Very good indeed, and worthy of being more widely planted. Most of them are native Americans and are of easy culture. Apart from their garden value, their spires of starry flowers are excellent for cutting purposes.

CHIONODOXA

Does the bulb glory-of-the-snow (chionodoxa) need any special care? One of the easiest and loveliest of hardy spring-flowering bulbs. Plant in the fall in any fairly good soil, 3 ins. deep, 2 or 3 ins. apart. Do not disturb for many years after planting. Top-dress every 2 or 3 years with fertilized soil. They will increase and improve with passing of years. Excellent for planting in low-growing ground covers such as vinca or bearberry.

COLCHICUM

How deep should colchicum be planted; and how often divided? Cover the tops of the bulbs with not more than 3 ins. of soil. Divide every third or fourth year.

What soil and situation are best for colchicums and when should they be planted? Soil should be rich and reasonably moist (but not wet). Light shade. Plant in early August.

Is it difficult to raise colchicum (C. autumnale) from seed? Not difficult, but it requires patience. Sow when ripe in pans of humusy soil and plunge in shaded cold frame. Keep uniformly moist.

CONVALLARIA (LILY-OF-THE-VALLEY)

Can lilies-of-the-valley be grown in an absolutely shady place? Yes. They will grow in dense shade if the soil is fairly good, but will probably not bloom so freely as when in partial shade.

When should the ground be made acid for lily-of-the-valley? This may be done at planting time, by incorporating generous amounts of leafmold or peatmoss with soil. Each year the bed may be top-dressed with sifted leafmold.

Should lilies-of-the-valley be fertilized to have more blossoms? If so, when and with what? They appreciate a top-dressing of well-rotted cow manure in fall. Do not allow them to become overcrowded.

How can I grow lily-of-the-valley? What kind of soil? I have no success. A moist, but not wet, soil that contains generous amounts of humus. Improve soil by spading in rotted manure, leafmold, peatmoss, etc., and by adding bone meal. Lily-of-the-valley prefers light shade. Plant in spring.

The bed in which I have very fine clumps of giant lilies-of-the-valley has been okayed as to soil, sunshine, and shade; they have splendid foliage. Why is it they do not multiply, and produce only a few stems of bloom? The soil is basically clay, though it has been enriched. If the soil is very rich, the foliage will be good, but flowers scarce. Let the plants become firmly established, then they will flower when the excess nutrients are used up.

Is there any difference in size of lilies-of-the-valley, or can you make them grow to be a good size? How? The largest-flowered variety is named *fortunei*. Old, worn-out plantings usually produce few small flowers. Lift, separate, and replant in newly fertilized soil every 3 or 4 years.

Why don't my lilies-of-the-valley bloom? They look thrifty. Probably in too-dense shade; or the plants are too thick, and need dividing and replanting.

How do you grow clumps of lily-of-the-valley for forcing for cut blossoms? Plant clumps in very rich, sandy loam. When pips are ¼ to ⅜ in. thick and ⅞ to 1 in. long, cut away from clumps with as much root as possible. Wrap in bundles and place in cold storage, 28° to 32° F., for at least 3 months. Best results however are obtained from specially prepared pips.

Are the roots of the lily-of-the-valley poisonous? Yes. The druggists' convallaria, which is used as a heart tonic, is made from lily-of-the-valley roots.

CROCUS

When shall I plant crocuses, and how? Spring-flowering kinds in September and October. Plant in light, fertile soil, in sunny place. If among grass, only where grass can remain uncut until leaves have died away in late spring. Plant 2 or 3 ins. apart and about 3 ins. deep. Fall-blooming kinds should be planted in July or August; or transplanted in June or early July.

Should crocuses be planted in beds, or with grass, to look natural? They appear best when planted among grass or some low ground cover, such as creeping thyme, mazus, or *Veronica repens*. A good method is to throw handfuls of the corms over the ground surface so that they fall in natural drifts, and then plant each corm where it falls.

DAFFODILS (NARCISSI)

Many of the early spring-blooming plants would not be worth a second glance if it were not for the fact that they are harbingers of spring. Daffodils, on the other hand, would be important even if they bloomed in June or August.

The daffodils belong to the genus *Narcissus,* and while all daffodils are narcissi, it is not quite correct to say that all narcissi are daffodils. In a general way the term is the common name for the genus, but certain species, like *Narcissus jonquilla* have a special common name, and in this case it is jonquil. Some 10,000 varieties have been introduced. The color range of the group is limited largely to yellow, orange and white, but apricot tones and a few clear pinks have recently been created. Perhaps other colors will sometime be available.

Daffodils have much to recommend them. While a given species may not succeed in all parts of the country, there are types that do well in warm climates, and others that thrive where the winters are severe. They are highly prized in rock gardens, borders, and in small intimate gardens, and they may be naturalized in woodlands and meadows. They are also of value as cut flowers.

Daffodils border a woodland walk. Ideal for the purpose because they take care of themselves.

Soils; Fertilizers

What type of soil is needed to grow narcissi? Any garden soil is suitable providing it is deep, well drained, and fertile. Avoid planting in hot, barren soils, or where the soil remains wet for long periods.

Will narcissi thrive in wet soils? No. The water table (level below which all spaces in soil are filled with water) should not stand nearer the surface than 18 ins. for any appreciable length of time.

What is correct preparation of soil for planting narcissi? Spade to a depth of 12 ins. and place rotted manure in bottom of bed. Cover so that at least 2 ins. of soil separates the manure from bases of bulbs. Incorporate 4 to 5 lbs. of 5–10–5 fertilizer per 100 sq. ft.

Can you tell me how to prepare a bed in which to grow daffodils for exhibition? The classic recommendation is to excavate a trench 18 ins. deep, dig into the bottom an 8-in. layer of well-rotted manure, and on this spread a generous sprinkling of bone meal. Cover with

6 ins. of good topsoil (without manure), set bulbs on this, and cover with any fairly good soil.

How should one fertilize narcissi that do not need lifting and replanting? Top-dress in early fall with bone meal and in early spring with a complete fertilizer and compost or old, well-rotted manure.

Is superphosphate a safe fertilizer to use on narcissi beds? Yes. It may be forked in at planting time, or applied as a top-dressing just as the foliage breaks ground in spring.

With what can I feed my daffodils to increase size of blooms for exhibition? Dilute liquid cow manure judiciously applied at intervals in spring, from the time flower scapes appear, helps immensely. Keep beds well watered. If reduction in size and quantity of bloom is caused by overcrowding of bulbs, fertilizer does not help. When foliage becomes crowded and bloom falls off (4 to 6 years after planting), dig after foliage matures, separate bulbs and replant.

Planting

What type of situation is best adapted for daffodils? A lightly shaded slope, sheltered from drying winds, with deep and well-drained soil.

Can daffodils be naturalized among trees? Light woodland affords an ideal location for daffodils which, under such conditions, thrive and increase abundantly.

A good way to use daffodils: informal or naturalized planting under tree.

When is the best time to plant daffodils? August, September, or early October, with preference for the earlier dates.

Daffodil bulbs ordered from seedsman usually do not arrive until fall, yet I am told to transplant those that are in my garden in July. Why? Bulbs in storage remain dormant for some considerable time after those in the garden have developed new roots. Bulbs are harmed by moving after root growth is far advanced. Early planting is always advisable.

I transplanted narcissi bulbs in October. They all died. Why?
If transplanted later than October 1, the root system, then in active growth, is severely disturbed; serious injury may result.

Can daffodil bulbs be planted as late as December? Yes; dormant bulbs can be planted any time before the ground freezes solid. Well-stored bulbs have been planted with success as late as February. Earlier planting, however, is much to be preferred.

Is it possible to plant narcissi in spring right after frost is out of ground? The immediate results may be quite unsatisfactory. If sound bulbs are available at that time, plant them, as they may improve the following year.

Is it true that if you transplant narcissi in spring, they will not bloom? If so, why? It is scarcely possible for them to bloom satisfactorily if removed from the soil. By spring the bulbs have a fully developed root system and the disturbance of transplanting causes a serious setback. If taken up in clumps of soil, with roots intact, they may bloom fairly well.

About what distance should be left between full-sized daffodil bulbs when planting? It depends upon the effect desired, and also upon the variety, because bulb sizes vary considerably. A minimum distance of from 3 to 6 ins. should be allowed. For colonizing, the bulbs should be set in a pleasingly informal pattern rather than evenly spaced.

How deep are daffodils planted? In light soils large bulbs are set with their bases 6 to 8 ins. deep; in heavier soils, 5 to 7 ins. deep. Small bulbs should be planted shallower than those of larger size.

Does deep planting encourage daffodils to multiply? No. On the contrary, it checks rapid division. Shallow planting induces rapid multiplication. Deep planting tends to build up strong-flowering bulbs.

Can daffodils be interplanted with tulips to produce early flowers and thus extend the blooming season of the planting? Yes. This is an entirely satisfactory combination.

Culture

How are daffodils cared for? Plant in good deep soil. Water during dry weather, especially after flowering, to keep foliage green as long as possible. Remove faded flowers. Fertilize yearly. Lift and separate every third or fourth year.

What are the moisture requirements of narcissi grown outdoors? They need ample supplies during the growing season, particularly in spring, when the flower scapes are developing.

When should daffodils be lifted for storage through the summer? Or is it better to leave them in the ground all year? Summer storage is not recommended for daffodils. If they must be dug, July is the best time. Store in dry place, as cool as possible down to 50°.

What time of the year should daffodils be separated? July; by then the foliage has fully matured and the bulbs are quite dormant. After separation, replanting should be done at once.

Do narcissus bulbs naturalized among trees have to be dug and replanted at intervals? Yes, do this whenever they become so crowded that the quantity and quality of the blooms have deteriorated. This may be as often as every third year, or as infrequently as every 5 or 6 years.

Daffodils left in one place too long (right) produce grassy foliage and poor flowers. Dividing old clumps and replanting will produce blooms like those at left.

Will daffodils bloom the spring after they have been divided and reset? Yes, if of blooming size: 1½ to 2 ins. diameter for trumpet varieties, 1 to 1½ ins. for smaller varieties; and ⅝ to 1 in. for the *triandrus, cyclamineus,* and *jonquilla* types.

What should be done with clumps of narcissi and daffodils that won't bloom? After the foliage has died down, dig them up, separate the bulbs, fertilize the soil, and replant.

How can I get miniature daffodils to bloom every spring? Plant in a sheltered place in moist, but not waterlogged, soil. Water freely during dry periods whenever foliage is present. Dig up, separate, and replant every 3 years.

Can daffodil bulbs which have bloomed indoors in pots be stored after blooming, to be used next year? Not for forcing again. If kept well-watered until ground is in satisfactory condition, they may be planted outdoors and will bloom in future years.

Do narcissi bloom the second year? Under favorable conditions yes, and for many successive years. Bulbs that are forced into bloom early indoors cannot be forced satisfactorily a second year.

I have heard that it is harmful to cut the foliage off narcissi when they have finished blooming. Is this so? Yes; the leaves are needed to produce food to plump up the bulbs in readiness for next season's flowering. Never remove foliage until it has died down, or at least turned yellow.

Daffodils planted the end of September are now (late October) through the ground. Will they survive? They probably will. Throw an additional 2 ins. of soil over them. They were undoubtedly planted too shallowly.

Can you tell me why double jonquils do not mature their blooms? Hundreds of stems come up with empty cases at the tops. They are overcrowded and are robbing each other of nutrients and moisture. Dig up the bulbs, separate them, enrich the bed, and replant. Water thoroughly during dry weather in the spring.

Propagation

What is the simplest way for an amateur to increase a limited stock of a choice narcissus? Plant bulbs shallowly (about 4 ins. deep) in a well-prepared bed—preferably in a cold frame. Give good cultural care and lift, divide, and replant every second year.

Is there any rapid method of vegetatively propagating daffodils? In summer large bulbs can be sliced vertically into many sections (each containing a small portion of the basal plate). The sections are then planted in peatmoss and sand. Mild bottom heat stimulates production of new bulblets.

How are narcissi raised from seeds? Sow in late August in rows 6 ins. apart in a well-prepared seedbed in a cold frame. Cover seeds ¾ in. deep. Shade the bed, keep uniformly moist, weeded, and covered with salt hay or other protection during winter. Allow seedlings two summers' growth, then lift and replant with wider spacing.

Why can't I get daffodil seeds to come up? It is possible that the seeds are not fertile, or perhaps your cultural care is incorrect. Hand pollination of the flowers should result in fertile seed. See previous question.

Pests and Diseases

Are daffodils subject to pests and diseases? Several diseases and some insect pests may be troublesome, but these usually do not appear in garden plantings. If trouble is suspected, remove affected bulbs and send samples to your State Agricultural Experiment Station for diagnosis and advice.

Is the hot-water treatment of narcissus bulbs effective? Yes, as a control for eelworms, bulb flies, and mites. The treatment consists of soaking for 4 hours in water maintained at 110 to 111.5° F. One pint of formalin to each 25 gals. of water is added if basal rot is present. Bulbs must not be treated too early or too late in the season. There are now many new chemical miticides on the market.

Varieties

What is the difference between a daffodil and a narcissus? These names are interchangeable, although "daffodil" is applied particularly, but not exclusively, to those kinds which have large, well-developed trumpets. The Latin name for the entire group is *Narcissus*.

What is a jonquil? A jonquil hybrid? The true jonquil is *Narcissus jonquilla,* a species that has slender, rushlike foliage and sweet-scented flowers in clusters. Jonquil hybrids are horticultural developments of this species, usually with larger flowers. The large-trumpet narcissi, or daffodils, are sometimes miscalled jonquils.

What are the names of some white and bicolor trumpet daffodils? White: Beersheba, High Sierra, Mount Hood, President Carnot, Roxane, Ada Finch. Bicolor: Jefta, Sylvanite, Spring Glory, Queen of Bicolors.

Can you tell me some good varieties of large-cup daffodils? Francisca Drake, Dick Wellband, Scarlet Leader, white perianths, orange cups; John Evelyn, E. H. Wilson, South Pacific, white perianth, yellow cup; Scarlet Elegance, Krakatoa, Fortune's Bowl, yellow perianth, orange cups.

What are some of the best small-cup narcissi? Alcida, white and yellow, Lady Kestevan, Firetail and Limerick, white and red; Sunrise, white with golden rays in pale cup; Nette O'Melveny, white with lemon cup edged orange; Hera, white with pale lemon cup.

Are there any small-flowered white narcissi for a rock garden? The following are *triandrus* hybrids: white or cream, Moonshine, Shot Silk and Thalia, with starry perianths, bell-like small trumpets; Agnes Harvey, white; *triandrus albus* (Angel's Tears), 6 ins. white, 2 to 3 flowers to a stem.

What are the names of some of the Jonquil Hybrids? Trevithian, fragrant, golden, starry, 2 to 3 flowers per stem; Golden Sceptre and Golden Perfection, golden yellow; Tullus Hostilius, yellow; *campernelli odorus,* single, golden, very small.

Please give me names and descriptions of some late-blooming daffodils. Azalea, pink cup; Bridegroom, white, yellow crown; Cover Girl, pink cup; Daphne, double fragrant white; Geranium, red-crowned cluster-flowered, fragrant; Gremlin, white, starry with lemon cup; Moonshine, white with bell-shaped trumpets.

Please name some mid-season daffodil varieties. Gertie Millar, white with flaring primrose cup; L'Innocence, white poetaz; Moonglow, sulphur yellow trumpet; Mount Hood, white trumpet; Trevithian, fragrant yellow jonquil hybrid.

What is the double white narcissus that looks like a gardenia, smells sweet but does not bloom very freely? *N. alba plena odorata* is a notoriously shy bloomer. It prefers a moist situation. Try instead, Daphne, Cheerfulness and the even newer Swansdown, all white doubles.

Can you suggest some very early daffodils? February Gold, small yellow trumpet, a *cyclamineus* hybrid; Ada Finch and High Sierra, white trumpets; Grapefruit, lemon trumpet; Hallowe'en, yellow trumpet; Riootous, two-toned double; South Pacific, white and yellow; Twink, primrose and orange double.

ERANTHIS (WINTERACONITE)

I have not had success with winteraconites, although I planted them in a favorable situation early in October. Can you suggest cause of failure? Too late planting. They should have been planted at least 2 months earlier. They quickly deteriorate when kept out of ground.

What conditions do winteraconites (eranthis) need? A woodsy, non-acid soil in light shade. They often do well on gentle slopes, and once planted should be left undisturbed. Set tubers 3 ins. deep and about same distance apart.

EREMURUS

Are Foxtail-lilies hardy? These stately (5 to 12 foot) members of the lily family produce from star-shaped, fibrous rootstocks, rosettes of narrow leaves which send up blooming stalks bearing heavy racemes of bell-shaped white, pink, yellow or orange flowers in late spring. They are hardy to Zone 4 if heavily mulched after ground freezes hard. Do not remove mulch until late spring frosts are past as early spring growth may be frost-nipped. For this reason a northern exposure is desirable.

ERYTHRONIUM

What are the habits and culture of dogtooth-violets? *Erythronium dens-canis* is a woodland plant which likes a constantly moist position in partial shade.

What is the proper depth for planting dogtooth-violet bulbs, and how late may they be planted for spring blooming? Plant with top of bulb 3 ins. below surface. September is latest month for planting. They quickly deteriorate if kept out of soil long.

Are the troutlilies or dogtooth-violets easily grown in gardens? They are among the most lovely of plants for lightly shaded places where soil is deep and humusy, and possibly moist. Unfortunately many of them gradually deteriorate when planted in Eastern gardens, but they are well worth replanting from time to time.

FRITILLARIA

What is the guinea hen flower? *Fritillaria meleagris.* The speckled, pendant blooms are curious rather than beautiful. A good rock garden subject.

What is the culture for crown imperial? *Fritillaria imperialis,* like many others of its genus, is capricious, sometimes doing well, and then again, for no apparent reason, failing to thrive. Plant in July in deep, limy soil, in light shade. Leave undisturbed as long as it continues to thrive.

GALANTHUS (SNOWDROP)

I am very fond of snowdrops. Where and how shall I plant them? Plant in early fall, setting bulbs 3 to 4 ins. deep and about 3 ins. apart. If possible, choose a porous soil that contains fair amount of humus, and a lightly shaded position. They multiply fairly rapidly if congenially located.

How often should snowdrops (Galanthus nivalis) be lifted and transplanted? Do not disturb them unless absolutely necessary; they thrive best when left alone. If transplanting becomes imperative, do it after foliage dies down. Do not keep bulbs out of ground longer than necessary.

HYACINTH

Can hyacinth bulbs be planted outside in November for spring flowers? Yes, but a month earlier is preferable.

Can I plant hyacinth bulbs in the spring? If so, will they bloom the first summer? Only the so-called summer-hyacinth (*Galtonia candicans*) can be planted at this time. It blooms the first summer. The spring-flowering Dutch hyacinths are planted in fall.

Will hyacinths be injured if moved after the leaves show? Yes, they will suffer somewhat. If absolutely necessary it can be done, providing every care is taken to keep a large ball of soil intact about the roots.

Will Hyacinthus amethystinus grow in light shade? When does it bloom? Yes. It blooms end of May and early June in vicinity of New York. A fine species for the home garden. It looks like a grape hyacinth. Plant bulbs in fall, 3 to 4 ins. deep.

LEUCOCRINUM

Are starlilies annuals or perennials? I have had them in the house summer and winter so far, but they increase so fast, I won't have room for them all another winter. Will they stand the winter in the flower bed? Starlilies or sandlilies (leucocrinum) are hardy perennials. They are native from Nebraska to the Pacific coast.

LEUCOJUM

A friend gave me a clump of leucojum which I greatly admired in

her garden 2 years ago. **They have never bloomed in mine. Why?**
This plant dislikes root disturbance and the transplanting may have
caused it to skip blooming for a couple of years. Leucojums enjoy a
soil rich in leafmold and a sunny or very lightly shaded position.

**I bought bulbs of Leucojum vernum, which books say grows 6 ins.
tall. Mine grew 2½ ft. Was the soil too rich?**   The plant often sold
as *Leucojum vernum* (Spring Snowflake) is the later-blooming and
much taller *L. aestivum* (Summer Snowflake). The former has but
2 flowers on each stem; the latter usually 4 to 6.

LILIES

Lilies have been called both the most fascinating and the most
exasperating of all garden flowers: fascinating because of their beauty
of form and coloring; exasperating because of frequent failures and
disappointments. However, few ornamental plants have as great decorative value or are better adapted to garden planting design. Because they are closely linked with art and religion, they are interesting
for sentimental reasons.

In nature different species are found under the most diverse conditions: some grow at high altitudes, others at low; some inhabit the
desert, while others are found in damp meadows. They come from
both dry and humid climates, and from cold and warm regions. Is
it any wonder that as a group they used to appear capricious when
included in a garden planting?

While lilies have been cultivated in gardens for a long time, it is
only within the past decade or so that they have really been domesti-
cated. For centuries efforts to hybridize the wild species had proved
almost futile. Once a few hybrids were obtained, however, these
intercrossed readily. The result has been new races or groups of man-
made lilies which are infinitely easier to grow in gardens than were
their progenitors. Today lilies have become flowers for every garden.
They are invaluable for cutting as well as for the landscape effects.

Soils; Fertilizers

How should soil be treated before planting lilies?   Well-drained
garden soil that is in good condition requires no special treatment.
Spade it well, allow it to settle, and plant the bulbs. It is desirable,
but not necessary, to mix some peatmoss with the soil for the eastern
American lilies, and for *Lilium hansoni*.

Do lilies require sweet or acid soil?   In most cases the acidity of
the soil is not important. The foliage of a few kinds, however, becomes chlorotic or yellowish in alkaline soil. *Hansoni, speciosum, canadense,* and *superbum* are some of these. Where this occurs the lilies
benefit if a layer, several inches thick, of peatmoss is spaded into
the soil.

What kind of fertilizer is best for lilies?   A good garden fertilizer, or almost any complete fertilizer that is relatively high in potash. One good formula is 5–10–10. Manure should not be used, as it may encourage losses from basal rot.

Can bone meal and cottonseed meal be used in ground where lily bulbs are to be planted?   Yes, these are excellent.

When is the best time to fertilize lilies?   Early spring.

Planting

How and when should hardy lily bulbs be planted?   The ground should be dug and leafmold or peatmoss added. Plant stem-rooting kinds, such as *L. regale,* with the tops of the bulbs about 6 ins. under ground; bottom-rooting kinds, 2 or 3 ins. Sand placed below and above the bulbs helps drainage. Most lilies are best planted in autumn.

How deep should Easter Lily bulbs be planted?   With a 4- to 6-in. cover of soil over the tops of the bulbs. They are hardy, of course, only in mild climates.

When is the best time to plant Regal Lilies?   Early fall. They may be planted in spring providing the bulbs have been carefully stored.

When is the best time to plant Madonna Lilies? And how deep?   Late August or early September. Somewhat later planting will do if the bulbs are not available earlier. Set them in a sunny site and do not cover the top of the bulb more than 2 ins.

When is the best time to divide and transplant various kinds of lilies?   When the tops begin to die. Somewhat earlier or somewhat later lifting will not materially affect the performance of the plants the following year.

I find it necessary to move Madonna Lilies to another place in my garden. When should this be done?   Shortly after the flowers have withered.

How often should Regal Lilies be divided and reset?   Only when the number of stems indicates that the plants are becoming crowded.

Can you tell me how to take up Regal Lilies? The leaves often stay green until cold weather. Also, how about the roots? I was always afraid to cut off roots, so I just took the plants up and set them in a new place, although I wanted to ship them.   If necessary to replant, do so in fall about a month before ground freezes hard. Ship with roots intact.

Should lilies be moved in spring? How deep should they be planted?   They may be moved if taken up with considerable soil about their roots. Plant at the same depth in the new site as they were before being moved.

Problems

What should a beginner look for when purchasing lily bulbs?
Try to get mosaic-free bulbs of reliable species, and avoid kinds
known to be difficult. A well-grown Maxwill or *henryi* is much hand-
somer than a diseased *auratum* or *japonicum*.

Just what is a "stem-rooting" lily? Most garden lilies are stem-
rooting; that is, they produce most of their roots from the stem that
grows upward from the bulb. For this reason most lilies are planted
deeply so that they will have a long portion of their stem underground.

**Why do lilies become spindly after a season or two? If this is
caused by lack of food, what is it best to do?** The Sunset Lily increases rapidly and becomes so crowded after 2 or 3 years that it is
necessary to dig, separate, and replant the bulbs, otherwise only weak,
non-flowering stems are produced. Many other lilies eventually become crowded and need separating.

**I have a lily which does not bloom every year. One year it blooms
with 7 or 8 blossoms, the next it fails to flower, and grows only about
1 ft. tall. Can you give me any information regarding this?** Some
lilies fail to bloom because they become crowded; others because of
disease or because of frost injury to the growing point.

Meadow Lily (Lilium canadense) *and Regal Lily*
(L. regale), *two of the most satisfactory for garden
use.*

**Does Lilium speciosum rubrum bloom in August; and can it be
planted in spring?** It blooms in late August or September. It may
be planted in spring.

I cannot grow Auratum Lilies. What do they need? They usually
fail because they become infected with mosaic disease. Try again with
mosaic-free bulbs, planted away from other lilies, in ground that has
not grown lilies recently.

**I have planted 12 Formosa Lilies and not a one to show for it.
I've tried to do just as nurserymen say, but no luck. Is something
wrong with soil?** Probably not. *L. formosanum* is susceptible to

mosaic disease and also to basal rot, which is caused by a soil fungus. Try some of the new disease-resistant hybrids.

If different kinds of lily bulbs are planted in the same bed, will the different species mix?   They will not mix if by mixing is meant that the pollen of one kind will influence adjoining plants so that their characteristics change. Varieties with wandering, underground stems may invade the territory of other near-by species.

Should Easter Lily bulbs be taken up and dried before replanting? (Texas.)   No. If it is necessary to move them, take them up late in the season and replant promptly.

Two other good lilies for amateurs—Hanson and Shuksan.

I planted Regal and Madonna Lilies 4 years ago. Should I have taken them out since and transplanted them?   Lilies that are doing well need not be transplanted until they become crowded, which condition will be manifested by their numerous short, weak stems.

Why do lilies "run out" in this section? (Pennsylvania.)   Because of their susceptibility to obscure virus diseases certain lilies, such as *L. auratum,* are not long-lived in many sections. Others, such as the Tiger Lily, thrive despite the diseases. Try some of the new horticultural types, such as the Mid-century Hybrids and Centifolium Hybrids.

Culture

How shall I plant and care for lilies of various kinds?   Plant Madonna Lilies in late August or September; all others when bulbs are received. Madonna Lilies are covered 2 ins. deep to top of bulb; most others 6 ins., more or less, depending upon the vigor of the plant. Mulch for winter with straw or marsh hay. After ground freezes mulch during the growing season with peatmoss or lawn clippings. Keep down weeds, fertilize with a complete fertilizer, and water if season is dry.

Will you give me some information about growing Madonna Lilies? Mine have always failed.   Deep planting is a common cause of failure. The top of the bulb should not be more than 2 ins. from surface of the ground. Any good garden soil, well drained, and a sunny site are suitable. Use organic fertilizer but no manure or peatmoss near the bulbs. Spray, if necessary, against botrytis blight, which see.

The Regal Lily is considered easy to grow, but mine are small. Do they like lime or an acid soil? Dry soil, or a fair amount of water? Failure may be due to plants being infected with mosaic disease, from which they will not recover. Soil conditions may be unfavorable. The Regal Lily prefers a fertile soil, well supplied with organic matter. Watering during dry weather and mulching to conserve moisture are beneficial. The presence or absence of lime is not important.

What are the cultural requirements of Lilium speciosum rubrum? What ground cover shall I use over them?   Any good, well-drained garden soil in full sun or light shade. Low-growing, shallow-rooted plants such as pansies, violas, Scotch pinks, canterburybells and low-growing ferns are the best ground covers for lilies.

Would you please give me information on culture of the Mount Hood Lily?   This is a form of *Lilium washingtonianum* which is rather difficult in gardens. Plant 10 ins. deep in well-drained soil that is supplied with an abundance of organic matter; provide a surface mulch to conserve moisture.

May ground where lilies are growing be hoed?   Yes, but with extreme care. Many lilies appear late in spring and careless hoeing may result in chopping the shoots off below ground. Lily roots are near the surface and are damaged by deep hoeing. A summer mulch of leafmold, lawn mowings, peatmoss, or bagasse will eliminate the necessity for much cultivation.

What sort of mulch should be used around Madonna Lilies? Lawn clippings, leafmold, or peatmoss.

Does it harm lily bulbs to cut the flowers?   Unfortunately, yes. One can scarcely avoid removing a considerable proportion of the foliage together with the blooms, and these leaves are needed to manufacture food to build up the bulbs for the next season's growth. Some kinds can be cut every second year without serious damage.

How do you get long stems on Regal Lilies?   Long stems are produced on well-grown plants that are free from disease. Cultural requirements are a fertile soil well supplied with organic matter, mulching to conserve moisture, and the annual application of a complete commercial fertilizer. Old plants with numerous stems should be divided, and the bulbs replaced in enriched soil.

Should lily blooms be left on plants, or should they be picked off before seeding?   Remove flowers as they fade. This favors the development of larger plants the following year.

Should lily stems, after they have dried up and died, be left, or

should they be cut off or pulled off? They should be removed. They may be pulled up gently if it is desired to save the bulblets which are found at the bases of the stems of certain species; otherwise they may be cut off.

At what time of year should lily bulbs be dug? Do not dig unless it is necessary to move them to another location or divide them. Take them up when the tops begin to die.

Should Regal Lilies be lifted every spring? Absolutely not. Lilies should never be dug unless they are overcrowded or unless it is desired to move them to another location.

Do we cover Madonna, Regal, and philippinense lilies because they are not quite hardy, or to prevent freezing and thawing? Lilies are mulched to prevent damage to the bulbs from low temperatures and to prevent injury to the roots from alternate freezing and thawing.

At what temperature should lily bulbs (Regal) be kept during winter? They are hardy and should be left in the ground over winter. In cold regions protect with a 6- or 8-in. straw mulch. (See next question.)

My lily bulbs arrived too late to plant outside. I have buried them in sand in a cold fruit cellar. Will they be all right? Yes, if temperature is kept just above freezing. It would have been better, however, to have potted them before storing in the cellar.

Propagation

Can lilies be grown from seed? Seeds of such lilies as *regale, tenuifolium, amabile, concolor, formosanum, henryi,* and *willmottiae* germinate promptly. Plant in early spring in flats of good soil, and leave in a cold frame, under lath shades, for 2 seasons. Water and weed regularly, and mulch or cover the flats with boards during winter. At the end of the second summer plant the seedlings out in nursery beds for another year or two, mulching the beds for winter. Plant seeds of *auratum, speciosum, martagon,* and native American lilies in spring. They will not send up leaves until the following spring. If the flats are stacked during the first summer no weeding, and only occasional watering, will be necessary. At end of the third season the plants should be large enough for the nursery bed.

What is the most successful way to propagate Regal Lilies, and how long before blossoms may be expected from seed? By seed. The larger seedlings should bloom during their third season.

Our Madonna Lily set seed after it bloomed. Could I plant the seed this winter in a box in the house? Madonna Lily seeds may be started in flats in the house any time during the winter.

I have some Lilium formosanum started from seeds sown last March. The bulbs are still pinhead size. How can I make them grow

faster? Water them every 2 weeks with water in which commercial fertilizer has been dissolved at the rate of 1 tablespoonful to 1 gal. of water.

When and how should lily bulblets be planted? Remove bulblets borne at bases of the stems when stems are cut down in fall. Plant them in a nursery row for a year or two until they are large enough to transplant to the border. Bulbils borne in the axils of leaves of some varieties may be planted about 1 in. deep as soon as they begin to drop from the plants.

How can I propagate the Gold-banded Lily (Lilium auratum)? Remove the bulblets from the bases of the stems in the fall and plant them out in a nursery for a year or two until they are large enough for the border.

I have three Madonna Lily bulbs grown from scales I took from large bulbs last August. What should I do with them until next August? I have them potted in the house now. Keep them growing in the pots until next August, when they may be planted in the garden.

Can small bulbs of Regal Lilies, that appear almost on top of the ground, be separated from the main plant and be planted deeper to increase the stock? Yes.

My Lilium umbellatum formed new bulbs on top of the ground. I covered them with 4 ins. of soil and mulched them with leaves. Will they come through the winter? Yes. To prevent crowding, bulblets which form near the surface of the ground on the bases of the stems, should be removed every year or two, and planted elsewhere.

How do you separate lily bulbs when you wish to start new plants? Dig, and break up the clumps in fall. The small bulbs on the bases of the stems may also be saved. Lilies which do not increase by bulb division nor by stem bulblets may be propagated by removing a few of the scales from the bulbs as soon as the flowers fade and planting these an inch deep in a light soil.

How do you propagate Regal Lilies from the flower stems? As soon as the last flowers fade, jerk the stems from the bulbs and "heel them in" (plant them) so that their lower quarters are covered with soil. In fall, when the stems are dead, remove the small bulbs from the bases and plant them 2 ins. deep.

Pests and Diseases

What is the best way to avoid mosaic disease in lilies? Plant only bulbs known, or guaranteed, to be free from mosaic. Or grow the bulbs from seed away from all lilies and other bulbous plants. When you see any sign of disease, dig up the plant and burn it at once.

What is the treatment for basal rot in Madonna Lilies? It is caused by a fungus. If detected before the bulbs have rotted much, remove decayed tissue, dip bulb for 20 mins. in 1 part formaldehyde to 50 parts water, and replant in a new location.

What is the recommended treatment for botrytis blight of lilies? Spray at weekly intervals with Bordeaux mixture. This disease is most serious in wet seasons.

How can I prevent field mice or moles from destroying Regal, Madonna, and other lily bulbs? Plant the bulbs in cages of wire netting of a large enough mesh to let the stems grow through.

Is it true that L. philippinense and Tiger Lilies are disease carriers and should be removed from the garden? They may or may not have mosaic disease. *L. philippinense* is usually raised from seeds and is therefore mosaic-free, but it may acquire the disease later. The Tiger Lily in the trade often, but not always, has mosaic. The health of these lilies is determined only by an examination of the leaves in the spring or early summer.

Varieties

Please tell me what new hybrid lilies to choose for my garden for bloom from June to September. I am not a specialist. Aurelian Hybrids; Bellingham Hybrids; Fiesta Hybrids; Golden Chalice Hybrids; Mid-century Hybrids; Olympic Hybrids, Rainbow Hybrids.

What lilies are long-lived? Healthy bulbs give long life. Buy only from a reliable dealer. Some of those most likely to live long in your garden are *hansoni, regale,* Maxwill, *superbum, henryi, speciosum, candidum* and *tigrinum.* Try also some of the new hybrids.

Which are the best lilies for dry soils? *Pumilum* (*tenuifolium*), *regale,* Maxwill, *formosanum, candidum, umbellatum* varieties, *tigrinum* and *princeps.* It is helpful, in conserving moisture in dry situations, to mulch the soil with peatmoss, lawn clippings, or some similar material.

What is the botanical name of the commonly used Easter Lily? *Lilium longiflorum.* Several varieties of this lily are grown by florists, among them *giganteum, harrisi, formosum,* Erabu, and Creole.

LYCORIS SQUAMIGERA

Which lily is it that shows its leaves in the spring, then dies, and in August sends up stalks which have a pink-lavender bloom? *Lycoris squamigera,* sometimes sold as *Amaryllis halli.*

How shall I care for Lycoris squamigera? Plant in September in light, loose soil, either in full sun or light woodland shade. Set bulbs so that their tops are 5 ins. deep and spaced 5 or 6 ins. apart. Leave undisturbed for many years.

Why did Lycoris squamigera fail to bloom since transplanting 2 years ago? It is in sunny, well-drained location. Bulbs multiplied, but

sent up no flower stems. It often happens that transplanted bulbs of this species refuse to bloom for 2 or 3 years after transplanting.

I have 2 Amaryllis halli, now 4 years old. They came up in the spring, and the leaves are healthy and long; they die down in July but never bloom. Can you help me? Maybe you planted small bulbs. If in a suitable soil (deep, light, well drained) and location (full sun or light shade) they should grow and eventually flower.

When do you dig Amaryllis halli? Some seed houses say after the foliage dies and before they bloom; others, after they bloom. Correct name of this plant is *Lycoris squamigera*. Best time for transplanting is immediately after they have bloomed.

MUSCARI (GRAPEHYACINTH)

How late can grapehyacinth (muscari) bulbs be planted? They may be planted any time before the ground freezes hard; but it is better to plant them in early fall.

Do grapehyacinths multiply? If so, when can one transplant them? Yes; they multiply freely. Self-sown seedlings come up in great numbers. Lift bulbs as soon as foliage has died down and transplant immediately; or store in cool, dry place until fall.

Can I keep grapehyacinth bulbs, without planting, till next spring? No. If you cannot plant them in open ground, plant them closely together in shallow boxes of soil. Stand outdoors and cover with leaves or hay during winter.

When should grapehyacinths, which have been undisturbed for years, be reset? To what depth? They may be lifted and replanted when the foliage has died and become completely brown. Plant 2 ins. apart, and cover tops of bulbs with 3 ins. of soil.

I have 2 varieties of muscari; one sends up top growth in fall. Which variety is it? How do I care for them over winter? The nomenclature of the species and varieties of muscari is very confused. Several of them produce foliage in the fall. They are quite hardy and require no special winter attention.

ORNITHOGALUM

Can you give me some information about ornithogalums? (Texas.) More than 100 kinds exist. They are natives of Europe, Asia, and particularly Africa, belonging to the lily family. Many kinds should be hardy in Texas. They need a fertile, sandy soil. See article in Bailey's Standard Cyclopedia of Horticulture, available in most libraries.

Is the very fragrant Ornithogalum arabicum hardy in the vicinity of New York City? Not generally so, although it will winter and bloom if given a very sheltered position, porous soil, and winter protection.

OXALIS

Will oxalis survive the winter months? *Oxalis violacea* and *O. acetosella* are hardy, and are sometimes grown as rock-garden plants.

PUSCHKINIA

Will you give me directions for growing a scilla-like bulbous plant called puschkinia? Plant in early fall about 3 ins. deep and same distance apart, in light, well-drained, fertile soil, either in full sun or very light shade. Do not replant more often than necessary. Need for this is indicated by reduction in number of blooms produced.

SCILLA

What is the best way to plant and care for the blue scilla? Plant *S. sibirica* in fall in deep, loose soil that is fairly fertile. It thrives for years without disturbance. Do not remove foliage until it has completely died down. The scillas, with large, potatolike bulbs (*S. hispanica* and *S. nonscripta*), are set 5 ins. deep. Other kinds about 3 ins. deep.

In the rock garden at a botanical garden I saw a pink scilla (squill) blooming in late August. What could this be? *Scilla chinensis* (sometimes known as *Scilla japonica*), an easily grown kind that self-sows freely. It thrives in ordinary garden soil in sun or light shade.

Which scillas are best adapted for planting in a shaded situation, in soil containing lots of leafmold? The Spanish Bluebell (*Scilla hispanica*) and the English Bluebell (*Scilla nonscripta*). Both may be had in blue-, pink-, and white-flowered forms.

STERNBERGIA

What is the name of the rich golden-yellow flower that looks like a crocus (but more substantial) and blooms in September? *Sternbergia lutea*. Plant bulbs 4 or 5 ins. deep in August, in quite porous soil and sheltered situation. Cover lightly during winter. This species resents root disturbance.

TULIPS

The May garden would indeed be dull without tulips. They are one of the "musts" of the mixed perennial border because they are unsurpassed in their wide array of harmonious colors and in their reliability. The range of hues covers the entire spectrum and all its tints and shades except pure blue. What artist would not revel in tubes of tulip colors as a medium for painting garden pictures?

For generations tulips grew in the fields and gardens near Constantinople before they found their way to Holland in 1571. Few plants have been molded to such an extent into the economic and social life of a nation. Even though grown in all the temperate regions they are still thought of as Dutch.

In the course of history, tulips have had their ups and downs. Soon after their introduction into Holland they reached a peak of popularity never before or since achieved by any plant. Men speculated and gambled with them as is done today in cotton, corn, and oil. The prices of new varieties soared to staggering heights. A single bulb of the variety Semper Augustus once sold for 13,000 florins, the equivalent of $6,500. Then came the crash; and the economic and financial structure of the entire nation was threatened. The popularity of tulips vanished, and for years they were hidden in the small home gardens of the poorer people of Holland only to rise again and become a leading industry.

Tulips are valuable in many kinds of garden plantings. Their best use is in the border, where they combine beautifully with all other plants. They may be planted in formal beds, where they take on an appropriate quality of stiffness and constraint. In small, intimate groups about the garden, they offer friendliness and charm. Because they are so easy to grow, they force well in the window garden. For flower arrangements, their form is distinctive and their coloring delightful.

Soil and Fertilizer

What kind of soil suits tulips best? A fertile, well-drained, light loam, at least 12 ins. deep. They will grow satisfactorily, however, in a wide variety of soils.

Will tulips grow well in a bed that is located in a wet spot in my garden? No. Good subsurface drainage is of the utmost importance in growing tulips. The bulbs will quickly rot in waterlogged soil.

Is it necessary to change the soil yearly in beds where tulips are planted? Desirable, but not essential unless disease is present. Changing the soil every 3 years should control fire blight, basal rot, etc.

What can I add to my garden soil to make my tulip bulbs grow larger? Coarse bone meal and commercial fertilizer, mixed with the soil at planting time, and well-rotted manure, set 2 ins. under the bulb with a soil separation layer between the bases of the bulbs and the manure, will aid.

How should soil be prepared for a tulip bed? Dig to depth of 10 or 12 ins. Place 2 ins. of well-rotted manure in the bottom. A dressing of bone meal or commercial fertilizer, worked into the bed, is also beneficial.

What common fertilizers are good for tulips? Bone meal, superphosphate, dried and shredded cattle manure, sheep manure, and commercial fertilizers, such as a 4–8–4 or 5–10–5.

Is it worth while to put commercial fertilizer on a tulip bed in late fall? Yes, but better in spring. Apply and water it in immediately.

What is the best fertilizer for tulips? Bone meal is probably best, because of its slow-acting properties. Complete commercial fertilizers, of low-nitrogen content, and superphosphate are also satisfactory. Avoid all fresh manures. Liquid manures should be used only in weak dilutions.

Is it well to put manure on my tulip bed? Manure is practically wasted when put on the surface. It should be used only in the bottom of the bed. Best winter covers for tulip beds are salt hay, clean straw, peatmoss, and rough compost.

Planting

When is the best time to plant tulips? October 15 to November 1, except where a short growing season makes earlier planting necessary. A good general rule is to plant 2 to 4 weeks before the ground freezes.

How late can one plant tulips and still hope for fair results? (Ohio.) December 15 in your section. However, if bulbs are sound they may be planted later.

How can I save tulip bulbs which are not in the ground at the time of the first hard freeze? Build a fire over the frozen ground and thaw it out, or else chop through the crust and plant. Tulips cannot be held a full year out of the ground.

Could tulip bulbs be planted in January or February if the weather permits? Yes, if sound and well preserved. By February the flower buds contained in the bulbs are usually dead. However, this procedure may result in saving the bulbs so that they will flower the following year.

What happens if tulips are planted in early spring? They grow very short, and usually do not flower the first year.

On December 2 I planted tulip bulbs in a prepared bed. Is this too late for them to make root growth? How will their spring growth be affected? They should grow and bloom. Their stems will be shorter, and their blooms not so large as those of earlier-planted bulbs.

My tulip bulbs are very soft. Would it be advisable to plant them? Soft tulips result from too early digging or hot, dry storage. They can be planted, and should recover by the second growing season.

How does one obtain even results from tulip plantings? Flowers all the same height, and all of one kind blooming together with flowers of the same size? By planting good-quality, even-sized bulbs at the correct season and setting them all at the same depth. Professional gardeners accomplish this by removing soil from the bed, placing the bulbs, and then refilling with soil. For the very best results new bulbs of the same variety or the same type should be planted each fall.

Will tulip bulbs just thrown in any way grow? They may grow but will not be satisfactory. They should be set properly on their bases, and at a suitable depth.

Is it true that tulip bulbs do better when planted 10 or 12 ins. deep as stated by some bulb growers? Deep planting prevents tulips splitting up and saves the task of digging and separating them every 2 to 3 years. Large bulbs may do well planted with their bases at this depth but shallower planting is usually more advisable if bulbs are small. Deep planting retards breaking up of each bulb into several smaller ones and therefore makes it possible to leave the planting undisturbed for several years.

Do you agree that if tulips are planted 9 ins. deep they'll never have to be moved? No; but they will need replanting less frequently than shallowly planted bulbs. They will eventually have to be transplanted.

Do you favor very deep planting for tulips; 10, 12 or 14 inches to the bottom of the bulb? Only if the bulbs are unusually large. Top-size bulbs should be planted 6 to 10 ins. Oversize Jumbo bulbs (13 to 14 centimeter or larger) may be placed deeper.

Will tulips planted less then 6 ins. deep bloom next spring? They should, providing they are not subjected to too much frost.

What happens if you plant tulip bulbs too deeply or too shallowly? If planted too deeply, small bulbs will waste their strength pushing through to the ground level. If too shallowly, they may heave out of the ground, or freeze completely.

How shall I plant Darwin tulips to get the best results in this climate? (Pennsylvania.) Obtain top-size bulbs. Plant in October in fertile, well-drained soil, covering the bulbs 6 or 8 ins. deep. After the ground freezes hard, mulch lightly with leaves, salt hay, or evergreen branches. Remove this covering gradually in spring. Feed with diluted liquid fertilizer and water freely during dry spells.

In planting 1,000 tulips in beds 36 ins. wide should I dig the dirt out to a depth of 6 or 8 ins. and replace after setting the bulbs? I want to plant annuals without lifting tulips. Your method is quite satisfactory, but it is quicker to prepare the bed and then plunge the bulbs into the ground, using a long-shanked trowel. Annuals can be planted over bulbs planted 6 ins. deep or deeper.

How soon will it be safe to plant tulips in the same bed again after they are lifted? They occupied the bed for 3 years. Unless the soil is changed, or unless bed has been sterilized, allow a 3-year period between tulip plantings.

What causes the "dropping" of tulip bulbs? (By this I mean that

the bulbs grow lower than the parent bulbs.) **Will the bulbs growing up on the stem produce true to variety?** Tulip bulbs "drop" when planted too shallowly. Bulblets on the stems can be used for propagation and will come true to the variety.

Culture

Is it true that American-grown tulips are very poor and that only about 40 per cent will grow? Definitely false. Good-quality, American-grown tulips bloom 100 per cent, and usually are earlier blooming. They are preferred by commercial growers for early forcing.

How can I grow tulips successfully? (Tennessee.) Plant bulbs, in your section, from October 20 to November 5, in beds that have been dug to a depth of 12 ins. and are enriched with bone meal and humus. Cover the bulbs to a depth of 6 ins. If a drought occurs in spring, water frequently and thoroughly.

How can I get larger tulip blooms? I plant only top-size bulbs obtained from a reputable dealer. Fertilize each September with 5 lbs. of a 4–8–4 fertilizer to each 100 sq. ft. of bed. Water freely during dry periods in spring. Do not remove leaves when cutting flowers. Remove faded flower heads to prevent seed production. Never remove leaves, or dig bulbs, until tops have dried completely.

What extra steps can I take to keep my Darwin tulips in fine condition, now that tulip bulbs are so expensive that I can't replace the present supply? Top-dress beds with compost and bone meal. Feed in spring with commercial fertilizer. Water frequently during growing season. Cut flowers high up on stem as soon as they begin to fade. Dig up and separate every 2 or 3 years, and replant in enriched soil.

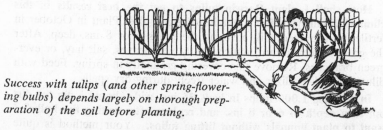

Success with tulips (and other spring-flowering bulbs) depends largely on thorough preparation of the soil before planting.

Will tulips bloom as well the second year after planting as they do the first? If the soil is well prepared, moisture is provided during the growing season, and the flowers are removed immediately after blooming (but the foliage left intact), there will be very little difference between the quality of the first and second year's blooms.

Could tulips be satisfactorily grown in a porch box 5 ft. long, 15 ins. wide, and a foot deep; northwest exposure? Not unless the box was packed around, bottom, sides, and top, with straw, salt hay, or other material to prevent the soil from freezing solid. It would be better to plant the bulbs in shallow pots or bulb pans and set them out in window boxes filled with damp peatmoss.

Can bulbs which have been forced be made to produce flowers outside? If so, how? They can be planted outside if the soil is well fertilized, but the number of flowers as well as their size is usually disappointingly small. If you intend to try this, be sure to keep the forced plants watered and growing so that they retain their foliage as long as possible.

Is it good policy to leave tulip bulbs in the ground all summer? It is quite practical. Tulips can remain 2 to 3 years without disturbing. Do not remove foliage until it has died down.

Can tulips be left in year after year? I have some that have been in for some years and they look very good. As long as the bulbs continue producing satisfactory blooms, keeping them in the ground is a good time-saving practice. It is usually better, however, to dig them and separate them every 3 years.

What is the best treatment for a planting of tulips which are to be left in the ground? Cut flowers off as soon as they fade. Keep watering the bed in dry weather until the foliage has completely died down. Fertilize in spring.

I had beautiful beds of Darwin tulips. I left one bed in the ground and covered it with manure. Will the tulips ever bloom again? If so, when? They should bloom again, in normal fashion, next spring.

Will tulip bulbs bloom again if flowers are cut? They should bloom the following year providing most of the foliage is left to die down naturally.

If all that comes up from a tulip bulb is one large leaf and no bloom stalk, will that bulb, or the increase from it, ever bloom? This indicates the need for digging and separation. First-year bulblets produce only one big leaf. Both the bulb and its increase may eventually bloom if planted in enriched soil. This "growing on," however, may prove tiresome, and for practical purposes it is often better to discard such weakened bulbs and start afresh with new stock.

Last year I lost about 1,000 tulips. Do they run out? One bed was replanted after bulbs were lifted and separated, but many died. Would lack of snow affect them thus? (Minnesota.) No. Losses may be caused by disease, rodents, or lack of fertility. In your section, shallowly planted bulbs need the protection of a winter mulch.

What is the best method of producing tulips from bulbs which have bloomed 2 years and now show nothing but leaves? Dig up the bulbs in July or early August. Replant only those having a diameter of 1 in. or more. Set small bulbs in rows, in vegetable garden or elsewhere, to grow on.

Is it advisable to prevent small tulip bulbs from blooming the first year, thus to obtain larger bulbs for the next year? Yes; but do not remove buds until they show color.

Can tulips be lifted and packed in dirt until the tops are dry so as to save the bulbs; or should they be planted deeper so that I can plant "glads" above them? Tulips can be lifted and carefully "heeled in" in a shallow trench until their tops are fully dried. They may then be separated and stored, and be replanted in the fall.

Should tulip bulbs be taken up each year and separated? Should they be covered with leaves in the fall? No. Dig them up and separate them every 2 to 3 years unless the ground is wanted for other purposes. (See answer above.) A winter mulch is desirable where temperatures go much below zero.

Is it wise to dig up tulip bulbs in May or June, and store them away to replant in fall? (Missouri.) This is too early. In your section July 1 would be better. When the bulbs are thoroughly dried, give them a good dusting with sulfur and store in a cool, dry place.

How often should tulip bulbs be removed from the soil and replanted? In light soils, every 2 years; in heavy soils, every 3 years. Bulbs planted 6 to 10 ins. deep require separation less frequently than those planted 4 ins. deep.

Is it all right to dig tulips in the fall for transplanting? Tulips can be dug and transplanted as late as October 1. An earlier date is better, however, as vigorous new root growth begins in October and continues until hard freeze.

How should tulip bulbs be handled after digging in fall? Tulips should not be dug in fall unless absolutely necessary. If they are, they should be immediately replanted.

Can tulips be moved in spring before blooming? No, it is impractical and will prevent the bulbs from blooming. It is also dangerous to the future welfare of the bulbs.

Do tulips need to be cured in the sun after digging? They should not be exposed to the sun, even a 30-minute exposure to full sunshine may crack the coats on the bulbs. Cure them by storing in a cool, dry place protected from sunlight.

What is the best way to store tulip bulbs through summer? Dry them thoroughly, dust well with sulfur, and hang them in ventilated bags from the rafters of a cool, dry cellar, shed, or garage.

I expect to move this winter and have taken my tulips out of the ground and have them stored in my basement. I covered them with soil. Would it be better to keep them dry and in a bag? Store them dry. Dust the bulbs with sulfur and keep them in open boxes or ventilated bags.

How can I keep tulips over winter, to plant in spring? This is not a good practice. If it must be done, store at 34° to 40° F. Tulips cannot be kept over safely for periods longer than 6 to 8 months.

When do you reset tulip bulbs that have been lifted and stored through the summer? No sooner than September 15. October 15 is better, if the bulbs are storing well.

What should be done with small tulip bulbs taken up in spring but not planted the following fall? Will they grow in size if planted next spring—not for bloom but for bulb growth? They are hardly worth bothering with. Small bulbs will have wasted most of their substance by being stored so long.

Winter mulch is applied after the ground freezes.

Is it important to cover the ground after planting tulip bulbs when the weather is freezing? (Long Island.) In sections as cold as Long Island it is wise to cover tulip plantings with salt hay or a similar protection. Apply this after the ground is frozen. Do *not* use manure for mulching tulips.

When should strawy manure be placed on tulips? Any manure may be a dangerous covering for tulips, as it sometimes harbors botrytis blight. Use only clean straw and apply it after a hard freeze.

Propagation

How is the crossing of tulips accomplished by the amateur? By the same methods used for most other flowers. Ripe pollen is transferred, with a camel's-hair brush, from the stamens of the male parent to the receptive stigma of the seed-bearing parent. All stamens are removed from the female parent before they ripen and shed pollen, and the flower is covered with a paper or plastic bag, to prevent accidental pollination.

Is it true that it takes 7 years to grow tulips from seeds? During this time is there any top growth? No. Tulips often produce blooms in 3 years from seed. Top growth appears on the young seedlings.

Is it worth while for the amateur to attempt growing tulips from seeds? No. The chances of getting desirable flowers are very small. The growing of seedlings for breeding work is a tedious job, best left to the specialist.

Could you give detailed directions for growing tulips from seeds?
Seeds should be planted in light, well-drained soil in a cold frame in
summer. Dig the bulblets the following year when the foliage has
died down, and plant them 3 or 4 ins. deep in nursery beds in fall.
The soil should be enriched for the young bulbs. It is a tedious
process that appeals only to the most interested amateurs and to
breeders of new varieties.

How do tulip bulbs multiply? By offsets (young bulbs), which
grow from the base of the mother bulb. These are separated and are
grown on to flowering size in specially prepared nursery beds.

**How can the little tulip bulbs be taken care of so that they can
produce full-size bulbs that will flower? When tulip bulbs are dug up,
there are so many little ones.** Immediately replant the small bulbs
3 to 4 ins. deep in good soil, or they may be stored in a cool place
in a mixture of *slightly* moist peatmoss and sand to be replanted in
fall. Allow flower buds (if any) to develop until they show color,
then nip them off. Allow foliage to ripen, then dig bulbs and store
until following fall. Have soil well enriched at all times.

**Why, after large clusters of tulip bulbs are dug, do the small bulbs
completely wither after a short period in storage?** Small bulbs are
often immature when dug. They have high water content and little
stored food. Loss of water causes withering. See previous question.

Diseases and Pests

Are tulips subject to disease? Tulip diseases include fire blight,
gray bulb rot, shanking, root rot, and mosaic. For all of the above,
destruction of infected stock and a change of soil or sterilization of
the infected soil are the only effective remedies.

**Last year some of my tulips had small greenish spots on the leaves;
the spots grew larger and many of the leaves turned yellow. Some
buds failed to open. What was the trouble; and what can I do?**
Botrytis or "fire" blight. Remove and burn infected leaves; dig bulbs
each year, and burn all showing infection. Replant in a new location,
where no tulips have been grown for several years.

**What causes new colors and varieties to appear in tulip beds after
a few years? Do the bulbils or offshoots produce other varieties? Are
the new forms seedlings?** Change of color is usually due to disease
mosaic. Infected plants should be removed or the virus will spread
through the entire planting. It is unlikely there would be any self-
sown seedlings.

**I have a number of named tulips that have bloomed every year,
and now some of them are striped. I move them every 3 years. Is
this a disease?** Striping and splotching of tulips are the results of
a virus disease. There is no cure. See question above.

Do moles eat tulip bulbs during winter or early spring? This is a moot question. Many gardeners believe moles do eat bulbs. Others contend mice and other pests follow the mole runs and destroy the bulbs.

What can I do to keep pocket gophers from eating tulip bulbs? (Idaho.) Use commercial rodent repellents, poisons, or cyanogas, in the form of dust forced through a special air pump made for the purpose.

How do you prevent mice and squirrels from eating tulip bulbs? There are many good commercial rodent repellents and poison baits. Avoid applying winter mulch until *after* ground has frozen. In extreme cases surround and cover plantings with fine wire netting spread beneath ground.

Varieties

What tulip types are generally available? What are their characteristics? Species or botanical and their hybrids: most of them low-growing and very early; a few, like Red Emperor, very large. Single Earlies, blooming just after Species: many fine yellows and oranges in this group and many are fragrant—10 to 16 inches in height. Double Earlies: double form of Single Earlies, long lasting, especially when cut. Triumphs and Mendels bloom next: they are crosses between Single Earlies and Darwins, 20 to 24 inches. Peony-flowered are double Triumphs, resembling peonies; long lasting. Cottage: tulips with tall, flexible stems, yellows and oranges but no purples, lavenders or bronzes. Darwins: the largest and most important group with large, globular flowers on very tall stems; colors range from white, yellow and orange through pinks, salmons and reds to lavenders and deep purples. Breeders bloom after Darwins and produce large, stiff-stemmed cup shaped flowers in golds, bronzes, browns, purples. Parrots are late flowering tulips with lacinated and twisted petals, excellent for arrangements. Lily-flowered; blooming late, with graceful, goblet-shaped blooms with pointed, recurved petals.

Which tulips make a good garden, but are not too expensive? Glacier, white; Mrs. John T. Scheepers, gold; Insurpassable, lilac; Lafayette, deep violet; City of Haarlem, red; Crimson Giant; Pride of Zwanenburg, rose; Clara Butt, pink.

How shall I select varieties of tulips for May flowering? From the catalogue of a reputable dealer select kinds which appeal and which are within your price limit (the highest-priced varieties are not necessarily the best). Make your selection from the Darwin, cottage, and breeder sections. If possible, visit tulip plantings in May and make your selections then.

Are the single, early-single, and early-double types of tulips satisfactory for spring bedding? Yes. They are lower-growing and earlier-flowering than the Darwins, breeders, and cottage tulips, but their flowers usually do not last so long in good condition. Many of the Single Earlies are delightfully fragrant.

What is a parrot tulip? One of a group with petals curiously twisted, frilled, and colored so that they are thought to resemble the plumage of a parrot. Fantasy is one of the best-known varieties.

Is there a black tulip? This name is applied to a very dark, maroon-black variety called La Tulipe Noire.

Is there a yellow Darwin tulip? Yes. Niphetos Sunkist, Mrs. John T. Scheepers and Yellow Giant. The cottage tulip Inglescome Yellow is often known as the yellow Darwin. It is a fine, inexpensive variety.

Which of the "botanical" tulips are most satisfactory for an ordinary garden? *Kaufmanniana* (the Waterlily tulip); *clusiana* (the Lady Tulip); *sylvestris* (the Florentine Tulip), *Fosteriana,* red, large; *praestans,* red.

Please name some desirable Species Hybrid Tulips. *Fosteriana* Cantate, Princeps and Red Emperor, all red; *Kaufmanniana* Caesar Frank, Elliot, Gaiety, The First and Vivaldi, all white or cream with red or rose exterior stripes; Scarlet Elegance, multiflowered; *praestans* Fusilier, red, multiflowered.

TENDER BULBS, CORMS, TUBERS

GENERAL

How often should bulbs be watered when being forced in a dark, cool room? Until growth starts, just enough to keep soil moist. All forced bulbs, while in active growth, require constant supplies of moisture, and should never be allowed to dry out.

Do the following need to be placed in dark to form roots: freesias, St. Brigid Anemone, ranunculus? Freesias, no. Anemone and ranunculus preferably, but not necessarily. All should be started in cool temperatures.

How long a rest period must bulbs that have been forced in pots have before being replanted? Hardy bulbs, such as narcissi, tulips, hyacinths, etc., should be discarded or planted out of doors after forcing. Tender subjects, such as hippeastrums, haemanthus, oxalis, lachenalias, etc., should be rested from the time the leaves have died away naturally and completely, until they show evidence of starting into growth again.

Can I store bulbs in an old-fashioned cellar which is damp? If too damp, many bulbs will rot. Suggest you make provision for better ventilation, which should result in drier conditions.

Can bulbs which are nearly, but not quite, hardy in Northern states be successfully wintered by mulching heavily before the ground

freezes? Many of them can. Plant them in a border on south side of a building when frost occurs. Before severe weather sets in, surround border with boxlike frame 12 ins. deep, fill with leaves, and cover with tar paper to shed rain.

SPECIFIC TENDER BULBS

(See also under House Plants.)

ACHIMENES

How are achimenes grown? Pot rhizomes about 1 in. apart and ½ in. deep in pans of sandy, humusy soil early in spring. Water carefully at first, more freely as growth develops. Temperature 60° to 65° F.; atmosphere moist. Keep air dry and cooler when flowers appear; shade from strong sun; feed when actively growing. Gradually dry off at end of growing season, and store when dormant.

Achimenes died after blooming. How long do bulbs remain dormant, and where shall I keep them during this period? From late summer until March or April plants remain dormant. Keep rhizomes mixed with dry sand, stored in temperature of 45° to 50° F. during this period.

ACIDANTHERA

Can acidantheras be grown outdoors, like gladioli? Yes, where the growing season is long; but in most parts of the country it is better to plant several bulbs together in good soil in large pots or tubs; or plant outdoors in a lightly shaded garden bed rich in humus after all danger of frost is past. Dig, dry and store when frost threatens. Grow outside during summer and bring into cool situation indoors before frost. After blooming, dry off and rest.

AGAPANTHUS

Is the blue Africanlily hardy, or must it be protected (in New Jersey)? Agapanthus is not hardy where more than very light frosts are experienced. In New Jersey it should be wintered in a light, cool, frostproof cellar, or some similar situation.

ALSTROEMERIA

Are alstroemerias hardy in New York? How are they grown? *A. aurantiaca* survives on Long Island when established; however, most kinds need protection of a cold frame, or may be grown by planting out in spring and lifting and storing in cool cellar through winter. They need an abundance of moisture (without stagnation) during growing season.

AMARYLLIS

What is an amaryllis? *Amaryllis belladonna* of South Africa is the only plant to which this name truly belongs. It is tender north of Washington, D.C. Requires deep planting and full sun. The name is commonly applied to hippeastrums, which hail from South America, as well as to sprekelia (Mexico), lycoris (Asia), sometimes to vallota (South Africa), and occasionally to crinum and other genera.

AMARYLLIS (HIPPEASTRUM)

Will red and white amaryllis bulbs bloom in summer garden? The florists' amaryllis, or, as it is more correctly named, hippeastrum, cannot be successfully grown as a garden plant except in warm sections, such as Florida and California.

Is there a way to have amaryllis (hippeastrum) bloom at a more desirable time? They are winter and spring bloomers. The exact time of flowering can be controlled to some extent by varying the temperature in which they are grown, and also by the methods employed to ripen them off in the fall.

Do amaryllis (hippeastrum) bulbs absolutely need to rest? Yes. However, some individual bulbs exhibit much less of a tendency to go completely dormant, and lose all of their foliage during the rest period, than others.

During the past summer my older amaryllis (hippeastrum) bulbs have grown some new bulbs. I will soon have to rest the large bulbs. How can I save the small ones? Would it be safe to separate them? Rest young bulbs with mother bulb, and separate at potting time. Plant young bulbs individually in small pots of sandy soil, and give same treatment as older specimen.

Is there a blue amaryllis? The "Blue Amaryllis" is *Hippeastrum procera* from Brazil, a plant rare in the United States. In recent years it has bloomed in the New York Botanical Garden, in Florida, California, and perhaps elsewhere. The flowers are lavender-blue or violet-blue, and very handsome.

BABIANA

I have a bulb called babiana. Will you please tell me how to care for it? Exactly same treatment as freesia, which see.

BEGONIA (TUBEROUS-ROOTED)

Are tuber-rooted begonias annuals? They are tender perennials. They bloom the first season if seed is sown early indoors.

Do tuberous-rooted begonias need any special attention except shade? The stems on mine seemed so brittle, the flowers fell off almost before they were open, and the tubers diminished considerably in size.

They need a loose, woodsy soil containing plenty of humus, even moisture, good drainage, and shelter from strong winds. They like well-rotted cow manure.

Where can I plant, and how can I start and care for, tuberous-rooted begonias? Purchase tubers in early spring. Plant in pots of light soil indoors for 6 or 8 weeks before plants are to be set outside. Set plants in open ground when all danger of cold weather has passed. Sheltered, shaded position necessary and soil enriched liberally with humus. Keep moist throughout summer.

What is proper soil mixture for tuberous begonias, for boxes placed on ground outside? One part good garden soil, one part sand, one and one half parts flaky leafmold, one half part old, rotted manure. Add bone meal, 1 pint to a bushel of compost. You may vary this mixture somewhat, but result should be a rich, but porous, humusy soil.

Will growing plants of tuberous-rooted begonias, set out in May or June, do as well as the tubers? Well-established plants set out from pots after the weather has become warm and settled should do as well as, and will produce earlier flowers than, tubers set in the open ground.

Should tuberous begonias be lifted before or after first hard frost? Before the first killing frost. A light frost that just touches the foliage will not harm them.

What should be done to tuberous begonias in the fall? (Outdoor grown.) Dig them up before severe frost, and spread out in flats (leaving soil adhering to roots). Put in sunny, airy place, and allow to ripen off. When stems and leaves have died, clean off and store the tubers in dry sand, soil, or peatmoss, in a temperature of 40° to 50° F.

My tuberous-rooted begonias "run out." Is there a way to grow them so they will bloom year after year? Too heavy a soil, strong competition from the roots of other plants, lack of fertility, or any other factor that discourages growth may account for this. If grown under favorable conditions, they will last for many years.

How can I grow tuberous-rooted begonias indoors? Start tubers in flats of leafmold or peatmoss in temperature of 60° F. in spring. When growth is 2 or 3 ins. high, pot into 4-in. pots, using loose, rich soil. Later pot into larger pots as needed, but *avoid overpotting*. Keep moist at all times; feed established plants; shade from bright sunshine; keep atmosphere moist; protect from wind.

Can tuberous begonias be used in house when taken from garden? No, at least not the same year. After a season's growth in the garden they need a winter's rest. They may be started into growth again the following spring.

Do tuberous begonias grown as house plants need a rest period?

Yes indeed. They must be dried off and completely rested during the winter. At end of summer, plants begin dying back naturally.

How can one propagate tuberous begonias? From seed. By rooting cuttings made from the young growths, or by carefully cutting the tuber into pieces. This last operation is done in spring just after growth has started. Be sure that each piece of tuber retains a growing sprout. Dust cut surfaces with fine sulfur before potting up.

Will a cutting from a tuberous-rooted begonia grow a bulb or tuberous root, and will it bloom? Cuttings taken in early spring (they are made from the very young shoots) will bloom well the first season and will form tubers that may be stored in the usual way through the winter.

Can you tell me if there is any way to increase tuberous begonias? By leaf or other cuttings? They can readily be propagated from cuttings made from the young growths, which are taken (when a couple of inches long) from the parent tuber and inserted in a moist, warm sand propagating bed.

CALADIUM

I bought a beautiful potted plant of fancy-leaved caladium, but it began to die in fall. What did I do wrong? It is natural for this plant to die down in fall, remain dormant, through the winter, then start into growth again in spring.

Would it be practicable to plant the beautiful colored-leaved caladiums out of doors in summer and dig them up in fall and store them in cellar through winter? Entirely so. Select a partially shaded location. Prepare soil well and incorporate humus with it. Plant tubers after ground has warmed up. Water freely in dry weather.

How can I care for bulbs of colored-leaved caladiums that have been dormant through winter in pots of dirt in which they grew last season? To start into new growth, remove tubers from old soil and place in shallow boxes of moss, leafmold, or peat, just covering tubers. Keep moist and in temperature of 70° to 80° F. When growth has started, pot up again, using a light, rich, humusy soil.

CANNA

Will you please let me know how to cut cannas to plant in spring? Use a sharp knife and cut so that each division consists of one good eye on a substantial piece of rootstock.

How early should cannas be started? They can be started indoors as early as February 1, and then potted into 4-ins. pots. For roots that are to be planted outdoors, without potting, start 4 to 6 weeks before planting (after danger of frost).

What is the proper method of starting cannas in the house? Plant divisions separately, in 4-in. pots. Water sparingly until growth has started, and then heavily. Use bottom heat to start.

What is the best soil for cannas, and how deep should they be planted? Any ordinary soil. Plant so that the "eye" is less than 2 ins. below the surface.

How shall I care for canna roots during winter? Dry thoroughly after digging. Dust lightly with sulfur and cover with clean sand or peatmoss kept slightly moist. Store in cool, dark cellar, and inspect often to see if drying occurs. If too dry, sprinkle sand or soil with water occasionally.

How can I keep canna roots over the winter? We have no basement. Dig a pit 3 ft. deep. Line bottom with 6 ins. of ashes, put roots in, and cover with 6 ins. of sand. Pack down litter, such as leaves, straw, etc., and cover pit with burlap bags, or an old rug.

How should canna roots be divided before storing for the winter? Do not divide in fall. Store whole, and cut in spring.

Cannas planted last year grew large and healthy, but very few developed flowers; they were small and poor. Why? Poor, runout planting stock is most likely responsible. Too much nitrogen could also be the cause. Cannas need fertilizer containing high phosphoric content. Lack of sunshine may also be responisble.

Is it a good plan to dig cannas and store the roots over the winter? (Georgia.) No. In the lower South it is a good practice to allow cannas to grow without moving until the clumps become very matted. Every 3 or 4 years dig the clumps, sometime during the winter, separate the roots, and set the divisions in new beds of well-enriched soil.

CLIVIA

Will you please tell how to grow clivias in pots? Pot in rich, well-drained soil. Do not repot oftener than absolutely necessary. Water to keep soil always moist; shade from sun; feed when growing actively. Give winter temperature of 50° to 60° F. In summer keep outdoors in shade.

COLOCASIA (ELEPHANTSEAR)

Is the elephantsear a kind of caladium? How do you grow it? Often sold as *Caladium esculentum,* but correct name is colocasia. Plant tubers in pots indoors in spring. After all danger of frost has passed, set outdoors in moist, rich soil. After first frost, dig up, dry off, and store in a cellar or similar place.

CRINUM

Is the Milk-and-wine-lily (Crinum fimbriatulum) hardy? (Pennsyl-

vania.)   It is not generally hardy in Pennsylvania. If planted in light, well-drained soil against the south side of a building, and well covered, it may survive.

Can you recommend some good varieties of crinum for growing in North Carolina?   A grower in that state reports best success with the following kinds: *kirki, kunthianum, erubescens, fimbriatulum, longifolium, moorei,* Powelli, and Cecil Houdyshel.

DAHLIAS

Few flowers have attained such wide popularity as the dahlia. Yielding readily to the handiwork of plant breeders, it has produced innumerable forms and colors. In the early days the breeding work was aimed at increasing the size of bloom. When flowers were obtained as large as dinner plates, the gardening public began to feel they were coarse, and too big to be artistic. The hybridizers were not disheartened, but proceeded to develop miniature types. Today the size of different varieties varies from ½ to 15 ins. in diameter, and the plants are from 18 ins. to 7 ft. in height!

The colors, clear and rich, include all the hues except clear blue. The petals have a crystalline texture which gives a luminous or translucent quality to the color. In addition to the pure spectrum hues they embrace the rich, warm tones of the sunrise and the soft, full tints of the sunset. There are flower forms to suit any fancy. Some varieties are dense, full, and formal; others are loose, shaggy, and carefree. There are ball-shaped types, singles, and some even mimic the forms of other flowers, such as the peony, orchid, and anemone.

The dahlia hails from Mexico, where it may be found growing at altitudes from 4,000 to 8,000 ft., among the broken rocks of lava beds, and where the temperature is moderate and rains are frequent. As with other plants, its native habitat suggests many clues to successful culture: good drainage, plenty of moisture, cool temperatures.

In garden plantings dahlias are not combined with other plants to the extent they might well be. Many gardeners feel that they are difficult to use except by themselves in mass plantings. Yet when skillfully placed in the perennial border, or in front of shrub plantings, they give a magnificent effect. Dahlias should be more generously used in the flower gardens of America to give added color in the late summer and fall.

Soil and Fertilizer

What type of soil do dahlias need?   They will grow in a wide variety. Important points are porosity and free drainage, reasonable humus content, and sufficient retentiveness, so that the plants do not suffer from lack of moisture. Any good vegetable garden soil is satisfactory.

What is the best way to prepare soil for dahlias?   A week or 10 days before planting spade and leave surface rough. Then broadcast to every 100 sq. ft., or to every 10 dahlia hills, 5 lbs. raw bone meal mixed with 1 lb. of muriate or sulfate of potash. Leave until day of planting, then thoroughly rake in the fertilizer, breaking all lumps and making the ground smooth.

I have been told that coal cinders are good to add to soil for dahlias. Is this so?   The porosity and texture of heavy soils are appreciably improved by the addition of gritty coal cinders. They have no value as fertilizer and should not be used on light soils, nor to excess on heavy soils.

Can dahlias be planted in the same place every year? What is best to plant to enrich the soil? (Pennsylvania.)   Yes. After roots are dug, spade and plant winter rye. If your soil is acid, broadcast ground limestone. Cow manure spread over the winter rye and turned under just before it goes into stalk (usually in Pennsylvania about the first week in May) would be beneficial.

Will you suggest a fertilizing program for dahlias?   At planting time broadcast 5 lbs. bone meal mixed with 1 lb. muriate of potash to each 100 sq. ft. of ground, or to each 10 hills. About July 10 give each plant a handful of a complete fertilizer (4–10–10). Finally, about August 25, when buds appear, mix 3 lbs. raw bone meal, 4 lbs. dried manure, and ½ lb. muriate of potash together and rake this amount into every 10 hills. Do not apply closer than 6 ins., nor more than 18 ins. away from stems.

Is bone meal preferable to Loma or Agrico as a fertilizer for dahlias?   All 3 are good. The bone meal is rather slow-acting.

Have saved wood ashes from my fireplace. Should I use them on my dahlia bed?   Yes indeed; they are a valuable source of potash. Be sure to store in a dry place, then either dig the ashes into the ground at planting time, using up to 10 to 15 lbs. per 100 sq. ft., or apply them as a top-dressing in early September.

Is liquid manure good for dahlias?   Excellent. A diluted solution made from either cow manure or chicken manure, and applied at weekly intervals while the flower buds are developing, increases both size and quality.

Planting

What is best location for dahlias?   They need free circulation of air, direct sunlight for at least 6 to 7 hours each day, freedom from competition with roots of large trees or dense shrubbery, and a fertile, well-drained soil.

Do dahlias thrive best in full sun or part shade?   Full sun.

Will miniature dahlias grow in a partially shaded place?   They require direct sunlight at least 6 or 7 hours each day. More is desirable.

In planting dahlias, should they be kept a certain distance from other flowers?   Not more than is necessary to permit both the dahlias and the other flowers to grow and develop satisfactorily. Dahlias should not be crowded.

What distance apart should dahlias be planted?   From 3 to 4 ft. for the taller kinds; somewhat less for the miniatures and pompons.

How soon can dahlias be planted in pots indoors before they are transplanted outdoors?   For May planting outdoors, pot during April.

What is the proper planting time for dahlias?   After all danger of frost has passed, usually about May 15 in the vicinity of New York City.

Can the tubers that develop on dahlia plants be replanted with success?   Yes. This is the most common method of perpetuating dahlias.

Can the tubers formed by the dahlia that one buys in pots and sets out in late spring be held over and used the following year?   Yes. They are entirely satisfactory.

Which is better, to leave dahlias in bunches or to plant the tubers separately? I have mine put away in bunches for the winter.   Always divide the clumps before planting.

If the necks of dahlia tubers are injured, will the plants bloom?   Dahlia tubers with broken necks will not grow.

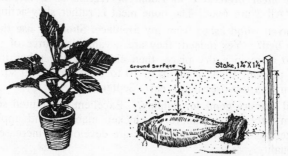

Left—pot-grown dahlia plant. Right—correct method of planting: one root, with strong eye, cut from clump.

Can dwarf or "bedding" dahlias be started in 3- or 4-in. pots and be planted out after tulips are dug?   Start seed, sowing in flats or bulb pans, indoors in March. Grow on, transplanting into pots of suitable size, and set out in open garden beds when all danger of frost is over and ground has warmed up.

Dahlia catalogues list plants as well as roots of certain varieties. I would like to try plants next season. How do you handle them? When received, remove from carton but leave in pots. Soak in shallow water to freshen. Set out in late afternoon or on a cloudy day. Dig holes 6 ins. deep; remove plants from pots; set so that root-balls are just covered with soil, and leave finished surface around plants 3 ins. below grade. If following day is sunny, shade. Plants will take hold in a few days. Gradually fill holes with soil as plants grow.

How are dahlia tubers planted, after clumps have been divided? First set stout stakes in place; at base of each stake, dig a wide hole 6 ins. deep; loosen up bottom. Lay tuber horizontally, with neck near stake and with eye pointing upward. Cover with soil so that tuber is just hidden. As eye grows, keep filling in soil so that it is kept just covered until surface grade is reached.

Culture

I am afraid my method of tying up dahlias is not very successful. They are always damaged in storms. What do you suggest? Plant in a position not too exposed to wind. Sisal binder twine is good for tying. Make 2 tight half hitches around stake; twist ends of twine twice around each other in front of stake; loop around stem tightly enough to afford support but not to cut, and tie with a square knot. Tie each stem separately and securely; do not bunch together like sheaf of wheat.

Is it necessary to hoe or cultivate around dahlias? Early in the season frequent surface cultivation is very beneficial, but it should be dispensed with about 10 weeks after planting, at which time beds should be mulched with peatmoss, bagasse, buckwheat hulls or other similar products which may be locally available. Do not cultivate when plants are in bud or bloom.

How do you prune dahlias in summer in order to get fall blooms? Allow only one main stalk to grow. When plants reach about 10 ins. in height, pinch out their centers just above the second pair of leaves. Side branches which develop should be pinched also. Remove any flower buds that appear before August 1.

How much water do dahlias require? Unless weather is very dry, they need none until they commence to bloom. Then water thoroughly, soaking the ground every week or 10 days whenever rainfall is insufficient.

Is mulching dahlias a worth-while practice? Yes. Early in the season maintain a "dust mulch" by frequent cultivation. At beginning of August cover surface of ground with a 2- or 3-in. layer of litter, salt hay, grass clippings, peatmoss, or similar material.

How are dahlias disbudded so that they have large blooms? When the buds appear (usually in clusters of three), pinch out all except the central one of each group. New lateral shoots will appear. All of these below the remaining bud, except the 2 nearest to the main stalk, should be pinched out. This will not only produce large blooms, but will keep plants low and bushy and will encourage the development of long stems.

What is the proper method to produce strong-stemmed dahlias that will support large blooms when cut? Remove all but 1 stalk from each plant. After 3 sets of leaves develop on this, pinch out its tip. Laterals will soon grow and eventually become main branches. All laterals and sublaterals other than the 4 main branches should be pinched out, except for the 2 sublaterals that develop near the base of each flowering stem.

How are exhibition dahlias grown? By planting healthy stock of suitable varieties, and by intelligent attention to cultivation, watering, spraying, disbranching, disbudding, and fertilization.

How many days should one allow from planting time for blooms of giant dahlias to develop for show? From 80 to 120 days, depending on the variety. A hot, dry season may cause blooms to mature from 10 to 15 days later than normal.

When and how do you cut dahlia flowers for exhibition? After sunset on the evening before the show. Cut with long stems, trim off any leaves not needed, and immediately stand the stems in water. Carry indoors and then trim the base of each stem by cutting it slantwise under water. Keep in a cool, dark place until they are packed for transportation.

Storage

How soon after digging should dahlia bulbs be divided and stored? After clumps are dug allow them to dry in the sun for 4 to 5 hours before storing. Do not divide until some months later (March or April).

At what temperature should dahlia roots be kept over winter? I always lose half my roots each year. From 40° to 55° F.

What care do you suggest if part of the dahlia bulb is injured in lifting? Remove injured tubers with a sharp knife or pruning shears. Sprinkle the cut surface with sulfur.

I planted dahlia tubers (pompons and giants) and now have 12 plants each with a cluster of from 5 to 7 tubers. How shall I store them? In a cool (45 to 55°) cellar, or in barrels or boxes lined with newspaper and placed where the temperature is not more than 55° nor less than 40°. Examine periodically to see that they are not becoming mildewed, nor drying up.

Should dahlia roots be wrapped in paper or packed in earth for

winter storage? Either. Allow soil to cling to clumps to prevent excessive drying. Peatmoss makes a good material in which to store them.

Will you tell me how to store dahlia roots in a modern basement? After digging, turn upside down and dry in sun for 4 to 5 hours; pack in barrel or box lined with newspaper. Allow soil to cling to clumps to guard necks from breaking and to prevent excessive drying. Keep as far as possible away from furnace.

What is your opinion of the practice of washing dahlia tubers as opposed to leaving on dirt? Either may be satisfactory. If soil is left, it tends to prevent excessive drying and reduces danger of necks of roots being broken. If tubers are washed, make sure that they are well dried before storing. Pack in peatmoss.

May dahlias be stored out of doors if buried below the frost line? Yes, if well below the frost line.

What makes dahlia roots rot after they are dug up? We put ours in the garage, and in about 3 weeks they had all rotted. Probably the temperature went down below freezing. There are also several rot organisms which affect stored dahlia roots.

A short time after digging my dahlias the roots shriveled and became soft. What was the reason? They were dug after the first frost. You probably kept them in a warm place and thus dried them out too fast.

Why do my dahlia tubers sprout after storing? They were put away in peatmoss in the cellar. Storage place is too warm. Take care they are not near a heater. Temperature during storage should not be above 55° F.

My dahlia bulbs in storage are beginning to sprout. I have them packed in sand. Will this harm them? Not if it happens in spring when planting time is approaching. Sprouting in winter weakens roots and should be prevented by storage at 40° to 55°.

My dahlia bulbs were not dug this fall. Will they die? Snow is on ground now, and lowest temperature has been 5° above zero. They will not survive if the tubers are frozen.

Problems

What causes large dahlias to wilt as soon as cut? Large-flowered dahlias always wilt if cut during the day. Cut in late evening, well after the sun is down, or *very* early in the morning. Dipping ends of the stems in boiling water for 1 or 2 minutes has a tendency to keep the flowers fresh.

We have dahlias which never bloom. Does their age have anything to do with it? Not if they are healthy. Dahlia "stunt," a virus disease, and tarnished plant bug often prevent flowering.

Why do dahlias with large flowers have very thin stems? The excess buds were pinched out. Some varieties naturally have weak stems. Excess nitrogen and too little potash also cause this condition.

My dahlia garden is between two buildings. I get very good plants, but the frost kills the buds before they bloom. Is there any way to speed the blooming of dahlias? Your plants may not receive sufficient sun. Plants in shade tend to become soft and to bloom late. Possibly you have late-flowering varieties. These should be planted early.

Why do my dahlias have so many leaves and so few flowers? Probably because of too much shade, or too much fertilizer. Attention to pruning and disbudding may help.

Can Coltness Gem Dahlias be carried over from year to year? I want particular colors; otherwise the ease with which they are propagated from seeds would make winter storage foolish. Yes, treat the roots exactly as you do other dahlias.

Why do some dahlias, of varieties supposed to be tall, stay low? Very possibly because they are infected with mosaic disease or "stunt." Check with a skilled grower or with your State Agricultural Experiment Station. Destroy diseased plants.

One of my choice dahlias had no tubers this fall. Why? This may be because it received improper fertilization. There are some dahlias, particularly choice varieties, that are very poor root producers. If the plant was grown from a cutting made *between* the joints, it would bloom, but would not form tubers.

My dahlias make good growth and lots of flowers but never form tubers. What can I do to encourage the plants to grow large, plump bulbs that will keep over winter? Probably you use an unbalanced fertilizer. Excess nitrogen will cause the condition you describe. Try more potash and phosphate. (See preceding question.)

I planted dahlias, took great pains with them, and although they were very thrifty they did not flower. They bloomed last year. What is the cause? Lack of blooms may be caused by not enough sunshine, surface cultivation continued late in the season, too much nitrogenous fertilizer, insects or disease.

Some years my dahlias bloom; other years they don't. What is wrong? Weather conditions have some effect on the blooming of dahlias. If water is not supplied artificially, a dry season may cause poor blooming. See other questions.

How can I stop my dahlias from growing 9 ft. tall, with very little bloom? Probably too much shade, or fertilizer containing too much nitrogen. Allow only one main stalk to grow from each plant, disbranch, and disbud as described in other answers.

Why do my dahlias refuse to bloom? They have plenty of water

and fertilizer and are planted in good garden soil. They have southern exposure. The plants grow strongly but have few, poor blooms. Is the air circulation good? Dahlias should not be planted along the side of a house or close to a hedge. They may be infected with insects such as thrips, leaf hoppers, borers, or tarnished plant bug; or with mosaic or "stunt." Try a change of stock. Dahlias planted in same soil year after year sometimes deteriorate.

I have a dahlia that grows about 8 ft. tall and has lots of buds, but they never open up. Why? It grows lots of nice tubers. These symptoms are suggestive of tarnished plant bug injury.

What causes imperfect dahlia blooms? Diseases, as stunt; pests, as leaf hoppers, tarnished plant bug and thrips; unfavorable weather conditions.

Has anyone discovered the cause of the variation in color in some bicolored dahlias? The exact cause is not definitely known. Bicolored varieties seem to be particularly unstable and tend to run back to solid colors.

What dahlia has the record of growing to the greatest height? Complete records are probably not in existence. The tallest reported by a well-informed source is a plant of One Grand, 13 ft. in height.

Do the tubers of the Coltness Hybrid dahlias store successfully, and, if so, are the flowers as good? They do; and will bear good blooms when planted the following year.

For what particular purposes are dwarf dahlias suited? For decorative garden beds or borders, for providing cut flowers, and for exhibiting at flower shows.

I have heard that dahlia bulbs were used as a food. Is there any reason why they should not be so used; are they habit-forming or harmful in any way? According to the authoritative Sturtevant's *Notes on Edible Plants,* "it was first cultivated for its tubers, but these were found to be uneatable." It is reported that sugar can be made from them.

Propagation

How are dahlias propagated? By division of the clumps of roots; by cuttings; by seeds; and, much more rarely, by grafting.

How are dahlias increased by cuttings? Undivided clumps are planted in a cool greenhouse in January or February. Cuttings, each with sliver of tuber attached at the base, are prepared when shoots are 3 ins. or so long, and are inserted in a propagating bench (bottom heat 65°; atmosphere, 5° lower), or in a flat. Shade and a "close" atmosphere are supplied. When roots are an inch long, cuttings are potted up individually. Ordinary stem cuttings may also be used, but the basal cut should be made just below a node.

Can I increase my dahlias in the house by cuttings? It is scarcely practicable. They need rather special conditions, and for best results should be made early in the year when it is difficult to provide a correct environment in the average home.

What types of dahlias bloom the first year from seed? All types. The Coltness Hybrids and others that are grown chiefly for mass-color effects in the garden, rather than for perfection of their individual blooms, are the kinds most commonly raised from seeds.

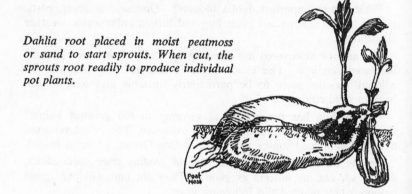

Dahlia root placed in moist peatmoss or sand to start sprouts. When cut, the sprouts root readily to produce individual pot plants.

How can I save seeds from my dahlias? After petals have fallen, allow the flower head to dry on the plant (wax paper or plastic is sometimes wrapped around heads so that they dry quicker). Gather heads before killing frost and place them in a dry cellar until they have fully dried out.

Do dahlias grown here (Mount Vernon, New York) have a long enough growing season to make good seeds? As a rule seeds saved from dahlias grown in the vicinity of New York are not fertile. The best seeds are produced in California, where the growing season is much longer.

How should dahlia seeds be started? Sow in pots or flats of light, sandy soil, February to March, in temperature of 60°. Transplant seedlings (when second pairs of leaves have developed) individually into small pots. Grow on in a sunny location, with temperature of 55°. When roots crowd small pots, replant into 4-in. pots.

Is it necessary to remove the tubers from seedling dahlias, and when? No; the small tubers are left on, and set out with the seedling plants.

How can I hybridize dahlias? Some large dahlia growers maintain beehives in their gardens, and the bees carry the pollen from plant to plant. Others employ hand pollination, which involves using a camel's-hair brush to transfer the pollen of one variety to the pistil of another.

How are new varieties of dahlias developed? They are selected from seedlings. Some responsible dahlia growers make a specialty of raising and selling dahlia seed saved from the leading exhibition varieties.

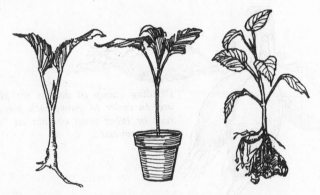

Left—dahlia cutting rooted, ready to pot up; right —dahlia seedling, ready for transplanting. (Note small tuber already beginning to form.)

How were the giant dahlias developed from smaller ones? By systematic breeding, based on hand cross-pollination, and by carefully selecting the most promising seedlings. This work has been carried on over a long period of years.

Can dahlias be divided immediately after they are dug in fall, or must they wait until spring when they are sprouted? Is any special instrument used for this purpose? It is better to wait until spring, when eyes are visible. Use any good, sharp knife with a stout, fairly long blade.

How should dahlia clumps be divided? By using a sharp knife and pruning shears. Each division of a clump should include a portion of the old stem attached to the neck of a tuber; on each should be a visible eye capable of developing into a sprout.

Is there any danger of dividing dahlias too much? Yes; unless you are experienced there is a danger of cutting into undeveloped eyes.

How can I divide dahlia bulbs when absolutely no eyes are visible? *Do not* divide until eyes appear. If clumps have a tendency to be slow in "eying up," put them in a flat with damp peatmoss and place near the furnace. This will cause eyes to develop in a few days. If eyes fail to appear, the stock is "blind" and will not produce plants.

Should each clump of dahlia roots be separated so as to plant only 1 root in a place? Yes. Be sure each division has an eye (bud) from which a shoot will develop.

Are dahlia bulbs which shrivel up after division any good? They will probably produce weak plants. After dahlia roots are divided, they should be kept in slightly damp peatmoss until planting time.

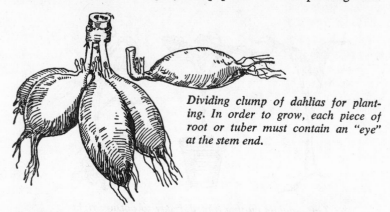

Dividing clump of dahlias for planting. In order to grow, each piece of root or tuber must contain an "eye" at the stem end.

How can I know a live dahlia tuber from one that will not grow, when dividing for spring planting? Roots that will grow possess eyes (buds) which usually appear on part of the stalk or old stem of the clump. Many clumps produce "blind" roots. These should not be planted.

Diseases and Pests

My dahlias are not growing well. I suspect mosaic disease. What are the symptoms? The plants are usually dwarfed; the leaves are smaller than normal and show a yellowish mosaic, or spotting. Pale-green bands are often developed along the midribs and larger secondary veins.

Is there any cure for mosaic disease of dahlias? No. Ruthlessly dig out and destroy affected plants. Under no circumstances propagate from them. Spray to control aphids, as they transmit the disease from plant to plant.

What is the cause of dahlia "stunt"? A temporary dwarfing, not carried over from year to year, may result from attacks of such insects as tarnished plant bugs, leaf hoppers, thrips, and aphids. Virus diseases may cause real stunting, which is not curable. Virus-infected plants should be promptly destroyed.

What is the recommended treatment for dahlia wilt disease? Two wilts attack dahlias—one caused by a fungus, the other by a bacterium. Destroy all affected plants. Use only healthy tubers for propagation. Move dahlias to new ground, or sterilize the soil with formaldehyde or chloropicrin.

How can I recognize and control red spider on dahlias? It is commonest in hot, dry weather. The leaves become yellowish or pale brown. With a hand lens the insects, usually covered with a fine web, can be seen crawling on the under sides of the leaves. Forcible spraying with clear water is helpful. Spray also with wettable sulfur. (See Red Spider.)

My dahlias are attacked by small bugs that jump off the leaves when disturbed. The leaves are turning yellow and becoming brittle. No holes appear in the leaves. What is insect, and what remedy do you suggest? This is leaf hopper. Spray at weekly intervals with a pyrethrum, DDT, or all-purpose spray. Keep all weeds cut down in vicinity.

I have had a lot of trouble with corn borers in dahlias. How can I check their ravages? Spray or dust twice a week with DDT or rotenone from August to October inclusive. Pick off infested blooms. Burn old stalks at end of season. (See Corn Borer.)

Does more than one kind of borer attack dahlias? Yes. The common stalk borer hatches out in May, eats a hole in the stem, and usually remains until August. Watch for holes in stems and probe with fine wire to kill borers. Destroy all coarse weeds in the vicinity.

I have found large shell-less snails eating dahlia flowers. Can I do anything other than hand-pick? Clean up all rubbish and debris. Slugs hide under stones, bricks, boards, etc., during the day. Spread poison bait around. (See Slugs.)

Varieties

What are the names of some of the leading varieties of large-flowering dahlias? New Look, Director Carl G. Dahl, Jane Cowl, Lois Walcher, Mrs. Geo. Le Boutillier, Murphy's Masterpiece, Sunrays, Volcano, and Yellow Glory.

Can you recommend some good exhibition dahlias? Jane Cowl, Jack of Hearts, Fanny Levy, Florence M., Murphy's Masterpiece, Sunrays, Maffie, Crowning Glory, Alabaster and The Real Glory.

What are some good varieties of miniature dahlias? Easter Greeting, Elsie, Gertrude, Kate, Marie, Park Yellow, Tacita, Red Head, Sunburst, Coltness Hybrids and Unwin Dwarfs.

Can you name a dozen good pompon dahlias? Atom, Betty Ann, Betty Malone, Dot, Ebony, Little Edith, Little Herman, Little Red Wing, Little Snow White, Morning Mist, Sherry.

What are 2 or 3 of the best dahlias for cut flowers? Jersey Beauty, Bishop of Llandaff, Newport Wonder, Dr. J. Beyer, Venita.

Is there a definite trend toward small-flowering varieties of dahlias?
Yes; largely because they require less space and less attention in regard to disbranching, disbudding, and staking. In many ways they are more useful than the large-flowering types both in the garden and as cut flowers. They are listed in catalogues as "miniature" dahlias.

EUCHARIS (AMAZONLILY)

Will you give me the recommended method of growing the Amazonlily? *Eucharis grandiflora* bulbs should be planted, several together, in large pots containing rich, well-drained, fibrous soil. Avoid repotting unless necessary. Give temperature of 65° to 75° F., plenty of moisture when growing, and shade from bright sun. Foliage is evergreen, so plants should never be dried off completely.

FREESIA

What conditions are necessary for growing freesias successfully?
Well-drained but fertile soil; strict care in matter of watering; cool (45° to 55° F.), airy, growing conditions; and fullest possible exposure to sunshine. Sound, healthy bulbs of fair size are a prerequisite.

What is the secret of watering freesias? When first potted, give thorough soaking; place in cool situation; and cover with several inches of moss or leaves. When growth starts, remove moss, and water to keep soil only just moist. Gradually increase supply of water as leaves develop, and water generously when well rooted and in full growth. After blooming, water freely until foliage begins to fade, then gradually reduce, and finally withhold water entirely.

Do freesias need a high temperature? Quite the contrary. They thrive best where the night temperature does not exceed 45° or 50°, with a daytime rise of 5° to 10° permitted.

How shall I fertilize freesias grown in pots in winter? Mix bone meal with potting soil. When flower buds begin to show, feed at weekly intervals with dilute liquid cow manure. Vary this occasionally by using a good complete fertilizer.

My freesias grew at first, but before they were very high they died, and green scum grew on top of soil. What was the cause? Poor drainage, overwatering, or both. Freesias abhor too much water during their early stages of growth.

GLADIOLI

The gladiolus species, from which the modern garden varieties have been developed, grow wild along the shores of the Mediterranean Sea and in South Africa. The true species are of little significance as garden plants. The flowers are small, the colors often harsh, and the forms uninspiring. It is a far cry from the unattractive wild-lings to the glorious flower we know today as the gladiolus.

Always popular as a specialist's flower, particularly with men, the gladiolus now takes its place beside the rose, the camellia and the iris in that an All America Gladiolus Selections Committee has come into being (1956) to test and study new varieties and to grant each year awards to those considered most outstanding. The first variety so honored was Royal Stewart in 1956.

The ease with which gladioli can be grown anywhere in the United States undoubtedly contributes to their popularity. They are not particular in their soil requirements. They do well in warm exposures. While they tolerate neglect better than many other plants, they also respond to good treatment. Of upright growth, they require little room, so that large quantities of flowers can be produced in a limited area. They are therefore ideal for small gardens.

Usually they are grown in beds or in rows in the cutting garden. However, if combined with other plants in the mixed border they will add much color interest. Gladioli are more important as cut flowers than as decorative garden plants. They keep exceptionally well, and the form of the spike is especially well adapted for use in various types of arrangements.

Soil and Fertilizer

Do gladioli take the strength out of the soil? I have 20 acres on which gladioli have been planted for the last 2 years, but the soil has been fertilized each time they were planted. Gladioli do not exhaust the soil, particularly if fertilizer is used, but repeated growing of "glads" in the same soil may result in an increase in prevalence of disease, and this may make bulbs unsalable.

I am interested in raising gladiolus bulbs. Does the soil have to be very fertile for best results? Fertile, but not excessively rich.

What is your suggestion for the best fertilizer to be used for gladioli? A 4–10–5 mixture. Avoid animal manures, as they are apt to cause disease in the corms.

Which fertilizer shall I use when I plant gladioli in my flower border? Providing the soil is in good condition, almost any complete fertilizer will be satisfactory. Bone meal and unleached wood ashes mixed together are excellent. Avoid fresh manure; leafmold and of course commercial fertilizers are satisfactory.

What type soil should "glads" have to be most successful? A well-drained, sandy loam in which gladioli have not been grown for the past 3 years.

Will "glads" grow in sandy soil? Fine specimens can be grown in sandy soil if enough moisture is supplied.

Planting

How am I to pick out the right kind of gladiolus bulbs to plant?
Best for planting are clean No. 1 bulbs, or corms 1½ ins. or more
in diameter, with small scars, which proves they were grown from
small corms. Very large, flat corms are less desirable than moderate-
sized ones with greater depth.

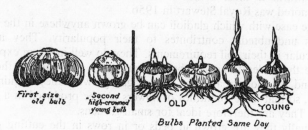

First size old bulb   *Second "high-crowned" young bulb*   OLD   YOUNG

Bulbs Planted Same Day

Gladioli corms: small, "high-crowned" young
corms are preferable to larger-sized, old flat ones.

Do gladioli prefer sun all day, or partial shade? Full sun, although they can be grown in partial shade.

How early can "glads" be set out? As soon as frost is out of the
ground. Little is gained by extra-early planting, and sometimes later
plantings bloom first.

When is best time to plant gladioli; and how deep? Make first
planting about May 1, and follow with successional plantings up to
early July. Set corms 4 to 6 ins. deep.

Trench method of planting gladioli: corms are set
in deep furrow (with fertilizer mixed with soil in
bottom) and the trench is gradually filled in—
thus smothering small weeds—as the plants grow.

**When should I plant "glads" to bloom in September and mid-
October?** Between June 15 and July 1.

**Will the flowers of late "glads" be as large as if the bulbs were
planted early?** Late flowers should be larger than early ones of the
same variety, because cool nights produce larger flowers and better
color in gladioli.

How deep do you advise planting gladioli; and how far apart in rows? Four ins. deep in heavy soil and 5 to 6 ins. in light, sandy soil. Three ins. apart is close enough in the rows for good spikes. Space rows 18 to 30 ins. apart.

What is the best method for planting gladioli? In rows, like vegetables. They can then be given better care and will produce better spikes.

Can gladiolus bulbs be planted too closely to each other? The old rule is to plant the diameter of the corms apart, but small sizes, at least, should be given more room.

Is it advisable to cut large gladiolus corms in two when planting? How deep should the cormels be planted? They can be cut in two providing each piece has part of the root base and an eye; little can be gained by so doing, however. Cormels should be planted about 2 ins. deep.

The gladiolus bulbs which I planted along the borders of my shrubbery failed to grow well. What is wrong? Gladioli are not able to compete successfully with the roots of strong-growing trees and shrubs. Try planting in well-prepared soil away from the influence of roots.

Can gladiolus corms be used after not having been planted one year? Gladiolus corms are of little use the second year; but bulblets are still good the second year, and those of hard-to-sprout varieties grow better then.

Culture

What is the best way of supporting "glads" so they do not fall over? Tie to individual slender stakes, or place stakes at intervals along both sides of the rows and stretch strings from stake to stake. Hilling up soil around the bases of the stems is also helpful.

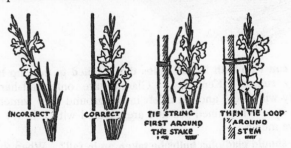

Method of staking gladiolus spike to prevent injury by wind.

Do "glads" need much watering? The soil must be well drained, but they need an abundance of moisture, and if the season is at all dry they should be watered liberally, particularly after the sixth or seventh leaf begins to develop.

How are gladiolus bulbs grown to such mammoth sizes as 4 to 5 ins. in diameter? Some varieties under good conditions make 4- and 5-in. corms, but a good, thick 1½-in. corm is more satisfactory.

Do gladiolus bulbs need to be taken up every year? They are killed by freezing, and so should be dug and stored in a cool, dry cellar over winter.

How can I keep my late "glads" from sprouting? To keep your corms from sprouting store them in a cool, dry, dark place, in slatted or screen-bottom trays. The temperature should be evenly maintained, at as near 40° as possible.

Taking up gladioli for winter storage. Plants are loosened in the soil, pulled up gently to save the cormels, and placed in flats to dry before cleaning. Tops may be cut off just above corms to save space.

What can I do with "glad" bulbs that I failed to take up last fall? Are they ruined? (Kentucky.) Gladioli are only half-hardy and ordinarily will freeze and rot if left in the ground over winter, unless they are in a well-drained soil and are covered with a heavy layer of protective mulch.

When should gladiolus bulbs be taken up in fall? When the leaves start to turn brown. A good new corm is formed 6 weeks after blooming.

When is it best to take up gladioli, and what is the proper way to keep them—in a basement; in sand, or in earth? Lift with a fork after the first frost, taking care not to damage the corms, and store not over 2 or 3 corms deep in trays in the basement. Do not cover with sand or earth.

Should gladiolus corms be trimmed close before storing?   The tops should be cut off close to the corm at digging time. The husk should never be removed while in storage, as it helps the corm to retain its moisture.

How can I store gladiolus bulbs to keep them from shrinking and drying out in winter?   If stored in a cool cellar, they will not shrink or dry out.

What about temperature for "glads" in winter?   The ideal temperature is 40°. Never allow them to freeze.

Problems

Will a light frost on gladiolus bulbs ruin them; and how can I tell if they are still all right?   A light frost will not harm the corms. If they are badly frosted, they will dry out and become very light in weight.

How does one develop larger gladiolus bulbs for larger blooms instead of having the bulbs multiply? Where 1 bulb is planted, 2 or 3 grow from it, all about the same small size.   To prevent gladiolus corms from splitting all the eyes but one may be cut out before planting. However this is a practice seldom resorted to.

Why do gladiolus bulbs produce large blooms one year and none or very poor ones the next?   Possibly your bulbs were dug too soon after blooming, or perhaps you cut the stems too low when picking flowers. Corm diseases or thrip may be factors.

Why do glad bulbs keep getting smaller from year to year?   Too-early digging; taking too much foliage when flowers are cut; or poor growing conditions.

Why do my gladiolus bulbs exhaust themselves within 2 or 3 years and produce inferior blooms?   Varieties vary greatly in this respect; some will produce good spikes for a number of years, others for only a single season. Gladiolus scab is often responsible.

What makes my gladiolus flower stems develop crooked necks?   Not all varieties of gladioli "crook," but those which do should be planted so that they bloom in the cool weather of fall.

How can I prevent my gladiolus bulbs from becoming flat, rather than high-crowned?   A high crown was at one time considered a mark of perfection, but Picardy and its children are never high-crowned, and there are few good "glads" today not related to Picardy.

Will small "glad" bulbs, such as No. 6 size, bloom the first season if planted early enough?   No. 6 size corms of most varieties will bloom, although the spikes will be short and the flowers few.

I have 200 gladiolus seeds planted and they have grown 8 ins. tall and have fallen over. They look healthy. Will they be all right? Gladioli, the first year from seed, look like grass. They should form small, mature corms in about 12 weeks.

Why don't gladioli bloom all at one time? Blooming time varies according to the size of the corms and the variety. A large bulb of Maid of Orleans will bloom in 60 days, and a small bulb of Bagdad, a late variety, will take 150 days.

Are gladioli true to color? They normally come true to color, although color sports often appear among the smoky shades.

Why did my assorted-color gladioli all turn yellow after the first year? Gladioli do not normally change color. Your yellow-flowered kind must be a robust variety and the only one to survive.

What makes gladioli of different colors gradually change to one color after a few years? Many people think that gladioli change color. What actually happens is that the more robust-growing varieties in a mixture outlive and out-multiply the weaker-growing ones.

My gladiolus bulbs end up with a growth on the bottom. Is this natural, or is it a disease? If so, what is the treatment? Gladioli in growing form new corms on the tops of the old ones; the old corms remain attached to the bases of the new ones; they are easily removed 3 or 4 weeks after digging. Often a cluster of tiny cormels grow from the base of the new corm.

Propagation

What is the best way to increase gladioli? By saving and planting the small bulblets that form around the large corms.

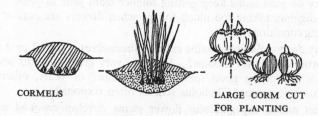

CORMELS   LARGE CORM CUT
FOR PLANTING

The cormels, planted early in spring, like peas, produce by autumn small corms, some of which usually flower the following year. Right—large old corms, with more than one sprout, can be cut before planting, to increase stock of a favorite variety.

How are gladiolus bulbs raised from many small bulbs that develop on each large one? The small corms are stored through the winter, and are planted in rows in well-prepared soil much as are larger corms (except that they are not set so deeply). They are then grown on to flowering size.

What is the best way to get gladiolus bulblets to sprout quickly and evenly? Soak them in tepid water for 2 or 3 days, before planting. Also plant them as closely together as 20 to the foot as they seem to like company.

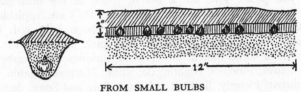

FROM SMALL BULBS

Small gladioli corms are planted out in nursery rows, to grow on into flowering-sized bulbs for another year.

In the propagation of "glads," what is the procedure of handling the bulblets or cormlets gathered from old bulbs, until the next planting season? Treat them with flake napthalene, and store in a cool, dry place in an open crate.

How are new varieties of gladioli developed? They are raised from seeds. Most improvements are obtained from seeds collected from hand-pollinated flowers.

How can "glads" be raised from seeds? Plant them in a light, friable soil in an outdoor bed early in spring, while the ground is still cool. Sow the seeds rather thinly in shallow drills, spaced so a cultivator can be used between them. Cover about ¼ in. deep. Corms the size of a pea or smaller should develop the first year, and most of these will bloom the second year.

Pests and Diseases

Should gladiolus bulbs be treated before planting? Certain fungous and bacterial diseases are sometimes carried on the corms. If these are suspected, disinfect by soaking for 20 minutes, just before planting, in a solution of 1 part mercuric chloride in 1,000 parts of water, by weight. Rinse thoroughly in clear water immediately before planting.

What should be done to stop wireworms from damaging gladiolus bulbs? Wireworms are usually bad only in newly made gardens, or where trash is allowed to accumulate. (For control, see Section VIII.)

How can I check the ravages of cutworms among my gladioli? Clean the ground of all weeds and other unwanted growth in fall. Use a poison bait. (See Cutworms, Section VIII.)

What is the most satisfactory method of combating gladiolus thrips?
In fall after corms are dug, dust with 5% DDT or with malathion
dust. In spring when plants are 6 inches high, spray or dust every
10 days with the same.

Varieties

**Will you please give me a list of some of the best gladiolus
varieties?** A.A.G.S. Selections for 1957 and 1958 are Appleblossom,
white flushed pink; Royal Stewart, very large light red; Carib-
bean, blue-violet, Maytime, ruffled deep pink and Emperor, rose-
purple with a white blotch. Other good varieties are Elizabeth the
Queen, mauve; Florence Nightingale, white; Margaret Beaton, white,
scarlet throat; Picardy, flesh; Red Wings; Spic and Span, deep pink;
Vagabond Prince, mahogany and bronze; and Voodoo, smoky.

What are the uses of Miniature Glads? Please name a few varieties.
Miniatures are generally useful in mixed border plantings and espe-
cially as cut flowers. They are more informal than the standard
varieties and the spikes are more graceful for use in arrangements.
BoPeep, salmon-pink Loveliness, shrimp pink; Golden Frills and
Little Gold; Massasoit, crimson; Atom, vermillion with white picotee;
Starlit and Snow Baby, white; Pint Size, lavender.

GLORIOSA

Can gloriosas be grown out of doors in summer? Yes. Plant
strong tubers in pots of light, humusy soil in March or April.
Transfer started plants to sunny border after all danger of frost has
passed. Place stakes or brushwood for support. Dig up tubers in
fall and store in dry sand or peatmoss through winter, in temperature
between 50° and 60° F.

HAEMANTHUS

Are haemanthus adapted for growing indoors? They are both
interesting and beautiful as house plants or greenhouse plants. Some
of the best are _katharinae, coccineus, multiflorus,_ and _albiflos._

How should I care for Bloodlilies (haemanthus)? Water freely
when leaves are in evidence; keep dry at other times. Give full sunshine, well-drained soil, and repot every 3 or 4 years at beginning of
growing season. Feed when in active leaf growth. Temperature 50°
to 60° F.

HEDYCHIUM (GINGERLILY)

**Is the Gingerlily (hedychium) adaptable for growing outdoors in
the North?** Only in sheltered, warm situations, and then the roots
must be lifted in fall and stored in sand in a frostproof cellar over
winter. Plant outdoors after all danger of frost has passed, and give
abundance of water when growing.

HYDROSME (SNAKEPALM)

Can snakepalm—the one that has a flower like a big purplish callalily, and a huge, finely cut umbrella leaf—be grown outdoors in summer? Yes, and its foliage is both distinctive and decorative. Plant in good soil in sun or light shade and it will quickly grow. Its name is *Hydrosme rivieri*.

ISMENE (PERUVIAN-DAFFODIL)

How can I raise Ismene calathina? Plant out after ground is warm, weather is settled, and all danger of frost has passed, in sunny, well-drained border in fertile soil. Cover to depth of 3 times the diameter of the bulb. Dig after first frost; remove foliage and store *with fleshy basal roots intact* at a temperature of about 60 degrees.

I planted Peruvian-daffodils—bulbs as large as those of amaryllis. On taking up this November, the bulbs were very much smaller. Why was this? Unsatisfactory cultural conditions. Soil perhaps too heavy, or not fertile. They probably will not bloom so well next year.

Should Ismene calathina (Peruvian-daffodil) be stored in dry sand over winter, or left spread out? Either way is satisfactory. It should be kept in temperature of at least 50° F.

IXIAS

Will you give me cultural directions for ixias and sparaxis? Read answers under "Freesia." Ixias and sparaxis need exactly the same treatment.

LACHENALIA (CAPECOWSLIP)

Will you give me the detailed cultural needs of lachenalias (Cape-cowslips)? Plant bulbs close together in early fall, in pots or hanging baskets containing light soil. Treat same as freesias.

Which varieties of lachenalias would you recommend to a beginner? *Pendula* (red and yellow); *tricolor* (red, yellow, and green); *tricolor nelsoni* (yellow); and *roodeae* (blue).

LEUCOCORYNE (GLORY-OF-THE-SUN)

What is Glory-of-the-sun, and how is it grown? A tender, bulbous plant from the uplands of Chile named *Leucocoryne ixioides odorata*. It is handled indoors like freesias. Avoid high temperatures and grow in sunny, airy situation. Blooms late winter and spring.

LYCORIS RADIATA

I have 3 bulbs of Lycoris radiata in a pot in the house. They have been potted since September. Why haven't they bloomed? Is there anything I can do to encourage bloom? *Lycoris radiata* often passes its bloom season. July and August are best months to plant these. Work a tablespoonful of bone meal for each bulb into the surface soil.

MONTBRETIAS

Will you describe culture of montbretias?   They need essentially the same care as gladioli. They are, however, rather hardier, and in favored places may be left in ground over winter if given a very heavy mulch.

OXALIS

How should one grow the tender kinds of oxalis bulbs?   Pot during August in light, fertile soil. Space bulbs 2 or 3 ins. apart just below surface. Water carefully at first; freely when growth has developed. Give plenty of sunshine; temperature of 50° to 60° F. Feed when pots are filled with roots. After flowering, gradually reduce water, and finally dry completely and rest.

POLIANTHES (TUBEROSE)

Will you give me some information on tuberoses? (Washington, D.C.)   Purchase good bulbs of tuberose (*Polianthes tuberosa*), plant outdoors in light soil that is fertile, after ground has warmed up. Lift in fall, and store dry in temperature of 60° F.

RANUNCULUS

Ranunculus bulbs sent from California arrived after ground was frozen. Can I successfully plant them in spring? How should I treat them during winter?   Store in dry sand or peatmoss in cool but frostproof cellar or shed. Plant 2 ins. deep, 6 ins. apart, as soon as ground can be worked in spring. Make soil friable with plenty of leafmold and sand. Position should be moist and lightly shaded. Tuberous-rooted varieties are dug and stored through winter.

SCHIZOSTYLIS (KAFIRLILY)

Will you give me instructions for growing the Kafirlily (schizostylis) in New Jersey?   Plant in spring in well-prepared, light, fertile soil in a deep cold frame. Keep sash off in summer, but protect in fall and winter. Water freely during growing season.

SPREKELIA (JACOBEANLILY)

In California I saw a lily called Jacobeanlily that looked like a curious crimson orchid. What is it? How can one grow it?   *Sprekelia formosissima* (sometimes sold as *Amaryllis formosissima*). Plant bulbs 6 ins. deep in light, fertile loam, in a sunny position. Water freely when foliage is above ground. In cold climates mulch heavily; or lift and store bulbs through winter; remove tops, but *leave roots on*.

I bought Amaryllis formosissima bulbs that bloomed well the first year. The next 2 years I planted some in semi-shade, and in sun, yet they don't bloom. I take them up every winter and store them in a cool place. Bulbs look good. Why don't they bloom? They need a very fertile soil. When you dig them in fall, remove tops but leave roots on. Leave in ground until after first frost.

TIGRIDIA

What soil and situation do tigerflowers (tigridias) prefer? A warm, well-drained soil and a sunny situation. Plant same time as gladioli. Take up and store in same way.

OTHER BULBS

I understand there are a number of South African bulbs that need very much the same treatment as freesias. Will you please list some of these? Ixia, sparaxis, babiana, antholyza, tritonia, crocosmia, lapeirousia, ornithogalum, and lachenalia.

What is the best way of propagating ixias, sparaxis, tritonias, and similar South African or "Cape" bulbs? They all multiply quickly by offsets. These can be removed and planted in bulb pans, about an inch apart, at potting time. They are also very readily raised from seed.

SECTION III-C

Roses

INTRODUCTION

BY F. F. ROCKWELL

ROSES ARE so closely associated with the painting, literature, music, and even the politics of the world that they have for many centuries been an integral part of our culture. The rose is the very symbol of beauty and loveliness. Since the dawn of history it has been admired, appreciated, and linked with all kinds of human activities. It would be difficult to find an individual who could not recognize a rose—the best known and most loved of all our cultivated plants, and truly the "queen of flowers." Its majestic form, gorgeous colorings, and delightful perfume are unsurpassed. Even the thorns command respect. It is the standard of perfection by which all other flowers are judged.

More than 200 species of wild roses have been described and named by botanists. They are distributed from the Arctic Circle to the equator, and there are types that will thrive in any climate. Few flowers have received so much attention by plant breeders and few have exhibited such potentialities for development. The number of varieties that have been introduced is almost limitless; in the United States alone nearly 5,000 different species and varieties are available.

Contrary to widely held opinions, roses are not difficult to grow. Their presence around long-deserted houses is evidence of their tenacity. A judicious selection of types and varieties and an understanding of their cultural requirements will enable anyone to grow roses successfully.

Many new home owners harbor the mistaken idea that roses are specialists' plants, and that the beginning gardener, with very limited space at his disposal, would do well not to attempt growing them—except of course, for the ubiquitous Climber or two at the front door or along a fence.

It is quite true that such roses are better than none at all, but no true flower lover will—or should—be content until he has in his garden at least a half dozen or so of the modern bush roses to provide flowers for enjoyment both in the garden and as cut flower decoration indoors.

The often-heard argument that roses "require so much care" scarcely seems to hold when one considers that the modern garden varieties give flowers almost continuously from late May into October or November, while most other hardy flowers are in bloom for little more than two or three weeks. And many of the splendid new varieties developed during the last decade or two, especially in Floribunda and the new Grandiflora groups, have remarkable vigor and hardiness. The development of improved "all-purpose" controls for insect pests and diseases has greatly simplified rose culture for the amateur and gone far to assure success even to the least experienced beginner, so we have really reached the day when there should be roses in *every* garden.

SELECTING PLANTS

What are the main types or classes of roses?   1, tea; 2, hybrid tea; 3, hybrid perpetual; 4, polyantha; 5, hybrid or large-flowered polyantha (floribunda); 6, grandiflora; 7, baby (miniature); 8, climber; 9, shrub.

What do the abbreviations HT., HP., etc. used after rose varieties mean?   They indicate the class to which the variety belongs: HT.—hybrid tea; HP.—hybrid perpetual; Pol. (Poly)—polyantha; HPol.—hybrid polyantha (floribunda); Cl—climber; R.—rambler; CHT.—climbing hybrid tea; T.—tea.

What are the standard rose grades?   No. 1. Three or more strong canes 18 ins. or more long; No. 1½. Two or more strong canes at least 14 ins. long; No. 2. Two or more canes at least 12 ins. long; No. 3. One cane with few or no branches.

What age plants should be purchased?   Two-year-old field-grown plants are best for planting in the garden. The actual age, however, is of less importance than the size. The largest plants, known as the No. 1 grade, usually give the best results.

Is it advantageous to buy climbing roses that are 5 or 6 years old?   No. In fact, a younger plant, 1 to 2 years old, becomes established sooner and is more successful.

Are cheap roses offered by nurseries a good investment?   Usually not. They are likely to be undersized plants, held too long in storage; or they may be "bench" roses from a greenhouse which have been forced for a year or more. As with everything else, you get what you pay for.

Should one buy budded or own-root stock when planting a rose garden? Approximately 99 per cent of the rose plants sold are budded stock. Good own-root plants are more difficult to obtain, and they are slower to become established. A few varieties may prove more satisfactory on their own roots.

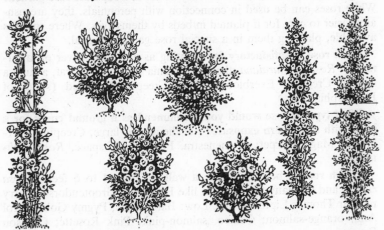

Types of roses: left, Climbing Hybrid Tea; center top, Hybrid Perpetual and Polyantha; center bottom, Hybrid Tea and Floribunda; right, Large-flowered Climber and Rambler.

Are Southern-grown rose plants as hardy as those grown in the North? In general, yes. Northern-grown plants can usually be planted earlier in the fall than those from the South, and therefore have a little better chance to become established.

PLANNING

What roses will be satisfactory in semi-shade? Roses need at least 8 hours of full sunlight per day. The hybrid teas, polyanthas, and floribundas do well in semi-shade; in fact, are better if they have a little shade during the hot part of the day.

Will a climbing rose do well on the northeast corner of a house? Such a situation would be unfavorable. It would be better to use a clematis, honeysuckle, or other vine that can get along with less sunlight.

Should rose plants be grouped together, or placed in separate parts of the yard? The best effects will be achieved if grouped, or, better still, planted in beds. The large shrub roses may be planted with other flowering shrubs. The climbing varieties need the support of fences, arbors, walls, or posts.

What flowers can be combined with roses in a rose garden?   Lilies, delphiniums, pansies, peonies, irises, tulips, daffodils, forget-me-nots, etc., can be used. A border of low growing flowers like pansies or sweet alyssum, edging the rose beds, is often the most satisfactory use of other flowers in combination with roses.

Will it be satisfactory to transplant some old rosebushes to a corner of a perennial garden, or should they be set in a separate rose garden? While roses can be used in connection with perennials, they are usually easier to care for if planted in beds by themselves. Where space is available, planting them in a special rose garden is ideal.

What rose is satisfactory for planting as a ground cover on a terrace?   *Rosa wichuraiana,* the Wichuriania Rose; Max Graf, a rugosa hybrid; Creeping Everbloom; Coral Creeper; Mermaid (south of Philadephia).

What type of rose would you recommend as a ground cover for a bank with a southern exposure?   If the area is large, Creeping Everbloom; Magic Carpet; Clymenestra. For a small space, *Rosa wichuraiana.*

Which rose is best to border a walk?   Tall (4 to 6 feet): *Rosa rugosa* and its many fine hybrids like Flamingo; Grootendorst, cherry red; Sir Thomas Lipton, white. Low: Baby Blaze; Pygmy Gold; Carol Ann, orange-salmon; Cameo, salmon-pink; Pink Rosette; Crimson Rosette.

I have a low rock retaining wall in front of my house that is 175 ft. long. Should roses be planted on the inside, which is on a level with the yard, or on the outside, so they would have the wall for support? Plant on the inside so the rose stems may overhang the wall.

What rose varieties would you suggest for a low rock retaining wall? (Kansas.)   *Rosa wichuraiana* and Max Graf, *Rosa rugosa repens alba.*

What type of roses are best for a week-end summer home?   Shrub roses like Fruehling's Gold, Mabelle Stearns, The Fairy; Belinda; Lipstick, Flamingo, Nearly Wild and Harison's Yellow. These are all iron-hardy and resistant to neglect and plant troubles.

Can I have Climbers which bloom every month like Hybrid Teas? (Northern New York)   Climbing Hybrid Teas are not hardy with you. Among newer, hardy everblooming climbers are Golden Showers; Dr. Nicholas, pink; Inspiration, pink; Parade, rose-red.

What roses are suitable for the rock garden?   Any of the Miniature or Baby Roses which are tiny Hybrid Teas growing only a few inches tall. For the large rock garden, Charlie McCarthy, China Doll, Carol Ann and Pinkie, all 18 inches.

What roses can I plant for very early bloom? *Rosa hugonis* and *R. rugosa* hybrid Sir Thomas Lipton.

SOIL

What type of soil is best suited to roses? While any productive garden soil can be improved to grow good roses, the ideal type is a well-aerated, slightly acid, medium heavy loam containing an abundance of organic matter.

What kind of soil is best for climbing roses? Climbing roses do well in a wide variety of soils. The ideal type is a moderately rich, well-drained garden loam that is high in organic matter and slightly acid in reaction.

Is it necessary to have a clay soil for success with roses? Not at all. Some of the best rose gardens are found in regions where the soil is light and sandy. Almost any type of soil may be improved for roses by proper treatment.

Can roses be grown in light, sandy soil if clay is added? The clay will have very little beneficial effect. The sandy soil may be improved by adding some form of organic matter, such as peatmoss, well-rotted manure, or leafmold.

What special treatments do roses growing in a sandy soil require? Working into the soil an abundance of organic material; watering during dry periods; and 2 or 3 applications of a mixed commercial fertilizer during the growing season.

What is the treatment for roses when soil is alkaline? (Texas.) Roses require a slightly acid soil—pH 5.5 to 6.5. Sulfur and alum are used to acidify soils, and the amounts required will vary with the free lime present. Apply 5 lbs. of sulfur per 100 sq. ft., *and check the* pH after 2 or 3 months. As much as 30 lbs. of sulfur per 100 sq. ft. *may* be needed; 10 to 20 lbs. is more frequently required in very alkaline soil.

Is a gravel soil good for roses? While it is not an ideal type it can be made satisfactory by incorporating organic material.

Do roses like wet or dry feet? Roses require good drainage. If water tends to stand around the plants, they should be moved to another location, or tile drains installed, if the condition is very serious. However, wet areas can oftentimes be improved by breaking up the subsoil, mixing coarse cinders with it, raising the level of the bed, and —if the soil is heavy on top—mixing in screened cinders to ⅓ the volume of soil.

Do old rose beds wear out? This is a serious problem and the answer is not well understood. It is often observed that roses planted in virgin soil do much better than in old beds. Just why is not known, but there may be a number of contributing factors, such as disease infestation, changes in the chemical and biological composition of the soil, etc.

PREPARING THE SOIL

How deep should the soil be prepared for a rose bed?   Experiments have shown that the deeper the soil is prepared the more vigorous the growth and the greater the production of flowers. However, it is questionable whether preparing the soil deeper than 18 ins. is worth while. Twelve ins. is considered the minimum.

What method should be followed in preparing a soil mixture for roses?   When a new bed is being prepared, dig the soil out to a depth of approximately 18 ins., keeping the topsoil and subsoil separate. Next put back a 6-in. layer of the topsoil in the bottom of the bed. Add 3 ins. old manure, peatmoss, or other type of organic material; fork it in thoroughly. Shovel in another 6-in. layer, and work in more organic matter; last, fill the bed with the subsoil mixed with more organic matter.

How may one prepare the soil for individual plants set in to fill out a bed?   Dig a hole large enough to accommodate the plant. Mix the required amount of peatmoss with the soil that was removed, and use the mixture to fill in around the plant.

Can the soil be made too rich for roses?   Yes. For example, too much nitrogen may be harmful and injure the roots; too much potash may cause a hard, stunted type of growth.

What is meant by "trenching" in connection with rose planting?   Trenching is the term used for the practice of digging a trench (a bed) 18 ins. or more deep and filling it in with especially prepared soil in which the rose plants are set.

Should lime be used on roses?   Only if the soil test shows the need for it. (See Soil Testing.)

How much lime should be used to correct an acid soil?   If a test shows that the soil has a pH value of 5 or lower, lime should be incorporated. Ground limestone (not hydrated lime) is best for the average garden because there is less danger of applying too much. Use the ground limestone; or common agricultural lime, at the rate of 3 to 6 lbs. per 100 sq. ft. of ground area, depending upon the degree of acidity.

Do roses want acid soil?   A slightly acid soil is considered optimum. Roses will tolerate a somewhat wider range of reaction if the soil contains a high percentage of organic material. Roses do best if pH value of the soil is 5.5 to 6.5.

Why will roses not do well in a sweet or alkaline soil?   The iron in an alkaline soil is insoluble, and thus is unavailable to the plants.

All garden plants require iron to form chlorophyll (the green coloring matter in the leaves); absorption of iron is interfered with in a highly alkaline soil.

What is the appearance of rose plants when the soil is too sweet or alkaline?   The veins of the leaves become dark green and the areas between mottled with yellow. In severe cases, the leaves may become almost pure white.

If the soil is sweet (alkaline), what can be done to make it slightly acid?   Such a soil may be made slightly acid by mixing in finely powdered sulfur. If the pH value is 8, use 6 lbs. per 100 sq. ft.; pH 7.5, 3 lbs.; pH 7, 1 lb. Have the soil tested after 2 months to make sure it has become slightly acid.

Is peatmoss useful for acidifying soil?   Peatmoss, if used in large enough quantities, will temporarily increase the acidity of the soil. Its effect, however, is not permanent, since the peatmoss-soil mixture gradually returns to nearly the pH value of the original soil. If the soil is neutral, or only slightly acid, the use of peatmoss will be found very satisfactory. It improves the mechanical condition of the soil as well.

Can aluminum sulfate be used to acidify soil for roses?   Aluminum sulfate is less desirable than powdered sulfur. It is more expensive, less easy to obtain, and more has to be used. If large quantities are applied, there is danger of the aluminum being harmful.

Is it a good idea to put tile under a rose bed for subirrigation?   If the subsoil is heavy, the method usually works satisfactorily; if the subsoil is porous, it will not work. Four-in. tile is used and is laid 12 ins. below the surface.

IMPROVING SOILS

How should a hard-packed soil be treated?   A soil that packs very hard is usually the heavy type. Working in organic material, especially peatmoss, will make it more friable.

How can a very loose, porous soil be improved?   Such soils are often lacking in nutrients and require additional fertilizer. Watering during dry periods will improve the growth and quality of the flowers. Permanent improvement can only be brought about by incorporating plenty of organic matter.

What should be done to soil that does not hold enough moisture?   Add organic material. Peatmoss is the best, but leafmold and well-rotted manure may be used. Water beds thoroughly during dry periods.

How can a red clay soil be improved for roses? (Georgia.)   Incorporating Georgia Peat, or a combination of the peat and well-rotted manure will improve such a soil.

FERTILIZER

When is the best time to fertilize roses? Fertilizer is most effective if applied in the early spring, when the new growth is about 4 ins. long.

How often do roses need fertilizer? If the soil has been well prepared, 1 to 2 applications yearly are usually sufficient. If the soil is light, low in organic matter, and not very fertile, 3 to 4 applications, at monthly intervals, are desirable. In wet seasons more fertilization is needed than in dry ones.

Is fertilizer put in the hole when setting out a rose plant? Additional fertilizer is not necessary if the soil has been previously well prepared. Where the soil is poor, a mixture of commercial 5–10–5 fertilizer, or a similar grade, may be mixed with the soil used to fill in around the plant. Not over 1 teacupful to each bushel of soil should be used.

Should any fertilizer be added at the time the soil is prepared? Incorporating 3 lbs. of superphosphate and ½ lb. of muriate of potash for each 100 sq. ft. is desirable. A mixed commercial fertilizer may be substituted, in which case 4 lbs. of the 5–10–5 may be used for each 100 sq. ft.

How can one tell when roses need fertilizer? The leaves are a uniform light yellowish green; plants fail to make lush, vigorous growth.

Are commercial fertilizers good for roses? Almost any fertilizer that contains an appreciable quantity of plant nutrients is satisfactory. A mixed commercial fertilizer, 5–10–5 or comparable grade, can be used at the rate of 4 lbs. per 100 sq. ft.

What can be done if roses have been overfertilized? Very heavy watering on several days in succession will leach out some of the excess nutrients. Working in peatmoss, chopped straw, or shredded sugar cane will also help.

How do roses look when they are overfertilized? Usually the growth is stunted, the stems short, and the flowers small. New shoots fail to develop promptly after the first blooming period. The midsummer and fall bloom is reduced. The tips of the feeding roots, normally white, appear brown.

Can manure be used as a fertilizer? Well-rotted manure is a satisfactory form of fertilizer and should be used at the rate of 3 to 5 bu. for each 100 sq. ft., applied in either early spring or late fall.

Should manure be mixed with the soil for roses? If the manure is well rotted, it is an excellent form of organic material. Fresh manure may do more harm than good.

How much manure may be mixed with the soil? Ten per cent by volume, or 1 bu. of well-rotted manure to 9 bu. of soil is satisfactory.

Should hen manure be used on roses? If so, when? Hen manure is a satisfactory fertilizer if it has been allowed to rot somewhat before using. It is advisable to put it on in the late fall or very early spring.

How much hen manure can be used on roses? One bu. for each 100 sq. ft. can be used with safety.

Is horse manure satisfactory for roses? If well rotted, it is nearly as good as cow manure.

Is peatmoss good for roses? Peatmoss is an excellent soil amender for roses, especially if the soil is heavy.

What is the value of peatmoss in a rose soil? It increases the organic matter content, aeration is improved, the water-holding capacity is increased, and the soil reaction (pH) may be made more favorable for growth.

How much peatmoss should be used? On very heavy clay soils as much as 50 per cent by volume may be incorporated. Ordinarily 25 per cent by volume is satisfactory. This means 1 bu. of peat to each 3 bu. of soil.

How should peatmoss be used in preparing the soil for roses? It is best to mix it thoroughly with the soil if a new bed is being prepared. Where individual plants are set in to replace those that have died, mix the peatmoss with the soil that is used to fill in around the plant.

Should the peatmoss be moistened before it is mixed with the soil? It is not necessary.

What kind of peatmoss is best? Any of the commonly available brands of peatmoss (sphagnum moss peat) are satisfactory. It should be fibrous, clean, free from sticks and other debris, and thoroughly granulated. The more thoroughly decomposed sedge and muck peats are less beneficial.

Will peatmoss improve a light, sandy soil? While the benefit of peatmoss is most striking in a heavy soil, it also greatly improves light, sandy soil.

Can both peatmoss and manure be used? Yes, they make an excellent combination. A mixture of 1 bu. of manure, 2 bu. of peatmoss, and 10 bu. of soil is ideal.

What kinds of organic material can be used in preparing rose soil, other than peatmoss and manure? Leafmold is satisfactory and may be used at the rate of 1 bu. to 5 bu. of soil. Compost, muck, and various commercial organic materials can be used.

Is bone meal better on one type of soil than on another? It is most satisfactory on medium acid or strongly acid soils.

Is there any danger in using bone meal on roses? Bone meal contains a large proportion of lime, which tends to sweeten the soil.

If the soil is already neutral or alkaline, the addition of bone meal may make it too sweet for the best growth of roses.

Is it desirable to put bones beneath rose plants? This practice is a very ineffective way to supply fertilizer and is not recommended. It does neither harm nor good. Raw ground bone, however, makes a good fertilizer, with the exceptions noted above.

Is there anything better than bone meal as a fertilizer for roses? Superphosphate is cheaper and more effective as a source of phosphorus. It should be used at the rate of 3 lbs. per 100 sq. ft.

Are wood ashes good for roses? Wood ashes are satisfactory in regions where the soil is acid (pH 5.5 or below). Where the soil is near the neutral point, wood ashes may make it too sweet or alkaline because of the lime they contain.

Can cottonseed meal be used as a rose fertilizer without danger of making the soil acid? While it's a comparatively expensive type of fertilizer for roses, cottonseed meal is effective. It should be used at the rate of 5 to 10 lbs. per 100 sq. ft. There is little danger of the material making the soil too acid unless it already is near the danger point.

PLANTING AND TRANSPLANTING

Should rose plants be pruned before setting out? All small, slender, weak, dead shoots should be cut back to approximately 9 ins. above the union between the understock and scion. Bruised or broken roots should be removed just back of the point of injury. Some nurserymen send out pre-pruned plants ready for planting.

Should roses be pruned when they are transplanted? Unless they are moved with a large ball of earth, they should be pruned like plants obtained from a nursery. (See preceding question.) Even when transplanted with a ball of soil, it is advisable to remove the weak canes and branches, and cut back moderately the strong canes.

What is the best time to plant roses? Fall is the best season to plant roses throughout most of the United States. In the extremely cold regions, where the ground freezes before plants can be delivered by nurserymen, spring planting is preferred.

Can roses be planted in the spring? While late fall is the preferred season, roses can be planted in spring with good success. It is very important, however, that the planting be done just as early as the ground can be worked.

Will spring-planted roses bloom the first year? All the bush or bedding types of roses bloom well the first year. The climbing and shrub varieties seldom bloom to any extent the first season because most of the flowering wood has been removed to facilitate shipping.

Are potted roses satisfactory and how late in the season can they

be planted? Rose plants grown in large tarpaper pots or gallon metal cans are now available from many rose growers and at wayside garden stands the country over. Though more expensive to buy than dormant plants, these are perfectly satisfactory. If correctly planted in a well prepared and enriched hole and adequately watered, a potted rose may be transplanted at any time. They are of particular value to those who have late losses in the rose garden which must be replaced after the leaves are out, and to those who are trying, for one reason or another, to establish a garden late in the season.

How deep should roses be planted? The union between the bud and the understock should be about 1 in. below the ground level.

How far apart should roses be planted? The planting distance depends somewhat on the growth the plants are expected to make. In very favorable climates they may be planted much farther apart than in regions where they do not make vigorous growth. The average planting distance for the hybrid perpetual varieties is 24 to 30 ins.; for hybrid tea, polyantha, and floribunda varieties, it is 18 to 24 ins. Climbers should be spaced 6 to 8 ft. apart.

How large a hole should be dug for a rose plant? The dimensions will depend upon the size of the root system. In all events, it should be big enough to accommodate the roots without cramping or bending them. Usually it will need to be about 18 ins. across and about 12 ins. deep.

Should the roots be placed straight downward or spread out horizontally? Rose roots tend to grow more or less horizontally and should be so placed in the hole. They should not overlap one another, nor be forced into too small a space.

Is it necessary to firm the soil when planting rosebushes? The soil should be very carefully firmed as the hole is filled in. It is best to do this with the fingers to make certain that every root is in close contact with the soil, and that there is no air space under the center of the plant. Where the soil is loose or somewhat dry, it may be firmed by tramping around the plant just before the hole is completely filled. This should not be done if the soil is wet.

In planting roses, the soil should be thoroughly firmed about the roots.

Should rose plants be watered when first planted? Where the soil is loose or dry, watering is always necessary. A space should be left and filled with water 2 or 3 times before the remainder of the soil is put in.

Can roses be planted in midsummer? Not unless potted plants are available. These may be obtained from roadside nursery stands and from a few nurseries which specialize in them.

Can hybrid tea roses which are 4 or 5 years old be successfully moved to a different location? If moved carefully and pruned back severely, they are not likely to suffer.

Can old rosebushes be transplanted? Transplanting old rose-bushes (10 to 15 years) is advisable only on a limited scale. Very old plants do not send out new roots readily, and it may take them several years to become re-established. The transplanting is best done in the fall, and the plants should be moved with as much soil as possible.

Should rosebushes be moved periodically? No. Once a rose plant is established, it is best not to move it.

How can I move a large climbing rose without danger of losing it? Do not try to move the plant without first pruning it. Transplanting should be done in the fall. Cut out all but 4 or 5 young, vigorous canes. Lift the plant carefully with a ball of soil.

When is the best time to transplant a large Dr. Van Fleet rose? The fall is the best season for transplanting roses.

How should potted roses be planted? It is best not to break the soil-ball any more than is necessary. Merely remove the pot and place the root-ball in the hole. Be sure the hole is large enough to accommodate the plant. If the ball of roots looks dry, immerse the whole ball in a pail of water until it is thoroughly soaked. Be careful that no air pockets are left between the root-ball and the walls of the hole when the soil is filled in. If the ground is at all dry, the plants should be watered frequently for a period of at least 3 weeks. Shading the plants during the hot part of the day helps in getting them established.

Is it better to try to move an old rosebush than to buy new ones? Old roses often do not move well. It is usually better to obtain new plants.

Can roses be transplanted after the ground begins to freeze, or should they be stored over winter in the basement in case it is necessary to move them? It is best to move them to the new location even though the ground is frozen a little. If the necessity for moving them can be anticipated, the ground in the new location may be mulched with 6 ins. of straw to keep it from freezing. After transplanting, soil should be mounded as high as possible around the bases of the plants, and it is well to prune the tops as for new plants. Move the plants with as much soil as possible.

Can rosebushes be taken up in the fall and stored until spring? It is possible, but seldom practical in the average home garden. If they must be kept over, pack close together in a deep trench, and mulch heavily after soil freezes.

When one has to move to a new house in midwinter, is it possible to dig roses and store them in burlap bags in the cellar? It is possible, but not usually practical, unless the cellar is cold and the air is not extremely dry. While the root-ball may be wrapped in burlap, it is much better to remove the soil and pack the roots in moist peat-moss. Some of the tops should be removed to facilitate handling. The important thing is to store them where the temperature is 35° to 40° F., and watch the canes to see that they do not dry out or shrivel.

Is it true that roses sold in the spring are dug in the fall, and kept in cold storage over winter? This is the usual method and the most practical one for the nurseryman. It enables him to supply plants in the very early spring.

Should rose plants be "heeled-in" if they cannot be planted immediately? If it is necessary to keep rose plants for more than a week before they can be planted, they should be heeled-in. To do this, dig a trench about 12 ins. deep. Remove the plants from the package and pack them closely in the trench, placing them at an angle of about 45°. Cover the root system and several ins. of the tops with soil. They should be set out in their permanent location within 3 weeks.

How may roses be kept if they arrive before planting time? Most nurserymen try to deliver rose plants at the proper planting time and it is best to set them out immediately. The plants will keep satisfactorily for 5 to 7 days in the package in which they arrive if kept cold (33° to 40° F.). Always open and make certain that the packing material is moist, but not soaked. Water if dry.

How shall I care for the rose plants during the operation of planting? Do not let the plants lie around in wind and sun with their roots exposed, for even a few minutes. Take the wrapped packages to the planting bed and unwrap only when you are ready to begin planting. While pruning roots and broken branches of one plant in a package, keep the others wrapped in damp sphagnum moss, or plunge the roots in a bucket of water.

Will the roots of fall-planted roses take hold before freezing? Many experiments give evidence that rose roots grow as long as the soil temperature is above freezing. The fact that some root growth takes place, enabling the plants to become established in the soil, is one of the important reasons for fall planting.

GENERAL CULTURE

PROBLEMS

Is there a rose on the market that does not require any attention? No. In fact, taking care of plants is part of the fun of having them.

Rugosas, the species (wild) roses, and the brier roses need very little care.

Why don't rosebushes grow after giving them the best of care? There is often a great difference between what roses like and what human beings think is good for them. As many plants are killed by improper care as by neglect. It is necessary to understand their basic requirements and then to provide for them. No treatment should be given unless there is a reason. Much is to be gained by letting well enough alone where the plants are making satisfactory growth.

Why do my roses fail to bloom even though they make some growth? There are many possible reasons: shoots produced by the understock, incorrect pruning, insect infestation—especially rose midge—severe winter killing, too many flowers picked, and presence of diseases are a few.

What makes rosebushes gradually die out? Poor location, poor drainage, diseases, winter injury, too much lime, too much fertilizer, not enough moisture, too severe pruning.

Why is it many of our roses have no fine feeding roots? Often the feeding roots are so fine that they are lost when the plant is dug. Certain understocks do not tend to produce many fine roots.

How long after spring planting before fibrous roots will develop? In properly prepared soil they will start in about 1 week. If the soil is too sweet or alkaline, contains too much fertilizer, or is too dry, the fine roots will not develop for some time.

Should rosebushes be taken up and the roots treated? There is nothing to be gained by such a practice under ordinary circumstances, and many of the plants may fail to recover from such a treatment.

Will competition from tree roots prevent roses from flourishing? Roses will not stand such competition. The beds should be located far enough from trees or other large plants to prevent the roots from entering the bed and exhausting the moisture and nutrients of the soil.

How can tree roots be kept out of rose beds? About the only way is to put a concrete or metal barrier between the tree and the bed. Such a barrier should extend about 3 ft. down into the ground.

Why should our climbing rose fail to bloom? Some varieties are naturally shy bloomers. If the canes are killed back to the ground level each year there will be no bloom. The variety may have reverted to the understock. Improper pruning will discourage flowering. It may be in too shady a location.

What is the matter with my New Dawn when it produces only pure white flowers? The variety was probably mislabeled in the nursery, because New Dawn always has light-pink flowers.

Is the fact that my climbing roses fail to grow due to the soil? Most likely not. Lack of success with climbing roses is usually due to some factor other than the soil. Poor drainage, unfavorable location, disease and insect pests, improper winter protection, etc., are more common causes of failure.

What is the trouble with a climbing rose that never gets taller than 5 ft.? The variety may not be a true climber. Perhaps more careful winter protection would prevent losing part of the canes from freezing.

What can be done to keep hybrid tea roses blooming and their foliage perfect, and not inclined to drop from the branches during hot weather? Many of the Pernetiana roses (the orange, bronze, and yellow sorts) have the inherent habit of dropping their foliage in summer, and no cultural treatment will stop it. Black spot (see Diseases) will defoliate roses, some varieties being more susceptible than others. It will not be easy to keep hybrid teas in full bloom in summer heat. Feeding, watering, removal of spent flowers, and a regular weekly all-purpose spray or dust program from the time the leaves develop until frost, will retain vitality and assure a good display during late summer.

Is it true that more can be expected from new rose plants than established ones? It is true of the weaker varieties, which are best the first year or two after planting. The more vigorous ones, however, usually are much better when well established.

How can one grow climbing roses in Vermont? Set the plants in as protected a place as possible. Remove the canes from the trellis, fence, or other support late each fall, after a few frosts have ripened the canes; pin them close to the ground and cover with soil. Put them back on the trellis in the spring. This method of winter protection prevents severe killing of the canes. Do not bend the canes while they are in a frozen condition.

CULTIVATING

Should the soil in a rose bed be stirred or worked every few days? Keeping the surface of the soil stirred by very shallow hoeing is beneficial. Deep cultivation should not be practiced except possibly in the very early spring or late fall.

Is it better to hoe or mulch rose beds? Mulching is preferable because it reduces the amount of labor, helps to retain soil moisture, keeps the soil cool, and does not disturb the roots.

WATERING

Is it a good plan to water roses in dry weather? Roses like plenty of water. They will make more growth and produce more flowers if thoroughly watered during dry periods.

What is the best way to water roses? It is essential to soak the soil to a depth of at least 5 or 6 ins. A light sprinkling on top does more harm than good. It is best not to wet the foliage, because this helps to spread the black-spot disease.

How can roses be watered without wetting the foliage? There are several devices on the market that are practical. The Soil-soaker Hose, Water-Wand, and others are satisfactory. Or the water may simply be allowed to run from the hose onto the bed.

What is the best method of watering standard or tree roses? Allow the open hose to run near the base of each plant until the soil is thoroughly soaked. Place a board under it so the soil will not wash.

SUMMER MULCHING

Should roses be mulched during the summer? Mulching is a good practice. It helps to keep down weeds, conserves moisture, and keeps the soil cool.

What materials are best for mulching rose beds? Peatmoss is ideal because it looks well, is easy to apply, stays in place, improves the soil as it decomposes, and becomes incorporated with it. Buckwheat hulls, sawdust, ground corn cobs, shredded sugar cane and similar waste materials are satisfactory in regions where they are available. Rice hulls make a good mulch, but their light straw color is less attractive. Partially decayed leaves may also be used. Straw and similar materials are usually unattractive and contain weed seeds.

How can one keep a peatmoss mulch from blowing away? Soak it and spread it on the bed damp. After it is in place, sprinkle it lightly with a hose or watering can. When it dries out, it will form a crust and that will hold it in place.

Trellis support for climbing and semi-climbing (pillar) roses.

SUPPORTS

How can I support my climbing roses? With a trellis bought or made for the purpose; over an arch; or on cedar posts with crossbars added for extra support (the later method is especially suited to pillar-type roses).

How can an overgrown rambler be attached to the side of a house? The plant should be properly pruned, by cutting off, at the ground level, all but the new basal shoots. These may be trained as desired by tying them with soft twine to nails driven into the side of the house, or to a lattice attached to the wall.

Are climbing roses satisfactory if attached to the side of a house? While they will grow satisfactorily, the wall of a house is not an ideal form of support. They interfere with painting and other types of maintenance work and are difficult to support on the flat wall without some form of latticework, which should be held out from the wall itself at least 6 inches, and preferably a foot.

DISBUDDING

Should roses be disbudded?   Stems that are to be cut for use indoors or for exhibition purposes should be disbudded.

What good does disbudding do?   It eliminates competition between the main and the secondary flower buds for nutrients, food, and water. The main or terminal bud of the cluster develops into a larger, more perfectly formed, and better-colored flower.

When should disbudding be done?   Just as soon as the secondary buds become visible.

How does one disbud roses?   Most varieties produce 3 to 7 buds in a cluster. All the secondary buds should be picked off, leaving the largest one to develop into a flower.

What types of roses should be disbudded?   The hybrid teas, hybrid perpetuals, and some varieties of climbers that bear well-formed flowers in small clusters that are useful for cutting.

How can the number of flowers and length of stems be increased?
Select free-blooming, vigorous varieties. Plant in a favorable location. Prepare the soil properly. Give adequate fertilizer. Supply plenty of water. Do not disbud.

How many blooms should a standard (tree) hybrid tea variety give the second year after planting?   The number will vary widely according to the variety. The average will be around 50 flowers.

CUTTING AND EXHIBITION

What time of day should roses be picked?   In the early morning, or late in the afternoon.

Is it best to cut all the flowers?   No, unless the plant is large it is best not to cut more than 3 or 4 flowers from a single plant at each season of bloom.

Should a rose bloom be cut at the second bud above where the stem joins the main cane?   It is better if it is cut higher up. Robbing the plant of foliage tends to weaken it.

At what stage should roses be picked for best keeping quality?
Roses will keep longer if picked when the bud is just starting to unfurl. If picked at too early a stage, the bud may not open. Mature flowers are likely to wilt or drop their petals in a short time.

How long a stem should be taken with roses?   Only as long as will actually be needed for a vase or in an arrangement. The less foliage is removed from the plant, the better.

What treatment should be given newly cut roses to make them last

longer? Immediately after cutting, place in a deep container of water in a cool room for 3 to 6 hours before arranging. Keep out of drafts and bright light.

Why do hybrid tea roses lose their petals as soon as they are brought into the house? The blooms were too far developed when cut. Try cutting them in the bud stage and placing them in a dark, cool room in deep water for a few hours before using them.

Are the flower preservatives, like Floralife and Bloomlife, sold by florists, satisfactory for keeping roses? Some of them are quite effective in prolonging the life of cut roses, as they supply essential nutrients.

Why do roses have weak necks? Weakness of the stem just below the flower is characteristic of some varieties in certain localities. Nothing can be done about it except to grow stiffer-stemmed varieties.

CUT POINTED BUDS WHEN FAIRLY TIGHT   GLOBULAR VARIETIES WHEN PARTLY OPEN   2 LEAVES AND EYES LEFT ON STEM   TO DEVELOP NEW BUDS

How to cut a rose.

What causes rosebuds to open before they are fully grown? High temperature is the most important factor.

When should roses wanted for exhibition be cut? Cut the roses if possible the night before; immerse the stems ⅔ their length in cold water; stand in a cool cellar over night.

What precautions should be taken when cutting roses for exhibition? Select those with good stems. Cut when the buds are slightly open. Avoid stems with injured or spray-spotted foliage. Cut several more than are needed. Set the stems in water as soon as possible, and handle them with extreme care. If they must be transported, wrap each bud in waxed paper, and pack very carefully.

When should roses be disbudded for exhibition? When the buds are very small. Bend them over, and the little stem will part at the axil of the leaf and leave no stub. A bud stem in the axil of the leaf is a mark against the rose.

What are the most important things to keep in mind when exhibiting cut roses? The things that count most are length and firmness of stem and sound, unblemished foliage. The flower must be held well up and not have a weak neck. Have the rose ⅓ open when put on the stage. The flower should have no blemishes. When arranging several roses, do not force them into a container so that they are clustered together. Let each rose stand out as an individual.

SUCKERS

What is a sucker? A sucker is a rose shoot arising from the understock of a budded or grafted plant.

How can one tell the suckers from the variety? Usually the foliage and habit of growth of the sucker will be quite different from the variety and invariably the suckers spring from below the swollen "bud" or graft at the base of the plant. The presence of 7 leaflets to a leaf is an indication that the shoot comes from the understock, but it must be remembered that many varieties, especially climbers, also have 7 leaflets. It is much safer to look for differences in size and shape of leaves and leaflets, texture of the foliage, size, shape, and number of thorns, and similar characteristics.

How can you prevent suckers coming up from the root? There is nothing to do but repeatedly cut them off below the surface of the soil.

Can salt be used to stop suckers from coming up? It is not safe. The suckers are growing from the same root as the variety. To eliminate the suckers you must kill the root which would, of course, kill the plant. Keep cutting them off.

Why do the shoots that start from below the ground on my rosebushes never produce blooms? They are suckers coming up from the understock and sometimes produce blooms characteristic of the stock on which the variety was budded.

REVERSION

Can you prevent roses from turning back to the wild form? Reversion of a plant occurs only when the bud has died or suckers from the understock have crowded it out. Protect the plants from winter injury and keep any suckers cut off *below* the surface of the soil.

Are hybrid teas getting ready to revert to the original stock when 7 instead of 5 leaflets appear on the stems? No. Reversion is the result of suckers coming from the understock. Many hybrid teas produce leaves with 7 leaflets, especially late in the season.

What makes a rosebush grow very tall and bushy without blooming? Probably the bud has died out and the understock has developed.

Should I keep tree roses on which the top has died out but which are sending up new shoots from the base? These basal shoots are coming from the understock. The plants are worthless and should be discarded after the top has died.

CHANGE OF COLOR

What causes roses to be lighter colored at some seasons than at others? The more foliage on the plant the brighter and more intense the coloring. Cool weather increases the color because less of the food from which the pigment is manufactured is used up in respiration.

Will the blossoms of very light climbing roses be darker if iron is added to the soil? No. The color is pretty largely controlled by the genetical make-up of the plant. Iron is rarely lacking in the soil, but it may be insoluble and therefore unavailable to the plants when the soil is sweet or alkaline. Increasing the acidity will increase the availability of the iron.

Will iron or rusty cans have any effect in changing the color or shading of a rose? None whatever.

Will sulfur or yellow ochre make yellow roses darker? Such materials affect flower color only in so far as they improve or hamper growth. Neither of these materials will alter the color.

Why are my Talisman roses pale yellow instead of their real color? Perhaps the plant was incorrectly labeled. Talisman is seldom as brilliant out of doors as in the greenhouse. Too-bright sun causes colors to fade. Flowers on plants defoliated by disease are lighter colored.

GROWING IN GREENHOUSE, TUBS, AND POTS

Is it possible to grow hybrid tea roses in a greenhouse? Yes, but you should use plants budded on *Rosa manetti,* which is an understock better suited to greenhouse conditions.

How do you grow roses in a small greenhouse? Plant in bench in good soil. Keep moist, but not soaked. Keep the temperature as near 60° F. at night and 68° F. during the day as possible. Use plants propagated for greenhouse work rather than those used out of doors, because they are budded on *Rosa manetti* understock and are better adapted for growing in a greenhouse.

Can I grow roses in tubs? If so, how? The chief difficulty will be carrying them through the winter. Fill the tub with well-prepared soil (see rose soil preparation) and set in the plants. They will need to be watched carefully during the summer to see that they do not dry out. They should be brought inside and stored, where the temperature is below 40° F., for the winter.

How shall I treat a rosebush that has been kept outside all summer in a large pot? Must I bring it indoors? Your best plan will be to leave the plant outside all winter. When all the foliage has been shed, dig a trench in the soil and bury the entire plant, still in its pot, on its side. Before really severe weather comes, put extra covering on the soil over the pot to prevent the soil from freezing, which might cause pot to break.

How large a box would be necessary to grow a Paul's Scarlet plant?

A strong box 2 ft. square and 18 ins. deep would be large enough to accommodate the roots for several years.

Is it possible to grow a climbing rose plant in a large box? (Maine.) It is possible, and practical, if one wishes to go to the trouble of handling such a plant.

MATERIALS FOR WINTER PROTECTION

Should tar-paper collars be placed around rose plants to hold the soil higher around the stems? The results of some experiments carried out at Cornell University demonstrated that a tar-paper collar filled with soil is harmful rather than beneficial.

Is manure satisfactory for mounding around roses? It is not quite so good as soil, because it does not conduct heat as rapidly. Horse manure is the best type.

Can coal ashes be used to form a mound around rose plants? Coal ashes are not so desirable as soil, because they do not conduct heat as well. They also tend to make the soil sweet or alkaline.

Is it all right to use peatmoss around roses for winter protection? It is better as a summer mulch. For winter protection it is not so effective as soil, because it is a poor conductor of heat.

Are leaves and grass good for covering roses? While they are reasonably satisfactory, salt hay or clean wheat straw is preferable.

Are oak leaves satisfactory for protecting roses? In general leaves are less satisfactory than straw, because they hold too much moisture. When they are used, soil should first be mounded around the base of the plants.

Are leaves, especially maple leaves, useful as a mulch for roses? Leaves will not take the place of a soil mound. Neither are they as good as straw for a mulch. They tend to hold too much water.

Does wrapping sheets of newspaper around rose plants and covering them with burlap do any good? Such a method affords little protection. If the temperature drops much below the killing point, 0° F., it is quite likely that canes so protected will not survive.

Is it all right to cover rosebushes with peach baskets during the winter? Such a treatment offers some protection, but it will not keep the tops alive if the temperature goes very low. Soil should be mounded around the base of the plant before the peach basket is put on.

WINTER INJURY

What kills rose canes during the winter—cold, or drying out? Experiments conducted at Cornell University under the auspices of the American Rose Society have shown that low temperature is the chief factor. Under some conditions drying out may cause injury.

Why do my roses die back each year after I cover them?   Merely covering the plant is no guarantee that the temperature of the canes will remain above the critical point in very cold weather. They should be protected with a soil mound; this conducts heat from the lower layers of soil.

Does it hurt roses to be killed back to the ground level?   It does them no good, because the plants will be weakened, due to the loss of stored food. If vigorous varieties are selected, they will make sufficient growth during the summer even if they kill back each winter.

How does one keep roses from freezing back of the graft?   Mounding or hilling soil around the base of the plant is a reliable method.

How can a Doubloons climbing rose be kept from winter killing?   Take the canes from their support and pin them close to the ground. (See Winter Protection.)

Why did the new shoots wither and die when the canes looked green and healthy when I pruned them in the spring?   This is an effect of winter injury. The outer bark is the most cold-resistant tissue of the stem. Often shoots will begin to grow but soon die because the inner tissues have been killed even though the outer bark looks perfectly healthy in the early spring.

Why did the rosebushes I planted fail to come up in the spring?   Winter killing, poor drainage, improper protection, poor-quality plants, improper planting—any of these might have caused their death.

HILLING AND WINTER MULCHING

What is meant by mounding or hilling?   The practice of placing, or hoeing, soil up around the base of rose plants as a winter-protection measure.

Is it good practice to mound soil up around the base of plants, as some growers recommend?   Yes. Where plants are set out in the fall, it serves as winter protection; with spring-planted stock it keeps the canes from drying out until buds have begun to develop. Soil should be mounded as high as possible. Usually enough can be obtained from between the plants without exposing the root system; otherwise it should be brought from another part of the garden. If plants are planted in the fall, the mound should remain all winter; when set out in spring, it should be leveled out 2 or 3 weeks after planting, or when the buds on the canes show signs of making growth.

Which is more successful: hilling the plants, or digging them and burying them for the winter, and replanting in the spring?   Mounding or hilling the soil around the plants is the simplest and generally the most reliable method.

How does a soil mound protect the base and crown of a rose plant?
Soil, even though frozen, conducts heat from the lower layers of
warmer soil and keeps the temperature above the killing point.

**Is it all right to cut monthly roses (hybrid teas) to about 8 ins. from
the ground before protecting for the winter?** Yes. This facilitates
mounding up the soil. Even pruning them back to 8 ins. will not
eliminate the necessity for spring pruning, because some of the remaining wood is likely to be injured.

**When should the soil be hilled or mounded around the base of
rose plants?** After frost but before the ground freezes. After the soil
settles or washes away, more should be mounded up. For this reason
the first hilling should be done during early October.

**Is there any particular date on which hybrid tea roses should be
hilled and protected for winter?** Hill before the ground freezes and
while soil is in good workable condition. Usually the mulch is not
put on until after cold weather arrives.

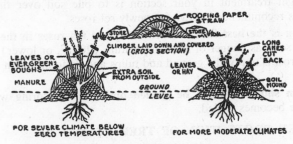

*Protecting roses for the winter. Manure, unless
very thoroughly rotted, should not be allowed to
come in contact with the stems.*

How is the soil mounded around the base of a rose plant? Usually
it can be hoed from between the plants, but care should be taken not
to expose any of the roots. Where plants are large and close together,
it may be necessary to bring additional soil from some other part of
the garden. This will have to be taken off again in the spring.

How high should the soil be hilled or mounded? As high as
possible. Usually to a height of 6 ins. above the soil level.

How are newly set rose plants protected during the first winter?
Mound soil over the plant, covering as much of the canes as possible.
Later a straw mulch may be put on.

Is it necessary to hill up soil around hybrid tea roses? (Nebraska.)
Yes, in your climate to a depth of 12 ins. Cover with 10-in. to 12-in.
straw or hay mulch after ground freezes.

Will you give information on covering and uncovering roses? First
tie the stems in with soft string, then hill up around the base as

described above. When soil freezes, fill the hollows with manure if possible. Later on, if the situation is much exposed, place evergreen boughs among plants to help protect them from the fierce combination of bright sun and cold wind in March. When this period is past, remove the top cover during dull or showery weather. A few days later break down the mounds of soil to cover the manure.

Where a straw mulch is used, when is it put on? When freezing weather arrives. If put on too early, it encourages mice and other rodents, which chew the stems.

Should a straw mulch be put over the soil mound? A straw mulch is of little value in keeping the stems above the soil mound from being killed. In very cold climates, it does help to prevent loss of heat from the surface of the soil and thereby insures a higher temperature in the soil around the stems and roots.

Is it necessary to straw-mulch tea roses in the winter in Illinois and Indiana? A straw mulch alone affords little protection for tea roses. The right treatment in your section is to pile soil over the entire plant as recommended above for newly set roses.

When is the best time to uncover hybrid tea roses in the spring? Just as soon as danger of low temperature (20° F. or lower) is past; when frost is out of the ground and tulips and daffodils begin to come up.

When should the soil be leveled out? In the spring when the weather becomes settled.

WINTER PROTECTION OF TREE ROSES

How may tree roses be protected in cold climates? Lay them down on the ground and cover with soil.

How does one lay down a tree rose? Remove the stake, and, if the trunk cannot be bent down without danger of breaking, lift one side of the root-ball so that it will. Cover the top, trunk, and exposed roots with soil, and later mulch with straw.

Is wrapping with burlap sufficient protection for tree roses in New York State? Not unless the winter is very mild and the plants are in a very sheltered situation. The only safe way is to lay them down and cover as described above.

Why did my tree rose die—even though the buds had started to grow—when it was straightened up in the spring? The trunk may have been infected with the stem canker disease, or a portion may have been winter killed.

WINTER PROTECTION OF CLIMBING ROSES

What protection can be given climbing roses to keep them from freezing if too big to lay on the ground? Nothing can be done except to reduce the size of the plants by pruning so that they can be laid down.

What can be done to prevent climbing roses from freezing out during the winter months? (Illinois.) They must be laid down and covered with soil to protect them from low temperatures. Few climbing roses are winter hardy in Illinois (without careful protection). Lay the canes on the ground (growing them on a hinged trellis is an advantage). Cover canes with at least an inch or more of soil and then cover with branches. Uncover in spring before growth starts.

How should climbing roses be protected? When the temperature does not drop below 0° F., no protection is needed for the hardy varieties. Where temperatures between zero and 10° below may be experienced, mound soil over the base of the plants. In more severe climates remove the canes from their support and pin close to the ground. They may be covered lightly with straw, soil, or leaves, but if so, they must be protected from mice.

What can be done to prevent climbing roses, after being uncovered in spring, from dying back to within 2 to 3 ft. of the ground? Buds are on canes, yet canes die back. Canes were wrapped with marsh hay and waterproof paper. (Minnesota.) Such protection is insufficient. Pin canes close to ground and then cover each cane with 2 ins. of soil; lay branches on top. Uncover *gradually* in spring and before growth starts underneath cover. Lower parts of the canes are more resistant to low temperatures. Developing buds die because inner tissues of stems suffered winter injury.

PRUNING

Is it necessary to prune roses each year? Yes, if the best quality plants and flowers are to be obtained.

What happens if roses are not pruned? The plants become masses of brambles which are very unattractive. Disease and insect pests are encouraged. Flowers will be of inferior quality.

Should roses that were planted in the fall be pruned the following spring? Usually it is unnecessary if they were pruned (as they should be) before planting. Sometimes the tops will be killed back a little above the soil mound; if so, the dead portion should be removed.

Are all types of roses pruned at the same time and in the same manner? No. The different types or classes are pruned at different seasons because of variations in their habit of growth and flowering. While the basic principles involved in pruning all classes of roses are essentially the same, the details of the practice vary.

When is the best time to give the different classes or types of roses major pruning? Hybrid teas (monthly roses)—early spring; hybrid perpetuals (June roses)—early spring; polyanthas (Baby Ramblers) —early spring; floribundas (large-flowered polyanthas)—early spring; climbers—immediately after flowering; shrub roses—continuous blooming types—early spring; others immediately after flowering.

Should roses be pruned in the fall before winter protection is given?
If the plants are large and tall, it is often advisable to partially prune
them by cutting back the long canes. It prevents them from whipping
in the wind and makes it easier to hill and mulch the plants.

**How heavily shall I prune roses in fall that were set out in the
spring?** Hybrid teas may be cut back to 18 ins. above ground before mulching.

Should one cut off the new shoots that develop in the fall? If one
has the time and patience, it is a good thing to do, since the young
shoots are prevented from using up the stored food in the stem. From
a practical point of view it is questionable whether the practice
warrants the effort.

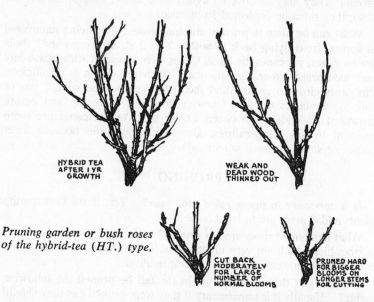

HYBRID TEA
AFTER I YR
GROWTH

WEAK AND
DEAD WOOD
THINNED OUT

*Pruning garden or bush roses
of the hybrid-tea (HT.) type.*

CUT BACK
MODERATELY
FOR LARGE
NUMBER OF
NORMAL BLOOMS

PRUNED HARD
FOR BIGGER
BLOOMS ON
LONGER STEMS
FOR CUTTING

Is it desirable to pinch out the tips of rosebushes? With shrub
roses it may be done to make a denser, more bushy plant. With
bedding types (hybrid teas, etc.) it tends to delay flowering, but
is sometimes practiced to encourage more continuous blooming.

**How should roses be pruned to produce more buds and longer
stems?** Experiments have shown that the less pruning the more
flowers will be produced. Contrary to the popular idea, pruning has
very little effect upon the length of rose stems. Proper soil preparation,
fertilization, and watering are much more important.

Does severe pruning cause more vigorous plants? No. On the
contrary, severe pruning, especially in climates where winter killing
occurs, tends to reduce vigor. Removing more healthy, vigorous wood

than is necessary only robs the plant of stored food. The stored food insures a vigorous plant with large, well-developed flowers.

How can you prevent roses from coming up between the branches with short stems (2 ins.)? Prune out all weak shoots in the spring.

How can you control the spreading shoots of roses? Cut them off.

When pruning roses, how far above a bud should the cut be made? About ¼ in.

Is it always necessary to make the cut where a bud points outward? It is not necessary, but it is desirable wherever practical. The branches will be better spaced, so that sunlight will strike all the leaves. The practice is thought to decrease disease, and it certainly produces a better-appearing plant.

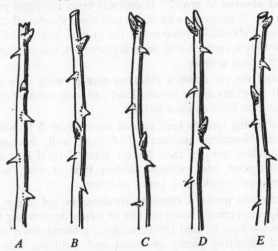

How to prune a rose. A – ragged cut, won't heal. B – cut too far above bud. C – cut too close to bud. D – cut too slanting, comes below bud. E – Right! Slight slant about ¼ inch above bud.

How can one prune roses without getting scratched by the thorns? Protect the hands by wearing heavy leather gloves of the gauntlet type.

Should roses be pruned with a knife, or pruning shears? A good pair of sharp pruning shears will greatly simplify the work and enable one to do a better job.

PRUNING CLIMBING ROSES

Are the large-flowered climbers pruned any differently from the ramblers? As a group the large-flowered climbers do not send up so many new basal shoots each year. For the most part, only the old flower clusters are removed, back to the first well-developed vegetative bud. This is usually where the first normal leaf joins the branch. As new shoots come from the base, the older canes should be cut out. (See illustration, page 506.)

Is it better to prune climbing roses in the fall or spring—or both? The best time is immediately after flowering. Occasionally a little pruning may be necessary in the spring to remove wood that has been winter killed.

How should an everblooming climbing rose be pruned? Very little real pruning is necessary. Merely remove the withered flower clusters back to the first well-developed shoot bud. When growth becomes too thick, cut out a few of the old main canes at the ground.

Should all old wood be pruned out of climbing roses, and just the new shoots allowed to grow? It depends upon the habit of growth of the variety. If vigorous, with many new basal shoots, all canes that have flowered should be removed at the ground level. With weaker-growing varieties, remove only as many canes as will be replaced by the current year's growth.

How shall we cut down a climbing rose growing over an arch? Cut off all old canes at the ground level and save the new ones from the base to train back on their trellises.

Can a climbing rose be kept pruned down under 5 ft. without destroying its blooming qualities? Not very well, because many climbers produce most of their flowers above 3 ft. If it is necessary to keep the plant low, perhaps another type of rose, such as a hybrid perpetual, would be a better selection.

How can you prune a climbing rosebush to get larger blooms? Pruning does not greatly affect the size of flower on climbing varieties. Some increase may be had by disbudding, growing fewer canes per plant, and supplying plenty of water and fertilizer. Select large-flowering varieties.

Should I prune out all branches that have leaves with 7 leaflets because they are throwbacks to the original stock? Definitely no. Practically all climbing roses have 7 leaflets. They often vary from 5 to 9 on the same shoot.

How should an American Beauty climbing rose be pruned? This variety is moderately vigorous; several new shoots come from the base each year. When the plant is as large as desired, remove the older canes to the ground as new shoots come up to replace them.

Should the climbing rose Blaze be pruned? Blaze tends to flower a second time during the summer. Only the withered flowers and seed pods should be cut off. As new shoots grow from the base, the oldest canes may be cut off at the soil level.

How should a Climbing Cecile Brunner be pruned? Each summer, after the blooming period is past, cut out the oldest canes if new shoots are developing from the base to replace them. Otherwise, remove only the withered flower clusters.

Why would a Dr. Van Fleet die after pruning in the fall? Pruning would not kill a climbing rose plant. Its death must have been caused by some other factor, possibly winter killing.

How should one prune Golden Climber (Mrs. Arthur Curtiss James) to make it flower more freely? This is naturally a shy bloomer in most situations. Train the canes horizontally so that more blooming shoots will be produced. Remove only the dead flowers. When it becomes too thick and tangled, cut off some of the fine, whiskery shoots which it often produces.

How many clusters of flowers can be expected on a Paul's Scarlet Climber the summer following planting? Probably not more than 3 or 4 on each cane, because they are usually pruned back before shipping.

How does one prune a Climbing President Hoover? As with other climbing hybrid tea varieties, keep old flowers removed. When the plant becomes too thick, take out a few of the oldest canes at the soil surface.

How do you prune a Silver Moon Rose? This variety is an extremely rank grower. It must be pruned at least once a year, and sometimes oftener, in order to keep it under control. Cut out canes that have flowered. Remove as many of the new slender side shoots as are necessary to maintain neat growth.

How should my Climbing Souv. de Claudius Pernet, which doesn't bloom more than once a year, be pruned? Climbing sports of hybrid teas seldom bloom as continuously as the original varieties. Keep withered flowers and seed pods picked off and prune only as necessary to prevent growth from becoming too thick.

Should Climbing Talisman and Flame be pruned back to 6 ins. from the ground every year? No. As much vigorous wood as possible should be left on Climbing Talisman. With Flame, remove only the shoots that have flowered, cutting them off at the surface of the soil after blooming. Pruning this variety back to 6 ins. will prevent it from flowering.

How and when should I prune the climbing rose Tausendschon, commonly called Thousand Beauty Thornless? Prune back to ground all old canes after it has ceased blooming. Keep the best of the new canes for following year's flowers.

PRUNING RAMBLERS

When, and how often, are rambler roses pruned? The main pruning is done each year immediately after flowering. Sometimes it is necessary to cut out in the spring wood that was killed during the winter.

How do you prune vigorous ramblers that send up many new canes from the base each year? Cut off at the ground level all canes that have produced a crop of flowers.

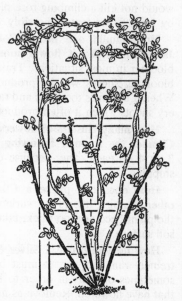

Climbing roses of the rambler type, which flower on new wood of the current season's growth, are pruned, just after flowering, by cutting old canes back to the ground (as indicated by dotted lines in sketch), thus leaving room for the husky new canes.

How many of the new canes should be left on a rambler rose? From 5 to 12.

What pruning is done to ramblers if no shoots grow from the base? Only the withered flower clusters, and any weak growths, are removed.

How and when can an overgrown rambler be pruned? Immediately after flowering cut out at the surface of the ground all but the new vigorous shoots that arise from the base of the plant. These may be trained as desired. Each year remove the old canes that have flowered, and save the new canes.

How can we get a Dorothy Perkins that has not been pruned for years back into condition? After it has completed flowering, cut out at the ground level all old canes. Leave only new canes that are growing from the base.

PRUNING FLORIBUNDAS AND HUGONIS

How are the large-flowered polyantha (floribunda) varieties pruned? This type is pruned in the same manner as hybrid teas and polyanthas.

Is it possible to transplant a large Rosa hugonis (7 ft.) without pruning it? Even if the plant is moved with a large ball of soil and well watered after planting, some pruning will have to be done. Remove about ⅓ of the canes; head the remainder back to 5 ft. Move in the fall.

How and when should Austrian Copper and Hugonis roses be pruned? Austrian Copper and Hugonis should require little or no trimming except to remove very old or dead wood. If they get too large and coarse, they may be cut back to the ground immediately after flowering. Fall or early spring is the proper time for ordinary pruning.

PRUNING HYBRID PERPETUALS

How are hybrid perpetuals pruned? In early spring cut out all dead, weak, or injured wood and leave 4 to 8 well-spaced, vigorous canes on each plant. Where plants have not suffered any winter injury, the strong canes should be cut back to about 2 ft. above the ground.

Should June roses that are 6 or 7 ft. tall be cut back? Unless they are attractive at this height, cut them back in the early spring. (See previous question.) Take out all weak shoots to the ground level and cut back strong canes to the desired height (2 to 4 ft.).

To what height should hybrid perpetual roses, that grow 6 to 7 ft. tall, be cut back? Two to 3 ft. is a good height.

Are hybrid perpetuals ever cut back during the summer? Ordinarily, only when their growth needs to be restricted for the sake of the appearance of the plant.

Should roses such as Frau Karl Druschki and Else Poulson be pruned like everblooming roses? Frau Karl Druschki belongs to the hybrid perpetual class. (See preceding questions.) Else Poulson is a large-flowered polyantha or floribunda and should be pruned in the same manner as other varieties of that class.

PRUNING HYBRID TEAS

How close to the ground should hybrid tea or other bedding roses be pruned? The exact height above the ground is not important. In cold climates, where plants suffer from winter killing, leave as much of the vigorous, healthy wood as possible. Usually all wood above 4 to 8 ins. from the ground is killed, and must be removed. Where there is little winter injury, the canes are cut back to 12 or 18 ins. to develop uniform and free-flowering plants.

What type of pruning can be done to encourage more continuous bloom in hybrid tea varieties? Pinching out the tips of a few shoots on each plant will force them to send out new branches. While a few of the first crop of flowers is sacrificed, these new shoots will bloom later and in between the main crops of flowers.

Is it advisable to prune hybrid tea roses after the first bloom in

June? Pruning in the true sense of the word is unnecessary and undesirable at this time. However, withered flowers should be removed.

How should hybrid tea roses be pruned in climates where the canes are killed back in winter? As early in the spring as possible remove all dead, weak, or injured wood. Cut back the strong, vigorous canes to just below where injury is evident.

How much should hybrid teas be cut back in mild climates where there is little or no winter injury? All dead, weak, or unhealthy wood should be cut out. Strong canes should be cut back no farther than necessary to produce an attractive plant. Eighteen ins. above ground is about right to insure vigorous, productive plants.

How much of the stem should be removed when old flowers and seed heads are cut from hybrid teas and other everblooming roses? Cut off the withered flowers and seed heads just above the uppermost 5-leaflet leaf, or where a plump, well-developed bud appears in the leaf axil.

PRUNING OLD-FASHIONED, POLYANTHA, AND SHRUB ROSES

How are moss roses pruned? Cut out a few of the oldest canes each spring; shorten the tops of the remainder.

Should old-fashioned roses like Rosa centifolia be pruned? Keep plants rejuvenated by removing a few of the very old canes to the base of plant; shorten back the long canes.

How are polyantha or baby-rambler roses pruned? Essentially the same as hybrid teas, but less severely. In cold climates, where winter injury is severe, remove in the early spring only the dead, weak, or injured wood. If not injured during the winter, trim back the strong canes to 12 to 18 ins. above ground.

Should new long shoots on the Cecile Brunner variety be trimmed back? Ordinarily Cecile Brunner does not produce long shoots. The variety is a hybrid or large-flowered polyantha and the shoots always terminate in a cluster of flowers. It is probable that the long shoots are suckers from the understock and should be cut off *below* surface of the soil.

When is the best time to prune rugosa roses? Rugosas bloom more or less continuously during the summer and are therefore pruned to the best advantage in the early spring.

What is the correct way to trim rugosa roses planted on a bank? It is important to keep plants rejuvenated and to prevent them from becoming "leggy." Each spring remove a few of the oldest canes to the ground level. Thin tops by cutting out some of the branches.

How can one make a hedge 4 to 5 ft. high of the rugosa variety

F. J. Grootendorst? The bushes are 2 ft. apart. Prune back to the ground level each spring several of the older canes of each plant. Cut new canes at the desired height, if they grow too tall. Keep plants well fertilized.

How should shrub roses be pruned? A few of the older canes should be cut back to the ground each spring to encourage the growth of basal shoots. This helps rejuvenate the plants. If growth becomes thick, remove some of the upper branches to thin out the plant.

How can the shrub and old-fashioned roses be pruned so that foliage will be produced on the lower part of the plants? Cut off the top of young shoots when they are about 18 ins. tall, thus forcing the canes to branch. Cut a few of the outside canes back to 2 or 3 ft. in spring.

PRUNING TREE ROSES

Just how are tree roses pruned? Remove all weak or dead wood from the top, and cut back the main canes to about 6 or 8 ins. from the crown. Take off all suckers that start to develop on the trunk, or from the base.

To what extent can tree roses be pruned? The top of a tree rose is pruned as though it were on the ground instead of on the tall trunk or stem.

PROPAGATION

What different methods can be used to propagate roses? Rose varieties may be propagated by budding, grafting, cuttings, and layering.

Are own-root rose plants propagated at home as satisfactory as budded stock? They are much slower in getting started, but will usually develop into equally good plants. Some gardeners consider them longer-lived and more productive.

What is the "union" of a rose plant? The place where the bud of the desired variety was inserted on the understock in the propagation of the plant. It can usually be seen as a jointlike swollen area 2 or 3 ins. above the roots. It is just below the region from which all main branches of the plant arise.

BUDDING

Are roses propagated by budding, or grafting? Most outdoor roses are budded.

What is meant by budding? Budding is a method of vegetative propagation. It means to graft by inserting a bud of one variety into the bark of another. (See Section II—Budding and Grafting.)

Why are outdoor roses budded instead of grafted?   It is the simpler method for large-scale production and requires less greenhouse space and equipment.

What is the best time to bud roses?   Usually in July and early August, but it can be done at any time when the bark slips readily.

How do you bud roses?   Grow or procure an understock of *Rosa multiflora* or some similar species. Make a T-shaped slit in the bark just at the ground level. From the stem of the desired variety cut out a well-developed bud with the petiole of the leaf attached. Pick out the wood attached to the bark. Open the slit on the understock and insert the bud so that the bark fits close to the wood of the understock. Wrap firmly with raffia or soft twine, but be careful not to injure the shoot bud. After 3 or 4 weeks remove the binding.

Should an amateur gardener try to bud roses?   Yes. It is fun to do. Do not be discouraged if unsuccessful at the first attempt. Do not try to produce all your own roses in this way at first. Try budding as an experiment.

CUTTINGS

Can roses be grown from cuttings or slips?   Yes.

When is the best time to root rose cuttings?   Rose stems will root best about the time the petals fall.

Where can one find the best cuttings on a rosebush?   The flower stems make the best cuttings.

How long should a rose cutting be?   Four to 5 ins. is the right length. It should contain 3 nodes.

Will a slip from a grafted plant be like the variety or the understock?   It will be the same as the variety.

Will all varieties of roses root readily?   The hybrid teas, polyanthas, floribundas, and most of the climbers will root easily. Hybrid perpetuals and many of the shrub and species roses do not root so well.

Should the leaves be removed from rose cuttings?   Leaves that will be below the surface of the rooting medium (usually sand) in which the cuttings are placed should be removed; others should be left on.

Should the blossom be left on a rose cutting?   Never. The middle and lower part of the stem make better cuttings.

What is the best material for rooting rose cuttings?   Clean, sharp, medium coarse sand or a mixture of sand and peatmoss.

What conditions are necessary for rooting rose cuttings?   Keep the rooting medium moist. Shade during first few days with newspaper or cheesecloth. Take out any cuttings that appear to be rotting, and any leaves that fall off.

Are root-growth substances helpful in rooting roses?   Yes. They usually cause cuttings to root more quickly and to produce a better root system.

Can rose cuttings be rooted in soil under a glass jar?   Yes, if only a few plants are needed.

What special precautions need to be taken in rooting cuttings under a fruit jar?   Select a place where the jar is shaded during the hot part of the day. Keep soil moist at all times. Do not put more than 3 cuttings under a single jar.

How long before cuttings rooted under a jar can be moved?   If the cuttings are taken early in the summer, they are usually large enough to move by fall. They will need to be protected by mounding soil over them.

How does one go about removing the glass jar?   Don't let too much growth develop before removing it. Select a cloudy day. Remove the jar. If the sun comes out, shade the cuttings with newspaper for a few days.

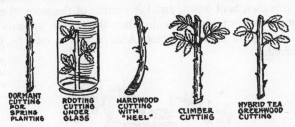

DORMANT CUTTING FOR SPRING PLANTING   ROOTING CUTTING UNDER GLASS   HARDWOOD CUTTING WITH "HEEL"   CLIMBER CUTTING   HYBRID TEA GREENWOOD CUTTING

New rose plants from cuttings or "slips."

Can cuttings be rooted in a cold frame?   Yes. The soil should be removed and clean, sharp, medium coarse sand put in to a depth of 4 ins. or so. It may be necessary to keep the cuttings shaded with cheesecloth.

Can seed flats filled with sand be used for rooting rose cuttings?   Yes, but they must be watched very carefully to make sure the sand doesn't dry out.

Will spring rose cuttings withstand the winter if left in the garden?   Yes, if completely covered with soil and if they are in a place where the drainage is good.

How should rose cuttings rooted during the winter be cared for?   Plant out of doors in the early spring in good soil. Keep them well watered.

Where should one transplant rose slips (cuttings) after they are rooted? They may be planted in their permanent location, or in a nursery bed or cold frame.

How long before a cutting from a climbing rose will bloom? Ordinarily some flowers can be expected the second year after the cutting was rooted.

Can a new shoot which has come up about a foot from the original plant of variety Blaze be moved? If possible, this shoot should be allowed to bloom before it is transplanted to make certain it is the same variety and not a sucker from the understock. Cut the root connection between it and the main plant the spring before it is moved. It will then develop a good root system of its own and will transplant easily.

GRAFTING

What does grafting mean? Grafting is a method of vegetative propagation by which a piece of the stem of the variety is made to grow on another plant. (See Section III—Grafting.)

LAYERING

How are roses layered? A branch is cut a little more than halfway through. It is then bent down, and the portion of the stem where the cut was made is buried in the soil. When the branch appears to be rooted, it is severed from the plant. After a year it may be moved where desired.

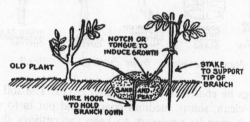

Propagating a rose by layering. New plants of many climbers can readily be obtained by this method.

SEEDS

Do roses come true from seed? Only wild species. Named varieties are hybrid plants, and every seedling will be different.

How may roses be made to set seeds? Some varieties are comparatively sterile and will set little or no seed. Try putting pollen from other varieties on the stigmas.

How does one germinate rose seed?   Place the seed in small, unstoppered bottles in moist peatmoss and store in a refrigerator for 3 months at 41° F. Plant seeds in soil containing ⅓ peatmoss, ⅓ sand, and ⅓ soil. Keep moist and at a temperature of about 68° F. Sometimes seed planted in a protected cold frame in the fall will germinate the following spring and summer.

HYBRIDIZING

How do you "cross" roses?   While the flower is still in the bud stage carefully remove all stamens before the pollen is shed. Cover emasculated flower with a cellophane or paper bag. When stigmas have developed, place some pollen of the plant selected for the male parent on them. It is desirable to repeat the pollination on several successive days. Remove the paper bag when the seed pod starts to develop.

UNDERSTOCKS

What is meant by a rose understock?   Garden roses are not grown on their own roots but are budded on the stem of a wild rose grown for the purpose. The stem, upon which the rose is budded or grafted, is called the understock. (See Budding and Grafting.)

How can one propagate his own understocks?   Make hardwood cuttings 6 to 8 ins. long of smooth 1-year-old shoots of *Rosa multiflora* or other species. Remove the 2 lower eyes to prevent suckering. Callus in moist peatmoss or sand at 45° F. Plant out of doors in the early spring, or root inside and plant out later. Bud during July or early August.

Where may understocks be obtained?   Few rose growers offer them except in large quantities. Try rose-growing concerns.

What understocks are used for tree roses?   *Rosa rugosa, Rosa canina,* and occasionally *Rosa multiflora.*

PESTS AND DISEASES

What are the main pests, insects, and diseases that trouble roses? See Section VIII—Insects and Diseases.

What are the most common and harmful diseases of roses? What treatment should be used? How often?   If a regular spray program is adhered to in the treatment of roses, using Triogen or some similar all-purpose spray, pests and diseases will be kept under control. Aphids, plant lice, leaf hoppers, rose bugs, Japanese beetles, leaf rollers, etc., attack roses, while black spot and mildew are the most destructive diseases.

How can mice be controlled in the rose garden?   Poisoned grain should be placed under the mulch, at frequent intervals, in small open containers that protect it from becoming wet. A jelly tumbler laid on its side and covered by a piece of board serves the purpose.

BLACK SPOT   MILDEW   COMMON CANKER   OLD BARK WOUND   BROWN CANKER

Some common diseases of roses.

What causes roses to bloom one-sided?   Usually insect injury from aphids, rose slugs, thrips, or weevil, which see.

I read an article on roses which said they should be sprayed with a 4–4–50 Bordeaux mixture. What is that?   Four lbs. of copper sulfate, 4 lbs. of lime, 50 gals. of water. The copper sulfate and the lime should be dissolved separately in a small amount of water, and then added to the rest of the water.

Does spraying give better control of rose pests than dusting? Either method will give good control if a regular control program is adhered to. With either method it is most important to cover the undersides of leaves.

Why does my baby-rambler rose fail to bloom? I have never been able to clean the plant of mildew. As soon as the clusters form they wither and die.   Start spraying early in the season, or dust with fine dusting sulfur. (See Mildew.)

TYPES AND VARIETIES

AUSTRIAN BRIAR

Are Austrian Briars old-fashioned roses?   Yes. They are hardy and bright-colored; some are shrub types, some climbers. Some varieties are Austrian Copper, single; Austrian Yellow; Parkfeuer, single scarlet.

BLACK ROSE

Is the so-called "Black Rose" really black? Where did it originate? There are several roses for which claims have been made for their black color. Among these are: Zulu Queen, Matador, and Nigrette. The color is not black but dark red to dark maroon.

CABBAGE

Can you give me any information about the Cabbage Rose. Is it suitable for the garden?   The Cabbage Rose (*Rosa centifolia*) is one of the oldest roses to be cultivated. It is an excellent garden plant, being fragrant, hardy and producing quantities of bloom during June.

CLIMBING

What is the difference between a rambler and a large-flowered climber? Any tall-growing rose that requires the support of an arbor, trellis, or similar structure, or can be trained to one, may be classed as a climbing rose. A rambler is one type of climber and is distinguished by its very long, slender canes and dense clusters of small flowers. The variety Dorothy Perkins is a good example of the rambler type.

Are there everblooming climbing roses? For the milder climates, the climbing forms of hybrid teas and polyantha varieties are satisfactory. They are not hardy enough, however, for general use in regions colder than Virginia. For the North, a number of hardy, everblooming Large-flowered Climbers have been recently introduced. Dream Girl, Inspiration, Temptation, Golden Showers, Parade and Coral Dawn are among those which produce flowers every month during the growing season.

What Large-flowered Climbers are especially hardy? All of the standard varieties have similar degrees of cold resistance. See previous question for recommended varieties.

What are some of the best ramblers? Chevy Chase, rose-red; American Pillar, single pink, white center; Hiawatha, crimson, white eye; Minnie Dawson, pure white; Ghislaine de Feligonde, yellow buds, creamy flowers; Dorothy Perkins, pink.

What climbing roses are best to plant on a steep bank with Hall's Honeysuckle? Almost any of the ramblers, such as Dorothy Perkins, Evangeline, Hiawatha, and Minnehaha are satisfactory in such a situation. Coral Creeper, Creeping Everbloom, Little Compton Creeper are large-flowered varieties for such use.

What is the red climbing rose, somewhat like Paul's Scarlet Climber, that blooms in the fall? The variety Blaze.

Are the climbing forms of World's Fair, Pinocchio and Summer Snow really everblooming? None of the climbing sports of dwarf varieties seems to bloom as freely as the original varieties. These 3, however, produce flowers more or less continually through the summer, although never in the quantity they do in June.

What climbing roses are recommended for northern Vermont? Any of the hardier varieties are satisfactory if properly protected by removing the canes from their support and pinning them close to the ground for the winter. Dorothy Perkins, Chevy Chase, American Pillar, New Dawn, Mary Wallace, and Purity should be tried with the suggested method of protection.

What climbing rose would be best for the arch on my garden gate? (Kansas.) Blaze, red; Inspiration, pink; Summer Snow, white; Dream Girl, salmon-pink.

DAMASK

Can you give me some information on the Damask Rose? The Damask Rose (*Rosa damascena*) is native to southeastern Europe, where it is used for making the celebrated attar of roses. It is one of the oldest roses in cultivation and is second only to the Cabbage Rose in the strength of its perfume. It makes a good garden shrub which is hardy. The real *Rosa damascena* has double rose-pink flowers. There are also many varieties, such as Damas officinalis, Kazanlik, and Marie Louise.

How tall does the rose of Damascus (Rosa damascena) grow, and is it hardy? The Damask Rose is one of the hardiest species. It grows to a height of about 5 ft.

FLORIBUNDA

What are floribunda roses? Technically they are hybrid or large-flowered polyanthas. They originated through hybridizing polyanthas with hybrid teas. The flowers are larger than those of the polyantha group, but in growth and flowering habit are much like them.

What are some good Floribunda Roses? Anne Poulsen, scarlet-crimson; Poulsen's Bedder, pink; Gruss an Aachen, soft salmon-pink; Golden Fleece; Gold Cup; Spartan, orange-coral; White Bouquet; Glacier; Corcorico, and Frencham, red; Fashion, salmon; Vogue, cherry-coral; Betsy McCall, pink.

FRENCH

Will you please name some French old-fashioned roses? Cardinal de Richelieu, dark purplish-red; Duc de Valny, large, double red to rose pink; *Rosa gallica,* large single, dark pink; *Rosa mundi,* semi-double, white to pale pink, striped red (also incorrectly called York-and-Lancaster).

GRANDIFLORA

What are Grandiflora Roses? Please name a few. A new class of very large flowered Floribundas. Outstanding varieties are Queen Elizabeth, rose-pink; and Buccaneer, yellow.

GREEN ROSE

I have been told that there is a rose called the Green Rose. What is it like? The Green Rose (*Rosa chinensis viridiflora*) has been cultivated for a long time. The petals are just narrow green leaves. The flower is very disappointing and not attractive. Sometimes used in flower arrangement before the buds open, as the foliage has a tint of bronze.

Is the Green Rose a climber? No. It belongs to the group of China roses. Aside from its interest as a curiosity, it is of no garden value.

HYBRID PERPETUAL

How do hybrid perpetuals differ from hybrid teas? The hybrid perpetuals were the progenitors of the hybrid teas and in their heyday ranked first in popularity. They have a decided Victorian quality in the largeness, fullness, and boldness of their blooms, but lack the refinement in form of the hybrid teas. The colors include purest white, deepest crimson, and the innumerable hues linking these two extremes. The plants are vigorous, rather coarse, and quite hardy. Most varieties bloom but twice during the season.

What are a few of the best hybrid perpetual varieties? Frau Karl Druschki, white; Henry Nevard, velvety scarlet; J. B. Clark, red; Mme. Albert Barbier, clear salmon-pink, almost yellow; Mrs. John Laing, clear pink; General Jacqueminot, crimson.

HYBRID TEA

What are hybrid tea roses? As a class they are moderately vigorous and with protection sufficiently hardy. Their chief merit is their frequency of bloom, a character that has given them the common name "monthly roses." In the variety, richness, and delicacy of their coloring, and in their perfection of form and pleasing fragrance, they are unequaled by any other type.

What is the difference between hybrid tea and a monthly rose? They are one and the same thing.

What are some of the best of the newer hybrid teas? Chrysler Imperial, President Eisenhower, Konrad Adenhauer, red; Confidence, Show Girl, Linda Porter, Helen Traubel, pink; White Swan, Sleigh Bells, white; Mojave, orange-red; Chief Seattle, apricot-buff.

What are some of the leading older pink hybrid teas? Betty Uprichard, Dame Edith Helen, Margaret McGredy, Miss Rowena Thom, Mrs. Henry Bowles, Radiance.

What are a few good red hybrid teas? Ami Quinard, Charles K. Douglas, Etoile de Hollande, Red Radiance, Heart's Desire. See previous question.

What are some of the most popular yellow hybrid teas? Golden Scepter, Golden Masterpiece, Lowell Thomas, Peace.

What white hybrid teas are satisfactory? Kaiserin Auguste Viktoria, McGredy's Ivory, Mme. Jules Bouche, Neige Parfume, Pedralbes, White Swan, Rex Anderson, Sleigh Bells.

What are a few of the best bicolor or two-toned hybrid tea varieties?

Pageant, coral-rose and gold; Forty-niner, crimson and creamy yellow; Huntsman, red and orange-yellow; Contesa de Sastago, copper and gold.

What single varieties of hybrid teas are worth while? Cecil, pale yellow; Dainty Bess, ruffled soft pink; Innocence, white; Isobel, flaming orange-pink, Irish Fireflame, buff, flame; Lulu, salmon; Vesuvius, crimson.

Are the new varieties of hybrid teas as hardy and strong as the older ones? With a few exceptions, yes. In fact, there is evidence that in general the new varieties are somewhat more hardy than those introduced 20 years ago. Old varieties grown today are a rather select group that have stood the test of time. It is likely that a larger percentage of the newer ones will stand the test, and of course it is quite probable that varieties much hardier than any we have today will be produced.

Are roses which win All America Rose Awards sure to give good results? No rose can be guaranteed to do well in any one individual garden. Roses honored by the A.A.R. Selections Committee have been tested in special test gardens in many parts of the United States. Their behavior, disease-resistance, bloom quantity and quality, foliage, etc. have been closely observed and on this basis they have received enough points for excellence from qualified judges to merit an award. Therefore they should give good results and will do so unless climate, soil or some other local condition is unfavorable; or unless they are poorly handled by their owner.

What types of roses do you recommend for the rank amateur? Hybrid Teas; Floribundas; Large-flowered Climbers; Shrub Roses.

I know nothing about hybrid tea roses, but wish to have a rose garden. What are the best varieties to purchase, as a beginner? (Nebraska.) The best roses for you are shrub types like *Rosa rugosa* and its hybrids; Harison's Yellow; Rosa hugonis; Belinda; Fruehling's Gold and the roses produced by Dr. Hansen of Brookings, South Dakota (Alika, red; Lillian Gibson, pink; Sioux City, red). If you live farther south, try the following Hybrid Teas, giving heavy winter protection. Red: Crimson Glory, Christopher Stone; Pink: Pink Radiance, Mme. Butterfly, Numa Fay; Yellow: Eclipse, Peace; bicolor: Pres. Herbert Hoover, Countess Vandal, Condesa de Sastago.

I have only a few hours a week to spend in my garden, but I want some roses. Can I grow hybrid teas? Why not? Get a few of the well-established varieties. Only plant what you can conveniently take care of. Or if you prefer less work, plant only iron-hardy, disease-resistant Shrub Roses like Mabelle Stearns, The Fairy, Flamingo, Lipstick, etc.

MINIATURE

What are "Fairy Roses"?   "Fairy Roses" is another name for the miniature roses which are forms of *Rosa chinensis minima.*

What are miniature roses?   They are very tiny forms of *Rosa chinensis* var. *minima,* or hybrids between this and other species and varieties. The plants are seldom more than 6 to 9 ins. tall, with the flowers proportionately small.

Are there many varieties of miniature roses?   Yes, quite a large number. Some of the best are: Tom Thumb, Red Imp, Oakington Ruby, Dwarfking, red; Tinker Bell, Bo Peep, Rouletti, Sweet Fairy, Cutie, pink; Pixie, Twinkles, white; Baby Masquerade, bicolor; Baby Gold Star.

MOSS

What are moss roses?   A type of the Cabbage Rose, *Rosa centifolia.* The bud of the flower is enclosed in a mossy envelope. Much of the great fragrance comes from the mossy glands. Moss roses are very old, having been in cultivation for centuries. Many kinds are still to be had from nurseries. Among them are Crested Moss (found on a convent wall in Switzerland in 1827), Blanche Moreau, Comtesse Doria, Eugene Verdier.

Is there a reliable old-fashioned moss rose?   The variety Communis, sometimes called Old Pink Moss or Common Moss, is one of the best. Others are Capitaine John Ingram, dark red, and La Neige, pure white.

PILLAR

What is a pillar rose?   The term "pillar" refers more to a method of support than to an actual type of rose. Varieties adapted to a post or pillar are called pillar roses. Certain climbing varieties that do not develop excessively long canes (such as Paul Scarlet climber) are classed as pillar roses. Some of the tall-growing hybrid perpetual varieties which lend themselves to being supported by posts are included in this group.

POLYANTHA

What are polyantha roses?   The term "polyantha" (meaning many flowers) well describes the class. The plants are dwarf, and give a continuous profusion of small flowers in large clusters. They are especially hardy, but less adapted for cutting than other types. For garden display they are unequaled. They were formerly called "baby ramblers" because the flower clusters were similar to those produced by the older varieties of ramblers.

What varieties of polyanthas are worth while?   Cameo, salmon; Katharina Zeimet, white; Mlle. Cecile Brunner, light pink; Chatillon

Rose, vivid pink; Ellen Poulsen, soft rose-pink; Gloria Mundi, orange-scarlet; George Elger, yellow; Ideal, red; Marie Pavic, blush (fragrant); Triomphe Orleanais, crimson.

RUGOSA

Will you tell me something about Rugosa Roses? This hardy species and its many fine hybrids are among the toughest and most long-lived of all roses. They are suitable for planting at the seashore where they make themselves thoroughly at home; in the very cold sections of the West where few roses can survive; and as large shrubs or hedges anywhere that there is room for them. The species is deep rose or white. For some of the best hybrids, see the second question under Shrub Roses.

SCOTCH

What are Scotch roses? A strain of old-fashioned roses with fine foliage and spiny growth. Hardy, disease resistant. Can be planted with shrubs or as specimens. Harison's Yellow, 6 to 8 ft., is semi-double; Stanwell Perpetual, pink, constant bloomer. Scotch roses are varieties or hybrids of *Rosa spinosissima.*

SHRUB

What are shrub roses? They are shrubs of varying heights and dimensions and in the garden are used as any flowering shrub. As a group they contain many beautiful plants, usually blooming in early summer. Some, such as *Rosa rugosa,* have stiff prickles and are used as barriers. Others, such as *Rosa hugonis,* for their beauty of bloom. The group is a large one, embracing many species and varieties, most of which are perfectly hardy.

Would you please give a list of some good shrub roses with their colors? *Rosa hugonis,* pale yellow; Harison's Yellow, golden yellow; *Rosa rugosa,* red, pink or white: (Agnes, yellow; Conrad Ferdinand Meyer, pink, and Mme. Plantier, white; Sanguinaire, red; F. J. Grootendorst, red; Pink Grootendorst;) *Rosa spinosissima, white, R. spinosissima fulgens,* pink; Stanwell Perpetual, pink.

SPECIES

What are species roses? Please name some. The species are the wild roses from which cultivated types have been bred. Some of those most suitable for the garden are *Rosa alba* or York Rose, white, semi-double; *Rosa hugonis,* yellow, early, 6 to 8 ft.; *Rosa setigera,* (Prairie Rose) large, single, pink, 6 to 8 ft.; *Rosa multiflora* (Thunberg), small white flowers in large trusses, red hips which attract birds, *Rosa rugosa,* red or white single. Others are *Rosa centifolia, Rosa chinensis, Rosa foetida, Rosa gallica, Rosa spinosissima, Rosa damascena.*

SWEETBRIER HYBRIDS

What are the hybrid sweetbriers? They are hybrids of *Rosa rubiginosa*, or Eglantine, having scented foliage, single or semi-double flowers on arching canes, and are strong growers. Lady Penzance, copper; Lord Penzance, fawn colored; Eglanteria (*R. rubiginosa*) pink, small clusters.

TEA

Why are varieties of roses called "tea roses"? The term refers to the true tea roses. They are not widely grown in American gardens, especially in the North. The flower odor is suggestive of the odor of fresh tea leaves. Harry Kirk, Lady Hillington, Maman Cochet and Bon Silene are members of this tea rose group. They are remontant (repeat bloomers), with well-formed, high centered buds and fine flowers but are tender.

Where did the "tea" in tea rose originate? Varieties allied to a Chinese species, *Rosa odorata,* are called tea roses. The odor of the flowers was thought to smell like fresh green tea leaves (not the beverage). At one time this species was called *Rosa thea.*

What is the difference between the tea rose and a hybrid tea? The hybrid tea rose is descended from the tea, the tea being one of the parents of the hybrid tea. In appearance the tea and hybrid tea look alike, but the hybrid tea is more vigorous and hardy, and has a wider adaptation. The true tea rose is seldom grown except in the South.

TREE ROSE

What is a tree (standard) rose? Instead of the bud being inserted close to the ground (as is done in propagating other types), tree roses are budded near the top of a tall understock cane. The plant that develops from the bud is therefore on a trunk or standard.

What is the difference between a standard and a tree rose? They are the same thing.

Can tree roses be grown in cold climates? They are difficult to grow in cold regions because they are hard to winter. In regions where the temperature does not drop below 10° F. they are usually satisfactory.

SECTION III-D

Perennials

What is a hardy herbaceous perennial?   A plant which lives for several years, whose tops die in winter, but are renewed, from the same roots, each spring.

What is the average age of perennial plants sold by leading nurseries?   About 1 to 2 years old.

WHAT TO GROW

Can you suggest a selection of 24 perennials of easy culture, for succession of bloom?   Spring: lily-of-the-valley, forget-me-not, coralbell, violet, bleedingheart (tall and dwarf), dwarf iris, mertensia, *Phlox divaricata,* ajuga. Summer: *Campanula carpatica, C. carpatica alba, C. lactiflora,* and *C. persicifolia;* astilbe, coreopsis, eupatorium, gaillardia, hemerocallis, bearded iris (tall), rosemallow, plantainlily, platycodon, hollyhock. Late summer and fall: plumbago, rudbeckia, chrysanthemum, hardy aster, helenium.

What are some of the more colorful perennials?   Balloonflower, Carpathian bellflower, chrysanthemum, columbine, coreopsis, dianthus, *Erigeron speciosus,* gaillardia, perennial flax, rudbeckia. *Heliopsis scabra incomparabilis.*

What bright-colored perennials can I use on the north side of my red brick house, to make an attractive rear terrace?   Aquilegia hybrids, *Anchusa myosotidiflora, Monarda fistulosa, Anemone hupehensis* and *A. magellanica, Dianthus deltoides* and *D. arenarius, Phlox subulata* varieties, *Plumbago larpentiae, Veronica incana.*

Can you list a few perennials that will bloom well with little or no care, and that will not look unkempt before and after blooming?   Any variety of hosta (funkia), any of the numerous hemerocallis, peonies, phlox, *Eupatorium rugosum, Aster novae-angliae,* ajuga, artemisia, baptisia, thermopsis, coreopsis, echinops, *Iris sibirica, Rudbeckia speciosa, Sedum spectabile.*

Will you give the names of the most suitable and inexpensive perennials for one quite busy on a farm?   *Silene maritima, Dictamnus* *fraxinella, Linum perenne, Papaver orientale* varieties, peonies, dianthus, Physostegia Vivid, *Platycodon grandiflorum,* heliopsis; gaillardia, coreopsis, *Helenium autumnale.* New varieties of these will cost more than the old established ones. The price, too, will vary with the nursery.

What would be an interesting layout for a perennial bed that is backed with shrubbery? First set out groups of delphiniums—3 or 4 to a group—spaced at irregular intervals over the bed 8 to 12 ft. apart, depending upon size of bed. Then set out hollyhocks in same manner—2 to 3 plants in each group. Intersperse in the same way varieties of summer phlox, then various hardy asters. This will give distribution of bloom. If spaces are left, fill in with Oriental Poppy, achillea, aconitum, *Anemone japonica, Campanula persicifolia,* cushion chrysanthemums, dianthus species and varieties, gaillardia, Gypsophila Bristol Fairy, heleniums, heliopsis. These will lend support to the 4 main kinds at different parts of the season. The principle is to weave the pattern back and forth across the border.

What are good combinations of ordinary perennials in border? The over-all border plan should be based upon the distribution of bloom over the planting and over the season. Color combinations, although effective at the moment, leave gaps in the planting unless planned to be followed up with other plants. Some good color combinations are lupines, Anthemis Moonlight and *Oenothera missouriensis;* Poppy Mrs. Perry, Shasta daisy, and *Linum perenne;* purple iris and *Aquilegia chrysantha;* delphinium hybrids, *Thermopsis caroliniana* and pyrethrum. These are but a few of the countless combinations possible. Be sure that all flowers selected for a combination bloom at the same time, as usually their season is short.

I have a collection of 24 varieties of hemerocallis for continuous bloom during the season. They are all in shades of cream and yellow. Which hardy perennials do you suggest for harmonizing bloom from early spring to fall in a border? Siberian iris, bearded iris, astilbe, cimicifuga, delphinium, *Salvia azurea,* Regal Lily, Veronica Blue Spires, goatsbeard, (*Aruncus sylvester*), *Platycodon grandiflorum,* liatris.

FOR SPECIAL PURPOSES

Which perennials can be planted around Oriental Poppies, to cover their unsightly fading foliage? *Anemone japonica, Gypsophila paniculata* Bristol Fairy, *Thalictrum aquilegifolium,* hardy chrysanthemums, *Eupatorium coelestinum.* This latter perennial starts very late in spring and bushes out by midsummer.

My yard is made up of rock and ashes. Which perennials will grow well here? Everything seems to burn up from heat of sun. *Euphorbia myrsinites, Tunica saxifraga, Sedum acre, Silene maritima, Saponaria* *ocymoides, Nepeta mussini, Lathyrus latifolius, Coronilla cappadocica, Echinops ritro.*

What makes the best plant or flower (perennial) for cemeteries? For shade: *Ajuga reptans, Dicentra eximia,* Vinca Bowles variety. For sun: *Dianthus plumarius, Sedum spectabile, Sedum acre.*

Which perennial can I grow in a small bed bordering my porch? The porch faces north, and I want something at least 1 ft. high. *Dicentra eximia* or *Phlox laphami.*

Which are the best perennials to grow in a border along an active cedar hedge? If there is at least a half day of sun: hardy asters; *Eupatorium coelestinum,* helenium, *Heliopsis scabra, Nepeta mussini, Ophiopogon jaburan, Oenothera youngi, Phlox arendsi* hybrids, and summer phlox are some of the most satisfactory.

Which perennial flowers can be satisfactorily grown in a city backyard garden where there is practically no sunlight? *Ajuga reptans* and *A. genevensis, Dicentra eximia, Mertensia virginica,* hemerocallis, *Pulmonaria saccharata,* and *P. angustifolia azurea, Phlox arendsi* Hilda, and *Phlox divaricata.*

Can you suggest perennials for small plot of ground facing the east? House is the background. Violets and lily-of-the-valley not successful. Aquilegia, anemone, *Phlox arendsi* and *P. divaricata,* anchusa, epimedium, monarda, *Hosta (Funkia) sieboldi* and *H. coerulea.*

What are some easily grown blue-flowered perennials? Veronica Blue Spires, *Veronica longifolia subsessilis,* Delphinium Belladonna, Tradescantia James Stratton, *Plumbago larpentiae, Platycodon grandiflorum, Campanula persicifolia grandiflora.*

What should one plant on north, east, and south fences to act as a screen, and also as a background for perennial borders? *Clematis montana rubens, Lathyrus latifolius, Polygonum auberti,* Bignonia Mme. Galen.

Will you name some very hardy perennials? Achillea, ajuga, aquilegia, artemisia, coreopsis, dicentra (bleedingheart), eupatorium, hemerocallis, lythrum, mertensia, *Nepeta mussini,* peony, platycodon.

I am interested in perennial flowers that require little work, after once being started, and are also good for cutting. Will you name a few? Bearded iris, hardy chrysanthemum, *Helenium autumnale, Coreopsis grandiflora,* peonies, hardy asters, *Gypsophila paniculata* Bristol Fairy, lily-of-the-valley, *Platycodon grandiflorum,* gaillardia.

Am interested in a small flower garden, including some for cutting. Which flowers would you recommend as of easy culture, and hardy? Any good varieties of bearded iris, any good varieties of hardy phlox, *Heliopsis scabra* Incomparabilis, *Gypsophila paniculata, Helenium peregrina* and *H. autumnale,* delphinium belladonna and delphinium hybrids, *Dianthus plumarius, Dicentra eximia* and *D. spectabilis.*

Are there any shade-tolerant perennials? Aconite, ajuga, anemone, aquilegia, astilbe, aubrietia, bleedingheart, bugbane, Carpathianbluebell, daylily, doronicum, eupatorium, lily-of-the-valley, *Lobelia cardinalis* and *L. siphilitica,* mertensia, *Monarda didyma,* phlox, plantainlily, plumbago, primula, thalictrum, vinca, and viola.

What are the best types of hardy flowers for a sunny, dry place? *Alyssum saxatile, Veronica incana, Cerastium tomentosum, Plumbago larpentiae, Aethionema grandiflorum, Arenaria montana, Arabis albida* (*alpina*), *Linum perenne,* dictamnus, heliopsis, iris (bearded), hemerocallis, *Oenothera fruticosa* (sundrops).

Can you give me the names of some low-growing perennials that can be used for a border? *Iberis sempervirens, Alyssum saxatile compactum, Plumbago larpentiae, Aster novi-belgi* dwarf varieties, polyanthus, primrose, *Sedum hybridum* and *S. sieboldi, Veronica incana.*

What low-growing, neat, easy perennials with good foliage can be used for edging? Ajuga, either with deep green foliage, or variety Metallica, with bronze leaves, is a good choice; it has blue flowers in the spring, husky foliage all season, spreads rapidly, and stands shade and city conditions. Several varieties of sedum may be used for edging, if controlled from spreading too much.

Will you name some bushy edging perennial plants for along walks? *Epimedium rubrum,* best in part shade; *Plumbago larpentiae, Campanula carpatica, Lamium maculatum, Iberis sempervirens, Aegopodium podagraria variegatum,* hosta (various kinds), *Lirope muscari* and its striped variety, *variegata; Sedum hybridum, S. spurium* and *S. sieboldi.*

Can you give a list of low perennials to be grown in beds along a flagstone-walk? *Achillea tomentosa, Ajuga genevensis, Alyssum saxatile citrinum, Anemone japonica,* Aster Countess of Dudley, *Campanula carpatica,* cushion chrysanthemums, dianthus, various species and varieties, *Nepeta mussini, Phlox subulata* varieties, *Plumbago larpentiae,* pyrethrum varieties, *Veronica incana.*

Will you name some perennials for planting along the front of the border? *Alyssum saxatile compactum, Dianthus plumarius, Statice longifolia, Plumbago larpentiae,* dwarf asters, *Veronica spicata nana, Arabis alpina, Silene maritima, Tunica saxifraga, Veronica rupestris, Nepeta mussini.*

What are some medium-height perennials for the center of the border? *Campanula persicifolia* varieties, Artemisia Silver King, *Achillea ptarmica, Aquilegia coerulea, Paradisea liliastrum major, Dicentra eximia, Eupatorium coelestinum, Veronica longifolia subsessilis, Gypsophila paniculata compacta.*

Which are the best tall-growing perennials for a border? *Bocconia* *cordata, Thalictrum aquilegifolium, Phlox paniculata* hybrids, *Helenium autumnale, Rudbeckia purpurea,* delphinium hybrids, asters (tall named varieties), *Cimicifuga racemosa, Campanula pyramidalis.*

Will you give list of plants for a small perennial border, with succession of bloom as long as possible and no plants which are difficult to obtain? *Arabis albida fl. pl., Phlox subulata,* bearded iris, Veronica Blue Spire, hemerocallis, heuchera, dianthus, Phlox Miss Lingard, Shastadaisy, *Nepeta mussini,* delphinium belladonna, hardy asters, coreopsis, gaillardia, *Heliopsis scabra,* helenium varieties, cushion chrysanthemums.

Can you give me a list of perennials to use in a border 2 to 3 ft. wide and 50 ft. long, that would keep it looking well all season? *Anchusa myosotidiflora, Dicentra eximia,* delphinium belladonna, *Dianthus caesius,* gaillardia, geum, *Gypsophila repens* Bodger, *Nepeta mussini,* pyrethrum, summer phlox, *Heliopsis scabra, Eupatorium coelestinum,* hardy asters (novae-angliae and novi-belgi types), cushion chrysanthemums. Constant color can be secured only by introducing annuals for later summer bloom.

Will you suggest varieties for a perennial bed 30 × 10 ft., so as to have continuous bloom from early spring to late fall? Make a selection from the following: March: crocus, snowdrop, squill, winter aconite. April: rockcress, goldentuft, hepatica, moss phlox, marshmarigold. May: perennial candytuft, columbine, globeflower, iris, Virginia cowslip, bleedingheart, polyanthus primrose. June: Japanese iris, early phlox, Shastadaisy, painted daisy, pinks, coralbells, Oriental Poppy, hybrid columbines, lemonlily, delphinium, hollyhock. July: babysbreath, false dragonhead, butterflyweed, loosestrike, Carpathian bluebell, perennial sunflower, balloonflower. August: plantainlily, rosemallow, sneezeweed, coneflower, cardinalflower, hardy asters, sea lavender. September: Japanese anemone, hardy asters, perennial sunflowers, goldenrod, showy stonecrop, hardy chrysanthemums. October: monkshood, hardy asters, leadwort (ceratostigma), hardy chrysanthemums, helianthus, *Salvia pitcheri.*

Is there a perennial that blooms nearly all summer? *Heliopsis scabra, Gaillardia aristata, Nepeta mussini,* and *Dicentra eximea* all come very near it.

Which perennials should I plant to provide flowers all summer? *Anchusa azurea* Dropmore, *Phlox suffruticosa* and *P. paniculata* varieties, *Penstemon heterophyllus,* gaillardia varieties, *Dianthus plumarius* hybrids, delphinium belladonna, Veronica Blue Spires, *Coreopsis grandiflora, Heliopsis scabra, Nepeta mussini.* (See also preceding questions.)

Which dwarf border plants bloom over the longest period of time? *Silene maritima, Dianthus deltoides* Brilliant, Viola Jersey Gem, *Tunica saxifraga florepleno, Nepeta mussini.*

SOIL PREPARATION

How deep should soil be prepared for new border? For best results, the soil should be dug and prepared not less than 18 ins., and preferably 24 ins., deep.

How shall I prepare new ground for perennials? Dig the ground to a depth of at least 18 ins., mixing in well-rotted cow manure, leafmold, peatmoss, or old compost, with bone meal 5 to 7 lbs. to 100 sq. ft.

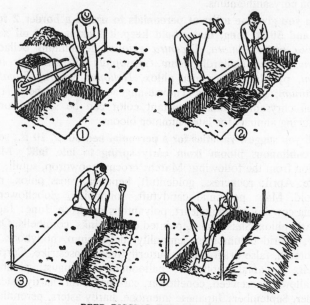

DEEP DIGGING FOR BIG CROP

(1) Soil is removed, a spade deep, from first section of garden plot. (2) Manure is spread on bottom of trench and forked in. (3) Next strip is measured off. (4) Soil removed from second section is thrown over into first trench. Operation is repeated to end of plot, when soil from first trench is used to fill the last one.

In preparing a border, should all stones be removed? Should soil be screened? For perennials, annuals, and shrubs, stones the size of a lemon or smaller may be left in the soil. Only for seedbeds should soil be screened through ½-in. mesh screen.

Is sand or clay better subsoil for perennial border? If sand is too loose and porous, drainage will be excessive; if clay is hard packed, drainage will be stopped. Generally speaking, a sandy subsoil is preferable. Hard clay should be broken up and lightened with coal ashes, gravel, or sand.

What element is lacking in the soil when perennials have good color and flower well but lack sufficient strength to stand upright and spread all over the beds? Possibly insufficient phosphorus and potash; but crowded planting, too much watering, and overfeeding with nitrogenous manures will cause weak stems. However, many perennials need support either by staking or using brush.

For 20 years we have had a perennial border. The last 5 years it has deteriorated; replacements, fertilizer, etc., have not solved the problem. Maple and elm trees grow near; sunshine is one hour a day. Can any soil be improved to overcome lack of sunshine? Nothing can be done to improve the soil so that it will overcome the lack of sunshine and greedy tree roots.

Why don't my plants near cedar trees thrive? Are there any perennials that will grow fairly well in the shade of cedar trees? The soil may be "poisoned" by accumulation of years of dead cedar foliage. Try removing this periodically. Give the surface a light application of slaked lime and a generous supply of rotted manure or leafmold. Work till the ground is in good "tilth." Most shade plants, especially the "woodsy" ones, will grow well if soil is friable and not super-acid. Some are ferns, dicentra, *Mahonia repens, Vinca minor,* hepatica, *Pachysandra terminalis,* primula, *Plumbago larpentiae, Phlox divaricata, P. carolina* and *P. ovata,* aquilegia.

FERTILIZERS

Which is the better time to put fertilizer on perennials—spring or fall? Apply manure or bone meal in the fall. Chemical fertilizer is best put on when plants are actively growing.

Will fresh sheep manure hurt perennials? No; providing it is not put on too heavily, and is not allowed to come in contact with the roots. Use 1 lb. to 10 sq. ft. and cultivate into surface soil.

What is a good fertilizer for asters, larkspur, peonies, and delphiniums? Well-rotted barnyard manure, supplemented during the growing season by a balanced commercial fertilizer. A little lime may be needed if the soil is acid.

Is there anything to be gained by fertilizing perennials during the growing season? In some cases, yes. Many kinds—phlox, delphinium, chrysanthemums, etc.—are helped by supplementary feedings of liquid manure or quick-acting commercial fertilizer, applied when flowers are about to be formed. Whether or not this is necessary depends on character of soil, the initial preparation of the border, and annual routine practices to maintain its fertility.

How do you prepare and fertilize perennial beds in the spring so as

not to disturb the plants?   By forking in the manure or fertilizer lightly.

Do all flowers of hardy varieties need lime? My soil is cleared-off pine woodland.   Most garden flowers need a soil near the neutral point. (See Lists, pH—Section I.) Your county agricultural agent probably would be glad to advise you on how much lime to apply to your soil.

PLANTING AND TRANSPLANTING

What is the method of planting perennials?   Make a hole of sufficient size, with spade or trowel (depending on the size of the root system), to accommodate the roots without crowding. Put plant in hole no deeper than it grew in nursery. Work soil between and over the roots, and pack *firmly* with hands, feet, or tamping stick. Soak with water if soil is on dry side.

Is it all right to plant perennials when soil is sopping wet?   No. Soil structure may be harmed as a result. Wait until soil is crumbly but still moist.

When is the best time to remake perennial border?   September and early October. Early spring is also good, but early-blooming plants should be replanted in the fall, except for those on the border line of hardiness in the region.

Is August a good month to revamp borders?   Definitely not. It is the hottest and driest month as a rule, and newly transplanted stock (with the exceptions noted below) is likely to suffer.

Which perennials should be moved in midsummer or early fall?   Bearded iris can be moved in July and August; bleedingheart, Christmasrose, narcissi, peonies in late August and September; Oriental poppies in August; Madonna Lilies as soon as tops wither.

Should all perennials be cut back either after replanting or transplanting in fall?   Tall perennials are better if cut back before being moved. Whatever foliage remains down near the soil matters little in the fall.

How can one transplant perennials without harming their growth?   By taking proper care in lifting, and transplanting at the proper time. For most kinds this is autumn or early spring.

What is the time for dividing and transplanting old-fashioned perennials in northern Maine: fall, or spring?   Fall, if it can be done at least 4 weeks before heavy freezing. It can be done in spring, too; but as early as possible.

In making over perennial borders, which plants should not be disturbed in the fall? What can I do about them?   None of the late-blooming ones, such as chrysanthemums, hardy asters, toadlilies, etc. Replant all early and midsummer bloomers, except those likely to suffer winter injury. Dig around others without disturbing them; transplant in the spring.

Should flowers be planted in straight rows or staggered? The effect is better in a staggered planting. When they are grown for cut flowers only, it is more convenient to have them in rows.

When is the correct time to plant perennials in the spring? Will they bloom the same year? Plant as early as the soil can be worked. Plants, if large enough, will flower the same season.

CULTURE

What constitutes good year-round care of a perennial border? In spring (when frost has left the ground) remove winter mulch. If manure or partly rotted leaves were used, leave finer portions and lightly fork into soil, along with top-dressing of complete fertilizer. Reset any plants heaved out of ground by frost. Hoe throughout season to kill weeds and prevent formation of surface crust. Support those plants which need it. Water thoroughly when necessary. Put on winter mulch after first severe frost.

What is the best way to keep down weeds in a border of perennials? Use a narrow scuffle hoe frequently to chop off weeds before they attain much size. Run the hoe through the soil about an inch below the surface. Weeds among the flowers must be pulled out by hand. Certain mulching materials also help to keep down weeds.

How close and how deep shall I keep soil worked around different plants, etc.? Depth depends on the type of plants; shallow-rooted plants need shallow cultivation; deep-rooted plants will take deeper cultivation. All can be worked close, but with care not to cut stems.

Will straw mulch help in weed control and hold moisture? If not, what will help besides pulling and hoeing? A straw mulch or any like material helps in summer to keep down weeds and hold moisture.

Which flowers should be pinched back to become bushy? Can poppies or lilies be so treated? Chrysanthemums, hardy asters, helenium, some tall-growing veronicas and penstemons. Most plants that tend to send shoots from the axils of the leaves can be pinched. Poppies and lilies may not be pinched.

When is best time to cut back perennials; and how far? This may be done in the late autumn, when the herbaceous stems have died down. Cut down to within an inch of the soil for most plants. Some plants have a clump or rosette of green leaves which should not be cut off; just cut the old flower stems. Some good gardeners prefer to wait until spring before cutting off the tops of the perennials. Their argument is that it helps to prevent winter injury because snow and tree leaves are held by the stems.

Why do hardy perennials die off after 1 or 2 luxuriant seasons?

Most perennials need dividing and transplanting after 2 or 3 years. Many are short-lived. Some do not overwinter very well; still others succumb to diseases or insects. Stick to those that are dependable.

How often should perennials be watered?   No definite time can be set; the kind of soil, the needs of the various plants, as well as other factors, have an influence. See that at all times during the growing season the soil is kept moist. This is the safest rule in mixed plantings.

Can plants be watered too much to bloom? I have some shade from maple trees and my soil gets hard if I don't water often. I have very little bloom on my perennials and roses. Iris do quite well.   Shade, rather than too much water, is responsible for lack of bloom. Use shade-tolerant plants. Improve soil by adding humus-forming materials.

Is it true that water should not touch leaves of perennials?   There is scant danger from water on the leaves doing any harm.

Do you have to water perennial flowers in the winter, or do you just cover them?   No watering is then needed, there being no activity. Merely cover them after the ground is frozen.

WINTER PROTECTION

What is the theory back of covering plants for the winter?   The theory varies with the kind of plant. Plants that are not hardy are covered *before* hard freezing to protect them from low temperatures which would destroy the cells and thus kill the plant. Truly hardy plants are covered *after* the ground freezes; not to protect them from cold, but to keep them cold. The theory here is to prevent fluctuation of ground temperature, resulting in alternate freezing and thawing, which cause the injury. A mild spell in late winter followed by a sudden hard freeze is dangerous. In some cases merely shading plants from the winter sun is sufficient. Most winter killing occurs in late winter or early spring.

Shall or shall we not let Mother Nature blanket our border garden with maple and locust leaves and if so, when shall we remove the leaves?   This is not the best way of protecting most garden perennials. Maple leaves tend to make a sodden mass and smother to death any but the more robust plants. Light, litterlike material, through which air can circulate, is best. Covering should be removed gradually when signs of pushing growth are observed underneath. Take off the final covering on a dull day.

Is it necessary to protect newly planted perennials for the winter? What is best method?   It is advisable, in colder regions, to protect plants for the first winter. Salt hay, peatmoss, evergreen branches, or cornstalks can be used. Lay loosely, so as not to smother plants; do not put on until after first hard freeze.

I planted perennial seeds in my cold frame in July. They have made good growth. Can I leave them in the frame until the spring? Should I put a mulch in the frame after December? A mulch will help. You may want to cover them earlier than December, depending on when you get heavy freezing. Seedlings from seed sown in July ought to make strong plants by late fall, particularly if planted out in a bed. If they are hardy perennials and are well grown, they do not need cold frame protection.

How much winter coverage is needed on established perennial beds of iris, phlox, tulips, and various small plants? How early should this be put on? What is best type? (New York.) A covering of about 3 ins. is sufficient for the average planting of perennials. Wait until the ground has frozen before putting it on. Use some litterlike material that will not pack down, such as salt hay, pine needles, or cranberry tops.

Is peatmoss a good winter covering for my garden of peonies, iris, hollyhocks, delphiniums, nicotiana, dicentra? Peonies and bearded iris should not be covered in winter. This favors rot. Delphiniums are better if covered with several inches of coarse ashes. Nicotiana is treated as a half-hardy annual. Hollyhocks and dicentra are the only ones that might benefit from the peatmoss.

Is it advisable to use littery material as a winter cover for plants near the house? In general, no. The appearance is untidy, and there is some risk of fire. Not all cigarette smokers are careful about the discards. Half-rotted manure or leafmold can be used on the ground, and evergreen branches for top cover.

In mulching plants and shrubs, do you wait till the ground is frozen? As a rule it is best to wait until the ground has frozen before putting on a protective mulch. Delay up to this point helps to harden the plants somewhat and also encourages rodents to find winter quarters elsewhere.

Should perennials be carefully covered in very changeable climates in the fall? It seems that we always cover or uncover at wrong times, and plants are more tender. It is really the changeable conditions in winter that make covering advisable. The covering is not to keep out cold but to protect against bad effect of alternate spells of freezing and thawing. Delay it as long as possible in the fall; at least until the ground freezes. With the approach of spring, partially remove the covering; watch the plants and the weather; complete it on a dull day if possible.

Which perennials need a winter mulch, and which prefer none? And what kind of mulch? Most perennials—except those with heavy green tops like tritoma—are the better for a winter mulch, particularly in regions of alternate freezing and thawing. Leafmold, salt hay, and evergreen boughs are some of the better materials. Light covering is to be strictly observed.

PROPAGATION OF PERENNIALS

SEED

When is the best time to sow perennials under glass? In late February or early March, in a greenhouse of moderate temperature. With most kinds seedlings will soon be large enough to be transplanted into flats, from which they can be set outside in a nursery bed in May. In this way only the usual summer cultivation is required and strong plants will be available for fall planting in the border if need be.

Can perennials be raised successfully from fall-sown seed? Where winter is severe and a cold frame is available, seeds of perennials could be sown as winter starts, so as to remain dormant for an earlier start in spring than would be obtained from spring sowing under similar conditions. Losses would be great in trying to carry small seedlings over winter.

Can you provide specific list of best planting dates for popular perennials from seed? If greenhouse space is available, in March; if only a cold frame, in April; if no glass protection, outdoors in May. Some growers prefer to sow in August, thus securing the advantage of fresh seed of the current season; but sowing in the first half of the year insures huskier young plants, better able to face their first winter.

What is the latest date for planting perennial seeds for bloom in following spring? Possibly in early August; but May sowing is better.

If you have no sunny window available, can you start perennial seedlings indoors? Perennial seedlings could be started indoors without a sunny window, but they would be a forlorn-looking lot. Better wait and sow outdoors in May.

Is it advisable to sow seeds of perennials in the open ground? Fair results could be expected if a special seedbed was made by mixing in fine leafmold and sand in the top 3 or 4 ins. of soil. Sow as early in May as possible and keep the soil nicely moist. A good method would be to sow in seed pans or flats, bury these to the rims in sand or coal ashes, and cover with panes of glass until germination.

Can any perennials be grown from seed by simply scattering the seeds where they are to bloom? There is no doubt it could be done with certain kinds; but it is not the best, nor, in the long run, the easiest method.

Should perennial seedlings be transplanted? If the seeds were sown during the summer, transplant when they have developed their first true leaves. Water immediately, and if possible provide light shade for a few days. Cultivate and water when necessary to promote growth.

Why do seeds I save come up so well, while seeds I buy, especially perennial, do so poorly? Because, being home-grown, they are fresh; and they may be sown soon after ripening if need be. Buy only from a reliable dealer.

Which perennials grow from seed easiest? Aquilegia hybrids, *Campanula persicifolia* in variety, Chrysanthemum "September Jewels," delphinium hybrids, *Coreopsis grandiflora,* erigeron, *Gaillardia grandiflora,* heliopsis, *Heuchera sanguinea, Lilium regale,* and *Lupinus polyphyllus* hybrids.

Can Thalictrum dipterocarpum seeds be planted in late fall or early winter? Will they bloom the following season? Yes, under glass; but they probably would not be strong enough to flower the following season.

What is the best method of raising thermopsis from seed? Sow the seed when ripe in a flat of sandy soil, and keep it in a cold frame over winter. If seed is at hand in March, sow in a greenhouse then, first placing it in hot water to soak overnight.

How can I raise trollius from seed? Sow the seed when ripe in a flat of rather porous soil. Keep it in a shaded cold frame, and as far as may be possible maintain cool, moist conditions. It will probably not germinate until the second year.

CUTTINGS

How are perennials propagated by cuttings? Cut off young shoots in spring when they are about 3 ins. long, making the cut below ground if possible. Insert in sand in hotbed, or in propagating case in cool greenhouse. Also, by non-flowering shoots in summer.

Will you tell me how to start slips in sand—such as chrysanthemum, carnation, and hydrangea? Use a box about 10 ins. deep; make drainage holes in the bottom; put in 1-in. layer of coarse cinders, and cover this with moss; add 3 ins. sand, tamped firm. Cover the box with a sheet of glass, and keep it where there is good light but out of sun. Chrysanthemum cuttings are taken from the base of old plants in spring; carnations may be rooted in August; hydrangeas either in spring or in August.

DIVISION

What is the best way to divide perennials? Dig up the plants and pry the rootstock apart into pieces of suitable size with the help of *two* digging forks; or hand forks if the plant is small.

When should perennials be divided? Early bloomers in early fall, late bloomers in spring. Bearded irises and Oriental poppies in summer.

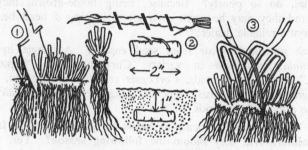

PROPAGATING HARDY PERENNIALS

Clumps or crowns can be cut apart with knife or spade (1); or torn apart with two digging forks (3). Root cuttings (2) of some subjects (Oriental poppy, phlox, platycodon), buried about an inch deep, quickly form new plants.

HYBRIDIZING

How are flowers crossed by hand? Remove anthers from the flowers you want for the seed bearer before the pollen is ripe. Cover flower with transparent bag. When stigma is ripe (or sticky), put on the ripe pollen from the male parent, return the bag, and tie securely.

How does one go about producing a new color in a perennial? By taking the pollen from the flower of one species or variety and placing it upon the stigma of another. Both should belong to the same genus.

SPECIFIC PERENNIAL PLANTS

ALYSSUM

What soil is needed to raise Alyssum saxatile compactum? It grows best in a light, porous soil with good drainage.

Alyssum saxatile lives but one year for me. Why is this? It needs a well-drained soil and full sun in order to live from year to year.

Does Alyssum saxatile compactum need full sun for growing? It does best in full sun; will grow in part shade but not flower so freely, nor live so long.

How do you make cuttings of Alyssum saxatile that will root and grow? Take cuttings soon after plants have flowered. Make them about 3 ins. long, or more, with about 1 in. of bare stem below the leaves; cut just below a leaf scar. Put in sand; water; keep shaded for a few days.

Will you explain how Alyssum saxatile compactum is raised from seed? I have had no luck with it. It may be raised from seed sown in summer and wintered over in a frame or bed and planted out in spring; also, sow in spring and plant out early in fall.

ANCHUSA

Will you please give cultural care of Anchusa Dropmore variety? Good garden loam, with fair moisture and full sun. Divide roots every 3 years.

Is Anchusa italica Dropmore a true perennial, or should it be treated as an annual? Is it hardy in Massachusetts? It is a perennial and should be hardy in Massachusetts. However, it is not a long-lived perennial.

ASTERS

When should hardy aster seeds be planted? May be sown in a greenhouse in March; cold frame in April; or outdoors in May.

When is best time to put out hardy asters? In spring before they have more than an inch or two of growth.

How can I keep wild aster (Michaelmas daisies) from growing too high? Pinching them back in early summer should help them stay dwarf and bushy.

Will you please name some red and pink perennial asters? Red: Beechwood Beacon, Red Rover. Pink: Harrington's Pink, Survivor.

Which are good white hardy asters? Mount Rainier, Mount Everest.

Which are good purple hardy asters? Amethyst, Violetta.

Will you name several kinds of dwarf hardy asters? Lady Henry Maddocks, Niobe, Constance, Ronald, and Blue Bouquet.

Which is a strong-growing hardy aster—preferably blue? Climax grows to 6 ft. or more, with lavender-blue flowers up to 3 ins. in diameter under favorable conditions.

BABYSBREATH (GYPSOPHILA)

How do you care for the soil when growing perennial babysbreath? It will grow in any reasonably good soil; it does not have to be rich, but should be well drained and deep, and not more than slightly acid.

Can perennial gypsophila be successfully transplanted? Yes, if care is taken not to break the fleshy roots. It is best done in the spring.

What's wrong when gypsophila petals are so small you can barely see them? Probably you have a poor seedling or another plant, *Galium aristatum,* which is sometimes sold as babysbreath which it resembles.

I have a Bristol Fairy Babysbreath that grows beautifully but never blooms. Can anything be done to make it bloom? Some do not bloom when planted in too rich a soil. Try transplanting it (being careful not to break the long roots), and lime the soil.

How is Gypsophila Bristol Fairy propagated? Propagation is done by division, by cuttings, or by grafting on pieces of roots.

Does Gypsophila Bristol Fairy come true from seed? No.

BLEEDINGHEART (DICENTRA)

I had a large bleedingheart die last winter; was this because I covered it with leaves? Probably you used too many leaves and smothered the plant; or perhaps you covered it too early. Wait until the soil is frozen, then cover lightly. Remove gradually in spring.

My bleedingheart plants grew to large, healthy bushes but would not bloom. Why? Probably planted in too dense shade, or in too wet a soil.

When is the best time to move bleedinghearts? In early autumn, or very early spring.

When is the correct time to divide bleedingheart? September.

CANDYTUFT

How can I propagate Iberis sempervirens (evergreen candytuft)? By seeds sown in spring; by dividing the old plants in autumn or spring; or by cuttings made in summer of the young growth inserted in a cold frame.

What is the best way to get a quantity of evergreen iberis for edging, from seed? Sow in an outdoor bed in May or June. Transplant seedlings to nursery beds, allowing 6 to 8 ins. between plants. Set in flowering quarters in fall, or following spring.

Will you give me proper culture for iberis? Mine is all dying. Iberis usually grows satisfactorily in any well-drained garden soil not too acid, and needs no special care. There are perennial and annual iberis. The perennial kind sometimes does better when plants are cut back to within a couple of inches of the crown after they have flowered. (See also Rock Garden.)

CARNATIONS (DIANTHUS)

Is it possible to grow the English border carnation in the Eastern states? The heat of our summers is not favorable to their culture, and they are not winter hardy here. Some success can be attained by sowing seeds in a greenhouse in February, potting the seedlings, and planting out in May in as cool a spot as possible; a little shade in July and August will help. Pinch them several times to make them branch; give some support to keep the plants from sprawling. Keep nearly all the buds removed until late summer, and let them flower in fall. Summer flowers are inferior.

What kind of fertilizer is best for carnations? The basic need is for some kind of humus; rotted manure is the best. Peatmoss, compost, or leafmold may be substituted, but to these lime and fertilizer must be added. To a bushel of any of the above add ½ lb. of pulverized limestone and 1 lb. of complete fertilizer. Mix thoroughly and spread this 3 ins. deep and mix with the soil. When plants begin to bloom, feed with pulverized sheep manure, dried blood, or tankage, ½ lb. per sq. yd.

The soil here is sandy. Water supply very limited. Will Chabaud Carnations get along on natural rainfall? It will not be possible to get the best returns under these conditions. Set the plants out as early as possible, while the weather is cool. In July put on old leaves, grass clippings, or weeds as a mulch, and maintain it. This will assist in keeping the roots cool. Don't let the plants exhaust themselves by overflowering. Remove most of the buds until cool weather sets in.

Will you give the culture of hardy carnations? Fertilizer needs, etc.? Sow seeds indoors in March in a soil mixture containing equal parts of loam, sand and leafmold. Transplant the seedlings into flats 2 ins. apart. Plant outside in May, about 12 ins. apart. Prepare the bed by forking in leafmold or peat; add 10 lbs. dried cow or sheep manure to 100 sq. ft. Water after planting; pinch out the tips to induce branching. Keep the soil stirred until the end of June, then mulch with old leaves or grass. Keep the plants watered; disbud for larger blooms.

What is the follow-up care of carnation seedlings; also winter care as far North as Pennsylvania? After hardening off the seedlings in a cold frame, set them out in the open in May in a well-prepared bed. (See previous questions.)

How can I grow pinks and carnations in upright clumps instead of spreading all over the ground? Pinks and carnations have a tendency to spread, although some of the improved Marguerite strain are less inclined than others. Insert small pieces of twiggy brush among the plants while they are still small. This will tend to hold them upright. A little tying here and there will keep them tidy.

I am able to raise most all kinds of flowers except hardy carnations. Just what do they need to do well? They need a well-drained soil. The plants should be set out early to become well developed before hot weather. Give them plenty of moisture during hot weather. Some believe in keeping the buds removed until late summer because they flower best in cool weather. Select a good strain like the hardy border, Improved Marguerite.

Why do my carnations have thin stems? The flowers are large, but the stems are so small they will not stand up. Try applying superphosphate to the soil, 4 oz. per sq. yd. Look to the variety; this sometimes is a vital fault that no amount of care will eliminate.

I have 2 choice carnation plants now 2 years old, one is full of buds and blooms, the other has not even a bud. Why? The fault in the non-blooming plant is in the way it was propagated—hard growth from non-blooming stock. Discard it, and propagate from the plant that blooms.

I read in a magazine that if you take cuttings from perennial pinks in October they would grow indoors. Did this, but they are not thriving. Why? What the article probably meant was to take the cuttings in October and winter the young plants over in the house and plant out in spring. They are not house plants. They need full sun, and bloom only in summer. In any case, cuttings are better if taken in August.

Our pinks formed large plants their second year but did not blossom. In the same soil sweetwilliams did very well. What do you suggest? The soil may be a little too rich or too wet, or lacking in lime. A well-drained soil, full sun, and the chance to ripen off in fall are necessary. Do not feed or water after August.

Which dianthus species are dependably hardy? *Dianthus arenarius, arvernensis, plumarius* (Cottage Pink), *deltoides* (Maiden Pink), *petraeus, caesius* (Cheddar Pink).

Which kind of pinks are perennial? Is it better to sow new seed every spring? The most important perennial pink in the garden is *Dianthus plumarius,* of which several varieties, both single and double, are grown. *D. alpinus, D. caesius, D. deltoides, D. knappi,* and *D. neglectus* may be grown in rock gardens. It should not be necessary to sow seed every spring. Named varieties of *D. plumarius* are propagated from cuttings or divisions.

The Scotch or dwarf pink in its usual form is too straggly. Can you name a dwarf compact variety that is better in this respect? *Dianthus deltoides* "Brilliant," *D. arvernensis, D. subacaulis, D. caesius.*

CHRISTMASROSE (HELLEBORE)

What is the botanical name of the Christmasrose? *Helleborus niger.*

How should I start a bed of Christmasroses? Select a position in partial shade where the soil is rich and moist; dig in some well-rotted manure or leafmold. Obtain young plants from dealers and set out in early spring.

I have a Christmasrose that I have had for 3 or 4 years, and last February was the first time it bloomed. Now I would like to move it. Will that set it back again for 3 or 4 years? The Christmasrose does not like to be disturbed, and if you move it again it will in all probability set it back for a few years. Moving carefully with a very large soil-ball would help.

What location should I transplant my Christmasrose to? It doesn't do anything on the south side of the house. The southerly aspect is too warm. Put in a cooler spot, and let it get established. Never allow it to become dry. See preceding answer.

Do Christmasroses need much sun? Christmasroses do best in partial shade, where they are not subject to being dried out in summer.

What makes my Christmasrose die down, then get new leaves, but no bloom? Has not bloomed this year. The plant failed to set flower buds due to some factor like drying out in summer, or poor soil. It may have been disturbed during cultural operations.

Will you tell me how to divide a Christmasrose? Mine is doing wonderfully well, but I would like to give some away. Best divided in late summer or autumn by taking a spading fork and lifting the side shoots without disturbing the main plant. It resents any disturbance, and when well established should be left alone.

I planted a Christmasrose in spring a year ago. It seems to be showing no signs of buds; in fact, no new shoots have come up this fall. It is in a well-drained spot, partially shaded, and covered with a box, one side of which is glass. What is the proper care? How early shall I cover it? What kind of fertilizer? Put fertilizer on in spring. Do not cover the plant at all. A few leaves drifting in among the stems is enough covering. Let the plant become well established, and avoid all disturbance. (See answers to preceding questions.)

How can I start Christmasroses from seed? Sow, as soon as ripe, in a mixture of soil, leafmold, and sand in cold frame, and keep moist. They are slow to germinate, and will probably take from 3 to 5 years to reach flowering size.

CHRYSANTHEMUM

The garden chrysanthemum, originally an oriental plant, has been so changed through centuries of cultivation that it scarcely resembles the species from which it was derived. In the year 1750 it was introduced into English gardens but at that time created very little interest. About a century later it was brought to America, and for years was grown only as a greenhouse plant. Within the last quarter of a century it has become a prominent garden flower—a result of the successful development of hardier and earlier-flowering types and varieties.

Chrysanthemums in the garden give a profusion of bloom in bright autumn colors as a grand finale to the gardening season. Light frosts do little damage to either the flowers or the foliage. If planted in protected spots, they will often remain attractive until mid-November in the latitude of New York State. Farther South, and in other milder climates, they are even better adapted, and a much larger selection of varieties can be used.

While hardy mums are comparatively easy to grow, they will not stand neglect. They need to be divided and reset every second or third year, and kept well fertilized and free of disease and insect pests. Considerable care should be given to the selection of varieties for outdoor planting. There are thousands of kinds in the trade, but only relatively few of these bloom early enough in the fall, or are sufficiently hardy where winters are severe, to be dependable garden plants.

Soil Preparation

What type of soil is best for hardy chrysanthemums?   Any friable, free-working soil is satisfactory. It should be well drained yet reasonably retentive of moisture and of goodly depth.

How should a bed for chrysanthemums be prepared and fertilized? Spade it deeply (without bringing up large quantities of unkind subsoil), incorporate a 3- or 4-in. layer of rotted manure and a dressing of superphosphate. If manure is not available, substitute compost and commercial fertilizer. Lime, if necessary, to keep soil approximately neutral.

How shall I prepare a bed for chrysanthemums? My ground is quite low and has a heavy clay subsoil.   Spade or plow in fall, adding manure, compost, or leafmold. In early spring apply a dressing of lime, and a week or so before plants are set out, fork in a light application of complete fertilizer. Chrysanthemums will not succeed in waterlogged soil.

Fertilizer

Do hardy chrysanthemums like lime or limestone in the soil?   They prefer pH 6 to 7. They have much the same requirements in this respect as the general run of garden vegetables.

What should chrysanthemums, carried over in a cold frame for winter be fed? And when?   Do not feed while in cold frame. Add manure and bone meal, or complete fertilizer, to outdoor beds prior to planting; possibly a light side dressing of complete fertilizer when half grown. Liquid manure applied in late summer and early fall works wonders.

What are "azaleamums"?   This is merely a trade name for a dwarf bushy type of chrysanthemums, more accurately termed cushion chrysanthemums.

How may manure be used on azaleamums? How freely?   Around second-year plants work a 2-in. covering well into the soil together with some bone meal and a dusting of wood ashes. When preparing soil for new plantings, manure and fertilize as for other hardy chrysanthemums.

Do azaleamums need summer feeding?   No. Not if soil is fairly good.

Planting; Transplanting

When should one plant chrysanthemums?   As soon as the ground can be worked in spring.

Where should mums be planted?   Any location that receives sunshine at least ⅔ of the day, providing soil and air circulation are good. Avoid overhanging eaves, walls, and stuffy corners. Don't crowd them among other plants.

What is the best way to plant hardy chrysanthemums?   In well-prepared soil make a hole with a trowel or spade, of ample size to accommodate roots. Set plant in position; spread out roots; work soil in among them and press soil firm with fingers. Do not plant when soil is wet and sticky. Water after planting if soil is at all dry.

How often should chrysanthemums be replanted?   Strong-growing mums should be divided every year; moderate-growing kinds every second year.

Would it be advisable to divide and reset chrysanthemums in fall after they have finished blooming?   No. It is safer to do this in spring. (See following questions.)

When is best time to divide hardy chrysanthemums? How?   Early spring, as soon as shoots are 3 to 4 ins. high. Dig up clump; discard old center portion; separate young offshoots; plant as single divisions, 10 or 12 ins. apart, in carefully prepared soil.

Is spring or fall the best time to transplant chrysanthemums that are in a too-shady place?   Spring is best, but if necessary they can be moved any time during the growing season if thoroughly watered first and carefully lifted with a good ball of soil.

Can hardy border chrysanthemums be moved when in bloom?   Yes. Be sure soil is moist; take up clump with a good root-ball; replant immediately. Firm soil around roots; shade for 2 or 3 days; and *don't neglect watering.*

When is the proper time to plant azaleamums?   In spring, just as new growth appears.

Should azaleamums be transplanted every year?   Divide and reset them every 2 or 3 years.

How often should Northland Daisies be lifted and divided? Every second year, in early spring when young growth is appearing.

Winter Care

What is the best way to store early chrysanthemums during winter in Washington? Lift plants and place in cold frame. If left in garden, cover lightly with evergreen branches, leaves, or similar protection.

What is the best way to care for chrysanthemums after they stop blooming in fall? Cut stems back close to ground. If brown foliage appeared during summer, burn stems and all dropped leaves—they harbor insects. Cover lightly with evergreen branches and dry leaves.

Should mums be wintered outdoors or in a cold frame? (New Jersey.) They should overwinter in New Jersey with a blanket of evergreen branches intermingled with leaves. Covering should be light.

What is winter care for chrysanthemums, without a cold frame, in southern Vermont? A blanket of evergreen branches intermingled with leaves would make best covering. Apply when soil is slightly frozen. Good soil drainage is an important factor.

Can well-rotted manure be placed on top of chrysanthemums as a winter mulch? Yes, but not close to the crowns. Pack dry leaves immediately around the plants themselves.

When should hardy chrysanthemums be covered, before or after frost? After the first killing frost and when the soil is slightly frozen.

Will azaleamums thrive in a northern exposure? Yes, if winter protection is provided. They must have full sun for at least ⅔ of the day.

How can I keep a cushion chrysanthemum over winter? (Minnesota.) Cushion chrysanthemums should winter over in Minnesota with a light blanket of evergreen branches and dry leaves applied when ground is lightly frozen.

How may I protect large-flowering chrysanthemum blooms in the outdoor garden? A double-thick cheesecloth covering stretched over a framework affords considerable protection. Avoid growing varieties that are late in flowering.

Will Northland Daisies winter satisfactorily in the East without protection? They are hardy, but benefit by light protection.

Can you take a non-hardy chrysanthemum, cut it off a few inches from the ground, keep it inside until spring, and then set it out? Yes, if you pot the roots and carry the plant over in a cool, well-lighted cellar or sun porch. Soil must be kept slightly moist. There are, of course, many reliable hardy chrysanthemums that do not require this attention.

Is December 1 too late to put a chrysanthemum plant outdoors that has been in bloom in the house for about 4 weeks? Too late for sure results. If planted in a sheltered corner and covered lightly, it has a fifty-fifty chance.

Would semi-hardy chrysanthemums winter in dirt in a barn cellar? Should the cellar be dark or light? A well-lighted barn cellar that is cool should do. Be careful that soil does not dry out.

Culture

Just how do you care for azaleamums? I know they are heavy feeders and I care for them very well, but why do they bloom one year and not the next? Divide every second year. Water copiously, but only when needed during dry periods. Reasonable feeding should be sufficient. Tarnished plant bug and other insect injury may prevent flowering.

How should chrysanthemums (cushion type) be cared for to bloom freely so they look like pictures in the catalogues? Choose sunny location. Don't crowd together or among other plants. Dig in barnyard manure, bone meal, and leafmold to a depth of 15 ins. under your plants. Cultivate frequently but lightly and water copiously when needed. Divide plants every other year.

What is correct care of English-type mums out of doors? They respond to same treatment as other types, but should be overwintered in a cold frame or given careful protection.

Will you give me information on how to grow large chrysanthemums out of doors? Use greenhouse varieties. Grow 1 to 2 stems only to each plant; remove all side buds. Shading with black sateen cloth to hasten blooming, or special protection, will be necessary.

Have read that covering chrysanthemums with black cloth for a certain time during the day brings them into bloom earlier. Will you give me detailed instructions for its use? There is a special black sateen cloth made for this purpose. Starting in mid-July, completely darken the plants from 5 P.M. until 7 A.M. Discontinue when the buds show color.

Can the blooms of large, exhibition chrysanthemums grown outside in the garden be hastened by enclosing them in darkened frames? If so, when should these frames be applied? I am an amateur but sell quite a few flowers to florists. Yes. Build framework of wood and cover with black cloth so as to be as nearly light-proof as possible. (See reply to previous question.)

What care should be given exhibition chrysanthemums? They require careful attention to all details of cultivation, such as propagating, soil preparation, watering, staking, disbudding, etc. When buds appear, apply liquid manure every week or 10 days until the flowers begin to open.

How do you care for Korean hybrid mums? Exactly as for other hardy chrysanthemums, but as they are more vigorous and inclined to spread more than older sorts, they should be divided every year. Light winter protection is advisable.

Will you please give culture on pompon chrysanthemums? Pompons are easily grown in the garden. Good rich soil, thorough watering when needed, and frequent cultivation are the essentials. Only tallest varieties require pinching.

How should I care for chrysanthemums in the spring? Divide and replant if they have been growing 2 years in same place; if possible give them a different location. Otherwise fork some manure or fertilizer into surface soil.

My chrysanthemums have been in 3 years and are large clumps. Should they be thinned out? Into what size clumps? Strong-growing mums should be divided every year; moderate-growing kinds every 2 years. Do this in early spring, leaving each division with 1 or 2 shoots.

How do florists manage to keep the foliage on chrysanthemums green down to the ground? By starting with young plants, taking care that they are never allowed to dry out, but are not overwatered. Most florists do not spray with water but use a rotenone mixture, spraying the plants every 10 days so that insects cannot get a start. (See Section VIII.)

How can I grow many-branched chrysanthemums? Keep plants young by frequent division and pinch them back 2 or 3 times during growing season. Keep staked up; and watered during dry periods.

What is the correct way to disbud chrysanthemums? Many garden mums produce larger flowers if just 1 (the terminal) bud remains on each branch. Remove unwanted buds by rubbing them out with thumb and finger when they are ⅛ in. or so in diameter.

When should chrysanthemums be pinched back? Tall-growing types, at intervals during spring and early summer. Give first pinch when 9 to 12 ins. high, second when about 15 ins. high, and possibly a third in late July. Cushion-type varieties require no pinching.

Should I pinch every shoot on a fall chrysanthemum, or just the center one? All strong shoots are pinched early in season to cause low, bushy growth.

What is the proper method to use for pinching back chrysanthemum plants? Pinch off an inch or so from the tip of strong shoots, using the finger and thumb.

How late in the season should azaleamum plants be pinched back? Azaleamums branch naturally and require little or no pinching.

Should cushion and pompon mums be pinched back in spring? All cushions and many pompons branch naturally and do not require pinching. A few of the taller pompon varieties should be pinched.

What is the best method of pruning and disbudding hardy mums? "Pruning" consists of pinching out the tips of the shoots when plants are 9 ins. high, and the tips of all subsequent side branches when they are 6 ins. long. This practice is discontinued in late July. Disbudding consists of removing many of the young flower buds so that the one or more allowed to remain on each stem will develop into especially fine blooms.

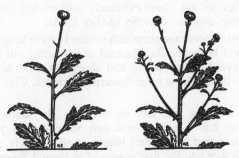

Disbudding a chrysanthemum. In order to secure a flower of large size, the top terminal bud (of the several which form) only is left.

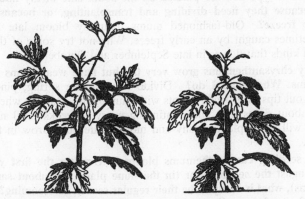

Pruning or "pinching" a chrysanthemum. In order to throw the plant's strength to the terminal bud, or a crown bud, side shoots or laterals are removed.

Do Northland Daisies require pinching back? Pinch once or twice, as needed, before end of June.

What is the proper way to tie up garden chrysanthemums? Each year the weight of mine bends over the stems. Wooden or bamboo stakes may be pushed into the ground near the plants and the stems neatly tied to these. Place supports *before they begin to flower*, and try to preserve the natural habit of plant. Avoid tying so that plant is bunched together like a shock of corn. Brushwood pea stakes inserted so that shoots grow up through the sticks are also very satisfactory.

Problems

Are hardy mums reliably hardy throughout the United States? Most varieties are not where extremely cold winters are experienced. Work is being done to develop hardier kinds.

How do you encourage chrysanthemums to have larger blooms, and stand up until blooming time instead of spreading out and laying on ground? Avoid overcrowding and shade. Provide neat stakes and tie plants to them. Grow large-flowering varieties. Give good cultural treatment.

Is there anything one can do to make chrysanthemums bloom earlier in the fall? I had several new varieties this year and they budded so late that they didn't bloom at all. Newly planted mums are apt to flower late the first season. Try them 1 more year without disturbing. When selecting new varieties choose early-flowering kinds.

Why didn't my chrysanthemums bloom this fall? They are the old-fashioned type and are planted on the south side of my house. Was it because they need dividing and transplanting, or because of an early freeze? Old-fashioned mums naturally bloom late and are sometimes caught by an early freeze. Why not try some of the many good kinds that flower in late September and October?

My chrysanthemums grow very tall but have weak stems and few blooms. What shall I do? Divide them in the spring; pinch back (nip out tips of growing shoots with thumbnail), starting when plants are about 6 ins. tall and continuing every 2 weeks until mid-July. This will make plants bushy and more floriferous. Grow in full sunlight.

If seedling chrysanthemums bloom in October the first year and in August the second year (in the same place and about same conditions), what is likely to be their regular season of blooming? From mid-September on if your plants are divided and reset every second year, as they should be.

What makes my hardy mums bloom so early (while summer flowers are still in bloom) that in the fall they are done? I have several varieties. (Pennsylvania.) You must have only early-flowering varieties. Obtain later-blooming kinds. Or hasten blooming by shading during part of the day. (See Culture)

Two chrysanthemums, full of buds that seemed ready to burst several weeks prior to freezing weather, did not bloom. Can their blooming season be hastened in any way? Your varieties are too late for your particular locality. Try earlier kinds. The *buds* of some varieties are not frost hardy, even though the flowers may be.

How can I keep chrysanthemums from growing out of bounds? Both hardy and exhibiton types are 5 to 6 ft. tall. Use phosphates rather than nitrates for fertilizing. Grow in full sun and do not crowd. Pinch back vigorous shoots during May, June, and July.

Are azaleamums hardy? Yes.

Do azaleamums bloom constantly? Reasonably so, from July on.

Our azaleamums have very few blossoms. This is their second year. What is wrong? Azaleamums should be at their best in their second year. Don't crowd. Prepare soil deeply and water copiously whenever needed during summer. They do best in full sun. Tarnished plant bug may prevent flowering.

Why do my azaleamums get taller than a lot of others I have seen? Perhaps the soil is too rich in nitrogen; plants too crowded or lack sunlight. Are you sure you have the true type?

Azaleamums, when originally planted, bloomed during late summer and were of proper color. During second year plants bloomed intermittently all summer and flowers were of mixed shades. Is there any special reason for this? Azaleamums are usually at their best in their second year. Poor soil or dry conditions will cause light and irregular coloring. Frequent cultivation and copious watering when needed will help. Divide plants every other year.

I had a fine collection of Korean chrysanthemums, but each blooming season I find that I have more bronze colors and less yellows, reds, etc. Do they revert? Chrysanthemums do sometimes exhibit the phenomenon known as mutation; but more probably self-sown seeds have germinated and reverted to other colors. The bronze varieties are especially vigorous, and would take the lead.

Do different chrysanthemums mix and change color if planted closely together? (Louisiana.) No. But seedlings which differ in color may spring up among the parent plants. This would be very likely in your climate.

Propagation

How can I best increase choice chrysanthemums? If hotbed or greenhouse facilities are available, take cuttings (in February or March) from stock plants kept over winter in a cold frame. Root in sand, transplant to pots or flats of soil, and set outdoors in April. Plants wintered outdoors can be taken up and divided in early spring.

What is the method of splitting or dividing an azaleamum plant? Same as any hardy chrysanthemum. (See previous and following replies.)

Will you please tell me how to divide or thin out chrysanthemum plants? Lift just as new growth appears in spring. With hands, knife, or a small hand fork pry off from outsides of old clumps small divisions, each consisting of 2 or 3 shoots, with roots attached. Plant divisions 1½ to 2 ft. apart in well-prepared soil.

Is it better to start new chrysanthemums from slips, or to divide old plants? Slips or small healthy divisions give equally good results. The former are better, however, if stock plants are infested with nematodes.

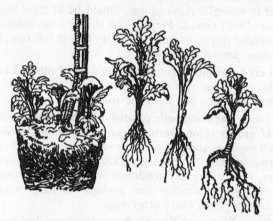

Old chrysanthemum plant, and young growths with roots removed to provide new plants.

Will chrysanthemums grow from cuttings made from tips of shoots that are removed when plants are pinched back? Yes.

When is the proper time to start to root mum cuttings for best results? For large plants, cuttings should be started indoors in late February and the cuttings taken in March. Cuttings taken in April and May are quite satisfactory, but plants are smaller.

How can I graft several colors on a single chrysanthemum plant? Grow a strong, early-started, young plant to a single stem. At the desired height, say 2½ ft., pinch the tip out to promote side branches. On these insert the grafts. A humid atmosphere should be maintained after grafting and the grafts should be kept sealed with polythene plastic film until they have formed a good union.

How can chrysanthemum seeds be saved? Early varieties may produce seeds in the garden. Better results are obtained from pot-grown plants kept under glass from late September on. This is the only satisfactory way of securing seeds from late-flowering varieties.

Can one buy seeds of the large-flowering type chrysanthemums?

They are seldom catalogued. One of the large seed concerns might be able to get them for you.

How can I grow chrysanthemums from seeds to get blooms first year? Start seeds indoors during March. Transplant once to flats or a cold frame before planting in outdoor garden.

Pests and Diseases

What insects and diseases commonly attack hardy chrysanthemums? See Chrysanthemums—Section VIII.

Why didn't my hardy chrysanthemums bloom this year? The leaves turned like dusty-miller leaves. Evidently the plants were badly mildewed. Do not plant too closely together or in shade. Dust with dusting sulfur or mildex, at first sign of appearance of mildew.

What spray do you recommend for black aphids on outdoor chrysanthemums? Use Bordeaux mixture to which Black Leaf 40 is added at rate of 1½ teaspoonfuls to each gallon. This spray, used at frequent intervals, kills aphids, controls certain fungous diseases, and repels the leaf nematode. Systox is a new control.

How can I control chrysanthemum leaf-spot disease? First be sure you have this disease. The effects of leaf nematodes are often mistaken for it. Leaf-spot produces in the diseased areas masses of white spores which are easily seen with a hand lens. To control, pick off and burn infected leaves; spray with Bordeaux mixture or with Ziram; avoid wetting leaves when watering.

What is care of fall-blooming chrysanthemums? Mine die down every fall, lose their leaves (which turn black or brown), and flower very late. They are probably infested with leaf nematodes (eelworms). After blooming, cut back close to ground. Remove and burn all stems and leaves, which harbor this pest over winter. In spring propagate from tip cuttings and set plants in new location in good soil, or in soil disinfected with formaldehyde, chloropicrin or systox.

My chrysanthemum blooms turn brown before fully opening. Why? Foliage is in good condition. Send a few affected leaves to your State Agricultural Experiment Station to be checked for leaf nematodes. (See previous reply.)

Varieties

Will you name the best double early-flowering varieties of garden chrysanthemums which are hardy and which will flower in September? Eugene A. Wander and Algonquin are good early yellows; Seminole, a small early white; Dean Ladd, bronze, My Lady, orange; Canary yellow.

Will you suggest outdoor chrysanthemums to have bloom from earliest to latest date? Try the azaleamums and the cushion pom-

pons, Summertime, September Bronze and September Gold, for early
flowering. Any varieties dated in the catalogues to bloom by October
5 will be good for later flowering.

**I want a collection of really hardy chrysanthemums—improved
plants of the old-fashioned sorts. Can you tell me what to ask for?
(Virginia.)**   Granny Scovill, Jean Treadway, Vivid, and the double
Korean hybrids, King Midas, Lavender Lady, and Mrs. Pierre S. du
Pont III should be hardy in Virginia.

Which variety or type of chrysanthemum is hardiest?   Cushion-
type varieties (such as Amelia, King Cushion, and Dean Kay) are
both early and hardy. The newer varieties originated by the University of Chicago are good.

**What varieties of mums are hardy? We dug and stored some and
they died, and those we tried to protect didn't thrive.**   For the many
hardy varieties now available read other replies and consult catalogues
of firms specializing in these plants. In severe climates they can be
wintered in a cold frame if covered with dry leaves after the soil is
lightly frozen. The glass should be shaded or covered with a wooden
shutter.

**What are the best large-flowering chrysanthemums—both hardy
and tender? (Kentucky.)**   The early-flowering, large commercial
mums, such as Betsy Ross, Detroit News, Golden Bronze, Mrs. H.
E. Kidder, and Sunglow should do well in Kentucky. For hardy decorative varieties, try Avalanche, Lavender Lady, Mrs. Pierre S. du
Pont III, King Midas, Granny Scovill, and Burgundy; or you could
make a selection from the "Bird" varieties.

What chrysanthemums are best for our location? (Idaho.)   There
are many good early kinds available. Try the cushion varieties, such
as Dean Kay, King Cushion, September Bronze, and September Gold.
For larger varieties, Eugene A. Wander, My Lady, and Early Wonder.
It would be a good idea to consult a local authority if possible.

What are the best early-blooming yellow chrysanthemums?   Algonquin, Eugene A. Wander, King Midas, and the pompon, September Gold.

Is Astrid correct in denoting a class of chrysanthemums?   No.
The variety Astrid was the forerunner of the named *arcticum* hybrids,
such as Good Morning, and also of the Northland Daisies. The name
"astermum" has been used in connection with a type that has aster-
like flowers.

**Is there any chrysanthemum that is low-growing and spreading,
that could be used along the top of a wall?**   Yes; Golden Carpet,
which grows about 18 inches tall, and spreads to 3 feet or more.

**Azaleamums and astermums—what is the difference, if any? Give
colors.**   Azaleamums are a class of the cushion type, and may be had

in white, yellow, pink, and bronze. All are low-growing and early. Some mums having aster-like flowers have been described as aster-mums, but they do not form a recognized type.

What are the names and where can I get large-flowering ball-type mums? Varieties such as Pink Chief, Silver Sheen, Alameda, and others could doubtless be furnished by your local florist who grows indoor mums, or you could purchase them from chrysanthemum specialists.

What are the best types of cushion mums to provide a good color range? Amelia, King Cushion, Golden Cushion, and Marjorie Mills.

What are Northland Daisies? Where did they originate? What is their history? Originated by Mr. and Mrs. J. Franklin Styer. They are descendants from Astrid, which is either a seedling or sport of *C. arcticum*. Pollen from other types has also been used.

COLUMBINE (AQUILEGIA)

My columbines never grow into healthy plants, as I have seen others do. They have full sun, and the other plants around the columbines grow very well. Why? They need a well-drained sandy loam, neutral or slightly acid. Prepare ground at least a foot deep; incorporate a 2-in. layer of rotted manure; space plants at least 9 ins. apart.

What is the best location for columbines? What fertilizer? Most any location except a hot, dry, windy one; light shade, too, is beneficial. Top-dressing of leafmold, with well-rotted manure or bone meal, in early spring, is good.

What is the proper way to plant columbines? I planted them in rich woods dirt in a spot that got sun in the morning, shade later in the day, fairly well drained. They never came up. The soil and position should be all right. You probably planted them too deeply, and the crowns rotted. They are subject to a soft rot.

From a planting of 15 columbines only 2 bloomed. Could you supply any information as to their culture? See preceding answers. When established, the others probably will bloom.

Can columbine seedlings, coming from seed planted in August, be transplanted next spring? Yes.

Is it possible to transplant old columbine plants? When? Yes. Best done in early spring. Water until established. Don't plant too deeply.

How shall I divide columbines? Lift the clumps, shake off the soil, and gently pull the plant apart, taking care not to break the roots.

DAYLILY (HEMEROCALLIS)

When is best time to plant lemonlily? How? Either autumn or spring planting is all right. Dig soil deeply, adding well-rotted cow manure; dig holes deep enough when planting so that roots are not crowded, and set plants with crown just level with soil.

Do daylilies have to be planted in the shade? No. Daylilies will grow in full sun if the soil is rich and moist, but otherwise do better in partial shade.

Can hemerocallis be successfully grown planted among other perennials in a border? Yes, providing you give them space enough to grow.

What is the cause of hemerocallis failing to blossom? Failure to bloom is most commonly due to too-dense shade, or plants being overcrowded and the soil exhausted.

How can I get lemonlilies to bloom? Divide and replant in full sun in soil that has been dug deeply (18 ins.) and enriched with a 3-in. layer of rotted manure, plus bone meal at the rate of 6 oz. per sq. yd.

How shall I divide hemerocallis, especially Hyperion? Hemerocallis sometimes are hard to divide, especially old clumps. The best method is to first dig up clumps, then push two spading forks through the clump, back to back, and pry the clump apart.

Can you give me the name of an exquisite, dainty, lemon-yellow lily, which blooms profusely in early spring, then on and off through summer? Foliage same as dark daylily, only light and much daintier. In all probability the lemonlily, *Hemerocallis flava*. This species is fragrant.

Will you name some good varieties of hemerocallis that will give a succession of bloom, from the earliest to the latest? Hyperion, July to August; Mikado, June to August; Waubun, June to July; Theron, July to September; Bagdad, July; Midas, June to July; Tangouni, May to June.

I am interested in hemerocallis. Will you name some of the most popular ones? Below are listed the first 25 of 100 in the latest list poll—1956—conducted by the American Hemerocallis Society. The numbers in parentheses is the number of votes received by each variety. The names on the right are those of the introducers. 1. Evelyn Claar (150), Kraus; 2. High Noon (126), Milliken; 3. Prima Donna (124), Taylor; 4. Salmon Sheen (122), Taylor; 5. Naranja (119), Wheelor; 6. Garnet Robe (118), Milliken; 7. Painted Lady (112), Russell; 8. Pink Damask (112), Stevens; 9. Pink Dream (110), Childs; 10. Cibola (109), Hill; 11. Colonial Dame (102), Milliken; 12. Jack Frost (97), Lester; 13. Pink Prelude (96), Nesmith; 14. Ruffled Pinafore (92), Milliken; 15. Potentate (86), Nesmith; 16. Dauntless (85), Stout; 17. Show Girl (84), Wheelor; 18. Georgia (79), Stout; 19. Revolute (77), Sass, H. P.; 20. Caballero (73), Stout; 21. Brocade (70), Taylor; 22. Neyron Rose (68), Kraus; 23.

Colonel Joe (67), Lester; 24. Picture (67), Lester; 25. Summer Love (65), Milliken.

Is there such a thing as a double daylily? I have one and thought maybe it was a freak. Yes, there is a double daylily, *Hemerocallis fulva* variety Kwanso.

Can you tell me how to hybridize hemerocallis? The flowers which are to be used as the seed bearer should be emasculated (remove anthers) and enclosed in a waxed or cellophane bag; when the stigma becomes sticky, the ripe pollen from another variety is transferred to it.

What is the best time of day to hybridize the hemerocallis? From about 12 noon until 2 P.M., as the pollen will be dryest at that time.

DELPHINIUM

The modern delphinium is one of the most spectacular and valuable of our garden flowers. The common garden hybrids are tall-growing, and are best used toward the back of a mixed border where they create strong vertical lines and accent points. While the clear blue colors are most highly prized, sparkling whites, rich violets, and soft, pleasing mauves are available. Some species have yellow or red flowers, but they are not so easy to grow in the average garden; nor are the flower spikes as showy as those of the more common types.

The geographic distribution of delphinium species is more or less limited to the Northern Hemisphere, but they are used in gardens on every continent. While their culture varies in different regions, they are grown successfully throughout the United States and Canada. Much of the horticultural development has occurred within the last 20 years, and improved colors and forms are rapidly replacing the earlier introductions.

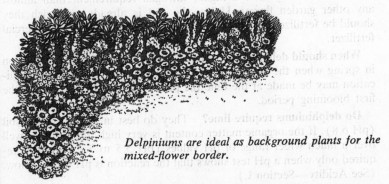

Delpiniums are ideal as background plants for the mixed-flower border.

There are 4 main types of delphiniums. The erect and tall-growing elatum or garden hybrids bear single or double flowers in dense spikes.

The belladonna and bellamosum strains are dwarfer, with more finely cut foliage and looser spikes. The two are essentially much alike in habit of growth, but the belladonnas have light-blue or white flowers, while in the bellamosum type the flowers are dark blue. The Chinese delphinium is comparartively dwarf, seldom attaining a height of more than 3 ft. The foliage is finely cut and the clear blue or white flowers are borne in a loose, informal arrangement. They are the easiest to grow, and especially valuable for cutting, to be used with other flowers in mixed bouquets or arrangements. There are also several annual species which are well adapted to many regions.

Soil and Fertilizer

What kind of soil is desirable for delphiniums? A rich, friable loam containing a high percentage of organic matter.

How can one increase the amount of organic matter in the soil for delphiniums? Experiments have shown that thoroughly decomposed leafmold is the best organic matter to use. Oak leafmold is less desirable than other types. Mix the leafmold with soil at the rate of 8 to 10 bu. per 100 sq. ft.; or 1 bu. of leafmold to 8 bu. of soil.

Is peatmoss good for delphiniums? In some experiments carried out to determine the best type of organic matter, peatmoss was found to be less desirable than leafmold.

What soil mixture is best for starting delphinium seeds? A mixture of 1 part good garden loam, 1 part sand, and 1 part leafmold is satisfactory. Sift through a sieve having ¼-in. mesh.

Can manure be used on delphiniums? Manure, if well rotted, is excellent. It may be mixed with the soil at the time it is prepared or it may be used as a top-dressing. Apply about 5 bu. per 100 sq. ft.

Do delphiniums need fertilizer? Yes. They require an abundance of nutrients. They have a higher nitrogen requirement than almost any other garden flower. Unless the soil is already very rich they should be fertilized at least twice a year with a complete commercial fertilizer.

When should delphiniums be fertilized? Make the first application in spring when the new shoots are about 4 in. tall. A second application may be made at the time the plants are cut back following the first blooming period.

Do delphiniums require lime? They do best in a slightly acid soil (pH 6.8). If the organic matter content is very high, they will do well over a much wider range of pH values (pH 5.5 to 7.2). Lime is required only when a pH test shows that the reaction is pH 6.5 or below. (See Acidity—Section I.)

What type of lime should be used for delphiniums; and how should it be applied? Ground limestone is best. Where soil is very acid or very heavy, hydrated lime may be used. Spread it evenly over soil surface and work it into the top 3 or 4 ins.

Should lime be applied to delphiniums every year?   No, only when a soil test indicates it is necessary.

How can one tell by observing the plants when the soil is too sweet for delphiniums?   The leaves appear mottled with yellow or, in severe cases, with white. The veins usually retain their dark-green color. A pH test of the soil will confirm the plant symptoms.

Planting and Replanting

In what situation should delphiniums be planted?   In full sun or very light shade and, if possible, with some protection from strong winds.

How far apart should delphiniums be planted?   In perennial borders, 2 to 3 ft. each way. In cut-flower garden, 3 to 4 ft. between rows and 2 ft. between plants in rows.

When should delphiniums be transplanted?   Very early spring is best; but they may be transplanted with success in fall, or immediately after their first period of bloom.

When should full-grown delphiniums be moved?   In very early spring, if possible before growth starts. Move with a large ball of soil.

Culture

How can I keep my delphiniums healthy?   Give them a rich, well-drained soil. Cover the crowns in winter with leached coal ashes to discourage crown-rot. Fertilize occasionally.

How can delphiniums be made to bloom in the fall as well as during their regular season?   By cutting the flowering stems back to the ground as soon as possible after they have finished blooming. New shoots will then come up and flower in the early fall.

How can delphiniums be staked?   Begin when the plant is about 3 ft. high, and place 3 6-ft. stakes in the form of a triangle around it. Tie a band of raffia or soft twine around the stakes about 1 ft. above the ground. As the plant grows, tie additional bands around the stakes. If desired, individual stakes can be used for large-flowering spikes. This latter method is to be preferred in decorative plantings.

Should delphiniums be watered?   Delphiniums require large quantities of water, especially during, and just prior to, the flowering period. They will be improved by thorough watering when the weather is dry.

Is there any advantage in spreading coal ashes around delphinium plants in the fall?   Many successful delphinium growers follow the practice with good results. Just what the benefits are has never been scientifically studied.

What winter care should be given delphinium seedlings started in a cold frame in August?   Cover with about 2 ins. of medium-coarse clean sand. Later mulch with straw or salt hay. Put sash on the frame to keep out snow and rain.

Should young delphinium plants, set out in the fall, be mulched? It is always well to protect seedlings transplanted in the fall from heaving. Covering the plants with about 2 ins. of sand, and later mulching lightly with salt hay or straw, will give the necessary protection.

Should established delphiniums be covered over winter?   In all but the coldest climates this is unnecessary. Delphiniums are more likely to be killed by poor drainage, smothering, or diseases than by low temperatures.

Problems

Should an amateur buy delphinium plants or start them from seeds? Either is satisfactory, but most delphinium growers prefer to start their own plants. Purchase only the best plants or seeds. Inferior strains are unsatisfactory.

Do seeds from hybrid delphiniums produce desirable plants?   If seeds are saved from superior plants they will probably be satisfactory. It is usually best to buy seeds from reliable growers who have taken special pains in producing them.

Why have my delphiniums failed since I moved them and replanted them 1 foot from a hedge where they get south sun?   Probably the moving is responsible. They may do better when they become re-established. However, you have set them too near the hedge. They should be at least 2 or 3 ft. away and kept well fertilized and watered.

How can I prevent my delphiniums from growing tall and having brittle stems even though I withhold nitrogen?   Vigorous delphiniums are likely to be brittle and to break off during wind- and rain-storms. Withholding nitrogen will not make the stems less brittle; in fact, it may make them more so. (See Nitrogen—Section I.) Nothing can be done except to stake the plants adequately.

Can delphiniums have their tops pinched out, like zinnias, to make them branch?   No, the shoots that arise from the bases of the plants terminate in flower spikes. When the growing point is removed, the lateral buds do not develop as they do with zinnias.

How can I keep delphiniums alive during the hot summer months? They may be grown in light shade or cloth houses. In the open keep them well watered and free of crown-rot diseases.

Why do delphiniums freeze out in winter?   Delphiniums are really very hardy plants. It is seldom that they are killed by low temperatures. They are more likely to be smothered by snow, ice, or water.

Diseases, especially crown-rot, may develop during the fall, winter, or early spring, and kill the plants. Heaving is another hazard.

How long will delphiniums live?   Where the crown-rot diseases are not serious, they live indefinitely. However, since these organisms are widespread over much of the United States, from 3 to 5 years is the expected life of the ordinary plant.

How can Delphinium cardinale be wintered in cold climates?   It can't. This species is tender and will not stand freezing. It can be carried over winter only in a greenhouse, and even then it is not very successful.

Is there any reason why good delphiniums cannot be grown in Connecticut?   No. In fact some of the best delphiniums in the country have been grown in Ridgefield, Connecticut, by a former president of the American Delphinium Society.

How can delphiniums be grown in a warm climate, such as Florida? Grow them as annuals by sowing seeds early each spring. The plants are not usually successfully carried over a second year.

Is there a truly perennial delphinium?   In their native habitats many species persist for years, but under garden conditions they are more subject to diseases and are less long-lived.

Why do some delphiniums live longer than others?   Natural variation in vigor, disease resistance, etc., account for the difference in longevity.

Propagation

What is the best temperature for germinating delphinium seeds? The optimum is 55° F.

What is the best way to raise delphiniums from seed?   Many different methods are successful; it is difficult to state which is best. Where many plants are needed, sow in well-prepared soil in a cold frame in August. Leave the seedlings in the frame over winter and transplant to the garden in spring.

What conditions are necessary for growing delphinium seedlings? Good light, plenty of moisture (but the soil must not be kept soaked), and a temperature of 55° to 60° F.

Can delphinium seeds be sown in the open ground?   Yes. If you do so, prepare a bed with special care where the tiny seedlings can be protected. It is really better, however, to sow in a cold frame or in seed flats.

When should delphiniums be started indoors?   Seeds may be sown any time between February 1 and May 1. If started early, many of the plants will bloom the first year.

How thick should delphinium seeds be sown and how deep should they be covered?   Sow in rows spaced about 2 ins. apart. The seeds in the rows should be about ¼ in. apart. Cover so that seeds are barely out of sight.

Should delphinium seeds be disinfected? And how? Disinfecting is desirable, especially where the soil is not sterilized. The use of Semesan or a similar product is satisfactory. Merely place a pinch of the powder in the seed package and shake until seeds are evenly covered.

Is it necessary to sterilize soil in which delphinium seeds are sown? Not necessary, but it is good insurance. Measure out 2½ tablespoonfuls of formaldehyde (40 per cent strength) for each bushel of prepared soil; dilute with 4 or 5 times its volume of water; add to soil, and mix very thoroughly. Place soil in seed boxes, saving a little for covering the seed; stack the boxes one above the other to confine the fumes for a day or two, then uncover them. When the odor is no longer perceptible it is safe to sow the seeds. Soil-fume caps will destroy nematodes in garden beds.

Will delphinium seeds sown indoors in spring produce flowers in summer? If sown indoors before April 1 most of the plants will bloom in late August or early September.

Should delphinium seedlings grown indoors be transplanted, or may one wait until they can be planted outdoors? Transplant to flats as soon as big enough to handle conveniently. Use a soil mixture of 1 part leafmold, 2 parts garden loam, and ½ part sand. Good drainage must be provided so that soil never remains soggy.

Is it wise to divide delphiniums that have grown to a large size; and how often should this be done? Ordinarily it is better to start new plants from seeds, but old clumps can be divided if they have become too large; this will usually not be until they are at least 3 years old.

How are delphiniums divided; and how large should the divisions be? Dig the plants, shake off the soil, and cut the clumps apart with a strong knife. Replant immediately in well-prepared soil. Each division should contain 3 to 5 shoots.

Diseases and Pests

My delphiniums suffer from "blacks"; they are deformed and stunted and marked with black streaks and blotches. What is wrong? This "disease" is caused by an infestation of an exceedingly minute pest—the cyclamen mite. Cut off and burn badly infected shoots. Spray from early spring to flowering time with rotenone or nicotine spray or, use a miticide such as Dimite about once a week. Avoid planting delphiniums near strawberries, which are also host to this mite.

What is a cure for crown-rot of delphiniums? Crown-rot is really a name for a group of diseases. All are very difficult to control. Sterilization of the soil with formaldehyde or chloropicrin is the surest method. In small gardens destroy infested plants, drench the soil with Semesan solution or mercury bichloride (1 to 1,000 parts of water). When possible, plant delphiniums on new ground.

I planted out some delphiniums but several were eaten off by cutworms. How can I prevent a recurrence? See Cutworms—Section VIII.

Is mildew on delphiniums caused by the soil? No. Mildew is a fungous disease that infects the leaves. It is controlled by keeping the plants dusted with sulfur. Avoid setting plants too closely together. (See Mildew.)

Types and Varieties

How many colors of delphiniums are there? If all the species are considered, they cover an unusually wide range. The garden hybrids (*Delphinium elatum*), the belladonna, bellamosum, and Chinese types contain white and tones of blue, violet, and mauve. *Delphinium nudicaule* is orange and red; *D. cardinale* is clear red; *D. sulphureum* and *D. zalil* are yellow.

Is there a true pink perennial delphinium? The variety Pink Sensation comes nearest to this description.

What delphiniums are bred especially for hardiness? Giant Northern Hybrids. They can be had in light blue, lavender, violet, white, blue, and pink-lavender, in named varieties.

How can I get the colors I want by growing my own delphiniums from seed? The Pacific Giant Hybrids can be had in blue and light blue, violet and dark blue, white, and in pastel and mixed shades.

EREMURUS

When is the best time to plant eremurus (foxtaillily), spring or fall? Will 2- or 3-year-old plants bloom the first season after planting, or must they be older? (Wyoming.) Plant in fall, since top growth begins early in spring. Usually plants younger than 4 years bloom little, if at all. For first season results 4-year-old plants are set out. They will require a winter mulch (10 or 12 ins. of coal ashes) to protect the roots from too-severe freezing in Wyoming.

Does eremurus (foxtaillily) require a special kind of culture? It is best to give it a deep, well-prepared soil but see that it is well drained. Work in some fine bone meal each fall.

How do you plant foxtaillily (eremurus)? Do you spread the roots out or do you plant with the roots down, like Oriental poppy? They should be planted with the roots spread out flat. The roots will snap off if bent when planting.

How deep should 4-year-old eremurus roots be planted?   Plant so that the crown is about 2 ins. below the soil surface. Too-deep planting is apt to cause the crown to rot, especially in a heavy soil.

I have some 3-year-old eremurus in a lining-out bed. What care do they require; and do they prefer light or heavy soil?   Plant in sheltered position in rich, well-drained soil, in full sun, with the fleshy roots spread out and the bud 2 ins. under the soil. Plant in late September, and cover before winter with leached coal ashes 6 ins. to a foot deep.

Can eremurus be divided, and when?   They may be divided only with difficulty, unless they make offsets freely. Early fall is the best time. Each division must have a bud, or eye.

Can eremurus be raised from seed? When and how long until bloom?   May be raised from seed sown in flats or pots in late autumn or spring. Will bloom from seed in about 4 to 6 years.

EUPATORIUM (HARDY "AGERATUM")

How deep should the hardy ageratum be planted?   It is shallow rooting; plant about 2 ins. deep. The roots are stringy; merely spread them out and cover.

When should hardy ageratum be moved?   It is best done in spring before growth starts.

How often do you have to move hardy ageratum?   Probably best lifted and transplanted every year or two, as it grows into quite a mat which usually dies out in the center.

HARDY FUCHSIA

Is hardy fuchsia a shrub, or can it be included among herbaceous perennials?   It is really a low-growing shrub, but in Northern climates it is often killed down to ground line by the winter, making it in effect an herbaceous perennial.

In what kind of soil should a hardy fuchsia be planted? I had no luck with mine.   A light, well-drained garden loam with some leaf-mold added. It is often planted in rock gardens. Keep it out of exposed situations, and try a light winter cover.

What might cause the buds of a hardy fuchsia to drop off before opening? The plant seemed healthy and many buds formed, but all failed to develop.   If spring planted, the exposure probably was too hot and dry. Fuchsias as a whole are not good garden plants in the East or Midwest, and the so-called hardy sort is far from being so under winter conditions.

Will Fuchsia riccartoni (or the variety Scarlet Beauty) live through

the winter in south central part of Maine? Don't believe all you hear about the hardiness of this fuchsia. Even in the neighborhood of New York its survival is exceptional. At 15° F. it will kill to the ground; and in Maine, unless buried deeply in snow, it's 100 to 1 against the roots surviving.

GERBERIA

What care does gerberia require—including cultivation, pests, and diseases? (New York.) This South African perennial is not hardy, although it may be grown outside in sheltered situations if given winter protection, or lifted in fall and wintered over in a cold frame. More commonly grown as greenhouse plant. Grow in well-drained, fairly rich soil; keep crowns just above soil level. Fertilize in spring with liquid manure. Propagate from seeds (slow to germinate) or, better, by cuttings of side shoots. Spray for leaf roller and green fly, two of its worst enemies. (See Section VIII.)

What garden soil, exposure, moisture, food, for gerberia? (They are hardy here.) (Delaware.) Best in well-drained soil in full sun. Water only in dry weather. Apply weak manure water in spring and early summer.

I have some gerberia roots. I have them in a box 18 ins. underground covered with leaves and dirt. Will they smother, or will I have to install an air vent pipe? The covering is too deep. Tender plants cannot be wintered over by burying them. Without a cold frame or like protection it is difficult to winter gerberias over. An air vent would be of little help. Plant them next to a building; erect a wooden frame around them. Cover with hay and give air in mild weather.

How can I grow gerberia outside? Should be grown in full sun in well-drained soil. Plant only in spring and give cold frame protection for the winter. They are not hardy in Northern gardens.

Do gerberia roots need dividing; and when? They do not require dividing very often; but when the clumps get large and begin to fail, divide in spring.

HELIOPSIS

Where should heliopsis be planted? In what type of soil? Plant in full sun, in any garden soil. Will probably flower better in a fairly dry situation.

HOLLYHOCKS

Do hollyhocks take an excessive amount of moisture away from surrounding plants? Not enough to harm near-by plants. The ground around hollyhocks usually looks dry because their large leaves shed a lot of rain.

IRISES

Like roses, irises have been a part of our historical and legendary heritage. Because of their delicate texture and sparkling hues it is appropriate that they should have been named in honor of the Goddess of the Rainbow, the messenger of Zeus and Hera. In medieval times the fleur-de-lis became the emblem of France. Its abstract form has been widely used as a motif in many forms of art.

Irises have always been popular as garden flowers. The many species are distributed throughout the Temperate Zone and are therefore adapted to culture in most of the civilized world. While some iris species have not responded to the efforts of plant breeders as readily as many other kinds of plants, considerable development has taken place, particularly in the tall-bearded iris group. The size, coloring, and garden value have been greatly improved. Many of the different species used in American gardens are the same as they appear in nature. They have not needed to be improved to make them worth-while garden subjects.

Most of the species and varieties bloom through early and late spring. They are especially useful in the flower border, in the rock garden, and in association with pools and streams.

Soils

Do irises grow better in low, moist ground, or in dry soil? In sun or shade? Bearded irises require sharp drainage. Beardless kinds (such as Japanese varieties) need plenty of moisture but not waterlogged soil. The Yellow Flag of Europe and our native *Iris versicolor* succeed even in swamp conditions. Most do best in full sun.

What is the correct soil for bearded irises? Any good garden soil. Add bone meal and gypsum when remaking the beds. If heavy, lighten with sand or ashes. They require good drainage.

Do Japanese irises require acid soil? Yes, or at least a soil that is not alkaline.

For Japanese and Siberian irises, what soil preparation is required? Spade deeply; incorporate plenty of humus—old rotted manure, leafmold, peatmoss, or compost. Also, if the soil is somewhat poor, add a dressing of cottonseed meal, pulverized sheep manure, or general fertilizer. Do not use lime or gypsum.

What kind of soil is good for Dutch irises? Any fertile, well-drained garden soil other than heavy clay. This is true for all bulbous irises.

Fertilizer

Is manure good for irises? Animal manure should not be used on bearded irises, but the beardless species (including the Japanese and Siberian irises) appreciate well-rotted manure.

What is the best time of year to feed ordinary bearded irises; and how? It is usually better not to feed established plantings, but to rely rather upon fertilizer that is dug in when beds are made. However, if additional fertilizer is applied, use any good garden type of low-nitrogen content in early spring.

Should beds of bearded irises be fertilized each spring? Not if ground was well prepared and fertilized at planting time.

What fertilizer do you recommend for ordinary (German) irises? Bone meal and unleached wood ashes together with a commercial fertilizer low in nitrogen. Mix with soil when beds are made.

Do bearded irises require lime? Only if the soil is decidedly acid.

What is the best fertilizer to use on Japanese irises? Rotted cow manure (or if this is not available leafmold or peatmoss fortified with a light dressing of complete fertilizer). Apply as a mulch in May or early June. In fall, mulch with manure, leaves, or peatmoss.

Planting

Are irises more attractive planted together or scattered in clumps throughout the garden? By themselves they are not attractive over the greater part of the year. Clumps of one variety in front of evergreens are very effective. Many people interplant irises with daylilies.

When, where, and how do you plant German (bearded) irises? In June or July, in good garden soil. Plant rhizomes level with surface in well-drained, sunny beds. Buy your stock from a reliable dealer so that you will recieve good, healthy rhizomes.

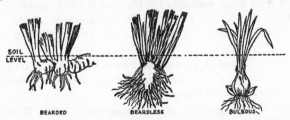

Planting depth for bearded, beardless, and bulbous irises.

Should irises be planted so as to cover up the rhizomes; or should they be left exposed? In light, sandy soil the rhizomes may be covered an inch or so; but in heavy soils they should be left with the tops exposed.

What distances should be allowed between irises when planting? Tall-bearded, 9 to 18 ins.; dwarf-bearded, 6 to 9 ins.; Japanese and Siberian, 18 to 24 ins.; bulbous, 4 to 5 ins. with 12 ins. between rows.

At what distance apart should purchased divisions of German irises be set? For a substantial effect the first year after planting, 8 or 9 ins. A better spacing is 16 or 18 ins., but this takes 2 years to produce a good display.

Should iris rhizomes be dried out before replanting? Not unless diseased, because if the feeding roots are dried no new growth results until new ones develop. Irises may be divided and transplanted without much setback providing their roots are kept out of the sun and they are replanted immediately.

I have been told that bearded irises can be planted only in June. Is this true? No. Many growers favor June, but entirely successful planting can be done in fall, or even in early spring. June planting (just after flowering) has the advantage of affording the divisions the longest time to recuperate before the next blooming season.

Will irises bloom if they are moved early in spring? The Japanese and Siberians usually do; the tall-bearded sometimes (but with short bloom stalks). If possible, avoid moving bearded irises until after the blooming season.

How late can bearded irises be planted in northern Virginia and still have good spring bloom? September. They must have sufficient time to make new growth and become established. Planting in July or early August is recommended.

When and how deep should Japanese irises be planted? Early spring, before growth starts, or late August. Crowns should be set 2 ins. below the surface.

Culture

Can we grow irises successfully? We have a lot of shade. Ordinary garden irises will not thrive in shade. Certain wild species, such as *cristata, gracilipes, verna,* and *foetidissima,* are satisfactory in partial shade.

How often should I transplant irises? Whenever they become so crowded that the rhizomes are growing over one another. This will usually mean about every 3 years.

Can irises be replanted in the same bed? Yes, if redug and fertilized. If disease is present, soil should first be sterilized.

Should irises be thinned out if not blooming freely? If lack of bloom is due to crowding, lift and replant. If some other cause, get diagnosis and be guided accordingly.

What culture do Japanese irises require? Bed must be well drained (it is fatal to select a location where water stands during winter). Enrich soil with leafmold, well-decayed manure, or garden compost. Plant in August; replant every 3 years. They like plenty of water before and during blooming season.

What are the conditions favorable to the growth of Siberian irises?
Plenty of sunshine, well-drained, rich, slightly acid soil. They like
plenty of rotted manure, also plenty of moisture from spring until
blooming is over.

Do the Dutch, English, and Spanish irises all get same culture?
In general, yes. Plant bulbs 4 to 5 ins. deep, October to November,
in sunny location and in good, well-drained loam. Let remain for
2 years, then lift and replant in a new location. They are gross
feeders and deplete the soil very quickly. In severe climates a winter
mulch is beneficial.

How are bulbous irises handled in the South? Dutch, English,
and Spanish irises are dug after blooming and are stored in a cool
shed until late fall, when they are replanted. This because they make
fall growth, and if left in ground the flower stalks are usually killed
by a freeze in late winter. When lifted and replanted in late fall,
stalks do not develop until spring.

Do Dutch irises have to be dug up each year? Not unless they
have suffered winter losses. In that case try planting as late in autumn
as weather permits. The following year dig the bulbs when the foliage
dies down, and store in a cool location until autumn. In extreme
climates a winter mulch is beneficial.

When is best time to move Dutch irises? As soon as the foliage
has died down. In the South many people lift them at this time and
store in airy containers in a cool shed until late fall.

What is correct culture of oncocyclus irises? These natives of the
Near and Middle East require a dormant season, without moisture.
Grow them in pots or cold frames so that they are kept dry from
mid-June to mid-December.

When do you divide and replant Siberian irises? Late August or
September.

**I have a large garden of Japanese irises set 4 years. When should
I divide and reset? They seem to be getting crowded.** Immediately
after blooming season, in September, or just before growth starts in
spring.

How much watering and cultivating do irises need? Bearded irises
ordinarily need no watering. Japanese and other beardless types need
plenty of moisture until flowering is through. Cultivate shallowly and
sufficiently often to keep surface loose and free of weeds.

What care should be given iris rhizomes after the blooming season?
If overcrowded, divide them. Remove flower stalks immediately after
flowering, and be on the alert for signs of borers or rots. Keep all
dead foliage cleaned off.

Does it injure iris plants to take green foliage off in the late fall?
Leaves turning brown should always be removed promptly. Green

foliage should not be removed nor cut back in late fall because this may adversely affect next year's bloom.

When leaves are forbidden as protection for bearded irises, what can be used?   No protection is necessary unless rhizomes have been planted in late fall. Evergreen boughs then make the best protection. Salt hay or excelsior may also be used.

Would you cover iris roots? I have over 400 different kinds and it would be quite a task to cover them all.   No. They only need protection if planted in late fall, and then only because their root growth will not be sufficient to keep them from heaving. A few irises of Californian origin need to be planted in sheltered spots.

Problems

How can I transport irises to shows?   Obtain large florists' boxes. String tape across them in several places so that stalks can be suspended without blooms touching bottoms or sides. Keep boxes level; or if this is impossible, then tie each stalk to the tapes.

How should I prepare irises for exhibition at my local garden-club shows?   Bloom stalks should have at least 2 open flowers. Three would be better. These should be the first blooms. After cutting, stand in water for 30 minutes or longer. Foliage should be displayed with flower stalks. Dead or torn blooms count heavily against you. Varieties should be correctly labeled.

What colors of irises look best in the garden?   This is a matter of personal taste. Soft colors usually fit best into general garden schemes. In large plantings, deep purples (such as Sable) and reds (such as Red Gleam) may be scattered in small clumps as accent points. Brassy yellows are sometimes difficult.

Is there any special organization of iris growers?   Yes. The American Iris Society. Each member receives the society's well-illustrated bulletins. The address of the secretary of the Society is 2237 Tower Grove Blvd., St. Louis 10, Mo.

I have tried for many years to raise red and pink irises, but can't make them live over winter. What is the reason?   Try planting earlier in summer, so that plants become established before winter. China Maid and Miss California (pinks of Californian origin) are sometimes tender. Try Angelus, a pink that originated in the Middle West. Christabel (red) is extremely vigorous, and should do well.

Why won't Japanese irises bloom for me?   Too much shade? Alkaline soil? Dry soil? Water settling around crowns in winter? Any of the above may be responsible.

My bearded irises grow and look well, but bloom rarely. What is the reason? They have been established more than 2 years. They get full sun at least half a day.   Most likely they are overcrowded and need dividing. Some varieties of tall-bearded irises require dividing every year for good bloom.

Are all bearded irises robust growers?   No. Certain varieties, especially dark-colored ones, are less vigorous than others. Some that have originated in southern California are tender, and do not do well in cold parts of the country.

Do irises change colors from year to year?   No. But in different gardens the same iris may vary somewhat in color intensity, due to cultural and environmental conditions. Slight variations may occur in different locations in the same garden.

After a few years does a mixed planting of irises gradually lose color and turn white?   No. What sometimes happens is that the faster growers crowd out slower-growing varieties.

Why do irises stop blooming after being separated, even though carefully taken apart at right season? They are free of pests and were planted at right depth.   Perhaps soil is deficient or exhausted. Try remaking beds and adding bone meal and perhaps gypsum. Sunshine is important.

I planted irises two years ago, half of them grew to enormous size and bloomed, but the others remained small and spindly. How can I make these perk up and bloom?   Robust varieties produce a representative bloom stalk the first year after planting, others take 2 years to become established. Furthermore, varieties vary in height; it may be that you have some of the intermediate varieties growing together with tall-bearded sorts.

My irises (early dwarfs and Siberians) bloomed the first year but not the following 2 years. What is wrong?   Perhaps they do not get enough sunshine, or they may be too crowded, and in need of dividing. Siberians are gross feeders; they require plenty of fertilizer.

My irises do not do well; they have decreased in size and stopped blooming. The soil is stiff clay. What would you advise?   Perhaps your soil is so heavy that just enough feeding roots develop to keep your plants alive, but not enough to build strong plants. Lift, divide, and replant in well-drained beds improved by addition of coal cinders or sand, bone meal, and a dressing of gypsum or agricultural lime if soil test shows need of it. Incorporate organic matter.

What is the difference between the Dykes Medal and Dykes Memorial Medal?   No difference. The complete name is the Dykes Memorial Medal, but it is generally spoken of as the Dykes Medal.

Propagation

How should I divide tall bearded irises?   After flowering cut the leaves back halfway, lift the clumps, then with a sharp knife cut the rhizomes into pieces so that each has one (or, if preferred, 2 or

3) strong fan of leaves attached. Be sure divisions are disease-free before replanting. Divide every 3 or 4 years.

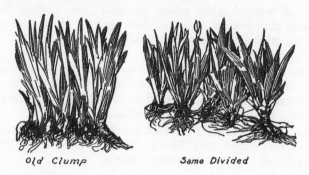

Ol̥d Clump   *Same Divided*

A clump of bearded iris, divided for replanting.

How are Japanese irises divided? When?   It is quite a job if the clumps are large. A heavy-bladed knife or billhook is the best tool. Cut the leaves halfway back and then chop the rootstock into pieces each having 3 or 4 growths. Discard old, lifeless material. Save only young, vigorous portions. Do this work in September, in shade, and keep the roots from drying out.

Should iris seeds picked in fall be planted fall or spring?   In fall; if planted in spring they will not germinate until following year. Plant in open ground or in a cold frame—the latter preferred. In a cold frame they start coming up in late February, and should be transplanted in late June to nursery beds.

Typical divisions of tall-bearded, dwarf-bearded, and beardless irises.

How do you grow irises from seed?   After seed is harvested plant immediately in a cold frame, or save until late fall and plant in open ground. If sown earlier outdoors, young seedlings come up and are heaved out during winter. Be sure soil is well prepared and on light side. Transplant the seedlings, in late June, to a nursery bed, spacing at least a foot apart each way. Nearly all should bloom the following year.

Diseases and Pests (See also Section VIII)

My iris leaves are spotted. What shall I do? This is leaf-spot disease. Cut back diseased foliage and burn it. If this is not done, it will spread disease through garden. Be sure and keep all dead leaves picked off, and in 2 years you will have eliminated disease.

Are irises subject to virus disease? Iris mosaic disease attacks both bearded and bulbous kinds, causing mottling or yellow striping of leaves, and lack of vigor. Destroy all infected plants.

My iris roots have rotted, and watery streaks appear on the leaves. What is the cause? Bacterial soft rot. It often gains entrance through wounds made by the iris borer. Dig and destroy rotted plants; sterilize soil by soaking with 1 oz. Semesan to 1 gal. water. Avoid planting diseased rhizomes. Sterilize knives and tools with Semesan solution, as disease is spread by these. Clean off and burn dead leaves and rubbish in fall.

How can I control thrips on Japanese irises? By spraying or dusting with DDT, lindane or dieldrin.

Grayish plant lice have attacked my iris roots underground. What control measures shall I take? Root aphids are destroyed by soaking the soil with nicotine sulfate, 2 teaspoonfuls to 1 gal. water; or by the use of malathion (follow directions on the package.)

What controls are recommended for iris borers? Clean up and burn all old leaves and debris in fall, and if winter covering has been used burn this in early spring. In severe infestations spray with dieldrin or lead arsenate ¼ lb. to 6 gals. water with a little wheat flour added as a sticker.

Varieties

How are irises classified? Into 3 groups. Group 1: bearded irises (Pogoniris) are derived from species native to southern Europe and Asia Minor. Distinguishing characteristics are a conspicuous beard on the lower petals and thick, fleshy rhizomes. Group 2: beardless irises (Apogon) are derived from species from Europe, Asia, and America; with thin rhizomes and grasslike leaves; they include *fulva, kaempferi* (Japanese), *sibirica* (Siberian), and *spuria*. Group 3: bulbous and miscellaneous, including English, Spanish, and Dutch irises.

Which group of irises is most useful in the home garden? Undoubtedly the tall-bearded (often miscalled German irises). The Japanese and Siberian groups are also very useful.

Which is better, cheap collections with many irises or a few good new varieties? Not always are high-priced varieties better than older, inexpensive kinds. Unless immediate effect is imperative, there is no doubt that a few good irises are to be preferred to a lot of poor ones. They soon multiply.

What are the "best" irises to date?   Below are the first 25 of the 100 listed by members of the American Iris Society in the Iris popularity poll. The numbers after each name indicate the votes received. Truly Yours (928); Ola Kala (742); Happy Birthday (726); Mary Randall (683); Palomino (662); Argus Pheasant (627); Chivalry (625); Elmohr (621); Blue Rhythm (552); New Snow (547); Lady Mohr (541); Pierre Menard (537); Pinnacle (526); Blue Shimmer (487); Desert Song (455); Sable Night (427); Minnie Colquitt (420); Snow Flurry (416); Blue Sapphire (414); Limelight (405); Amandine (403); Char Maize (389); Inca Chief (384); First Violet (375); Helen McGregor (367).

Which are the most popular white irises?   New Snow, Snow Flurry, Spanish Peaks, Winter Carnival, Samite, White Wings.

Will you give me a selection of good yellow irises?   Truly Yours, Ola Kala, Pinnacle (white and yellow), Spun Gold, Mohr Beauty.

Is the bulbous iris Juno known by any other name? Can I obtain hybrids in the Juno group?   No. It and other species of the Juno group are rare in American gardens. They are only suited for skilled growers and comparatively mild climates.

Which are the 12 best varieties of Japanese irises?   Probably unobtainable, even if it were possible for 2 persons to agree on the "12 best." Following are good: Aspasie, Betty F. Holmes, Elbrus, Fanny Hamlet Childs, Goldbound, Koki-no-iro, La Favorite, Light-in-the-Opal, Mahongany, Pluton, Satsuki-bare, Violet Beauty. The "Marhigo" series of seedlings (judging from the colored pictures in the Walter Marx catalog) are as good as any of these named varieties.

LUPINE

What can I use to build up soil for lupines?   They need a well-drained and medium soil. Use sand, leafmold, and well-rotted manure. Lime should not be used on lupines.

One authority says acid soil, another a lime soil for perennial lupines. What is your opinion?   Most lupines seem to do better in an acid or neutral soil.

What should I use to fertilize lupines?   Well-rotted compost, cow manure, or any general garden fertilizer.

Will you give soil and cultural direction for Russell Lupines?   Russell Lupines thrive in any good garden soil in full sun. Seed should be planted in August, about ½ in. deep, and soon after it has ripened. The spikes do not grow so large here as in England.

It is, however, one of our finest perennials. Lupines are short-lived and may not persist after the first year. Give adequate winter protection.

What is the best way of raising the improved types of perennial lupine from seed indoors? I have had poor germination. Sow individual seeds in small pots of sandy soil, first nicking the hard seed coat with the point of a knife. Sown in March and started in a greenhouse the seedlings will show in a week and be ready to plant outdoors, without the roots being disturbed, in May. Or nick the seed or place in hot water for an overnight soak, and sow thinly outdoors in April if the soil is in friable condition.

Will lupine seeds "stratified" come up following year? They should. If kept over winter in a seed container germination is aided by making a nick in seed coat with a sharp knife.

Can lupines be transplanted? Do they last many years? Old plants do not like to be disturbed and are very hard to transplant. Young plants can be transplanted in very early spring if care is used to protect the roots. Lupines are short-lived. For a constant supply sow seed each year.

MONKSHOOD (ACONITUM)

How often should aconitum be divided? These plants flower very freely when they are in established clumps, and may be left undisturbed for years.

How deep shall I plant aconitum, and in what kind of soil? They are best planted with the crown about one inch down, in rich, moist soil, neutral or slightly acid.

Do aconitums need winter protection? They are hardy but should be protected for the first and second winter after planting.

When should I sow seed of monkshood? In late autumn, using fresh seed.

What soil and site do monkshood need? They require a rich, moist soil, and do best in partial shade.

Will you name several kinds of monkshood that would be successful? *Aconitum fischeri, A. napellus* Sparks Variety, *A. wilsoni,* and *A. uncinatum.*

Is it advisable to plant monkshood? I have heard it is poisonous. Monkshood does contain poison. It is said to have been mistaken for horse-radish on occasions and eaten with fatal results. But it is widely grown in gardens.

PENTSTEMONS

I have several pentstemon plants which stayed green long after frost. Is it hardy? You may have plants of the bedding pentstemon, which is not hardy but which stay green until late. The other kinds are hardy, and, with the exception of the alpine sorts, are treated like ordinary perennials. Many of them remain green until long after frost.

How do you trim and care for large pentstemons? They need no trimming. The wiry stems of the tall kinds need support, best supplied by using twiggy brush inserted among the plants when they are about a foot tall. Growing up through this, with loose stems tied up and the tops of the brush cut away when flower buds form, they will be held neatly and securely. Cut the stems after flowering, and top-dress with bone meal.

How is it best to divide pentstemon plants? Lift the plants in early spring, pull them gently apart, and replant.

PEONIES

The modern peony is the achievement of years of steadfast devotion and effort on the part of plant breeders. For more than 2,000 years the peony has been cultivated in China, not alone for its highly prized flowers, but for its roots, which in early times were used for food and medicinal purposes. It was named in honor of Paeon, the physician of the gods, who—according to mythology—received the first peony on Mt. Olympus from the hands of Leto.

Present-day gardeners are inclined to take the peony for granted because it has become so common. The very fact that it is common only serves to emphasize its many worth-while qualities. Hardiness, permanence, ease of culture, and freedom from pests are but a few of its merits. Diversity in flower form, attractive colors, clean habit of growth, and deep-green foliage combine to produce a plant of exceptional value for mass plantings or for the mixed border. Peonies rank high as cut flowers because of their extraordinary keeping qualities. They are primarily plants for the North, for they require the low temperatures of winter to break the dormancy of the buds before spring growth will take place.

Some horticulturists consider that the interest in peonies is on the wane; that their potentiality for further improvement is exhausted. This does not seem to be the case, however, for within the last few years several new varieties have been introduced that eclipse all previous originations in perfection of form and color. They have always been garden favorites and will continue to be so.

Soil; Fertilizers

What type of soil is best for peonies? They grow well in a wide range of soil types. Any rich, friable garden soil is satisfactory.

Is a very heavy soil satisfactory for peonies? Yes, providing it is well-drained. Some form of organic material, such as well-rotted manure, peatmoss, or leafmold, should be added to make it more friable.

Will peonies thrive in a sandy soil? Sandy soil is well suited to peony growing if its fertility is maintained. Well-rotted manure and commercial fertilizer should be used.

What is the proper method of preparing the soil for peonies? Spade it to a depth of 12 to 18 ins. Thoroughly work in some well-rotted manure or other form of organic material at the rate of 4 bu. per 100 sq. ft. Incorporate 3 lbs. of superphosphate to each 100 sq. ft. If the soil is acid apply lime (5 lbs. per 100 sq. ft.) several weeks before planting.

How deep should peony soil be prepared? Because they may remain in one spot for many years, it is desirable to thoroughly prepare the soil to a depth of from 12 to 24 ins.

Do peonies need lime? Peonies grow best in a slightly acid soil (pH 5.5 to 6.5). If the soil is very acid (below pH 5), the addition of lime is beneficial.

What kind of lime and how much should be used for peonies? If a soil test shows a pH value below 5, apply ground limestone or ordinary agricultural lime at the rate of 5 lbs. per 100 sq. ft.

What kind and how much fertilizer should I use for peonies? A mixed commercial fertilizer of 4–12–4 or 5–10–5 analysis is satisfactory. Use 4 lbs. for each 100 sq. ft. Well-rotted manure is also satisfactory. Avoid the use of fresh manure.

When peonies are planted in the fall should they be fertilized then, or the following spring? Work fertilizer thoroughly into the soil before planting. No additional fertilizer will be needed the spring following; but each succeeding spring use a mixed commercial fertilizer.

Do peonies need fertilizer; and when should it be applied? Yes. Apply commercial fertilizer in spring. When growth is about 4 ins. high work it into the soil around the plants. Rotted manure makes a good fertilizer to put on in the fall.

Planting

Should peonies be planted in full sun? The best results are obtained when the plants are exposed to full sunlight. It is desirable, however, to put them where they are somewhat protected from strong winds.

Can peonies be grown in partial shade? While they do best in full sun, they will grow satisfactorily in partial shade. They require at least 6 hours a day of direct sunlight for good results.

Does the peony plant need to be kept away from other flowers in the beds? Providing they are properly spaced and cultural conditions are right, other plants exert no influence whatever on the blooming of peonies. They are often used in mixed perennial borders, and are excellent for the purpose.

When should peonies be planted?   September 15 to November 1.

How deep do peonies need to be planted?   The crown, from which the buds arise, should be only 1 to 2 ins. below the soil level.

Does it matter whether the eye of a peony is 1 in. or 2 ins. below the surface?   No. It is important, however, not to exceed 2 ins. If planted too shallowly, there is danger of the roots being heaved out during winter.

I planted peonies the last of November; was it too late?   Planting may be done any time until the ground freezes, but the ideal months are September and October. This gives them an opportunity to become partially established before winter.

I planted peonies in a temporary location in late November. When and how should I transplant them to their permanent place?   It would be desirable to leave them where they are until October, when moving would be much easier. However, if you feel you must move them in spring, dig them with a large ball of soil as soon as the ground has thawed, and replant immediately.

Can peonies be shipped and planted in spring?   It is not recommended as a general practice, because the results are seldom satisfactory. Only in special instances should this be done.

If I move peony plants in spring will they bloom the same year?   Yes, if moved *very* early, before growth starts. The soil must be kept moist at all times. (See previous question.)

Will peony roots, which have been kept in the cellar all winter, grow satisfactorily?   It is never advisable to treat them in this manner. However, if they have not dried out, and appear to be in good condition, they will survive. It may take 3 or 4 years before they regain their full vigor.

Will peonies bloom the first summer after transplanting?   Usually; if the plants are vigorous and were not divided into small pieces; and if the transplanting was done at the right time. The blooms may not be so large and perfect as those produced in succeeding years.

Why does it take peonies so long to bloom after dividing?   Dividing the clumps is a severe operation; it results in the loss of roots in which food is stored. Dividing at an improper time causes recovery to be especially slow. If the divisions are very small, it may take 2 to 3 years before the plants are sufficiently vigorous to bloom.

How do you recognize healthy peony roots suitable for planting?   They should be approximately 1 in. in diameter, smooth, free from bruises, and each containing at least 1 plump bud and several smaller ones. No decay should be evident near the cut surface.

Culture

How can you bring an old peony border back into bloom? If the plants are very old, it is advisable to divide the clumps and replant them in well-prepared soil. Keeping the bed free of weeds by shallow cultivation, and applying fertilizer in the spring, will increase the quality and quantity of the flowers.

Is it necessary to dig up peony roots every year and break them up to obtain more blossoms? No. It is best not to divide and transplant peonies any oftener than is necessary to maintain vigorous growth. Ordinarily every 5 to 8 years is often enough. Better-quality blooms may be had by fertilizing and making certain that the plants do not lack moisture at the time they come into flower.

Should peonies be disbudded? Size and quality of flowers are improved by disbudding. The practice is advisable if blooms are to be used for cut flowers, or for exhibition purposes. In the garden, where mass color effects are desirable, it is not important.

When should peonies be disbudded? The earlier the better. Ordinarily it can be done when the plants are about 18 ins. tall. Just as soon as the secondary buds become visible they should be removed.

How are peonies disbudded? A peony stem usually has from 3 to 7 buds. The main or terminal one produces the largest and most perfect flower. All of the buds except the terminal one should be picked off, leaving but 1 on each stem.

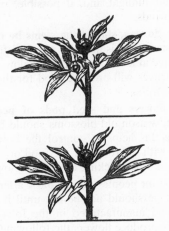

Disbudding peonies.

Should the flower buds of newly planted or transplanted peonies be removed the first year? Some growers do this to help the plants recover from shock, but it is not absolutely necessary. Most gardeners allow their plants to bloom even though the flowers are not so large and perfect as they will be later.

Do peonies need to be cultivated?   Very little cultivation is necessary except to remove weeds. The best time to destroy weeds is very early in the spring before the plants have made much growth, or late in the fall after the tops have been cut off. During summer the top 2 ins. of soil should be kept loose by shallow hoeing.

Do peonies require much moisture?   A moderately moist soil is suitable. In spring when the flowers are developing, if the natural rainfall is not abundant, thorough watering increases the size and quality of the flowers.

Does irrigating peonies when in bud bring the flowers on sooner, or does it hold them back?   It tends to hasten flowering. If the soil is very dry, irrigation also greatly improves the size and quality of the blooms.

How can I keep the stems of peonies from falling over?   Support with special, circular wire "peony stakes," or use individual stakes to each stem. Good growers shake the water out of peony heads after each rain. Planting in a location sheltered from wind helps to prevent damage.

Is there any way to make the stems of peonies stronger?   Some otherwise fine varieties naturally have weak stems. There is little that can be done except to give them artificial support. It is also well to plant them in full sunlight and, if possible, where they are protected from strong winds.

In picking peony flowers, should the stems be cut at ground level?   Do not take more stem than is actually required for the arrangement. It is advisable to leave at least 2 or 3 leaves below the point where the stem is cut. These leaves will produce food for the production of the succeeding year's flowers.

Should the old flowers and seed pods of peonies be removed?   During the flowering season old blossoms should be picked off before the petals fall since this helps to control the botrytis blight disease. Seed pods compete with the roots for the food produced in the leaves. Do not remove leaves when picking off the old flowers and seed pods.

Should the foliage on peonies be cut back after the blooming season?   No. The foliage should not be cut until it has been killed by hard frosts. The food manufactured in the foliage is stored in the roots, and thus helps produce flowers the following year. If the foliage is cut back shortly after blooming, the plants are deprived of their next year's food supply.

Should the dried foliage of peonies be cut off to the ground in the fall, or left on until spring?   In fall. Its removal helps to prevent the spread of disease.

When is the proper time to cut down a peony? After the foliage has been killed by frost. The autumn coloring of peony foliage is usually quite attractive.

Problems

Should peonies be protected in winter? Peonies should be mulched the first year after planting to prevent heaving. After they are well established, no protection is necessary.

Will peonies do well in warm climates such as Florida? No, they require low temperatures to complete their rest period.

Are peonies hardy in cold climates? They are among the hardiest of garden flowers.

Why do peonies, several years old, fail to bloom? The following conditions may prevent blooming: too deep planting; too shady a situation; poor drainage; plants need dividing; disease, especially of the roots; botrytis blight disease; roots infested with nematodes; lack of fertilizer; lack of moisture; lack of sunlight; injury to buds due to late frosts.

I have peonies, about 12 yrs. old, that only have a blossom or two a year. The soil is black, sandy loam. They are not planted too deep. Are they too old, or what can be the trouble? An application of complete fertilizer at the rate of 4 lbs. per 100 sq. ft. may correct the trouble. Nematodes also may cause failure to bloom. If infested with nematodes, the best thing to do is to discard roots.

Is there any way to tell the color of peonies from the roots or from the buds on the roots? No. Experienced growers can recognize certain varieties by root and bud coloring, but there is no general rule to follow.

What would you do with peonies that have been in the ground for many years and are not doing well? Dig and divide them during October. Replant them in well-prepared soil in a good sunny location.

What can I do to make peonies bloom as they did for the first 5 years? They were divided 4 years ago and are growing in a sunny situation in well-drained clay soil. Try fertilizing them each spring with a mixed commercial fertilizer.

I have some very old peonies. Last summer the flowers were almost single, and many did not bloom well. Why? Old plants often fail to produce perfect flowers. They should be dug, divided, and replanted in well-prepared soil.

When should peony flowers be cut for use indoors? Preferably in the early morning. Select, for cutting, buds that have just started to open.

How are peonies scored or rated? On a scale of 10. A rating of 10 represents the highest possible excellence, or absolute perfection, in both plant and bloom. Varieties rated at 9 or above are very high in quality. Between 8 and 9 they are considered good. Few varieties are grown that rate less than 7.5.

Propagation

Can peony roots be divided in spring with as much success as in fall? No, *early* fall is the best time.

How are peony plants divided? Dig the clumps carefully so as not to injure or bruise the roots. Wash off all soil. With a heavy, sharp knife cut each clump, through the crown, into several pieces. Each division should have several plump buds, which in the fall are approximately ½ in. long. Roots without such buds rarely produce plants.

Would it be advisable to separate a peony root with a spade, leaving part in the ground and removing part? This method can be used and has the advantage of not interrupting the bloom of the portion that is left in place. However, it is usually better to dig the entire plant and divide it carefully. Before replanting there is an opportunity to prepare the soil to improve growing conditions.

Can peonies be raised from seeds? Yes, but this method is used only for the production of new varieties; it is slow and tedious.

How should seeds of peonies be sown? Collect when ripe. Keep in damp moss until November. Sow in a cold frame or protected bed. Cover the seeds to their own depth, and mulch with peatmoss the following spring. Keep the bed shaded and reasonably moist. They usually take 2 years to germinate.

How long does it take peonies to bloom from seeds? They ordinarily germinate 2 years after sowing. After 3 years' growth, a few flowers may be expected. This means 5 or more years from seed-sowing to bloom.

Diseases and Pests

What can I do to control ants that are eating the flower buds of my peonies? Ants do not eat peony buds; they feed on the sweet, syrupy material secreted by the developing buds. They do no harm to the peonies except, possibly, to spread botrytis blight disease. (See Ants—Section VIII.)

Why do peony buds dry up without developing into blossoms? The plant seems disease-free. The leaves do not dry nor is there any sign of bud rot. Probably botrytis blight. This may be prevented by carefully cleaning the bed in the fall and by keeping it clean of dead leaves all seasons. Spraying with Bordeaux mixture every 10 days from the time the leaves show until the flowers open is a good control measure. Late frosts in spring may kill buds.

Is there something lacking in the soil when peony leaves turn brown at the edges early in July? Usually this is the result of drought, or of infection with some root disease.

Varieties

What are the names of the different types of peony flowers? The most distinct are single, Japanese, anemone, and double.

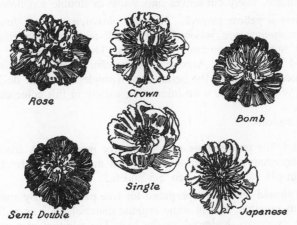

Peonies—various flower types.

What is the difference between single peonies and the Japanese type? Singles have 5, or possibly a few more, true petals around a center of showy, fertile stamens. Japanese types have a single row of large petals, but the center consists of much enlarged stamens which bear very little, or no, pollen.

What is the anemone type of peony? It somewhat resembles the Japanese but the centers of the flowers are composed of much enlarged, petallike stamens which bear no pollen whatever. These center petals are long and narrow, more or less incurved, and imbricated.

What varieties of anemone-flowered peonies are desirable? Aureolin, rose-pink; Golden Dawn, ivory; Red Bird, dark red; Laura Dessert, pale pink.

What are a few good single peonies? L'Etincelant, pink; Le Jour, white; Pride of Langport, pink; Scarf Dance, light pink; and Verdun, crimson.

Which are some popular varieties of the Japanese type? Alma, pink; Ama-No-Sode, rose-pink; Charm, dark red; Hakodate, white; Mikado, crimson; and Prairie Afire, cream-rose.

Which are a few of the best double peonies? A. B. Franklin, white; Baroness Schroeder, white; Cherry Hill, red-maroon; Cornelia

Shaylor, pale rose; E. J. Shaylor, deep rose; Festiva Maxima, white; Hansina Brand, pink; James Boyd, flesh pink; Karl Rosenfield, red-crimson; La France, light pink; Longfellow, red; President Wilson, rose; Reine Hortense, rose; Sarah Bernhardt, deep rose; Therese, pale rose; and Walter Faxon, pink.

Which peony flowers 2 weeks before the common ones? The Fernleaf Peony (*Paeonia tenuifolia*) is a very early-flowering species with delicate, finely cut leaves and single or double red flowers.

Is there a yellow peony? *Paeonia mlokosewitschi, P. lutea,* and *P. wittmanniana* are yellow-flowered. All are early-flowering, low-growing sorts not common in gardens. There are several yellow-flowered tree peonies. Argosy, Chromatella, La Lorraine, and L'-Esperance are some of the better-known singles. Souvenir de Maxine Cornu, yellow-orange, is an interesting variety in this color class.

Tree Peonies

What is the proper type of soil for tree peonies? A friable rich soil is necessary. Incorporate well-rotted manure or leafmold. The optimum pH value is between 5.5 and 6.5.

How should the soil be prepared for tree peonies? By spading as deeply as possible. Mix in some organic material, such as well-rotted manure, peatmoss, leafmold, or the like. The addition of a complete commercial fertilizer is also desirable. If a 5–10–5 or some similar grade is available, use it at the rate of 4 lbs. per 100 sq. ft.

Can tree peonies be planted in spring? While October is the best season, success may be had from *very* early-spring planting.

How old do tree peonies need to be before they will flower? Tree peonies are often slow to begin blooming. Normally, however, they produce a few blooms the second or third year after planting.

How can I propagate tree peonies? The usual method is by grafting in August or September. The scion should have at least 2 eyes. Its base is cut wedge-shaped and is inserted in a piece of root about ½ in. in diameter, and 3 or 4 ins. long, taken from an herbaceous peony plant. The scion is held in place with raffia or with a rubber band. The grafted roots are placed in good soil, in a cold frame, where they can be protected during winter. If a cold greenhouse is available, the grafts may be placed in a deep pot and kept indoors over winter. One of the eyes of the scion should be below soil surface. Tree peonies may also be propagated by layering, division, and by seeds.

Which are some of the best tree-peony varieties? Carolina d'-Italie, flesh-pink; Madame Stuart-Low, salmon-red; Blanche De-chateau Futu, white; and Reine Elizabeth, salmon and copper; Oriflame, cherry-red; Osirus, chestnut-brown.

PERENNIAL PEA (LATHYRUS LATIFOLIUS)

How do you start what is called "wild sweetpea"? I have tried planting seeds and roots without success. The perennial pea (*Lathyrus latifolius*) is best started from seeds sown in autumn, preferably where they are to grow permanently. The plant has long, fleshy roots and resents disturbance.

What is the best way to plant and care for everlasting peas? If by "everlasting" peas you mean the perennial kind, they rarely need special soil preparation or care. A sunny location and average good garden soil that is not acid are about all they require.

I have a well-established perennial sweetpea, which failed to bloom last year. What can I do to it, to produce bloom? The perennial pea usually flowers freely when established, even in poor soil. Try mixing superphosphate with the soil, 6 oz. per sq. yd.

Should hardy sweetpeas be cut back in the fall? How far? They may be cut back to just above the ground level any time after the tops have dried up.

Is the perennial pea a good plant for a large lattice fence? Yes, if the slats are not too large for the tendrils to grasp. It will grow to a height of about 8 ft.

PHLOX

How is soil prepared for phlox? Soil should be dug to a depth of 1 ft. to 18 ins. and mixed with a 3-in. layer of rotted manure.

When is the best time to plant garden phlox? Either in early fall or early spring. If fall planting is practiced, the plants should be mulched with a 3-in. layer of rough litter, hay or straw, to prevent possible heaving as a result of freezing.

What is the best exposure for phlox? They thrive in full sun, but will grow in partial shade. A minimum of 3 to 4 hours of full sunshine is desirable.

What are some good varieties of garden phlox? Red: Leo Schlageter, Africa, Colorado, and B. Comte. Pink: Daily Sketch, Nordlicht, Elizabeth Campbell, Jules Sandeau, and Painted Lady. White: Snowcap, Mary Louise, and Tapis Blanc. Other colors: Count Zeppelin, George Stipp, Silvertone, and Widar.

Can you name 6 varieties of phlox for continuous bloom? Miss Lingard, Leo Schlageter, Columbia, Atlanta, Charles Curtis, and Cheerfulness.

How far apart should phlox be planted? Set them 15 ins. apart and allow 3 or 4 shoots to grow from each plant.

Do phlox require much water? They need plenty of water during the growing season, but the soil must be well drained.

Do phlox require summer feeding? If the bed was well prepared by deep digging and the incorporation of manure, it may not be necessary; but they do respond to side dressings of fertilizer or to applications of liquid manure when flower buds are about to form.

How can I handle phlox to get more perfectly shaped heads of blossoms? They now grow ill shaped. Probably your plants are old and need lifting, dividing, and replanting. Good trusses are obtained by thinning out the shoots that appear in spring, leaving several inches between those left. Apply a mulch of grass clippings around the plants, and give liquid manure weekly. Perhaps you have a poor variety.

Would appreciate some tips on raising phlox. Is it advisable to reset plants, and how? Phlox grow best in a well-drained rich soil; need a fair amount of water. Lift, divide, and replant about every 3 years. Cut off old flowers. They are subject to mildew; spray or dust regularly. (See Section VIII.)

In transplanting phlox, how deep should they be set? Is bone meal and peatmoss good for them? Phlox should not be planted deeper than 1 to 2 ins. Bone meal and peatmoss are all right for phlox; mix them thoroughly with the soil when planting, or work in around plants in early spring if established.

How deep should phlox crowns be planted? Just about one inch below the ground surface.

Do you spread out the roots when planting phlox, or leave them straight? Phlox roots should be planted straight down, so dig the holes deep and give them plenty of space.

My yard is on a slope. I have trouble with hardy phlox. They don't seem to bloom as they should. Is the soil the cause? May be. Phlox need a rich, moist, but well-drained soil. It might be the variety— some are poor bloomers. Disease or a pest like red spider may be responsible. It might be due to drying out of the roots, which are close to the surface.

Why don't my phlox thrive? Foliage is sometimes whitish looking, turning to brown, lower leaves drop off, and blooms are poor. (New York City.) Phlox are subject to red spider mite infestation, which causes a whitish appearance at first, then leaves turn brown; also mildew and a disease which causes the lower leaves to drop. Deep, rich, moist, but well-drained soil and periodic dusting with sulfur will help. Phlox is extremely difficult to grow in the city.

Do phlox run out? Yes. Phlox will deteriorate if not lifted, split up, and replanted in good soil every 3 or 4 years.

Should phlox be pinched back, thus preventing top-heavy plants while in bloom? Pinching would induce branching, resulting in smaller heads of flowers.

Could I plant hardy phlox at the base of poplar trees to follow

tulips? Phlox may do there all right, especially the arendsi hybrids, which grow very well in part shade. The regular summer phlox will have too much competition from the tree roots.

What is the procedure in propagating perennial phlox by cutting up the roots into small sections? When is best time to do this? The plants are dug in September, and the roots cut into lengths of 1 to 2 ins. They are scattered in a cold frame and covered, ½ in. deep, with a half-and-half mixture of sand and soil. The young growths are kept in the frame until spring, and are then planted out in nursery-bed rows.

How should I start the better varieties of phlox? Mine always die. Phlox is propagated by lifting and dividing in the fall. Choose the new divisions from the outer edge of the clump, and discard the old center, which is too woody for good growth.

Why did my phlox change color? Many plants which were white, salmon, or deep red, are now a sickly magenta. You probably allowed seeds to ripen and self-sow. Unfortunately, self-seeded phlox revert to their ancestral purplish color; and, as they are usually exceptionally vigorous, they crowd out the desirable but less sturdy varieties. Weed out seedlings and do not permit plants to go to seed.

Should the seed heads be cut off the new hardy phlox? Yes, because that will help the plant conserve its energies and also prevent seedlings from self-sown seeds, which may smother the original plants.

I have been told that unless phlox seed heads are kept cut off they will revert back to the original lavender. Is it possible for roots of any plant to change like that? The reason for the so-called reversion is self-seeding. The seedlings are always different in color, are very vigorous, and in time will displace the original variety. The original roots normally do not change. Cut off faded flowers to prevent reseeding.

Does dwarf phlox reseed itself? Please name a few kinds. Yes, some of the dwarf phlox seed themselves but will probably not be the same color as the original plant. *Phlox subulata* varieties alba, rosea, lilacina; *P. stolonifera, P. divaricata,* and *P. d. laphami.*

PLATYCODON

Do platycodons need a rich soil? No; any garden soil will suit them in the open.

When should platycodon plants be set out? In the spring.

How do you keep platycodon in bloom? Keeping the old flowers pinched off to prevent seed formation will help.

Should platycodon be pinched back? It is not necessary, but permissible if a more bushy plant is desired. It must be done when the plants are about 6 ins. tall.

Do platycodons need winter protection? They are perfectly hardy and need no protection.

How is platycodon propagated? By division, in spring; or by seed, sown in fall or spring.

PLUMBAGO

What perennial of easy culture has blue flowers late in the season? *Plumbago larpentiae* (*Ceratostigma plumbaginoides*). It is tolerant of city conditions, thrives in sun or shade, and blooms until frost.

POPPIES

What fertilizer for perennial poppies? Any balanced one will give good results. Take your pick of the several special garden fertilizers offered by responsible supply houses, or a farmer's 4–8–4 or similar formula.

Will you give full planting instructions and care of Oriental poppies? Should be planted out in August or September, making the hole big enough so that the fleshy roots are not broken or twisted upward; water well if weather is dry; protect in winter with salt hay or dry leaves to prevent crown rot.

How shall I care for Oriental poppies? (Maryland.) They don't need much attention. Cut off flowers as they wither; keep the soil around them constantly raked shallow; occasionally work in side dressings of balanced fertilizer. A mulch of manure or leaves after first heavy frost in autumn would prevent bursts of growth in winter, which may happen in your locality and would not be helpful to the plants.

My Oriental poppies come up and grow well, but never bloom. They get afternoon sun. Should they be in a different place? Transplant in April or August into a sunnier spot.

When is the best time to plant or transplant Oriental poppies? In August, after the leaves have withered, and early in spring before growth commences. They dislike being transplanted, so injure the roots as little as possible; don't keep them out of the ground long, and water in thoroughly. If you grow them from seed, transfer the seedlings from flowerpots with the ball of soil intact.

When is the best time to thin out plants such as Oriental poppies? Thin out seedlings whenever the young plants tend to crowd. In growing practically all plants, thin out so carefully and continually that seedlings do not touch each other. If you mean dividing the roots of large plants, August is the time.

Will Oriental poppies planted in the spring bloom the same year? Yes, but you should buy large established plants. Plant them in March or early April, give them good care, and you are quite likely to get some flowers.

Can I sow Oriental poppy seed in May, to bloom next year? Yes, if the plants are given good care. Transplant seedlings into individual pots to avoid root disturbance when they are planted in their flowering positions.

How do you protect Oriental poppies in winter? I have lost 3 different settings. They may be set out in very early spring, but the best time is in August, when they are dormant. Is the soil well drained or waterlogged in winter? They resent the latter. Little protection is needed. A light covering of salt hay or coarse ashes over the crown will suffice.

Is it necessary in this section to mulch fall-planted Oriental poppy before December? (South Dakota.) Tuck excelsior around the crown beneath the leaves; then mulch them with rotted manure or compost after the soil freezes.

Is there any danger of Oriental poppy plants mixing if they are planted close together? Occasionally parent plants will mix, and after a few seasons you can hardly help having in your group of plants some which are self-sown from seed dropped from the parents. These will be mixed.

PRIMROSE

What kind of soil do primroses need? A fairly rich and moist but well-drained soil; the addition of leafmold is good. Should be planted in partial shade. Some, such as *P. japonica* and *P. rosea,* will grow in full sun where the soil is constantly wet.

Do primroses need fertilizer? Yes, they need a fairly rich soil. Well-rotted cow manure is probably the best.

What do you advise as a fertilizer for cowslips? (Virginia.) Well-rotted cow manure. Maintain the soil near neutral point by applications of pulverized limestone, if necessary.

What summer care and winter protection do primroses need? (Virginia.) Should be given shade and not allowed to dry out in summer. They are hardy and should not require any winter protection in Virginia.

What time of year is best for splitting up primulas? After they have finished flowering in late spring.

Are primroses easily raised from seed? When is seed sown? Primroses come readily from seed sown in spring. Use fresh seed. Protect the seedlings in summer by shading.

PYRETHRUM

How do you separate pyrethrums? Should be divided after they have finished flowering. The clumps are dug up and pulled apart, or pried apart with two spading forks.

ROSEMALLOW (HIBISCUS)

How shall I treat hibiscus (mallow) before and after flowering? In spring dig in some old rotted leafmold and bone meal. Cut off faded flowers, and prune back to the ground in the fall after frost.

Should rosemallow be left in ground all winter? Yes; the roots are perfectly hardy.

How can hibiscus (mallow) be grown successfully from seeds—how many years before plant will be large enough to bloom? Hibiscus seeds are best sown, 2 in a pot, and then planted out from the pot in permanent position. Will take about 3 years to bloom.

Rosemallows are beautiful plants, but attract Japanese beetles in droves. Are there any means of keeping the beetles off them? Use a spray especially designed to repel Japanese beetles. (See Section VIII.)

SALVIA

What extra care would you advise for salvias? *Salvia pitcheri* grows well in good garden soil with a reasonable amount of moisture, and in full sun. Lift and divide the plants about every 3 or 4 years.

Are there any perennial salvias? Yes; there are many. The ones usually found in gardens are *Salvia farinacea, S. officinalis, S. pitcheri, S. pratensis,* and *S. nemorosa. S. farinacea* is often treated as an annual in Northern gardens.

SCABIOSA

When and how do I divide my scabiosa roots, grown from seed planted last spring? Your plants would hardly have grown enough from seed last spring to be divided now; plants 2 or 3 years old may be divided by cutting or pulling the plants apart in early spring and replanting.

FLOWERING SPURGE (EUPHORBIA COROLLATA)

When should Flowering Spurge (Euphorbia corollata) be planted? Spring or fall? Best in spring.

SHASTADAISY

What is the best way to protect Shastadaisy plants in the winter? Cover with salt hay after ground is well frozen, and gradually uncover in spring.

How should Shastadaisies be divided? By digging up, in early spring, the outside rooted shoots either singly or in clumps. Shastadaisies are usually short-lived in the North and should be divided every year or two.

TRADESCANTIA

What is the botanical name of "widows' tears"?   *Tradescantia virginiana*. It is also known as common spiderwort and snake-grass.

TRITOMA

Can you grow tritomas from seed in the winter and transplant in the spring?   Yes; transplant the seedlings into 2½-in. pots, and plant out in early May.

Should tritoma be cut down to the ground after blooming?   Just the flowering stems should be cut away after blooming. The foliage usually persists through the winter and affords some protection to the crown.

Do tritomas have to be taken up, or can they be left out in the open all winter?   In very cold sections it is better to lift them. Pack the roots in earth and store in a tight frame or in cellar until early spring.

How do you prepare tritomas for winter along the north Jersey coast? When is the best time to separate tritomas?   Give winter protection with salt hay or some other suitable material; do not cut off their leaves until spring. Separate tritomas in spring only.

Is it possible to divide tritomas? How should it be done?   Divide them in spring only. It may be done by division of the roots, but much easier to dig up the offsets which come on the side of the main crown. See that these have roots.

VERONICA

The crowns of my veronica are rising above the surface. Can I remedy this?   Veronicas tend to raise their crowns if left in the same spot for some time. Dig up and replant every 2 or 3 years.

Why does my veronica, variety Blue Spires, sprawl instead of growing upright as the spicata and subsessilis varieties do? I have it from 3 different nurseries and all plants do it.   It is characteristic of this variety to have weak stems. Little can be done to overcome this, other than to support the stems. This is best done by sticking twigs in the soil around the plants before the shoots begin to sprawl. Try variety Blue Peter.

VIOLA

What is the proper time to plant viola seed for spring blossom?   In latter half of August, or early September.

Will you discuss culture of violas? I planted good plants last year, but blossoms didn't form till frost.   Nearly all violas need cool conditions, moisture, and partial shade. Hot, exposed locations are not conducive to good results. Provide a moist soil containing plenty of leafmold and the above conditions.

Does Viola pedata bicolor prefer sun or shade? Grows naturally in full sun and in an acid, sandy soil.

VIOLETS

Is the wood violet a perennial? I grow it as a house plant. It is difficult to say which violet you have, as several are known in different regions as the wood violet. All of these are perennials.

I am very much interested in growing English violets. Have a cold frame, and yet don't seem to have any success; had good roots and thrifty leaves; flowers very small and few. Will you give me some information? Remove sash, and shade the frame with lath screens in summer to keep plants cool; cut off all runners as they appear; feed and water to build up vigorous plants for late fall. Ventilate freely in fall, winter, and spring whenever temperature is above 35° to 40° F.

What is the proper method to water English violets? Water only when foliage can dry off before night. They need plenty of water during their growing period, but the soil must be well drained so that water does not collect in pools.

Should the runners be clipped off violet plants? Why do the plants grow up out of the soil instead of staying in it? How may large blooms and long stems be secured? In commercial culture the runners are cut off as fast as they appear in order to build up the plants for flowering. The plants root at the surface, with the crown above; as they develop, the crown rises still higher above the soil. Young plants give the best bloom, hence a number of these must be kept coming along. Long stems and good flowers are produced on young, well-developed plants in a rich but well-drained soil. Thin out old plants in spring.

Why do English violets, growing for 3 years, refuse to bloom? These are planted on west side of house. Violets need moist conditions and some shade from a hot sun. If you can supply these and keep the soil covered with a mulch of old compost, peatmoss, or grass clippings, they may bloom. They should be watered when necessary, and fed liquid manure. Renew part of the planting annually with strong, rooted runners. Our hot climate is not the best for violets.

My English violets produce seeds, but I never see any blooms; or maybe they bloom without petals, for they never come out of the ground like a flower, but develop into seed pods. Can you explain? Violets produce cleistogamous flowers, which are mostly on or under the ground. These are small, self-fertilizing flowers which never open.

YUCCA

How old must a yucca plant (from seed) be to blossom? Will it

bloom frequently?   About 4 to 5 years old; then the clump should bloom every year or at least every second year after that.

Is it necessary to mulch a yucca plant?   No; the common yucca is very hardy and prefers a dry, sandy soil.

What is the preferred time for moving yuccas?   Best done in early spring, when plant is dormant.

Have several yucca plants that were on the place when we moved here 5 years ago; why don't they bloom?   Probably planted in shade, or too heavy a soil. They prefer a light, sandy soil, good drainage, and full sun.

When can I separate yucca?   Detach young suckers in early spring; or divide old clumps immediately after flowering, or in the spring.

SECTION III-E

Annuals and Biennials

INTRODUCTION

BY F. F. ROCKWELL

AND ESTHER C. GRAYSON

THERE HAS BEEN a tendency on the part of many gardeners during recent years to look down their noses a bit when annuals are mentioned. The fact remains that annuals offer the beginning gardener the means— when it comes to beautifying his or her new home with flowers—of getting the fastest and the mostest, for the leastest.

By no means, however, should annuals be considered merely as stop-gap plants, to be used for temporary results until one can obtain something better. For many purposes, and for many special effects, there *is* nothing better. Many of the famous gardens of England make lavish use of annuals to obtain the breath-taking color displays for which they are noted.

While most annuals are so easily grown that they present no great challenge to the gardener's skill as a grower, they do test his skill— and offer him endless opportunities—in the employment of color and design in ways that will give his place individuality as well as beauty. And they do possess the great advantage of *flexibility*. Shrubs and perennials, once established, become more or less permanent fixtures. Annuals, used to supplement them, make it possible to shift the emphasis as one wishes, from year to year, or even during one season, and thus to obtain a series of interesting focal points not otherwise possible.

The flower arranger too, will find that some annuals are almost indispensable in enabling her to maintain a really constant supply of blooms for cutting, and for supplementary foliage.

So in planning the all around garden, annuals should never be eliminated from the picture. There is no necessity of selecting only the usual kinds, such as zinnias, marigolds and petunias. Any gardener who feels that he has outgrown annuals should try some of the kinds with which he is not familiar. He will find some amazingly interesting subjects.

ANNUALS; AND PLANTS COMMONLY TREATED AS SUCH

What is an annual?   An annual is a plant that lives but one season from seed sowing to flowering, setting of seed, and death.

What is meant by a hardy annual? A half-hardy annual? A tender annual?   Hardy annuals are those the seeds of which can be planted in fall or very early spring. Half-hardy annuals are cold resistant, and seeds of these can be planted early in spring. Tender annuals are easily injured by frost and must be planted only after the ground has warmed up and all danger of frost is past.

WHAT TO GROW

Can you give me a list of a few annuals (flowers) that will stand early planting in the spring? (Vermont.)   Sweet alyssum, scabiosa, candytuft, sweetpeas, cosmos, cornflowers, larkspur, shirley poppy, pricklypoppy (argemone).

Will you give list of annuals requiring least care for home gardens?   Marigold, verbena, gaillardia, cosmos, spiderflower (cleome), calliopsis, petunia, zinnia, salvia, scabiosa, annual phlox.

What annual flower would you recommend for planting in a completely shaded area?   There are no annual flowers that will grow well in *total* shade. A perennial ground cover such as *Pachysandra terminalis,* English Ivy, *Ajuga reptans,* and periwinkle (*Vinca minor*) would be more suitable for such conditions. Your best choices, if you want to try annuals, would be cleome, cornflower, godetia, lobelia, nasturtium, nicotiana, wishbone-flower (*Torenia fournieri*), and balsam.

Which annual flowers are best for flower beds—along sidewalks and on side of house?   Ageratum (dwarf forms); *Begonia semperflorens* varieties; dustymiller (*Centaurea cineraria*); *Lobelia erinus;* marigolds (Tagetes) dwarf varieties; petunia (dwarf varieties); sweet alyssum.

Which are the easiest annuals to grow in a sunken garden? Fragrant species preferred.   Ageratum, alyssum,* calendula, centaurea, dianthus,* iberis,* lobelia, dwarf marigold, matthiola,* mirabilis,* nicotiana,* petunia,* phlox,* portulaca, torenia, nasturtium,* viola, dwarf zinnias, if low-growing plants are desired, otherwise any variety.

Will you give me the names of a few unusual annuals, their heights, blooming dates and uses?   Bells of Ireland (*Molucella laevis*), green, 24 inches; late summer; flower arrangements. Nemesia, various (ex-

*Fragrant

cept blues), 18 inches; edging, bedding. Nierembergia, lavender-blue, 12 inches; window boxes, edging.

TRANSPLANTING

When should flat-raised seedlings be transplanted? How many times? First transplanting should be done when seedlings have formed their first true leaves. Many plants benefit from a second transplanting, when 2 or 3 ins. high, to individual pots, before they are moved outdoors.

What is the best mixture of soil for transplanting seedlings from flats to pots, or to the cold frame? Sandy loam mixed with ¼ well-rotted manure (or dried manure or rich compost), and 4-in. potful of a complete fertilizer to a wheelbarrowful.

What annuals to you recommend as foliage plants for use in arrangements? Castor bean; sideritis, gray; coleus, variegated; prickly-poppy, white-veined foliage; *Amaranthus tricolor,* variegated.

What are the best tall annuals for background planting? Celosia, cleome, cosmos, datura, hollyhock, larkspur, marigolds (tall varieties), salvia, tithonia, snapdragons (tall varieties), zinnias, (tall varieties).

I have difficulty in removing annuals from flats without ruining their root systems. Any pointers? Water thoroughly a few hours before transplanting. With an old knife, or a small mason's trowel, cut soil into squares, each with a plant in the center. The plants can easily be removed with root system almost intact.

What is the right technique in setting out annual plants? Remove plants from flats with as little root disturbance as possible. Stab trowel in soil, pull toward you, set plant in hole, remove trowel, push soil around roots, *press soil* down firmly, and leave a slight depression around stem to facilitate watering.

How does one "thin out" seedlings? Choose cloudy weather when soil is moist, and spread operation over 2 or 3 weeks. Pull up weakest seedlings before they crowd each other, leaving 2 to 6 ins. between those remaining, according to their ultimate size. When those left begin to touch, again remove the weakest, leaving the remainder standing at the required distance apart.

How much space should be given annuals, when thinning them, or planting them out? Distance varies according to variety and habit of growth. A rough rule is a distance equal to ½ their mature height. Swanriverdaisy, Virginia stock, and similar weak growers, 4 ins.; marigolds, Shirley poppies, etc., 1 ft.; strong growers, such as spiderflower and sunflower, 2 to 3 ft.

When can seedlings raised indoors be transplanted into the open?
Hardy annuals, as soon as large enough. Tender annuals, when all
danger of frost is past. First harden them off by placing them in a
cold frame or protected spot for several days.

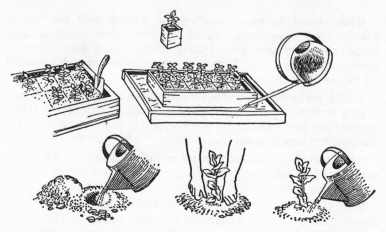

*Steps in transplanting. Plants in flats or in plant bands (as shown)
are kept moist by watering from the bottom. When setting out
(preferably on a cloudy day) dig holes, apply water and after
it has soaked away insert plant and pack soil firmly about roots.
If soil is dry apply more water at surface.*

CULTURE

**Is it wrong to plant the same kind of annuals in the same space,
year after year?** So long as the soil is well dug each year and the
humus content maintained there is nothing wrong with the practice.
China asters, snapdragons, and marigolds may well be changed each
year.

What type of soil, and what fertilizing program, is best for annuals?
Most annual flowers do best in a well-drained, rather light soil in full
sun. Unless it is really run-down and deficient in plant nutrients, only
a light annual application of rotted manure, plus some standard commercial fertilizer, is advisable.

What is the best fertilizer for the annual and perennial flower beds?
For most annuals and perennials a 4–12–4 or 5–10–5 fertilizer is
recommended. For perennials with fleshy roots a 2–10–10 fertilizer
may be substituted.

How deep should the soil be prepared for annuals? Nine ins. for
good results. Some growers go twice this depth to assure maximum
growth.

Do popular annuals have decided preferences for acid or alkaline soil?   Most popular garden flowers tolerate either a slight acid or alkaline condition and thrive in a neutral soil. (See lists under pH, Section I.)

My 3-year-old garden is on a slight slope, with sun all day. The first year, cosmos and pinks did fine. Now everything dwindles and dies. Even petunias won't grow. What can I do?   Dig deeply and add 3-in. layer of well-rotted manure or leafmold. Set the plants as early as you can, depending upon your conditions. Sloping site and a hot sun are not conducive to good growth because of the moisture conditions. Get moisture down around the roots of the plants; keep a heavy mulch of partly decayed leaves or grass clippings over the soil in summer.

How shall I top annuals to make them bushy? What does one do, pinch them or cut them with a knife or scissor?   Pinch out no more than the growing point with thumbnail, if possible, so as to avoid wasted energy on the part of the plant.

Exactly what is meant by "pinching back"?   Pinching back is the removal of the tip of a growing shoot to induce branching.

Which annuals, and at what stage, should be pinched back for better growth and more flowers?   These annuals may be pinched to advantage when from 2 to 4 ins. high: ageratum, antirrhinum, carnation, cosmos, nemesia, petunia, phlox, salvia, schizanthus, tagetes, and verbena. Straggly plants of sweet alyssum may be sheared back in midsummer for better growth and to induce flowering later in the season.

Is it true that if flowers are picked they bloom better?   On plants that continue to make flowering growth it is best to pick off flowers as soon as they fade, to prevent the formation of seed, which is a drain on the plant's energy.

What would cause annuals to grow well but come into bud so late in the summer they are of little use? Seed was planted late in April.   Most annuals are blooming at midsummer from April-sown seed. Lobelia, scarlet sage, torenia, and tithonia are examples that should be sown under glass in March for good results. The late, older varieties of cosmos usually do not have time to flower in the North, even if sown early under glass.

Why do I have to tie up so many plants—zinnia, marigold, and other common plants? They grow fine, bloom generously, yet if not tied do not stay erect.   May be insufficient phosphorus in soil; or perhaps they are exposed to too much wind; or heavy rains may have beaten them down.

Most of our annuals pass out about August, leaving few flowers for fall. Is there any way we could renew our plantings so that flowers

are available until late in the season? There are numerous annuals which, sown in summer, will provide bloom right up to frost. These are *Browallia americana* (*elata*), calendula, candytuft, celosia, globeflower, the little fine-leaved marigold (*Tagetes signata pumila*), *Phlox drummondi*, sweet alyssum *Torenia fournieri*, verbena and all types of zinnias. The dates for sowing must be closely adhered to. These apply to the vicinity of New York City and would suit a rather large region. The date of the first killing frost in fall must be allowed for in the more northerly sections. With care, seeds can be sown outdoors and seedlings transplanted direct to their flowering quarters, or potted up and held over, and used as needed. The latter plan is better for torenia and browallia. Sow these the first week in June; transplant to 3-in. pots. At the same time sow celosia, nicotiana, dwarf scabiosa, and tall marigolds. Third week in June, sow California Poppy (sow where to bloom or in pots), globeflower, candytuft, *Phlox drummondi*, and tagetes. None of the above will grow to the size of spring-sown plants. Last week in June to first week in July sow calendulas, sweet alyssum, and zinnias of all types, including Haageana hybrids and *Z. linearis*. Alyssum and calendula and verbena will survive light frosts.

How long from planting of seed to cutting of flowers on asters, stock, snapdragons? (California.) The length of time required will vary somewhat according to the type and variety, the time of year, and conditions under which grown. Early varieties of either might be ready in 14 to 16 weeks. Snapdragons will be bushier if pinched when about 3 ins. high, but pinching delays flowering.

How can I save the seed from annual flowers? Select healthy plants of the best type, allow the seeds to mature on the plant, but gather before they are shed, then dry in an airy, rainproof place safe from mice.

Will seed from hybrid annuals flower the following year; if so, will they come true? Seeds of the so-called annual hybrids saved one year should give flowers the next. They would most likely come pretty true, but some variation could be expected.

I have looked and looked for the answer to this question and haven't found it yet. When different shades of the same flower are planted together, which ones may I save seeds from and have them come true to their parent? Which ones not? You have not much chance of getting seed which would come true from any of them.

Do the following come up without replanting? Bergamot, ageratum, ladyslippers, four-o'clocks, sweet alyssum, morningglories, moonflowers. Of this group only bergamot is a perennial; this will come up each year. All the others are annuals. They come up from the seeds dropped from the plants the previous year. However, to be on the safe side it is best to sow seeds each spring.

PROPAGATION (INDOORS)

Is one seed disinfectant satisfactory for use on all seeds? No. There are special disinfectants for certain seeds. (See Section VIII.) For annual seeds use semesan or rootone.

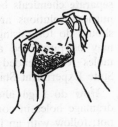

Seeds of many vegetables and flowers are benefited by being dusted with a disinfectant before planting. The operation is simple—a mere thorough shaking up with a pinch of the dust. The cost is infinitesimal.

What is a flat? A shallow, topless box (usually about 3 ins. deep) with holes in the bottom to allow for drainage of water from soil. It is used for sowing seeds, inserting cuttings, etc.

Is there any rule about the dimensions of flats? There is great variety in flat sizes. Usually they should be not less than 2½ ins., nor more than 4 ins. deep. If more than 14 × 20 ins., they are likely to be too heavy to carry with comfort.

Can cigar boxes and cheeseboxes be used instead of flats for starting seeds indoors? Usually cigar boxes are too shallow. Cheeseboxes are all right when only a few seedlings are to be raised and they can be accommodated on narrow window sills. Bore small holes in the bottom for drainage.

What soil mixture is preferable for seeds sown indoors? One part good garden loam, 1 part leafmold or peatmoss, and 1 part sand, screened through ¼-in. mesh screen; or half sand and half peatmoss; or pure fine sand, or vermiculite, watered with nutrient solution.

For starting seeds, rooting cuttings, potting seedlings or small plants, soil or compost should be sifted through screen of ¼-in. mesh.

What is the procedure in raising seedlings in sand, with the aid of nutrient solutions? Take a flat 3 to 4 ins. deep, with provision for drainage. Place a piece of burlap or sphagnum moss over the holes and fill with clean sand. Soak it with water, then with the nutrient solution diluted 1 part to 5 parts water. Sow seeds thinly; cover with sand; firm well. Keep the sand moist with the dilute solution. When the seedlings have made true leaves, use equal parts nutrient solution and water.

Can ready-to-use nutrient solutions be purchased, or must the separate chemicals be obtained and mixed at home?   Ready-mixed nutrient solutions are obtainable from garden supply houses, and should do for raising seedlings. For more extensive use, chemicals may be purchased and dissolved to make solutions according to tables recommended in books on the subject, or obtainable from State Experiment Stations. (See also Soilless Gardening—Section I.)

How do I go about sowing seeds of annuals indoors?   Cover drainage holes in containers with moss or pieces of broken flowerpot; follow with an inch of "rough stuff"—flaky leafmold, moss, or screenings; fill with screened soil mixutre (¼-in. mesh); press down level, and sow seeds.

How deep should seeds be planted in flats and pots indoors? How deep in rows outdoors?   Indoors, very small seeds are merely firmly pressed into soil with a tamper, or covered with a dusting of fine soil or sand; medium-sized seeds covered ⅛ to ¼ in.; large seeds about 3 times their diameter. Outdoors, seeds are customarily covered a little deeper—half as much again.

What is a tamper?   An oblong piece of board with a handle attached (similar to a mason's float) for tamping soil firm in flats. For use in pots or bulb pans the base of a tumbler or flowerpot can be used.

Is it better to scatter the seeds, or to sow them in rows?   When flats are used, it is preferable to sow in rows. You can judge germination better, cultivate lightly without danger of harming seedlings, and transplant with more ease. When pots are used, seeds are generally scattered evenly and thinly.

How can very small seeds be sown evenly?   Mix thoroughly with sand before sowing. Use of a small gadget known as the sow-rite seed sower also helps.

When starting seeds in the house in the winter, what do you put in the soil, so that the plants will be short and stocky and not tall and spindly?   No treatment of the soil will prevent this. Good light, moderate temperature, and avoidance of overcrowding are the preventives. Turn pots daily to keep the plants from "drawing" to the light.

When would seeds for annuals be planted in seed flats in spring?   Mid-March usually is soon enough, in the North especially, if raised under space limitations. Allow from 6 to 8 weeks before it is safe to plant the seedlings outside.

STARTING SEEDS INDOORS

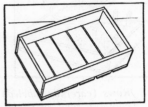

*Compost is sifted, ready to go into flat, with cracks
(for drainage) in bottom.*

*Sifted compost is placed in flat, pressed down in
corners, and leveled off.*

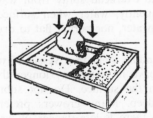

*It is then pressed down firmly and thin layer of
fine soil sifted over surface. Small seeds are barely
covered from sight.*

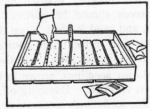

*Rows are marked off (2 to 3 ins. apart) with label
or pencil, and seeds sown thinly.*

Rows (carefully labeled) are covered with sifted compost, sand, or sifted sphagnum moss.

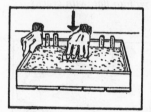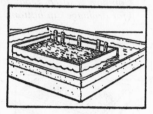

Surface is pressed down firm and flat watered (from beneath) by placing in tray or sink, until moisture shows on surface.

How should seed flats be watered after the seed is sown? Water thoroughly after seeding with a fine overhead spray from watering can until soil is saturated. Subsequently, water when surface soil shows signs of dryness. Do not overwater, nor permit flat to dry out. (See following question.)

Can seed flats be watered by standing them in a vessel of water? Yes, if more convenient. Do not leave in water any longer than is necessary for moisture to show on the surface. Do not submerge flat; place in water about 1 in. deep. Many growers prefer this method to watering the surface, as there is less danger of washing out fine seeds.

I have tried starting annuals indoors but without much success. Is there some trick about watering, or soil, that I should know? I've always used ordinary wooden flats and bought good seeds. The soil for seeds should be porous. A mixture of equal parts loam, leafmold, and sand is good. Keep the soil just moist, but not sodden. Sometimes poor germination comes from covering seeds too deeply. Sow them no deeper than twice their diameter.

Why do my seedlings, grown in the house, grow to about an inch, bend over, and die? Damping off, a fungous disease. Prevent it by disinfecting seeds with semesan or rootone, thin seeding, not overwatering, and giving seedlings fresh air without drafts. In severe cases, disinfecting soil or sand is advisable.

The seedlings in my seed flat get very tall and leggy, and very light

in color. Why? Seedlings in this condition are said to be "drawn." The causes are insufficient light and too-high temperature. Overcrowding may result in insufficient light.

What is the best germinating temperature for annual nicotiana and annual gaillardias? I have planted both late in the spring with dubious results. Must they have a cooler temperature to start? Indoors in April a night temperature between 50° and 55° F. is suitable. Annual gaillardia germinates well outside in late May or early June. Self-sown nicotianas often germinate in early June, but are a bit late for best effect.

What is proper time to plant indoors seeds of pansy, petunia, and other annuals, that should be started early, but not too soon, as we often have frost here in May? (New Hampshire.) Pansy may be sown inside in January, but the best plants for spring display come from seed sown in August. The pansy can stand some frost; March or April is a good time to sow petunias for good plants to set out as soon as the weather is warm enough.

How can I start seedlings indoors to prevent too-rapid growth and decay? When shall I plant outdoors? Too-high temperatures and too early a start often account for conditions described. Few plants need starting indoors around New York before late March. Most of these are ready for planting outdoors in late April or early in May.

How do you make new plants blossom early in spring? There is not much that can be done to make them bloom early unless they are forced in a greenhouse. Most plants have to reach a certain age before they will flower.

PROPAGATION (OUTDOORS)

What should the temperature be before planting annuals in the garden? (New York.) There can be no set temperature figure. Hardy annuals may be seeded as soon as the ground is ready to work; half-hardy annuals about 4 weeks later; tender ones when all danger of frost is past for the region. In and about New York this is usually during the second week in May.

How early may annuals be planted in the Philadelphia, Pennsylvania, area? Hardy annuals late March to April 1; half-hardy kinds mid-April to end; tender kinds from first week in May to end of month.

What does this mean: "Sow seeds when the maple leaves are expanding"? The unfolding of the maple leaves in the spring indicates that the season has sufficiently advanced for the gardener to sow certain of his hardier seeds outdoors.

How does one sow seeds for annuals in patches outdoors? Rake surface soil to break lumps and remove large stones. If seeds are small (alyssum, petunia, portulaca), scatter evenly, and pat down soil. For medium-sized seeds, rake soil again lightly *after* sowing, and pat down. For seeds which have to be covered ¼ in. or more, scrape off soil to required depth, sow seeds, and return soil removed.

English sparrows take dust baths in my newly planted seed patches. How can I prevent this? Lay pieces of burlap or of fine brush over the seeded areas. Remove when seeds have germinated. Keep seedbed constantly moist.

What is the best method of insuring germination of small flower seeds in heavy clay soil, which consists mostly of subsoil, due to excavation for house? It grows plants very well once they get started. Hoe out rows 2 ins. wide and deep, fill with good screened compost, and sow the seeds in that. Before sowing work in a generous amount of peatmoss, sifted compost, or old manure, if possible, to improve the general texture of the soil.

Which annual seeds are suitable for autumn planting? Larkspur, poppy, gilia, sweetpea, portulaca, nicotiana, salvia, celosia, cleome, alyssum, centaurea, petunia (robust kinds), coreopsis, kochia, euphorbia, cosmos, candytuft. They must be sown sufficiently late, so they will *not* germinate before freezing weather.

Which seeds can be sown out of doors, not later than November, to germinate next spring? (Ohio.) Annual poppies, balsam, California Poppies, cornflower, portulaca.

Can larkspur, centaurea, and other seeds which are recommended for planting in the fall, be planted in February? (Maryland.) Seeds of these plants can be sown outdoors just as soon as the soil is dry enough to work in the spring. For a broad naturalistic effect the seed could be scattered in February even if the ground was not fit to rake.

Is it advisable to sow seeds of annuals, such as cosmos, zinnias, and marigolds, in late autumn, so that they can germinate the first warm days of spring? Cosmos is the only one of these likely to come up if sown outdoors in autumn, and there is nothing to be gained by this for early flowering, if seed can be sown in a cold frame in April.

How late is "late" when we are told to plant seed in late autumn? Usually about the average time of killing frost for your locality. Consult zone map in back of book. Some seeds (sweetpeas and other hardy annuals) may be sown after frost, provided the ground is not frozen.

Is it necessary to prepare the soil for seed planted in the fall? Yes. Soil should be just as carefully dug, fertilized, raked, and graded for fall planting as for spring planting.

Which flower seeds should be sown where they are to grow because

of difficulty in transplanting?   Poppies, annual larkspur, calendulas, nasturtiums, dwarf lupines, portulaca, mignonette, Virginia stocks.

If such plants as petunias, phlox, etc., are permitted to self-seed, is there a true-to-color reproduction?   Not usually.

PROPAGATION-CUTTINGS

How are plants like snapdragon, petunia, verbena, and other annuals started as slips from the original plant?   These may be rooted if short side shoots, 3 to 4 ins. long, are placed in sand in a

Cutting of patience-plant, with leaves trimmed from base, ready for insertion in rooting medium. Cutting of tradescantia or wanderingjew.

closed container, in July and August. If the slips have flower buds, these should be pinched off. (See Cuttings.)

Why does coleus wilt so badly when I try to start new cuttings in soil?   The air about the cuttings is too dry. Cover them with a bell-jar, battery-jar, or preserving jar until they have formed roots. Trim large leaves back one half.

How are geranium slips rooted?   Geranium slips may be rooted in sand at almost any time of year indoors during cold weather. The cuttings should be about 4 ins. long, and about ⅓ of the stem should be in the sand. Make the basal cut ¼ in. below leaf attachment. They can be rooted readily out of doors in September. Keep sand moist but not soggy.

What is the best method of handling lantana cuttings—our cuttings this year rooted well and got off to a good start after potting, but after a short time wilted and died. We kept them on the dry side, and shaded.   After potting them, water thoroughly and keep in a closed, shaded propagating case for a week or two. Then gradually admit more air and remove the shade.

SPECIFIC ANNUAL PLANTS

AGERATUM

How is ageratum started for outdoor planting?   Sow seeds in a protected cold frame in early April, or outdoors early in May when danger from frost is past. The best method is to sow them in seed pans or small pots of fine-screened soil. Sow on a level surface and press the seeds in. Set pan in water until moisture shows on the surface; cover with glass and shade; remove when germinated; transplant 2 ins. apart when first true leaves show.

Can I sow seeds of Ageratum Irwin's Beauty or how are the plants raised?   Ageratum Irwin's Beauty does not come true from seeds. It is propagated by cuttings. These are usually taken from outdoor plants in late summer, rooted in sand, and kept in a cool greenhouse during the winter. From these plants cuttings are taken in spring to furnish material for outdoor planting.

What is the proper care of ageratums over the winter?   Young plants, started late in the season, may flower as house plants during late winter. Cuttings are taken from the young growth in September and rooted in sand.

ALYSSUM

Why does white sweet alyssum come up year after year when yellow and purple don't?   The white alyssum reseeds itself; the purple will not, as the seeds do not live over the winter; both of these are annuals. The yellow is a perennial and probably is winter killed.

ARCTOTIS

Would appreciate instructions for success with African-daisies (arctotis). Mine achieve the bud stage, but never blossom, falling off at that point. Can it be too much water, or are they perhaps pot-bound? (Kentucky.)   Dropping of buds can be caused by extremes. Too much moisture around the roots or their drying out; warm, humid conditions or a sudden chill. Use fine bone meal for fertilizer; have the soil open and well drained. Don't plant in very large pots.

ASTER

How can I grow annual asters?   Select wilt-resisting seed. Plant indoors in flats or pots in late March or April; transplant into the open when danger of frost is past. Or sow seed outdoors in May. Select "early," "midseason," and "late" varieties for continuous bloom. If in a region where aster "yellows" are prevalent, grow under cheesecloth screens.

What culture do asters require?   The types best suited for sowing outdoors are American Beauty, American Branching, California Sunshine, Giants of California. Get wilt-resistant varieties of these types. Prepare seedbed by forking over the soil and working in peatmoss or leafmold. Draw drills 2 to 3 ins. apart and ¼ in. deep; sow seeds

6 or 8 to the inch about mid-May. Cover with a half-soil, half-sand mixture, and water with a fine spray. A light covering with hay or strips of burlap will help retain moisture until germination; then remove *immediately*. Keep the soil stirred between the rows and keep the seedlings watered. Transplant when seedlings have formed their first true leaves. Soak the soil a few hours before, lift seedlings with all roots, and keep them wet. If wanted for cut flowers, set in rows 18 ins. apart, the plants 9 to 12 ins. apart in the rows. Set the seedling in the soil so that the bottom leaves are resting on the surface. Give a good watering; keep soil cultivated until plants get large. Enrich the soil prior to planting by digging in 3 ins. rotted manure; or use compost or peatmoss mixed with dried cow or sheep manure —6 lbs. manure to 1 bu. of compost or peatmoss. When flowers show, feed liquid manure weekly.

Will you please give information on the raising of asters in New Jersey? Early Branching and Queen of the Market types for early flowering (July) should be sown toward the end of March, either in the greenhouse or a protected cold frame. The later-flowering kinds (Sunshine, Giants of California, Late Branching, Crego, and American Beauty) can be sown directly outdoors early in May. (See preceding question.)

Which are the best annual asters for cutting, for a small garden that does not recieve more than the average amount of care? The soil is reasonably good. Varieties of American Branching, Burpeeana, Giants of California, and California Sunshine.

Which are the best varieties of winter asters? (Illinois.) You are probably referring to the practice of forcing the annual aster by growing the seedlings under light in January. The types used are Early Branching and Ball Branching. Any of the varieties within these 2 types are suitable.

We have China asters. Do they reseed themselves? (New York.) Yes, occasionally, especially the single-flowered kinds. However, it is better to raise new plants under controlled conditions annually.

Can't asters be planted in the same spot each year? Better not. They are subject to several diseases that collect in the soil, making it desirable to select a new site each year unless special precautions are taken. (See next question.) The ground, of course, can be used for other plants.

Is it true that asters cannot be planted in the same space a second year? No—not literally. Asters can be grown in the same spot by using disease-resistant strains, by disinfecting the seeds, by mixing tobacco powder with the soil to discourage root aphis, and by screening with cheesecloth to keep out leaf hoppers which transmit the virus disease known as aster yellows.

What is the best procedure in disbudding asters? Should the top be pinched out when they are young to make them branch? Asters usually are self-branching, producing a number of branches, and do not need pinching. Each branch will bear a terminal flower, together with numerous other buds on small side shoots. All these must be removed, retaining the main bud only.

Do annual asters come true from seed collected from a flower bed? If several varieties were growing together, variation could be expected.

BALSAM

Is Balsam worth growing? Yes, especially for positions in part shade. Try the new camellia-flowered double strains on bushy, branching plants.

BELLS OF IRELAND

How are the seeds of Bells of Ireland germinated? Mine don't come up. Sow in a carefully prepared seed frame in May when soil has warmed up. Keep constantly moist until germination. Transplant to garden beds in late June.

My Bells of Ireland don't look like the ones in the flower show arrangements. Why? Flowering stems are "groomed" by removing all the foliage, leaving only the bell-like bracts with the little flower "clappers" in the center of each.

BROWALLIA

When should browallia be sown for outdoor flowers? Which varieties should I use? For early flowering, sow in late March indoors, or in a cold frame after mid-April. Outdoor sowing can be done about mid-May. These dates apply in the vicinity of New York City; farther North it would be 7 to 12 days later and correspondingly earlier farther South. *Browallia americana* (*elata*) and *B. speciosa major* are the best for summer.

What is the method of growing browallia for the house; and what is the best variety to choose for this? Sow seeds in August; transplant into 2½-in. pots; as the plants grow, shift to 4-in. then perhaps to 5-in. pots, but don't overpot; water sparingly after November. Sow again in January for early-spring bloom. Use *Browallia speciosa major*.

CALCEOLARIA

Some years ago I saw a hardy annual about 6 ins. high, with lemon-yellow blossoms about the size of a fingernail, shaped like the calceolaria. Leaves were quite lacy and fernlike. What is its name? It may have been an annual calceolaria. The species *mexicana, scabiosaefolia,* and *pinnata* all more or less agree with your description.

CAMPANULA

Are annual Canterbury bells easy to raise from seed? Yes, annual types bloom in less than six months from seed. Colors are the same as in biennial strains.

CANDYTUFT

My annual candytuft only bloomed a short time, then died. Why? Annual candytuft blooms very quickly from seed but only for a short time. Plant seeds at 2 or 3 week intervals for constant bloom during cool spring and fall weather. Candytuft does not do well in the heat of summer.

CLEOME

I have seen lovely pink and white spider plants. Are they something special? Pink Queen is a fine variety which won a silver medal for excellence. Helen Campbell is a pure white. If your plants self-seed, pull up all purplish-red volunteers.

CASTORBEAN

I always grow a few castorbean plants and am interested in them. Can you tell me more about them, their cultivation, and if there is a market for the bean? (Ohio.) Castorbean plants grow best in a rich, well-drained loam soil. Seeds may be planted in May where they are to grow, or started earlier indoors and then set out later. There is a market for the seeds, of course, but it is well supplied by commercial growers. The commercial crop is produced in the South, where a long season allows for maximum production.

Is it advisable to plant castor-oil-bean seeds around the lawns to prevent molehills and mole runs? Castorbean plants have very little if any effect on the mole population.

Is there anything poisonous about the castorbean plant? The seeds contain a poisonous principle called ricin. They are best planted where children cannot get at and eat the beans. Fatalities have been reported from eating as few as three seeds.

CORNFLOWER (CENTAUREA)

Why do our bachelor buttons or cornflowers show retarded growth, with feeble flower stalks? Sow the seeds on a finely prepared soil in the fall or as soon as you can work the soil in spring. Sow thinly; cover about ¼ in. Thin out the seedlings to 9 ins. apart when large enough. Yours probably were too crowded.

What treatment do you prescribe for bachelor-buttons for large blossoms and long period of bloom? If by bachelor-buttons you mean the annual cornflower (centaurea), you should get excellent results by giving them a moderately rich, well-drained soil and extra watering during dry weather. Keep faded flowers picked off. (See preceding answer.)

COSMOS

When should early cosmos be started from seeds? Sow in a cold frame in early April and transplant directly to the place to flower, or sow outdoors in late April.

I like and grow cosmos. Pink plant blossomed in early July—very unusual to me. Why should this happen? The rest of my plants blossomed in fall as usual. I know of the yellow early bloomer. There are several forms of early-flowering cosmos, including pink varieties. The Sensation type blooms in 8 weeks after the seed is sown. You probably have an early kind.

DAHLIA

Is it true that some dahlias flower the first year from seed? Yes, especially the dwarf bedding dahlias like Unwin Dwarfs and Coltness Hybrids. See Dahlias, page 451.

DIANTHUS

What are the best annual pinks? Double: Chinensis; Fringed. Single: Westwood Beauty; Heddensis.

DIMORPHOTHECA

How long can dimorphotheca be expected to stay in bloom? The plants I had last summer bloomed from about June 1 to July 15 and then died. Six weeks of bloom is about all you could expect, though the time might be lenthened somewhat by snipping off all withered blossoms to prevent seed formation. It is a good plan to make a second sowing of seed 4 to 6 weeks or so after the first, to provide blooming plants for the second half of the summer.

What are the requirements for African-daisy (dimorphotheca)? It just never comes up. Can it be planted early? I buy good seed. (Washington.) Sow the seed outdoors in spring when the ground has warmed up, or indoors 4 to 6 weeks earlier. Give the plants light, well-drained, and not specially enriched soil. Be sure they get plenty of sun.

EVERLASTINGS

I want to grow some everlastings for winter bouquets. What shall I select? Acroclinium; globe amaranth; helichrysum; statice; honesty; xeranthemum.

FOUR-O'CLOCK (MIRABILIS)

I have been told you get larger bushes and greater amount of flowers from four-o'clock roots the second season. Are they to be left in the ground, or dug up and dried like certain bulbs? (Missouri.) Mostly used as annuals; the roots would be very unlikely to live through winter outdoors in your region. The large, tuberous roots can be lifted before hard frost and stored indoors for the winter, like dahlias. It is the prevailing opinion that they will flower earlier and produce better bloom. Try it, but sow some seeds outdoors in May to be sure of a crop of flowers.

GODETIA

I have no luck with satin flower. Can you help me? These lovely, bushy, 18 inch annuals with their masses of hollyhock-like salmon, orange, pink, red and lavender flowers, prefer part shade and a cool, moist location. They thrive on Cape Cod in a well watered garden but cannot stand areas where nights are hot and humid.

KOCHIA

I have heard of an annual which can be used instead of a real hedge. What is it? Burning Bush or Kochia. The rounded plants, like sheared evergreens, grow 3 feet tall. During hot weather the foliage is light green but in autumn it turns a rich red.

LARKSPUR

How early should larkspur be planted? (Virginia.) As early in the spring as the ground becomes workable, or in late fall about November.

What month is best to plant larkspur and raggedrobin? (Virginia.) Larkspur and raggedrobin (lychnis) can be sown in November for spring bloom, or as early in spring as possible.

Will larkspur do well if transplanted? It transplants very poorly; sow the seeds where the plants will flower, and thin out the seedlings to 9 ins.

When shall I transplant annual larkspur? Only when the seedlings are small—just large enough to handle; large plants do not transplant successfully. Better to sow where they are to bloom and thin them.

What is the secret for successful larkspur? Ours start well, but fade away before flowering. Sow seeds in well-drained, moderately fertile soil, in full sun or light shade. Thin seedlings to stand 9 ins. apart. (See preceding answers.)

LOBELIA

Will lobelia grow in part shade? Yes, the low-growing varieties are ideal for window and porch boxes or hanging baskets as well as for partly shaded edgings. Choose Gracilis Blue for boxes and dwarf varieties for edgings.

MARIGOLD

What types of marigolds do you suggest for a garden of annuals? African (tall, double including carnation-flowered, chrysanthemum-flowered, dahlia-flowered, peony-flowered; French Single; French Double; Dwarf Signet (*Tagetes signata pumila*).

What marigolds shall I grow for variety in color? Man-in-the-moon, very pale yellow; Glitters, canary yellow; Fluffy Ruffles, gold; Limelight, lime-yellow; Mayling, primrose yellow; Tetra, deep orange. Dwarf: Butterball, yellow; Lemon Drop, lemon; Red Head, gold and maroon; Cupid, yellow.

Would you kindly tell me why my marigolds didn't blossom well last summer? Could it be the fault of the ground? It may have been any one, or several, of a number of reasons: too late sowing; too much rain; too heavy or too-rich soil; insufficient sun; overfeeding or over-watering.

Are seeds good which have not been picked until after a killing frost, such as marigolds? The first killing frost would probably not be severe enough to harm the seeds.

NASTURTIUMS

What nasturtiums shall I grow to produce seeds for pickles and salads? What shall I do to keep them free of the little black bugs? The old-fashioned singles, either dwarf or tall. The much more beautiful and attractive sweet scented doubles produce few seeds. Keep young plants sprayed with Black Leaf 40 to keep off aphids.

NICOTIANA

I have seen flowering tobacco in mixed colors. What variety is this? The Affinis Hybrids or Sensation Mixed. Crimson Bedder is deep red. All are delightfully fragrant, and will grow in part shade.

NIEREMBERGIA

How shall I grow nierembergia from seed? Start indoors in March for early bloom. Purple Robe is a fine violet-blue variety.

PERIWINKLE

How and where shall I plant the annual periwinkle? Periwinkle (*Vinca rosea*) is a native of the tropics and practically everblooming. Sow seeds in January in a warm temperature. The seeds are sometimes difficult to germinate, and at first the seedlings are slow of growth. Have the soil well drained and don't overwater. When these seedlings produce the first true leaves, transplant to 2¼-in. pots, later on to 3-in. pots. From these transplant to the open ground when all danger of cold weather is past. Provide a fairly rich soil. Once established they need little care beyond watering occasionally.

PETUNIAS

Can petunias be grown successfully with only 4 hours of afternoon sun? Yes, provided other conditions are suitable.

How can I prepare seedbed for petunias? When shall I plant in St. Louis area? (Missouri.) Have the soil well drained, moderately rich, and very thoroughly cultivated, so that its texture is fine and light. Sow thinly in spring when soil is in good workable condition.

When is the best time to plant petunias? In what soil? (New York.) The new Hybrid F_1 and F_2, Fringed Giant, Ruffled, Double and other improved petunias are best started indoors in March in the vicinity of New York. See Propagation Indoors, this section.

When is the best time, and what is the best way, to plant petunia seed? (Alabama.) In your region, outdoor sowing of petunia seed is likely to be the most satisfactory. It may be done as soon as the soil has warmed up in spring. Have the soil very well and finely prepared, and barely cover the seed.

Can petunias be sown in the fall? (Ohio.) Fall-planted petunia seed sometimes comes through the winter and germinates in the spring—this depends chiefly on climate, location, and the character of the winter. Spring sowing is preferable in middle and northern sections of the country.

How long does it take petunia seeds to germinate, and when should one transplant them? Good petunia seeds sown on prepared soil, only lightly covered, and kept at greenhouse temperature, should germinate in from 8 to 12 days. Transplant when the first *true* leaves appear. (The leaves that show at germination are only seed leaves.) This might be approximately 10 to 14 days after germination.

Should petunias always be transplanted, or will they bloom well where originally planted? If the soil and other conditions are favorable, they should do well where originally planted. But thin the seedlings to 6 ins. or so apart if they come up thickly.

Set out petunias in bed with partial shade when they had just begun to bloom; plants withered and died until 90 per cent were gone. Soil analysis said nothing was wrong. Gladioli did well in same bed. What was wrong? Probably root injury when transplanting, plus too much water. Petunias will stand some shade but not too much.

I'd like a mass of petunias for borders but have no success growing from seed. How can this be done? How early to start, etc.? (Connecticut.) Petunia seed for a mass planting is best sown as soon as the soil has warmed up. Have the soil very thoroughly pulverized, and barely cover the seed. Keep watered, and thin out plants to 6 or 8 ins. apart when they are a couple of inches tall. For earlier bloom, start seed in flats indoors in March, and transplant outdoors early in May.

Is there any way to prevent petunias growing lank during late summer? I keep seed pods picked off pretty well, still they look straggly by August. This tendency is hard to prevent in some varieties unless the flowers are cut quite often; prune back the longer stems to encourage stockiness. Use compact-growing kinds.

Why can't I raise petunias? They are the only plants I have a complete failure with. I buy good seed, but the plants that do grow just get tall (leggy), with very small bloom, if any. A hard question to answer without more information. The plants may be too crowded, or the soil may be too heavy and shaded. Try careful thinning and pinching back young plants.

Why can't I raise any petunias? They come up but die. Perhaps the soil is too heavy and claylike, or it may be too wet. A light, well-drained soil in practically full sun is best, and it should be only moderately rich.

What makes petunia plants turn yellow, especially if grown 2 years in succession in the same soil? Petunias are subject to several virus diseases that discolor the leaves. The condition may also be due to a highly alkaline soil. Dig in peat or leafmold, change the location, and prepare the soil deeply.

Why do petunia plants grow large but have no blooms? Soil probably too rich, thereby forcing excessive stem and leaf growth at the expense of blooms. Try them in another place where the soil is poorer. Don't overwater.

Can you explain just how to snip off a petunia plant (brought in from outdoors) so that it will have many blooms instead of spindly stems? Cut back about half of the stems to 4 or 5 ins. When these have developed new growth, cut back the remaining stems in the same way.

How can I force petunia (giant and ruffle types) under average conditions as to light and heat found in a home? Your chances of raising petunias under home conditions are slight. In greenhouses, cuttings are taken in September from summer plants, the young growths being used. These are rooted in sand and then potted up in small pots. They do not bloom much in the winter but begin about February. Seeds can be sown in January and February for early flowering. Petunias need plenty of light and a fairly even temperature—about 55° F. at night. You might try digging up old plants in fall, cutting them back, and planting in pots.

Will petunias reseed successfully? (Indiana.) Sometimes they will; it depends on conditions. The more common kinds reseed freely, but the colors will be unsatisfactory. For good petunias secure good seed each year.

How can I root cuttings from double petunias? If the plants are growing outdoors, take the cuttings in August or September. Select young growths about 2 ins. in length that grow from the older stems. Trim off the bottom leaves and insert them ½ to 1 in. deep in pure, moist sand in a cold frame in a warm atmosphere. Shade and keep the sash on for about a week. Give light when they are rooting; this will be indicated by the foliage remaining erect. Keep the sand moist.

Dwarf, compact-growing annuals (such as the Gem Petunias) are used for the foreground of mixed borders and for edging.

How can I root petunia cuttings in winter? About February take young side growths, trim off the lower leaves, and set them firmly in moist sand. (See previous question.)

Which kind of petunias shall I get to grow against a small white fence? Something not tall, but rather bushy. F₁ Hybrids like Ballerina, Comanche, Prima Donna, Red Satin, Flamingo. Dwarfs: Cheerful, Blue Bird, Peach Red, Improved Rosy Morn and Snowball. Doubles, like Burpee's Salmon, White, Orchid, and Mrs. Dwight D. Eisenhower; the F₂ Hybrids, in mixed colors; Balconies, Salmon, Black Prince, etc.

What type of petunia is best for garden work—for all summer beauty? The regular "bedding" and "balcony" types are generally the most satisfactory.

POINSETTIA

What is the best treatment for annual poinsettias? Have some, but they appear weak, and are having a hard time. Not very easy to germinate the seeds outdoors. Suggest you sow in a small pot or seed pan indoors last of April. Use a soil mixed with sand and leafmold or peatmoss screened through ¼-in. mesh. Cover with glass and shade but remove when seed germinates; give all light and air possible; transplant outdoors when first true leaves appear.

POPPY

Do California and Shirley Poppies reseed themselves? Yes, usually; but much digging of the soil in the spot where reseeding took place will bury the seed so deep it may not germinate.

When is best time to plant the (annual) peony-flowered poppy? Can it be successfully planted on top of the snow? (Kansas.) If in your region the poppy usually reseeds itself, and plants come voluntarily the following spring, you can very well sow on the snow. Otherwise sow just as early as you can get on the soil.

When is the correct time to plant poppy seed? How is it best sown? Just as early as you can work the ground in spring. Rake the soil as fine as possible; make level and firm it slightly; scatter the seeds thinly, press them firmly into the soil but don't cover. Thin out the seedlings when 2 ins. high, spacing 3 ins. apart. Two weeks later thin again to 6 or 9 ins. apart.

PORTULACA

How can I make portulaca catch and grow? Portulaca is usually easy to grow from seed sown outdoors in either October or early spring. It should have a well-drained, light, and not rich soil, in full sun.

SALPIGLOSSIS

How can I grow large, healthy salpiglossis plants? (New Jersey.) Sow seeds in a well-prepared bed in May. Work peatmoss or leafmold into the surface, sow the seeds thinly in rows 2 ins. apart. Cover them not more than ⅛ in. deep. Transplant 12 ins. apart in soil deeply dug and enriched with old manure or compost; or with peatmoss mixed with dried cow or sheep manure, 10 lbs. to a bushel of peat, plus ½ lb. of ground limestone. Spread an inch deep and dig in. Do not soak the soil until the plants are steadily growing and have some size. Cultivate frequently. When flower stalks form, feed with liquid manure; or apply sheep manure, about 1 lb. per 40 sq. ft.; hoe and water in; repeat every 2 weeks during bloom.

SALVIA

How do you start red salvia seeds? (South Dakota.) The seed should be sown indoors in a warm temperature, about the latter part of March or beginning of April, in small pots or seed pans. Cover seeds ⅛ in., and set pot or pan in water until moisture shows on surface. Cover with glass and newspaper, but remove as soon as seed germinates.

Are there other colors of bedding salvia besides the red and blue? Yes, the so-called Welwyn Salvias, and others, can be had in white, salmon-pink, purple, mahogany, and lilac.

SCABIOSA

What is the best method of culture for scabiosa? (New Jersey.)
Sow seeds outdoors about April 15 or indoors in March. Give the
plants a sunny position where the soil is rather light in texture, moderately rich, and in full sun. Do not cover the seeds deeply; not more
than ⅛ in. Transplant when the seedlings have made their first true
leaves, setting them in the soil so that the lower leaves are resting on
the surface. Set 9 ins. apart each way.

SNAPDRAGONS (ANTIRRHINUM)

Do snapdragons require a rich, shady place? (Idaho.)   They should
have full sun and a light, well-drained soil that is only moderately
enriched. Early planting is desirable for best bloom.

What is the best fertilizer for snapdragons?   Rotted manure or
leafmold when preparing the soil, which should be neutral or slightly
alkaline. Feed liquid manure when coming into flower, or give a
dressing of complete chemical fertilizer.

Can snapdragon be sown in the fall? (Kentucky.)   Yes, in your
part of the country but it must be done sufficiently early to provide
young plants which will be large enough to withstand the winter with
protection. Sow in August.

When shall I plant snapdragons? (Wisconsin.)   The best time to
set young plants out is in the spring when the ground has begun to
warm up. Seeds should be started indoors in March.

**When is the best time to set out snapdragon plants? (North Caro-
lina.)**   Early in spring, when the ground has really started to warm
up.

**Are snapdragons strictly annuals? Mine bloomed after several frosts
and continued in leaf. (Virginia.)**   No; in the South they are often
treated as biennials. Generally speaking, they are handled as hardy
annuals (more cold resistant than most). Botanically they are perennials.

**Must snapdragons be supported by stakes at planting time? Mine
were all in curlicues, and staking them after 8 or 10 ins. tall didn't
help at all.**   It is a good idea to put in the stakes at the time the
young plants are set out, and start tying as soon as signs of flopping
over begin. A better plan is to use twiggy brush and insert pieces 18
ins. long among the plants. The growths will work up among the
twigs. In an open situation, with proper care of soil, they ought not
to need much support.

**Can you tell me how to grow snapdragons? I buy the plants and
they bloom a little while, then die. (Mississippi.)**   Perhaps the soil is
too rich, too heavy and claylike, or poorly drained. Or there may be
too much shade. Snapdragons like an open situation, light soil, and

not too much feeding. They dislike a hot situation and bloom best in cool weather.

How can I attain many-flowered snapdragons in my summer garden? I get good plants but there are many stems and few blooms to a stem. Thin out weakest shoots, apply superphosphate and pulverized limestone to the soil at the rate of 8 oz. per sq. yd., and scratch into the surface. Full sunshine is necessary. Set out well-developed plants in early May.

Why can't I grow snapdragons from seed? They never come up. (Kentucky.) Sow in late April in well-drained place where the soil is light and only moderately rich and has been raked into fine texture, free of stones and lumps. Cover seed with sand not more than ⅛ in. deep, and do not pack hard. Cover with burlap, which remove as soon as seed shows germination. Water regularly in dry weather. Disinfect the seed with Semesan before sowing.

Can snapdragons be carried over winter in a cold frame? (New York.) Yes, if they are less than 1 year old. Actually, these plants can be considered as biennials in the South, or in the North when frame protection can be given in the winter.

How shall I protect antirrhinum outdoors to survive sub-zero winters? (Kentucky.) Attempts to bring snapdragons through such winter weather outdoors often fail, whatever precautions you take. Try mulching with 3 or 4 ins. of coarse straw or salt meadow hay after ground freezes. A cold frame is about the only safe means of protection.

Can you give best method for protecting snapdragons through winter? Would it do to cover them with one of the glass substitutes? (Georgia.) A mulch of straw or salt meadow hay, 2 or 3 ins. thick, is the best winter protection for snapdragons in the garden. Or the plants could be carried over in a cold frame. A glass substitute, by itself, would not do.

Are there such things as perennial snapdragons? No, from the practical gardening standpoint. Technically, they are perennials, but in the North they are too tender to be treated as such. There are some species grown in rock gardens which are truly perennial in regions that have mild winters.

What are the best snapdragons for the garden? Please name one or two, tall or medium kinds, rust resistant or not. I do not have good luck with "snaps" of late years. By all means get rust-resistant kinds. Good varieties are: Tall: Tetraploid strains. Tip Top varieties; Colossals. Medium: Super Majestics; Extra Early Hybrids; Base-branching varieties. Dwarf: Magic Carpet; Miniature strain.

Could you tell me which are the largest and best snapdragons to plant? Size and quality are strongly influenced by the grower's skill and the cultural conditions he provides. Other things being equal, try the "giant" types listed in the catalogue of any leading seedsman.

STOCKS

What causes stocks to mature without blooming?   May have been the common stock (*Matthiola incana*), which acts as a biennial and does not flower until the second year. Ten-weeks Stocks are annual, and flower the first year if conditions are to their liking.

Of 100 Ten-weeks Stock plants in our garden, 20 of the smallest, most puny ones bloomed. The other 80 grew into beautifully thrifty plants from early summer until a hard freeze came, but did not bloom. Why?   Ten-weeks Stocks usually fail to bloom if subjected to constantly high temperature—60° and over. Yours were grown under border-line conditions, enabling a few individuals to bloom.

How can I make Ten-weeks Stocks bloom? (New Jersey.)   By starting them indoors in March and setting them outside late in April. This enables them to make their growth before hot weather comes.

Can stocks be wintered through? (Kansas.)   Yes, if you have the biennial kind, *Matthiola incana,* and a mild, dryish winter climate. For the average gardener, this type is not worth trying or bothering with.

SWEETPEAS

When is the best time to plant sweetpeas?   As early as the ground can be worked in the spring; or the seeds may be sown in a cold greenhouse or cold frame a month or more ahead of the time when frost may be expected to be out of the ground, and then transplanted.

When and how shall I plant sweetpeas to insure blooms?   If you have a frost-free frame, you can sow the seed in September or October in a flat or in small pots, and in March transplant where they are to flower. Or if you have a coolish porch or window, temperature not above 45° to 50° F., you can sow in February, shift into pots, and, after hardening, plant out in late March. If there are no such facilities, sow where they are to flower as early in March as you can; prepare the ground the preceding fall. (See question on preparation.)

Can sweetpea seeds be sown in the fall, for earlier and stronger plants in the spring? If so, at what time, and how deep?   Sweetpeas can be planted in fall just before ground freezes, putting them 4 ins. deep and mulching lightly with straw or litter after hard freezing. It is doubtful, though, whether the plants would be appreciably earlier or finer than if spring-sown as soon as ground can be worked.

Can sweetpeas be planted if the ground softens to a depth of 2 ins.?   No. Wait until all the frost is out; otherwise the soil will be too muddy to work.

What is the planting date for sweetpeas in Oklahoma? Sow in November and give protection during the coldest part of winter; or sow in late winter, as soon as it is possible to work the soil.

In our mountain climate, what is the best time to plant sweetpeas? When and how should I prepare the soil? (New York.) As early in the spring as it is possible to work the soil. If the soil could be prepared the previous fall, so much the better. (See previous and following answers.)

How shall I prepare ground for sweetpeas for cut flowers? Dig a trench 1½ ft. wide and deep. Mix with the soil a 3- to 4-in. layer of rotted manure, and bone meal at rate of 1 lb. to 10 to 15 linear ft. If possible, do this in the fall so seeds can be planted without delay early in spring.

I want sweetpeas in clumps in flower border. How do I go about it? Prepare soil as described in previous answer except that instead of a long trench you should make circular planting stations 2 to 3 ft. in diameter. Support the peas on brushwood or a cylinder of chicken-wire netting held up by 4 or 5 stakes. Or you can use a dwarf variety such as Little Sweetheart.

Will you let us know something about the cultivating of sweetpeas? How far apart should the plants be? Should they have commercial fertilizer? See preceding answers for soil preparation. The plants should not be closer together than 4 ins. Commercial fertilizers, used according to manufacturer's directions, are good for application along the sides of the row after the plants are 4 ins. high.

How deep should sweetpea seeds be planted? Usually about 2 ins. Some gardeners prefer to sow them in a trench 6 ins. deep, covering them at first with 2 ins. of soil. As the plants increase in stature, the trench is gradually filled in. This works well in sandy soils.

How early must I place the supports for sweetpea vines? When they are about 4 ins. high. If left until they topple over, they never seem to grow so well as they do when staked early. Twiggy branches stuck in on both sides of the row, or in among the plants if they are grown in clumps, make the best supports, but chicken-wire netting, or strings supported by a frame, will do.

How much sun for sweetpeas? Soil? How to combat lice? General care? Full or nearly full sun is best; some shade is tolerated. Soil should be deep, well drained, rich, and well supplied with humus material. Be sure it is neutral or somewhat alkaline—never acid. Spray with nicotine sulfate for plant lice. Keep weeded and cultivated; water regularly; feed weekly with liquid manure when buds begin to show.

Will sweetpeas do better in part shade? Is it right to plant them in January? (North Carolina.) They are likely to remain in bloom somewhat longer if shaded during the hottest part of the day. Seed can be sown in January if the soil is well drained and free from frost.

How can I raise sweetpeas? Formerly had no trouble, but can't seem to grow them now. Perhaps the soil needs enriching. Sweetpeas need a rich soil. Prepare as described in previous answers, side-dress the row after the plants are 4 ins. high with a complete fertilizer. Feed liquid manure when the plants are in bud. Plant as early as possible.

I have never been successful with sweetpeas, my favorite flower. I get about 3 bouquets, and then they die. Can you help me? I have used a number of methods with no success. (Oklahoma.) Maybe the summer sun is too much for them; try shading with cheesecloth as soon as really hot, dry weather starts. Water thoroughly and regularly. Try preparing the soil and sowing in November, or December, giving a little protection in cold weather. Spring-flowering type is somewhat heat resistant.

Had very healthy-looking sweetpea vines, but no blossoms. Why? Soil may be deficient in phosphorous; or they may have been planted too late for buds to open before hot weather blasted them.

How can the blooming season of outdoor sweetpeas be prolonged? By picking the flowers as fast as they mature and by shading from hot sun with cheesecloth or similar material, plus abundant, regular watering. Usually hot weather limits the season.

Sweetpeas that are planted in November usually make some winter growth or early-spring growth. Will it be advisable to shear this top growth and let the base of the plant start new and tender growth? (Virginia.) Yes, pinch the growth back to where the stem shows signs of sprouting at the base. This later growth produces better flowers.

Is there any way to keep birds from eating my sweetpeas and ranunculus as they come up? (California.) Lay a few pieces of garden hose or rope alongside the rows; birds are afraid of snakes. Or cover with cheesecloth. Strings with white rags hanging from them may also help.

How can I successfully grow sweetpeas in a greenhouse? (Texas.) For your region the seed should be sown in late August. These plants should give a crop the greater part of the winter. Try another sowing in late September. Prepare soil 18 ins. deep, with old manure ¼ the soil volume. Add 1 lb. ground limestone and ½ lb. superphosphate per 20 sq. ft. Sow in rows 36 ins. apart, 1 ounce to 35 linear ft. Thin to 4 plants per linear ft. Support the vines by stretching a wire at ground level along the row, another at 10 to 12 ft. in height. Stretch strands of string between and train the vines up the string. Watering and feeding must be related to growth and flowering. In winter water only when moisture is low, as seen by examining the soil 1 to 2 ins.

below the surface. After flowering begins, feed every 2 weeks with liquid manure. Use only the greenhouse varieties.

Is the Spencer Sweetpea the same as the sweet-smelling variety that had a place in Grandmother's garden? Essentially it is the same, though greatly improved in size, form of blossoms, and range of colors.

Which varieties of sweetpeas are the best for a hot, dry climate? What is best method of planting? (Kansas.) Sweetpeas rarely succeed outdoors in a hot, dry climate unless sown very early. Your best chance is to plant in earliest spring, keep well watered, and shade with cheesecloth from direct sun. There are, so far as known, no varieties especially adapted to your conditions. The giant heat-resistant and spring-flowering types are quite heat resistant but need abundant moisture.

TORENIA

What can I use instead of pansies in late summer? *Torenia fournieri,* an attractive little plant, very bushy with purple, lavender and gold flowers like miniature snapdragons. Foliage turns plum-colored in late autumn. Start the seeds in May in a seed bed as they are very tender.

TITHONIA

My tithonia plants never bloom. Can you tell me why? This Mexican sunflower with its handsome, single, brilliant orange blooms, must be started early indoors to give generous bloom before frost. The variety Torch grows only 4 feet tall as against the type which reaches 6 feet. Torch also blooms earlier. Use it at the back of the border or as a screen plant.

VERBENA

How can I raise verbenas? I have not much luck with them. (Kansas.) Verbenas are not easy unless you have facilities for raising them. The seed is variable in its germination. Requiring a long season, seeds must be sown about March 1 in a temperature of 60° F. at night and 70° to 75° F. during the day. The seedlings are pricked off (transplanted) into flats, after the first true leaf appears, using equal parts loam, sand, leafmold and rotted manure. Keep in same temperature until established (10 days), then harden off the plants in a cold frame before planting outside. Set out in the ground when danger of frost is past.

When is the season to plant verbena? The plants should be set out when warm weather is established. Seeds are best sown indoors 2 months prior to setting out plants. (See previous question.)

ZINNIAS

What soil is best for zinnias?   Zinnias appreciate a fairly heavy, rich loam. Additions of rotted cow manure and commercial fertilizer will produce sturdy plants.

We have been unable to grow zinnias. Our soil is rich and well drained. We are able to grow asters, but they attain no height or size. What could be the cause?   Maybe soil is too acid. Have it tested, and if below pH 6 bring it up to neutral.

Is the middle of April too early to plant zinnia and marigold seed outdoors in central Pennsylvania?   It might be suitable for marigold, but May 1 would be better for zinnia.

Should zinnias be transplanted?   Zinnias are very easily transplanted. They may, if desired, however, be sown where they are to grow, and then thinned out.

How should I gather zinnia seeds?   Select healthiest plants with the best flowers. During late August or early September allow the flowers to mature on the plant and when the seeds are quite dry and dark, harvest them. Spread on paper in a dry, airy place. When thoroughly dry, discard chaff and place best seeds in sealed envelopes or jars. Label and store until planting time.

Why did seeds from a certain zinnia, when planted the next year, not come true to color?   Because it was a variety not capable of transmitting its characteristics by seed, such as the new hybrids; or the flowers were fertilized with pollen from other plants of a different color.

How can I get zinnias which will fit into my color scheme?   Buy named varieties like Apricot, Riverside Beauty, azalea-pink; Daffodil; Eskimo, white; Glamour Girls, pastel shades, to name a few.

Which zinnias do you suggest for a small garden?   Cut and Come Again varieties; Fantasy; Cupid; Lilliput; Navajo; Mexican; Persian Carpet; *Zinnia linearis*.

BIENNIALS

Biennials—plants which start their life cycle one year, pass the winter in a state of dormancy or "suspended animation", and then grow on to complete their lives in the following year—are comparatively little used by amateur gardeners. Even pansies, best known of the biennials, and one of the easiest of all flowers to be grown from seed, are usually bought in spring as plants in full bloom, instead of being raised from seed—at a fraction of the cost of plants—by the gardener himself.

One of the chief reasons why biennials are not more generally grown by the home gardener is that seed should be sown at a time when he feels that the planting season is over. Biennials sown in May or early June—or, in the case of some of them, such as pansies and Siberian Wallflower (*Chieranthus alloni*), as late as late July—can be transplanted as soon as the true leaves develop. By mid-September or October the little plants are ready to be transferred to their allocated positions in the garden, or (in severe climates) carried over winter in a frame, under a protective covering of straw, rough compost or evergreen boughs, applied after the ground has frozen slightly. Covering with glass sash, except in *very* severe climates, is not necessary.

One of the great advantages of using some biennials in the garden scheme is that they provide very early color out-of-doors, and also cut blooms for bringing indoors, weeks before spring sown annuals will be in flower. They are unsurpassed for "filling in" wherever color may be lacking in the spring garden, for they produce almost immediate results.

When is it best to sow seeds of most biennials? July and early August are considered the best times. This gives a fairly long season to produce good-sized plants for blooming the following year. Hollyhocks, for extra-heavy plants, are best sown in June; but pansies and forget-me-nots are best sown in August, as very large plants of these may winter kill. Others fare very well from July sowings.

How are the so-called biennials best used in the garden? They are valuable in the mixed border for early-summer bloom. Solid plantings can be made of such kinds as foxgloves, with early lilies, such as Madonna and Hansoni. Combinations like Canterburybells in different colors, faced down with sweetwilliam, pansies, English daisies, and forget-me-not, are valuable as a ground cover for a bulb bed. The biennials must be followed with annuals to fill the bare spots left when the biennials die. In the mixed border they are best used in small groups near later-blooming perennials that will tend to cover the bare spots left. The later-blooming biennials (like hollyhock) can be given due prominence in a mixed planting.

Will you give a list of biennials, with their time of bloom? This will include many that are perennial but which in garden practice are grown as biennials. Canterburybells (*Campanula medium*), cup-and-saucer (*C. calycanthema*), steeple-bellflower (*C. pyramidalis*), June and July; English daisy (*Bellis perennis*), April and May; foxglove, June–July; hollyhock, July; honesty (*Lunaria*), May; hornpoppy, July; rosecampion, May to June; pansy, April to June; Siberian-wallflower (*Cheiranthus allioni*), May to June; sweetwilliam (*Dianthus barbatus*), June to July; forget-me-not (*Myosotis alpestris* and *M. dissitiflora*), April to May.

Do any of the biennials self-sow? Yes, quite a few, such as foxglove, forget-me-not, rosecampion, steeple-bellflower, and hollyhock. But if the soil is too assiduously cultivated, the seedlings may be killed.

Are biennials winter hardy in Northern gardens?   The hardiest are the campions, foxglove, hollyhock, steeple-bellflower, honesty, horn-poppy, sweetwilliam, Siberian wallflower. Most other biennials (see list) need considerable protection, preferably a cold frame.

At what time of year should biennials be planted outdoors?   Plants started the preceding year are set out in very early spring for blooming the same year.

SPECIFIC BIENNIAL PLANTS

CANTERBURYBELLS (CAMPANULA)

What is the best time of year to plant seed of Canterburybells and foxglove?   June is a good time to sow seeds of these plants. If sown later, the plants may not be big enough to flower the next year.

Will Canterburybells grow well in upper New York State? When should the seed be sown?   Yes, they will do very well but must have adequate winter protection. Do not stimulate growth by watering or feeding after mid-August. After a hard freeze, cover with brush over which spread a layer of marsh (or salt) hay or similar covering. Sow seeds in June.

How can I grow Canterburybells and cup-and-saucer?   The cup-and-saucer type (*Campanula calycanthema*) is a variety of the regular Canterburybell (*Campanula medium*). The cup-and-saucer requires the same culture and conditions as the regular Canterburybells.

What is the best winter mulch for Canterburybells? (Wisconsin.) Light, littery material that will not pack to a sodden mass over the leaves. Before covering, remove any bad basal leaves that might rot. Tuck the material in around the plants, and stick a few twigs among them to keep a light covering from lying directly on the leaves.

Why is it that Campanula medium sometimes does not blossom? This spring I had two dozen nice-looking plants, transplanted in fall last year; but none of them blossomed.   Plants of Canterburybells, unless they reach a good size, may fail to bloom the first summer. Many, however, will persist through the second winter and set bloom the second summer. Biennials will occasionally, for some unknown reason, do this.

I planted Canterburybells in July, expecting them to bloom the following season, but they did not. Why?   The plants were old enough to bloom. Did you notice if the crown was attacked by any disease? Sometimes virus diseases will attack the plants, causing mottling of the foliage, and possibly prevent blooming. Root lice also will check development.

FOXGLOVES (DIGITALIS)

Can you give us information on growth of Digitalis purpurea, or references from which it may be obtained? (Michigan.) For details of culture consult *Farmers' Bulletin 663,* "American Medicinal Plants," or *Miscellaneous Circular 77,* "American Medicinal Plants of Commercial Importance." These 2 works are obtainable from Superintendent of Documents, United States Printing Office, Washington, D.C.; *Bulletin 663* is 5 cents; *Circular 77* is 30 cents.

What do you do with foxgloves that do not bloom the second year? Will they bloom the third year if kept on? Yes, they probably will; foxgloves frequently behave in this way.

Should we cover our foxglove plants heavily in winter? (Vermont.) In your region they will need adequate protection. Mulch soil with decayed leaves, lay cherry or birch branches over the crowns, and on top of this spread an inch or two of marsh hay or straw. If covering packs on top of the crowns it will cause rot, hence the branches. Evergreen boughs—not heavy ones—are also valuable. These are used alone.

Will foxglove, if separated in winter, bloom the following year? If you refer to the common foxglove, *Digitalis purpurea,* from seed sown the previous summer—probably no. The perennial kinds may be separated in spring.

What parts of foxglove are poisonous, if any? Probably all parts. The drug digitalis (poisonous in overdoses) is obtained from the second year's young leaves, so presumably the poisonous principle is most abundant in them.

What is the best method of gathering foxglove seed? Gather the lower seed capsules from the stem as soon as they show brown, but before they open to shed the seed. Select from the best type.

PANSIES

What is the best location for pansies, for good bloom? A cool, moist, well-drained soil, in a sunny location.

What is the best soil for pansies? Any soil which contains plenty of humus. Well-rotted manure, peatmoss, or leafmold, mixed with the soil, will help. Neutral or slightly acid reaction is best.

When is pansy seed sown? (Minnesota.) In August, to produce plants large enough, before cold weather, so they can be wintered in a covered cold frame.

What is the best method of growing pansies? (Iowa.) Plant seed in cold frames in August, transplanting 6 × 6 ins. when second set of leaves appear. When freezing weather arrives, cover plants with straw, and keep frames closed. About March 1 remove straw, but keep glass on, and ventilate freely. Remove glass about April 1, and set plants in permanent position between April 1 and May 15. Best soil is a good loam with plenty of humus and moisture.

What conditions are necessary to get pansy seed to germinate? (North Carolina.)   First obtain *fresh*, plump seeds. For the seedbed use a mixture of 1 part each of soil, sand, and leafmold or peatmoss, put through a ¼-in. mesh screen. Select as cool a spot as you can—a cold frame that can be heavily shaded is ideal. Level and lightly firm the soil. Broadcast the seed on the surface (or sow in rows 4 or 5 ins. apart), and cover with ⅛ in. of fine soil, press lightly, and shade, but leave space for ventilation. As soon as seeds have germinated remove the shading, except during the hottest part of the day. Give full sun when seedlings are well through.

Would pansy seed sown in the open in April come up and bloom by June 15?   Pansy seed sown the first of April might possibly show a few flowers by June 15 if growing conditions were favorable. The finest spring display comes from seed sown in August.

Are pansy seeds, if sown outdoors in September, likely to survive the cold weather during winter and flower next summer? (New York.)   No; the seed should be sown early in August. In vicinity of New York City young plants will live outdoors with light covering. Farther North they should be grown in cold frames.

Will you tell me when to transplant pansies? (Texas.)   Presuming you mean pansy seedlings, you should plant them in their permanent locations (from seedbeds, flats, or pots) in September or October for bloom during the following spring. Young plants, grown in cold frame or in open beds, may be transplanted in the early spring.

Is it better to purchase pansy plants for autumn planting, or for very early-spring planting, if one desires them for sale purposes around Mother's Day?   Purchase seedling plants in September, and grow these on to blooming size.

Why don't pansy plants bloom and grow all summer when planted in spring in full bloom? Mine don't.   They bloom best in the cool weather of spring and early summer. In an exposed place they deteriorate in the heat; also the earlier heavy bloom exhausts the plants.

What would be the cause of pansy plants growing long stems and very small flowers?   Too much shade, or overcrowding. A good strain of seed, August sowing, winter protection, a good soil, and not too much shade are the prerequisites for good results.

Why do blue pansies often have petals streaked blue and white?   The seed strain is not good. Blue pansy seed that comes true to type is offered by reliable seedsmen.

When wintering pansies in a cold frame, should one wait until the soil in the frame has frozen, then close the frame and keep it covered with a mat or leaves until spring?   No. Best plan is to give plants light, ventilate whenever frost on glass melts, and cover with mats only on coldest nights. Do not remove snow from frames.

What is considered a foolproof winter mulch for pansies? (Wyoming.) Branches of spruce, fir, or pine; straw or hay held down with chicken wire. If hungry mice or rabbits abound, spray pansies first with aluminum sulfate.

When is the best time to apply winter protection for pansies? (Wyoming.) As soon as the surface inch or two of the ground freezes.

When is it safe to remove the winter covering on pansies? (Wyoming.) When severe freezing is past. It is well to remove this (and all such mulches) on a cloudy or rainy day. Sudden exposure to sun and wind is unkind to leaves and buds.

Last year's pansies did such a wonderful job of self-seeding for this season that the resulting plants are lovelier and stronger than the new ones we grew from seed with great care. Any particular reason? Probably due to some cross-pollinizing which developed strong, healthy plants. However, continuous intercrossing year after year will result in deterioration. To maintain the strain, weed out poor plants and poor colors as soon as flowers open.

What are the best varieties of pansies for fall planting? Use separate colors of the Giant Swiss strain.

What is the name of the really giant pansies (4 ins. across)? Are they grown indoors or out? For indoors in winter, use Don's Winter Flowering strain. For outdoors in spring, Super Swiss Giants in separate colors. These can be obtained from any reliable seed firm.

ROSECAMPION (LYCHNIS)

Will you please give botanical name of mullein pink or rosecampion. *Lychnis coronaria,* of easy culture and hardy.

SWEETWILLIAM (DIANTHUS BARBATUS)

When shall I plant sweetwilliam? What kind of soil is required? In a sunny spot, or in shade? (Missouri.) Set plants out as early in spring as the ground can be worked. They like a well-prepared soil with plenty of humus-forming material (like old manure, leafmold, or peatmoss) in addition to a good dressing of dried sheep or cow manure. They prefer a sunny location.

Can seeds of Dianthus barbatus be planted in late fall or early winter? Will they bloom the following season? This is a biennial normally sown in summer for bloom the following year. There is an annual strain which would blossom the following season if planted under glass.

Sweetwilliam will not live through the summer for me. Why? Sweetwilliam is grown as a biennial. It usually dies after flowering.

Do foxglove and sweetwilliam (Dianthus barbatus) come up a second year? The common foxglove (*Digitalis purpurea*) is a biennial. Sweetwilliam is used as such. Rarely do they appear the second year except from self-sown seedlings. It is best to sow seeds of these kinds every year to insure a supply of plants.

WALLFLOWER

What is the difference between wallflower and Siberian Wallflower? Wallflower, (*Cheiranthus cheiri*), grows to a height of two feet and produces yellow, mahogany and brownish flowers in spring and again in autumn. Siberian Wallflower *Cheiranthus allioni* or *Erysimum asperum* is only about a foot tall and produces fragrant yellow flowers in early spring. Golden Bedder is the best variety.

Can you tell me how to grow wallflowers? Both types of wallflowers require cool nights and moisture in the air during the growing season to thrive. They are supposedly lime-lovers but sometimes grow well in acid soil, as near the seashore, when other conditions suit them. *Cheiranthus cheiri* is quite tender inland, but grows well near the coast in New England. Wallflowers need full sun and a sandy soil. Both are usually grown as biennials.

Lawns and Turf Areas

INTRODUCTION

BY P. J. MCKENNA

AND F. F. ROCKWELL

IT IS THE DESIRE of every homeowner with some ground to have a good lawn. A lawn enhances and improves the whole aspect of the property. It ties together in a common unit the various scattered landscape features, and adds considerably to the keen enjoyment of the home and garden.

Setting about the task of making a lawn brings one face to face with numerous problems. Some of these are local in character, others are general, and apply almost wherever lawns exist. Among the latter are insect pests that annually take a heavy toll of numberless turf areas; diseases that, under the influence of certain weather conditions, suddenly make their appearances; drought periods in summer; unusually cold spells in winter; and weeds like crab grass, plantain, and others that, getting a hold, increase the difficulties of maintaining a lawn.

Basic Requirements

In making a lawn a few basic factors (too often overlooked) must be considered. Every blade of grass is part of a complete plant, each with its own root system, and capable of manufacturing its own food. During the growing season this plant is continually drawing on the soil for the materials necessary to sustain itself. When you consider that in a square foot of good sod there are over 400 of these plants competing for food and moisture, you begin to appreciate that the most important phases of lawn making are, first, to provide the soil conditions necessary for the best growth of the turf; and second, to maintain these conditions thereafter.

Lawns made in the fall are the most successful. Then grass makes its best growth, roots have a chance to become established and to penetrate deeper than is the case with a lawn sown in the spring, when high temperatures force constant top growth. In late fall, even after the grass tops are dormant, root development goes on until the ground is frozen many inches deep.

Types of Turf, and Their Uses

It is well at the outset to realize that there are several kinds of turf, and that success depends largely upon selecting one to fit the soil and the situation. It would be folly to attempt to create a lawn of

An unbroken stretch of lawn, with appropriate planting around the edges, is always more effective and pleasing than when the turf area is broken up by flower beds or trees placed in the center.

Velvet Bent on poor, infertile soil, or to try to form a turf of Kentucky Blue Grass in deep shade, or even on a steep slope. Each situation demands its own treatment, for the problems involved are not the same.

Turf of Creeping Bent, such as is generally used in putting greens, is a high-maintenance type of turf requiring frequent cutting, watering, and top-dressing. It is best suited to good, fertile soils that must be given more than average preparation. The kinds of turf most generally used are the strains of Creeping Bent, Velvet Bent, and Seaside Bent. All have the same growth habit in that they spread by surface stems ("stolons"); hence the need for frequent cutting and for top-dressing to keep the stolons in close contact with the soil.

Kentucky Blue Grass and Merion Blue Grass, two of the best for lawns in temperate regions, also require a good, fertile soil. They grow best in cool, moist weather. The tops will brown in midsummer heat, but come back in fall with renewed vigor as the roots, which spread by underground stems, are uninjured.

The fescues, another group frequently used, are the toughest of the lawn grasses. Most of them possess wirelike tops, making them difficult to mow. However, they will grow on poor, dry soils and are fairly successful in shade. They do not spread much by creeping roots, however, as do the other grasses. The best of the fescues is Chewing's Fescue. Spreading but slowly, it is best used in combination with transient grasses like Red Top and rye grass. When established, it makes a durable sod and is used in mixtures for growing in shade and on terraces. Meadow Fescue grows well in sun or shade and will stand up fairly well under dry conditions. It makes a loose sod, however, and should not be mowed too often.

Of the other grasses used in lawns, Rough-stalked Blue Grass grows well in shade, but requires a good soil well supplied with lime. This grass will not persist under close and frequent mowing. Periodical feeding is necessary, and even then a dry summer may end its career.

Among the few rye grasses (rye grass is often confused with rye for grain), Perennial Rye is the best. Good seed germinates at once. The grass grows fast, but is short-lived, lasting only about two years. It is used in mixtures where it is designed to hold until the more permanent grasses become established. It can be used alone and will create a green sward in a short time—a fact of importance if one is trying to cover a poor soil by sowing in early summer with a view to improving the soil before putting in a permanent lawn later on.

Preparing the Soil for Turf Areas

The most important of all lawn operations is the initial preparation of the soil. At no other time in the life of the lawn is it so easy to create (as far as possible) the conditions necessary for good turf. To be favorable, soil conditions must not only encourage root formation, but also depth of penetration. The rooting depth is influenced by two factors: good drainage and deep working of the soil.

Drainage is the first prerequisite. In wet soils, air—which is very important to roots—is excluded. Under wet conditions lawn grasses will not long survive: either they are winter killed, or crowded out by coarser-growing grasses. Poor drainage is associated with low-lying sites in which the water table is near the surface, and with soils of clay texture through which water moves too slowly. Aeration and the water travel in clay soils are improved by mixing screened cinders, the size of beans or peas, with the top 12 ins. A layer 1 to 3 ins. deep is not too much. Low-lying sites are drained by installing tile pipes, or by raising the grade sufficiently and providing enough pitch for surface drainage.

Foundation for a good permanent lawn.

The soil should be worked (dug or plowed) 10 to 12 ins. deep, but the subsoil must not be brought up to the surface or bare spots will result. Organic matter, without which a good lawn is not possible, must be used in some form and incorporated at the time of working the soil. It improves the whole physical condition of the soil, especially its moisture-holding qualities, and promotes root action. There are several sources of humus. Farm manure and good compost contain valuable nutrients, while peatmoss, humus, muck, and leafmold contain but little. All, however, improve the soil. The material used is spread on the surface 2 to 4 ins. deep. Bone meal is scattered over this 4 to 6 lbs. per 100 sq. ft. All is then dug or plowed under, or, if the soil has been dug, thoroughly worked into the surface.

This is also the time to get grub-proofing material into the ground to check the beetle grubs, using chlordane 5% dust ½ lb. per 100 sq. ft. For an even covering mix the powder with sand or fine soil, using 10 lbs. to 1 lb. of powder. After the soil has been roughly leveled, spread the material evenly and rake it into the surface. A few weeks before seeding broadcast a combination nitrogenous fertilizer and a weed seed killer such as Lawn and Garden Cyanamid or Aero-cyanamid, carefully following the directions on the package as to when and how to apply it. The area should be fairly even, merely needing a few operations with a rake to finish the grade. Plowing, on the other hand, may leave much unevenness, needing more than raking to level the grade. Soil may have to be moved from high to low spots. Even after this, it is better to roll the area to take out further unevenness. Other things to be considered are trees or areas reserved for beds and borders. The grade should be adjusted to blend with these features.

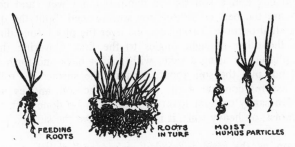

A square foot of turf contains some 400 individual grass plants, each of which must be well fed. An abundance of humus in the surface soil is especially important in maintaining the moisture supply.

Terraces

Terraces present different and sometimes difficult problems. The all-important factor of moisture supply is the main consideration. If the slope is steeper than one foot in three, and with a southerly aspect, the problem of getting a turf started from seed, and then maintaining it, is a particularly difficult one. Here fertile topsoil is even more important than on level ground. Not less than 6 ins., preferably more, of prepared soil, with old rotted manure (or well-dampened peatmoss) constituting ⅓ of its bulk, is used for surfacing. If the slope is long, place strips of sod, 8 to 10 ins. wide. at right angles across the slope at 3-ft. intervals, and seed the lawn grass in between. To prevent washing, cover the seeded area with hay or loosely woven burlap; remove gradually as seed germinates.

Grass Seeds and Turf Mixtures

Good seed is the first consideration. Avoid cheap mixtures. They contain grasses such as timothy, totally unsuited to lawns. Besides, the percentage of germination is poor, and much chaff and weed seed is pretty sure to be present. Deal with seed houses that have a recognized reputation for quality. Many lawn-seed specialists have excellent mixtures designed to fit particular situations.

The rate of seeding will depend upon the kind of grass to be used. For an area of 1,000 sq. ft. (20 × 50 ft.) 5 lbs. of a mixture in which Kentucky Blue Grass predominates is needed. Of the bent grasses (the seeds of which are much smaller), 3 lbs. is ample.

Fescue seeds are larger, and in addition their germination is poorer than that of most other grasses. It is therefore best to use as much as 6 lbs. per 1,000 sq. ft.

Seeding and Sodding

A calm day and a soil that is damp but not wet (and certainly not dry) are the best conditions for sowing seed. Split the quantity into two equal portions. Broadcast one over the plot in one direction, and sow the other at right angles to the first. Covering the seed is accomplished by using a rake, with a light back-and-forth motion that will not pull the soil about. Firming the surface by rolling or tamping assures contact of the seed with the soil, and even germination. On sandy or light loam soils this can be done with the soil slightly moist; on heavy soils, it is better to have the surface perfectly dry.

As soon as the area is seeded, raked and rolled, a thorough watering is given, preferably with an oscillating sprinkler, or one which produces a fine mist spray. The usual rotating type is apt to deliver too much water to some areas and not enough to others. "Puddling" of the surface is almost sure to wash the seed into the low spots, the result being an uneven germination with many bare spaces. The object should be to soak the lawn thoroughly and evenly to a depth of at least 4 inches. To insure even germination, the lawn area must be kept consistently moist until after the seedling grass is well up. If it is permitted to dry out even for a day some of the germinating seedlings may be burned out.

Sodding. The advantages of sodding are that results are immediate, and the work can be done equally well in spring or fall. Its drawbacks are the expense involved and the difficulty of securing weed-free turf to use for sodding. The soil is prepared and leveled as for seeding, the surface inch being kept loose to embed the turves (sods) which, for easy handling, are usually 12 by 12 ins. They are set close together, tamped into place, and loose soil, in which seed is mixed, is worked into the joints. The area is then rolled and, if the weather is dry, watered frequently. Sodding is particularly valuable on terrace slopes because, in addition to the immediate effect, the danger of the soil and seeds being washed out is avoided. Beginning at the base of the slope, the sods are laid as for a lawn, and each sod— or, if the slope is not too steep, each alternate row of sods—is fastened to the slope with wooden pegs. The area is then treated as for the lawn.

Early Care of the New Lawn

The first mowing of a fall-seeded lawn should take place when the grass is about 2 to 3 ins. high, but close cutting should be avoided. Another cutting may be necessary before winter, but it is essential that the lawn go into winter with a good top growth to afford protection to young roots from the drying action of freezing winds. In March, even before the frost is out of the ground, seed down any bare spots that may appear. Later, as growth is beginning, top-dress with sifted soil mixed with turf fertilizer, 3 lbs. to the bushel. Apply a bushel of this to every 100 sq. ft., and with the *back* of a rake work it down among the young grasses. When the surface is dry, firm with a roller.

Begin cutting when the grass is over 2 ins. high but do not cut close the first summer. Rake off all mowings to prevent disease until the dry, hot weather of July and August, when the mowings may be left on. The machine should then be adjusted to cut at a height of at least 2 ins.

How to Maintain Good Turf

Feeding. Keeping the turf thrifty is the first step in lawn management. This means supplying nutrients in abundance and at the right time. The only period during the growing season when nutrients are useful is when there is plenty of moisture in the soil. Spring and fall are the two best seasons for feeding. Although fertilizer supplies the nutrients that grass needs, the best form of spring feeding is a top-dressing of compost. This is especially important on lawns of Creeping Bent. (A mixture of soil with ¼ its bulk of rotted manure, peatmoss, or leafmold will do.) One cubic yard will cover 1,200 sq. ft. With this quantity mix 30 lbs. of grass fertilizer, of a 5–10–5 analysis, if it can be obtained. The top-dressing is spread evenly with a shovel, worked into the grass with a wooden rake, and the area is then rolled.

Mowing at 1½ ins. should be frequent in early summer, the cut grass being removed. In July and August the mower should be adjusted to cut at about 2 ins., depending upon the kind of grass. Creeping Bent lawns will have to be kept below the 1½ ins.

Watering—an important factor in maintenance—will depend upon the kind of soil and the exposure. For best results, water must not be withheld until the soil is completely dry, for then it is difficult to raise the moisture content. Examine the soil *beneath* the turf, and if after 4 or 5 days of hot sun it is showing a tendency to become dry, water immediately, *giving a thorough soaking*. Sandy soils will dry out much sooner than loam soils that are well supplied with organic matter, and a lawn that has been cut at about 1½ to 2 ins. will not dry out so quickly in midsummer as one that is kept shorter.

Weeds and How to Control Them

The maintenance of a dense, thrifty turf is the best insurance against weeds. If any appear, they should be eradicated at once. Allowed to secure a hold, their elimination is difficult. Deep-rooting weeds, like dandelion, if not too numerous, are best dug up. Merely cutting out the crown will not kill them. Dandelion spreads by roots and by seeds. Constant close cutting to prevent flowering will, after a time, reduce their numbers, gradually weakening the old roots.

Large-scale eradication is best done with chemicals, spraying with iron sulfate (copperas), 1½ lbs. in 2 gals. of water. (This will cover 350 sq. ft. of area.) It will also kill plantain, chickweed, and others. Several applications will be necessary at 2- to 3-week intervals during the season. Iron sulfate will blacken the grass, but this will disappear in a few days, especially after the grass is cut. This chemical will also stain stone, cement, metals, and clothes. A stronger solution (3 lbs. to 2 gals.) squirted into the heart of dandelion and plantain with a pressure oilcan, or applied with a pointed stick dipped in the solution, is also effective.

Crab Grass. The most insidious weed of all is Crab Grass. The pest is an annual and dies with the first frost; but the abundantly produced seeds start into growth the following May or June as the weather becomes warm. Crab Grass thrives only in full sunshine. Keeping the grass at 2 ins. high and maintaining a close turf are the best preventives. Young plants must be removed as soon as recognized.

Preventing the formation of seed is important in controlling Crab Grass. Raking the lawn to bring up the creeping stems where the mower can catch them will help. Removing the whole plant is better. Where Crab Grass has become well established, only drastic measures will eradicate it. In this event the lawn may have to be entirely remade. Using a portable kerosene torch about the time the seeds are ripening will consume the plant and scorch any seeds that have fallen on the ground. Good control has also been obtained by using sodium chlorate or sodium arsenite. The latter is a deadly poison; the former, although not poisonous, is highly inflammable. These salts can either be sprayed on, or mixed with sand and spread dry. One pound of the salt mixed with a 2-gal. bucket of sand will treat 1,000 sq. ft. To complete the eradication, two further applications, at double this strength, will be necessary. Apply from the end of July through August, if there is considerable moisture present.

New chemicals now available are most helpful. Several of these, sold under such trade names as Lawn and Garden Cyanamid are calcium cyanamid compounds which may be applied to the bare ground some weeks before seeding, and which kill the ungerminated seeds of crabgrass. In using an herbicide of this sort it is most important to follow exactly the directions on the package.

Other crabgrass killers such as Alanap, Crag 531, PMAS, Scutl and KOCN, kill in the seedling stage.

The growth on a fall-planted lawn is usually dense enough by the following May to prevent the germination of crabgrass seeds which require full sun. This is another good reason for making your lawn in autumn.

Diseases and Insects

Besides the grubs which eat the roots of grasses, and are controlled with chlordane (as advised above, in making a new lawn), the other serious pest is the chinch bug. There are usually two infestations, the first in June, the second in August. Timing the control is important, but this pest can be handled with a single treatment of chlordane dust or spray, applied between June 1st and 15th.

The chinch bug sucks the juices out of the grass stalks, leaving brown, dry, injured areas, circular in outline. The bugs usually are found at the outer edge of the circle working on the live grasses. The insecticide must be forced down into the grass where the pest is working.

Fungous diseases sometimes cause trouble. The worst of these are brown patch and dollar spot, which look much alike. The conditions conducive to an infestation are high temperature, excessive humidity, and a soft, lush growth of grass. Circular brown patches appearing in June, when the grass is wet, are indications of the disease. Mercurial preparations, of which there are several (such as PMAS, Tact-c-lect, Semesan, and Nu-green), are the best controls. A homemade mixture consisting of two parts calomel and one part corrosive sublimate, applied at the rate of 3 ozs. per 1,000 sq. ft., may be used. Mixed with 2 to 3 gals. of water, it is applied as a spray; or it may be mixed with a bucket of sand and spread dry. If the weather remains humid, repeat the treatment every 10 days.

Calendar of Lawn Operations

Late winter (February or March). Sow all bare spots with a lawn-seed mixture and cover with ¼ inch of sifted soil.

Spring. When frost is out of the ground, top-dress with compost, as previously advised, and work in with a rake. Roll, using a roller 150 to 300 lbs. in weight, but not so heavy as to pack sod. Roll when the lawn is *moist but not wet.*

Remove any dandelions or plantains that show, or treat the plants with a spot weed killer.

Mow when 2 to 3 ins. high, maintaining the height at 1½ ins. Remove clippings and put on compost heap.

Summer. In June, if weather is hot and humid, watch for brown patch and treat as advised. If there has been previous injury from chinch bug, or if bent grass predominates in the lawn, dust during the most vulnerable period. Watch now for young Crab-Grass plants, and *remove while small.*

In midsummer raise the cut to 2 ins. Watch the moisture content of the soil and water if needed.

Fall. In August, inspect for chinch bug. Toward the end of August or beginning of September cut the grass close, removing the clippings. Rake the sod with an iron rake to remove weeds. Apply turf fertilizer, 10 to 25 lbs. per 1,000 sq. ft.

Repair all bare or injured patches, digging up if necessary. Seed, and cover with sifted soil. Keep the cut at 1½ ins. and mow regularly. As cold weather approaches, raise the cut to 2 ins. until top growth stops.

LAWNS

GRADING

How should a lawn be graded? What operations are involved? Grading first depends upon the particular site and whether paths or driveways are to be laid out. Existing trees and areas for planting must also be considered. Outline the paths and drives with stakes. Remove the topsoil from these and spread it over the lawn area. If the dwelling is much higher than the street, slope the grade gradually down to meet the lower level. Do not terrace unless the situation demands it. If the dwelling is on a level area, give the lawn a slight pitch from the house to the street.

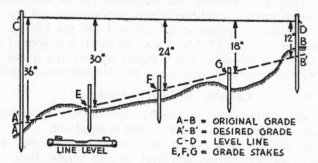

A-B = ORIGINAL GRADE
A'-B' = DESIRED GRADE
C-D = LEVEL LINE
E,F,G = GRADE STAKES

Establishing a grade line where an uneven surface is to be regraded. A–B—original grade; A'–B'—desired new grade; C–D, cord stretched level between two stakes (it is leveled by means of a little instrument known as a "line level"); E, F, G—grade stakes set at equal distances between points A and B. The grade stakes are marked, as indicated, and the soil is cut down or filled in to establish the new grade.

How much pitch must be given a lawn, and how is the pitch determined? A pitch of 1 ft. in 20 ft., or even 30 ft., unless the soil is heavy clay, is sufficient to give surface drainage. The grade can be established by using a line and a line level, and thus determining the difference, in height, between the high and the low points.

If there is much unevenness in the ground, should it be dug or plowed before grading? The soil, of course, will have to be loosened to move it. The practical thing to do is to remove all the topsoil, loosen the subsoil, and do the grading; then finish the grade with the topsoil. This insures an even depth of good soil over the entire area. If the existing topsoil is not sufficient to give about 4 ins. covering, provision should be made for the adding of extra soil.

Our house sets quite a way back from the street and several feet above it. How should the front lawn be graded? A low, sloping terrace, 10 to 15 ft. wide, across the house front will tend to give it a feeling of stability. Work the soil down to a gradual slope from the bottom of the terrace to the street.

What is the procedure to follow if much soil has to be moved around? In large operations the easiest way to move quantities of soil is with a bulldozer, or a team of horses and a drag scoop can be used. In small areas, soil can be loosened with a rototiller and moved in a wheelbarrow.

How is the soil leveled to make it even for seeding? Several rakings are sometimes necessary. Rake first with an iron rake to remove stones, sticks, and other debris, at the same time filling in as many hollows and smoothing down as many hills as possible. Some shoveling may be necessary to get rid of the worst of these. Then rake with close-toothed wooden hay rake to remove smaller stones and break up lumps. Roll lightly. Ridges and depressions will then be apparent and can be leveled off by raking or shoveling. Rake again before seeding.

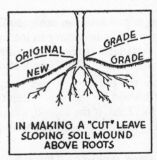
IN MAKING A "CUT" LEAVE
SLOPING SOIL MOUND
ABOVE ROOTS

IN MAKING A "FILL"
PLACE A WELL OF STONE
OR CONCRETE
AROUND BASE

Grading around an established tree to obtain a properly sloped lawn surface.

We need to fill in to get a good slope for a lawn, but there are large trees in the way. Will the grading injure them? If the grade is to be carried much over the existing level, some protection must be given the trees. It may be necessary to build a dry well of stone around the trunks to allow air and moisture to reach the roots.

How high can the soil be raised around a tree without injuring it? This depends somewhat on the variety of tree. In general however, where the soil is light and well drained, the grade may be raised around trees a foot or two without appreciable injury. If the soil is heavy and not well drained, raising the grade as little as 6 ins. may cause injury.

How large should a tree well be? (Maryland.) Generally speaking, the diameter of a tree well should be four times the diameter of the tree. Deep wells should be provided with tile drains running out laterally from the bottom. They should not be narrowed in at the top, since it may be necessary to get down into them to clean out leaves.

PREPARATIONS FOR SOWING

When is the best time to prepare the soil for a lawn? It should be prepared at least 2 weeks before seeding. This is one of the reasons for fall sowing. Not enough time is available in spring. Much will depend upon the extent of the preparation. Time should be given for a thorough working of the soil and for allowing it to settle.

What is the proper method of making a lawn? See Introduction for directions. Adjust these to the conditions existing in your own locality as to kind of soil, site, and exposure. Consult a seedsman about proper mixture.

Is it necessary to make the soil for a lawn fine, or can it be left rough? The top surface must be made very fine, so that when the seed is planted the earth will come in close contact with it; root action is promoted in well-tilled soil.

Can I get information on building a new lawn on sandy soil? To produce a successful lawn on sandy soil it is necessary to incorporate large quantities of humus-making materials. Humus is the deciding factor in establishing a lawn on a sandy soil. (See Introduction.)

How may I start a new lawn from my old one? It was completely ruined by Jap beetles and severely burned by the sun. Remove all weeds. Dig or plow to a depth of 9 to 12 ins. if the topsoil will permit. Then proceed as outlined in the Introduction concerning grub-proofing, seeding, etc.

Can I get a good lawn on very stony ground? This is a difficult problem. Remove as many of the larger stones as possible. Seed with 1 part each Red Top and Perennial Rye Grass, and 2 parts Chewing's Fescue. Gradually build a new surface by top-dressing with fine soil and compost. Reseed in spring and fall to promote a thick turf. Because of stones, the grass may have to be cut higher than the ordinary lawn (see top-dressing, seed quantity), until a new surface has been established.

How deep must I prepare soil for a lawn which has never been cultivated before? See Introduction. The instructions given there will have to be adjusted to the depth of topsoil and the kinds of plants that now occupy it. Provide, if possible, 4 ins. of topsoil. The initial work is all important.

How much topsoil is needed for a lawn? At least 4 ins. of good topsoil is needed to insure the grass getting a hold. Six to 8 ins. is better.

Should the soil be compacted before seeding? The type of soil and its condition will have to be considered. If the soil is heavy and very damp, it would be better not to compact it. On a light soil, yes, especially if there has been much grading. The compacting will then reveal depressions that can be corrected before seeding.

Preparing surface for sowing grass seed. After grading and raking, the ground is rolled, and again raked to fill in uneven spots. On new or filled-in ground, it may be necessary to repeat these operations two or three times, until a perfectly smooth, even surface is secured.

How should a lawn be treated to discourage weeds before seeding? If the soil has been prepared for seeding, there is little that can be done against weeds before they germinate. Chemicals will have no effect either. If the lawn is to be sown in the fall, a good seeding (as discussed in Introduction) and good fall growth will be a factor in weed control. In spring, little advance control can be attempted. If a season can be devoted to the cover-crop method, this will eliminate many weeds. The best insurance is to stimulate a dense turf.

Our land was once covered with clover hay. To raise a crop of grass (lawn), will it be necessary to plow the ground in order to sow the grass

seed? If the land is properly graded, it is possible to make a lawn without plowing. Perennial weeds, such as thistles, teasles, and plantains should be removed. Use a good seed mixture 3 lbs. per 1,000 sq. ft., and cover with soil. Under constant mowing many of the former grasses and clover will disappear. Reseeding and top-dressing annually will gradually build up a good turf.

How do you supply drainage to a lawn on heavy clay soil? Water stands for hours after a rain. Dig the soil at least 12 ins. deep; incorporate a 4-in. layer of screened cinders; mix thoroughly with the soil. Pitch the grade several inches to facilitate surface flow. If the area needs more extensive treatment, dig trenches 20 to 30 ft. apart, 12 ins. wide and 18 ins. deep and lay agricultural tile, with a pitch of 6″ to 100′, with 1 or 2 ins. gravel or cinders on top. Then fill the trench with soil.

Can I make a temporary lawn? Our season here is short and I do not wish to undertake the work involved in making a permanent one. Yes, a temporary lawn can be made, but some work will have to be done even for a temporary lawn. Dig the area 3 to 4 ins. deep and break the soil down fine. If the soil needs lime, apply 50 lbs. of ground limestone to 1,000 sq. ft. As recommended elsewhere give a dressing of chemical fertilizer or dried manure. Sow Perennial Rye Grass 10 lbs. per 1,000 sq. ft. Make the first cut when the grass is 4 ins. high. Keep the height at 3 ins. if possible.

How soon after sowing the average lawn-seed mixture should we expect to see grass? The purity of seed, the temperature and moisture conditions, and the physical condition of the soil exert much influence on this matter of germination. Given pure seed and with the temperature between 65 and 75°, Perennial Rye Grass, fescue, and Red Top will be up in 5 to 10 days, bent grass in 10 to 20 days, and Kentucky Blue Grass around 14 to 28 days.

Is a layer of topsoil 4 in. deep sufficient on top of a base of ashes to grow a good lawn? Much will depend upon the kind of topsoil. Be sure it contains at least 15 per cent humus. A 2- to 3-in. layer of peatmoss, leafmold, or partly rotted leaves placed over the ashes before putting on the topsoil will further assist the moisture-holding qualities.

Could you tell me how to get a good lawn? Have used the best seed available, also the best fertilizer. Had ground dug up twice, and I still grow mostly all Crab Grass and very coarse grass. Your soil is fully impregnated with weed seeds. Grass has too much competition. Two courses are possible: (1) Allow the weeds to grow in summer and before they seed eliminate by burning them off with a torch, grubbing them out, or treating with chemicals (see Weed Control); the lawn will look unsightly. Late August prepare to remake the lawn. (2) Prepare soil in May. In early June sow a cover crop. (See Cover Crops for directions.) Remake lawn in fall.

GRASS-SEED MIXTURES

What is Mascarene Grass, and what is it used for? Mascarene Grass (*Zoysia tenuifolia*) was found in the Mascarene Islands. It makes a turf much like Red Fescue but produces quantities of short root stalks which in places will force the turf up in ridges. It has been used to some extent in lawns in California and along the Gulf Coast. In the latter region it remains green all winter.

Why are mixtures of several kinds of seed advocated instead of just one kind? Soils differ in their structure and fertility, there are light soils and heavy soils. Growing conditions are always fluctuating, are never stable; at one time they will favor one grass, at another time other grasses are encouraged. Sunny exposures need one mixture, a shady location another. The lawn mixtures put out by reputable seedsmen are the result of experience, study, and trial. The "one-grass" lawn is seldom if ever a success.

What is meant by "nurse grass"? What is it used for? The term "nurse grass" is applied to such quick-growing grasses as Perennial Rye Grass, Red Top and even to such crops as oats and rye. A nurse grass is used in the grass mixture to occupy the ground quickly until the more permanent grasses, which usually are slow, become established. Nurse grasses, too, are short-lived and give way to the more permanent grasses.

Is annual Blue Grass the same as Kentucky Blue Grass? No. Annual Blue Grass (*Poa annua*) is an annual grass starting early in the season and usually going to seed in midsummer. In some places it is a weed. Kentucky Blue Grass (*Poa pratensis*) is a perennial grass that comes up each year from its own roots and is one of our valuable lawn grasses. Merion Blue is an improved variety of Kentucky Blue, the seed of which is more costly. Less is needed to cover however, and the grass is more disease resistant, and makes a better lawn.

Is Timothy Grass suitable for lawns? Timothy is not a lawn grass, although it is found in some of the cheaper lawn mixtures. It is a bunch grass and spreads but little.

I have an area that is damp all season. Is there any grass that will grow here successfully and compete with the weeds? When should it be planted, and how often cut? Sow Meadow Foxtail and Red Top in equal parts, and use 5 lbs. per 1,000 sq. ft. Although these grasses are tolerant of wet soils, it might be better to sow in spring, as winter conditions may injure a new seeding. Allow the grass to grow to 4 to 6 ins. and have it mowed a few times with a scythe or a machine that will leave a high cut.

Is there any ground cover that can actually take the place of grass on an open plot of ground in full sun? There have been reports (notably from California) that such substitutes are available. No satisfactory substitute has yet been found for grass. The claims occasionally made about certain plants as grass substitutes have not been borne out by experience. The latest is a plant called *Dichondra repens* (sold as Dewdrop Grass). This is a low-creeping plant resembling clover, but related to the morningglories. It spreads rapidly, and, once established, is difficult to control. Certain other plants have been offered under the same guise, such as camomile with fern-like leaves and small daisy-like flowers; *Lippia canescens* with gray-green foliage and lavender flowers; lily-turf, (Mondo "grass") (*liriope muscari*) with narrow grass-like leaves; and turfing-daisy, (*matricaria ichihatchewi*). Most of these do best in mild climates. Dwarf Dutch White Clover is probably the best substitute for grass in the north. Some are good ground covers but they are not grass substitutes.

What kind of grass should be used on heavy red clay soil? Two parts Canada Blue Grass and 1 part each of Perennial Rye Grass and Red Top. Use 5 lbs. per 1,000 sq. ft.

What is best grass seed to sow for orchard (small lot) with semi-sandy soil? Use a mixture consisting of equal parts of Red Top and Sheep's Fescue; failing Sheep's Fescue, use Red Fescue, or Perennial Rye Grass. Seed at the rate of 6 lbs. per 1,000 sq. ft.

What kind of grass could be planted in an orchard, that would not have to be cut, and would look like a lawn? There is no grass that will quite fill these requirements. The nearest to it would be Kentucky Blue Grass, and this should be cut at least twice during the season.

What grass can be sown in June on a poor soil and make summer growth? Sow Perennial Rye Grass when the soil is damp.

What is the best mixture of grass seed? (Maryland.) Grass seed should be selected to fit your particular need. Soil condition, moisture and site, as well as the particular region and the kind of lawn desired, govern to a large extent seed selection. For an all-purpose lawn around the average home, use 50% Chewing's Fescue, 35% Merion Blue Grass and 15% Rhode Island Bent. For shade use 50% Chewing's Fescue, 30% Rough Blue Grass, 10% Astoria Bent and 10% Kentucky or Merion Blue Grass.

Why are patches of fine, wiry grass appearing in my lawn? Probably one of the fescue grasses; most likely fine-leaved fescue.

Is fescue a harmful weed and likely to spread? It is not a weed nor does it spread very much, if at all. The fescues tolerate dry soil conditions.

I have a bank in which there are a few rocky outcrops. The soil is sandy. What kind of grass would grow there? After improving the soil with fertilizer, sow a mixture containing 3 parts Chewing's Fescue, 2 parts Colonial Bent, 1 part Perennial Rye, with white clover 1 ounce for every lb. of seed. Sow 6 lbs. per 1,000 sq. ft.

What grass-seed mixtures do you recommend for shady places? There are several standard mixtures on the market. Consult an experienced seedsman about your particular location, as conditions differ. If the soil is good and the trees are the deep-rooting kind, try the following: 3 parts Rough-stalked Meadow Grass, 2 parts Chewing's Fescue, 1 part Rhode Island Bent. Use 6 lbs. per 1,000 sq. ft.

How can I have a nice lawn with poor, sandy soil? It is impossible to get good topsoil. Apply bone meal and tankage in equal parts, 20 to 30 lbs. per 1,000 sq. ft., or one part bone meal and 3 parts dried manure, 30 to 40 pounds per 1,000 square feet, and mix with top 6 ins. Sow a seed mixture of 3 parts Chewing's Fescue; 2 parts Colonial Bent; 1 part Red Top; 1 part Perennial Rye Grass.

Which, in your opinion, is better for a large lawn—blue grass and clover mixture, or bent grass? Bent grasses in general are suited to special conditions and demand greater attention than do other types of grasses. A mixture in which Kentucky Blue Grass predominates would be better. Clover can be used, if desired, at the rate of 1 oz. per lb. of the seed mixture. But sow the clover separately.

What kind of lawn grass shall I plant in places where it is sunny all day? Sow a mixture consisting of 3 parts Kentucky Blue Grass, 1 part Perennial Rye Grass, 2 parts Chewing's Fescue, 1 part Red Top, 1 oz. white clover per lb. of seed. Use 5 lbs. per 1,000 sq. ft.

What grass grows best on sandy soils? A mixture containing 2 parts Chewing's Fescue, 1 part Red Top, 1 part Perennial Rye Grass, and 2 parts Colonial Bent, sown at the rate of 6 lbs. per 1,000 sq. ft. should give a good turf.

What is the best kind of grass for an ordinary lawn? Experience has taught that the planting of one kind of grass in an ordinary lawn is not practical. If the soil is in good condition, sow 2 parts Kentucky Blue Grass, 2 parts Chewing's Fescue, 2 parts Rhode Island Bent, and 1 part each Perennial Rye Grass and Red Top. If white clover is desired, add 1 oz. per lb. of seed. Sow at the rate of 5 lbs. per 1,000 sq. ft.

White Clover

Is a clover or all-grass lawn the more desirable? Most of my neighbors have a clover lawn; they seem to get best results. My lawn

is all grass in spring and summer but in fall it turned brown, while the clover kept green. Will the clover return in spring? It is possible that your lawn is a Crab Grass lawn, which would turn reddish brown as cold kills the grass for the year. Clover would be preferable to this, and a mixture of good lawn seed with 5 per cent white clover added should be satisfactory. Be sure to apply lime every late fall (see lime), and top-dress with compost and bone meal at least once each spring and autumn.

May I use grass and white clover seed purchased in late summer and fall this year for next spring? Yes, but use about ¼ more than the recommended allowance to make up for possible reduction in germination. This would occur mostly in any fescue grass seed that may be in the mixture and which does not live so long as other sorts. The clover will be little affected, assuming that the seed has been kept dry and not too close to a radiator.

Is white clover useful in a lawn? Yes, owing to its withstanding drought and to its being little affected by fungous diseases.

Will white clover grow on most any soil or does it require a rich soil? On almost any soil, but it does best on a rich, *deep, neutral* soil.

How much white clover seed should be used in a seed mixture to insure a good stand of clover in the lawn? Ten per cent by weight will give a thick stand.

What quantity of white clover seed should be used in an average lawn mixture? About one ounce of clover to every pound of grass seed.

Do you recommend the use of white clover in the lawn? The use of white clover in the lawn is a matter of personal preference. Some like it; others dislike it. It will grow in dry weather and often covers areas where the grass has been killed.

What are the objections to the use of white clover in the lawn? It is objected to mostly in turf used for games. Golf balls are lost in it, tennis balls are stained by it, as also are white shoes. White clover is very slippery when crushed, and accidents in football, tennis, and polo are not uncommon on it.

Does white clover become a pest in lawn? In the opinion of some, it does.

I pulled out the Crab Grass, sowed Kentucky Blue Grass, but white clover came up. Does clover remain green all winter? In regions of mild winters, white clover will give occasional bursts of growth as warm spells occur. On a small area, in such regions, a clover turf can be kept very much greener during winter by watering it from time to time. Top-dressing and fertilizing would help too.

HOW AND WHEN TO SOW

Would it be O.K. to sow lawn seed in January or February if the snow leaves the ground clear? (Ohio.) In winter, it is good practice to seed while there is a *little* snow on the ground. On slopes, where the seed might wash in a thaw, it is better to wait until the ground is clear.

Is spring or fall better for lawn seeding? (Illinois.) The best possible time for lawn seeding is in the fall, September 1 to October 15 being the general range. Grass seed germinates well in this period with cold nights and sufficient moisture. Fall-sown grass becomes firmly rooted. There is no weed competition, and the grass has an early start in spring. In spring sowing the danger is that the young grass will not be strong enough to withstand summer droughts because of inadequate roots and fast-growing tops.

When is the best time to sow grass seed? (Indiana.) In the section of the country extending from southern New York west to Omaha the first half of September is the best. Farther southward somewhat later; farther North somewhat earlier.

How early in spring can lawns on Long Island be seeded? As early as the soil can be worked; late March if possible.

Is it advisable to plant grass seed in December? (New York.) If earlier planting is impossible, and there is little danger of the seed washing away, December planting might be tried. The better course would be to wait until late winter and sow just as the ground starts to thaw and is "honeycombed" on the surface. (This assumes, of course, that the soil was prepared in the fall.)

Is it best to wait until warm weather to sow grass seed? (New Jersey.) No, grass seed thrives best during the cool, moist periods of very early spring and early fall.

What practices or methods are generally used to insure sowing seed evenly over the lawn? A calm day is the first requirement. Seed cannot be sown evenly when a wind is blowing. Practices vary from dividing the seed into 2 parts and sowing each part at right angles to the other, to splitting the quantity into 4 parts and sowing it from 4 different angles. Marking off the area to be sown with parallel strings, stretched between small stakes placed at regular intervals of 5 to 10 ft., is helpful. Throwing the seed forward with a circular sweep of the arm aids in getting even distribution. On large areas the seed is usually spread with a machine made for the purpose. This can be adjusted to sow any quantity and give an even distribution.

QUANTITY OF SEED NEEDED

Why is there so much difference in the quantity of seed suggested

for sowing? What factors determine the quantity of seed to use?
The season of the year, the location, whether shady, sunny, or sloping, and the vitality of the seed have much to do with the matter of quantity to sow. Not all the seeds sown will germinate and it is essential that enough be sown to insure a good stand of grass. One of the factors involved is the size of the seed and number per pound. Bent grass seed runs from 4,000,000 to 8,000,000 seeds to the pound; fescues around 500,000; Kentucky Blue Grass 2,000,000 and rye grass about 250,000. The more seeds per pound, the less the quantity needed.

SOWING SLOPES AND TERRACES

What is the best way to grow grass on a bank, near the house, on the north side? I have found it almost impossible. Have good soil, and add limestone if soil is acid. Sow a shade mixture obtained from a reliable seedsman, or make up a mixture yourself consisting of 60 per cent Chewing's Fescue, 25 per cent Canada Blue Grass, 10 per cent Red Top, 5 per cent Colonial Bent. Use 5 lbs. per 1,000 sq. ft. Top-dress with sandy soil mixed with fertilizer spring and autumn. Sow additional seed every spring and autumn also. Do not mow more often than once a week; water copiously in July and August; only sparingly rest of the year. Broadcast wood ashes every spring, up to 25 lbs. per 1,000 sq. ft.

What is the best procedure when seeding slopes? The greatest danger is from washing out of seed and seedlings. If the slope is long, lay rows of sod at 3- to 4-ft. intervals across the slope and seed between the rows. Logs of wood 6 to 8 ins. in diameter laid along the slope and supported by wooden pegs will do instead of sod. The interval between the logs must be reduced according to steepness of the slope. Mix the seed with soil before sowing, or cover the seed with soil after sowing. Sow when the soil is moist and roll lightly if practical. If not, the seed should be firmed into the soil with the back of a spade, or a tamper.

Should any added protection be placed over newly seeded slopes? Protection should be given until the seed has germinated. Old burlap may be stretched over the area, or grass clippings, hay, or straw spread over it. Coverings must be removed after germination.

The slope of my garden is 1 to 1. Could you suggest a grass, shrub, or vine to stop erosion? The temperature in winter is occasionally 20 to 30° below zero. Use the seed mixture recommended for terraces. But before doing so sow and rake in some rye seed. Use equal weights of rye and grass seeds; sow rye first and cover about one inch deep, then sow the grass seed. Mow the rye as soon as it is long enough for a mower to cut it, and turf will gradually change from one of rye to one of grass. (For other suggestions see Ground Covers.)

What is the cheapest and best way to replant a sloping, sunny front lawn? I have reseeded and used new topsoil, but only a part looks good. Unless the soil is good, it is impossible to keep moisture on a slope. Probably your lawn is struggling along on a very thin layer of topsoil. Best procedure would be to remake it in early September, but cheapest scheme would be to renovate it. Open the soil without unduly spoiling what you have; scratch it with a sharp rake, or hold a garden fork vertically and work it up and down, filling soil full of holes. Spread 1 to 2 ins. of good topsoil, smooth with the back of a rake, and sow seed. Do this every April and September, and in addition apply fertilizer twice a year and limestone every year in late fall, unless you are in a section where there is naturally a large supply of lime in the land.

Should the soil for a grass terrace be rich? As rich as you can make it. Terraces and slopes need plenty of humus to hold moisture, as it is a big factor.

What kind of grass is best for a terrace? Get a mixture for the purpose from a reliable seedsman, or make up your own mixture of 35 per cent rye grass and Chewing's Fescue, 20 per cent blue grass, and 10 per cent white clover if you wish.

When should a terrace be planted? (Connecticut.) September 1 and April 15 would be two most desirable dates in your section, weather permitting.

How can I get grass started on a terrace? The degree of slope must first be considered. If the slope is less than 22½°, sow the seeds directly when the soil is moist and conditions are right for quick germination. If between 22½ and 45°, you can also seed it, but before sowing the grass seed sow rye (the grain, not rye grass) and rake it under, completely covering it, then sow the grass seed on top and roll it in or tamp it with a spade. If the slope is over 45°, the grass seed will have to be sown in holes. Make the holes 3 ins. deep, 3 ins. wide, and 10 ins. apart; fill them with a mixture of seed and soil, using 1 part seed to 10 parts soil. There should be at least 4 ins. of good soil on the surface. Until terrace is well established it will be necessary to resow spots washed out by erosion.

How often should the grass on a terrace be cut? At least once a week, unless slope is so severe that mowing is difficult. In this case, as often as you can.

SODDING

I have some old pasture turf I wish to use for sodding but it has stones in it. Do you think it will be all right? Sod that has stones in it cannot be cut evenly nor will the sod hold together. When stripping the sod, the tools are continually being obstructed; when the sod is lifted, the stones fall away, leaving nothing but a mere shred of turf which even with the best of care would hardly resume growth on a terrace.

My terrace was repaired with sod in spring, and now some of the sods are turning brown. What could be the cause?   There are several reasons. Sections of the sod may have been very thin with little roots left to help renewed growth; they were uneven and extra soil was not used to imbed them properly, thus leaving air pockets; they were not firmly embedded and tamped into the soil or the watering after the sod was laid was uneven or insufficient.

Establishing a new lawn by means of sodding. The ground is prepared as for seed sowing, and the sods (cut to an even thickness of 1½ ins. or more) are carefully fitted into place, firmed with a tamper or the back of a spade, and kept thoroughly watered until new roots form.

I wish to cut a section of good sod from my lawn to cover a small terrace. How must I go about cutting the sod? How should I sod the terrace so that it will be even?   To sod the terrace evenly, the sod must be even in size and thickness. To get an even size, lay a 12-in. board on the turf and, standing on it, cut the turf along both sides of the board. When the whole section has been cut in foot-wide strips, with a lawn edging knife, make another series of 12-in. cuts *across* the strips. This will leave the section cut into 12-in. squares each of which can easily be cut under with a sharp spade. To get an even thickness of sod, proceed as follows: Secure a shallow box 1½ ins. deep and 12 ins. square but with only 3 sides. Slide a sod into the box through the open side, grass side down, and, using an old sickle, the blade of a scythe, or a heavy knife, rest the blade on the sides of the box and slice off any soil that is higher than the 1½-in. sides. Treat each sod the same way. Prepared thus, the sods will be even in width and thickness. With the surface of the terrace level, lay the sod as directed in the Introduction. Have a barrowload of soil handy to fill up uneven spots as sodding proceeds. Slightly overlap each sod as it is laid and vigorously tamp it in with the back of a spade. Spike each sod with a wooden peg and water several times at intervals of 3 to 4 hours, so that plenty of moisture is available to the new roots of the grass.

How do you prepare a lawn plot for transplanting sod? Prepare the soil as advised for a lawn. Remove all stones and adjust the grade and have the surface loose. (See Introduction.)

Will sodding eliminate patches of Crab Grass? Perhaps, if there are only a few patches and the Crab Grass has not seeded. Otherwise it might be a questionable practice. Crab Grass seeds itself beyond the area occupied by the plants.

LAWNS FOR SPECIAL CONDITIONS

Shaded Areas

Can you suggest an aid to sparse lawn around our oak-tree trunks? Perforate the soil to several inches with a spading fork. Top-dress with good soil and fertilizer and sow a standard mixture of shady grasses. (See Fertilizer, Seed Mixtures.)

Does the lawn area close to trees need any special care in order to keep it in good growing condition? Because of the competition of the tree roots, grass near trees requires more fertilizing and watering than in open areas. Also the grass should not be cut so low.

Under a European linden tree on my lawn the grass in early spring and summer grows reasonably well. Toward late summer it thins out. What suggestion would you make to remedy this situation? Soil is slightly acid. Grass under trees needs more maintenance than grass on lawns. To maintain grass under trees a regular program of feeding, top-dressing, and watering must be kept up. Do not cut the grass so low nor so frequently as the regular lawn. (See Applying Fertilizer.) Apply 50 lbs. pulverized limestone per 1,000 sq. ft. in late fall.

Will clover grow under trees, or will it be necessary to plant a special mixture for shady lawn? It is better to plant a shady-lawn mixture. Clover will not survive under trees.

What grass seed do you suggest to make a lawn under maple trees? Grass is not successful under maple trees. Maples are surface-rooting trees, and grass could not compete with the large roots for food and moisture. By midsummer the grass usually disappears.

What type of grass will succeed under elms, hackberry, linden, and other trees with surface-feeding roots? Please state variety, not just shade mixture. A mixture is much more successful than one kind. Failure is not due to a mixture but to inadequate preparation and to the lack of attention that grass in shade requires. The only lone kind that has given results is Rough-stalked Blue Grass, also called Rough-stalked Meadow Grass. Use 5 lbs. per 1,000 sq. ft.

Play Areas

How should the soil for a playground lawn be prepared? More than the average amount of humus is needed to maintain a spongy surface to prevent packing. As much as a ton per 1,200 sq. ft. of old rotted manure, spent hotbed manure, or compost should be worked in by plowing, disking, digging, or by rototiller, to mix it thoroughly with the soil. With the humus use 75 lbs. of ground limestone. If the soil is heavy, incorporate a 3-in. layer of very coarse sand, or screened cinders, about the size of peas, in conjunction with the manure. Failing manure, use a good grade of cultivated peat which must first be dampened down, spread on 4 ins. deep, and then mixed in as advised for manure. In this case 100 lbs. of lime will be needed. With the peat use a 10–6–4 fertilizer, 30 lbs. per 1,000 sq. ft., but a 4–8–4 or something similar is better if manure is the source of the humus. Grading and getting an even, compact surface are essential. These are accomplished by alternate harrowing, or raking, and rolling to eliminate depressions and form a true, even surface.

What grass do you recommend as most durable for a playground? What rate of seeding is necessary to secure a good turf? Because of the conditions of growth and the wear to which grass is subject, the seed mixture and the manner of seeding on a playground are different from those of the ordinary lawn. Consult an experienced grass seedsman about your particular site and the kind of sports for which it is to be used. The following mixture is typical of the kinds used on sports fields: 35 per cent Chewing's Fescue, 25 per cent Kentucky Blue Grass, 20 per cent Red Fescue, 10 per cent Red Top, and 10 per cent Perennial Rye Grass. Sow 6 to 8 lbs. per 1,000 sq. ft.

How should the seed be sown on a playground lawn to get an even covering? Use the wheelbarrow type of seeder or a mechanical grass seed sower. Split the quantity of seed into equal portions and sow the portions at right angles to each other. Cover with a light seed harrow, or by raking and rolling.

How high should the grass be allowed to grow before its first cutting? Allow the grass to grow to 3 ins., then reduce it to 2 ins. Maintain the length of the grass at 2 ins. thereafter.

What are the most important operations concerned with the upkeep of a playground lawn? The maintenance of the right moisture conditions is a critical factor. The soil should not be allowed to dry out; neither must it get soggy through over-watering. By keeping the soil moisture constant, the grass will be kept in continuous growth and all food materials that are applied will be more efficiently used. Top-dress in spring and again in fall. (See Applying Compost.) Reseeding is another important operation. This differs from the practice on the average lawn. Keep the turf constantly supplied with seed. Wash seed in when watering; the seed will be pushed into the soil by treading or by shoe spikes. Grub-proof for beetle grubs as advised in the Introduction. Keep a sharp lookout for fungous diseases, especially during hot, humid weather. (See Diseases.) Avoid the overuse of highly nitrogenous fertilizers or grass will become soft. Do not allow heavy trucks on frozen sod.

Service Areas

The front part of my lawn is subject to much treading down. What kind of grass would stand this wear, and how would I maintain it?   The soil, if heavy, must be well supplied with humus combined with coarse sand or screened cinders, to keep the surface from packing. Annual top-dressings and reseedings when traffic is not too bad will also be required. It may be necessary every few years to perforate the surface to encourage aeration. (See Spiking.) Sow with 3 parts Chewing's Fescue, 1 part each of Red Top and Perennial Rye Grass, and 2 parts Kentucky Blue Grass. Seed at 6 lbs. per 1,000 sq. ft.

City Lawns

I have a typical New York City back yard which gets about four hours of sun daily. Grass grows well until August, when it dies out although liberally watered. What is the cause?   The fault lies with the soil which, without improvement, is not capable of supporting a stand of grass in summer.

Can I do anything to my soil to help it retain moisture? This is a city lawn.   Soil in city lots is often heavy. Incorporate to a depth of 8 ins. a 2-in. layer of dampened peatmoss. Apply 12 lbs. of ground limestone per 100 sq. ft. and rake it into the surface. Use a 5–10–5 fertilizer at the rate of 4 lbs. per 100 sq. ft. and thoroughly mix with the soil before seeding.

Is a single kind of grass better on a city lawn or would you prefer a mixture?   A good grass mixture is to be preferred to a single kind. Conditions are not always suited to one kind of grass.

What lawn seed will grow under city conditions?   Two parts Chewing's Fescue, 2 parts Colonial Bent, and 1 part each Red Top and Perennial Rye Grass. Add white clover if desired, 1 oz. per lb. of seed. Use 5 lbs. per 1,000 sq. ft.

For a city lawn, when should the seed be sown for best growth? Early September is the best time to get the lawn started to take full advantage of fall growth and assure a good start in spring.

Will a city lawn be permanent after one planting? No. It will be necessary each fall or spring to reseed. Use half the original quantity over grass; full quantity on bare spots.

How often should the grass on a city lawn be cut? At least once a week, perhaps more often in early summer. In July and August the cutting must be adjusted to rate of growth.

What height would you leave grass on a city lawn? It is best kept cut to about 1½ ins. in early summer, increasing to 2½ ins. in mid-summer.

How often should a city lawn be watered? This is the prime cause of much disease, which is more prevalent under city conditions because of poor air circulation. Cut the grass a little shorter before watering. Soak thoroughly and, if possible, choose a windy day. (See Control of Brown Spot.) Avoid constant sprinkling, and do not flood. Water once a week.

My lawn is completely surrounded by concrete, close to a subway with filled-in soil. I have used topsoil, lime, and regular blue grass seed mixture. In spite of conscientious watering, the grass burns up because of the sun beating down all day. Is the grass hardy? Blue grass is hardy. Although the tops die back in the excessive heat of midsummer, the roots are not so easily injured. Look to the watering practice. Does the water penetrate deeply, or is the water merely sprinkled on, evaporating in the heat and providing ideal conditions for brown patch? Topsoil should be good and at least 4 ins. deep.

BENT LAWNS

Is bent grass lawn expensive to start? Every new lawn should be on soil prepared with meticulous care; so a bent lawn from seed should cost but little more in preparation, the difference being mostly in the cost of seed. Bent stolons cost more than bent seed, and their preparation and planting are more expensive.

Is a bent grass lawn hard to maintain? Yes. Don't think of a bent lawn unless you are prepared to take every care of it. Mow twice weekly; watering, when necessary, must be generous; apply fungicides at first sign of brown patch. Fertilizer and top-dressing, should be given spring and autumn. Weeding should be continuous, as bent grass does not crowd out weeds. The holes made when they are removed heal over quickly.

Must the soil for a bent lawn be very rich? Yes. Bent lawns require a soil rich in humus and high in fertility. Good drainage, too, is very important to a well-aerated condition and root growth.

How early in spring is best to start a new lawn with Creeping Bent grass? Immediately frost is out of the ground and land is dry. Autumn is another good time. *Late* spring is to be avoided.

Will the treating of bent grass seed with certain chemicals stimulate growth? There is little evidence to prove that these preparations have any effect on growth. Put your emphasis upon obtaining first-grade seed and insuring the conditions for germination by good soil preparation.

How do you sow Creeping Bent lawn seed? The 2 to 4 lbs. of bent seed per 1,000 sq. ft. that you will use may be divided into 2 equal parts. Broadcast ½ over the entire area, and rake once only and in one direction; broadcast the second half over the entire area also, and merely roll, making no attempt to cover it. Select a still day, take half handfuls, and throw them horizontally with a circular motion, stooping as you do so.

Must the soil for a bent lawn be grub-proofed? If the application of arsenate of lead for grub-proofing does not delay your work of preparation, it may be applied before your final raking to prepare the surface for seed. If you are pressed for time, however, broadcast it after the lawn is established and repeat every 3 to 5 years. Allow 10 lbs. per 1,000 sq. ft.

How should I take care of my bent grass in spring? Mow, first with a high-set mower, then gradually lower the adjustment each time you use it, so that at the end of 2 weeks you have it at its normal height. Spread fertilizer and top-dressing.

Should bent grass be rolled? Yes, but not until all frost has gone and the soil has dried. Use as light a roller as you can get results with. (See Rolling.)

Should the first mowings of bent grass be raked off? Yes, if they are long enough to rake together. But aim to mow so frequently thereafter that your clippings are short and powdery and you could not rake them up if you wished to.

How often should bent lawns be cut? Twice a week at least. Golf putting greens are often pure bent, and are examples of exquisite turf; at certain times they are mown every day.

I have a bent grass lawn. How short should it be cut? One person says as short as possible; another says 1½ to 2 ins. It is important, first, that you cut it regularly and often. A height of 1½ ins. would be all right. The standard on a golf putting green is ¼ in. Do not cut as short as this.

Would there be any serious effect if the grass on my bent lawn were not cut for a while? Yes. When you *do* get around to mowing it, you will injure it, perhaps permanently, besides encouraging weeds. If the grass gets tall, cut with the mower set as high as you can mow with it, then lower it and use it the next day, continuing until you have *gradually* brought the lawn down to its normal height.

How late in the season can cutting of bent grass be continued?

Right up to winter. Raise mower to maximum height in October, so that the grass is somewhat longer before winter.

Does bent turf require much watering?   Yes. The soil should never be allowed to become dry during the growing period: spring, summer, and autumn.

Is Creeping Bent advisable in the country when water has to be obtained by electric pump?   This should not be an obstacle provided there is a good supply. However, if the water is very cold, better use it as late as possible in the evening or early morning; never in sunlight.

In watering my bent lawn is it all right to flood it?   Avoid flooding; use a nozzle or sprinkler that delivers in small droplets. If the lawn still puddles, turn off the water for half an hour and then sprinkle again.

How often should bent lawns be fed?   At least once in spring and once in autumn. In most sections of the Northern states (bent is rarely successful in the South) an application of limestone in late fall or earliest spring will be desirable also. (See Lime.)

What is the proper kind of fertilizer for bent lawns?   A balanced one, like 3-8-2, 4-8-4, or 5-10-5 is to be preferred; it should be a mixture of organic materials and chemical fertilizers. Acceptable compounds are made up by leading supply houses.

How can I fertilize a thick turf of Creeping Bent without burning it?   Use ½ the quantity that the maker recommends. Give a similar half-rate application a week later. Spread the material at a time when the grass is dry; immediately knock the powder off the grass leaves by drawing the back of a rake across the lawn; water thoroughly. Many turf keepers mix fertilizer with compost or screened soil, thereby lessening the chances of burning. Grass is sensitive in July and August; much less so at other times. Never apply more than 1 lb. of nitrogen per 1,000 sq. ft. at any one time. The first figure of a fertilizer analysis indicates the pounds of nitrogen in a 100-lb. bag of the fertilizer; be guided by this. (See Fertilizer.)

Is a mixture of hardwood ashes and bone meal applied heavily on a bent lawn in February and March good or bad for the grass? How much of each would I use?   Excellent. April 1 to 15 would be better. Two dressings may be given, one in September and one in April, unless you note an increase in clover. If the clover becomes excessive, change to a balanced fertilizer high in nitrogen. Allow 25 lbs. of bone meal and 50 lbs. of ashes per 1,000 sq. ft. at each application.

What about top-dressing bent lawns?   Very helpful. Fertilizer is mixed with screened rich topsoil, and spread. Quantity of soil is as much as possible without hiding the grass, usually about ¼ in. thick, and is raked in. Amount of fertilizer is determined by the nitrogen factor in the analysis. In a 4-8-4 formula the first figure indicates that in 100 lbs. there are 4 lbs. of nitrogen. We do not apply more than 1 lb. of nitrogen per 1,000 sq. ft., otherwise turf will be scalded; so 25 lbs. of this mixture is the most that could be used on 1,000 sq. ft. Instead of screened soil, compost is often used. (See Compost.)

Can bent lawns be top-dressed any time? Yes. But top-dressing is best omitted in July and August.

What is the minimum number of top-dressings that must be applied to a Creeping Bent lawn to keep it healthy? Minimum annual top-dressings would be two: one in spring and one in fall. But aim for four if possible: the first very early in spring, another in June with the others put on in early September and October.

This spring I planted Astoria Bent seed and it came up and grew very well, but there have been no signs of creeping or of stolons. Does this type of bent grass creep, or don't the stolons start the first year? It creeps, but slowly, because the stolons are normally very short. They usually appear the second year.

Does Colonial Bent Grass spread by underground stolons or surface stolons; or both? Its stolons, which are above ground, are short. It spreads so slowly that it may be regarded almost as a non-spreading grass. Strongly creeping kinds for latitudes north of Washington, D.C., are Creeping Bent and Seaside Bent. For points south of Washington, D.C., except where altitude produces conditions similar to the Northern states, the typical creeping grasses are Bermuda and Carpet.

Is it practical to sow Creeping Bent grass seed with regular lawn mixture and let it eventually crowd out ordinary grass? Highly practical. Good grass-seed mixtures put up by reputable supply houses often contain as much as 10 per cent by weight of bent seeds. Whether it crowds out other grasses or not depends upon the treatment given the lawn. Feeding, regular and frequent mowing, and watering when necessary, will encourage the bent; neglect the turf and the bent will disappear.

What quantity of bent grass seed should I use with regular grass mixture to insure a good stand? The 10 per cent usually contained in mixtures may be increased to 25 per cent.

I have a blue grass lawn. Could I convert it to a bent lawn? Yes, but it may take a year or more. Add Seaside Bent to some screened soil, 1 part by measure of the seed to 10 parts of the soil. Broadcast this every spring and fall, allowing ½ lb. of seed to each 100 sq. ft. Spread fertilizer 1 week before or 1 week later.

If I sowed a few pounds of bent grass when fertilizing in spring, would it grow and gradually work into a bent lawn? If the soil is fairly rich and there are not many weeds, this could be accomplished over a period of time (for quantity to use, see previous question). To succeed, you will have to encourage the bent grass to become established by close mowing twice weekly, fertilizing spring and autumn, top-dressing, and watering generously when needed.

I planted Creeping Bent in my front yard, which is quite shaded. I had no luck with it; brown spots appeared, and it doesn't seem to spread. What can I do?   Creeping Bent is not very tolerant of shade; sow instead a shady-lawn seed mixture containing Chewing's Fescue, Velvet Bent, and Canada Blue Grass, or *Poa trivialis,* known as Rough-stalked Blue Grass, if it can be obtained. These four are shade tolerant.

From Stolons

How is the soil prepared for starting Creeping Bent grass from stolons?   Have at least 6 ins. of good topsoil, broadcast 100 lbs. or more of sheep manure or similar desiccated animal fertilizer over 1,000 sq. ft. Work it into the surface and rake the soil smooth. (See Soil Preparation—Introduction.)

How do you estimate the quantity of stolons needed?   One sq. ft. of plants taken from the nursery bed or nursery row will plant 8 to 10 sq. ft. of new lawn.

The bent grasses spread by means of stolons which form new individual plants.

In planting a bent lawn with stolons (instead of seed) the mass of stolons and roots is cut up into short lengths.

When is it best to plant the stolons?   Either in the early spring or late summer.

How are the stolons spread over the ground?   Best way is to cut them into 1-in. lengths, broadcast them by hand, taking care that nowhere is there a space of more than ½ in. between pieces.

Are the stolons covered with soil or rolled in?   Both. Roll them into the surface; cover with ½ in. screened soil; and roll again.

How can stolons be inserted in an old lawn which is being renovated?   Pot-grown stolons are now available together with a cylindrical metal planter which cuts out the turf to exactly the size of the pot-grown plants, which are inserted in the holes, pressed firmly into place, and watered thoroughly.

Should the ground be watered after the stolons are planted? Keep continually moist until young grass shows through. Use a fine nozzle; if soil covering is displaced, add more.

Planting a lawn with stolons. The cut-up pieces are spread over the prepared surface and rolled in; sifted compost is then spread over them to a depth of ½ in., and the surface again is rolled.

How high should the grass from bent stolons be for the first cutting? As soon as a mower, adjusted to cut medium long, can effect a cut; approximately about 2 ins.

Should a bent lawn from stolons have any winter protection? Only if you happen to live in a region where from experience this type of lawn is known to be subject to winter kill; then a few inches of covering may be applied. Tobacco stems held in place with birch or maple branches are sometimes used; so are branches alone.

Weeds and Pests

What do you put on a bent lawn to make ground more acid and thus stop growth of weeds? The standard chemical is ammonium sulfate 3 to 5 lbs. per 1,000 sq. ft. But it can be overdone, so occasionally apply a balanced fertilizer. Liquid manure, made by steeping rotted cow manure in water, discourages many weeds. Aluminum sulfate, too, is sometimes used to make soil acid, also at 3 to 5 lbs. per 1,000 sq. ft. *Ammonium* sulfate stimulates growth; *aluminum* sulfate has little effect on the grass. An application of lead arsenate (for grub-proofing) to some extent discourages weed growth.

How can I get rid of White Clover in a Creeping Bent lawn without killing the bent, or resorting to the laborious backbreaking, hand-pick-

ing method? I have tried aluminum sulfate and frequent dressings of
ammonium sulfate, but clover seems to thrive on them.   Try raking
quite harshly once a month with an iron rake, with the teeth filed sharp.
Continue with applications of aluminum and ammonium sulfate; alternate them with cottonseed meal, castor pumice, or shredded cattle
manure. With cow manure made liquid to the color of beer drench
the turf every six months. A more drastic way is to scald the turf with
a solution of sodium arsenate, 2 ozs. in 4 gals. water per 1,000 sq. ft.;
grass is injured temporarily, and clover more seriously; several treatments may eliminate the clover.

**What causes, and how can I get rid of, mushrooms and toadstools
in a sunny bent lawn?**   Usually fragments of manure, and sometimes
pieces of rotting wood, are to blame. Fungi of this type do little harm,
and the growth may be rubbed away with a rake. If serious, punch a
number of holes with a vertically held garden fork; then saturate the
soil with Thiosan, 4 ozs. in 10 gals. of water; repeat weekly if necessary.

**I have a bent lawn. Last summer we had heavy rains. But from
July to late September my grass turned to brown spots and died out.
Can you give me information?**   If condition showed within 3 days of
excessive rain, possible reason (1) is "damping off" or pythium; (2)
if in hot spell, probably brown patch, dollar spot, or copper spot; (3)
if hot sun followed heavy rain, might be "scald" when water in puddles
cooks the plants; (4) if spots were like burns and reddish brown,
suspect chinch bugs; (5) if dead grass lifts up readily, like a piecrust,
look for May beetle grubs. Also consider wear, dogs, fuel oil. (See
Disease and Insect Control.) Dust with chlordane for chinch bug.
Correct surface drainage so that no puddles form.

**Does Astoria Bent Grass from seed always get brown patch and
die out?**   If conditions are right, you should have little of this kind
of trouble, although all bents are sensitive to fungous injury the first
year or so. Possibly your soil lacks porosity and remains wet too long
between rains. Also, in grading operations, was subsoil brought to the
surface? Did you immediately apply fungicides when you first saw
brown patch, continuing with further applications every 10 days? Is
the lawn under trees? Astoria Bent is not shade tolerant.

**What is the proper yearly care for bent grass lawns? How avoid
brown spots?**   Broadcast fertilizer and top-dressing twice in spring
and twice in autumn; roll in spring; remove weeds as soon as you
see them, and water generously in July and August. Try to do without
water in spring and autumn, but avoid letting the grass suffer through
dryness. Mow twice weekly. (See Disease Control for Brown Patch.)
Repeat at 10-day intervals until September 30.

**We have bent grass and there is a small gray grubworm eating the
roots of it. We have found about 12 in a space of about 5 ins. square.**

What remedy will destroy them? These are undoubtedly grubs of the Japanese beetle. (See Grub-proofing—Introduction.)

What shall I do for chinch bug in beautiful large front lawn which is mostly bent grass? It got quite a start before we knew what it was; now we want to prevent its spoiling our lawn another year. See Insect Control—Introduction.

Have started a Creeping Bent lawn from seed this fall. Worms are coming up through it at night causing eruptions in the soil which kill the grass in these spots. **What should I do about it?** Carefully use a bamboo rake to distribute the material in the worm casts, or drag a flexible steel mat over the grass, or "swish" the surface with a very long bamboo. Never mow until you have first done this. There is a substance sometimes used as a fertilizer called mowrah meal, which usually kills earthworms. Chemical worm killers are also available such as bichloride of mercury (one ounce dissolved in 15 gallons of water will cover 500 square feet). Water in after sprinkling the chemical over the area.

What is the best way to prevent damage to young bent grass by worms? Possibly the sod webworm, the infestation of which is affected by weather conditions. Mix 7 lbs. arsenate of lead with twice its bulk of sand. Spread over 1,000 sq. ft. Work it in with a broom. Water with a hose.

MOSS LAWNS

What is the name of the moss that is used for planting lawns? Will it grow anywhere? Its botanical name is *Sagina subulata,* commonly called Lawn-moss. It is used extensively in the Pacific coast states. It will grow almost anywhere in the United States except the Rio Grande Valley and the region south of Fort Pierce, Florida. In extreme Northern latitudes, it usually winter kills. It is not a true moss.

Does the moss used for lawns need a good soil? It thrives best on a fertile soil, but it has grown well on the "dobe" soils south of San Francisco. Having a shallow root system, it can be surface fed like bent grass.

Is the moss that is used in lawns grown from seed? How is it planted? Lawn-moss is planted from divisions. Two-in. squares are planted 6 ins. apart. A quicker effect can be had by planting them 3 or 4 ins. apart. In planting the roots are well covered and firmed, and the crown (sprig) kept above the surface.

Does moss make a level, green lawn? Lawn-moss does not remain level. Being of very vigorous growth, it rises in small mounds or knots. In order to keep the surface even, these mounds must continually be compressed by rolling. Occasionally the lawn must be cut with a disk harrow and top-dressed.

How many years can I expect a moss lawn to last? In a climate where no great winter cold occurs, and if rolling, disking, and top-dressing are consistently carried out, Lawn-moss will last for several years. A disease similar to brown patch will at times infect it, destroying areas in the sod. This is controlled by the same agents prescribed for brown patch. The rapid growth of the moss soon covers the bare spots.

Would the fact that moss has flowers add to its value in the lawn? True, it blooms very prolifically in early summer with tiny flowers on 1-in. stems and it is very pretty. The flowers, however, do not last long.

Will the planting of a moss lawn relieve me of all the work involved in caring for a grass lawn? There will be little difference in the amount of work involved in the upkeep. You will have to roll a moss lawn as often as you would have to cut a grass lawn, and the danger of the moss dying out is greater than that of grass, especialy if the moss is overfertilized.

REHABILITATION OF OLD LAWNS

Could one gradually create a new surface on an old lawn by top-dressing? Annual or semi-annual top-dressing of rotted compost would, in a few years, build up a new surface.

What materials would I use for surfacing a lawn? Surfacing materials are best obtained by composting good garden soil, manure, and old leaves. Build a pile 4 ft. high with the soil, manure, and leaves in alternate layers 6 ins. thick. A sprinkling of chemical fertilizer over each layer and watering to keep materials moist will help decompose the pile more rapidly. Allow at least 6 months before use. For immediate use, make a compost by thoroughly sifting and mixing together 3 parts loam, 1 part pulverized peatmoss and 1 part dried manure.

How and to what depth is compost applied? Compost must be screened before applying. One cubic yard is needed to add ⅓ in. of surface over 1,000 sq. ft.

Is it possible to renew an old lawn by adding fertilizer and some seed? Provided the turf has not deteriorated too seriously, a program of this sort coupled with weed eradication consistently kept up would go far to restore an old lawn. Annual dressings of compost would still further improve it.

What is spring and fall treatment for an old lawn, badly run down and grub eaten, as to fertilizer and seed? Remove weeds and all dead grass; dig bare areas, and break up the soil. While digging, work in arsenate of lead, 10 lbs. to 1,000 sq. ft., and apply a complete fertilizer. Sow 2 parts Chewing's Fescue, 2 parts Colonial Bent, 1 part each Red Top and Perennial Rye Grass; cover, and roll. Fall treatment: Top-dress. (See question on Top-dressing.) Reseed again any spots that are bare or thin.

In reseeding an old, established lawn, is it sufficient to scratch the topsoil? If not, how deep should I dig the ground? If the soil is in poor condition and weeds have taken hold, the mere scratching of the topsoil would hardly suffice. The only permanent course would be to dig up the area, clear out the weeds, and remake the entire lawn.

What fertilization should an old lawn be given between spring and fall? If the turf is good and if there is considerable bent grass present, top-dressing about the end of June might be desirable if sufficient water is also available. On the whole, a good spring and fall feeding should be adequate.

What can I do to improve the appearance of my lawn in winter? (Atlantic City, N.J.) Near the seashore or in the south where no deep freezing of the soil occurs, a program of monthly lawn feeding with a complete plant food (of 10–6–4 formula for sandy soils or 8–6–4 for heavy soils), or with an organic fertilizer such as milorganite or agranite, will go far toward maintaining a handsome lawn through the colder months. Zoysia lawns, for instance can be kept green most of the year in such locations by resorting to winter feeding.

Is it safe to burn grass that has grown tall on a lawn which has been neglected for 2 years? If so, what time of year is best to do burning? If you can find it dry enough in late fall, burning it off then would destroy many insects and weed seeds before they have a chance to get deep into the soil. Burning may be done in early spring also. It will not injure the roots.

What is the best fertilizer for spring for an old lawn of 14,400 sq. ft.? Last fall we spread 330 lbs. of bone meal, 100 lbs. of lime, and 55 lbs. of seed. A nitrogenous fertilizer would be best for early spring growth. Use either dried cow manure or tankage, 30 to 40 lbs. per 1,000 sq. ft.

CARE OF NEW LAWNS

Having no roller last spring we just tamped the soil down. Is that the cause of the holes in the lawn? The uneven firming by tamping may be partly to blame. The condition is more likely the result of poor grading. If hard and soft areas were left, the soft spots would settle.

The fall sowing of my lawn resulted in patchy growth. Can the spots be filled in by spring planting, or should I wait for another year? Early spring patching is usually satisfactory. Loosen the soil, apply seed liberally, and use some nitrogenous fertilizer, such as sheep manure, to give the young grass a quick start.

When is the best time to put manure on a lawn seeded in fall? Apply well-rotted and sifted manure in early spring.

How late can one make a new lawn in fall and still get good results in spring? Lawns should not be planted later than the middle of October. In the East, later plantings sometimes become established enough to winter well, but results are uncertain.

Can a new lawn be made in spring? Yes, although the grass will not have as good a root depth as fall-planted grass.

About 2 years ago I made a new lawn. Each spring it is reseeded. It grows for a while, then it gets full of weeds and looks like a hayfield. I'd like to know what to do. Weeds must first be eradicated. (See Introduction and questions on Weed Control.)

Will spreading a thin layer of black dirt over my new lawn, which is seeded in sand, help to enourage its growth? This will help very much, provided it breaks down easily and will work into the surface and is not just a plastic material that will lie on the top and bake in the hot sun.

Would manure on fall-planted grass seed help to protect grass and fertilize the grass in spring again? If seed was sown late and the grass is very short, a thin layer of manure, if well rotted, would give protection and at the same time add some fertilizer. If the grass was sown early in fall, it would not need manure but an application of complete fertilizer in early spring would be very beneficial.

I am having trouble to get a nice yard—have planted the best of grass seed and fertilizer, and still it dies. What is the trouble? Your seed mixture may not be adapted to your soil requirements. Thorough preparation as outlined in the Introduction is the most important step. Poor drainage, poor soil texture, and lack of humus may be the trouble.

Made a new lawn in spring. Used new topsoil and the best grass seed. Now it is full of Crab Grass and brown spots. What causes this? The Crab Grass seeds were in the topsoil. The brown spots probably were the fungous disease by that name. (See Diseases.)

Have had no results with my lawn after using an expensive mixture of grass seed. What procedure must I follow to insure a better lawn? Should I have the soil tested? If so, please advise where. Expensive grass-seed mixtures alone will never make a lawn unless the seeding has been preceded by adequate soil preparation (as outlined in the Introduction). Except for determining lime requirements, the soil test is of little use. Your Agricultural College will test your soil.

My lawn has small, hard mounds in it. Can I correct this without completely rebuilding the whole lawn? There are two approaches to the problem? (1) Slice the mounds off with a spade and remove enough soil to put the sod back level; or after slicing the mounds off, loosen the soil and sow seed. (2) If the mounds are not too numerous, level up to them with fresh topsoil and reseed the areas.

What causes moundlike humps in a new lawn? Caused by poor grading and sowing the seed before the soil had settled sufficiently to reveal unevenness in the grade; or by mole runs.

MAINTENANCE OF ESTABLISHED LAWNS

How can I make my lawn look nice? It has sun and good soil. Use fertilizer in spring and fall to invigorate the turf. Make a yearly top-dressing of compost. Eradicate weeds before they seed. Adjust the cutting to the season, and supply sufficient moisture before the soil supply is exhausted. Constant reseeding of poor spots and liming will aid.

Areas in my lawn die out each winter; is this because some of the grasses are not hardy? The more permanent of the lawn grasses are winter hardy. The condition may be due to lack of drainage, poorly aerated soil, or Crab Grass. The latter dies after the first frost. (See Crab Grass.) Dig all poor spots, work in humus, and sow seed in late winter.

Why is my lawn, in a sunny location facing south, full of bare spots? Have patched with new seed, but this has not been successful. Probably the soil where the bare spots appear is too shallow or not fertile enough to support a good stand of grass. Remove the soil to a depth of 4 to 6 ins. Fill with good soil, and reseed.

All summer my lawn was beautiful, but this fall it turned brown while other lawns were still green. What is the cause? Probably your soil is shallower than that of your neighbor's. Hence when dry weather comes yours suffers first. Summer watering would help. Top-dressing with humus-making material would be more permanent.

At the point where my lawn touches the sidewalk I have been unable to grow grass. Have you any suggestions? The grass roots were dried out on coming in contact with the concrete in summer. Try putting a layer of peatmoss 1 inch thick next to the sidewalk. Keep it well watered.

Our house has a field of grass on which we look out. We enjoy the daisies and first stand of young grass. After that, when should it be cut, and how often per year, to keep it attractive? It is now full of red bunch grass. Cut the first grass before the seed ripens in the heads. Two more cuttings at monthly intervals during the summer should keep it orderly.

Should grass clippings be removed? Remove in the early part of the season if the grass is long, and especially during wet periods. Short clippings during hot, dry periods can be left on.

Should my lawn be rolled in midsummer? No; this compacts the soil and causes quicker drying out.

Our lawn is full of deep holes. How shall we go about renewing

it this coming spring? The only practical plan is to fill the holes with topsoil, level off with a rake to even the grade, and then reseed. More than one treatment may be required.

Is it advisable to repair bare spots in the lawn in fall? Yes; all bare spots should be repaired in early fall. Inspect them again in spring for reseeding.

Would appreciate some information on the reason for spiking lawns. How is spiking done? Spiking is carried out for the purpose of opening up a heavy soil or very thick turf to permit air, moisture, and plant nutrients to reach the grass roots. The turf is perforated by rolling with a spiked roller on large lawns, or by a hand spiker on small areas. The tines of a digging fork plunged into the turf will answer as well.

Will spiking improve a poor soil? Spiking the soil alone will not improve it. The amount of top-dressing that can be worked in, together with fertilizer, will bring the improvement.

Under what conditions should spiking be done on a lawn? If the turf is thick or compacted through the use of heavy mowers or by rolling, or if the soil is a heavy clay and the grass is being starved even though fertilizer and water are applied, spiking has been found to be beneficial.

Is spiking practical on a small lawn? Yes, if the soil is heavy and the other conditions indicate a need for it.

What is the best time of the year to spike the lawn? As early in spring as it is possible to begin operations and the soil is not wet.

How late in fall can you cut a lawn? This will depend on the region and the severity of the winter. Throughout the East growth slows up in September; close cutting after that should be avoided, especially where winters are severe or lawn is new.

Will grazing the cows on the grass injure it? Grazing late in the fall would be the same as late mowing. It would deprive the grass of a winter top.

Will cows tramping on a lawn in the fall, leaving hoofprints, do any damage? If the sod is thin or the ground wet, the surface will become full of small depressions in which water will lodge, to the detriment of the grass.

Is it good practice to allow tree leaves to remain on the grass all winter? The leaves should be removed from the lawn. An accumulation of wet leaves on the grass in many instances will be harmful.

We are going to lime our lawn in December; in March use lead arsenate for beetle grub; in early May chemical fertilizer. Will this

be all right? This is a sound program. It might be better to apply fertilizer in April, particularly if its nitrogen content is largely organic.

How should a lawn be treated each spring and fall so as to assure a good carpet of green all through the summer months? Spring and fall treatments with fertilizers and humus-forming materials, while they will promote the vigor of the lawn grasses, will not overcome the effects of a long drought. Only a constant supply of moisture can assure this. (See Maintenance; Watering.)

If exceptionally good care is given to a lawn, will it last indefinitely or will it need to be redug and seeded? A well-cared-for lawn will normally last many years.

How do you increase the fertility of an established lawn? By top-dressing with humus-forming materials and fertilizer. (See Top-dressing.)

MOWING LAWNS

I have been told that the reason for my lawn not thriving is that the grass is cut too short. It is kept at 1 in. and sometimes less. Is this too short? What is the proper height at which to cut a lawn? One inch is too short. The food upon which the grass depends for development of root and top is manufactured in the green leaves (tops). In proportion as the grass top is restricted the roots also are restricted. Lawns in general would be in better shape and weeds less a problem were the grass allowed to grow longer; 2 to 2½ ins. is none too high for the average lawn.

How often should a terrace be mowed? This will depend upon the rate of growth. If the grass is kept vigorous through feeding and watering, mowing will be done more often than if grass is thin and is not so vigorous. If the height of the cut is maintained at 2 ins. the grass must be cut when it exceeds 2½ ins. Also, mowing will be more often done in early summer than through midsummer.

Should grass be left cut short for the winter? It would be better to allow 2 to 3 ins. of growth on the average lawn before winter sets in. This, however, would not apply to bent lawns. These are usually top-dressed in late fall.

In mowing a lawn must you use a catcher for the grass? The catcher would avoid the necessity of raking if the grass is heavy early in the season. When the cut is light, as in midsummer, the clippings are just as well left on the lawn.

The lawn was cut in October, and since then the grass has grown quite long. What should I do in spring with the grass? Before growth begins comb out the dead grass with a rake and if possible mow the area to give all possible light to the new grass.

Should grass clippings be saved? Certainly. They should be added to the compost heap, or used as a mulch under broad-leafed evergreens or shrubs. They are a source of some plant food elements and good humus.

Lawn Mowers

I wish to keep the grass on my lawn more than 2 ins. high, but my machine is not constructed to cut above this height. Is there any way I can get around the problem? Wind a small rope around the roller, or have special attachments adjusted to the wheels.

How can you check the height a lawn mower will cut? How is the cut adjusted? Place the machine on a level pavement and with a rule measure the height from the pavement to the iron plate against which the revolving blades cut. The height of cut is adjusted by raising or lowering the roller.

I seem to have difficulty adjusting my lawn mower to cut evenly. How can you tell when a mower is properly set? The cutting blades are adjusted by screws which are found on each side of the reel blades, on the bearings. The adjusting of these screws will adjust the evenness of cut against the plate at the bottom. The tightening of one side more than another will after a time wear that side down, causing an uneven cut. In this case the blades will have to be ground and set by someone who understands this and who has the equipment to do it.

Power Mowers

I have a country place with a large lawn bordered by open woodland and pasture. What power mower do you recommend? A rotary type mower, powerful enough to keep blackberry vines, seedling trees, grapevines etc., from encroaching on the lawn area.

My home is on the outskirts of town and I have a beautiful rolling lawn of well-established bent grass. What power mower shall I buy to

take care of this? By all means purchase a reel-type mower which will do as good a job as a well-sharpened hand mower.

We have a large, general purpose lawn, formerly mowed by hand. This has become too costly. What type of mower should we get? You would find a rotary mower completely satisfactory, and easier to maintain in good condition than the reel-type mower.

WATERING LAWNS

What is the best method of watering the lawn? Should one use a hose or a sprinkler? Should the ground be flooded? I have been given so much conflicting advice that I am confused. Avoid flooding the ground if possible. Flooding compacts the soil and invites disease. There is no doubt that a sprinkler designed to throw a fine spray over a large area is better than a hose. There is a more even distribution of water and this sinks in gradually without flooding. It is not the amount of water that is applied to the surface that helps the grass but that which reaches the roots 4 to 6 ins. below. If when watering the water collects in pools, shut the supply off for a few hours and water again. Once the pores of the soil have been opened the water will penetrate much faster. Flooding will occur when the soil is dry and especially if the water is applied too rapidly, as from a hose.

How can you hit the happy medium in lawn watering to avoid both burning out and scalding out? Watering should be started before the soil becomes dry. This will give better penetration, and food materials will be kept available in the soil. Enough should be given to moisten the soil for several inches deep.

How soon after the grass seed germinates would you water a slope? How often should water be applied in the first stages of growth? Slopes and terraces dry out faster than level areas, especially if the aspect is sunny. The period after germination is a critical one until the roots of the young grass take hold. If the surface looks dry, water with a fine spray. Do not play the water on too long and thus cause washing; just enough to moisten the soil. How often to water will depend upon the weather. If dry, water every 2 or 3 days until the grass is tall enough to shade the roots. Afterward adjust the watering to the weather.

How should a terrace be watered so that the water will soak in? The water I apply just runs off and does not penetrate. The top portion of the terrace will dry out sooner than the lower portion because of the moisture moving downward. Apply the water in a fine spray, moving back and forth with the hose and distributing the water evenly over the whole area. Only enough should be applied to soak in. After a few hours apply some more and repeat until the soil is moist to a depth of 4 ins.

Although watered 2 or 3 times a week my lawn in some places is drying out. Does it need more water? The lawn is not being watered; it is merely being sprinkled. The water it receives remains on the surface and evaporates. The soil down at the root area is always dry. When watering is needed, give the area a good, deep soaking; water again when examination of the soil shows the need for it. Do not wait until the soil is dry.

Is the chlorine in city water harmful to grass? No, not at all.

EDGING

What is the most practical way to edge the lawn along the path and driveway and around shrubbery beds? Mine were left as steps 3 in. or more high and now they are crumbling. High edges around paths and drives are difficult to maintain unless the turf is compact and the soil fairly heavy. If the path and drive are hard surfaced and not loose gravel, remove the sod from a space 3 ft. or more back from the lawn edge and grade the soil down to meet the surface of the path, leaving no step. Make the slope so gradual that the mower, when going over it, will catch all the grass. Turf edge along the beds should be kept about 2 ins. high to prevent the soil from being washed over the grass.

Is there some means of keeping the margins of my lawn neat without always taking a slice from the sod edge? Use edging shears. These are similar to a hedge shears except that they have long handles and the shears instead of being straight are turned at right angles to the handles. They are designed to trim the lawn edgings along paths and beds which a mower cannot catch.

Is there any material I can obtain that will make a permanent edging to the lawn? How about a strip of concrete? Concrete edgings are quite practical and can be stained a dark color to harmonize with the turf. However, unless they are sufficiently reinforced they will crack in winter. Concrete absorbs moisture. If the situation is exposed to full sun, the grass will dry out near the concrete. Wood strips, too, are used, but they must be constantly renewed. The low iron aluminum or asbestos corrugated edging strip, designed to be installed in sections, is a good answer. It is also inconspicuous.

ROLLING

Is the purpose of rolling a lawn to level the bumps? Not at all. Irregularities due to construction should not be corrected by rolling. The purpose is to settle the turf back after the winter action of freezing and thawing and to press the grass roots into contact with the soil.

What weight roller should be used? A light soil can stand a much heavier roller than a heavy soil. A very general rule for a ballast roller is 75 lbs. per foot of width. Better a light roller than a heavy one any time.

Is it best to roll the lawn when it is wet to obtain a good level surface? On a heavy soil that would be fatal, for the surface would dry out hard. Roll when only slightly damp, or even when the lawn is on the dry side.

How frequently should a lawn be rolled? Normally, one rolling in spring to settle the turf after winter freezing is all that is necessary.

COVER CROPS

What is meant by cover cropping? Cover cropping is the planting of a quick-growing, lush vegetation that can be turned under. The purpose is to build up the vital humus content of the soil and to crowd out weeds.

Can you tell me what to use for cover cropping? For very early spring planting rye, rye grass, common vetch. For summer (sown in June), buckwheat, cowpeas, soybeans. For fall, to hold over winter, rye, Rye Grass, Crimson Clover, Alsike Clover.

Is it better to sow lawn seed early in spring on our 100 × 200 ft., or sow buckwheat, soybeans, clover, or rye to combat weeds first and then seed to grass later in fall? Used to be a nursery; soil light, sandy muck. Without a doubt the cover-crop plan is to be preferred for weed control and the supplying of humus.

If you advise a crop to sow first, which would be best and why? It is possible to get two cover crops before fall. Sow rye or rye grass as early as possible in spring, and turn it under about June. Seed again to buckwheat or soybeans; preferably the latter, because it is a legume and will add nitrogen.

Should I use fertilizer? How much? Use fertilizer on summer crop to stimulate a thick growth. A 5–10–5 or similar complete fertilizer, 20 lbs. to 1,000 sq. ft.

How much seed would I need? Use 3 lbs. rye or rye grass seed, 1 to 1½ lbs. buckwheat, or 2 to 2½ lbs. soybeans per 1,000 sq. ft.

When should the crop be turned under? Turn the summer cover crop under about mid-August, approximately, or when it is still green.

Can anything be done to prevent weed seeds from germinating in the new lawn? Yes. After turning under the cover crop, treat the area with Lawn and Garden Cyanamid, a nitrogenous fertilizer which also kills weed seeds. See introduction.

How long after turning it under could I sow the lawn? Two to 3 weeks after turning under the summer cover crop prepare the lawn for seeding.

HUMUS AND PEATMOSS

Would a covering of peatmoss over the grass in summer help to hold the moisture and do away with watering? In actual practice this does not obtain. If the peatmoss becomes dry, it will absorb the moisture from the soil. Besides, the peat may encourage surface rooting unless it is incorporated *in the soil* at the time it is prepared for seeding. Peatmoss does much to retain moisture as it holds sixteen times its own weight in water.

I bought some black material which I was told was a good lawn food, but it did no good. Was this a fertilizer? No, it probably was not fertilizer. A lot of dark materials are being sold as lawn food. Most of them are waste from manufacturing plants and some of them may be injurious. Lawn food materials should be purchased only from reliable firms.

FERTILIZERS

What kind of chemical fertilizer is best for grass? We have part shade and part sunshine in our yard. A chemical fertilizer having 10 per cent nitrogen, 6 per cent phosphorus, and 4 per cent potash (10–6–4). Same for shaded area. Half of the nitrogen should be in organic form.

Is commercial fertilizer good for lawns? Yes, commercial fertilizer is excellent for lawns. The nutrients in it are fairly quick acting.

Can commercial fertilizer be used at any time? It is best applied in early spring or in late fall.

How is commercial fertilizer best applied? In dry form, either by hand or by a spreader. Mixing it with ⅓ its volume of fine soil or sand helps to get even distribution. Water in thoroughly.

What quantity commercial fertilizer should be used over a given area? Thirty lbs. per 1,000 sq. ft. is a good application.

Can you advise me the best top-dressing to use on a very sandy lawn to enrich the soil? Use good, screened topsoil, and add rotted manure, leafmold, or peatmoss—1 bushel to 8 bushels of soil. Broadcast fertilizer, as suggested above.

When and how should top-dressing be applied? Scatter over the lawn in spring as growth is beginning, using 2 bushels per 100 sq. ft.

Would you advise the use of superphosphate on the lawn? Superphosphate will prevent the grass from becoming too soft, a condition inviting disease; it also stimulates root action. Use 2 to 3 lbs. per 100 sq. ft.

When using only bone meal to fertilize the lawn, how much should I use in the spring, and how much in the fall? I want to make 2 applications for 1,000 sq. ft. If it is steamed bone meal (and this is the best), use 15 lbs. in spring and 10 lbs. in fall. For finely ground bone meal, 20 lbs. in spring and 10 lbs. in fall.

May bone meal be put on a lawn without injury to the grass? Yes, at any time.

May superphosphate be used at any time? Although there is little danger of injury from superphosphate, this would be better applied when the lawn is moist in spring to insure its being of value to the grass.

What value is tankage on a lawn? Tankage is valuable for its content of organic nitrogen that becomes gradually available to the grass as it is needed; also for the stimulation of bacterial action.

Are hardwood ashes good or not good for lawns? Hardwood ashes promote growth and hardness of grass stems. Applied as a top-dressing, 5 to 10 lbs. per 100 sq. ft., it is a good grass fertilizer.

When should lime and wood ashes be put on the lawn? It would not be necessary to put both on at the same time. Wood ashes contain a high percentage of lime as well as potash. Apply the lime in late fall and the wood ashes in April.

In applying lime, fertilizer (bone meal), arsenate of lead, and grass seed on lawns, can any two or more be safely applied simultaneously? Soil conditions and temperature exert considerable influence on these materials and their action at the time of application, making it advisable to apply them separately. Suggested procedure: Arsenate of lead followed by fertilizer at a week or 10-day interval; a few days later apply lime. If pulverized limestone is used, the seed may be applied simultaneously with it.

Should you sprinkle fertilizer over snow on lawns, which have bald spots, to restore the grass? Fertilizer will not restore grass if it has died out. Only reseeding would restore the bald spots. The seed may be sown in late winter, even on top of snow. In the South and elsewhere in areas where there is no deep freezing, a monthly application of a 10–6–4 formula complete fertilizer through the winter months will help keep the grass green and healthy.

The soil of our lawn is composed of sand covered thinly with black dirt. This has hardened. Would an application of fertilizer this spring help to open it up? Lime would open it up better than fertilizer. Use 60 lbs. ground limestone per 1,000 sq. ft. Follow some time later with fertilizer. Loosen soil with a spiked tamper, or tines of a fork, before applying.

How is fertilizer best applied to grass under trees? Do the tree roots use it up? The most complete method is first to feed the trees by placing fertilizer down in the root zone. This is done by removing pieces of sod and making holes by plunging a crowbar to a depth of 18 ins., the holes being about 2 ft. apart. Use a funnel and pour about ¼ to ½ lb. of fertilizer into the hole, water well, fill up with soil, and replace sod. Proceed to fertilize the lawn by broadcasting fertilizer in the usual way.

What will promote the growth of fall grass?   It is best promoted by using rich, screened topsoil to which has been added the fertilizer suggested in the Introduction. Thoroughly mix the fertilizer at the rate of 1½ lbs. of fertilizer to 1 bushel of soil. At the end of August apply 2 bushels to 100 sq. ft. and, using the back of a rake, work the material down among the grasses. Water thoroughly.

When is the best time to feed the lawn, spring or fall?   This depends on the type of fertilizer used. A quick acting one is best for spring use while one which releases nitrogen slowly like Golden Vigoro is best suited to use in fall. Spring *and* fall feeding is advised.

COMPOSTS

Should sifted compost be used to top-dress an established lawn? This is excellent practice. Apply in either spring or fall, first cutting the grass short so that the compost will work down to the roots when broadcast over the lawn surface.

How is compost applied to the lawn for top-dressing?   It is usually taken on to the lawn in wheelbarrows and spread roughly with a shovel at first. The final spreading is done by using the blunt teeth of a wooden rake. The back of an iron rake or a coarse broom may be used to spread the compost evenly over the area and at the same time work it down around the base of the grasses.

How is compost prepared before being applied to lawns?   The compost, when well rotted down, is first put through a ¼-in. wire screen. In large operations a power-revolving screen is used, but in small areas a section of ¼-in. wire mesh 4 × 3 ft. is nailed to a wooden frame which is tilted at an angle and supported by a prop. The compost is thrown against this to remove all foreign material like pieces of wood, stones, and coarse, unrotted compost. The screened compost is then thoroughly mixed with active fertilizer at the approximate rate of 4 to 5 lbs. of fertilizer per bushel of compost.

MANURES

What proportion organic fertilizer per 1,000 sq. ft.?   Apply 30 lbs. of dried poultry manure or 15 to 20 of tankage per 1,000 sq. ft.

To what depth must fertilizer be mixed with the soil?   Fork the material in and mix thoroughly with the upper 4 in. of topsoil.

What about the use of chicken manure on grass as a top-dressing? Chicken manure is a good grass stimulant. Use the dried product at the rate of 5 lbs. per 100 sq. ft.

Would you advise using well-rotted cow manure in preparing a lawn? How much on 1,500 sq. ft. of area? Because of its beneficial action on the soil and grass, rotted cow manure is the best of all materials to use in preparing soil for a lawn. If the soil is poor, apply a coating 2 to 3 in. deep.

How is cow manure best applied? Spread over the ground and dug into the soil. If used for top-dressing turf, it should be well pulverized, sifted, and a complete fertilizer added. (See questions on Top-dressing.)

Is mushroom manure for lawns? Mushroom manure, although not too rich in nutrients, is a splendid source of humus for lawns. It gives maximum results when worked into the soil at the time of preparation.

Can cottonseed meal and manure be used together when making a lawn? What proportion of cottonseed meal to manure? Yes, the combination is quite practical. The action of the cottonseed meal may be hastened somewhat by mixing with the manure. 1 part cottonseed meal to 15 parts manure is a good proportion.

Is sheep manure suitable for lawns? When is it best applied? Yes, a good grade of sheep manure makes a fine top-dressing for lawns. It may be applied any time during the season and is particularly valuable when applied early in spring and again in fall.

How much sheep manure should I use for 1,200 sq. ft. of lawn? Sixty lbs. is a good dressing. This is at the rate of 5 lbs. per 100 sq. ft.

I am told that if rotted cow manure is placed on my lawn in the fall I will not have to use commercial fertilizer on it for about 5 years. Is this true? Rotted manure is excellent material, but it should be used on the lawn in fall only after it has been so completely broken down that it can be worked in among the grasses and not merely left on top. One dressing in 5 years without any other fertilizer would not be enough to maintain the lawn. An annual dressing coupled with the use of a complete fertilizer would be better for keeping the turf in vigorous growth.

Do you suggest the use of farm manure for a grass lawn? If it is not fresh and if it spreads easily, farm manure can be applied lightly before the grass gets into very active spring growth. When growth is well under way, the surplus manure should be raked off.

I can get old hotbed manure. Is this good to dig into lawn? See question on mushroom manure. This is the same material.

Should lawns be covered with stable manure in the fall? As an agricultural practice, covering grass with manure in winter is an accepted one. On lawns it is sure to bring in weeds, and may injure the grass. It also makes a spotty lawn.

I have a large pile of gravel to dispose of. If I sift it, how much would I dare use to build up my lawn as a top-dressing and keep from rebuilding it? From the point of view of nutrients, sifted gravel would have no value as a top-dressing for a lawn.

What is the best time to fertilize the lawn with manure and commercial fertilizer? Apply in fall, but only if the manure is well rotted.

LIMING

What is the action of lime on lawn? If the soil is heavy, lime will help to keep it porous, permitting air and moisture to penetrate. Because of many decayed roots, lawns tend to become acid. Lime will correct this tendency and will release plant-food materials for the grasses.

What kind of lime is best to use? Pulverized limestone, also known as ground limestone, is the safest kind to use.

How much lime should be used on the lawn? Fifty lbs. per 1,000 sq. ft. is a maximum application for lawns at any one time. If a test reveals the need for more lime, put it on in two separate applications at an interval of several months.

How often should you lime a lawn? Frequency of liming will be determined by the type of soil, the grasses, and the amount of fertilizing materials used. The most accurate check is a yearly soil test for lime needs.

When is the best time of the year to put lime on the lawn? Late fall is best. When applied at this time, lime penetrates the soil to a greater depth than at any other time of the year.

Can lawns be limed in December satisfactorily? Yes, in fact December is a very good time to apply lime.

Is field lime good for lawns? When is it applied? Field lime is also known as agricultural lime, both being the same as ground or pulverized limestone.

I understand that "liming" an established lawn is ineffective, and may be harmful. Is there any way to correct an acid condition in such cases? Calcium in some form must be used to correct acidity and lime is the best form. Lime is not ineffective on an established lawn. It is needed. (See question on lime.)

DISEASES

What is the best prophylactic program to prevent brown patch or dollar patch? Keep the grass in steady growth, never allowing it to get a check by drying out. Keep regular mowing program with the length of the grass at 1½ to 2 in. If a bent lawn, do not exceed 1 in. Use a balanced fertilizer with a compost. In hot weather, especially when the humidity is high, rake with a wire rake twice a week. Every morning swish off the dew with a long bamboo pole. During June and July, and at other periods when fungus is feared, spray with a disinfectant. (See Introduction.)

What causes brown and dingy spots on our bent lawn grass? This is probably brown patch, a fungous disease that attacks most lawns in hot, humid weather but is more prevalent on bent lawns. The tops are injured, and in severe cases the roots, too, are killed. For control, see Introduction.

What is the best way to repair a lawn damaged with small spots? The grass seems to have died completely. The lawn was treated with arsenate of lead last year and with a combined fertilizer and grub killer this fall. This is probably dollar spot. It is not associated with grub-proofing treatment. Remove top 6 inches of soil and replace with fresh compost. Reseed (see Introduction). Or treat lawn area with crabgrass seedling killer, loosen soil with rototiller, and reseed.

What causes dollar spot, and what is the treatment? A fungus *Sclerotinia homoeocarpa*. See Control for Brown Patch, in the Introduction.

What is snow mold? This is a disease of closely cut turf observed at the edge of melting snowbanks. The disease will spread in high humidity at temperatures below 40° F. without snow. It is more prevalent on bent lawns (control same as brown spot).

Each spring I have a good grass lawn in a semi-shady location until we have a wet humid spell, then algae form and grass dies. Do you know of any treatment to prevent or lessen the damage caused by formation of algae? Algae or scum is usually related to wet-weather conditions or to wet areas in the lawn. Spray the infected spots with one of the preparations recommended in the Introduction. In a day or two rake the area over thoroughly and apply a dressing of sand.

What makes lawn grass turn yellow? We planted our lawn this fall. It came up very green, and now it has turned yellowish in spots. Spots where seeds fall too thickly and where extra fertilizer is concentrated will show this. Yellowing is also common in fall when too much moisture is present, evaporating too slowly from some areas. Run an iron rake through the spots and scatter sand mixed with a disinfectant. (See Introduction.)

What causes the ground to have white moldy spots after sowing grass seed? A common occurrence on newly seeded ground and somewhat related to the moisture conditions and the use of fertilizer. There is no indication that it is harmful. Should it increase before seed germination, sweep it with a broom to disturb it, allowing air to dry the surface. If it persists after germination, comb the spots once with a sharp-toothed rake.

INSECTS

What causes the lawn to have a yellow-brown color in late mid-summer, continuing until snow? This is probably due to the action of beetle grubs which hatch out during the latter part of summer and begin feeding upon the grass roots. Dig up some of the brown area about September. If this is the cause, the grubs will be found under the sod. (See Introduction for control.)

While working on my lawn this fall I discovered several beetle grubs working their way into the ground. How can I get rid of them and when is the best time to do it? The best control is to apply arsenate of lead in August or in April to poison the grubs which are hatched from the eggs deposited by the beetles in the sod. (See Introduction.)

Is there any point in watering down arsenate of lead into my lawn if the neighbors do nothing about the beetle grub? The grubs of the Japanese and Asiatic beetles feed on the grass roots. You will be protecting your own lawn from damage through the use of arsenate of lead.

How can I grub-proof my lawn? We have Japanese beetles. See Introduction.

Is there any more effective way to eliminate a bad infestation of chinch bugs, in a beautiful lawn, than tobacco dust, and when is the proper time to combat this pest? A 1 per cent rotenone dust is equally effective, using 25 lbs. per 1,000 sq. ft. for each brood. (See Introduction.)

PESTS

What should be put on lawn full of earthworms? Bumps all over lawn. The use of arsenate of lead (see Grub-proofing) will eliminate worms. If arsenate of lead is not available, try the following: Lime water made by dissolving lime and allowing the liquid to settle and clear poured over the lawn in the evening. This will draw the worms to the surface. They can then be brushed off the following morning.

I was advised to use mowrah meal to poison worms in my grass. What is it, and how should it be used? Is it poisonous to children? Mowrah meal is used in cases where earthworms are injuring young grass seedlings and the use of any other chemical might injure the young grass. Mowrah meal is made from the butternut tree of India. It is an effective worm killer when fresh, but it deteriorates with age, especially if stored in a damp place. Apply it dry at the rate of 15 lbs. per 1,000 sq. ft. and water it in with a hose. It can be handled with safety and is harmless to human beings.

Are ants harmful to a lawn? Yes, in the sense that they form galleries in the soil and disturb the grass roots. Besides, they throw up mounds of soil, covering the young grasses and killing them.

What is a good way to get rid of ants in the lawn? Mix one part of tartar emetic to 10 parts powdered sugar and sprinkle a little around the ant heaps. Repeat for a day or two. If tartar emetic is unavailable, use thallium sulfate or Antrol.

Our lawn is overrun with ground moles. Could you tell us some way to get rid of them? We have tried trapping and gas, but can't seem to get them. Try (1) carbon disulphide, a teaspoonful at points 5 feet apart; (2) household lye a teaspoonful inserted every 20 feet; (3) paradichlorbenzine; drop in the runways every 6 to 10 feet; cover with soil. Apply cyanogas by pumping into mole runs with dust gun made for the purpose by the American Cyanamid Co.

How can I keep the skunks from digging in my lawn? The skunks are looking for the grubs of the common June bug. The grubs which are close to the surface are relished by skunks. (See Control of Grubs.)

WEED CONTROL

I have started a new lawn and used pure seed. I want to keep it free from weeds. Can you outline a program for weed control? Top-dress the lawn each spring (see Top-dressing); fertilize again in fall. Do not mow too close, not below 2½ ins. Repair poor and bare spots immediately and eliminate weeds before they have a chance to become well established and before they seed. Treat for beetle grubs and other insects and be on the alert in June for fungous diseases, especially if the weather is moist and hot. (See Introduction.)

We have an established lawn that is becoming so infested with Crab Grass that eradication by hand is impossible. Can you suggest any method of control? It is known that Crab Grass will not thrive under the slightest shade, therefore allow the grass to grow after the first of June to shade the young seedling Crab Grass. Cut when 6 ins. tall, but only reduce it to 3 ins. Allow grass to grow tall before another cutting and repeat until the end of August, then gradually lower cut. Reseed and top-dress.

Crab Grass has taken my lawn. Grass was planted 2 years ago in about one inch of good soil on top of dirt and shale rock from basement excavation. Can I rebuild lawn successfully without much expense? How? The soil now is probably well supplied with seeds of the Crab Grass that will germinate when the weather is warm. An inch of topsoil is not enough to grow a turf so thick that it will crowd out the Crab Grass. In August treat with Lawn and Garden Cyanamid to kill ungerminated crabgrass seeds. Loosen surface with rototiller or hand cultivator. Add 2 inches of compost to surface. In September reseed with Red Top and Perennial Rye Grass in equal proportions, 4 lbs. to 1,000 sq. ft. These will grow fast. Keep height of grass at 3 ins. If Crab Grass shows up next spring, increase height of grass to 5 ins.

Lawn is patchy, with Crab Grass; very thin layer of topsoil; many stones from excavation of cellar. Topsoil very difficult to obtain. What would you do? (1) Allow Crab Grass to grow in July to form seed heads. Burn with a kerosene torch. Cut lawn, rake prostrate stems, cut again or burn. Repeat when necessary until September. (2) Rake off all stones; prepare for seeding. Seed with mixture for poor soils.

Will frequent reseedings of good lawn seed discourage Crab Grass? A vigorously pursued program of seeding and fertilizing in spring and fall to maintain a dense turf is the best means of controlling Crab Grass.

What method would you suggest for eradicating Crab Grass from a new lawn? Feed in spring to promote vigorous growth. Reseed all bare patches. Watch for seedling Crab Grass in June. Eradicate by hand if possible. Allow grass to grow to 2 ins. in July. Rake the lawn to bring up Crab Grass stems; pull out or cut with a mower. Prevent seeding the first year. Fertilize. Reseed in early September.

My new lawn, made in April, became infested with Crab Grass in July and August. Can anything be done in spring to prevent reappearance? The Crab Grass undoubtedly seeded itself, ready to reappear when warm weather arrives. The best spring preparation to combat Crab Grass is to promote a thick growth of lawn grass by fertilizing and seeding. Do not cut grass below 2 ins.

Why does Crab Grass spread to a healthy Kentucky Blue lawn when the Crab Grass was cut regularly to ½ in. and wasn't given a chance to flower? Crab Grass, when regularly cut, will form seed heads on stems that lie close to the ground, or on stems so short the mower cannot catch them. Hence the advice about raking to bring up the prostrate stems.

Since Crab Grass is perpetuated only from seed, how early in the summer will all of the last season's seed be cropping up? Crab Grass seed germinates when hot weather arrives—approximately about June, but often much earlier. Presumably any seeds that are lying on the surface will then grow. Where conditions are unfavorable, the seed may remain dormant even for a number of years before germinating. Some will spring into growth through the lawn if patches of grass die from dryness, disease, or injury.

Why is it always deemed necessary to remove Crab Grass from lawns? Even though this dies down annually, and is of coarse texture, it provides a thick mat of green all summer, and its removal is some-

times almost impossible. Crab Grass doesn't start to grow until June. This means that the lawn would be bare, or filled with other weeds, until the Crab Grass becomes thick enough to form a carpet. Crab Grass turns an ugly color in fall and with an early frost it disappears again, leaving an unsightly area that exists all winter. Control of Crab Grass is necessary to an orderly place.

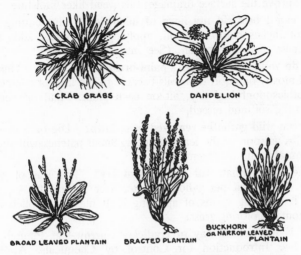

CRAB GRASS   DANDELION

BROAD LEAVED PLANTAIN   BRACTED PLANTAIN   BUCKHORN OR NARROW LEAVED PLANTAIN

SOME COMMON LAWN WEEDS

How is Crab Grass spread? Do you think it is possible that it is spread through the water hydrant? Does it come in grass-seed mixtures? It is spread by birds, and by animals that eat the grass and seeds; by wind, and by surface flooding. One plant is hardly noticed until it has seeded itself. Tests of several water-supply systems gave no indication of the presence of the seeds. New York State Experiment Station by test found it only in a few of the cheap seed mixtures.

What other names are usually applied to Crab Grass? Wire Grass, Summer Grass, Fall Grass, Water Grass.

We were told that White Clover in our lawn would die out the third year, but it's still going strong. Why? White Clover will be reduced when it builds up enough nitrogen in the soil to stimulate the grass, but it will return when the nitrogen supply in the soil is exhausted. This phenomenon has been called the clover grass cycle. (See Clover Control in Bent Lawns.)

How may I eradicate White Clover which is gradually covering my Blue Grass lawn? See Clover Eradication from Bent Lawns.

What other method than mowing can be used to eradicate a troublesome lawn weed which resembles a young pine tree and has deep, stringy, tough mats which have tremendous runners? This probably is

Cypress Spurge, a weed of sandy or gravelly soils. Full control is possible only when the roots are entirely removed from the soil, or crowded out by dense grasses.

Is there any way effectively to get rid of Creeping Jenny from a lawn without digging up the whole lawn and starting afresh? Raise the creeping stems with an iron rake and pull out or mow them close. Improve the surface drainage; this weed likes moisture.

How can I best rid my lawn of dandelions? By cutting top a couple of inches below the soil; applying a chemical adds to the effectiveness of the operation. (See Introduction.)

How do you get rid of devil's paint-brush in the lawn? This weed is found mostly on poor, thin soils because of the lack of competition. Try a tablespoonful of dry salt on each plant. Final answer is to build up the soil and reseed.

How can wild garlic be removed from lawn? Dig or hoe out the little bulbs as soon as the leaves appear. Small patches will succumb to sodium chlorate treatment.

In the lawn, what will kill ground ivy? The use of sodium chlorate, 1 to 2 ozs. per gallon of water over 100 sq. ft. A pressure sprayer is the best means of applying it. It may be applied in late fall without discoloring grass.

What is the easiest way to eradicate Narrow-leaf Plantain from lawn? See Introduction for Control by Chemicals. Apply the chemical about the time the seed stalk is forming.

How does plantain spread? By new shoots from the roots and by seeds. The seeds, coated with a sticky substance, adhere to shoes, clothes, and tools. They are thus carried and disseminated.

Is there any means of controlling quack grass growing on an embankment edging my garden? I haven't been able to keep it under control by hand. The only effective control for quack grass is to smother it out by laying boards over it, spreading tar paper, or heaping soil over it. Several weeks will be necessary to complete the process. Try disodium methyl arsenate.

What is the cause of sow-grass in lawn although calcium content is good? Sow-grass, sour-weed, or sorrel is not related to the alkaline or acid condition of the soil. This weed thrives in acid, alkaline, or neutral soils. Sow-grass commonly thrives on poor soil and in soils low in nitrogen. In good soils it cannot withstand competition with other plants.

How can a lawn be rid of sorrel, sow-grass, and chick-weed? It is too large to remake and it is but 4 years old. Has had some lime and a good fertilizer every year. Spray in June with iron sulfate, 1½ lbs. to 2 gallons of water. A second application may be necessary to complete the job. (See Introduction.)

How can weeds be kept from my lawn? I have 2 vacant lots on each side. (1) Burn the margins of the lots in spring and fall. (2) Cut down the weeds in the lots in June. (3) Maintain a close turf by seeding and fertilizing, so that no spots of bare soil appear.

Is there any method of eliminating weeds from a lawn other than by cutting out each individual root? Cover crops; turf building by top-dressing and seeding. The use of such chemicals as Crag 531, KOCN and PMAS is another means used in the battle to control weeds.

What is the cause of moss on a lawn? Moss is caused by poor drainage that keeps the areas damp; by poor aeration due to a hard, compact soil; and by a lack of fertility. It doesn't always indicate an acid soil.

My lawn does not do well. The soil packs hard and green moss appears on it. We dug it up twice and added peatmoss, fertilizer, and sand. We water and seed it, but no success. What would you advise? Spray the moss with a solution of iron sulfate. (See Introduction.) In a day or two rake off the moss. Dig the area at least 12 ins. deep. If the soil is heavy, work in small screened cinders. Lime, 5 lbs., and tankage or steamed bone meal, 4 lbs. per 100 sq. ft., will improve the soil texture and supply some lasting plant nutrients. If soil is sufficiently moist, do not water when seeding.

There are toadstools growing in my grass plot. What causes them, and how can they be eradicated? They appear in moist, warm weather and are usually associated with soils that are rich in organic matter, especially animal manures. Soak the ground thoroughly with Bordeaux mixture. Perforating the ground with a fork will help the solution to penetrate.

WEED KILLERS

Is there any chemical preparation that will kill weeds in a lawn? When temperature amd moisture conditions are right, iron sulfate has given good results. It is neither inflammable nor poisonous. Others are Crag 531, Scutl, Sodar and PMA. (See Introduction.)

Will the chemicals that are recommended for killing weeds in the lawn also kill the weed seeds? No, these chemicals, although successful under certain conditions in killing the weeds, have no effect on the weed seeds.

Can weed-control chemicals be used on all types of lawns? No, chemicals should not be used on new lawns, on bent lawns, nor on areas where Rough-stalked Blue Grass is growing.

Are weed-control materials dangerous to humans and animals? Sodium chlorate in contact with clothes and shoes becomes a fire hazard. It should not be spilled on wooden floors or other such places. Sodium arsenite, lead arsenate, and calcium arsenate are strong stomach poisons. The person handling them is safe if a dust mask is worn and the hands are thoroughly washed after using them. The treated turf is safe for man and animals after the material has been washed into the soil.

Will the chemical preparations that are used on lawns to kill weeds do so without injury to the grass? There is bound to be some injury to the grass following the use of chemicals, and if too much is applied, the soil may be made sterile. The moisture conditions of the soil, as well as the temperature prevailing at the time of application, will largely influence the result. There are many factors over which the operator can exert no control. Chemicals, therefore, are not to be entirely depended upon. *When using commercial preparations, adhere strictly to the manufacturer's directions.*

Temperature Zone Map
of the United States

On the following pages there is a map, marked off in zones extending from coast to coast. These different zones indicate variations in temperatures—from the highest in summer to the lowest in winter—that may normally be expected.

(*continued on page 690*).

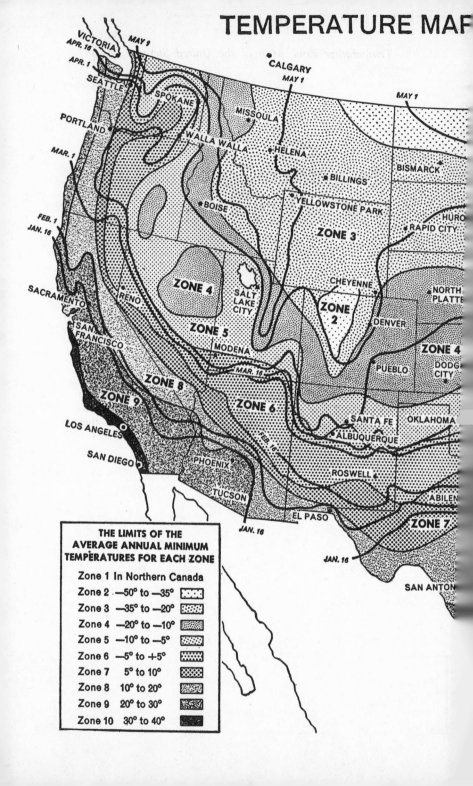

TEMPERATURE MAP

OF THE UNITED STATES

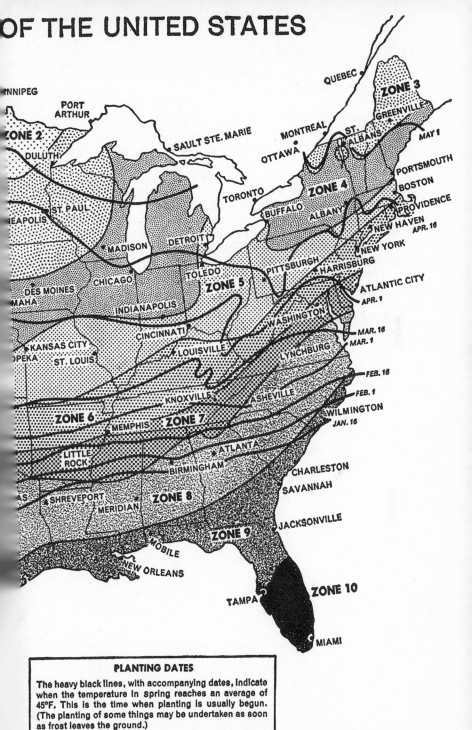

PLANTING DATES

The heavy black lines, with accompanying dates, indicate
when the temperature in spring reaches an average of
45°F. This is the time when planting is usually begun.
(The planting of some things may be undertaken as soon
as frost leaves the ground.)

(Page 690—zone map text)

No zone map small enough to be reproduced in a book can begin to cover in any great detail the many temperature areas that exist. It would be impossible to indicate accurately those of even a single state. There are many conditions, quite aside from latitude, which affect temperatures: altitude, for instance. The proximity of large bodies of water; prevailing winds and their velocity; the general terrain; the presence or absence of neighboring forests, are others.

The gardener, therefore, can find in a zone map only a very general sort of reference chart. He must be guided by local conditions. These he learns from personal experience, which takes a long time; or from the experience of others in his vicinity—which, while it may be less accurate, is immediately available, and hence is invaluable to the beginner.

Then, too, one can do much in the way of *creating* micro-climates on his own grounds. He can utilize existing shelters; and he can make others with fences, hedges, and tree and shrub plantings. By adding pools and other water features he can increase humidity and lower high temperatures.

The Home Vegetable Garden

INTRODUCTION

BY F. F. ROCKWELL

DESPITE the fact that it receives very little publicity in newspapers or "on the air", home vegetable gardening continues to hold an important place in horticultural circles. A recent readers' survey made by America's leading garden magazine indicated that more than 40% of its readers grew vegetables.

By far the most important reason for "growing your own" is that only by so doing can one be certain of getting vegetables of the finest quality. The local market gardener, who used to provide really fresh vegetables to neighborhood stores, is all but extinct. Vegetables that have to be shipped hundreds or thousands of miles before being graded and repacked for chain store distribution, lose much in quality and flavor. Many of the best quality *varieties* are never grown for market because they lack eye appeal, or do not mature uniformly so that a crop can all be harvested at one time; or because they do not keep well when shipped. Lettuce is an example. The real quality varieties, such as Mignonette and Oakleaf, are seldom if ever to be found in a market; the shopper must go without lettuce or be satisfied with the coarse and tasteless "cabbage-head" sorts which possess about as much flavor as a piece of aluminum foil. Such things as cantaloupes and tomatoes must be picked "firm" (a euphuism for half-green) in order to be safely shipped to the wholesaler, and by him distributed to the retailer. They may "color up" by the time the consumer gets them, but they never gain their full flavor, or their full value as food. Sweet corn that is picked not more than an hour or two before it reaches the table is very different from the semi-withered article in the super market bins.

Even if one does not have space for a full scale vegetable garden (say 50 × 30 feet) a supply of some of the most productive things—such as tomatoes, pole beans, broccoli, bush squash and lettuce—can be grown on a very small plot; or even in combination with garden flowers. In addition to getting better quality, the home gardener will find—after deducting the very few dollars expended for seed, fertilizer, spray materials—that he has made a considerable saving in dollars and cents.

Location

The location of the vegetable patch is important, but in the home garden plot there is not likely to be much choice as to where it can be placed nor as to the type of soil to be selected. One thing, however, is absolutely essential—an abundance of sunshine.

The shade of a tall tree that casts a constantly shifting shadow upon the vegetable rows will not be too serious; but every square foot of the vegetable patch should get daily at least 5 or 6 hours of full sunshine, and preferably more. Asparagus and rhubarb, which make their most rapid growth in early spring, will stand considerable shade later in the season; lettuce in hot weather is rather benefited by slight midday shade; but as a general rule—the more sun the better.

Size of Plot

"How large a plot should I have to make it worth while to grow vegetables?"

That is a question often asked by the beginner, and it is a very sensible one. The answer, however, cannot be too definite. A well-worth-while supply of quick-growing, closely planted crops—such as lettuce, onion sets for green onions, beets and carrots, radishes, mustard, cress, New Zealand spinach for a summer-long supply of "greens," and some tomatoes and beans (both bush and pole)—can be grown on an area as small as 10 × 10 ft., or in a long border 5 × 20 ft.

A larger plot, however, is advisable, if it is at all possible to secure one. On many a small place a plot at least 10 × 25 ft. can be provided for vegetables by the simple expedient of transplanting some of the existing shrubbery and possibly doing away with a shade-casting and root-hungry tree or two not really needed to maintain an attractive landscape planting around the house.

A plot 30 × 50 ft. (or its equivalent) is recommended by government experts as desirable where the object of the gardener is to grow an important part of the family's food supply. Unfortunately the prevailing "lot" system used in subdividing suburban real estate makes it impossible, in many cases, to allocate even this moderate amount of space to home food production. But very often it is possible for the homeowner to obtain the use of additional land at a not-too-inconvenient distance.

Drainage

"Can vegetables be grown on wet ground?"

Drainage is another important factor in the growing of vegetables. Soil in which the average run of flowers and shrubs grow will prove suitable for the vegetable patch; but a boggy or a swampy location, in which the water has a tendency to remain, after heavy rains, at less than 12 ins. below the surface, should be drained before any attempt is made to employ it for vegetable gardening.

Low-lying ground that has a tendency to collect and hold surface water, but is not actually swampy, can often be made suitable for vegetable growing by the simple process of using raised beds in which to plant. Such beds—made up into shape and size convenient for planting—are formed by merely digging out paths 4 to 6 ins. deep and distributing the removed soil over the surface of the beds. It is desirable, but not essential, to have the paths slope slightly to a low spot, so that surplus moisture draining from the beds into the paths will in turn be drained out of the paths.

Protection

Many a first-year gardener has seen much of his efforts go for naught because his plot was not adequately protected from mechanical injury—damage by dogs, rabbits, woodchucks, chickens (his own or his neighbors'), gophers, or children not trained to have a proper respect for plants. Without such protection the experienced gardener would not think of attempting to plant a garden where injuries from such sources are possible; but the average beginner will go gaily ahead and "take a chance"—only to regret it later.

The only positive protection from rabbits and other small animals is a substantial wire fence.

Chicken wire with a 2-in. mesh, and at least 2 feet (and better 3 or 4) in height, supported by posts firmly set in the ground at intervals of 8 or 10 ft., will supply adequate protection. The lower edge of the wire should be buried 2 or 3 ins. deep, and firmly pegged down to prevent small animals from burrowing under it.

Such protection will of course make an additional item of expense the first year, but it is a worth-while investment, and if kept in repair will last for many seasons. A 4-ft. fence will also serve as a permanent and space-saving support for tomatoes, peas, cucumbers, or (with some additional support) for pole beans. It is quite worth its cost for this purpose alone.

Equipment

The equipment required in caring for a moderate-sized vegetable garden need not be extensive or expensive, but it pays to have tools of the best. A spade, spading fork, or trowel of poor quality not only will be quite likely to break or wear out within 2 or 3 years, but will fail, while it is in use, to do as efficient work as a first-class one. The cost of a cheap garden tool, per year of service rendered, is likely to be 2 to 5 times as great as that of a good one.

For a small plot a spading fork, an iron rake, a hoe, a trowel, and a watering can are the essential implements. A hand duster or a small sprayer (preferably both) will be needed in the control of insects and diseases.

In addition to these tools for working the soil, *provision for watering* is most important. An adequate supply of water, used intelligently, will, in 3 seasons out of 4, increase the yields of many crops 50 to 100 per cent. (See Introduction to Section I.)

What Vegetables to Grow

"What vegetables shall I grow in a small garden?"

In arriving at the answer to this question, several things must be considered.

How small is the garden?

What vegetables does the family like?

What crops will do well in your locality?

Is it planned to grow some crops for canning, freezing and storing, or only summer supplies?

Without knowing the answers to these questions, it is not possible to suggest a definite list of what vegetables to grow. It is possible, however, to give the beginner some guidance. Here are 5 lists that will help him.

I. Vegetables That Yield Most

(In Proportion to Space They Occupy and the Time Required to Grow Them)

1. Tomatoes
2. Pole beans
3. Broccoli
4. Onions (from sets)

5. Beans, bush
6. Beets
7. Carrots
8. Chard
9. Chinese cabbage
10. Spinach, New Zealand
11. Mustard

12. Lettuce
13. Turnips
14. Rutabagas
15. Cabbage
16. Radishes
17. Spinach
18. Cress

II. Requiring Least Space

1. Tomatoes
2. Pole beans
3. Beets
4. Carrots
5. Leeks
6. Turnips
7. Rutabagas
8. Onions

9. Lettuce, leaf
10. Chard
11. Chinese cabbage
12. Beans, dwarf
13. Mustard
14. Radishes
15. Cress
16. Tampala

III. Requiring Considerable Space

(Those Marked "X" Should Be Provided with 30 Inches or More of Space Between Rows)

  1. Broccoli
  2. Cabbage
  3. Cauliflower
  4. Spinach, New Zealand
x 5. Corn
  6. Eggplants
  7. Peppers

    8. Parsnips
x 9. Potatoes
x 10. Sweet potatoes
   11. Peas
x 12. Cucumbers
x 13. Melons
x 14. Squash

IV. Short Season

(Can Be Followed by Other Crops)

1. Beans, bush
2. Beets
3. Early cabbage
4. Carrots
5. Kohlrabi
6. Lettuce

7. Mustard
8. Onions (from sets)
9. Peas
10. Radishes
11. Spinach
12. Turnips

V. Difficult to Grow in Many Sections

1. Cauliflower
2. Celery
3. Cucumber
4. Onions (from seed)

5. Peas
6. Potatoes
7. Pumpkins
8. Spinach

9. Squash (winter varieties)   11. Chinese cabbage
10. Melons

The Planting Plan

It will be seen from all this that the planting of a vegetable plot, *if it is to yield maximum returns,* is not merely a matter of walking into a seed store or a department store, picking out, more or less at random, a dozen or two packets of vegetable seeds, and then starting in at one end of the vegetable plot and sowing each as far as it will go.

A carefully thought out *plan* for the vegetable garden should be made before any seed is bought—and this is even more important for a small plot than for a large one.

Making such a plan is not difficult, and it is a lot of fun; quite as interesting as solving a crossword puzzle. The first step is to make an outline plan, showing the shape and dimensions of the plot. It will help greatly if this is drawn to scale—say ½ in. equaling a foot for a small plot; or ¼ in. or less to a foot for a larger one. On the former basis, a garden plot 20 × 30 ft. would be represented by a rectangle 10 × 15 ins. Each row of vegetables to be planted is then indicated. "Planting Tables" showing the proper distances between rows of the various vegetables and the amount of seed required for each 50 or 100 running feet of row are issued by State Experiment Stations, the United States Department of Agriculture, and many newspapers and magazines. The two plans reproduced herewith show how the finished planting plan should look.

Planning for Winter Supplies

In making up the planting plan it must be borne in mind that if vegetables for winter use are wanted—for canning and for storing—

Seed sowing in July and August provides vegetables for late fall and winter.

these must be provided for in the planting plan. Depending entirely on "surpluses" from the summer garden will *not* give satisfactory results.

If, for instance, canned tomatoes and tomato juice are wanted for winter, at least twice as many tomato plants should be set out as would be required to provide a summer supply alone. Beets and carrots to be stored for winter are not sown in early spring, but planted in late June or July, thus utilizing space from which quick-growing early crops have been removed.

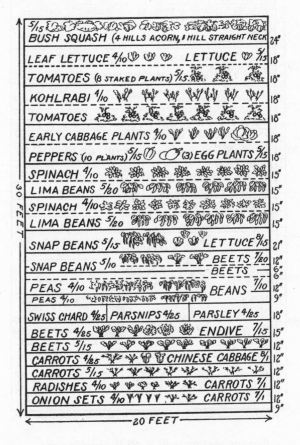

PLAN FOR A 20 × 30 FOOT GARDEN
Here full advantage has been taken of all available space by "interplanting"—note lettuce (sown April 10 and May 15), between rows where bush squash and tomatoes are to be planted May 15; also kohlrabi between rows of tomatoes. Space is also conserved by "succession" crops—beans after early peas, and Chinese cabbage after early carrots.

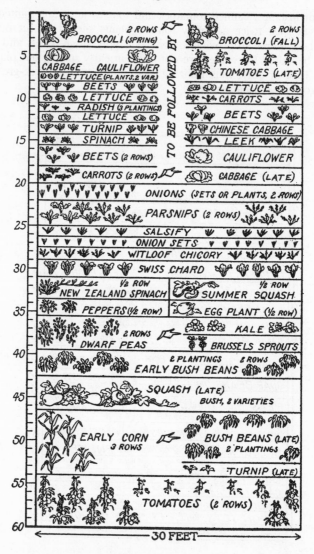

Planting plan for a 30 × 60 ft. vegetable plot.

Preparing the Ground

The beginner with vegetables is very likely to make the mistake of planting in ground that has not been thoroughly prepared. Most vegetables, to produce a full crop of first quality, must have conditions that enable them to grow rapidly and without a check. This means extremely thorough soil preparation, both mechanically and in the supply of plant foods.

Individual small gardens usually must be dug by hand. Proper digging involves slow, hard work. The longer in advance of planting the ground can be turned over, the better. Many gardeners dig the soil (where the earliest crops are to be planted) the preceding fall, turning it up roughly and thus getting the benefit of the pulverizing action of alternate freezing and thawing during the winter. A further advantage of digging in advance of planting is that weed seeds have a chance to germinate. The tiny weed seedlings are destroyed when the soil is worked over before sowing or planting.

Details of how to dig the soil, apply plant foods, and prepare for planting will be found in Sections I and II.

Sowing and Planting

"When should the vegetable garden be planted?"

In the well-arranged vegetable garden, planting is a more or less continuous operation from the time the frost is out of the ground until 6 to 8 weeks before hard frost is to be expected. The 3 most active planting periods, however, are very early spring, when the hardy, frost-resistant vegetables are put in; 4 to 6 weeks later, when the tender ones are planted; and 4 to 8 weeks later than this, when many crops for late fall and winter use are sown. North of the Mason and Dixon line these dates are normally:

Mid-March to mid-April for early, hardy crops.

May 1 to June 1 for tender crops.

Mid-June to late July for "succession" crops for fall and winter use.

The *hardy* vegetables include beets, carrots, turnips, lettuce, onions (sets, plants or seed), leeks, radishes, parsnips, salsify, witloof; the cabbage group (cabbage, broccoli, cauliflower); mustard, spinach, and chard; parsley; early celery; peas; potatoes.

The *tender* sorts include beans of all types; corn, tomatoes, eggplants, and peppers; the vine crops (squash, cucumbers, melons, and pumpkins); okra; sweet potatoes.

The *late* sorts (some of which are hardy and some tender) for fall and winter use include bush beans; beets, carrots, turnips, rutabagas; lettuce, Chinese cabbage; cabbage, broccoli, Brussels sprouts, kale.

Information covering the details of seed sowing, transplanting, cultivating, is given in Section II.

PLANNING THE GARDEN

Is it advisable to make a ground plan of the vegetable garden before planting? By all means. It will save time, seed and mistakes later on. However, seasonal developments may make minor changes necessary.

Should plant rows run east and west?   The direction of the rows is of minor importance. Other factors being equal, there is a slight advantage if the rows run from north to south.

When the land slopes from north to south, should the rows be made across the slope, or down it?   When the land slopes perceptibly, so that there is a tendency for heavy rain to run down the slope instead of soaking in, rows should always be run across the slope. If this makes the rows too long, a path can be run down the center of the plot cutting the rows in half. On steep slopes it is desirable to make a series of terraces, held in place by stone or permanent sod, so that the ground under cultivation will be fairly level.

In what direction is it best to plant a vegetable garden, north and south, or east and west?   It makes very little difference. What is more important is the location of the tall-growing vegetables with reference to the low-growing kinds. Plant the low plants on the east or south sides. Keep tall ones in the back where they will not shade the others.

Leaf Lettuce	Radishes	Green Onions From Sets
Early Peas 2 rows 4' apart	Late peas 2 rows 4' apart	
Earliest Spinach	Later Spinach	
Early Turnips	2nd Lettuce	2 Radishes
Early Cabbage and Cauliflower (Transplant)	Later Cabbage (direct seeding)	
Early Carrots	Early Beets	
Swiss Chard	N. Zealand Spinach	Parsnips - Salsify
Spanish Onions from Seedlings	American Onions from Seed	
Early Snap Beans	Later Variety of Snap Beans	
CORN Earliest Sweet Corn	2nd Early Sweet Corn	A very late Sweet Corn
TOMATO Earliest Tomatoes	2nd Early Tomatoes	Late Baltimore Type Tomato
Peppers	Eggplant	Bush type Summer Squash
Bush type Lima beans or Pole 'Lidaas on' slyplants		
Asparagus	Rhubarb	
Snap Beans First year only		

When, for any reason, it is desirable to run the rows the long way of the vegetable plot, they may be broken up into sections. Usually it is better to have the rows parallel with the short dimension.

Should root vegetables and leafy sorts be planted in alternate rows?   Since the fertilizer requirements differ—the leafy vegetables needing considerable nitrogen and the root vegetables a higher percentage of phosphorus and potash—it is usually more convenient to group the two types rather than to plant them in alternate rows.

Shall I plant rows of tall vegetables between those which are low growing?   So far as is practicable, tall growers should be together at the north end of the garden and low growers at the south or east. Often, however, rows of lettuce, radishes, or other low growers car be grown between tomatoes or other tall growers and can be harvested before the latter attain much height.

My garden is 22 × 30 ft. Should the tall vegetables, like corn and climbing beans, be on the south side of the garden; or where, to prevent shading smaller plants? Always plant tall-growing vegetables on the north or west side of the garden, if it is possible to do so.

On what sides of the garden should trees or shrubs be planted as a protection against winds? Ordinarily on the north and west sides, unless prevailing spring winds are from some other direction.

Shelter on the north or west aids materially in hastening growth of early crops.

Which vegetables are easiest to grow in a beginner's garden? Explain how to arrange beds. For vegetables easiest to grow, see Introduction to this section. It is not necessary to make beds in a vegetable garden. Practically all types do best planted on the level surface. Merely mark off rows for sowing the seed after ground is well worked and prepared. A narrow path may be left through the center or along the sides of the garden.

Have an area 50 × 15 ft. What is the best way to plant it? How can I obtain extra crops, earlier and later? Plant rows crosswise; 14 ft. of carrots, beets, leaf lettuce, or other greens are enough for one planting. For beans and other vegetables of which larger amounts are wanted, plant 2 or 3 14-ft. rows. Keep tall-growing sorts, like tomatoes, corn, or pole beans, at one end, preferably north or west. Set out *plants* of as many things as possible, such as cabbage, broccoli, lettuce, tomatoes, eggplant, beets, to get extra-early crops. Be ready to plant succession crops *at once*, when early crops are finished.

What are the so-called warm-weather plants? The warm-weather plants will be killed by even light frosts and cannot be placed in the garden until all danger of frost is past. The following may be grouped under this heading: beans (all types except Broad Beans), cucumbers, eggplant, muskmelon and cantaloupe, okra, peppers, pumpkins, squash, sweet corn, sweet potatoes, tomatoes, and New Zealand spinach.

Where can I get a chart on various vegetables—telling how long from seed to table? These vegetables are listed in tables in pamphlets on vegetable growing issued by most state experiment stations or in vegetable gardening books now on the market. Most of this information is given in seed catalogues but is not listed in tables. The information is given with the description of each vegetable. See individual vegetables, this section.

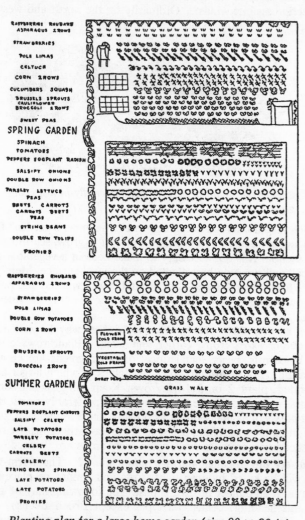

Planting plan for a large home garden (size 90 × 90 ft.), showing the spring crops, and the same area after replanting with late summer and fall crops.

What are the frost-hardy vegetables? Certain vegetables will live through a light frost after they come up or after they are set out. The following may be grouped under this heading: beets, broccoli, Brussels sprouts, cabbage, carrots, cauliflower, celery, chard, collards, dandelion, endive or escarole, kale, kohlrabi, leeks, lettuce, mustard greens, onions, parsley, peas, potatoes, radishes, spinach, and turnips, also Broad or Windsor Beans.

What are the planting and maturing times of different vegetables for a vegetable garden? See list of frost-hardy and warm-weather vegetables given in previous answers. Get length of growing season of each from the seed catalogues, garden manuals, or individual vegetables in this section, and plan crops accordingly.

On an edge of the city plot that gets hard in the hot summer and isn't very fertile, what crops would you suggest? Can more than one crop come off through the year? (Oklahoma.) Sweet potatoes, peanuts, bush beans for use dry, and soybeans. You would get only one crop of these. Any crop will take moisture. These will take the minimum amount of care.

What types of vegetables grow best in a sandy soil? While sandy soils are not recommended for commercial growing of some vegetables, satisfactory crops of most of them for home use can be obtained. The soil, however, must be kept well supplied with humus, and fertilizer in small amounts applied frequently.

What vegetables would grow best in ground that has never been cultivated before? This ground contains a lot of quack grass. More or less clay soil. This would depend largely upon the character of the soil. In general the root crops—beets, carrots, parsnips—do not do so well on new ground as on that which has been worked for a few seasons. This is especially true of onions. Turnips, however, often do excellently on new soil. Corn and the various vine vegetables, if generously manured, should do well. Also potatoes if the ground is suitable for them. However, the quack grass is likely to prove troublesome.

What is best to plant on newly cleared land; soil is a little sandy? Would potatoes do well? (Rhode Island.) Potatoes need good soil. This is especially true of the Chippewa variety. Snap beans and sweet corn and sweet potatoes would probably be all right. Other vegetable crops are heavy feeders and would require very thorough soil preparation.

Which of the common vegetables can satisfactorily be grown in clay soil? Practically all of the usual home garden vegetables can be grown in a clay soil if it is properly handled.

What small vegetables can be successfully raised to mature before September 15 on the north shore of Cape Cod? (Northeast storms are frequent and devastating.) Most of the frost-hardy plants, including cauliflower and turnips, or rutabagas.

What could you recommend for a vegetable garden 50 × 100 ft., having in mind northern New England? This will make a very big garden which should produce a surplus for sale unless you decide to grow a large area—say one half—in potatoes. That leaves a lot of space for cabbage, broccoli, cauliflower, carrots, turnips, rutabagas, lettuce, Swiss chard, and sweet corn. If you grow tomatoes, you probably should have at least two dozen plants.

What varieties of vegetables are suitable for home garden? We would like some that are best quality even though not practical to grow commercially. (New York.) These varieties are listed in literature which you can get from your local Agricultural College. Varieties are adapted to local conditions, and any general list would not necessarily be suited to your locality.

What are the best vegetables to plant in new ground? Vegetables that have a low-fertilizer requirement like turnips, rutabagas, peas, snap beans, radishes, and greens. With an application of lime you can grow almost any vegetable in the list but you may not get a big crop. How they will produce depends on the preparation of the soil.

We own a vacant lot on a hillside—the soil is heavy yellow clay (brick clay). What sort of garden should we contemplate? Tomatoes do well enough, but what else? If tomatoes do well on this soil, most other crops, except asparagus and melons, will do better. You will have to grow a short, stubby variety of carrot. You probably cannot grow parsnips. This soil needs considerable limestone, and the addition of plant refuse and coal cinders would tend to loosen it. Use limestone freely. Start out with a 25 × 25 ft. garden and grow tomatoes, cabbage, broccoli, and Brussels sprouts as well as lettuce, carrots, and beets. Then add to it each year.

What vegetables would you recommend for the garden of a person who works all day and has a minimum of time to work his garden? Most people work all day and have an hour to spend in their garden in the evening. It isn't a question which vegetable takes the least effort, but how big a garden you have. Radishes and turnips can be grown by sowing seed and forgetting them until it is time to pull them out of the weeds. Timely control of weeds when they are small will save much labor, regardless of the crop.

What kind of vegetables can be grown over a wire fence? Tomatoes, cucumbers, melons, squash, pole beans.

ROTATION

Is rotation of garden vegetables important? Yes, changing their location in the garden is desirable. If space permits, it is a good idea occasionally to give the whole garden a rest for a year or two.

**What is the difference between planting crops in "rotation" and in

"succession"?   Rotation cropping is the practice of planting, in a given area, different crops each year. Succession planting means following one crop with another in the same season—as the planting of snap beans in the row from which early carrots have been harvested.

Can you give me a good general rule for crop rotation?   Whenever possible avoid planting successive crops of the same botanical family on the same ground. Root vegetables should follow vegetables grown for their leaves or seeds, as chard, beans, etc. And vice versa.

How rotate plantings of vegetables to get the most out of them?   Simply change the location of the different vegetables from year to year. However, in a small garden most vegetables can be grown in the same spot for several years in succession, if ground is kept fertile.

Can you suggest a rotation of crops for the small garden?   If you can use a big enough area, a garden planted every other year or every third year makes a good rotation. The vacant years the garden may be seeded to green-manure crops which are plowed under or put into a permanent sod. If weeds are permitted to grow and are mowed down when they begin to blossom, they will make a good green-manure crop. Rotating the vegetable crops in a small garden, except in a limited way, is not practical.

How would you rotate a home garden, size 30 × 100 ft.?   If not all the area is needed, allow ¼ to ½ of the area to grow up to weeds each year but cut them off before they go to seed; or, better, sow a green-manure crop. If you need all the space (this is a large garden), shift the vegetables around so that those that grow in the north half this year would grow in the south half the next year.

What is the best method of practicing rotation in a small vegetable garden?   The best method on a small plot is to plant in one strip of the garden all crops which will remain for an entire season, such as onions from seed, parsnips, oyster plant, and witloof chicory; in another strip the cabbage group, such as cabbage, broccoli, cauliflower, Brussels sprouts, and kale; and in another section the short-season crops, such as lettuce, radishes, early peas, spinach, and mustard. The following year the location for each of these *groups* of crops may be shifted to another part of the garden.

In a small vegetable garden (16 × 40 ft.) do you recommend growing tomatoes in exactly the same location year after year? The same question in regards to corn?   It is better to change the location occasionally; if necessary they can be grown in the same place for 2 or 3 years.

Is it advisable to plant the same vegetable in the same space in the garden year after year?   No. See answer to previous question. Onions are a possible exception.

SUCCESSION PLANTING

What vegetables can be planted in the same area in a current season, one following the other? (New York.) There is no fixed rule for the use of succession crops. In general any vegetable that is removed from the ground sufficiently early in the season may be followed by any other which will have time to mature. Crops which are out of the way in time to be followed by others are early cabbage and cauliflower, lettuce, peas, beets, radishes, carrots, kohlrabi, turnips, and spinach; also onions from sets that are used green. These may be followed by peas (in cool sections only), late celery, and late plantings of lettuce, beets, carrots, and turnips; cabbage and cauliflower, and early varieties of sweet corn. Chinese cabbage, mustard, kale, and collards for late autumn and winter use may also be grown after early crops.

Define "intercropping." Is it desirable; and if so, why? The planting of rows of quick-growing crops, such as lettuce, radishes, or spinach, between widely spaced, slower-growing items, such as celery, peas, and tomatoes. It is desirable because, if carefully planned, it results in producing more food from a given area.

What are the combinations for intercropping vegetables? In general intercropping vegetables in the small garden gives less yield per square foot of space than extra-close planting without intercropping. There are some exceptions. Early cabbage, for instance, can be set between the rows where tomatoes are to be set out later. Bush beans can be planted between the rows where peppers and eggplant are to be set later. With close planting (12 in. between rows for many crops) the ground will be so completely covered that there is not room for another crop in between. In general two crops can be grown on the same ground only when one of them will be removed *before the other needs the entire space;* or when long-season crops are widely spaced to permit intercropping.

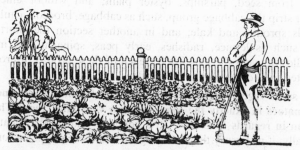

*The carefully planned and well-cared-for garden provides
a summer-long succession of fresh vegetables.*

How can I get the largest number of vegetables from a small plot of ground? By intensive culture. This implies careful planning, thorough soil preparation, adequate fertilization and irrigation, succession and companion cropping, proper selection of varieties, constant control of pests and diseases, and keen attention to details at all times.

What is the trick to intensive gardening? I have about 4 × 15 ft. to devote to vegetables. There is no trick or magic involved. Lay out 3 rows 13 ft. long. Plant 1 row of beets, 1 row of carrots to be followed by 2 rows of snap beans planted after roots are out. Plant ½ row radishes or onion sets to be followed by Swiss chard, and ½ row leaf lettuce to be followed by late turnips or other roots. Plant a staked tomato at each end of each row, allowing 1 ft. from stake to planting of other vegetables.

Is the custom of planting beans, corn, and pumpkins in the same space a good procedure? While this practice is often followed on farms, in the home garden it is better to keep them separate. In the small garden pumpkins have no place unless they can be planted near the edge of the plot and allowed to run out over the grass or climb along a fence.

USE OF SPACE

How many square feet will I need to supply each member of my family with vegetables for one year? No exact answer can be given because much depends upon soil fertility, crops grown, methods of cultivation, as well as varying needs of different families. From 500 to 1,000 sq. ft. per person would perhaps be a fair answer. This would include crops for storing and canning for winter.

What is the size of the smallest plot one can use for a vegetable garden? You can use a porch box and grow radishes and lettuce. An area 4 × 20 ft. is practical.

Would it pay us to have a garden in a space 10 × 17 ft.? There are just two of us. Yes, if you like to work in a garden. Highly perishable crops like lettuce and greens are always worth growing. You can grow a large part of your green vegetables in this area if you plan carefully.

Which are the five or six most practicable vegetables for an inexperienced person to try to raise in a little home garden (20 × 25 ft.) in New England? Tomatoes, pole beans, onion sets, radishes, Swiss chard, carrots, beets, broccoli, cabbage, and head or leaf lettuce. Follow one crop with another. Snap beans could follow radishes and lettuce.

What would you put into a 20 × 30 ft. garden so as to keep it working all season? For possible arrangement of crops, see plan on page 697; also Introduction to this section.

What vegetables shall I plan to grow in a medium-sized garden?

Anything you like with the exception of kinds which are known to be uncertain in your locality (consult local growers or your State Experiment Station) and such space consumers as corn, potatoes, squash, and pumpkins. (See Introduction.)

How would you plan a vegetable plot 60 × 90 ft. using principally the ordinary, easily grown items: corn, beans, peas, potatoes, tomatoes, radishes, etc.? Use 30 ft. of the 90 for potatoes and divide the remainder among other crops, giving most space to those the family likes best.

What vegetables shall I plan to grow if I have ample space? With ample space and limited labor grow any kinds you like that are known to thrive in your locality. (Consult local growers or your State Experiment Station with regard to these.) With sufficient labor (sometimes enthusiasm will substitute for this) try, in modest amounts, even the difficult kinds. (See Introduction.)

What is the best way a plot 50 × 200 ft. can be utilized so that it will include a home 20 × 32 ft.; a little orchard of about 18 trees, a vegetable garden, and space for housing chickens? I would suggest that the chickens and the orchard occupy the back 50 × 100 ft., with the poultry house in the center. The area between the house and the orchard could be the vegetable garden. If the house used up 75 ft. it would still give you a 25 × 50 ft. vegetable garden.

How can I plan my garden 90 × 100 ft.? My husband died and I want to make a garden for myself and two children. This is almost a quarter of an acre, which would require a tremendous amount of work unless you possess a small power cultivator or rotary tiller. An area 25 × 50 or 75 ft. will give you all the vegetables you need for your family. You might use that much for the garden and use the other land for some crop like tomatoes, potatoes, or sweet corn which you could sell to the neighbors.

What is the most profitable crop on an acre lot (part sandy and part loam and clay)? Have raspberries and strawberries, corn, and most garden vegetables. (Ohio.) This depends on local weather and market conditions. Any crop is profitable if it will grow in your locality and you have a market for your produce. Strawberries, with irrigation and mulching, are usually profitable. If your vegetables are good and you live in a section where you can sell good produce, a general assortment may be profitable. Usually the more you have to do to grow a crop the more you will get out of it. First you must learn to grow the crop well, and then sell it to good advantage.

What is the proper arrangement and size of a good, substantial vegetable garden for a family of three? A garden 25 ft. wide by 50 or 60 ft. long probably will be large enough. Don't plant too much of any one thing. See answers to previous questions.

Which vegetables would you recommend for planting in a small

area (10 × 12 ft.) that would produce the best yield? Onion sets, leaf lettuce, carrots, beets, 6 staked tomato plants, and 2 rows of snap beans. Make more plantings after the first crops are finished.

What vegetables could I plant in a sunny place where I have dug an extra foot of border on my flower bed; also in an old rose garden about 9 ft. square? Radishes, leaf lettuce, carrots, and beets in the narrow border; staked tomatoes and snap beans in the rose garden. Plant the beans between the tomato plants.

What is the usual size of a town back-yard garden? What vegetables could best be grown in that size? What could be used for second-crop or succession planting? An average-size back-yard garden would be 20 × 25 ft. This will grow most vegetables for a family of four, and give some to can. Lettuce, beans, beets, carrots, cabbage, tomatoes, and onions (from sets) are good to start with. You can make several plantings of everything except tomatoes. Rutabagas, turnips, spinach, and lettuce are good for fall.

Would you advise planting a few vegetables in border flower beds? We have very little rainfall, must irrigate most of year. This is easily done. Plant tall vegetables north and west so they won't shade the low-growing plants. Keep the low-growing plants near the edges on the east or south side. Tomatoes may be set 2 ft. apart and trained to stakes set alongside the plants. Asparagus makes a good background for a flower garden. Low-growing plants may be set or planted in rows in the borders. Avoid crowding for vegetables which set pods or fruits.

We are planning to convert some of our flower garden into a vegetable garden. Will you suggest suitable vegetables to plant against a brick wall—space 4 ft. wide, facing south? Tomatoes, pole beans (especially limas), and cucumbers trained on trellis would do well in such a situation.

What vegetables can be grown in flower beds in limited space? Half-a-dozen tomato plants scattered along the back of the flower beds, tied to stakes so they won't sprawl. Radishes and lettuce may be planted in the border toward the front. Asparagus may be planted so that the summer growth will serve as a background. Snap or pole beans may be planted between later-flowering plants. Rows of carrots and beets may be grown between rows of flowering plants, as they do not take much space. Onions may be grown from sets. There is always the possibility of growing a few cucumber vines in a tub or barrel in a vacant corner.

What steps must one take to start a home garden? (Massachusetts.) (1) Decide on your crops and how much you want of each. (2) Select the ground and make your plan. (3) Sow seed for plants 5 to 7 weeks before you plan to set them outside. (4) Get your ground ready with lime and fertilizer. (5) Plant frost-resistant crops (see list) about 3 weeks before the last spring frost (usually about mid-May). (6) Get warm-weather plants started, to have them ready by the middle of May.

LOCATION

What exposure should I choose for my vegetable garden?   Providing the site is sunny, the precise exposure is less important than soil and other details. A south or southeastern exposure will produce earlier crops. Even a north exposure has advantages for cool-weather crops, such as late peas and summer lettuce.

What is the ideal location for a vegetable garden?   A well-drained, gentle slope facing the east or southeast, in full sunshine throughout the day and protected by shrubbery or a fence on the north and northwest.

Can I have a successful vegetable garden in a low, wet spot on my grounds? The soil is rich.   Vegetables must have good drainage. The only way you can successfully grow them in the location mentioned is to drain the area thoroughly by ditching, or tiling if necessary. (See Section I, also Introduction to this section.)

What food plants can be planted in wet places such as undrained muck ponds, bayheads, etc.?   There are no vegetables which will grow in undrained soil. Of course you must stay away from salt water. Make beds 4 to 6 feet wide and at least a foot higher than the paths to get rid of the free water. Then you can grow lettuce, carrots, beets, collards, and similar types. If the soil stays fairly dry, celery, tomatoes, and beans will grow well.

Can my vegetable garden be made on the west side of my house?   This is not a good spot for vegetables. Try to find a place that has full morning sunshine and as much in the afternoon as possible. West side would do if not too close to house.

How much sunshine is necessary for vegetables?   Vegetables need all the sunshine they can get. A minimum of 5 to 6 hours of direct sunshine per day.

What's the best vegetable to plant in the shade?   There are none that will grow well without some sunshine. With partial shade, but sunshine in the morning, some of the leafy vegetables grow fairly well.

What vegetables are most suited to a shady garden? Will any of them yield successive crops, or is each good for only one crop?   Vegetables to amount to anything must have sunshine during the morning. The leafy vegetables are the only ones that will stand any shade. If they will grow, they may be planted in succession.

What vegetables will grow close (5 ft.) to the north side of a house?   Only leafy vegetables, providing the wall isn't concrete. Concrete walls draw the moisture from the soil. These vegetables will not grow well unless there are 5 to 6 hours of direct sunshine.

I have a plot of 36 × 50 ft., one side of which lies in the shadow of my house. What vegetables (if any) can I plant in those shadows? If the garden is to the south of the house, you will have little difficulty. If it's on the west side, your only chance is some greens that may grow in the shadow.

We have a large space of fertile ground underneath our fruit trees which gets the sunshine only part of the day. Have not planted anything that has grown satisfactorily. Will you please inform me as to which vegetables will grow well in partial shade? Leafy vegetables are the only ones that will do well. Your difficulty may be that the tree roots rob the vegetables of water and fertilizer.

Would it be worth while to dig up a partially shaded area to plant vegetables such as beans and tomatoes? No, absolutely not. Some of the leafy vegetables might make a fair growth but not tomatoes and beans.

How can I raise a vegetable garden surrounded by oak trees 25 ft. or more in height? Hardly worth trying unless trees are 20 ft. or more from vegetable plot. Plants must get morning sun at least, and the roots of the trees would rob the vegetables of water and nutrients.

What vegetables will grow near maple trees, in dry earth? With water and morning sun and some liquid fertilizer, beans and tomatoes; but the ground would have to be thoroughly watered frequently. Such a location is not suited to vegetable growing.

Our new home was built on land which formerly was occupied by many tall trees, mostly oaks. We have some trees left which shade all parts of our grounds at some part of the day. The soil is acid and heavy. We have turned over half of the back yard and removed stones, roots, etc. Some we left rough, and another section we planted to rye and vetch, intending to turn it under in the spring. Can you suggest vegetables which we might grow under these conditions? To grow good vegetables stay at least 10 feet from the outer edge of the branches, and where the vegetables will receive at least the morning sun. The biggest problem is to keep the roots of the growing trees from robbing the water and fertility from the vegetable plants. Put on sufficient pulverized limestone to sweeten the soil. If this soil is very heavy, it should have considerable leaf mold or manure, or even coal cinders, mixed with it.

What flowers and vegetables will grow close to the shady side of a privet hedge? Most vegetables, if the privet does not rob the vegetables of water and fertilizer. The shading effect is not serious unless it is on the south side of the vegetable plants, when it may produce too much shade.

Are there any vegetables that will grow and produce in a plot 4 × 20 ft., which gets only morning sun and is within a few feet of pine

and birch woods? The main problem here would be water and nutrients for vegetables. The shading is not so serious. Probably frequent watering would be required.

How do you develop a hillside garden? This requires the building of terraces, the width of which will be determined by the steepness of the slope. Rows must run crosswise of the slope.

What vegetables may be grown in sandy soil where wind and salt spray attack them? We have grown kale, broccoli, and lettuce fairly well. What others would you suggest? This can only be answered by your experience. Any smooth-leafed vegetable, including asparagus, should grow well. Plants with hairy or rough leaves probably would be injured by any appreciable amount of spray.

What vegetables grow and produce best in sandy and decomposed granite soils? This depends on how well the soil has been fertilized previously. If the soil has some lime in it, most vegetables may be grown, providing sufficient water and plant nutrients are added. Dissolving a teacupful of a mixed fertilizer in 3 gallons of water and watering the plants with this every 2 weeks will help. These usually are good soils.

SOIL PREPARATION

PLOWING

What's the case for fall plowing versus spring plowing? Plow in fall, leaving furrows turned at an angle. Winter weather breaks up clods and aereates soil through freezing and thawing. Many overwintering insect enemies are turned up, and there is less liability of leaving air pockets in the turned soil. Light, sandy soils may suffer from washing by winter rains and usually are best left until spring for plowing.

When plowing up a sodded plot of ground for the first time, to be used for a vegetable garden (in the spring), how should the ground be treated? Plow in the fall, leaving the furrows on an angle instead of turning them over flat. This is done to avoid leaving a layer of sod between the subsoil and the surface soil. If lime is needed, apply that also in the fall, harrowing or raking it in lightly so that rains will not wash it into hollows and low spots. If the sod is heavy, the plot should be plowed again in the spring at right angles (if replowing is necessary) to the direction in which it was first plowed, in order that the decomposing sod may be more thoroughly broken up and mixed through the soil.

When should spring plowing be done? Plowing or digging should not be undertaken in the spring until the ground has begun to dry up after spring frosts are out. A simple test is to squeeze a handful of soil into a firm ball. If this ball under pressure from the fingers crumbles apart readily, the soil is ready for plowing. If it tends to remain in a sticky mess, plowing or digging should not be attemped until it has dried out further.

Correct and incorrect methods of digging under manure. It should be thoroughly mixed through the soil (as at right) instead of being covered in a solid layer (left).

Should the vegetable garden be spaded up after the harvest in the fall and then again in the spring before the new planting? Or is spading in spring sufficient? Spading or plowing in the fall is of advantage on most soils, except very light, sandy ones. Ground thus prepared in the fall will need much less work done on it in the spring to get it ready for seed sowing and planting.

When should the new vegetable garden be plowed or dug? Any time before seed-sowing time. Heavy or medium soils are better plowed or dug in the fall; very sandy soils in the spring. But if you have missed out on fall preparation, don't hesitate to begin a new garden in spring.

When should the established vegetable garden be plowed or dug? If the soil is at all clayey, it should be turned over in the fall and left in a rough condition all winter. Very light, sandy soils should be plowed or dug in early spring.

Rolling the newly made garden plot, especially if the soil is light, aids in preparing a level, even bed for seed sowing.

How deeply do you think ground should be turned in plowing or digging for a vegetable garden? As deeply as possible providing (1) that not more than an inch or so of unkind subsoil is turned up; (2) that labor is available. From 8 to 12 inches is a fair depth, but a somewhat greater depth is by no means excessive as the ultimate goal.

Does deep preparation of the soil help to make long, sturdy roots?
Yes indeed. All crops benefit from deep soil preparations. Onion roots
have been traced to a depth of 5 ft. Parsnips may be grown that are
3 ft. long, with roots extending deeper.

*In digging soil with shovel or spading fork, thrust blade or
tines straight down instead of at an oblique angle. Hoeing or
cultivating while weeds are very small is easy work that will
save backbreaking "chopping" later on.*

Should ground be more deeply plowed in dry areas?   In general,
yes. Some sandy soils are exceptions. Especially in dry locations is it
necessary to encourage roots to strike deeply in search of moisture.

**What do you think of the theory that ground should not be plowed,
but only lightly disked?**   It is good to see that you regard this only
as a theory. It may work on a few special soils (perhaps on extremely
sandy soils) but it should not be recommended as a practice for the
ordinary gardener or farmer to follow.

**Do you advise plowing old sod ground, not used for 15 years, in
late fall?**   By all means plow in the fall if possible. Leave the ground
in ridges rather than turning it over flat; this will permit alternate
freezing and thawing during the winter to pulverize it more thoroughly.
If the ground slopes, plow it across the slope of the land, to check
any tendency to erosion. If you live in a suburban area where plowing rigs
cannot be readily rented, a man with a rototiller may usually be hired
to turn over small pieces of ground. These small machines do an excellent job. If your grounds extend to even as much as an acre or two
and the actual creation of your garden is still ahead of you, the purchase of a rototiller is often a wise move.

LIME

What is the best ground conditioner?   For most soils raw ground
limestone is the best conditioner, as it both improves the mechanical
condition of the soil and corrects acidity. For most vegetables, however, lime should not be applied to soil that is alkaline. Under such

conditions gypsum or land plaster is better. Ashes and sifted cinders improve the physical condition of any heavy soil.

Should lime be spread over the vegetable garden early in the spring or in the fall? It is much better, if possible, to apply lime in the fall after the ground is plowed or dug; or upon the surface. Then cultivate it in so that heavy rains will not wash it to low spots.

What are the relative lime requirements of the common vegetables? With few exceptions most vegetables do best in a soil which is slightly acid—that is, a soil showing a pH reaction of 6 or 6.5 to 7. (See Acidity.) The vegetables most tolerant of a somewhat acid soil are potatoes, sweet potatoes, watermelon, (to a somewhat less degree) eggplants, peppers, and tomatoes. Those least tolerant of acidity (and therefore most in need of lime) are asparagus, cauliflower, celery, leeks, lettuce, onions, and spinach.

SOIL PROBLEMS

What soil treatment do you recommend for a lawn dug up for a vegetable garden? If the sod is very heavy, it may be desirable to remove the turf, cutting as shallow as possible and making a compost heap of the sod thus obtained. However, if the sod can be dug under (mixing it thoroughly with the soil so that it does not remain in unbroken lumps), that is preferable. On soil so prepared an application of 3 to 5 lbs. per 100 sq. ft. of a complete fertilizer should give good results the first year.

Do you think removing all the stones from a vegetable garden a good idea? Our garden was cleared of every stone for some 10 ins. down; lots of manure was spread over the ground in the winter. My theory is that the fertilizer sank too far into the ground, as there was no foundation, and was lost to the crop. Year before we had a fine crop—only second time for using this garden. Removing stones is not at all essential, except as their absence makes it easier to work the soil. But taking them out would not injure the soil, nor make fertilizers leach away more quickly. Roots of most vegetables go down 2 ft. or more.

How can I prepare a 10-acre plot to good advantage? First supply sufficient liming material to bring the pH up near the neutral point, and plant some cover crop to plow under. Then fertilize for the vegetable crops.

What types of vegetables can be grown in clay-loam soil? How can that kind of soil be made to grow any kind of garden? This is a cold, late soil, best suited to frost-hardy plants like members of the cabbage family. Such soil should be well limed and have coal cinders and organic material mixed with it. After a year or two of use it should be suitable for most vegetables.

Our vegetable garden has a rather heavy clay soil. What treatment would you advise?   Manure, compost, and humus supplied by growing green-manure crops will all help to lighten a clay soil. Applications of lime or of land plaster (gypsum) will also help greatly in improving the mechanical condition and make it less likely to form hard lumps. Clay soil should never be dug or cultivated while wet.

Have never done any vegetable gardening; want to dig up part of my lawn to plant a vegetable garden. Only about 2 ins. topsoil, the rest sand. How go about it?   Your problem is a difficult one, as very shallow soils are not the best for vegetable growing. Dig about 4 ins. deep, breaking the sod up as thoroughly as possible and mixing it through the soil. If well-rotted manure can be obtained in the spring, apply a heavy coating—2 to 4 ins. deep—and dig this under just sufficiently to cover it up so that the surface will be clear for planting. Your problems will be to keep the soil well supplied with humus to absorb and hold moisture; sandy soils dry out too rapidly. In using fertilizer, make frequent small applications while the plants are growing instead of putting it on in advance of planting, as is often done on heavier soils.

How is newly spaded soil prepared for vegetable garden?   If the soil is acid, lime should be added and cultivated in. Unless the soil is already in very good condition from previous applications of fertilizer, 4 to 5 pounds of complete fertilizer per 100 sq. ft. is broadcast and raked in before planting. Before seed sowing the surface of the soil should be gone over with an iron-toothed rake, removing all small stones and trash and leaving it as smooth and level as possible.

What is the best time to prepare the ground for early planting of potatoes, corn, and various vegetables?   As a general rule it is best to prepare the ground for planting a month or more in advance. This is particularly true if sod or a green-manure crop is to be turned under. Advance preparation makes possible partial decay of the green vegetable matter before the vegetable crop is planted, otherwise the decaying plant material will temporarily draw upon the nitrogen in the soil, thus robbing the planted crop, unless additional nitrogen is added when the crop is planted. Wherever very early planting is to be done, it is of advantage to plow the ground the previous autumn if it is possible.

How do I prepare a former flower garden for a vegetable garden and what are the best vegetables for an amateur to grow?   A flower garden which has been well fertilized should be in excellent shape to grow vegetables. Thorough and deep digging and the application of a complete fertilizer will put it into condition. The vegetables which it would be advisable to grow will depend on the size of the plot and the gardener's experience (see lists in the Introduction to this section).

If clay soil is turned over in the fall, how early can the first vege-

tables be planted in spring? (In northern Ohio.) Clay soils plowed or dug in the fall can usually be planted much earlier than if the preparation of the ground is left until spring. The hardy crops (see Introduction) can be put in just as soon as the soil is sufficiently dry to be cultivated and raked without sticking to the tools and forming hard lumps. Ordinarily this would be in early April, but will vary with the season.

Is it necessary to have different types of soil for the common vegetables, such as carrots, lettuce, cabbage, etc.? No. In a well-prepared garden plot practically the complete list of vegetables can be grown satisfactorily. It is important, however, that the soil be slightly acid in reaction. If it is too acid or too alkaline, many vegetables will not do well. (See Acidity.)

We live near the salt water; our soil is not very good. The only flowers that we seem to grow successfully are marigolds and zinnias. If this soil agrees with them, what vegetables could we grow? If protected from high winds and salt spray, most vegetables can be grown.

In our vegetable garden we always have excellent results with green beans, tomatoes, butter beans, cucumbers, but poor results with English peas, carrots, spinach, beets, and turnips. The soil is sandy, with pine trees in adjoining pasture. Does this experience suggest something lacking? (Texas.) This indicates that the soil may be low in lime, boron, and potash. A complete soil test should be made, and if calcium is low, some pulverized limestone (preferably dolomitic) should be spread on the surface when the soil is prepared.

Why did my carrots, beets, and turnips grow only to about ¼ normal size? My flowers also mostly stayed very short with small blooms. Ground hadn't been turned over in 75 years. Does it require some special care? Few vegetables (particularly the root crops) do well on soil not previously cultivated. With good culture you will undoubtedly see an improvement each year for two or three seasons. Other than the usual cultivation, the incorporation of humus, and fertilizing, the soil probably does not require any special treatment.

I have heard that poor soil can be improved by adding something called Krilium. Is this true? There are a number of so-called "soil conditioners" now on the market of which Krilium is one of the best. These materials are valuable in keeping soils in good mechanical condition *after* they have been improved by the application of lime, and the incorporation of humus. Some of the companies selling these "conditioners" claim that—simply by applying them to a poor soil— it can be magically transformed into fine loam. Tests have proved however, that their use is of little permanent value unless the soil is first put in friable shape.

FERTILIZERS

What is the difference between "fertilizer," "manure," and "plant food"? In a general sense, any material added to the soil which will aid plant growth is a fertilizer. As more commonly used, the term "fertilizer" refers to manufactured products in dry form sold in bags; "manure" to such animal products as cow, horse, or sheep manure. "Plant food," as usually employed, is an incorrect term; the only true plant foods are manufactured or developed *within the plant*. However, the term "plant food" is frequently employed as a polite word for fertilizer or manure.

What is the difference between organic and inorganic fertilizer? The former is made from animal or vegetable sources, such as bone or blood or cottonseed meal; the latter from mineral or synthetic substances, such as phosphate rock, nitrate salts, or potash salts.

What is meant by the term "complete plant food"? As used by manufacturers, a commercial fertilizer containing all three of the main elements which are required for plant growth, i.e., nitrogen, phosphorus, and potassium. "Complete fertilizer" is the correct term, rather than complete plant food.

What is the meaning of the three numbers which appear on every package of complete fertilizer, such as "5–10–5"? The first number always stands for the percentage of nitrogen, the second for the percentage of phosphorus, and the third for the percentage of potassium.

What is meant by "trace elements"? Do any complete fertilizers contain these? Trace elements are substances such as manganese, boron, sulfur, and iron, required for plant growth but in smaller quantities than the three main elements (nitrogen, phosphorus, and potassium) and usually present in most soils. Yes, most complete fertilizers do contain some of the trace elements, either in the raw materials from which the fertilizer mixture is made, or added purposely to supply them.

What is the best all-round garden fertilizer—one which is of high, medium, or low percentage in plant nutrients? A medium-percentage fertilizer such as 5–10–5 or 4–12–4 is usually recommended for general garden use.

What is a "starter" or "transplanting" solution? This consists of a small amount of high-analysis chemical fertilizer dissolved in water. A teacupful is poured directly on the roots of plants when they are transplanted or a teacupful is poured directly on the seed for every 3 ft. of row. An ounce of 13–26–13 fertilizer, or 3 ozs. of a 5–10–5, in a gallon of water, makes a starter solution.

What is a "side-dressing" solution? This is merely the same as a starter solution, but sometimes made stronger, used to pour around the plants after they are well established and growing. Two to three times as much fertilizer is dissolved in the water. It gives a quick response and there is somewhat less danger of burning the plants than when a dry fertilizer is used.

Liquid fertilizer is made by dissolving the dry material—at the rate of a level tablespoonful or two (depending on the strength of the fertilizer) to a gallon of water.

How should nitrogen be applied to the soil?   In complete fertilizer, or in the form of ammonium sulfate, nitrate of soda, dried blood, or tankage; usually at time of transplanting or in early stages of plant growth: 2 or 3 lbs. per 100 sq. ft. of row. Helps in development of leafy vegetables.

When and how should phosphorus be applied to vegetable garden? Apply phosphorus in complete fertilizer, or in superphosphate, at time of soil preparation, at rate of 3 to 5 lbs. per 100 sq. ft. Superphosphate is especially valuable in preparing new ground.

When should I apply potash, and in what form?   In a complete fertilizer, 3 to 5 lbs., or in the form of muriate of potash 2 to 3 lbs. per 100 sq. ft. Or add this material to the manure or compost used in the garden. Especially helpful in building up soils which do not grow good root crops or produce satisfactory stem plants, such as celery.

When should dried blood be used as a fertilizer?   Dried blood is used when nitrogen is needed more slowly than it is supplied by nitrate of soda to stimulate vigorous growth. Usually applied at rate of 4 lbs. per 100 sq. ft.

What is "superphosphate," and what is its chief use in the vegetable garden?   Superphosphate is ground and treated phosphate rock that carries (usually) about 20 per cent of phosphorus. ("Treble" phosphate carries about 45 per cent.) Used in almost all complete fertilizers. On most new soils can be applied separately in addition to other fertilizers, being thoroughly mixed with the soil, in advance of planting, 4 to 6 lbs. per 100 sq. ft.

Is nitrate of soda of any particular advantage in vegetable growing? Yes, because it is one of the quickest-acting sources of nitrogen, carrying 15 per cent nitrogen. Particularly valuable as a side dressing (see Index) in early spring, when nitrogen in soil becomes available slowly. Should *not* be used on most crops as they approach maturity.

Apply dry, 2 to 3 lbs. per 100 sq. ft. of row; or at same rate, diluted in water, 1 tablespoonful to 10-qt. can.

Side-dressing applied (in rings)
to young eggplant and cabbage.

What is the difference between nitrate of soda and ammonium sulfate? The latter is used like the former; contains about 20 per cent nitrogen; tends to increase soil acidity.

I find "tankage" and cottonseed meal listed in some catalogues. What are they, and how used? Like nitrate of soda (see above), they are nitrogen fertilizers, the former made from slaughterhouse refuse, the latter from cottonseed. Used like nitrate of soda, but as they carry only about half as much nitrogen, can be applied more generously. Safer to use, but slower in effect. Tankage contains some phosphates. Cottonseed meal is a *complete* fertilizer with a 7–3–2 analysis.

Can a successful garden be made using only complete fertilizers and peatmoss or humus without manure? If manure is not obtainable, a successful garden can be had by planting and turning under cover crops yearly, maintaining compost heaps to be used in the garden when rotted, and adding complete fertilizer when preparing ground at planting time, and as side dressings during plant growth.

If both are available, which do you recommend, manure or fertilizers? Use *both:* manure when preparing ground and when planting many crops; complete fertilizers just before planting and as side dressing during growth of plants.

Is there a good general fertilizer for the vegetable garden? Most fertilizer companies put out a "Vegetable Formula" fertilizer designed for use with most vegetable crops. This varies somewhat in different sections, according to soil and climatic conditions. To get the best for your particular needs, it would be well to consult your county agent. In general, a 5–10–5 mixture (see Fertilizers, Section I) is a good general-purpose fertilizer for vegetables. For root crops, a 2–10–10 fertilizer, if available, is better; or supplement the 5–10–5 with extra potash.

What are food needs of different vegetables? While there are many special formulas made up for different vegetables that are grown on a commercial scale, in the home garden it is not practical to attempt to work out these differences. Animal manure, if it can be obtained, plus a generous application of a high-quality complete fertilizer, will produce good crops. Where some special need exists, this can be provided by an additional application of one of the several materials that carry nitrogen, phosphoric acid, or potash. These are described in the Introduction to Section I.

What is a good general fertilizer that can be used on potatoes, celery, tomatoes, and cabbage? A 5–10–5, or a 2–10–10, or a 5–10–10 if your soil needs the extra potash. The first is better for cabbage and celery.

What fertilizer (grade of mixture) should be used on plants such as potatoes, tomatoes, corn (sweet), cabbage, cauliflower? See answer above. A general-purpose fertilizer can be supplemented by other materials for particular crops. For instance, lettuce, cabbage, and cauliflower during their early stages of growth are benefited by an abundance of nitrogen, and this can be supplied in the form of nitrate of soda or ammonium sulfate applied around the growing plants in addition to the general-purpose fertilizer which has been used.

How best to fertilize new ground for vegetables? If the soil is acid, spread lime over the surface, and apply at least 25 lbs. of 5–10–5 on a 1,000-sq.-ft. area before the ground is plowed or spaded. Then set all plants and plant all seed with starter solution.

How shall I fertilize small space to produce largest possible crops of different vegetables? (North Dakota.) In sections where water is at a premium, it is difficult to use chemical fertilizer in the dry form. Keep the soil limed only if needed, and use animal manure if possible. Then use a starter solution (which see) for setting plants and when sowing. If more fertilizer is needed, use a side-dressing solution.

What can I do to enrich a vegetable garden plot 20 × 20 ft. which has been planted regularly for 15 years and does not produce very

Manure is spread on the ground and mixed through soil in the process of plowing or digging.

good crops?   Very likely the soil is deficient in humus. If this is the case, commercial fertilizer alone will not produce good crops. Dig in a generous coating of well-rotted manure, applied 2 to 4 ins. deep over the surface, or half that amount of compost.

Can you tell me the fertilizer necessary to make an active producing vegetable garden soil out of former woodland?   This would depend upon the type of soil. It is best to make a test for acidity (see Section I), then apply sufficient lime to bring the soil to a "slightly acid" condition—the best for most vegetables. Phosphoric acid is almost sure to be needed. Suggest consulting your local county agent or State Experiment Station for general requirements of soil in your vicinity.

What should I use on a leaf soil in the woods to be able to grow a vegetable garden? I tried squash; it flowered, but never any squashes; blossoms all fell off. Cucumbers the same. Please tell me what kind of fertilizer to use.   The falling off of flowers without setting fruit usually indicates a deficiency in phosphoric acid and potash. Probably these should be used, in addition to a complete fertilizer, for two or three seasons, until the plant nutrients in your soil are more evenly balanced. Full sun is needed for all vegetables.

Does rotten manure have any effect on root crops, like scabbing or stunting?   Manure that is not thoroughly decomposed does sometimes make rough or scabby root crops. Other conditions, however, may be the cause. Potatoes grown in soil too heavily limed are almost certain to be scabby although no manure was used on the ground for years.

Is there a connection between fertilizer and taste of vegetables or fruits?   In general there is not. There have been reports of extra-heavy applications of manure, particularly pig manure, affecting the taste of resulting crops, but there do not seem to be any authentic cases of this kind.

I have room to place tomato plants between my rows of daffodils during the month of May. What would be the best fertilizer to use? Would manure dug in be injurious to the bulbs?   Thoroughly decayed manure (which would be best for the tomatoes) would not injure the daffodil bulbs. In addition to a general-purpose fertilizer used for the tomatoes, bone meal might well be added, as this would not only help the tomato crop but would also be of decided benefit to the daffodils.

What causes rindy and very small carrots and beets grown in same ground that grows excellent tomatoes?   Some deficiency in the soil, such as lack of phosphorus, which builds strong roots. Apply super-phosphate, 4 to 5 lbs. per 100 sq. ft. If possible, have soil tested by your county agent. He will give you advice on its improvement.

Our soil is sandy. What amount of fertilizer? Have heard so much of the damage of too much fertilizer that we are confused.   Sandy soil usually requires larger additions of humus and nutrients, in the form of manure or fertilizer, than heavy soils. The method of application, moreover, is different. Sandy soils are likely to leach badly. Several light applications during the season give better results than one heavy application. Everything possible should be done to increase the humus content of sandy soil by using manure, humus in the form of compost, or green crops for turning under.

Side dressings of fertilizer during growth are helpful to most crops. Fertilizer with a high nitrogen content is desirable for leaf crops, such as lettuce and chard; while seed- or fruit-producing crops, such as beans or tomatoes, require abundant potash.

Which is the best time to fertilize a vegetable garden, fall or spring? Slow-acting materials such as rough manure, lime, and coarsely ground bone meal may best be applied in the fall; or, if in the spring, as early and as far in advance of planting as possible; the more quick-acting materials (such as the ordinary "complete" fertilizer), thoroughly decayed manure, and compost, in the spring. The very quick-acting fertilizers, like nitrate of soda or sulfate of ammonia, and the somewhat slower dried blood or tankage, at the time of planting, or around plants after some growth has been made.

Is it best to put stable manure on a vegetable garden in the fall or spring? This depends largely upon the condition of the manure. If thoroughly decayed, it is usually best to apply it in the spring. If in a rough state, in the fall. If manure is applied long in advance of planting, there is a considerable loss of nitrogen, especially in light soils.

If a vegetable garden is covered with manure in the fall, is fall plowing really necessary? Fall plowing is highly desirable unless there is danger of erosion. The manure will decay more thoroughly and evenly instead of merely drying out; and it will also increase the bacterial action in the soil. Earlier planting is made possible.

Is there anything I can do in the fall to improve a plot to be used for vegetables in the spring? A heavy application of manure dug into the ground in the fall will put it into good condition for spring planting. Even if manure is not available for plowing or digging, leaving the ground in ridges and furrows will help put it into better mechanical condition. If lime is needed, fall is the best time to apply it.

Is it a good thing to use wood ashes on a vegetable garden plot? When is the best time to apply them? Wood ashes contain potash, and are also an excellent soil conditioner. Usually it is preferable to apply them in the fall, as they are not as "quick acting" as most commercial fertilizers. However, if this cannot be done, they may safely be applied in the spring.

Do wood ashes on the ground make parsnips woody, and if not, what is the cause? Wood ashes, which add both lime and potash to the soil, are excellent for almost all vegetables. It is much more likely that woody or fibrous parsnips are the result of conditions causing a slow growth. All root crops, to be brittle and tender, must develop quite rapidly and without a check. Lack of sufficient nitrogen, or a prolonged period of dry weather, would cause a woody condition.

Is soot from a furnace motor stoker beneficial for vegetable garden? This depends entirely upon the type of soot. The so-called "Scotch soot" is highly prized by many gardeners. However, chimney soot and the fine ashes produced by a motor stoker are two quite different products. The material you have would probably be beneficial to the soil mechanically, even though it helps in no other way. Don't expect it to take the place of fertilizer.

Should coal ashes be used on the vegetable garden? If so, when? Sifted coal ashes are beneficial to most soils, especially to heavy ones. The winter's supply of ashes, screened and spread over the surface as they are produced in the winter, can be dug or plowed under in the spring.

In growing vegetables, is there much difference in results in broadcasting commercial fertilizer before planting, or spreading it in the rows when planting? Formerly most fertilizers were applied broadcast before planting, or in the row at the time of planting. Modern practice is to use a half or two thirds of the fertilizer in one, two, or three side dressings along the sides of the rows during growth. This has been found to produce bigger yield and to maintain growth at a more even rate of development—highly desirable for most crops.

How should fertilizing be done when transplanting vegetable plants from frame to open garden? Fertilizer is applied about a week previous and thoroughly mixed in with the top 3 or 4 ins. of soil. Or manure or a complete fertilizer is thoroughly mixed with soil in bottoms of holes in which plants are to be set.

Should vegetables be fertilized after sowing or transplanting into open garden? If so, when and how? If the soil is rich and fertile, this may not be necessary. Otherwise many vegetables benefit from a side dressing applied when about half grown. Use 3 to 5 lbs. of fertilizer to each 100 ft. of drill. Spread it thinly down each side of row, 3 or 4 ins. from plants, and cultivate in.

ACIDITY

What is meant by an "acid" soil? One in which the chemical reaction is acid instead of alkaline, as measured by the pH scale. This scale corresponds, in a way, to the thermometer scale for measuring temperature.

What is the meaning of "pH"? See Introduction to Section I. A pH reading of 7 indicates the neutral point. Figures below pH 7 (pH 5.5, for instance) indicate the degree of acidity; figures above pH 7, the degree of alkalinity.

Is it worth while to have my soil tested before planting vegetables? It is well to have the soil of an untried piece of ground tested before starting to improve its condition, especially if you have reason to think it is worn out or unfertile. Your county agent or nearest State Agricultural Experiment Station will test your soil and give advice on how to improve it.

How can I tell if my soil is acid? There are available inexpensive testing kits which any amateur can use.

Do vegetables prefer acid or alkaline soil? Most vegetables are grown most successfully in slightly acid soil; i.e., soil with a pH of 6 to 7. Soil with a pH 5 to 5.6 will grow potatoes, sweet potatoes, watermelons; pH 5.2 to 6—eggplants, peppers, tomatoes; pH 5.6 to 6.8—beans, carrots, corn, parsley, parsnips, pumpkins, salsify, Swiss chard, turnips; pH 6 to 7.2—beets, broccoli, cabbage, cucumbers, endive, leaf lettuce, muskmelons, peas, radishes, rhubarb; pH 6.4 to 7.6—asparagus, cauliflower, celery, leek, head lettuce, onions, spinach.

What are the alkalinity or acidity requirements of our common vegetables; i.e., the ideal or optimum pH values? See previous question.

What vegetables are good for a very acid soil? We cannot raise peas. Potatoes, sweet potatoes, and watermelons. Liming the soil (see Soil Preparation) would make it suitable for peas.

What treatment is necessary when beans, carrots, and beets are stunted, when ten feet away they grow fine and strong? If poor drainage is not the cause, there may be an extremely acid spot in the soil. A soil test would prove this. If not, an additional application of a complete fertilizer should correct the trouble.

What steps can I take to correct the condition of my vegetable plot, which is very acid? See Introduction to Section I, and Soil Preparation, this section.

GREEN MANURES

When a garden writer advises the use of "green manure," just what does he mean? Any crop grown for the purpose of digging or plowing it under to decay in the soil—and thus add humus—is called a green manure. Long used in farm practice, green manuring in the home vegetable garden is rapidly gaining favor.

Is the practice of green manuring worth while for the home garden? Most decidedly: especially in sections where it is difficult to procure animal manures. This is the best way to build up the humus content of the soil.

Do you advise the use of green manures for conditioning the vegetable plot? Yes, by all means. By putting in a cover crop in late summer or autumn, as soon as vegetable crops are harvested, and digging it under in spring when 6 to 10 ins. high, the humus content in the soil will be maintained. (See Section I.)

What is the best way to handle a green-manure crop (rye) that has grown too tall to be dug under conveniently? Mow the tops and add them to compost heap, or use for mulching; dig under stubble and roots, which will add considerable humus.

What is the best way to maintain garden fertility? One of the most important factors in maintaining fertility is to keep up the humus content of the soil. This can be done by using manure or compost, and by growing green crops whenever possible to be turned under to decay. (See Section I.) After the soil is once producing well, the practice outlined above, plus moderate yearly applications of a complete fertilizer, should maintain the fertility indefinitely.

What should I sow after plowing my garden plot in the fall? Unless ground is plowed or spaded by the first of September (in the latitude of New York) there is little use in sowing a green-manure or cover crop where early planting is to be done. Rye and rye grass are the two most satisfactory crops for fall and winter growth to turn under for green manure. In the latitude of Washington, D.C., and farther south these crops will make considerable growth during the winter months, and can be sown in late September or early October.

Which makes the better green-manure crop for the vegetable garden —rye or rye grass? Both Winter Rye and Perennial Rye Grass make excellent green-manure crops. Both can be sown any time from midsummer until frost, and are perfectly hardy through the winter. Rye germinates somewhat faster and makes a more rapid early growth. It is coarser and more difficult to dig under in the spring if the job is not done early. Rye produces more bulk in a shorter time than Rye Grass, but both are satisfactory.

What is the best time to plant, and when should these two cover crops be turned under—a, sweet clover; b, soybeans? Sweet clover (Melilotus), a biennial, may be sown early in the spring but will make a suitable growth for green manuring even if sown as late as mid-June. Turn under when 8 to 12 ins. high, or any time before stalks become hard; sow in midsummer to turn under following spring. Sow soybeans after danger of frost, and turn under any time after sufficient growth has been made, until main stems begin to get hard.

What are several good summer and winter cover crops? Summer: Cowpeas, soybeans, oats, buckwheat, and Huban or annual sweet clover. Winter: Rye, perennial rye grass, or (if sown not later than mid-August) crimson clover or vetch.

Is there any evidence that growing vetch on land will inoculate peas? Yes. The bacteria left in the soil from the vetch roots will help the growth of peas.

My vegetable garden is covered with leaves; because of furrows it is difficult to rake them off. Shall I burn them or plow them under in the spring? By all means plow or dig under the leaves instead of burning them. Anything which will decay that can be turned into the soil will help add humus.

What vegetables or flowers will grow in 100 per cent humus? A shallow pond drained many years ago is dry, black humus that I am told should be mixed with topsoil, now hard to get. Undoubtedly topsoil mixed with the humus would improve it. Many humus soils, however, will grow good crops of most vegetables, provided a complete fertilizer is applied. Such soils are used by many truck gardeners. Would try it for one season before adding topsoil, and then use that only for such vegetables as may not do well in the humus.

SEED SOWING

SEEDS

How can I be sure that I am buying good vegetable seed? By making your purchases only from reliable houses that specialize in seeds. The great skill and effort which go into producing high-quality seeds are not apparent in the seed packet—only in the crop that results.

Is it important to ask for improved varieties in ordering seeds? Ask for the best varieties of the various kinds that are suitable for your locality. Try out new varieties in a modest way, until you have proved they are useful to you. Not every "novelty" is a real improvement.

For how many seasons are vegetable seeds good? There is considerable variation in the length of time that different vegetable seeds maintain their vitality. Onions, okra, and parsnips, for instance, can be counted on for only one year. Beans, beets, members of the cabbage family, and most vine crops for 3 or 4 years. Any seeds held over should be tested before planting. (See Testing Seeds.)

Will seeds that are purchased for one season, and not used, germinate the following spring? What can be done to help them? If they have been stored in a dry place they probably will germinate fairly well if the germination was good when they were bought. There is no treatment that will improve their germination but the germination can be tested before planting.

I have considerable green bean seed left. Can it be used next planting season? The seeds usually germinate well for several years. However, to make sure that germination will be satisfactory, it is best to sprout a few of them on moist blotting paper (in a saucer) before planting. The percentage of germination can then be accurately determined.

What vegetable seeds can the home gardener save without risking deterioration or cross-pollination, and what steps can he take with the more difficult varieties? This is a big question to answer here. In a dry season, with good, clear weather, many kinds can be grown. Tomatoes, peppers, eggplants, lettuce, endive, and onions are self-pollinated. Most of the others are cross-pollinated, and for good seed would have to be hand pollinated under bags.

What is the proper method of saving and treating seeds from the vegetable garden so that they will grow the following year? In general, vegetable seeds are gathered as they begin to reach maturity, indicated by the seed pods turning brown and hard. They may then be spread out on trays or in flats until they ripen further. During this period they must be protected from moisture. When completely ripened, they are stored in tight containers. In general, it does not pay the home gardener to attempt to save seeds, as the varieties are likely to be mixed the following year, even if the germination is satisfactory.

INDOOR SOWING

What vegetable seeds can be started in the house, greenhouse, hotbed, or cold frame in spring? Tomatoes, peppers, eggplants, early lettuce, sweet potatoes, celery, celeriac, early cabbage, early cauliflower, and early broccoli; beets also transplant readily, if a few extra-early ones are wanted.

What is needed in the soil to start vegetable seedlings indoors? The soil for starting seedlings need not be rich. The mechanical condition is more important. A mixture of ⅓ garden soil, ⅓ sand, and ⅓ peatmoss or compost, thoroughly mixed and passed through a sieve, gives good results.

Is it possible to have any amount of success in starting vegetable seeds indoors if there is no direct sunlight? Seeds will start but will not progress satisfactorily unless they have long hours of direct sunshine. Would not advise starting vegetable seeds indoors unless you have a very sunny south or southeast window.

When is the best time to seed vegetables in a flat before transplanting in the spring? This depends on what vegetables you are growing, whether they are hardy or tender, and the length of time these take from seed to food crop. In general, seeds are planted in flats in late

February and early March to be set out in April and May. Cabbage and broccoli started in February can be set out in early April. Tomatoes started at the same time are transplanted first into 2- and then into 3- or 4-inch pots before they can be set out in May. Peppers and eggplant seeds, which are very tender, can be sown in March as the plants cannot go into the open garden until all danger of frost is past and the ground has warmed up.

Treating seeds with a disinfectant before planting often means full rows instead of loss from damping off, or some other seed-borne disease.

How thickly should seeds of cabbage, broccoli and other crucifers, peppers, eggplants, and tomatoes be planted in flats for growing on under glass? Sow thinly in straight marked rows in flats (so seeds do not touch each other) in order that the seedlings will not crowd each other when they germinate. The larger seeds—such as tomatoes—should be about ⅛ in. apart.

Should vegetable seedlings in flats, pans, or seedbed be thinned before they are transplanted? If seeds are sown thinly enough, thinning will probably not be necessary. If the little plants are much crowded, however, thinning is advisable, *just as soon as they are well up.*

What temperature should one have to start plants from seed indoors or under glass? Night temperature for hardy plants: 40 to 50° F.; for tender plants (tomatoes, peppers, eggplants): 50 to 60°. These are minimums; 5 to 10° higher will do no harm. To *germinate* the seeds, 60° for hardy plants (cabbage, etc.), and 70° for tender sorts.

How can lettuce, tomatoes, peppers, cabbages, and other plants from seeds be grown in the house? (New York.) To grow vegetable plants successfully indoors from seed you must have a very sunny window, or a sun porch with south or southeastern exposure. Start hardy vegetable seeds (cabbage family, lettuce, etc.) February 15 to March 1 in flats of prepared soil. Tender vegetables (peppers, eggplants, and tomatoes) about March 15, also in flats. Transplant to other flats when true leaves are formed, and (for extra good plants) finally to small pots. Harden off the hardy vegetables outdoors in cold frame from about April 1 to April 15 before setting in open garden. Tender vegetables are hardened in frame, beginning about May 1. For other localities, seeds are started about 2 months before they can go out into the frame for hardening off.

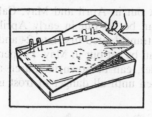
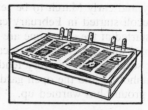
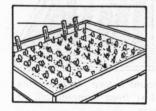
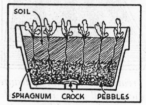

STARTING VEGETABLE SEEDLINGS
*Pane of glass over planted flat keeps soil moist. News-
paper shading, removed as soon as seeds germinate. Seedlings, if not transplanted, should be thinned out before
crowding. If transplanted, they should be placed deep in
the soil—almost up to the seed leaves.*

Should newly planted seeds be labeled, and if so, how? Each group
of seeds planted should be labeled. Place a small wooden label with
name of plant, variety, source, and planting date in pan or at end of
row in flat or bed.

**What is "bottom" heat? When is it used in growing vegetable seed-
lings?** Warmth applied beneath the soil in which the seeds are grown,
as by placing a flat of seeds on the heater or on a radiator. Used to
hasten germination of tender or difficult seeds. *Should not be continued
after seedlings are well up.*

**How long can newly sown seeds in pans, flats, or seedbeds be kept
covered from the light?** Until germination takes place. They must
then be uncovered *immediately.*

*Two methods of germinating "difficult" seeds: seed pan
covered with glass to hold moisture; inverted bulb pan
over seeds planted in center of small flat.*

How can I water young seedlings to keep them from being beaten down by the spray of water? If grown in flats, pans, or pots they should be watered *from the bottom,* by placing container in a tray or pan partly filled with water. If grown in a seedbed or in open garden, they should be watered with very fine spray, but long enough thoroughly to soak soil; water early in the morning, so they can dry off before night.

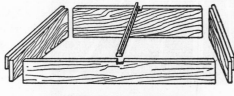

A ready-made frame for hotbed or cold frame can be put together in a few minutes.

New type of hotbed, with lightweight sash, each 2 × 4 ft., is convenient for women gardeners to handle.

The use of a cold frame or a hotbed gives the vegetable garden a running start in spring.

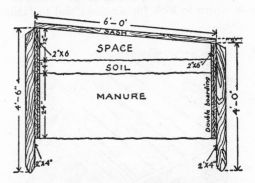

Cross section of a manure-heated hotbed.

What would be the cost of small outfit for sprouting seed before planting? You can grow your own plants (to be set out in the garden) in a one-sash hotbed built against a cellar window if you have some heat there. Otherwise four 100-watt light bulbs placed in the sash along the sides, and lighted on cold nights, would give sufficient heat to keep the plants growing. You can cover the sash in late afternoon to hold in as much heat as possible from the sun. Grow the frost-tolerant plants first and the warm-weather plants later. If you are concerned only with sprouting seed, use shallow enameled pans. Soak the seed for 3 hours in water, then drain off free water, leave seed in pan and cover top of pan with newspaper until seed sprouts.

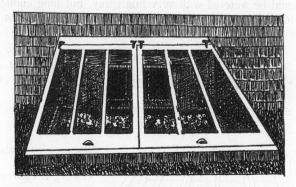

Hotbed heated from a cellar window.

How can I prevent seedlings in flats from turning to the light so that their stems are crooked? Give them all the sunshine possible. If they still "draw" to light, turn flat or pan daily.

In planting seeds (in the open) for later transplanting to permanent positions, shall I broadcast or plant in rows? Plant in rows so that you will know where to look for seedlings and to facilitate weeding and transplanting.

End of cold frame marked off for seed sowing.

OUTDOOR SOWING

How should ground be prepared for seed sowing of vegetables? Spade or plow. Lime if necessary. Fertilize. Rake or harrow to a fine, crumbly surface, tilth immediately before seeds are sown. Surface should be even. If in doubt consult local gardeners or State Experiment Station with regard to your lime and fertilizer needs.

*Commercial fertilizers are cultivated or raked
in after the ground is plowed or dug. A
second raking is usually needed to provide a
suitable seedbed.*

**Should vegetable seeds be treated with a disinfectant or root
stimulant before planting?** The root stimulants are of questionable
value in the garden. Seed disinfectants may be used because they do
provide a measure of insurance against certain diseases of the seedlings.

**How many different kinds of chemicals are needed for treating seed
for the average home garden? What are they?** One or more of the
following: Cupricide, Rootone, Semesan, and Semesan Jr. (for corn),
Nitrricin for legumes.

**How can I hasten the germination of hard-shelled seeds like peas,
New Zealand spinach, celery, and parsley?** By soaking them in tepid
water for 24 to 48 hours before they are sown. Then dry off, and sow
at once.

What vegetable seeds are planted in the open garden in early spring?
Peas, radishes, lettuce, spinach, onions and leeks, parsnips, salsify,
dandelion, early beets and carrots, kohlrabi, turnips, and Swiss chard.

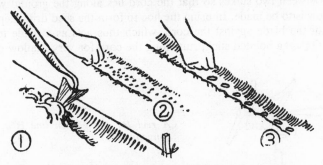

*Seed sowing. (1) A hoe—or a pointed stick—is drawn
along a tightly stretched cord to mark the row or open
a furrow. (2) Small seeds—such as lettuce, carrot, or
onion—are sown thinly and barely covered from sight.
Larger seeds—peas, beans, corn—are placed 2 ins. or
so apart, and covered 2 to 3 ins. deep.*

Some seeds are sown in hills. In the bottom of a hole (4) 5 or 6 ins. deep, manure or compost and fertilizer are thoroughly mixed with soil. The hole is then filled level with the surface and the seeds sown.

Which tender vegetable seeds cannot be safely planted until the soil is thoroughly warm? String beans, lima beans, corn, cucumbers, squash, pumpkins, okra, and New Zealand spinach.

What is a trench, a furrow, a drill, and a hill? *Trench*—a ditchlike excavation 6 ins. or more wide and a foot or more deep. Used in digging. Also applied to deep drills in which celery or peas are planted. *Furrow*—The hollow between the ridges of soil thrown up in the process of plowing or of digging. Also, a very deep drill (such as a "furrow" for planting potatoes). *Drill*—A shallow mark in the soil in which seed is sown; usually less than an inch deep. *Hill*—A low, broad, flat mound in which seed is sown. Also spot where a few seeds are sown when the rows are not continuous but have spaces between a group of plants—as a "hill" of corn or of beans—even though the ground is perfectly level.

How can I get my seed rows straight? By stretching a stout cord taut between two stakes so that the cord lies along the ground where the row is to be made. In using the hoe to form the seed drill keep one side of the blade against the cord, which thus acts as a guide to the hoe. Or use a pointed stick, run along the cord for very shallow drills.

A reel for the garden line is a great convenience.

How should rows be fertilized before seeds are sown? In the intensively cultivated garden it is better to broadcast the fertilizer over the surface and rake it thoroughly into the top 2 or 3 ins. of soil a few days before seed is sown. Where rows are 2 ft. or more apart the fertilizer may be worked in only along the rows.

How deep should seeds be covered with soil? From 2 to 4 times their own smallest diameter. For early sowings, and in clay soils, cover somewhat less than normal depth.

I planted lettuce and dandelion seed last spring and they did not grow. Got it from our best seed store. Can you tell me why they did not grow? Mustard seed did. The trouble may have been too deep planting. Lettuce seeds should be scarcely covered, and sown in very well-prepared light soil. Lettuce seedlings cannot push up through a hard surface. Dandelion seeds also should be planted very shallow. Often the germination is low. Mustard, which is an unusually strong grower, will generally sprout even under unfavorable conditions.

How thick should vegetables be sown? Small seeds, 4 or 5 times as thickly as the plants will finally stand. Thus, if turnips need 3 ins. of space between plants to develop, sow from 12 to 20 seeds per foot. This permits proper spacing after thinning out. Large seeds (as pole beans or squash) may be sown 1½ to 2 times as thickly as plants are to stand after thinning.

How thick should the following seeds be planted to get the best and biggest yield: carrots, beets, Swiss chard, cucumbers, bush beans, and lettuce? Sow carrots and lettuce 15 to 20 seeds to the foot of row, and make first thinnings (as soon as plants have made two or three leaves) from 1 to 2 in. apart; beets and Swiss chard 10 to 15 seeds to the foot, and thin out to 2 to 3 ins. apart; bush beans an inch apart and thin to 3 ins.; as the plants grow, a second thinning should be made, removing the weaker plants. To form heads, lettuce plants should stand at least 8 to 10 ins. apart. Cucumbers are usually sown in hills 3 ft. or more apart, 8 to 12 seeds to the hill. They may be grown in rows, placing the seeds 2 to 3 ins. apart and thinning to 1 to 2 ft. as the plants develop.

Is it advisable to water vegetable seed rows after sowing? If the ground is at all dry, it is very much better to water the seed rows *before* sowing. After the drill is made, run a slow stream of water from a hose or watering can along the bottom. Let soak in, then sow the seed.

Will soaking seeds in coal oil keep worms and beetles away from sweet corn and cucumbers? Soaking in coal oil or kerosene would kill the seeds. Crow Repellent (sold by most houses) is effective and protects the seeds from worms as well as from crows. A generous amount of tobacco dust sprinkled around the seeds when planting will act as a repellent.

What seasons and how deep should vegetable seeds be planted? (Maryland.) In most parts of Maryland the planting of hardy vegetables (see Introduction) can be begun by the middle of March. This, however, will vary with the season. Practically all seed packets contain directions for depth of planting for the varieties enclosed. For more complete instructions would suggest your getting the bulletin on this subject published by the State Agricultural Experiment Station at College Park.

What time should a garden be planted in western Suffolk County, Long Island? See questions on frost-hardy and warm-weather plants. Frost date probably will be around middle of April.

How late in the season can you make a second planting of such vegetables as string beans, beets, radishes, and lettuce? (Pennsylvania.) Eight to 10 weeks before a killing frost for string beans and beets; 7 to 9 weeks for lettuce; and 4 to 5 for radishes. See frost-resistant vegetables and warm-weather vegetables.

Is there anything gained by planting by signs—such as the phases of the moon? Many gardeners believe so, but there is no scientific evidence to this effect. Planting by such a sign as "when white oak leaves are the size of squirrels' ears" (for corn) is quite different, as the size of leaves is determined by seasonal weather conditions.

ROUTINE CARE

THINNING

What is meant by "thinning" vegetables? This is the term applied to the practice of pulling out surplus seedling plants so that those left

Vegetables sown in rows must be thinned out to allow room for remaining plants to develop. Above, seedling beets before being thinned.

Seedling beets after being thinned out.

may have room to develop properly. In order to be sure of having rows without skips, gardeners sow extra seeds in the row. If germination is good, a surplus of plants is the result.

How can one tell how many plants to remove when "thinning out"? In directions for growing vegetables, the distance apart at which they should stand is given. Carrots, for instance, are usually thinned to about 2 in. apart; onions, 2 to 3; beets, 3; beans, 4 to 5, etc.

Can any use be made of thinnings? Thinnings of many vegetables can be used. Young beets, for instance, make excellent boiled greens; small onions may be used as "scallions," for eating green. Baby carrots may be canned. Or the thinnings of many kinds may be used for transplanting, if additional plants are wanted.

After being thinned, my plants wilted badly; can anything be done to prevent this? Yes. First of all, begin thinning just as soon as seedlings are well up—the bigger they get, the more those left will be disturbed. Thin when soil is moist, after a rain or a good watering. If plants start to wilt, water, and shade with newspapers for a few days.

How soon should rows of small vegetable plants be thinned? Just as soon as the individual plants begin to crowd each other and before there is the slightest chance of their becoming "leggy" for lack of light and air.

Is more than one thinning advisable? With plants that grow closely in the row—such as onions from seed, carrots, and beets—two or three thinnings are often made as the plants grow; this leaves a margin of safety in case of injury or loss among the plants that are left.

TRANSPLANTING

How large should seedlings be before transplanting? Seedlings should be transplanted as soon as they form their first true leaves (these are the third and fourth leaves to form) and before they become crowded in the flat, pan, or seedbed.

How many times should vegetable seedlings grown under glass be transplanted before being set in the open garden? Preferably twice: first into a second flat, at a sufficient distance from each other to prevent crowding, usually 3 to 4 in. apart each way; and, second, into a small pot or plant band to form a good root ball before setting out.

Should seedlings be transplanted direct from the flat or pan to the open garden? It is better practice to transplant to a second flat or to pot up seedlings from the pan or seed flat. These can be grown on in the greenhouse or frame until they are well rooted and strong. If grown in greenhouse, they should be "hardened off," for a week or more, in a cold frame before being set out in the open garden.

What are the advantages of pot-grown plants over young plants cut out of the flat and planted in the garden? Pot-grown plants suffer little or no shock when they are set in the open garden, while plants removed from flats or seedbeds have to recover from the disturbance to their root systems.

A pot-grown eggplant plant.

When are tender plants set out in the vegetable garden? When the ground warms up and weather is settled. Tomatoes about May 15 to June 1 in vicinity of New York, or about the time white oak leaves are the size of squirrels' ears; peppers and eggplants a little later.

When can hardy vegetable plants be set in the open garden? Just about the time the last expected hard frost is past. Many amateurs delay planting much longer than necessary.

How can I prevent newly set vegetable plants from wilting? Set after sunset, or on a cloudy or rainy day. Water well after setting. If necessary, cover during hours of high sun for a day or two, using newspapers, hotkaps, or baskets. Uncover as soon as sun is low.

Should newly transplanted vegetables be watered after the plants are set? Yes, they should be thoroughly watered. Leave a slight depression around the stem when planting, and fill this with water.

When transplanting, does it help to trim back vegetable plants? Such plants as lettuce, cabbage and other crucifers, and beets may have their outside leaves trimmed back before setting. This practice is particularly helpful in setting plants which are apt to wilt.

What are hotkaps? Are they useful in transplanting? Hotkaps are miniature paper tents to be set over seeds or young plants in the

Cross section of hotkap in place.

open garden to protect them from frost, wind, and insects during the early part of the season. They are of use in transplanting. They must be removed, however, before plants are crowded; preferably as soon as they are established and begin to grow after setting.

Are "hot caps" made of plastic better than the old-fashioned ones made of paper? Yes. Plastic caps or domes are clear and so admit sunshine to the young plants. They are more substantial and may be used over and over again. In order to admit fresh air to seedlings while using plastic domes, however, it is necessary to tip them, propping up the rim on one side with a stone or a block of wood, during the hottest part of the day.

If a late frost is forecast after setting young plants in the open garden, can anything be done to save the plants? Yes, they may be covered with hotkaps or with newspaper tents until the weather warms up.

CULTIVATION

Just what is meant by the term "cultivation" as used in garden articles and bulletins? Cultivation is the breaking up and stirring about of the soil around and between growing plants.

How do "deep" and "shallow" cultivation, often advised, differ? Shallow cultivation is stirring the soil to a depth of 1 or 2 ins. Deep cultivation may penetrate the soil as much as 5 or 6 ins., but usually less.

The prong hoe, a useful tool for quick, light cultivation.

Should plants be cultivated to the same depth throughout the season? No. Usually deep cultivation is given just after transplanting, or when plants from seed are still small. As they grow, and the roots spread out into space between rows, the depth of cultivation is reduced.

What tool do you recommend for hand cultivation? The scuffle hoe is the most useful tool for hand cultivation. Sometimes known as the Dutch hoe or the English scuffle hoe, this tool, with various minor modifications, is now manufactured in the United States.

The Dutch or scuffle hoe—a light tool excellent for shallow surface cultivating.

How long should cultivating be kept up? As a rule, the longer the better; and at least until crops have neared maturity and pretty well cover the ground.

What are the advantages of frequent cultivation? Weeds are killed. Air is admitted to the roots. Soil moisture is conserved.

How often should I cultivate my vegetable garden? After every rain or artificial watering, beginning as soon as the soil has dried to the extent that it does not stick to the shoes. Whenever a crop of young weed seedlings appear.

Is a wheel hoe or cultivator worth while for use in a small vegetable garden? Its use is not justified in gardens that are quite small, but it is a mighty useful implement in a garden of a quarter-acre or so.

Frequent stirring or cultivating the soil surface, with a scuffle-hoe or a wheel hoe (shown), breaks up hard crust, destroys small weeds, admits air, and aids plant growth.

How can I prevent heavy crops of weeds from developing among my vegetables? By clean cultivation. This means carefully digging out perennial weeds from newly broken ground and the repeated use of the hoe or cultivator throughout each growing season. Also cut down weeds on adjoining wasteland before they go to seed.

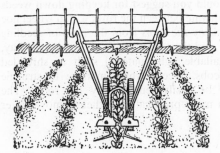

Wheel hoe with hoe-blade attachments set for working close to both sides of row.

What is meant by "hilling"? Drawing the soil up around growing plants with the hoe for the purpose of (a) covering small weeds; (b) supporting the plants; or (c) blanching the stems to make them more tender.

What vegetables require hilling? In the home garden, very few (in farming the practice is more general). Potatoes, corn, broccoli, and bush beans are often hilled for support; celery, leeks, and sometimes asparagus for blanching. As a rule—except in heavy soils— the less hilling the better.

In hoeing, it is important to stir soil between plants as well as that between rows.

WEED CONTROL

Are there weed killers which are safe to use in the vegetable garden? KOCN may be sprayed on young weeds in onion rows; 2, 4–D on asparagus, beets and strawberries for young annual weeds; and a dinitro selective weed killer such as Knox-weed 55 for young weeds in pea rows. Stoddard Solvent takes care of annual weeds in carrots. A "spot" weed killer is now available which can be used on individual broad-leaved weeds without danger of killing desirable plants nearby.

What general procedure would you suggest for keeping down weeds in the vegetable garden? Cultivate between the rows with a wheel hoe or rototiller and remove weeds *by the roots* from the rows of seedling vegetables. Water thoroughly and then mulch with grass cuttings, hay, salt hay, straw or other available light material such as shredded sugar cane, or ground corncobs. Weeds which manage to struggle up through the mulch may be easily removed by the roots. The prevention of weeds is much more practical than their removal after they are well established.

WATERING

Which vegetables need water in dry weather? In prolonged droughts all vegetables benefit from artificial watering. Those most susceptible to drought injury are peas, celery, spinach, and lettuce.

Does it harm plants to water in the heat of the day? Not if water is fed slowly and deeply into the soil from the end of a hose from which the nozzle has been removed. Lightly sprinkling the surface of the soil and the leaves in high sunlight does no good. Small seedlings may be destroyed. Growing crops are often watered with overhead irrigation in full sunshine, but early morning or evening is better, as less water is lost by evaporation.

An effective method of applying water to vegetable rows: it is allowed to run slowly into shallow trench from open end of hose, supported upon brick or block of wood.

Does artificial watering tend to bring plant roots to the surface and thus weaken plants? Only if the watering is insufficient. If a "rain machine" or rotary sprinkler is used it should be left on long enough in each area to really moisten the soil several inches deep, just as when watering slowly with the hose.

How often should an area be watered in dry weather? About once a week, or when the soil is found to be dry and powdery several inches down. A thorough watering should last at least a week, except on very sandy soils.

How deep should the soil be moistened by watering? Water long enough to moisten the soil to a depth of at least 4 ins. One watering will then last a week to 10 days.

Some authorities contend that watering vegetable plants weakens their root systems and makes them "soft." Is this true? If it is possible to get water to the vegetable garden, the crops harvested on watered areas will well repay the gardener for his effort and expense. Vegetables which do not receive any water are better fitted to withstand long drought than watered vegetables, but the quality will be less succulent and the yield smaller.

SUPPORTS

What supports do you recommend for pole beans? Use 8- to 10-ft. poles driven 1 to 1½ ft. into the ground and made into a "tepee," using 3 poles for each support. Plant beans at foot of each pole. If single poles are used, have at least 2 ft. in the ground.

On what support shall I grow my lima beans? These will grow readily on a fence with additional wires or cords added above to give sufficient height. Poles may also be used. (See above.)

Tomato plants with side shoots removed (indicated by arrows) and tied up to wire trellis.

Methods of supporting tomato plants without using upright stakes.

How shall I stake or support tomatoes? Use stout stakes, 7 ft. long, driven 2 ft. into ground, with crossbars nailed at 1-ft. intervals. Or make a trellis by driving 10-ft. stakes 2 ft. into the ground at ends of row with 8-ft. stakes driven 1½ ft. into ground at 10-ft. intervals between end stakes. Stretch heavy wires from post to post at 1, 3, and 5 ft. from ground. Plant tomatoes along row and fasten to wires as they grow. Stout cords may be stretched from post to post between wires at 2 and 4 ft. from ground for additional support.

What are the best kind of frames to make for keeping tomatoes off the ground? If not trained to stakes or trellis, the plants may be supported by some device such as barrel hoops supported on stakes, or short brush placed under the vines.

How shall I grow my tall peas to support them adequately? Peas may be planted along a 4- or 5-ft. fence. Encourage vines to climb by setting in pea brush as soon as vines begin to form. Set brush *outside* row of peas, on an angle to fence. Peas may also be planted along a row of tall pea brush driven firmly into ground. Place brush, then plant along both sides as close as possible.

Should dwarf peas be supported? If dwarf peas are held up with pea brush cut about 3 ft. long and driven firmly into ground, they will bear more heavily and be easier to pick.

When brush is not available to support peas, what is the best substitute? A special coarse netting of cord, made for the purpose, is available. Chicken wire will do, but it is well to use some small brush to start the vines up the wire.

Can vine crops be grown on supports and thus save ground space? Yes, cucumbers, melons, and even squash do well on trellises or fences.

MULCHING

What is meant by a "dust mulch"? This is merely the layer of dust-dry soil—usually 1 to 2 in. deep—produced by frequent shallow cultivation with a scuffle hoe or a hand cultivator. Most gardeners believe such a mulch conserves the soil moisture, but some modern investigators deny this.

What can be used for mulch in vegetable garden in place of peatmoss? There is no real substitute for peatmoss, because most other mulches are less absorbent. However, there are many other mulches which may be used in its place. Select a material locally available in your vicinity such as sawdust, ground corncobs, or buckwheat hulls. See also previous question.

When should mulching be applied in the vegetable garden? As soon as plants are well started, ground may be cultivated, weeds removed, area thoroughly watered, and mulch applied.

Is a summer mulch advisable in the vegetable garden? It can be used successfully to keep weeds under control with crops which do not need frequent cultivation. It also serves to conserve soil moisture, to absorb rain where it falls, and to keep the soil beneath it loose and friable.

Is paper mulch gardening practical for the average vegetable garden? Not under average conditions; it is expensive, and very difficult to keep in place. Peatmoss, peanut shucks, or other similar material is much better and more practical.

HARVESTING

How can I tell when vegetables are ready to pick, such as onions, potatoes, beans, and squash? This depends upon the purpose for which they are wanted: whether for immediate use, for storage, or for canning. Onions can be pulled when small for green onions. For storage, they should be picked when the tops have fallen over. For pickling, you want them when an inch in diameter. For immediate use, potatoes may be used as soon as they are big enough to make it worth while to dig. For storage, they should be dug when the vines are practically dead. Snap beans should be picked before the pods show the location of the seeds. Cabbage and head lettuce should be picked when the heads are solid. Fruits should be picked green or ripe, depending on the use you wish to make of them. Green fruits, such as tomatoes, are best when they are full grown, just before they begin to turn color.

Midsummer products of the home garden.

What vegetables may be gathered after frost? There are two types, those that will withstand a light frost without being injured and those which will survive after fairly hard freezing. Among the former are cauliflower, lettuce, chard, celery, and such root crops as beets and carrots. Celery well banked up will stand fairly hard frost. The real tough ones, which resist quite heavy freezing, are Brussels sprouts, cabbage, kale, broccoli, parsnips, salsify, rutabagas, turnips, leeks, and spinach.

How can one tell when melons are ripe? As soon as they can be lifted easily from the stem.

When New Zealand spinach grows too fast and gets ahead of us, what can be done with it? Use the tips for pot greens, or can. Cut back the old stems to within a few inches of crown to stimulate bushy new growth.

Our okra grew well, but was woody and tough. What was wrong? You did not harvest it soon enough. Pods should be barely finger length.

When are edible soybeans ready to cook green? When are they harvested to be used dry? As soon as the pods have filled out. They remain edible as green shell beans for about 2 weeks. After the pods turn brown they must be dried for use as dried beans. Harvest these before the pods burst open, as this will result in the beans shelling out on the ground. Pull up the plants and strip off the pods into a basket. Keep in a dry, warm place until they shell out.

When should summer squash be picked? When very young, less than half grown, and while skin is very tender. Though edible when better developed, the flavor and texture are inferior.

When should sweet corn be picked? When in the full milk stage, i.e.: while kernels may still be readily punctured with a thumb nail, releasing the juice or "milk"; and as short a time as possible before it is to be cooked.

When should sweet potatoes be harvested? After first killing frost blackens vines.

When are winter squash and pumpkins harvested? Before frost.

WINTER STORAGE

Is there any simple and inexpensive method for the small gardener to use in storing his vegetables for winter? The simplest method for storing vegetables is pit storage. Dig a pit in a well-drained location. Place a layer of gravel or sand in bottom. Line pit with straw. Store vegetables in pit. Cover with straw and then at least 6 in. of soil, or deep enough to insure safety from freezing in your climate. A 3- or 4-in. pipe sunk into the storage space and extending well above ground gives ventilation.

How are root crops and cabbages stored outdoors in a barrel? An excavation is made in a well-drained spot and a tight barrel is buried

Cabbages, pulled up by roots, are stored upside down to prevent moisture collecting in leaves.

in an upright or tilted position with its top 6 to 10 ins. below ground level. Vegetables are packed in barrel. Opening is covered with bag thickly packed with dry leaves, peatmoss, or sand. Soil is then filled in to a depth to make contents of barrel frostproof.

How should vegetables be stored for winter use in a root cellar? How should a root cellar be properly constructed? An ideal root cellar can be constructed by making a double wall with an air space between, and an insulated roof. An 8-in. terra-cotta flue is placed in the bottom and run through a trench to a point well outside the root cellar, where it is brought up to the surface and hooded with a wind-operated ventilator several feet above soil level. The roof also has a ventilator with a damper. The action of the wind forces air (which takes on the temperature of the soil) down through the terra-cotta duct to the storage. This maintains a constant temperature in the storage house and at the same time maintains good aeration. Root cellar must be well drained to prevent water standing on floor or gathering in low spots.

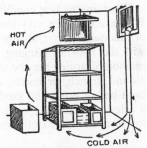

Arrangement of shelves and ventilation in cellar storage room.

How can celery be stored out of doors? Dig a trench or pit 2 ft. deep in a well-drained location on a gentle slope facing southeast or south. A 6 × 4 ft. trench will accommodate 250 plants. At the low end of the trench dig a sump (a pit filled with stones) to receive excess water in case of extra-heavy rains. Lift celery plants (roots and all, with dirt adhering to them) and pack closely in pit. Add a little soil if necessary to keep roots covered. If weather is very dry, water the roots slowly, by giving water at upper end. Keep water from foliage. Next build a peaked roof of boards over the pit, closing in the ends. Secondhand boards may be used, but if the structure is well made to begin with, it can be used year after year. Pack the earth up to the roof on each side. Until very cold weather, leave cracks in roof for ventilation, but when hard freeze comes, cover roof thickly with salt hay. Remove celery on warm, sunny days only, opening for a short time and closing again tightly. (Heads of cabbage may be hung, roots up, from ridgepole.)

What are the proper temperature and moisture conditions for fruit and vegetable storage? The best temperature for winter storage of root crops, cabbage, and most fruits is 35 to 40°. The cellar, pit, or other storage space should be dark, with a dirt floor, but well drained. Though humidity is needed, no water should collect and stand on the floor or in the bottom of the pit or barrel.

How do you store carrots, beets, and turnips to keep them from shriveling? Store in a cool, dark place, 35 to 40°, packed in sand or slightly moist peatmoss, or in boxes covered with bags containing sand, leaves, or peatmoss.

What kind of vegetables can be kept in a dirt cellar; and for how long? Root crops will keep through winter at 35 to 40°. Cabbage will keep about 3 months if hung, roots up, from nails in ceiling.

Can Chinese cabbage, leeks, kale, and celery be stored indoors? Yes, in a basement room or root cellar at a temperature of 35 to 40°. They will need moderate air circulation and plenty of moisture. Leave some dirt about the roots and pack closely in boxes placed on the floor. Kale can be kept growing in a covered frame in the garden through most of the winter.

What are the best conditions for the winter storage of raw cabbage? We have not been very successful and would appreciate a discussion of this question. Cabbage may be stored in a cool cellar 35 to 40° with dirt floor, by hanging, roots up, from a nail in ceiling. The same method of storing may be used in an outdoor cellar. In an outdoor pit, mound, trench, or barrel, cabbages are piled in a mound, roots up, on a bed of sand, and sand is packed around and over the heads. In a celery trench (see question on celery) cabbage may be hung, roots up, from the ridge of the roof.

Convenient type of box for storing root vegetables in sand or peatmoss in cellar.

How can squashes, pumpkins, and onions be stored? These vegetables require dry storage. The vine crops should be "cured" for a week or two in a temperature of 80 to 85°, then stored on a shelf in a dry cellar at 45 to 60°. Onions should be kept in the dark, in a dry place, at 35 to 40°, after they have been dried off in trays or boxes, under cover, but with free circulation of air, for several weeks after harvesting.

How to store sweet potatoes to keep them through the winter? Sweet potatoes are dug when vines are killed by frost, and are handled with care to avoid bruising. Perfect tubers are cured at a high temperature (80 to 85°) for 2 weeks. They are then stored in a dry place at 45 to 50°.

What is the best care for parsnips and salsify? Can they safely be left in the ground all winter? If so, should they be covered? Parsnips and salsify may be left in the ground all winter uncovered by a mulch. Or they may be dug, piled in a sheltered place against the north side of a building, covered with a light layer of soil, and mulched with hay or leaves, so they can be reached when desired.

We have strong, healthy roots of French Endive. We do not wish to force until spring. How shall we winter the roots? Leave them in the ground in the open garden. Dig when ready to force. Hard freezing does not injure French Endive.

Can parsley be stored, and if so, how? Parsley can be kept green in a cold frame until late fall. When hard freezes come, cover frame with leaves or mats and open on warm, sunny days.

Where one does not have a place cold enough to keep potatoes from sprouting, is there any other method one can use to prevent them from sprouting while in storage during winter months? A frostproof pit is most satisfactory for storing potatoes. They need to be kept in the dark, just safely above freezing, in a humid but not too moist atmosphere. Otherwise, they will sprout; rubbing the sprouts off is of some benefit. Or they may be treated with a chemical "sprout inhibitor."

What is the best way for the urban grower to store vegetables during the winter months? He cannot store vegetables unless he has a cool cellar, or ground enough to build an outdoor root cellar. It would be necessary for him to can or freeze his vegetables for winter use. A thoroughly insulated container which would be frostproof can be used outdoors to hold stored vegetables until needed for use.

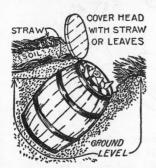

Barrel type of outdoor storage pit. (Cover must be tight to keep out moisture.)

My family has a farm in northern New York. They harvest beans, and about two bushels of them are allowed to dry for winter consumption and for seed. These dry beans are infested by worms which render them unfit for consumption and for seed. Can you tell me what can be done to remedy this condition? After drying, place beans on screened trays in cold oven. Heat very gradually to 180°. After 10 minutes at 180°, cool and store.

How are dried peas and beans stored for winter? If possible, in airtight containers of tin or glass, in a dry, cool room at a temperature from 45 to 60°.

How should canned goods and jellies be stored for winter? In a dry, cool, dark room, at a temperature of 40 to 60°. Jars are stored on shelves, not touching each other.

Is sand the only suitable material in which to store cabbages and other crops in an outdoor pit? Vermiculite, peatmoss or pulverized volcanic rock (pelonex) may be used instead. These materials should be *very slightly* dampened.

EXHIBITING

In what condition should vegetables be picked for exhibition purposes? In prime eating condition. The overgrown specimens often shown by beginners will not win prizes on size alone.

How should vegetables and fruits be prepared for exhibition? Root crops are washed. Tomatoes, eggplants, peppers, squash, apples and pears are wiped and polished. Onion tops are cut off, and outer, discolored skins are removed. Celery, leeks, and Chinese cabbage are washed and the roots cut off neatly. Cabbage stems are removed, together with outer imperfect leaves. Strip husk from a section of each ear of corn and cut it off near the base.

Root crops, such as beets and carrots, make a better appearance on the show table with foliage attached, provided it is fresh, clean, and undamaged by insects.

How can greens and the tops of root vegetables be kept fresh for exhibitions? Harvest well in advance and harden overnight, in a cool place, in water, or sprinkled with water. If they are unwilted and of good color at end of hardening period, they will probably stand up through the show.

In showing vegetables it is important to select specimens of even size and uniform shape.

How are vegetables displayed in harvest shows? Try to have each exhibit made up of items of uniform size. The schedule usually calls for a specific number of potatoes, tomatoes, beans, etc. Select perfect specimens of uniform size and place each group neatly on a paper plate. Lay out pea or bean pods side by side where they can be counted and seen easily by the judges. Turn tomatoes stem end down; fruits stem end up. Carrots, beets, and other roots may be displayed with tops if they can be kept fresh, but usually with tops removed.

Is it important to show only perfect vegetables in an exhibit? Yes, in order to win a prize each item shown must be of high quality, well grown, and well displayed. Uniformity of size also is important.

How shall I display a vegetable collection in a show? Make an arrangement of the vegetables, placing squash, melons, and other large items at back center with corn, root vegetables, etc., radiating from the center. Smaller kinds are placed in foreground.

EQUIPMENT

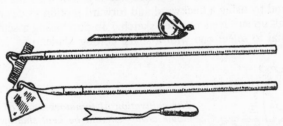

Some convenient garden tools: seed sower for frames or small gardens; narrow-bladed onion hoe, which for most uses is much more convenient than the regulation large hoe (shown just below it), and an asparagus knife—also useful for cutting deep-rooted weeds.

What tools are needed for a vegetable garden? The tools for a small garden need be but few. The most important are a spade or a flat-tined spading fork, an iron rake, a hoe, and a hand weeder. It is highly desirable to have two hoes, one with a fairly large blade for "hilling" and heavy hoeing and one with a small, narrow blade for cutting out small weeds. In a vegetable garden of considerable size a wheel hoe will be found a great timesaver. There are several types. The more simple ones cost but a few dollars.

Is a spading fork essential equipment for the vegetable garden? Many people consider the fork indispensable. It is useful in breaking up the soil when digging and in lifting roots or other crops. If only a small number of tools are to be purchased, however, get a spade first and a spading fork later.

What sort of spade do you recommend for the vegetable garden? A strongly made one with a D-handle and with reinforcing strips extending from the blade well up the handle. A good spade will outwear three or four cheap ones, so costs less in the end.

What sort of knife shall I use to cut asparagus? An asparagus knife with a fishtail blade is best for the purpose; cuts stalks below ground without injuring new stalks that are developing.

What type and make of power machinery do you suggest for plowing, cultivating, etc., to lighten hand labor and suitable for a woman to use in a garden 50 × 100 ft.? There is no power machine particularly suitable for use in a plot as small as 50 × 100 ft., especially if the area is fenced in. Probably the nearest thing to it is a small-sized Rototiller. This is for preparing the land but not for cultivating. It would be much more satisfactory to have the garden plowed or dug by hired labor and depend upon a wheel hoe to lessen the work of cultivating.

What is a scuffle hoe? A scuffle hoe is a tool used for cultivating the ground by using a backward and forward motion to destroy weeds and break up surface soil. (See sketch.) In purchasing a scuffle hoe it is essential to select one with a sharp cutting blade.

The cultivation of tomatoes—and of most vegetable crops—should be kept shallow after the plants begin to grow vigorously.

Which is the more useful in the vegetable garden, a wheelbarrow or a garden cart? A wheelbarrow is stronger and better calculated to carry the large quantities of humus, manure, compost, weeds, and refuse which must be transported to and from the vegetable garden.

What type of wheelbarrow do you recommend? A light metal barrow is more generally useful. It can be easily dumped and is easy to handle.

Where can I get "flats" or shallow boxes for planting early vegetable seeds? Order these knocked down from greenhouse companies or seedsmen, and nail them together yourself. They can be had at a higher price, set up and ready for use, from department and seed stores.

Are seed sowers worth buying? Yes, they are very helpful to the vegetable gardener. There are a number of different sorts. A seed-sowing attachment for the wheel hoe drops vegetable seeds in rows. A small hand sower helps to drop seeds evenly in flats, seedbeds, and even in the garden.

What is the best piece of equipment for measuring space between vegetable rows? Secure a long, narrow strip of wood about 1 × 2 ins. and 8 or 10 ft. long. Mark it off at 3-, 6-, and 12-in. intervals with a heavy carpenter's pencil.

Are rotary sprinklers helpful in the vegetable garden? As a rule it is better to water slowly about plant roots with the hose, without a nozzle.

What is a "porous" hose, and how is it used? This is a canvas hose to be attached to the end of the rubber hose. It can be had in 25- or 50-ft. lengths. Water seeps through the canvas very slowly and is at once absorbed by the soil. It is especially good for watering vegetables in rows and in soaking the bottoms of drills before sowing seeds in very dry weather. Three-ply or two-ply plastic, perforated hose throws many fine jets of water along its length, watering a 25-foot or 50-foot row or length of border at one time.

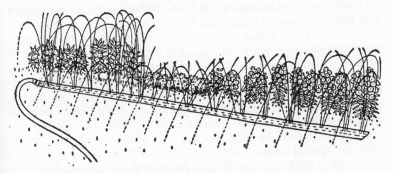

Sprinkler type of hose applies water through minute holes, in a rain-like spray that soaks deep into soil without packing surface or spattering mud.

Is a fence necessary for the vegetable garden? See Introduction to this section.

Would creosote-treated fence posts affect vegetable plants very near them? No. The creosote will not spread through the soil.

Are hotkaps satisfactory, and will they pay? Hotkaps, properly used, are of great assistance in getting an early start in the garden. Not only do they make possible earlier planting, they also furnish protection from insects and from wind and heavy rains while the plants are small and struggling to get a start. They are particularly useful in starting vine crops such as cucumbers and melons, and protecting tender plants such as tomatoes, eggplants, and peppers when they are first set out.

MISCELLANEOUS

What edible foods can be raised in a basement or cellar and sold at a profit? As practically all vegetables require full sunshine for several hours a day, they cannot be successfully grown in a basement. Witloof chicory, a salad plant (formerly largely imported from abroad) can be grown in the dark from roots which have been produced by sowing the seed in early spring and gathering the roots in the autumn. A local market for this crop might be developed. Another possibility might be mushrooms, but this crop requires quantities of horse manure or a special mushroom compost handled in just the right way, and would not prove feasible unless the manure were readily available.

What are practical suggestions for a vegetable garden in a large attic for a winter hobby? Unless the attic had a glass roof, thus practically converting it into a small greenhouse, no vegetables could be satisfactorily grown. If there were sufficient light, radishes, parsley, and lettuce would be the best ones to try.

How to build and manage a cold frame? What vegetables can be kept in it for winter use? (Ohio.) See Cold Frame. In a tight frame in a well-protected spot lettuce can be grown until late December or January, if the plants are started in August or September. Root crops, such as beets, carrots, and turnips, can be stored for the winter, but they should be covered with several inches of soil, leaves, or other mulching when the ground begins to freeze. Boards instead of glass are used to cover the frame when used for storing purposes. Celery taken from the garden on the approach of freezing weather, with the roots on and replanted in the frame close together, will blanch nicely and remain crisp for several weeks. Cabbage, Chinese cabbage, and cauliflower replanted in the frame may be held for several weeks longer than out of doors.

What vegetables would you suggest for raising in boxes, pots, and tubs, on a city roof that is very high and exposed to wind and sun? One difficulty is in obtaining sufficient earth. Except as a "stunt," it is not practical to attempt to grow vegetables in boxes on a high city roof. Little success can be expected, and the cost is out of all proportion to the return. Parsley, onion sets, lettuce, and tomatoes (if they can be protected from the wind) would be some of the best things to try.

What vegetables can be eaten from the garden in winter? My basement is too warm for storing. (Michigan.)   About the only vegetables which can be used direct from the garden in cold weather in the North are kale, collards, and Brussels sprouts; these will stand quite hard freezing and can be picked through December and often into January. Also parsnips, salsify and leeks are so hardy as not to be injured by severe freezing. To use the latter during the winter, they should be heavily mulched to prevent the ground from becoming too hard to dig. The Jerusalem artichoke is also perfectly hardy and the tubers may be dug and used any time they can be got out of the ground.

I have learned by experience that there are two kinds of fruits and vegetables. (1) Those that can stand shipping. (2) More delicious and delicate ones for home gardens. How can I select the latter?   A recent increase in the interest in home vegetable growing has focused attention on this point. The leading catalogues now take these differences into account in their descriptions. Consultation with local home gardeners within your vicinity will prove most helpful in the selection of high-quality varieties.

Is there any danger of germ contamination in having a vegetable garden over a septic-tank drainage system?   There is some question as to whether contamination may occur in soil over a septic-tank overflow field. In theory it cannot. The natural drainage of the soil is, however, an important factor. I know of several gardens so planted and have never heard of any undesirable results. However, if another location for the vegetable plot could be found it would be better.

What is organic gardening?   Organic gardening or farming is the growing of vegetables without the use of chemical fertilizers. It is accomplished by keeping the soil limed to a near neutral pH and following a rotation of crops where a good leguminous crop like clover or a sod crop occupies the land 2 out of 3 or 4 years. Animal manures are used to maintain the fertility of the ground. Also plant refuse is composted, and this is applied to the soil. Organic fertilizers are also used. The economics of this method may be questioned. Sometime there may be a day of reckoning, when some elements of the fertility balance become deficient. If so, it will be necessary to add chemical fertilizer, particularly potash and phosphoric acid.

What kind of soil will produce the best vegetables containing the most vitamins and minerals; or is commercial fertilizer necessary to obtain such vegetabls?   Any garden soil in good tilth. While commercial fertilizer is usually used, it is not essential; minerals exist in the soil.

What vegetables are considered helpful to nearsightedness and astigmatism? Vitamin A is supposed to improve eyesight, and carrots, broccoli, and all the "greens" are fairly high in this vitamin, provided they are used fresh soon after they are harvested.

Can we have a garden on a sandy soil that is full of ants? Most sandy soils, if improved with humus and fertilizer, will grow excellent vegetables. If ants have made nests or hills, they can readily be eliminated with cyanide gas applied according to directions.

Do large seed companies have contracts with private parties for raising seeds for them? For example, the raising of pansy seed? Yes, frequently they do; but such contracts are usually made with established seed growers upon whom they can rely for deliveries and quality.

PESTS AND DISEASES

See individual plants, and Section VIII.

INFORMATION ON INDIVIDUAL CROPS

ARTICHOKE, GLOBE

In what section of the country can globe artichoke be grown successfully? As a winter crop, in California, between San Francisco and Los Angeles; on the Gulf Coast, and in the South Atlantic states. In the Eastern states (as far north as Massachusetts) as a summer crop, the roots being mulched over winter. A difficult crop for the home gardener, requiring two seasons to grow if started from seed.

How does one grow the large globe artichokes? (Pennsylvania.) They cannot be grown satisfactorily in Pennsylvania, unless you can protect them against winter freezing. They require a fertile, well-limed soil; the plants are grown from slips from old plants. They are vigorous growers and need at least 16 sq. ft. for each plant. The part used is the bud of the flower, which should be picked before it is open.

Should artichoke plants be thinned down to three or four shoots? Not unless they are too crowded. It is better to leave them and feed the plants.

ARTICHOKE, JERUSALEM

Can you tell me something about Jerusalem artichokes grown as a garden root vegetable? The tubers are started like potatoes, from cut tubers set 18 in. apart. It is really an American sunflower, and ought to be known by its Indian name of sun-root; grows 5 to 6 ft. tall. No attention is required until the roots are dug in late fall or early spring, *when they must be thoroughly removed from the soil,* or plants will spread and are likely to become a pest. Best planted by themselves, outside of the garden.

Jerusalem artichokes are native to swamps. Will they grow in average garden soil? Yes, vigorously even in upland soils.

Are Jerusalem or American artichokes desirable as a garden vegetable? They are easy to grow and produce a heavy crop of non-starchy tubers. However, they spread rapidly and may become a weed. The plants are subject to black aphids and mildew, and so should be kept at a distance from choice flowering or vegetable plants.

I should like to get a planting of Jerusalem artichokes started. Can they be treated in any way to make them less tempting to moles, squirrels, rabbits, etc.? Treat tubers before planting with "crow repellent," but it's a messy job!

What time of the year should Jerusalem artichokes be dug? Does freezing improve them? Freezing does improve their flavor and therefore they should be dug as late as possible in the fall, during a winter thaw, or early the following spring before they have a chance to sprout.

How are Jerusalem artichokes prepared for the table? Boiled and served with cream or Hollandaise sauce. Diced raw, chilled, and added to mixed salads. In numerous other ways as glazed, au gratin, etc.

ASPARAGUS

Where can I purchase roots or plants of asparagus? Most seedsmen offer asparagus roots. In many cases they are rather small in size. It is advisable to order about twice as many as needed, and plant only the best.

How should new asparagus bed be fertilized? See that there is plenty of humus in the soil, preferably by turning under a cover crop or manure the fall before planting. When preparing trenches for planting, enrich thoroughly with manure or manure compost and coarse bone. Be sure the pH is not below 6.5. If it is, add lime to sweeten the soil.

What is the proper procedure for starting an asparagus bed from plants? Since asparagus is to occupy the ground for a long time, it is well to have the land in good fertility and tilth and free of weeds. Asparagus does well in a fairly wide variety of soils, from sandy to moderately heavy; good drainage is important. In early spring make trenches 4 or 5 ft. apart and about 8 ins. deep, in well-prepared soil. The very deep planting that was formerly recommended is not now considered necessary; if the soil is heavy, planting shallower than 8 ins. may be better.

How should asparagus roots be planted? Plant roots 18 ins. to 2 ft. apart, in a well-enriched trench 8 to 10 ins. deep. Place each plant on a rounded mound of soil; spread roots out carefully in a horizontal position. Cover roots with a few inches of enriched soil. Fill trench in gradually as growth appears above surface. By the first autumn the trench should be filled to the soil level.

Is it advisable to attempt to plant a bed of asparagus roots in the fall of the year? Early spring is better. If plants are home grown (from seed), leave in ground, or dig and store in soil in cold place over winter, then plant early as possible in spring.

How many asparagus roots should be planted per person? Under favorable conditions 10 plants or 15 ft. of row may be expected to furnish asparagus for one person through the season.

How many 3-year asparagus roots (or plants) should I buy for a family of four? (See above.) It is considered better to buy 1-year-old asparagus roots than 2- or 3-year-old roots.

If young asparagus is covered too much, would that stop its growing? Yes, especially if soil is heavy and planting is deep. Eight inches is deep enough for asparagus roots, and the first covering should be only 2 ins., gradually working soil in as the season advances.

If I transplant asparagus that has been cut before, can it be cut the first year after it is transplanted? It is not ordinarily best to move old asparagus roots, but if this is done it would probably be best not to cut the first year. Good top growth is necessary to re-establish the crowns. After that, judgment can be based on the vigor of shoots as they come up.

Is it possible to purchase asparagus roots to plant in the spring and have the shoots to eat the following spring? If asparagus plants are set out in the spring, the shoots should not be harvested until the second spring following, then they may be cut for a period of about 4 weeks, and for a full crop the next year.

How late in the season can asparagus be cut? For an established bed, 8 weeks is about the usual cutting period. If the shoots become spindling, quit cutting so that good growth may be made for the following year. The tops have the job of storing food for next year's crop in the enormous root system under ground.

I started an asparagus bed this year. Next year, when it's time to use the spears, how are they cut? Asparagus should not be cut the year of setting, nor the year after. The third year it should be cut for only about 4 weeks unless you have a long growing season providing rapid growth of crowns. Asparagus is best cut with a special asparagus knife (see Index) just below the surface of the soil. Care must be exercised not to jam the knife into the crown or to injure buds of shoots that may be coming up. The knife should be slipped down fairly close to the shoot that is being cut, and then tilted to avoid injury to other shoots.

Is it necessary to bank or ridge asparagus each year? Most people prefer green asparagus to white or blanched, hence banking is not necessary. Slight ridging may be effective in smothering young weeds just when they appear in the row.

Should asparagus be deeply cultivated?   Asparagus should not be deeply cultivated, as this practice damages the roots and crowns and so hinders growth.

How do I care for and harvest asparagus plants (roots) set out last spring?   During summer pull weeds and give shallow cultivation; mulch with manure in autumn and work it lightly into the surface soil in early spring, keeping a little away from plants and remembering that their roots are shallow and spread horizontally. In fall, when the old plants have lost their green color, cut the tops a few inches above ground and burn them.

Why do some authorities advise cutting asparagus stalks in fall, while others prefer leaving them until spring to help hold the snow and form a winter mulch?   Cutting the stalks in fall before the seeds mature and sow themselves prevents an infestation of seedling plants in the bed. These may become troublesome weeds. If cut 6 or 8 in. high, the stems will help hold mulch or snow.

When should asparagus be fertilized and what fertilizer should be used?   Once a year is often enough to fertilize the asparagus bed. It doesn't make a great deal of difference whether it is done in early spring or at the end of the cutting season, when plants are allowed to grow up. Fertilizing before cutting is generally preferred. In sandy soils use a 5–10–10 fertilizer, at the rate of 35 lbs. per 1,000 sq. ft. In heavier soils, a 5–10–5 would probably do as well. Stable manure also is first-rate for asparagus.

How does one apply salt to asparagus?   The use of common salt on asparagus beds has long been traditional, but there is little scientific support for this practice. If it is used in large quantities, it is effective for control of weeds. This would require around 2 lbs. per square yard. Use of a complete fertilizer will meet requirements of the plants for sodium and chlorine.

How do you protect asparagus during the winter?   Asparagus winters over very well even in Northern climates. Leaving tops on to help hold snow cover is desirable. If winter injury is noted, a light mulch of coarse manure may be helpful.

How often should asparagus beds be reset?   Resetting is not practical. Asparagus beds remain in good production from 10 to 25 years or even longer, according to conditions, if a bed is well maintained as to fertility and weed control.

Is it natural for asparagus plants to turn brown in the fall of the year?   Yes, the tops of asparagus plants turn brown and die in the fall.

Do asparagus crowns gradually come to the surface of the soil?
This is true, not because the crowns actually move, but because the
new growth of the root stocks which make up the crowns is nearer
to the soil surface than the old growth. This, however, is of little
harm since most people prefer green asparagus. When they come
within 2 or 3 ins. of the surface, cultivation over the row before and
after cutting is likely to injure the buds.

**What is best to do to revive an old asparagus bed? The yield is
light now, and stalks small.** If an asparagus bed is in good shape
except for lack of fertilization, it may be revived by starting a good
program of fertility maintenance. If the crowns have become spent,
or the stand is poor, it is better to start a new bed.

Is it practical to interplant between asparagus rows? No. Roots
of asparagus are not deep and spread horizontally. Interplanting would
injure these spreading rootlets.

How are asparagus plants grown from seed? For growing asparagus roots select a fertile soil in good tilth. Mark out rows 18 ins.
apart. Sow seeds 2 ins. apart in the row and cover ½ to 1 in. deep.
Soaking the seed in lukewarm water for 3 to 5 days will hasten germination. Then plant at once; in late April or early May.

Does asparagus do well in the far South? Asparagus is successfully
grown commercially in South Carolina, but in such states as Florida
and Louisiana it does not do well. Under these conditions the plants
seem to continue to produce shoots and do not build up adequate
reserve in the storage roots.

What causes asparagus to be tough and pithy? Insufficient fertilizer; poor soil preparation, a pH below 6.5; allowing it to get too old
before cutting.

How can I avoid asparagus rust? Purchase seeds or roots of a
rust-resistant variety, such as Mary Washington.

What is the control for asparagus beetle? Dust with rotenone.

**What asparagus varieties are suitable for the Washington, D.C.,
metropolitan area?** Mary Washington, which is partially resistant
to asparagus rust, is the leading variety everywhere.

**What is your opinion of the new Paradise asparagus compared
with Mary Washington?** Indications are that Paradise is very
similar to a good strain of Mary Washington. Cannot be expected
to give full crop a year ahead of other varieties, as is sometimes
claimed.

BEANS, SNAP AND POLE

**What is the difference between string beans, stringless beans, and
snap beans?** All older varieties of beans had strong, fibrous, stringy
growths running the length of the pods. The removal of these strings

was a tedious job. Many years ago plant breeders began producing varieties in which these "strings" were eliminated. These were called stringless beans. Stringless beans are easy to break or "snap" into pieces; hence they are called snap beans.

How should ground be prepared and fertilized for planting snap beans and shell beans? Beans need a well-prepared, thoroughly drained soil. Use a 5–10–10 complete fertilizer, 2½ lbs. per 100 sq. ft. of row. Apply as a side dressing, 3 ins. from row or hill. Beans do well on soil too poor for most other vegetables. Fertilizers high in nitrogen are to be avoided.

How are bush beans planted? At intervals of 2 or 3 weeks, beginning as soon as danger of frost is over until 2 months before first fall frost may be expected. Sow 1 in. deep in rows 18 to 24 ins. apart, seeds about 1½ to 2 ins. apart in row.

How are snap beans best grown in the home garden? Bush snap beans are planted after danger of frost is fairly well past, say 2 or 3 weeks after average date of last killing frost, or a week before tomatoes are set out. They will not withstand frost after they are above ground. They thrive in a wide variety of soil types. Leaf diseases are controlled by getting seed that is disease free. Dusting is necessary in areas where Mexican bean beetles prevail.

How many plantings of snap beans shall I make each year? That depends on the length of your growing season. Beans require about 60 days to mature. The last planting should not be made later than 70 days before the first killing frost. Therefore you can plant every 2 weeks until that date. If you make a planting May 1, you can plant 5 or 6 times.

Why do the new stringless green beans lack the flavor of "string beans"? It is doubtful if there is much connection between stringless-ness and stringiness on the one hand and flavor of beans on the other. Some of the old varieties were thin-walled and less succulent than the newer ones, and so would presumably have more pronounced flavor. The stringless or nearly stringless pole beans, Burpee's Golden, Blue Lake, Scotia, and the Old Kentucky Wonder, would be described by some as richer and more flavorable than such varieties as Tender-green.

Is there really a bean, either string or lima, that can be planted early, and perhaps stand cool weather? No. Lima beans are hot-weather, long-season beans. Snap beans will grow in somewhat cooler weather; however, they are not frost resistant.

What varieties of yellow wax beans will ripen in rotation? All the bush beans bear in about the same time. They can be planted, however, for succession crops, at intervals of 2 to 4 weeks. You can grow the pole varieties and have beans over a longer period.

Do varieties of beans mix when planted in a garden near each other?   Some degree of crossing in the field occurs among beans, differing with varieties and conditions. However, this would not affect the immediate crop. It might result in contamination if seed were to be saved for the next year.

Can beans be grown in the same place two successive years?   Yes, but it is preferable not to grow beans in the same ground within 2 or 3 years as diseases are likely to harbor in bean refuse.

Could one plant pole beans around a live tree or would the roots of the tree kill the plant?   Not advisable, on account of shade and the drying of the soil by the tree roots. Set poles, say 10 ft. high, then plant the beans in a circle around each pole, running strings to little stakes in the circle. Another good way is to set poles 6 or 7 ft. high, rather firmly anchored, at the ends of a row; string a heavy wire on top of the poles and another wire about a foot from the ground; weave binder twine (or stout string) between the two wires, averaging about a foot apart. Beans will climb such a trellis like nobody's business.

How and when should I plant Kentucky Wonder or other pole beans?   Plant when danger of frost is past. Where seasons are very long, a late planting may be made for fall. Sow seed along a fence or trellis 3 or 4 seeds per ft. and an inch or 2 deep. If hill system is preferred, plant 6 to 8 seeds per hill; set poles at least 3 ft. apart.

Can pole beans be grown successfully along a fence about 4 ft. high?   Yes, on a wire fence. A higher fence is better. A little trellis can be set above the fence to allow for greater height of plants. If the fence is of stone or boards, it will be desirable to use strings or poultry wire from the ground to the top of the fence.

Tepee support for pole beans made by tying three light poles together at the top.

When do you harvest kidney and other shell beans for use in the dry state? Should they be shelled right away?   Dry beans are harvested when the pods have matured and begun to dry up but before they open and begin to drop the beans. One has to strike a happy medium for minimum loss from immaturity on the one hand and shattering on the other. Leaves ordinarily turn brown to considerable degree. Vines may be harvested entirely and allowed to dry on a shed or garage floor, and then the beans may be flailed out. Of course in small quantities they may be picked by hand. They will shell out easier after the pods have become dry.

How should I care for snap, lima, and soybeans in the fall so as to get seed for planting or winter eating? Conditions in the northeast are not very favorable for saving seed of beans. Commercial production has moved West to irrigated areas where there is bright, dry weather at curing time. On a small scale one can pick the pods, dry them, shell them, and put the seeds away. On a larger scale the whole plant may be pulled when leaves begin to drop and taken in to a barn floor, garage, or other suitable place. Then they may be flailed out, cleaned, and put away. Plants from which seed is saved should be free of anthracnose and bacterial blight. Seeds should be treated with carbon disulfide to control bean weevil. Put beans in tight vessel with a cover. Put 1 oz. of carbon disulfide (inflammable) per bu. in a dish on top of beans inside of vessel to vaporize. For table use, heating for 30 minutes at 125° F. will kill the weevils but also the germ of the seed and it will not sprout.

When bean vines turn yellow is it an indication of too much water, cold weather, or lack of fertilizer? This could be an indication of either lack of fertilizer or cold weather.

What beans for use green or dry are not bothered by the bean beetle? There seems to be little difference in susceptibility of bean varieties to Mexican bean beetle. People are sometimes confused because there are early and late broods of the beetle with a period of relative immunity between. The beetle is not particularly difficult to control with rotenone, pyrethrum, or magnesium arsenate. Magnesium arsenate should not be used while plants are in bloom.

What is the best control for Mexican bean beetle? Rotenone dusted on the under side of the leaves when the grubs hatch from the orange-colored eggs. Don't dust until you see the grubs or beetles as the dust does not last long. (See Section VIII.)

What are the names of really honest-to-goodness stringless bush beans, both green and wax? Tender green, Tender Pod, Stringless Valentine and Wade for green; Pencilpod, Brittle Wax, and Black Wax for the yellow.

What is the best green bean to plant for canning? Bountiful is a heavy bearer. Tendergreen is of better flavor and retains its tenderness even when quite fully grown.

What variety of green stringless beans would you recommend for freezing and storage in lockers? Tendergreen, Topcrop or Tenderlong.

What beans are resistant to the blight? Bountiful and Tendergreen.

In a small vegetable garden would you recommend pole beans instead of bush beans? The question of bush *vs.* pole beans is largely one of choice. Bush beans are less trouble to take care of, bear considerably earlier, and succession plantings may be made to give a supply throughout the season. On the other hand, pole beans bear over a longer period of time, and a good many like the pole varieties such as Blue Lake, Scotia, and the old Kentucky Wonder. Decatur and Potomac are two new ones. Burpee's Golden is a distinct new type, with yellow pods of fine flavor.

BEANS, LIMA

Do large lima beans need to be planted right side up to grow? Lima beans do not need to be planted right side up (or, more correctly, with the eye down). Experiment has shown small difference in results when planting in this way. But in heavy soil in the home garden it is probably worth the extra trouble.

How can I grow lima beans successfully? Lima beans (bush type) can be grown on well-maintained garden soil, planting after danger of frost is past. Seed at the rate of 3 or 4 per ft. 1 to 2 ins. deep, with rows 2 to 3 ft. apart. Dusting for Mexican bean beetle may be necessary.

How long will pole lima beans grow and produce? Pole limas will yield edible beans over a longer period of time than bush beans—say 4 to 5 weeks, or even more, depending on climatic conditions.

When are lima beans ready to eat? When they are about full grown but still green. If they stay on the vines long enough to begin to turn white they are usually too hard.

Do large limas require acclimating? No. Acclimating a stock of seed generally means breeding for adaptation to a specific soil and climate. Lima beans seem to be about as widely adapted as most of our vegetables.

How and when do you harvest lima beans? If left till dry they mold; and if green, they shrink. I have too many to go over them every day or so. Most gardeners prefer to harvest lima beans when the seeds have reached full size in the pods but are still young and tender; eating, freezing, or canning them at this stage. Most of the dry lima beans are grown in western areas where conditions are particularly favorable for their production and curing. If left to mature in the garden, they may be harvested when the pods have dried, but if the climate or weather at this time is humid, there is likely to be trouble in drying and curing.

What can I do to pole limas to make them mature? Lima beans, especially the pole varieties, require a fairly long season for maturity of the crop—90 to 120 days. Thus in northern climates it is important that they be planted as soon as possible after danger of frost is past. They can be started earlier if hotkaps are used.

Will pole lima beans mature in Massachusetts? The growing season in Massachusetts varies from 150 to 200 days. Pole limas require 90 to 120 days for maturity, so it is possible to grow them. (Length of season is measured between average date of last killing frost in the spring and average date of first killing frost in the fall.)

I have been trying to raise pole lima beans for 3 years and have had no success. Vines grow 10 to 12 ft. long, lots of bloom, but beans fall off when they are about ½ in. long. A few will get full-size pods but no beans. My garden is sandy loam and I use the best seed I can obtain; also use 5–10–10 fertilizer at the rate of about 1,000 lbs. per acre, applied in the hill. What is wrong? Lima beans do not set well when there is a period of hot, dry, sunshiny weather with low humidity during the blossom period. Fordhook, a large lima, is more susceptible to these unfavorable conditions than the Henderson, or the Bush Sieva type. One study showed also that under certain conditions, where there is boron deficiency in the soil, applications of 15 lbs. per acre of borax made increases up to 40 per cent in yield of limas. Whether this is directly associated with set of pods or with other factors is not clear. Use of a hormone spray, such as Blossom-Set is recommended. Factors such as insect injury, unbalanced nutrition, and others are probably involved.

How can I raise lima beans without blight? The best insurance against blight (including both anthracnose and bacterial) is the use of clean seed which has been grown in territory free from the disease. Some progress has been made in developing resistant strains. Cultivating beans when wet will spread anthracnose if it is present. Bean refuse in the garden is likely to harbor and carry over the disease.

Why can't we raise lima beans? They come to full bloom then blight. Crop rotation, burning old vines, and spraying with Bordeaux mixture are the best controls for blight. Of course clean, healthy seed is important.

Do Mexican bean beetles attack lima beans? Yes, very much so. Control by dusting with rotenone dust.

What are best varieties of lima beans? Leading varieties of lima beans are: Bush, potato type: Fordhook U.S. 242, bush, flat-seeded; Burpee bush, and similar ones. Small or Sieva type: All green, Baby Fordhook, Cangreen, and others; some of these maintain green color until ready to harvest. Pole, potato type: Challenger; Pole, flat-seeded: Giant Podded, King of the Garden, and Ideal. Small-seeded: Sieva, or Carolina Small White.

What variety of lima beans will produce the most? It is difficult to say what variety of limas will do best under the widely different conditions of the country. In general, large-seeded limas, such as Fordhook and Burpee Bush, do well in the more humid climates. The Sieva type (including Baby Fordhook, Baby Potato, and Cangreen) do well under hotter, drier conditions, but it is a good deal more trouble to pick and shell them.

SOYBEANS

What type of soil is needed to grow soybeans? Soybeans are among the thriftiest of plants and will make the most of any soil in which they find themselves. But better soil means more and better beans.

Where can I obtain United States bulletins on the culture of soybeans? Publications of the United States Department of Agriculture may be obtained from Office of Information, United States Department of Agriculture, Washington, D.C. Other publications on soybeans are: W. C. Sherman and H. R. Albrecht, *Edible Soy Beans,* Alabama (Auburn). Experimental Station *Bulletin 255.* United States Department of Agriculture *Farmers' Bulletins 1520, 1617,* and *Leaflet 12.*

Do soybeans require any special care? Soybeans should not be planted too deep, say about 1 in. Rows 2 to 3 ft. apart; 5 to 8 seeds per ft. Protect from rabbits and Japanese beetle.

Should soybeans be inoculated? When growing soybeans for the first time it is wise to get inoculating material with the seed or from a seed store. They may be grown on the same soil for a year or so, and from that point on inoculation should not be necessary. Even though not inoculated they will usually make a fair crop.

Please give some idea of production of soybeans. I understand the pods average 2 beans each but have not been able to determine to what extent each plant produces pods. Is it wise to include a planting of soybeans in a small garden? Garden soybeans are certainly worth trying, but make sure to sow an edible variety. Variety, soil, and season are some of the factors determining the number of pods per plant; it may vary between 20 and 50.

Are edible soybeans satisfactory in the home garden? Yes, if you have use for them and you like them. They are used as green shell beans or dry, but require 3 to 4 months to mature and more space than snap beans.

Is it feasible to grow edible soybeans as a green-manure or cover crop, to be plowed under after harvesting the beans? One of the advantages of growing soybeans is that the roots gather nitrogen and leave it with the soil. Usually, however, the plants are cut or pulled with the pods on them; in that case they would not supply much humus, unless used in the compost heap.

What are the chief pests attacking soybeans? Japanese beetles and rabbits are the only bad pests.

We had a lot of soybeans. It was a big job to pick them but fa' worse to shell them. Is there an easier way? Soybeans should be blanched in boiling water, 3 to 5 minutes, before shelling them out. This makes the process much less difficult.

How do you cook soybeans? Green soybeans may be scalded in the pods to make shelling easier. Shell, boil until tender (like limas), and serve buttered. *Baked:* Soak dried soybeans overnight; bring to a boil in fresh water, and boil ½ hour; then use same as pea beans for baked beans. *Soy Loaf:* To one pint of cold, boiled (dried) soybeans add a beaten egg, a cup of bread crumbs, 1 tablespoon chopped onion, 2 tablespoons tomato catsup, and salt and pepper to taste. Form into loaf and bake 1 hour. Serve with tomato sauce. *Salted:* Soak dried beans overnight; boil 1 hour in fresh, salted water; spread in shallow pan (after removing excess moisture) and roast in oven at 350° until light brown; butter and sprinkle with salt. Or French fry dried, boiled beans in deep fat, and sprinkle with salt.

Can soybeans be canned successfully? And how? Yes. Eighty minutes at 240° F. of 10 lbs. pressure in the cooker. (See canning directions for fuller instructions.)

Which varieties of soybeans are suitable for the North? Giant Green, Bansei, Mendota.

What are some good Southern varieties of edible soybeans? Willomi, Rokusan or Hokkaido.

Which variety of soybeans is best for home garden? Giant Green is the earliest—about 90 days from seed to picking. Hokkaido and Jogun are good varieties requiring about 110 days. Willomi is late and requires a longer season than most of New York or New England affords, but it is a good variety.

BEANS, BROAD

What soil is preferred by Broad Windsor beans? A heavy, well-drained soil, limed and manured.

When should Windsor (or Broad) beans be planted to crop before hot weather? Broad, Windsor, or Fava beans thrive under cool conditions. They can be planted as soon as soil is dry enough to work —2 or 3 weeks before snap beans would be planted. They mature in about the same time as bush lima beans; somewhat quicker than pole limas, or about 80 to 90 days.

How can black aphids be avoided on Broad beans? Plant early, as soon as danger of hard frost is past. Spray with Black Leaf 40 or use Lindane or Aphis Dust or Spray (Niagara Chemical Company) according to directions on the package when first aphids appear; repeat as frequently as needed.

BEANS, MUNG

What is the botanical family and species of the small mung beans

used by the Chinese for sprouts, and how do they compare with soybeans in protein and vitamin value? (California.) The small-seeded or green mung bean used for bean sprouts by the Chinese is *Phaseolus aureus*. Like other beans, the family name is *Leguminoseae*. The mung bean, although belonging to the same genus as our common field beans, is of a different species. The protein content of the mung bean is about the same, or slightly higher, than that of our common beans. The comparative figures on percentage composition are 23.3 and 22.7 per cent respectively. For soybeans the protein value is about 50 per cent higher. No comparative figures on vitamin content seem to be available.

How do you grow bean sprouts used to make chop suey? (Oklahoma.) The bean usually used in the production of bean sprouts for chop suey is the mung (*Phaseolus aureus*). This is a small, green-seeded type grown most extensively in this country in Oklahoma. The method of producing mung beans commercially is best described in Oklahoma Station *Circular C-104,* "Mung Beans for Oklahoma." Bean sprouts are usually produced by placing a layer of the dry seed on a rack in the bottom of a moist chamber, preferably in a large earthen jar. (The beans should not lie directly in water, hence the advice to place them on a screen or rack above the water.) The vessel should be covered to exclude light and maintain a moist chamber. A minimum of 5 to 7 days is the period usually required to produce sprouts 2 to 4 in. long. Room temperature will promote rapid sprouting. In the winter, water should be added twice daily; in the summer, preferably three times a day. Before placing the beans in the jar for sprouting, the seed should be thoroughly washed and the jar made sterile to prevent molding.

BEETS

How shall I sow beets and when? Sow as soon as ground can be worked, in rows 12 to 15 ins. apart, a dozen seeds to the foot, ½ inch deep. For late beets, sow deeper, up to 2 in., to secure moisture in very dry, light soil.

What fertilizer for beets? Beets require very fertile, well-limed soil, not deficient in potash, and in good tilth. *Do not use fresh manure.* Apply old manure, or complete fertilizer (preferably 5–10–10), at rate of 3 lbs. per 100 sq. ft. of row.

Why are there spaces in the beet row where seed did not come up? Possibly the seed did not germinate because it was too old. Or damping-off organisms may have been at work. Use a seed disinfectant (Cupricide) before planting to prevent damping off.

Is it profitable to transplant beets? I have never had them grow so well as the ones left in the row. However, I don't seem to be able to prevent the seed from coming up too thick. Each beet seed (so-called) contains several true seeds, hence the thick growth of seedlings. Those thinned out may have been damaged at the roots, or when transplanted the taproot may not have been set vertical. Carefully transplanted plants grow well.

Why do beets, apparently healthy, fail to produce large roots? Possibly because the plants are getting too much nitrogen and too little potash. Better have your soil tested.

Heard over the radio that beets need boron. Could I put some borax in a watering pot and add it to the soil that way? My beets were a failure. Carrots growing beside them were fine. This may have been lack of boron. One ounce of borax in 16 qts. of water will prevent it. Trouble may have been due to a lack of potash. Use wood ashes where you grow beets.

What variety of beets do you recommend for winter storage? Detroit Dark Red is a standard variety for late keeping. Winter Keeper and Lutz Green Leaf are others.

BROCCOLI

How is Italian Broccoli grown? In exactly the same manner as cabbage. The spring crop is started in the greenhouse or hotbed in early March, taken to the field in mid-April, and harvested in June. The fall cut may be directly seeded in the field about July 1 to 10, thinned out about August 1, and harvested in September or October.

How do you fertilize for broccoli? Broccoli requires a lot of nitrogen, especially if it is planted in the spring and is permitted to grow all summer. If it is kept fertilized well, it will grow until freezing weather. Side-dress the plants every month or so.

Cabbage and broccoli, two important crops for the home garden, can be set out as soon as frost is out of the ground.

How can I get early broccoli for the table? Grow plants from seed under glass, planting in late February. (See Seed Sowing.) Or buy young plants from a local grower and set out as soon as ground can be worked and danger of hard frost is over.

When should broccoli be planted? Because of its highly nutritious nature broccoli is becoming more popular every year. It may be started with plants set in the garden as early as the ground can be prepared. These plants will produce good broccoli all season. If second crop is wanted, sow seeds outside in May.

Is there any way to hurry along broccoli? I planted some late in April and September arrived and still no blooms. Up until severe freezing it was still growing, but no heads. Late April is not the time to plant broccoli seed. Sow seed May 15 to June 1 and set out plants in July; or sow in February or March for early crop. Early strains are now available.

What treatment of Sprouting (or Italian) Broccoli will cause them to produce thick clusters of buds rather than sparse clusters? Plant in rich, deep, friable soil. Cultivate constantly. Water during dry periods and side-dress with nitrogen or liquid manure when plants are established. The side sprouts never produce heads as large as those that first form at top of main stalk.

When and how should broccoli be cut? When flower heads have formed, but while florets are *in tight bud*. Cut with sharp knife a few inches below head. New heads will form from side shoots, and cutting can continue as heads form. Keep heads cut regularly.

How can I keep broccoli producing all summer? *Keep the heads cut off* as soon as they are ready to use. When cutting broccoli cut 2 to 4 ins. of stem. If cut too close to the heads the plant will send out too many small side shoots.

What is the cause of apparently healthy broccoli suddenly turning yellow and wilting? It could be caused by any one of a number of things: lack of water or food, cabbage yellows, or root maggots. (See Section VIII.)

Can you give me some information on the preparation of broccoli for the table? Broccoli is cut when flower heads are close and green. All but small leaves about head are removed. Wash, and place upright in deep kettle, heads above water. Boil, uncovered, until stems are almost tender. Then immerse heads and cook until these are tender. (Entire cooking time 15 to 30 minutes.) Serve with browned butter, cream, cheese, or Hollandaise sauce.

BRUSSELS SPROUTS

When should you plant Brussels sprouts seed? Sow seeds May 15 to June 15. Set plants out about August 1.

What cultivation and type of soil are needed for Brussels sprouts? Set plants out in rich, friable soil; cultivate constantly; water in dry weather, and side-dress with nitrogen or liquid manure during early stages of growth.

How can I raise Brussels sprouts? They grow up, and I break off outer leaves, except top few. The little balls start, and there they sit! Try an application of liquid manure or water-soluble fertilizer when sprouts begin forming (see preceding answer).

Can Brussels sprouts be grown in the climate we have in St. Louis? (Missouri.) Not too well. Seed should be sown in your section June 1, plants set out July 20, in cool soil, and watering should be frequent.

Should we cut the leaves off Brussels sprouts when heads start to form? Remove lower leaves only, to facilitate cutting of the sprouts.

Brussels sprouts have beautiful plants, but the sprouts are not firm, just loose and leafy. How can I get firm sprouts? (South Carolina.) Heat may be the cause of this trouble. Try an application of liquid manure or water-soluble fertilizer when sprouts begin forming.

When and how are Brussels sprouts harvested? Brussels sprouts are harvested by cutting the "sprouts" (like tiny heads of cabbage) off the stems with a sharp knife after the leaves have been broken off. The leaves will usually snap off easily as far up the stem as the "sprouts" are ready to cut.

CABBAGE

What kind of soil is suitable for cabbage? In the home garden cabbage may be grown successfully in a wide variety of soils. For commercial culture, a rather heavy loam is usually preferred, although early varieties are frequently grown on fairly light soil. All of the cabbage group are heavy feeders and do best when two or three applications of fertilizer are given during the growing season.

What kind of soil and fertilizer are required for growing cabbage successfully? (California.) Any soil that will not bake too hard is suitable for cabbage. Frequent cultivation is essential. Fertilizers high in nitrogen are preferable when setting plants out, plus a side dressing of nitrogen or liquid manure when they are half grown.

How can I make cabbage head early? (New Jersey.) Set out in early April, soon as ground can be worked. Apply good fertilizer immediately. Side-dress with nitrogen or liquid manure one month later. Water frequently in dry weather.

I cannot raise cabbage or cauliflower in my garden. Why? If soil is not poor, it may be infested with club root, which attacks cabbage and cauliflower. Try new soil in a different part of the vegetable garden. Dig to a depth of 12 in.; use plenty of rotted manure. Cultivate frequently; water during dry spells; side-dress with nitrate of soda or liquid manure when plants are established.

Why do our cabbage and broccoli plants, carefully tended in newly turned soil that is rich and black, form foliage instead of heads? (Illinois.) Probably a lack of lime, phosphorus, or potash. Boron deficiency may cause the heart to die out. You can see this by examining the leaves in the center of the plant.

I have been planting cabbages for four years, but they do not do well; make long stems but few heads. What is the trouble? Seed purchased may be of doubtful quality. Plants may be held out of ground too long before planting. Soil may be deficient in phosphorus and potash, or not be sufficiently cultivated.

We have a small plot of Savoy cabbages. Some of them are large and some very small. Why? Evidently seed obtained could have been higher quality; soil fertility may be spotty. Buy the best seed and distribute fertilizer evenly.

Why do cabbage heads crack? How can I prevent this? Usually due to rapid growth during warm weather on early cabbage, causing premature formation of a seed stalk when the head is maturing. Heads should be cut as soon as full grown. With the fall crop there is less difficulty. If the heads tend to split, plants should be pulled up by the roots, allowed to dry, placed in paper bags, and hung in the storage room with the roots up. Loosening the roots by pulling will check splitting for several days.

When should cabbage seed be started? (Missouri.) For spring crop, 60 to 90 days before danger of last hard frost. For fall crop, May 15 to June 20.

When is the best time to plant cabbage for early setting? (New Jersey.) Sown indoors 60 to 90 days before danger of last hard frost in spring, usually late March to mid-April.

How is fall cabbage grown? When planted? (Missouri.) Sow seed May 15 to June 20. Set out plants August 1. Harvest before hard freezing.

How do you control worms on cabbage and other crucifers? Dust the foliage with rotenone dust when the worms make their appearance. In the home garden, catching the yellow or white butterflies, which lay the cabbage worm (see Index) eggs, with a net is helpful.

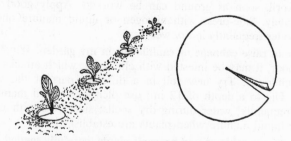

Tar-paper discs placed snugly around stems of cabbage plants prevent injury from root maggots.

What insects and diseases attack crucifers? Root rots are the most serious diseases. Cabbage yellows is serious in some sections but there are resistant varieties to overcome this disease. The main insect trouble is the cabbage worm, which eats the leaves; the harlequin plant bug, and aphids (plant lice), which suck the juices. On early cabbage the root maggot does much damage, unless controlled by using tar-paper discs around stems when setting out plants.

How can cabbage be stored for winter? A few heads of cabbage may be stored by pulling the plants out by the roots and covering the head with a paper sack, tying the sack shut around the stem, and then hanging the head up by the roots. A cool cellar is best. For large quantities cabbage should be stored in pits out of doors and covered with layers of straw and dirt so that it won't freeze.

What are good early and late varieties of cabbage? Early: Jersey Wakefield, Golden Acre, Cornell Savoy. Mid-season: Glory of Enkhuizen. Late: Danish Ball Head. Red: Red Danish.

CARROTS

What soil is best for carrots? Well-limed and aerated sandy loam soil. Incroporate plenty of humus.

Do carrots need plenty of water to grow large, or is fertilizer more important? Carrots need a well-limed soil and average moisture conditions. Use a 5–10–10 fertilizer if the soil is poor.

Does the flavor of carrots vary with the condition of the soil? The carrots which I raised last year had a flat, unsavory flavor. They were grown in ground uncultivated for 10 years. A well-grown carrot is sweeter than a stunted carrot. You may need more lime, humus, and potash in the soil. Too much nitrogen as well as continued hot weather will cause poor flavor.

How does the market gardener plant carrot seed and cultivate to keep down the weeds? What are the newest ways of carrot growing? The market gardener's soil is freer of weeds because he cultivates his ground so much. He thins the rows while plants are still very small, and he may use Stoddard Solvent to control annual weeds, not later than 50 days before harvesting.

Can never get a good stand of carrots. Why? Probably the ground bakes too hard. Try sprinkling some pulverized magnesium limestone over the seed before you cover it. Don't plant the seed too deep; barely covering from sight is sufficient.

How should carrots be planted for succession crops? Make 3 plantings: early spring, early summer, and midsummer—mid-July to August.

Why doesn't carrot seed germinate? It may be too old. Or it may be due to a lack of lime in the soil. Use pulverized magnesium limestone and sprinkle it over the seed in the row before covering with soil.

When is it best to thin out carrots?   When the seedlings are about 2 in. tall. Thin them when the soil is moist—soon after a rain or a good watering.

How are carrots transplanted?   This cannot be done satisfactorily. Anything that breaks off the main taproot causes them to produce branched or forked carrots.

Why do my carrots so often lack color?   The soil may be too dense, contain too much nitrogen, or lack lime. On black soil 20 to 50 lbs. per acre (1 to 2 ozs. per 100 ft. of row) of copper dust will improve their color.

What would make carrots (good seed) which grew rapidly very tough, even the baby ones?   Probably a deficiency of potassium, or insufficient lime in the soil.

What makes forked carrots?   Failure to pulverize thoroughly the soil in which they are to grow; the use of manure which is not well rotted; or perhaps allowing seedlings to grow too big before thinning, which is apt to make their roots twist around one another.

Have read of treating soil with borax for carrots. When advisable, how is it done? Is regular kitchen borax used?   One ounce of ordinary borax to 16 qts. of water, poured along the row, is enough for 50 to 75 ft.

My carrots sometimes have many roots instead of one straight one; or sometimes they are full of little nodules like root bumps. How can this be prevented?   This sounds like nematode injury. Try to grow them where carrots have not been grown before. Fall plowing will tend to minimize the trouble. A lack of lime sometimes causes forked carrots.

Carrots grown during the past season have sprouted many smaller roots from around the main root. Main roots are healthy, about 7 or 8 ins. long, with as many as 6 or 8 smaller carrots all around the main stem. Only some of these in the same row showed this peculiarity, while others were normal. Soil tests were: slightly alkaline, good nitrogen content, deficiency in potash. A good dose of 20 per cent superphosphate was given soil three weeks before planting sandy loam soil in southern Connecticut. What is the matter?   Try some magnesium limestone as well as more potash. It is doubtful whether the high pH is due to lime in the soil.

Do carrots poison the ground?   No, but they do use up nutrients which cause deficiencies for other crops. This is not poisoning, but does affect following crops.

Carrots come up and grow very well until first week in July, then tops die down rather suddenly. About middle or last of August new shoots appear. Carrots get no bigger than middle finger, although tops

look healthy. **Above has occurred every year for 5 years. Other things grow on. What is it?** This sounds like leaf blight. Many commercial growers spray with Bordeaux mixture (which see) to control this disease.

What is proper time to plant carrots for small size for winter storage? (Iowa.) Plant seed June 1 to 20, for usual table size. If de luxe "baby" carrots (about half grown) are wanted—2 or 3 weeks later.

We replanted the carrots in a box of dirt in the cellar this fall. Now they are developing new tops and rootlets. Will the rootlets spoil the carrots for use as a raw vegetable? Not unless they make considerable growth, in which case they will be bitter. The soil should be air dry when used for storing roots. *Very slightly* dampened peatmoss, sand or vermiculite are better than soil for packing around roots in winter.

When shall I dig carrots for winter storage? Just before hard freeze; early frosts do not injure them. Storing them too early may cause them to sprout.

At what stage of development should carrots be pulled for canning? In the "baby" stage—finger size—for best table quality.

What is the best carrot to plant on a rather heavy soil? Oxheart, Chantenay, Danvers, or Nantes Half Long. Use plenty of magnesium limestone.

Can you name a good sweet brand of carrots for the home garden? Tendersweet Nantes, and Hutchinson are the sweetest, according to chemical tests.

CAULIFLOWER

What is the best method for growing cauliflower? Get high-quality seed. For spring crop sow indoors in February or early March. Set out plants as soon as danger of frost is over. Soil must be deep and very rich. Cultivate constantly, and side-dress with a high nitrogen fertilizer. Fall crop: sow seed June 1 to 15; set out plants in August.

Why didn't some of my cauliflowers form heads, while the others did? Also Brussels sprouts? Apparently the seed used was not very high quality. Good cauliflower and Brussels sprouts seed should produce at least 90 to 95 per cent true.

What causes cauliflower heads to turn yellow or purple? The heads turn yellow or purplish if not protected from sun. Pull leaves together over the top of the head as soon as it begins to form, and tie them together at the tips to hold them in place. This will keep the heads perfectly white. Early Purple Head and Royal Purple do not require tying; they turn white when cooked.

How do you bleach cauliflower? When I tie the heads together they turn black and rot. I have been told to use lime, but hesitated to do so.

Do not tie the heads until about 2½ in. in diameter. Never tie too tightly or too closely over the head.

I planted cauliflower and grew nice, snowy-white heads, the first one in 62 days. When they were cooked, they turned a light brown color. What was wrong? Evidently your water contains a considerable amount of iron. Cauliflower should be steamed rather than boiled.

What are better kinds of cauliflower, early and late, for our climate in Wayne County, Pennsylvania? The best varieties are Extra Early Snowball, Early Dwarf Erfurt, and Snowcap. Any reliable seed house can supply high-grade seed of these varieties.

CELERY

Can celery be grown in the home garden? If so, what variety is recommended? It *can* be grown, but requires so much care, patience, and space, that most home gardeners prefer to buy it. Golden Self-Blanching is one of the best for the home garden, though—despite its name—it requires blanching. Emperor (Fordhook) is another.

How should early celery plants be started? Good potting or plant-growing soil should be used for celery. Sow seed in flats or bulb pans. Mark out rows ¼ in. deep and 2 ins. apart. Sow seed 10 to 15 per in., cover very lightly by sifting on not more than ⅛ in. soil. Cover flats with burlap and water moderately. As soon as seedlings break ground, remove burlap. When seedlings are 1½ or 2 in. high, transplant to other flats, spacing them about 2 in. each way. Firm well, with the crowns just about even with the soil but not above. Watering should be managed to give steady but not too rapid growth; temperature between 55 to 65° F. is about right. Plants should be hardened by watering sparingly, instead of by subjecting to cold, as this is likely to cause premature seeding when they are set out in the garden.

Flat of celery plants ready for transplanting into garden.

What is the best time to start celery seed for early planting? Celery seedlings start slowly and seed should be sown under glass 8 to 10 or even 12 weeks before outdoor setting. Celery will withstand moderate frost, and it may be put out about the average date of last hard killing frost, or 2 to 3 weeks before tomato-setting time. Celery plants for a fall crop may be started in a well-prepared outdoor seed-bed about 8 weeks before field setting. Celery will withstand light frost but not hard freezing in the fall, and 100 to 125 days should be allowed from time of *setting out plants* until harvest or storage.

How should celery be spaced and transplanted in the garden? Celery plants should be dug with minimum breaking of the fine root system. In transplanting, avoid doubling up or bunching of roots; pack the soil firmly and set the plants at about the depth they were growing in plant box or seedbed. If set too shallow, roots are exposed; if too deep, dirt is likely to get into the crowns. Rows may be 2 to 3 ft. apart and plants spaced 6 in. apart in the rows. For partial blanching, celery may be planted in rows 18 in. or 2 ft. apart. For blanching with earth, 3 to 4 ft. between rows should be provided.

Kind of soil best for celery? Should it be planted in sun or shade? The soil best for celery should be fertile, well filled with organic matter. The soil range is from moderately sandy to sandy loam to moderately heavy soil, provided the other requirements are met. Muck or peat soils are especially suitable. Rich, well-maintained garden soil usually serves well. It may be fertilized with liberal applications of well-rotted manure (1 lb. per sq. ft.). It responds well to liberal applications of commercial fertilizer—up to 1 lb. per 20 sq. ft. A 5–10–5 fertilizer will not be far wrong on most soils. On peat soils a high potash fertilizer may be desirable. Celery does not do well under shady conditions.

How is celery grown for home use? Buy seed of a good variety of celery. Start the plants under glass or in a carefully selected and prepared seedbed. Choose soil and fertilizer as indicated in answer above and supply adequate moisture—celery is a glutton for water. Control leaf diseases by thorough spraying or dusting with Bordeaux every week or ten days, according to conditions and prevalence of disease. (Blanching and storing are discussed in other answers.)

How much water does celery require? A great deal. The root system of the celery plant is not spread far or deep and a liberal water supply is needed, more so than for most vegetables. Soil should be kept nicely moist throughout the growing season.

Can an outdoor seedbed be used for late celery plants? Yes, but it should be well prepared, rich, friable soil. If seed is sown thinly, transplanting may be omitted, but this uses up garden space. Watering is likely to be necessary, but it should not be overdone, so that plants will not be soft and spindly. Good plants for setting out are about 6 in. high and should be managed so that leaf pruning will not be necessary. It takes about eight weeks to grow them.

How to grow and care for celery in southern California? Celery is not likely to do well in the hotter, dryer parts of California, but a good deal is grown near the coast. Cultural methods are not greatly different from other places. Ample irrigation is likely to be necessary.

Grew our first celery this year. It seemed to thrive, became good size, blanched well, but is hollow and tough. What does it need to grow large and tender? In fall, stalks were soft and stringy. Quality in celery is very much dependent upon favorable growing conditions, especially fertility and moisture. Nor is it likely to be good if the weather is hot and dry. Pithiness or hollow stalk is generally traceable to poorly bred seed. Stringiness varies widely with varieties, being more prominent in the Golden Self-Blanching group than in the late green celeries. It is much more prominent where celery has been grown under unfavorable conditions of fertility, moisture, or heat.

I planted celery in April, and by September it had grown no larger than when planted. It did not die, however. Tomatoes and carrots do well in the same locality. What is wrong? Celery requires soil of high fertility and ample water supply, and it does not do well in hot, dry climates. It is possible that you may have had disease (such as fusarium wilt) without recognizing it.

How does one grow the celery that develops large hearts to be used for braising or eating raw? The proportion of "heart" in celery depends a good deal upon variety. The Golden Self-Blanching strains are good in this respect, the old Giant Pascal not so good, but a number of green celeries of high quality (such as Emperor and Utah) have been developed. The heart comes up and becomes more prominent late in the growth of the plant, or even in the storage space.

How should celery be blanched? Commercial growers use boards or stout paper along the rows; home gardeners may slip a tube over each plant, or tie paper around it. The old method of pulling up earth around the plants involves much washing in the kitchen. Only the stalks, not the foliage, are to be blanched.

Is it necessary to tie up celery, or just let it spread as it grows? Celery is not ordinarily tied up; drawing moist earth up against the plants as they grow will help to keep them from spreading.

Would like to know what causes celery blight. What can I do to check it? Celery "blight" (there are three different leaf diseases) is controlled by faithful dusting or spraying with Bordeaux, taking special pains to cover the lower leaves, especially the under sides. Soil should be free from celery refuse, and it is best if it has not grown celery for a period of 3 years. Spraying or dusting may well begin in the plant bed, especially if disease has been troublesome in the past. Treatment every week or 10 days is necessary, unless the season is very dry and disease is not developing.

What will prevent celery from rotting in the ground after it has been hilled up? Celery for storing and hilling ought to be practically free from disease. Hilling should not be done until really cool weather, and the plants should be dry.

Celery stored in trench (cross section) for fall use.

How can celery be stored, and for how long? Plants are lifted complete with roots (which are light and should be disturbed as little as possible) and replanted in a shallow trench, or in boxes in the storage house or cool cellar, or in a cold frame. The roots should be kept moist *but the stalks dry*. The plants may be kept for a good many weeks. Temperature should be just above freezing.

Why do stalks of celery become yellow after being placed in storage? It was stored in a pit and covered with sand and the roots and leaves over it. Yellowing of celery is the result of the blanching process. It is pretty hard to prevent it under storage conditions. It represents the disappearance of chlorophyll from the leaves and leaf stalks. Temperature just about 32° helps retard yellowing or blanching.

Which is best celery to grow? Recent trend is strongly toward green celeries, with thick leaf stalks which are relatively stringless. Among the most commonly grown of these are: Utah 52–70, Summer Pascal, Fordhook, Emperor, and Masterpiece. The old Giant Pascal is rather lacking in heart, although some strains have been improved in this respect. Cornell 6 and Cornell 19 have the thick leaf stalks and high quality of Pascal but much of the self-blanching character of Golden Self-blanching. If self-blanching celery is desired, use the Dwarf Golden Self-blanching or Golden Plume. Under very favorable conditions these afford good celery but are tougher, more stringy, and have thinner leaf stalks than those mentioned above.

CELERIAC

How to grow celeriac; what soil; shade or sun? Does it have to be blanched? How long can it be left in the ground? Is it subject to celery blight? Celeriac (also known as root celery or knob celery) is grown by the same methods as other celery, with about the same type of soil and light requirements. It doesn't need to be blanched and seems to be more resistant to disease than ordinary celeries, but it may require Bordeaux dusting. It can be left in the soil until danger of freezing weather. The roots will not freeze quite so quickly as the leaf stalks of ordinary celery. It does require good soil and ample irrigation to develop large, smooth roots of fine quality. These, with tops removed, can be stored in sand or soil for winter.

CHAYOTES

What is chayote?   A perennial tropical vine, native to America. Grown as an annual in cooler climates, where 150 days may be counted on between killing frosts. Fruits, which are melonlike, are edible baked or steamed. The tuberous roots are also edible in climates where the vine is perennial and so able to produce small tubers. Young shoots also edible.

What is culture for chayote?   Plant entire fruit on its side, with point slightly exposed, where vine is to grow; or plant shoots from base of an established plant. A rich, well-fertilized soil is needed and a support on which to climb. Fruit may be expected in late fall from spring planting.

Can the chayote be grown in Maine?   Chayote is a tropical perennial vine. It may be grown in greenhouses, or as an annual for its fruit, in sheltered places where the growing season is at least 150 days between killing frosts.

CHICORY (WITLOOF; FRENCH ENDIVE)

Why does my chicory seed, planted in spring, fail to come up? Much of the seed used in this country is often several years old. Fresh seed should come up readily no matter how early it is planted. Buy seed from a reliable seedsman.

How is chicory grown in the garden for winter forcing?   Plant out of doors in early spring in rows 18 in. apart; thin out to 4 in. apart; grow on through entire summer. Summer foliage is not used but permitted to grow and feed roots. Dig roots just before hard freeze for forcing indoors.

How force chicory? What should be done with roots saved for successive forcing?   Dig roots just before hard frost, and trim to a uniform length of 6 to 8 in.; cut tops off just above roots. Pack in a box 12 to 16 in. deep, in peatmoss and sand (or peatmoss and loam), close together, and cover with 6 in. or more of soil. Place in a cool, dark cellar, water well, and cover with a board. When shoots appear at surface, reach down through soil and cut just above roots with sharp knife. Save roots wanted for a second crop by planting— as above—*in dry soil; do not water* until ready to force crop.

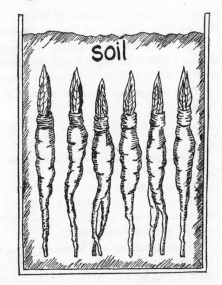

Roots of witloof chicory packed in deep box of moist soil or peatmoss and sand for forcing for winter salad. (Cross section.)

Growing chicory in the cellar, how do we take off the leaves—cut or tear off? We seem to be having good growth, and the leaves are very good eating. If the chicory is forced properly, you shouldn't have to remove any leaves. The "heads" are cut. If the outer leaves are loose, it is an indication that the soil above the crowns is too loose. This should be compact and firm. (See previous question.)

CHINESE CABBAGE

How should soil be prepared for planting Chinese cabbage? Soil should be well drained but moist, thoroughly prepared and fertilized, especially with nitrogen.

How is Chinese cabbage seed planted, and when? Sow where the plants are to grow, very thinly, in rows 18 to 24 in. apart. Thin to 3 in. apart, then to 6 or 8 in. Fall crop is planted 2½ to 3 months before frost. Chinese cabbage is a cool-weather plant and must be grown quickly.

How can one keep Chinese cabbage from going to seed instead of heading? Plant in late midsummer for fall crop; it doesn't like heat. Plant late as possible to mature. Keep soil moist, plants growing without check—80 to 90 days from seeding to maturity.

Why does my Chinese cabbage not form heads? Some pointers on its cultivation. Chinese cabbage requires cool weather to make heads. It should be grown on very fertile soil with lime and plenty of moisture. Thin to 8 in.

What is the trouble with our Chinese cabbage? It grows well until ready to head, then begins to wilt; then the leaves begin to rot. This is probably due to a crown or heart rot. A specimen should be sent to your State Experiment Station for diagnosis.

Why is our Chinese cabbage so buggy? Plant lice or aphids are bad on Chinese cabbage. Spray the plants with Black Leaf 40 just as soon as the lice appear. Repeat as frequently as needed.

What is the best way to store Chinese cabbage? (See Winter Storage.)

CHIVES

How to grow chives: what soil; shade or sun? In view of the fact that seed may not be too good, it is best to start with plants, dividing them into sections, and setting these in the ground as one would onion seedlings. They need a well-limed, loamy soil, and must be grown in full sunlight. Divide and replant old clumps every 2 or 3 years to prevent overcrowding.

Is it necessary to cut blossoms from chives in order to keep tops (foliage) good for use? Removal of the flowers makes new growth easier to cut, because old flower stems are tough. This also encourages growth of new foliage instead of letting strength go into seeds.

How are chives used in cookery? Young foliage and bulbs are both used for flavoring, in soups, salads, on vegetables—wherever a very delicate onion flavor is desired.

CORN, SWEET

How is ground prepared for corn planting? Thoroughly dug or plowed and soil along rows or in hills well pulverized when fertilizer is being added prior to planting.

How should corn be fertilized? Corn needs a 5–10–5 complete fertilizer and/or well-rotted manure to make soil fertile. Rotted compost is also good. Fertilize when preparing ground a week or more before planting. In good garden soil, in good tilth, pour a cupful of starter solution over seeds in a hill before covering with earth and omit other fertilizer.

Does sweet corn need lime? Corn likes pH of 5.6 to 6.8: that is, slightly acid.

How should corn be planted? Either in rows 30 in. apart, 3 or 4 kernels to the foot, 1 to 2 in. deep, 3 or 4 rows being planted at once to insure cross-pollination; or in hills 3 ft. apart each way, 5 or 6 seeds to the hill, planting always 2 or more rows of hills, for cross-pollination.

When should sweet corn be planted? Plant sweet corn a week before the probable date of the last killing frost in the spring, if early crop; 10 days or so later for main crop. A late planting (of *early* varieties) can be made 80 to 90 days before probable date of first fall frost.

Can sugar corn be successfully started in pots indoors for transplanting? Yes, providing they are not kept too warm and set in the ground too early. This method has limitations but will give you earlier corn. Dirt bands (see Index) made of thin wood veneer and 3 or 4 in. square are better for this purpose than pots.

In order to have a supply of young corn fairly late into the fall, what is the latest date it should be planted? (New York.) July 4 to 15, depending on length of growing season (between last spring and first fall frosts) in the locality.

Is there any advantage in planting sweet corn in blocks instead of single rows? When planting three varieties of sweet corn at one time for succession it is better to plant a third of each of three rows in a little block than to have single rows of each variety. This makes for better pollination, since each row helps pollinate the others and so ears are better filled.

How should corn be cultivated? Cultivation should be frequent to control weeds, but should be shallow. Hill up as plants grow.

How many stalks of sweet corn are left to a hill? Usually only 3.

How many corn plants are left to the foot when planted in rows? Thin to 1 ft. apart.

My sweet corn was a complete failure this season. It grew heavy, tall stalks but no ears. Planted 6 rows at a time, about 6 in. apart in row. Rainfall was exceptionally heavy, which was the only unusual thing. What was wrong? (Soil analysis shows deficiency of potash.) Used commercial fertilizer with heavy percentage of this; small amount of nitrogen. Stalks were too close together. They should be a foot apart.

I have never succeeded in growing good corn. The stalks grow well but the ears are few and small. I buy seed from a good house and plant in accordance with instructions. I have planted the seeds in three very widely separated locations; in fact, one garden is 7 miles away from the others. This sounds like too close planting or too much nitrogen and too little lime, phosphorus, or potash. The soil may be too dense below the plowed layer.

Last spring I planted corn (two kinds) and it tasseled when about 2 or 3 ft. high. That was all we saw of corn. Why? Sounds like an acid soil, dry weather, or a lack of fertilizer; possibly all three.

What is the cause of incomplete development of kernels on an ear of corn? All around the ear the kernels may be plump, sweet, and full of juice, but 2 rows or more may be dry and flat. Plant in blocks rather single rows, in order to assure cross-pollination and development of every kernel. It may also be the result of the corn borer working in the stalk just below the ear.

Can the fact that my corn failed to produce one single ear, when planted in 2 250-ft. rows, as per directions, be due to the fact that the 3–8–7 fertilizer used was too poor in phosphate? Fertilizer should be O.K. Perhaps stalks too close together. Ten 50-ft. rows would insure better pollination than 2 250-ft. rows.

Should suckers be removed from corn? If so, when? Nobody has been able to prove that there is any advantage in removing the suckers from sweet corn. From a physiological point of view, to do any good the suckers should be removed when they are not over 3 in. tall. Most people sucker corn when it is a foot high. This is too late and injures the parent plant when the suckers are removed.

How keep crows from stripping sweet corn after it is in ear? Hang up tin cans, or other nose makers. Scarecrows may help.

What can I do to control corn borer? Dust the plants every 5 days with ryania dust. They should be dusted from the top, so that the dust gets into *the axils of the leaves*. The use of rotenone dust once a week is the usual control. All infested stalks should be burned in the fall, as the pest winters over in the plant refuse.

How can I prevent the corn-ear worm from ruining the ears? You can put 10 to 20 drops of mineral oil, containing rotenone, on the silk about 3 days after the silk comes out of the ear. Or you can cut off the silk close to the ear every 5 days. Or grow varieties developed with close-tipped husks, to prevent entry of worm.

Why do we usually find only one worm in an ear of corn? There are many eggs laid on the silk and many worms hatch, but one of them survives and grows by devouring all the others, so that there is only one left.

Is there any method of controlling corn smut during the growing period? No complete control except to remove and burn as soon as discovered and *before* powdery spores are released into air to spread disease. Smut is a fungous growth which comes through the stem into the ear or tassel.

Are there any varieties of sweet corn absolutley smut proof? No. You might try spraying the plants with Bordeaux mixture when the ears are beginning to form. Be sure to destroy smutty ears before the powdery spores are released into the air.

What is hybrid sweet corn? A hybrid is the first-generation progeny resulting from the crossing of two inbred lines. The breeder first works several years purifying and fixing the character of his inbred lines. He then crosses two of these, hoping to secure a combination of several desired characters and more vigorous growth.

What kind of sweet corn is best for home garden? One of the

Golden Bantam hybrids, such as Golden Cross. Lincoln has a tight tip which discourages ear worm.

Which variety of sugar corn should be planted to obtain the best results? (Massachusetts.) There are many varieties of sweet corn, some of them bred to suit particular conditions of growth in differing areas, but the most widely adapted and most extensively planted in recent years is the yellow hybrid, Golden Cross Bantam, derived from the famous old Golden Bantam.

What is the earliest and best yellow sweet corn to raise for market? (Connecticut.) Marcross or Spancross. The Connecticut Experiment Station at New Haven has many good new varieties.

What variety of yellow sweet corn, frost resistant, will mature early in July? There is no frost-resistant corn. There are some varieties that will grow at lower temperatures. North Star, Sun-up and Spancross are early yellow varieties but they may not mature early in July. Miniature is a very early, small-eared variety.

What six kinds of corn are best for succession crops? Varieties that would give you corn over the longest period might be the following from earliest to late: Sun-up, North Star, Golden Beauty, Golden Sunshine, Northern Cross, Golden Cross Bantam. And for still later Stowell's Evergreen, Country Gentleman, and Golden Colonel.

How can I get succession crops of sweet corn? Take any one variety and make plantings every 2 weeks. If you make only small plantings (a dozen hills or so), make plantings every week. Or you can pick a group of varieties that will mature at different dates.

What varieties will give a good succession of sweet corn? For a succession, a first early variety such as Spancross, Seneca Dawn, North Star, or Extra Early Yellow may be used. Plant at the same time Marcross, Carmel Cross, Lincoln, or similar varieties; and also Golden Cross Bantam or Golden Colonel. These will come on far enough apart for each planting to clear the other. Then when the Golden Cross Bantam is 2 or 3 in. high, another planting may be made, and so on, as long as maturity can reasonably be expected. This means up to 90 or 100 days (early varieties 80 to 90 days) before average date of first killing frost in the fall.

Where can I get seed for vari-colored Indian corn? (Michigan.) Western seed houses carry Black Mexican and Calico corn.

CUCUMBERS

How is cucumber seed planted? In the open ground after danger of frost is past. Rows may well be 4 to 5 ft. apart, with a plant every 2 to 4 ft. in the row. Many gardeners plant seeds too thick and fail to thin out.

How are cucumbers fertilized? With plenty of well-rotted manure placed under the soil in which the seed is planted, either in hills or rows.

How are cucumbers cultivated? Cultivate carefully for weeds until vines spread, when hand weeding is necessary. Mulching between rows or hills can be used to keep weeds down.

Should cucumbers be picked regularly? Yes, to insure production through full bearing period, pick regularly, the younger the better. If fruits are allowed to mature, vines soon stop bearing.

Can cucumber plants be transplanted? Cucumbers may be started inside, 3 weeks ahead of garden setting, using any good greenhouse or plant-growing soil in 3- or 4-in. veneer bands, or clay pots, or other containers. Sow 4 to 6 seeds per pot and thin out to 2 or 3; keep at a temperature of about 65° F., water moderately so that plants grow vigorously but will not have started to vine before field setting. Care must be taken in setting them out not to distrub the root system, as they do not stand transplanting so well as cabbage or tomatoes.

Should cucumbers be trained up? If so, how? They may be trained on a fence or over a wall, but are usually allowed to run over the ground.

Can cucumbers be planted near melons? Cucumbers can be planted close to melons without fear of "crossing." When muskmelons taste like cucumbers, it is likely the result of poor growing conditions, poor variety, or diseased vines, rather than cross-pollination.

Do cucumbers and muskmelons cross? No. However, the belief that they cross is widespread, and many experiences are related that seem to confirm it. The most carefully conducted and scientifically correct experiments have been made in vain attempts to cross them.

How can I prevent cucumbers from being burned by sun? Burning or scalding of cucumbers is not a common trouble. Ordinarily, if plants are healthy, the foliage gives sufficient shade not only to prevent scalding but to make the cucumbers hard to find.

Should cucumbers be picked when foliage is wet? What makes cucumber vines turn yellow before all fruit is mature? Cucumbers are subject to several leaf and vine diseases which would probably be spread somewhat more freely when the plants are wet. These diseases are best controlled by rotation of land and by seed treatment as mentioned in following question.

Why do cucumber vines die too soon? Because of diseases such as bacterial wilt, scab, anthracnose, and angular leaf spot. Seed should be treated by dipping for 5 minutes in corrosive-sublimate solution, 1 tablet per pint water. Rinse, dry, and plant at once, after dusting with Spergon or red copper oxide. As cucumbers come up they should be dusted with rotenone, pyrethrum, or arsenical dust for striped beetles, which are carriers of bacterial wilt. Use of hotkaps will protect small plants from the cucumber beetle, which spreads the wilt.

Where do cucumber beetles come from? Cucumber beetles pass the winter as adults. Some are in the garden under old cucumber or melon vines and unharvested fruits and some are in fence rows, ditch banks, wood lots, and rubbish piles near the garden. They come out of hibernation about May 1 and feed on weeds for a few days while waiting for the cucumbers and melons to come up.

My problem is growing cucumbers and squash. I can grow the plants but they get many empty blossoms; and when the fruit comes on the plants, and I get a few small ones, the plants start to die. I use plenty of well-rotted manure and give them lots of water when needed. What is the trouble? Probably wilt spread by striped cucumber beetles. (See previous questions.) "Empty" blossoms may be male.

Is bacterial wilt of cucumbers recognizable by little green "egg masses" on under side of leaves? No. Bacterial wilt is evidenced by discoloration and wilting of the leaves. It is checked by controlling the striped cucumber beetle.

Are there wilt-resistant cucumbers? Some results have been achieved in breeding mosaic and mildew resistant strains, but so far none have been developed resistant to bacterial wilt. Burpee Hybrid is resistant to both mosaic and downy mildew; Ashley to the latter and Niagara to the former. Of the pickling sorts, Ohio MRM, Wisconsin SMR 12 and Yorkstate Pickling are resistant to mosaic, and Wisconsin to scab as well.

What are good varieties of slicing cucumbers? Straight Eight, China, Marketer, Colorado, Burpee Hybrid.

What variety of small cucumber can I plant that will be just right for pickling? For small pickles use Ohio MR 25, Double Yield, Chicago, West India Gherkin, Wisconsin SMR 12. Slicing varieties may be used for dills and cut pickles.

DANDELION

How grow tame dandelions? You can buy dandelion seed and sow it in drills in late summer and harvest them the following spring. They require a fertile soil that is well limed.

Would dried dandelion leaves make good winter eating? What about other edible weeds? Most of the common non-poisonous weeds, if harvested when young, are quite nutritious from the standpoint of vitamins. They may be dried and used later. The main question is their palatability. Lawn grass and young alfalfa are very nutritious if you like them.

DASHEEN

I have heard about the "dasheen," the rival of the potato, and I

wish to try it. Can you tell me of its cultural necessities and if it is possible to grow it at an altitude of nearly 5,000 ft., with a relatively short season? You cannot grow this crop under your conditions. It is tropical and requires heat during a prolonged season. You might be able to force some of the roots to get the tender sprouts which are quite delicious. You cannot grow the tubers. Tubers may be bought from the commission houses dealing in tropical fruits and vegetables. The roots may be set in sand or light soil and grown with little difficulty if the temperature is above 70°.

EGGPLANT

How is soil prepared for eggplant? The soil should be well drained and rather sandy; well worked with compost or rotted manure.

What is the secret of growing eggplants successfully? Plants free from wilt on clean soil and free of red spider and other pests. Don't grow the young plants too fast until the fruit is set. Grow them on well-aerated soil that is amply supplied with lime. Use plenty of compost in holes when setting out, and keep well watered.

Which is best culture for eggplants? Buy young, healthy plants or raise from seed under glass. (See Seed Sowing.) Set out when ground is thoroughly warmed up. Set 2 ft. apart in rows 2½ to 3 ft. apart. Work in 5–10–5 complete fertilizer around each plant as it begins to grow. Cultivate often.

How in the deuce do you make eggplants have eggplants? If they are healthy, don't force them too much. High temperatures when the flowers are open will cause the flowers to abort. Watch for insect pests which may get into the flowers. The use of Blossom-Set is helpful.

Why do the blossoms of eggplants continue to drop off? Care is taken they do not get frostbitten, manure has been applied, the ground kept cultivated, but the blossoms still will not hang on. You probably grow the plants too soft with manure. Grow them slower, with less nitrogen.

What makes eggplants develop a rot all over them in spots while only half grown, resulting in practically no crop? This is a bacterial or fungous spot and is caused under conditions where the fruit tends to stay moist on the surface. This often happens on poorly prepared soil. Check soil acidity. It may need more lime.

Eggplant in this territory was destroyed by a "wilt." Modern dust and sprays failed completely. Can any helpful information be given? (Kansas.) There is no control for eggplant wilt after it has once got into the plants. The prevention is to grow seedlings in soil which has not grown them before and set the plants in fields which have not grown eggplants for at least 10 years. Some varieties, such as Black Beauty, are more resistant than others.

How do you keep bugs off eggplants? Dust the plants with rotenone if the bugs eat the foliage; or spray with nicotine spray if plant lice are present.

Which are the best varieties of eggplant? Black Beauty is the old stand-by. New Hampshire Hybrid and Burpee Hybrid are early, for Northern growing. Florida High Bush is especially suited to the South.

ENDIVE

How is endive grown? Culture of endive is the same as that of lettuce. When it reaches maturity, it is usually blanched by tying the outside leaves around the heart as with cauliflower. After tying, the head may be covered with waterproof paper to prevent rotting. Endive is frost resistant and provides salad greens late in the fall. It can be stored in a cool cellar like celery, where it blanches in the dark.

How can endive be kept from rotting after tied for bleaching? Endive that is tied up will rot in wet weather, particularly if the soil is not well limed. It is better to lay a board over the heads to bleach them than to tie them up, or cover heads with waterproof paper as described in previous question.

FENNEL, GARDEN

What is garden fennel, and how is it grown? Garden fennel (or finocchio) is a celery-like vegetable with an anise flavor. It matures quickly and is sown in garden rows, thinned to 6 ins., and grown on without special attention until approaching maturity. Then it is hilled up by having the soil drawn high on either side of the row to blanch the stalks. The blanching process takes about 3 weeks.

GARLIC

How does one grow garlic? Garlic may be grown just like onions, either from the "cloves" (divisions of the bulb) or from seed.

How do you divide garlic to plant? I want to grow large bulbs. You divide the garlic bulb into cloves and plant the individual sections. The size of the bulb is determined by soil and weather conditions. A fertile soil in good physical condition with ample rainfall will produce large bulbs.

When is it best to plant garlic, spring or fall? It may be planted either time. Spring planting is best where the soil freezes.

How deep should one plant garlic? Cloves are planted with tops ½ in. below the surface. Seed should be planted not over ¼ in. deep. Plant in moist but not wet soil so that the ground over the seed does not bake.

How prepare garlic for market? Do you wash the soil off or strip it? (Orgeon.) Garlic should be grown on soil that does not discolor the bulbs and which will rub off readily when dry. The bulbs should not be washed, and the outer leaves should not be taken off unless absolutely necessary.

HORSE-RADISH

How do you raise horse-radish? What kind of soil do you use? Horse-radish must be grown on a well-limed, sandy loam soil that has a subsoil which is well aerated to permit deep penetration of the tap-root. The crop is grown from root cuttings which are set (large end up) 10 to 12 ins. apart in rows 2 to 3 ft. apart. The roots may be set in deep trenches covered 2 ins. over tops.

When to plant horse-radish, spring or fall? Set horse-radish roots in the spring for that season's crop.

Interested in growing horse-radish. Find plants 1 year old show no signs of root deterioration. However, plants 2 to 3 years and older show excessive dry rotting of roots. To your knowledge can this be remedied? This is a natural sloughing off of tissue which cannot be prevented. The best horse-radish is 1-year roots from small root cuttings which are planted every year.

When do you harvest horse-radish? Should it be dried before grating? Horse-radish is harvested in the fall and the grating is done while the roots are in their natural fresh state.

KALE

When and how is kale planted? Kale is improved by a touch of frost and should therefore be sown in the open, about 2 months before freezing is expected. A packet of seed should be thinly sown, as the plants will eventually stand 18 to 24 ins. apart. While kale will grow almost anywhere it will be of better quality on good soil.

How long can kale be cut for table use? Until heavy frost kills all leafy vegetables. Cut the bottom leaves first, and before they get tough. Neglect of this point has given kale a worse name than this vitamin-richest of the potherbs deserves.

I have planted kale two different years. In all about 3 plants have appeared. How do you make it come up? Buy high-grade seed. Seed should be covered ⅜ to ½ in., and the seedbed should never be allowed to dry out.

How can I keep kale in the garden from freezing? (Ohio.) Kale is considered hardy in your section and nothing but extremely low temperatures should cause damage. The leaves are improved by hard frost.

Can kale be kept green for table use during cold weather? By taking up plants and growing on in a covered frame it is possible to have kale through most of the winter.

How should kale be cooked? Kale can be chopped, boiled as a green and served buttered. It can be cooked with ham hocks or ham, which flavors the kale. *Scalloped Kale:* Boil chopped kale until tender. Drain. Mix with chopped hard-boiled egg. Place in baking dish. Moisten with soup stock or bouillon. Cover surface with slices of process cheese and sprinkle with seasoned bread crumbs. Bake in oven about 15 minutes, until heated through and crumbs and cheese are browned.

KOHLRABI

How should one plant and care for kohlrabi to get best results? Plant early on a well-limed, fertile soil. Easy to grow and should give no trouble on a good soil. On poor soil you need some fertilizer and liquid side dressing should be used. Thin out to about 3 ins. Harvest when not over 2 ins. in diameter.

How should kohlrabi be harvested? Many gardeners plant kohlrabi but few eat it. Kohlrabi should be harvested while the bulb is still growing and tender. When growth stops, the bulb quickly becomes hard and woody in texture, bitter in flavor, and entirely inedible.

LEEKS

How to grow leeks: soil; shade or sun? Leeks are grown from seed in well-limed, very fertile soil with ample water. They must be grown in full sunlight. Shade in the morning will not produce good growth. Culture similar to that of onions, but leeks require hilling.

What is the proper way to transplant leeks? Make a trench 5 to 6 ins. deep; enrich bottom with old manure or compost and fertilizer. Set young plants (trimmed back, both tops and roots) in the bottom, 5 to 6 ins. apart. As they grow, fill the trench, and draw earth up to blanch them. (See illustration, p. 799.)

Part of my crop of leeks is still in the ground. I have been told they could be left there and used next spring. Is this information correct? (West Virginia.) Yes, this is true for the home garden where the appearance of the leaves is not so important. For market the leaves will be ragged, which will hurt their sale.

LETTUCE

How should soil be fertilized for head lettuce? Lettuce has a scanty root system, therefore must have good soil with enough humus to hold the moisture so necessary for such a crop and to provide equally necessary nitrogen. Old, well-rotted manure is the proper addition, and as much lime as is needed to counteract any acidity.

When can lettuce seed be planted outdoors? Loose-leaf lettuce should be one of the earliest crops sown and is to be preferred, for several reasons, by the average home gardener. Head lettuce should be started indoors and transplanted (after hardening off), so that the heads may be well grown before hot weather comes.

Lettuce for extra-early use is easily grown in a cold frame.

How soon should lettuce be thinned? How far apart?   Leaf lettuce, sown in the open, may be thinned a couple of times while still very small, until the final plants stand 8 to 10 ins. apart. The larger head-lettuce varieties should stand 10 to 12 ins. Small varieties, such as Mignonette, Bibb and Burpeeana which are among the best, need only about 6 ins.

How can I be sure to get good head lettuce?   By growing it in ideal conditions; namely, a fertile soil, well drained but not dry, in a climate where the nights are cool and the days warm. Raise seedlings indoors or in a frame; harden off by gradual exposure to the outdoors; transplant them on a cloudy day and protect them from strong sunlight until well established in the garden.

How can I raise large heads of delicious, crisp, tender, loose-leaf lettuce? (Vermont.)   You should have no trouble in your climate. Prepare soil with plenty of lime and well-rotted manure if available, and sow the seed as soon as the ground can be prepared in the spring; thin so that the plants stand 8 ins. apart; or start seed indoors, side-dress with liquid fertilizer if needed. Grand Rapids and Oakleaf are good varieties of the type you describe.

How can an amateur gardener, with Missouri soil conditions and without replanting, raise head lettuce rather than leaf lettuce?   Head lettuce requires a good, well-limed soil with ample moisture and cool nights. You can't grow head lettuce if the weather gets hot. Sow the seed as early as possible and thin the seedlings to stand 8 ins. to 12 ins. apart. See that the ground has plenty of humus—in the form of well-rotted manure, if available.

How can I get lettuce to grow faster?   Lettuce requires a limed soil with a good balance of nutrients, especially nitrogen in early spring. The soil must have a clean odor and drain easily. You probably need lime and humus.

How can head lettuce be grown for small family to have plenty all summer?   You may not be able to grow head lettuce during the summer months because of hot days and nights. During the season of cool nights you should have good heads by making plantings at 2-week intervals. Matchless is a heat-resistant variety of head lettuce. Leaf lettuce is more nutritious and is usually grown during the summer months.

In growing head lettuce I have succeeded in growing only loose leaves, 10 ins. in diameter. How can I successfully grow this type of lettuce? You may not have the soil in good condition. Head lettuce must be planted *very early* in the spring. If the weather is hot and humid when it is ready to head, it won't form a head.

Why doesn't lettuce grow in our soil? (Pennsylvania.) Perhaps you have insufficient lime in the soil, or too little phosphorus. Have your soil tested and if necessary add lime to bring it up to pH 6 to 7. Use well-rotted manure as a fertilizer.

What makes lettuce heads rot in center, and why does first early crop seed before heading? This may be due to a lack of available calcium, or to one of the lettuce diseases that cause the heart to decay. Head lettuce goes to seed because of hot weather or some other conditions that check normal growth. It needs cool nights to head well.

What causes "tip burn" in head lettuce? Tip burn is usually caused by uneven growth where the leaves get too soft. It may be due to too little calcium in the soil or to the too free use of nitrate of soda as a side dressing, especially if hot sunshine follows a cloudy, moist spell.

Can lettuce be planted in the house? Not unless you have sunshine and cool temperatures. The temperature should not be above 55°. It can be grown in a cold room in a south window.

Would appreciate suggestions for vegetable window boxes. Can lettuce be grown in pots or boxes? Yes, if you have sunshine and the night temperature is not too high. Head lettuce requires cool nights to make it head. Leaf lettuce will grow in any window box. Keep the plants 6 to 8 in. apart. Use a soil with plenty of lime and humus in it.

Where can I obtain the lettuce seed which produces a plant for all winter? (Pennsylvania.) No varieties are hardy in the Northern states unless grown in greenhouse or frame. Mignonette, Boston, Thanksgiving, and Oakleaf are good varieties for late fall crop. Endive, similar to lettuce and used for salads, is considerably hardier.

Recommend some lettuce varieties for the home garden, including some which are heat resistant. Grand Rapids and the two varieties which go by the name of Simpson are about the best of the loose-leaf types, which is easiest to grow and give a plentiful yield of leaves which are higher in vitamin content. Mignonette makes a sweet, smooth-textured head but is too small for markets. Imperial No. 44 and Imperial No. 656 are bred to head in hot weather. Matchless is especially heat resistant.

Oakleaf Lettuce (at left) and Mignonette, two splendid home-garden varieties.

What members of the lettuce family (or other salad greens) may be planted throughout the summer months? Use head lettuce in the early spring and late fall. Mignonette is a good very early variety. Oakleaf is another. In summer grow leaf lettuce, mustard greens, and such heat-resistant head lettuces as Matchless; in autumn, Grand Rapids, Oakleaf, and Thanksgiving head lettuce, and endive, which is frost resistant. Witloof chicory (which see) can be forced indoors for winter salad.

What is Bibb lettuce? Bibb lettuce is a semi-heading or bunch-heading variety having very thick, smooth, dark green leaves quite different from any other variety. It is especially adapted to growing in cold frames in the Southern states during the winter months and makes a good spring lettuce in the open garden in the North. Burpee-ana is similar, more easily grown and does not "bolt" to seed so quickly.

MUSHROOMS

I would like to know about growing mushrooms in the cellar. How do you start a bed? Is there a special temperature you have to keep? Can you be sure of having non-poisonous kinds? Use composed horse manure; pack in beds 6 ins. deep; inoculate with pure-culture spawn; cover with an inch of soil; grow at 55 to 60°. Sounds simple but really very difficult. Write to your Agricultural Experiment Station for detailed information; or purchase prepared flats with the spawn already planted. Water and care for according to directions.

How can a home mushroom bed be made under a front porch? You would have to close the area so that you could maintain conditions described in answer to previous question.

How can mushrooms be grown outside? You will have difficulty in doing this. Wild mushrooms grow only when weather conditions are favorable. You would have to provide those favorable conditions; therefore mushroom growing in the open is not practicable.

How tell edible wild mushrooms? Write to the Bureau of Plant Industry, U.S.D.A., Washington, D.C., for their bulletin on the subject.

MUSKMELONS; CANTALOUPES

Please give information on raising muskmelons. Muskmelons do well in lighter soils and need a warm, sunshiny season for maturing quality fruits. Seed may be sown out of doors, but in northern sections it is better to start them under glass or under hotkaps. Set 3 to 4 ft. apart in rows 4 to 5 ft. apart. Cultivate frequently; some pulling of weeds will be necessary after the vines spread. Paper mulch works well with muskmelons. Where the season is short, early varieties such as Emerald Gem, Harper Hybrid, Champlain, and Delicious 51 may be used.

How are muskmelons fertilized? They need a well-manured soil, light and thoroughly prepared, and a complete fertilizer. Two to 4 shovelfuls of well-rotted manure are usually worked into the soil under each when planting.

When can I plant muskmelons? After danger of frost, about tomato-setting time. About the middle to the last of May in most of the Northern states.

How can an early crop of muskmelons be achieved without starting under glass? Use plant protectors such as hotkaps. In this way seed or plants may be put out 2 or 3 weeks earlier than would otherwise be advisable. As plants begin to make growth the protector should be torn to provide ventilation.

Can muskmelons be started under glass? Yes, 3- to 4-in. veneer bands, clay pots, paper pots, or the like may be used with a good plant-growing soil. Sow seed 3 to 4 weeks before setting out of doors.

Cucumbers, melons, and squash may be planted earlier if the hills are covered with hotkaps.

Grow at a temperature of 65 to 70° F., watering to provide vigorous growth; but plants should not start to run before they go to the garden.

How can I tell when muskmelons are ready to pick? Most varieties of muskmelon develop a yellowish color as they mature. Watch the place where the stem joins the fruit. When this begins to crack and the stem comes off cleanly and freely, the melons are ready to harvest. Some varieties are not quite ready for the table at this stage but should be kept a few days in a sunny window-sill, until they become a little soft at the blossom end. Varieties differ considerably in the application of these tests.

Can you please tell me how to grow good quality muskmelons? I planted some last summer on a pile of old sod. I had melons all right, but they were quite tasteless and flat. Lack of sweetness and flavor in muskmelons may be due to cool, moist weather during the maturing period and to loss of leaves by disease. Active foliage is required to make sugar. Varieties also differ in quality.

Our muskmelons grow only as large as an egg. Why? This may be due to a lack of phosphorus and lime in the soil. There are, of course, many possible reasons for this. It may be due to a lack of water or the presence of insects. On sandy soils it may be a lack of fertility. If the vines are vigorous, it may be due to a lack of potash.

Can I raise muskmelons in the clayey but well-drained soil of this region? (New Jersey.) Yes. Add humus, do not plant until the soil is warm. Try variety Hearts of Gold.

How can I fight muskmelon diseases? Seed should be treated with corrosive sublimate solution of 1 tablet per pint of water for 5 minutes. After treatment, seed should be dusted with red copper oxide or Spergon. When plants come up, they should be faithfully dusted for striped cucumber beetle. Keep free from weeds; some of them carry mosaic, which injures the crop.

How can I keep cantaloupe vines from wilting about the time the fruit starts to grow? This is due to the work of the cucumber beetle when the plants are young. As they feed on the foliage they inoculate the plants with the wilt organsim. A frame with mosquito netting over it placed over the plants until they are well started will keep the beetles off and thus prevent the wilt.

What can be done about crickets eating muskmelons? Try using poison bran mash. (See Index.)

I live on the north shore of Long Island; I should like to grow some melons. What kind is best? Muskmelons generally do not do their best in a maritime climate although some growers on Long Island and in Connecticut have had good success with Delicious. Other good varieties are Hearts of Gold, and Honey Rock, Harvest Queen and Burpee Hybrid.

What are the best varieties of muskmelons? Muskmelon varieties vary widely in their adaptation to regions. In the southern half of the country the Hale Best group does very well, but it does not thrive under the cooler, more humid, conditions of the North. Emerald Gem is one of the earliest and best quality home-garden melons, but it is not good for market. Delicious 51 is a good early. Milwaukee Market, Honey Rock, Harvest Queen, Hearts of Gold, Burpee Hybrid, and the Marvel group all do well in various sections of the North. This latter group includes Pride of Wisconsin and Queen of Colorado.

OKRA

How much seed is necessary to plant 30 ft. of okra? One half ounce of okra seed will plant 100 ft. of row, usually enough seed in a packet for 25 or 30 ft. The plants should stand at least 12 or 15 in. apart.

How and when should okra be planted? I have been unsuccessful in trying to raise them. When the soil is well warmed—that is, about the same time as beans. The soil should not be acid, and better plants and pods will result if it is fertile. Okra needs, in addition, lots of sun and a location where there is little risk of cold winds.

What caused most of my okra to grow to immense size but to set only a few pods? In all probability some fertilizer too rich in nitrogen has been used. Unfavorable weather conditions, however, may have been the cause. Long periods of rain often result in poor pollination.

In a fairly good soil where other vegetables grow well, for 4 years in succession okra has done poorly. The leaves turn yellow, wither, and die. This sounds like either a disease working in the stems, or root lice or other insects working on the fine roots. The soil should be well limed. Dig up a plant next time and see whether root lice are causing the trouble. They infest okra at times.

At what size should okra pods be picked? When they are young and tender—finger length, and not too thick through. Large pods are too pithy and tough to be palatable.

ONIONS

What is the correct way to raise onions? Grow onions from sets for summer, or from seed or plants for winter storage. Soil should be well limed, fertile, and abundantly supplied with nitrogen; work in 5 lbs. of a complete fertilizer to 100 sq. ft. Harvest when the tops begin to break over and die. Use small sets to prevent large neck and seed stalks.

What is the best way to grow onions in the small garden? From onion sets—very small onions which made their limited growth the previous season. These will furnish the early onions. Those for later use and winter storage may be grown from seed. The soil must not be acid, and should be extra well fertilized.

For fall and winter use is it best to plant seed, plants, or sets of onions? Sets for early onions, and plants for late onions for storage. Growing from seed is much more difficult and uncertain.

When should onion sets be planted? How deep? As soon as the soil can be made ready in spring. Push into prepared soil, leaving ½ in. above top of sets. If large onions are wanted, the sets should be 3 to 4 ins. apart; for scallions, or bunch onions, about 1 in. apart. Do not plan to thin out and use alternate onions for scallions, as this disturbs the roots of those left to form large bulbs.

How do you raise onion sets for the following year? Onion sets are grown by sowing seed thickly, 50 to 60 lbs. per acre, in drills or rows 2 or 3 ins. wide. The seedlings should be grown on fairly clean soil. The tops will begin to turn yellow in July. When mature, they are pulled and the tops cut off. They are piled in the field in shallow piles for a week if the weather is dry. Then they are stored under cover in shallow trays with good ventilation.

Please give the easiest way for the home gardener to raise onion sets for the following year. Or is it better to raise onions from seed in one season? There is no easiest way. Sow seed (see previous question) about ten times as thick as usual. Curing properly and storing over winter are the difficult parts and best left to the commercial grower. For home use it is better to buy sets or plants in the spring and raise a crop of bulbs from these.

How should onion sets be kept through the winter? They should be kept in shallow, slat-bottom trays in a dark building where the temperature remains at 35 to 40°.

What is the proper way to grow onions from seed? Plant the seed in drills early in the spring as soon as the ground can be worked. Make rows 12 to 15 ins. apart; sow 8 to 10 seeds per inch; cover ¼ in. deep; thin to stand 2 to 3 ins. apart in the row. Use fertile, well-drained soil, liberally limed, then cultivate to keep out weeds. Watch for thrips (see Index) on the young seedlings. Harvest when the tops begin to die after they break over. Cure thoroughly under cover before storing for winter.

What kinds of onion seed do I need for my truck garden to supply good green onions all summer? What kind of fertilizer do they require? (Michigan.) White Bunching is grown for this purpose, but any variety recommended for the Northern states is good for growing green onions. In order to have them all summer it is necessary to make successive plantings of seed at 2- to 3-week intervals. An 8–6–6 fertilizer at the rate of 400 lbs. to the acre broadcast over the surface when the ground is prepared should be ample for green onions.

Can I raise Bermuda onions from seed? (Ohio.) Yes; but unless the seed is sown early (under glass) and transplanted, the onions will be much smaller than those sold in stores.

How and when should Bermuda onions be planted to grow large? Get plants from a Southern plant grower, or from your seedsman. Set the plants, as soon as the ground can be prepared, in rich soil, and make provision for watering during dry weather.

How should Bermuda onions be stored for best results? It is important to grow the onions well and have them properly matured and cured. They can be stored in ventilated crates or trays, in a dark room of 35 to 45° temperature with a good circulation of dry air.

What fertilizer is best to use in a sandy soil to grow big onions from sets? A 7–7–7 or an 8–6–6. Well-rotted manure, plus a complete fertilizer (such as 5–10–5), usually gives a satisfactory crop. Wood ashes are excellent for onions.

Do onions need lime? Onions should be grown on soil with a good lime content; not because the onion actually needs so much calcium but because the presence of lime helps to aerate the soil, enabling the plants to grow better.

What is the botanical name of the onion that bears little bulblets at the top? This is the Perennial Tree (or Egyptian Tree) onion, *Allium cepa, viviparum*. It is winter hardy.

What are "multiplier" onions good for? The multiplier onion is probably a sport of the regular onion, *Allium cepa* variety *solaninum,* and is used for flavoring just as regular onions are used. Often confused with species mentioned above.

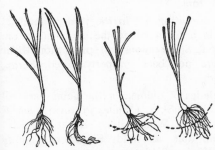

Onion seedlings ready for transplanting. Tops and roots are trimmed back as indicated at right.

What is the botanical name for shallots, and how are they grown? The shallot is *Allium ascalonicum*. It is propagated by planting the sections or cloves of which the large bulb consists.

I had very bad luck with onions. They were no bigger than seed

onions at the end of the season, and the green onions were very thin. What was wrong? If they did not stay green, it may have been due to thrips on the leaves, lice or maggots on the roots, poor soil, a lack of lime in the soil, or too much nitrogen.

Could onion seeds be sown in fall, or February? Especially interested in Sweet Spanish. (Missouri.) Both seed and sets may be planted in the fall and winter months if the soil can be prepared properly. The large Spanish onions are usually sown in seedbeds and then transplanted.

Should blossoms of onions be cut? If the flower stalks are forming, they can be recognized when the neck of the onion is small. They should be cut at once to prevent the neck of the onion from getting too large. A big-necked onion does not keep well in storage.

How grow large onions? When should they be taken up? Size depends on the weather, how well the soil has been prepared, adequate thinning (2 to 3 ins. apart while plants are small), and keeping the crop absolutely free from weeds.

What causes onion tops to fall over and turn brown? This is normally the sign that the bulbs have attained maturity. The tops, then of no further service to the plant in manufacturing its food, naturally shrivel and collapse. If the onions are not matured, drought may be cause, or thrips.

Does planting onions near gladioli increase the possibility of the latter being attacked by thrips? It would not make much difference; if thrips are bad, it is because of weather conditions being favorable for their multiplication. Any crop that harbors the thrips will increase the population for crops that follow.

How can I prevent onions from becoming sunburned? White varieties sometimes sunscald or turn green. Gather as soon as tops begin to die; spread out thinly, under cover, but with good ventilation until tops dry up, then remove tops.

How keep dry onions from sprouting out in the winter months? If onions are kept too warm in a room where the air is moist or where light enters, they will sprout. Some onions will sprout more than others because the bulbs have not been properly cured. Some varieties keep better than others.

Please name some good varieties of onions for the home garden. Early: Crystal White Wax, Silver Skin (White Portugal) early Yellow Globe mild. Late: Southport White Globe, Sweet Spanish, Iowa 44, Epoch, Gigantic Gibraltar, all mild; Ebenezer, Yellow Globe, medium mild; and Red Wethersfield, extra strong.

PARSLEY

How should parsley be grown? Does it tolerate shade? Parsley does not do well in a shady place. As a matter of fact, there are very few vegetables that do, not even the ones that do not tolerate too much heat and drought. Parsley may be sown in good, friable, well-enriched garden soil as soon in the spring as the ground can be prepared. Make rows shallow and cover lightly with fine soil. Seed may be sown about 10 or 20 to the foot or thicker if it is desired to use the thinnings. If sizable plants are wanted, they should be thinned from 5 to 8 ins. apart. Adequate water supply is important.

Should the parsley bed be covered during the winter? If so, what material should be used? Excelsior or dry leaves or some other material which will not become wet and form a mat will keep the plants green well into the winter. Still better, transfer some of the plants to a tight frame; if the latter is reasonably frost-proof, they should last through the winter.

My parsley plant stops growing when taken indoors, ball, root, and all, even though it stands with other plants that thrive. Why does it do this? This sounds like the turnip-rooted parsley, which will become dormant. It is better to use the regular parsley, which is fibrous-rooted.

How can I successfully transplant parsley from outside beds for winter window gardening? Soak the ground around the plants the day before you wish to move them. Dig the plants by leaving a small ball of soil around the roots, and set in the window box in soil that has not been treated with chemical fertilizer. Trim off at least half of the outside leaves.

Why does my parsley, brought in from out of doors and potted, turn dark at edge of leaves and look as if it were dying? Parsley brought in from out of doors should be cut back to the crown so it can make new growth. Old leaves will wither. Water sparingly at first, increasing as growth starts. Requires several hours' sunshine a day to do well indoors. Young plants started in August are much better for winter use than old roots.

Are the bottoms of parsley plants good to eat? If so, how would you use them? Only the leaves of fibrous-rooted parsley are used for the table.

How can I make my parsley seed germinate more quickly? The natural germination period is long. Soak the seeds for 24 hours in tepid water before planting to soften the hard shells.

PARSNIPS

How can I have long, fleshy, well-developed parsnips? Soil for parsnips should be very well and deeply worked to a depth of 12 to 18 ins. If perfect roots are desired, all stone and hard clods must be removed from the soil, which should be enriched with very well-rotted manure or with compost. Plant seeds early in spring in rows 18 to 20 ins. apart, covering ¼ to ½ ins. deep. Thin to 4 ins. apart. Grow on through entire season, cultivating ground as needed. Crop will be ready in autumn and can be stored, or some left in ground (as they are perfectly hardy) for digging in spring.

How are exhibition parsnips grown?   Deep holes, 4, 5, or 6 ins. apart, are made with crowbar, in well-prepared, pulverized soil. These are filled with sifted soil and compost, and 3 or 4 seeds are planted on top of this. When seedlings develop, all but one are removed. Such roots are often 3 to 4 ft. long when dug at end of season.

What variety of parsnip is best to grow?   Though Hollow Crown is the standard, All American is newer and preferable because the roots are thick through but chunky and so can be well grown without quite such deep preparation. Harris' Model is a reliable newer variety.

PEANUTS

What is proper time for planting and care, cultivation, and harvesting of peanuts?   The nuts (removed from the shells) are planted an inch deep and about a foot apart in well-prepared, light soil. Manure and nitrogenous fertilizers are avoided. Rows 3 ft. apart. Give clean cultivation till after the blossoms at the base of the plant (and not readily found) are produced. Mulching around the base of the plant at this time is beneficial and helps keep down weeds for balance of season. Plant about the same time as first sowing of sweet corn. At least 4 months are required to produce the crop.

What should one do to make peanuts give better yield in sandy Michigan ground?   This may be a water and a fertility problem. Perhaps the season is too cool for peanuts to grow satisfactorily. They require warm nights for a considerable period.

Do you think it possible to grow peanuts successfully as far north as I live, in Spokane, Washington?   The season in your section should be amply long even if the seed is sown outdoors in the usual way. While peanuts do not transplant readily, they may be started in small pots and the young plants set out after danger of frost. The time thus gained results in a larger crop.

PEAS

Are green peas very hard to raise?   In sections where hot weather, and especially hot nights, is likely to come suddenly, they are difficult. Peas are easy to grow if the soil is in good condition and the seed is planted very early in the season. (See Introduction.)

What sort of weather and climate do peas prefer?   Cool nights with bright, cool days.

**What kind of soil, weather conditions, etc., are necessary for growing green peas in a home garden? What variety is best? A good soil that is well limed and does not contain an excess of nitrogen. The subsoil should be open so the roots can penetrate it. Peas should be planted as early as possible to get them to set pods before hot weather. Little Marvel, Blue Bantam and Notts' Excelsior are good dwarf varieties. Freezonian, Midfreezer, Mammoth Podded Extra Early and Lincoln are good 2½ footers. Alderman (dark-podded Telephone), an excellent tall one.

Do garden peas require a new soil to do their best? Not unless the soil is infected with root diseases. Lime will work wonders for peas. Don't overfertilize them. Use a starter solution. Water in dry weather.

What fertilizer is necessary to produce a good growth of peas? If the soil is properly limed and generally fertile, you do not need any fertilizer. In a garden a starter solution poured on the seed when it is planted should be enough. (See Index.)

What particular soil feeding do peas need? I have good loam soil that produces excellent beans, tomatoes, etc., but peas do not do well. The plot is well manured each year though I haven't used any commercial fertilizer. You may need some lime. Also the soil may have too much nitrogen. Peas must be planted as early as the ground can be prepared.

Is hen manure good fertilizer for growing peas? What causes pods to dry up instead of maturing properly? No. Peas do not need the nitrogen that is present in the chicken manure. If peas grow too rapidly because of too much nitrogen and water, the pods may start to grow without being fertilized and will dry up, as there is no seed in them. Hot weather also causes them to shrivel.

When should peas be planted, both smooth and wrinkled sorts? Either type may be sown just as early in spring as a good, mellow seedbed can be prepared. The sole advantage of the smooth-seeded sorts is that they are a trifle hardier and can be planted a few days earlier; usually this is scarcely sufficient compensation for their lower quality.

How would it be to plant garden peas March 17 as we do sweet peas? Excellent, for smooth sorts. Wrinkled kinds about a week later.

When is best time to plant garden peas? As soon as the ground can be prepared in the spring. The earlier the better.

When is the proper time to plant peas on the Eastern Shore of Maryland? Late fall, or very early spring.

When is the right time to plant garden peas, also sweet peas, in this locality? (Missouri.) Fall, or as early as the ground can be prepared in the spring.

Is it possible to raise wrinkled peas in the fairly well-drained, rather

clayey soil of this region? (New Jersey.)   Yes, if the soil is properly limed. Don't use too much nitrogen. Plant the peas before the first of April, if possible. Try Little Marvel for early peas and Laxton's Progress for a little later.

Can you tell me if it is possible to raise peas on light soil?   Yes. Be sure that the soil has sufficient lime and humus, then use a starter solution on the seed when it is planted.

Is it possible to grow peas near salt water? (Massachusetts.)   Yes, if the spray does not hit them and the ground does not contain salt.

How early can garden peas be started in my locality? Also will peas grow in practically full shade or do they require some sunlight? (New Jersey.)   Plant as early as possible. This may be April 1 or even earlier. Peas will not grow in shade; require full sunshine, especially in morning.

Why are peas a poor crop in northern Virginia?   This may be due to a lack of lime in the soil, or to hot, dry weather when the pods are ready to set. Peas must be planted in the fall, or very early spring.

Is there any type of garden peas that can be planted in the fall or winter for an extra-early crop? (New Jersey.)   Any variety of garden peas can be planted in the fall if they are planted late enough so that they won't germinate until spring. Drainage must be perfect; how they will come through depends largely on the winter weather.

Do dwarf peas need support? If so, what kind?   While they do not need support, it is well to use it if possible in the home garden; rows may be planted closer (24 ins. or so), and the crop is more easily tended and picked than when the vines are allowed to sprawl.

What is the best support for peas and sweet peas?   Brush, if it can be obtained; if not, wire or string. Support should be 15 to 18 ins. for dwarf peas; 5 to 6 ft. for tall peas and sweet peas.

What makes pea vines wither and turn brown before they mature?   Hot weather; aphids; soil in poor physical condition or with poor aeration.

What insects are most common on peas?   Plant lice or aphids. (See Section VIII.)

What to do for garden pea weevil?   Place seed in airtight container, drop a few drops of carbon disulfide in the can, and cover tightly.

What fungous diseases attack garden peas? How can they be identified? How can they be prevented or controlled?   Powdery mildew on the leaves; control with dusting sulfur. Root rots causing brown roots; caused by poor aeration of the soil; corrected by deeper plowing and more lime in the soil.

What is the most effective way of protecting young peas and other succulent seedlings from slugs during wet weather in the spring?

Sprinkle some hydrated lime on the ground under the vines and even on the lower leaves on the vines.

What treatment do you recommend for mildew on peas?   Dust with flowers of sulfur or a sulfur-lime dust.

How can sparrows be kept from eating the peas and beans as they come through the earth?   Some short pieces of rope should be placed where the birds will see them. Birds fear snakes; or cover the row with a strip of close-mesh wire.

What is the difference between smooth-seeded and wrinkled peas? Smooth-seeded are hardier for very early sowing, but the crop is inferior in quality. Smooth-seeded peas take two months to mature. Superb is the best variety, though Eight Weeks is earlier. Wrinkled-seeded are a little less hardy, the seeds being more apt to rot in cold, wet ground, but the quality and yield are superior. For varieties see following questions.

Which are the best early and best late garden green peas?   Mayflower, World's Record, Little Marvel, Laxton's Progress, and Freezonian for early; Alderman, Fordhook Wonder, and Lincoln for late.

What are the best kind of garden peas to plant for home use? Little Marvel for garden and Mayflower for early. See previous questions for later varieties.

Which peas give the best yield?   Late varieties such as Alderman (dark-podded Telephone) or one of the Giant Stride types.

What varieties of peas are best for freezing?   Freezonian is the outstanding variety for freezing. Little Marvel, which is one of the best home-garden varieties, is also a very good freezing variety, as are Lincoln and World's Record.

PEPPERS

How can I have early sweet peppers?   Buy plants from a local grower, or start seeds under glass in March. Set out when all danger of frost is past—just a little later than you set out tomatoes in your locality.

How do you make pepper plants bear? Mine grow beautifully but bear late and little.   Grow them with little or no nitrogen. Use only lime and an 0–12–12 fertilizer.

Why do I have no success with sweet peppers? The plants have loads of flowers and tiny peppers but very few that can be used, yet the plants are nice and big.   Plants are too vigorous. Try growing them on less fertile soil, and do not put any nitrogen or manure on until the peppers are set and partially grown. Try using a liquid fertilizer side dressing.

What makes fruit drop off pepper plants in summer?   Too much nitrogen, boron deficiency, or high temperatures when the flowers are setting fruits. Grow them slower until the fruit is set.

Should green pepper plants be pinched back?   No; this would make them late.

If sweet pepper plants are brought indoors in the fall, will they continue to bear during the winter?   Yes, if moved carefully and with sufficient soil. It would be difficult. Peppers need high temperatures, humidity and sunshine.

What peppers shall I grow?   Sweet: Early Pimiento, Pennwonder, Sunnybrook, Fordhook, or California Wonder, and Morgold. Hot: Long Red Cayenne, or Hungarian Wax (yellow).

POTATOES

Are there any tricks about raising enough Irish potatoes for our own use next winter? How many potatoes should we plant to get about seven bushels?   Potatoes are somewhat more difficult to grow for home use than most other vegetables. A few fundamentals must be observed. These include choosing a loamy soil, using healthy seed, and practicing a thorough program of weed control and of spraying for insects and blight. To raise about seven bushels of potatoes, plant about 30 to 50 lbs. of seed. The former figure assumes a fifteenfold increase, which is somewhat above the average.

Is it profitable to grow potatoes in the home garden?   It depends on whether potatoes grow well in your locality, on the size of the garden, and similar considerations. In the suburban garden of a family with a normal liking for potatoes and located near a store, the answer is probably "No." Potatoes are a big commercial crop efficiently distributed and do not suffer in quality by being stored and shipped.

Are home-grown potatoes of superior eating quality?   Definitely yes. Fresh dug potatoes are tender, mealy and delicious, with an especially fine flavor.

What soil do you suggest for potatoes?   Potatoes are not adapted to heavy and poorly drained soils. Farmers who do not have good potato soil grow other crops. A good potato soil is one which is loamy or friable to a depth of at least 12 ins. In choosing a soil for potatoes, it is fortunate if one can be found which is naturally quite acid in reaction. Otherwise, there will be trouble with potato scab. It is fairly easy to sweeten, by liming, a soil which is too acid, but it is difficult to acidify a soil which is naturally within the range favorable to scab; i.e., anything above pH 5.6.

What are the best commercial fertilizers on a sandy loam for a potato crop? For clay soil?   Sandy soils are particularly deficient in soil nutrients, especially in potash. For this reason potato growers on the sandier soils usually use large applications of such fertilizers as 5–10–10 and 4–8–12. For heavier soils use a fertilizer relatively high in phosphoric acid, such as 4–12–4 and 5–10–5. Soil with a high clay content tends to tie up or make unavailable the phosphorous element, thereby increasing the danger of deficiency unless supplied in excess.

Will horse manure make potatoes scabby? Can chicken manure be used for potatoes? Among the types of manure used on potato land, chicken manure is most likely to cause scab. Horse manure also will do so to a lesser degree. Both of these are more dangerous than ordinary mixed stable manure because of their relatively high ammonia content. Where these manures are used, it is advisable to apply them several months ahead of potato planting, and to use them rather sparingly. Six to 8 tons to the acre of horse or chicken manure are suggested as compared to 10 to 15 tons of mixed stable manure.

Is Vigoro a complete fertilizer for potatoes? Vigoro is one of the patent fertilizer preparations marketed at retail in small packages, principally for home gardeners. It is a complete fertilizer and should give as satisfactory results as other complete fertilizers.

What is needed in fertilizer for potatoes in home gardens? My soil has a good deal of oak-leaf humus. Since such soil is well supplied with humus, the principal need for nutrients would be phosphoric acid and potash. It may be desirable to add some form of commercial nitrogen to hasten decomposition of the humus—such materials as nitrate of soda or sulfate of ammonia. Whether or not this garden soil needs lime depends on its present reaction. Probably is acid enough, but would have soil tested.

Do seed potatoes differ from the ordinary table potatoes? No, except that they are usually certified as free from diseases.

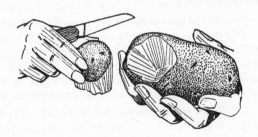

Large potatoes may be cut up into seed pieces;
these should have at least two good strong eyes.

What are certified seed potatoes? Certified seed potatoes are potatoes stored, treated, planted, and harvested under definite rules of sanitation. Twice during their growing period they are inspected by trained men employed by the state. These men watch carefully for symptoms of any virus disease. There is a final bin inspection before the potatoes are bagged for shipment. If the potatoes pass these three inspections, they are certified by the state as being free from virus diseases.

How should seed potatoes be prepared for planting? Cut the seed potatoes into several pieces, each of which should have one strong eye, or two, and a good piece of the tuber. The "eye" is a dormant bud from which a new plant will grow, and its first food will be derived from the piece of tuber. Plant only *certified, disease-free seed potatoes.*

Are seed potatoes planted immediately after cutting? They may be, but it is better practice to lay the cut pieces out in flats or shallow trays, skin side up, and leave them in a sunny but airy place for from one to four weeks until the "eyes" sprout. Or the whole potatoes may thus be sprouted *before* cutting. Unlike sprouts produced in the root cellar on stored potatoes, these sprouts will be dark green and closely clustered in the eyes close to the tuber. They are then planted, eyes up of course.

Should I use large or small seed potatoes? If the potato tubers are small because they came from diseased plants, they are unfit for seed. If they came from healthy, high-yielding plants, they are as valuable for seed as cut pieces from large tubers. In many sections of the United States growers are paying and receiving a premium for small, whole tubers for seed because uncut tubers are less likely to rot under unfavorable soil conditions and do not involve cutting. The important thing to observe is that small seed should be free from virus diseases; i.e., certified seed.

Will I get more potatoes from seeds or potatoes? Except in breeding work, potatoes are not propagated from seed. The common practice is to plant either whole or cut tubers; these produce plants.

How many pounds of seed potatoes are needed for planting ½ acre? (Illinois.) Most potato experiments which have been made to determine the optimum amount of seed indicate that 18 to 20 bushels of seed to the acre are desirable on upland soils; 25 to 30 bushels on muck soils. Therefore, 9 to 10 bushels of seed would be the approximate amount needed to plant ½ acre of potatoes on upland soil.

How many potatoes should be planted in a hill? The best way to plant potatoes is in a trench 5 to 6 ins. deep. Place one piece of tuber every 12 ins. and cover with 3 ins. of soil. As the plants grow and the soil is cultivated to keep down weeds, the trenches are gradually filled up.

When is the best time to plant early potatoes? About a month before the last spring frost is expected. By the time the young plants have come up through 3 ins. of soil any frost likely to hurt them should then be past.

When should late potatoes be planted?   The word "late" as applied by gardeners means late in reaching maturity, not late in time of planting. Your seed catalogue will show approximately the number of days for the variety you select; count back this number from the expected date of first frosts in fall.

When is it time to plant potatoes? (New York.)   Depends on latitude and location. In upstate New York, any time after the first of May, when the danger of hard freeze is past and the seedbed can be properly prepared. It is important that the potatoes be planted sufficiently early, so that the plants will blossom and set tubers during relatively cool, moist weather. By planting as early as May 15, the period of blossoming will normally come 6 weeks later, or about July 1. The season on Long Island is about six weeks earlier.

How deep should potatoes be planted?   In most soils, from 3 to 5 ins. Many beginners do not plant deep enough to provide ample soil moisture for the developing tubers and to prevent sunburn. For a deep, loamy soil, 4 to 5 ins.; in a shallow, heavy soil, 3 ins. Although deeper planting means harder digging, it usually results in increased yields.

How deep should early and late potatoes be planted?   Early varieties of potatoes (planted early) should be planted shallower than late potatoes. Shallower planting results in earlier emergence, which in turn tends to hasten maturity. However, most potatoes, regardess of variety, should be planted 3 to 5 ins. deep, depending on the soil type. (See question above.)

Is it better to plant Irish potatoes deep (so the weeds can be kept down by frequent harrowing) or shallow, and count on plowing dirt up to them to prevent sunburn?   Inasmuch as ridge culture is practiced in the majority of potato fields, deeper planting affords a better method of weed control than a shallow planting. Shallow planting as practiced in Maine and on many farms of New York and Pennsylvania subsequently requires extreme ridging to control weeds and prevent sunburn by covering. By planting deeper, weeds can be controlled by harrowing without danger of pulling out plants and with less danger of injuring root system.

Do potato plants need any water after being planted? If so, how much? How often do they need it? (California.)   The potato tuber is nearly 80 per cent water. In many parts of California, particularly the inland valleys, irrigation water is absolutely necessary for profitable yields. The equivalent of 10 to 12 ins. of rainfall is necessary for good yields of potatoes. In the East, rainfall usually supplies 2 to 3 times the water actually necessary to produce a good crop. In irrigating potatoes in California, the water is let into every other furrow every alternate day early in the season. Early season irrigation is far more useful than late.

Since July–August droughts almost regularly injure late potato plantings in the Central States, would it not be well to plant the late potatoes early, along with the early potatoes? The late potatoes are varieties which take longer to mature, and the drought will affect them no matter when they are planted. Early planting would be better. Try spreading a mulch of straw 4 to 6 ins. thick between the rows. This will conserve moisture and keep down weeds.

Is it practical to mulch potatoes in this area? (Southeast Kansas.) How do I do it? Yes, entirely practical. Before dry weather, spread straw to a depth of 4 to 6 ins. between the rows and close up to the plants.

Should potatoes be grown under straw? The effect of the straw mulch is to maintain a lower soil temperature, to conserve moisture, and to control weeds. The straw should be applied about the time the potato plants are emerging. If applied too early, growth is retarded; if too late, the plants already started will be injured by the straw. Often as much as 12 ins. of straw is used, when entire growing area is covered. This must be removed before the crop is dug.

Is it practical to grow the Idaho potato in New York State? New York is a large state and has many types of soil and many variations in climate. Consult your county agricultural agent or local seedsman as to which variety of this type will do best in your particular area.

Is it possible to plant potatoes in January, February, and March? Frosty nights but sunshine daytime; no snow. (California.) Plant the seed potatoes 4 or 5 weeks before the frosty nights are expected to end.

What is lacking in the earth that our potatoes don't grow normal size? They are perfect and good flavor but remain very small. They seem to grow well and have plenty of top. There are two probable reasons. Your soil may be deficient in nitrogen, phosphoric acid, or potash. Too little fertilizer or too little orgainc matter in the soil may be responsible. If in your judgment neither of these factors is involved, the most likely explanation is that the seed you have planted is infected with virus disease. The principal virus diseases are mosaic and leaf roll. Purchase certified or disease-free seed.

Why is it I cannot raise potatoes? It is difficult to see any reason for failure to grow potatoes successfully, if soil is deep and manure and fertilizer have been used. One explanation would be that seed potatoes have not been healthy or that they have been so stored that the sprouts are weak. Ordinarily there is no advantage in liming soil for potatoes unless it tests so acid that it will naturally grow only such weeds as daisies, paintbrush, and berry briars. Perhaps soil has been limed too much.

I grow wonderful potato vines in my garden, but the tubers are seldom larger than marbles. What can I do about it? Large potato vines and poor yields may indicate an excess of nitrogen or a deficiency of potash and phosphorus. This can be corrected by an increased application of phosphoric acid and potash. If the garden has had an abundance of manure, the difficulty might be corrected merely by using superphosphate, broadcasting it and working it in when preparing the plot. Another possibility is that the garden does not get enough sun. Too much shade causes an excessive ratio of top to tuber in potatoes.

Could we grow potatoes in our garden? Do they need a sandy soil? Unless potatoes are difficult to purchase in the market, they are not recommended as first-choice crop for the home garden. Many garden soils are not adapted to potatoes, the result being poor yield and low quality. See previous questions.

In potato growing, how long after plants have wilted do spuds continue growing? Or don't they? What I want to know is when to harvest. When the vines have completely died down. The tubers make no growth after that.

When should potatoes be dug, and how? The tops wither when the tubers are mature, and most home gardeners dig them with an ordinary flat-tined fork, but special "potato hooks" are made for the purpose. In either case careful digging is necessary to avoid injuring the potatoes. The late crop for storage should be dug in cool weather.

Is light harmful to potatoes after they are dug? Yes, they acquire an unpleasant flavor and should be exposed to the sun only long enough so that the adhering soil may be easily removed. Then they should be taken to cellar or other storage, in complete darkness.

How should potatoes be stored? In a very cool cellar, and so piled or arranged that a little air can circulate around them; otherwise they are likely to sweat. The loosely woven potato sacks are satisfactory, or slat crates—much better than solid boxes or bins.

What does the word "culls" on a bag of potatoes mean? New York is one of the few potato states in which the grade "culls" is legally defined. According to New York State standards, any potatoes which contain more than 2 percent of soft rot or more than 15 per cent of defects which cause serious damage are culls. In general, culls are potatoes or other products not good enough to make standard market grades such as United States No. 1, United States No. 2, United States Commercial, etc.

What causes potato plants to lose color and fall to the ground in midsummer? More of the symptoms would need to be known before answering this question. Potatoes are subject to many plant enemies, both diseases and insects, therefore seed potatoes should be certified disease free, the beetles should be kept down by dusting, and the blight by spraying with Bordeaux mixture or a copper dust or spray such as Bonide Coprqure, Copper A or Carbola Copper Spray.

How can flea beetle and potato beetle be controlled on homegrown potato plants? When insect pests appear, use an all-purpose potato dust or spray such as Liberty Copper DDT Dust Mixture or Garden Master Three Way Spray which controls both pests and diseases. Agricide Potato Dust is a specific for beetles. Also look at the back of leaves for their little clusters of orange-colored eggs and destroy these.

What causes scab on potatoes? A fungus, *Actinomyces scabies,* which thrives best in light, alkaline soils. It can be brought into the garden by infected seed potatoes; if it is already in the soil, be very wary of using lime on the potato patch. This organism does not endure acid conditions.

How often should potatoes be sprayed, and with what, to control late blight? The best safeguard against this disease is Bordeaux mixture applied either as a spray or a dust. As plants increase in size, more Bordeaux spray is needed for thorough coverage. Bordeaux can be made at home or bought as a prepared powder mixture. The spray should be applied often enough to keep all of the new growth completely covered throughout the season. Under conditions favoring rapid growth, this means an application of Bordeaux at least every week after the plants are 6 ins. high.

Potato Varieties

What are early, medium, and late varieties of potatoes? First the type of soil, climate, and other local conditions should be considered. In general, Irish Cobbler is the favorite early, though many prefer Chippewa or Early Ohio. For midseason, Katahdin and Kennebec. Green Mountain does well on heavier soils. For the late crop, Jersey Red and Russet are among the best.

What are the best-tasting potatoes to raise? Plant Early Ohio for the first crop, Katahdin for the second, and if your soil, culture, and climate are good, the potatoes will be of fine flavor.

Am planting 3 acres of potatoes. What kind are best? (New York.) For a planting of this extent it would be well to consult your County Agricultural Agent, who will advise not only on conditions of growth but also on the preferences of local markets and other factors.

Does the Katahdin potato do well in the corn belt? (Illinois.) When grown as a late potato, the Katahdin does as well or better than the members of the Rural group in the northern part of the corn belt. Trials in the southern part of the corn belt have been inconclusive.

What experiments have been made with Sebago potatoes, and with what result? Sebago has proved widely adapted and very satisfactory as a late variety in the New England states and in New York. Sebago is definitely later in maturity, white skinned, lower in starch content, and much more resistant to scab, blight, and mosaic, than is Green

Mountain. Experience to date would indicate that it is also more widely adapted to adverse potato soil and climate than Green Mountain. Seed-spacing tests both in Maine and New York indicate larger seed pieces and more seed to the acre are desirable with Sebago than with Green Mountain.

Has there been any real improvement over the Early Rose and Green Mountain potato? No variety exists today which has a higher starch content than Green Mountain. Such new varieties as Chippewa, Katahdin, Sebago, and Sequoia are lower in starch content but much more resistant to disease and more productive of yield. However, some of the new varieties, such as Houma and Mohawk, have as much starch content and are as mealy as Green Mountain and Early Rose. The public has readily accepted newer varieties because they are impressed with their fine shape and white skin and their tendency to remain white after cooking.

PUMPKIN

What is the best way to grow good pumpkins? Soil for pumpkins should be well enriched. If good garden ground is used, it is not necessary to make up special hills, but if the soil is a bit poor, work a forkful or two of well-rotted manure into each hill. Plantings should be made after frost danger is past, with rows 8 ft. apart and hills 4 to 8 ft. apart in the row. Cover the seed about an inch deep. Dusting for striped beetle will be necessary during early growth.

What kind of soil should pumpkins have? Are they planted in sun or shade? Pumpkins grow in a wide variety of soils; should have little or no shade. (See previous question.)

Is it good to plant pumpkins with corn? It is an old custom to plant pumpkins every 8 or 10 ft. in each third row of corn. However, if the corn makes a strong growth, it is likely to shade the pumpkins, resulting in reduced yields. If corn is planted thinly, the scheme may work fairly well, but it is better to plant them separately.

What method does one follow to force or produce super-sized pumpkins or squash? Does it help to cut off branch tips and keep them in a dish of milk? The plants should be grown under favorable conditions of soil and climate. Soil should be fertile and moisture holding. If rainfall is short, water frequently. Plants are spaced widely, about 8 to 12 ft. Allow the whole plant to grow, but remove extra fruits, leaving only 1 or 2 per plant. Side-dress the plants with a little sodium nitrate or complete fertilizer as the season goes along. Nothing is gained by cutting off the tip of the branch and keeping it in a dish of milk.

What are some good pumpkin varieties? Connecticut Field is the usual variety of large pumpkin, but Winter Luxury, New England Pie, and Small Sugar are considered better for cooking quality and pies. The Cushaws (including the Green Striped, Tennessee Sweet Potato, Golden Cushaw, and Large Cheese) are favored in the South.

RADISHES

What soil and plant food are necessary to produce good radishes? Any soil that does not bake too hard will produce good radishes. Use fertilizers low in nitrogen. All organic materials such as leaf mold, rotted manure, and humus are beneficial. Sprinkle land plaster (gypsum), 3 or 4 lbs. to 50 ft., along row and work into soil before planting.

Why can't we raise radishes of any kind? This is hard to understand. Radishes are very easy to grow. Plant seed from April 1 to May 15, using early varieties. Thin seedlings to stand 1½ ins. apart when the first set of true leaves appear. They are a cool-weather crop.

What should be done when radishes all grow into tops instead of radishes? You are probably not thinning your radishes early enough or severely enough. Radishes should be thinned as soon as seedlings produce first true leaves.

What happened to my second crop of radishes and lettuce planted in July? They came up 2 ins. and would go no farther. First crop was fine. I have sandy soil. (Indiana.) July is a poor month to sow radishes and lettuce. Midsummer temperatures are not conducive to the production of these crops in your section.

I have a small greenhouse and the radishes I planted have long, thin red stalks between the green leaves and the radish itself. What is the remedy for this? Evidently the soil is too rich in nitrogen, the night temperatures are too high, and they are not being thinned out sufficiently.

What are the names of some improved radish varieties? Cherry Belle, Champion, Comet, Sparkler (red with a white tip); Crimson Giant (very large, and remains long time in good condition); Long Scarlet and White Icicle, both long and narrow, the latter less peppery than the former. Winter radishes: White and Scarlet Chinese and Long Black Spanish.

RHUBARB

How do you prepare the bed for rhubarb roots? Make sure that the soil is rich and well drained. If you have barnyard manure, it should be liberally spread and dug in. Set roots in holes 6 ins. deep and 18 to 24 ins. apart, with crowns just below the surface. Firm dirt about them with the feet, applying full weight.

What yearly care is needed for established rhubarb roots? In autumn mulch entire surface of bed with well-rotted manure. In spring, dig this into the bed lightly, being careful not to cut roots. An application or two of nitrate of soda (or some other high-nitrogen fertilizer) will hasten spring growth and produce tender, juicy stalks.

How is rhubarb propagated? Rhubarb is usually propagated by dividing the older roots. This is best done in the early spring just as the first buds appear. Use a sharp spade to cut the old root into pieces, having at least 1 and preferably 2 or 3 buds at the top. Set the cut pieces in the new location immediately, with buds just at the surface of the soil; water in well.

Do rhubarb roots ever need to be divided? Yes, about every second or third year for best quality stalks.

When is best time to reset pie-plant (rhubarb)? Fall or early spring? Reset rhubarb in the early spring, as the first buds appear.

When is the best time to take up and move rhubarb? How many roots are placed in a hill, and how do you fertilize? I have plenty of barnyard manure. (See above.) Barnyard manure on a well-limed soil will grow good rhubarb. Divide old roots (free from any rot) into 2, 3, or more sections and place 1 section in a hill.

How do you cut rhubarb? Rhubarb is not cut, but *pulled,* as the whole leaf-stalk is usable. When young, vigorous leaves come up during the summer, rhubarb makes just as good sauce as in the spring. Pull only a few stalks for the first season, however, to give plants a chance to get well established.

When should you divide rhubarb in California? Soon after it has stopped growing and has become dormant. If under irrigation, it should be made dormant by withholding water. After the leaves have dried, the plants may be divided and moved.

In forcing rhubarb, does it kill or injure plants for outdoor garden use? Some growers force rhubarb in forcing sheds and then plant sections which still have buds on them in the garden or field. However, this is not a sure method. Many of the roots may die, depending on how much they were forced.

I have tried to grow rhubarb several times and in several locations. It always starts out well and grows part of a season, then the stalks seem to begin to rot, fall over, and the plant dies. Can you tell me what is wrong? This is due to a crown rot. If it once gets into the plants and the soil there is not much you can do except to get clean plants and set them where rhubarb has not grown before. The soil should not be acid. Rhubarb does better in the cooler parts of the country.

What is the best variety of rhubarb? MacDonald, Valentine and Victoria are considered tops.

SALSIFY

What information can you give on the growing of vegetable-oyster or oyster-plant? Oyster-plant (salsify) requires 120 days of growing weather, and a fertile, sandy loam soil. Sow seed early, in rows 18 to 20 ins. apart, and thin plants to 4 ins. It requires a well-aerated subsoil to get long, fleshy roots. The flavor of the root is improved by freezing. It is better taken directly from the soil than if dug and placed in storage.

How hardy is salsify? Perfectly hardy. The roots can be left in the ground over winter and dug during a thaw or in early spring.

I planted salsify last spring, but it did not come up. Why? Salsify seed has a low germination at best and if it is several years old will not germinate. It should be grown in well-limed soil. Obtain seed from reliable source; sow thickly enough for the seeds to touch; if thinning is needed, *do it early.*

What caused my salsify to go to seed? It also rotted. Anything that causes a dormant period or a stoppage of growth processes due to dry weather may cause it to go to seed. The decay may be due to boron deficiency in the soil or a lack of sufficient calcium. Usually a small percentage of roots will throw seed stalks; these should be pulled out.

Why does salsify grow 3 or 4 sprawly roots instead of one good root? This is the nature of the plant. The roots can be made to grow deeper and longer by extra-thorough and deep preparation and by loosening the subsoil. Make sure that the calcium supply is adequate.

How is salsify cooked? Scrape roots; boil or steam until tender, then: (a) Serve with cream, cheese, or Hollandaise sauce; (b) braise in butter; (c) run through food chopper, add seasoning, beaten egg, and bread crumbs. Form into small cakes and fry in butter; or French fry in deep fat. Serve with tartare sauce. (The flavor somewhat resembles that of oysters.)

SPINACH

What are the soil requirements for spinach? Any fine, friable soil that can be worked up in a mellow seedbed, and which is well supplied with organic matter and nitrogen, will grow spinach. The optimum pH level is 6.0 to 6.7, mildly acid.

When should spinach be planted? *Very* early in spring, making 2 or 3 sowings, timed so that the last will mature before hot weather comes. Sow again in late summer 50 to 60 days before frost for the fall crop. Seed should be treated with red copper oxide or zinc oxide, to prevent damping off.

What varieties of spinach are satisfactory for the home garden? There are two principal types: the smooth, thicker leafed, of which Nobel is about the best; and the savoyed or crumpled, of which Bloomsdale Long-standing is preferred, as it does not throw up seed stalks quite so readily as some others.

Can you expect more than one cutting from spinach? Ours usually turns yellow after cutting once.   No. The whole spinach plant is cut at soil surface—not picked off a leaf at a time.

Can spinach be grown in midsummer? If not, suggest substitute greens.   Spinach bolts to seed in hot weather. The best substitute—and a very good one too—is the so-called New Zealand spinach, which resembles spinach only when cooked. It loves heat and is very easy to grow, but makes a slow start. Soak seed 2 or 3 days before planting; sow 8 to 10 seeds to the foot in rows at least 24 ins. apart; thin to about 8 ins.

What is summer spinach?   New Zealand spinach, which is not spinach at all but is used as such and is often called summer spinach. Seeds planted about April 15 will yield a harvest from about July 1 until frost. The plant is a tremendous yielder and only a few feet of rows are necessary for the average family. Like beets, there are a number of seeds in each seed pod. Though germination may be poor, seedlings may be readily transplanted to fill out a row, especially as the seed pods which do germinate are apt to produce quite a large group of seedlings growing close together. (See preceding question.)

SQUASH

How should summer squash be planted to produce abundantly?   Summer squash is not difficult to raise. Start with good seed. Seed may be sown when danger of frost is past, with rows 4 to 5 ft. apart and plants thinned to about 3 ft. apart in the row. Soil should be well fertilized. Plant protectors will permit planting 2 or 3 weeks earlier, or plants may be started under glass as with cantaloupes. Faithful dusting for a few weeks will be necessary to control the striped cucumber beetle.

Are squash grown more successfully in hills or rows?   In gardens where fertility is well maintained, the practice of making hills with manure has been largely abandoned. This practice may be good where soil is not rich, stirring a couple of forkfuls of well-rotted manure into the soil under each hill.

When should summer squash be picked for best table quality?   When the skin of the fruit is soft. On vigorous vines the fruit will be about 6 ins. long. They should be a lemon-yellow color. When orange yellow, they are too old and the flesh gets coarse and tasteless.

What kind of soil should I use to grow winter squash? When and how should the seed be planted?   Winter squash thrive in a rather wide variety of soils. Moderately heavy soils retain moisture better, are likely to be somewhat more fertile, and give good results. Seed should be planted about the time tomatoes are set, when danger of frost is past. In Northern climates practically the full season is required to mature them, for they need 100 to 130 days. They must be harvested before frost in the fall. Hills should be at least 6 ft. each way; or thin to single plants 4 ft. apart in rows.

How should squash vines be trimmed to keep them bearing longer? It is not desirable to trim the plants of squash or similar plants. With cucumbers, muskmelons, and summer squash it is best to remove the fruits when they are ready; failure to do this is likely to hamper development of others.

How are winter squash harvested and stored? Winter squash should be harvested as late as possible before a fall frost. Cut with an inch or so of vine, either side of stem. They must have a hard rind to keep well. You should not be able to dent them with the thumbnail. If well matured, they should be kept near the furnace for several weeks to cure them. After that they may be placed on shelves in a single layer in a dry place at 45° to 60° F. Don't pile them up. *Handle like eggs!*

How can striped cucumber beetle be controlled? By dusting the plants with rotenone-copper dust or DDT.

What can I use on the "stink bugs" that infest the squashes? The squash bug, commonly, and not without reason, called the "stink bug," is troublesome in home-garden plantings. The bugs may often be trapped by laying a shingle or little board on the ground near the plants. This shelters the bugs at night and they can be destroyed in the morning. Watching for egg masses or colonies of young insects and removing and destroying them are also helpful. Pyrethrum or rotenone dust may be used, though heavy and repeated applications are required. Dust must be applied to the *under side* of the leaves as well as the surface. If you have only a few hills, make cases 2 × 2 × 1 ft., covered with mosquito netting, and keep these over the hills until the vines crowd the cases. This will give the vines a good start before being subjected to insect injury.

How can I protect my vine crops from stalk borers? Stalk borers are very difficult to control. Vines should be examined occasionally for borers. If found, they must be removed by carefully slitting the vines and removing. Also keep joints of vines covered with soil to encourage the joints to root. If rotenone dust is not available, spray with Black Leaf 40 (at rate of 1 pt. to 25 gals. of water). Cover small plants completely, or areas 3 ft. in diameter around center of larger plants. Make 4 applications at weekly intervals, the first about the last week in June. Drench base of plants. Soap chips will help make the spray stick.

What can be done about root maggots in vine crops? Root maggots are probably the larvae of the cucumber beetle. Keep the vines covered with rotenone dust or some dusting lime while they are young, and the beetles won't come near them.

Can Acorn squash be grown in southwest Ohio? What is its culture? The Table Queen (Des Moines or Acorn) squash grows under a wide range of conditions, matures in 60 to 75 days from seed, is prolific, and is not difficult to grow. Grow in the same way as other squash but with somewhat closer spacing of plants.

Can Table Queen or Acorn squash be stored through winter months? Table Queen squash may be stored successfully for several months, using the same method as with Hubbard or other winter squash. It probably will not keep in good shape as long, say, as Blue Hubbard.

Will Buttercup squash produce satisfactorily if staked up in garden to save or conserve space? The added exposure to heat, sun, and wind might be damaging. Saving space would be offset, at least partially, by shading other crops. However, they are sometimes grown this way.

What is the best small early squash to grow in northern Michigan? Yankee Hybrid is early and prolific. It matures in about 60 days from seed; an early start may be gained by starting plants indoors as with muskmelon or by using plant protectors. For winter use, such small varieties as Table Queen, Fordhook, and Delicata require only 60 to 75 days to mature from seed.

What are some satisfactory summer squash? Yankee Hybrid, yellow. Fordhook (Black) Zucchini and Cocozelle.

What is the best variety of Zucchini squash? The new Black Zucchini is very dark green, a heavy bearer, and edible until quite large. Many people consider it the best of the summer squashes in flavor and quality.

What are the best winter squashes to grow? Delicious, Quality, Buttercup, and Butternut are good for fall and early winter; Golden and Blue Hubbard for winter.

Where can seed of new high-yield squash be obtained? The new Yankee Hybrid is the heaviest yielding summer squash. Fordhook Zucchini is a heavy bearer. Of winter squash, Blue Hubbard and Butternut will probably outyield most of the others. These varieties can be obtained from most large seed stores.

SWEET POTATOES

Can I grow sweet potatoes? If so, how? Yes, if you have lots of room and a long, hot summer. Buy slips (young, rooted plants) from a reliable source to avoid transmission of diseases, and set them out 18 ins. apart, with 4 ft. between the rows. They prefer a rather light soil.

How should soil for sweet potatoes be prepared? No other preparation than for the usual vegetable crops is required. A sandy soil is best, and it should not have a hard subsoil, which would prevent the roots from reaching down to moisture.

Should sweet potato vines be trimmed?   No; injury to the vines would cause loss of nourishment to the potatoes. If the vines grow too large, it is better to loosen them from the soil, where they root at the joints.

Sweet potatoes are started in a covered box or frame to supply "sets" for the garden.

Will sweet potatoes grow in the North, just for an experiment? (Illinois.)   This is by nature a tropical plant, but it can be successfully grown where the summer is warm and free of frost for 5 months. As the vines spread extensively, culture is more for the field than the garden.

Sweet potato "sets"—young rooted sprouts started in a frame and then transplanted to the open.

How do you grow sweet potato plants?   Growing the slips, or plants, to set out for sweet potatoes is rather tedious, and the home gardener would be better advised to buy them. They are started in hotbeds or cold frames, the sprouts or "slips" being removed, with adhering roots, from the old potatoes.

When should I start sweet potatoes in the house for sprouts? When should I plant the sprouts outside in the garden? Start 6 weeks before the date when frost is sure to be over for the season. Set out the plants only when the soil has become well warmed.

During the past season I have raised delicious, large sweet potatoes in my garden, but my great difficulty was in digging. How can I best dig without breaking them? This problem has never been satisfactorily solved because the tubers are so very tender. There is nothing for it but to exercise great care—start digging a little way off and approach from the side instead of the top.

Do sweet potato tops die when ripe? How are sweet potatoes "cured"? The tops survive until cold comes. The potatoes are cured by storing 2 to 3 weeks at 75° to 80° F., after which store in a temperature of 50° to 60° F. until the tubers are used. Do not handle them while in storage. At all times handle with greatest care to avoid bruising. Broken or injured ones should be used first.

SWISS CHARD

How is Swiss chard grown? This is really a leaf beet, and is grown in the same way as beets, but only the leaves and stalks are used. It is a "cut-and-come-again" crop.

How is Swiss chard harvested? A leaf or two at a time may be cut from several plants. These should be outer leaves; they will be replaced as the plant grows. Or the center top is cut off, 2 ins. or so above crown, so that all new growth will be tender.

Last year my Swiss chard was covered with small brown spots. How can this be controlled? Probably potash deficiency if they occurred along the margins; or magnesium deficiency if in the body of the older leaves. Magnesium, lime, or wood ashes will correct the deficiencies. If serious, send a specimen to the Experiment Station in your state for diagnosis.

*Two good vegetables for summer-long crops
—Swiss chard and bush squash.*

What insecticide can be used on Swiss chard and beet leaves to keep insects from eating leaves? Rotenone dust is the only safe thing to use.

What are good varieties of Swiss chard? Rhubarb Chard, with crimson stalks; Fordhook Giant, dark green leaves with white stalks; Dark Green, and Lucullus.

TOMATOES

What is surest way to get a crop of tomatoes? High points in tomato culture are: using seed of a good variety; planting on fertile, moisture-holding soil; buying or starting strong plants; and keeping the weeds under control. Tomatoes thrive under a very wide variety of soil and climatic conditions.

Is it advisable to plant tomato seeds in the garden, or is it best to have a hotbed? It is generally best to start tomato plants in greenhouse, hotbed, or kitchen window; or buy plants. Some cannery growers sow seed in the open, but the practice is not recommended for the home garden. Starting under glass gives earlier maturity than outdoor sowing of seed, and is necessary in most parts of the North.

Do tomatoes thrive best on alkaline or acid soils? Tomatoes seem to thrive under a fairly wide range of soil reaction. Experiments have not shown much benefit from liming when the crop is grown in acid soil. It also seems fairly tolerant up to a pH of 7.5 or so (7.0 is neutral).

Do tomatoes require much fertilizer? Tomatoes need to be well supplied with nutrients, whether this is achieved by the use of stable manure, manure and phosphorus, complete fertilizer, or a combination. Phosphorus is particularly important for tomatoes, contributing to good yields and to earliness. Oversupply of nitrogen under some conditions, and with some varieties, may result in overgrowth of vine and poor set of fruits.

How many tomato plants will I need per person? Just for the table, 3 plants are plenty. For canning, 6 average plants are needed.

How far apart should tomatoes be planted? Spacing of tomatoes depends a good deal on soil and variety. Heavy-growing varieties, such as Rutgers, need more space than small-growing sorts like Pritchard and Victor. Wider spacing is needed in rich soil where vines make large growth. In general, most varieties, if allowed to run on the ground, may be spaced at about 4 × 4 or 4 × 6 ft. Many prefer 4 × 6 to 5 × 5 ft., because it leaves wider space between rows for cultivating and picking. Pritchard may be planted 3 × 4 to 4 × 5 ft., and Victor 3 × 2½ ft. If tomatoes are to be trained to a single stem, rows may be 3 to 4 ft. apart and plants 1½ to 2 ft. apart in the row.

When is it safe to set out tomato plants? Except in the far South, they are set out when danger of killing frost is past. This is usually 2 to 4 weeks after average date of last killing frost in the spring. Local experience is valuable; talk to other gardeners.

Is it best to buy tomato plants or plant seed yourself? Growing plants require a suitable place and a little equipment, and the gardener must look after the plants regularly. With care, better plants can be grown at home; *and they are on hand when planting conditions are right!* It is easier to buy plants—if good ones are available at a reasonable cost—but many poor plants are offered for sale, and if one needs as many as 100, the cost becomes significant.

Growing Tomato Plants

Is February too soon to start tomato seeds in the house? In most climates tomatoes are set out in the garden about 3 weeks after the average date of last killing frost. For much of the northeast this means setting the last week of May. Seed may be started about 8 weeks ahead of this to get good-sized plants, though 10 weeks is preferable.

How should one manage the starting of tomato plants? Use a little box or flat, 2 to 3 ins. deep, filled with good potting or plant-growing soil well firmed around the sides and corners. Sow seed in rows 2 ins. apart, 8 to 12 seeds per inch. Seeds may be treated with red copper oxide or one of the special dusts to control damping off. Keep the box in the window, greenhouse, or hotbed at a temperature of about 70° F. Water so that the soil is moist, but not so heavily as to result in tender, spindly growth. As soon as seedlings come up, give full sunshine.

How should tomato seed be planted in cold frame? Tomatoes cannot be started as early in cold frame as in hotbed, a greenhouse, or in the house. It is a good plan to start a flat of plants where there is artificial heat, and then transplant them (spacing from 2 × 2 to 4 × 4 ins.) in the cold frame for further growth and hardening. Somewhat more time may be required by this method than if hotbed or greenhouse is used.

Young tomato plants—about four weeks old—at right stage for transplanting.

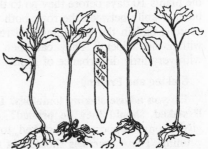

How should I prepare the soil for starting tomato plants? Should they have sun all day, or part shade? Prepare the soil for tomato plants as for other early plants. A bushel of potting soil can often be bought at a greenhouse. One good way to provide it is to make a compost pile a year ahead. A sandy, loam garden soil makes a good starting base, piling it in alternate layers with an equal volume of half-rotted or even fresh manure. The heap should be kept reasonably moist and the soil should be turned 2 or 3 times during the season. In the fall it should be put in a cellar or other place where it will not freeze up hard and be inaccessible. It is not usually necessary to add commercial fertilizer to a mixture of this sort. If soil has not been prepared in advance, 4 ozs. of garden fertilizer may be added to a bushel of soil. Or mix 2 lbs. of good sandy garden loam with 1 lb. of fine, well-rotted manure.

What kind of box or pot is best for growing tomato plants? Clay pots, preferably of 4-in. size, are excellent. If one wants plants at the stage of first bloom at transplanting time, 5- or 6-in. pots may be used, starting seeds a little earlier than otherwise recommended. Veneer dirt bands and boxes are excellent. Berry boxes and tin cans are also commonly used.

When should tomato seedlings be transplanted under glass? When seedlings are about 2 ins. high and showing the first true or rough leaves, transplant with spacings of 2 × 2 up to 4 × 4 ins. Set the plant almost down to the seed leaves, and firm the soil securely about the roots. If only a few plants are involved, they may be kept in a window in the house, or they may continue their growth in greenhouse, hotbed, or cold frame. Temperature should be 65° to 70° F. and plants should have benefit of full sunshine. Water just enough to insure steady, vigorous growth without plants becoming soft. If this is well managed, little hardening is necessary.

What is meant by "blocking" tomato (and other) vegetable plants? Seedling tomato plants are often transplanted into greenhouse benches, or into the soil in a hotbed or cold frame, spaced 3 × 3 up to 4 × 4 ins. When planted this way (or in flats), it is good practice to "block" the plants 10 days before they go to the garden. This means running a butcher knife between the rows both ways. This results in gentle root pruning and in the branching and re-establishing of the root system within the "block." They can then be transplanted to the garden with very little disturbance of roots.

Staking and Pruning

Do you advise staking tomatoes? Does this cause sun blister? And if staked, should they be pruned? Tomatoes are always better if given some support, and staked tomatoes benefit from intelligent pruning. These practices should not result in sun blistering.

Is it best to stake tomato plants individually or tie them to row lengths of heavy chicken wire or iron posts? If time can be spared, individual stakes are preferred. Wooden trellises are also excellent.

Chicken wire and iron posts are probably less satisfactory, but any support is better than none.

How shall I stake my tomato plants to keep them off the ground? One method is to make tripods and set a tomato plant at the foot of each leg. The tripods should stand at least 6 ft. tall. The main stem of a plant is then tied to each leg with pieces of cloth. Barrel hoops, supported about 18 ins. above the ground by stakes (3 to each hoop), are sometimes used.

What is the best method of training tomatoes? Most common method of training tomatoes is to trim the plant to a single stem, taking out all side branches. Plants set 18 to 24 ins. apart in rows 3 to 4 ft. apart may be tied to stakes 4 or 5 ft. high, one to each plant. Another method consists in driving heavy posts at each end of the row, then stringing a stout wire over the top, anchoring well at the ends, and giving light post support every 10 ft. or so along the line. Tie binder twine or other string around the base of the plant, using a bowline knot so that it will not slip and bind the stem; then tie to the wire overhead. By twisting the plant around the string, it is not necessary to do any other tying. This saves stakes and labor and works very well. Using a second wire, 8 or 10 ins. above the ground, to hold lower end of string is an improvement on this method.

Should tomatoes be pruned? Depends on circumstances. Where comparatively few plants are grown and labor can be spared, it is advantageous. Where an extensive area is given over to the crop, it is often uneconomical to prune.

How should tomato plants be pruned into one tall plant instead of a bush? Remove every side shoot (lateral growths that develop in the angles formed by the leaves and main stem) when not more than 3 or 4 ins. long. Also remove leafy growths that develop on fruit trusses. Continue this throughout season.

Can tomato plants be pruned at the top to keep them low and bushy? If the tops are pinched out in late summer, the plants will remain lower than otherwise. They may also be kept low by tying them to low trellises, training the growths to go more or less in a lateral direction.

Does pruning and pinching back tomato plants make for more fruit? If properly carried out, staked and pruned tomato plants yield less per plant but more from a given area than untrained plants.

Is the theory sound that two tomato plants, given intensive care and trained to grow upright, will produce more than a dozen plants with only moderate care? No, this is not true. Good cultivation increases yield, of course, but scarcely sixfold. (See preceding question.)

Does pruning tomato plants result in larger fruits? The size of the fruit is not materially increased by pruning, but the proportion of clean, healthy fruit produced by pruned and staked plants is higher than from untrained plants.

How should tomatoes be trimmed to keep them from growing tall and large vines, with few tomatoes?   Trimming (pruning) ordinarily tends to make plants taller rather than to dwarf them. Grow plants in full sun, and do not overfeed with nitrogenous fertilizers.

Can new growth pruned from tomato plants be rooted to make new plants?   Yes, if the growth isn't too watery. Cuttings should be firm, but not too old.

My tomato plants went all to foliage. How should I prune them? This may be due to too much shade (perhaps from planting too closely) or to too much nitrogen in the soil. Cut surplus growths away *when quite small,* so that not more than 3 stems develop from each plant.

General Culture

How far from the growing plants should tomatoes be cultivated? My tomatoes were a failure this year.   Cultivation of tomatoes (as with most vegetables) should be shallow and may go close to the plants. The idea is to destroy weeds, avoiding damage to roots from deep cultivation. There may be many causes of failure. Get local advice on cause of failure.

Would you hill up the soil around tomato plants?   It is now generally agreed that there is little to be gained by hilling up the soil around most vegetables. It results in damage to roots, which spread wider than the tops. Under some field conditions a little hilling may be desirable to smother weeds.

Applying summer mulch to tomatoes trained to stakes. Ground should be cleared of weeds and lightly culitvated before mulch is put in place.

Is mulching of tomatoes a good idea?   When tomatoes are allowed to run on the ground, mulching is good practice. A 2- or 3-in. layer of hay, straw, old leaves, lawn rakings, or anything of the sort serves to retain moisture in the soil, smother weeds, keep fruit clean, and the material is a good addition of organic matter for the next year. A little extra nitrogen on the soil may be necessary to balance the demand of organisms which decompose the mulch material.

Our tomatoes play out by September 1. How can we have good ones later in the fall? It is good practice to set some tomato plants a bit late for fall maturity. Seed for these may be sown in the open May 1 to 15. This also furnishes good mature green tomatoes to put away for fall use.

Our tomatoes had an acid taste. Testing indicated ground had too much potash. Could this account for it? It does not seem very likely that the nutrients in the soil would have very much to do with the acidity of tomatoes. Varieties differ a good deal in this respect. Varieties of the Ponderosa group and also the yellow tomatoes are milder in flavor and acidity than most varieties.

Will tomatoes do well if planted in the same location several consecutive years? In general, rotation of crops, avoiding planting the same thing in the same place from year to year, is advisable. However, tomatoes do not seem particularly sensitive on this point, unless disease infestation accumulates in the soil. The fusarium wilt or yellows is a soil disease, and long rotation helps in the control. It is best to use fusarium-resistant varieties, of which there are now many.

We have grown tomatoes in the same plot for several years; find that we get a tremendous growth of vine but not very large or many tomatoes. Would you advise what to add to the soil? Probably too much nitrogen. Use superphosphate of lime and wood ashes as fertilizers.

How can tomatoes be ripened in very high altitudes or in the extremely cold northern sections of the mid-west where the growing season is very short? Varieties Sioux, Valiant and Valnorth have been especially developed for growing under these conditions. Get the plants to the flowering stage in 4-in. pots by the time the ground is ready to receive them. Have the soil in good condition with respect to lime. Use a mulch. If fertilizer is needed, use it in liquid form.

What shall I use to control flea beetle on tomatoes early in the season? Dust rotenone on the plants, or keep the leaves covered with lime dust.

What causes tomato leaves to curl? Plants that are soft and succulent and growing rapidly require a lot of water. If suddenly exposed to very dry and hot weather, the leaves curl in an effort to reduce the loss of water from the leaves. Leaf curl usually is not a disease, though there is also a virus disease so named.

Should tomatoes be sprayed or dusted? If leaf diseases are prevalent on tomatoes, use an all-purpose dust such as Miller's Tomato Dust D–1 C–7 or Liberty Copper DDT Dust Mixture.

Why do tomatoes get black spots at the blossom end? This trouble is ordinarily called blossom-end rot. It is not caused by a definite disease organism, but seems to be physiological in its nature: a failure of moisture to reach the tender tissues at the blossom end. The trouble may be due to lack of rainfall, drouthy soil, or some condition within the plant preventing proper movement of moisture. The trouble is often followed with secondary mold or fungous infection. It sometimes occurs when the soil is not particularly dry, either because the root system is defective or because there is not enough oxygen in soil for proper moisture intake. Control is by any measure that insures adequate water supply, such as irrigation, maintaining organic matter in soil; in some cases, improved drainage.

Can tomatoes be saved after frost? Healthy, mature green tomatoes (that is tomatoes that have attained full size but have not begun to show color) may be kept for 4 or 5 weeks in the fall. They will keep longer at a temperature of 45° F., but will ripen more quickly at temperatures up to 70° F. Precaution should be taken against evaporation and shriveling; that is, the storage place should be fairly humid. Tomatoes at the half-ripe and turning stage will also ripen up nicely in a few days.

How may partly ripened tomatoes be saved from freezing? As danger of frost approaches, pick all partly ripened fruits and lay them on boards on a table, or even on the floor in a basement or shed where they are protected from freezing. If the room can be kept at 40° to 45° F., the nearly ripened tomatoes will ripen with normal color and flavor. The less-ripened ones will ripen with some loss of flavor, color, and texture.

Are vine-ripened tomatoes more nutritive than those picked when only partially ripe? Vine-ripened tomatoes are of better quality and flavor, and are much better for canning. It is probable that they are more nutritious, although some authorities dispute this.

Why do tomatoes grown in northern United States lack the flavor and brightness of color of those grown 500 miles farther south? (Wisconsin.) Tomatoes like warm weather, but with careful cultivation you can grow Northern tomatoes of equal merit.

Varieties of Tomatoes

Is the acid and food content much different in various varieties of tomatoes, such as white, yellow, and red kinds? Most yellow types of tomatoes are less acid than the red, while white tomatoes are almost free from acid. Food content is about the same in all types.

For late tomatoes should one plant late varieties, or is it as well to plant early varieties at a later date? It is better to plant late varieties for late tomatoes. Most home gardeners plant very few, or no, extra-early sorts, as but a few days are gained at best, and the quality and yield are inferior.

What is the earliest tomato for home or market? Chalk's Early Jewel, Earliana, Big Early, Burpeeana, Early Hybrid, Fireball. For very cold sections use Sioux, Valiant and Valnorth.

Which main crop tomatoes are considered best for the home garden? Harris' Early Hybrid, Moreton Hybrid, Vancross, Glamour; Burpee's Hybrid, Big Boy, Big Early and Burpeeana Stokesdale, Marglobe, and Rutgers are main-crop varieties of merit. Jubilee is the best yellow.

Which tomatoes do you advise for table and home use? Marglobe and Rutgers are considered two of the best varieties for home use.

What kind of tomato plants would you recommend for a very small place, where I have room for only 4 or 5? What can be done to make the tomatoes less spindly, outside of pruning, which did not seem to make much difference? Marglobe and Rutgers are excellent for home use. Your spindly plants are evidently caused by lack of sun, or poor soil. Add humus to the soil if possible.

Which tomatoes are best for staking in limited space? Rutgers, Marglobe, Michigan State, Bonny Best, or John Baer. (Last two are early sorts.)

What are several recent improved varieties of tomatoes? Moreton Hybrid, Glamour (crackless), Burpee Hyrid, Big Boy.

What is the best tomato variety for low, sturdy plants and early fruit? Earliana is the earliest sizable tomato. Fruits tend to be rough and soft. Victor and Bounty have recently come into use. Reports as to their earliness vary widely; quality is second rate. These should be grown on rich soil that retains moisture well. Since vines are very dwarf, plants may be set 30 ins. apart with rows 3 ft. apart. They produce a large number of fruit close to the center of the plant, and the crop is soon cleaned up.

What is meant by "resistant" varieties of tomatoes? These varieties have been bred to resist the attack of the common fusarium wilt. They are attacked by the disease but do not succumb to it. There are no immune varieties. Among the resistant varieties are Marglobe, Pritchard, Early Baltimore, Rutgers, Norton, Pan America, Roma, Marvel, Columbia, Arlington, and Louisana Red.

What are the best varieties of non-acid wilt-resistant tomatoes for main crop in a small garden? Marglobe and Rutgers are wilt resistant and not highly acid. John Baer is non-acid, but not wilt resistant. The most non-acid tomatoes are the yellow or orange type. Good varieties of these are Mingold, Yellowstone, Yellow Aberdeen, and the new golden Jubilee.

In this locality, due, probably, to late spring and much rain, to-

matoes do not mature. **What would you suggest to overcome this difficulty? If caps were used, would they tend to rot in wet ground? (Minnesota.)** Grow an early variety in pots to the flower stage or early fruit stage, and set them in the ground as soon as it is ready. Put up some protection on the north and west sides of the plants. Grow an early variety.

What tomato (meaty, not acid) would you recommend for this area? We use 15 plants—small garden. Ponderosas didn't do well last year. Give best culture. (Minnesota.) Try Rutgers. Grow plants in pots. Have the soil well limed and feed with liquid fertilizer as they need it. A mulch would be advisable.

What is the best all-around tomato for this climate? How should the seed be planted? (Missouri.) Marglobe is an excellent selection for all-around use. Start seeds in flats in a greenhouse and transplant when well sprouted, then replant into a cold frame. (See directions for starting tomato seeds, this section.)

Where can I get the so-called "cherry" tomato plants—those tomatoes that grow only as large as a cherry? Most commercial growers or seed houses have a good selection of cherry-type tomatoes.

Are so-called "climbing" tomatoes a success? They are successful, so far as growth and yield are concerned, but are late, and the quality is inferior. More valuable as a curiosity than for practical purposes.

What is the best canning tomato? Glamour, Burpee Hybrid, Rutgers and Marglobe.

What type of tomatoes is best for juice? Stone is often used for juice, but any of the more common types may be used. Marglobe, Moreton Hybrid and Rutgers are excellent. Jubilee (yellow) makes mild juice of a distinct flavor which most people like.

TURNIP

How do you grow large, yet tender, rutabagas, turnips, etc.? Plant the seed in late July in a well-limed soil that is thoroughly aerated. Don't use too much nitrogen, but plenty of potash.

When should turnips (yellow) be planted for a fall crop? (New Jersey.) About August 1.

I was perfectly successful in raising large crops of lettuce, carrots, beans, beets, tomatoes, and mint, but my white turnip, seeded in two different places, refused to ball up, and grew long like carrots. Why? Probably due to a lack of potash. Put on some wood ashes, or muriate of potash at the rate of 2 lbs. per 100 sq. ft. Be sure that the lime content is satisfactory.

When do you dig turnips? Turnips may be dug at any time when they are ready and one feels like eating them. For winter storage they can be left until the first light frosts have come, then they should be lifted, topped, and stored in the root cellar.

What makes small marks on the outside of turnips? It may be due to growth cracks or bugs that rasp the young roots, leaving scars. Also, insufficient lime may cause this condition.

What makes turnips grow corky? Too much nitrogen or hot weather. If they grow too fast, they get pithy. Plant late enough so that they may develop during cool nights.

Our turnips, which grew fine, are hard and bitter when cooked. What is the cause? This is probably due to hot weather when they matured, or they were allowed to remain in the ground too long.

What is the best variety of turnips to grow for winter storage? The Swede turnip, also known as rutabaga. If you prefer yellow, use American Purple-top, but if you think, as some do, that the white sort is milder and better flavored, try Macomber.

WATERCRESS

How should watercress be started? Seeds may be germinated in a flower pot set in a pan of water. Thin out to avoid crowding, and, when large enough, transplant to a shallow stream. Plants may also be grown in moist soil if watered frequently enough to prevent the surface from becoming dry.

WATERMELONS

How would one manage a watermelon planting in the garden? Watermelons need well-drained, sandy or light soil. Use manure or commercial fertilizer, or both, liberally. Seed is planted outdoors after danger of killing frost; or plants may be started under glass, as with muskmelons. Rows should be about 8 ft. apart and plants thinned (or hills made) 4 to 6 ft. apart, according to variety and how well they grow under local conditions. Careful dusting to control striped cucumber beetle is usually required. Shallow cultivation is practiced as long as possible to control weeds; some pulling of weeds after that may be necessary.

How do you tell when watermelons are ripe? If the sound, on snapping with the finger tip (or knocking with the knuckle), is sharp and high, the melon is immature. If there is a dull, *hollow* sound, it is more likely to be ripe. When the tendril or curlicue by the melon is alive and green, it is almost certainly immature. If the curlicue is dead, the melon is at least approaching maturity. Another test is to watch the change in color—a yellowing of the spot where the melon rests on the ground. A ripe melon when pressed with a bit of weight will usually "crackle," but this is not good for ones that are to be kept.

How would you raise watermelons in the North? What varieties

are best here? (New Jersey.) Watermelons are very much at home in South Jersey, less so in North Jersey. However, they can be grown successfully much farther north than is ordinarily supposed. To grow watermelons successfully in Northern regions, use an early variety. One of the finest is Honey Cream. This variety will mature as early as most muskmelons (in about 80 days from seeding) and thrives under Northern conditions. Other early varieties are: Congo, Rhode Island Red, Fordhook Early, Early Canada, White Mountain, Early Arizona, and Early Kansas. Watermelons may be started under glass, like muskmelons (which see).

Can watermelons be raised in this climate? (Massachusetts.) Yes, in the warmer parts of the state, particularly in the eastern and Cape Cod sections. The sandy soils are best suited to them. Some of the small-fruited varieties should be tried where the growing season is less than 120 days.

Please name some good new midget melons. Midget or Ice-box varieties maturing in from 80 to 85 days include Takii Gem, a Japanese import; New Hampshire Midget, both 82 days; and Sugar Baby, 85 days.

Is it true there are now seedless watermelons? Yes, Seedless Hybrid 317 matures in 90 days, a triploid producing 8 to 12-lb. striped, round fruits with solid, red, seedless flesh of excellent flavor. In starting and growing them, however, particular care is required.

SECTION VI
Home Grown Fruits

BY C. H. CONNORS AND GEORGE L. SLATE

WILD FRUITS formed an important part of the diet of primitive peoples. Some fruits—as dates, bananas, and plantains—still supply a considerable part of the food supply of certain races. Even today tremendous quantities of wild fruits, such as cranberries, blueberries, grapes, plums, crabapples, elderberries, blackberries, and others, are gathered in the wild, not only to increase the food supply but to make viands more palatable and to add pleasure to eating. What would turkey be without cranberries? Or roast pork without applesauce? We have come to think of these as concomitant. Originally they were used as condiments, to help subdue wild flavors.

As families migrated from one part of the world to another, an accompaniment deemed as essential as tools for work, or seeds of vegetables, were plants or cuttings or seeds of fruiting plants. Sometimes these would thrive in the new environment, and sometimes not. Then new varieties had to be sought as substitutes for those that could not be grown.

The nutritionists value highly the inclusion of fruits in the diet. Some of them, such as citrus fruits and strawberries, yellow peaches and apricots, are especially valued for their vitamin content. All supply sugars of several types in easily digestible form. Most are esteemed for the acids that add tone to the system. Minerals are found abundantly in many. Above all, the flavors and aromas that abound, while they may not add anything essential to the diet, certainly contribute something that makes of eating a little less of a chore that must be performed three times a day.

Why Grow Your Own?

Home-grown fruits, if properly cultivated and handled, are, as a rule, much superior to market fruits. Fruits for shipment must be picked in a slightly immature condition, so that they may be able to stand packing and handling. They must often be harvested before the sugars and flavors are developed up to the point where the ripening process will continue after the fruit is removed from the tree. This is especially true of the more perishable fruits, such as the berries. One has not really had peach ice cream until he has picked from the tree a suitable variety, so fully ripe that it would squash in the hand, and used this for the making of a most delectable dish, quite different from the drugstore product. Or, with blackberries, there is absolutely no comparison between the fruit as purchased in the market and those ripened on the canes to the point where a touch will make them fall off.

A fruit that is allowed to develop on the plant, under the proper environmental conditions, until it is fully ripe, has quality, flavor, and nutritional value that cannot be attained in fruits that must be picked for shipment.

Of course location with respect to production has a bearing. If the homeowner is situated in a region where fruits are harvested and delivered to a local market, the quality will more nearly approach that of home-grown fruits; but even for such local handling many sorts must be picked before fully mature.

Limiting Factors

The successful culture of fruits depends upon space, the time available for care, climate, soil, and site.

Space Limits. One having only a limited space which may be used for fruit will be wise not to attempt to grow any of the fruit trees, as these require much more space than the small garden affords. A standard apple tree, fully developed, occupies a space 35 to 40 ft. square; a pear, 24 to 30 ft. square; a peach, 20 to 25 ft. square, and so on. Not only is the space occupied to be considered, but also the effect of the tree upon the surroundings. The roots always extend beyond the spread of the branches. The shade cast by the tree may seriously affect plants grown near it.

In addition to the space required there is another factor, known as self-incompatibility. Most of the varieties of apples, pears, sweet cherries, and some of the plums will not set a satisfactory crop of fruit to their own pollen. Consequently, if there is not in the immediate neighborhood a compatible variety, in addition to the variety wanted, one must have 2 trees of the same fruit, of different but compatible varieties; otherwise the results will be very disappointing.

Dwarfing stocks have been in use for years. In general, these are suited for special situations. They require some space for cultivation. Dwarf apple trees require special attention; otherwise they are likely to become standard trees. Many situations may be suitable for cordon or espalier trees. These, too, are grown on dwarfing roots, and they require much more care in training than do standard trees. The yields, from the quantity standpoint, are apt to be disappointing.

It would be well, then, for the person with a small area to limit the fruit plantings to the small fruits, as they are called.

Strawberries are best for a small area. They can even be worked into a perennial border as an edging, or in other ways. A yield of about 40 quarts may be expected from a row 50 ft. long. The so-called ever-bearing varieties at present available are not so high in quality as the spring-fruiting sorts, nor do they produce so heavily.

The cane or bramble fruits are less satisfactory for very limited space. While they may be used in rows as separation between areas, they will spread by shoots arising from the roots, or by rooting at the tips. For this reason they should not be planted too near a property line, as they may become a nuisance in a neighbor's garden. Raspberries become very ragged in appearance after the fruit is harvested, as the fruit-bearing canes die. Blackberries are very rampant in growth. Dewberries do best in a light, sandy soil. Boysenberry is a variety of dewberry that is a little more tender to cold.

Currants and gooseberries are very prolific bearers and for the average family only a few plants of each would be required. These can very well be used in the shrub border, or as specimen plants, or at the edge of the garden.

Grapes can be worked into the landscape scheme about as well as any plant. They can be used to cover a pergola or to form a shaded arbor. On trellis or fence the vines form a good screen, or a separation between areas.

Blueberries are very exacting in their requirements of soil and moisture, so they do not fit into the general garden picture. However, if they can be given the proper environment, they are satisfactory. If space and proper provision for culture are given to rhododendrons and azaleas, blueberries may well be companions, for they have the same cultural requirements. And the blueberries, while they are deciduous, are handsome plants, both when in flower and when the foliage turns color in the autumn.

Time Limitation. No one should plant fruit on faith alone. Time must be available, at the proper seasons, for cultivation, for pruning, and, above all (especially in the case of tree fruits), for the spraying required in the control of insects and diseases. Such control also involves proper equipment, for ordinary garden equipment will not suffice for trees. Wherever dwarf fruits are grown, whether to develop normally or trained as cordons or espaliers, much more attention must be paid to both top and root. The top must be skillfully pruned and trained to secure maximum production. The roots must be given at least annual attention to make sure that the scion or top is not forming roots above where it joins the dwarfing understock.

Climatic Limitation. Climate has a very great bearing upon the kinds and varieties of fruits that may be grown; such factors as rainfall and temperature must be taken into consideration.

Rainfall, of course, is important. Where it is more than 20 ins. a year, fruits may be successfully grown. This embraces the region from the eastern margin of the Great Plains to the Atlantic Ocean and southward to the Gulf of Mexico. In the Great Plains region the rainfall decreases from more than 30 ins. to the east to 15 ins. on the western border. Where the rainfall is below 20 ins., irrigation must be practiced. In the plateau province (from the Great Plains to the coastal range) the rainfall is usually less than 20 ins., so no fruits, generally speaking, will be possible unless they are irrigated. On the Pacific coastal belt the rainfall may vary from 100 ins. in Washington to about 10 ins. in the San Joaquin Valley. The variation may be as great as this in California alone. In Washington the rainfall will be 100 ins. on the coast and 10 to 15 ins. east of the coastal range.

Temperature limits the distribution of fruit plants. Citrus fruits, pomegranates, and figs will not grow in Vermont; nor will the apples at home in Vermont do well in the deep South.

Low temperature affects fruit production by bud injury, by injury to woody parts above ground, and by root injury.

Buds of peaches will usually be killed at 10° to 15° below zero, depending upon the growth conditions of the buds. Flower buds of sweet cherry will probably all be killed at 15° below. Flower buds of apples may be killed at low temperatures, but there is a considerable variation among varieties. Susceptibility, according to the development of the bud, will have a bearing. Some varieties of grapes lose their flowers at low temperatures. Currants and gooseberries are very hardy. Apricot is very tender.

Wood injury at low temperatures will vary with the age of the trees, culture and latitude, soil moisture, wind velocity; apples are most resistant, peaches most susceptible, among the tree fruits. Of course the tropical and subtropical fruits cannot stand much frost.

Temperature affects fruit setting also. The varieties of peaches grown in the East and in the middle section of California will not develop flower buds unless they are subjected to chilling to complete the process known as after-ripening, so they do not do well in some parts of Florida, for instance.

Absolute and accumulated temperatures have an effect on initiation of growth and upon maturity. Baldwin may be a good variety of apple for Vermont, while Delicious will not do well in the colder parts of that state.

Soil and Site

In general, fruits require a loamy soil with good drainage, but retentive of moisture. Even though the cranberry must be flooded at certain times, the soil should be well drained. The dewberry does not grow well except in sandy soil. Apple varieties will vary somewhat; summer varieties in general do better on a sandier soil than do winter varieties.

A soil reaction that is slightly acid is best for most fruits. The blueberry, which does best in very acid soil, is an exception.

Site is important, as it affects drainage both of water and of air. A pocket or depression may be too moist. Peaches and other early-blooming fruits, such as the apricot, will be injured by late frosts in such a situation.

Where there are large bodies of water, the movement of air results in a warmer condition on the leeward side. This is notable in the Michigan fruit belt and along the shores of Lake Erie and Lake Ontario. In the latter area, the fruit belt is 6 to 10 miles wide. South of it, fruit cannot be grown for some distance.

Elevation is also important. Sometimes a difference in elevation of even less than 50 ft. may mean success or failure with peaches. Apples may be grown on high elevations in states which normally would not be considered suitable, as New Mexico.

Sunlight is an exceedingly important factor. Fruits must have plenty of sunlight, and do best when exposed to direct sunlight for the full daily period. Some varieties are affected in maturing by the total hours of sunlight. For instance, apple varieties adapted to growing in England will seldom prove satisfactory over most of this country, and vice-versa.

Planting

The season when planting may best be done varies with the climate. In regions of fairly early and severe winters, spring planting will usually be best for most fruits. In milder climates, fall planting seems to be best. There may be variations with kinds and within states. Sweet cherries in a fairly mild climate will do better if planted in the fall, while sour cherries may do better if planted in the spring. In other states, the reverse may be true.

With tree fruits, it is best to plant trees 1 or 2 years old. If they are older than that, there is a tremendous setback, unless great pains, at considerable expense, are taken in moving them. So-called bearing-size trees, if moved with bare roots, will probably have a high mortality and will not yield as quickly as young trees properly planted and handled.

Buy from a reliable nursery and as near home as possible. Most fruit plants lose a great deal in drying out during shipment, even though they may be carefully packed. Furthermore, especially with the brambles, there are mosaic diseases that will cause trouble. The reliable nursery will have rogued the planting to eliminate as thoroughly as possible the danger from this source.

Insects and Diseases

It is not possible to produce good fruits without careful attention to control of insects and diseases, but the seriousness of injury from these sources varies with climate and soil. Fire blight of pear, apple, and quince is usually less severe on heavy soils of good drainage and with a relatively low nitrogen content. Codling moth, which attacks apples, is so serious in a few sections of the country that a continuous coating of insecticide must be maintained on the fruits.

The pests may be seasonal or permanent. Many of the Agricultural Colleges and Experiment Stations issue up-to-the-minute information on the development of insects and diseases. All issue spray schedules, with time of application based on stage of development of the plants and of the pests concerned.

There are systemic diseases, such as mosaic and wilt diseases, which affect the whole plant. Here eradication is the only means of control.

Some diseases affect the leaves (cherry leaf spots, peach leaf curl, scab of apples), causing destruction of leaf tissue, the malformation of leaves, or premature leaf drop, thus reducing the power of the tree to manufacture carbohydrates. Other diseases affect the fruit, sometimes causing injury that may mar only the appearance (as sooty mold of apple, apple scab); or (as with brown rot of peach, plum, cherry) invading the deep tissue and resulting in the eventual destruction of the fruits.

Insects are of many different types. Some bore into the stem. Some, as the cane borers of the brambles, are controlled by the removal of the affected parts. Others, as apple-tree borers, are sometimes sought out and killed in place. Sucking insects—such as aphids, leafhoppers, and psyllas—may kill or cripple leaves and malform fruits. Various scales injure or even kill young wood. Leaf-eating insects—as currant worm, Japanese beetle, tent caterpillar, webworms—reduce the ability of the plants to manufacture sugars. Some destroy the fruits from within or without, as codling moth of pome fruits and curculio of stone fruits. These often cause premature ripening and dropping of tree fruits, which results in considerable nuisance on the home grounds, where an adequate spray schedule is not followed.

Generally speaking, the nearer home fruit plantings are to commercial plantings, or to where there are, or have been, abandoned commercial plantings, the more likelihood there is of damage by pests.

The Question of Varieties

The gardener desiring to grow fruits on his home place, in deciding which kinds to attempt, will be limited first of all by the controlling factors of climate and site. In the selection of varieties, the same natural factors will have a bearing. For instance, the Cuthbert raspberry, while subject to mosaic disease, might be hardy in one state and not in another. Delicious apple will do well in the climate of Philadelphia and under irrigation in the apple section of Washington, but will not do at all well in the colder parts of New Hampshire. Most of the Agricultural Colleges and Experiment Stations have available lists of varieties of fruits that are adapted to areas within their limits. The next consideration should be quality and yield. One of the objects of growing fruits on the home grounds is to produce specimens of really superior eating quality. So only the varieties producing fruits of the highest quality and capable of good yields should be selected. Then should come resistance to disease. If a strawberry variety is of highest quality and yield, but susceptible to the red stele disease, it would be folly to plant that variety in a situation where the disease is present. The Latham raspberry is susceptible to mosaic disease. It should not be planted unless assurance is given that the plants have been carefully selected for freedom from that disease, and then only where the disease is not prevalent.

Herewith are given some lists of varieties for home planting. They are merely suggestions, as all of them will not do equally well in all conditions under which the particular class of fruit will survive the climate. For this reason, in selecting a list of fruits for the home garden, the planter will do well to check with his state Experiment Station (see list in Section X) before sending in his order.

APPLE: Lodi, Melba, Early McIntosh, Wealthy, Cortland, Macoun, Delicious, Golden Delicious, Jonathan, Northern Spy, Stayman, Winesap.

CRAB APPLE: Hyslop, Dolgo.

PEAR: Tyson, Clapp Favorite, Bartlett, Flemish Beauty, Gorham, Sheldon, Seckel, Bosc.

PEACH: Dixired, Jerseyland, Redhaven, Golden Jubilee, Triogem, Halehaven, Summercrest, Elberta, Raritan Rose, Redrose, Champion, Laterose.

NECTARINE: John Rivers, Nectarose, Garden State, Nectacrest.

APRICOT: Moorpark, Blenheim, Geneva.

PLUM: *European:* De Montfort, Stanley, Italian prune, Reine Claude.
  Japanese: Beauty, Shiro, Abundance, Burbank, Santa Rosa.
  Hybrid: Underwood, Monitor.
  Damson: Shropshire.

CHERRY: *Sour:* Montmorency.
  Sweet: Early Rivers, Victor, Emperor Francis, Schmidt, Yellow Spanish, Napoleon, Hedelfingen, Windsor.

QUINCE: Orange.

GRAPE: Van Buren, Fredonia, Portland, Seneca, Buffalo, Concord, Steuben, Yates, Sheridan, Golden Muscat.
  Seedless: Concord Seedless, Romulus.

RASPBERRY: *Red:* September, Newburgh Latham, Taylor Milton, Amber.

Black: Logan, Bristol, Dundee, Cumberland.
Purple: Sodus, Marion.

BLACKBERRY: Hedrick, Bailey.

DEWBERRY: Lucretia, Boysen.

CURRANT: Red Lake, Wilder, White Grape.

GOOSEBERRY: Poorman, Downing.

STRAWBERRY: Midland, Catskill, Empire, Sparkle, Fairfax.
Everbearing: Gem, Arapahoe, Redrich.

BLUEBERRY: Earliblue, Bluecrop, Berkeley, Herbert, Jersey, Coville.

ORCHARD

SOIL

How can soil for orchard fruits be built up? Building up the soil is accomplished by increasing its content of organic matter to improve the physical condition. This may be done by adding large amounts, 20 tons or more per acre, of manure or peatmoss; or more cheaply by seeding the land to a green manure crop, grass, or a legume and fertilizing it heavily. Mow it several times a summer leaving the clippings to rot. Turn it under after 2 or 3 years.

Does sandy soil retard growth of apples and peach trees? Mine are 4 years old and only about 5 ft. tall. Will other soil put around the trees help any? Apple and peach trees will grow well in sandy soil if it is properly fertilized, provided it contains ample moisture. Adding heavy soil might help, but it would require a great deal. It would be more feasible to improve the soil by adding lime (if it needs it), then a 5–10–5 commercial fertilizer at the rate of about 800 lbs. per acre. If the soil is dry, either irrigate with a sprinkler system or mulch with some strawy material to conserve moisture. Heavy mulching will gradually increase the humus content of the soil.

Will fruit trees grow in a scrub-oak section on Long Island? The soil in question is probably low in fertility, but with good care might produce enough fruit for home use. Liberal applications of stable manure, annual fertilizing, and mulching to conserve moisture should make it possible to produce fruit on this soil.

Our soil is mostly sand. Would it be suitable for the raising of strawberries, red raspberries, and fruit trees? A sandy loam soil, or even a loamy sand, is suitable for these fruits if it has a reasonable supply of moisture. If it is very dry, sandy soil you will probably have poor results unless you irrigate. Coarse sands will probably need heavy and frequent fertilization with complete fertilizers. Peaches will thrive in sandier soil than is needed for apples.

Will fruit trees grow in muck ground? Yes, provided the muck is well drained, not too acid, and contains the necessary nutrient elements in sufficient quantities. Muck land is usually low; hence cold air may "drain" into such an area and result in frost damage. Frost damage to the flowers may be so frequent on muck that crops will be few and far between. Fruit trees should have good "air drainage," so are usually set on relatively high land.

Is there any reason why fruit trees will not grow on soil adjacent to black-walnut trees? Black walnut roots are known to excrete a substance that is toxic to the roots of many plants, including apples, tomatoes and alfalfa. Grass will grow under black-walnut trees, but other plants should be kept well away from the roots of the walnut.

FERTILIZER AND MANURE

Must fruit trees (such as apple and peach) be heavily manured? Fruit trees should have sufficient manure (or commercial fertilizer) to supply any nutrient elements which may be deficient in the soil in which they are growing. However, it is easy to overfertilize these fruits. They do not require as heavy fertilization, for instance, as is needed by most vegetable crops.

Should manure be placed on a new garden plot on which fruit trees and berries are to be planted? A good coat of manure would be about the best treatment you could give.

How is nitrate of soda applied when used for fruit trees? Nitrate of soda is usually used for fruit trees at the rate of ¼ lb. for 1- to 2-year-old trees, to 5 to 10 lbs. for trees 20 to 30 years old. Ammonium nitrate, which contains twice as much nitrogen, is used at one half this rate.

Can you give some data on fertilizer to help fruit trees produce well, and at younger age? (Illinois.) Good production will be secured only if the trees have the proper supply of nutrients, and that in turn will depend a great deal on the natural fertility of the soil. Check with your county agricultural agent for specific recommendations for your particular soil. No particular type of fertilizer will cause the trees to bear at a younger age. Age of bearing is influenced chiefly by the variety, the pruning, and by some rootstocks. The age of bearing can be delayed, however, by applying too much nitrogen, or by heavy pruning.

What type of fertilizer should be used for fruit trees in acid soil? Most fruit trees in the East are grown in acid soil; that is, soil which is below the neutral point of pH 7.0. If soil is very acid (below pH 5.5), lime should be added to bring the reaction to around pH 6.0, then use ordinary commercial fertilizer as required.

I have heard that fruit trees do not require lime. Is that correct? Fruit trees require lime as much as any other plants. Whether it should be used or not depends on the acidity and calcium content of the soil. The pH should be between 5.5 and 6.0.

PLANTING

What is the best age at which to buy apple, peach, cherry, plum, and pear trees for setting in the home garden? Apple, 1 or 2 years; peach, 1 year; cherry, 1 or 2 years; plum, 2 years; pear, 2 years. Larger trees are not recommended, and nothing is gained by planting so-called "bearing-age" trees.

How many fruit trees will be necessary to supply a family of 4 with an adequate amount for the year? This will vary greatly according to personal preferences. Six apple, 2 pear, 6 peach, 1 sour cherry, and 2 plum trees would provide about as much as the ordinary family would want, if varieties with a succession of ripening dates are chosen, and if the trees are on suitable soil and well cared for. Additional varieties may be grafted onto these trees to extend the season.

How early in spring should fruit trees and berries be planted? Plant just as early as the soil can be worked. There is no danger of planting too early, provided the soil has dried out enough to be worked into good tilth.

How far apart should fruit trees be planted? I plan to plant about 10 acres. Planting distances of fruit trees depend on the kinds of fruits, and, to some extent, on soil and climate. The following are average: Apple, 35 to 40 ft.; pear, 24 to 30 ft.; peach, 20 to 25 ft.; plum, 22 to 24 ft.; cherry (sour), 22 to 24 ft.; cherry (sweet), 24 to 30 ft.; apricot, 22 to 24 ft.; quince, 18 to 20 ft.

Just how should I go about planting a fruit tree? How big a hole should I dig for an apple tree? A hole 12 to 15 ins. deep and 15 ins. across should be large enough for the average nursery tree. If the roots are too long to fit in a hole this size, cut them back. As the soil is filled in, jiggle the tree up and down a little so that all the roots will make contact with the soil. When the hole is half full, and again when it is full, step on the soil around the trunk of the tree in order to compact it. Finish filling the hole. If the soil is at all dry, pour in a pail of water before the hole is quite full.

How should nursery-grown trees be treated upon receipt? Remove from packing at once and plant immediately or heel in. Examine carefully. If the plants are dried out, soak in water, completely immersed, if possible, for 24 hours. If they do not plump up, return them.

Received nursery-stock fruit trees in fall. What is best way to hold until spring? If they cannot be planted at once, heel them in in a shaded place. Dig a trench wide enough and deep enough so that the root systems will almost go in them. Place plants in the trench, packed close together, at any angle of about 45°. Place loose soil about roots, work down and pack tight, then mound. No grass or weeds against roots. Object is to keep roots moist during winter.

How large does a body of water have to be to cause conditions to be favorable for fruit growing? The moderating effect of the body of water is caused by the changes in temperature occurring in air masses as they move across the water toward the fruit-growing section. If prevailing winds do not blow across unfrozen water long enough to have their temperature raised, then there will be no effect on temperatures in the orchard. This means a body of water will have to be several miles wide and remain unfrozen in order to have very much effect.

Can fruit trees be used as decorative specimens on the home grounds? Quite often crabapples are used to good advantage. Some people use peach, cherry, and apple trees as part of the decorating scheme.

Is locality taken into consideration with regard to the types of trees which should be planted? Yes indeed. Fruits which thrive in Louisiana would not survive the winters in New England, and New England varieties would not do well in Louisiana. Cultural methods also vary greatly in different localities.

SPRAYING

We have a new orchard of fruit trees. What should they be sprayed with, and when? The damage likely to be caused by certain pests varies a great deal in different localities, hence spraying recommendations vary from one producing section to another. Unless the trees are sprayed regularly and intelligently the fruit will be worthless and the trees severely injured by diseases and insects. Each Agricultural Experiment Station has developed spraying directions to fit conditions within the state. These directions may change from year to year as new methods are developed. Get on your station's mailing list to receive spray schedules.

How and how often should orchard trees be sprayed? The number of sprays varies according to the locality, the insects and diseases, and whether one wants perfect fruit or will be satisfied with fair control. They should have a minimum of 4 sprayings, with a good pressure sprayer. One dormant spray should be given, and at least 3 before and while fruit is forming. Commercial growers use as many as 11 sprays in one season.

Does the Japanese beetle do much harm to fruit trees? What spray can be used against it? The regular DDT sprays for fruit trees are fairly effective in controlling the beetles, but must not be used on ripening fruits. In this case use a rotenone spray or dust before the fruit ripens.

MULCHES AND COVER CROPS

How does a mulch of straw or peatmoss provide more water to young trees? No more water is provided, but what is already there is conserved. The mulch prevents wind and sun from striking the ground and evaporating moisture from the surface. It also prevents the growth of weeds and grass which would compete for water with the trees. During a very hard rain the mulch prevents or lessens surface runoff.

How should fruit trees be mulched? They were 3-year-old trees when planted, and have been growing in a yard for 3 years. By mulching is meant the placing of enough strawy material around the tree to keep down weeds and grass and thus conserve moisture. The mulch is usually applied from the trunk to a point under the tips of the branches, hence the area mulched increases as the tree increases in size. Straw, spoiled hay, lawn clippings, or leaves may be used. If leaves are used, place some hay or brush over them to prevent their blowing away. Mice often injure mulched trees, so it is best to rake the mulch away from the trunk in the fall (a distance of 3 or 4 ft.) and spread it again in the spring.

Should the ground under orchard fruit trees be kept cultivated? Apples and pears are often grown in sod ground, but most other fruits do better where the ground is cultivated. Cultivation is kept up during the early part of the year. It ceases about July, or when cover crop is sown. Mulching is an excellent substitute for cultivation in the home orchard.

Is the growing of fruit trees in grass sod satisfactory in a small orchard? Peach trees are better with cultivation or a mulch, but the other tree fruits may be grown in sod if it is mowed frequently to reduce competition for moisture. Thick vigorous sods may need occasional partial breaking up with a disk-harrow or a rototiller to reduce competition.

What is the best ground cover for a young orchard of 2-year-old trees? If the soil is sandy or rather level, cultivate during the summer, and seed a cover crop (such as rye) in the fall. If the soil is rather heavy or moist, start a permanent grass sod; cultivate just around the trees, or mulch them to conserve moisture.

What are the advantages of mulching trees? Moisture is conserved, weeds are controlled, plant food is added by the decaying mulch and drop fruits do not bruise much when they fall on the mulch.

What are the disadvantages of a mulch? It creates a fire hazard and should not be used if there is danger of fire. Mice are much worse under a mulch and they should be poisoned and the tree trunks protected by a wire collar or a mound of gravel around the trunk.

If I grow my trees in sod how should I manage it? Mow it frequently, several times a summer, to reduce competition with the trees. Leave the mown grass to rot under the trees.

PRUNING AND TRAINING

How and how often should fruit trees be pruned? Trees are pruned during the dormant season, preferably towards spring in severe climates. The object of pruning is to produce a structurally sound tree that will not experience limb breakage from a heavy crop or ice storm. The scaffold branches should be about 6 to 12 inches apart and pointing in different directions. Crotches with each member of equal size should have one member cut back a little each year until it becomes a branch of the other. Interfering and broken branches should be removed as well as those with disease. Pruning should be a little each year rather than a lot at longer intervals. It is better to err on the side of too little rather than too much pruning.

When and how much should I cut back fruit trees planted this Fall? The tops should be reduced about one half leaving 4 or 5 branches 6 to 12 inches apart and pointing in different directions. It is better to wait until spring to cut back the newly planted trees, especially in the northern states.

Is it advisable to cut the heart or center limb out of a fruit tree to prevent its growing too tall? Peach trees are usually trained to an open center, so the central leader is cut out. Apple trees are well adapted to the modified leader system, in which the leader is allowed to grow to a height of 8 to 10 ft. before it is cut out.

How should fruit trees be pruned so that branches will not bend down or break off when fruit gets large? We would like to make the branches stronger and not lose more fruit than necessary. The branches are bound to bend down if a crop is being produced. However, heading back the long, leggy branches will reduce their length in relation to their diameter. Such branches will not bend or break so badly because the leverage exerted by the load of fruit is not so great. Breakage may also be prevented by propping with poles and by thinning off excess fruit.

Is root pruning the proper way to reduce wood and leaf growth on a fruit tree? Root pruning is seldom justified unless the tree is growing in a greenhouse, or is used as an ornamental where its size must be strictly limited. If a tree is making too much wood growth, it can usually be checked satisfactorily by withholding nitrogen from the fertilizer application, or by growing it in a grass sod.

What is meant by "ringing" of fruit trees? Taking out a ring of bark around the trunk or one or more main limbs of a tree—usually an apple tree. This causes carbohydrates synthesized in the leaves to stay in the top of the tree, above the ring. The result usually is a heavy set of fruit buds followed by a large crop, but the roots are starved for carbohydrates, so the tree is weakened. It will die if the ring is too wide to heal over in one season, therefore scoring by cutting through the bark in one or more places, all around the trunk, but without actually removing any bark, is a safer method. Ringing or scoring is usually used only on filler trees which are to be removed in 2 or 3 years anyway.

PROTECTION

Does it harm a young fruit tree to have its branches tied together in a compact column when covering them with burlap to protect them from winter sunscald? If the branches are flexible and not frozen, they may be tied up. When frozen, they are brittle and will snap off.

Is whitewash beneficial to fruit trees? How should it be applied? Whitewash was once considered of some benefit in preventing sunscald of fruit trees, but it is rarely used by fruitgrowers now and is probably of doubtful value.

Would it be advisable to use a good white-lead and oil paint on fruit trees? No paint should be used on fruit trees except possibly on pruning wounds over 2 ins. in diameter. Most commercial growers do not paint wounds unless they are much larger than that. The paint does not cause the wound to heal faster but may help to keep the exposed wood from decaying before the new bark grows over the wound and seals out decay organisms.

Small wounds, 2 inches in diameter or less do not need painting. Larger wounds may be painted with an asphalt emulsion in water. "Tree Seal" and "Tree Heal" are paints of this type.

Young apple trees protected against injury from rabbits by tar-paper cylinders tied around them.

How are young fruit trees best protected from mice in the winter? Remove mulch and loosen plant material from around the trunk for a foot or more. Use strychnine-poisoned oats in the runways under matted grass. The county Agricultural Extension Service can advise as to the best poison baits and where they may be obtained.

What is the best protection against rabbits, for young fruit trees, other than using wire netting? A home-made rabbit repellent is described in United States Department of Agriculture Leaflet 396. Another material known as 96a may be purchased from the Pocatello Supply Depot, 238 East Dillon St., P.O.B. 749, Pocatello, Idaho.

POLLINATION AND FRUITING

What is cross-pollination? Cross-pollination is the transfer of the pollen of one variety to the pistil in the blossom of another variety.

What is meant when you say that a plant is self-sterile or self-unfruitful? The two terms are commonly used synonymously, but there is a difference. Self-sterile means that a variety will not form seeds with its own pollen. Self-unfruitful means that it will not form fruits with its own pollen.

Is there any explanation why a variety may be self-unfruitful? It is based on genetic factors. Sometimes the pollen may be sterile, i.e., not capable of germinating. In other cases it will be able to germinate but will fail to function on its own pistil, but will function on the pistils of other varieties.

Which fruit trees are not self-fertile? Fruits that are not self-fertile are many apples; all varieties of the European pear and its hybrids; a few varieties of peaches; all sweet cherries and Duke cherries; many of the European plums, most of the Japanese plums, and many of the hybrids arising from American plum species.

Will any variety of apple cross-pollinate another? No. There are certain varieties that definitely will not pollinate themselves, nor will they act as pollinators, because of a weakness in the pollen. Varieties that bear a close relationship, as Delicious, Starking, and Richared (the last two being bud sports of Delicious), will not cross-pollinate each other.

Are there some varieties of apples and cherries that will act as pollinators for one variety and not for another? Delicious forms good pollen but will not cross-pollinate its bud sports, Starking and Richared. Among sweet cherries there are a number of varieties that are cross-unfruitful.

Why do seedlings of fruit trees differ so much from the parents in fruit quality? Nearly all of our fruits are of complicated parentage, so that when seeds are sown all sorts of variations may be expected to occur. Often the weakest qualities of the genus show up, or susceptibility to disease. Some do come relatively alike; Elberta peach seedlings, for instance, may all resemble Elberta in shape and color, but many will be clingstones and many will be of poor quality.

For how many years can the following fruit trees be expected to bear heavily: apple, pear, peach, sour cherry, sweet cherry, plum, quince? Will depend somewhat upon variety, and definitely upon climate, site, soil, culture and control of insects and diseases. Apple, 50 to 75 years; pear, 35 to 50 years; quince, 25 to 30 years; peach, 15 years; plum, 30 years; sour cherry, 30 to 40 years; sweet cherry, 50 to 60 years. Profitable commercial production may be less.

Can I have young transplanted fruit trees bearing in a year or two?

The age at which a young tree begins to bear fruit depends on the variety (some are early bearing, some may take a number of years), the rootstock and the care, especially pruning. Many tree fruits should begin bearing at 4 to 6 years of age. Frosts and disease or insect troubles may cause delays.

My fruit trees were set out 2 years ago but seem to show small progress. What should I do to get more rapid growth? (Tennessee.) Give them good growing conditions by cultivating and applying fertilizer, and lime if the soil needs it. It may be necessary to spray to control pests. Dry weather may have been a factor; if so, mulching will help. As they become well-established and older they will grow faster.

How can I develop fruit trees quickly? I set out 15 trees 2 years ago and have had poor results. Fruit trees normally develop rather slowly; apple trees, for instance, taking 4 to 12 years, depending on the variety, to come into bearing. Give them good growing conditions, full sun, sufficient moisture, and the fertilizer needed by your particular soil.

I have a few fruit trees: peach, pear, and plum; none bear any fruit. Why? There might be several reasons: too young; weak, because of faulty nutrition; over-vegetative, because of too heavy pruning or too much nitrogen in the fertilizer; injury to buds or blossoms by low temperatures; injury by pests, and possibly because cross-pollination is not provided.

I have a home fruit orchard: apples, peaches, pears, plums, and cherries. The fruit seems small. How can the size be increased? Size will depend on the variety, planting distance, natural fertility of soil, fertilizer treatment, moisture supply, and amount of pruning and thinning. Overbearing is a common cause of small size. Severe thinning of plums, peaches and apples is necessary for good fruit size. Try to determine which factors were responsible, then improve conditions with respect to those factors. The system under which they are grown is a factor, whether on sod, cultivated, or mulch. Build up the humus content of the soil by the use of cover crops if the trees are on cultivated soil. If the soil is light and tends to dry out, use the mulch system and apply fertilizer early in spring. Trees in their first years should be well grown to eventually make vigorous trees.

Can I get quick returns from berries and grapes? Second season for berries, third for grapes. Strawberries fruit the second year and raspberries a little the second year and nearly a full crop the third year. Grapes bear some the third year and nearly a full crop the fourth year.

Does covering berry bushes with cheesecloth to keep birds away retard growth and ripening of fruit? Cheesecloth to keep birds away from berry bushes should be put on just as the fruit starts to ripen, and at this stage it will not appreciably retard growth or date of ripening.

How may heavily laden branches of fruit trees be prevented from breaking? Proper thinning of the fruits should be done after the so-called "June drop"; if still heavy, prop with stout crotched stakes.

HARVESTING AND STORING

What is the right time to pick apples, cherries, pears? For home use summer and fall apples may be left on the tree until ripe enough to use, or until they start to drop. Winter apples are picked before eating-ripe and stored until they are ready to eat in late fall or early winter. Most varieties of pears should be picked when fully grown but still relatively hard—when the first few specimens begin to acquire a yellowish tinge and start to drop. Cherries are picked when fully ripe.

How should fruit be harvested which is to be stored for winter? Each apple or pear should be picked from the tree, by hand or with a picker, before it is dead ripe. Avoid bruises, scratches, and cuts. Store only perfect fruits.

Where apples are stored in fruit cellar and temperature is controlled only by opening windows to outside air, but where humidity can be controlled, what degree of humidity should be maintained? Give as much ventilation as possible, and a relative humidity of 85 per cent.

Should the door of a fruit house (built into a bank, with stone sides, wooden roof, ventilating opening in roof, concrete floor) be kept closed in early fall for apple storage; or open? Close on warm days and open at night on cold days, to bring the temperature down close to 32° F.

Should apples in storage be kept dry or moist? The air should circulate, and the room should be ventilated. The air should, if possible, have a relative humidity of around 85 per cent.

Should apples in storage be sprayed with water? The floor of the storage, rather than the apples should be sprayed to maintain the humidity.

Will apples keep longer if waxed? Commercial-wax emulsions will reduce shriveling in storage but may increase "scald" if not properly used. Moisture-proof cellophane wraps will also reduce shriveling. The best assurance of good keeping is to store a long-keeping variety where the air is moist and as near 32° F. as possible.

Should apples be wrapped when stored? Wrapping will help to prevent shriveling and will keep decay from spreading if a few bad apples are mixed with the good ones. Special oil-treated wraps will prevent scald. Most apples stored commercially for any length of time are wrapped in oiled paper or have oil-impregnated paper strips scattered through the package.

Apples placed in a cold storage room looked fine when they came out, but 2 days later they looked as if they had been dipped in hot water. Why? This is a storage trouble known as apple scald. It is worse if the fruit is picked before it is fully matured and colored. Some varieties are much more susceptible than others. Good ventilation in the storage will help to some extent. Wrapping the apples in thin paper impregnated with oil will prevent scald almost entirely. The immediate cause seems to be certain gases given off by the apples themselves, and the oil in the wraps will absorb these gases.

I have had some very fine apples, but no place to store them; cellar too warm, attic and garage too cold. How can they be stored inexpensively somewhere outdoors? You could build an insulated storage room in the cellar, about a window. Or they can be stored in a barrel pit. (See Storage.)

Can I successfully store fruit in a cellar with a central heating system? The cellar is much too warm. You should construct an insulated room which can be ventilated through an outside window. Try to keep this room as close to 32° F. as possible. A bulletin from the United States Department of Agriculture describes several simple types of home fruit and vegetable storage.

EXHIBITING

How are tree fruits selected for shows? Usually shown as plates of 5. Select fruits that are typical in form, size, coloring for the variety and vicinity; that are uniform in form, size, and color, and free from insect and disease injury. Do not wash or polish: dirt may be wiped off, but even this may mar the natural appearance.

PROPAGATION

What are Malling rootstocks? Apple rootstocks were formerly mixed in the trade so that variety names were meaningless. The East Malling Research Station in England collected all the types, classified them according to their effect on tree growth and assigned Roman numerals to each distinct clone. They are now being used by several nurseries for propagating apple trees. Some produce very small early bearing trees, others large trees. Malling IX produces the smallest tree, 6 to 8 feet tall and best for garden use. Malling VII is popular for small trees for commercial planting.

Can grapes, peaches, cherries, and apples be grown from seeds obtained when you get them from the fruit you buy? All fruits are originally grown from seeds. They seldom resemble their parents, and more often than not are decidedly inferior.

Would it be practical for me, as an amateur, to attempt budding

or grafting named varieties of apples on some young wild apple trees growing on my place? Yes indeed; neither process is very difficult, though in this, as in most things, "practice makes perfect." For details of the operations, see illustrations below and on page 852.

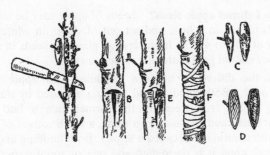

BUDDING

Budding is the simplest method of propagating a desired variety upon another of the same (or a closely related) species. (A) Bud stick; (C and D) different views of bud, after being cut from bud stick; (B) T-shaped cut in bark, on stock (stem or branch that is to be budded); (E) bud inserted; (F) bud bound in tight with raffia or rubber band.

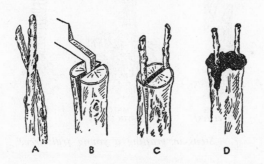

BARK (CLEFT) GRAFTING

A simple method of grafting for the amateur. (A) Scions, or sections of small branches of the variety it is desired to obtain. (B) Heel of grafting tool holding open the split or cleft in the end of branch on which graft is to be grown. (C) Scions cut to wedge shape and inserted so that bark layers of branch and scions come into direct contact. (D) Grafting wax applied to protect wound and prevent drying out.

How and when should seeds of cherry, peach, plum, apple, and pear be planted? Mix with sand in the fall and place outdoors, where they will be kept moist. Freezing is not essential; however, the temperature should not rise above 51° F. The optimum temperature is about 36° to 40° F.

How can I sprout apple seeds? Seeds of apple may be mixed with moist sand, placed in a box, and set out of doors in winter or in a refrigerator at 36° to 40° F. In the spring, plant the seeds in a nursery row and they should germinate that same season.

What is the difference between "budding" an apple tree and "grafting" one? Both budding and grafting are used by nurserymen in growing young fruit trees. In the former case a bud (with a sliver of bark attached) is used; in grafting, a small section of a branch or shoot, with several eyes (called a scion). Both budding and grafting are also used when it is desired to add one or more varieties to an older tree. Budding is done in mid-summer when the tree is in full growth. Grafting is usually done in spring just as growth starts, but may be done later if dormant scions are used.

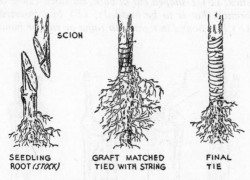

SCION

SEEDLING
ROOT *(STOCK)*

GRAFT MATCHED
TIED WITH STRING

FINAL
TIE

Steps in grafting a young fruit tree.

WHAT TO GROW

Can I grow orchard fruits on a small place? Yes, if you are willing to do the spraying necessary to protect the trees from insects and diseases. Apples on Malling IX require very little space and you can graft additional varieties to provide a succession. Plums and peaches are small trees naturally, but sweet cherries are too large for the small place. Pears are kept small by propagating them on quince stocks.

Which are the best kinds of tree fruits for home gardens in northern New Jersey? This will depend somewhat on the personal preferences of the gardener. If there is room for only 1 or 2 trees, the apple would probably be most generally satisfactory: it makes a fair shade tree and can stand neglect better than the peach. Most pear varieties blight badly, except Seckel and Kieffer. The sour cherry Montmorency is fairly easy to grow, but birds are likely to get a good share of the fruit.

What kinds of fruit trees shall I plant in a space 75 × 150 ft. to give our family of 5 the best selection of fruit and assure fertilization of the blossoms? (New York.) The varieties, and to some extent the kinds of fruit to plant, will depend on how cold it gets during the winter. If you are in a part of the state where peaches can be grown, try the following plan: Row 1 (4 ft. from fence), strawberries. Row 2 (8 ft. from first row), raspberries, currants, or other bush fruits. Row 3 (10 ft. from second row), grapes. Row 4 (20 ft.), 4 peach, 2 sour cherry, 2 pear. Row 5 (23 ft.), 6 apple trees. This will make the apple row 10 ft. from the edge of the plot, which may be too close or not, depending on who owns the adjoining land and the purpose for which it is used. There will be no pollination problem with the small fruits or sour cherries. With peaches and pears, planting of more than one variety will practically insure a satisfactory supply of pollen. McIntosh, Delicious, Cortland, Grimes, and many others are good pollinizers for other varieties of apples.

We plan to put in a few fruit trees. What would be a good selection for an amateur? Our soil is fairly good but somewhat shady. Do not plant fruits in the shade. Suggested kinds are listed in Introduction, and in questions on Kinds of Fruits. These, however, require open, sunny situations.

In planting a new orchard (of as few as 6 trees) on a place having no fruit at present, what would you advise? (Illinois.) Your choice of fruits should be governed by your soil and climatic conditions. Plant what is already growing well in your community, or consult your county agent.

What fruits can be grown in cold and short-growing season? Elevation 5,700 ft. (Montana.) Only the hardiest varieties such as some of the new fruits produced by breeding at the Minnesota and South Dakota Experiment stations. Write to your own Experiment Station for a list of recommended varieties.

What fruits are best for the home garden? The small fruits require less space, bear early, have less trouble from insects and diseases than tree fruits, and need less equipment for their care. Strawberries are first choice, with red raspberries, currant, gooseberries, blackberries and blueberries nearly as good.

SPECIFIC TREE FRUITS

APPLE

Planting

When is the proper time to plant apple trees? Some say fall, others spring. Either spring or fall. If you can get the plants and you live in a region where the autumn is long, fall will perhaps be better, as the soil can be handled and the trees planted when there is not much pressing work.

Can an apple tree be transplanted without injury to it if it has borne its first crop of fruit? Transplanting any tree is a shock, and if a tree has been bearing, transplanting (unless the entire root system is taken with it) may result in rapid vegetative growth that will retard fruiting. If the tree is 4 or 5 years old it will be better to set a new young tree.

What is meant by a frozen ball? After trenching, when one growing season has elapsed, the tree may be moved in the late autumn or early winter. Dig a trench at the edge of the previous trench wide enough to work in, at the same time digging an inclined place so the ball can be pulled out of the hole. Now cut the soil off the ball, uniformly, until roots can be seen. Undercut at the bottom so that the ball is resting on ⅓ or less of its diameter. This cannot be done unless there is enough moisture in the soil to hold it together. Put some straw or other material in the bottom so the connecting section of soil will not freeze too hard. Wait until the ball is frozen solid, and will remain frozen, before attempting to move it. The new hole will have been dug, the soil placed under cover or protected so it will not freeze, and some straw placed in the bottom of the new hole to prevent deep freezing. If the distance is only a few feet, a trench can be made between the old hole and the new and the ball drawn through this. Otherwise, put it on a sledge or platform to move.

How should a 13-year-old apple tree be fertilized? Apple trees require a complete fertilizer treatment containing the important nutrient elements. The amount of each element needed is determined by the natural fertility of the soil and its past treatment. Therefore the requirements of a 13-year-old tree might vary from nothing in a very fertile soil to 20 lbs. of a 5–10–5 formula on a light sand. (See Fertilizer.) Most soils will need nitrogen in the form of ammonium nitrate or nitrate of soda. A few soils are deficient in potash.

What is the best time to plant apple and pear trees in state of Connecticut? Also best time of year to prune such trees? Prune and plant in very early spring before the buds begin to swell.

Should an apple tree be fertilized at planting time? No, it is too easy to burn the limited root system with chemical fertilizers. If fertility is needed work manure into the soil before planting the tree, making sure that no raw manure comes in direct contact with the roots. Or use dehydrated manure and bone meal.

How can I improve a heavy soil at planting time? Mix the soil removed when digging the hole with a pail of wet peatmoss and work this mixture around the roots as the hole is filled.

Pruning Apples

When is the best time to prune apple trees? Any time during the dormant season is satisfactory. Actually the best pruning weather is likely to be in late fall, just after the leaves have dropped, and before the weather becomes too cold. In regions where unusually severe cold, (25° to 30° F. below zero, or lower) may occur, pruning should be delayed until the severe cold of winter is past, as winter-injured trees may experience much more damage if pruned, than if not pruned.

What are the main points to keep in mind when pruning a bearing apple tree? Do not remove a branch unless there is a good reason why it should come off. Some varieties will require very little pruning. Take out limbs that are dead, broken, or badly diseased, too low, or too high; remove water sprouts from trunk and main limbs, thin out a little in the top, if necessary, to admit light to the lower limbs; remove slender, obviously weak twigs.

How can I prune so there will not be a lot of water sprouts? If large branches are to be removed, take them out gradually, over 2 or 3 years. This will result in fewer water sprouts, and these can be detected and rubbed off before they become large.

Is it true that fall pruning of fruit trees cuts down sucker growth? Fruit trees react the same to dormant pruning regardless of whether it is done soon after the leaves fall in the autumn or just before growth starts in the spring.

What happens when apple spurs are pruned off? Most of the fruit in certain varieties is borne on short, crooked growths known as spurs. These spurs start to form on 2-year-old wood and grow very slowly. If spurs are pruned off a particular section of a limb, they will not be replaced, and that part of the tree cannot produce any fruit.

Is summer pruning of trees advisable to make them bear fruit earlier? Most experiments have indicated that dormant pruning is preferable. The reduction in leaf area from summer pruning may be a disadvantage to the tree. Certainly summer pruning is not of any practical value as a means of hastening fruit production by young trees.

How often should apple trees, just planted, be pruned? Prune at planting time, and early each spring thereafter.

Should bearing-age apple trees, which were pruned when shipped from nursery, be further pruned when planted? It may be necessary if the trees are shipped bare root. If there appears to be any drying out,

more pruning may be necessary—back to live wood. The top should
be reduced proportionately to the size of the root system. Heavily
pruned large trees are really no better than young trees.

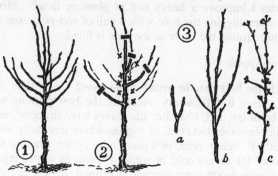

APPLE TREE PRUNING

*(1) A 2-year-old nursery-grown tree, as received
and planted. (2) The same tree after being pruned.
The "X" signs indicate branches removed entirely.
(3) Effects of cutting back compared with thinning. (a) Twig severely cut back. (b) Growth from
cut-back twig is all vegetative (no flowers). (c)
Growth from tree with thinning pruning only;
nice balance of twig growth and flowering spurs
is clearly evidenced.*

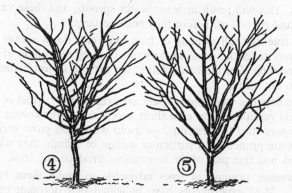

*(4) Neglect of early training results in poor frame-
work. A Stayman apple about 6 years old with three
"leaders" (very undesirable), pole-like growths,
and bad crotch. To correct these faults now means
a high head. (5) Early training results in good
form. Stayman apple about 6 years old; good spacing of scaffold branches. Central leader still present.
Note development of secondary branches.*

How should I prune apple trees that are in their second or third season? Apple trees of this age should receive only corrective pruning. In other words, do not remove any branches except those which especially need to come off. This would include branches that are broken, too low on the trunk, crowding other branches, or that make a narrow angle with the trunk. Crotches with narrow angles (less than 45°) are more likely to split apart than are wide-angled crotches. Keep the central leader dominant at this stage by shortening branches that may be competing with it for dominance. Head in (prune moderately) very long, leggy limbs to make them develop side branches.

After planting a Dolgo crab tree 3 ft. high, does one prune it the first year, and how much? What care does it need in winter? Crabapples are hardy. They don't require winter care. Only pruning needed is to remove those branches not needed for the framework. Select the 3, 4, or 5 branches that are to form the frame so they are spaced 8 to 12 ins. apart on the trunk, thus avoiding crotches. Remove the rest.

Culture

Can mulching an apple tree be overdone? Seldom. If a mulching material that will pack down too much is used, it might prevent root aeration. Loose material to a depth of 4 to 12 ins. is good. Heavy mulching for several years with a hay mulch relatively high in nitrogen, or a legume mulch, may make the tree over vegetative. The apples may color poorly, drop prematurely and lack keeping quality. Susceptibility to injury from low winter temperatures is another possibility.

What special care do apple trees need in the spring? Proper pruning and spraying, and then attention to the fertilization of the soil. (See Fertilizer.)

How should the fruit of an apple tree be thinned? What is the best method and time? Thin when the young apples are about the size of hulled walnuts. Leave at least 6 or 7 ins. between fruits. The small apples may be removed by snapping the stem with thumb and finger, being careful not to injure the spur. Special thinning shears are available, and very useful.

Can bearing-size fruit trees, such as apple, cherry, or peach, be purchased at a nursery? "Bearing age" trees may be nursery scrubs that were not large enough to sell at 1 or 2 years of age. They experience such a shock from moving that they are not likely to bear much fruit any earlier than the 1 or 2 year old trees customarily planted. They should not be planted in spite of claims of early bearing.

I have just purchased a 6-ft. McIntosh apple tree. How many years, approximately, until it bears fruit? With good care it should bear in the 6th year, in the orchard.

How much should a Red Delicious apple tree grow a year if planted at 2 years of age? The first year it should increase its height about

2½ ft.; the next year 2 ft. Ordinarily, 3 to 6 shoots, 30 to 48 ins. long may be produced in the first year.

An apple tree bears fruit by halves—that is, first one side bears apples and the next year the other side. How do you explain this? (New York.)   Some varieties bear a full crop in alternate years. In the case of your tree, something happened to upset the periodicity on one side. This is a desirable condition.

We have an Astrachan apple tree that bore no fruit last year. It is about 12 years old and bore abundantly the previous year. Would you have any explanation?   Red Astrachan is generally an alternate-year bearer.

Have two early apple trees bearing only every other year, but together. Can I change the bearing years of one of them?   The only certain way is to remove practically all the flowers, or small fruits from one of them. If you change the bearing year of one you must be sure that there is another variety near enough to provide for cross pollination of each variety. A spring frost by destroying the blossoms might throw both trees back into fruiting the same year.

What can be done to an apple tree (about 5 years old) to get it to blossom and bear fruit? It is now about 10 to 11 ft. high.   Any variety of apple must reach a particular state of internal development before it will set fruits. Do only corrective or formative pruning, and do not fertilize too heavily with nitrogen. When the proper balance is reached, the tree will fruit; to use means to hasten this might prove dangerous.

What causes a young medium-size apple tree to have only one large flawless apple?   Probably it is a self-unfruitful variety and needs to be pollinated by a compatible variety.

We have a Wealthy apple tree about 8 years old that seems to produce a lot of foliage but few apples. What is the reason?   Wealthy is one of the earliest varieties to bear. Probably too much nitrogen, or too heavy pruning. Inexperienced persons have been known to prune off the fruiting spurs also. Lack of cross-pollination could be the answer if there are no other apple varieties nearby.

Have a Grimes Golden apple tree in yard 8 years old. Has been pruned by experienced nursery 1940 and 1941, yet will not bloom; hence, no fruit. Why?   Grimes Golden should bear at about 5 or 6 years in the orchard. Probably the pruning was too heavy and encouraged vegetative growth.

I have a Golden Delicious apple tree 10 years old which has had only 5 apples on it. Tree looks fine; 12 ft. high. Why no apples?   Delicious apples will not set a crop of fruit to their own pollen. Some compatible variety must be grown nearby.

I have 10 apple trees, 16 years old, which do not bear any fruit.

This is a small orchard by itself. Can anything be done to make it bear? (Wisconsin.) This may be due to winter injury; if so, there is little chance of correcting the condition. If a tree is making a very vigorous growth and does not form fruit buds, it may be caused by pruning too heavily, or by using too much nitrogenous fertilizer, in which case the remedy is evident. If the trees are all of one variety lack of cross-pollination is a possible reason. Severe injury to the foliage from disease (apple scab) or insects is another.

How can immature apples be prevented from dropping? Nearly all species of fruiting trees lose some fruits by dropping when the fruits are small; this is called the June drop. The reason is that more fruits are formed than the tree can support. Sometimes the drop is because of imperfect fertilization by pollen. Sometimes it is caused by codling moth or curculio, which can be prevented by spraying. (See Section VIII.)

What new spray is used to prevent premature dropping of apples? Various commercial brands of hormone sprays or pre-harvest sprays may be obtained. The active agent in most of these is napthalene acetic acid. These are for prevention of premature dropping of nearly mature fruits.

My 2 apple trees have full bloom, but when the apples form they fall off. Spraying helps very little. Can you offer a solution? If the fruits attain a size of ½ to ¾ ins., the spraying may be with the wrong material, or applied at the wrong time, or otherwise inadequate. If they drop at smaller size, it may be a question of incompatible pollination or too rapid growth.

How old must a Northern Spy apple tree be to produce fruit? What is the matter if an apparently healthy tree does not yield? Northern Spy apple requires the longest period of any variety to reach the stage of fruitfulness. This may be as much as 15 or 20 years in some instances. Try to reduce its vigor by growing it in sod. Do not prune the tree.

What is best method to make apple and pear trees 50 to 60 years old profitable? Pruning, spraying, soil enrichment, etc. If they have been long neglected, might be better to start anew. They may be too tall for profitable handling, and then many new and better varieties have come along since these were planted. If in fair condition, a renovation pruning, together with lime and fertilizer and spraying, may bring them back.

How about apple trees that have been neglected for several years and no longer bear fruit fit to eat? Can these trees be brought back to a normal condition? If so, how? Renovation pruning, lime (probably), fertilization, and proper spraying are indicated. These measures will gradually restore the trees to vigor, provided, of course, they are not too old.

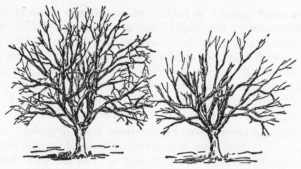

Old neglected fruit trees can be cut back severely to form new, lower heads, thus making them easier to care for.

How can I preserve an old apple tree that is beginning to decay? Cut and scrape off all decayed material down to sound wood, and paint large cuts with a good tree paint. If there are bad crotches, it will pay to secure the limbs with a chain or a bolt brace. It seldom pays to fill large cavities.

How can I tell flower buds from leaf buds on apple trees in the summer? Apples form most of their flower buds at the ends of short spurs. Some varieties may form them laterally, on longer twigs of the current season's growth. Flower buds are plump and more rounded than the narrow-pointed leaf buds.

Is there any way to keep apple trees from blooming too early? Frost always gets our blossoms. There is no practical way to delay the blooming date. Certain varieties, such as Rome Beauty, Ralls, Northern Spy and Macoun bloom later than most. Consult your State Experiment Station as to hardy varieties for your locality. You may be in a place where the climate does not permit apples to be grown successfully.

Is it possible to determine the variety of apples by the appearance of the leaf on a "Quintuplet" apple tree? Probably only a few men in the country are qualified to determine, negatively or positively, some varieties of apples by their foliage. It would require an unusual knowledge in this field.

What varieties should I look for on a "Quintuplet" apple tree? Whatever the nurseryman chooses to put on. (Usually the varieties are stated.) However, he should select these, as far as possible, so that they are practically uniform in growth, because there is great variation in the growth of various varieties. There must be at least one good pollinator in the lot.

What special care do dwarf apple trees require? Apple trees on Malling IX, the most dwarfing rootstock, should be planted with the bud union (indicated by a swelling) 4 inches *above* the ground. Soil must not be allowed to get above this point or the top may develop roots, and soon become a full-sized tree. Dwarf trees should be tied to a stout stake as the roots are brittle and the tree may topple over with a heavy crop.

Multiple-Variety Trees

Is an apple tree that bears several kinds of apples good to grow? If there is space for only one apple tree, one with several varieties may be used, provided the varieties are carefully selected. Several trees on Malling IX rootstock will occupy no more space than one large tree and because of their lower height, 6 to 8 feet, they are easier to manage.

About how much room is needed for a "5-in-1" apple tree? Since these are grafted on standard roots, they will require a space about 35 × 45 ft.

How soon can I expect fruit from a 5-in-1 apple tree? Depends upon the varieties used. Some varieties will produce fruits in 3 to 5 years after planting; others require 5 to 8 years, and sometimes more. Growth conditions, as governed by site, soil, and fertilization will also have an effect.

Will a "5-in-1" apple tree continue to bear heavily over a long period of years? If properly cared for, it should bear as long as if the same varieties were planted individually.

What precautions should be taken in pruning a non-bearing "Quintuplet" apple tree? Try to secure as uniform a development of each variety as possible. If one is weaker than the others, prune it more lightly than the more vigorous kinds. Only prune in winter, but pinch back rapid growths in summer to act as a stopper.

My "Quintuplet" apple tree is lopsided. Why? The varieties are such as do not grow at a uniform rate, or the union on one may not be as good as with the others. The exposure as related to shading may affect one more than another. (See page 860.)

Insects and Diseases

See Section VIII.

My apple tree is turning green around the trunk. What is the cause? What is the remedy? The green color is probably caused by moss or lichens growing on the dead outer bark. It will do no harm, but may indicate poor circulation of air, or too much shade. Possibly pruning has been neglected. This condition usually does not occur on sprayed trees.

What causes hard brown spots in apples? The trees appear healthy, but the apples are not fit to use. Probably "bitter pit," usually associated with excessive tree growth late in the season. Some varieties especially susceptible, such as Baldwin or Northern Spy. In some localities lack of boron in the soil may cause brown spots in the flesh of the apple.

Is it the same kind of aphis that we have on other plants that curl up apple leaves? These are "green" and "rosy" apple aphids. If they are present, the eggs may be killed by a dormant spray of dinitro cresol or dinitro phenol compound, which is miscible in oil or water. This spray also kills scales and mites. A summer infestation may be controlled with a nicotine spray or TEPP, parathion and malathion.

Are there borers that attack apple trees? There are 3 that may: Round-headed apple-tree borer, flat-headed apple-tree borer, and leopard-moth borer. The round-headed usually attacks young trees, and the laying of eggs may be prevented by means of repellent paint, or covering the trunks with fine-meshed wire or with paper. The flat-headed usually works in old, neglected trees. The leopard moth attacks young trees or branches. Examine the trees frequently, and if sawdust is seen near the trunk, look for the hole. Sometimes the larvae may be killed in the hole with a fairly stiff wire; but carbon disulfide or a nicotine paste made especially for the purpose will usually be effective.

My apples all have worms in them. What shall I do? The worms are codling moth, the most serious insect pest of apples. Consult your Agricultural Extension Service as the spray program is rather complicated and new insecticides vary the program from year to year.

What causes young apples to fall off? They have crescent-shaped marks on them. This is the egg-laying mark of curculio. Arsenate of lead is the control, used with other materials for additional insects and diseases. Parathion and methoxychlor are also effective in controlling the curculio. Pink-bud and petal-fall spray are important, but others may be necessary in different localities. Consult your county agent, Agricultural College, or Experiment Station for spray schedule.

In July, when I approach my apple trees, myriads of little flies come out. What are they? They may be leaf hoppers. Keep watch just after bloom. The nymphs cannot then fly, but are very shy and sidle away. This is the time to kill them with a nicotine spray. DDT at the rate of 2 pounds of the 50 percent wettable powder in 100 gallons of water is also used for leaf hopper control. They are not as easy to kill as adults.

What is San Jose scale? A sucking insect which forms a hard circular covering that attacks orchard fruits and related plants, especially apple, peach, pear. It may kill young trees in 2 or 3 years. It is indicated by scurfy appearance when the scales are thickly clustered on young twigs. There may be a reddish discoloration along veins of leaves, or small circular red spots on fruits. Control is lime-sulfur or miscible oil as dormant spray. Which to use depends upon whether other insects or diseases need to be controlled with the same application.

How can I get rid of tent caterpillars? Apple-tree tent caterpillars east of the Rockies, and a similar species west, infest wild cherries, apples, etc. In regularly sprayed orchards they are usually no problem, but in home fruit gardens they may be. Do not burn them, as this will injure the tree. Spray with arsenate of lead when the nests are about the size of a silver dollar. DDT at the rate of 2 pounds of the 50 percent wettable powder in 100 gallons of water will also control the caterpillars. Better still, follow the regular spray schedule for your state.

What are the brown and somewhat star-shaped spots on my apples? This is apple blotch, prevalent in the South and Southeast. Spray with Bordeaux mixture, if the variety will tolerate it, during petal fall. A regular spray schedule with wettable sulfur and lime sulfur usually gives control.

Why do they order cedar trees cut down near apple orchards? The Red Cedar and the apple are alternate hosts for the so-called cedar rust which is indicated by light-yellow spots changing to orange on apple leaves and fruits in spring and summer; cedar "galls" on cedar in winter, developing to release spores in early spring. If there are only a few red cedar trees destroy all within half a mile to protect the apples. If too numerous to destroy, ferbam sprays on the apple will give good control.

What makes the leaves on some of the twigs of my apple trees turn black and dry up, just as if they had been burned? This is fire blight, a bacterial disease. Cut these off well back from the dead part. Use a solution of zinc chloride to sterilize tools after each cut. Look for cankers on the trunk or limbs and clean these out. Regulate the growth of the trees so that it is not too vigorous. Spraying with Bordeaux mixture while the trees are in full bloom will often prevent infection through this means. Antibiotic sprays are proving effective in controlling fire blight in some areas.

What is apple scab? Apple scab is the most serious fungus disease of apples in the North. It partially, or sometimes nearly completely defoliates apple trees thereby greatly reducing them in vigor and productiveness as well as making them susceptible to winter injury. The scab lesions, if numerous, also disfigure and spoil the fruit. Ferbam, captan, mercurial compounds, elemental sulfur, and other materials are used in controlling scab. Because of the importance of this disease the county Agricultural Extension Service issues special bulletins and radio information on the latest control measures. These should be followed for best results as careful timing is important in securing good control.

Varieties

What is best and quickest-growing apple tree? If you want apples in a hurry plant an apple propagated on the Malling IX rootstock. Most varieties will start bearing on this root in 2 or 3 years. Golden Delicious, Jonathan, Wealthy and Lodi are good varieties. However, unless you plan to spray you will not get many usable apples.

Which varieties of apples have proved suitable in New York? The McIntosh family of apples are all good in the Northeastern states. Melba ripens in August, Milton in September, McIntosh, Cortland, and Macoun in early winter. Rhode Island Greening and Northern Spy are good winter varieties.

For a family which likes crisp, hard, slightly tart, and very juicy, old-fashioned apples, and which has room for only 2 or 3 trees, which varieties would you recommend for central New Jersey? You might try Wealthy for medium early, Jonathan for early winter, and Stayman for a late variety.

What is the best all-round or all-purpose apple tree to plant in New England? Baldwin.

APRICOT

Can apricots be grown in central Massachusetts? Yes. The Russian types, although inferior to the better types, are more apt to fruit in the East. Doty and Henderson are suitable. Geneva is better and hardy in New York.

We have 2 apricot trees 8 to 10 years old. What can I do to prevent fruit rotting just before it becomes ripe? (California.) Spray with wettable sulfur when calyx or shuck splits, again in 10 days, and twice more at 2- to 3-week intervals. Removal and destruction of all rotten fruits is a worthwhile supplement to spraying.

CHERRY

Soils and Planting

Under what conditions of soil and climate can sweet cherries be grown successfully? They need a sandy loam, deep and well drained. Climate is even more important. The shores of the Great Lakes, the Hudson Valley of New York, and the Pacific coast are the areas where sweet cherries are grown commercially. They are susceptible to winter injury and late frosts and do not like extremely hot summers.

Are sour cherries fussy as to soil and climate? These can be grown over most of the Atlantic coast and in the Mississippi Valley. Commercially, they are grown in New York, Wisconsin, and Michigan. They are hardier than the sweet varieties. They can be grown on sandy or heavy soils, if well drained, and can stand drought better than sweet cherries.

When should young cherry trees be fertilized to bring them most quickly into bearing? If young cherry trees need fertilizing, do it in early spring. As a general rule they would start bearing at an earlier age if they were grown a bit slowly. It is desirable to grow good-sized trees as quickly as possible, in order to get a large crop; hence the trees are usually forced while young, thus sacrificing very early bearing for the larger size of tree.

What is a good fertilizer for cherries and how should it be applied? On sandy soil of average fertility a complete fertilizer such as a 5–10–5 might be used at the rate of 300 to 500 lbs. per acre. Then use nitrate of soda or some other readily available nitrogenous material in quantity sufficient to maintain good, vigorous growth. Broadcast complete fertilizer in early spring, the nitrate of soda later as needed.

What is the best age to buy cherry trees and when should trees be planted? One- or 2-year-old trees. Plant in early spring in the North. Farther South, in late autumn.

What rootstock is best for cherries? Cherries are propagated on two rootstocks, mahaleb and mazzard. Sweet cherry trees on the mazzard root are longer lived than trees on the mahaleb root and generally more satisfactory, especially on heavy soils. Mahaleb roots are used generally for sour cherries. To get cherries on mazzard roots you must specify them and pay more as they are more expensive to produce.

Pruning; General Culture

Should cherry trees be pruned and at what age? Cherry trees should be pruned each year, but removal of a few undesirable twigs may be all the pruning needed. They require less pruning than the apple or peach.

When is the best time to prune cherry trees? The best time is in early spring—during the latter part of March. They may, however, be pruned at any time during the dormant season.

How should cherry trees be pruned? With sweet cherries little need be done except to remove dead or injured branches and twigs that are growing in an undesirable position as too high or tending to make a weak crotch. Sour cherries should be started as delayed open-center trees with a short trunk about 6 ft. high and several well-spaced scaffold limbs. Besides the "corrective" pruning as recommended for sweet cherries some thinning of tops will be needed to keep trees from becoming too dense and so shading out fruit-bearing wood in lower part. If trees are pruned every year, not a great deal of cutting will be needed at any one time.

I have been told a Bing sweet cherry will not produce fruit when planted by itself. What variety will? I don't want more than 1 tree.

No sweet cherry will produce fruit to its own pollen. Nearly all sweet varieties will pollinate others. You might top-work (graft) Windsor or Black Tartarian on a branch of the Bing. This will provide enough pollination for 1 tree.

I have a Black Tartarian cherry tree surrounded with plums, peaches, Oka cherry, Rocky Mountain cherry, and apples. Does it need any other cherry for fertilization? None of these is an effective pollinator. You could use Bing, Windsor, Napoleon, and Wood.

What do you recommend doing for white cherry tree when very small green cherries fall off before maturing? Plant another variety to act as a pollinator.

What causes the small green cherries (sour cherry) to drop off the tree? May be lack of pollination, attacks by curculio, or frost injury during bloom or shortly after. (See Cherry—Chapter VIII.)

I planted 3 cherry trees and 2 days later we had frost. How should I protect these trees from frost? If the trees were dormant, as they should have been for transplanting, frost a few days after planting would not hurt them.

I have a 15-year-old sweet cherry tree. Why does it bear only a few large fruits? This tree is located in a strip 4 ft. wide separating two cement driveways. This is a very poor location for a tree. Probably there is no other sweet cherry variety in the near neighborhood to act as a pollinator.

How long does it take for a cherry tree to blossom? A sour cherry should produce its first blossoms 3 or 4 years after planting. A sweet cherry tree may take 1 to 3 years longer.

How can I retard the blooming of cherry, peach, plum, and apricot trees? There is no practical method of retarding blooming dates of fruit trees in order to avoid frost injury. Some varieties naturally bloom a little later than others.

We raised a cherry tree from a pit; it is 3 years old. Will it bear fruit? It will bear eventually but is not likely to resemble the parent.

A sour cherry tree bore fruit 1 year and none the next. Why? The blossoms or buds were probably injured by cold weather.

I have 4 cherry trees which bloom but have only a dozen or so cherries. Why? Probably because of imperfect pollination. If your trees are all of one variety, plant some other. There are 7 distinct groups which will not pollinate each other, so the variety must be selected with care and also as to possibility of frost injury.

I accidentally broke a branch in the lower part of a cherry tree that left a groove in the bark; the sap keeps running out at foot of tree. What must I do to correct this? Sap will run from any kind of an injury on a cherry tree. There is no practical method of repairing an injury such as the one described. If the tree is growing vigorously, the wound may heal over eventually.

Pests and Diseases

How can I keep my cherries free of insects and diseases? Plum curculio and brown rot are worst. (See Section VIII for control.) Cherry leaf spot appears first as yellow spots—in the leaves. These turn brown and fall out. They look like shot holes. Leaves turn yellow and fall. Sometimes tree is completely defoliated. Lime sulfur or wettable sulfur sprays in the regular schedule should control this.

I have a cherry tree that blooms every year; the cherries start forming, then wither and fall off tree. Sounds like injury by plum curculio, which attacks the small fruits. It may be controlled by spraying with arsenate of lead, parathion or methoxychlor soon after the blossoms fall. Ask your Experiment Station for spraying recommendations.

How can I keep birds from eating my cherries and other fruits? This is a hard question to answer. The only 100 per cent way is to build a cage around the tree or stay and guard it from sunup until sundown. Scarecrows of various kinds will help some, especially if put up before the birds get a taste of the fruit. Tethering a captive hawk in or near the tree is one method which works well—if you can find the hawk. Hanging up objects, such as inflated paper bags, which will blow about in the wind, is sometimes successful but not always. Covering branches with large cheese cloth bags will save a few of the fruits for you.

I have heard of virus diseases of cherries. What can I do to avoid them? As the result of an extensive search for virus-free trees of the important cherry varieties nurseries are now propagating virus-free trees. These should be specified when ordering trees. They are superior to stock of uncertain virus status.

PEACHES

What kind of soil is needed for peach trees? Any good soil that is well drained. They prefer sandy loam, however.

Should I mix fertilizer with the soil when I plant a peach tree? Do not mix fertilizer with soil used to fill in around roots, as it might cause some injury. Dig it under before the tree is planted or work into soil around newly planted tree, but outside limits of the hole in which it was planted.

Should I plant a peach orchard in spring or fall? In general, except where winters are quite mild, spring planting is best. (See Introduction.)

Is it wise to plant new peach trees in the same places from which the old ones have just been removed? It is not. Peaches so planted often fail. The trouble is not well understood, but it may be nematodes, root aphis, or possibly something else from the roots of the old trees.

I have a bearing peach tree. When can I move it?   Moving a bearing-age peach tree is hazardous. It must be pruned heavily and might be as long coming into bearing again as a new tree. It can be moved in fall, but very early spring would be better.

How does one care for a peach tree in a suburban back yard?   Ideal treatment would include cultivation of soil around tree; use of a complete fertilizer; lime if necessary; adequate pruning; some spraying and thinning of fruit whenever a heavy crop is set. Control of peach borer, which works in the trunk just above level of soil, is very important.

I have 3 5-year-old, thrifty peach trees: Early Crawford and Hale. Why do they bloom well but bear only 5 or 6 peaches?   The variety might be self-sterile, as J. H. Hale. If other varieties are near to furnish pollen, then there must be some other reason for failure. Blossoms may have been killed by frost. Give them another chance.

My peach tree has 3 main trunks at ground level, forming a sort of cup which is filled with gum. How shall I treat it?   Probably result of killing the leading shoot when tree was a year or two old. Best cut away 2 of them as close as possible and arrange drainage so water will not stand in "cup" if one is left. Paint the wounds.

I have a Halehaven peach tree which has had only ½ doz. peaches. Could you explain why and what to do to improve fruit?   The tree may be too young to bear a full crop. It should have a full crop by the fourth year if it is making good growth and has not been injured by cold weather.

Why do some peach trees fail to bear? (California.)   Might be due to any one or more of these factors: lack of enough winter cold to complete the rest period, frost injury to buds or flowers, lack of pollination (if a self-sterile variety), or faulty nutrition.

I have a 3-year-old peach tree about 8 ft. high with no blossoms on it yet. It grew from a Halehaven pit. When will it bear fruit, or must I graft it?   Peaches usually bear at 3 or 4 years of age. Whether a seedling will bear good fruit is a matter of chance. Some seedling peaches are good enough for home use. Seedlings are budded in their first season's growth to standard varieties. (See Budding.)

Have 6 peach trees which grew from Elberta seeds. What could I do to them to assure successful blooms and fruit?   The best method would be to bud them to some desirable variety.

What is the approximate life of a peach tree?   With good care peaches can be made to produce for about 20 to 25 years.

I have a young peach tree about 12 ft. away from a large oak tree. Will it grow and produce fruit there as well as it would in the open, or

should it be moved? You have two handicaps: competition of roots, and shade. Better move it. Peaches need full sun.

Will a peach tree which came up from seed ever bear good peaches? It may or may not. If it is a seedling of Elberta, it will resemble that variety.

My peach tree is simply loaded with fruit but it never gets large enough to amount to anything. The fruit should be thinned when a little larger than a robin's egg. Take off all small or stunted peaches, leaving at least 6 ins. between the fruits that remain on the tree. Thinning will result in larger size, better color, and less breakage of limbs.

What is the best method of "domesticating" wild grown or neglected 2- to 3-year-old peach trees? Probably better to start anew if badly neglected. If not too bad, plow, lime (if needed), fertilize soil, prune, and give good spraying. Take out very bad trees and replace.

How can a peach tree 4 years old be changed to another variety? Peaches can be top-worked (see Grafting), but cleft grafting used for apples or pears is not successful with peaches. The way to proceed is to cut off branches 2 or 3 ins. in diameter in late winter. During the summer, shoots will appear, and these can be budded in July, August, or early September, just as seedling peaches are budded. (See Propagation, pages 849–852.)

Will peach-tree roots block up a drain or sewer? Peach roots will not seek out a drain or sewer; but roots of any tree planted above or very close to a loose-joint sewer will enter it.

Pruning Peaches

When and how should I prune newly planted peach trees? Prune just before the trees are planted or just after. Small nursery trees, 3 to 4 ft. high, should be pruned to a "whip" (a single stem) and cut back to a height of 24 to 30 ins. Larger trees, 5 to 6 ft., should be cut back to about 30 to 36 ins., but instead of cutting off all side branches leave 3, suitably spaced to be used as scaffold limbs, and cut them to stubs 4 to 6 ins. long.

What is the proper way to prune a young peach tree? Develop an open center, bowl-shaped type of tree with lowest scaffold limb at least a foot from the ground. Remove limbs that are too low, that head in and tend to fill up the center, or that crowd other limbs and make any part of tree too dense. Tallest limbs should be headed to side branches pointing outward in order to get maximum spread and keep center open.

What time and method should be used in pruning old peach trees? Pruning is best done in late winter or early spring after the time is past when dangerously low temperatures may occur. Old peach trees have general type of tree already established, hence pruning at this stage is to maintain vigor, thin crop, and remove weak twigs. Pruning should be more severe than for younger trees. Cut out weak twigs and limbs, thin out year-old shoots by taking out weaker ones. Cut back shoots that are longer than 12 ins. As tree gets older, severe pruning needed to maintain vigor may cause it to be smaller than it was as a younger tree.

When is the best time to remove a limb from a peach tree? Any time it seems necessary, although it is usually done during the dormant season.

What is the best way to fix a peach-tree limb which was broken because of the heavy crop? If the branch can be spared, cut it off. If it is split in the middle, prop it up and put in a few small bolts with washers.

Should one cut all dead limbs from peach trees? All dead limbs should be removed from all trees, as they present a disease and insect hazard. You should have no dead limbs if you prune peach trees properly.

How do you prune a nectarine tree? A nectarine is essentially a peach without fuzz, and is pruned in the same way as a peach.

Special Problems

Must peach trees be cross-pollinated? Only varieties that have poor pollen need other varieties near to provide good pollen. J. H. Hale, Mikado, Vimy and Pacemaker have poor pollen.

When I cut open peaches that appear to be sound, why are there little pink worms in them? These are the larvae of the Oriental fruit moth. It may be controlled by spraying the trees with parathion, or DDT, following manufacturer's directions for amounts and the Agricultural Extension Service for timing.

Do peach trees need a mulch for winter? Mulching soil about peach trees will have no appreciable effect on their susceptibility to injury by cold weather.

What is the best method to protect young peach trees from freezing in winter and from rabbits? There isn't much that can be done in a practical way to protect peach trees from freezing. If they are of a hardy variety and in good growth condition, they will be as resistant to cold as it is possible to make them. Rabbits usually are not so likely to bother peach trees as apple trees. Mechanical protection by use of wirecloth, building paper, or even newspapers wrapped around trunk is probably most satisfactory.

What is the best method of propagation for peaches? Peaches are usually budded on seedlings grown from wild peach seeds. (See Budding.)

What are the main insects and diseases that trouble peaches? See Section VIII.

Varieties

What are the best varieties of peach trees to plant? See Introduction.

PEAR

When does one fertilize young pear trees to bring them into early bearing? The trees will bear earlier if making a moderate growth than if growing too vigorously. Overfertilization is also conducive to fire blight. If soil is poor, make a light application of a complete fertilizer in early spring. Otherwise, if tree is making good growth, do not use fertilizers.

What soil is best for pear trees? Heavy sandy loam or clay loam with plenty of humus which will hold moisture, yet assure good drainage.

When is the best time to plant pears? Plant trees as early in the spring as the soil can be prepared. Planting should be completed by time fruit-tree buds begin to expand.

How can I plant, care for, and prune Bartlett pear trees? Am setting out 100 trees this spring. A hundred trees of Bartlett pears will involve considerable care and expense. It would be advisable, therefore, to get rather complete information from your Experiment Station as to fertilizing, spraying, etc., under your particular local conditions. When making planting plans, some provision should be made for cross-pollination by planting at least 5 or 6 trees of another variety which should be something other than Seckel, as Bartlett and Seckel do not pollinate each other.

Why has a pear tree which bore fine pears when first planted 3 years ago had none since? A pear tree would not be expected to bear until 3 to 5 years after it is planted. Give it good growing conditions and it will start producing at the proper time, barring damage by frost and pests provided a suitable pollinating variety is nearby.

Our 5-year-old Bartlett pear has twice borne fruit sparingly. It is of good size and leaves look healthy. Why are leaves very small and few? This tree is doing well to have borne fruit twice the first 5 years. Bartlett leaves are normally rather small, so perhaps the tree has nothing wrong with it. If you stimulate its growth too much, you may have trouble with the disease known as fire blight.

Are there dwarf pear trees? Are they worth planting? Pear trees are dwarfed by propagating them on quince roots. They are suitable for the home garden.

Will one pear tree alone in a garden bear fruit? Most varieties of pears will bear a much better crop if cross-pollinized, so in making a new planting it would be highly desirable to include at least 2 varieties unless there are other varieties growing in the immediate neighborhood. However, single trees sometimes prove to be fairly reliable croppers.

Is Bartlett pear self-fertile? If not, what variety should I plant near it? Bartlett will set a much better crop if cross-pollinated. Any of the common varieties, such as Sheldon, Bosc, or Anjou would be satisfactory pollinizers.

Does a Duchess pear need cross-pollination? Experiments in New York and in California indicate that this variety may bear a fair crop if self-pollinized but a better crop if cross-pollinated.

Pruning Pears

How should mature pear trees be pruned? Mature pear trees of most varieties require very little pruning and are likely to be injured by fire blight if pruned too heavily. Simply remove dead and broken branches. If trees become too high, leaders may be cut back a little to a side branch.

How do you prune pear trees at planting time? One-year trees will be unbranched whips. Head a 5-ft. tree back to 3½ or 4 ft. Two-year nursery trees will have 2 to 6 side branches; remove all side branches below 30 ins., save 2 to 4 of the stronger ones well distributed around the trunk and spaced at least 4 ins. apart. Remove the rest, head the leader back by about ⅓.

Our pear and plum trees have not had very much fruit for several years. They have never been pruned. How and when should this be done? The lack of fruit is probably due to other factors than lack of pruning, such as frost injury, insects, or diseases. Pruning would probably result in larger fruit. Remove dead, very weak, or broken branches, limbs that are too low or that rub and crowd other branches. If trees are getting too high, tallest limbs should be cut back to side branches. Avoid overpruning. The pear may be injured by blight if cut too hard. If there is a great deal of cutting needed, spread it over 2 or 3 years. If soil is fairly fertile, withhold fertilizers during years when heavy pruning is done.

How should I prune a young Seckel pear tree? The Seckel pear makes a rather dwarfish, compact tree which requires very little pruning. Remove only dead or broken twigs and those branches which are definitely out of place (too low, rubbing, too high, etc.).

When pruning pear trees, is it harmful to remove some of the branches which had borne fruit during the past summer? It is claimed that this helps the growth of trees. Pruning will stimulate growth, but if tree grows too vigorously, it will be more susceptible to fire blight. Pear trees usually need very little pruning. Just remove dead and broken branches and those which are too low or interfering with other branches. Tips of main limbs may need to be cut back slightly from time to time to prevent tree from growing too tall. No effort should be made to remove those branches which have borne fruit, as they should continue to bear for many years.

The trunk of our 20-year-old pear tree has produced 3 off-shoots this year. If I cut them off and set them in a container of mud and water, will roots develop? No.

Insects and Diseases

Is it necessary to spray pears to secure good fruits? Pears are attacked by San Jose scale, codling moth, and fire blight. (See Apple for control.) Fire blight is serious. Pear psylla is sometimes called a jumping plant louse. A black fungous grows in the excreta on leaves. Apply a dormant spray of lime sulfur; and also summer sprays of Black Leaf 40 (1 to 1,000) with soap after showers. Consult your Agricultural Extension Service for instructions.

Varieties

What pear varieties are suitable for home-garden planting? See list in Introduction.

Can you give information on the Du Comice pear? The Doyenne Du Comice pear has excellent fruit but the tree is a poor grower, subject to blight, and not very hardy. It is a valuable commercial variety on the Pacific coast but likely to prove disappointing in the East.

What is the best pear for the Lake George region? (New York.) Flemish Beauty and Clapp Favorite both of which are more winter hardy than most other varieties, are suggested for the Lake George region. Two varieties are necessary to provide cross-pollination.

PLUM

Do plums require a special type of soil? Heavy soils are preferred for the European types and lighter soils for the Japanese varieties; but they will all do well enough for home use on a fairly wide range of well-drained farm soils, if the site is otherwise suitable.

How should young plum trees be fertilized to bring them into early bearing? Young fruit trees usually make a rather vigorous growth if soil is reasonably fertile. Addition of fertilizer, if not carefully regulated, may make growth too vigorous and delay bearing instead of hastening it. Fertilize only enough to maintain good growth and trees will bear early. On sandy soils, of course, fertilizer will be needed every year if good growth is to be secured. The fertilizer program must be adapted to local soil conditions.

What is proper way to plant plum trees? Order 1- or 2-year-old trees and plant in early spring 20 ft. apart (or a little less for Damsons).

Can a single plum tree bear fruit?   A few varieties such as Stanley, Italian prune, Reine Claude and the damsons will set fruit if self-pollinated. Most varieties of plums, however, will set a very poor crop, or none at all, unless blossoms are fertilized by pollen from another variety of the same species of plum. Bees will carry the pollen for some distance, but it is better to have trees close together to insure cross-pollination.

I have a young plum tree which bloomed last spring but no fruit followed. Can you tell me the reason?   There are various possible reasons for the failure to produce fruit. The variety may be self-unfruitful and require another variety to pollinize it. Frost may have injured blossoms and prevented them from setting fruit. A young tree may sometimes be overvegetative and fail to set on that account. Pruning would make the tree more vegetative and would not induce fruiting.

We have a plum tree that blooms but never sets fruit. What causes this and what can be done to set fruit on this tree?   It is probably a self-unfruitful variety requiring pollen from a tree of another variety. If this is a Japanese plum, plant another Japanese variety near and let the bees do the rest. If it is a European variety plant another European as the European and Japanese plums are not satisfactory pollenizers for each other.

Does the purple-leaf plum bear fruit?   Yes, if pollinized by another variety of the same species.

Why does my Elephant Heart plum tree not bear fruit? It is healthy, almost 5 years old.   Sterility unless some of the other plums near are of the Japanese type. If they are, they should provide cross-pollination and some other explanation would have to be formed. If it blooms and fails to set fruit it is because it is self-unfruitful and needs cross-pollination by another Japanese variety. Redheart is recommended. If the tree is in good vigor and fails to bloom wait another year or two, but be sure that suitable pollination is provided.

I have a plum tree and think it needs pruning. Should I cut the branches short or just thin them out?   Some cutting back may be needed to prevent the tree from getting too tall and "leggy." Most of the pruning should be a thinning out to remove undesirable branches and keep top from becoming too dense.

How should a Japanese plum tree be pruned?   This type of plum grows and bears much like the peach and should be pruned a good deal like it. Train young tree to an open center and practice fairly heavy annual pruning to keep top from becoming too dense. This will help maintain vigor of tree and size of fruit.

I have several year-old plum trees grown from pits. May I expect these to bear in time, or should I have planted only grafted trees?   As the seedlings may not bear fruits worth having, it is much better to plant trees of known variety.

When and how should sand (or cherry) plum seed be planted? If you want named varieties of plum, they must be budded onto seedlings, as seedlings do not "come true." To produce seedlings for budding purposes, plant seed in the fall in furrows about 2 ins. deep. If only a few seeds are to be handled, it will be better to stratify (that is, mix the seed with sand and bury in a well-drained place). It may be protected against rodents by wirecloth. Take up seed in early spring and plant in shallow furrows.

What causes my plums to rot and fall off? This is the brown rot of stone fruits. More difficult to control on plum than on peach (which see) because of smooth skin.

Why are my plums wormy? See Control of Plum Curculio under Peach.

What caused my Italian plums all to drop off? The tree is 6 years old. The trouble may be frost injury to the young fruits, and plum curculio if they are wormy. A virus disease may also be responsible. If the trouble continues the tree should be replaced with one of known freedom from virus troubles.

DWARF AND ESPALIER FRUIT TREES

What is an espalier fruit tree? It is a tree trained in formal shape to a given number of branches, usually in a vertical plane. The tree is planted against a wall, building, or trellis where it takes up little space and provides decoration as well as fruit. It may be trained to a single shoot or to 2 shoots opposite each other, or in fan or other shapes. The training is begun when the tree is very young. Espalier fruit trees have always been popular in Europe, where the protection afforded by wall training makes it possible to grow orchard fruits in climates less favorable than those in this country.

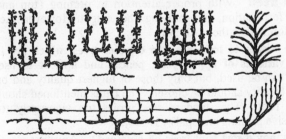

Various forms of espalier (or trained) fruit trees. These are usually grown against walls, or secured to very strong wires or trellises.

Are espalier trees practical for the average home garden? If you want fruit trees on a small place, they may do. But most of them are on dwarfing stocks and require a great deal more time and care in pruning and training. The yields are never plentiful.

What is the place of espalier fruit trees in the garden picture? Where there is limited space or if novelty design is wanted or in climates where severe weather changes prevail, this type of tree has its place.

What part of the season is fertilizer applied to dwarf fruit trees? Two to 4 weeks before trees come into bloom.

How much fertilizer and how is it applied to dwarf trees on sod land? One lb. chemical fertilizer per 1,000 sq. ft. for sod and ¼ lb. for each year's growth (age of tree). Broadcast under tree, beginning 2 ft. from trunk and extending to the outer spread of the branches. Chicken manure, 3 lbs. for the sod and 1 lb. for each year's growth of tree, may be used instead.

What fertilizer materials are used to feed dwarf fruit trees? Nitrogen has been found to be the main element in the growing of tree fruits. Apply a complete fertilizer high in nitrogen, such as 5–10–5. If unable to obtain this, apply dried chicken manure.

How is feeding applied to dwarf fruit trees on cultivated land? Same quantity as advised for age of tree for sod land, but omit the quantity for the sod.

How is feeding applied to dwarf fruit trees under the mulch system? Broadcast the material on top of mulch as per the suggestions given for cultivated land. Water in if dry weather is encountered.

How should espalier trees be pruned? The object is to maintain the skeleton form into which the tree has been trained. This means frequent pruning at an early stage to prevent undesired branches and suckers from getting a start.

Will dwarf fruit trees continue to bear as many years as regular-size fruit trees? With proper attention to pruning (top and root), training, fertilization, and spraying, they might. However, the general expectation is that they will not.

If one wishes to train his own espalier trees, which are the most suitable varieties of apple, pear, peach, and apricot to use? Any varieties can be used, but only those of highest quality and best yield for your locality should be chosen. The fruits mentioned should be on dwarfing roots. The standard tree grows too vigorously to permit the intensive pruning an espalier is subject to.

Where may dwarf fruit trees be obtained? Any first-class nursery in your neighborhood should be able to supply them.

SMALL FRUITS

STRAWBERRY

In what sort of soil should strawberries be planted? What advance

fertilization is necessary? A sandy loam soil is good, but any well-drained soil that is fairly retentive of moisture can be made to produce good strawberries. Turn under manure or commercial fertilizer before the plants are set.

Do strawberries require an acid soil? I have a patch that does not do very well, as my soil has a tendency to be alkaline. Would it be O.K. to use aluminum sulfate? The alkalinity of the soil probably has very little to do with the failure of your strawberry bed to do well. Various diseases and insects are more likely to be causing the trouble. Aluminum sulfate is not likely to be of any value in your case.

Is lime needed for strawberries? There is a popular belief that lime may be injurious to strawberries, but actually they will respond to lime about as well as other crops. If the soil is alkaline or only mildly acid (pH 5.6 or above), then lime won't be needed, and might even be harmful. But if the pH is down around 4.0 to 5.6, then by all means use lime.

Should you use fertilizer on strawberry plants? What is the best kind to use? A complete fertilizer, such as 5–10–5, at the rate of 2 to 4 lbs. per 100 sq. ft., should be broadcast and worked into the soil before planting.

Is animal manure too alkaline for dressing strawberries for winter? A straw mulch after the ground is frozen is better for winter. Manure is best used in fitting the soil for planting the strawberries.

How can a strawberry planting be tied in with a vegetable garden? A good plan is to have it adjacent to the vegetable garden, with strawberries next to vegetables. When an old row of strawberries is removed, vegetables may take their place, as it is not desirable to keep strawberries in one place too long. Strawberries should not be grown on land that has grown tomatoes, peppers, eggplants and potatoes during the previous 2 or 3 years. A few feet between them is enough.

How much space should be planted in strawberries for each person in the family? Twenty-five ft. of row per person in fruit, and another 25 ft. of young plants coming along for the following year.

I have a slope in the back of my yard which I wish to have covered with strawberries. If I plant them at the bottom, will they climb? Do the leaves stay green in winter? Better to plant in rows 2 ft. apart across the slope. As runners form, you can place them where needed, to cover soil. The leaves remain more or less green over winter, depending upon site; in cold regions, will need to be covered.

I plan on starting a strawberry patch for a family of 2. I want some for canning. How many plants do I need? One hundred ft. of row would take 40 plants, set 30 ins. apart, and would yield 30 to 40 quarts if all goes well. Decide how many quarts you want and compute the number of plants needed. Don't forget that you will want some for preserves, or to give to your friends.

How far apart are strawberry plants set? Varieties which do not make runners freely (especially the Everbearers), about 18 ins. apart;

SETTING OUT STRAWBERRY PLANTS

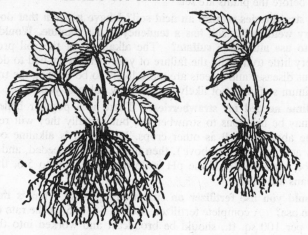

Old leaves removed and roots trimmed back.

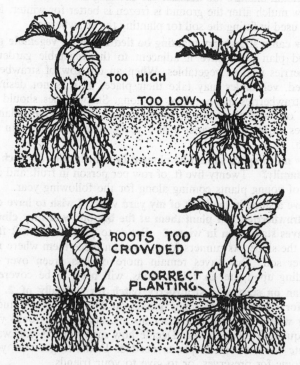

fair plant takes 24 ins.; good plant takes 30 ins. The rows 36 to 48 ins. apart.

When should strawberry plants be set? Strawberry plants are usually set in the spring as soon as the ground can be worked. If dormant plants from cold storage are used, then later planting is all right. Late October and early November is also a good time to plant. Fall-set plants should be mulched the first winter, the mulch removed in the spring and the blossoms removed to prevent fruiting the first summer. Care is then the same as for a spring-set bed. Mid-summer is not a good time to plant strawberries.

How should strawberries be planted? Have soil in good tilth. Scoop out a hole with a garden trowel to a depth of 4 or 5 ins.; plant firmly, being sure that roots are well spread and extend down into the hole and are well covered. Plants should be set as deeply as possible without covering the crown. If set too deeply, plants will be smothered; if not deeply enough, part of roots will be exposed and dry out.

What is considered the best system of setting strawberry plants in small gardens—200 to 250 plants? The matted-row system is the easiest to develop and is favored by most commercial growers as well as home gardeners. Many home gardeners, however, like the hill system, as it produces a higher percentage of fine, large berries.

Setting out a narrow border of strawberry plants to be grown by the hill system.

What is the hill method of strawberry growing? The plants are set a foot apart and all runners removed as they appear. Single rows are often used, but much higher yields will be obtained if 2 to 4 rows are set a foot apart with an alley between each set of rows.

What is the matted-row method of strawberry growing? Plants are set 18 to 30 ins. apart in rows 30 to 48 ins. apart. The runners are allowed to develop and take root, forming a "matted row" 18 to 30 ins. wide, of plants which will produce fruit the following season. Matted rows are often overcrowded with a consequent reduction in yield. Runner plants as they develop should be spaced about 6 inches apart until the row is 18 inches wide. Thereafter the runner plants should be considered weeds and removed.

How long is a strawberry bed good for when using hill method of planting? If properly cared for, a bed may be kept productive for 3 or 4 years; the first crop will be the best, and later crops will be successively poorer. It is best to set new plants each spring, let them fruit the following spring, and then spade them under.

Is it necessary to plant more than one variety of strawberries? All modern varieties are perfect flowered and do not require another variety for pollination purposes.

How often should strawberries be renewed to maintain an abundant yield? At least every 2 years, and better every year.

Culture

Should strawberry runners be removed to prevent them from sapping the strength of the plants? The production of runners by strawberry plants is a perfectly natural process and is not necessarily devitalizing. The severe competition from overcrowding in a matted row is the reason for removing runner plants in excess of those needed to form a fruiting row. In the hill systems of growing, all runners should be removed in order to keep the plants properly spaced. In the common matted-row system the only runners removed are those in excess of the number required to produce a matted row with plants spaced at least 7 to 8 ins. apart. Each runner soon produces leaves and roots of its own, and becomes a "self-supporting," individual plant.

When is the best time to thin out strawberry plants? Begin to space and thin out as soon as the first runners take root. To get a properly spaced bed, go over it every 2 or 3 weeks for rest of growing season.

How many runners should be allowed to develop from each mother plant in the matted-row system? Allow at least 7 or 8 ins. (in all directions) between runner plants. If plants are 30 ins. apart in rows, allow 12 to 14 runner plants to develop from each mother plant. The excess runners should be cut off, preferably before they take root.

What shall I do when my June-bearing strawberries grow too thick? Keep the runners spaced and thinned so plants will stand at least 7 or 8 ins. apart in matted row. Usually beds are replanted every year or two, setting runner plants in a new location.

We have been advised to cut strawberry leaves off in the fall. Is this correct? The leaves definitely should not be cut off in the fall. They are the organs in which are manufactured those foods which feed the plant. Cutting off the leaves "starves" the rest of the plant.

How can I distinguish sex of strawberries? All modern varieties are "perfect" flowered; that is, they have both stamens and pistils. When such varieties are in bloom, center of flower will consist of a rounded mass of light-green pistils surrounded by large yellow anthers (full of pollen) at ends of stamens. The "imperfect" or pistillate varieties at the same stage of development will have only the pistils; no anthers.

Can strawberries be weeded in the spring? Most strawberry beds need weeding in the spring unless the ground is unusually free from weed seeds. Some weed seeds come in the mulch. Many of the weeds should be pulled by hand to prevent damaging the strawberry plants.

Why did my strawberry plants bloom so profusely but set no berries? Just a few tiny ones. Set new bed just last year. The variety may be pistillate and unable to set fruit without being pollinated by another variety. If it is a perfect flowered variety, then the blossoms may have been touched by frost, which, without injuring the petals, often kills the part which will develop into fruit.

My strawberry plants blossom and set berries, but they do not develop after being half grown. Why? Misshapen and knotty berries are often caused by the feeding of the tarnished plant bug, an insect which feeds on the blossoms. It is easily controlled by spraying the plants, just before they bloom, with DDT at the rate of 2 pounds of the 50 percent wettable powder in 100 gallons of water. Direct some of the spray into the straw and weeds and fence rows alongside the bed as the plant bugs stay there on chilly days.

I seem to have no luck with strawberries. They do not bear very heavily. First be sure you have a productive variety and one *suited to your soil and climate;* set a new bed frequently and keep the soil well, but not too heavily, fertilized. Do not let the plants crowd in the matted row.

How are strawberries propagated? Strawberry plants produce in summer long, stringlike growths called "runners," at the tips of which grow new plants. These send roots into the soil. They are allowed to develop until the following spring, when they are dug up and set out in new beds. Some varieties make many runners, others but few.

How should strawberry runners be cared for before they are set out in a new bed? If using runners from your own beds, dig only when ready to plant. Thin off old ragged or dead leaves, leaving the small leaves at the tip of the crown. If you purchase plants, try to plant them as soon as received. If this cannot be done, "heel in" in a shallow trench and keep them well watered until planting time.

Pot-grown strawberry plants for August setting.

Method of rooting strawberry runner in pot buried in soil.

How can runners be rooted in pots? Fill 2½- or 3-in. pots with a good composted soil and sink them in the ground about the mother plants. Place a runner tip over each pot and hold in place by putting a stone or clod on the runner near the tip, or bend or twist wires into hairpin shape and peg the runners down, or use clothespins. When new plant is well developed, the runner may be severed from the old plant.

Are potted strawberry plants any better than those runner plants which have been allowed to become well established in the garden before transplanting? For starting a new bed in late summer or early fall only potted plants will stand transplanting satisfactorily. However, spring planting of ordinary runner plants is to be preferred.

Can strawberry seeds or plants be started in spring and produce worth-while results the same year? There are certain small-fruited European varieties which "come true" from seed and will fruit the same year the seed is planted. The common garden strawberry of North America, however, does not "come true" from seed. Plants do not produce full crops until the second year.

Mulching

Should strawberries be mulched during the winter? Mulching is advisable to prevent winter injury, conserve moisture, and keep the berries clean the following spring. Plants are more likely to heave out during alternate freezing and thawing on heavy soils than on sandy soils, hence mulching is more essential on the heavier soils. Apply the mulch after 2 or 3 sharp freezes, but before temperatures drop below 20° above zero. Temperatures lower than this when the ground is bare may injure the strawberry plants.

What is the best material to use as a winter mulch on a strawberry bed? Wheat, oat and rye straws, and marsh or salt hay, are all good mulches. Pine needles are good. Sawdust has been used satisfactorily but supplementary nitrogen may be needed with it.

How is mulching material applied to a strawberry bed? The straw is scattered over the bed with a fork to a depth of 3 or 4 inches. In windy situations, weight it down with brush.

What are the advantages of mulching strawberries with salt hay, and when should it be applied? Salt hay is freer from weed seeds than wheat, oat, and rye straws, and may be easier to get in coastal areas.

Is it all right to mulch the strawberry plants with tree leaves? Tree leaves are a fair mulch, but if too thick may mat down and make it difficult for the leaves to push through in the spring. If most of the leaves are pulled off the plants into the space between the rows they may be used safely.

How soon is the mulch removed from the strawberry bed? The mulch is removed in early April when inspection of the plants shows the new leaves beginning to grow from the crown. Part of the mulch is pulled off the plants into the space between the rows and part is left over the plants. The leaves and flower clusters push through the mulch and the berries rest on the straw which keeps them clean.

Everbearing Strawberries

What are "everbearing" strawberries? These are varieties that form a crop of fruit in the spring and another in late summer. The total yield is smaller than that of one-season berries, and most of the varieties are not of so good quality.

Are everbearing strawberries successful? They do not live up to the descriptions in some of the catalogues, but if you like strawberries well enough to put up with the faults of everbearing varieties, then they may be termed "successful." One of the faults is that crop is produced over such a long period that only a very small picking can be made on any one day.

Are everbearing strawberries as prolific as the ordinary kind? If the plants are grown in hills and mulched with sawdust and the blossoms removed until the middle of July, most varieties will produce a fairly large crop per plant. The fruit will then ripen over a period of 2 to 3 months but the picking on any one day will be rather small. If the blossoms are not removed, plants will exhaust themselves by producing heavily during the hot midsummer months. Fruit produced in cooler fall weather will be of better quality than that produced in midsummer.

Should the runners be removed from everbearing strawberry plants? A maximum fall crop will be produced if plants are set close together, about 12 to 15 ins. apart, in rows 2 ft. apart, and all runners removed as they form. This is known as the hill system.

How, and when, are everbearing strawberries thinned? Most varieties will need no thinning unless grown in hills, in which case all the runners should be kept off. Set a new bed each spring rather than try to rejuvenate the old one.

Should the first blossoms be removed from everbearing strawberry plants? When should they be allowed to bear? Best results will be secured if all blossoms are removed up to the latter part of July. The first fruit would then ripen about the middle of August.

If I transplant everbearing strawberry plants in the spring, will they bear the same season? Yes, they should bear their maximum crop in the fall of the year in which they are planted.

My everbearing strawberries do not have the flavor of standard strawberries. Are there any that compare with usual spring berries? Most of the everbearing varieties are of rather poor quality. Rockhill (Wayzata) has good quality, but makes very few runners and in the East is not so productive as some of the poor-quality sorts, such as Gem. Redrich is of good quality. Arapahoe, a new sort, is also of good quality and otherwise a good variety.

What care should be given everbearing strawberries to keep them bearing from year to year? It can't be done. You could get some fruit for 2 or even 3 years, but many plants would die and the others would get progressively weaker. Don't count on one planting to produce more than one fall crop, followed by a spring crop.

What care should be given everbearing strawberries through winter? Do they thrive better in moist ground or dry? They should be winter mulched like any other strawberries. Everbearers are getting ready, during hot, dry weather of midsummer, to produce a fall crop, hence they must have ample moisture or the results will be disappointing.

What are several varieties of everbearing strawberries? Gem, also sold as Superfection and Brilliant, is widely grown, although very acid. Redrich and Arapahoe are others.

I have a 50-gal. oak barrel in which I want to grow strawberries. How would I prepare the soil and set the plants? How far apart for the holes? Beginning 1 ft. from the bottom, bore holes, at irregular intervals, 9 ins. apart and large enough to hold a plant without cramping. Bore a number of smaller holes in the bottom for drainage, and set the barrel on flat bricks. Put in 6 ins. of drainage material—

coarse gravel or cinders, topped with finer material. Mix good garden soil with ⅓ its bulk of old rotted manure or the like and ⅓ screened cinders. To every bushel add 1 lb. of a complete fertilizer. It is not necessary to fill whole interior with this soil. Maintain a 6-in. thickness around the inside, and fill center with any old gravelly material available. Planting and filling are done at the same time. Begin by covering the drainage with soil to level of first holes. Push plants through from inside, spread roots, and cover with soil. Repeat to within 12 ins. of the top; fill this with good soil and plant entire top. See that moisture conditions are uniform.

What variety should be used in a strawberry barrel? How should the plants be wintered over? Select a variety of high quality adapted to your climatic conditions. If you like a sweet variety, try Fairfax. It is desirable to use potted plants if you can get them. Mulch with straw over the top; protect side plants if possible with straw or burlap after the first heavy freeze. Check moisture conditions occasionally to prevent drying out.

What is the proper way to handle strawberry plants in a strawberry jar after they are through bearing? Remove the old plants and replace a little later with newly formed runner plants rooted in small pots.

Insects and Diseases

Do strawberries need to be sprayed? Probably not—only if certain pests (such as leaf roller or weevil) are bad. Most strawberries in the home garden do quite well without being sprayed.

What causes the purplish spots on the leaves of my strawberry plants? One of two diseases—either leaf spot or leaf scorch. During most seasons the modern varieties will not be injured enough to make it worth while to spray.

What causes the buds to drop from my strawberry plants before they bloom? The strawberry weevil, a tiny insect, lays an egg in the bud and then cuts the stem just back of the bud. Control is by dusting the bed with a 3 to 5 percent DDT dust. The first application is made when the weevils first begin cutting the buds. A second is made a week later. Very thorough coverage is important.

Are any strawberry varieties resistant to the red stele root rot? Sparkle, Fairland, Vermilion, Redglow and Surecrop are resistant.

What are "virus-free" strawberries? They are plants which tests have shown to be free of virus diseases. They are much superior to the old stock, most of which was infected with a virus disease that reduced the vigor and productiveness of the plants. Most good strawberry plant nurseries are selling them. Plants that are obtained from sources that are not attempting to produce virus-free plants should be avoided.

Varieties

What are some good strawberries for the home garden? Good standard varieties of satisfactory quality are Midland, Catskill, Fairfax and Sparkle. Empire is a new variety of promise for home use. Gem, (Superfection, Brilliant) Redrich and Arapahoe are everbearing varieties. New varieties of lower quality for the region south of New York are Pocahontas, Earlidawn, Redglow and Surecrop.

What are the best strawberries for freezing? Sparkle, Midland and Eden.

What are "runnerless" strawberries? These are a strain of the Alpine strawberry, *Fragaria vesca,* that produces no runners so must be raised from seeds. The berries are small, pointed and have a distinctive flavor. The plants fruit throughout the summer.

Can wild strawberries be transplanted in a regular bed? If so, do they give a good crop? Wild strawberries in cultivation, that is, fertilized and weeded, will give better yields than in the wild, but it requires a good many to fill a quart basket.

GRAPES

What soil is most suitable for cultivation of grapes? A good loam or sandy loam is probably ideal, but grapes will grow satisfactorily on a wide range of soil types provided the moisture supply is adequate. Extremely dry or extremely wet soils are to be avoided.

Do grapes like alkaline or acid soil? Grapes thrive on soils showing rather wide ranges of soil reaction. On the whole, acid soils seem preferable to alkaline soils.

Will grapes grow on muck soil? Grapes are never grown commercially on muck soil. Grapevines are usually planted on slopes because they will not tolerate poor drainage, and most muck soils offer drainage problems at some seasons of the year. Also, grapes should have good air drainage, and the level surfaces of muck soils do not favor air drainage.

What fertilizer is best for feeding new grapes? Where it can be obtained, barnyard manure is as good a fertilizing material for young grapevines as any, and is safer to use than commercial fertilizer. It should be applied in the winter or early spring, and worked into the ground around the young vines. It is not wise to place manure in the holes when grapes are planted.

When should I fertilize young grapevines to bring them into bearing early? Applying 1 to 2 oz. of nitrate of soda or sulfate of ammonia to each vine about the time the growth starts in the spring will stimulate growth and hasten their reaching bearing size. If these materials are not available, a good covering of barnyard manure should be applied to the soil around each vine, in winter or early spring, and worked into the soil. Hoeing and cultivating to keep down weeds are also necessary. Mulches are good for grapevines.

What is a good fertilizer for grapes? Grapes on the average soil are most apt to respond profitably to nitrogen at the rate of 60 or more pounds to the acre. This may be obtained by applying 200 pounds of ammonium nitrate or 400 pounds of nitrate of soda. Per vine this would be ¼ pound of ammonium nitrate or ½ pound of nitrate of soda. On light soils a need for potassium may be indicated by a marginal browning of the leaves. Here sulfate of potash may be used. A hay or straw mulch will supply potassium too.

What is the best way to apply fertilizer to grapes? Broadcast the fertilizer, covering an area from a foot from the trunk out to 4 or 5 ft. away from the trunk. Spade fertilizer under or cultivate it in.

My Caco grapevine is 5 years old, has made wonderful growth, but it bears no grapes. What fertilizer should I use on it? The fact that your grapevine is making wonderful growth indicates that it does not need more fertilizer, but, on the contrary, needs to have all such materials withheld from it. It is possible that you have been pruning it too closely. Leave at least 40 buds on it the next time you prune it. If it is still too vigorous and non-fruitful leave 60 buds a year later.

What location is best suited for grapes? Do they grow well near trees? The ideal location for a vineyard is gently sloping land. Air and water drainage must be good to avoid danger of late spring frosts and "wet feet." Steep slopes should be avoided because they favor erosion unless rows are planted on the contour. Southern exposures favor earlier starting of growth in spring and earlier ripening of fruit, but are more susceptible to late-spring frost injury and to summer drought. Northern slopes are less susceptible to injury from late-spring frosts and summer droughts, but ripen their crops later than southern slopes. Deep, sandy soils that contain a good amount of organic matter will give best results for grapes. Soils too poor for other crops are not good grape soils. Planting grapes close to trees is usually not a good practice because the trees compete with the vines for water and soil nutrients as well as furnish cover for insects which may attack grapes. Shade from trees may favor diseases, delay ripening of the fruit, and reduce productiveness of the vine.

Where should grapes be planted? On fences, trellises that mark boundaries, or on arbors especially constructed for the purpose.

Do grapevines need much sun? Grapes are sun-loving plants, as is shown by their tendency to climb over tops of tall trees. The outstanding grape regions of the world are in areas which have much clear, sunny weather and few fogs. Lack of sunlight favors the spread of mildew and black rot and retards ripening of fruit. However, grapevines will do fairly well if they receive direct sunlight at least half of the day. The vines will require more constant care under such conditions.

Will grapevines grow well in shade? Though grapevines may grow fairly well in partial shade they will not produce well under such conditions. Shading favors the spread of diseases, delays ripening, and gives fruit of lower sugar content and quality.

How far apart should grapes be planted? A suitable spacing for most varieties is 8 feet between rows and 8 feet between vines in the row.

How should grapevines be planted? After the ground has been prepared and the rows have been marked, dig holes of sufficient size to accommodate the roots of the vines after they have been cut back to within 8 ins. of the trunk. The top should be cut back to a single strong cane of 2 buds' length. The vine is then placed in the hole and the roots spread out evenly. A few shovels of dirt are then thrown in on roots while the stem is shaken gently to sift fine dirt in around the fine roots. More topsoil is then thrown into hole and thoroughly tamped into place with the feet. Holes should then be well filled.

My Concord grapevines, now 5 years old, should be moved to a better location. When is best time? Will it destroy them if their root systems are cut? Any time in the fall after the vines are fully dormant. A good-sized ball of earth should be moved with the vine, so that as many roots be kept intact as possible. The tops should be cut back severely in order that the top growth be kept in balance with the greatly reduced root system. Vines should not be allowed to bear fruit the first year after moving, and only a light crop the following year.

How many grapevines will a family of 4 need? This will depend on how you use the fruit. For table use, etc., include 2 plants of very early varieties, 2 early, 6 to 10 mid-season for jelly and juice, and 2 to 4 late to very late.

Is it necessary to dig around grapevines? In a moist, fertile soil grapes may make a satisfactory growth with no cultivation. If they do not make satisfactory growth, however, soil should be cultivated out to a distance of 3 ft. from the trunk. In sandy soils, cultivation is imperative during early summer. Mulching is a good substitute for cultivation.

What treatment should I give my grapes? They are fruiting poorly on clay soil. The fact that grapes are not fruiting well on clay soil indicates that vines are probably not making enough growth to permit heavy fruiting. As a rule, grapes prefer lighter and sandier soils, but many good vineyards are found on clay soils. Fertilize vines with ⅓ lb. of nitrate of soda or sulfate of ammonia per vine. Apply when shoots are starting growth in spring. Apply barnyard manure about vines during winter or early spring, and work into soil. Frequent cultivation to keep down weeds and close pruning will encourage more vine growth and eventually result in heavier fruiting. Be sure that insects and diseases are not responsible for the poor cropping.

What can I do to make my grapevines bear heavily? An application of proper fertilizers, plus cover cropping and cultivation, should result in vigorous vines capable of bearing good crops of fruit. Pruning vines properly to not more than 40 buds per vine should enable them to set good crops. Spraying to control mildews, black rot, and leaf hoppers favors ripening of such heavy crops.

How soon, and how much, will grapes bear? Grapevines should not be allowed to bear any fruit until their third season, and then only a small crop. The fourth season may be expected to give a good crop of fruit, and by the fifth season, if vines are well grown, they may be expected to have reached full production. This may be from 10 to 20 lbs. per vine. An average of 10 lbs. per vine would give about 3 tons per acre for vines spaced 8 to 10 ft. apart.

Why do grapes grow all to vines and bear no fruit? How often and at what season should they be trimmed? Vines have probably been thrown into an overvegetative stage by being grown on too rich a soil, by overfertilization, or by being pruned too closely. Very vigorous vines should have from 40 to 60 or more buds left to fruit. Grapevines require pruning only once each year, when the vines are fully dormant. Dense shading encourages excessive vine growth and tends to discourage fruiting.

Concord grapevines, 15 years old, in recent years have ripened fruit very unevenly, with green and ripe berries of uneven sizes on each bunch. What is the cause and remedy? Causes for the production of the small green berries on Concord grapevines and uneven ripening are not fully understood. It is thought that cool, rainy conditions at blossoming time, which interfere with fertilization of flowers, are usually responsible for the trouble. Vines having an insufficient supply of nitrogen often show more of this trouble than those more vigorous. Other than to keep vines in good, healthy condition there is little that one can do to correct this trouble inasmuch as one can do nothing to control the weather at blossoming time.

What is necessary to have grapes grow in nice bunches and have all the grapes ripen near the same time? Uniform ripening of fruit is more likely to occur when vine does not bear too heavy a crop. This is controlled by pruning vines each year so that no more than 40 buds are left on such vigorous varieties as Concord or Fredonia, and about 30 buds, or fewer, on less vigorous varieties such as Delaware or Diamond. Spraying to prevent leaves from being attacked by mildew, black rot, or leaf hoppers will also favor uniform ripening.

How can I recognize flowers of grapes? My 3-year Caco vine has

shown wonderful growth but no grapes. If you will look at the young shoots on grapevines when they are 6 to 10 ins. long, you will find tiny green structures which have much the appearance of a small bunch of grapes. These are rudimentary flowers and are borne opposite the lower 3 or 4 leaves on each of the shoots. As shoots grow, the flower clusters enlarge and expand. About 6 weeks after the shoots start to grow, individual blossoms appear. In opening, the petals, which remain greenish in color, are shed, leaving only pistil and anthers. The reason for non-fruiting may be overfertilization, which produces lush, soft growth at expense of fruit. Perhaps your vine is not Caco, but is another variety that may produce poor pollen and hence require another variety with good pollen to pollinate it.

We have Tokay grapes that crack open before ripening and are sour; also some dry up. The bunches are very large and crowded. Cracking of the berries followed by souring is due to clusters being too compact. The only remedy is to reduce the cluster by pinching some of the berries from each cluster soon after they are set in the spring. A good plan is to remove ¼ to ⅓ of the branches of the cluster. This will reduce the size, and should loosen it enough to prevent cracking.

What pre-winter care should be given to grapevines? In regions where grapes are not injured by winter temperatures, no special fall treatment, except possibly sowing of a cover crop, is necessary. In the far North, if tender varieties are grown, they will need to be laid down and covered for winter protection. In such regions it will probably be more satisfactory to grow a hardy variety, even though such varieties may be of somewhat lower quality.

What causes my grapes to remain red instead of getting blue as they are supposed to do? Grapes color normally if they have sufficient leaf surface in proportion to fruit being produced. Therefore, failure to ripen may be due to pruning too lightly, which will result in an excessive crop or to loss of leaves caused by grape leaf hopper or Japanese beetle.

Can good fruit be grown on an arbor, or must there be more sun available? It is the sunlight on the leaves, not on the fruit, that determines whether grapes can be grown. The shade of nearby trees and buildings should be avoided. An arbor can produce heavy crops of fruit if the vines are sprayed and pruned regularly.

Pruning

When is the best time of year to prune grapevines? Grapevines should be pruned when vines are fully dormant, in late fall, winter, or early spring. Pruning in late winter, the canes which have suffered from winter injury can easily be detected and cut out, thus leaving only sound canes on the vine. Spring pruning is not recommended, because as buds begin to swell they become brittle and break off easily, thus reducing size of crop.

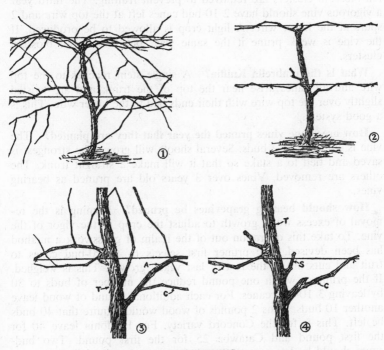

GRAPE PRUNING

(1) *Concord grapevine (several years old) before pruning.*
(2) *Same vine, pruned back during winter (Kniffin system).*
(3) *Detail, before pruning. T—main stem or trunk; A—arm, or lateral, 2-year-old wood; C—cane, 1-year-old wood. (4) Detail, after pruning. T—trunk; C—renewal cane, 1-year-old wood, tied to wire; S—spur, 1-year-old wood, cut back to 2 buds.*

What is the difference between grape training and pruning? Training is the arrangement of the trunk and canes to facilitate care of the vines. Pruning is the removal of excess wood growth to adjust the number of buds to produce a crop that the vine is capable of maturing.

How are grape vines trained? The single stem 4-cane Kniffin system is a good method. A vine trained this way consists of a trunk 6 feet tall with two arms 3 feet from the ground and two at the top of the vine. A two wire trellis with the lower wire 3 feet from the ground and the top wire 6 feet from the ground is used.

How are young vines pruned after the first year?   The second year the best cane is cut off at 6 feet and tied to the top of the trellis. All blossom clusters are removed to prevent fruiting. The third year a vigorous vine should have 2 10-bud canes left at the top wire and 2 spurs at the lower wire. A light crop is allowed to be produced. If the vine is weak prune it the same way, but remove all blossom clusters.

What is the umbrella Kniffin?   A single stem reaches to the top wire and all canes arise near the top of the trunk and are twisted slightly over the top wire with their ends tied to the lower wire. This is a good system.

How are grape vines pruned the year that they are planted?   The vine is cut back to 2 buds. Several shoots will grow. The strongest is saved and tied to a stake so that it will make a straight trunk. The others are removed. Vines over 3 years old are pruned as bearing vines.

How should bearing grapevines be pruned?   Pruning is the removal of excess wood growth to adjust the crop to the vigor of the vine. To take this operation out of the realm of guesswork a method has been devised. The pruner first selects 6- to 10-bud canes to fruit and cuts off all the rest of last year's growth. This is weighed. If the prunings weigh one pound reduce the number of buds to 30 by leaving 3 10-bud canes. For each additional pound of wood leave another 10 buds. Thus 2 pounds of wood would require that 40 buds be left. This is for the Concord variety. For Fredonia leave 40 for the first pound and Catawba 25 for the first pound. Two bud-spurs should be left near the trunk for canes for the following year.

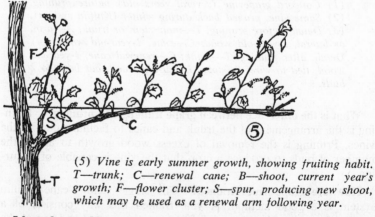

(5) *Vine is early summer growth, showing fruiting habit. T—trunk; C—renewal cane; B—shoot, current year's growth; F—flower cluster; S—spur, producing new shoot, which may be used as a renewal arm following year.*

I have been told to prune my grapes in the summer to let the light in to the fruit. Is that necessary?   It is not only unnecessary but undesirable. The fruit will color normally even if no light at all gets to it—quite different from the apple in this respect. Furthermore, removal of leaf surface at this time of year will delay or prevent normal ripening; hence defeat the very purpose for which it is done.

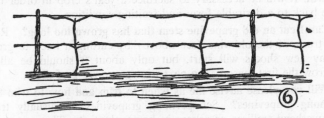

(6) *Trellis for Kniffin system; wires 3 ft. and 6 ft. above ground; posts 15 to 20 ft. apart.*

Would you recommend thinning foliage on grapevines in fall to hasten ripening of fruit before frost? Thinning the foliage would not hasten ripening of the fruit but would delay ripening, inasmuch as leaves are the food-manufacturing organs of the plant. Nothing can be done at this stage of the season to hasten ripening of fruit. Thinning crop shortly after blossoming might have speeded up ripening of remaining fruit if vine had set too heavy a crop.

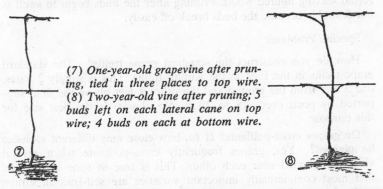

(7) *One-year-old grapevine after pruning, tied in three places to top wire.*
(8) *Two-year-old vine after pruning; 5 buds left on each lateral cane on top wire; 4 buds on each at bottom wire.*

How do you trim grapevines which have been neglected for years? Neglected grapevines should be renewed by cutting the old trunk back to the ground. New shoots will start from roots. Only 3 of these should be allowed to grow, and at the end of first season the strongest one should be selected for a new trunk and the others removed. The new trunk should be cut back to desired length and 4 side branches, of about 10 buds' length each, are then selected.

How can I best revitalize an old, neglected grapevine? Cut back the old vine severely. If the old trunk is in bad shape, cut it back to the ground and start a new trunk from one of the new shoots. If you do not care to cut it back that severely, and if the trunk and old arms are still in fair condition, cut vine back to point from which most vigorous shoots, closest to trunk, are arising. Leave a few, preferably 4, spurs of 2 buds each when the vine is cut back to provide new growth. It will be necessary to sacrifice a year's crop in order to get vine back to a desirable form and fruiting condition.

Can I cut an old grapevine stem that has grown too long? Renew the trunk of the old vine (see above) by cutting it back to ground. Many new shoots will start, but only about 3 should be allowed to grow the first season. The next winter remove 2 of these.

Will you please advise me as when to trim and how to trim Scuppernong grapevines? Scuppernong grapevines are usually trained on overhead trellises or arbors in home plantings. This system calls for a single trunk running to overhead trellis. At that height 8 arms, radiating from trunk like the spokes of a wheel from the hub, are selected and trained to grow out over trellis. After arms have been established they are pruned by cutting back all side branches on them to short spurs 2 or 3 buds long. As arms become older it may be desirable to renew some of them by cutting them back to a strong lateral cane near trunk. It is a good plan to renew one arm each year in this way. The best time to prune is in late winter, after danger of severe freezing. At that time one can easily tell which wood is alive. Avoid leaving injured wood. Pruning after the buds begin to swell is not desirable because the buds break off easily.

Special Problems

How do you construct the standard grape trellis? The standard grape trellis in the East in the Kniffin trellis. This is simply 2 wires, one 3 feet from the ground and the other 3 feet above the first, supported by posts every 18 to 20 ft. No. 9 wire is the best size for this purpose.

Do grapes cross-pollinate? If so, how close may different varieties be planted? Yes, grapes frequently cross-pollinate when several vines are planted near each other. This is true in spite of the fact that most commercially important varieties are self-fruitful. Grape pollen is very light and fluffy and is easily scattered about by winds and is carried about by many small insects. However, you need have no fear that the pollen of one variety will in any way influence the fruit of another variety. It has been shown many times that there is no immediate effect produced by pollen of one variety being placed on pistils of another variety. Only the seedlings produced from such cross-pollination will show any effect.

How should grape cuttings be handled? Make cuttings during February or early March of vigorous 1-year-old canes with 3 nodes or buds per cutting. Cut at base of cutting just below a bud, at tip about 1 in. beyond the bud. Tie in bundles like asparagus with butts all the same direction and bury upside down in a sandy soil, with about 2 ins. of soil over the cuttings. As soon as soil warms up take cuttings out, open up the bundles, and put the cuttings about 6 ins. apart in the nursery row, right side up, of course. Cuttings should be set deeply enough so that only tip bud is above surface of soil.

Should all grapevines be grafted? In some sections grapes should be grafted on rootstocks that are resistant to the grape phylloxera or root louse. Where this insect is not prevalent, vines may be grown from cuttings. Consult your Experiment Station concerning your own locality.

How can I get another vine started from the one I have? The easiest way is to lay a cane on the ground, peg it down if necessary, and cover a portion of it with soil. Roots will form at joints which are covered, and cane can be cut loose from old vine and used as a new plant. Most vines are propagated commercially by means of cuttings.

What is the best way to get grape cuttings started and set out so they will grow? Should grafting wax be used? Select straight, vigorous, well-matured, 1-year-old wood of pencil size. Cut into sections 3 buds long, making lower cut through node opposite lowest bud and upper cut about an inch above third bud. Tie cuttings in bundles of 50 and bury them in a trench, butt ends up, and cover with 6 ins. of soil during winter. After ground has warmed in spring, set cuttings in well-prepared soil so that they are about 3 ins. apart and with only upper bud above the soil. Hoe, cultivate, and water them during summer as needed. On good soil they should make enough growth in one season to permit transplanting them to the vineyard the next spring. No grafting wax or other materials need be used on cuttings handled in the manner described.

Pests and Diseases

My grapes turn to mummies right on the vines. Why do they look like raisins but don't taste like them? Your grapes have been affected by the black rot disease which is caused by a fungus. It can be controlled by spraying with Bordeaux mixture. The most important times to spray are when new shoots are about 1 in. long, when they are 12 ins. long, right after blooming, and again 10 days later. (See Grapes—Section VIII.)

How can I protect my grapes from birds? Cover the clusters with 2 pound paper sacks such as are used in grocery stores. Do not use the brown sacks as they give the grapes an unpleasant flavor. The sacks are put on as the grapes begin to color and are folded around the cluster stem and fastened with a stout pin.

How can I keep bees and wasps from destroying my grapes?

The bees and wasps are secondary; the birds puncture the skins and the insects move in. Sprays that will poison them will poison the grapes and spoil them for food. Bag the clusters as described above.

Varieties

Is there a seedless Concord grape on the market?   There is a variety of grape available to growers which is known as Concord Seedless. It is thought that it originated as a sport or mutation of Concord grape. The berries are much smaller than those of Concord and have only very rudimentary seeds which are hardly noticeable. It is fine for grape pie and for small children.

How is the new Sheridan grape compared with our Concord grape? Where it can be grown properly the Sheridan grape is an improvement over Concord. It has a larger berry and cluster, a more compact bunch, is more attractive, has a finer flavor, tougher skin, and will keep in fine condition in common storage until January. It requires a long season to mature, however, ripening about 2 weeks after Concord in central New York.

Are there any varieties of grapes which will keep better than Concord, either on the vine or after picking?   Long keeping grapes are Seneca, Buffalo, Yates, Sheridan and Steuben.

What grape variety is usually made into grape juice?   The most common sweet grape-juice variety throughout the East is the Concord. Good grapes are the old varieties, Concord, Niagara, and Delaware. Recent good varieties are Seneca, Ontario, Buffalo, Yates, Steuben, Sheridan and Golden Muscat.

What varieties of grapes should I plant for a long season of harvesting?   In order of ripening from earliest to latest the following are good varieties. Van Buren, Fredonia, Seneca, Buffalo, Delaware, Concord, Yates, Steuben, Sheridan, Golden Muscat and Catawba. Unless you have a long season you may not be able to grow those ripening after Concord.

What are some good varieties of hardy seedless grapes?   The new seedless grapes—Himrod, Interlaken and Romulus—originated at Geneva, N.Y., will endure winter temperatures down to about 15° below zero. These three varieties are much like the Thompson Seedless of California. Concord Seedless, not new, is like Concord in flavor, but the berries are much smaller. The vine is as hardy as Concord.

I should like to grow some of the California varieties of grapes in New Jersey. Do they require special culture?   Not so much special culture as special climate. Winters are too cold and summers too cloudy in New Jersey for most California varieties. American varieties or hybrids between American and European (California varieties are mostly of European origin) are most satisfactory in the East. Some varieties of this type are Fredonia, Niagara, Concord, and Delaware.

Will Scuppernong grapes grow in Pennsylvania? You are too far north for this type, which is widely grown in the South. The northern limit of the Scuppernong or Muscadine type is southern Virginia.

Do ordinary table grapes make good wine? Some varieties that are good table grapes—Delaware, Iona and Catawba—make excellent wine. Generally speaking, the best wines are made from grapes suitable only for wines. Recently French hybrids have been planted a little in New York for wine and several have considerable promise, but their usefulness has not fully been determined and exploited.

What kind of grape will pollinize with California Tokay grape? The vine is no more than 10 years old and covers Jasper Walnut tree. (Michigan.) The Tokay grape is self-fruitful and does not require cross-pollination. This California variety is not hardy enough to withstand the winters in Michigan. Therefore, I doubt whether you have a Tokay grapevine. My opinion is that you planted a vine of this variety which was grafted on a hardy American rootstock. Probably the Tokay graft has been killed and the vine has sprouted out from the hardy rootstock. Many of the hardy rootstocks used for grafting are male vines and never set fruit. This may account for the fact that your vine fails to bear a crop even though it may blossom profusely. If this is the case, there is nothing you can do except to replace the vine with another vine or to cut it off at the ground and graft a scion of the desired variety onto it. If another Tokay scion is grafted onto it, the Tokay top would need to be given winter protection to prevent it's being killed.

Can the California grapes like Tokay, Malaga, etc., be grown in eastern United States? No, for two reasons. The root louse (phylloxera) will destroy vines on their own roots; and the season is not long enough to ripen the fruit. Certain new hybrids between the American varieties and the European vinifera vines, however (notably the new Golden Muscat), can be depended upon to ripen their fruits if a season 10 days longer than the normal season for ripening Concords can be expected in your locality.

Are there any grape varieties hardy enough to be grown in northern Minnesota? Beta is one of the hardiest of all grapes. The Minnesota Agricultural Experiment Station at University Farm, St. Paul, Minn., can supply information as to the best grapes for northern Minnesota.

CANE FRUITS

What is meant by the term "bramble or cane fruits"? This group includes the fruits belonging to the genus Rubus; the red, black, and purple raspberries, the dewberry, and the bush and trailing blackberries. The loganberry, boysenberry, etc., may be classified as dewberries.

Have the "brambles" any preference as to soil? Raspberries and bush blackberries do best in heavier soils; dewberries like sandy soils and will not thrive on heavy soils. If the soil is well-drained and in good physical condition the brambles will grow satisfactorily on a fairly wide range of soil types.

Can cane fruits be grown successfully in a sandy soil? A sandy loam soil is satisfactory, but coarse sands are too subject to drought and are low in fertility.

What fertilizer should be used for brambles? Stable manure is excellent if available; otherwise, use a nitrogenous material such as ammonium nitrate or nitrate of soda. If marginal burning of the foliage is present sulfate of potash should be used.

Where should cane fruits be planted? They should be planted on fertile well-drained soils that are well-supplied with organic matter. The black and purple raspberries should not be planted on land that has grown tomatoes within the past three years or near wild raspberries or runout cultivated raspberries which often harbor diseases and insects that may ruin the new planting.

Can you plant berry bushes during the winter when ground is soft? It could be done, but if soil has much clay in it it will be too sticky to do a good job. If there is much freezing and thawing afterward plants might heave out of ground unless mulched and surrounded with soil. Fall or early-spring planting would be preferable.

How much space should be planted with cane fruits for a family of 4? Personal tastes must be considered, of course, but here is one suggested assortment: plants 3 ft. apart in row, in rows 6 to 8 ft. apart. Red raspberries, 50 ft. of row; black raspberries, 24 ft. of row; blackberries, bush, 50 ft. of row.

Can raspberries be planted near pine trees? If there is distance enough between them so that there is no root competition or shade.

What berry bushes thrive in shade? No plants that bear fruit will thrive in much shade. The more sun they receive, the better the crops.

When do you plant everbearing raspberries? Everbearing raspberries may be set either in the fall or spring and should have the same care that the ordinary one-crop varieties receive.

What bramble or cane fruits could be grown in a very small city garden? None of them are really adapted to such conditions as they will all spread, either by suckering or by tip rooting. Possibly black raspberries would be easiest to keep under control.

Do cane fruits need support? Cane fruits do not require support, but most growers use some means of training to keep them from growing too "ragged" and occupying too much space in the garden.

How would you construct a trellis for dewberry vines? A 5-ft. stake driven 1 ft. into the ground beside each plant will be quite satisfactory. Cut out old, dead canes and tie up new, vigorous canes in early spring, cutting them off at top of the stake.

How should I care for the September raspberries which I set out last spring? How should they be pruned and sprayed? (Vermont.) September raspberry is pruned in the same manner as the one-crop varieties. (See question on pruning raspberries.) Spraying is not necessary. The season in Vermont is too short to ripen the fall crop of September.

What is correct yearly cultural care of established cane fruits? Constant shallow cultivation to control weeds is important. Mulching is a good plan, using well-rotted manure. Prune living canes only where necessary for training of plants. Prune out all dead canes after fruiting season. Apply nitrate of soda (or a similar high-nitrogen fertilizer) in spring, 1 to 2 lbs. per 100 ft. of row.

How often should berries be picked? Pick red raspberries every day, blackcaps and blackberries every third day.

What pre-winter care should be given raspberries? Raspberries should have cover crop sown between the rows.

How can I increase my stock of raspberries? Black and purple raspberries are propagated by tip-layering. The tips of the new canes are inserted vertically in the soil in late August to a depth of 4 inches. Roots form on the tip in late fall and in the spring the tip is dug, severed from the mother plant and planted where desired. Red raspberries send up many sucker plants which can be dug in late fall and early spring for planting.

How often should the brambles be planted? Usually in 5 to 10 years, but if weeds are not bad and diseases are kept under control the planting may last longer.

VARIETIES OF CANE FRUITS

What kind of fruit bushes can I grow on a strip 3 × 40 ft.? (New York.) If the area is exposed to full sunlight, you could grow any of the small fruits; such as grapes, strawberries, raspberries, currants, or gooseberries, or combinations of the ones you like best. For instance, 3 currant bushes would take up about 10 ft., leaving 30 ft. for strawberries if you particularly like these two fruits; or all may be planted to raspberries or blackberries.

Our garden is in Maine, rather far east on the coast. Can you give information on varieties of small fruits? Sparkle, Catskill, and Fairfax are good home-garden strawberries. Latham, Newburgh, September and Taylor are good red raspberries. Bristol and Dundee are the best black raspberries. Sodus is the best purple variety.

What would be a profitable fruit planting, producing in about 3 or 4 years, which could be tended on week ends and will produce for at least 10 years without replanting? There are 2 acres and full sun, ½ mile from ocean. The acreage is too small for tree fruits. A combination of red raspberries and strawberries has been profitable for some growers, but strawberries have to be planted each year for best results. You might make a miscellaneous fruit planting for your own and sell the surplus. In that case, choose the fruits you like and take a part of your "profit" in personal satisfaction. If profit is the main objective, secure enough land to make an economic farm unit.

What different kinds of berries should be planted in order to have a continuous supply from late spring until frost? Start off with strawberries, then raspberries, currants, gooseberries, bush blackberries, trailing blackberries. These will cover the season until early August. Everbearing strawberries and raspberries will fill out the rest of the season. It might be better to depend on grapes during the fall.

Are boysenberries worth an amateur week-end gardener's efforts? Boysenberry is a form of dewberry that requires sandy soil. It is not reliably hardy in the North. It must be given adequate winter covering.

What kind of everbearing raspberries are suggested for south of Boston? The best variety is September. This is really fall bearing. The fall crop is produced at the tips of the new canes and next summer the same canes bear another crop.

Can we grow the Oregon Evergreen blackberry in this state? (Massachusetts.) It would kill to the ground during any but the mildest winter.

What is the best variety of blackberry for Maine? Bailey or Hedrick.

What is the best variety of raspberry for Maine? Latham raspberry.

What are the best varieties of cane fruits to grow? See Introduction.

BLACKBERRY

Will blackberries grow on any soil? They do best on good sandy loam soil containing plenty of humus, but well drained.

Can manure be used on blackberries? Yes, manure or complete fertilizer can be used to improve poor soils on which blackberries are grown. A yearly cover crop, turned under in spring, or the turning under of summer mulch adds needed humus to the soil.

When is the best time to transplant blackberry or raspberry bushes? Early spring, although fall planting may be successful if plants are set rather deeply and mounded somewhat to prevent heaving during winter. This applies to red raspberries; black raspberries should be set in the spring.

How far apart should raspberries and bush blackberries be planted? Three ft. apart in the row and rows 7 to 8 ft. apart are standard distances.

How far apart should blackberries of the trailing type be planted? Trailing blackberries such as Black Diamond (called Oregon Evergreen in the West) need plenty of room. Set plants at least 6 ft. apart in rows 6 to 8 ft. apart.

When and how should blackberries be pruned? In June tips of new shoots are pinched off at a height of 3 ft. to make them branch. The following spring the branches are cut back to a length of about 15 ins. After crop is harvested, canes that have borne fruit are removed.

Why do some blackberries blossom and not have any berries? There are two possible causes. A sterile blackberry has been widely distributed by nurseries. It produces no fruit although it blooms. Another cause is the feeding of the tarnished plant bug on the flowers causing them to develop into sterile or partially sterile fruits. The plant bug is easily controlled by spraying the plants with DDT at the rate of 2 pounds of the 50 percent wettable powder in 100 gallons of water. This is applied just before the plants bloom.

Are the trailing blackberries, that is, dewberry, boysenberry, Himalaya blackberry, etc., propagated the same way as the regular blackberries? These are usually propagated by tip layering.

Can the suckers that come up from the roots of blackberries be used to make plants of the same variety? Yes. Usually the nurserymen use root cuttings 3 to 4 ins. long and the thickness of a lead pencil. (See Division.)

Why do blackberry leaves get a bright orange color and then seem to die? The orange color is made up of spores of a disease known as orange rust. Infected plants will die. The only control is to dig out diseased plants before spores have been discharged to infect other plants. Be sure to dig out the roots, as shoots coming up from these would be diseased.

Is it satisfactory to transplant wild blackberry bushes for home use? This is all right if you can find really superior wild bushes, otherwise you will have much better results by planting named varieties. Wild blackberries sometimes do not do so well under cultivation as they do in the wild. Try such varieties as Hedrick or Bailey.

Is the thornless Black Diamond blackberry as good as the thorny type? Much better, as it is practically identical with the older type of Black Diamond, and thornlessness is a very valuable asset, as can be attested by anyone who has pruned the thorny type.

Would raspberry and blackberry plants make a good ground cover for a steep embankment? Raspberries and blackberries will grow satisfactorily on a steep bank if the soil is fertile and the ground is mulched to prevent washing. Steep banks, however may be cut or badly eroded in which case the soil is not suitable for the brambles.

BOYSENBERRY

Are Boysenberries worth growing in the East? Boysenberries are not winter hardy north of Washington, D.C. and even though protected the crops are very light. The other small fruits will produce much more fruit with less effort. Boysenberries are an excellent fruit in California and Oregon.

How should boysenberries be fed? Boysenberries may be fertilized with nitrate of soda or sulfate of ammonia at the rate of 1 lb. per 100 sq. ft. Failing these fertilizers, use 5 lbs. dried chicken manure.

Have some boysenberries, set out last spring, which I would like to move. When can this be done? (Washington.) Boysenberries can be moved in late fall or early spring before growth starts. In mild climates, they may be moved any time during the winter.

How are boysenberries pruned out and trained? Boysenberries are a trailing vine. The canes grow one year, bear fruit second, and then die, another crop taking their place. To facilitate harvesting of fruit and tillage operations fruiting canes are tied up to a trellis at beginning of second season. A suitable trellis consists of a wire 3 or 4 ft. above the ground. Canes are gathered together and tied at top to this wire. The ends are cut off or tied along wire. Canes may also be tied up to 5-ft. posts, ends being cut off at top of post. After crop is off, fruiting canes are removed and new canes, that will fruit following year, tied in.

Have 6-year-old boysenberry bushes, which were planted close to young shade trees and now are shaded too much. Can I transplant this coming spring? The plants are very large and strong. Can I divide them and make more plants? (Oregon.) Old berry plants do not transplant and re-establish themselves readily. Either buy new plants or cover tips of new canes with soil in late summer. Roots will form at tips. New plants may be severed from parent plant following spring and moved to their permanent location. Dividing old plants is hardly practical.

DEWBERRY

What are dewberries? Are they a desirable cane fruit for the home garden? Trailing or procumbent blackberries. They are a week or two earlier than other blackberries, with large berries but of a poorer flavor than high-growing types.

Where should dewberries be planted? Dewberries are happiest on sandy soils south of central Pennsylvania. In the Northern states winter protection is advisable where reliable snow cover is lacking.

What is the planting distance for dewberries? The plants are set 5 ft. apart each way for training on stakes or 7 × 2 ft. if they are to be grown on a trellis.

Can dewberries be trimmed in some way so that the branches do not cling so close to the ground? The dewberry naturally trails on ground. The second or fruiting year canes may be tied to a 5-ft. stake and cut off at top. Sometimes they are tied to a wire 3 or 4 ft. from the ground.

How far should dewberry branches be allowed to spread? During the first season, when canes are trailing on ground, they are not restricted. (See next question.)

Last spring I planted some dewberry plants along the edges of my vegetable garden. How do you care for the straggly growth, to keep it within bounds? Dewberry canes are tied up to a trellis or a stake for the fruiting year. The first year canes trail on the ground.

RASPBERRY

Will young black raspberry bushes grow well if planted in fresh brown sandy loam fill? If the soil used in filling is subsoil, it is hardly suitable for berries of any kind. If it is topsoil, berries should do well in it.

When is the best time to plant red raspberry bushes? Red raspberries may be set in late fall if soil is mounded around plants to a height of several ins. to prevent heaving from frost action. In spring soil is worked down level. Raspberries may also be set in early spring.

When is the best time to transplant black raspberries? Tip plants are set in spring, but "transplants" may be set either in spring or in fall.

How far apart should raspberries be planted? Plant suckering varieties 3 ft. apart, in rows 5 or 6 ft. apart; blackcaps, 4 or 5 ft. apart, in rows 6 or 7 ft. apart.

Can raspberry bushes which were not planted in the fall be held over until spring without heeling them in? They must be heeled in, or packed in moist material such as sphagnum moss, and stored in a cellar where the temperature stays near 32° F. Roots must not be allowed to dry out, and temperature must be low enough to prevent canes from sprouting.

Is it possible to plant between the rows of raspberries? It seems as if there is space going to waste. Small vegetables, but not tomatoes, pepper, eggplants or potatoes may be planted between the rows the first season, but not close enough to the raspberries to compete with them.

Should raspberries and blackberries be pruned in the summer? Red raspberries should not be summer pruned. Blackcaps and bush blackberries should have their canes pinched back when they reach the height at which branching is desired. This would usually be at 24 to 30 ins. for black raspberries, and 30 to 36 ins. for bush blackberries. If pinching is done at proper time, it will consist of merely nipping out growing tip of cane with the fingers.

How should red raspberries be pruned and trained? Red raspberries are commonly tied to stakes or a wire trellis in the garden, but support is not necessary. Plants should be grown in hedgerows not over 1 ft. in width. In early spring canes which grew previous season are cut back about ¼ of their height. Weaker canes should be removed so that remaining canes are spaced about 6 ins. apart in rows 1 ft. in width. Canes which fruited previous summer should be removed if this was not done after the crop was harvested. Red raspberry plants send up a multitude of suckers between rows and unless these are subdued by vigorous use of hoe a veritable thicket will result.

How should black raspberries be pruned? Remove canes that are dead, broken, obviously diseased, or that grow at such an angle that they will bend to the ground when in fruit. Cut back good canes to about 24 to 30 ins. and then shorten the lateral branches to about 4 ins. in length.

Do red raspberries need a trellis? Not necessarily. If they are pruned rather short (cut back about ½ if 5 to 6 ft. tall), they will hold themselves up. However, a trellis of one wire on each side of row, supported by posts and crosspieces, will hold canes up during storms, prevent breakage, and keep berries from getting into mud.

Last summer I planted some Sodus purple raspberries. They have grown to a length of 9 to 12 ft. How far and when should they be cut back? In early spring canes should be cut back to a length of 4 or 5 ft. and tied up to a stake or wire trellis. To eliminate need for support, pinch off tips of new shoots when they reach a height of 30 ins. This makes canes branch and they are sturdier and self-supporting. The following spring cut branches back to a length of 10 or 12 ins. and no support will be needed.

What, if any, winter protection should be given 1-year-old black raspberry bushes? (New York.) Black raspberries are hardy without winter protection except in the coldest parts of the country like northern New York.

How can I protect raspberries over winter? (Massachusetts.) Hardy raspberry varieties should not need protection in Massachusetts. If protection is desired, bend canes down and cover tips with soil. In this position snow will provide protection. Where snow blows off, straw or earth may be used to cover the canes.

Are leaves or natural fertilizer better as a mulch dressing for raspberry bushes? Straw, old hay, or leaves are good mulching materials for raspberries. Manure, if used in sufficient amounts to be of value as a mulch, will stimulate such a strong growth that winter injury may result. Manure is, of course, an excellent material for fertilizing raspberries.

At about what date in spring should mulch be removed from raspberries? The best time to remove mulch is when unmulched plants begin to start growth.

Do everbearing raspberries bear more than once in a season? Two crops are borne, the first in July on canes which grew previous season, second or fall crop in September and October on tips of current season's canes.

My red raspberry patch has grown so profusely. Would it be wise to take out every other row and start a new patch? It is rather difficult to subdue and restore order in a raspberry patch that has run wild. It will be easier and more satisfactory to take up healthy sucker plants and set a new patch, resolving to take care of it and keep suckers in bounds. Have rows in the new patch 6 or 7 ft. apart and keep rows of plants about 1 ft. in width.

Can shoots of red raspberry be cut away from parent plant and transplanted in the spring? If so, how and when? New shoots of red raspberries may be taken up in June after they have reached a height of 6 or 8 ins. Care should be taken to get part of the old root. Cloudy, moist weather is essential and the plants should be watered in. This method of starting raspberries is not successful in hot, dry weather.

When is the best time to propagate wild red raspberries? Red raspberry sucker plants may be taken up and set either in late fall or early spring.

How can I get new plants to renew my raspberry planting? Red raspberries are propagated from suckers from the roots of old plants. These are dug up, the large root severed, and new plants set in place. Black and purple cane raspberries are propagated by tip layers. (See Division.)

Will red and black raspberries mix if planted close? No, not at all.

Pests and Diseases

How can I keep the birds from devouring my red raspberries? Cover plants with netting or cheesecloth.

How can I keep rabbits from gnawing raspberry bushes during the winter? Fence them out with poultry netting 30 ins. high.

What causes the so-called mosaic disease of raspberries? This is a virus disease spread from one plant to another by aphids. The only remedy is to keep digging out and destroying diseased plants. Be sure to take out roots, as all the shoots coming up from roots of a diseased plant will also be diseased.

What causes a hard, woody knot to grow at the ground level on my raspberry bushes? This is caused by the disease known as crown gall. There is no cure for a diseased plant, and the disease will live in the soil for some time. So set clean, inspected plants in soil that has not recently grown any of the bramble fruits.

What causes tips of my Latham raspberry plants to wilt over? The raspberry cane borer, a beetle, lays an egg near the tip of the cane, then cuts a girdle just above and just below the egg which usually causes the tip to wilt and die. The most practical control consists of breaking off wilted tips and burning them. Break or cut a couple of inches below the girdle in order to get the larva, which will start to bore down through the pith of the cane as soon as it hatches.

My blackcap raspberries have gray spots on the canes and on the fruit. What can I do? This is the disease known as anthracnose. A delayed dormant spray of lime sulfur, 1 to 20, when the buds are out about ½ in. in the spring, will usually give control. In seasons favorable for anthracnose (prolonged wet spells) ferbam at the rate of 2 pounds to 100 gallons of water should be applied when the new shoots are 12 to 15 inches high and again just before bloom.

Why aren't red and black raspberries supposed to be grown together? Because of certain diseases, mosaic in particular, which are carried by the reds and readily transmitted to the blacks. Mosaic infection may not injure a red variety very rapidly but will kill a blackcap in a much shorter time (that is, the reds act as carriers of the disease). The blacks would be much safer a couple of hundred yards away, far enough so aphids will not get from one to the other.

Why aren't the purple raspberries more widely grown? They are susceptible to the mosaic disease. They are not very attractive in the box and do not sell well. Those who know them frequently prefer them to the reds and blacks.

Varieties

Are everbearing raspberries more desirable than standard sorts? For the home gardener, everbearing sorts are desirable to extend the season. They should be used to supplement the regular sorts rather than in place of them. September is considered the best everbearing variety.

What black raspberries are the best producers for home use? Bristol and Dundee are both productive, high-quality varieties.

What red raspberry do you consider best for home garden and

market garden? (Wisconsin.) For Wisconsin, Latham is a standard variety. Newburgh and September should also be tried.

Is the Columbian the best purple raspberry? (Pennsylvania.) It used to be the standard variety of this type, but the newer varieties Sodus and Marion are better.

What are good early and late red raspberries? September for early and Latham for late would make a good combination.

What is a good everbearing raspberry? September is the best variety. It produces good summer and fall crops. Durham is earlier for the fall crop, but the summer crop is not satisfactory.

BLUEBERRY

Soils and Fertilizers

What is an ideal blueberry soil? A well-aerated mixture of sand and peat with the water table 14 to 22 inches below the surface. In such a soil there is excellent drainage near the surface, but water is always available within reach of roots. A plentiful supply of peatmoss means plenty of organic matter and usually the required acid reaction of pH 4.5 to 5.5. Such soil conditions are seldom available in the home garden, so they have to be approximated by spading in peat or leafmold, and by mulching or irrigation, or all three.

How can I make the soil sufficiently acid for successful blueberry culture? Soil should be moist, full of peat or other organic material, and with a reaction of about pH 5.0. Soil may be made acid through the use of acid peatmoss, oak leafmold, and chemicals. Most chemicals are dangerous, as an excess is apt to be harmful. Sulfur and aluminum sulfate are among the best, but the quantities necessary have to be calculated in relation to the composition of the soil and its pH reaction.

How can hybrid blueberries be grown on neutral soil? Limestone soils vary. Sometimes, if the underlying rock is limestone, the topsoil may be acid. If the soil is deep and of limestone origin, the conditions are different. Investigate. Why try something that may be troublesome in later years? For instance, you might make the soil acid enough originally, but if it is necessary to irrigate, and the water is hard, trouble will develop. Excavate a bed 4 ft. wide and 2 ft. deep, put in a layer of 6 or 8 ins. of acid peatmoss or acid leafmold. Fill with soil that has been acidified chemically or by being composted with acid peat or leafmold. Use water that does not contain lime.

What is the pH requirement for Rubel Blueberry, Juneberry and Highbush Cranberry? The ideal pH range for the highbush blueberry is usually from 4.5 to 5.5. The Juneberry and Highbush Cranberry do not require an especially acid soil, although (so far as we know) no experiments to determine optimum pH for these plants have been conducted, whereas several workers have studied the pH requirements of the blueberry.

Having limestone soil, how shall I prepare for growing blueberries successfully? First get your soil tested, for it may not be as alkaline as you think. If it is not more alkaline than pH 5.5, no special treatment will be needed. If it is around pH 6.0, you can probably get satisfactory results by using ammonium sulfate as a fertilizer. If the pH is about 6.5 or 7.0, you will have to acidify by bringing in a plentiful supply of acid organic matter, or by chemical means. Acidity isn't the only soil requirement, however. Proper fertilization and a relatively constant and ample supply of moisture are necessary.

Just how is ordinary soil prepared for growing blueberries? Is there any way to test it? Most State Agricultural Extension Services will test soil for residents of the state. Methods of acidifying the soil are elsewhere discussed. In many cases it will not be necessary to acidify artificially, and then the main requirement is assurance of a uniformly plentiful supply of moisture. If the soil is dry, it may be necessary to irrigate. If it is fairly moist, a permanent mulch of straw or hay will give best results by conserving what moisture there is.

Our soil is too rich for blueberries. What can we do about it? It probably isn't too "rich," as blueberries will grow in very fertile soil provided other conditions are right. Your soil may be alkaline, deficient in some one or more elements, or it may be too wet or too dry.

Would you recommend blueberries for an acid garden section? Blueberries will do excellently in an acid garden, and will usually be an asset to it. They require the same cultural conditions as azaleas and rhododendrons.

Is the soil in Cleveland all right to raise blueberries? Ground quite clayey. (Ohio.) Blueberries probably will not grow successfully in unmodified Ohio clays. They are lowland plants that like acid soils stuffed with humus and with a strong acid reaction. To grow them successfully will probably require the use of a good pH indicator. (Consult your county agent for details.) Dig a trench about 5 ft. wide and at least 2 ft. deep. Fill with a mixture of ⅓ soil, ⅓ rotted oak leaves or peat, and ⅓ sand. Maintain a pH of between 4.9 and 5.6, if possible, but always below 6.0.

We are much interested in trying to raise blueberries in an ashy soil in a dry climate; have plenty of water to irrigate, but the atmosphere is very dry. Can it be done? (Idaho.) Your main difficulty would be in getting your soil acid enough. It would be best to start in a small way first.

How should blueberries, already planted, be fed and cared for? Assuming that the soil is acid apply a sawdust mulch to a depth of

2 to 4 inches and renew as needed to control weeds. Fertilize with sulfate of ammonia at the rate of one ounce for each year of age of the plants up to 8 years. During the first years of the mulch double this amount may be necessary.

What is the best fertilizer for blueberries? I have a field of very fine native lowbush berries in Maine, which I wish to improve for marketing. Experiments at the Maine Agricultural Experiment Station have indicated the value of a complete fertilizer for lowbush blueberries provided weeds are kept under control. Since this is to be a commercial venture, write for the latest recommendations from the Maine Station.

Culture

How and when should blueberry shrubs 3 years of age be pruned? Prune during late fall, winter, or early spring. Three-year-old bushes will need comparatively little pruning. Remove small, rather weak lateral twigs to prevent their fruiting. Long shoots, well covered with fruit buds, may need to be cut back to leave only 2 or 3 fruit buds. Remember that 1 fruit bud will produce a cluster of flowers and of fruit. If the fruit buds are not thinned by pruning, too many berries will be set, the fruit will be small and late in maturing, and the bush will be weakened.

When is the best time to make blueberry cuttings, and how are they cared for? Make hardwood cuttings in late winter or early spring and place them in peatmoss, or ½ sand and ½ peat, in ground beds under a lath house, or in a special raised propagating frame. Cuttings should be about 6 ins. long of good 1-year-old twigs, preferably without fruit buds. Place them at an angle in the moss, with at least ⅔ of the cutting covered. Great care must be taken in watering and ventilating, especially in raised frames which are covered with hot-bed sash and kept closed in the early stages of rooting.

Are 2 blueberry bushes sufficient to assure fruit, or is it necessary to have more than that number? If so, how many? Two bushes are enough if they are different varieties which bloom at the same time. If only 1 variety is planted, a fair set might be obtained, but the berries would probably be a little smaller than if they had been cross-pollinated.

Is any progress being made in adapting blueberries to dry land? The only way this can be accomplished is by crossing those which require moist soil with one of the dry-land types. This work has been started. The cultivated blueberry has been crossed with the lowbush blueberry of Maine, a dry-land type, and also with 2 or 3 dry-land species of the South. Eventually there should be varieties adapted to ordinary agricultural soil and possibly even to the sandy coastal plains soils.

What are the requirements of hybrid blueberries? The so-called hybrid blueberries are essentially like other plants with respect to most of their requirements, the two principal exceptions being that they require a rather acid soil and an ample and uniform moisture supply.

Where should blueberries be planted in the home garden? Blueberries require acid soil, good drainage, and aeration. They need a space of 8 ft. between bushes.

Can blueberries be cultivated in a limited space under favorable conditions? Yes. Favorable conditions, however, include full exposure to sunlight, which is not always possible in a very limited area.

How can I promote faster growth of blueberry bushes? Be sure growing conditions are favorable with respect to soil fertility and moisture supply. Some varieties grow more rapidly than others, but all are rather slow growing compared, for instance, with a peach tree.

Will blueberries grow under tall, large oaks in semi-shade? They will grow in this environment, but the yield of fruit will not be equal to that of plants grown in the open.

How are weeds controlled in the blueberry regions of Maine where cultivation isn't practical? By burning over the blueberry fields every other year or every third year. Straw is spread thinly over the area and burned when conditions are right for a quick fire which will not injure the blueberry roots.

I have 2 acres of well-drained swampland; how and when should I plant highbush blueberries? Be sure the swampland is well drained but not too dry; blueberries are very sensitive to moisture conditions. Plant as early in the spring as the soil can be got into condition. Set the plants carefully, slightly deeper than they were in the nursery row, about 5 ft. apart in rows 8 ft. apart.

We have very large blueberries in a pasture. Can they be moved to a garden with good results? Very large bushes would be difficult to move, but you could move smaller ones. Some would need to be split up to make several plants. The size, color, and quality of the fruit are not likely to be as satisfactory as that from the named varieties, plants of which you can buy. Be sure your soil is properly prepared before digging the wild bushes.

Cultivated blueberry plants have been neglected for approximately 3 years. Will transplanting and proper care revive these plants? Prune them to thin out the probably too dense bush; control weeds with shallow cultivation or a mulch; and fertilize with sulfate of ammonia.

How often should a planting of blueberries be renewed? Blueberries, with good care, should be as permanent as tree fruits, that is, 15 to 25 years or more.

Under ideal conditions are the leaves of blueberries light or dark green? Could yellowish-green color be due to any factor other than incorrect soil reaction? The leaves of blueberries that are doing well are large and dark green, although the intensity of the green may vary somewhat in the different varieties. The yellowish green color might be due to nitrogen deficiency; a too wet, poorly aerated soil; a too alkaline soil with which might be associated iron deficiency; or a virus disease known as stunt.

I have blueberries which are not doing well. What can be done? Check the following, which may be responsible: soil not acid enough; lacking in fertility, especially nitrogen; too dry; too wet; injury by low temperatures or by some pest.

How can I grow blueberries successfully in Ohio? For soil requirements, see previous questions. Plant 5 ft. apart in row, using balled and burlapped stock, either in fall or spring. Always plant 2 or more varieties to insure good pollination. Water once a week if rain does not fall for the first season. Cultivate shallowly or mulch the plants with sawdust, peat, or oak leaves. In the spring apply one ounce of sulfate of ammonia for each year of age of the plants. Use peatmoss or well-rotted oak leaves as a mulch. After plants are in full bearing, remove old, unfruitful branches during the winter.

Will the large blueberries grown in south Jersey do as well in northern New Jersey? Yes, if proper growing conditions are provided. However, there is not nearly so much good blueberry soil in the northern part of the state as in the southern part.

Does the blueberry make a good ornamental shrub? Yes, it is attractive in bloom, when the fruit is ripe, and when the leaves turn red in the fall. The twigs in winter are also striking. Results will be disappointing, however, if growing conditions are not right. If they are favorable, it may be possible to raise a nice crop of fruit on a border of ornamental shrubs, but because the birds will take the crop the bushes must be covered if the berries are to be harvested.

What are the advantages of mulching blueberries? Blueberries are shallow-rooted, so that the advantages of mulching are very substantial and greater than with many other plants. The mulch conserves moisture, eliminates most of the weeds, keeps soil temperatures lower and prevents injury to the roots from too deep cultivation.

How hardy are the new high-bush blueberries? They will stand temperatures down to 20° to 25° below zero and sometimes even lower. When in bloom they will stand more frost than other fruit blossoms. Injury may be expected in bloom when temperatures drop below 22° above zero.

How are blueberries protected from birds? The plants should be covered with cheesecloth or a cage made of poultry netting small enough to keep out birds. Scaring devices are of little value as the birds soon become used to them. Unless the bushes are covered birds are likely to take all of the berries from garden plantings.

Varieties

What is meant by hybrid blueberries? The term is commonly used to designate the named varieties of the type known as the highbush, swamp, or cultivated blueberry. The first varieties to be cultivated— Rubel, Sam, Grover and others—were merely wild highbush blueberries that were somewhat superior to the general run of wild blueberries. All of the good cultivated varieties now are several generations of breeding removed from their wild ancestors.

What is the difference between blueberries and huckleberries? The term huckleberry is often erroneously applied to blueberries outside of New England. Blueberries have many small seeds, 60 or 70, that are not noticeable, while huckleberries have 10 comparatively large seeds that are very noticeable and crackle between the teeth. Huckleberries have small yellowish dots on the underside of the leaves; blueberries have none.

What are the best blueberry varieties for the home garden? Ripening from early to late the best varieties are Earliblue, Bluecrop, Berkeley, Herbert and Coville. The older Stanley and Dixi are of fine quality. Jersey is still a good variety and one of the hardiest.

I have seen blueberries growing in western Florida. What kind are they? These are a different species than grows in the North. It is known as *Vacciuium ashei,* the rabbit-eye blueberry. It is suited to the deep South and makes a much larger bush than the northern types. Improved varieties now being grown are Coastal, Callaway, Tifblue, Walker and Homebell.

What is the difference between the cultivated blueberries and the ones that grow in Maine? The species usually meant when the term "cultivated blueberries" is used is *Vaccinium corymbosum,* otherwise known as the highbush or swamp blueberry. The ones commonly seen in Maine belong to the species *Vaccinium angustifolium,* the lowbush type, which grows in dry upland.

What are the important blueberry-producing states? New Jersey, North Carolina, and Michigan produce the most cultivated blueberries. There are some commercial plantings in Massachusetts, New York, and Maryland. Maine is in the lead in the production from wild lowbush blueberries. Nurseries in New Jersey, Michigan, Massachusetts, Maryland, and North Carolina, are propagating blueberry varieties.

CRANBERRY

Is the American cranberry worth planting for jelly? The highbush cranberry, *Viburnum trilobum* is not a true cranberry, but is a red-fruited viburnum of about the same size and color as the true cranberry. It makes a fair jelly, but is not equal to jellies made from currants, grapes, quince and several other fruits. It is most useful in regions too cold for these other fruits.

Where is the cranberry native? There are 2 species used for jelly, sauce, etc.: *Vaccinium oxycoccus,* native to northern Europe, northern Asia, and North America, as far south as Pennsylvania, Michigan, and Wisconsin; and *Vaccinium macrocarpum* (the kind mostly sold), native to Newfoundland, south to North Carolina, Michigan, and Minnesota.

What are the soil requirements of the cranberry? Cranberries are grown in acid peat bogs which can be flooded. A level peat bog with a clay subbase is selected. Growth of weeds is killed by flooding for a year. Clear sand is added to a depth of 2 or 3 ins., and cuttings are thrust through this into the peaty soil beneath, 12 to 18 ins. apart. They fruit in about 3 years. Bogs are flooded from December to April or May, and at other times to control insects, to prevent frost, and to harvest loose berries. Bogs are fertilized every year or two and are sanded at intervals to prevent too-rapid, tangled growth.

Can cranberries be grown from seeds? Cranberries can be grown from seeds stratified in the fall.

How should Highbush Cranberries be pruned? Highbush Cranberries require very little pruning. The method is to cut out, close to the ground, the oldest canes. This will permit the growth of renewal shoots from the base of the plant. Pruning is done in winter.

CURRANT AND GOOSEBERRY

Are currants and gooseberries particular as to soil? They may be grown successfully on the average good garden soil that will grow good vegetables and flowers.

How should currants and gooseberries be fertilized? Ammonium nitrate at the rate of about 4 ounces per plant, or nitrate of soda at 8 ounces per plant is most likely to be profitable. On light soils sulfate of potash at about 3 to 4 ounces per plant may be useful, but it will not be needed every year. Manure is an excellent fertilizer for these fruits. A hay or straw mulch is also good and may substitute for part of the fertilizer.

Where should bush fruits be planted? They are somewhat tolerant of shade and may be planted on the north side of buildings or fences and between young fruit trees and grape vines if space is limited. However, there may be spray residues on the currant and gooseberry fruits from sprays used on the trees.

When should currant and gooseberry bushes be planted? These plants start growth very early in the spring, so they should either be set in the fall or by the latter part of March.

How far apart are currants and gooseberries planted? In the garden 4 to 5 feet in the row and 5 to 6 feet between rows.

May gooseberries and currants be planted near pine trees? In regions where white-pine blister rust is serious, and White Pines are important, the planting of gooseberries and currants may be forbidden. (See also same question under Raspberries, this section.)

How many currant and gooseberry bushes should be planted per person in the home garden? Currants—2 plants. Gooseberries—2 plants.

What care do currants need? Annual pruning, fertilization and cultivation or mulching to control weeds. A dormant spray to destroy aphid eggs and summer sprays if the need arises.

Do red currants need to be cultivated? Currant bushes sometimes struggle along in sod and produce some fruit, but they will do much better if weeds and grass are suppressed by cultivation or mulching.

Should I purchase bearing-size currant bushes? Good 1- or 2-year plants are much superior to bearing-age transplants. They are cheaper and more likely to survive.

How often should currants and gooseberries be picked? For jelly currants are all picked at once, as soon as ripe, but for dessert they may be picked as needed for 3 or 4 weeks as they remain in good condition for sometime. Gooseberries may be picked when half grown to make green gooseberry pie or sauce, delicious dishes known to very few. This early picking of part of the crop amounts to a thinning which makes the late berries much larger. Gooseberries are sometimes scalded by unusually hot weather (90° F. and above) so should be harvested promptly.

I planted 6 gooseberry bushes 3 years ago; gave each plant lots of space, but never a blossom or berry on them. What is wrong? Most gooseberry varieties should bear by the time the plants are 3 years old. Do not overfertilize, and if the plants don't bloom next spring send a branch to your Experiment Station. Some kind of pest might be causing the trouble. It is possible the nursery made a mistake and sent some ornamental shrubs instead of gooseberry bushes.

My gooseberry bushes are about 5 years old and produce hardly any fruit, despite good attention. What could be wrong? Most gooseberry varieties should be in full production at 5 years of age. Possibly you are "killing them with kindness." It would be possible by heavy pruning plus heavy fertilization to keep them in an excessively vegetative and unproductive condition. If you have been doing that, try no pruning and no fertilizers for 2 years.

Can gooseberries be successfully handled by a small gardener? Gooseberries are easy to grow and have few pests. The plants are very compact, so that the few needed by an average family will not require much room.

Why are gooseberry bushes not grown more in Massachusetts? Currants and gooseberries are alternate hosts for white-pine blister rust, a serious disease in New England as well as other parts of the country. Various state and federal laws provide for eradication of these plants in certain areas, and in Massachusetts state authorities have the right to remove them when deemed necessary, thus aiding in the control of this disease.

At what time of year should currant bushes be pruned? Late fall, winter, or very early spring. Since so many things have to be done in the spring, autumn is the most practical time.

What is the best method of pruning red currant bushes? Remove canes 4 years old or older; low-growing canes that droop to the ground when heavy with fruit; broken or diseased canes; the weaker 1-year shoots. After pruning, an ideal bush might consist of about 5 1-year shoots, 4 2-year canes, 3 3-year canes, and possibly 2 or 3 4-year canes, if they are vigorous.

Do red currant bushes that have borne heavily for 3 years have to be trimmed? They don't seem to have any dead wood. When the canes get to be about 4 years old they usually weaken and become unproductive. Such canes should be taken out, down to the ground, before they actually die.

Do gooseberry bushes need pruning? They may continue to produce for a long time without pruning, but the bushes will be more vigorous and the fruit larger if they are pruned.

When should gooseberries be pruned? At any time during the dormant season; that is, after the leaves fall and before growth starts in the spring.

How does one prune gooseberry bushes? Remove dead or broken canes, then those branches that are borne around lower part of bush, low enough to touch ground when loaded with fruit. Canes more than 4 years old usually are too weak to be productive, so they should be cut out. This will usually be all the pruning needed, although it may be desirable to remove a few twigs here and there to shape up the bush, or open up a crowded part of it.

Are currants raised from cuttings? That is the usual method—hardwood cuttings taken in late winter. Cuttings are made of 1-year canes, and are usually 6 to 8 ins. long. Currants can also be propagated by layers; that is, low-growing branches covered with soil except for the tips. After roots have formed, cut branch from plant and set where desired.

Will gooseberry bushes root from cuttings? Hardwood cuttings are usually used, but they will also root from half-ripe cuttings in summer. They are easily layered: often branches resting on the ground will root. (See Section II.)

What causes currants to have distorted, crinkly leaves? Aphids feeding on the leaves cause them to become distorted. These are best controlled by spraying the bushes in early spring before growth starts with a dinitro compound such as Elgetol, Dinitrosol, or Krenite. This is used at the rate of 1½ quarts in 100 gallons of water. If this is not used spray the bushes at the first sign of leaf distortion with nicotine sulfate, being sure to hit the underside of the leaves.

We have found our currant bushes stripped entirely bare of leaves. What causes this? This is undoubtedly the work of the imported currant worm, which usually works in large numbers and can strip a bush in a very few days. Watch your bushes carefully in early summer, and when the greenish worms appear dust with rotenone. Pyrethrum sprays or dusts are also effective. Bordeaux sprays used for disease control may kill many of the worms. Follow directions on the package.

Do early browning and dropping of leaves from currant bushes mean the bushes have died? Or will they come out again next spring? The leaf-spot disease and injury by the currant aphis may make leaves turn brown and drop prematurely. If the twigs are still plump and the bark, when scraped, is bright green, you can expect the leaves to come out again next spring. However, premature defoliation weakens the plants so that they are less productive next year.

We have been told that currant and gooseberry bushes and pines do not mix. Must one or the other necessarily be host of attacking disease? Currants and gooseberries are the winter host for the white-pine blister rust, which attacks only those species of pines that have 5 needles in a bundle. The disease is limited in areas, and where not present, the fruits may be grown. Black currant is the worst, gooseberry next, and the red currant is permitted except in seriously infested areas. State laws should be consulted.

What varieties of currants are recommended for the home garden? Try Red Lake, one of the newer varieties.

What is a good gooseberry variety? (Pennsylvania.) Poorman is a good red-fruited variety. Chautauqua is very large fruited and yellowish green when ripe.

ELDERBERRY

Is the Adams Elderberry worth planting for fruit for pies and canning? Yes. Elderberries are ornamental, and many people like the blossoms for wine and the fruits for pies and jelly. They are of easy culture, growing almost anywhere. Some elders, including Adams, need cross-pollination so more than one clone, or type, should be planted. Can be used as a hedge.

Does the Adams Elderberry spread and become a nuisance? All elderberries spread by means of suckers from the roots. With watchful care these can be eliminated. Adams is not so aggressive as the wild types.

JUNEBERRY

Is the juneberry worth planting? The dwarf juneberry or serviceberry (*Amelanchier canadensis*) bears heavy crops of bluish black fruits about the size of wild blueberries. The flavor is insipid, but if they are cooked with lemon juice they make fair pies. The bushes grow 3 to 4 feet in height, are covered with white flowers in early spring and are very hardy, which makes them useful in the cold Great Plains region. Birds are very fond of the berries.

CHINESE JUJUBE (OR DATE)

What is the Chinese Date fruit like? How old are the trees before they fruit? (Kentucky.) Fruit of the Chinese Date, more commonly called the Chinese Jujube, is a drupe (stone fruit) oblong up to 2 ins. long with a sweet, whitish flesh of applelike flavor. The trees bear early, second or third year, where growing conditions are favorable. (See United States Department of Agriculture *Bulletin 1215,* "The Chinese Jujube.")

MISCELLANEOUS FRUITS

FIGS

What is the best fertilizer for a fig tree in acid soil? One of the best fertilizers is well-rotted manure. A good garden fertilizer, such as 5–10–5, used at the rate of 1 lb. per 50 sq. ft., will probably supply sufficient nutrients.

What is the best time to prune a fig tree growing in a tub? If it's in a forcing house, at any season when it is not maturing fruits. If out of doors, prune in early spring.

How are fig trees pruned? (Maryland.) Figs require very little pruning. Most of this is done in training the tree while it is young. It is especially desirable in regions where winter injury is probable and the trees must be protected. If trained to 3 or 4 branches, low, it is easy to lay these down and cover them with soil, mounding up over the center point, for protection from cold.

How can one keep a fig tree from freezing in the winter? (New

York.) Many methods are used, depending upon the protection afforded by buildings. One way is to tie up the branches and wrap them with several layers of burlap. Or heavy waterproof paper may be used. Surest way is to train the plant so it branches close to the ground. These branches may then be pressed to the ground, fastened, and covered with a foot or more of soil, with soil mounded over the central point.

Should fig tree on Long Island, on side of house, be covered for winter? Fig trees will need good winter protection on Long Island. (See previous questions.)

What is method of propagating fig tree by layering? (Pennsylvania.) Bend a branch over in the early spring until a portion that is 2 years old may be fastened down and covered with soil. A notch in the underside of the covered portion, held open by a sliver of stone, may help. Keep this covering of soil moist. Roots should form by the middle of summer, when the new plant may be detached and planted.

In what parts of the country will figs bear successfully for the home garden? In the southeastern Atlantic and Gulf states, in parts of California, much of Arizona, and New Mexico. In Northern states figs need winter protection, and usually bear little fruit.

What is treatment for fig trees under glass? The soil should be a good compost, and it is advisable to keep this mulched with well-rotted manure. Early temperature, 50° F. night, 65° F. day. Later increased to 65° F. night and 70° F. day. Figs must have plenty of air and moisture until the fruit is set.

Have a fig tree, which is covered every winter, but only few of the figs ripen before frost. Is there any way of forcing them to ripen earlier? (Ohio.) The variety factor enters here. Some varieties, such as Brown Turkey, mature fruits earlier than others.

How may I learn the variety of fig trees I have? (California.) Your State Agricultural College could probably identify the variety.

MULBERRIES

What are the chief uses of the mulberry? The fruit is good to eat, although somewhat insipid. The trees grow fast and bear large quantities of fruit ripening over several weeks, which makes it a fine tree to attract birds. Since the fruit is messy the mulberry should not be planted near the house, or a sidewalk.

Are mulberries easy trees to grow? Yes, they like almost any soil, and thrive under varying conditions.

How many kinds of mulberries are there in cultivation? Probably not more than 5 to 10 species although about 100 have been described. Two species, *Morus rubra* (Red Mulberry) and *M. celtidifolia* or *M. microphylea* (Texas Mulberry), are native to the United States. There are, of course, numerous varieties mostly belonging to *M. alba* (White Mulberry). This is the species used in feeding silkworms.

Did the so-called Russian mulberry actually come from Russia, or is it just a name?   Yes, it really came from Russia. It was brought to the Western states by Russian Mennonites in 1875 to 1877.

Is it true that there are male and female mulberry trees? Must you have both to have berries? Also is there a difference in the foliage?   Yes, the sexes are separate, but there is little difference in the foliage. Both should be present to insure fruiting.

We have 2 mulberry trees planted about 30 ft. apart. They are over 15 years old. Why are they full of blossoms every spring but never set fruit?   Mulberries are often dioecious, that is, staminate (male) and pistillate (female) flowers on separate trees, though generally both sexes are borne on the same tree. The failure to set fruit is undoubtedly due to lack of pollination. Both your trees may either have all flowers of one sex, or the male and female flowers do not mature at the same time. If you cannot judge, cut a small branch of each tree just before the flowers open and submit them to a botanist for examination.

How can a mulberry tree which has sprouted from the bottom (top dead) be cultivated to grow right? It is about 2 years old.   Cut off all but the strongest sprout. If the stub of the original stem remains, cut this (with a sloping cut) close to the shoot which was selected to carry on.

What are best varieties of mulberry for fruit production?   Mulberry varieties true to name are hard to get. New American and Downing are good sorts.

PERSIMMONS

Are persimmons reliably hardy?   The native American persimmon, *Diospyros virginiana* is native from Connecticut to the Gulf of Mexico. Selected varieties are hardy at Geneva, N.Y. and some mature early enough to ripen fruits nearly every year.

Is the native persimmon worth growing for its fruit?   Most of the wild trees produce fruits that are small and very astringent. However, there are a number of selected varieties that produce large, sweet persimmons that are well worth growing. Garrettson, Early Golden and Josephine are some that are available from nurseries.

Do persimmons need frost to make the fruit edible?   Frost does not hasten the ripening of the persimmon or make it edible. On the contrary, a hard frost before the persimmons are ripe will spoil them. After they are ripe the frost will not spoil the fruit. Probably many persimmons ripen about the time of the first frost, hence the idea that frost is needed to ripen them.

Is the persimmon tree fussy about soil?   No, they often grow on very poor soils. In the south on abandoned eroded farm land, the persimmon is one of the first plants to come in. They respond to good soils and care, however.

How should a persimmon tree be transplanted?   With a burlapped ball of earth, even if the tree is of small size; in early spring.

How should persimmons be cared for in order to insure fruits? Very little care is needed. Reduce competition from competing trees, shrubs, grass and weeds. Be sure that a male tree is nearby to pollinate the flowers, or there will be no fruit.

Are persimmon trees staminate and pistillate varieties?   Persimmons are usually dioecious; that is, staminate and pistillate flowers on different trees. Some pistillate trees produce parthenocarpic (seedless fruits) without having been pollinated.

I have some persimmon seeds. How should I start them?   Plant the seeds about 1 in. deep as soon as they are ripe.

QUINCE

Does the quince make a good home garden fruit?   If it is sprayed thoroughly to control the oriental fruit moth to which it is very susceptible, and if it is not allowed to grow vigorously, thereby making it subject to fire blight, it is a good garden fruit. In the kitchen it can be used to make some very fine dishes, jelly, quince honey, etc.

What soil does the quince require? How are trees planted?   Quince needs somewhat heavy, moist soil. Set 1- or 2-year specimens, in early spring, 8 to 10 ft. apart.

Are the quinces of an ornamental flowering quince bush edible? Or useful for jelly or quince honey?   They can be used in any way the ordinary quince is used. The jelly is not equal to other jellies in flavor. In addition, they may be dried and used among linen for their aroma.

How and when are quince trees pruned?   Pruning should be very light to avoid stimulating vigorous growth that may be attacked by fire blight. Remove dead twigs and those which are growing "out of bounds"—too low, too high, etc. The bush form is probably preferable to the tree form. Prune in early spring.

I wish to cut back a tall quince tree. How many branches should I leave? It is difficult to spray as is.   Remove a few of the tallest branches one year and a few more the next, so as to reduce the height gradually. Too-severe pruning all at once will probably result in an outbreak of fire blight.

How do you graft a quince bush?   It is not necessary to graft quinces, as they can be propagated by cuttings—a much easier method of getting new plants.

NUT TREES

What is the best soil for nut trees? I have an open field. Any well-drained soil that will produce good farm crops is suitable for nut trees. The native walnut especially prefers fertile bottom-land soil, while the Persian (English Walnut) is thought to need limestone soils. Poor, eroded soils are not suitable for nut trees.

What is the general care for nut trees? The principal care required is to eliminate weed competition by cultivation or mulching. If the soil is not fertile, an annual application of nitrate of soda or sulfate of ammonia, at the rate of ¼ lb. for each inch of trunk diameter, should keep the trees growing.

Will the planting of nut trees in a fruit orchard react against either the fruit or nut trees in the presence of each other? Nut trees are too vigorous and grow too large to be grown in the same orchard with fruit trees.

Can nut trees be grown as far North as Brunswick, Maine? Those best suited are the native hazelnuts, the shagbark hickory, and butternuts.

How can nut trees be grafted? Several methods of grafting are used in nut-tree propagation. Splice grafting or whip grafting (see Grafting Section) is used when propagating young Persian Walnuts in nurseries in the West and for young pecans in the South. Scions are grafted onto a 1-year-old seedling understock. In the Persian Walnut the union is waxed but not tied; in the pecan, the union is tied with raffia. Soil that was removed from around the seedlings before grafting is pushed back, and the scions completely covered to a depth of 2 ins. When trees are being top-worked to another variety, the cleft graft method is used. This method, however, has been largely supplanted by that known as bark grafting (See Grafting).

Is there a miniature nut tree? No dwarfing stock for nut trees has as yet been introduced.

What kind of nut trees will grow in the East? (New Jersey.) Black walnuts and Chinese Chestnuts are probably the most satisfactory. Hickories are slow growing, and the hardy varieties of pecans are not especially satisfactory. The growing season is too short and too cool for most pecans north of Washington, D.C. The trees are hardy.

What kinds of nuts can be successfully grown in south Pennsylvania climate? How to get such an orchard started? Is it necessary to purchase trees from nurseries, or can they be grown successfully from nuts? Southern Pennsylvania has suitable soils and climate for all of the common nut trees of the eastern states. Black and Persian walnuts, shagbark hickories, Chinese chestnuts and filberts are the best. The heartnuts and Japanese walnuts grow well, but the nuts are not of high quality. The practicability of commercial nut culture in this region has not been demonstrated, and plantings should be experimental or for pleasure. The named varieties available from nurseries as grafted trees are much superior to seedlings. Seedlings should be used only for reforestation or as food for game.

What are several quick-producing nut trees that can stand cold and strong wind? (New York.)   Filberts will bear nuts in 4 or 5 years, and are about as hardy as peaches. Grafted black walnuts also bear young, but will not produce many nuts until the trees develop sufficient bearing surface, which takes 8 or 10 years.

ALMOND

Can almond trees be grown in this country?   Commercially, only in California. They are almost as hardy as the peach, but because they bloom earlier, they are especially susceptible to damage by late spring frost. Care and culture are the same as for peach.

Will almond come true from seeds? (Oregon.)   No. Named varieties are increased by budding them on to seedling almonds or seedling peaches.

BUTTERNUT

Would you advise the home gardener to plant butternut trees?   Butternut (*Juglans cinerea*) belongs to the walnut family but is hardier than our native black walnut, growing from New Brunswick to Arkansas. It is a good choice for the home garden in the north. The oblong nuts have a rich but delicate flavor, preferred by many to the stronger-flavored black walnut. Trees reach 50 to 75 ft. in height.

CHESTNUT

What kind of soil do chestnuts need?   Well-drained, acid soil, preferably sandy.

Are the blight-resistant Chinese Chestnuts hardy?   Less so than our native chestnut. They may suffer injury in winter in northern United States. Oriental chestnuts have smaller nuts of inferior flavor, but since the native tree has been all but destroyed by blight, the blight-resistant Oriental sorts offer our only opportunity to grow healthy chestnuts today.

Have the Chinese Chestnuts which I see advertised been definitely proven to be blight resistant?   Chinese Chestnuts are generally sufficiently resistant to blight to permit their culture in regions where the blight has destroyed the native American chestnut. Many of the Chinese Chestnuts in the trade are seedlings instead of grafted trees, and exhibit considerable variation in blight resistance. Several named varieties are available from nut tree nurseries. Abundance, Nanking, Kuling and Meiling should be tried.

Where can I get Chinese Chestnuts and the thin-shelled black walnut and pecan? A list of nurseries specializing in named varieties of nut trees may be had from the Northern Nut Growers' Association, Experiment Station, Geneva, New York.

Will any chestnut stand the climate of Montreal, Canada? It is doubtful if any chestnut trees are hardy enough for Montreal.

I have in my garden a chestnut tree severely afflicted with blight. Is there any effective treatment which might be applied to save this tree? If this is an American Chestnut, it is useless to attempt to save it.

We have an American Chestnut tree which bears many false (empty) burs. If a Chinese Chestnut were planted, would it fertilize the American? This tree has died down several times, but sent up a few shoots, which would live about 3 years and then die. No treatments will save the American Chestnut. It will send up shoots for many years, but these will die as they become infected with blight. Planting another tree alongside this one would have no effect whatever on it.

FILBERT (HAZELNUT)

Will filberts grow in this country? What are the best varieties? The European filbert is grown commercially in Oregon and Washington. Barcelona, DuChilly and Daviana are good varieties for that area. In the northeastern states near the Great Lakes where peaches are hardy filberts may be expected to grow well. They will grow as far south as southern Pennsylvania at least. At Geneva, N.Y. Italian Red, Cosford and Medium Long are the best varieties. Hybrids between the native American hazel and the European filbert grow well in the north. Potomac, Reed, Bixby and Buchanan are named hybrids that should be tried.

Where should filberts be planted? Any good well-drained soil is suitable. A north slope or the north side of buildings and a site protected from cold winds is desirable.

Should filbert (hazelnut) trees be trimmed to tree shape, or allowed to grow as bushes? They may be grown either as trees or bushes; the former is thought to be more productive.

How should filberts be pruned? Prune them like peaches only not as severely. Severe pruning may result in winter injury. A moderate thinning is sufficient.

HICKORY

Are hickories worth growing? The shagbark hickory nut is of very fine flavor being excelled only by the best pecans. Wilcox,

Fox and a few others are being propagated by nut nurseries are well worth growing and they are much superior to seedling hickories. Hickory trees are difficult to transplant and establish because of the long taproot.

Where should one report good nut trees, when found, that they may be preserved? Such, for instance, as hickory or black walnut? Northern Nut Growers' Association, Experiment Station, Geneva, New York.

MACADAMIA

What is the macadamia nut? This is an edible nut of a species of Australian tree (*Macadamia ternifolia*). It is commonly called the Queensland Nut.

Is the macadamia nut tree grown in this country? Yes, these nut trees are cultivated in California and in parts of Florida. They thrive in rich, loamy soil with plenty of moisture, although they have been reported as growing in dry sections as well. The tree is an evergreen, and is ornamental as well as useful.

PECAN

Are pecans successfully grown in the North? Pecan trees are hardy in the North, but the growing season is too short and too cool to mature the nuts. Several Northern Pecans, as they are called, will mature nuts as far north as Washington, D.C. and the Ohio river valley. The nuts are good, but are not as large as the southern varieties. Some of them are Butterick, Busseron, Major, Green River and Chief.

Of several small pecan trees planted, all have died but one. Is there some special way to dig holes or set them out to make them live and grow well? (Georgia.) Vigorous pecan trees that have been carefully dug and not allowed to dry out should not be difficult to establish. Set the trees in the fall; firm the soil tightly against the roots; keep down weeds; and water and mulch the trees when drought threatens during the first year or two.

What should be done for pecan trees when the nuts do not fill properly? They hull themselves as they should, but do not fill out. (Virginia.) Try fertilizing the trees with a complete fertilizer at the rate of ¼ lb. for each inch of trunk diameter. The 6–8–4 formula is suggested, and the rate of application is 40 lbs. to a 10- or 12-year-old tree, or 600 to 800 lbs. per acre.

How old does a soft-shell pecan tree have to be before bearing nuts? Do you know of a nursery that has these trees for sale? A list of nurseries supplying pecan trees may be had from the Northern Nut Growers' Association, Geneva, New York. Age of bearing depends on the variety of tree, but not many nuts will be had until the trees are 6 to 8 years of age.

How should pecans be grafted? (Alabama.) Varieties of pecan are propagated almost entirely upon seedling stocks of pecan species. Stocks of certain varieties are said to have some influence upon the growth of the grafted tree. Various pecan stocks are used in Texas. In Louisiana some use is made of the water hickory as a stock. Study local conditions as to stock used. (For grafting process see Section II.)

PISTACHE

In what part of the country can the pistachio nut tree be grown? Only in California and Mexico. It needs a climate like that required by olive trees.

BLACK WALNUT

Is the black walnut a good tree for the home garden? If you live where winter temperatures do not drop too low and want a handsome specimen tree which will produce nuts, the black walnut is a good choice. The tree requires lots of room, and many plants will not grow within reach of its roots as these produce a substance toxic to these plants. Grass will grow all right under a black walnut. Though individual specimens live for years in New York State and similar sections, black walnuts are not considered reliably hardy where winter temperatures drop below 20° F. Butternut (which see) is hardier.

What special requirements has the black walnut? Wild specimens are often found growing in dry, rocky upland pastures as well as in woodland. To produce nuts, this tree needs good soil, well drained, with regular supplies of moisture. A wild tree, in a dry, unfertile location, if subjected for a few years to fertilization and sufficient moisture, will increase its yield tremendously. If caterpillars defoliate the tree they should be destroyed. They gather in clusters on the trunk at night at which time they may be destroyed by rubbing out the colony with a broom. Spraying the foliage with DDT or arsenate of lead is also effective.

What are the dirty-white worms all through the outer shells of my black walnuts? What can I do to get rid of them? (New York.) These are the maggots of the walnut-husk fly, distributed throughout the East to the Kansas-Nebraska line, on black walnuts and butternuts. A closely related species attacks the central and western black and English Walnuts. Flies, a little smaller than house flies, with transparent, black-banded wings, lay their eggs in the husks in August. The maggots tunnel through the husk for several weeks, drop to ground before or with nuts, and pupate several inches down in soil. They emerge as flies the next summer, or wait until second or third summer. They do little injury to kernels, but they stain surface of nut. Trees may be sprayed with cryolite in July. Drop infested nuts in water to drown the worms.

How can I grow native walnut seedlings from walnuts? So far have had no luck. (Missouri.) Plant seeds in the fall about 2 ins. deep. If squirrels are troublesome, store nuts in a box of moist sand outdoors and cover with wire netting to keep out rodents. Plant nuts in the spring.

PERSIAN (ENGLISH) WALNUT

Is the Persian walnut hardy in the Eastern states? Many seedling trees have been grown for years in the fruit growing regions of the Great Lakes, but occasionally a severe winter that injures peach trees may kill or seriously injure many of these trees. The winters of 1933–34 and 1956–57 were particularly damaging to Persian walnuts in New York. Several superior varieties, supposedly of greater than average hardiness, are now being propagated by nut tree nurseries. Among them are Metcalfe, McKinster, Broadview and Littlepage.

What are the soil and cultural requirements of the English Walnut? Good, deep loam, well drained but with plenty of moisture to produce large crops of nuts. Where peaches are hardy in the North, the walnuts are worth trying. Farther south many of them start growth too early and are injured by frost.

Are Persian Walnut trees harmful near shrubs? The Persian (English) Walnut is not considered to be harmful to shrubs, but of course it will compete with them for plant food and moisture.

I have a Persian Walnut tree 14 years old. Never bore until last 2 years. All nuts fell off both years when they were quite small, but nuts inside were formed. Why does this happen? The nuts may not have been pollinated. If no other Persian Walnut is near this tree, another should be planted to provide pollination.

What can I do to have more walnut nuts mature? The tree sets plenty of fruit, but nearly all drop off when they reach the size of large cherries. Lack of cross-pollination may be the cause of the trouble. Another variety of the same species should be set near by. The tree may need fertilizing to increase its vigor. Nitrate of soda or sulfate of ammonia at the rate of ¼ lb. for each inch of trunk diameter may be tried.

Is the Persian Walnut self-pollinating? Persian (English) Walnuts usually require cross-pollination by another variety, since its own pollen often is not shed at the time when the pistils are receptive.

Must 2 (male and female) Persian Walnut trees be planted side by side? No hard and fast variety recommendations can be made as there is very little definite information on which to base recommendations. The following are considered among the best and worth trying for home use: Metcalfe, McKinster, Broadview, Littlepage and a few others being propagated by nut tree nurseries.

How are Persian Walnuts washed and dried to be stored for the winter? Remove the husks promptly and wash the nuts immediately. Lay the nuts out one layer deep in an airy room until they are thoroughly dried. Keep them in a cool, dry place.

We have a Persian Walnut tree. Is there some way to treat the nuts to prevent mold while drying and to keep nut meats white? The nuts should not mold if they are husked promptly, washed, and thoroughly dried in an airy place.

Do you know a good soft-shelled walnut—better than Manchurian —that will stand 10° or 20° below zero if need be? Usually 10° above. (Washington.) The Broadview variety of the Persian Walnut, and the Carpathian strain of the same species are thought to be somewhat hardier than the usual varieties and may be worth trying.

What variety of Persion Walnut will thrive in the vicinity of New York? The Carpathian Walnut is the hardiest of these, and is the one to grow.

JAPANESE WALNUT

Can you give some information about a Japanese Walnut? The Japanese Walnut is a rapid-growing, very handsome tree. The nut is elongated, smooth, cracks poorly, and is inferior in quality to other walnuts. The Heartnut, a supposed sport of the Japanese Walnut, is much superior in cracking quality.

SECTION VII

House Plants

INTRODUCTION

BY HELEN VAN PELT WILSON

AND ESTHER C. GRAYSON

THE ATTRACTIVENESS of plants indoors depends first of all on their health, and then upon how they are grouped or arranged. To be satisfactory, potted plants should be green and flourishing and, in the case of flowering types, in bloom for as long a period as possible. To attain these ends, the selection of varieties tolerant of special unalterable conditions of light, heat, and humidity is most important. Only after this problem has been solved comes the artistic arrangement of plants at windows, so that as a group they may present an effective, arresting, even a changing and colorful picture as the autumn weeks give way to winter, and winter passes into the life-stirring months of early spring.

Although plants suitable for indoor culture have to a degree different requirements, there are certain basic needs shared by them all. There are conditions of light, heat and humidity, moisture, food, and rest, which are common to all. The window-garden enthusiast, therefore, keeps these basic factors in mind, while yet interpreting them for each plant as observation reveals its special and individual nature. Sometimes contradictions develop. Thus the general practice is to pot flowering plants "closely" (that is, in pots that keep their roots restricted), since a little root cramping tends to promote bloom. The African-violet, if crowded, however, fails entirely to keep in blossom. Another idiosyncrasy of some plants is a great need for water. Thus "do not let standing water remain in the plant saucer" is another general rule contradicted by the calla, and cyclamen. These appear at their best when there is a constant inch of water always at their disposal in a pebble-filled saucer under the pot.

So it happens that the gardener often learns but to unlearn; and the printed word becomes but a guide which only the actualities of experience can make valuable.

Light

All plants require a fully light location. Fresh-from-the-greenhouse specimens hung on a bracket in a dark hall or set at the mantel ends of a dim living room are destined, no matter what their original condition, for a short life—and not a very merry one. Light permits the plant organism to work effectively in transferring certain substances into usable foods. There are, of course, a number of excellent foliage plants which need no direct sun. The wax begonia and the patience plant will bloom to some extent in a fully light location, without direct sunshine, but for most flowering plants sunshine is required—not an occasional hour or so, but every bit a southern or eastern window can afford. Without a maximum of sunshine, the geranium will fail to bud, while the gardenia and cactus will tend to enduring green.

Temperature

Most house plants flourish at a temperature much cooler than that of the modern home with its efficient central heat and consequent low humidity. Grown at 60° to 65° F., almost every house plant is better off than at 70° or 75° F., while a night drop to 55° F., similar to nature's outdoor falling of temperature after sunset, is a further cultural benefit. Many of the most decorative plants can be grown in a really cool house window where the average is 50° to 60° F. For this reason a sunporch makes an ideal location for indoor gardening, since temperatures are usually lower there than in the house itself.

On record, for example, is one where night temperatures dropped to 35° and 40° F., and where only a small amount of electric radiation supplemented the effects of the sun during the day. Here begonias and geraniums bloomed incessantly. The cyclamen, with never a yellow leaf, opened bud after bud for a full 3 months. Primroses and Paperwhite Narcissi kept fresh for extra weeks, while ivies, waxplants, *Asparagus sprengeri,* many ferns (even maidenhairs), and strawberry-begonias, maintained marvelous health. Of course these plants were all set back somewhat from the glass and, if outdoor temperatures threatened to go below 20° F., they were covered at night with newspapers.

When plants develop weak, soft, spindly growth, foliage color is light, and buds blast or fall prematurely, it is very often because they are suffering from too warm an atmosphere.

Humidity

The greatest foe to successful indoor gardening, however, is lack of humidity. Outdoors the air is moist. Inside, with modern heating devices what they are, it is usually much too dry. This results in parched foliage, especially on English Ivy, even when the owner has never neglected moistening the soil.

Now how can humidity be increased? Various makeshifts are helpful when no real humidifying devices exist. If one has a hot-air central-heating system, a bucket or pan of water may be suspended under the register, and kept filled with a long-necked watering can. Supplying the window garden with a galvanized-iron or zinc tray fitted to the sill and filled with pebbles is probably the most effective means of increasing humidity. Where it is possible, the plants are set in the tray on top of a 1- or 2-in. layer of little stones. Excess water from the pots runs through to these, and more is added as needed. This serves as a source of evaporation for constantly moistening the air circulating about the plants.

An occasional cleansing of the foliage with a forceful stream from the hose is important in keeping house plants in good condition and free from insect pests.

Keeping deep bowls of water on the radiators is also a good plan; or extra-large, pebble-filled saucers or water-holding fiber mats may be set under each plant. Furthermore, humidity as well as cleanliness is increased if plants are frequently sprayed from a bulb syringe, or set under shower or faucet. Usually this can be managed only weekly, while a light syringing may be a daily matter. But again there must be interpretation according to individuals. The hairy-leaved African-violet, gloxinia, and Rex Begonia, and the tightly crowned cyclamen or pandanus, are more often harmed than benefited by showering or syringing.

Watering

The question most often asked by house-plant growers is, "How often should I water my house plants?" or, "Is there a rule, so much water for so much soil?"

Only in a very general way can a rule be offered. *When the topsoil feels dry to the touch, then is the time to water.* Then water so thoroughly that the entire root system is saturated and in a little while excess seeps out into the pot saucer. Except in a few cases, it is best immediately to empty this excess from the saucer.

The most important "Beware" in connection with watering applies to the little-and-often method. Pouring water on plants just for the fun of it does them no good. Often it results in a too-wet upper half of soil and a too-dry lower. Especially is this true of thick-rooted plants such as palms; or very large specimens of almost any plant, particularly those of the shrubby type—gardenias, azaleas, and the like. All such are wisely set, about once a week, in a pail filled with water to within an inch of the pot rim. Here they remain until enough moisture has been drawn up to make the surface *feel* moist. Then they are removed in a thoroughly refreshed condition.

Daily attention to every plant in the window garden, with a moderate amount of water applied where needed, is one of the secrets of success with house plants.

Most plants are safely moistened by applying water at the edge of the pot rim. Some with thick crowns, like the cyclamen or birdsnest-fern, are better moistened from below by pouring water into the saucer and letting the plant draw it up according to its need. Saved rainwater is better than faucet water, especially in places where the local supply has been treated with chemicals, the residue from which often collects on the soil and discolors the containers. Room-temperature water also is better than cold, which may have a retarding effect on growth. Most plants, however, are fairly tolerant, and, given *regular* care, will not be too fussy about the type of water supplied, only the amount. Actually, most amateurs tend to overwater rather than to neglect. Experience reveals which plants, like the gardenia or cyclamen, want a "just-moist" soil at all times; while others, notably the jadeplant, many of the cacti, the sansevieria, and geranium, thrive only when allowed to become quite dry between drinks.

In addition to the drinking habits of the plant itself, other factors influencing the amount of water required are: the size of pot (little ones dry out faster); the type of pot (glazed ones permit less evaporation); the stage of plant growth, whether active or resting; and the temperature of the room. The weather is also a factor: on sunny days more water is required than during dull ones. All these conditions are to be taken into consideration. Complicated as all this may sound, however, it soon becomes second nature to water the tiny poinsettia twice a day and the big jadeplant but once in 10 days, when the *feel* of the soil is made the actual guide.

Ventilation

A close atmosphere is very hard on house plants. Even when the weather is definitely cold, they require some fresh air. The best plan then is to admit fresh air indirectly through a window or door in an adjoining room, or through a canvas ventilator in the same room, but not directly beside the plants. It is most important to provide an abundance of fresh air for several weeks after plants are brought in in autumn; and again in spring, as the midday hours become increasingly warm.

Where manufactured gas is used for heating and cooking, plenty of fresh air is especially necessary; but even this will not counteract the effects of escaping gas, the fumes of which spell ultimate death to most plants. Some of them are extremely allergic to gas. The Jerusalem-cherry, for instance, is one of these. First they drop all their fruit, then the leaves shrivel, and finally the plant dies. Such plants as the aspidistra, sansevieria, and Bostonfern will prove more tolerant, especially where there is good daily ventilation.

Air is essential to the roots as well as to the tops of plants. A constant loose condition of the surface soil, and hence aeration of the roots, is readily obtained by a weekly stirring with a discarded kitchen fork.

Pruning and Training

Plants are kept shapely by being turned frequently so that all sides receive an equal amount of light, and by the cutting back of overlong growth which tends to make ungainly specimens. Sometimes, too, a drastic pruning back is necessary to promote health. Thus in autumn the summer geraniums are cut back to stubs 3 to 6 ins. long, while the dormant poinsettia in spring is started all over again by hard pruning.

Fertilizing

Extra fertilizer is not nearly so important as good texture and structure of soil and proper potting. Sickly plants especially are more likely to be suffering from too much heat and water, or from some insect pest, than from starvation. Usually a plant from the florist requires no extra nutrients for a month or more. If a plant is at a standstill when, by all the rules of its own nature and the time of year, it should be growing, or when its buds are not maturing, or its foliage color is poor—although a proper system of culture is maintained—then extra feeding definitely is to be considered. Generally speaking, flowering plants require more nutrients than foliage ones, at least up to the time the buds show color. For slow-growing plants occasional light top dustings of complete fertilizer are good. Plant tablets, or one of the "complete" fertilizers especially prepared for house plants, are excellent, provided directions are carefully followed and it is not assumed that because a little is good for a plant a lot will be better. Nor should a resting plant be "pushed" with a quick-acting fertilizer when the need is for quiet and not for action. Thus the summer-weary geranium or waxplant in fall requires not fertilizer, but coolness and time to resuscitate itself.

Certain items are *not* suitable fertilizers—notably tea, coffee, cigar ashes, and castor oil.

Repotting

When a plant has actually outgrown its living quarters (when, after the pot is removed, a fine web of roots is seen on the outside of the earth ball), that plant needs another container, but probably one only a size larger. Usually established plants need shifting but once a year; some but once in 2 years. Often wornout soil can be carefully washed from the roots, and the plant then repotted in the same size pot.

Repotting is not a panacea. A too-large pot with unneeded amounts of soil and moisture more often kills an ailing plant than cures it. The best general policy is to keep plants in as small pots as possible. Over-large antique specimens of plants, dear as they may be sentimentally, are rarely, when dispassionately viewed, very attractive in themselves or as part of the general window-garden arrangement. Institutional-size plants do not belong in people's houses, nor do sickly plants which, outside a greenhouse, will be unlikely to regain health under the trying conditions of our houses in winter.

The best time for repotting is in spring; then the resulting shock is offset by months of ideal outdoor life. In May, when the weather is settled, a practical plan is to take all the plants outdoors, discard some, divide others (repotting the divisions into *smaller* pots), and then shift the remainder into larger pots.

Arranged in a row, small to large, with a few pots on hand larger than any already in use, plants are easily repotted—the largest plants going into the new pots (which have first been soaked in a pail of water for 24 hours), and the others, successively, to the outgrown pots, which are thoroughly scrubbed out before receiving new occupants.

Plants are readily depotted for examination or repotting if they are first watered and then inverted on the gardener's left hand, with the main stem placed between the index and middle fingers. The pot rim is then knocked sharply against table or step. So loosened, the pot is lifted off by the right hand, and the root condition examined.

When needed, a larger pot is fitted with an arching piece of broken flower pot above the drainage hole and, if it is above a 3-in. size, a few more pieces of broken crock over this. In very large pots a handful of gravel or small cinders or pebbles is placed above the "crocking." (When pots have no drainage hole, a drainage layer of some of this coarse material is especially necessary in the bottom; also a bit of charcoal to insure sweetness.)

When the drainage layer is in place, a sifting of soil is added. Then the plant is centered in the pot, and extra soil firmly pressed around it with a potting stick—a piece of lath or an old ruler. The soil is kept ½ in. or so below the rim of the pot, this space being needed to receive water.

Potting Soil

Although there are almost as many soil formulas as there are types of house plants, it is a matter of experience that plants try to accustom themselves to any soil which is of proper texture or friability, and well drained. A generally good formula (which may be altered in its proportions according to type of plant to be grown) consists of 2 parts loam from vegetable or flower garden and 1 part well-rotted cow manure, leafmold, commercial humus, or peatmoss, with enough sand to make the mixture porous. Unless cow manure is used, add 2 qts. commercial cow manure to each bushel. For further enrichment, a 4-in. pot of complete fertilizer or bone meal to a wheelbarrowload of soil, or 1 teaspoonful to an 8-in. pot of soil.

The loam contains nutrients, sand facilitates drainage and aeration of roots, while the other elements increase the water-holding capacity and thus prevent too-rapid evaporation of moisture and caking of soil. Humus also helps to produce a light, mellow mixture which roots can easily penetrate. To these essentials may be added, when convenient, a little charcoal to sweeten the soil (especially in pots lacking a drainage hole), and tobacco dust to discourage root aphis. Apartment gardeners can procure ready-made soil mixtures from florists or 10-cent stores.

If the plants have heavy roots—such as those of pandanus, sansevieria, or palm, also the geranium—less sand and more loam is used, because such roots have force enough to penetrate a firm mixture, and the plants prefer it. The fibrous-rooted ferns, begonias, and fuchsias thrive in a lighter medium—about ½ leafmold or peatmoss, ½ loam, and plenty of sand.

Acid-loving plants—the blue hydrangeas, camellias, heaths, and azaleas—require equal parts of soil and *acid* peat or hardwood leafmold, while bone meal is omitted.

Summer Quarters

Summer is the ideal time for all plants with real *future* possibilities to be resuscitated after the trying months indoors. Summer quarters may be established on porches, in window boxes, or in garden beds. (Even a cool, light window indoors will do, if plenty of fresh air is afforded.) Wherever placed, the plants are out of the way of strong winds, and are grouped to facilitate watering and syringing. Pots are not removed because house plants, freed of their containers, develop in an open garden bed such ranging root systems that autumn repotting becomes almost impossible.

Plunging in a garden bed which offers suitable gradations of light for the varying needs of the sun-loving geraniums and shade-requiring fern is, in general, the most healthful procedure. A location under some open-leaved tree, like an apple or an elm, with branches not too low, is ideal. Nearest to the trunk, where the shade is deepest, go the ferns; below the open branches in light shade are set resting geraniums and heliotrope, vines, foliage plants, and most of the flowering subjects: gardenias, azaleas, fuchsias, and shade-loving begonias; near the edge, but not under the drip, where sun daily penetrates, are placed the young geraniums, semperflorens begonias, and poinsettias.

A bed is dug deep enough to contain the largest pot to be plunged, plus a 3- to 6-in. layer of stones, cinders, or other worm-deterring drainage material. Here the plants are arranged according to their light requirements, and around them is packed light soil containing plenty of water-holding humus, preferably peatmoss. When plunging is completed, pot rims remain slightly above the soil surface. About once a week each plant is turned. This prevents anchoring roots from taking hold through the drainage hole, and also facilitates the development of shapely tops.

House plants cannot be forgotten in summer. Even when plunged, they require, because of their restricted root systems and location under tree branches, more frequent watering than average summer rainfall supplies.

The best procedure is to let a hose with nozzle removed trickle slowly into the bed for a period long enough to moisten it completely to a depth of 6 inches. This will suffice for a week or 10 days even in hot weather. During long, hot, dry spells, an oscillating watering machine or "rain machine" played on the bed through the late afternoon hours will give the plants a lift. The cool night hours to follow should revive them completely.

An ordinary rotary sprinkler should not be used unless it produces a fine spray, for heavy drops falling successively in the same spot or on the same leaf or flower over a long period may do more harm than good.

Some pruning may be required to promote shapely growth, and insect pests must always be watched for. Usually frequent hose syringing deters them but sometimes, as in winter, aphids or mealy bugs must be sprayed with an insecticide.

Lifting Plants in Autumn

Plants are prepared for winter well before frost. It is a good precaution to remove the pot from each specimen and, if necessary, to renew the drainage arrangements. At this season, however, roots are disturbed as little as possible.

Plants are brought inside before the first touch of frost. Many of the best ones, such as the poinsettia, are from the tropics, and hence are easily harmed by cool fall weather. During the first weeks indoors much attention is given to ventilation and syringing. Now more than at other times plants are particularly inclined to resent the dry, close air of the house. Falling leaves and blossoms are signs of unfavorable reaction. A thorough drenching under a faucet will often immediately check leaf dropping. This is also the time for insect pests to attack. A sharp eye should be kept out for these and an all-purpose *house plant* aerosol bomb used if any are discovered.

Rest Period

All plants have growth cycles which include periods of rest. As trees lose their leaves in fall and enter into a dormant period, so do house plants at some time rest in greater or lesser degree. In winter, ferns and palms are less active and produce fewer new leaves than in spring. In early fall many of the cacti remain utterly quiet. After flowering, poinsettias and cyclamens appear on the point of death, when really they are only going to sleep.

All plants which are resting require less water and warmth than when they are in a period of active growth. Many can be left entirely dark and dry. None are fed at this time. The resting condition of plants is not always an easy one to identify, but constant observation of each variety eventually reveals it, and the indoor gardener is accordingly guided in the treatment he gives them.

HOUSE PLANTS

SOIL

Are all house plants potted in the same soil mixture? No, there are variations in soil mixtures for various types of plants. (See following questions.)

What is a good standard potting mixture for house plants? Two parts good garden loam, 1 part leafmold or peatmoss, 1 part sharp sand. For general use add 1 pt. complete fertilizer (or bone meal) and 2 qts. dried cow manure, or well-rotted cow manure, to each bushel of mixture. For plants requiring special soils see following questions.

What mixture of soil is best for azaleas and other acid-loving plants? An *acid mixture*. Add to standard potting mixture (see previous question) 25 per cent in bulk acid (hardwood) leafmold and to each bushel add 2 qts. commercial or well-rotted cow manure and 1 pt. complete fertilizer.

What mixture of soil do I need for ferns grown indoors? A *fibrous mixture*. Add to the standard potting mixture 25 per cent in bulk humus or peatmoss, 2 qts. well-rotted or commercial manure and 1 pt. complete fertilizer.

How shall I sweeten the potting mixture for house plants which need an alkaline soil? Herbs, for instance. Make an *alkaline mixture*. To each bushel of standard mixture add 1 qt. raw ground limestone, 1 pt. bone meal, and 2 qts. well-rotted or commercial cow manure. Make up mixture 2 weeks or more before use to permit limestone to alkalize soil.

What potting soil shall I use for cacti and other succulents? A *sandy mixture*. Add 25 per cent in bulk sharp sand or crushed soft stone (or crushed flower pots) to standard potting mixture (see previous question). Add to each bushel 1 qt. raw ground limestone and 1 pt. complete fertilizer, or bone meal. Make up mixture 2 weeks or more before use. (See Cacti.)

Do tender bulbs, such as amaryllis, tuberous-rooted begonias, etc., need a special potting soil? Yes. Place 1 to 2 ins. of well-rotted cow manure in bottom of pot, and as potting soil use sifted, well-rotted compost. If compost and cow manure are not available, use 1 part garden loam, 1 part peatmoss or leafmold, and add to each bushel 3 qts. commercial cow manure and 1 pt. complete fertilizer.

Which house plants prefer peatmoss in the soil? Please add information concerning its use. All house plants like peatmoss in the soil except those which prefer an alkaline soil. (See previous questions, for information concerning its use.)

What do you think of the prepared potting soils sold by garden shops, Woolworths and other stores? Most of these are well balanced mixtures suitable for African-violets, begonias, ferns, etc.

How shall soil on house plants be prevented from getting solid? Is there danger of cutting rootlets if soil is dug in, to loosen it? Stir the surface frequently. Use soil mixtures recommended in previous questions.

POTTING AND REPOTTING

What size pots are best for winter-blooming plants? Depends on the plant. Good primroses can be grown in 4½- to 5-in. pots. Wax-type begonias the same. Most flowering plants give more bloom if grown in pots just big enough to hold the roots.

Should the soil on a potted plant be changed? If so, how often? See Introduction to this section.

When should house plants be repotted? Varies with kind of plant. Good general rule is to repot at beginning of growing season. Fast-growing plants (as geraniums) may need a second or even third shift during season. Some (as agapanthus) need attention only every few years.

How can I tell when my plants need repotting? When plants are knocked gently from pots (see Introduction) root system shows whether repotting is necessary. If roots have formed a thick, dry web on outside of root ball, repot. If visible roots are few and appear succulent and healthy, repotting is not needed.

When repotting house plants, how much larger should the new pot be? Usually one size larger. In the case of very fast-growing plants, two sizes larger can be used. Gently remove a little of the old soil in order to make room for more fresh potting mixture. (See Introduction.)

What size pots should I use when repotting in spring so my house plants will not have to be repotted again in autumn? Use pot two sizes larger in spring for plants which are to be sunk in garden beds in their pots. Cut back when they are brought into the house in the fall. Fast-growing plants may need fall repotting in spite of this precaution.

How should tender bulbs be potted for indoor bloom? Most of these bulbs, such as amaryllis, callas, and tuberous-rooted begonias, are planted with the top of the bulb exposed.

With some bulbs (such as amaryllis) and other plants in large pots, the soil is renewed, without repotting, by removing as much as possible of the old soil, and then refilling with new soil.

How can I provide good drainage in the pots of my house plants? Place a bit of broken flower pot, convex side up, on the bottom of small pots before potting plants. For medium-sized pots, use several pieces of this "crocking"; for large bulb pans and large pots, cover the entire bottom with broken bits of pot, always being sure the piece which covers the drainage hole is so placed as to allow free ingress and egress of water. In forcing bulbs and other plants which like manure, placing large pieces of well-rotted manure over the crocking before adding soil will help to assure good drainage.

I have a lot of house plants. Is there a suitable paint for covering flower pots to make them colorful? Ordinary paints peel off. Doubtless the Duco type of enamel will last if it is applied when pots are dry. Ordinary house paint is not suitable.

FEEDING

When shall I feed my house plants? See Introduction.

When shall I give fertilizer to flowering house plants? See Introduction.

What fertilizers are best for house plants? In the questions on Soil in this section and in the Introduction, recommendations are made for fertilizing the soil mixtures. In addition to this, complete fertilizers may be given in liquid or tablet form according to package directions, or liquid manure (which see) may be used. (See Culture of Specific Plants.)

Do you think liquid manure is a good fertilizer for house plants? Yes. It gives excellent results. Use it sparingly once a week on plants which prefer a pot-bound condition (amaryllis, pandanus, palms, nerine, etc.) and on flowering plants until blooms show color.

How is liquid manure prepared for use on house plants? Place a bushel of cow manure in a burlap bag and steep it in a tub of water for 3 weeks. For use on plants, dilute to the color of weak tea.

Why does Vigoro kill my begonias? Properly used, Vigoro or other complete fertilizers will not kill begonias or other house plants. Your begonias may have been unthrifty before you applied the fertilizer, or too much may have been given. Vigoro is a reliable complete fertilizer which, if properly used, gives consistently good results.

Several of my house plants look very sick indeed. Shall I give them fertilizer? No. Cut them back; withhold water. Repot if pot-bound. Examine for pests. When new growth begins, a complete fertilizer can be given sparingly, according to directions on package.

What is the proper means of feeding plants that were slipped as house plants to carry over until spring? Plants propagated for carrying over to spring, or old plants cut back and potted for the same purpose, don't need feeding during winter. Keep cool and don't encourage growth. Water no more than is necessary to prevent wilting; much depends upon the kind of plant.

What fertilizer is best for house plants (cacti, ferns, begonias)? Cacti: sandy potting mixture with fertilizer suggested. Ferns: fibrous potting mixture with fertilizer suggested. Begonias: standard potting mixture with fertilizer suggested.

Is black tea of any value to ferns? No.

WATERING

What is a good general rule for watering house plants? Water only when plant *needs* water, not whenever it seems that it may stand watering. Whenever water is supplied, give enough to saturate thoroughly the whole ball of soil. Never merely sprinkle the surface.

How often does one water house plants, namely, ferns, wax begonias, and geraniums? Watering is governed by the temperature and humidity of a room. Keep geraniums on the dry side if not actively growing; begonias and ferns in a room of 60° to 70° F. will need water almost every day. Feeling the soil, judging the weight of the pot, or rapping the pot with the knuckles are other ways of telling when to water. A pot of soil that is wet sounds dead; if dry, it gives an empty ring.

Can you tell me why growing house plants rot or decay from the roots up? This sounds like overwatering. Do not permit the plants to stand with their roots soaking in water. Surplus water should be poured from saucer after each watering, and water given only when surface of soil feels dry.

What can be done to counteract the effect of watering house plants with the hard water we have in this locality? If the hardness of the water is merely due to lime, use an acid fertilizer such as sulfate of ammonia.

Do flowers kept in cellar in winter need much water? If the cellar is poorly lighted and not warm, plants should, as a rule, be kept fairly dry. If they are not actively growing, keep on the dry side.

How can I give enough water to azaleas, hydrangeas, and other house plants which seem to dry out completely? Once a week place potted plant in bucket of water until soil is thoroughly soaked. (See Introduction.)

How can I keep my house plants from having "wet feet"? Place a handful of large pebbles or gravel in the saucer under each pot, or in the tray or on the shelf on which pots are set. If there is surplus water, the pebbles will provide good drainage.

Must all flower pots have drainage? Plants can be grown in pots without drainage and no outlet for surplus water, but they won't thrive for long because of lack of air. During the winter and spring narcissi and some other bulbs can be grown in pebbles in pots without a hole at the bottom.

How should house plants in glazed pots be watered? More sparingly than those in unglazed pots. Though glazed pots hold water longer, they do not provide aeration of the soil. A quart of finely broken bits of charcoal added to each bushel of potting soil helps keep mixture "sweet".

TEMPERATURE

What temperature is best for most house plants? Most flowering house plants are happiest at 55° F. or lower. Cinerarias and calceolarias prefer 45° F. That's why so many people fail with house plants in hot rooms. It also explains why cyclamen, Jerusalem-cherry, decorative peppers, etc., last such a short time after coming from the florist. If your home is kept at 70° F. or above, day and night, grow semitropical foliage plants, cacti and succulents, African-violets, and poinsettias. If a low night temperature can be maintained, many plants preferring a cool temperature will do quite well.

Why do my house plants die within a short time? All except Chinese Evergreen and some ivy, both in water. I tried different soil, plant tablets. I put them in the sun and in the shade with no result. They grow nicely outside in summer but die in the house even in summertime. Probably too high temperature, poor drainage, or too much water. (See previous questions.)

What house plants thrive in a day temperature of 70° F. or more? Poinsettias, African-violets, and other tropicals such as most of the foliage plants; cacti and succulents. Begonias and geraniums if night temperature drops to 60° F.

What house plants, if any, will survive a night temperature of 26° F., day temperature of 50° to 60° F.? No house plant will continue to show green foliage if it must endure a night temperature below freezing. Only hardy perennials will stand this (lavender, thyme, dianthus, viola, etc.). You might have a few very dwarf or seedling evergreens, either coniferous or broad-leafed, and English Ivy for a bit of green through the winter.

What plants can be grown in unheated sun porch? I am trying geraniums, sweet marjoram, parsley, sage, winter savory, and ivies. Your suggestions will be appreciated. (New Jersey.) Such a porch in winter is hopeless, as in severe weather everything will freeze solid. Even the hardiest of plants will give up when in pots and exposed to fluctuating temperatures day and night.

Will house plants survive in a home with a modern heating system? They may survive or even do well if the temperature is kept below 70° F. in the daytime, below 60° F. at night. But if high temperatures are the rule, house plants are apt to develop many difficulties such as falling leaves and buds, pests and diseases, and general unthriftiness. Tropicals such as African-violets, poinsettias, semi-tropical foliage plants, etc., are exceptions to the rule.

Why do house plants do best in country farmhouses? Because the temperature is low, especially at night, and the humidity high, due to lack of central heating. The steaming kettle on the farm kitchen range is a first-class humidifier.

Is a very cool sun porch suitable for house plants in winter? If the night temperature is safely above freezing, house plants which prefer coolness (see individual plants) will be far happier there than indoors. (See previous questions.)

VENTILATION

Do my house plants need fresh air in winter? Yes, decidedly. See that fresh air is admitted daily to the room where they are kept, but avoid direct drafts. A window or door opened for half an hour each day in an adjoining room will provide the needed ventilation. (See Introduction.)

How can I give my house plants fresh air without chilling them by a direct draft? If air must be admitted from a near-by window in the room in which they are kept, use a window ventilator or a screen to prevent drafts.

SUMMER CARE

What shall I do with my house plants in summer? See Introduction.

How can I arrange my house plants outdoors in a garden bed so that they will receive the right amount of sunshine and shade? Choose a location near a water supply where part of the bed receives morning sun and part shade. Place geraniums, Semperflorens Begonias, and other flowering, sun-loving plants in sunniest location. Ferns, foliage plants, and other shade lovers go in the shade.

What house plants suffer from being sunk in a garden bed in summer? African-violets, Calla Begonias, and other "difficult" plants which cannot endure beating rains and winds. Place these on a sheltered porch or in an open window.

What house plants prefer a bed of cinders to garden soil when placed outdoors in their pots in summer? Cacti and succulents.

Will house plants take care of themselves if sunk in garden beds in summer? Yes, if there is adequate rainfall. In drought, they must be watered slowly and deeply by letting the hose run into the ground about them with the nozzle removed. Keep weeds down and cultivate soil occasionally.

AUTUMN CARE

When should house plants be brought indoors in autumn? At least 2 or 3 weeks before you plan to turn on the heat, and of course before frost. This permits the plant to acclimate itself gradually to the new environment.

How shall I prepare my house plants for the autumn move to the house? Two weeks before they come in, loosen the pots in the ground. Prune back long, unsightly branches. If plants tend to wither, prune more severely. At the end of a week, lift the pots and place plants on a sheltered porch or against a retaining wall where they will have outdoor light and air. At the end of 2-week period from first loosening pots in ground, remove to house.

Do house plants need special care when they first come indoors in autumn? Yes, the leaves of glossy-foliaged plants should be frequently syringed. Water moderately. Ventilation should be good. Pests are apt to appear now. Keep a close watch and have a spray gun handy.

Is it possible to leave coleus, geraniums, and begonias in the ground during the winter (covering them for protection), or should they be taken into the house? (New Jersey.) Positively will die however well you protect them. There is only one begonia that is hardy with protection, the tuberous *B. evansiana*.

What shall I do with fuchsias, lantanas, and other summer bloomers when they come indoors in fall? Place in a cool cellar window. Water very sparingly until new growth appears. Then cut them back and bring to light and give more water.

What shall I do for house plants that turn brown when brought in the house during winter? I am losing all of my plants. Keep them cool. Do not overwater. See that they get fresh air. Cut back withered portions.

EXPOSURE

What flowers and vines are suitable for a sunny window? Geraniums, abutilons, shrimp plant, Baby Roses, crown of thorns, kalanchoe, oxalis. Vines: tradescantia, Kenilworth-ivy, *Campanula isophylla*, nasturtiums and morningglories.

Which house plants will grow in a window in winter? It has all of the morning sun. Flowering plants that will keep blooming if the temperature is not high (55° F. at night) are primulas in variety, callas, bouvardias, begonias, impatiens, and all kinds of bulbs which potted in the fall will keep up a succession, including Paperwhite and other narcissi, amaryllis, veltheimia, etc.

What house plants will blossom with only 2 or 3 hours of sunshine during the winter months? The small-flowered begonias are dependable; also various bulbs potted in the fall will help out. Saintpaulia and Bromeliads will bloom without direct sunshine.

What house plants would you suggest for east windows partially shaded most of the time, and in a steam-heated room which is consistently overheated? Why expect the impossible? Plants will not tolerate extreme heat unless they are tropical subjects which require high humidity, which almost never prevails in overheated rooms. About the only things we can suggest are sansevieria (Snake-plant) and the Kangaroo-vine (*Cissus antarctica*). Both can stand dryness and warmth to an unusual degree.

What house plants are suitable for rooms having little sunshine? Much depends upon the temperature maintained. Dry, hot rooms will kill anything, but if temperature is moderate and you maintain fair humidity, you can grow small palms, ferns, ivies, *Philodendron cordatum,* many large leaved begonias, bromeliads, tropical foliage plants and many of the so-called dish plants florists use.

What plants can be grown in a sun porch without southern exposure? Almost anything you fancy if there is sufficient heat during winter to keep the night temperature around 45° F. Both blooming and foliage plants from the florists will get along in such a porch.

What flowers and vines are suitable for a shaded window? Begonias, lobelia, English Ivy, German-ivy, variegated panicum, Strawberry-geranium, trailing fuchsia, Creeping Fig, Grape-ivy, Kenilworth-ivy, ceropegia, chlorophytum, palms, Chinese-evergreen, dracaena, dieffenbachia, nephthytis, rubber plants and ferns. Keep the night temperature down to 55° F. if possible.

What flowering house plants may be grown successfully without a great amount of sunshine? Other than wax begonias, bromeliads and saintpaulias you won't find many that will bloom in poor light. The room temperature counts for a lot, and if never above 65° F. in day and 50° to 55° F. at night, you can expect all kinds of ferns, palms and ivies to get along nicely.

Can I keep house plants in a west window? Yes, plants which do not need full sunlight, such as African-violets, large-leaved begonias, foliage plants, ivies, etc.

What plants other than Chinese-evergreen and nephthytis will grow in water in a northern exposure? Philodendron, tradescantia, English Ivy, Grape-ivy, redwood burls, and Umbrella-plant (*Cyperus alternifolius*).

What can I grow in a north window? All kinds of ferns, ivies, philodendron and other foliage plants; African-violets; large-leaved begonias; pick-a-back plant; bromeliads; strawberry-begonia.

ENVIRONMENT

What are the conditions under which my house plants will flourish in winter? See Introduction.

I have a steam-heated house and have difficulty getting house plants to live. What is the trouble? Place humidifiers on your radiators, or stand open dishes of water near your house plants to increase humidity. See that they get fresh air daily, without direct drafts.

Does coal gas injure house plants? Yes, it is deadly, even in very small amounts.

Does cooking gas affect house plants? Artificial or manufactured gas has a bad effect on house plants. Natural gas does not effect them adversely, according to statistics.

I use gas for heating and cooking. The gasman says there are no leaks, but my house plants don't thrive. It is not too hot and dry nor too cold or dark where I have them. What is wrong? If the temperature and humidity as well as light are right, there may be a gas leak too small to be detected by human beings. Raise some tomato seedlings, or get some sizable, healthy tomato plants from your florist. If they hang their leaves and look sad after a short time, you can be sure gas is present.

What is the easiest flowering house plant to raise, having to use gas for cooking in the house? Geraniums, fuchsias, shrimp plant, bromeliads and semperflorens begonias are pretty easy, but a lot depends upon where you grow the plants, and the temperature. If you have a room that is 50° to 55° F. at night, 10° higher by day, with plenty of light and not too dry, your chances are good in spite of gas cooking, but don't expect plants to thrive in a kitchen that is 80° or more in the daytime and 20° or 30° lower at night.

What climbing plant, such as ivy, can one grow in the house with

gas furnace? The Kangaroo-vine is about the toughest house vine we know. If that won't thrive with you, nothing will.

Our new home has gas hot-air heat. Will I be able to keep my gardenias, palms, and other house plants healthy during the winter? If there is no leak of unburned gas. If you maintain high humidity, you will find it good for the plants as well as yourself.

How can one grow house plants in a chimneyless house where the only available heat is from open natural gas stoves? The atmosphere may be too hot and dry. Keep shallow pan filled with water near plants. If the temperature is 70° F. or more, humidity low, few plants will last long. *Natural* gas is not injurious to plant life.

Is the cold from windows injurious to plants? Definitely so if the plants are tender kinds; take out of the window at night or place thick paper in front of the glass. Cold drafts are very bad.

Do oil stoves in rooms injure house plants? The temperature varies from 40° to 80°. I do not have much luck with house plants. The fumes of oil stoves are not good for house plants. If stove is kept in first-class working condition, plants will suffer less. Give them as much fresh air as possible without direct drafts. Eighty degrees is too high a temperature. (See questions on Temperature.)

What house plants can be easily kept in a hot, dry room with only a small amount of diffused sunlight? No plant can thrive in a hot, dry room, but some of the cacti and succulents can put up with a lot if not kept too moist.

Do plants grow under electric light? Yes, electric light can be used as a substitute for sunlight, though plants do better under natural conditions.

How do you grow house plants under artificial light? Install fluorescent light fixtures over the bench or table on which the plants are to be grown. Tubes should be 14 inches above the tops of growing plants and long enough to illuminate the entire growing area. Leave lights on 12 to 14 hours a day for optimum results. Use "daylight" or "white" fluorescent tubes or a combination of the two. Water, feed and otherwise care for plants as though they were growing in natural light.

What house plants grow best under artificial light? African-violets and gloxinias seem particularly happy under these conditions. House plants like pothos, philodendron, ferns and ficus which do not require full light can be grown in a dark part of the living room if an ordinary 60 or 75 watt incandescent bulb is placed above them for from 4 to 6 hours a day. Planters are available commercially with "built-in" light fixtures above them.

Why do my house plants have luxuriant foliage but the buds dry up and fall off before opening? This may be due to high temperatures, irregular or too heavy watering, or gas fumes. (See Watering, Temperature, and Sanitation.)

What causes the lower leaves on a small palm plant to turn brown and then die? What is the remedy? Unsuitable soil. Dryness at the root. Dry atmosphere. If possible have local greenhouseman or florist diagnose trouble, then correct offending condition.

How can I prevent plants, grown indoors from seeds or cuttings, from growing spindly? This is caused by too much warmth and not enough light and humidity. Direct sunshine is needed by most plants.

INSECTS AND DISEASES

How can I prevent pests from getting a start on my house plants? Examine all house plants before bringing them in. If any specimens from the garden or purchased from a florist are infested with pests of any sort, segregate them and get them entirely clean before letting them join other healthy plants. Make it a habit to look all plants over weekly for possible pests.

How can disease and pests be well controlled in growing house plants? By providing the best possible cultural conditions. Sponging with soap and water at intervals checks such pests as scale, mealy bugs, and red spider. Keep all dead leaves picked off. Use a pressure-bottle all-purpose *house plant* spray as soon as pests are discovered and keep infested plant segregated until clean.

What shall I use to get rid of aphids on house plants? Black Leaf 40, used according to directions on bottle. (See Section VIII.)

Mealy bug, one of the most annoying of house-plant pests, is controlled by applying alcohol with a small swab.

What is the best method to clean mealy bugs off plants? Place plant in bathtub, and wash off bugs by directing a spray of water at them forcibly. With very hairy-leaved subjects brush off bugs with small, soft paintbrush dipped in 60 percent alcohol.

How can I get rid of red spider on my house plants? Syringe with clear, cold water forcibly applied. If badly infested, dip the tops of the plants quickly, 2 or 3 times in succession, in water heated to 140°. Or spray or dust with an all-purpose house plant spray.

A small bulb syringe is very convenient for keeping the foliage of house plants clean and healthy.

What is the brown scalelike pest which adheres closely to the leaves and stems of ivy, and which seems to attract ants? What will kill this pest? Have used nicotine sulfate and pyrote but neither one was successful. Brown scale is the name of the pest. It may be removed by sponging the leaves with soapy water to which Black Leaf 40 (nicotine sulfate) is added at the rate of a teaspoonful to a gallon).

What is the pin-point black insect that attacks nephthytis and causes the leaves to turn yellow and then dry up? Sounds like a small scale insect. If adult insect is incapable of movement, this diagnosis is correct. Remove scales by sponging with Black Leaf 40 used according to manufacturer's directions.

What can be done about white jumping insects in soil of house plants? These usually breed in the organic matter in the soil. Try standing the pots in a vessel of water kept at 110° F. for a few minutes. This temperature is fatal to many insects, and most plants are unaffected by it even when completely immersed.

How can one kill white flies? Do these flies hatch in the earth or on the leaves of plants? They are difficult to control on house plants. Repeated sprayings with an all-purpose house plant spray is the best procedure. The eggs are small, translucent bodies laid on the under sides of the leaves. (See Section VIII.)

SANITATION

How often should house plants be syringed or washed under spigot? Glossy-leaved plants profit from a weekly syringing or sponging. Fuzzy-leaved plants should be dusted with a camel's-hair brush.

In washing of leaves of house plants, should soap be added to water? Many green-fingered gardeners do use soapy water in sponging off the foliage of glossy-leaved house plants. Plain water is just as good if all dust is removed, unless the plant is infested with red spider, scale, or other pests, when soapy water helps to remove them.

How can house plants be cleaned without injuring the plant, as certain plants are not to be touched with hands or most instruments? Brush dust from fuzzy-leaved plants with a fine camel's-hair brush.

What causes the white and brownish moldlike substance on the outside of flower pots? The white film is the lime or alkali in the clay. Wipe the pots occasionally; use wire brush if necessary.

Why does the soil of house plants get moldy? It is not mold, but algae, the spores of which are in the air and perhaps in the water. Keep the surface stirred, and once a month water with permanganate of potash, ½ teaspoonful to 1 gal. of water. Wipe off the pots occasionally.

Why does the soil in my house-plant pots smell sour and musty, and sometimes have a green, mosslike coating on the top? See Introduction to this section on Potting Soils. Bits of charcoal mixed through the soil will help keep it sweet. Do not overwater; try to admit fresh air daily, without direct drafts.

How can small seeds, such as orchid and begonia, be disinfected before growing them in cultural media of agar-agar? Calcium hypochlorite, 10 gm. to 160 c.c. of distilled water. Shake several minutes, and filter. Place seeds in tube and enough filtrate to wet all. After shaking and allowing to soak 15 minutes, transfer from solution with a platinum needle to the agar-agar.

Should the dirt be heated so as to kill bugs and worms before using for house plants? No, this should not be necessary if you have good clean garden loam. This precaution is sometimes taken when preparing a soil mixture for starting difficult seeds or rooting cuttings, of such plants as African-violets which are readily attacked by disease. For directions for sterilizing soil see pages 79–81, Soil and Fertilizers.

PROPAGATION (See also Section II.)

How should I take slips from house plants and make them grow? Take shoots or tops of plants 4 to 6 ins. long with firm, but not hard, stem growth. Fill a pot with sandy soil, vermiculite or other rooting medium, dip lower ends in Rootone and insert cuttings around the edge. Make the holes with a stick and press soil around cutting firmly. Sink about 1 in. Shade from sun and keep only just moist. When growth starts, pot singly. (See also Section II: Propagation.)

Is there any way of dividing very large house plants so they will not take up so much room in the house? It is usually better to root cuttings, discarding the unwieldly parent plant. Geraniums and many others can be pruned back very severely. Large tropical foliage plants such as dieffenbachias, monsteras and rubber plants can be air layered. See question on following page.

What can I feed house plants that will encourage blooms? I have a fairly cool room and southern exposure. My geraniums and fuchsias refuse to bloom during the dreary winter months. I have taken my rosemary indoors, but it will not grow in spite of all my efforts. If your geraniums and fuchsias have been in bloom outdoors in summer, they are now resting. Start slips in summer for late winter bloom. Rosemary can also be readily rooted by slipping, and the young plants will grow more thriftily than the old, sometimes even coming into bloom.

Which blooming house plants can be started in March? If you have ample light, a temperature not above 60° F., and understand the rudiments of plant raising, you can have fair success with begonias, African-violets, gloxinias, and primulas. For lower temperatures, cinerarias and calceolarias can be tried.

What is the procedure for starting house plants from seeds, rather than from the usual slips? Use light, sandy, not overrich soil. Sow each kind thinly in a pot, making soil fairly firm and level beforehand. Water by standing in a vessel of water and then cover with glass. Give shade, and temperature of 60° to 70° F. Always water from the bottom. Transplant into other pots or boxes when true leaves show. Best time for sowing such seeds is between January and March; but some, like primroses, can be sown in June, and cinerarias and calceolarias in August or September.

Can seeds, taken from the garden in the fall be used indoors during the winter, or do they have to be dormant for a certain period before they will grow? Seeds can be planted immediately.

Can the soil in which seeds are planted indoors be permitted to dry off? Keep constantly moist, until the seed has germinated.

What is "damping off," and how can it be prevented? This is a fungous disease prevented by sterilizing the soil or treating the seed with a disinfectant such as Semesan or copper oxide. (See Section VIII.)

How can one start bougainvillea cuttings in the house? Take short side growths or tips 6 ins. long. Insert in sandy soil in a small pot, or several around the edge. After watering, stand in a box or big pot and cover with a sheet of glass, giving a warm position. Don't overwater but never allow to dry.

How can one take slips from a rubber tree? *Ficus elastica* can best be propagated by air-layering. Make a slanting cut halfway through the stem with a sharp knife; insert a toothpick to keep open, and bind around with a ball of damp sphagnum moss and bind tightly with a sheet of plastic film, fastening near each end with twistems. While rooting, stake the branch to avoid breakage. When moss is filled with roots (three months or more), cut from parent plant and pot in soil.

How can I propagate "Pick-a-back" plant? The small plants on the leaves will quickly root if the leaf is taken off the plant and pegged on the surface of soil in a pot. About the easiest of things to propagate.

PLANNING AND ARRANGING THE WINDOW GARDEN

How can I make a window garden? Have a wide shelf built to fit in a sunny bay or deep-silled window. Line the shelf with metal, or give several coats of bathtub enamel, after the cracks have been puttied up. It is well to have a rim built around the shelf to keep pots, pebbles, etc., from falling off. If entirely waterproof, the shelf may be lined with pebbles in which the pots are set. Pebbles are kept moist. If not completely waterproof, set pots on shelf, each in its own saucer. A "fountain" or a wide dish of water in the center will help keep a humid atmosphere if the shelf is not waterproof.

What sort of indoor window box do you recommend? A box with a metal lining. Fill the container with damp peatmoss or with standard potting soil (which see) in which bits of charcoal have been mixed. Sink potted plants to the rims in the soil or peatmoss.

Fancy-leaved caladiums, streptocarpuses, and gloxinias are three of the less well-known plants which the experienced amateur will find interesting to grow.

Which flowers may be grown in the house throughout the year? I have an inside flower bed about 8 × 4 ft.; the earth being about 3 ft. deep with drainage. A box of this size needs to be in a glassed porch or greenhouse. In any ordinary window the light would be insufficient to permit healthy growth of all the plants the box would hold. Unless your room is especially well provided with windows, don't expect all plants to be a success. In such a box, in a dwelling room, trouble is certain. At best, a room is only a makeshift for plant growing. Window plants are best grown in pots, which permits moving them around.

What are sure-to-bloom winter window garden flowers? Semperflorens begonia, crown-of-thorns, and impatiens.

What are ten good plants for providing a long succession of blooms during the winter? Begonia Preussen, *Begonia froebeli,* zonal geraniums, Paperwhite and Soleil d'Or Narcissi, Christmas Cactus, *Begonia feasti,* shrimp plant, cypripediums, veltheimias, amaryllis and primroses.

What blooming flowers may I put in my fernery to keep in the house during the winter? I have it in front of south windows, but have Venetian blinds which I keep tilted just a trifle—the sun is not there all day because of the next house. Better give up the idea of flowering plants in a fernery that gets no sun, but you might try the African-violet (saintpaulia) or some of the winter-blooming begonias (which see). Forced bulbs are also a possibility though they will not last so long as though they had some sun.

What flowers and other plants can be grown in a window box in the heart of the city? Begonias, geraniums, lobelias, chlorophytum, English Ivy, Japanese Honeysuckle, sansevieria, German-ivy, and Kenilworth-ivy.

What house plants will survive in a city apartment with little or no sunshine? Snake-plant, aspidistra, Chinese-evergreen, English Ivy, pothos, tradescantia, bromeliads, palms, fatsia, dieffenbachia, Grape-ivy, dracaena, rubber plant (*Ficus elastica* and *Ficus pandurata*), pandanus, monstera, and peperomia.

What house plants require a great deal of moisture? Callalily, Chinese-evergreen, ferns, spireas, hydrangeas, primulas, cinerarias, cyclamen, Jerusalem-cherry.

Which house plants do well if kept on the dry side? Aloe, bromeliads, agave, crassula, sedum, sansevieria, and other succulents including most cacti (excepting the orchid cactus).

How can I supply needed humidity in the room where I keep my house plants? By fitting humidifiers to the radiators; by placing shallow trays or wide saucers filled with pebbles or sand (which must be kept moist) beneath the pots; by spraying the plants each day with a fine atomizer.

Is there any way of safely leaving house plants during a vacation of a week to 10 days without care? Would it be harmful to leave them standing in saucers of water so that they do not dry out? This would not be harmful in most cases. An alternative is to water the plants well and then stand the pots in a box packed around with wet paper or peatmoss. Place in a shaded place not subjected to drafts.

What are the names of some house plants that are easy to raise? (Washington.) If your rooms have ordinary windows and in winter are heated to 70° F. or more, plant growing is not easy. All depends on light, temperature, and humidity, plus careful watering. For winter and early spring, various bulbs are relatively easy to flower, but their season is brief. If you want all-year-around plants, grow ferns, ivies, sansevierias, cacti, and succulents. Geraniums, fuchsias, and similar flowering plants are easy to raise from cuttings.

Which low-growing plants would be suitable for house use in small containers without drainage holes? (Michigan.) Containers without drainage or vent at the bottom will soon sour the soil. If not carefully watered, air is driven from the soil, and no plants can stand that. With care you may, for a time, keep ivies, saintpaulias, cacti, and succulent plants in variety in good shape. Succulents and cacti need very little water. Mix finely broken bits of charcoal in your potting soil and place a layer of pebbles in the bottom of each container.

What plants would be good to plant in fancy china figures like rabbits, etc. What kinds would stand the shade? For sunny positions, Baby tears, cacti, and succulents in small sizes. For shady windows, various small ferns, peperomias, cryptanthus, pilea, small-leaved ivies, *Saxifraga sarmentosa*.

What dwarf plants are best suited for growing in small containers to keep on glass window shelves? (Maine.) Small leaved ivies, Kenilworth-ivy, grevillea seedlings, various ferns, small crotons and other tropical foliage plants, cacti, and succulents in variety; saintpaulia and many others according to fancy, room conditions, light, etc.

How shall I place the house plants in a window garden with a southern exposure? Put the flowering plants which need full sun close to the glass. On the edge of the shelf, facing the room, use small-leafed ivies or other vines which do not need sun. Against the walls on each side can go foliage plants with colored leaves to give variety of color. When the forced bulbs are ready for bloom, these can be placed just behind the ivy away from the full heat of the sun. Such flowers as callas, amaryllis, primulas, and fuchsias can also occupy this less sunny space when they are in bloom.

The only place I have for a window garden gets little sun. Is there any special way to arrange the plants? If plants are used which do not need sun, these can be placed to give the best effect. Large plants can go against the walls or be silhouetted against the glass. Vines are trained around the window frames and along the edge of the garden facing the room. Low plants are placed just behind this edge. Use foliage plants with variegated and colored leaves.

MINIATURE GARDENS

TERRARIUMS

What type of soil should I use in planting a terrarium? Half sandy loam, half peatmoss, or leafmold, with bits of charcoal added.

How can one make a terrarium? Use any large glass container and cover top with sheet of glass in the day; open at night. Place small rocks or coarse gravel on bottom of container, covered with soil, as above.

How should the interior of a terrarium be arranged? After the drainage layer and soil have been placed in the bowl, a grade may be established which will make it possible to have all the plants visible at one time to the eye of the observer. Perhaps stones, moss, or lichens can be used to give the effect of a miniature landscape. By arranging a slope instead of a flat surface, seedling trees or shrubs and other erect growers can go in on the low side, with creeping and low-growing plants on the higher level and between the taller ones.

What cultivated plants are suitable for terrariums? Various ferns, small palms, pellionias, selaginellas, *Begonia imperialis,* cryptanthus, small ivies, pileas, *Saxifraga sarmentosa, Festuca glauca* (grass), fittonias, marantas, ferns, small crotons, peperomias and saintpaulias and whatever plant appreciates humid conditions. Some of the plants soon outgrow their quarters, so remaking at intervals is necessary.

What wild plants can be used in a terrarium? Wood wildings such as partridge-berry, wintergreen, pipsissewa, rattlesnake-plantain, hepatica, ground-pine, moss, lichens (on bits of bark or half-decayed wood), seedling evergreens, and tiny wild ferns do very well in a glass garden.

What seed can I sow in a woodsy terrarium? It is not customary to sow seeds in a terrarium, but such a container is ideal for raising ferns from spores. The spores usually found on the back of fern fronds shaken in a terrarium will start as green flattened growth from which tiny ferns will duly emerge.

What is the proper way to care for a terrarium? Keep in a not-too-sunny position and cover with a sheet of glass during the day; partly open at night. Water very sparingly, especially if the container is topped with glass. Don't wet the foliage when watering. Wipe glass top dry each day, also the sides if there is a great deal of condensation.

ORCHIDS IN TERRARIUMS

Can I grow orchids in the house? If so, how? Providing you have a suitable terrarium and give the plants careful attention, a wide variety will thrive. Excellent results have been obtained with cattleyas, cypripediums, calanthes, *Odontoglossum grande,* and others.

How can orchids be raised in the house? Satisfactory results are obtained by growing them in a terrarium built so that ventilation can be given both at top and sides. The orchids are grown in pots which stand on slat shelves over a tray holding water. Terrarium is placed near window. Temperature should average 55° to 65° F.

How often must I water a potted orchid growing in a terrarium?

On an average about once a week, but this will vary somewhat with prevailing weather conditions, amount of artificial heat in room, and the condition of the plant itself. Most orchids have a resting period during which they need little water.

DISH GARDENS

What plants are suitable for dish or tray gardens? Cacti, succulents such as small specimens of crassulas, gasterias, echeverias, kalanchoes, and sedums. *Saxifraga sarmentosa,* cryptanthus, ferns, myrtle, seedling evergreens, pileas, small *Begonia semperflorens,* peperomias. Go to the florist and select any very small potted plants which will fit in your dish or tray. Or try small plants from your own garden or window garden.

How is a dish or tray garden arranged? A shallow dish or tray is lined with coarse gravel or small pebbles, over which is placed a thin layer of light garden loam, sandy for cacti and succulents, mixed with peatmoss or leafmold for woodland plants. The plants are set in to simulate a miniature landscape and earth is packed firmly about their roots. Moss can be used to cover the bare soil of the surface.

How should the tray or dish garden be watered? When the garden is made, enough water should be given to moisten thoroughly the roots of the newly set plants, but not enough to leave them soggy and waterlogged. After first watering, give water sparingly when soil feels dry to the touch. Pour water directly to the roots with a small pitcher or long-spouted watering can.

How can I keep the soil sweet in my dish garden? Mix small pieces of charcoal through the soil mixture which you are using.

How long will the plants survive in a dish garden? That depends on the plants used and the care given. Cacti or succulents often live for months or even for years if planted in sandy loam and watered sparingly. Foliage plants do not last quite so long, but if given proper care will remain fresh and green for some weeks.

LIVING PLANT ARRANGEMENTS

What is a living plant arrangement? An arrangement of flowers and foliage, or of foliage plants, actually growing in a container instead of cut and placed in water, as with the usual flower arrangement.

How should a living plant arrangement be made? Place gravel or pebbles in the bottom of the container which you select—preferably a bowl or dish deep enough to receive comfortably the roots of the plants. Arrange the flowers and foliage plants to make an interesting design, just as you would in arranging cut flowers. Fill in with soil around the roots, covering soil with a ground cover such as myrtle or moneywort.

What flowering plants are suitable for living plant arrangements?
Fuchsias, African-violets, semperflorens begonias, browallias, torenias, minor bulbs (grapehyacinth, crocus, snowdrops, species tulips, sternbergias, colchicums).

What foliage plants are suitable for living plant arrangements?
Small specimens of any of the foliage plants with decorative leaves (see Foliage Plants), myrtle, moneywort or creeping jenny, baby tears, partridgeberry, small-leaved ivies, tradescantia, pteris ferns.

What wild plants can I use in a living plant arrangement? Violets, hepaticas, springbeauties, arbutus, marshmarigolds, pipsissewa, partridgeberry, wintergreen, ferns; seedling blueberries, evergreens, and deciduous trees; also moss and lichens. Use a mossy rock or lichen-covered root or piece of stump to give a natural effect in placing the wild material.

THE KITCHEN-WINDOW HERB GARDEN

What herbs can I grow in my sunny kitchen window? Annuals: parsley, sweet marjoram, basil, anise, coriander. Perennials: mint, chives, thyme, sage, lemon balm, tarragon. Tender perennial shrubs: scented geraniums, lemonverbena, rosemary.

Should annual herbs in the kitchen-window herb garden be started from seed? Not unless seeds have been planted in summer so that the plants have a good start before going indoors. Before being brought to the kitchen they should be well established and happy in the pots or boxes in which they are to grow on through the winter. The double shock of transplanting and bringing indoors is apt to be too much for them.

What kitchen-window herbs can be grown from seed? If planted early enough to produce plants before cold weather, sweet marjoram, parsley, basil, anise, coriander.

What kitchen-window herbs must be purchased as plants? Rosemary, lemonverbena (tender shrubs), tarragon, mint, chives, thyme, sage, and lemon balm are perennials and must be purchased as plants or grown on in advance from seed so that you have plants ready to bring in for use during the winter.

Where can I purchase herb plants; seed for growing indoors in winter? Most leading seed houses now carry lists of herbs.

What kind of soil is necessary for herbs grown indoors? See alkaline potting mixture in Soil, this section.

Can herbs be grown in a window box or should they be kept in pots? In general, pots are more successful. Basil or parsley may be grown in a box, especially if started from seed during summer. To be reasonably successful, the room must be cool—below 60°, preferably 50° to 55° F., for all but the tender perennial shrubs. (See previous question.)

Can chives be grown indoors in winter? If so, how? Yes, chives do well in the kitchen herb garden. Bring in a clump of bulbs from the garden, setting it in a bulb pan of light, sweet soil. Cut back the foliage and let new growth start. Grow on in a sunny window, at a low temperature—preferably 55° F. Keep on the dry side.

Can I grow scented geraniums in the kitchen herb garden? Yes. See Geraniums.

Do you think one should bring in lemonverbena during winter? I did, potted it and kept in basement near a window, watered once a week. Am I doing the correct thing? (Michigan.) Being a native of Argentina and Chile, the lemonverbena would not winter over out of doors in Michigan. You are doing the right thing with it, if it stays alive all winter in the basement. It can be cut back when brought in from the garden and grown on through the cold weather in a sunny window. It can stand a higher temperature than that preferred by most herbs.

Can I leave my rosemary plant outdoors the year round? I have seen plants as big as shrubs in gardens on Cape Cod but my friends tell me to bring it indoors here in the vicinity of New York City. Rosemary is unreliably hardy in the North but where humidity is high and temperatures not too frigid, as along the seacoast, it survives outdoors surprisingly far north. You were well advised to take it in. When pruning it back in fall preparatory to bringing indoors, root some of the cuttings in moist sand or vermiculite. They are easy to propagate.

How can parsley plants be grown in the house during the cold months? Cut back, lift, and pot strong plants in the fall and give them a well-lighted window with a temperature never above 55° F. Don't overwater and don't feed with fertilizer.

Why does house-grown parsley become very pale, with long, weak stems? I give fertilizer every 2 or 3 weeks. It probably lacks sun and is grown too warm. Parsley grown indoors is almost always weaker and less thrifty than that grown in the garden. It wants plenty of sun, a temperature of not more than 55° F., enough but not too much water (keep it rather on the dry side), and *no* commercial fertilizer.

Should parsley and chives be kept very moist grown in a kitchen window? No. Be careful with watering; with a little practice you can tell by the weight of the container or the feel of the soil if it needs water or not.

Does it injure tarragon, rosemary, and pot marjoram to pot them every winter for use indoors? It does not injure them if they get the proper care and the plants are not too large. They should be set into the garden again in spring to recuperate. Eventually they will get too big to pot up, and cuttings should be propagated to produce young plants, leaving the parents in the herb garden out of doors. If the young plants are left in their pots, plunged in the garden through the summer, they will sustain less shock when brought indoors in autumn.

What is the truth about growing herbs indoors? The truth is that few herbs do well indoors unless they have the conditions which they prefer; namely, a night temperature of not over 55° F., plenty of light and sunshine, sufficient humidity, good air circulation, and regular care. These conditions are hard to provide in the average centrally heated home. A sun porch, cool window, or lean-to greenhouse offer more possibilities.

FLOWERING PLANTS

ABUTILON

Does abutilon or flowering-maple make a good house plant? Abutilon was one of Grandmother's favorite house plants. It also makes a good garden subject, growing tall and bushy and blooming freely in sunny, open beds. In autumn it may be so large that cuttings must be taken for rooting instead of bringing in the overgrown parent plant. Cuttings root readily. If the old plant comes in, cut it back very severely to prevent wilting and to encourage new growth. The variegated foliage and bell-shaped flowers are most attractive. It rapidly becomes pot-bound and therefore needs a lot of water. It is subject to white fly (which see). Repot in standard potting mixture. (See Soil, this section.)

I have a small plant with leaves almost exactly like a maple. Set it outdoors in July, it thrived, producing orange-colored flowers like "Japanese lanterns," on long, fine, drooping stems. What is it? What winter protection does it need? (Pennsylvania.) The plant is abutilon or flowering-maple. Not hardy, and must be grown as a pot plant in your section. Give average room conditions in winter, at 50° to 60° F. Flowers freely in winter. Root cuttings to make new plants. Grows quite large.

How can abutilon or flowering-maple be raised from seed as a house plant? Sow the seed in a pot in February or March, in sandy soil, barely covering. Place sheet of glass on pot and keep in a warm room. Give some light when germination starts, but use care in watering, as the seedlings are tiny. Transplant into another pot 1 in. apart when in rough leaf, and grow on like any other tender plant.

AFRICAN-VIOLET

Culture

Please suggest the best soil mixture in which to grow African-violets.

Mix 2 parts (by bulk) good garden loam, sterilized (see below)
  1 part vermiculite or sterilized sand
  1 part peatmoss
Add 1 quart broken bits charcoal per bushel
  2 quarts commercial cow manure per bushel
  1 quart bone flour per bushel

Is it necessary to sterilize African-violet soil? If so, describe method. Yes, it is advisable as African-violets are susceptible to a number of soil-borne pests and diseases. Only loam, sand and pots need be sterilized as vermiculite and peatmoss are sterile. Soil must reach and maintain a temperature of 140 to 160 degrees for a full 2 minutes. Place mixture of loam and sand in scrubbed pots on rack in pressure cooker and bring to 10 pounds pressure for 10 minutes. Hot soil smells very unpleasant!

What is the best temperature for African-violets? The minimum night temperature in winter should be 60° to 65° F. At 50° to 55° F. saintpaulias only struggle along. The day temperature is immaterial so long as it is not below night figures.

Will an African-violet thrive with no sunshine? Frequently these plants bloom even at north windows, but more prolific results are obtained with plants grown at a sunny eastern exposure, with pots set back a little from the glass.

How should African-violets be watered? Because of its thick crown and velvety leaves, moisture is avoided around the heart of the plant, and water supplied from the saucer or on the edge of the pot. Do not water again until soil surface in pot feels dry to touch. Pour any excess water from saucer after soil is thoroughly moist, or stand pot on bed of pebbles.

If African-violets require water in the saucer constantly, how do you avoid damping off and loss of plant? Care is taken not to allow moisture on the leaves. Regardless of what some claim, saintpaulias do not want to be soaking wet all the time. Soil in such a condition lacks air and the roots will go bad.

Is cold water bad for African-violets? Lukewarm water is better.

My African-violet has white rings and spots on the leaves. Is this a disease, or fertilizer deficiency? Neither. It is caused by application of cold water on the leaf. If you must water the leaves, use lukewarm water. Otherwise, apply water only to the soil. It is not necessary to water African-violets from below, but it is important to avoid wetting the crown or heart of the plant.

Please tell me how to get African-violets to bloom. My plants remain green and healthy, but shortly after they leave the florist they cease flowering. Shall I repot them? The difference in humidity between a greenhouse and ordinary living room is probably the reason for non-blooming. Best flowering is had on plants kept standing on moist pebbles which afford a constant "aura" of humidity. Faded flowers must also be promptly snipped to prevent seed formation, which is always a deterrent to further bud development. Plenty of fresh air indirectly admitted in cold weather is likewise important. Repotting may be necessary, but other factors in culture are first considered. An African-violet plant food or one of the several reliable house plant foods may be applied according to directions on package when buds begin to appear. *Do not* feed during the short periods when plants are resting and producing no new growth.

Should African-violets be kept "root-bound," and in small pots? Unlike many flowering plants which tend to bloom more freely when the potting is close, African-violets flower better when somewhat overpotted. A plant entering its third year should flower well in a 6- or 7-in. pot. Young flowering plants do well in 3-, 4-, or 5-in. pots, depending on size of plant.

Does keeping an African-violet plant in a glazed flower pot prevent it from blooming? In such a pot, even if it has a drainage hole, the plant will not dry out so readily; but it does not do so well in glazed pots as in porous clay pots, because air circulation in the soil is poorer. Wick-fed plastic pots are very satisfactory but care must be taken with these not to overwater.

What is the best location for African-violets in summer? They are either set in a light north window in a room where windows are kept open over long periods, or else on the sheltered porch; never are they "plunged" in the garden.

How are plants kept free of dust, if spraying is harmful to the hairy leaves? Dust is removed with a soft brush. A flat camel's-hair paintbrush is ideal. Leaves may be sprayed occasionally with a fine mist of room-temperature water. Until completely dry, plants must remain in complete shade, away from drafts.

What makes the blossoms of an African-violet fall off while they are still fresh? It is natural for them to do so. They fertilize or pollinate readily, and after that happens they slide off.

Why do African-violets drop their blooms before they open? Probably the temperature or the humidity is too low. They want 60° F. or higher at night.

Will gas heat cause the buds to fall from African-violets? Leaking manufactured gas, however slight, will make any plant drop its leaves or buds.

How can one keep the leaves of African-violets from drooping onto the edge of the pot and thereby rotting away where contact is made? This condition is now believed to be caused by surplus deposits of chemical fertilizer salts on the rims of clay pots. Reduce fertilizer, scrub pot rims, protect stems from direct contact by inserting a cardboard or lacepaper doily "collar" until condition is corrected and stems regain crispness. Overwatering which produces soft growth may also contribute to the trouble. Do not permit night temperature to go below 60°.

My African-violet develops 10-in. stems which break in pieces. How can stronger stems be developed? Such stem growth is most unusual. Very likely plants are in too cold or too shaded a location, with the center of the plant overcrowded with leaves. The overlarge foliage could be cut away and the plant divided.

Insects and Diseases

See Section VIII.

What causes a gnarly condition on African-violets? New leaves and blossoms have no stems, just grow out from the base of the plant. Need of division might be the explanation, but more likely the cyclamen mite is at work. Use a pressure bottle house plant spray recommended for red spider or containing a miticide.

How can I clean up mildew on leaves and mold on stems of African-violets? What causes these? These thick-leaved velvety plants are often a prey to mildew and mold without any apparent cause, although poor ventilation and insufficient sunlight seem to be contributing factors. Badly affected sections are sharply cut away and the plant, upper and under side, dusted with fine sulfur, or one of the dusts with sulfur as an active ingredient. The "mold" on stems may be mealy bug. See next question.

Why do mold spots form on the stems of my African-violets? Your "mold" spots are mealy bugs. (See following question.)

How can mealy bug be cleaned up on African-violets? The end of a skewer or matchstick is wrapped with cotton and dipped in wood alcohol (or in a little toilet water). This is applied to all affected sections of the plant. Repeat as needed.

I have 7 African-violets which had blossoms steadily for 3 years, but now are infested with a webby substance on the under side of the leaf. Leaves are spotted yellow. What causes this? This sounds like red spider, a minute insect forming colonies of red dots on the under side of the foliage where webs are formed for protection. Increase humidity in room. Forceful syringing with clear, lukewarm water or with a rotenone preparation, to break the web and wash away the insects, is effective. Spray with a house plant pressure bottle spray which contains a miticide.

My African-violets have developed pale, limp leaves and the flowers blast before they fully develop. What causes this? Probably nematodes. Remove plant from pot and examine roots. If swellings are present and decayed areas visible, destroy plant and pour boiling water through potting soil before discarding it.

Propagation

Can African-violets be successfully divided? Readily. Indeed, as soon as the crown gets overthick, flowering usually wanes. Carefully reset, each fair-sized repotted section usually begins to flower again immediately. It is also easy to maintain your stock by rooting leaf cuttings. (See following questions.)

Which is the better time to divide African-violets, in the spring or the fall? The spring is better. The divisions then grow on into good plants by the following winter.

What is the best method of propagating a large number of African-violets? Leaves may be sharply cut with 1½ inch stems from the base of the plant at any time (although florists prefer October and November). These are inserted in small separate pots, in a large bulb pan of light soil, or in a Wardian case. Half sand and half peat-moss or vermiculite seems to give the quickest results. Leaves are

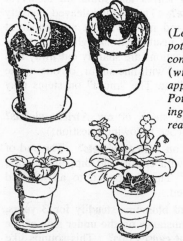

PROPAGATION OF AFRICAN-VIOLET

(*Left to right*) *Leaf cutting inserted in pot of sandy compost. Method of keeping compost moist, by inserting small pot (with bottom hole loosely plugged) and applying water through this. (Below) Potted young plant, with saucer for watering from beneath. Plant, repotted, has reached flowering size.*

inserted the length of the stem. Soil is kept warm, in light place, and moist, while roots are forming. Covering with a drinking glass or Mason jar helps to maintain ideally quick, humid rooting conditions; or pots may all be set in a box containing a layer of sand always kept moist. If warm weather makes outside growing safe, the plants are moved to a sheltered outdoor porch. When roots are formed, new leaves will begin to appear at the base of the old one. The glass is then removed and new "plants" are separated from parent leaves and potted up separately in an African-violet potting mixture in

2-inch pots. When these are root-filled, 4-in. pots are supplied, a good size for young plants of first flowering size. Generally speaking, it takes about 5 weeks for roots to develop, and 5 weeks more for the first new leaves to appear. The first blossom by this method will show at 4 to 6 months.

How can African-violets be rooted in water? Mature leaves cut with plenty of petiole or leaf stem will root if placed in a glass with just enough water to cover the end of the stem but not up to the leaf. As soon as roots develop, the "plant" is moved to a small pot of sandy soil. This method is slower than inserting leaves in a rooting medium such as vermiculite or sand.

Types and Varieties

How many African-violets are there, and what are their names? There are hundreds of varieties. The chief types or strains are: The Amazon or Supreme with very heavy, thick stems, large rounded leaves and large flowers; The DuPonts, like super-Supremes; Girl or My Lady with scalloped or deeply lobed leaves, white, yellowish or pinkish centers; Doubles, with double flowers; Fringettes, flowers with fringed, ruffled petals on long stems, roundish leaves, edges toothed; Spoons, leaves curling upward; Genevas, flowers edged with neat white line. Colors are white, pink, fuchsia-red, purple, violet, lavender, blue, blue and white, pink and white.

Where did the African-violet originate? *Saintpaulia ionantha* was first discovered in East Africa in 1893 by Baron Walter von Saint Paul. Forms of it introduced at that time were *purpurea,* dark purple; *grandiflora violacea,* large flowered; and *albescens,* white tinted pink. These forms seemingly were all lost, as up to the time Blue Boy was originated in California the only form known was *S. ionantha,* the species, usually grown from seed in a small way, and *S. kewensis,* a hybrid.

ANTHURIUM

What are the requirements of an anthurium plant to make it bloom? In an ordinary room you have as much chance to flower this plant as you have with cattleya orchids. Anthuriums are tropical and demand high humidity and heat while in active growth with cooler conditions while in flower. The pot must be well drained and compost of sphagnum, peat, fibrous loam, and sand should be used. Crown must be above soil, and as stem base rises it should be wrapped with moss. If you succeed in flowering it, you are good.

BEGONIAS

Soil and Fertilizer

What is the best soil mixture for begonias? A loose, humusy mixture suits most begonias best. One part good loam, 2 parts leaf-mold, 1 part sand, ¼ part small lump charcoal, ¼ part dried cow manure, plus bone meal at the rate of 1 pt. to the bushel is satis-factory.

What type of soil do rex begonias need?   Mellow, porous, and rich in humus. One part good loam, 1½ parts leafmold, 1 part sand, ½ part old, rotted cow manure, and a generous helping of broken charcoal mixed in.

Fibrous-rooted begonias: type of soil and amount of moisture? Room temperature and humidity? Should they be kept in a sunny window or shaded?   Light, humusy, well-drained soil. Never permit soil to become really dry, but avoid saturated condition, 55° to 70° F. Sun in winter; shade in summer.

How should I feed begonias growing in pots?   They respond best to organic fertilizers, one of the best of which is diluted liquid cow manure; but any complete standard fertilizer that will dissolve in water may be used. Never feed plants that have not filled their pots with healthy roots.

How often should begonias grown as house plants be fertilized? Providing the plants are healthy and their roots are matting around the insides of their pots, about once a week during the active growing season and once every 2 or 3 weeks during the winter.

Potting, Care, and Culture

What are the rules for repotting a healthy, fibrous-rooted begonia that has filled pot with roots?   (1) Water thoroughly few hours before repotting; (2) new pot should be only an inch or two wider than old; (3) put crocks (drainage material) in new pot; (4) avoid damaging roots; (5) moderately firm soil about root ball; (6) water thoroughly; keep warmer. Shade and spray with water for few days.

What is the proper care for begonias? They grow well but hardly ever blossom. About once a year they bud and then drop off.   Bud dropping suggests lack of light, or too low temperature. Most begonias need a minimum of 55° F., and a good light position. In summer, shade from strong sunshine is needed.

Can begonias in the house be pinched back severely to prevent them from growing leggy, or does this condition indicate some cultural defect?   Pruning back can be done. Some varieties (the coccineas, for example) send up long, canelike growths. Lack of light and too high temperatures may also be responsible for legginess.

Where in the house do begonias do best?   A sunroom where the night temperature is not below 50° F. and the day temperature not above 65° F. is ideal. Otherwise a light window (with the plants not too close to a radiator) is best.

How should fibrous-rooted begonias be watered? Soil should be kept moist but not waterlogged. When water is given, thoroughly saturate whole ball of soil (preferably by immersing pot in pail), then give no more water until soil begins to show signs of dryness. Use water at room temperature.

How do you take care of begonias? My plants are withering up. Begonias that have tuberous roots die down and rest for a period each year. Most others thrive in 55° to 70° F., providing atmosphere is not too dry and light is reasonably good. Soil should be light and humusy and moderately moist.

Should begonias have a rest; if so, when and what care should follow? Impossible to generalize. The tuberous kinds need a complete rest through the winter. *Socotrana* and some South African kinds rest during summer. Many benefit from a partial rest (but are not dried off), while others continue growth the year round.

What is your method for growing a Callalily Begonia? One person's directions contradict the others. (New Jersey.) Place the plant in the window of a New England home and have the housewife care for it! This prima donna seems to do best under these conditions. Professional gardeners often fail, especially south of New Haven, Connecticut. A west window in a room with a night temperature not below 60° F., reasonable humidity and fresh air, with moderate watering from below (or without wetting heart of plant), may keep it alive.

Why is it so difficult to grow the Calla Begonia south of New England? This seems to be due to the extremes of summer weather. Like sweetpeas, delphiniums, and some other garden plants, this house plant abhors spells of weather when both days and nights are hot and humid.

How can I keep a Christmas Begonia over summer so it will bloom next winter? Rest for few weeks after blooming; cut back and repot in light soil in spring; grow on in humid atmosphere (minimum temperature 60° F.). Shade from bright sunshine; repot as becomes necessary during summer. Control pests. You can scarcely expect success without a warm greenhouse.

How do you care for Lorraine (Christmas) Begonias after they are through blooming? They are usually discarded, because young plants develop into better specimens for following year. If you wish to grow on old plants, rest awhile by reducing water supply somewhat. In spring, cut partly back, repot, and start into growth again.

How can I make my angel-wing begonia bloom? Providing plant is growing well, it should bloom after it attains a reasonable size if it is not kept in too dark a place.

Why do my angel-wing begonias after a few days' growth dry up and

lose the leaves? I keep them well watered and cool. Common causes of leaf dropping are too much or too little water, low temperatures, exposure to drafts, too dry atmosphere, and careless repotting. Minimum temperature should be 55° F.

What disease causes begonia leaves to turn yellow? This is usually not due to any organic disease but to the plants receiving a check to their growth due to dryness, too strong sunshine, arid atmosphere, or too low temperature.

Why do begonias bloom in hothouses and not after I get them home? I have one now, it grows just fine, but no flowers. Possibly too little light. Begonias need light shade from intense summer sun, but good light is necessary for flower production, especially in winter.

Begonias kept on the porch during the summer, brought in the house in the fall, dropped all their leaves. What can be the cause or causes? We have gas in the house. Leaking gas may be the cause, but much more probably the dry air inside (especially after heat is turned on) is responsible. Install humidifiers. Stand plants on trays in moist gravel.

My potted, everblooming begonia blooms on one side branch only. What can I do with it? It is about 9 ins. tall, has 4 stalks full of foliage, smaller one coming from the bottom, so it should be bushy. Needs good light to bloom well. Will stand more sunlight than any other begonia.

I have a begonia named Loma Alta that sends up huge bunches of blossoms but they always blast before opening. I keep them just moist. What causes this? It may be due to keeping the plant *too* dry. Loma Alta makes a heavy foliage growth, and a healthy plant needs liberal supplies of moisture.

When a rex begonia droops, is it going into a rest period? It has just finished blossoming. Should I water it less often? When grown in the house, this often happens at the approach of winter. Reduce water supply (but keep soil somewhat moist). Repot, and water more when signs of new growth show in spring.

My rex begonia never seems to increase in size. As soon as a new leaf comes on, one turns yellow and dies. What is wrong? Wrong soil; too low temperature or too dry atmosphere. Soil should be humusy but porous; temperature not below 60° F. A humid atmosphere such as is provided by a terrarium suits these plants best.

Propagation

Why do my begonia slips rot instead of root when I try to start them in water? While some people report success with *some* varieties of begonias in water, a generally preferable method is to use moist sand (not sea sand) or vermiculite as a rooting medium. If water is used, add a few lumps of charcoal.

Can Calla Begonias be made to grow from slips, and how? (New York.) Yes. You must be careful to select the greenest slips for cuttings. The white ones are devoid of chlorophyll and will not grow. The green ones produce white tips later. Root under glass dish.

When is the best time to take cuttings of double-flowered begonias? At the same time as cuttings of single-flowered varieties belonging to the same section would be taken, thus: of most fibrous-rooted and tuberous-rooted kinds in spring; of most winter-flowering hybrids in early winter.

How can rex begonias be propagated? May be increased by seed, division, or from leaf cuttings. Cuttings are best made from mature leaves in spring. Insert them in sand, or sand and peatmoss. Keep moist and shaded from direct sunlight. Young plants should develop in a few weeks.

How do you start new plants of a Christmas begonia? Most commonly from single leaves treated as cuttings and inserted in a bed of moist sand in December. They need 70° temperature and moist atmospheric conditions to succeed. Can also be grown from ordinary stem cuttings inserted in spring.

My Begonia sutherlandi has developed swellings or lumps on its stems. Can these be used to start new plants? Yes. If planted in the spring, these bulbous growths will develop into new plants.

Which is the best way to propagate the hardy Begonia evansiana? Collect the small bulblets that form so freely on the stems in late summer. Store them in a cool place for the winter, and plant them in boxes of light soil in spring. Also by division of old plants.

What precaution should be observed in sowing begonia seed? Use a light, woodsy soil mixture, finely sifted—upper layer through a piece of window screening. Water well *before* sowing. Scatter dustlike seed evenly, and press in lightly. Do not cover with soil. Cover pot with glass and place in dark—temperature 60° to 70° F.—until seed germinates. Never allow soil to become dry. Water by standing pot in dish so that moisture seeps up from below.

How may begonias be grown from seed? I have difficulties; they always damp off. Damping off is caused by a fungus that thrives when conditions for the seedlings are unfavorable. Treat seed with disinfectant such as Semesan or Rootone. Avoid overwatering, too heavy shade, extreme fluctuation of temperature. Try using sterilized soil. Be sure soil is well drained. Water only on sunny days.

How should seedling begonias be transplanted? They are such tiny things. Prepare shallow boxes or pans by placing drainage material in bottom and filling with mixture of 1 part soil, 2 parts leafmold, 1 part sand sifted (the surface layer through window screening). Loosen seedlings and lift with roots intact (use wooden label with V-notch) and plant with leaves on surface, roots covered. Water with fine spray, or from below. Keep warm and shaded.

Insects and Diseases

See Section VIII.

What causes the younger leaves on begonias to crinkle and become hard or brittle? Mites (microscopic insects) which suck the juices from the plant. Spray repeatedly with Black Leaf 40, or all-purpose pressure bottle house plant spray recommended as miticide. Keep covered thoroughly with fine dusting sulfur.

My begonias fail to grow. Have been told they have root knot. What shall I use? Root-knot nematode causes swellings on roots, and, finally, decay. Only control is to repropagate, throw out old plants and keep new ones growing in sterilized soil.

Little green plant lice are on my begonia plants. What shall I do? Make a sudsy solution with Ivory soap; add 1 teaspoonful of Black Leaf 40 to a gallon. Invert plant, and dip foliage and stems so they are thoroughly wetted.

Varieties

What are varieties, names, and kinds of begonias, and their care, and when they bloom; also resting time? This subject is much too extensive to discuss briefly. You will find *Begonias,* (Hale, Cushman and Flint, 1939), and *Begonias and How to Grow Them* (Oxford University Press), both by Bessie Raymond Buxton and *Begonias for American Gardens* by Helen K. Krauss, (The Macmillan Company) most helpful.

Begonias: what kinds are best in the house? A good selection of easy-growing kinds includes: *B. feasti* (beefsteak), *B. semperflorens* (Wax), *B. argentea-guttata* (Trout), *B. coccinea* (Angel-wing), *B. heracleifolia* (Star), *B. scharffi* (*haageana*), President Carnot, and *B. fuchsioides.*

What are several varieties of begonias for winter blooming in house —hot-water heat? *Feasti, manicata, heracleifolia, nitida, roseagigantea, Sunderbruchi, verschaffeltiana.*

What are Lorraine begonias? Commonly known as Christmas begonias, they are the result of hybridizing *B. socotrana* and *B. dregei.* The first hybrid produced was named Gloire de Lorraine.

What is the name of the begonia with green-and-white, and some all-white, leaves; small red and deep pink flowers? Often called Calla Begonia. It is *Begonia semperflorens* var. "Callalily."

Can you tell me the name of a hardy begonia? *Begonia evansiana,* a native of China, is the hardiest species. In a sheltered position it will live outdoors in New York. It comes in both pink- and white-flowered varieties.

CAMPANULA ISOPHYLLA

There is a plant common in Cape Cod homes, which is generally called Star-of-Bethlehem. This is not the same as the one that grows in our garden from a bulb. It is a larger plant with beautiful blue or white flowers. Can you give me some idea of the right name? This is *Campanula isophylla,* a native of Italy. It is a trailing plant with beautiful gray-green foliage; a winter bloomer. It can be purchased from florists.

How can Star-of-Bethlehem be grown in the house? See above. Grow in sandy soil that has humus added. Sunny window in winter; light shade in summer. Keep moderately moist in winter; water freely in summer. Feed with diluted fertilizer when in growth. Propagate by cuttings in spring.

CALCEOLARIA

How can I grow calceolarias from seed? If you propose to do this in an ordinary window, you have chosen a tough subject. Like cinerarias, the spotted and other hybrid calceolarias want coolness. Sow the fine seeds on the surface of level sandy soil in a pot in July or August; full shade and never dry; transplant the tiny seedlings to a flat and keep in a shaded cold frame. Pot later and keep in the frame till late fall, then move to a light place with a temperature around 40° to 45° F. at night. If temperature runs above 50° any time during the winter, failure is almost certain. Beware of aphids and white flies.

CINERARIA

Can cinerarias be grown in a south window in a home with vapor heat? Can they be carried through summer for flowering again the next season? Cinerarias are short-lived plants in a warm room. They are grown at 40° to 45° F. and never above 50° F. When through blooming, discard them, as they don't like summer weather.

How can I raise cinerarias from seeds? I used moist sand and covered with a glass, but one by one they died. As cinerarias have to be sown in July or August to get sizable plants for winter or early spring, damping off in hot weather is always a menace. Use very sandy soil and don't use glass cover. Stand the pan where it is shaded, and keep as cool as possible. Sow late in August or early September, to escape the hot days and nights. Cinerarias must at all times be grown cool, 40° to 45° F.

Will cinerarias bloom in a warm room? 70° to 80° F.? No. If you can't give them a night temperature of 45° to 50° F., little more during day, don't try cinerarias either from seed or as blooming plants.

What causes cineraria leaves to curl and dry at edges? Probably too hot and dry an atmosphere; possibly plants are dry at the roots.

Cinerarias don't last long in a hot, dry temperature; 45° F. at night is plenty. Aphids are prone to attack them.

How should cinerarias be cared for in the window garden? Cinerarias with their masses of purple, red, or rose-pink flowers and dark, heavy foliage can be purchased from a florist's ready for late fall and winter bloom. They like a cool but sunny window. Watch for aphids.

FUCHSIA

How are fuchsias handled as house plants? Cuttings are rooted in spring, taken from old plants that have been started after a winter rest. If you keep them growing all year around in a warm room, you won't get flowers. They are spring and summer bloomers. Like full light but not full sun; rich soil and plenty of moisture and humidity when in growth.

Stable manure is usually advised for fuchsias, but this is hard to obtain. Is there any substitute? Fuchsias, if grown in pots, require the standard potting mixture. (See Soil, this section.) If rotted manure is impossible, use leafmold or peatmoss with good loam, and add a little dehydrated manure. Feed like any other pot plant when in full growth.

What fuchsias will bloom indoors in winter? *F. magellanica gracilis* is a winter bloomer. It will look well in a hanging basket, as it is a drooping, almost vinelike variety. The small flowers are ruby red. Most fuchsias are summer bloomers. By taking slips from larger plants in summer and having them well rooted by early winter, you may get bloom in late winter or very early spring. Or buy young blooming plants from a florist who has forced them.

I have a fuchsia that blossomed in May and June. What should I do so it will bloom during the winter months? Fuchsias are not naturally winter bloomers. The winter is their resting season. (See other questions.)

Should fuchsias be given a rest period, or may they be kept in bloom the year around? Fuchsias are not ever-blooming, and in winter old plants are best kept dry and cool until early spring. They should be potted and rested in a cool cellar or room, and watered very little. Cut back in February or March and give warmer quarters, watering more when new shoots begin to appear. If you can't accommodate growing plants so early, keep practically dry and cool till April, then stand outdoors on warm days; indoors at night. Don't plant outside until all danger of frost is past.

What is the cause of buds and blossoms falling off fuchsia plant on window shelf indoors? Too hot and/or dry an atmosphere, resulting in red spider; or white fly attack. Possibly either too wet or too dry at the root. Root injury always causes leaf drop. Spring and summer are the blooming seasons. Don't expect flowers in winter. The plants should be resting unless they are young plants. (See previous questions.)

Can fuchsias be wintered in cold frame? If the frame is absolutely frostproof and the fuchsias are kept dry and dark until March, they might survive. The so-called "hardy" variety Magellanica is the only sort that will stand real frost.

GERANIUMS

Which kind of soil should be used for geraniums to get good flowers? A mellow, loamy soil (not a sandy soil) is best. It should be well drained and enriched with bone meal. Avoid excessive use of nitrogenous fertilizer.

Do geraniums like a rich soil? When grown in pots, a rich and rather heavy soil is best. In beds or borders too rich a soil induces rank growth at the expense of flowers.

What is the best fertilizer for geraniums? Plants in outdoor beds respond to bone meal or superphosphate and wood ashes. Avoid nitrogenous fertilizers unless soil is poor. Pot-grown plants appreciate cow manure, bone meal, or any complete fertilizer used in moderation.

What do you suggest feeding geraniums for Christmas blooming? Providing you have a good winter-blooming variety, and have grown it specially for winter bloom, any good complete fertlizer that is moderately quick acting may be used after final pots are well filled with roots.

Culture

What must I do to start geraniums left to hang in cellar (root upward) when spring arrives? Take them down, prune them back somewhat (cut back roots as well), and pot in sandy soil in pots just large enough to hold the roots. Give one good soaking and put in light, warm place. Avoid watering frequently until new growth is well started.

When is it safe to plant geraniums from window into open garden? After all danger of frost has passed and ground has warmed up. About time lima beans are planted. Harden plants gradually before planting by standing them for few days in cold frame, on porch, or in sheltered place outdoors.

Should I break the soil and spread out roots of potted geraniums when I plant them in garden? No, leave ball intact. Thoroughly soak it an hour before planting. Make hole plenty big enough, press soil firmly about ball; water well. Top of ball should be half inch below finished surface.

What window is best (in house) for geraniums? The sunniest one, where a minimum temperature of 50° F. is maintained.

Should geraniums be always kept toward windows, one side always facing the window, or may they be moved? (Maryland.) They may be moved if desired, but it is not advisable to change them around frequently.

How should one care for geraniums in the house? What about using milk on them? What size pots? Do *not* use milk. Pots must be adjusted to size of plant. Avoid pots too large for plant. When pot is well filled with healthy roots, transfer to pot a size or two larger, using soil mixture suggested in first question on geraniums.

How shall I water my potted geraniums? Watering must be adjusted to individual plant and environment. Aim to keep soil moist (but not wet and boglike) throughout. When water is given, saturate whole ball of soil. Sunshine, high temperature, breezy weather, vigorous growth all make more frequent watering necessary.

I have potted my garden geraniums. What procedure do I follow to keep them blooming in the house? Please give directions for watering, sunlight, clipping tops, and temperature. See other questions. Cut tops about halfway back at potting time. Give all available sunlight, and fresh air, without drafts.

Can anything be done about correcting the growth habit of a peach-blossom geranium which is growing too tall and not sending out any side shoots below a distance of about 10 ins. from flower pot? Yes. You may "stop" the plant by pinching out the tips of the growing shoots, or, if necessary, you may prune the stems back to force new growth nearer pot.

Is it true if geraniums bloom continuously outdoors in the summer they seldom bloom freely in winter? Also, is the temperature of the room indoors important? Yes. All plants need a season of comparative rest. For the best winter bloom grow plants through summer in pots and pick off all flower buds until late fall. Give night temperature of 50° F.

How can I make my geraniums bloom through the winter? By preventing them from blooming in summer by picking off all flower buds. Also by keeping them in a light window. Some varieties are better winter bloomers than others.

Should geraniums be repotted, and how often? Mine are scrawny and do not blossom since being brought in from outdoors. Plants that have given a good display all summer can scarcely be expected to continue throughout winter. Prune back severely when you bring them indoors. Rest them somewhat by keeping them drier, but not completely dry, until new growth begins in late winter.

How do you treat and store geranium plants through the winter?

The best procedure is to cut the plants back part way and pot them a couple of weeks before killing frost may occur. Winter in a sunroom or window where temperature does not drop below 55° F. Water with care through winter.

Have geraniums in flower boxes now in the basement. Last summer they developed rather long stems and I want to cut them back this year. How shall I do it? I had these boxes in the unheated porch, but when the weather got too cold I put them in the basement for protection against frost. They lost all their leaves while in the porch (which I wanted to happen, to give them a rest over winter), but now in the basement they are producing small buds all over and it will not be long until they have new leaves. What shall I do? Prune away ½ to ⅔ the length of each shoot. Repot into new soil, put in light place, and they will develop nicely by summer.

Can geraniums planted outside be successfully wintered by storing plants in peatmoss or similar material, or must they be potted? They probably could be planted in peatmoss and sand, but potting in a sandy soil mixture would undoubtedly be surer and better.

Will geraniums keep all winter if pulled up by the root and kept in a cool fruit cellar? Have some beauties I would like to keep. Yes, under the conditions you mention. Hang them up by the roots from the ceiling and pick off all leaves that decay.

What is best care for Ivyleaf Geranium? Mine becomes straggly and root-bound in spite of being cut back and continuously changed to larger crocks. Perhaps your plant is so old that it would be wisest to start afresh from a cutting. When plants are well rooted, feed with liquid fertilizer at weekly or biweekly intervals. Pinch the tips out of growing shoots occasionally to induce branching.

What is the proper treatment of Ivy Geranium? Soil, exposure, watering, etc.? Pot in rich, mellow soil that is well drained. Grow in full sun; light shade is desirable during hottest part of day in summer. Water to maintain soil always evenly moist, but not wet and stagnant.

Why do Ivy Geraniums always have some dead leaves during blossoming season? This seems a common complaint except with plants grown in a comparatively humid (and perhaps lightly shaded) greenhouse.

What are conditions favorable to growth of the Martha Washington Geranium? Soil and moisture required? Cool, airy, sunny conditions (minimum night temperature 45° F.). Porous, fertile soil with some lime added. Plenty of moisture when growing rapidly; little or none when resting.

How do I care for my Lady Washington Geranium that bloomed this summer? After blooming period, gradually dry off, laying plants on their sides out of doors. In August prune back, shake old soil out of roots, pot into smallest possible container, water, and start into growth again.

Why do the leaves of my normally blooming geraniums turn brown and drop off? Many possible causes: too dry atmosphere; lack of water; too much water; damage to roots when repotting; or too strong fertilizer or spray.

What causes brown edges on geranium leaves? Probably wrong cultural conditions such as faulty soil, improper watering, or a parching atmosphere.

What causes my geranium leaves to turn pale green (almond-white) and not thrive? Have been recently repotted; long enough to be growing and thriving. Probably you are growing them with too little light. Low temperature could also be a factor. Try full sunshine and minimum temperature of 55° F.

Will geraniums thrive inside in a window box when the house is heated by gas? Unless gas is escaping into room atmosphere, method of heating will make no difference. Good light, reasonable temperatures, proper soil, and good care are the factors that count.

What makes our geranium house plants thin and spindly instead of short, stocky plants as they are outside? Would having bottled-gas cookstove effect plants? Too high temperature, coupled with too little light. Pinching tips out of plants occasionally will help. Read other questions and answers on this subject.

My geraniums won't blossom. They are in a southeast window, the room temperature is between 75° to 80° F. most of the time. What is wrong? Temperature is much too high. Ideal temperature for geraniums is 50° to 60° F.

What causes buds of a geranium to turn brown and dry up? May be due to leakage of manufactured gas; to general poor health of plant; to insufficient light; or to a very dry atmosphere.

What causes a geranium to have flowers of different colors? First red, and then pink? Plants sometimes "sport" or mutate. A red-flower geranium may produce a branch that bears pink flowers, and vice versa.

When I cut off pieces of my Rose Geranium and put them in a bunch of flowers, they start wilting almost at once. What can be done to prevent this? Very little. It will help to cut the geranium ahead of time and plunge it in cold water in a dark cool place for a few hours.

Propagation

What is a good method for propagating geraniums? By cuttings. (Terminal pieces of stem 4 or 5 ins. long with lower leaves removed and bases cut cleanly across just beneath a joint.) Plant firmly in clean sand; keep shaded from direct sunshine and in a fairly moist atmosphere at about 60° F.

What is the best way to start geraniums from cuttings? What kind of soil should be used, and how much water? Start with good, clean cuttings made of shoots that are neither hard and woody nor yet very vigorous and watery. Plant in sand. Keep just moist (not sopping wet). When roots have formed, pot singly in small pots, using for this first potting a very sandy soil.

What is the recommended time for slipping Rose Geraniums? Cuttings will root any time, but the most favorable months are May, August, and September.

When is the right time to take cutting of geraniums so they will flower for Decoration Day? August or September.

When should geraniums be started for spring outside boxes? From August to February, depending on size of plants needed. Early cuttings will finish in 5-in. pots; late cuttings in 3½- or 4-in. pots.

Why don't my geraniums bloom in the house before February? I usually start them from slips in August. They are very beautiful otherwise, with very large, thick, glossy leaves. The flowers are large and beautiful when they do bloom. For early bloom propagate in May.

Is it better to root geraniums in water or in sand? What is the best time to root them for early blossoming? Moist sand is best. Take cuttings early in September for late spring blooming; in May for winter blooming.

Before frost in October I take geranium clippings and plant them in sand in pot indoors for rooting. About 90 per cent eventually rot at the dirt line. What is wrong? You will stand a greater chance of success if you take your cuttings in late August or early September. Keep the sand moist but not wet. (See Insects and Diseases of Geraniums.)

My geranium slips looked very healthy at first, but now leaves are turning yellow and dying. No gas in house, and plants in south window. What is the trouble? Cuttings are losing water faster than they can take it up. Reduce the transpiration by shading from bright sun and by placing them in box covered with pane of glass. Allow small amount of ventilation.

When and how do I pot geranium slips rooted in sand? As soon as roots are ½ to 1 in. long plant singly in small pots, using very sandy soil without fertilizer added. Do not press soil too firmly. Water well immediately; syringe for a few days.

Have an Apple Blossom Geranium and can never start a new slip. When and how should I try? May or August. Make cutting 4 or 5 joints long; cut with sharp knife below joint; remove lower leaves; plant firmly in moist sand; keep moist, shaded from strong sun, in a moist atmosphere at 60° F. or more.

How does one slip Martha Washington Geraniums?   Very much as any other geranium. The shoots that root with greatest ease are young ones produced after plants have been started into growth in late summer, but tips of older shoots may also be used.

How may geraniums be grown from seeds?   Sow seeds in spring in pots of light, sandy soil. Cover very lightly, keep moist (and shaded until seedlings appear) in temperature 60° F. If seed is good, it will soon germinate, and under favorable conditions, the transplanted seedlings make rapid growth.

Why don't my seedling geraniums bloom?   Possibly they are growing too vigorously because of too-rich soil. Too much shade also reduces blooming. Try keeping some plants in pots.

How long after geranium seed is planted may blooms be expected? From 6 months to 1 year.

How can large geranium plant be divided into smaller plants? What fertilizer is recommended?   Geranium (*Pelargonium zonale*) plants do not lend themselves to this method of propagation. Increase stock by means of cuttings. Any commercial fertilizer may be used advantageously.

Insects and Diseases

See Section VIII.

I have an Ivy Geranium that is almost 3 ft. tall. It was a slip last spring; now the leaves are starting to curl down. What is the cause of this?   It may be due to a severe attack of aphids. Examine young shoots and under sides of leaves; if plant lice are found, spray with any good contact insecticide.

Have a pelargonium 6 years old; bloomed once with gorgeous red and brown blooms. It has never blossomed since. I've changed dirt and pots, started new slips, but none will bloom. White flies bother it all the time. What shall I do for it?   This is a Martha Washington variety. To control white flies, spray at weekly intervals (until trouble is cleared up) with a nicotine insecticide used according to manufacturer's directions, or with a pressure bottle house plant spray recommended for the purpose. For cultural details, read answers to other inquiries.

Why do geranium cuttings rot while in the sand and turn black and die without rooting?   The fungous disease known as Black Leg causes these symptoms. The rot begins at base and works upward to leaves. Use clean flats and sand that has been thoroughly baked, or sterile vermiculite. Propagate from healthy plants only.

Varieties

There is a small-leafed geranium similar to Rose Geranium, with a most unusual and delightful emanation from the leaves. What is its name? Perhaps you mean *Pelargonium citriodorum* (lemon-scented), *P.* Dr. Livingston (lemon-rose-scented), *P. denticulatum* (pine-scented), *P. fragrans* (nutmeg), *P. odoratissimum* (apple-scented), or *P. tomentosum* (peppermint-scented).

What varieties of geraniums are best for outdoor planting? How and when should they be propagated to bloom for Decoration Day? What soil and fertilizers should be used? Beaute de Poitevine, S. A. Nutt, Red Fiat, Pink Fiat, Radio Red, and Ricard. By cuttings, rooted in sand bed in September. Good ordinary soil and any standard fertilizer is O.K.

I have seen a geranium on the market in both red and light pink. The green leaves have a white border around. What is the name of this geranium? Silver-leaf S. A. Nutt (red-flowered), Madam Languth (pink).

GERBERA

Do gerberas or African-daisies, when brought indoors from the garden, get a rest period; or should they continue to show leaves? Gerberas do best when kept growing during the winter at 55° F., as that is their real flowering season. They are not likely to prove good window plants at ordinary room temperatures.

HELIOTROPE

Is heliotrope a satisfactory house plant? Heliotrope can only be made to bloom in winter by purchasing plants forced by the florist, or by starting cuttings in summer which are ready to bloom by late winter. To force winter bloom on mature plants, they must be kept pinched back and disbudded through the summer. Heliotrope must have a very sunny position in a cool window garden. Water moderately. Cut back long, sprawling branches occasionally. Watch for white fly (which see).

Can a heliotrope potted from the garden be kept over the winter to set out again in summer? Yes. Cut back a bit and keep cool— not above 55° F. Cuttings can be rooted in February to make more plants to set out in late May.

Can heliotrope and lavender be treated in the same manner? No. Lavender is a hardy plant and thrives outdoors the year around. Heliotrope is tender, and is grown either from seed or from cuttings. It is used either as a pot plant indoors or as a bedding plant outdoors in summer.

IMPATIENS

What varieties of patience-plant shall I get, and how should it be cared for indoors? The Latin name is *Impatiens*. *Impatiens sultani* has bright red, single blossoms. Hybrids of this variety are white and pink or salmon; one has variegated foliage. *I. holsti* is a stronger grower, with large scarlet flowers. *Impatiens* is a willing house plant. Give plenty of water, but pour surplus from saucer after soil is soaked. Prune in spring; root cuttings from pruned branches. It blooms constantly through the winter. Use standard potting mixture. (See Soil, this section.)

MARGUERITES

Are marguerites satisfactory as house plants? Yes. Purchase blooming plants from florist. They will do well in a sunny window. Sink pots in garden bed in summer where they will do almost equally well. For winter bloom, keep plants disbudded through summer. New plants root readily from cuttings. Marguerites need ample water. Watch for aphids. Use standard potting mixture. (See Soil, this section.)

MARICA

Is the marica sometimes called Twelve Apostles? Does it make a good house plant? Yes, the maricas are sometimes given this nickname because of the number of their irislike leaves, which sometimes reaches twelve. *M. gracilis* is the smaller leaved of the two generally grown, and has white and violet, irislike fleeting blossoms which appear at the tips of leaflike peduncles in late winter. *M. northiana* has larger leaves and blooms about the same time, having larger violet and white fragrant blossoms. It blooms less freely than *M. gracilis, M. caerulea* has 4-in. violet-blue flowers. New plants can be started from the peduncles, which produce young plants after bloom. Maricas need sunshine and warmth for early bloom. Sponge the glossy leaves to keep them free from dust. Use standard potting mixture. (See Soil, this section.)

I have a Marica gracilis which grew lustily and increased greatly in size. Why didn't it blossom? Perhaps you kept it too cool. At 50° to 60° F. bloom is considerably delayed. The flowers should appear in late winter if plants are kept at a day temperature of about 70° F. Pot-bound specimens seldom bloom well. Yours may need division; or discard the old plant and start new stock. (See previous question.)

Is it safe to divide old plants of marica? Yes, they can be easily divided. Or start new plants from those which develop on blooming stalks.

How old does the Twelve Apostles have to be before it blooms? This plant (marica), if grown from a small offshoot, may take 2 to 3 years to reach blooming size. Put the plant outdoors in partial shade during the summer. Bring in before frost.

Does the Twelve Apostles require much sun and water? Marica presumably is meant. It can take its full share of sun and light in a window, but use care in watering at all times; placing outside in partial shade during the summer is desirable. It blooms in late winter or early spring, depending on the species.

What makes the tips of my marica leaves turn brown? Probably watered too much. This plant is related to the iris, and, while ever-green, it has its resting season. When the leaves go bad, the best thing to do is to repot in fresh soil (after cutting away dead roots) and give only enough water to prevent wilting until it becomes active again.

PANSIES

Will pansies bloom indoors in winter? Seed must be sown in late July; seedlings transplanted to rich ground. If for pots or boxes, plant in September and bring inside before hard freezing. Unless you have a light, frost-free porch or big window with temperature not above 45° F., don't try. Rather plant in cold frame, lift, and pot in March, and you will get some flowers.

PRIMROSES

What primroses can I grow indoors in winter? *P. sinensis* or Chinese Primrose, single or double. Can be purchased from a florist. Bears pink, magenta, or white blooms. Long blooming period. *P. malacoides,* or Fairy Primrose, has small, frothy violet blossoms throughout winter. *P. obconica,* with vigorous hairy leaves, has larger flowers. *P. grandiflora fimbriata* (Giant Fringed Primrose) has flowers more than an inch across in white, through pink to deep rose. Water daily, in the saucer. Keep in cool east window, with a dish of water near by to provide humidity. Use fibrous potting mixture. (See Soil, this section.)

What can I do to make my primrose bloom? It is about 3 years old. Not knowing the kind of primrose, we can't advise. There are several types grown in pots for winter and spring flowers in greenhouses, and dozens of hardy kinds that bloom outdoors in the spring and early summer if conditions are right. The greenhouse kinds are discarded after one season.

What conditions are best for primroses as house plants? How much water? How much light and sun? How much heat, and how cool at night? For *P. malacoides* and *P. sinensis,* not above 50° F. at night; even less is better. *P. obconica,* 50° to 55° F. at night. All like partial shade, ample water, but plenty of drainage in the pots. Soil should not be very acid.

What care does the Christmas-blooming primrose require?   If you mean *P. obconica,* this is raised from seed sown in February or March, grown on in pots in moderate shade through the summer, and from fall on kept at 55° F. or so. Don't give too much water, yet never allow to wilt for lack of moisture at the roots. Discard the plants after blooming.

How can I propagate a Chinese Primrose?   The Chinese Primrose (*P. sinensis*) is raised from seed each year. Choice double sorts that do not seed usually produce side growths which can be cut off with a knife and rooted.

STRELITZIA

How is Bird-of-paradise (strelitzia) handled in winter? Should I take it out of pot and plant in ground in summer?   The strelitzia is a big subject for a house plant, needing a tub—since it won't bloom until of some size. In winter, give only a moderate amount of water; good rich soil with plenty of drainage; full light but no feeding while semi-dormant. Don't take out of pot or tub in summer, sink to rim, and feed regularly. Blooms generally in late summer and fall. Winter temperature, 45° to 50° F.

Whenever my Bird-of-paradise makes a new leaf the old one dies. Why doesn't it bloom?   You won't get blooms until the plant has 10 or more healthy leaves. The dying leaves indicate something wrong at the roots. Either insufficient size pot, poor drainage, not enough water while in active growth during summer, or too much water in winter when it should be semi-dormant.

SWEET-OLIVE

How shall I care for a sweet-olive (*Osmanthus fragrans*) as a house plant?   Sweet-olive does well in an east or west window if you can give it a day temperature of 60 to 65 degrees. It needs plenty of water and a humid atmosphere. Syringe the leaves weekly and feed occasionally with a complete plant food after the pot is filled with roots.

ANNUALS AND BIENNIALS

Is it possible to raise annuals indoors in winter without the plants becoming stalky?   You can germinate the seed but will not be able to grow them satisfactorily unless you have an abundance of light and a temperature not above 50° F. for most sorts. Still less chance to flower them. All the annuals florists grow in winter are kept at the above night temperature and no higher in the day except through sun heat.

Dwarf varieties of many garden annuals—such as marigold, ageratum, and zinnia—supply color for the indoor garden in late fall or late spring, if seed sowing is carefully timed.

ALYSSUM

Can I make alyssum bloom indoors? Yes, if you have enough sun and a really cool window or sun porch. Sow the seeds in late summer in pots or boxes.

BROWALLIA

Is the browallia an annual? I potted mine in the fall and about January the leaves withered and it died. *B. elata* is an annual for outdoor use. *B. speciosa* is a biennial or perennial, but not hardy. The variety known as Sapphire is sown in the fall, carried along in a greenhouse through the winter, and planted out in the spring; or sown in spring to flower indoors in winter.

Are browallias suited to the window garden? Yes, *B. speciosa* makes a most satisfactory house plant. The tubular flowers, rather like small petunias, are blue, violet, or white, and literally cover the plants through a long blooming season. They are easily grown biennials which form shrubby, compact plants. Purchase them in bloom from a florist, or grow them yourself from spring-sown seed.

FORGET-ME-NOT

Can forget-me-not be made to bloom indoors? Yes. It needs a cool but humid atmosphere and, unlike most other annuals and biennials, can stand some shade, though not much indoors. Plant the seed in spring for the following winter's bloom. This is really a greenhouse subject for winter bloom, but with the right conditions you may have flowers.

LOBELIA

Is lobelia a plant which can be made to bloom indoors in winter? Yes, you can grow lobelia from seeds or cuttings to produce winter bloom. Since it does not need as much sun as many other flowering plants, you will have pretty good chance of success if the window is cool. There are many fine blue varieties, and White Gem is a pure white.

MORNINGGLORY

Can I have morningglories in my window garden? Yes, if you have a cool, sunny window. Plant seeds in individual pots in August. Transplant to larger pots as needed. Have strings ready near the glass to encourage the vines to climb. Heavenly Blue is the most beautiful variety. Pearly Gates is similar, but pure white.

NASTURTIUM

How can nasturtiums be grown indoors in winter? They must have a cool, sunny window or sun porch. Plant seeds in late summer in pots of soil without too much fertilizer. Or slip some of the summer bloomers in the garden, keeping them cut back to prevent bloom until winter. Of course black aphids will attack them indoors as well as out. Use some of the double fragrant varieties.

PETUNIA

How can I grow petunias in the house during the winter? I took a few in this fall and they wouldn't grow. Petunias are not winter bloomers, nor can they be classed as good house plants.

SNAPDRAGONS

Are snapdragons practical house plants? If you have a very cool sun porch or bay window (40° to 50° F. night temperature), you may be able to have blooming snapdragons (*Antirrhinum*) through the winter. Though these are perennial in the South, they are grown as annuals in the North. Buy budded plants from a florist, or grow your own from seed planted the previous spring. Select dwarf, rust-resistant varieties. Or you can start plants in summer for winter bloom by slipping those growing in the summer garden. Whether plants are started from seeds or slips, they should be kept pinched back to encourage winter bloom.

FOLIAGE PLANTS

GENERAL

What temperature is best for foliage plants indoors? No one temperature is best for all. The majority grow well in night temperature 55° to 60° F. with a rise of 10° in the daytime permitted. For cooler rooms try English Ivy, Leopard-plant, Australian-silkoak, eucalyptus, aspidistra, baby tears, pick-a-back plant, strawberry-geranium, spider-plant, and Norfolk-Island-pine.

Does it help to spray water on the leaves of foliage plants grown in the home? Daily sprinklings with atomizer syringe benefit all plants having leathery leaves, such as rubber plants, palms, and pandanus.

On the mornings of bright, sunny days syringe plants with thin or hairy leaves such as coleus or pilea.

Some people tell me to wash my foliage plants with milk, others to wipe the leaves with olive oil. Which is better? Both are harmful, they merely result in an artificial gloss due to the oil or to the fat of the milk. When you sponge leaves, use lukewarm, soapy water. Leaves can be treated with a gloss such as Plant Shine to make them glossy.

My foliage plants indoors do well in summer, but in fall their leaves turn yellow and drop off. What is the cause? When artificial heating is used, air becomes too dry for plants. Lack of atmospheric moisture is one cause of failure with house plants. Install humidifiers. Stand plants on shallow trays of sand or gravel kept moist.

Can you give a list of foliage house plants that can easily be raised from seed? *Eucalyptus globulus* (Blue Gum), *Eucalyptus citriodora* (Lemon-scented Eucalyptus), *Grevillea robusta* (Australian-silkoak), coleus, *Asparagus sprengeri* and *Asparagus plumosus* (asparagus ferns), and *Cordyline indivisa* (*Dracaena indivisa*).

ARALIA

Is Aralia sieboldi a house plant? An easy subject to grow in a light window where the temperature ranges between 55° and 65° F. Shade from bright summer sunshine is desirable. Water to keep soil always evenly moist but not waterlogged.

How can Aralia sieboldi be raised from seed? The correct name is *Fatsia japonica*. Sow seed in pots of light, sandy soil in spring; cover seeds to own depth with sifted soil. Keep moist; temperature, 65° F. When an inch or two high, transplant to small pots of sandy soil. Grow in light window.

ASPARAGUS

What kind of soil does Asparagus plumosus like, acid or alkaline? More on acid than alkaline side. It likes a garden soil that has both peat and sand in it (2 parts soil, 1 part peat, 1 part sand); this should be enriched by ⅛ part (in bulk) of dried cow manure mixed with bone meal.

What are asparagus "ferns"? Two are commonly grown: *A. plumosus,* with flat sprays of fine foliage, and *A. sprengeri,* with coarser and less regular leaves. These foliage plants are *not really ferns.* Both are subject to red spider, so spray once a week with cool water. Transplant once a year, or whenever pots become filled with roots. They like plenty of light and air. Water regularly and feed once a month. (See next question.)

What are the water requirements of Asparagus sprengeri? Is it the moisture or temperature conditions that turn foliage yellow? *A. sprengeri* likes adequate and regular watering once a day. Once or twice a month substitute liquid manure. Leaves turn yellow from lack of food, if plant is pot-bound, or if temperature is above or below 55° to 65° F.

How do I raise asparagus "ferns" from seed? Very easily. Soak seed in tepid water for 24 hrs. before sowing, then plant 1 in. apart and cover to a depth of ¼ in. in light, sandy soil, in a pot or pan. Keep moist, dark, and in temperature of 65° to 70° F.

ASPIDISTRA

What is the common name for Aspidistra lurida? Parlor palm and cast-iron plant are two common names for the aspidistra.

Why do the leaves of my aspidistra turn yellow? Yellowing leaves mean either red spider mites are sucking the life out of them, that you have watered too much or have exposed plant to extreme drought. If red spider is the trouble, spray or sponge the leaves with any good contact insecticide.

Does the aspidistra plant ever bloom? Old, well-established plants sometimes do. The flowers are relatively inconspicuous, being reddish-brown in color and borne at soil level.

Can aspidistra be increased in any other way than by division? No. In nature it may propagate by seed, but these do not seem to form in cultivation. Divide in spring and keep newly potted divisions in warm room and moist atmosphere until new roots become established.

AUSTRALIAN-SILKOAK

What kind of soil does Australian-silkoak (Grevillea robusta) like? A sandy and rather peaty mixture that does not tend to become water-logged. Very heavy soil is unsuited to this plant, particularly in its young stages.

AVOCADO

Should avocado seed be dried before attempting to root it in water? Mine have always formed a slimy coating in water and never rooted. Do not use water; plant seed in a pot of porous soil; keep moist and in a temperature of 60° to 70° F.

BABY TEARS

What is the plant called Baby tears and how can I grow it in the house? Baby tears, or creeping-nettle, is *Helxine soleiroli,* a native of Corsica and Sardinia. It looks like a fine green moss; grows well in sandy soil, kept moist, in morning sun or very light shade. Easily propagated by pulling apart and setting pieces in soil.

BAY TREE

Are there several varieties of bay trees, and how should they be

treated? Mine were given me as a gift. I am at a loss as to how to keep them growing. There is only one true bay tree. It is not hardy in New York. It eventually grows to large size. Tubbed specimens are best wintered in a cool, light, frostproof cellar.

CAMPHOR

How can a camphor plant be raised? The camphor tree, (*Cinnamomum camphora*) can be raised from cuttings under a bell glass with bottom heat and a sandy peat medium. But since it grows to tree size and needs a winter temperature of around 55° to 60° F., it is not particularly suitable as a house plant. Camphorosma is a group of small shrubs or herbs with camphor-like odor, some of which are grown in herb gardens. They are not hardy and have to be brought indoors in winter.

CHINESE-EVERGREEN

What is the real name of Chinese-evergreen, so often grown indoors in water? What are its requirements? *Aglaonema modestum* is a very satisfactory house plant for rooms with little sun. Grown in water to which a few small pieces of charcoal have been added to keep the water sweet, it behaves well in average living-room conditions.

COLEUS

Can I dig up coleus plants from the garden and put them into pots for winter decoration indoors? If plants are cut back at time of potting, they may grow into decorative specimens by late winter; but a much better plan is to take cuttings from outdoor plants in August, root them in sand, and pot up to provide young new plants for your indoor garden.

How can coleus be raised as house plants? Mine always become sickly. Coleus are raised from seed or cuttings but are not A-1 house plants. They like full light, temperature not above 55° F. in winter, and careful protection from mealy bugs.

Mealy bugs on my coleus are a constant source of trouble. What shall I do? Mealy bugs on coleus are difficult to eradicate because forceful syringing with water is apt to damage leaves. Try brushing them off with a soft camel's-hair brush dipped in soapy water or denatured alcohol.

CROTON

I have a croton (codiaeum), potted in fibrous loam, but while the plant in general does well, sometimes leaves wilt and drop. What causes this? If plant is growing outdoors, cool spells may be the cause. This plant loves heat and lots of it. Not a good house plant unless high humidity with heat is provided.

CRYPTANTHUS

What is a cryptanthus, and how should it be grown? It is a minia-ture bromeliad (pineapple relative) that is grown for the beauty of its stiff little leaves. It grows best in a terrarium or in a warm room where air is not too dry. Pot in sandy, humusy soil with charcoal added, or in orchid peat and leafmold mixed.

DUMB CANE

I have a dumb cane (dieffenbachia) in the house and the lower leaves turn yellow. What shall I do? Too low a temperature or lack of moisture in air are commonest causes of yellowing. Excessive dryness at root may be a contributing cause. This plant likes warmth, a moist atmosphere, shade from strongest sunshine, and a fair amount of moisture.

Why is dieffenbachia called dumb cane? Is it poisonous? Not poisonous, but, like its relative, the Jack-in-the-pulpit, it contains sharp crystals of oxalate of lime. If the stem is chewed, these pierce the tongue, causing it to swell with intense pain. Speech may be im-possible for several days.

Can a "leggy" dieffenbachia be successfully air-layered? The plant is 30 ins. high? Cut halfway through, slanting and upward. Insert a tooth pick and bind with a large ball of damp sphagnum moss. Then wrap tightly in pliofilm, binding at each end with twistems. A thick stem may take a year before it is rooted enough to cut below the moss and placed in a pot.

HOLLY

I have a dwarf holly plant in a pot. Can it be made to fruit indoors? Holly is not a house plant, but some species are not hardy except in the South. Most hollies are unisexual and fruit is not possible unless both types (a male plant and a female plant) are grown near each other.

LEOPARD-PLANT

Is the Leopard-plant classed as a foliage or a flowering plant? Like most "foliage plants," *Ligularia kaempferi aureo-maculata* blooms (and the yellow flowers are quite attractive); it is grown primarily for the beauty of its large, rounded leaves, which are conspicuously spotted with yellow markings.

Under what conditions does the Leopard-plant grow best? How is it propagated? It likes a rather cool room with full sun or partial shade. A freely drained soil, but enough water to keep it always moist. In summer plunge outdoors in a partially shaded position. Propagate by dividing up the old plant in spring.

MANGO

Am raising mango tree from seed. Do you think it will bear? No, it will not. The mango is a large tropical tree that sometimes attains a height of nearly 100 ft. Is only hardy in the most tropical parts of the United States. Fruits of seedling mangoes are very inferior to named varieties.

MARANTA

How should Maranta leuconeura and kerchoveana be cared for? Marantas, grown chiefly for their unusual foliage, are semi-tropical plants which flourish in a warm greenhouse. However, the maranta does unusually well in farm kitchens where the range and steaming kettles provide the needed humidity. It is often called Prayer Plant because it folds its leaves at night. Keep warm and moist. Use fibrous potting mixture. (See Soil, this section.)

MONSTERA

What is the foliage plant, of climbing habit, with large, heart-shaped, cut leaves? You are probably referring to *Monstera deliciosa* (*Philodendron pertusum*), a very showy foliage plant which looks well in modern rooms and which can be grown in good light without direct sun. Though a climber, it grows rather slowly and is usually treated as a foliage plant, trained on cork bark.

NEPHTHYTIS AFZELI

What are the requirements of nephthytis indoors? Nephthytis is a tropical vinelike foliage plant which usually comes from the florist trained on cork bark. It does not need full sunlight and stands ordinary living-room conditions well. Trailing portions cut from the main plant do well grown on in water.

NORFOLK-ISLAND-PINE

How do we take care of Norfolk-Island-Pine during the summer? *Araucaria excelsa* makes a good but slow-growing pot plant. During the summer sink pot outside in light shade and syringe and water regularly. In winter it wants 55° to 60° F., and even light to keep it shapely. Spray regularly to prevent spider and mealy-bug attack.

I have had an araucaria house plant for the past 4 years. It is now 40 ins. high. The branches are starting to droop. Can you suggest the reason? It is natural for lower branches eventually to droop. If plant is wilting, you have either overwatered or given too much fertilizer with perhaps not enough light and too much heat. Stimulants are not called for when plants droop.

PALM

How shall I take care of date palm? (1) Temperature from 55° to 65° F.; (2) soil—ordinary loam, peatmoss, and sand, proportions 5–3–1; (3) watering—never completely dry but not too wet; just moist at all times, soaking thoroughly and not again until surface feels firm; (4) exposure—never expose to full sunshine if grown as a pot plant.

Is there any special fertilizer or treatment to give palm trees and how often must they be watered? Palms need full shade and must never be dry, yet not constantly soaking wet. No feeding is needed until pots are full of root.

What possibility is there of growing palms? Palms are good house plants if given shade but full light and are not subjected to dry, hot rooms in winter.

PANDANUS (SCREWPINE)

How should I care for a pandanus plant? Keep out of bright sunshine and use care in watering. It is easy to kill this plant with overwatering.

My pandanus leaves are turning yellow, especially at the tips. What is the cause? A sure sign of root trouble; you probably have overwatered. Keep on dry side and don't use too large a pot. Don't expose to bright sunshine.

How should shoots from pandanus be rooted, and when? Cut off the suckers at base and insert in sandy soil. If you can place the pot in a box and cover with a sheet of glass, all the better. Do this in the spring, when growth is active.

PEPEROMIA

How can I grow the striped peperomia successfully? Peperomias require fairly warm, humid conditions and protection from direct sunshine. A humusy soil (well drained), kept uniformly moist, is desirable.

Rooted leaf cutting of Peperomia.

What causes small brown spots on the under side of peperomia leaves? Spots on the under side suggest injury from thrips or other insects. Poor foliage generally is due either to sunburn, lack of moisture in the atmosphere, or too much water on the leaves.

My peperomia gets large, irregular brown spots on the back of the leaves. Can you tell me why and what to do? Such spots or patches are usually an indication of disease brought about by atmospheric conditions. These plants do best in a terrarium or a shaded greenhouse. Keep out of the sun.

PICK-A-BACK

What is the pick-a-back plant? *Tolmiea menziesi,* a native of our Pacific Northwest. It has the curious habit of producing young plantlets on its leaves from which new plants can be grown. It is an interesting, worth-while house plant.

The Pick-a-back plant (Tolmiea menziesi) *is one of the few which forms new plants on the growing leaves instead of by runners.*

How shall I care for the pick-a-back plant? Grow in pots of light, rich soil. Keep quite moist at all times. Thrives in full sun or part shade. Although a hardy plant, it seems not to object to ordinary room temperature. Propagate by planting well-developed plantlets that are borne on mature leaves.

PINEAPPLE

What can I do with a pineapple plant that is nearly 2 years old and does not seem to grow any more? It stands nearly 8 ins. high now. Doesn't it flower? If a true pineapple, grown from the tuft of the fruit, flowers will not develop. If some other member of the bromeliad family, flowers are apt to be quite attractive. Don't overwater, and give full light. They are naturally slow growers.

What care is needed for the pineapple plant? The true pineapple needs plenty of warmth, light, and sun, and very careful watering, as it quickly resents very wet conditions at the root. Frequent feedings (2 a week) with liquid manure or fertilizer are of great help to a healthy plant.

POMEGRANATE (PUNICA)

Can pomegranates be grown from seed? Yes, they can, and if wanted merely as house plants are quite satisfactory. For fruit production (when they can be grown outdoors) named varieties are used, and these will not come true from seed.

How are pomegranates propagated?   By hardwood cuttings planted in open nursery beds in February; by taking rooted shoots directly from base of plant; by layering; by green cuttings taken in summer.

POTHOS

What care is needed for Pothos aureus?   It likes shade, a uniformly moist (but not a boglike) soil, temperature of 60° to 70° F., and occasional sponging of leaves with lukewarm, soapy water. Correct name is *Scindapsus aureus*.

REDWOOD BURL

How long will a redwood burl last? Also can a sprout of it be rooted and grown as a pot plant?   A burl kept with its base in a shallow container of water lived and thrived for many years at the New York Botanical Garden. Sprouts cannot be rooted.

RUBBER PLANT

What care is needed in watering and feeding rubber trees grown as house plants?   *Ficus elastica,* the recognized rubber plant of early days, and *Ficus lyrata,* like part shade and lots of room, as they eventually become very tall, rarely branching. Give plenty of water and food once a month when root-bound.

How does one encourage the rubber plant to branch out, rather than grow as a single upright stem?   *Ficus elastica* is not very responsive to cutting back, but if done after the plant has 6 or 8 leaves, removal of the point will induce 2 or 3 breaks. The natural habit is to grow single stemmed for many years before branching.

Can I cut back large rubber plant when the trunk is thick?   *Ficus elastica,* if cut back, may die from the shock if it is treelike and has no lower leaves. The regular method of propagation is to slit the stem partly through, wrap with moss, and keep constantly moist. If your plant has a branch with ½-in. stem, you can so treat the branch, but if there are no branches and the trunk is really heavy, 1 in. or more, it's too large for air-layering.

What is the name of the rubber plant with leaves that widen out toward the tips? What culture does it need?   This is the Fiddle-leaved Fig (or rubber plant)—*Ficus lyrata,* or *pandurata.* It requires the same general care as the common rubber plant—*Ficus elastica.*

SAGO-PALM

I have a sago-palm in a pot. It is about 20 years old, but I've had it only 5 months. It isn't doing well since I brought it inside. Can you

suggest proper care? *Cycas revoluta* likes sunshine with only moderate shade from strong summer sun. Avoid overwatering but never allow to dry out completely. In fall don't be alarmed if the lower leaves turn brown and drop. It's natural for them to go as new ones are produced.

SENSITIVEPLANT

How can I grow a sensitiveplant in my sunny window? Sow seeds of *Mimosa pudica* in pot of light soil in March. Transplant seedlings into 2½-in. pot when second set of leaves is well grown. Later pot into 4-in. pot. Grow in well-drained soil, minimum temperature 60° F. Never permit to suffer from dryness.

SNAKE-PLANT

Under what conditions will sansevieria do best? Dry, moderately warm rooms with full light. Water carefully once a week. This is enough under ordinary conditions, as it is easily killed by overwatering.

I can never get the sansevieria to grow and do well. Why? Too much water and not enough light. This plant, when well rooted, can go for weeks without water. Shade also is detrimental.

My sansevieria plant had flowers on it this summer. Is this unusual? Not so unusual as is sometimes thought. Old, well-established specimens are apt to bloom, and once they begin, they repeat the performance year after year. The flowers are light greenish, in feathery spikes, and are very fragrant.

How does one increase sansevieria? These are grown from divisions of roots or rhizomes. Pieces of leaf planted in moist sand will root and make plants, but if you so treat the variegated sort, the young plants will come green leaved.

SPIDER-PLANT

Is the spider-plant a house plant? Yes, it is a species of chlorophytum (*C. variegatum*). It has green-and-white-striped leaves and sends out long, slender stems which bear young plants at their extremities.

STRAWBERRY-GERANIUM

What will encourage growth of strawberry-geranium? Should it be kept on the dry side? In sun or shade? This is *Saxifraga sarmentosa,* which is almost hardy. Don't try to grow it in a hot, dry room, or it will become infested with red spider. Sun or shade, providing light is good. Moderate supplies of water. If you want runners bearing young plants to develop, grow it in a hanging basket or on a wall bracket.

UMBRELLA-PLANT

What conditions does the feathery green plant called umbrella-plant require? *Cyperus alternifolius* is really a bog plant and needs a moist or wet soil. It does well if the pot is kept standing in a saucer of water; prefers plenty of sunshine.

How are young plants of the umbrella-plant raised? *Cyperus alternifolius* is easily raised from seeds sown in soil kept constantly moist. Another method of increase is to cut off the leafy top with about an inch of stem attached. When roots have formed, plant in pot of soil.

VELVET PLANT

I have a foliage plant with velvety purple leaves. What is it and how shall I care for it? This is *Gynura aurantiaca* or velvet plant. Place it in an east window and water freely. It is of easy culture.

GIFT PLANTS

AZALEAS

What is the proper soil for azaleas and other ericaceous plants? It must be lime free, definitely acid, and well drained. The addition of liberal amounts of oak leafmold or peatmoss to the mixture is recommended. (See Soil, Acid Potting Mixture, this section.)

How shall I care for a tender azalea after blooming? Keep well watered, in full light, in a room at 50° F. If overlarge for pot, shift to one 1 in. larger, soaking soil well after repotting. Use acid potting mixture. Pot firmly but do not ram earth down hard.

Should I cut back my indoor azaleas, and when? No, merely pinch back any extra-long shoots, but don't prune in the usual way for shrubs or the plants may die. Azaleas make but short growths each year.

What care is needed for an azalea plant grown indoors? Pot azaleas should only be indoors during the winter and while in bloom. From mid-May on pot should be sunk in ground, with light shade, regular watering and spraying, pinching back of overlong growths. A level teaspoonful of ammonium sulfate in a gallon of water twice a month will keep the soil acid. Use a general fertilizer occasionally. Bring indoors before severe frost.

How should I treat my tender azalea after bringing indoors in autumn? Keep just moist, in a light, cool room at 40° F. until 4 weeks before you want full bloom, then bring into warm, sunny room, water plentifully. Give complete fertilizer until color shows on buds.

Should an azalea plant have a rest period during the winter? Yes. After being brought indoors before severe frost, a potted azalea must be kept cool (40° to 60° F.) and just moist until after Christmas.

Experts can bloom them at Christmas, but the window gardener should not attempt it.

How can I tell whether my tender azalea is going to bloom? The buds should be well set when brought indoors in the fall.

An Easter azalea plant was put aside and forgotten after blooming until discovered in November, in dry, warm cellar. Is this plant dormant or really dead? An azalea so treated is dead—or it ought to be! Don't waste time on it. Azaleas after flowering need a cool place, moderate water, and good light before being sunk outdoors. The plants that are flowered in pots are practically evergreen and should never be bare of all leaves.

How are greenhouse azaleas propagated? The small-flowered Kurume sorts are easily rooted from cuttings, using the short shoots that come after blooming. Root in sandy soil in a box with a piece of glass on top. The Indica types of azaleas have to be grafted, entailing both skill and hotbed facilities.

I was presented with a fine azalea plant. Why has it shed all its leaves? You either let it get dry at the roots or the foliage became infested with red spider (which see). Both will cause defoliation, and, if complete, the plant cannot be revived.

I have an azalea which I purchased in a florist shop 2 years ago. Last year it bloomed beautifully. Now it is dying. Can you give me any help in the care of the plant? The soil is probably over-alkaline and of a dry nature. Frequent watering and an application every 6 weeks of a solution of 1 tablespoonful of aluminum sulfate to 1 gallon of water should help.

Should I plant outdoors a pink-flowered azalea purchased in a florist's shop? (Vermont.) If your azalea is small flowered, it is a Kurume, and there's little chance of its surviving a winter outdoors. If large flowered, it is an Indica, and positively will winter kill. If you want garden azaleas, plant sorts listed as such. For correct care of your azalea, see previous questions.

I have a small-flowered and a large-flowered house azalea. Can you tell me what they are? The small-flowered type is Kurume. The large-flowered is an Indica. There are many named varieties of each type.

CHRYSANTHEMUMS

How long can chrysanthemums be kept flowering indoors? Two weeks is average. Spraying daily with cool water will help to keep foliage fresh looking and prevent its turning brown and dry before the flowers fade. Keep in a cool location.

Are any of the potted chrysanthemums used for gift plants hardy enough to be transferred to the garden? Yes, those that flower the end of September and early October are usually hardy varieties. The large-flowered kinds at Thanksgiving time are not.

Is there any way to save chrysanthemum plants sent in the fall from the florist? They don't winter over outside. After blooming, cut stems down, store pot in cool, light cellar or shed. Propagate by cuttings or division in March. Keep potted on or plant in garden in April. Lift in September and bring into very cool sunroom or porch to bloom.

How can one best grow mums to bloom during months of November, December, and January? We have the severe cold of Lake Erie and a long winter. Could they be brought into the house when winter comes and so bloom during these months? (New York.) Pinch plants well in early season. Pot from the garden in early October. Use late varieties. Give a sunny location in a cool room.

CYCLAMEN

Why does cyclamen always die a few days after it comes from the florist? The florist grew the plant in a moist atmosphere and temperature 40° to 50° F. Living-room conditions are too warm and dry; however, you should be able to keep the plant for a few weeks if you can find a window where its ideal requirements are more nearly met. See following question.

The leaves on the cyclamen I received for Christmas are turning yellow. What caused this? Sudden change from greenhouse to dry, hot atmosphere of house is responsible. Cyclamen should be kept cool, well watered, and away from too much sunlight. An east or west window is best. At ordinary living-room temperature, watering twice daily may be needed.

How cold is it safe to have cyclamen when flowering, and when not flowering? At 40° to 45° F. a plant in flower will be far happier and last much longer than in a room of 60° to 70° F. After blooming, gradually dry off and rest in the cellar, or in cold frame outdoors. Repot in July, and with luck you may get the corm to start again.

How shall I water cyclamen plants during their flowering period? If cyclamens are kept cool enough—40° to 50° F.—they will not dry out quickly. If kept in a hot room, watering freely and frequently may prolong their lives for a week or two, though it will not take the place of a low temperature. Water from below, keeping soil moist but not soggy. (See following question.)

How long must you let a pot of cyclamen soak in a pan of water to wet it thoroughly? If the water in pan is halfway up the pot and the soil is moderately dry, allow to soak 10 to 15 minutes, then stand in sink to drain off surplus.

Are cyclamens difficult as window garden plants? Cyclamens are among the most difficult of all plants for the living room. Old corms that have blossomed can be dried off and kept dormant in a cool place until July, but it's a 50–50 chance to get them to start up strongly again.

Is it worth while to save cyclamen corms over? If so, what care should be given during rest period? It can be done, but is not generally considered worth while.

Can one keep cyclamens for years, or do they die after they are a year or so old? Cyclamens seldom are worth keeping after they flower, and it takes about 18 months to get a sizable plant from seed. Corms normally go dormant after blooming and frequently refuse to start up again in late summer, but experts carry them in active growth for 2 years. The wild species will live for 20 years or more, and corms as large as a plate have been found.

How can I make a cyclamen plant bloom the second year, having got it from a florist when in flower? Cyclamens are not easy plants to keep over a second year, and even expert gardeners seldom attempt it. Gradually reduce water after flowers finish, but spray regularly to prevent mealy bug and mite attack. When leaves have died down, keep in cool place and quite dry. Shake out in July, and repot in fresh soil and lightly water and spray regularly. Give full light, but shade from sun. If the corms push up leaves freely, all's well; if only 2 or 3 leaves start, don't waste time on them.

How long should a cyclamen bloom? Cyclamen should flower either in a greenhouse or under favorable home conditions from Christmas-time until March. Eight to 12 weeks is average. Remove faded blooms.

Should faded blooms be removed from cyclamen with a knife or scissors? Neither. Get a firm grip on the stem of a dead flower or yellowed leaf and give a sharp pull. It comes out cleanly.

How is a cyclamen repotted? Do not disturb earth about the corm more than is necessary. Place it, with adhering soil, in larger pot, using standard potting mixture. Top of corm should be well above soil level when potting is completed. After potting, soak from below.

I have heard that cyclamens are subject to mite. Can anything be done to prevent them? Spray with pressure bottle house plant spray recommended as a miticide.

How can one keep the leaves of cyclamens clean? Dust can be sponged off, or water can be applied with bulb spray; but constant spraying with insecticide is necessary, otherwise mites and mealy bugs will ruin the plants.

How shall I slip a cyclamen? Cyclamens cannot be "slipped," but experts sometimes have divided large corms in two. The only successful method of raising new plants is from seed, which comes true to color of parent plant, but it requires skill, good facilities, and patience for 18 months.

Can one grow cyclamens from seed? What soil and how long a time before blooming? Seedlings are easy to start, if seed is sown thinly in July or August; but after that, troubles begin. If you can simulate greenhouse conditions for 18 months, and can keep the plants free of mites and other pests, you might succeed. Even florists usually procure their cyclamens from specialists. They like a compost of good loam, sand, rotted manure, and peatmoss; shade during the summer yet full light; careful watering; high humidity and frequent spraying; and in the fall and winter a temperature not above 55° F.

Why do my seedling cyclamens get only one leaf at a time? Some are over a year old. Cyclamens are specialists' plants, and it is almost too much to expect to grow them from seed in a window when many florists don't attempt to raise them, preferring to buy plants when 1 year old and carry on to the blooming stage. See previous question.

GENISTA

Can anything be done with a genista after it has stopped blooming? Genistas (the greenhouse kinds) are strictly gift plants, not even good house plants for any length of time. They are not hardy outdoors in the vicinity of New York. Keep in a sunny window, water well, and see that there is circulation of air around them. In other words, don't crowd genistas in with a lot of other plants.

HYDRANGEA

Why did my hydrangea die the day after I received it as a gift? The hydrangea does *not* die that quickly. If leaves and flowers wilt, it is suffering from lack of water. Immerse the whole pot in a pail of water for 20 minutes. It will revive immediately.

How long should a hydrangea flower in the house? It should flower not less than 3 weeks. Keep it away from a hot, sunny window and radiators. Water *thoroughly* twice a day.

What care and treatment should be given pot hydrangeas? Florists' hydrangeas are propagated from cuttings in early spring grown on in 4-in. pots which are sunk in the open ground during the summer and well fed. Put into larger pots in September and place in a cold frame with sash but well ventilated. Bring inside before hard freezing and keep in cool cellar 40° F. till late December or January. Give just enough water to prevent drying, but leaves should fall off. Start in full light at 50° F.—never above 60° F. Give plenty of water at all times and lots of light. After blooming, cut back well and carry outside during summer if a large specimen is wanted the next season.

What must I do to make a pot hydrangea bloom in March or April? If you have only room facilities, don't expect to do what florists can't always manage. A hydrangea has to rest, dormant, in a cold cellar until late December. Start up at 50° F. and never above 60° F. Grow it cool, or you'll have a blind plant.

Will pot hydrangeas bloom again? Yes. Cut back a bit and keep watered till safe to sink pot outdoors. Feed and water in full sun to encourage growth. Bring indoors before hard frost and induce rest by coolness and very little water. Start up again in January. Give full light but little water at first. Temperature never should be above 60° F.

Can my hydrangea be planted in the garden after it has stopped flowering? Yes. After it has finished blooming, cut back stems about half their length, remove plant from pot, and plant in garden where it will have plenty of room. It will grow into a big, shrubby plant. Water well.

I would like to know something about hydrangeas. Are they hardy? The florists' hydrangeas are hardy, but in areas where hard freezing occurs the wood is killed to the ground. If you have a variety that will bloom on the new wood, well and good. If not, and the wood is killed back, you'll never see any flowers. Such kinds have to be kept in pots and brought indoors and rested during the winter.

Twice I have purchased plants of Hydrangea Bluebird, and after potting, new shoots appeared, but in a week or two the plants died. The potting mixture had a pH of about 4.5. Temperature, watering, and light conditions apparently perfect. What was wrong? If you bought actively growing young plants, why not in pots? Who told you to use such extremely acid soil? No variety comes truly blue unless the soil is neutral or on the acid side. Some sorts come blue more readily than others, but you undoubtedly overdid the acidity. Unless your soil is naturally alkaline, forget the pH stuff and use a good rich compost.

What element is it that makes the hydrangea flowers blue? Acidity of soil causes blue flowers, but some varieties come blue more readily than others. Repeated watering with alum solution or aluminum sulfate (1 level teaspoon to 1 gal. of water) will cause blueness.

JERUSALEM-CHERRY

Why do leaves and berries fall off a Jerusalem-cherry soon after I receive it? If your house is hot, Jerusalem-cherry will not survive. It likes a cool room (about 50° F.), plenty of water, and a location away from chills or drafts. Spraying the leaves daily may help. It is a poor house plant.

How shall I treat a Jerusalem-cherry after it has fruited? Unless you want to grow a big specimen, throw the plant away. Old plants can be cut back a little, kept on dry side until spring, then shifted into a larger pot and stood outdoors with slight shade during the summer. Give plenty of water and feed; bring indoors in September.

When shall seed of Jerusalem-cherries be sown for Christmas coloring? Sow seed in January or February. Grow on in pots and plant outdoors in late May. Lift carefully with ball in September, pot, and shade till established, then place in a bright window or greenhouse. Selected types can be raised from cuttings taken early in the year.

ORNAMENTAL PEPPER

How can ornamental peppers be kept small and full of blooms as you see them in the markets? Raise from seed annually and grow in full light. You can't expect plants grown in a window to equal those grown in a greenhouse, but pinching several times will induce bushiness. Plant outside for the summer and pot up in August. Grow in temperature of 50° to 60° F.

POINSETTIA

Why do the leaves of a poinsettia turn yellow and drop continually? Poinsettias are heat lovers. They thrive outdoors in the summer but want a temperature of about 60° F. constantly after early September. If you can't give them high humidity with a night temperature not much higher or lower than 60°, leaves will drop. Possibly plants became chilled or were in a draft.

Will my poinsettia bloom again? How should it be treated? Keep dry after it has bloomed and stand in cellar. Cut back halfway in May, and water. Give full light. Sink pot in ground outdoors in June, and keep watered and fed. Bring indoors end of August, and give sunny window and lots of water. Night temperature has to be 58° to 62° F., not lower or higher, or leaves will drop and it will not flower.

Will a poinsettia that has bloomed, bloom the next winter? For 2 years I have pruned mine and it grows beautifully green but does not bloom. Old plants will bloom the following year if conditions are right, but the plants grow large and will not tolerate severe pruning. If you don't give the right temperature—(see above) from September on, with full sun, it will not flower.

I carried over a poinsettia last year and it made good growth but never bloomed. What was wrong? One cause is keeping it near a light at night. The poinsettia is a "short-day" plant, and if placed in a room where the lights are on several hours every evening, it won't bloom.

I raised a poinsettia this summer in a pot in the yard and brought it in the house in October. Just as the buds for the blooms started, they dried up and fell off. I saw some fine web. Has some minute insect done the damage? Bring indoors earlier if in your section it gets cool at night after August. The web suggests red spider. Regular spraying is needed to prevent this and mealybug attack.

Why do my poinsettias, cut back and nursed through the summer, have only a few petals to each flower? Poinsettias will grow well outdoors during the summer, but if after late August you can't keep a steady temperature of 60° F., the leaves will drop, and if the day temperature is more than 70° F. poor or no flowers result.

After bringing in poinsettias from a summer in the garden (in September), how can one "hold them back" from blooming until about Christmastime? Yours is an exceptional case. The trouble with most people is to get them to flower. Temperature should not be above 60° F. at night. Too high a temperature will cause premature, poorly developed blooms.

I brought some dormant poinsettias from California in May, planted them, and they grew; when cold weather came, I carefully potted them. Why did they wither and die? Poinsettias in growth won't tolerate root disturbance.

If you cut poinsettias close to the soil, will they sprout again? Poinsettias may be cut back ⅔ while quite dormant, but when actively growing no cutting back should be practiced unless the young shoots are to be rooted as cuttings.

When and how does one make cuttings from poinsettias and grow them into blooming plants? After blooming, the plants are allowed to rest. Keep quite dry until May, then cut back and start in a warm temperature. The cuttings are taken off when 4 to 6 ins. long and rooted in sand between June and August—the latter date for small plants. They need a greenhouse to grow successfully.

Should poinsettia cuttings be started in part sand? What temperature is needed? Short 4- to 6-in. cuttings will root either in plain sand or a sandy soil. Successful growers use bottom heat at 70° F. with high humidity. They can be rooted outdoors in June or July if in a closed box with glass on top.

ROSES

Are roses good house plants? As a general rule, no. Some of the miniature ones, such as *Rosa rouletti,* Tom Thumb, or Pixie will do well. The gift plants received at Eastertime will flower for about 2 weeks and then should go into the garden. While indoors, spray the foliage daily with tepid water and give the soil plenty of moisture.

Some of the buds failed to open on the rosebush I received at Eastertime. Can anything be done to prevent this if I get another next year? Don't let the soil dry out, spray the foliage daily, and keep the plant in a sunny window, turning it around each day so that it will receive sun equally on all sides.

Are the climbing rosebushes hardy which I received in flower last Easter? Yes. After they have finished blooming, prune off dead flowers, remove from pot, and plant in a sunny location in enriched soil.

At flower shows I see Miniature or Baby Roses for sale in small pots. Can these be grown indoors and if so how? Miniature Roses do well in the window garden if properly cared for. Give them a sunny spot in a cool room or sun porch (not above 60 to 68° daytime temperature and 10° lower at night). Water daily but do not let water stand in saucers. Frequent syringing of foliage is helpful. Turn pots frequently to receive maximum sunshine. After bloom is over, prune as you would garden roses, and decrease watering, to encourage a resting period of two or three months. In spring when outdoor roses are starting, repot, sink in their pots in a sunny border. Or, if you prefer to grow them on as outdoor plants, remove from pots and plant in well enriched bed. They are perfectly hardy.

SHRIMP-PLANT

What exposure does shrimp-plant like? Shrimp-plants like plenty of sun, so keep them in a sunny window. Do not keep too near a radiator, as they should not dry out. They need plenty of water. This is a fine house plant, untroubled by any insect pests.

What will I do with my shrimp-plant when it gets tall and leggy? Cut the plants back each spring and root cuttings for new plants to bring indoors in the fall. Cuttings will root easily, either in pots of sand or in a cold frame.

Can shrimp-plant be wintered in a cold frame? No, it is too soft and will die, even with protection. Even at a temperature of 45° shrimp-plant is unhappy. It grows best at 55° to 60° F.

Can you tell me the native habitat of shrimp-plant and any legend or general information about the plant and its care? *Beloperone guttata* comes from tropical America. There are no legends, as it was practically unknown except to botanists up to 1905. Some of the species were discovered over 100 years ago.

SHRUBS

AZALEA (See Gift Plants)

CAMELLIA

How should a camellia plant be grown? If in a pot, stand in light shade in open in summer. Bring in in September. Night temperature should be 50° F. It requires sun. Keep soil always moist, but not waterlogged. In spring, after blooming, repot or top-dress as necessary. Feed once a week when good growth is being made.

When should I pot my camellia and in what soil mixture? Never repot unless soil is obviously unsuitable or unless pots are crowded with roots. Do this as soon as flower buds have set. Soil should consist of good loam, leafmold, sharp sand, with some bone meal and dried cow manure added. After potting, spray frequently with clear water. Avoid overwatering.

What about pruning camellias? Only prune sufficiently to keep plant shapely. Thin crowded plants by removing weak growths. Cut back any long, straggly shoots. Do this immediately after flowering. Remember flowering shoots for following year arise from base of flower; to cut back flowering shoots destroys following year's bloom.

How can the buds be kept from falling off a camellia plant? It was just loaded with buds when I took it in this fall and all but 3 fell off. Indoor camellias ordinarily lose buds: (1) because the indoor temperature is too high and the atmosphere too dry; (2) lack of sufficient moisture; (3) lack of light.

Can a camellia be grown in the house? How old must it be to bloom? Camellias are not satisfactory house plants unless, perhaps, you can keep them in a cool sunroom. In wintertime they are harmed by temperature higher than 50° to 60° F. Plants often bloom when quite young—3 or 4 years old.

Indoor camellia plant has conditions in my home similar to gardenias. Is this right? Is it a sun-loving plant? (New York.) Camellias need cooler growing conditions than the florists' gardenia. They enjoy sunshine and a free circulation of air. It is important that the soil be always reasonably moist.

Can one start camellias from a bud in the winter? Not from a flower bud. Camellias are propagated by cuttings, grafting, and layering. July is a good time to take cuttings. (See Propagation—Section II.)

What are the best varieties of camellias for growing indoors? Alba Plena (white), Donkelaari (red and white), Sarah Frost (light red), Candidissima (white), Compt de Gomer (pink), Debutante (flesh pink).

What shall I do to prevent scale on my camellia plants indoors? Spray once in early spring with Volk or other oil emulsion spray. Frequent syringing of the leaves with cool water is helpful.

CITRUS FRUITS

What sort of potting soil shall I use for citrus fruit trees grown as house plants? A standard potting mixture. (See Soil, this section.)

Grapefruit

Have a grapefruit tree grown from seed, now 10 years old, 8 to

10 ft. tall, in good condition. I plant it out of doors during the summer and in a wooden tub in the winter. Why has it never bloomed? Seedling grapefruits are capricious as to time of blooming, particularly when grown as house plants. In winter they should be grown in cool temperature 40° to 50° F., and light, airy conditions.

Lemon

Can you give me information about indoor culture of dwarf Ponderosa Lemon trees? Type of soil, exposure, room temperature? Soil should be rich, rather coarse, and well drained. Expose to maximum sunshine. Night temperature should be 45° to 50° F. with a 5° to 15° rise permitted in daytime. Plunge plant (pot and all) in outdoor garden bed in summer.

Will a lemon tree planted from seed ever bloom without grafting? Is about 5 ft. tall, trunk diameter 1½ ins. It may bloom with age. Seedlings often take many years from time of seed sowing until they bear flowers.

What fertilizer could I use to feed a lemon tree? Any complete commercial fertilizer will be satisfactory. It is not necessary to select one having a particular analysis. Fertilizers of organic origin are to be preferred to non-organic materials.

Orange

What is the correct care for orange trees? Temperature and fertilizer? Can they be grown as other house plants with success? Essentially the same as for grapefruits and lemons. See replies to inquiries on these subjects. The plants grow well as house plants, but often they fail to bloom or develop fruits.

How can I treat an orange tree, as a house plant, to always have oranges on it? Don't expect the impossible. Oranges of all kinds, including the dwarf Otaheite (inedible sort), need lots of light and to be kept free of insect pests. Plant the pot outdoors in summer, as this may induce flowers to set fruit.

Why do blossoms on dwarf orange and lemon trees drop and bear no fruit? Lack of light, or improper water relations within the plant (due to unsatisfactory environment) is probably responsible. Take care the plant is not kept too dry when flowers and fruits are developing.

Can a small orange tree, grown from a seed, be grafted to bear? If so, how? Yes. The operation should be done in spring. A whip graft is probably best. For details read discussion on grafting, Section III.

What varieties of citrus fruits can be grown as pot plants? Ponderosa lemon, Otaheite orange (inedible), Satsuma and Kumquat orange.

CRAPEMYRTLE

Could a crapemyrtle be grown in a tub like an oleander? Outdoors in summer, indoors during the cold months? Yes, very easily. Store it in wintertime in a frostproof place and at that season keep soil very nearly dry.

GARDENIA

Can gardenias be grown as house plants? *Gardenia veitchi* (the one that blooms in winter and early spring) is not adapted for house culture. Much more suitable is the summer-flowering *Gardenia florida*.

What type soil do gardenias thrive best in—acid or alkaline? Acid, very definitely. A pH of 4.5 is generally considered best. Chlorosis (yellowing of the foliage) results from alkaline-soil conditions.

Can you recommend a good soil mixture for gardenias? Two parts mellow loam, 1 part peatmoss, ½ dried cow manure, ½ sharp sand. To this add a 4-in. pot of bone meal and a heaping tablespoonful of iron sulfate (copperas) to each bushel.

What kind of food should be given gardenias? A 4–12–4 fertilizer is recommended. Particularly suitable are fertilizers that provide nitrogen in the form of ammonia such as tankage, dried blood, and sulfate of ammonia.

The gardenia that I received for Christmas has developed yellow leaves at the tips of the shoots. What is the trouble? This is a deficiency of iron. To prevent as well as cure, apply ½ teaspoon of iron sulfate to the soil and water thoroughly. To keep the plant growing, apply ½ teaspoon of 4–12–4 or 5–10–5 every 6 weeks. Never apply lime.

When is the best time to repot my gardenia house plant? It appears pot-bound to me. Any time from April to August inclusive that the plants show evident need of this attention. The final pots should be filled with roots before winter begins.

When and how should gardenias be pruned? Pruning of the florists' *Gardenia veitchi* consists of "stopping" (pinching out the tips) growing shoots each time they attain a length of 6 ins. or so from spring to mid-August.

What causes gardenias to dry up? The leaves become brittle and drop off and the plant seems to be dead. I've had 3 plants do the same. Gardenias, and particularly the variety grown by florists for decorative purposes, need high atmospheric humidity. This cannot be provided in the house and is one of the major causes of failure.

What is the correct application of water to the gardenia? Because of varying environmental factors, no exact answer is possible to your question. *Gardenia veitchi* must never be subjected to dryness at the root. The Capejasmine (*Gardenia florida*) is kept rather on the dry side during winter.

Any helpful suggestions for gardenias in this climate? (Connecticut.) Only variety recommended if you have no greenhouse is *Gardenia florida*. Grow as tub plant, storing in winter in light cellar or sun porch at temperature of 45° to 50° F.; place outdoors, in sunny position, in May. Water freely and feed during summer. Bring in before killing frost. Keep much drier in winter.

I have a beautiful gardenia bush. In summer it bloomed. Now, indoors, the buds turn black and yellow at bottom and don't get larger. Why? It has loads of buds, but they never get to bloom. (New Jersey.) If your plant is *Gardenia florida* (Capejasmine), it should be wintered in a cool, light, frostproof place. Dwelling-house atmosphere is too dry for gardenias.

How would I treat a gardenia plant that was hit by frost or cold air in house? If severely damaged, it probably won't recover. If damage consists only of moderate injury to leaves, keep in warm place. Water with great care, so that soil is not kept in saturated condition, and lightly spray branches with atomizer 2 or 3 times daily.

I have 2 lovely gardenia plants, one with 17 buds and the other with 7. I also started 6 small plants. How can I produce large blooms like the florists do? The variety *veitchi* thrives only under expert care in carefully controlled greenhouses. You are probably growing *Gardenia florida*, which naturally has much smaller flowers.

Year-old gardenia plant has never bloomed. Would sinking the pot in ground outdoors in summer help? Plunging outdoors is a satisfactory procedure with the Capejasmine (*Gardenia florida*). *Gardenia veitchi* is best grown in a greenhouse with high temperature and high atmospheric humidity.

How do you make gardenias bloom? No simple method can be given. You must provide conditions that are to the plant's liking, so that it grows vigorously and ripens its wood satisfactorily. (Read replies to other inquiries about gardenias.)

I have a beautiful gardenia which I raised from a flower. It blooms almost constantly. I think it should rest more. What care should it have? We know of no gardenia that blooms throughout the year. *Gardenia florida* (Capejasmine) blooms over a long summer period. It is rested by being kept cool and nearly dry in winter.

Can limbs be cut off a gardenia plant and rooted, and, if so, when is the best time? Large branches that have become woody are not suitable material for propagation. Cuttings of the young terminal shoots that are firm but not hard and woody are started in winter and spring. (See following question.)

What is the most successful way to root gardenia cuttings? They are not easy to handle unless greenhouse facilities are available. Cuttings 3 or 4 nodes long are inserted in sand or sand and peatmoss from December to March. The sand is maintained at a temperature of 75° to 80° F. and the surrounding atmosphere 70°. A humid atmosphere is necessary.

What are the white, woolly insects that cluster on my gardenia? How to kill them? Mealy bugs, one of the worst pests of this plant. Wash them off with a forceful stream of water, or with a sponge dipped in soapy water to which Black Leaf 40 is added at teaspoonful to a gallon.

Are there different kinds of gardenias? Yes, those commonly grown by the florist, and unadaptable as house plants, include *veitchi*, Hadley, and Belmont. The only kind really useful to the home gardener is *Gardenia florida* (more correctly but more rarely called *G. jasminoides*).

HIBISCUS

How shall I care for hibiscus house plant? Presumably you have the Chinese Hibiscus. If so, prune plant back hard in spring and repot in any good, well-drained soil. Spray lightly with water each sunny day. Keep soil moist but not waterlogged. Give full sunshine. In winter keep soil just moist in temperature about 50° F.

I have a Chinese Hibiscus growing in a pot, as the cold here would kill it if I planted it outside. What is the best plan for keeping it safe all winter? Keep in a light cellar or sunroom where the temperature is not less than 40° F. nor more than 50° F. Give only sufficient water to prevent soil drying out completely.

HYDRANGEA (See Gift Plants)

LANTANA

How are lantanas handled to bloom in winter? Buy small plants in summer and sink the pots in soil out of doors until autumn. Bring in before danger of frost. *Do not repot* at this time. Keep in a cool, sunny window or sun porch at not more than 60° F. Give water sparingly at first, then more water and liquid manure. They should start into fresh bloom in December or January. In spring, repot in standard potting mixture (see Soil, this section), and sink outdoors in garden bed. If winter bloom is desired a second year, keep summer bloom pinched back. It would be better, however, to buy new small plants for winter bloom. See next question for usual way of handling lantanas in winter.

I have a weeping lantana. When does it bloom? Lantanas are naturally summer-to-fall bloomers. Must be brought indoors after

September. Keep moderately dry and cool throughout winter. Cut back and give more water and warmth from March on; plant out in late May.

LEMON-VERBENA (See Kitchen Herb Garden)

OLEANDER

How can oleanders be grown successfully in tubs? Prune back old growths and top-dress in spring and increase temperature and water supply. Feed occasionally in growing season. Give full sun. After midsummer keep somewhat drier. Store in winter in light, cool, frostproof place and keep nearly dry. Spray to keep clean of scale and mealy bugs.

My oleanders look perfectly healthy, but never bloom. I keep them on a glass-enclosed porch in the winter and around an outdoor birdbath in summer. What else do they need? This is often due to insufficient ripening of the wood. To induce ripening, make sure plant has ample light and air and rather dry conditions at the root after the season's growth is completed.

ROSEMARY (See Kitchen-Window Herb Garden)

SWEET-OLIVE (See Flowering Plants)

FERNS

SOIL AND FERTILIZER

What soil is recommended for indoor ferns? Mix together 2 parts good loam, 2 parts leafmold, 1 part sand, ¼ part dried cow manure, ¼ part broken charcoal, and add ¾ of a pint of bone meal to each bushel.

What is the best fertilizer for ferns? There are many good commercial preparations on the market now. Plant tablets, dry commercial fertilizers, or liquid commercial fertilizers are all satisfactory if used according to manufacturer's directions. Liquid manure is always good; some growers prefer sheep manure.

Do vitamin tablets for ferns really do much good? No. Although many claims (supported by unscientific observations) have been made to this effect, both practical growers and scientists are now satisfied that green plants are able to manufacture all the vitamins they need for their own use.

PLANTING

Should house ferns have large, roomy pots or do they prefer to be pot-bound? How deep should plant be set in soil? Most plants thrive in pots just large enough. Too-big containers allow over-abundance of food and water, resulting in plant indigestion. Let crown of plant be level or just a little above soil level. Allow 1-in. space above soil to receive water.

Is good soil enough or is it necessary to provide additional drainage for ferns? Although moist soil conditions are appreciated, drainage must be perfect for ferns. Soil should be porous, there should be an inch or more of cinders over broken crock in the bottom of the pot, and finally ferns should not stand in a saucer or jardiniere in which water has been allowed to collect.

How often should ferns be repotted? Usually not oftener than once a year. Divide, if necessary, and always give them fresh soil. Young ferns that have filled their pots with roots by July may need a second potting but should not be divided.

When is the best time to divide and replant an old Bostonfern? In spring, just as new growth is beginning. Select younger and stronger crowns from outside of the plant for replanting rather than old woody interior parts.

CARE

Are there any tricks to watering ferns? Soil should never be allowed to bake out nor be kept constantly soggy. Keep soil medium-moist and when water is given, soak ball of roots and soil thoroughly. Never apply water in a stream heavy enough to settle in heart of the plant. The best way is to immerse pot in pail or tub of water, then allow to drain before replacing in saucer.

Do ferns like plenty of sunlight? Ferns prefer light but not direct sunlight. In fact, too much sun may be the cause of a sickly, light-green appearance.

What window is best (in house) for ferns? An east, west, or north window, or any place within a room where they receive plenty of light but not direct sunlight.

CULTURE

Is there a general routine for keeping ferns looking bright and crisp? Dry leaves form on my ferns right away. Probably lack of moisture either in the soil or air. Water regularly and keep away from radiators, in temperature above 55° F. When buying a new fern, look for a young one that has not been growing in a greenhouse too long.

How should ferns be cared for in the city apartment? Use same procedure as care of ferns in a house. They do not like direct sun and want plenty of light; moisture in air and soil, warmth, and to be kept away from drafts. Choose only the thriftiest ferns for apartment conditions, such as Rabbitfoot, Holly, and Birdsnest.

Will it help my fern to cut off fronds that have turned brown at the tip or have been broken off? Cut off brown or damaged fronds. Ferns must have plenty of room, for fronds are easily damaged either from close contact with other plants or people brushing past them.

Should one cut the runners on ferns grown in the house? A friend told me to cut them off my fern, and it doesn't seem to be growing so well since I did it. By all means cut the runners off house ferns. They never develop into fronds and only take strength from the rest of the plant. Perhaps your fern needs repotting in fresh soil.

What special care should be given a house fern to produce luxuriant foliage? Mine has a tendency to turn yellow frequently. Is it possible the pot is too small? Yes, it is possible the pot is too small. (See previous questions.)

Will ferns do well in a Wardian case or terrarium? Yes, many of them do better there than in the average living room. Pteris ferns are especially good for terrariums, the small rock ferns or polypodium, small Hollyferns, and possibly the Maidenhair.

Should ferns (house plants) be put outside during the summer? Many ferns benefit from being plunged (planted nearly to the rims of the pots) in an outdoor bed of ashes in a shady spot during the hottest months.

What causes the fronds of ferns to turn brown and fall off? This may be due to people passing by and injuring tips. It may also be due to growing conditions: too small a pot, too low temperature, too hot or too dry atmosphere, lack of water in soil, poor drainage. Check up on conditions.

How can I save my fern, just ordinary house fern, after an overdose of tablet fertilizer? Obviously, roots were burned from an overdose of fertilizer. Better charge it up to experience and start over with a new fern.

I left a fern in an unheated room and it froze. What can I do for it? If only tops and not roots were frozen, tops should be cut off and roots repotted in fresh soil to encourage new top growth. If roots as well as tops were frozen, plant is a total loss.

BOSTON

What is the proper care for a Bostonfern? Provide any good, well-drained soil, plenty of water, air, light (but not direct sunlight), and humidity in the atmosphere (steam-heated rooms are likely to be too dry). They love warmth and should never be where temperature drops below 55° F.

My Bostonfern does not send out sprouts, only long stems, and very few leaves. Should it get fertilizer in the form of cow manure? Cut off long stems, or runners, which do not turn into fronds and only take strength from plant. If otherwise healthy, diluted liquid cow manure may be given once a month. (For other cultural directions, see previous questions.)

How should lace ferns be grown? Probably you mean Whitman Fern, a sport of the Bostonfern. It needs essentially the same care as the common Bostonfern, but special care must be taken to keep any dead leaflets picked off and to prevent water lodging in the centers of the plants.

Mold is beginning to show around the topsoil of my fernery in which are several plants of the common Bostonfern. What does the soil need? Mold seems to indicate that the drainage is poor or that you are not providing sufficient ventilation. Are there drainage holes in the bottom of fernery and an inch of broken crock or cinders under soil? Better change soil and pay attention to drainage when repotting.

Why does a crossbred (Ostrich-Boston) fern revert back to Boston type? Your fern is a somewhat unstable "sport" from the Bostonfern. Such mutants often tend to revert to type. Unless the typical Bostonfern fronds are cut out, they will eventually displace the weaker-growing type.

HOLLYFERN

Is there such a plant as a Hollyfern? The Hollyfern is a cyrtomium. Its fronds are divided into small leaflets each one resembling a holly leaf in outline. It is one of the best ferns for the house and grows steadily. In summer, put it outdoors in a shady spot.

MAIDENHAIR

What are the best growing conditions in the house for the Maidenhairfern? Maidenhairfern is one of the most difficult to grow in the house. It likes a porous soil that contains plenty of humus, and more moisture in the air than is usually found in any house. A temperature of about 65° F. and shade from direct sunlight are necessary. A terrarium is most likely to provide the requisite conditions.

PTERIS

What is the best time to pot, and what is the best fertilizer for greenhouse pteris? Several varieties are available, all generally known as "table ferns." They grow rapidly under favorable conditions and should be repotted into the next size pot whenever their containers become filled with roots. Liquid manure or any good plant food, applied once a month to well-rooted specimens, is sufficient.

RABBITFOOT

How should Rabbitfootfern be cared for? Rabbitfootfern can stand higher temperature and drier air than any of the other house ferns. Should do well in the average living room. Keep it out of direct sunlight but see that it has plenty of light. Like all ferns, it needs a porous soil and plenty of moisture and should be kept away from drafts.

PROPAGATION

How are ferns propagated from the spores on the back of the leaves? The average person may find it difficult to do. Take a piece of soft brick and a clay saucer. Sterilize these by baking. Stand brick in saucer and wet thoroughly. Scatter spores over surface of brick. Keep a little water in saucer and cover with glass, leaving slight opening at bottom for ventilation. Keep in diffused light, temperature 60° to 70° F. First growth of fern looks like green scales.

Is it safe to divide fern plants? Yes, but not oftener than once a year. New crowns or heads which have sprung up around the original crown can be pulled or cut off gently and each piece potted in a pot of suitable size. Probably the original plant can go back into the same pot with fresh soil.

DISEASES AND PESTS

See Section VIII.

When ferns have black specks on the under side, is that fungi? If these black or brown specks appear in even lines or regular pattern on the under sides of the leaves, they contain the spores by which ferns reproduce themselves. They are not harmful to the plant.

My Swordfern has little black spots on stems. Is it a disease? If these black spots are on the stems, not on the back of the leaves, they are a scale insect. If it is a scale, half a teaspoon of kerosene to a quart of soapy water makes a good spray. Or purchase a whale-oil preparation and use according to directions. If there are only a few scales, hand pick them with a toothpick.

VARIETIES

What are the best ferns for indoor culture? Bostonfern (and its several variations), Hollyfern, Birdsnestfern, and pteris ferns. All of these will thrive in the average home if given reasonable attention.

Is Ostrich-plume-fern all right for the house? The native woods Ostrich Fern (*Pteretis struthiopteris*) is hardy and not suitable for indoor culture. If by Ostrich-plume-fern you mean one of the feathery Bostonfern types, it is a suitable house plant.

VINES

WHAT TO GROW

Will most vines do better in a conservatory than in the house?

Yes, if ideal conditions and care are given; yet remarkably good results are obtainable in the house with vines that are adapted to such conditions; this group is by no means a small one.

What kind of house plants grow long and trailing, in addition to ivy and philodendron? *Cissus antarctica* (Kangaroo-vine) is one of the best and longest growing; Grape-ivy, pothos, tradescantia, waxplant, and sweet potato.

What vines grow best in a light window? Can they be grown in water? Ivy, philodendron, and tradescantia are stand-bys to grow in water. They do not need sun. Pothos and nephthytis will grow in either water or soil. Grape-ivy, Kenilworth-ivy, German-ivy, passion-vine, creeping fig and Kangaroo-vine do well in soil.

What are the names of vines that will grow in water in the house? In a light place: English Ivy, philodendron, tradescantia, pothos, nephthytis, passion vine, sweet potato. In sun: trailing coleus and *Zevrina pendula,* whose leaves are purple on the under side and silver-striped on the upper.

What vines are best for a city apartment? The thriftiest vines are philodendron, pothos, Kangaroo-vine, with Grape-ivy a close runner-up.

What about growing vines indoors in water? Should the water be plain or are there solutions which should be added? Many vines grow satisfactorily in water—plain water plus small piece of charcoal to keep water sweet. Don't disturb roots by changing the water; simply add more as needed.

Is it safe to use foliage vines to frame the sides of a sunny south window used for other house plants? Yes, if the foliage vines are not kept in the direct sunlight of the window but are fastened or trained to the window frame facing in toward the room.

How should the leaves of vines be kept clean? Spray vigorously once a week with cool water on both the upper and the under sides of the leaves. This not only prevents insects but keeps the foliage fresh looking. Or sponge leaves with soapy water occasionally.

Can any vines be grown from seed for use indoors? Morningglory, especially the Japanese ones and Heavenly Blue; black-eyed-susan-vine (*Thunbergia alata*), cup-and-saucer-vine (*Cobaea scandens*), canary-bird-vine (*Tropaeolum peregrinum*).

How should Boston-ivy be cared for in the house? True Boston-ivy is *Parthenocissus tricuspidata.* This is a large-leaved vine which drops its leaves every autumn. It is an outdoor, not an indoor, vine.

CREEPING FIG

Can you suggest a creeping vine that will cling to a masonary wall behind a small pool in a sunroom? The Creeping Fig (*Ficus pumila*) will suit your purpose. It is small leaved, intensely green, and makes a flat mat against the wall, up which it creeps. A variegated variety is also available.

ENGLISH IVY

How can hardy ivy be grown in the house?   Keep in cool, light place, away from radiators and direct sunlight. Spray foliage once a week with cold water to keep clean and free from dust and red spider. Keep soil moist; feed monthly with pinch of complete fertilizer. It also grows well in water.

Does an ivy require sunshine when grown indoors?   No. Ivy should not be in direct sun. It does need good light. North window preferable.

We have been unsuccessful in keeping ivy cuttings alive over the winter in the house in water. What is the proper method?   Glass container best; be sure to have piece of charcoal in the water so that it will stay sweet and not have to be changed; add water as needed. A light but not sunny place is preferred.

My ivy, grown in water in the light, dries up and dies. How may this be remedied?   The location is either too sunny and hot, or the plant has red spider. Spray both sides of leaves vigorously with cool water once a week. Keep in a light but not sunny place.

What is the best method of starting indoor ivy?   Cuttings, rooted in water. Take tip ends of ivy, having at least 4 mature leaves. Remove 2 lower leaves and stand in water. Longer stems may be used but leaves must be removed from as much stem as is under water.

Why do the leaves of ivy turn yellow?   Too much sunshine perhaps, a too hot and dry atmosphere, or soil too dry.

My ivy (indoor) has a brown scale on its leaves. What causes this?   Brown scale is an insect. Most effective control is to sponge leaves and stems with soapy water to each gallon of which is added 1½ teaspoonfuls of Black Leaf 40. If necessary use a soft toothbrush to remove scale from stems.

How can variegated ivy be grown successfully?   Variegated ivies should be grown in north windows only, or in eastern exposures if shaded by larger plants. Good soil, moderate watering, and spraying of the foliage once a week to keep it clean are of basic importance.

I have a green-and-white variegated ivy. As the new leaves come out the old ones turn brown and die, beginning on one side. Why?   Probably due to too much sun. Keep in a north window. Check other general factors: soil, watering, and cleanliness of foliage, for additional causes.

What are some unusual and hardy types of English Ivy for indoor culture?   Baby Ivy (*Hedera helix minor*), two variations of Pittsburgh Ivy, Merion King and Little Beauty; *H. helix cordata* with rather large heart-shaped leaves; *H. helix palmata*, *H. helix digitata*, and *H. helix marginata*. Try local greenhouses for unusual types.

What are best kinds of English Ivy for indoor culture? The standard English Ivy (*Hedera helix*) and the Pittsburgh Ivy are the two thriftiest kinds. Many variations have been developed but their availability depends on local market.

GRAPE-IVY

I have a trailing house plant that looks like poison ivy. What is its name and of what country is it a native? *Cissus rhombifolia* (it used to be called *Vitis rhombifolia*). Its common name is Grape-ivy and it is a native of northern South America.

Is the Grape-ivy a satisfactory house plant? Yes, it is splendid and will thrive with any reasonable care in a warm room. It appreciates sunshine except for shade from the intensest of summer sunshine, a good rich soil, free drainage, adequate supplies of water, and feeding when pot-bound.

Is Grape-ivy a form of English Ivy? No. Grape-ivy is *Cissus rhombifolia,* which is quite different in appearance from English Ivy (*Hedera helix*). Its leaves are made of three leaflets while those of the English Ivy are merely lobed. It is less subject to insect pests than English Ivy and usually looks well longer.

GERMAN-IVY

I have seen German-ivy grown indoors in ferneries. Is this a difficult house plant? No, *Senecio mikanoides* does well in window boxes or fern stands, in full diffused light and without direct sun. Plant in standard potting mixture to which charcoal has been added to keep soil sweet. When growing well, water weekly with liquid manure. Cuttings root easily in moist sand.

KENILWORTH-IVY

Can I grow Kenilworth-ivy as an indoor vine? Yes, this dainty little vine (*Cymbalaria muralis*) with its violet flowers and leaves tinted with red beneath, grows well in a sunny window if the atmosphere is not too dry. It requires standard potting soil. Often it will seed itself in the soil about the base of other pot plants. In summer it grows riotously in a wall or rock garden out-of-doors and seeds itself freely (in the vicinity of New York City).

KANGAROO-VINE

Does Kangaroo-vine (Cissus antarctica) make a good house plant? Yes, this is one of the toughest and least temperamental of house vines. It does not object to living-room temperatures. New plants can be propagated from cuttings.

MYRTLE

Will myrtle grow indoors? Yes, it will, but it must be sprayed, without fail, once a week with cool water to ward off red spider, its greatest handicap to growing well indoors. It does not like too warm a location. Myrtle will root and grow in water, or larger plants may be potted in soil.

PASSION-FLOWER

Would passion-flower grow in the house during the winter months? Should it be cut back before being brought in?   Passion-flower (*Passiflora*) makes an excellent winter house plant. It grows luxuriantly outdoors during summer and it may have to be cut back before being brought indoors. Train to a bamboo stake and put strings against the window up which it can climb. To encourage growth of vine, it *must* be provided with something on which to climb. Growth depends on height of trellis or string provided.

My passion vine, kept in a south window, grows well during winter but does not flower. Will anything encourage blossoms?   Early winter should be a season of comparative rest (temperature 55° F.; soil on dry side). In late winter increase temperature 15° to 20°; give more water. Repot if necessary, or, if not, feed every 2 or 3 weeks. Rest season is important.

How can you propagate the passion-flower?   By tip cuttings rooted in sand kept constantly moist or in water in a glass container. Keep in a light but not sunny window. When well rooted, pot up in a rich, humusy soil.

PHILODENDRON

What are cultural directions for philodendron?   The philodendrons used as house plants are tolerant of warm rooms and some shade although they appreciate atmospheric moisture and sunlight. Give well-drained, humusy soil and avoid potting too frequently.

What is the proper method for growing philodendron? In water or soil?   Philodendron grows well in either. If in water, keep a piece of charcoal in the container to keep water sweet. Do not change water but add to it as needed. If soil is more convenient, any good garden soil that is porous is all right. See that it is watered regularly.

How does one obtain a cutting of philodendron?   By cutting off the tip ends or any side shoot. The piece cut off should have at least 4 leaves. Remove 2 bottom leaves so that the nodes from which the leaves grew can go under water. New roots will appear from these nodes. Sometimes cuttings can be selected with aerial roots already formed at nodes.

What can be done to make a philodendron branch and to prevent it from becoming stringy?   As soon as distances between leaves start to get longer than normal, pinch off the ends of the vine. The plant will branch out and the severed pieces, if long enough, may be rooted in water to make new plants.

What should be done with philodendron when leaves become too small? It is probably growing in too dark or too cool a place. It does not need sun but plenty of light and a temperature of 60° to 70° F. If roots are healthy, give it a plant tablet, or feed with liquid manure or good complete fertilizer once a month.

How should philodendron vine be taken care of? The leaves seem to dry off. Do I water too much? Dying leaves are evidence of root injury or too dry atmospheric conditions. Never water a plant if the soil is really moist. Shake out your plant, and if roots are decayed, repot and water carefully. Don't use much fertilizer. Perhaps you have been overfeeding.

POTHOS

What kind of exposure does pothos like? Pothos will grow in either sunlight or good diffused light. Good for a south window as well as for an east or west one.

SWEET POTATO

How start a sweet potato vine in water? Select a good-sized sweet potato and a glass container about 8 ins. deep and suitably wide. Thrust a toothpick in the middle of either side of the potato and let the toothpicks rest on the rim of the container. Keep water at a level so that the lower end of the potato is always covered.

WANDERINGJEW

What is the botanical name of the trailing indoor plant called Wanderingjew? Two plants of very similar appearance go by this name. One, *Tradescantia fluminensis,* produces white flowers, leaves often variegated; the other, *Zebrina pendula,* flowers pink or red-purple, foliage striped above, purple beneath. Both are of the very simplest culture and will grow under similar conditions.

What is best time to put in slips of Wanderingjew? They root readily at any time if planted about 2 ins. apart in pots of sandy soil. Stand pots in box with 1 in. sand or cinders in the bottom. Water well, cover with sheet of glass, and shade lightly from bright sunshine.

WAXPLANT

Could you tell me anything about the house plant known as "Parlor Plant"? It has thick waxy leaves and clusters of small, star-shaped waxy flowers. From your description this is *Hoya carnosa,* or waxplant. It is a native of southern China and Australia and is an old-time favorite. Botanically it is related to the milkweeds (*Asclepias*).

What kind of soil should be used for Hoya carnosa? Soil rich in humus. One part good garden soil, 1 part coarse sand, 2 parts leaf-mold, with the addition of ⅛ part of bulk of dry cow manure and a pint of bone meal to each bushel.

Should Hoya carnosa have sunshine or shade, plenty of moisture, or kept on dry side? It appreciates sunshine, good drainage, and plenty of moisture in spring, summer, and fall but should be kept drier and cooler (50° F. night, 60° to 65° F. day) in winter.

Why doesn't my Hoya carnosa (5 ft. long and 5 years old) bloom? Although slow to flower, your plant is large enough to do so. Does it get plenty of sun and has it filled its pot with roots? Plant must be pot-bound to bloom well, hence avoid overpotting. A partial rest in wintertime is very beneficial.

CACTI

SOIL AND FERTILIZER

Are cacti in the house grown in all sand? Cactus plants can be kept alive and will grow in sand for long periods but thrive better and are more permanent if planted in a loose, porous soil mixture.

What is the proportion of sand to soil for cacti grown in the house? From ¼ to ½, depending upon how sandy the soil is that is used.

What soil do cacti require? Cacti form a large family and there are some differences in soil requirements of individual kinds. In general, a loose, porous soil, fertile but not over-rich in nitrogen, is desirable. Many species benefit from the addition of lime. (See Sandy Potting Mixture.)

What kind of soil for night-bloming cereus? The soil must be very porous, so that water drains through quickly, even when packed together. Mix good garden soil, sand, and broken brick until you get this result, then add 1/10 part in bulk dried cow manure and a pint of bone meal to each bushel.

Is there any fertilizer suitable for cactus plants? Cacti do not need much fertilizer. Bone meal, wood ashes, and very old cow manure that has been well dried may be used with discretion.

Can liquid manure be fed to potted cacti? Yes, and with benefit, but only if the plant is vigorous, is in active growth, and has filled its container with healthy roots. It should be well diluted. (See Liquid Manure.)

Should we start feeding cacti, and what month? Never feed cacti unless they are strong, vigorous plants that have filled their pots with healthy roots. Feed only during growing season (usually late spring and summer) and then sparingly.

POTTING

When should cacti be repotted? The repotting of healthy cacti that have filled their receptacles with roots should be done at the beginning of their growing season (in most cases from March to May). A plant that is planted in unsuitable soil and is consequently unhealthy may be carefully repotted at any time.

CULTURE

How can a cactus be made to bloom? The cactus family is a large one. Some kinds flower regularly and with ease while others are much more capricious. Study the individual plant, provide it with the best possible environment, and see that it has a period of rest immediately before its season of active growth.

What temperature must be held to keep cactus plants healthy? A minimum of 50° F. for plants grown indoors. Some few kinds are hardy outdoors even in the North.

What is the best method of watering cactus plants? Submerge pots nearly to their rims and leave in that position until water entering drainage holes in bottom of the pots seeps through and wets surface soil.

Can you tell me something of the care of cacti so they will blossom? I have one that blossoms about July; last year the buds formed and then dried up. You probably kept plant too dry. Pot-grown cacti require moderate amounts of water over the greater part of the year. Supply quite a generous quantity when growth or flowers are developing.

How often should cactus plants in small flowerpots be watered? This depends largely upon prevailing weather and other environmental factors. In general, water often enough to prevent soil from ever drying out *completely,* yet soil should be allowed to become nearly dry before each watering.

How often should cacti in small pots be watered when they are in the house in wintertime? In winter most cacti are resting and soil should be permitted to dry out almost completely before water is applied. The frequency with which this occurs varies with the individual plant and its environment.

How can succulents and cacti be kept thriving in an apartment with not much sun? Grow them in a window where they will receive the maximum amount of light (even though this is not direct sunlight) possible. Attend carefully to watering, potting, cleaning, and other details.

Will cacti grow and bloom better if set outside in summer? Should they be left in pots or set directly in the ground? If their indoor position is a sunny one and otherwise satisfactory, it makes little difference whether they are left indoors or are set outside. If set outside, they should remain in their pots.

How can cacti be carried successfully through the summer out of doors? We have a lath house. Would that be better than the rock garden? Bury the pots nearly to their rims in a well-drained bed of soil or cinders located in a sunny position.

Why do my miniature cacti fail to grow? Because the soil or other environmental factors are not to their liking. Read with care the answers given to other inquiries and be guided accordingly.

I have 2 cacti 6 ft. tall that have never blossomed. Why? Some cacti do not bloom until they are several years old. Resting plants by keeping them decidedly on dry side during winter often helps blooming, as also does exposure to full sunshine at all times.

Will the Peanut Cactus plant blossom? The Peanut Cactus (*Chamaecereus silvestri*) normally blooms from May to July. Its flowers are tubular, nearly 3 ins. long, and orange-scarlet in color.

How can a model cactus indoor garden be assembled and developed? Purchase 10 or 12 easy-to-grow kinds from a reliable dealer. Grow them separately in pots. Read about cacti. Join the Cactus and Succulent Society of America. Increase collection by exchange and purchase.

NIGHT-BLOOMING CEREUS

What will make a night-blooming cereus bloom and keep the buds from dropping off? Good cultural care, good light, suitable soil, proper temperature; plenty of water and feeding when growing, little water during resting period; freedom from scale and mealy bugs.

How should a large night-blooming cactus be cared for through the winter? Would it do all right in a dark cellar? It should be kept in a light place at all times. Providing the soil is kept nearly dry through the winter, it may be kept in a temperature of 40° to 45° F. At warmer temperatures, more water is needed.

Could a cereus plant be cut back? I had one given to me and it had been broken in many places, but this past summer it put out new growth. When is blooming time? Yes. Dust the cuts with finely powdered sulfur. Summer.

A night-blooming cereus started from a slip bloomed once when 2 yrs. old but hasn't had a flower since. It seems healthy enough and is growing well. What is wrong? Young plants bloom either irregularly or not at all, especially when growing vigorously. Your plant will probably bloom when it is older. Avoid overfeeding or overpotting.

How long does it take for a night-blooming cereus rooted from a cutting to bloom? This cannot be stated with any degree of precision. Usually several years.

One of two night-blooming cactus plants blooms profusely, the other has only 2 or 3 blooms. Why? Assuming plants are of similar age and receiving similar care, this may be due to one being a shy-blooming type. Such shy bloomers are familiar to cactus fans.

When should a large night-blooming cereus be transplanted? In April or May.

PROPAGATION

I have two cactus plants that are night blooming, have a cream-yellow, waxlike flower about 5 ins. in diameter. Can you tell me the correct way of increasing these to make more plants? This is the night-blooming cereus. Cuttings of the stems, each a foot or so long, taken in the summer and set in clean sand which is kept moist, will soon form new roots.

How should cactus cuttings be made? Most cacti root readily from cuttings. Make cuttings spring or early summer. After cutting, leave lying in sun for few days to dry cut surface, then insert in sand bed. Keep sand just moist; atmosphere *not* close and humid as recommended for cuttings of most plants.

How should seedling cacti be grafted on larger or stronger stock? Have raised many from seeds. Seedling cacti are not usually grafted. Grafting is reserved for varieties that do not do well on own roots. While a simple process, this can scarcely be adequately described in a brief reply. (See Grafting—Section III.)

How can I start cactus seed? Plant seeds in pots filled ⅓ with "crocks" and ⅔ with very sandy soil that has had no fertilizer added to it and that has been passed through ¼-in. screen. Sow in spring. Cover seed to own depth. Keep soil moderately moist at all times. Temperature should be 60° to 70° F.

How long does it take cactus seeds to come up? From 1 to 2 weeks under favorable conditions.

DISEASE AND INSECTS

How can I remove mealy bugs and scale insects from my cactus plant? Mealy bugs are easily washed off with a forceful stream of water. Scale can be removed by scrubbing gently with a soft toothbrush dipped in Ivory soapsuds or in a pyrethrum or rotenone insecticide.

CHRISTMAS CACTUS

What kind of soil is best suited to Christmas or Zygocactus? Equal parts of turfy loam, leafmold, and coarse sand (not seashore sand) together with a pint of bone meal and a quart of wood ashes to each bushel is a good mixture. One tenth part by bulk of old dried cow manure may be added if loam is poor.

What fertilizer or procedure is used to blossom Christmas Cactus which has been grafted to Barbados gooseberry root stock? If healthy, use very diluted liquid cow manure monthly during growing season. Plunge plants in semi-shaded place outdoors June to September. Full sun indoors other times. Water moderately April–January. Keep nearly dry January–April.

How often should a Christmas Cactus be repotted? Ordinarily every two or three years, or whenever the pot is filled with roots and the soil appears to be worn out.

When should the Christmas Cactus be transplanted? In spring if the plant is healthy. A plant that is unhealthy because of poor root condition may be carefully repotted at any time.

Must the Christmas Cactus have sunshine to bloom? It needs full exposure to sunshine except from May to September; during this period shade from full intensity of strong sunlight.

How do I care for my Christmas Cactus after it blooms? Rest plant by keeping it nearly dry for 6 or 8 weeks. When new growth appears, repot or top-dress with fresh soil and water so that soil is kept fairly moist.

Why do Christmas Cactus leaves turn yellow and fall off indoors each winter and come out again on the porch in summer? Because the indoor atmosphere is too arid for these epiphytic plants. Attach humidifiers to radiators. Stand pots on trays of moist gravel or sand.

Why do leaves of Christmas Cactus turn yellow and eventually drop off? Two pots of same outdoors all summer; taken indoors September 15; one very healthy, the other in the above condition. May be due to poor root conditions. Take plant from pot, carefully remove old soil, and repot into fresh soil in pot just big enough to contain root mass.

What makes Christmas Cactus leaves turn yellow and grow very small? They do not grow broad as they should. They are planted in sandy soil. Soil is probably too poor. Try repotting into a richer (but still porous) mixture.

What care must I give to my Christmas Cactus so that the buds will not drop off? Out of 25 buds appearing on the plant about 7 or 8 develop into full-blooming flowers. Common causes of bud dropping are overwatering, exposure to cold drafts, a position too close to a hot radiator, and lack of sufficient potash in the soil. Syringe foliage frequently in autumn. Water plant sparingly. Feed a little liquid manure weekly.

I have a Christmas Cactus plant several years old, and it hasn't bloomed. Someone told me it must be a male plant. Are there male and female plants? How can you tell? The Christmas Cactus bears male and female parts in the same flower, not upon separate plants.

What can I do to have my Christmas Cactus bloom at Christmas-time instead of in March? Outside a greenhouse such regulation not possible. Varieties, however, differ on blooming time. Can you get a slip from a plant known to bloom near Christmas? Withhold water entirely in October and during that month keep in a cool place, then bring to sunny window at temperature of 65° to 70° F. Water very moderately. Feed with liquid manure.

Why does Christmas Cactus send out tiny hair roots at each leaf joint? This is quite a natural phenomenon and occurs particularly if the plants are grown in a moist atmosphere.

How can a Christmas Cactus be started from an old plant? By stem cuttings planted firmly in moist sand in spring. By grafting on to pereskia, cereus, or other suitable stock in early summer. (See Grafting —Section III.)

What is the botanical name of the Christmas Cactus? *Zygocactus truncatus.* It used to be called *Epiphyllum truncatum.* It is a native of southern Brazil.

ORCHID CACTUS (EPIPHYLLUMS)

What is a good potting mixture for an orchid cactus or epiphyllum? This needs a moister and richer soil than desert types of cacti. Two parts loam, 2 parts leafmold, 1 part sharp sand, and ½ part dried rotted manure plus a pint of bone meal to each bushel should be about right.

Would like some information on the orchid cactus. Does it like sun or shade, sandy or rich soil? Epiphyllums enjoy moister soil and a moister atmosphere than most cacti. The soil should be rich in humus but porous. Shade from strong summer sunshine is needed.

What is best fertilizer for epiphyllums? Dilute liquid cow manure and bone meal.

What time of the year does the orchid cactus bloom? Will it freeze in winter? The epiphyllums or orchid cacti bloom from April to July ordinarily. They are natives of the warmer parts of North, Central, and South America and are not adapted for outdoor culture where freezing weather is experienced.

What is the trouble when a night-blooming orchid cactus sets many buds which turn brown and wither when no larger than peas? The plant is well watered and sprayed with water after the buds appear. Lack of potash in the soil is said to cause buds to drop. Overwatering will also bring this about.

What is the reason my epiphyllums grow but seldom bloom? To bloom satisfactorily they must be given a rest each year. This is done by keeping them as dry as possible (without permitting the leaf-like stems to shrivel) for a period of 8 to 10 weeks during the winter.

SUCCULENTS

SOIL AND CULTURE

People speak of cacti and succulents. What is the difference? A cactus is any plant belonging to the botanical family Cactaceae. A succulent is any plant of a fleshy character adapted to conserve water and store same in its tissues. Nearly all cacti are succulents, but not all succulents are cacti. Century-plant, aloe, air-plant, stapelia, and many others are succulents that belong to families other than Cactaceae.

Do succulents need the same kind of soil as cacti? In the main, yes, but succulents that are not cacti form a much more diverse group than those that are, and, in consequence, their specific needs tend to vary more. Good, sharp soil drainage is of primary importance.

In what kind of soil should succulents be planted? This varies to some extent with the individual needs of the large number of species that comprise this group. It *must* be porous but should not, as beginners often think, be nearly all sand. The admixture of coarse cinders of finely broken brick is helpful. Many species appreciate lime.

Do succulents need a resting season? Yes, all do. As they come from many different parts of the world, their seasons of rest vary. Thus most South African succulents grow in our winter and should be rested in summer, while species that are native to lands north of the equator commonly rest in our winter. When resting, keep cooler and drier than when growing.

BOWIEA

How can bowiea be grown? *Bowiea volubilis,* or, more correctly, *Schizobasopsis volubilis,* is a South African with large onionlike bulbs from which is formed a tall, delicate, green vine-like growth. Pot in porous soil with only base of bulb buried. Give sunny window. Keep soil moist when green growth is in evidence; dry at other times. Goes many years without repotting.

BROMELIADS

What is the correct care for bromeliads? Bromeliads, of which there are many species, are relatives of the pineapple. Treat like most other succulent plants—sandy soil with leafmold, plenty of drainage in the pot, and careful watering. They like a winter temperature of 55° to 60° F. The common name is air-plant because they derive most of their nourishment from air and water, being tree perchers in their native habitats. A number make fine house plants including bilbergias, vriesias and aechmeas. The leaves of many species are vase-like, rising from a tight base and the exotic, colorful, long-lasting flowers on stiff stems are borne in winter. Vase-like bromeliads should be watered in the "vase" which holds moisture well. They may be planted in osmunda (orchid) fiber, a sandy soil mixture, or will even grow in a crevice of cork bark. They thrive equally well in sun or shade. Excellent for city conditions.

BRYOPHYLLUM

How can I make a bryophyllum or air-plant bloom? Good culture that has as its object the rapid production of a large, vigorous plant. It needs a rather warm temperature (60° to 70° F.), plenty of sun, rich but quite porous soil, rather ample supplies of water, and feeding when it has filled a 6-in. pot full of roots. Low temperatures, too dry soil, and lack of light prevent blooming.

What is the name of the house plant that produces many little plants along the edges of its fleshy leaves? Several species of kalanchoe (bryophyllum) possess this habit. They are easily propagated from the plantlets.

What is the botanical name for the airplane plant? We find no reference in literature to this name. Could you mean the air-plant, *Kalanchoe* (*Bryophyllum*) *pinnata?*

CRASSULA

What could cause a crassula (jade-plant) to drop most of its leaves? Too much water or possibly very extreme drought. This succulent plant should be treated like a cactus—plenty of drainage in the pot but water enough to prevent shriveling. The exact frequency of watering depends upon the size and condition of plant as well as upon the weather and position in house.

What can be done to encourage a jade-tree (crassula) to bloom? Kept it in good health for 10 or 15 years. The jade-tree does not normally bloom until it is many years old. Younger specimens sometimes bloom if pot-bound. (See next question.)

I have a so-called "rubber plant" about 10 years old; it bloomed 2 years in succession, the last time 3 years ago, and not since. Why? Your plant is probably the so-called Japanese Rubber, *Crassula argentea;* its failure to flower regularly is probably due to giving it too much water, so that it never rests. This plant is a succulent and needs to be kept on the dry side in late summer and early fall.

A friend has given me a plant of Crassula multicava. Is it a good house plant? One of the best for a sunny window where temperature is about 50° at night and 60° to 65° F. during the day. It blooms freely in early spring. The flowers are delicate pink and very dainty. Give a porous soil. Propagate by cuttings in the spring.

How can I propagate my jade plant? It is now so large I can no longer handle it. You can scarcely help doing so! Branches and leaves of *Crassula argentea* or jade plant, which makes a showy, treelike house plant, root so easily that if a piece is accidentally broken off and falls in the pot, roots soon form in the surface of the potting soil. The thick, glossy, rounded leaves will also produce roots if the bases are inserted in damp, sandy soil.

CROWN-OF-THORNS

How can I keep my crown-of-thorns (Euphorbia splendens) green? The leaves come on and drop off. It just refuses to bloom in the house. Probably you are keeping the plant too dry. It cannot produce leaves and flowers without a constant supply of moisture during its growing season.

Does crown-of-thorns require a dry soil? Soil should be exceedingly porous and well drained but should be kept moist whenever leaves are present on stems. When leaves fall off, keep soil nearly dry until new growth begins.

Which plant food is best for crown-of-thorns? Avoid the excessive use of fertilizer. A vigorous plant with a strong, healthy root system will respond to small amounts of any complete fertilizer applied during its active growing season.

What window should a crown-of-thorns plant stand in? Why do the buds blast? The sunniest possible. Bud blasting may be due to extreme dryness, gross overwatering, or low temperature. Ordinarily temperature should not go below 45° F.

Is the crown-of-thorns a constant bloomer? Yes, if kept in good growing condition, it will bloom much of the year. (See previous questions for culture.)

ECHEVERIAS

I have a tender succulent which resembles the common hardy hen-and-chicks. What is it? Probably an echeveria. The handsome rosettes of these succulents are often silver-gray, gray-green or almost white, touched with pink. Plant them in the rock garden in summer and bring indoors in winter, before first frost.

KALANCHOE

What is the proper soil and care for successful blooming of the Kalanchoe blossfeldiana? Soil should be moderately rich and quite porous. Grow in full sun. Propagate by cuttings in spring. Repot plants as roots fill pots. Water fairly freely when in active growth, and feed gently when final pots are root-filled.

Why do the leaves fall from my Kalanchoe coccinea, but it still blossoms? The leaves fall after I bring it in the house in the fall. This is due to sudden change of environment and particularly to the drier indoor air. Transfer plant to house at least two weeks before heat is turned on. Keep soil fairly moist, and on bright mornings spray foliage with clear water from atomizer syringe.

LITTLE-PICKLES

Can you tell me something about the plant called "Little-Pickles"? This is *Othonna crassifolia,* native of South Africa. A trailing plant with tiny green, sausage-shaped leaves and small, yellow daisy flowers. Excellent for a hanging pot or basket. Grow in cool, sunny window. Keep soil on dry side. Propagates very readily from cuttings.

LIVING ROCKS

How should living rocks (lithops) be treated? Plant closely together in shallow pans filled with exceedingly porous soil. Tops of plants should be well above soil level. Surface pans with gravel or small stones. Water freely October to May. Keep nearly dry at other times. Shade lightly from bright summer sun. Grow in temperature of 50° to 60° F.

SEDUMS

How can healthy small potted sedums be kept growing? Grow them in the sunniest window in a room where temperature is not excessive. Pot them in a porous, well-drained soil and keep moderately moist at all times. Sedums are easy to grow.

STAPELIA

I can never get stapelia to grow and do well. Why? They are sometimes rather tricky. They need an open, porous soil, rather more water than is commonly accorded cacti, and a light shade during summer. They should be kept nearly dormant in winter.

Concerning stapelias: mine are rested, kept fairly dry in summer, and form buds in late August or early September. Buds wilt, however, without maturing. How should they be treated? Perhaps you keep them too dry in summer. Usual practice is to rest by keeping nearly dry in winter and to water moderately and encourage growth in summer.

TYPES AND VARIETIES

What are some of the most interesting succulents, other than cacti, for the window garden? The list is vast. You might try euphorbias, echeverias, stapelias, haworthias, gasterias, kleinias, cotyledons, crassulas, kalanchoes, and some of the South African rock plants (lithops). *Succulents for the Amateur,* by Scott Haselton (Abbey Garden Press, 1939), is a good book on this subject.

BULBS, HARDY, FOR FORCING

IRIS

Can Wedgewood Iris be grown successfully in the house in winter? If you have a cool room (50° to 55° F.), plant the largest size bulbs in 6- or 8-in. pots; give full light and sun; keep free of aphis and don't disturb the roots. This iris may flower, but it really needs greenhouse or outdoor culture. Don't use small bulbs for indoors, as they won't bloom.

LILIES

Will regular garden lilies bloom indoors? The Regal Lily is a good pot plant but rather tall. Potted in late fall and given 55° to 60° F., with full light, it will flower in April or early May. Other hardy lilies are not likely to do well under room conditions.

Can Easter Lilies be raised in the house? If a bright, warm sun porch or conservatory is available, Easter Lilies can be grown successfully.

What is proper time to pot Easter Lilies for growing in house? Date depends on variety. Bermuda or *harrisi* Lily should be planted September 1 to October 1; Creole Lily, October 1 to November 1; Croft Lily, October 1 to November 1.

How can Easter Lilies be made to bloom in time for Easter? Starting temperature should be 50° to 60° F. After rooting, minimum night temperature, 65° to 70° F.; day temperature, 75° F. When plants are 3 to 4 ins. high, move to lower temperature (60°) for 14 days, then to high temperatures. Water frequently.

LILY-OF-THE-VALLEY

Can I make lily-of-the-valley bloom indoors? Yes. Order large, cold-storage pips sold for forcing. Plant in moist fiber, leaving tops exposed. Place at once in sunny window and give plenty of water.

DUTCH BULBS

Daffodils (and other spring-flowering bulbs) grown for winter bloom are planted in pots, pans, or flats, and then stored in cold, dark place (such as a bed made against north wall of house) for several weeks to make roots before being brought indoors.

What spring-flowering bulbs can be forced in pots of soil for winter bloom? Daffodils (suggested varieties): February Gold, Ada Finch,

Roman Candle, Golden Sceptre, Pearly Queen, Alasnam, King Alfred, Croesus, Diana Kasner, Cheerfulness. Tulips: Fred Moore, Tea Rose, Mr. Van Tubergen, Le Reve, De Wet; Species: *Clusiana* and *Kaufmanniana*. Minor Bulbs: grape-hyacinth, crocus, snowdrop, chionodoxa, scilla, lily-of-the-valley; Dutch hyacinths.

FORCING BULBS FOR INDOOR BLOOM

Bulbs are placed, close together but not touching, in bulb pan, and covered with soil. Bulb pans are placed in frame or trench and covered with leaves or litter.
After a period of several weeks to allow roots to form, they are brought indoors to make foliage growth and eventually to flower.

How are hardy (spring-flowering) bulbs forced for winter bloom?
In late October pot up in crocked bulb pans in standard potting mixture (see Soil, this section), 3 to 7 to a pot, according to size of bulbs. Tips of bulbs should be level with the surface of soil in pot. Soak well from below. Bury in trench outdoors or in empty cold frame, placing pots on 2-in. layer cinders or small stones covered with 1-in. layer peatmoss or humus. Pack damp peatmoss or dead leaves around and over pots 1 in. deep and mulch above with leaves, salt hay, or soil. Or store in cold, dark cellar where freezing occurs. Leave to freeze and root for at least 6 weeks, then bring in as desired for succession of bloom. Place first in half light at 40° to 50° F., with little water. Bring gradually to sunlight, warmth, and plentiful watering. When flower stalks appear, give complete fertilizer. When blooms open, remove from full sun.

Do you water daffodils or tulips which are potted and kept in a cold cellar for later forcing?　After bulbs are potted they should be thoroughly soaked. If conditions are right (i.e., if there is proper humidity in the cellar), they will not require additional watering. However, if pots dry out, they must be watered.

In how many days will tulips bloom after they are taken out of the cold-storage pit?　They will bloom in 5 to 8 weeks, depending on earliness of variety and temperature.

Can we plant tulip bulbs in indoor pots to bloom at Easter? How and where?　Yes. See previous questions.

What care is given to spring-flowering bulbs forced for winter bloom after they have bloomed?　Foliage is ripened as in garden, being kept green as long as possible. As spring comes, pots can be sunk outdoors until foliage matures. When leaves turn yellow and dry off, remove bulbs and store. In fall, plant outdoors for garden bloom. If more bulbs are to be forced, use fresh stock from bulb grower or from garden.

BULBS, TENDER, FOR FORCING

In what sort of soil should tender bulbs be forced?　Light, well-drained, and fertile. Avoid use of *fresh* manure. (See Soil, Fibrous Potting Mixture, this Section.)

AGAPANTHUS

What is proper care for an agapanthus both winter and summer?
In winter, rest. Keep nearly dry in temperature 45° F. In spring, increase water supply and temperature. In summer, stand outside in sunny position and water and feed freely. Repot in spring only when growths become crowded.

How deep should lily-of-the-Nile (agapanthus) be planted in pots to take into basement for winter?　The tuberous root stocks should be planted just beneath the soil surface, so that the crown of the plant is practically at the surface.

AMARYLLIS (HIPPEASTRUM)

Are amaryllis bulbs planted inside or out? If out, should they be dug out for winter? When do they bloom? (Ohio.) Plant in pots indoors, leaving upper half of bulb sticking out of soil. They bloom from January to April, but the same bulb does not produce bloom over this entire period.

What soil should be used for amaryllis? Heavy loam, enriched with bone flour (1 pt. per bu.) and well-rotted or commercial cow manure (2 qts. per bu.).

How shall I plant an amaryllis bulb? Select a pot just large enough to hold bulb, comfortably surrounded by soil. Pot up in potting mixture indicated in previous question, with top half of bulb exposed. Water well from below after potting.

When do I plant an amaryllis bulb? I planted it last year—no blooms. Plant new bulbs December to March.

Should amaryllis bulbs be kept in the dark until rooted? This is not necessary. A temperature of 60° to 70° F. and just sufficient moisture to keep the soil damp (all the way through) is needed.

How can amaryllis bulbs be kept from year to year? Keep plant growing by watering and feeding during season when leaves are developing or present. When leaves die down, keep dry. Repot every third or fourth year; top-dress at beginning of growing period other years. (See answers to other inquiries.)

How shall I top-dress a potted amaryllis? By scraping off the top inch of soil in the pot without disturbing the bulb and substituting good garden loam containing a complete fertilizer.

Is there some fertilizer that I may feed amaryllis to produce better and more blooms? When the plants are growing, and providing the pots are well filled with roots, use liquid manure (which see) or any good complete house-plant fertilizer.

What is the trick of raising amaryllis in the house? Make sure that it is rested in fall and early winter. Water freely, feed and otherwise encourage growth when leaves are growing. Plunge outdoors in shaded spot during summer. When potting, do not bury bulb more than halfway in soil.

How long do you leave amaryllis bulb in dry dirt before applying water? From time leaves yellow and die away until the first signs of new growth can be seen sprouting out of top of the bulb.

How long should amaryllis bulbs be dried off? I want mine to bloom in March. Individuals vary greatly. Some are nearly evergreen; others die down quite early in the fall. Six or 8 weeks would perhaps be a minimum.

When should I start to water amaryllis bulbs to have them bloom in January or February? They are now in a cool, dark room in pots. Pick out bulbs that went to rest early. Examine carefully in December, and if you can find any showing tips of flower buds out of top of bulb, start these up by watering and placing in temperature of 70° to 75° F.

Last Easter I bought an amaryllis. Left it outdoors without watering until September, when I brought it indoors and started to water it again. To date no sign of any growth. What is wrong with it? You dried it off too soon. It should be encouraged to grow as vigorously as possible through the summer to build up bulb and following year's bloom.

In what window should amaryllis be kept—south or east? Either exposure should be satisfactory. They need as much sunlight as possible during winter and spring, and light shade during the summer.

Have some fine hybrid amaryllis bulbs which bloomed the first year; now—in spite of following directions for resting, feeding, etc.—I get no more blooms though the bulbs are growing well with big leaves. Have had bulbs 2 years. What is the trouble? Amaryllis bought and flowered first year often fail to bloom second year. Their energy is used to establish a new root system. As good foliage has developed, your plants should bloom from third year on.

Why don't hybrid amaryllis bulbs brought home from Florida bloom? I have about 3 doz. bulbs and all bloomed before we got them. It may be that they have not established themselves yet. This may take a year. (Read other replies on this subject.)

How is the best way to grow amaryllis bulbs to a really large size? Mine seldom reach 3 ins. in diameter. Good cultivation over a period of years is the answer. This implies potting, watering, feeding, resting when required, suitable soil, temperature, and light conditions, as well as maintaining the plants free from pests. (See previous questions.)

Is bulb fiber as good as soil for growing an amaryllis bulb? No. To grow these successfully so that they will last from year to year nourishment is needed, and this is not contained in bulb fiber.

Is it unusual for an amaryllis to bloom in December? It was kept in a warm basement and manure water was used. No, it is not particularly unusual, although most bulbs produce their flowers later in the winter.

Do amaryllis often bloom more than once a year? Mine bloomed 3 times this year. The amaryllis (*Hippeastrum*) does not bloom more than once a season. Strong bulbs will sometimes produce more than one flower scape, however. If your plant blooms every 3 or 4 months, it is something other than *Hippeastrum*. There are many bulbs of the amaryllis family (*Amaryllidaceae*) with varying characteristics.

How may a fine hybrid amaryllis (hippeastrum) be propagated vege-

tatively to make a rapid increase in the stock of bulbs? By cutting bulb into segments, each containing small part of basal ring. These pieces are planted in sand and peatmoss and placed where bottom heat of 70° F. is available. Keep just moist and shaded and new bulblets should arise in few weeks.

I have amaryllis hybrids, from seed, already as big as marbles, but they have stopped growing. Should the bulb be nearly out of the soil? What fertilizer should be used and how often? What soil? Bulbs of young amaryllis naturally grow out of soil. They will cease growing for a period in late summer. Use bone meal in soil, which should be a medium porous loam. Feed when in active growth with liquid manure (which see) or other organic fertilizer.

ARUM PALAESTINUM

What is the plant history of the Black Lily-of-the-Nile? *Arum palaestinum,* also called the black calla, is native of Palestine, a relative of our common skunk cabbage, of the tropical anthurium, and of the white callalily. First discovered by the Genevan botanist M. Boissier near Jerusalem.

What can I do to make a black calla come into bloom? Have tried, but to no avail. Perhaps your tuber is too small and will bloom when older. Grow it in rich soil, keep moist and in light position during summer. Dry off completely during winter.

BRUNSVIGIA

How can brunsvigias be grown as house plants? They are often shy bloomers and plants will sometimes live for years without producing flowers. Pot bulbs in rich, sandy soil. Grow in sunny position. Water freely and feed when in active growth. Keep quite dry from time leaves die down until signs of renewed growth begin to show.

CALADIUM

How can I preserve fancy caladium tubers from season to season? My tubers deteriorate more and more each season, till finally there are none left. Apparently your growing conditions are unsatisfactory. These plants are gross feeders, and to build up a good tuber for succeeding year, a rich humusy soil, adequate supplies of moisture, and summer feeding are necessary.

What is the most dependable fertilizer for potted caladiums? Organic fertilizers are best. Bone meal and dried cow manure at potting time, followed by feeding with dried blood and liquid cow manure during growing season, are recommended.

Will caladium grow well in jardinieres with hole in bottom for drainage? Why do leaves wither quickly? Can soil be too wet? If properly cared for, they will. Withering of leaves could be due to excessive water. While they appreciate moist soil, a waterlogged condition is fatal.

Is it possible to keep the Fancy-leaved Caladium in the window garden all winter, or does it have to be stored in sand to rest?   Yes, providing the temperature is maintained at not less than 60° F. and the soil in which it has been growing is kept quite dry.

After getting caladium bulbs to start, leaves are small, but stems of leaves are abnormally long; growing in parlor window which gets some sun during day. What causes this?   This is usually true of the first few leaves. If the condition persists, it is probably because of lack of sufficient light.

When should Fancy-leaved Caladiums be started indoors in spring?   From March to June, depending upon facilities available and upon when the plants are wanted to be at their best. A temperature of 70° to 80° F. is needed for starting caladiums.

I have a Fancy-leaved Caladium. It grew rapidly at first, but the leaves drop off as soon as they get a good size; now there are but 2 new ones coming on. What shall I do?   In all probability this is due to a too-dry atmosphere. Perhaps you start the plants too early for house cultivation. Tubers planted in May will give better results.

I was told to cut my caladium down when it started to droop. Did I do right? Should I keep the roots damp while stored?   No. Growth should not be checked suddenly at the first sign of the plant going to rest in the fall. A gradual drying-off process should precede final dormancy. Keep tubers dry in storage.

How should a caladium which has finished blooming in the house be treated?   As soon as plant begins to lose foliage in fall, gradually reduce frequency of watering. When all leaves have gone, withhold water completely and store pots containing bulbs in dry place, at a temperature 60° to 70° F.

How can you divide caladium bulbs?   In spring cut well-developed tubers into sections, each containing a portion of the apex. Dust cut surfaces with powdered sulfur. Plant in mixture of sand and peatmoss. Temperature should be 70° F.

CALLALILY

What kind of soil grows callalily best?   They like a moist soil that is well supplied with humus and plant food.

How should callalily bulbs be cared for after blooming?   Keep feeding the plants (good organic fertilizer) and encourage strong growth until July, then gradually dry off and rest until September. Repot and start into growth at this time.

Should a callalily be given a rest period? If so, when?   A rest period is very desirable. Dry plants off in July and August, beginning by gradually reducing the water supply and finally turning the pots on their sides, so that the roots are kept dry for 5 or 6 weeks.

Two satisfactory house plants: the quick-growing but short-lived Paper-white Narcissus, and the slower-growing but long-blooming calla.

My white callalily forms a bud but never matures. Can you tell me why? This may happen if you are growing the plants in insufficient light; also if you have diseased tubers that do not produce a good, healthy root system.

I have a white callalily 5 years old which never has blossomed. What is the reason? This plant needs rich soil, ample moisture during growing season, at temperature of 50° to 60° F., feeding when in active growth, and a definite rest period during late summer.

After blooming time is over in summer my calla (Richardia albomaculata) forms bunches that look like seeds. Could they be planted? Seeds of this plant are clustered together after the manner of those of the skunk cabbage. Sow when ripe in pots of light humusy soil and keep moist, at temperature of 60° F.

CLIVIA

Can clivias be grown as window plants? Yes. Stand potted plants outdoors in summer; feed and water regularly. Bring indoors before frost and give a light window. Water enough to prevent shriveling, as the plant is evergreen. When buds push up, give more water.

I have had a clivia 6 years which bloomed only when I bought it. Are there any secrets of how to make it bloom? Clivias need cool growing conditions and full sunlight, except during summer months, when light shade is appreciated. They resent disturbance at roots. Soil should always be moist but not waterlogged. During summer, feeding at weekly intervals with diluted liquid manure is beneficial.

CRINUM

Can you give me information on crinum lilies?   When grown in large pots or tubs, they need good drainage and rich soil. Plant with base of bulb deep in soil. Store in winter in light place, at temperature of 50° F., water little. In spring, increase temperature and water more freely. In summer, water freely; feed generously; place outdoors in sunny location.

What is proper culture for Crinum fimbriatulum (Milk-and-Wine Lily)? Mine does not bloom but develops many bulblets.   Plant in very rich but well-drained soil in large pots or tubs. Set bulbs deeply. Water and feed established plants generously in summer and grow in sunny position (outside in hot weather). Keep in cool, frostproof place and nearly dry in winter.

FREESIAS

When is the best time to start freesias in the house and how should they be taken care of?   Plant bulbs in September in fertile, porous soil. Space 1½ ins. apart. Put in cool place. Give little water at first, more as growth develops. Place in a cool, sunny window when tops are 1 to 2 ins. high. Avoid overwatering. Feed lightly when flower buds appear.

How can I have a succession of freesia bloom in my window garden?   Plant bulbs at 2-week intervals from September to November; 3 months are needed from planting to flowering.

Freesias planted in pots grew well but did not bloom. Why?   After planting, freesias need a period in a cool, frostproof light place to develop root growth. When growth starts, the temperature should be 40° to 50° F. at night, with a 5° or 10° rise in daytime.

My freesias last year were more beautiful than all expectations, exceeding those at the Philadelphia Flower Show. This year I took advised care of them, and they are spindly and small-leaved; used fertilizer this year but not last. This has happened before. Why? I bought giant-size bulbs.   It is advisable to buy new bulbs each year. Quality of bloom depends largely upon cultivation bulbs receive *previous* year. In house or small greenhouse it is difficult to provide ideal conditions for bulb development.

Why are my freesia leaves turning yellow? They are 8 to 9 ins. high.   Overwatering will quickly cause freesia leaves to turn yellow. Lack of sufficient light or extreme dryness of the soil will cause a similar condition.

My freesias are growing spindly without blossoming and are drying up. Why?   Temperature too high. Atmosphere too dry and possibly lack of sufficient sunlight.

How should freesias that bloom in the house be cared for to have

bulbs for another year? Mine will bloom about Christmas time. If brought into bloom as early as Christmas, it may be difficult to provide conditions that will insure good bulbs for following year. Water and feed and keep growing in sunny, cool position until foliage fades, then gradually dry off.

How are freesia bulbs stored through their summer rest period? Either in the pots of soil in which they were grown (soil kept dry, pots on sides in cellar or shed), or shaken from soil and kept in cotton bags in cool, dry place.

I've grown freesias from bulbs and have lots of little bulblets. Will they produce? They are planted now. They will not bloom while very small, but if grown under good conditions they should soon make blooming-size stock.

Can freesias be grown successfully in the garden? This can be done only in the warmer sections of the country. They cannot be handled as summer-flowering bulbs.

GLOXINIA

What soil mixture should gloxinia bulbs have for best growth? Should gloxinias be watered from the top or bottom? A loose, humusy soil. Adding to the mixture flaky leafmold, very old rotted manure, sharp sand, and broken charcoal is helpful. They can be watered from top to bottom providing the soil is thoroughly wetted through and no water is splashed on the leaves.

What are cultural requirements for the gloxinia, from bulb planting to maturity, and back to rest again? Put tubers in pots just large enough to hold them, in light, humusy soil, February or March. Keep just moist in temperature of 70° F., increasing water supply as growth develops. Pot on into 5- or 6-in. pots when first pots are filled with roots. Feed liquid manure or complete fertilizer biweekly when in full growth. Shade from sun. Dry off gradually after flowering.

Will you please tell me if gloxinias grow best in a shady or sunny place? Shade from anything but weak early-morning and late-afternoon sunlight is necessary.

May I have some information about gloxinias? Do you water them and bring them to the window or in the sun right away, or do you wait and let them set awhile before bringing them into the sun? Flowers never developed from the buds mine had last year. Probably you gave them too much sun. (See answers to two previous questions.)

What is correct temperature for gloxinias? How should watering be done? During the growing season a minimum temperature of 60° F. (rising to 70° in daytime) is satisfactory. Watering should be done with caution until a good growth of leaves has developed, then it may be given more freely.

Why do my gloxinia buds turn brown and die?   The blasting of the buds may be due to an infestation of mites, but more probably the air is too dry. A moist, but not stagnant, atmosphere and freedom from draft provide congenial conditions.

Why do my gloxinias grow tall and lanky? Those I have seen at florist shops are bushy.   This may be due to too little light. They need shade from bright sun, but good light otherwise.

Why do gloxinia leaves curl and look limp? I drop no water on the leaves.   You probably are either keeping the soil too dry or you have watered it so much that the roots have rotted off. Gloxinia leaves normally die down after flowering.

What is proper care for gloxinias after they bloom?   Shortly after blooming is over, begin to reduce the moisture supply by increasing the intervals between applications. As leaves die down, intensify this drying-off process; finally store plants (leaving bulbs in the soil) in a dry place at a temperature of 45° to 50° F.

When can I take my gloxinia out of storage and start it growing?   From mid-February to end of March. Should it show signs of activity (new leaves appearing), it should be potted and started without delay.

What is the proper blooming season for gloxinias?   Under greenhouse conditions, with skilled cultivation, they may be brought to bloom at almost any time. However, they are naturally summer and early-fall bloomers, and it is easiest to have them in flower at those seasons.

Which gives the better satisfaction in starting a new gloxinia, to plant a leaf after it has rooted in water, or to plant the unrooted leaf in soil immediately?   The best plan is to root the leaf cuttings in moist sand or sand mixed with leafmold or peatmoss.

How and when does one start new gloxinia plants from their leaves? Are mature or immature better?   Leaf cuttings consist of partly matured, medium-sized leaves with some of the apex portion cut away. They are taken in early summer and planted in sand and leafmold, or sand and peatmoss, in a warm propagating bed. Keep only just moist until new tubers form.

In starting gloxinias from leaf cutting, what is done after you have a tuber and roots formed? Mine don't seem to start.   If cuttings are started late in the season, the young tubers are rested through the winter and started up in the spring. Even with early summer-rooted cuttings, a period often elapses between formation of the roots and tuber and development of leaves.

What is the best method of starting gloxinia from seed?   Sow in January or February in very sandy, humusy soil that has been finely sifted. The seed is exceedingly small and should not be covered with soil, but firmly pressed into the surface. Keep evenly moist at all times in a temperature of 70° F. Shade seedlings and transplant as soon as large enough to handle.

HAEMANTHUS

Can the bloodlily, native of South Africa, be started in the house in the winter and set out in the spring, then taken in the house again and repeat the same culture again? Haemanthuses should not be taken out of their pots and set in garden. If desired, pots could be plunged to their rims in bed of ashes outdoors (in light shade) during hottest months.

HYACINTH

I have seen hyacinths forced in winter in dishes of fiber or pebbles. What kind are they, and how should they be handled? These are the delicate, fragrant Roman hyacinths. Bulbs are delivered from the seed house in August, and if they are planted immediately and left for 10 days or 2 weeks in a dark cool cellar, then brought to a cool, sunny window, they will be in bloom by Christmas. General planting and care the same as for tender narcissi.

Left: bulb pan removed from pre-rooting storage, ready to be brought indoors. Right: paper cap, open at top, used during early growth to induce formation of longer flower stems of certain bulbs, especially hyacinths.

HYDROSME RIVIERI

What is the Sacred Lily-of-India? This name is applied to *Hydrosme (Amorphophallus) rivieri*—a relative of the callalily. It is a native of Cochin-China. In spring large tubers produce a tall, dark-colored, foetid, calla-like bloom; in summer, a single, stout leaf of umbrella shape finely divided into many leaflets.

Have been given a Sacred Lily-of-India, supposed to bloom black. Looks like a large potato. What is name and how do I care for it? *Hydrosme rivieri.* Grow it in pot of loose humusy soil, or plant it out in garden in summer. Leaf is produced in summer; flower in spring. In fall dig up and keep dry until following spring. Flower is exceedingly curious.

What is correct culture for a Snake-palm or Sacred Lily-of-India? Snake-palm is a common name applied to *Hydrosme (Amorphophallus) rivieri*. Plant large tuber in pot of fertile soil. Water when young leaf appears, and increase supplies as growth develops. Keep quite dry during resting season. Plant may be set outdoors in summer.

HYMENOCALLIS

How must I plant hymenocallis bulb outdoors? Can it also be forced indoors during the winter? Hymenocallis may be grown as a house plant. Winter-blooming kinds are *speciosa* and *caribaea*. For outdoor culture see Tender Bulbs.

IXIA

How can ixias be grown? I cannot make them live. Bulbs start, then die off. Treat exactly like freesias. Pot in early fall, spacing bulbs about 2 ins. apart. Water carefully at first, more freely afterward. Grow in cool, light position (night temperature 45° F.). Dry off gradually after flowering. Avoid overwatering and high temperatures.

NARCISSI

What tender narcissi are usually grown as house plants in fiber or pebbles for winter bloom? Is culture the same for all? Paperwhites, pure white, fragrant; Soleil d'Or, golden yellow, fragrant; *tazetta orientalis* or Chinese Sacred Lily, two shades of yellow, fragrant. Yes, all are forced in the same way.

How can I grow tender narcissi as house plants? Buy bulbs from a reliable house so that you will know that they have been well grown. Plant in moist bulb fiber, or place in dishes of moist pebbles to which bits of charcoal have been added; or, better, plant in bulb pans as described on page 1027. Place for 2 weeks in a cool dark closet or cellar until growth starts. As roots develop, bring to more light. Keep cool. When foliage growth begins to develop, place in *cool,* sunny window.

I bought narcissus bulbs. The directions say plant on 1 inch of gravel and fill around with garden soil. I always plant these in stones. The soil is to be kept very wet. Do you think this better than stones? Growing in stones is just as satisfactory if not more so than the method described.

I started some Paperwhite Narcissi the first of November, now they are about 3 ins. high. How long before I should bring them into the light and a warmer temperature? They should be brought into growing temperature immediately.

When narcissus bulbs are planted in the house, is there any way to keep them from getting so tall? My present ones are now 30 ins. high.

These are undoubtedly being grown at too high temperature. Best daytime temperature is 70° to 75° F., night temperature 60° to 65° F. The lower the temperature, the shorter and more satisfactory will be the plants.

Why do my narcissus bulbs have only leaves and not flowers (bulbs grown indoors in water)? If bulbs are good quality, failure is most often caused by excessively high temperature.

My Paperwhite Narcissi, growing in pebbles in a cool cellar, grow tall and fall over before blooming. Why? They must have been planted too early and kept in a dark place too long. They must have full light to mature.

I planted 18 Paperwhite Narcissus bulbs indoors in light soil. The bulbs were bought at 2 different places. I had a fine forest of foliage, but only one small bloom; why? I kept them in the dark 4 or 5 weeks, then in a sunny window. Excessively high temperature was the probable cause of this failure. Best planting date for Paperwhite is from October 15 to November 15. Two weeks in cool dark for rooting is sufficient.

What procedure should be used in keeping Paperwhite Narcissus bulbs for the next season? It is impractical to keep Paperwhite Narcissus over from year to year.

How do you restore bulbs of Paperwhite Narcissus after forcing indoors? (Pennsylvania.) These bulbs cannot be restored in Pennsylvania. They are tender bulbs, and outdoor planting revivification cannot be practiced in your section.

Can the Paperwhite Narcissi bulbs grown in water in the house be made to blossom again out of doors? (Washington.) If your section of Washington has a mild winter such as is found near Orting, Washington, these bulbs will produce blossoms again after the second year.

Do Paperwhite Narcissi, kept in the house, ever develop seeds that are worth planting? I have 2 that seem to be developing seeds. It is not worth while to save the seeds.

Is it possible to get bloom from Chinese Sacred Lily (*Narcissus tazetta orientalis*) and similar bulbs for house bloom, if stored after foliage matures and planted following fall? No, it is not possible. Polyanthus narcissi do not bloom the second year after forcing.

What does this mean—Chinese Sacred Lilies, price 14–15 cm per M $37.50? Cm means centimeters. Per M means per thousand. A centimeter is the international measure for bulbs. This is usually used in the wholesale trade.

ORNITHOGALUM

Have carefully followed directions for Ornithogalum aureum with poor results. Only one bulb out of 4 in the same pot has started and

that has blossomed low. What is the trouble?   This species needs considerably more warmth and moister conditions than most ornithogalums. A temperature of 60° F. at night and 65° to 70° F. in daytime is not too much.

OXALIS

How should I care for oxalis? I have several different kinds.   Tender oxalis are potted in September, 3 or 4 bulbs in a 4-in. pot or bulb pan in porous, fertile soil. Water carefully at first; more freely as growth develops. Repot into 5-in. pot when 4 ins. is filled with roots. When blooming is over, gradually reduce water and keep quite dry through summer. Grow in temperature of 60° F.

Why can't I grow oxalis successfully in the house?   Because the environment is not likely to be suitable. They need plenty of sunlight, ample water during growing season, none during dormant period, a loose, porous soil, and a temperature of 55° to 65° F.

How do you store, and where is the best place to plant, oxalis bulbs?   During dormant season leave bulbs in soil in pots, keep dry, and store in cellar or shed. They may be grown in pots or in hanging baskets in greenhouse, sunroom, or sunny window.

Why do my oxalis bloom for only a short time in my window garden?   Oxalis have a definite season of bloom. Unlike some geraniums, begonias, and fuchsias they do not produce flowers over a period of months.

Why don't my oxalis bloom? Have one in east and west window.   Possibly lack of sufficient light. These plants need full exposure to sunshine for good results. Overcrowding, or an unsuitable soil may be contributory causes.

RANUNCULUS

My ranunculus is drying leaf by leaf; it's in the north window. What is the cause?   Probably too warm and dry. This bulbous plant must be grown indoors in cool (night temperature 45° F.), moist conditions for best results. A cool sun porch would afford right conditions.

VALOTTA PURPUREA

What can you tell me about Valotta purpurea?   The Scarborough-lily is a tender evergreen bulb. It needs rich, porous soil. Repotting is resented and should be resorted to only when absolutely necessary. Never let soil become dry. Grow in full sun and feed plants vigorously.

VELTHEIMIA VIRIDIFOLIA

How shall I plant and care for my veltheimia bulb?   Pot in standard soil mixture in a 6- or 8-inch pot with the upper half of the bulb exposed. Give regular water and sunshine through autumn. The bloom should begin to develop around Thanksgiving and be open for Christmas. It lasts several weeks. After flowers fade, cut off the blooming stem but continue to give water and light while the handsome foliage remains green. As it dies back, toward spring, gradually reduce water. Store in pot turned on side on damp floor of potting shed or outdoors during summer. When new growth starts, increase water, feed with complete plant food and give full sunlight.

What shall I do with the small bulb which has appeared on the side of my veltheimia? When leaves die back, gently remove offset from parent bulb and pot up separately.

Plant Troubles and Their Control

INTRODUCTION

BY CYNTHIA WESTCOTT

DISEASES AND PESTS have taken their toll of food crops and ornamental plants since the beginning of history; often they have influenced the course of world events. Rust, for instance, is known to have been blighting wheat for more than two thousand years; the ancient Romans found it so important that they held a yearly festival and offered sacrifices to the rust gods for the protection of their grainfields.

Another rust disease is credited with keeping the British confirmed tea drinkers, for after practically all the Ceylon coffee trees were destroyed by rust the plantations were turned over to the growing of tea. The world's coffee production became centered in Brazil, and it was the Americans who took over coffee as their favorite beverage.

Potato blight, another fungous disease, produced the Irish famine of 1845, so disastrous that it caused mass emigration from Ireland and changed British political policy away from self-sufficiency to Free Trade. Even today, in the United States, that same fungus does untold damage in a bad blight year.

American grapes introduced into France for hybridization experiments brought with them a few phylloxera, and these plant lice in the short space of 10 years (from 1865 to 1875) nearly wrecked the wine industry. Two and a half million acres of vines were affected.

In 1868 there escaped from the laboratory of a scientist at Medford, Massachusetts, a few caterpillars which had been imported for experiments in breeding silkworms. Attempted eradication of the gypsy moth has cost the state of Massachusetts millions upon millions of dollars.

Shipments of broom corn from Italy or Hungary, about 1908, brought in the European corn borer, now familiar to everyone who has grown or eaten sweet corn, and one of our most serious insect pests. Corn plants, unprotected, may have an average of 3 to 5 borers apiece.

Every schoolboy has heard how the Japanese beetle arrived in New Jersey from Japan, sometime prior to its discovery in 1916, in soil around the roots of nursery stock; and every Eastern schoolboy has doubtless collected his quota of beetles at a nickel a quart.

Relatively recent is the Dutch elm disease, established about 1930 by means of bark beetles, some of which came in from Europe in elm burls imported for furniture veneer and others in the wood of crates used for shipping dishes. Although the full story has yet to be written, the disease has already caused the loss of thousands upon thousands of fine elms.

And so plant life goes on, from one generation to the next, with disease and pest control a continuing problem and not something that has suddenly descended upon us in the twentieth century. Increased transportation facilities and more crowded living may mean a few more pests in our suburban gardens, and perhaps one or two new ones unknown to our fathers, but the chief reason we hear so much more about pests nowadays is because, with improvement in methods of control, our standards are so much higher. We are no longer satisfied with a wormy apple or a half-rotten vegetable.

By now you are probably asking, "What has all this to do with my small home garden? Pest control is chiefly for the government and commercial growers, isn't it? If I am satisfied to grow some for the bugs and some for me, isn't that my own business?"

The amateur gardener may feel justified in asking this question. The answer is: "Unfortunately, no!"

Diseases aren't kept in place by a scarlet-fever sign, nor does a boundary fence or hedge mean anything to a beetle. Your neighbor suffers by your neglect. So do you! When rust first came to Ceylon it did not kill the coffee trees immediately: it merely weakened them a little and meant a smaller crop. The growers were satisfied with a little less than perfection and had scarcely begun to worry when they woke up one day to find themselves out of business. If you ignore pests in your home garden year after year, your crops will get progressively leaner. On the other hand, it doesn't help to get hysterically alarmed about pests and diseases. They are as natural as weeds, and control is merely another garden operation, like weeding or cultivating. It may require a little more intelligence and forethought, but it will probably take far less time and energy than other garden operations.

Importance of Diagnosis

In plant medicine, as in human medicine, diagnosis is 9/10 of cure. You must know what is wrong with your plant before you can select the right control measure. The wrong medicine, or even unnecessary medicine, may do more harm than good.

Some diseases and pests are readily recognized by layman gardeners; others are extraordinarily difficult even for a specialist to identify. If you are in doubt, do nothing until you get advice from some competent person. (Your neighbor is usually not qualified, even though his advice is profuse and free.) The most reliable source of advice is your county agent or your State Experiment Station. It is far better to send a specimen than a description, and to send a whole plant if possible, for the trouble you think is in the leaf may originate in the stem or roots. Diseased material travels best flattened out between layers of newspaper. Don't send live insects about the country, for they may escape and establish themselves in some hitherto-uninfested area. Insects may be quickly killed by dropping them into a cyanide collecting jar or into a jar of kerosene.

In making your own diagnosis, check the obvious things first. *The name of the plant is of primary importance.* Some insects and diseases are promiscuous, attacking a wide variety of plants; but others are highly selective, attacking only the members of a certain family, or even genus, so that the name of the host plant may mean almost immediate identification.

Consider also the time of year. A webby mass in a tree in the spring probably means tent caterpillars; in late summer it indicates fall webworms. An elm leaf perforated in May is probably chewed by a cankerworm; in June, by the elm-leaf beetle; in July, by the Japanese beetle. These dates are for New Jersey, where the writer lives. If you live in Florida, or California, or Maine, your dates, as well as your pests, may be quite different. That is one reason for you to keep in close touch with the information put out by your own State Experiment Station.

Diagnosis is a process of elimination. After knowing the plant that is being attacked and the time of year, look at the foliage. Holes in leaves are probably the work of some chewing insect, although there are one or two diseases that cause shot holes.

Disease is the term applied to the abnormal condition that comes from the work of bacteria, fungi, nematodes, viruses, one or two higher plants, or unfavorable environmental conditions.

Injury is the term applied to havoc caused by insects. The different chewing insects make their own patterns in the leaves. When all the leaves of a single twig or branch are chewed off down to the midrib, or, as in the case of pine, the needles are chewed down to the fascicles, then sawfly larvae may be responsible. Flea beetles make tiny round perforations; weevils produce rather typical angular openings; beetle larvae (grubs) more often "skeletonize" leaves, chewing everything but the epidermis and veins.

If the leaf is yellowish, or stippled white, or gray, the loss of color may be due to sucking insects. You may see them, or their cast skins, or brownish eggs, or excrement, on the underside of the foliage. Yellowed leaves that are cobwebby or mealy underneath indicate spider mites; while whitish streaks spell thrips. If there is no sign of insects, the yellowed leaf may be a symptom of malnutrition, perhaps lack of nitrogen, or unavailable iron. Leaves curled up, or cupped down, may harbor aphids; deformed leaves may be due to the cyclamen mite; blotches or tunnels, to leaf miners; round or conical protrusions, to aphids, midges, or gall wasps.

Leaf spots with definite outlines and filled with numerous minute dark pimples are of fungous origin; smooth spots are usually symptoms of a bacterial disease. Fungi may produce irregular blotches on a leaf, but if the black specks or pimples are missing, the blotches may be sunscald or windburn—the result of cells collapsing when water could not get up from the roots fast enough to replace that evaporated from the leaves. Spray injury also produces leaf spots. When phlox leaves die progressively up the stem, it very likely is due to some unbalanced water relation; but if chrysanthemum leaves die in the same fashion, it may be due to drought, leaf-spot fungus, a wilt fungus in the soil, or to leaf nematodes, the latter being more probable with Korean varieties. Reddish pustules on a leaf say rust; a white felty growth, mildew; and dark soot, a mold living on aphis honeydew.

A dark lesion, or canker, on a stem indicates a fungous disease; a sawdustlike protrusion is the sign of a borer; but a gummy substance exuding on a peach tree may be caused either by the peach-tree borer or the brown-rot fungus.

Wilt—the partial collapse and dying back of a plant—may result from any one of many causes: high temperature, lack of moisture, root injury from too-close cultivation, too-strong fertilizer, a soil fungus which invades the vascular system, or one which causes a crown or stem rot, large grubs, or microscopic nematodes working on the roots. Rots may follow physiological disturbances, and then millipedes and other small animals feast on the disintegrating tissues. *Determine, if you can, the primary cause, and don't worry about the secondary effects.*

It all sounds enormously complicated, but with a little practice you learn to recognize at a glance the signs and symptoms of common pests and diseases, just as you recognize your acquaintances when you pass them on the street. You don't stop to analyze why that is Mrs. Smith; you just know that it is. With a little more training you'll be noticing signs in spite of yourself and walking along the street muttering, "The lace bugs have certainly made Mrs. Smith's azalea look sick; I wonder why Mrs. Jones never sprays her junipers for scale; Mr. Brown's corn smut is a public menace. If the Board of Health makes me cut down my ragweed they ought to make him burn up his smut boils."

Types of Control

Having, so far as possible, diagnosed your plant trouble, how are you going to control it? There are four main avenues of approach: immunization, exclusion, eradication, and protection—and sometimes it takes all four.

1—Immunization means the development, by hybridization or selection, of varieties which are resistant to certain diseases. One hundred per cent resistance, or total immunity, is impossible, but if you can buy varieties reasonably resistant to the diseases most prevalent in your locality, that is the first, and easiest, control method to attempt. Some seed catalogues list resistant varieties, and your State Experiment Station will help you out with suggestions. Many resistant vegetable varieties are listed in United States Department of Agriculture *Leaflet 203,* which you may obtain from the Superintendent of Documents, Washington, D.C.

There is a theory, widely held by gardeners, that vigorous plants are more resistant to diseases and pests. This is more often due to coincidence rather than to any true relationship between lack of vigor and susceptibility. The same cultural practices which produce a vigorous plant often check the spread of pests. Spider mites flourish and plants languish in close quarters where there is little air circulation. Proper pruning and feeding of elm trees check the spread of Dutch elm disease only indirectly by reducing weak or dead wood in which the bark beetle, disseminator of the fungus, lays its eggs. Some fungi, weak parasites, can enter plants only through wounds, and thrive on decaying tissue; but other parasites, such as rusts, smuts, and mildews, can operate only on a vigorous plant. In corn-breeding experiments it has been found the hybrids of high vigor are more susceptible to smut than those of low vigor; but since vigor is more important than smut resistance, we must continue to control this fungus by eradication methods.

Japanese beetles definitely prefer young, succulent leaves to old and wilting ones, and you never find Mexican bean beetles waiting until plants are weakened before they move in!

There are some rather hazy theories about plant nutrition as a factor in disease resistance, but we have not yet gone very far along this line. No matter how well plants are cultivated and fed, one still cannot ignore their insects and diseases. The sooner this fact is recognized, the sooner the gardener will get over having nightmares about pests and learn to take them in his stride. He cannot have a garden without planting seeds; he cannot continue to have a garden, year after year, unless pest control becomes a routine operation.

2—Exclusion is practiced by counties, states, and countries by means of quarantine laws and regulations, backed up by careful inspections. You can apply the same principle to your garden by looking at every plant, whether acquired by gift or purchase, with a suspicious eye before allowing entry. If you insist on acquiring a diseased plant, either disinfect it or put it in an isolation hospital far removed from your healthy plants.

Buy certified seed when you can. That means that government inspectors looked at the seed plants in the field and certified them as being free from specific diseases. Treating seed with hot water or a disinfectant is another exclusion measure. Farmers through their co-operatives have been able to obtain treated seed more readily than the home gardener, but there is a present movement to encourage seed dealers to disinfect seeds sold in small packets. If you ask for treated seed often enough, you may get it.

3—*Eradication,* of course, means the destruction of a pest after it gets established in an area. It includes soil sterilization to kill soil fungi or nematodes, or treating the soil with chlordane, dieldrin or heptachlor to kill grubs; or putting cyanogas into an ant nest, or breaking off a tent caterpillar egg mass or wiping out the nest. It means getting after Japanese beetles with DDT, or picking them off into a can of kerosene, or putting milky-disease bacteria into the soil where their grubs develop. It may mean taking up an entire plant and its surrounding soil (as in crown rot), or cutting off a branch of apple or pear that has fire blight. It means removing and burning rose leaves infected with black spot; cleaning up peach or plum "mummies" (wizened, dried-up fruits), or maggot-riddled apples; or spading under or burning up all vegetable refuse after harvest.

Remains of any diseased plants should be carefully burned.

Eradication may mean crop rotation to starve out the insect or disease, or cleaning up additional weed hosts, or eliminating some plant which is an "alternate host" and so a necessary factor in the life cycle of a certain disease. Eradication measures were applied long before people understood the nature of the plant disease. The first barberry eradication law was passed in France in 1660, when it was noticed that wheat rust flourished when barberries grew near by. Nowadays we eradicate cedars to prevent the apple-rust fungus from completing its cycle, and take out black currants to save pines from blister rust.

To sum it up, eradication is really garden sanitation, the removal of all factors injurious to plant health. *It is probably the most important control method available to the home gardener.*

4—*Protection* involves the spraying and dusting of plants to kill or to keep away insects or diseases. (Some dormant spraying, however, is more properly an eradication measure.) When chemicals are applied in a wet mist, we call it "spraying"; and when they are applied as a dry powder, the operation is known as "dusting." There are many arguments as to the relative advantages of dusting and spraying; but each has its place, even in the small garden. The lazy gardener will use his small dust gun more often than his sprayer, which should be—though it seldom is—thoroughly cleaned after each use.

A spray or dust used against insects is called an "insecticide," and one against bacteria and fungi a "fungicide." In addition there are "fumigants" and "disinfectants," "attractants" and "repellents"; as well as materials to make the sprays spread and stick.

Sometimes one chemical serves two purposes. A dormant dinitro is used both as a fungicide and a dormant spray for scale insects and aphid eggs. Sulfur dust is effective against mildew and red spider. Bordeaux mixture—a copper fungicide—sometimes serves as a repellent for insects.

Insecticides may control insects when they are swallowed; when they hit their bodies or touch their feet: when their vapors enter the insects breathing organs; and when they repel them because of odor or taste. Just how any given insecticide affects insects may depend on its characteristics, when it is applied, how it is applied and the nature of the pests involved. Most of our newer insecticides will destroy insects in more than one of the above ways.

Insecticides and fungicides are sold under hundreds of different trade names, all variations in one way or another, based on a relatively small number of chemicals. The trade name is unimportant except as it indicates a reliable manufacturer; *it is important to read the label on each package and know you are using the right chemical at the right dilution for your particular purpose.* These chemicals are listed in the following pages with formulae for the small garden and cautions as to use. The possibility of spray injury is ever present. Some plants are at all times allergic to certain chemicals; others can stand them if it is not too warm, or too cold. There is grave danger of injury when two incompatible chemicals are mixed together.

It is not possible to cure all garden troubles with one general spray any more than one kind of pill will cure all human ills, from a sprained ankle to cancer. Sometimes, however, sprays or dusts may be combined to take care of both insects and diseases of certain kinds. Such combination sprays or dusts may be purchased under trade names or, occasionally, mixed at home.

The timeliness of the application is most important. Fungicides should be applied *before* rains, so that a protective coating will be present when the fungous spore or the bacterium starts to grow in the presence of moisture. For fungous diseases, spraying should start *well before the disease is expected,* and should be continued, at whatever intervals are needed, to keep it in check. For rose black spot in New Jersey that means weekly treatments from early May until the end of October; but July 1 to September 1 usually covers the spraying period for late blight of potatoes. The adult Japanese beetle is with us from mid-June to mid-September, but for the holly leaf miner there is only a two week period in May, during which the flies are laying their eggs, when spraying will have any effect.

Know your insects and know your diseases, and don't waste your money and your patience by spraying too early or too late, or with any material but the right one.

Recent Advances in Pest Control

Only a little more than a decade ago the home gardeners could count the number of pesticides available to them on the fingers of their two hands—there was lead arsenate, calcium arsenate, and cryolite for chewing pests; the combination of nicotine sulfate and soap for the sucking insects; rotenone and pyrethrum for both types; lime-sulfur for dormant pests and foliage diseases; and Bordeaux mixtures and the sulfurs for plant diseases, with the latter also good for spider mites. That was about it and the pests not taken care of by these chemicals had to be hand picked or just ignored. Today, we have many more compounds and new ways of applying them. Our modern organic insecticides and fungicides are not only generally much more effective but also much more specific in their effectiveness on certain organisms or groups of organisms. That means that gardeners must be much better informed in order to purchase the best materials for their needs. For dormant spraying gardeners now have the choice of miscible oils or dinitro compounds—both more effective for specific pests than liquid lime-sulfur.

One new series of summer insecticides are grouped together as chlorinated hydrocarbons. In it are DDT, DDD (TDE), methoxychlor, BHC (benzene hexachloride), lindane (a pure and odorless form of BHC), toxaphene, and endrin—used chiefly as foliage sprays or dusts; and chlordane, aldrin, dieldrin and heptachlor most useful for soil and lawn insects but also excellent for some foliage or fruit pests. Another series of summer insecticides are grouped together as phosphorus compounds. These are highly potent materials effective for many foliage or fruit chewing and sucking insects as well as mites. The phosphates include parathion, EPN, TEPP (HETP) phosdrin, diazinon, sulfotepp and metacide to be used as sprays or dusts by commercial growers only, familiar with their dangerous properties and safety measures; equally dangerous demeton (Systox, Systoban), thimet, and shradan (Pestox), systemic insecticides for plant sucking pests on ornamentals only; and malathion and chlorthion excellent general insecticides for the home gardener and safe to use with ordinary precautions. (See Question and Answer section for more details on these compounds.)

The gardener also has available a number of new spray compounds specific for mites (*miticides* or *acaracides*) as substitutes for the phosphate compounds, since spider mites in many places have built up a resistance to the phosphates. These miticides are known by such names as Aramite, DMC (Dimite), Ovex (Ovotran), Chlorobenzilate, Genite, and Kelthane. One or two applications in the spring before populations build up are usually sufficient to avoid damage during the summer. Nematodes too are now vulnerable to chemical attack by gardeners. For preplanting soil treatments (treatments made after the soil is prepared but at least 2 weeks before planting) there is a choice of the soil fumigants ethylene dibromide, D–D, chloropicrin, methyl bromide, or sodium methyl-dithiocarbamate (Vapam or VPM). The last 3 compounds will also destroy weed seeds, disease-producing organisms, and insects, giving almost complete soil sterilization. For either preplanting application or treatment of certain established plants and lawns a number of compounds (such as Nemagon and V–C13) easily applied with hose proportioners or in granulated form, are available or soon will be.

Parallel with the development of more effective insecticides better and more specific fungicides have appeared to replace the old standbys. The most useful group for preventive spraying or dusting are the dithiocarbamates. This group consists of thiram (Tersan), for lawn diseases; ferbam (Fermate Karbam Black) most effective for rust diseases, fruit diseases, shade tree diseases and black spot of roses; ziram (Zerlate Karbam White) for many vegetable diseases; zineb (Parzate, Dithane Z–78), for many vegetable and flower diseases; nabam (Dithane D–14, Parzate liquid) for many vegetable and flower diseases; and maneb (Manzate) excellent for black spot of roses and good for many vegetable, flower, and fruit diseases. Captan, a much publicized fungicide, is effective on a wide range of diseases. The phenyl mercury compounds (Puratized, PMAS, Tag, Puraturf) are used for apple scab control before the 1st cover spray, and for some turf diseases. Similar compounds for turf diseases containing cadmium and/or chromium complexes have such trade names as Cadminate, Crag 531, Caddy, and Kromad. In the group classified as quinone derivatives, dichlone (Phygon–XL) is used mainly for fruit diseases and chloranil (Spergon) is a seed treating fungicide. The glyoxalidine derivative, glyodin (Crag Fruit Fungicide), is also used for fruit diseases. Specifically for powdery mildews, we now have the dinitro crotonate, Mildex or Karathane, and a brand new product, Ortho Phaltan.

Besides the soil fumigants, mentioned previously, that destroy disease organisms in the soil before planting there are two compounds that show promise in controlling soil borne diseases on growing plants: Solutions of oxyquinoline sulfate are effective in controlling Rhizoctonia rot of hardwood cuttings and ericaceous plants: and PCNB (Terrachlor) solution looks good for club root, damping-off, and crown rot of flowers. The control of bacterial plant diseases, against which we have been more or less helpless until recently, is now also within our reach. Some of the antibiotics such as the agricultural grade of streptomycin (Agri-Strep, Agrimycin, Phytomycin) show promise against such bacterial diseases as fire blight of apples, and pears, bacterial wilt of chrysanthemums, and leaf rot of philodendron. Another antibiotic, Actidione, is effective for certain lawn fungus diseases and cedar-apple rust on red cedars.

Chemotherapy

The future successes in plant disease control probably lie in chemotherapy or the use of systemic compounds for internal chemical cure or disease prevention. This relatively new approach involves the absorption of curative or prophylactic compounds through the roots, trunks or leaves; their translocation throughout the vascular system of the plants; and selective fungicidal or bacteriacidal action to kill or inactivate the disease-causing organism without harm to the plant itself. In other words plants are made to take doses of medicine to cure their troubles in much the same way we take pills or injections of antibiotics to cure ours. Some success has been achieved to date in treating plants suffering from certain formerly incurable vascular diseases such as wilts, root-rots, and virus troubles, but the method has been most effective in the correction of nutrient deficiencies in plants such as lack of iron, zinc, copper, and boron, through the use of chelated compounds. For further details see under Chemotherapeutic Treatments for Diseases.

ALPHABETICAL LIST OF
INSECTS, DISEASES, AND CONTROLS

AEROSOLS

I have heard about aerosol sprays for insect control. What are they?
Aerosols are pesticides dispersed in the form of a fog or mist by means of a liquified gas or superheated stream ejected through an open valve; or in the form of a smoke by igniting a combustible material in which they are dispersed. Practically all pesticides (insecticides, fungicides, weedkillers) that can be dissolved in sufficient concentration in organic solvents may be applied in aerosol form. Generally

insecticides are much more quickly applied and more potent when used in this form, but how aerosols act on insects is determined by the nature of the insecticide and the amount deposited on the plants.

How do I go about selecting a suitable aerosol? It all depends on the pests involved and the area to be covered. Sprays in aerosol form are now available as combinations of insecticides and insecticides and fungicides. They are purchased in small to large hand borne metal containers (aerosol bombs) with a valve release for home, garden or greenhouse use; in cardboard or metal containers for combustion in greenhouse; and with a small to large mobile fog generator for space applications outdoors.

ALDRIN

Does aldrin have any advantages over chlordane, dieldrin or heptachlor for soil pests? It has some advantages and disadvantages. The advantages are that it is faster-acting with a soil life of not more than a year so no harmful residue is left or can accumulate. As little as 1 to 3 lbs. of actual aldrin per acre will control soil insects. Chlordane has a residual effect of 3 to 5 years in the soil; dieldrin may stay effective up to 10 years; and heptachlor ranks with aldrin. Its big disadvantage is its lack of long residual effectiveness in the soil, if that is desired. As little as 2 ounces actual aldrin per acre controls grasshoppers. (See also Grub-proofing).

ANTS

What can be done about ants in the garden? Ants are undesirable in the garden not so much because of their feeding but because they loosen soil around roots, causing plants to wilt and die, and they cart around and nurse aphids and mealy bugs for their honeydew. They may be fought either by applying chlordane, dieldrin or fumigants to the nests.

How can I rid my perennial flower beds of great colonies of big black ants, which destroy everything in areas of 3 to 4 ft.? Fumigate the nest with calcium cyanide granules; make holes with a pointed stick down into the nest to a depth of 8 ins.; pour in the granules and cover hole immediately with soil; or punch holes over nest and pour in chlordane emulsion as above.

Either apply 5% granulated chlordane to the flower beds while cultivating the soil prior to planting at the rate of 5 lbs. per 1000 sq. ft. or soak the soil around the plant bases with a chlordane emulsion (1 tsp. 72% chlordane emulsifiable concentrate to 1 gal. of water).

How can you exterminate the large red ant leaf eater, stripping the bushes clean? (Texas.) The leaf-cutting ant does not eat the leaves but carries them to its nest where it chops them up in pieces as a medium on which to grow the fungi it uses for food. Spraying the foliage with lead arsenate might have some deterrent effect, but fumigating the nest with calcium cyanide granules is surer. Ordinarily the injury by this ant is more interesting than serious.

How can I get rid of ½-in. long black ants that live inside trunk of my English Walnut tree? Entrance is narrow fissure 18 ins. long. Have tried filling with cement but they burrow around. This is the carpenter ant, which seldom works through living bark but can enter through a wound in a tree and play havoc in the interior. Easiest method would be fumigation with cyanogas if you can close up the fissure. Or spray the interior of the tree with chlordane emulsion.

APHIDS (PLANT LICE)

What year-round program would you suggest for aphids? Aphids are soft-bodied sucking insects controlled by contact insecticides; in general spray for them when you see the first few individuals. They are more numerous at certain seasons of the year, the time varying with the host plant, so that spraying is generally spasmodic rather than regular. Often an aphicide may be included in a spray put on for other purposes.

What should I use to destroy plant lice? Nicotine sulfate, 1 to 1½ teaspoons, and 1 cubic inch of laundry soap or 2 level tablespoons of flakes to 1 gal. of water is an old and successful spray for aphids.

Malathion is at present the most effective spray material for use on aphids, but pyrethrum, rotenone, or lindane may also be used.

Can anything be done to destroy the white aphids which feed on roots of plants? Malathion when used at 1 tbsp. a gal. and poured into a depression around the plant stem, is helpful. Root aphids are usually tended by ants, so that ant-control operations should also be started.

A dormant dinitro spray applied to fruit trees kills aphid eggs. The same spray will also kill aphid eggs on shade trees but would not be used unless needed for scale insects. The spray is not safe on evergreens. The fluffy white bark aphids on pine and the spruce gall aphid are best controlled with malathion applied on a warm day in the late winter or early spring.

ARMADILLOS

How do I get rid of the armadillos that root up my garden at night? (Florida.) Armadillos are as difficult as rabbits to control. The best method is a fence of 2-ft. chicken wire around the garden, otherwise shooting, if permitted, or trapping in rabbit traps put across their paths. They cannot be readily poisoned.

ARMY WORM

What is the dark-green, white-striped worm, similar to a cutworm,

which attacks grasses, corn, and grain crops, feeding at night and hiding under clods, stones, or leaves during the day? Army worm. Controlled by scattering poison bait in late afternoon or by spraying with DDT, TDE, or lindane. (See Cutworms.)

Army Worm: attacks corn, grain, and grass. Dark green, white stripes; feeds at night.

ARMILLARIA ROOT ROT

What is the fungous disease, especially prevalent in California, which kills trees, shrubs, and other woody plants, being most destructive on lands recently cleared of oak? It may be recognized by the white mycelial threads or fans, black shoestring strands extending through the soil, and honey-colored toadstools that grow near the base of the trunk. Remove dead trees and shrubs, taking out all roots. Rhododendrons and azaleas may sometimes be saved by exposing crowns and main roots for a season. Avoid planting in areas of high-moisture content. Disinfect soil where diseased plants have been taken out with methyl bromide. Apply under plastic tarpaulin over soil at rate of 1 lb. per 100 sq. ft. for 48 hrs.

ARSENICAL SPRAYS AND DUSTS

See Lead Arsenate; Calcium Arsenate.

ASIATIC BEETLE

How do you identify the Asiatic beetle? (New York.) There are two: the Asiatic beetle (*Anomala orientalis*) and the Asiatic garden beetle (*Aserica castanea*). They both are the size and shape of Japanese beetles and work on grass roots in the white grub stage. The adult Asiatic beetle varies in color from light brown to black, with or without mottled marking. It is sometimes found feeding on roses and other flowers but does not do much damage there. The garden beetle is a smooth copper brown, and has been described as an animated coffee bean. It stays in the ground during the day and feeds on foliage, bangs against windows, and flies into cars at night. The larvae injure grass roots and some vegetables. The adults injure leaves of asters, zinnias, and other low ornamentals and carrots, parsnips, turnips, beets, and pepper tops.

How do you combat the Asiatic beetle? (New Jersey.) Grub-proof lawns and spray foliage of ornamentals with chlordane or dieldrin. Rotenone may act as a deterrent on food plants. (See Grub-proofing; also Japanese Beetle.)

Are castor bean plants a protection from Asiatic beetle? (Connecticut.) Their efficacy has been greatly overrated. Entomologists claim tests in cages show that the foliage is practically nontoxic and they cannot be used as trap plants in the field because beetles do not go to the castor bean before their favorite food plants have been exhausted.

Last summer I found hundreds of young Asiatic beetles in a semi-dormant state around my garden plants. I grub-proofed the lawn with arsenate of lead. How do they hibernate? Will my garden be eaten up next summer? (Massachusetts.) They will hibernate in the soil under the grass roots of your neighbor's lawn, and the beetles may fly to feed on your plants next summer. However, treatment should reduce the infestation.

Is it possible the Asiatic beetles came from the roses and destroyed the bent grass in large spots? (Iowa.) The Asiatic beetle is not prevalent in Iowa. Lawn may have been injured by white grubs or chinch bugs or the fungous disease called brown patch, and your rose pest is probably the rose chafer. (See Rose.)

What should I use for the Asiatic beetle? (California.) Nothing. According to statistics the Asiatic beetle is not a problem in California.

BAGWORM

How do you destroy bagworms? (Georgia.) This pest, generally distributed in the East, is more severe in the South. Hibernation is in the egg stage in the female bags, made from interwoven twigs and leaves. The young hatch late in spring, spin their own bags, and immediately start feeding on evergreen and deciduous trees. Control by picking off and burning bags in late winter and by either a heavy arsenate-of-lead spray when feeding starts (use 4 tablespoons arsenate of lead to 1 gal. water) or toxaphene (4 tbsp. per gal. of water).

BEETLES

What are real "beetles"? Members of the insect order Coleoptera, with chewing mouth parts and hardened front wings forming convex shields. Except for a few beneficial types, such as ground and lady beetles, they are injurious both in their grub or larval stage and as adults. They are controlled by stomach poisons used in the ground (see Grub-proofing) or on the foliage.

Do beetles ever come through closed windows into the house in winter? They get in through very small cracks and crevices around the windows. Lady beetles are very frequent house visitors in winter while elm-leaf beetles enter houses in late summer to hibernate.

BENEFICIAL INSECTS

What bugs are harmful and which are harmless in the garden? (Ohio.) The harmful bugs are discussed under the different host plants. Of the harmless or helpful ones lady beetles, ground beetles, and praying mantes are most often seen in the home garden, although sometimes, if you look closely at a group of aphids, you will see a sluglike creature, larva of the syrphus fly, working among them.

BHC (BENZENE HEXACHLORIDE)

My peaches have a peculiar taste after canning. What might cause this? BHC sprays applied to fruits and vegetables after they are developed or to the soil are known to produce an off-flavor or taste. Use the material only in the early stages of growth or better yet substitute a less odiferous material such as lindane. Chlordane may cause a similar off-flavor in fruits or root crops.

BICHLORIDE OF MERCURY (MERCURIC CHLORIDE; CORROSIVE SUBLIMATE)

What is bichloride of mercury? A general disinfectant and virulent poison, to be used with caution. Of value in gardens for treating limited soil areas, where diseased plants have been removed, for some seed, rhizome, or corm treatments, and for disinfecting roots. Usual dilution is 1 to 1,000, or 1 7-grain tablet to a pint of water. Mix only in glass or enamel container.

Can corrosive sublimate be used around the roots of perennials in the fall to discourage fungous blights of various sorts? It is not a good idea to use any chemical as a general soil treatment around growing plants, but if 1 or 2 plants have been infected with some root or crown rot, then the area involved, including soil around nearby plants, may be treated. Treatment should be made immediately and not left until fall. The bichloride will check spreading mycelium but will not always kill the hard sclerotia or resting bodies. Great care should be exercised in removing diseased plants.

BIOLOGICAL CONTROL

What is biological control? The control of plant or animal pests by other living organisms. Notable examples include the work of the Australian lady beetle on the cottony cushion scale, ground beetles on gypsy moths and predacious wasps, and the bacterial milky disease on Japanese beetles. Biological control can never completely exterminate a pest and usually must be supplemented by mechanical measures.

Is there any biological control for codling moth? (Illinois.) Yes, birds and many insects work on the codling moth, but they have never been able to reduce it below the point of commercial damage. Other control methods must be used.

BIRDS

What is the best way to keep birds from eating vegetable seeds? Farmers' supply places sometimes sell a crow repellent for treating seeds, but some say that crows often work down a whole row of corn, hoping to find a kernel that is not treated and palatable.

Is there any known object besides old-fashioned scarecrows that will keep birds out of the strawberry patch? Cover the strawberries with coarse cheesecloth or netting.

Can you tell me anything that will poison sparrows? The baits used for cutworms and slugs sometimes kill birds by mistake. Do not put it out for sparrows; you may kill desirable birds also. Use a sparrow trap or a gun.

BLISTER BEETLES

What are those long bugs that attack Irish potatoes and gardens? (North Dakota.) Blister beetles. They are common in most states, feeding on vegetables and many ornamentals, especially asters and Japanese anemones. They are as much as ¾ in. long, plain black, or black with gray margins, or yellow or gray stripes, or brown or gray.

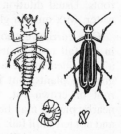

Blister Beetle: attacks asters, anemones, potatoes, and many other plants.

What is the best insecticide for blister beetles? They are hard to kill. Fluosilicates do a good job, either barium fluosilicate or cryolite mixed with 3 parts flour or talc, or DDT dust or spray. Knocking the beetles off into a jar of kerosene is a helpful measure.

BORDEAUX MIXTURE

What is Bordeaux mixture? An old fungicide still of great value in the control of plant diseases. The regulation formula is 4–4–50, meaning 4 parts copper sulfate, 4 lbs. hydrated lime to 50 gals. of water, but for many ornamental plants a weaker solution is needed. Bordeaux mixture may be purchased in dry powder form to be mixed with water at the time of spraying, or it may be made at home by preparing 2 stock solutions, one made by dissolving 1 lb. fine copper sulfate crystals in 1 gal. of water, and the other by dissolving 1 lb. lime in 1 gal. of water. Dilute only at the time of use, the amount of water determining strength of Bordeaux; never put 2 stock solutions together, but add the water to lime solution and then stir in copper sulfate solution. For a 4–4–50 mixture use 1 part of each stock solution to 10½ parts water; 3–8–50, 1 part to 14⅔ parts water; 2–2–50, 1 part to 23 parts water.

Please define 3–5–50 Bordeaux mixture or any such combination of figures. What do they stand for? They are a kind of shorthand to describe strength of spray. The first figure is for the copper, the second for lime, and the last water; in this case it means 3 lbs. copper sulfate and 5 lbs. lime to 50 gals. of water. Ordinarily lime and copper are used in equal amounts, as 4–4–50 or 3–3–50, but sometimes lime is increased to avoid injury to specific crops.

What can you substitute for Bordeaux mixture when you do not have an agitating sprayer? Will tribasic copper act the same? (Oregon.) There are several metallic copper sprays which may be used to replace Bordeaux mixture and they are safer when lime is undesirable. Tribasic copper is one of these, but you should get specific instructions from your county agent or Experiment Station.

What amount of Bordeaux mixture should be used per gallon of water? Directions come on the package, usually 8 to 12 tablespoons of prepared dry Bordeaux powder to 1 gal. of water. For most ornamental spraying about half this amount is safer, less conspicuous, and equally effective.

BORERS

How can borers be prevented from doing their deadly work? Borers are caterpillars or grubs, larvae of moths or beetles, that work in woody or herbaceous stems. Some, like the European corn borer or common stalk borer, are best prevented by cutting down weed hosts and burning old stalks at end of the season. Twigs infested with borers should be cut out and burned, but when the borer is in a woody trunk, such as rhododendron or lilac, it may be fumigated by squirting in some Bore-Kill or Borer-Sol and then plugging the hole with putty or gum. Newly set trees should be protected from borers by wrapping trunks with Kraft crepe paper wound spirally from crown to the first branch. Three or four applications at two to three week intervals of DDT, dieldrin, or malathion, to the trunks and branches of trees and shrubs beginning in mid-June will also protect them from borers.

BOX-ELDER BUG

What will destroy box-elder bugs? They infest the trees and eat my

fruits and flowers. **The young is red and the adult dark gray, with a red border. (Arizona.)** Since they are sucking insects, malathion or other contact insecticide may control them on the plants, but to prevent their swarming into the house, avoid planting the pistillate tree near by, for the eggs are laid on the fruits.

BUG

What is a bug, horticulturally speaking? A term used by the layman to denote any insect but by the scientist to mean a sucking insect of the order Hemiptera, which means half-winged. The basal half of the fore wing is stiffened and the other half membranous. They often have an offensive odor. True bugs include stink bugs, lace bugs, plant bugs, and chinch bugs.

What can I do to kill sucking bugs? Use a contact insecticide, which see. (See also Insects.)

CAPTAN

Is captan really as wonderful as some write-ups would indicate? It is an excellent general fungicide sold as a 50% wettable powder or a 7 to 8% dust for foliage and fruit diseases but it is not a "cure-all". Many general purpose spray mixtures contain captan. It will not control powdery mildew or rust diseases. Captan is widely used as a seed protectant; in drenches to control damping-off of seedlings and cuttings; and in dips for corms and tubers to prevent storage rots. Its toxicity to warm-blooded animals is quite low. Dogwoods, apples, and crabapples have had their foliage injured by early season captan sprays.

CATS

How can cats be kept out of the garden? (Massachusetts.) They can't, very well. Aside from a small city garden, where numerous cats may congregate, they do little damage to the garden itself, but of course they are enormously destructive to birds. They often are a great help to the gardener in the control of rabbits, mice, and moles.

CENTIPEDE

In digging I see quite a few slender orange-and-brown insects about 2 ins. long, that run fast and want to be in the dark, look like thousand-legged brown or tan miniature snakes. Are they injurious to plants? (Kentucky.) These are probably centipedes, meaning hundred-legged, although literally they have about 15 pairs of legs. They are usually beneficial in the garden, preying on other insects, but the larger ones may inflict painful bites on humans.

What is the color of a centipede in infancy? (New York.) The true centipede is yellow to brown, like the adult, but the garden centipede, so-called, but really a symphyllid, is small and white. This creature injures plants and has become an important pest in greenhouses and truck fields in some states.

CHINCH BUGS

How do you guard against chinch bugs? (Ohio.) Chinch bugs are very small black-and-white sucking insects, red when young, which injure corn and small grains for the farmer and lawns for the homeowner. In hot, dry seasons large brown patches in lawns are very commonly chinch-bug injury. A 5 per cent chlordane dust, applied in June and again in August, is the most effective lawn treatment. Growing soybeans between the corn rows will shade the base so that the chinch bugs will avoid the corn (they do not touch soybeans or any plant outside the grass family). They may be trapped as they migrate from small grains to corn by a barrier line of chlordane dust.

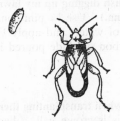

Chinch Bug: small black-and-white sucking insect destructive to lawns.

CHLOROPICRIN

What is chloropicrin? Tear gas, a soil fumigant usually sold as Larvacide. It is excellent for the control of weed seeds, nematodes, various soil insects, and some soil fungi, and may be purchased in a special dispenser with full directions for dosage. It should be used in a loose, moist soil, at a temperature above 60° F., and the gas should be held in the area by wetting down the soil or covering with impervious paper. It is deadly to living plants and should not be used within several feet of them.

COMPOST

Is there a way of combating insects and diseases by treating the compost heap and using it where plants are to be grown? The compost itself may be treated to insure against its being pest-ridden, but it will confer no immunity to the plants in the garden bed.

What is the danger of carrying over fungi and insect pests in compost? There is some danger, and that is why we recommend burning plant material known to be diseased or likely to harbor insects. If doubtful plant debris is included in the compost, it may be treated with chloropicrin or methyl bromide before use.

CONTACT INSECTICIDE

What is meant by a "contact insecticide"?   A material used to kill insects by direct contact. Used chiefly for sucking insects not amenable to stomach poisons, but contact sprays will usually kill those chewing insects that are actually hit with the chemical. Oils, nicotine sulfate, pyrethrum, or rotenone are most used as contact poisons. Sometimes the killing is quick, as with pyrethrum or nicotine, sometimes it takes 24 to 48 hours, as with rotenone. The newer chlorinated hydrocarbon insecticides (DDT, lindane, dieldrin, etc.) and the phosphate compounds, (parathion, malathion) act on most insects as both contact sprays and stomach poisons. In addition they have residual contact effectiveness on many insects—that is they kill insects that walk on the residue.

CRAWFISH

I am having considerable trouble with crawfish digging up my lawn. How do you exterminate them? (North Carolina.)   Use ¼ pint commercial coal-tar creosote emulsion in 3 gals. of water, and apply ½ cupful in each hole; or else 2 tablespoons carbon disulfide poured in each hole and covered with soil.

CROWN GALL

I noticed swellings on the roots of my roses when transplanting them —what shall I do about this condition?   This is crown gall, a bacterial disease that is soil borne as well as plant borne and gradually weakens and kills the plants. Take up plants and prune out all the galls, and dip remaining roots in a solution of 4 tablespoons of captan per gallon of water. Then plant in a new area or in sterilized soil.

CROWN ROT

What will prevent crown rot?   Crown rot is a disease causing sudden wilting of plants from a rotting at the crown or soil line. In the North *Sclerotium delphinii* and in the South *Sclerotium rolfsii* are the causative fungi. The best prevention is to put healthy plants in a new location. The fungus may live for several years in the soil in the form of reddish-tan sclerotia, which resemble mustard seeds. Therefore it is important to take out all surrounding soil when the diseased plant is removed. Unless soil can be dug out for 1 ft. deep and 2 ft. or more in area and replaced with fresh, terrachlor (PCNB) should be poured over the earth and crowns of near-by plants.

CUTWORMS

How shall a poison bait that will kill cutworms be mixed?   There are many formulae, but the following is a simple mixture. Thoroughly mix 1 tablespoon chlordane or dieldrin with 1 qt. of bran. Put 2 tablespoons molasses or syrup in 1 pint of water and moisten the bran until it is crumbly. Scatter bait thinly in late afternoon.

How about a remedy for cutworms that is not injurious to birds, animals, or children? Any poison bait left where young children or pets can reach it is dangerous. Scientists say there is little proof that songbirds are killed by cutworm bait, but gardeners often have sad experiences blamed on poison bait. The safest measure is a paper collar around each seedling as it is set out, 1 in. below the ground and about 2 ins. above. Five per cent granulated chlordane applied to plant bases is also safe and effective.

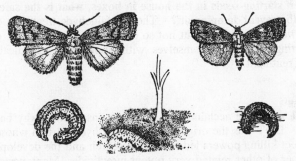

Cutworms: attack young cabbage and tomato plants and other seedling vegetables and flowers. Left, Greasy Cutworm; right, Dark-sided Cutworm.

Do cutworms stay in the soil in some form over winter? (New Jersey.) Usually cutworms winter as small larvae in cells in the soil, or under trash or in clumps of grass, although sometimes they winter as adult moths or as pupae. In spring the larvae feed, usually cutting off seedlings at the surface of the ground, and change to the adult stage in summer. Plowing at that time will prevent egg laying on broken land.

CRYOLITE

Is cryolite an effective insecticide? Sodium fluoaluminate, sold as Kryocide, natural cryolite, and as Alorco Cryolite, the synthetic form, is less poisonous to humans than the arsenicals. It is one of the older stomach poisons of especial value in control of blister beetles, cucumber beetles, and flea beetles, and may be used on beans up to the time the pods form. As a dust it is mixed with 1 to 3 parts of flour, talc or sulfur, but *never with lime*. For spraying use 2 tablespoons to 1 gal. of water.

DAMPING OFF

What would cause seedlings in flats to sort of rot at the stems just at the top of the soil? This is known as damping off—a disease caused by any one of several soil fungi. There are two types, pre-emergence damping off when the sprouted seeds rot in the soil; and post-emergence damping off, when the young seedlings wilt and fall over. For growing in flats either soil or seeds may be treated, but seed treatment is more practical for sowing directly in the garden.

What is the safest preparation for soil treatment to prevent damping off in seed flats? Formaldehyde, perhaps. Dilute 2½ tablespoons commercial formaldehyde with 6 times as much water and sprinkle over a bushel of soil, mixing thoroughly. Place in flats. Wait 24 hours before planting, and water well immediately after planting.

When starting seeds in the house in boxes, what is the safest thing to use to prevent damping off? The formaldehyde treatment outlined above would be all right but not so convenient for small lots of seeds as dusting the seeds themselves with appropriate chemicals. (See Seed Treatment.)

DDT

DDT was once acclaimed as a miracle insecticide, why has it lost favor? DDT was the original chlorinated hydrocarbon whose amazing insect killing powers led to more research and the development of a number of other related very potent insecticides. Many pests against which it had amazing effectiveness—such as houseflies, Colorado potato beetles, cabbage loopers, and flea beetles—have become resistant to it. In addition its use encourages red spider build up.

What pests is DDT still useful for? DDT is still very effective on Japanese beetles, many other foliage chewing pests, the codling moth (some resistance is beginning to show up), the European corn borer, the corn earworm and as a bark spray to protect trees and shrubs against borers.

Is DDT as dangerous to health as some people proclaim? An average sized adult would have to consume as many as 50 normal sized pills made of DDT to be dangerously affected. But, along with all the other chlorinated hydrocarbons, it is readily absorbed thru the skin and tends to accumulate in the body, especially the fatty tissue. Continued exposure or the intake of sublethal amounts will eventually lead to poisoning. There is no need to fear DDT, if all normal precautions are followed in its use. Methoxychlor and TDE (DDD) are the least dangerous of the chlorinated hydrocarbons. Fish and wildlife may be harmed by indiscriminate heavy spraying of forested areas and bodies of water.

How close to harvest is it safe to apply DDT on edible crops? About 3 weeks is the recommended safe margin for DDT, but some, such as lindane, methoxychlor and TDE (DDD), may be used up to within a week of harvesting.

DERRIS

What is derris? One of the plants used as a souce of rotenone. It is imported from the Far East.

DIABROTICA BEETLES

What do you do about the 12-spotted beetles? They ruin all the late blooms—roses, gerberas, carnations, chrysanthemums. (California.) These are the 12-spotted cucumber beetles, Diabroticas, very common in your state. They are hard to kill, but dusting with one of the chlorinated hydrocarbons or with pyrethrum, would be helpful.

DINITRO COMPOUNDS

I have tried to get a dormant dinitro compound and the clerk doesn't know what I'm talking about. Can you help me? Most clerks in horticultural supply stores are poorly informed about the basic names of newer pesticides. Dormant dinitro compounds are sold under such trade names as Elgetol, Krenite, Dinitro-sol, Dinitro-Dry, etc. Horticultural supply stores in fruit growing areas normally handle such products. They are excellent for aphid eggs, armored scales, and the suppression of apple scab in the dead leaves.

DITHIOCARBAMIC ACID DERIVATIVES

Are the fungicides in the dithiocarbamic acid group compatible with other spray compounds? They are not compatible with solutions containing lime, coppers, or organic mercury compounds.

DOGS

What are your views and advice on the dog-nuisance question? Owners should be willing to keep their dogs restrained and, when walking them on leash, should keep them curbed rather than allowed to ruin lawns and shrubs near the sidewalk. For advice I can only refer you to the letter symposium conducted by O. M. Scott and Sons Co., in *Lawn Care.* Moth balls around shrubs and BB guns in action seemed to get most votes. A barberry hedge and a few chopped twigs of barberry scattered about was one idea that might work. Wire shrub guards are usually quite successful. There are many dog-repellent sprays on the market but they all have only fleeting effect.

DORMANT SPRAYING

What is a dormant spray? A spray applied while plants are dormant, which means sleeping; that is, while deciduous trees are bare and before evergreens have started into new life. At this time the plant can stand a stronger spray than during the growing season, and a strong spray is needed to get hard-shelled insects like scales.

When and how should the dormant spray be applied to trees and bushes? (Illinois.) The safest time is toward the end of dormant season, just before new growth starts. In Illinois that might mean the end of March for lilacs and early April for evergreens. For dormant spraying the home gardener usually has a choice of lime-sulfur, either the commercial liquid or a dry mix; a dinitro compound; or an oil spray, either a miscible oil or an oil emulsion. The liquid lime sulfur should be diluted with 7 to 9 parts of water. It is safe, but unpleasant to use, impossible near painted surfaces because of the indelible stain, and leaves an objectionable residue on evergreens. Miscible oils—colorless oils which mix readily with water to form a white liquid—are sold under many trade names. Most manufacturers suggest a 3% dilution for deciduous trees and for evergreens. Oil sprays may be injurious unless they are used on a bright, clear day with the temperature well above 45° F. Do not use on beech, black walnut, butternut, Japanese or sugar maple, or magnolia. Do not use on such evergreens as retinospora, cryptomeria, Douglasfir, true firs, hemlock, Japanese Umbrella Pine, or yew.

DUSTER

What is a garden duster? Machine for applying insecticides or fungicides in dry dust form. For the small garden choose a squeeze duster, a hand rotary duster, or a dust gun, ranging in size from 1 pt. to 2 qts. capacity. Choose one with an extension rod and a flange which will allow you to stand up while using the duster and yet drive the dust from the bottom of the plant up through it. For the larger garden a knapsack bellows or a rotary duster will save much energy in operation.

DUSTING

What is "dusting" as used in the garden? The application of a fungicide or insecticide in dry powder form.

How do you know how much garden dust to use? Tried a dust gun which didn't cover the leaves sufficiently without extreme labor and when tossed out by hand seemed too much. Many plants wilted. I used sulfur and rotenone. (Virginia.) Apply only as much dust as will cover the plants with a thin, even coating. This can be done only with some sort of duster. If yours was too hard to work, it either was the wrong type for the number of plants or else needed adjusting. Coverage of the underside of the leaves is most important and can be done only with the right apparatus, never by throwing it on. Your method of application together with the sulfur in your dust would account for the plants wilting. Sulfur may be injurious to any plant in hot weather, but vegetables are particularly sensitive. Beans occasionally require sulfur, but cucurbits should never have it.

Do you dust plants when they are wet with dew or when they are dry? There is always an argument on this question, but if ornamental plants are dusted when they are wet, a better coverage will be obtained.

EARTHWORMS

It seems as though I have 10,000 or more saboteurs on my lawn, night crawlers, that tear the devil out of it. Is there any solution for their extermination? Yes, you may treat the lawn with bichloride of mercury, at the rate of 2 ozs. in 50 gals. of water sprinkled over 1000 sq. ft. Water the lawn well afterward. If arsenate of lead has been used in grub-proofing, that will suffice for earthworms also.

Do angleworms feed on and destroy peony, iris, and other tubers? I have dug them up and found worms imbedded in them and nothing left but the outer shell. Your peony probably succumbed to Botrytis blight and the iris to borer and rot. Earthworms do not feed on living plant tissue.

When garden worms are found in flower pots, do they feed on the roots of the plant? No. Worms in pots are chiefly a nuisance because they clog up the drainage holes. Watering with lime water will get rid of them.

EARWIGS

Is there anything possible on this earth to exterminate earwigs? (California.) Earwigs, beetlelike creatures with their "jaws" on the wrong end, are poisoned with the standard brand bait used for cutworms or a special earwig bait containing oil. To make the latter, mix 3 lbs. bran with ¼ lb. DDT or chlordane and then moisten with 1 cup fish oil.

How can the small home gardener combat the European earwig? (New York.) In New York State he usually does not have to. Earwigs appear occasionally in the East but are chiefly Western pests. The bait given above will cover 2000 sq. ft. The formula can be reduced to make a smaller amount.

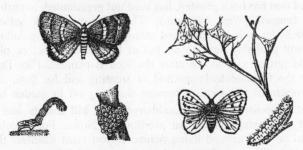

Fall Cankerworm (left) and Fall Webworm.

FALL WEBWORM

What is the difference, if any, between the fall webworm and the fall cankerworm? The fall webworm forms weblike nests in trees in August and September, somewhat like the nests of tent caterpillars. The caterpillars are yellow or green, about 1 in. long and hairy. Control by spraying with DDT or methoxychlor, or by dousing the webs with the same solutions. Fall cankerworms, prevalent early in the spring (usually May), are yellowish or green, and "inch" along, and for this reason are sometimes called inch-worms or measuring-worms. The best complete control is to spray the trees each spring with DDT or methoxychlor.

FERBAM

Can you give me some trade names under which ferbam is sold? Trade products containing ferbam are Fermate, Ferradow, Carbamate, and Karbam Black. It is a good general fungicide especially for rust diseases of plants. The usual dosage is 2 tablespoonfuls per gallon of water.

FLEA BEETLES

What about flea beetles? (Florida.) Flea beetles, that get their name from their habit of quickly springing several inches when disturbed, are small oval beetles which chew tiny shot holes in the foliage of most garden crops. Two species in Florida are most troublesome on beets, cabbage, and tomatoes. In the North potatoes and seedling tomatoes, peppers, eggplants, and crucifers are almost sure to be riddled by flea beetles early in the season. Dusting or spraying with DDT or TDE will control flea beetles. Weeds and other debris around the garden should be burned to destroy winter hiding places.

FORMALDEHYDE (FORMALIN)

What is formaldehyde? A useful soil disinfectant. (See also Soil Sterilization.)

Is it safe to use a weak solution of formaldehyde (1 to 50) on a seed bed that has been planted, but seed not germinated, to curb damping-off fungus? (West Virginia.) This is not a weak solution of formaldehyde; it is the standard strength for drenching *fallow* soil, which will probably have to air out at least a week before planting. It would not be safe to use after the seed is planted. (See Damping Off for the formaldehyde method of treating soil for flats, and see Seed Treatment for ways to prevent damping off in garden soil.)

What concentration of formaldehyde will kill insects and larvae without destroying foliage on seedlings? None. Formaldehyde is never to be used around living plants. If you must disinfect the soil, the plants will have to be moved out for a couple of weeks, and since you do not want to set infested or infected plants back in treated soil, you have to start a new batch of seedlings. So try some other method of controlling your insects.

FUNGI

What are fungi? Members of the Thallophytes or lowest plant group. Lacking the power of manufacturing their own plant food, they live as saprophytes on decaying plant tissue or as parasites on living higher plants. They are characterized by a vegetative stage, consisting of fungous threads or mycelium and fruiting bodies which contain the reproductive organs. Some fungi are readily recognized at a glance: mildew with its white weft of mycelium growing over a leaf; rust, which produces reddish dusty spore pustules, and smut with its masses of black spores; some can be differentiated only by microscopic examination.

What do you do for white fungus? (California.) Such a question is too indefinite. A white fungus may be the coating of mildew on a leaf, it may be the white weft of mycelium at the base of plants in crown rot or Southern blight, or it may be the fans of white mycelium peculiar to the Armillaria root rot, prevalent on woody shrubs in California. Then there is downy mildew and many other possibilities.

What do you recommend as treatment for mustard-seed fungus? (Missouri.) This question is almost as brief as the one above, but it can be answered definitely because there is only one fungus, *Sclerotium rolfsii,* that would be present in Missouri, known as the mustard-seed fungus. It causes the disease known as Southern rot or blight or crown rot and gets its name from the reddish sclerotia which look like mustard seed. (For control see Crown Rot.)

FUNGICIDE

What is a fungicide? A material used to eradicate bacteria and fungi in soil or on seeds, or, more commonly, used as a protectant to cover susceptible plant parts before the disease organisms arrive. Most of the older fungicides are compounds of either copper or sulfur. The most common newer ones are dithio-carbamic acid derivatives (ferbam, ziram, maneb, etc.) and captan. (See Introduction for more details.)

GOPHERS

What is the best way to poison California pocket gophers? There are many species of pocket gophers (ground rats) found in California, Oregon, and Washington. There are special gopher traps on the market, but poisoned carrot bait is simpler. Cut 1 qt. of fresh carrots into pieces 1½ ins. long and ½ in. square and dust over 1/16 oz. powdered strychnine alkaloid. Open the runways at intervals with a pipe probe and insert the pieces of bait. Use care in handling. This bait is extremely poisonous.

GRASSHOPPERS

We were almost ruined by a grasshopper wave last summer. I scattered poison bait. Is there anything else one can do? (Washington.) You can plow sod land where grasshoppers have laid their eggs. Poison bait, to be effective, must be put out for the young hoppers and broadcast early in the morning of a warm, sunny day. The bait formula given under cutworms is all right for grasshoppers but will be somewhat more effective if a sprinkling of salt and part of a chopped-up orange or lemon is added to it. An aldrin or dieldrin dust or spray on foliage is also effective.

GROUND BEETLES

Have found several June bugs in the ground this fall. Are they harmful? (New York.) You would not be apt to find June beetles in the ground. You probably found ground beetles, black or brown or iridescent large beetles with very prominent jaws that live in the ground or under stones. These are beneficial insects, feeding on cankerworms and other pests, and should not be disturbed.

GRUB-PROOFING

How do you kill grubs in the soil? Lawns may be treated with chlordane (5 lbs. of 5% dust, or granules, per 1000 sq. ft.); dieldrin (8 lbs. of 1% dust or granules per 1000 sq. ft.); or heptachlor (5½ lbs. of 1% dust or granules per 1000 sq. ft.). Water in well after treatment. The same chemicals may be applied in spray form, is desired. Practically all soil insects will be killed by any of these materials. Dieldrin gives grub protection for at least 5 years; chlordane for 3 to 4 years; and heptachlor for 1 to 2 years. Heptachlor gives the most rapid kill of grubs. (See also aldrin.)

Is there a safe chemical that can be worked into the vegetable garden for grub-proofing it? Yes, heptachlor as indicated above may be used. It will not impart any off-flavor to root vegetables.

GRUBWORMS

See White Grubs.

HARLEQUIN BUG

How do you get rid of Harlequin bugs? (Kansas.) This brilliantly colored red or yellow and black or blue bug causes the leaves of horse-radish, mustard, cabbage, and related crops to curl and turn brown. It lays clusters of black-banded eggs that look like barrels. Hand-picking before egg laying and removal of eggs are the best control. DDT or toxaphene dust or spray will kill the young nymphs, or rotenone dust may be used after the plants have started to head. Destroy all old plant parts.

HYDROXYQUINOLINE SULFATE

How is hydroxyquinoline sulfate used for the prevention of soil rots? For cuttings of succulent plants use the 25% material at the rate of 1 teaspoon per gal. of water, and soak cuttings for 5 minutes. Use the same strength for a seed bed drench and apply at rate of 1 gallon to 10 sq. ft. This compound acts as a chemotherapeutic or systemic fungicide.

INFORMATION

What we need is plenty of information on pests. We find some that are different from Eastern states. Are they pests or beneficial? (California.) Your own State Experiment Station is set up to give you exactly that knowledge. Not many gardeners realize what a wealth of information, applicable directly to their own state, may be obtained for the price of a post card requesting certain bulletins or circulars. In your particular case you can write to the College of Agriculture, Berkeley, California, and ask for a list of publications. You will find there such very useful bulletins as *Insects and Other Pests Attacking Agricultural Crops, Diseases of Flowers and Other Ornamentals, Diseases of Truck Crops, Diseases of Fruits and Nuts,* and many others. Practically every state has concise information ready for the home gardener as well as the farmer. Ask for it.

INSECTICIDE

What is an insecticide? Chemical compounds that are used in the control of insects are generally called insecticides. Any given insecticide may act on insects in one or more ways, however it is generally grouped according to its main mode of action: a *stomach poison* attacks the internal organs after being swallowed; a *systemic insecticide* is a stomach poison absorbed and translocated in the sap of plants, destroying sap-sucking pests mainly; a *contact insecticide* kills upon contact with some external portion of the insect's body; a *residual contact insecticide* kills insects by foot contact for long periods after application; a *fumigant* is a chemical that produces a killing vapor in the air; and a *repellent* is a substance that is distasteful or malodorous enough to keep insects away. Of the older insecticides the arsenicals are stomach poisons; nicotine sulfate, pyrethrum and oils are contact poisons; rotenone kills in both ways; and chloropicrin and methyl bromide are typical fumigants. The newer organic insecticides are generally effective for a variety of pests regardless of the way they feed. For example DDT works on most foliage chewers that have not become resistant to it, but will also control the boxwood leafminer adults, and some sucking insects such as leafhoppers, through body or foot contact. Many chewing and sucking insects are readily destroyed by either malathion or lindane. Chlordane is widely used for lawns and soil pests such as white grubs and ants, but dieldrin in addition is useful for leaf chewers, thrips, leaf miners and tree borers. See also Systemic Insecticides and Aerosols.

INSECTS

Just what are insects? Members of the animal group Arthropoda, meaning jointed legs. True insects, of the class Hexapoda, meaning 6-legged, are characterized by always having 3 pairs of legs and 2 pairs of wings in the adult form, except for flies, which have but 1 pair. The body is composed of head, thorax, and abdomen. Along the abdomen are small holes, spiracles, which form the breathing apparatus. Contact poisons work through their action on the spiracles or directly through the chitin. Chewing insects have jaws and bite holes in plant tissue, and hence can be controlled by spreading a stomach poison in advance of the insect. Sucking insects cannot bite but obtain their food through a beak which pierces the plant epidermis to get at the sap. Since they cannot be injured by stomach poisons unless they are systemics, contact sprays are necessary.

JAPANESE BEETLES

What are effective ways to eliminate Japanese beetles? (New York.) Chemical treatment of soil (grub-proofing) in lawn areas; biological control by distribution of natural parasites, especially the milky-disease bacteria; spraying foliage during the flying season; hand-picking; trapping in special beetle traps.

How and when do you fight the Japanese beetle—a month-by-month schedule? (Pennsylvania.) Grub-proofing (which see) is done either in May or September, and one treatment should last for 3 or more years. Summer spraying normally starts at the very end of June and may have to be continued until the end of September on plants like roses, although beetles often stop feeding on vines in late August. If shade trees are sprayed with lead arsenate at the end of June, one spraying will normally give protection for the season. Two sprays at 3 week intervals are necessary with DDT. With shrubs, vines, and flowering plants the number of applications depends on the rapidity with which new growth is formed. Roses and ampelopsis require a spray weekly to keep the new growth covered.

Is there any control, other than chemical, for Japanese beetle grubs in lawns? Yes. The spore dust of Milky Disease—a natural enemy of the beetles—is another means of controlling and eliminating this pest, and it is available commercially. Directions for use are printed on the packages.

Is there anything I can do to the soil in flower beds? The beetles destroy hollyhocks, cannas, petunias, roses, and geraniums. (New Jersey.) Soil treatment for flowers is ineffective. For flowers, the most effective control is picking off the beetles; for roses, cutting the buds when they show color and enjoying them in the house. Aerosol bombs for use on flowers, will paralyze or kill beetles without disfiguring blooms, but in general you have to rely on DDT in a spray or dust to take care of the foliage and hand-picking the beetles into a jar or can of kerosene.

Can you tell me something to get rid of Japanese beetles? I have tried traps and they seem to attract them. That is exactly the purpose of a trap: it is painted bright yellow and baited with geraniol just to attract the beetles. Unfortunately, the trap attracts more beetles than get caught in it, so that the near-by plants serve as beetle food and suffer proportionately.

What is the best method of exterminating Japanese beetles before they are hatched? Only by picking off or spraying for the adults before they can lay their eggs in the grass. The eggs will hatch into grubs even if the soil has been grub-proofed, but if the poison is in the soil, the grubs will gradually die, as they feed on grass roots.

Is it possible to recognize the Japanese beetle in the daytime? How can you fight the Japanese beetle on rosebushes? (Louisiana.) In Louisiana you probably will not have to fight Japanese beetles on rosebushes. If and when you do, DDT or methoxychlor or a combination spray will keep the foliage reasonably whole; but to save the flowers you should cut the buds and let them open indoors. The beetle is readily recognized. It works in the daytime and prefers hot sunshine. It is about ½ in. long, shiny metallic green with bronze wing covers and tufts of white hairs protruding from under the wing covers. It is a very handsome beetle.

What do you do with Japanese beetles? (California.) Nothing in California. It's not your problem yet. (But see preceding questions.)

What is the most effective repellent of the Japanese beetle? (Connecticut.) Rotenone, probably. Some of the special Japanese-beetle sprays have a derris base, sometimes with rosin as a sticker. Hydrated lime will serve as a repellent on grapes, and lead arsenate will serve as both repellent and stomach poison on ornamentals.

Can I check Japanese beetles with caster-oil beans? Probably not. (See Asiatic Beetle.)

Does fall spading help exterminate the Japanese beetle? Yes, especially if you take the trouble to destroy or throw out to the birds the grubs you turn up. Birds, by the way, are great allies. The holes you see in the lawn in late summer are where the robins, starlings, and other birds have gone in after the grubs. The starlings are given the most credit for eating the hard beetles, but some other birds work at them. In my garden brown thrashers will pick a beetle off a rosebush and then whack it down onto the cement path to soften it up for eating.

Is the Japanese-beetle nuisance likely to abate soon? Does severe cold tend to kill them? (Connecticut.) The menace will abate but never cease. The beetles stay wherever they have become established, but their numbers diminish after 4 or 5 years at peak abundance. Natural enemies and man-made control methods take effect. Any newly introduced insect does more damage than a long-established pest. Beetles will probably take their place with tent caterpillars and cankerworms as nuisances to be expected each season but not to be unduly excited about. The grubs go so far down in the soil severe winter cold has little effect.

Do Japanese beetles bother geraniums? They are attracted to them; indeed it is geranium bait used in traps, but there is some evidence that beetles are killed by eating certain varieties of geraniums.

Which plant is easy to cultivate, free bloomer until frost, and free as possible from Japanese beetles? (Connecticut.) Phlox and the Heavenly Blue morningglory answer your requirements. Roses, marigolds, and zinnias are favored food plants; delphiniums are not much bothered by beetles, but they are not easy to grow. Blue eupatorium will contrast with your phlox and give you color until frost. It has few insects; if it blights, you can always remove a plant and have plenty left. To replace marigolds, try Orange Flare cosmos. It has almost no pests and diseases and grows with no effort at all. Scatter the seeds broadcast in any odd corner; rake them in lightly. With no more attention they bloom from early July to November.

Japanese Beetle. Injury to silk on corn causes poorly filled ears.

Which vegetables would be least affected by Japanese beetles?

Most vegetables are little affected by Japanese beetles. They are extremely fond of soybeans and sometimes appear on snap and lima beans; they injure the silk of corn; they are numerous on, but seldom injurious to, asparagus foliage, and they often play havoc with rhubarb leaves.

JUNE BEETLE

What is a June beetle? See White Grubs.

KARATHANE OR MILDEX

How often is it necessary to apply Karathane to plants to control powdery mildew? Karathane (or Mildex as it is also called) should be applied about 3 times at weekly or 10-day intervals to stop the progress of this disease. The normal dosage is 2 level teaspoons in 3 gals. of water plus a spreader. It may also be obtained as a ½ to 1% dust. Mixtures with the common summer insecticides and fungicides are safe on foliage.

How do you kill lace bugs? (Iowa.) Lace bugs, small bugs with lacelike wings that work on the underside of leaves, sucking out the sap so that the upper surface becomes a stippled white, gray, or yellow, are readily killed by any contact insecticide applied with a good spreader and sufficient pressure. Malathion or lindane is effective.

LEAD ARSENATE

What is lead arsenate? A formerly widely used stomach poison, valuable for spraying ornamentals and for some food plants like apples. Because of the residue problem, lead arsenate being the most poisonous of the arsenicals, and because it burns some tender foliage, it is of little value in the control of vegetable pests. The strength of the solution varies with the pest to be controlled, but for normal spraying 2 level tablespoons per gallon is about the right proportion. It should be used with sticker, either casein, or some trademarked preparation, or ordinary household flour. As a dust it may be mixed with 4 to 5 parts of hydrated lime but it is more often added to sulfur to make a combination insecticide-fungicide dust. One part lead arsenate to 9 parts of sulfur, or 1 part lead, 1 lime, and 8 sulfur, are the usual combinations. Lead arsenate may be added to Bordeaux mixture or lime-sulfur sprays, but it should never be used with soap.

Have a pet cat. What spray will take the place of DDT on garden flowers and vines? Have Japanese beetles. There is no need to change from DDT on the cat's account, and this is the best choice for flowers and vines. In my 10 years of doctoring gardens with DDT there has never yet been a case of harming pets. Dogs and cats like to follow around when you are spraying and kittens want to play with the nozzle, but if you shut them in the house during the actual mixing and application of the spray, there is no problem with the residue on the plants. Of course you do not want to leave a pail of DDT standing where a dog or cat might mistake it for milk. Mix up your spray and dispose safely of what is left in your spray tank and you will have no trouble.

Is it harmful to put lemon oil on plants?   If you mean the furniture polish that goes by that name, yes; but there is a tried-and-true insecticide called lemon oil sold for years for use on house plants and perfectly safe when used according to directions.

LIME-SULFUR

What is lime-sulfur?   A fungicide, often acting as an insecticide also. Formerly valuable in dormant spraying for the control of fungous diseases and scale insects, but also useful as a summer spray to control apple scab and other diseases, boxwood canker, red mites on fruit trees, spider mites on evergreens. Liquid lime-sulfur is used at a 1 to 7 or 1 to 9 dilution as a dormant spray and 1 to 40 or 1 to 50 as a summer spray. It stains paint and leaves an objectionable residue, but is relatively safe. Do not use it within one month of using oil.

LINDANE

Is lindane safe to use on my vegetables?   Lindane is a highly refined form of BHC without BHC's disagreeable persistant odor. It can be used safely for many chewing and sucking pests up to within a week of harvest. It is especially useful in the control of melon and pickle worms and the European apple sawfly, a relatively new pest in southeastern New York and Connecticut.

MAGGOTS

What causes ground maggots and how can they be got rid of? (Maryland.)   Maggots are legless white larvae of flies that lay their eggs in plants near where the stem meets the ground or in crevices in the soil. The cabbage maggot is the one most bothersome to the home gardener. For control see Cabbage.

MALATHION

I have a cat and dog which roam around in my gardens. Will malathion sprays applied to the plants harm them?   Very unlikely. Malathion is about one-half as toxic as DDT to warm blooded animals and in addition loses its toxic properties rapidly on exposure to air moisture, so that in two days no toxic residue is left. The only precaution I would suggest is to keep pets and children away from freshly sprayed plants. Homeowners should leave parathion, TEPP and similar highly toxic phosphate sprays strictly alone.

MANEB

What is maneb? It is the "coined" name for the manganese salt of dithiocarbamic acid. This is another valuable general fungicide safe to use in combinations for fruits, vegetables and ornamentals, but like captan will not control powdery mildews or rusts. Delay applying to cucurbits until they are beginning to branch out. Trade names are Manzate and Dithane M-22.

MEALY BUGS

What are the fuzzy white bugs on my house plants? Mealy bugs, sucking insects closely related to scales; flattened, oval, with short projections from the body, and often looking like bits of cotton fluff because of the eggs carried by the females in a cottony sac. Mealy bugs are especial pests of house and greenhouse plants, and in the South on such outdoor plants as gardenias, azaleas, citrus fruits. In the North, Taxus is often heavily infested, and the Comstock mealy bug is an apple pest.

What is the life history of the mealy bug? How does it travel, etc.? The female mealy bug deposits her eggs in a cottony waxy sac attached to the rear end of her body. When she has laid 400 to 600 eggs, the sac is left at the axils of branching stems or leaves and the female dies. The eggs hatch in about 10 days, and the flattened, oval, yellow young crawl over the plants, sucking the sap, and soon a waxy covering is exuded from their bodies. They are sluggish and do not move much. The males transform into small, active 2-winged flies to mate with the females and then die. Mealy bugs are disseminated by ants, and by moving about infested plants.

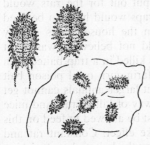

Mealy Bug; attacks many house plants; the small, soft bugs are covered with a cotton-like fluff.

How can I rid a small greenhouse of mealy bugs? Plants may be sprayed with or dipped into a solution of 1 lb. of soap to 3 gals. of water, but this must be washed off within 2 hours to prevent burning. Spraying with malathion is probably the easiest solution, provided manufacturer's directions are rigidly followed. (See Control of Ants.)

What is the best method of getting rid of mealy bugs and how long

does it take? (California.)   First wash off your plants with a strong spray from the hose, then use malathion at the rate of 3 tbsp. to 3 gals. of water. It may be necessary to spray 2 or 3 times at weekly intervals to clean up an infestation. For a few small plants an aerosol plant bomb is very effective.

What will destroy mealy bugs in the soil? (Ohio.)   Remove soil from around the roots and pour in some of the spray described above.

Can window boxes once infested with mealy bugs be used again? (Connecticut.)   There is no reason why not, if the soil is cleaned out and the box thoroughly washed with strong soap and water.

We are plagued with mealy bugs on our flower and vegetable plants. Can you recommend a safe spray so as not to harm the plant or poison the vegetables? (Pennsylvania.)   I cannot believe that mealy bugs in an outdoor garden would be that much of a pest in Pennsylvania, although I have occasionally seen coralbells and yew with bad cases of mealy bugs in this region. Perhaps you have root aphids. (See Aphids.)

METHOXYCHLOR

What advantages has methoxychlor over DDT?   It is much safer to warm blooded animals (about 24 times as safe), its residual toxicity lasts only about a week, it does not injure cucurbits, and it controls the plum curculio and the Mexican bean beetle which DDT does not.

MICE AND RATS

How can you keep rats from eating plants in a city garden where, because of lack of co-operation from neighbors, it is impossible to get rid of all of them? (Maryland.)   Poison put out for the rats would probably get a pet cat or dog, and even traps would have to be used cautiously to avoid maiming a pet. When the house plants on my window were mysteriously chewed I could not believe it was a rat until I caught it in the act one night. It was killed in a trap baited with sunflower seed. A pival-corn meal or warfarin-corn meal poison bait placed in a protected feeding station so that larger animals cannot get to it is a most effective and relatively safe way of killing rats and mice by internal hemorrhage. Rats and mice must be allowed to feed on this bait daily for at least a week for it to take effect. Constant rat and mouse protection will be obtained by leaving the bait and replenishing it when necessary. Fumarin and diphacinone are two newer anti-coagulants for use in baits. The last named one is the most potent of all, killing rats and mice within a few days. A most attractive bait consists of corn meal 65%, rolled oats 25%, granulated sugar 5% and corn oil 5% plus the anticoagulant.

What can be used in winter mulch to discourage mice? (New

Jersey.) Zinc phosphide rodenticide obtainable from county agents is a most effective poison for mice. Dust the poison on cubed apples and place in open tin cans under the mulch pile, preferable in mouse runways if you can locate them. The chemical is very poisonous and must be handled with rubber gloves. The anticoagulant baits recommended for rats as above and placed in open tin cans under the mulch is also effective. Mouse poisoning is best done in the late fall when other food is scarce.

What is a sure cure for moles and field mice? (Connecticut.) Set snap traps for the mice in the mole runways or use poison bait as above in the runways. (See also Moles.)

MILDEW

What makes mildew on plants? (Texas.) A fungus, of the type they call an obligate parasite because it must get its food from living plants. When the wind carries a spore (little seed) to a leaf and the moisture conditions are right, the spore sends out a germ tube that grows into white threads, mycelium, which branch over the leaf in a soft, white, felty coating. This fungus does not grow inside the plant but sends little suckers, haustoria, into the sap. In a few days chains of spores are built up from the mycelium which gives the powdery effect. Later black fruiting bodies with the sexual or overwintering spores are formed. Because it is on the surface, mildew is more readily controlled than many other fungi and may even be eradicated after the first signs of it appear.

How may one control mildew? (Minnesota.) Sulfur is a specific for mildew and the easiest way to apply it is in dust form, but sulfur or copper sprays may be used. The dinitro crotonate, Karathane or Mildex, is used specifically for mildew control.

MILLIPEDES

What is the best way to rid a garden of the dark-brown, hard-shelled, spiral variety of worm which eats root vegetables? (Massachusetts.) This is a millipede. The name literally means thousand-legged, but the number falls far short of that, although this animal comes in many segments and there are 2 pairs of legs on each segment (the centipede has only 1 pair to each segment). Ordinarily millipedes in the garden act more as scavengers than as a direct cause of injury, but they do some feeding on potatoes and other root vegetables. For control use heptachlor as for grubs. (See Wireworms; Sowbugs.)

MITES

What kind of spray is used to kill or cure possible mites? (New York.) There are 3 kinds of mites apt to be troublesome in the garden: red spiders, spruce mites, and cyclamen mites. Red spider is a good term because mites do belong to the spider group, characterized by 8 legs rather than the 6 of true insects, for all their almost microscopic size. Red spiders and spruce mites make a fine web underneath the leaves or between needles, and their sucking turns foliage yellow or needles rusty brown. They are best controlled by spraying with malathion, Ovex, aramite, Dimite, or Chlorobenzilate two or three times in the growing season. The cyclamen mite stunts and deforms plants, especially delphiniums, and causes blackened buds that never develop. Control with endrin spray weekly (1 tsp. per gal. water). Destroy seriously infected plants. Endrin is quite poisonous, so use carefully!

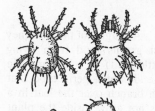

Red Spider: very tiny; makes fine webbing on under sides of leaves.

What is the best material to use for spider mites on my garden and greenhouse plants? There are several specific miticides on the market. Some such as aramite and malathion kill only the active forms and applications must be repeated a number of times to hold the mites in check; others such as Ovex, Dimite, Kelthane and Chlorobenzilate either kill the eggs or have a residual effect making only one or two applications in the spring necessary.

MOLE CRICKET

How do you get rid of cricket moles? (Florida.) Mole crickets are dark-brown burrowing insects, about 1¼ ins. long, with front legs enlarged for tunneling. They come out at night to feed and are destructive because they eat the vegetative parts of seedlings as well as disturb the roots. Any of the grub-proofing treatments will kill mole crickets.

MOLES

How do I get rid of moles? This is a very popular question. It was sent in by 91 gardeners in 32 different states. It is unfortunate that moles, which really do a lot of good in the world by eating white grubs and other insects, should also have the bad habit of making unsightly ridges and mounds in lawns and of disturbing the roots of flowers and vegetables by their tunnels. Actual feeding on plants is probably done by mice which use the mole runs. (See following questions.)

Do moles eat bulbs? That is a moot question. The gardener says "yes" and the scientist says "very unlikely."

How do you get rid of moles without traps or poison? (Pennsylvania.) There is not much left except patrolling the ridges and watching for movements indicating the mole is at work and then killing it with a spade or a fork. A dog after a mole is disastrous, but cats may catch moles without any extra damage to the garden. One cat of my acquaintance (not my own, which always turn out lazy) had an unbroken record of a mole a day. Flooding the mole runs with water in the spring will drown young moles and mice in some soils.

What is the best method of controlling moles? (Oregon.) Trapping. Fish and Wildlife Service in Oregon and Washington report negative results with poison baits and cyanide dust but success with traps correctly set. They also say that the skin of the Oregon mole, if properly prepared, may be sold for enough to pay for the time and trouble. Traps should not be set in the shallow runways but in the deeper main highways. Two types of traps may be used, the scissors, or the diamond-jaw. Both depend on a trigger, sprung when the mole follows its natural instinct of burrowing through an obstruction of loose earth placed in the runway. Use a strong trowel to set the trap in the runway, aligning it so the jaws of the scissors trap straddle the course or the choker trap encircles it. Pack the earth firmly under the trigger, so the mole cannot work through without springing it. In gravel soil the choker works best. Some success has been reported with peanuts soaked in thallium sulfate (Mo-Go) and placed at intervals in the runways. Skin the mole by slitting from chin to tail, peeling out the body, and cutting off tail and legs. Pin flat on boards in an oval shape and dry thoroughly in the shade. The Oregon mole is superior to the European mole and should sell for a fair price.

What will eradicate Townsend moles? (California.) These are Oregon moles. (See previous question.)

Can one ever get rid of moles? (Iowa.) Maybe, with persistence, but you don't want to get rid of those that are not actually injuring your garden. Think of your white-grub problem in Iowa. The loop or choker trap has been found to be very effective in Iowa soil.

How do you combat moles? (New York.) New York State has 3 different moles. The naked-tail mole does much of the damage to lawns and golf courses on Long Island and in the lower Hudson Valley. In central and western New York the star-nosed and the hairy-tail moles are working. The star-nosed throws up earth in a mound similar to a gopher mound, but the other two make the familiar ridges. Use mole traps for these, but snapback mousetraps for the star-nosed variety. Grub-proofing the lawn is often helpful in discouraging moles.

What are the best ways, supplementing traps, to discourage moles? (New York.) Calcium cyanide may possibly be effective in April and May when the young are in the nest. Or open the runways at intervals with a sharp stick and drop in a teaspoon of lye, paradichlorbenzene, or naphthalene. Some report success with trade-marked materials such as Mole-Nots or Mo-Go. Trapping remains the most effective method.

MOTHS

What is the difference between moths and butterflies? Both are adults of caterpillars, often called worms. Moths are night fliers and antennae are never clubbed.

I have a small golden moth infesting shrubs and grass and when I use the hose they fly up in great numbers. No one seems to know what they are or has noticed them. They last from June or July to September. What are they? (New York.) They are probably the crambid moth, adults of sod webworms. Webworms are not a major lawn pest in New York as they are in California and some other states, but sometimes the larva, a fat caterpillar which lives in a silk-lined nest, injures the grass roots. Sprays or dusts with chlordane, DDT, or dieldrin give good control. In your particular case the larvae of your moths may not be doing enough damage to bother about.

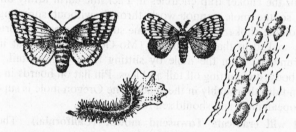

Gypsy Moth: attacks trees, and, occasionally, vegetables. Caterpillars, 2 in. long with conspicuous blue and red markings.

NICOTINE SULFATE

What is nicotine sulfate? Usually purchased as Black Leaf 40. A useful contact insecticide. It is poisonous but is readily washed off, and so may be safely used on vegetables and fruits to within a short time of harvest. It is used ordinarily in a soapy solution but it may be added to fungicides and some other insecticides. The dosage varies according to the insect to be controlled. A normal solution (1 to 800 dilution) is made with 1 teaspoon nicotine sulfate and 1 oz. soap (1 cu. in. laundry soap) per gal. of water. For more resistant insects the dosage is increased to 1½ to 2 teaspoons per gal. Ordinarily nicotine sulfate may be used without injury to plants, but caution is needed on a very hot day in the garden or in an enclosed greenhouse that is too warm.

NEMATODES

What are nematodes and in what manner does soil become infested? (Georgia.) Nematodes are roundworms or eelworms, too small to see with the naked eye, that live in moist soil, in decaying organic matter, or as parasites in living plant tissues. They can travel only a short distance in the soil by themselves but are spread by surface water, by moving infested soil from place to place, and, very commonly, by local transfer and shipment of infested plants. Nematodes are more serious in sandy soils in Southern states, or in California. In the North they may live over the winter in perennials, and can survive free in the soil.

How do you recognize the presence of nematodes? (Texas.) Injury to plants is slow to show up and not at all dramatic. Usually conspicuous above ground symptoms do not appear until a heavy population of nematodes has built up. Nematodes should be suspected when plants show a slow decline in vigor and growth, when they become stunted and unthrifty, when water does not help them much in drought, or when the foliage becomes discolored yellow or bronze as from a nutritional deficiency. Underground you may or may not find swellings on the roots. The feeder roots may be lacking and the root system stunted and sparse or matted and shallow. Washed roots may disclose abundant small reddish-brown lesions in the epidermis. A hairy root condition occurs in some plants. Often roots are partially to wholly decayed because of secondary fungus or bacterial infections starting in lesions made by the nematodes. Foliar nematodes, common in chrysanthemums, produce angular brown lesions in the leaves; and bulb and stem nematodes produce discolored streaks or rings in narcissus bulbs, thickened stems and crinkled leaves. The root-knot nematode most common in southern areas infests more than 1700 species of plants. The nodules formed by beneficial nitrogen-fixing bacteria on legumes should not be confused with the root galls produced by this nematode.

How can root-knot nematodes be destroyed without killing shrubbery and perennials in infested beds? (California.) Nematocides are now available that destroy nematodes without killing plants; however not all plants are tolerant to them so read directions carefully and use on the specified plants only. You may use either V–C 13, a complex phosphorus compound, or Nemagon, 1, 2–dibromo 30 chloropropone. Both may be watered directly into the lawn or under plants with a watering can or hose proportioner. Granulated formulations can be applied by hand or with a fertilizer spreader and then watered in.

What is the latest information on combating nematodes in the Southern garden? (Texas.) Either of the above nematocides may be used some 2 weeks previous to planting on prepared soil for susceptible plants or after planting on tolerant plants. An excellent preplanting treatment that may be used in any garden area after the soil has been prepared, but some 2 weeks before planting, consists in applying sodium methyl dithiocarbamate (Vapam or VPM). Just apply it with a watering can or with your hose and hose spray proportioner. This treatment destroys disease-producing fungi, and most weed seeds, as well as nematodes.

Is there a quick, economical method of ridding garden soil of rootknot nematode? (Georgia.) The chemical methods discussed above are quick but not economical for large areas. Both ethylene dibromide and methyl-bromide are more economical but not as easily applied. Ethylene dibromide may be applied as an undiluted liquid with special equipment on a field basis or in furrows six inches deep and ten inches apart by pouring a stream along the trenches at the rate of ½ cup for every seventy-five feet. A quart container with 2 nail holes in opposite sides of the lid will facilitate application. As the application is made another person should follow filling the trench with soil and tamping it down. Ethylene dibromide is also available in gelatine capsules (Soilfume-Caps, Fumi-Soil) specifically for home gardens. The capsules are dropped in holes, at the recommended intervals and depth, made with a stick and covered over. No water seal is required after the application, but wait two weeks before planting. Methyl bromide (Dowfume MC–2, Pestmaster Soil Fumigant, Bromex) is a volatile liquid that must be kept under pressure at ordinary temperatures. Small amounts of soil for use in flower pots, flats, and greenhouse benches, can be treated in a large garbage can with a tight cover. Use ½ oz. per cu. ft. of soil for 24 hrs. and allow 3 days for aeration before using. This treatment destroys soil fungi, weed seeds, and insects as well as nematodes. For larger prepared soil areas such as coldframes, gardens and seed beds a plastic tarpaulin is essential to confine the fumes for 24 to 48 hrs. The rate is 1 lb. per 100 sq. ft., and allow at least 2 days for aeration. The soil temperature should be above 60 deg. F. to make treatments effective. Avoid treating soil under trees and shrubs, and soil to be used for carnation growing.

Two other soil fumigants, D–D and chloropicrin (Larvacide), are used chiefly in commercial enterprises; the first for nematodes and insects, the second for all soil organisms including weed seeds. They are applied with special hand applicators or tractor borne applicators attached to plows or cultivator-like devices. A water seal is necessary along with a two to three week wait before planting.

OIL SPRAYS

Where can "miscible" oil be bought? At any seed store and in most hardware stores. Ask for a dormant oil spray (almost all those sold to small gardeners are of the miscible type—an oil that mixes readily with water). Miscible oils are procured under such trade names as Scale-O, Scale-Oil, Scalecide, etc. (See Dormant Spraying.)

PESTICIDAL FORMULATIONS

It is very confusing to determine whether a powder or liquid formulation of an insecticide should be purchased. Which is preferable? Insecticides and Fungicides may be purchased as dusts ready to use in dusters; as wettable powders to be made into water suspensions for spraying; as emulsifiable concentrates to form milky suspensions in water; or in a few cases as powders or liquids that go into water solution. The form to purchase may be influenced by the type of equipment you have, your personal preference, conspicuousness of the residue, effectiveness, or the safety to the plants. In general dusts are easier to use, give quicker coverage but have a more conspicuous residue, and a greater margin of safety to plants. Wettable powders rank next in plant safety and conspicuousness but require spray agitation or a sprayer with an agitator to produce an even spray concentration. Insecticides in the form of emulsifiable concentrates are most apt to burn tender plants, but are least conspicuous and usually give the best control. Fungicides are mainly available as dusts or wettable powders with only a few available as water miscible compounds. The wettable powders applied as sprays are generally more effective. (See also answer to question below).

I should like to apply dieldrin to my lawn to kill grubs. How is this best done? Many soil treating insecticides, fungicides, and weed killers are now available in what are known as granulated formulations, somewhat like sugar in texture. These formulations are especially adapted for application with fertilizer spreaders for lawns or garden areas. A good spreader is needed and should be adjusted to apply half the rate required so that half the dosage may be applied at right angles to the first for a more even coverage. Granulated formulations eliminate any danger from dust and on lawns they settle down to the soil eliminating residues on grass that may be dangerous to children or pets. Grub-proofing chemicals on lawns should be watered in after application; on garden soils they may be raked or cultivated in when preparing the beds for planting.

PESTICIDES AND PUBLIC HEALTH

How dangerous are the new organic insecticides and fungicides to man and animals? The new organic insecticides may harm warm-blooded animals when they are swallowed, when they come in contact with skin and are absorbed, or when they are inhaled. In addition the chlorinated hydrocarbons tend to accumulate in the body making repeated small doses dangerous. Repeated small doses of the phosphate insecticides sensitize the body to them making poisoning more likely. The home gardener not only faces the problem of handling these chemicals safely, if at all, but also the problem of avoiding poisonous residues on fruits and vegetables.

The Miller Bill or Public Law 518, put into effect in 1954, regulates the sale and use of pesticides and at the same time helps to protect the public from dangerous residues. It requires that all pesticides in interstate commerce must be label approved for specific crops and pests by officials of the U.S.D.A. and that a residue tolerance (amount of toxic chemical allowed at harvest) in parts per million must be established by the Food and Drug Administration for those to be used on food crops. A list of insecticides from least to most dangerous to handle is as follows: pyrethrum, allethrin, rotenone, methoxychlor, TDE (DDD), Malathion, chlorthion, chlordane, DDT, lindane, toxaphene, aldrin, dieldrin, nicotine, endrin, parathion, demeton, and TEPP.* The fungicides except the organic mercuries are not highly toxic and are safe to use with ordinary precautions. It is very important to follow all label directions carefully with regard to dosages, crops to protect, safe interval between last spray and harvest, and precautions.

PRAYING MANTIS

Can you tell me about praying mantis? I am planning to purchase an egg case next spring. (Illinois.) If the praying mantis is not naturally present in your neighborhood, it might not pay to spend much for an egg case, for these ferocious-looking beneficial insects are not commonly found much north of 40° latitude. The mantis belongs to the grasshopper family. It is very long and thin, with prominent eyes and enormous front legs used for preying on other insects but often held up in a praying attitude. The baby mantes look just like the adults, except for lack of wings. Their cannibalistic instincts are so well developed they often eat one another. Do not let the egg masses hatch in the house, for heat brings them out in the winter and there is no way to feed the young mantes until they can survive out of doors.

I have hundreds of praying mantes in my garden. What do the egg cases look like? I find so many tentlike formations. (Kansas.) The egg cases are a sort of dingy cream or yellow in color, shaped something like a round hatbox, but not especially regular, about 1 in. across, and made of a frothy gummy substance which hardens in that same frothy texture. They are usually attached to twigs of trees or shrubs.

PYRETHRUM

What is pyrethrum? A contact insecticide obtained from the

*TEPP is 125 times as toxic as DDT and must be handled with extreme care and the use of a special mask.

pyrethrum plant, mostly grown in Africa. It is especially effective against aphids and soft-bodied insects, but it will kill whatever chewing insects it hits. It is useful for spraying flowers where a stain would be objectionable. For use on the Mexican bean beetle, impregnated pyrethrum dusts are more efficient.

RABBITS

Other than by fencing, how can rabbits be kept out of the garden? (Pennsylvania.) Some sort of fence is still the best solution. If you cannot get the poultry wire ordinarily recommended, a picket fence may be substituted, or a low concrete wall built. The expense of either of these would be justified if the vegetable garden is to be permanent, and would look better than a wire fence. A temporary expedient sometimes used is a fence of 18-in. roofing paper. Properly braced between the corners, this works well for the first part of the season but after many rains is apt to sag enough to let in the rabbits. There are reports that a row of child's windmills, or glass bottles stuck in the ground neck down, will act as a fence in scaring rabbits away.

Will dried blood sprinkled around roots of beans or other vegetables prevent rabbits from eating them? (New Jersey.) Dried blood has long been listed as an effective rabbit repellent, as well as being good for the garden. Some gardeners report that it is not always effective.

What is a good rabbit repellent? (Illinois.) The New Jersey Fish and Game Commissioners has listed 9 repellents for harassed gardeners: 1, dust plants, when damp, with powdered lime; 2, dust liberally with dusting sulfur (some vegetables do not take kindly to sulfur); 3, sprinkle plants with red pepper; 4, spray with a solution of 3 ozs. Epsom salts in 1 gal. water; 5, spray with 1 teaspoon Lysol in 1 gal. water; 6, spray with 2 teaspoons Black Leaf 40 in 1 gal. soapy water; 7, spray with solution of common brown laundry soap; 8, spray with 1 oz. tartar emetic and 3 ozs. sugar in 1 gal. of water; 9, sprinkle naphthalene flakes between rows of plants. The commercial product No Nib'L is an effective spray on plants.

How can you keep rabbits from eating young soybeans? That is the $64 question. Soybeans are often used to keep rabbits away from other plants. They work that way in my garden, and I still get a lusty crop of soybeans. Formerly I credited moth balls with repelling the rabbits just enough to give the soybeans a fighting chance, but I visited a garden last summer where the rabbits had not allowed one soybean plant out of hundreds to get above 6 ins. high and the moth balls were so thick the garden looked white. Now I have come to the conclusion that it is my neighbors' cats, hunting young rabbits, that keep the population down to reasonable proportions.

How can we prevent rabbits from eating our shrubs and evergreens?

We have sprayed with copper sulfate, which is a waste of time. (Illinois.) Most repellents do not remain effective long enough. A box trap placed under shrubs in the winter and early spring when food is scarce may catch many rabbits. Rabbits are protected in some areas, and you would probably have to make arrangements with the game warden. With rabbits such a menace to gardens, a permit may sometimes be obtained for shooting them from the Fish and Game Commission, but one still has to get permission to shoot from the local police, and that is often denied in thickly settled suburban areas.

Is there any repellent which can be put on trunks of trees and shrubs? The U. S. Fish and Wildlife Service have developed a rabbit repellent for use on dormant plants, whose active ingredient is a trinitrobenzene-aniline complex. One application lasts all winter. Excellent results have been obtained on such trees and shrubs as apple, ash, crab, dogwood, euonymus, honeysuckle, holly, lilac, magnolia, maple, plum, tulip, and viburnam. This material may be obtained as a 5 oz. aerosol spray, or in pints, quarts and gallons from Panogen, Inc., Ringwood, Ill. One precaution—*don't smoke while using it!*

Rabbits have chewed the bark completely from the trunk of a young flowering crab planted this spring. Can anything be done to save the tree? (New Jersey.) You might try bridge grafting (which see), which has worked successfully for apple trees girdled by rabbits and mice. Unless you are acquainted with this art, it would be better to have the work done by a tree expert, and that might cost as much as a new tree. Next time, protect your tree with a cylinder of close-mesh woven wire, 24 ins. wide, sunk into the ground a few inches and held away from the trunk with stakes. Sometimes prunings left on the ground around the trees and bushes will feed the rabbits enough to keep them from injuring the trunks. (See page 846.) See answer to previous question.

RED SPIDER

What is red spider? See Mites.

RESISTANCE TO INSECTICIDES

DDT does not kill my potato beetles anymore—what is the matter? The phenomenon of insect resistance to insecticides dramatically showed up in houseflies a number of years ago to the then wonder insecticide DDT. Since then resistance has cropped up in mosquitoes, roaches, bedbugs, fleas, lice, lygus bugs, salt marsh caterpillars, potato beetles, cabbage worms, codling moths, and flea beetles. Other chlorinated hydrocarbons as substitutes are not always satisfactory as resistance to DDT usually means a quick build-up of resistance to these too. To overcome this resistance growers turned to a different group, the phosphate compounds. But mites in turn are becoming and have become resistant to the phosphates and new compounds such as Kelthane and chlorobenzilate have taken their place for these pests. All this results in an ever changing and confusing picture in our chemical control of insects and mites.

ROTENONE

What is rotenone? The principal insecticidal constituent in roots of derris, timbo, cube, or lonchocarpus. It acts as a stomach and contact poison for insects, kills fish and cold-blooded animals, but is not injurious to man except as a throat irritant. It leaves no poisonous residue on the plant. Rotenone formerly was obtained from the Far East and is now coming in from South America. Lonchocarpus is being established there to provide a new source of rotenone. Rotenone dust is used in a 1 per cent dilution, or derris analyzing 4 to 5 per cent rotenone is used for spraying.

RUST

What is a good spray for rust? (California.) That depends on whether or not you have true rust, a fungus that manifests itself in erumpent reddish-brown or reddish-orange pustules of spores, or, in the case of cedar and apple rust, in long, gelatinous spore horns. Sulfur and ferbam are the best fungicides for the control of rust. For ornamental plants they may be applied as a dust. Very often gardeners speak of "rust" when they merely mean a reddish discoloration of the tissue, which might be due to a variety of causes but never to the true rust fungus.

SCALE INSECTS

What is life history of scale? What plants are attacked? What are treatments? Do you mean indoors or out? There are many different scale insects, but 2 general types. Those found in gardens in New York would be mostly of the armored-scale type, that is, after they finish the young crawling stage a hard, separable shell is formed on their bodies and they stop moving around. In this group is the oyster-shell scale on lilacs, scurfy scale on apples, rose scale on roses, euonymus scale on euonymus and bittersweet, juniper scale, pine-needle scale, and many others. This group is controlled by spraying before growth starts in the spring (see Dormant Spraying) and malathion for the young scales in midsummer. The second group includes the soft or tortoise scales, represented in a Northern garden by maple, tulip tree, fruit lecanium and magnolia scales but more often seen on house plants, where they have to be scrubbed off or sprayed with an aerosol plant bomb or malathion. (See House Plants.)

How do you get rid of cottony cushion scale on trees? (Texas.) Ask your State Experiment Station where you can get a colony of

Australian lady beetles. In California they may be secured from the Citrus Experiment Station at Riverside. A malathion spray may also be helpful.

SEED TREATMENT

Should seeds be treated before planting?   Yes, the application of a chemical protectant is insurance against damping off, either in the seed flat or the garden row, and in addition it may prevent some diseases due to organisms carried on the outside of the seed.

What chemicals are used for seed treatment?   Semesan, an organic mercury; and Spergon, Captan or Arasan, synthetic materials.

Can you buy one dust and treat all kinds of seeds?   Not very successfully; there is a marked difference in response of seeds to chemicals. Spergon is particularly effective for peas. Possibilities are: Semesan for celery, cabbage and other crucifers; Semesan, Jr., for corn; Spergon for peas, beans, lima beans, lettuce; Arasan for onions, tomatoes, and beans, and Captan for practically all seeds.

How do you dust the seeds? Is it injurious to use too much of the protectant?   Using too much dust may be decidedly injurious, causing stunting or preventing germination entirely. The usual rule is 1 teaspoon per pound for small seeds and ½ teaspoon for larger seeds like cucumber and squash. For a small packet of seeds use about as much as can be held on the tip of a knife blade. Put seeds and dust together in the packet, shake until each seed is faintly coated, and then dump out onto a strainer so that all excess dust can be shaken off. Many seeds are pretreated before being sold.

What about the organisms carried inside the seeds?   They cannot be killed with external dusts. They must be soaked in hot water or bichloride of mercury—a treatment usually not given unless the disease organism is presumably present. Tie seeds loosely in cheesecloth bags and keep the temperature of the water constant: 122° F., 25 minutes for cabbage, 15 minutes for other crucifers; tomato seed, 25 minutes; 118° F., 30 minutes for celery. Seed potatoes are treated in 1 to 1000 bichloride of mercury 1½ hours, but seeds only 10 to 15 minutes, after which they are washed to prevent injury. Seed potatoes may also be dipped in nabam. (1 pint in 30 gals. water.)

SLUGS AND SNAILS

What is a certain positive method of ridding your garden of slugs? (California.)   Is there ever anything "certain positive" about gardening? Metaldehyde as the active principal in slug baits was tried out first in California and was so successful there that it has become more or less standard for the rest of the country. Many of the baits sold under trade names contain metaldehyde, which exerts a fatal attraction on slugs, and then, when they come close enough to touch it, liquefies them. The bait is put out in small piles, about the size of a silver dollar, and should be covered in some fashion to protect it from the weather, birds, and pests. Slug bait in the form of pellets is also available.

How can I best rid my grounds of the soft-bodied slug? (Vermont.) Use a combination of methods—poison bait, sprinkling lime or salt in the slug paths, dusting plants with fluosilicates DDT or lead arsenate, or dusting ground and plants with dry Bordeaux mixture as a repellent, trapping slugs by putting out shingles at night and destroying the catch in the morning. In the long run the most effective method is to keep your garden so cleaned up that slugs will have no daytime hiding places. Cleaning irises in late fall deprives slugs of a favorite winter home.

What is best method for combating slugs? We use lime but it whitens shrubs. They attack cherry trees, purple-leaf plum, and flowering quince. (Utah.) Put your lime on the ground in a circle, enclosing the tree trunk. Try spraying the slugs at night with a spray of ¼ to ½ lb. alum per gallon water. Try metaldehyde baits.

Will a boardwalk in a garden be the cause of an exceptionally large number of slugs? It would provide the protected hiding place favored by slugs, but it should also prove a help in getting rid of them, for poison baits put under the boardwalk would not endanger children, pets, or birds.

What is the best way to destroy slugs and snails without risk of poisoning birds or pets? (Ohio.) If poison baits are put out under little jar covers or pieces of board, there is little danger to pets, but to play absolutely safe, resort to lime on the ground, cleaning up plant debris, hand-picking, and probably spraying or dusting plants as outlined above. For hollyhocks I have found that DDT added to the dust used to control rust will take care of slugs sufficiently. There is practically no danger to pets when a poison is used on plants.

Are hard-shell snails or big, fat, soft ones harmful or beneficial in the garden? Have roses, iris, lilies, etc. (Pennsylvania.) They are not exactly beneficial. Roses will be little bothered by true slugs in Pennsylvania, but they have their special brand of false slugs or sawfly larvae. (See Rose.) Any plant with leaves close to the ground like iris or lily will be apt to have light-colored areas in the leaf where the slugs have eaten everything but the epidermis.

What do you do about snails? (California.) Snails are just slugs (soft molluscs) with a shell. Use poison baits in spring and summer in rainy weather or when there are fogs at night. Either metaldehyde slug bait or a mixture of 1 part calcium arsenate and 16 parts wheat bran may be used. Hand-picking is always successful. Lime around trees will act as a barrier to prevent snails from climbing the trunk in destructive numbers.

How can I rid my plants of snails? (Texas.)   Another bait, listed by a group of Southern nurserymen and entomologists, contains 1 qt. dry bran, ½ oz. Paris green, ½ cup molasses, and ½ cup water.

SOIL STERILIZATION

Isn't there some way to get the soil in such a healthy condition that insects and diseases will not bother a plant?   Disease organisms in the soil may be killed by soil sterilization, but there is no known way to render plants immune to attacks by fungi or insects. There are a few instances where fertilizing is somewhat linked up with resistance; there is little exact knowledge along this line.

How do you sterilize soil?   The usual aim is not a complete destruction of all living organisms but a partial sterilization which will control harmful organisms. Heat is one of the best means, but there are difficulties. Steam is excellent but practical only for the commercial greenhouse operator; hot water can be used, but it is apt to puddle the soil; baking is used for small quantities, but there may be toxic materials liberated; this may be true also when electricity is used. Formaldehyde is most useful for treating small lots of soil to prevent damping off of seedlings. Formaldehyde dust is used, but the liquid sprinkle method seems more generally satisfactory. For each 20 × 14 × 2 and ¾ in. flat of soil use 1 tablespoon formalin diluted with 6 tablespoons water. Sprinkle it over the soil and mix thoroughly. Let stand 12 to 24 hours; *after* the seeds are sown, water immediately.

How do you treat soil in the garden?   It is rather an expensive procedure recommended only for the control of specific organisms when crop rotation is not feasible. Formaldehyde is usually used for root-rot fungi. Dilute 1 part commercial formalin with 50 parts water and apply ½ gal. to each sq. ft. of soil. Cover for 1 to 2 days with burlap, paper, or boards. Spade to air out the gas and wait about 2 weeks before planting. Chloropicrin (Larvacide) is used against nematodes, weed seeds, and certain fungi in the soil, at the rate of 1 lb. to 140 sq. ft. The soil should be in a loose, moist condition and the temperature 60° to 85° F. The fumes are very injurious, and treatment must not be carried on near living plants. After the chloropicrin is injected into holes 6 to 8 ins. deep and about 15 ins. apart, the holes should be closed and the soil wetted with water, or else covered with impervious paper. Bichloride of mercury may be used fairly safely around living plants, but it has a rather temporary effect. For other chemical methods see under Nematodes.

SOOTY MOLD

I have had trouble in my greenhouse with a black sooty substance forming on the leaves. It is hard to wash off. What is it and how pre-

vent it from forming? (Wisconsin.)   This is a black fungous growth, called sooty mold, but the fungus is not parasitic on the plant; it is merely growing in insect honeydew that drops on the leaves; in your case very likely from white flies, but on outdoor shrubs very often from aphids or scale insects. There is not much hope of washing it off. You can prevent it by spraying to control your insect population.

SOWBUGS

How do you destroy hog bugs? The bug is flat and fairly round, hard legs along the side. (Virginia.)   They are ususally called sowbugs, probably named for female hogs because of their shape. But they are sometimes called pill bugs because of their tendency to roll up into little balls. Sowbugs are not true insects but crustacea, related to crayfish. They are grayish in color, segmented, with 7 pairs of legs about ½ in. long. They hide at the base of plants under clods of earth or manure. Dust soil with 5% DDT or chlordane to control them.

Do sowbugs eat seed in flats?   I am not certain about the seed itself, but they injure the seedlings by feeding on the stems and tender growth.

SPITTLE BUGS

What causes the white frothy substance that looks like white foam to come on plants?   This is the spittle bug, so named because the young nymphs have the habit of secreting a quantity of frothy material between molts. The adults leave the "spit" protection and look something like leaf hoppers, but because of their bulging eyes are often called froghoppers. In Michigan the pine spittle insect may be injurious to pines and other conifers by sucking the sap. Occasionally young trees are killed. Use contact insecticides at double the strength recommended for aphids, and apply the spray with great pressure.

What can I do to rid my plants of insect in a sort of bubble? Have heard it called spit bug.   Various species of spittle bugs may occasionally injure garden plants. In New Jersey several years ago a devastating attack on strawberries was repulsed with derris dust. Any fairly potent contact insecticide applied with enough pressure to penetrate the protective froth should be satisfactory. Spittle bugs do get around. They have been several times reported from penthouse gardens high over New York City.

SPRAYERS

What are garden sprayers?   Equipment to apply liquid insecticides or fungicides to plants in a fine mist. Sprayers vary from aerosol bombs and pint- or quart-size atomizers useful for house plants to huge power apparatus that will spray tall trees with 500-lbs. pressure. For the average garden a cylindrical compressed-air sprayer or a knapsack sprayer of 1½- to 3-gal. capacity, that fits on the back, will be sufficient. For small trees and shrubs a bucket or barrel sprayer mounted on wheels to move around the garden will be most convenient. Small motor-driven sprayers are also available. If a copper sprayer rather than a galvanized one can be procured it will be worth the extra price in longer life. No sprayer is better than the care given it. Rinse thoroughly immediately after use and occasionally take it apart for cleaning. Strain all spray mixtures into the tank through cheesecloth to prevent clogging. Extra parts can often be obtained from manufacturers or distributors to keep old sprayers in operation.

Is any single spray, such as the hose proportioner type, sufficient for all average conditions? Hose sprayers of the proportioner type are very convenient and easy to use and are suitable for shrubs and small trees as well as flowers and vegetables. They handle solutions and emulsions readily, but you may run into trouble with suspensions because of clogging. Not all types give a suitable dispersion of the active chemical in the spray. Those with a shut-off near the nozzle are much preferable to those that have no shut-off and require you to place your finger over a hole to start the chemical mixing with the water spray. The one to three gallon compressed air sprayers will handle all chemicals and will do a good job in most gardens. In addition gardeners should have a few aerosol plant bombs on hand for spot treatments of pests.

SPRAY MATERIALS

Spraying charts are usually given for the large farmer, not the backyard gardener. Will you furnish a simplified spraying chart where a gardener requires only a pint or a quart at most? So far as possible the directions in this section are given in small quantities, usually 1 gallon. One pint, or even a quart, will not go very far, even in a backyard garden. Moreover, anyone capable of filling out income-tax blanks should be able to do a little arithmetic on garden sprays. Remember that there are 3 teaspoons in 1 tablespoon, 16 tablespoons in 1 cup, or 8 liquid ozs., 4 cups in a quart, and 4 qts. in a gallon. Buy a set of kitchen measuring spoons and a glass cup marked off in ounces. When the recipe calls for 1 teaspoon per gallon and you need only a quart, use the tiny ¼ teaspoon measure.

What can I use on vegetables that is harmless to people or dogs and will kill the chewing bugs? Rotenone. Methoxychlor is also relatively safe, and may be used within a week of harvest.

What are the main spray materials to have on hand? I understand some of these sprays are the same, only going under different names. You understand correctly. Insecticides and fungicides are sold under hundreds of different trade names, but basically they depend on malathion, DDT, methoxychlor, chlordane, dieldrin, pyrethrum, rotenone, and oils for action against insects, and copper, sulfur and the new organic fungicides (captan, ferbam, maneb, zineb, and nabam) for diseases. Always read the label on your proprietary mixture and know what you are buying. Only the plants you grow and the diseases and pests you have can determine how many different materials are required in your garden. Theoretically, 1 fungicide, 1 stomach poison, and 1 contact insecticide would see you through, but not all fungi react to copper or to sulfur, and not all insects can be controlled by rule.

Isn't there some one spray I could use for all the garden ills to which the far South is heir? (Louisiana.) Unfortunately, no, but a general purpose garden spray comes close to taking care of some of the most important Southern pests. Send to the Department of Entomology, Louisiana Experiment Station, for *Insect Pest Control Service Leaflet No. 31.* It is excellent.

Would you suggest how to plan a spray schedule for a perennial border? It would take more than the space I am allowed here. There are a number of books telling you when and how to spray your ornamentals. Consult *Diseases and Pests of Ornamental Plants,* Ronald Press, 1948, etc., list on page 1315.

What ingredients would you advise in a general purpose spray mixture for use on fruits, vegetables and ornamentals? A good general purpose spray or dust may have malathion for sucking pests and mites; methoxychlor for chewing insects; and captan and sulfur for diseases; other combinations may be made or are available using lindane in place of malathion, DDT in place of methoxychlor, ferbam and sulfur in place of captan and sulfur, and a specific miticide such as Aramite. Where sulfur isn't used Karathane or Mildex are essential for powdery mildew control. General purpose sprays applied periodically eliminate the necessity for knowing what foliage or fruit insects or diseases to worry about on your plants.

STREPTOMYCIN

Do any of the antibiotic drugs for humans work on plant diseases? Yes, streptomycin has been found to effectively control a number of bacterial plant diseases such as fire blight of apples and pears, bacterial spot of tomato and pepper, and bacterial wilt of chrysanthemum. The formulations are sold under the names Agri-Mycin 100, Agristrep, and Phytomycin. Effective dilutions range from 50 to 100 parts per million.

SULFUR

How is sulfur used in the garden? A valuable fungicide with many uses but especially in the control of rust and mildew, and also of some value as an insecticide in the control of red spiders and other mites. In the home garden, sulfur is usually used in dust form, and it may be safely combined with insecticides. Wettable sulfurs are available to use as liquid sprays. In very hot weather sulfur should be used cautiously, for it is apt to burn the plants. It is incompatible with oil and should not be used within 30 days of an oil spray.

Is there a green dusting sulfur available for the amateur gardener? Yes, one may be purchased under the name of Pomo-green. Personally I do not find the green color of enough benefit to justify the extra expense. It is less conspicuous, but any that falls to the ground shows up more than the ordinary yellow sulfur. The green dye does, however, slightly increase the fungicidal value.

SQUIRRELS

How do I get rid of chipmunks? (Massachusetts.) It has been said, although I cannot prove it personally, that chipmunks are unsuspicious creatures readily caught in snap-back traps baited with a nut, pumpkin seed, or berry, and placed near their burrows. These ground squirrels eat some slugs and insects and should not be destroyed without reason. Bulbs may be planted in wire baskets to protect them.

Our corn patch was neatly devastated, a dozen ears per night, by some animal that shucked as it ate. Is it likely to have been squirrels? How can we combat such an unseen adversary? (Connecticut.) It may have been woodchucks or squirrels, but more likely raccoons if ears were husked. There is not much solution except to trap or shoot them or to plant enough for you and the animals too. In my garden they are satisfied with the outside row. (See Corn.)

How do you get rid of gray squirrels? (Virginia.) Get permission to trap them or to shoot them, which is easier said than done in many communities.

How do you prevent squirrels from monopolizing feeding stations? (New York.) If the feeding station is hung from a horizontal wire, metal guards may be placed either side; or if the feeding station is on top of a post, a guard may be placed underneath; but if the station is anywhere within leaping distance of a tree, the guard is useless.

SYSTEMIC OR CHEMOTHERAPEUTIC AGENTS

I understand that certain compounds can be absorbed by plants without harm to them but toxic to their insects pests. What are these compounds? This is a relatively new and promising approach to insect control involving the use of systemic insecticides. The chemicals are absorbed by the roots, stems or leaves and translocated throughout the plants. Those found useful as systemics are sodium selenate (P-40, Sel-Caps) on herbaceous plants; and the phosphorus compounds demeton (Systox, Systoban Granules), Schradan (Pestox), and Thimet on both herbaceous and woody plants. These systemics have given good control of mites, aphids, thrips, scale insects and certain leaf miners for a period of 3 weeks or more after application. Their use is limited to ornamentals and only sodium selenate and the granulated formulation of demetan, Systoban granules, are available for home-owners to use—the other materials and formulations are considered too dangerous.

TDE (DDD)

What are the virtues of TDE (DDD)? This compound (sold under the trade name of Rhothane) is closely related to DDT but is about 10 times as safe to warm blooded animals and is especially recommended for hornworms, budworms, tomato fruitworm and redbanded leaf roller on apples (resistance is showing up in the last named pest).

TENT CATERPILLAR

How can I control the tent caterpillar which attacks wildcherry and apple trees in the spring? As soon as the webs form, while worms are still very small, wipe them out of the crotches of branches with a pointed stick or a swab dipped in kerosene, or spray them with DDT. If webs must be destroyed after the caterpillars are well developed, do so in early morning or after sunset when they have returned to web for warmth. A preventive control is to cut off and burn the twigs bearing egg masses which can be seen after the leaves have dropped in autumn or winter.

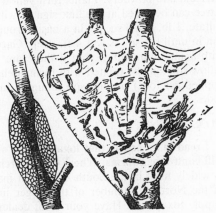

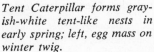

Tent Caterpillar forms grayish-white tent-like nests in early spring; left, egg mass on winter twig.

TERMITES

How can anyone treat their ground to get rid of white ants or termites which get into all woody roots and ruin plants? (Kentucky.) Use chlordane or dieldrin in topsoil as for grub-proofing.

Where termites are in cordwood, 50 feet from a brick house, is there

danger that they will get started in the house itself? (Maryland.) Not unless there is any woodwork on the building in direct contact with the ground. If there is, a metal shield can be inserted.

TERRACHLOR

My dealer does not have Terrachlor—Where can he get it? Terrachlor or PCNB is manufactured by the Olin Mathieson Chemical Corp., Baltimore 3, Maryland, as a 75% wettable powder or a 20% dust. It is very promising for some soil-borne diseases such as club root of crucifers, and crown rot of iris and many other plants. Use the wettable powder at the rate of 1⅓ lbs. per 12 gals. of water per 1000 sq. ft., or the dust at the rate of 5 lbs. per 1000 sq. ft. Work the dust into the upper soil before planting.

TEXAS ROOT ROT

Has there been anything found to control root rot? (Texas.) Texas root rot, also called cotton or Phymatotrichum root rot, is probably the chief problem in gardening in certain parts of Texas, Arizona, and New Mexico. The fungus *Phymatotrichum omnivorum* is a native soil inhabitant in semi-arid regions of low humidity, high temperature, and alkalinity. It attacks 1700 plant species. The monocotyledons are immune, so you can grow palms, irises, lilies, gladioli, and bulbs without trouble. During the period of summer rains dense circular mats of fungus mycelium appear on the surface of the soil, at first white, later tan and powdery. Plants turn yellow and die rapidly. Sometimes a tree can be saved at the first sign of wilting by applying ammonium sulfate, 1 lb. to 10 sq. ft., in a basin around the tree and letting water run in until the soil is wet 4 ft. deep. Garden soil may also be treated with ammonium sulfate, but if there are no shrubs within 20 ft., the fallow soil may be treated with formaldehyde (1 to 70 dilution, 1 gal. applied per foot) or with soil fumigant fungicides. (See under Nematodes.)

TOXAPHENE

I read in an article that toxaphene is one of the few chemicals that will control bagworms. Where can I purchase some? This insecticide is widely used in the South on cotton insects, but is not yet popular in the North. A number of the larger insecticide manufacturers can supply toxaphene. Have your local dealer obtain a supply for you.

WITCHES'-BROOMS

What are witches'-brooms and their cause? (Massachusetts.) Broomlike excessive development of twigs in response to an irritation caused by insects, fungi, or some virus. Hackberry is a notable example with often hundreds of brooms, each a mass of stubby twigs arising from a swelling at the base of a branch, on a single tree. A gall mite and a powdery-mildew fungus seem to be jointly responsible for this deformation. There is no control in this case, but cutting out the brooms improves appearance.

WHITE GRUBS

This spring I plowed and planted land that had not been farmed for 25 years; grubworms killed potatoes, cabbage, etc. What was reason? (Illinois.) Grubworms are white grubs in your area, soft-bodied white worms with brown heads, curved bodies ½ to 1 in. long. They look like Japanese beetle grubs but are a little larger. They damage lawns in the same way and are much more injurious to root vegetables than are the grubs we suffer from in the East. As you continue to garden your land, the injury should get less. It is most serious in areas neglected for a long time. White grubs are larvae of June beetles. There is a 3-year cycle, the grubs staying in the ground 2 years and the large brown beetles flying the third year and eating tree foliage. Injury from the worms is greatest the year after beetle flight.

White Grub: large, soft white grub with brown head—larva of the June beetle; attacks roots of grass and other plants.

How shall I rid my soil of grubworms? (Texas.) Prevent trouble, if possible, by not planting garden crops on sod land, or land grown up to weeds and grass the preceding year. If such land must be used, plow in the fall, or spade, and apply grub-proofing chemical (See under Grub-proofing). Legume crops will suffer less than corn or potatoes.

WIREWORMS

I have a pest in the soil about the thickness of a darning needle, light brown, very tough; have to cut off the head to kill it; ¾ to 1½ ins. long; seems to live in the roots. Is it harmful to plants? (Indiana.) You have described a wireworm, a chewing insect which feeds underground on germinating seeds and underground roots, stems, and tubers. Potatoes, beets, beans, cabbage, carrots, corn, lettuce, onions, turnips, and other vegetables may be injured. Damage is worse on poorly drained soil or on land that has been in grass sod. The adult stage of the wireworm is a gray, brown, or black click beetle, an amusing creature that clicks itself right side up when it falls on its back.

What is the best method for exterminating wireworms? (New Jersey.) If newly broken sod must be used, plow it thoroughly and then apply grub-proofing material. (See under Grub-proofing.) To help control wireworms, with a growing crop water grub-proofing material into the soil.

WOODCHUCKS

How do you get rid of woodchucks? The United States Fish and Wildlife Service has developed a special woodchuck cartridge, which may be obtained through county agents. When lighted according to directions and placed in a den mouth, this will diffuse a lethal gas through the den.

How prevent woodchucks from eating strawberries? A fence is the only sure protection, except a dog.

What can I do about woodchucks that eat my garden plants? Watch for them early morning and late afternoon and shoot them. Find the holes and poison them with cyanogas.

How is cyanogas used to kill woodchucks? A woodchuck usually has at least two openings to his home. Close these up with heavy stones and soil to keep gas fumes in. Put about 3 ozs. cyanogas into one opening and then close. This is an extremely fatal poison, so handle carefully. The fumes are given off when the crystals are in contact with moist soil. The gas is heavier than air, so it settles into the burrow.

ORNAMENTALS

ACONITE

Why do monkshood leaves and stems die? Cure? Bulbs look healthy. (Connecticut.) If the vessels are black when you cut across the stem, dying leaves are probably due to verticillium wilt, results of a soil fungus affecting the vascular system. No cure. Plant healthy roots in new or sterilized soil.

Can one prevent yellowing of leaves or complete defoliation of aconitum before blooming? (Ohio.) Since this is presumably the same verticillium wilt, nothing will prevent the disease except starting over with new roots in fresh soil.

Is there any other cause of blight of aconitum, except verticillium? (New Jersey.) Yes, sometimes the crown-rot fungus so destructive to delphinium attacks aconitum. In this case you usually see white threads or seedlike bodies on the soil, and the plant may topple over at the crown. Remove plant and surrounding soil. Disinfect area with bichloride of mercury or terrachlor.

Why do the flower buds of my aconitum turn black and not open? (New Jersey.) The cyclamen mite affects aconitum as it does delphinium. Remove infested portions and spray weekly with endrin (1 tsp. per gal. of water).

AGERATUM

What do you do for white flies on ageratum? The white flies usually come along when you get your plants from the greenhouse in the spring and cause minute white spotting of the foliage all summer, getting worse toward fall. Frequent spraying with nicotine sulfate and soap or malathion hitting the under side of the leaves, is helpful.

How can I keep mooly aphids or milk cows from my blue ageratum? I lose the plants each year. (Missouri.) "Mooly" is evidently mistyped for woolly, but the pun is too good to lose. Ants keep root aphids herded together so they can feed on the honeydew (milk) excreted. Make a shallow depression around each plant and pour in malathion solution. (See also Ants, for their control.)

AFRICAN-VIOLET

How can I get rid of the mealy bugs on my African-violet? It is difficult, because spraying injures the foliage. Watch for the first signs of these white woolly sucking insects and remove them with a small brush dipped in alcohol. Touch only the bug, not the leaf. Avoid a too-hot, dry atmosphere. A house plant aerosol bomb is also effective.

How rid my African-violet of a small insect that weaves a white web all over it? It is probably a mealy bug, and if the infestation is that bad you'd better burn the plant and start with a healthy one.

Is there a remedy for lice on African-violet plants? You probably refer to mealy bugs, for ordinary aphids are not so common on this plant. Constant vigilance is the remedy; pick off the first bit of cotton fluff you see, or touch each insect with a small swab of cotton on a matchstick (or a very small paintbrush) dipped in alcohol. A malathion spray will control mealy bugs.

What causes a moldlike covering over the topsoil of house plants, particularly African-violets? Insufficient aeration. Cultivate the soil occasionally with the tines of an old fork. Too much water compacts the soil and encourages the moldy surface growth. You may need to repot with a fresh mixture.

ALYSSUM

Why does Basket of Gold Alyssum die? Possibly because of wet feet. Good soil drainage is necessary; the foliage should be kept dry. This plant thrives on walls and other dry locations.

AMARYLLIS

Can mealy bugs be removed from scales of amaryllis bulb? Have tried alcohol sprays and enclosing pot in bag with napthalene flakes, but still mealy bugs. Be wary about alcohol *sprays*. You can remove bugs with a tiny cotton swab on a toothpick dipped in alcohol. Or try dipping in malathion solution.

What is the grub that gets into amaryllis bulbs? Probably larval form of greater or lesser narcissus bulb flies. Grub of the greater fly may be up to ¾ in. long, the lesser up to ½ in. Commercial growers often treat bulbs with hot water, but there is nothing for the home grower to do after the injury is noted.

Why do amaryllis leaves turn yellow and die? They do not dry up but have something like wet rot. If the rot is wet, it may be bacterial soft rot following work of bulb-fly larvae. If the bulb is not sound, do not save it for another year. Burn it.

AMARCRINUM

How do I get rid of thrips on Amarcrinum howardii and Urginea maritima? Have sprayed with nicotine and dusted with sulfur. Spray or dust weekly with DDT or dieldrin.

ANEMONE

How can one protect anemones from the blister beetle? Only by constant vigilance when the beetles appear in midsummer. Dust or spray with DDT or methoxychlor. Pyrethrum-rotenone sprays are also helpful, as is hand-picking of the beetles. (See Blister Beetle.)

ARBORVITAE

What is the best solution to use on arborvitae when the branches become a rusty color? (Illinois.) The rusty color is often due to spruce mite, similar to red spider. The most potent spray is a miscible oil, applied before new growth starts in the spring. (See Dormant Spraying.) During the growing season, monthly spraying with Ovex, malathion, aramite, or chlorobenzilate is very effective.

What might be the cause of arborvitae turning brown and dying? (Mississippi.) If the whole tree dies, it may be from prolonged injury from spruce mites, but the browning and dying of inner leaves are a natural shedding. Dying of the tips of the branches, twig blight, is a fungous disease, calling for cutting off and burning of infected portions.

How do you destroy little red bugs that suck the sap from arborvitae? (Arkansas.) You may mean the arborvitae aphid, a very small, hairy, amber-brown plant louse. Apply a good contact spray, such as malathion, with as much pressure as possible, for these aphids are covered with a powdery film which makes them hard to kill.

Why do the tips of arborvitae twigs turn white? (Connecticut.) This is the work of a leaf miner, which winters in the leaves and emerges as a moth to lay eggs in June. Spraying or dusting with DDT in late June and early July helps to kill larvae as they enter the base of the leaves.

ASPIDISTRA

What causes the white-looking fungus or scale or whatever it can be called on aspidistra leaves? How can it be cured? (Louisiana.) There is a fungous disease, anthracnose, characterized by white spots with brown margins. Spraying is seldom necessary or profitable. There is also a brown scale listed on aspidistra. Perhaps you refer to mealy bugs. (See House Plants, this section, for control.)

ASTER, CHINA

Will paper collars adequately protect transplants, aster particularly, from grubworms? (Oregon.) Collars will protect against cutworms (fat caterpillars which cut off plant stems near the surface). Collars offer no protection against the white grubs, larvae of June beetles, which stay in the soil and feed on roots of garden plants.

After being full-grown and flowering plants, asters dried up and died. What was the cause? (New York.) Aster wilt, a disease caused by a soil fungus, a species of fusarium, which grows into the roots and affects the vascular or water-conducting system of the plant. Young plants may be infected and not show symptoms until flowering, as in this case.

Why do some asters thrive until they are 7 to 8 ins. tall, then turn brown, rusty, and die? I can't find anything at the roots or on the tops. (Idaho.) This is an earlier manifestation of the same aster wilt. Infection often takes place at transplanting, with the leaves drying and dying somewhat later. Plant wilt-resistant seed, many varieties of which are now on the market.

When asters have blighted, how long a time must elapse before they can be safely grown in the same ground? (Illinois.) No one knows exactly how long the fusarium wilt fungus lives in the soil, but it is several years.

What can I do to prevent root rot in my aster bed? I plant wilt-resistant seed, disinfected with Semesan, without the desired results. (Illinois.) Certain soils are so infested with the wilt fungus that a certain percentage of "wilt-resistant" plants will succumb, the situation being worse in wet seasons. Try sterilizing the soil in the seedbed with methyl bromide and transplanting seedlings to a fresh location. (See Soil Sterilization.)

Is there anything to sterilize the ground for infected aster plants? It is a large space. (Wisconsin.) It will scarcely pay to treat a large space. For a small area try a formaldehyde drench, spading the soil, and then saturating with a solution of 1 gal. commercial formalin diluted with 50 gals. of water. Apply ½ to 1 gal. per sq. ft. of soil, cover with paper or canvas for 24 hours, and then air out for 2 weeks before planting. (For other methods see Soil Sterilization.)

What causes some asters to open greenish white instead of coloring up? (California.) Aster yellows, a virus disease transmitted from diseased to healthy plants by leaf hoppers. The leaves lose their chlorophyll and turn yellow, while the blossoms turn green. Plants are usually stunted. This is the most serious aster disease and occurs throughout the United States.

How can I prevent aster yellows? Only by preventing insect transmission. Remove diseased plants immediately, so there will be no source of infection. Spray frequently with contact insecticides to kill leaf hoppers. Commercial growers protect asters by growing them in cloth houses made of cheesecloth or tobacco cloth with 22 meshes to the inch.

How can I get rid of the small root lice that suck life out of aster and other annuals? (Illinois.) Make a shallow depression around each plant and pour in the same malathion solution used for spraying above-ground aphids.

What treatment will reduce damage to asters by the tarnished plant bug? (Kansas.) This small, light and dark brown sucking insect is hard to control. It is very active, occurs on many kinds of plants, stinging the flower buds and spotting the leaves, and has several generations a season. Contact insecticides such as DDT, lindane or malathion will kill those insects. Derris (rotenone) dust is effective. Cleaning up all trash and weeds will make hibernation difficult for the bug.

What is the control of the common black beetle on asters? (Michigan.) You probably mean the long, slim blister beetle, which is very destructive to asters. Dust or spray with DDT or methoxychlor. (See Blister Beetle.)

AZALEAS

What is azalea flower-spot disease? (Louisiana.) A relatively recent fungous disease which has spread from South Carolina through the Gulf states since 1931 and has been reported from California. Pinhead spots on the flowers enlarge to brownish blotches and the flowers collapse in about 3 days. Black resting bodies form in the petals and winter in the fallen leaves. The indica varieties are especially susceptible.

How do you control azalea flower-spot? Spraying has little permanent effect and injures the bloom. The best "cure" is prevention by placing a barrier between the fungus sending up its little spores from the soil and the petals. A thick mulch of Spanishmoss fiber has been quite effective. After blooming, clean up and burn the old contaminated mulch, and put on a new mulch for the summer, adding 4 to 5 ins. additional material when the buds break in January. Asphalt paper mulch proved effective in experiments at Louisiana State University.

What are cause and treatment of moldlike white threads and general decline of azalea plants? (California.)   Azaleas in California are subject to attack by the oak-root rot fungus (*Armillaria mellea*). Besides the white threads (*mycelium*) the fungus has shoestringlike black strands which go through the soil and produce honey-colored toadstools. Increase vigor of plants by feeding; remove some of the soil from crowns and roots; avoid too-high soil moisture content. Treat soil known to be infested with chloropicrin or methyl bromide. (See under Nematodes.)

My azalea buds blight before they open. Why? (Ohio.)   There is a fungus which blasts terminal flower buds in the summer so they do not bloom the following year and sometimes kills leaf buds and twigs. Prune out and destroy all diseased material. Spray with Bordeaux mixture after blossoming.

What bores holes in my Azalea mollis? It goes in near the ground and comes out at top of branches? (New Jersey.) (New York.)   Probably the azalea borer, but this starts at the top and works down. The beetle lays its eggs near the tip and the young larva enters near a leaf node and bores down through the twig into the crown. Cut off dead and dying tips; inject BHC paste into holes showing sawdust.

My azalea plants (outdoor) have been attacked by lace bugs. How can I get rid of them? (New Jersey.)   Spray with malathion or other contact insecticide when the young nymphs hatch, usually in early June. There are 2 or 3 broods of the azalea lace bug, and spraying may need to be repeated at 3-week intervals throughout the summer. Cover under surface of leaves very thoroughly. The sucking of lace bugs turns the leaves of evergreen azaleas coffee-colored and those of deciduous varieties whitish.

What kills black aphids on azaleas? (New Jersey.)   Aphids are not ordinarily so common on azaleas as on other hosts, but they may be killed with the usual malathion spray, or any other contact insecticide.

When and with what do I spray azaleas for red spider and other pests? (West Virginia.)   Malathion is the best all around material. Spray just after blooming and again in late May or early June to control lace bug, thrips, mealy bugs, and mites (red spiders).

What causes leaves to drop on a webby string from an azalea house plant? Is dry sulfur good for this?   Probably the work of red spiders. Water is more important than sulfur. If the plants are bathed frequently, or treated with a fine mist spray from an atomizer, and kept under sufficiently humid conditions, red spiders will never have a chance to cause this much damage. After the plant has been thoroughly washed and dried, spray with malathion.

BEGONIA

What makes the leaves of begonia turn brown on the edge and get lifeless?   Perhaps unfavorable environment and perhaps injury from leaf nematodes, which cause irregular brown blotches, enlarging until the leaf curls up and drops. Prune off and burn infested portions; do not let leaves of 2 plants touch; water from below instead of wetting the foliage. The nematodes will be killed if potted plants are submerged in hot water held at 115° to 118° F. for 3 minutes, but this may cause injury and is more for the florist than the home grower. Try watering-in Systox (Systoban granules).

Dry spots form on leaves of begonias until they are almost eaten up. What are cause and treatment?   Possibly sunscald, possibly the leaf nematode just discussed.

I have a Calla Begonia, healthy a month ago, now with leaves withering and tops of new branches falling off. Why? (Wisconsin.)   This is probably due to unfavorable environmental conditions rather than any specific organism. The Callalily Begonia is conceded to be difficult. Cool, moist air, fairly dry soil, and watering only from the saucer are recommended.

When my tuberous begonia was budded to bloom, the leaves, then the stalk, turned brown and dropped. What was the trouble? (Nebraska.)   It is hard to be sure without personal inspection, but there is a soil fungus, pythium, which causes a stem rot and may produce a soft rot and collapse of the crown and stalk. Avoid crowding of plants. Do not replant in infected soil without sterilizing.

A tuberous begonia rotted after a promising start. It wasn't overwatered. What could we have done wrong? (Ohio.)   Tuberous begonias are sometimes attacked by larvae of the black vine weevil, which destroy the roots so that the plants wilt and die. If the white grubs are found in the soil treat with chlordane or dieldrin as for grubproofing.

What blight or insect attacks tuberous begonias to keep them from developing properly? (New York.)   Insufficient light may be responsible, even though these are shade-loving plants. The cyclamen mite or possibly thrips may cause deformation. Frequent spraying with endrin (1 tsp. per gal. of water) before blooming may be of some benefit.

What spray shall I use for plant lice on a Lorraine Begonia?   Malathion before flowering; pyrethrum while in bloom.

What is the tiny white or transparent worm which gets in the stalks and roots of begonias?   It is probably only a scavenger worm feeding on tissues rotting from some other cause; possibly a fungous stem rot. If the plant is this far decayed, you should start over with a healthy plant in fresh soil.

What causes a sticky sediment on my begonia?   It is honeydew, secreted by sucking insects, aphids, mealy bugs, or white flies.

BIRCH

How can white birches be protected against a small worm that gets between the layers of the leaves? (New York.)   This is the birch-leaf miner, which causes a brown blotch on the outer half of the leaf. The worm is the larval stage of a black sawfly. Spray with lindane or malathion as soon as leaves are fully out.

How can I stop insects from eating leaves of cut-leaf birch? (New York.)   The birch aphid sucks sap from leaves of cut-leaved birch and may be controlled with malathion spray. Cankerworms chew holes in birch leaves in May. Spray with DDT or methoxychlor.

How can I eliminate bronze birch borer from a weeping birch? (New York.)   The flat-headed, light-colored grubs, ½ to 1 in. long, make winding galleries underneath the bark; the adult beetles feed on foliage. Trees growing under adverse conditions may die. Spray tree trunks with DDT or dieldrin in June and again in July and see that trees are well fed and watered.

BITTERSWEET

What is the treatment for scale on Oriental Bittersweet?   The euonymus scale often covers bittersweet vines with a heavy infestation of slim white male scales, and darker, rounder females. Spray before growth starts with a miscible oil, at a 1 to 25 dilution or with a dormant dinitro spray. Spray again in summer, when your scales hatch, with DDT and malathion combination.

BOXWOOD

What is good for boxwood with white scale? The leaves are dying on most of bush and spreading to others. (D.C.)   Oyster-shell scale may infest boxwood, but it is dark brown or gray in color. You may refer to nectria canker, a serious fungous disease which kills the leaves and twigs and produces pinkish-white spore pustules on the backs of the leaves and on the stems.

How do you control boxwood canker? (New Jersey.)   Chiefly by sanitary measures: cleaning out old leaves and dead twigs twice a year and getting rid of all material that can hold moisture. Never water boxwood so that the foliage is wet for long periods. Try a dormant dinitro spray directing the spray into the interior of the bush.

What should I do for my young boxwood, dying by degrees? (North Carolina.)   Probably the canker disease just discussed is responsible or possibly nematodes. This is somewhat more prevalent farther North, but it is sometimes serious in your state. Clean out; spray; avoid prolonged wetting of foliage. Try V-C 13 or Nemagon for nematodes.

What treatment will keep boxwood leaves from turning brown? (Delaware.) Winter injury, nectria canker, serious infestations of scale, nematodes or leaf miners will all cause brown, unhealthy foliage. Winter protection and sanitary measures are most important.

What about the orange flies that come on boxwood in May? (Connecticut.) These are the adults of the boxwood leaf miner. Spray with DDT when the flies first begin to emerge or with malathion in mid-June after eggs have hatched.

What shall I do for red spider on boxwood bushes? (Tennessee.) Spider mites turn the leaves a light, unhealthy color. Spraying with a miticide as recommended under azaleas should be effective.

BROWALLIA

How do you treat the black-spotty disease that infects foliage of browallia? (Mississippi.) Smut has been reported on this host, and would make black sooty masses over the leaves. The best thing to do would be to remove smutted leaves and burn them. However, you may merely be having sooty mold growing in insect honeydew, in which case you use contact sprays for the insects.

BULBS

What formulas have been used with known success in combating fungous diseases of newly planted bulbs? The most successful formula is to plant clean, healthy bulbs. Look them over carefully and discard any that show signs of black sclerotia. Look for these small, flat, hard bodies under the outer scales. Soaking for 2 hours in a 1 to 1000 solution of bichloride of mercury may kill fungi, but it is better to discard diseased bulbs. Plant in a new location or in treated soil if you have been previously troubled with much disease.

How can ants be destroyed which occur in clumps of bulbs? (Alabama.) Soak chlordane solution in around the bulbs. (See also Ants.)

What are the minute white worms found in and around rotting bulbs? Do they cause the decay or are they scavengers, cleaning up? (Minnesota.) They are scavengers, doing their appointed job. Don't worry about them, but do hunt for the primary cause of rotting.

CACTI

What shall I do for white furry web spots on small spiny cactus? The spots are doubtless mealy bugs, which may be removed with a toothpick, or small brush, by washing off with water applied as a fine spray; by spraying with an aerosol bomb, or with malathion, using caution. (See House Plants.)

How do you combat mealy bugs on cacti too spiny to use a brush on? Use an aerosol bomb or spray with malathion as above.

How do you cure cactus scab? Maybe you refer to a corky spot due to unfavorable conditions, often prevented by increasing light and decreasing humidity, but perhaps you are describing scale. Remove scale with a brush dipped in pyrethrum solution or scrape off with a small piece of wood.

What causes pricklypear cactus to get a white fungus or mold on it, and what can be done to prevent it? (Texas.) A white mold is rather improbable on cactus. You may be describing mealy bugs; or possibly one of the scale insects common on Pricklypear Cactus. (See previous questions for control.)

My Christmas Cactus is covered with a web, and large pieces drop off. How can I prevent this? The web is probably produced by red spiders, which flourish in a dry atmosphere. The Christmas Cactus does not need to be kept as dry as other cacti, and should be frequently syringed with water to keep spider mites in check. Try also spraying with malathion or an aerosol plant bomb.

How can I use sulfur on cactus with mildew? True mildew, a white powdery coating, would not be common on cactus. Perhaps you have a rot encouraged by overwatering. Cut out the diseased portions and dust the cut surfaces with captan.

What is the cause of cactus plants dying off at the base? Probably too much water. Cacti are very subject to rot caused by fungi which flourish in the presence of moisture. Infection often starts through wounds, which should be avoided so far as possible.

How do you overcome silver and brown rust on cactus? This "rust" is more likely due to unfavorable light conditions than to a fungus. Increasing the light and decreasing the humidity may help.

CALADIUM

Worms have appeared in the caladium plant and all the brightly colored leaves have withered and died. What can be done? Probably nothing at this stage. Worms in the soil can be flushed out with lime water, but they do no damage except to clog the drainage holes. It sounds as if the plants had either been drowned with the roots in too soggy soil, or else had dried out.

CALENDULA

Is there something that will kill black bugs on calendula? (Minnesota.) Malathion spray applied thoroughly and often should clear up the black aphids which are practically inevitable on calendula.

CALLA

What can I do for tiny black bugs on my calla? Strong soapsuds seem to do no good. Apply malathion. Repeat the spray at intervals.

Why didn't the flower on callalily I raised bloom? Had beautiful bud, but did not open. There are only two diseases of callalilies: a root rot which may prevent flowering, and a slimy, soft rot which starts in the rhizome, and spreads up into the flower stalk. Your plant may have been infected with the root-rot fungus, or some physiological condition may have prevented blooming. In either case, it would pay to start over with a fresh rhizome next year.

CAMELLIA

What do you do when camellias have root lice? (North Carolina.) If you are sure the trouble is root aphids and not from the root-knot nematode, a weevil grub, or other pest, scoop the soil away from the trunk somewhat and pour in a solution of malathion. There are also root mealy bugs. If they or root lice get too serious you have to take up the plant, wash off the roots carefully, and replant in fresh soil.

I have a camellia that has small spots on leaves, pinhead size, leaves are light green, sick looking. Growing in a tub in hothouse. What can I do for it? (Texas.) The soil may be wrong; or the plant may be in too strong sun or improperly watered, but the light spots indicate the tea scale working on the under side of the leaves. This is a white cottony scale, the most serious pest of camellias. Spray with malathion. Two treatments may be necessary to clean up a heavily infested plant.

CAMPANULA

Why don't I have success with campanulas? They rot away. Have a dry soil. (Delaware.) There are 2 soil fungi which may cause crown or stem rot under moist conditions, but your trouble may be physiological and due to insufficient water. Try another location and improve the soil with organic matter such as leafmold or peatmoss.

CANDYTUFT

What is the cause of candytuft turning white? Looks like mildew and is dying. (North Carolina.) A white rust is common on candytuft and other members of the crucifer family. White pustules appear on under side of leaves, which turn pale. Burn diseased plants or plant parts and clean up cruciferous weeds, such as wild mustard. Spraying with Bordeaux mixture may help.

CANTERBURYBELLS

What can be done to prevent canterburybells from rotting just before blooming? (Ohio.) Possibly growing plants in a new location, or disinfecting the soil with formaldehyde, perhaps merely by improving soil texture. Might be due to winter injury.

CARNATION

What causes me to lose my clove pink? Foliage turns brown in center of clump and spreads until entire bed is dead. (Tennessee.) It may be a fungous stem rot, partially controlled by spraying with captan. Try healthy cuttings or plant in a new location. They need a very well-drained soil.

Is there any pest that will cut carnations off at the joints? (Montana.) Cutworms, possibly. Try chlordane or dieldrin dust around the plants. A fungus, called branch rot, may girdle the nodes, or joints, and cause death of the branch. Remove infected parts.

What do you recommend for baby snails that feed on carnation buds? (California.) Hand-picking or a poison bait of 1 part calcium arsenate to 16 parts wheat bran. In New Jersey I can prevent slug damage on hollyhocks by dusting with sulfur-lead arsenate dust. It might work for snails on carnations.

My greenhouse carnations wilt and dry up. What shall I do to produce strong, healthy plants? (Rhode Island.) Several soil fungi cause wilts or stem rot, being more prevalent at high temperatures and in wet soils. Steam sterilize your greenhouse soil and bring in only healthy plants. (See also Soil Sterilization.)

What is wrong with my hardy carnations? I get them started and they bloom until August, then droop and die. (Iowa.) Are there rusty pustules on the under side of leaves and do the leaves turn pale? If so, try sulfur or ferbam dust to control rust. More likely soil fungi are to blame. Try a new location. Perhaps your carnations merely dry out and require more organic matter in the soil.

CEDAR

Do windbreaks of Maryland pines or cedar trees harbor diseases which may be transmitted to fruit trees near by? (D.C.) Pines are not dangerous to orchard trees, although I am not sure what you mean by Maryland pine. Redcedar harbors the cedar-apple rust fungus. Brown galls put out orange spore horns in the spring, and infective material is carried to apples as much as a mile or more away, although the amount of infection is roughly proportional to distance. In some apple regions cedars are prohibited by law.

Some of the cedars in my hedge are developing brown patches; I suspect red spider. Can you prescribe a remedy? (Georgia.) It is very likely red spider. Try forceful spraying with malathion or Ovex, or occasional drenching with a strong stream of water from the hose. (See also Juniper.)

CHINESELANTERN

What type of insecticide will kill the striped beetles which ruin our Chineselanterns? They resemble cucumber bugs but are much hardier. (Minnesota.) They probably are striped cucumber beetles which are certainly hardy, but should be killed by spraying the plants with methoxychlor. If you want to grow cucumbers you'd better get rid of the Chineselanterns entirely, because the beetles carry a virus disease, mosaic, from one host to the other.

A yellow-and-black bug lays eggs, hatching a slimy, sucking bug. What will destroy these? (Michigan.) If your "bug" is spotted, it is the tortoise beetle; if striped, it is the cucumber beetle. (See above.) The "slimy" bugs are the larvae, or immature beetles. Those of the tortoise beetle carry their excreta in a pack upon their backs. Spray with methoxychlor.

CHRYSANTHEMUM

What causes the leaves of an outdoor chrysanthemum to curl up and turn brown? This question, in one form or another, was asked most frequently of all the pest questions. Verticillium, or fusarium wilts, septoria leaf spot, or improper water relations, will all turn foliage brown, but in 9 cases out of 10 leaf nematodes are to blame.

What are leaf nematodes, and how do they work? They are eelworms—microscopic animals which live in the soil and in wet weather swim up the stems of chrysanthemums and enter the leaves through the stomata—small mouthlike openings in the leaves. Infection begins with a yellowish-brown discoloration bounded by the larger veins, so that the discolored area is usually pie-shaped. Later the entire leaf turns brown and brittle, and may fall.

How may leaf nematodes be controlled? First, by removing and burning seriously infested plants; next, by cutting off and burning all chrysanthemum tops after blooming. Make cuttings or divisions only from healthy plants or clumps, and either plant in a new location or sterilize the soil with a nematocide. (See nematode control.)

Will spraying control leaf nematodes? Yes, Parathion in 3 biweekly sprays, beginning in late July, has been used with success to control them but it is highly toxic to man and animals and must be used with great care.

Are any systemic treatments effective for leaf nematodes? Sodium selenate in capsule form (Sel-Caps) may be used effectively in the soil under plants. It is absorbed by the plants through the roots as a systemic and destroys the nematodes in the leaves.

How do nematodes spread from one plant to another? If the leaves touch, they can swim across in wet weather. They can also be carried by the gardener on hands, tools, or clothing. Do not cultivate or handle the plants when they are wet with rain or dew.

Some of my chrysanthemums have dried leaves halfway up the plant; others were all right. Why? (New York.)   Some varieties are much more resistant to nematode injury than others. Ask your dealer for varieties that will withstand nematodes. The Korean chrysanthemums are notoriously susceptible.

Early in summer my mum plants start turning yellow on lower leaves. The leaves turn brown and crisp. This moves up stem until entire plant is dead. Roots show no growth since planting. What should I do? (Utah.)   This may be nematode injury, but in your state it is likely to be verticillium wilt. Start fresh with healthy plants in a new location or in sterilized soil.

How do you prevent the lower leaves on tender mums from spotting and shriveling? (Ohio.)   If your trouble starts as definite black spots, rather than brown wedges, you probably are dealing with a fungous disease, septoria leaf spot, which is quite readily controlled by spraying with ferbam and picking off infected leaves. If the spotting is white and powdery, it is due to the mildew fungus, and you should dust with sulfur or spray with Mildex or Karathane.

What causes my mums to get black and wilted at the lower part of the plants? (New Jersey.)   If you are sure it is a black wilting it may be due to a leaf-spot fungus, or a soil fungus. If the color is brown, it is probably the work of leaf nematodes. (See answers to above questions.)

Will the fungus Sclerotium delphinii, which caused crown rot among the hybrid delphiniums, be likely to affect chrysanthemums planted in that bed next spring?   Infection is possible, since this fungus is known to occur on almost every garden plant, but the disease is far more prevalent on delphiniums. Play safe and treat the soil with Terrachlor or Vapam this fall or very early next spring. (See Soil Sterilization.)

What do you advocate for exterminating dodder on chrysanthemum plants? (Pennsylvania.)   This charming parasite seems to be increasing as a garden pest. Once a plant is entwined with the orange tendrils, there is no remedy except breaking off and burning the parasitized plant parts before the white dodder flowers set and drop their seed for another year.

What insect causes mums to open only partially? (Illinois.)   If the foliage is not brown and crisp, suggesting leaf nematode injury, it may be the gall midge, which lives in little conical projections of the leaves and flowers. Pick off and burn infested plant parts. Spraying with lindane will help. A fungous disease, ray blight, also deforms flowers.

What shall I spray with to kill those little black bugs that get on chrysanthemums? (Missouri.)   These are aphids, almost inevitable on chrysanthemum tips in late summer, and sometimes all summer.

They are readily killed with any contact insecticide, such as malathion. Spray often enough to protect the new growth.

I have a chrysanthemum plant with black insects creeping on it. If I cut the branches down, will it be all right to put it out in the garden in the spring? (D.C.) Yes, you may safely move your infested plant to the garden. Aphids are readily killed with any contact insecticide. (See previous question.)

Each year my indoor chrysanthemum gets covered with little green bugs. How can I get rid of these pests? The green bugs are undoubtedly aphids, or plant lice. Spray with malathion if they get numerous, but pure water will help in prevention. Wash the foliage frequently, or apply a fine mist from an atomizer.

What can I do to prevent root aphids? (New Jersey.) Scoop out the soil from a shallow depression around each stem and pour in about a cupful of malathion, 1 tbsp. per gallon of water. Control ants.

What poison can be used in a cold frame for a small green caterpillar which eats young leaves? (New Jersey.) Spray with DDT or methoxychlor; keep the glass sash off until the spray has thoroughly dried.

What is the little bug like a ladybug that eats the flowers of Astrid mums every fall? (Texas.) If the "bug" is green with black spots, it is the spotted cucumber beetle, known in your section as the diabolical diabrotica because it is so fond of so many garden flowers.

How do you eliminate diabrotica beetles? Control is difficult because sprays discolor the flowers. Pyrethrum or rotenone would be best. As a last resort spray or dust with DDT or methoxychlor.

What treatment shall I use for insects that eat centers of chrysanthemums? (Missouri.) Probably these are the 12-spotted cucumber (diabrotica) beetles discussed above.

What are the flying, hard-shelled, rather beetlelike bugs that attack some chrysanthemums during the blooming season? (Indiana.) Black-spotted green beetles are diabroticas; long, black beetles are blister beetles. For the latter try dusting with DDT. (See Blister Beetles.)

What do you do for a small beetle, yellow with black spots, that eats beans and chrysanthemum flowers? (New York.) The Mexican bean beetle is not ordinarily a chrysanthemum pest, but when it has devoured all the bean foliage in sight it may seek other fields. Try spraying or dusting chrysanthemums with rotenone or methoxychlor.

What can one use to keep grasshoppers from eating buds? (Kentucky.) Poison bran mash, as used for cutworms, is the recommended control for grasshoppers; but probably it would be easier to spray the chrysanthemums with DDT after the buds form but before they flower.

What is treatment for gall on garden chrysanthemums and disposition of infected plants? (New York.) Assuming this is the bacterial crown gall which appears at the base of the plant, and not the gall midge, there is nothing to do for infected plants except to remove and burn them.

Is the soil liable to harbor crown gall infection the succeeding year? Yes, the bacteria may live for some time in the soil. Plant in a new location or sterilize the soil.

What is the gall midge? A fly, which lays its eggs in foliage and buds, where the larvae stimulate the formation of small conical galls. This is primarily a greenhouse pest, controlled by DDT applications, but sometimes attacks outdoor plants. It is usually easier to remove infested chrysanthemums.

About July something attacked my chrysanthemums; they broke off about 3 ins. from ground, leaving piles of what looked like white ant eggs. What caused this? (Ohio.) The stalk borer was probably responsible, the "ant eggs" being frass excreted by the caterpillar inside the stem. When you see borer injury, it is too late to help the plant. Cleaning up weeds is best prevention.

What is the round black worm around roots of shasta daisies? (New Jersey.) Likely a millipede feeding on roots rotting from some other cause; perhaps a fungous stem rot. Remove and burn the diseased plant if the roots are destroyed.

How shall I exterminate termites in beds? (Texas.) Water with a chlordane or dieldrin solution into the soil around the plants.

CITRUS

How shall I care for scale on dwarf citrus fruits in the house? Spray with malathion or house plant aerosol bomb. (See House Plants for special precautions.)

My grapefruit tree has become infested since being taken in from garden. Same pest on cacti. What is it? The infestation is probably mealy bugs, which flourish on cacti. Use the same treatment as for scale.

What is the cause and cure of syrup substance on leaves of dwarf lemon and orange? The sticky material is a honeydew secreted by sucking insects, probably mealy bugs in this case, although possibly scale insects, white flies, or aphids. (For control see previous two questions; also House Plants.)

CLEMATIS

In late fall what attacks Clematus paniculata, which has flourished like a green bay tree? Hordes of beetles practically denude the vines overnight. (Georgia.) These are probably blister beetles. Dusting with DDT will be most satisfactory. (See also Blister Beetles.)

How can I kill blister bugs that eat vines in summer? (Louisiana.)

Blister beetles are more prevalent on clematis in the South than in the North. They are hard to kill, but spraying or dusting with DDT will be effective. Knock off the beetles into a can of kerosene.

My Clematis jackmani climbers, after getting several feet high, wilt unexpectedly. If dry stem rot causes this, what can be done? (Wisconsin.) It sounds like stem rot. After the fungus has girdled the stem so that the vine wilts suddenly, nothing can be done. Spraying or dusting with sulfur through the season may aid in prevention. Start cuttings from healthy plants.

COLEUS

Are mealy bugs on coleus caused by too much or too little watering? Mealy bugs, like most sucking insects, thrive in a dry atmosphere, but too little water cannot "cause" them. Also if the plants are unhealthy from a waterlogged soil they may succumb more readily to mealy-bug injury. Spray at the first sign of bugs.

What is one to do to get rid of the soft white fungous scale on coleus? I scrape it off, but this is not drastic enough. It is neither a fungus nor a scale you describe, but mealy bugs again. Spray with malathion or a house plant aerosol bomb. (See House Plants.)

What causes blistered or puckered leaves? It sounds like the work of the cyclamen mite, which attacks so many greeenhouse plants. (See Cyclamen.)

What can I do to stop a white moldy rot on coleus, kept as a house plant? There is no white mold on coleus, but you may have a combination of white woolly mealy bugs, very common on this plant, and a black rot, called "black leg" because it rots the stalks at the base. For the mealy bugs see House Plants; for the rot, destroy infected plants; pot new ones with fresh soil.

What causes white fungous growth? Changed from glazed to clay pot, but growth persists. Changing the pot won't affect mealy bugs on the foliage. Spray and spray again until you clean them up. (See answers to previous questions.)

COLUMBINE

How can one keep the roots of aquilegia from becoming infested with worms? (Minnesota.) The worms are probably millipedes, and usually they swarm around when a plant is weakened or dead from other causes, either disease or unfavorable cultural conditions.

What makes hybrid columbines pass out in a perennial bed where everything else is happy? (Pennsylvania.) Hybrid columbines, like hybrid delphiniums, are usually short-lived, but sudden passing out may be due to crown rot, a fungous disease; or to the columbine borer.

What remedy will prevent crown rot? (Alabama.) Crown rot in

Alabama is caused by *Sclerotium rolfsii,* a fungus that is generally prevalent in the soil and kept viable because it can attack so many different plants. Soil sterilization is difficult and not too satisfactory. Remove infected plants as soon as noticed and pour a terrachlor solution over the area.

What about the columbine borer? This is a salmon-colored caterpillar that works in the crown of the plant. All you can do is pull up and burn the victim and in the fall destroy all waste grass, weeds, and other debris which might harbor borer eggs over the winter.

The leaves of our columbine have little silvery-white lines all over them. Could you tell me the cause? (Rhode Island.) These are the serpentine tunnels of the columbine leaf miner. The larvae work inside the leaf and a small fly emerges to lay eggs for the next generation.

What is the cure for white line discolorations in leaves? (Illinois.) There is no cure, but picking off and burning all infested leaves as soon as noticed and cultivating the ground around the plants in fall and early spring will help prevent further infestations. Spraying with malathion may help.

What shall I do for plants turning brown because of a certain type of spider that gets on them? (Florida.) If this is red spider (the tiny mite which makes webs on the under side of the leaves), try sulfur dust, but not when the temperature is so high (above 90° F.) that the sulfur will burn the foliage. Malathion or other miticide is also effective.

COSMOS

What is the cause of annual cosmos turning brown and dying? (Nebraska.) It may be a bacterial wilt, but more likely a fungus stem blight. A grayish lesion girdles the stem and all parts above die. Spraying is of little value. Remove infected plants when noticed, and pull up and burn all tops after blooming.

CRAPEMYRTLE

How is mildew on crapemyrtle controlled? (Alabama.) Either by a dormant spray of 1 to 8 lime-sulfur when the buds start swelling; or by spraying with wettable sulfur, or Karathane, after growth starts. It is important to spray early; otherwise the white fungus will stunt the buds.

What spray formula will destroy white fly covering my crapemyrtles, causing smut? (Louisiana.) The smut is a fungous, sooty mold growing in the honeydew secreted by the white flies. Spray after blooming with malathion, 3 tbsp. to 3 gals. of water.

CRABAPPLE

Why do the leaves of a Bechtel's Crab curl up and drop in summer?

(New Jersey, Illinois.) Bechtel's Crab is peculiarly susceptible to the cedar and apple rust, a disease even more prevalent in the Middle West than in New Jersey. Spores are carried from the cedar galls in the spring and the resulting infection of orange spots on the crabapple leaves shows up in mid summer. Defoliation follows heavy infection.

How do you prevent rust? Never plant cedars and crabapples together. It is preferable not to have them on the same property, but at least get a windbreaker of a house or trees between the two as a barrier to windborne spores. Remove cedar galls in winter and early spring. Spray crabapples with colloidal sulfur or ferbam when leaves come out, and every 10 days until July.

I have sprayed my Malus floribunda but it is always full of aphids. What can I do? (Michigan.) Try spraying with a dinitro spray just before the buds break. (See Dormant Spraying.) If aphids appear during growing season, spray with malathion.

What treatment shall I give small flowering crab? No new growth, leaves shrivel, fuzzy white substance appears at crotches and twig intersections. (Rhode Island.) The fuzzy white substances are woolly aphids, controlled by spraying thoroughly with malathion. The tree is apparently dying from other causes—improper planting or some soil trouble.

What solution should be painted on trunks of young flowering crab trees in March to prevent green worms from climbing up and depositing their eggs? (Illinois.) None. No chemical should be applied directly to the trunk. If you have time and money to burn, apply a band of balsam wool and cover with Tanglefoot. This will prevent cankerworm moths from climbing the crabapples, but will not stop young worms from dropping onto crabapples from near-by shade trees. Spray with DDT or methoxychlor in May in any case, for the trunk treatment reduces infestation not more than 10 per cent.

CROCUS

Is there any method of preventing squirrels from eating crocus bulbs? (Massachusetts.) Plant the bulbs in wire baskets, which may be purchased for this purpose, or made at home from ½-in. wire mesh. A few naphthalene flakes may act as repellent, but too many will injure the bulbs with their fumes.

CYCLAMEN

What causes a cyclamen to become soft and die? I watered mine carefully through the bottom of the pot, but it died within 2 weeks. It sounds like bacterial soft rot, usually serious only when plants are too wet, or shaded, or not well ventilated. Your plant may have been infected when it came from the greenhouse.

What would cause a cyclamen to wilt suddenly and the bulb to rot?

Probably the bacterial soft rot suggested in the previous question. Possibly a fungous disease called stunt, although here the dying is usually gradual.

What is cyclamen mite, and how does it affect the plants? This mite is a microscopic spider, white to pale brown in color, that infests many varieties of ornamental plants causing puckering, curling, or other deformation of the leaves, and flower buds to become blackened and distorted. If plants are kept close together the mites can crawl from one to another. They can also be spread by hands, tools, clothing.

How do you control cyclamen mite? Once you get an infested plant in the home, it is best to discard it to save other house plants. Greenhouse operators should clean up their stock by endrin sprays (2 tsp. per gal. of water) applied weekly for several weeks. Pick off all deformed leaves at once.

DAHLIA

What causes dahlia roots to rot? (Florida.) Any one of several fungous or bacterial diseases. With verticillium wilt the lower leaves gradually lose their color, the roots are decayed, and the stem shows black streaks when cut across. With stem rot and soft bacterial rot, wilting is rather sudden.

How are the wilt diseases of dahlias cured? There is no cure. All you can do is remove infected plants immediately and plant healthy tubers in a new location, or sterilize soil with chloropicrin or methyl bromide.

When the tubers rot, is the soil too damp? (New York.) A heavy, wet soil encourages stem rot and bacterial wilt, but the organisms have to be present. Improving drainage and lightening the soil with sand or coal ashes will help.

There is a little brown worm about ½ in. long that eats my dahlia roots. How should I treat ground before I plant? (Ohio.) It is probably a millipede feasting on tissues rotting from one of the wilt diseaes just discussed. (See previous questions.)

When I dig my dahlias in the fall, the tubers are almost always rotted away. Why are gray-blackish insects present? (New York.) Doubtless millipedes again. They look brown to some, grayish to others. They are hard, with many legs, usually coiled into a circle, and almost always scavengers feeding on rotting tissue.

My bulbs are drying up and some show rot all through. How do you prevent this? (New York.) Botrytis, fusarium, and other fungi and bacteria may cause storage rots. Use care in digging to avoid wounds, store only well-matured tubers, avoid any frost damage, and keep at 40° F. in sand that is only very slightly moist. Too much moisture will increase rotting. Dusting tubers with captan before storage may help.

How is corrosive sublimate used to keep bulbs from rotting? (Missouri.) Wash the tubers to remove soil and then soak in a 1 to 1000 solution of corrosive sublimate (2 tablets to 1 qt. of water) for 30 minutes. Dry thoroughly before storing.

Some dahlia leaves have bright yellow mottling; is that mosaic, and what can be done? (Montana.) The mottling is a typical symptom of mosaic, a virus disease carried from one plant to another by aphids. There is usually dwarfing or stunting. Control aphids with contact sprays, and remove and burn infected plants.

What are the chief causes for dahlia "stunt"? (Illinois.) Either mosaic or the feeding of sucking insects, often leaf hoppers, but sometimes thrips or plant bugs. Stunted dahlias are short and bushy with an excessive number of side branches. Leaf hoppers cause the margins of the leaves to turn yellow, then brown and brittle—a condition known as hopper burn.

How do you control stunt caused by insects? Spray once a week with malathion, beginning early in the season and covering under side of leaves thoroughly. DDT will serve for leaf hoppers.

After plants are stunted, are the tubers good the following year? (New Jersey.) Yes, if the stunting was due to leaf hoppers and the tubers appear sound. But if the stunting was due to mosaic, a virus disease, the tubers should not be used.

What is the trouble with my dahlias, which start out grandly but then shrivel up, get curled leaves, and produce buds that do not open? (Illinois.) Probably stunt, due either to mosaic or insect feeding. (See preceding answers.)

My miniature dahlia is full of buds, but they rot. What is the matter? (Ohio.) It may be gray mold, the same type of botrytis blight that affects peony buds. Remove all diseased buds and spray with captan. Burn all plant tops in the fall.

How can I prevent mildew? (Pennsylvania.) Dust foliage with sulfur or spray with Mildex or Karathane especially in late summer.

If dahlias mildew badly at the end of the season, will the tubers be injured? (California.) Probably not, but mildew is a serious disease on the West coast, and dahlias should be sprayed or dusted with one of the above fungicides.

Is the borer which attacks dahlia stalks the corn borer? (New Jersey.) Yes, if the borers are flesh-colored when young, later turning smoky or reddish. If the caterpillar is brown, striped with white, it is the common stalk borer, also prevalent on corn, but using giant ragweed as its favorite food plant.

What can I do to prevent borers? (Illinois.) Clean up and burn stalks of all herbaceous plants in the fall. Include the weeds, for many of these harbor borers over winter. Spray or dust stalks with DDT once a week.

How do you prevent the little black flies from biting or stinging buds so they only partially open? (Vermont.) The tarnished plant bug is brownish rather than black, but it stings and blackens the buds. Control is difficult. Keep down the weeds and spray frequently with malathion or DDT.

European Corn Borer: adult, yellowish brown; larva, pink. Frequently attacks dahlias.

Last summer I found a lot of black bugs and some ladybugs on my blooms. The petals had holes in them. Were the little black bugs to blame? (Texas.) The black bugs were probably aphids or plant lice, controllable by spraying with malathion. If the "ladybugs" were green instead of red, they were diabrotica or cucumber beetles and responsible for the holes. (See Chrysanthemum.)

What can I do about aphids on roots? Have tried ground tobacco. (Wisconsin.) Tobacco dust in the ground should help, but pouring a solution of malathion in a shallow depression made around each dahlia stem will be a more potent remedy.

This year grasshoppers ate our dahlia blooms. Is there any way to prevent this? (Mississippi.) A poison bran bait scattered on the ground is the usual recommendation, but this is poisonous to birds and pets. Spray or dust the flowers with DDT or other stomach poison if the residue is not too objectionable. Keep down weeds. (See also Grasshoppers.)

How do you rid dahlias of snails? (Michigan.) A poison bait, made of 1 part calcium arsenate to 16 parts wheat bran, with enough water added to make a moist mash, scattered around plants, is said to be satisfactory in controlling snails in California, where they are a constant pest. Or try one of the metaldehyde slug baits, obtainable under commercial trade names such as Metameal or Snarol. (See also Slugs.)

How can I eliminate red spider? (California.) Dust with fine sulfur or spray with a miticide covering the under side of the leaves particularly.

Do thrips ever attack dahlia? How may they be protected? (Iowa.) They may infest the flowers, turning the petals whitish. Regular spraying with malathion or lindane for the control of leaf hoppers may discourage infestation by thrips. (See Gladiolus.)

How do I exterminate termites? (Texas.) Treat soil around the plants with chlordane or dieldrin. (See also Termites.)

DAPHNE

The leaves of my daphne are turning yellow. Why? (California.) This may be chlorosis, due to an alkaline soil which makes iron unavailable. Spray leaves with 2 teaspoons ferrous sulfate and ¼ teaspoon glue in a quart of water. Or treat the soil with iron chelates available under trade names. (See Chlorosis.) Your *Daphne odora* may also be dying from Armillaria root rot, which see.

DELPHINIUM

Last summer I lost a great number of my delphiniums. A creamy, seedy substance formed around the plants, making the roots rot off. Later it spread to the phlox and buddleia. What is it? (Ohio.) This is a good description of crown rot, caused by the fungus *Sclerotium delphinii* (in the South called *S. rolfsii*). White fungous threads, mycelium, form at the base of the stalk and spread over the ground. Seedlike bodies, sclerotia, are also formed, often in great numbers. The roots are attacked so that the plant is readily pulled up. This fungus attacks more than 100 species of ornamentals, and readily spreads to other plants in wet weather.

How shall I grow delphinium when the plants rot off at the ground and the earth turns white and rust color? (Kansas.) Another phase of crown rot. The sclerotia which are at first cream-colored turn reddish or rusty as they mature, and there may be so many crowded together at the base of the plant that it seems as if the earth itself had changed color.

How shall I keep delphinium from getting crown rot; how stop its spread to other plants? (Illinois.) Stopping the spread immediately is very important. Dig up an infected plant as soon as noticed, using a shovel so as to get all the surrounding soil harboring the sclerotia. If you pull up the plant and leave the sclerotia behind, they may live for months or years ready to infect other plants. Wrap the diseased specimen and soil in several thicknesses of newspaper and hurry it to the bonfire.

Will bichloride of mercury 1 to 1000 cure crown rot, or does the plant have to be destroyed? When is the best time to apply? (Massachusetts.) Usually it is not possible to save the plant already infected, but try to save neighboring plants by pouring 1 to 2 qts. of the solution into the space from which the diseased plant was removed and over the crowns of near-by plants. Sometimes a lightly infected specimen can be saved. Apply whenever the disease is noted.

Does the bichloride of mercury permanently sterilize the ground, or is crown rot likely to appear another year? You may expect crown rot every year in the same place. The bichloride apparently kills the mycelium but has no permanent effect on any sclerotia left beind in the soil. The disease reappears at the first sign of warm, humid weather. It is a good idea to remove soil over an area of 2 ft. across and 1 ft. deep, and replace with fresh earth.

Is there any other chemical to prevent crown rot? I have tried napthalene flakes. (Iowa.) Napthalene is somewhat effective in stopping the spread of the white mycelium, but it cannot be relied on to kill the sclerotia. Sulfur dust will likewise check the mycelial growth, terrachlor as a crown drench may be effective. The permanent remedy is to sterilize the soil, when all plants have been removed, with formaldehyde, methyl bromide, or chloropicrin. (See Soil Sterilization.)

Can delphiniums be replanted after sterilizing soil in bed where others died of sclerotium rot? (New Jersey.) Yes, if you use soil sterilizers according to directions and wait until all odor has disappeared from the soil before replanting—usually about 2 weeks. Naturally, put back only healthy plants. The treatment is not guaranteed; a new location is preferable.

What makes delphinium get a mildewed appearance and what can be done to prevent it? (New York.) This is powdery mildew, a fungus appearing as a white coating on the leaves. In the East it is seldom serious before late summer. Dust with sulfur, or use one of the combination sprays with copper as a fungicide.

Is it possible to prevent mildew? (Illinois, Minnesota, Colorado.) The mildew problem seems to increase in importance as one goes West, until a climax is reached in California. However, many of the new hybrid strains are fairly resistant to mildew, and dusting or spraying with sulfur or spraying with Mildex or Karathane gives reasonable control. There is no "prevention" except cleaning up and burning all old plant material.

Why do delphiniums mildew so badly? (California.) It's your famous California climate, which seems to encourage mildew on delphinium, roses, and other plants. But cheer up, troubles even up, and Easterners have to fight black spot and cyclamen mite as much as you do mildew. Try to get California strains of delphinium more or less resistant to mildew, and dust with sulfur or spray with Mildex or Karathane.

How do I prevent rust and white mold? (Wisconsin.) The white mold is mildew. (See answers to previous questions.) True rust is not very common on delphinium. Discolored patches on the leaves may be due to the broad mite or the leaf miner (which see).

How do you control black spot? This bacterial disease appears as tarry black spots on the leaves. It is not serious except in wet seasons, when it may be controlled by spraying with Bordeaux mixture or possibly streptomycin. In a normal season picking off infected leaves and cleaning up old stalks in autumn are sufficient.

How should dry Bordeaux mixture be diluted for spraying delphiniums when they come up in the spring? (Pennsylvania.) Use about half the strength recommended on the package, which usually gives directions for a potato spray. If your brand calls for 8 to 12 tablespoons per gallon, use 4 to 6, adding 2 tablespoons flour to the dry powder before stirring the water in very slowly. Strain through cheesecloth into the sprayer and use *immediately*.

Is there a remedy when the leaves curl and plants fail to bloom? Those that do bloom have green blossoms. (Utah.) This is a virus disease, probably aster yellows. There is no cure except taking out infected plants as soon as noticed and spraying with contact insecticides to control the leaf hoppers, the insect carriers of the virus. Such diseases are common in the Northwest.

Why do my delphiniums grow large and thrifty, have one blooming period, and then get a black rot? (Ohio.) There are various delphinium rots besides sclerotium crown rot, caused by at least 2 bacteria and several fungi. Rotting is usually worse in wet weather and with succulent tissue. Some growers feel that the act of cutting down the old stalks after blooming spreads the rot organisms.

What causes the yellowing of leaves on hybrids? When the plants were treated with nitrate of soda every 10 days, they took on a healthy green again. (Illinois.) You answered your own question: evidently your plants lacked nitrogen. But be careful about applying too much. Getting too succulent a growth will mean more rot diseases.

Why do my delphiniums turn yellow and dry? (Indiana.) Possibly due to fusarium wilt, this fungus being common in soils in the Middle West. There is usually a progressive yellowing of leaves from the base upward. But the yellowing may also be due to crown rot, lack of nitrogen, lack of water, or intense heat. Try a new location.

What causes delphinium buds to become black and wadded up? (Indiana.) The cyclamen mite, a light-colored spider mite too small to see with the naked eye, and a very serious pest on delphiniums. It deforms the leaves, blackens the flower buds, usually preventing bloom, and stunts the plant.

What can be done to overcome cyclamen mite on delphinium? (Wisconsin.) The treatment most generally approved is spraying weekly with endrin, 2 tsp. per gal. of water. Start spraying very early in the spring. Pick off deformed parts; discard severely infested plants.

Do coal ashes help in the control of mites? Some growers believe that a 2-in. layer of sifted coal ashes put on for the winter and left on for the shoots to come through in the spring aids in cutting down mite infestation.

What should be done for brown spots on under side of leaves of delphinium? (Illinois.) If these spots are rather glassy in appearance, they are due to the broad mite, which is not so harmful as the cyclamen mite and more readily controlled with sulfur dust or malathion.

What causes blighted areas in the leaves? The larvae of leaf miners feed inside the leaves, which collapse and turn brown over rather large areas, usually near the points. Remove and burn infested leaves. Spraying with malathion may help.

Why are there red lice during blooming time? (Michigan.) Why any calamity? These are the same aphids so prevalent on annual larkspur. Spray thoroughly and frequently with malathion.

Why do my young delphiniums get little red bugs and finally die? (Illinois.) These are aphids, plant lice. If you spray with a contact insecticide when they first appear, they will not get so numerous they will cause death. Your young delphiniums may die from other causes.

I have tried sulfur dust for the little red lice. How can I prevent them? (Michigan.) Sulfur dust will be of little benefit. You need a malathion spray.

My delphiniums always get orange lice on the under side of the leaves. When shall I start watching for them and what shall I do? (Michigan.) These aphids usually get serious toward midsummer, but sometimes appear in spring. When the leaves start cupping downward, looking like umbrellas, you always know red aphids are underneath. Use a spray rod with an angle nozzle so you can cover the under side of the leaves.

My delphinium leaves get infested with tiny red insects. Are they red spiders? (New York.) Probably they are red aphids. Red spiders are almost too small to see with the naked eye and form a mealy cobweb on the under side of the leaves. In either case malathion will work.

DOGWOOD

What can be done for bark borers on dogwood trees? (New Jersey.) Twig borers can be taken care of by cutting below the infested portion, but bark borers are best prevented by wrapping newly transplanted trees in Kraft crepe paper, extending from the crown up to the first branches. Leave on 2 years. After infestation borers may be surgically removed, but it is not always possible to save the tree. Spraying DDT or dieldrin on trunks monthly in summer will also help prevent borers.

I had 2 flowering dogwoods which I planted; 1 died, bark blistered, chipping off easily. Can the other tree be saved? (Ohio.) A crown canker disease might have that effect but I do not know of its occurring in Ohio. It may have been bark borers. (See previous question.) If you cut out all borers in remaining tree, wrap the trunk, and feed and water it; it may live.

Dogwood, pussy willow, other shrubs, and roses have some disease; are covered with scales of shell-like nature; trees finally die. What is the remedy? (Maryland.)   All these plants are subject to attack by scale insects, but they are of different types. Dogwood can have round scurfy scale or cottony cushion scale, white fluff under brown shell. Spray with miscible oil in spring before growth starts. (See Dormant Spraying.)

ELM

What is best to use for yellow striped bugs on Chinese elms in July? Little result from Red Arrow or Black Flag. (Ohio.)   This is the elm-leaf beetle, a chewing insect little affected by a contact insecticide like Red Arrow. Have your trees sprayed with DDT in June.

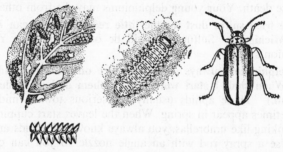

Elm Leaf Beetle: distinct yellow stripes; larvae black.

What spring care can be given to an elm which gets covered with small worms causing the leaves to turn brown and fall in midsummer? (New Jersey.)   Cankerworms chew foliage in May, but in June the dark, dragon-shaped larvae of the elm-leaf beetle skeletonize the leaves, causing the browning and defoliation. Two DDT sprays are best, the first after the leaves come out in May and the second in early June; otherwise, plan one treatment in late May. Power spraying by a tree expert is required.

What is a practical insecticide for Chinese elms? Affliction is a black caterpillar worm which attacks foliage. (New Jersey.)   This is the larval stage of the mourning-cloak butterfly, but readily controlled by power spraying with DDT.

What is the scale infecting the bark of my Chinese elms? (New York.)   Elm scurfy scale and 2 or 3 other scale insects may appear on elm bark, causing death of branches and occasionally of young trees. Use a dormant spray before growth starts, such as a miscible oil at 1 to 25 dilution. (See also Dormant Spraying.)

Why did the elm tree give off a black secretion so that the lily bed

under it looks like a city garden? (New Hampshire.)   The secretion was colorless honeydew from aphids on the elm, but when it dropped onto the lily leaves a black fungus grew in it. (See Sooty Mold.) There is no control except spraying the elm for aphids and the expense may not be warranted.

The leaves of the 5-year-old elm in our vegetable garden turn yellow and fall off in August. (Ohio.)   The elm-leaf beetle may be the cause, or the Dutch elm disease, or cephalosporium wilt, or a new virus disease, common in Ohio, called pholem necrosis. Call in a tree expert for diagnosis, or send specimens of twigs to your Experiment Station at Wooster.

What is the Dutch elm disease?   A wilt disease, first reported in Ohio in 1930 and in New Jersey in 1933. It is transmitted by bark beetles which came in from Europe on elm burls imported for furniture veneer, wood for dish crates, etc. Wilting is followed by yellowing, curling, and dropping of leaves. When the twigs are cut across, the vessels are black, but this is also true of cephalosporium and verticillium wilts, so that laboratory cultures are needed for a true diagnosis. So far there is no real control except destruction of infected trees to prevent spread. Keeping trees healthy by proper spraying, feeding, watering and pruning reduce infestation of the dark beetle carriers, which lay their eggs only in weakened or dead tissue.

What causes Chinese elm trees to bleed so long after pruning? Mine have been discharging for two years. (Illinois.)   Elms are subject to a condition known as slime flux, which means a continuous exudation from wounds due to positive pressure in the sap. Often this bleeding flux has an alcoholic odor and attracts insects.

What will dry up sap flowing from borer hole wound? (Oklahoma.)   It is slime flux. Sometimes it helps to drill a hole below the bleeding wound into the heartwood and insert a drainpipe. This carries the flux out beyond the tree trunk and gives the wound a chance to heal.

EVERGREENS

Is there any spray with an odor which will keep the dogs off my evergreens? (Tennessee.)   There are on the market many dog repellents with such descriptive names as Dawg-gone, Dogz-off, Dogsix, Scram, Anti-Dog, Marvel Dust. Black Leaf 40 is supposed to be a dog repellent, but whenever I spray with this nicotine sulfate the dogs persist in following me all around the garden.

Is there anything else I can do to keep dogs off evergreens? The repellent sprays have but a fleeting effect. (Wisconsin.)   Lasting and inconspicuous are the wire shrubbery guards, placed 3 or 4 around each shrub. If they are unavailable and you can spare some wire coat hangers, borrow some wire cutters and make your own guards. File one end to a point, make a right-angle bend so that the point sticks out from the tree, and put the other end in the ground.

Is it advisable to use a dormant spray of miscible oil for pines and junipers? What concentration of Scale-Oil or Scale-O?   Yes, if you have a serious infestation of scale insects. Spray only on a bright day, before new growth starts, with the temperature about 45° F., and follow manufacturer's directions for dilution, usually 1 to 30 or 1 to 35 for evergreens. Oil sprays should not be used every year but only when definitely needed.

Should evergreens have a dormant spray in early spring for red spider? (New York.)   Yes, if the infestation was serious the preceding year; otherwise, rely on Ovex or malathion and syringing with the hose during the growing season. If you use a dormant oil spray, wait 30 days before applying any form of sulfur.

What is the most effective control measure for bagworms on evergreens? (Illinois.)   Pick off the bags whenever you see them during the winter. Spray with lead arsenate, malathion or toxaphene when the young worms start feeding, probably in late May. (See Bagworms.)

What is the best treatment for gall on evergreens? (New York.)   Depends on the evergreen. If cedar, then cut out the rust gall before the spore horns develop; if spruce, spray to kill the gall aphids before new growth starts, using a malathion spray. Cut out the galls on blue spruce in early summer. (See also Spruce.)

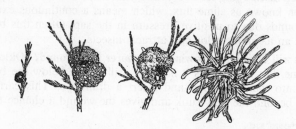

Stages in the development of rust galls on cedar.

What can I put on to prevent grasshoppers? They are destroying the evergreens around a new home. (Ohio.)   Grasshoppers occasionally are destructive to evergreens. The best control is a DDT or methoxychlor spray. (See Grasshoppers.)

The inside of my evergreens are brown with needles fallen off, but the outside looks all right. Could this be caused by grasshoppers in them all the time? (Maryland.)   Possibly (see Grasshoppers), or perhaps it is due to red-spider injury. If the browning occurs in late summer and fall, it is merely natural maturing of the needles. The individual leaves of evergreens do not stay on forever, but ripen and drop as any other tree. The new outer leaves stay green while the older inside foliage is lost each year.

What feeding procedure should be followed to revive dying evergreens? (Illinois.) Feeding may kill them off more quickly, just like giving a large meal to a person with high fever. Have the cause of the dying evergreen diagnosed by an expert before you try to revive it by feeding.

EUONYMOUS

Why do the stems of my Euonymus radicans, 15 years old, growing on cement garage, become white? (Massachusetts.) Your vine is completely covered with the euonymus scale. Look closely and you will see thin white sticks, the male scales, and brownish oval females. When the young scales hatch, they are yellowish and crawl slowly about, but the adults are motionless. Scale is always worse on a vine attached to a wall.

Oyster-shell scale, one of the most common pests on fruit trees, is controlled by spraying with a miscible oil spray; that is, one which will readily mix with water.

How shall I check or prevent euonymus scale? Use a dormant spray, miscible oil or dinitro in spring before growth starts; in summer, when young scales hatch, apply a combination of malathion and DDT. Temperature must be above 45° F. for spring spraying. Try to get the spray in back of the vine, close to the wall.

What is a satisfactory treatment for blight of evergreen shrub euonymus? (Virginia.) You probably have euonymus scale, treatment for which is given in previous question. Sometimes, in the South and West, euonymus foliage is covered with the white coating of the mildew fungus. A sulfur spray or dust will control this, but it must not be used within 30 days of an oil spray.

FERNS

What is wrong with a fern when it gets minute white specks all over it? Also brown ones which are larger? The white ones can be moved

but the brown ones are tight. A perfect description of the fern scale. The white bodies are male scales, and those that move are young ones; the brown pear-shaped objects are female scales, which stay put. A severe infestation ruins the fern.

I have used Black Leaf 40 and soap without success for the fern scales. What shall I try now? Try spraying with malathion, following directions carefully, and washing off with a pure water spray several hours later. Remove badly infested fronds.

Fern is covered with brown spots and a sticky substance on back of leaves. Friend insists these are not spores but living creatures. However, spots don't move. What are they? Probably the soft brown scale or the smooth brown hemispherical scale common on ferns. The sticky substance is honeydew. If you can't get rid of them with a brush dipped in soapsuds, try malathion or house plant aerosol bomb.

What should you do for moldy-looking spots on ferns? Your spots are likely mealy bugs. (See House Plants.)

What is the most effective treatment for white lice on ferns? Do you mean white flies, those tiny mothlike creatures? (See House Plants.)

My maidenhairfern gets brown places in the leaves; cause and cure? Nematode injury is a possibility; this may cause brownish areas in leaves, although more often they are black bands. Remove and burn infested leaves.

I have a staghorn fern attacked by worms each year; they eat foliage at night, hide in ground in day. What will kill the worm and not affect the fern? (Florida.) This is the Florida fern caterpillar, pale green changing to black, which feeds at night, and may strip a fern in a day or two. Dusting with DDT or methoxychlor will probably be effective.

What laces fern leaves? We can find no insect to cause it. (Kansas.) Possibly the Florida fern caterpillar, with its nocturnal habits, has come to Kansas. (See previous question.)

Will Bordeaux hurt Boston ferns? A weak 2–2–50 solution of Bordeaux mixture should be fairly safe. It is sometimes recommended to control the rhizoctonia damping-off disease which may rot the lower fronds of Boston ferns.

What causes rust on sword fern? (Washington.) Rust is a fungous disease somewhat common on outdoor ferns. In the Northwest there are 8 fern rusts which have fir as an alternate host, causing white blisters on the fir needles. Ferns and firs should not be grown close together.

FIR

The lower branches of several fir trees are dying. Is this usual in this type of evergreen? (New Jersey.) There is usually a definite reason when branches die, even though it may be unfavorable location, crowding, or injury from red spiders. Lower branches of firs are occasionally infected with a fungous needle-and-twig blight. Prune out and burn infected parts.

Four beautiful Douglasfirs have died on our property this past year. Is it caused by an insect between bark and wood and will it spread to more trees? (Washington.)   Firs in the Northwest may succumb to various rust diseases and to the dwarf mistletoe. Bark beetles are also a possibility. The latter will spread to other trees if infested dead wood is left unburned. Call in a tree expert for exact diagnosis.

FUCHSIA

How can small white flies infesting fuchsias be controlled? (California.)   White flies seem to be inevitable on fuchsia, whether it be a greenhouse plant or grown outdoors as in California. The important thing is to spray for the nymph stage, when the white flies look like pale-greenish scales. Spray weekly with malathion until eradicated.

Black spots appear on under side of fuchsia leaves which turn yellow. Cause and remedy?   There is a rust which comes in brown spots on under side of leaves, but yellowing of leaves is probably due to sucking by white flies and the black spots are insect eggs or excrement. (For control see previous question.)

What causes root rot in fuchsia? (Kansas.)   Probably a waterlogged soil, although a verticillium wilt has been reported from fuchsias growing outdoors in California.

GAILLARDIA

How can I keep grubs out of the stems of gaillardias?   Your grubs may be larvae of the common stalk borer, with the best control depending on cleaning up all weeds and woody stems in autumn. Frequent spraying with DDT may partly repel borers. (See also Dahlia.)

GARDENIA

What is the best insecticide for the mealy bugs on gardenias? Probably malathion. (See Mealy Bugs.)

My gardenia has a little white speck that looks like mold, but when you mash it, it is alive. What is it?   The specks are mealy bugs. Clean up the first you see, before the infestation gets serious.

How do you get rid of lice on gardenias?   You probably mean mealy bugs, which see. If you refer to aphids, the same spray will do.

My Capejasmine, which grows outdoors, had some sort of insect eat a fringe around the leaves, but I never can find the insect. What can I spray with? (North Carolina.)   It may have been some sort of weevil with nocturnal habits. Spray the foliage with DDT.

How should I rid my gardenia plant of beetles? (New Jersey.)
Depends on kind of beetles. Fuller's rose weevil, a gray-brown snout
beetle, is sometimes reported on gardenia. It feeds at night. Spray with
methoxychlor.

GERANIUM

**Is there any way to prevent geranium stalk rot? Some of mine rot
each winter, but I do not think they are too wet.** Stem rot is usually
associated with poor drainage or excessive watering. Start with cuttings from healthy plants placed in fresh or sterilized sand.

**About a third of my geranium slips have shriveled at the ground,
turned black, and died. What is the cause?** Either a fungus or a bacterial stem rot. Take cuttings from healthy plants and place in clean
new sand. Keep slips on dry side.

**What spray should be used to kill the tiny white insects on under
part of leaves of a rose geranium?** These are white flies, hard to kill
when they get to the moth stage. Spray with malathion using 1 tbsp.
per gal. of water.

**My choicest pelargoniums have green bugs. How can I get rid of
these pests?** Spray with malathion for aphids.

**After pruning geraniums and using a 45 per cent angle the stems
turn black and rot back for 4 or 5 inches. What can be done? (California.)** Try frequent pinching back instead of occasional heavy
pruning. When you prune, do it close to a node and disinfect your
knife between cuts in 5 per cent formalin, or denatured alcohol.

GLADIOLUS

How do I recognize thrips on my glads? (Wisconsin.) The gladiolus thrips is a small slender insect, 1/16 in. long and only as wide as
a small needle. When young, it is yellow, but changes to black as an
adult. It feeds by rasping petals and leaf surface. It is hard to find
because it hides under the leaf sheaths and inside the flowers.

**What causes gladioli to fleck or get speckled and the foliage to turn
whitish? (Wisconsin.)** These are typical results of thrips injury. Infested spikes may fail to bloom, or the flowers may be spotted, or they
may dry and shrivel.

**Does the planting of onions near the gladioli increase the possibility
of thrips on the galdiolus? (Illinois.)** No, the onion thrip is a different species.

**What is the best spray for gladioli to avoid the difficulty caused by
thrips? (New York.)** Spray or dust plants every 10 days with DDT,
lindane or dieldrin.

**How high should gladiolus plants be before you start spraying and
how often after the first time? (Wisconsin.)** Start when the plants are

not more than 6 ins. high and repeat weekly for about 6 weeks, or until flowering.

Why do my glads bloom only partially? Only 2 or 3 of the lower flowers open. Should the bulbs be left in the ground all winter? (Oklahoma.) Thrips are probably to blame. Take up the corms and treat them with 5% DDT or 1% dieldrin dust. Make sure also all old tops and debris are burned in the fall, for thrips may live through an Oklahoma winter. Plant in a new location if possible.

Is it harmful to next year's plants to leave thrip-infested gladiolus bulbs in ground during winter? (New York.) In New York, thrips would presumably be killed out over the winter, but the corms might harbor various fungous diseases. Why not clean up?

Will it be safe to plant new gladiolus bulbs in the same ground affected by thrips this past summer? (Minnesota.) I think you can rely on a Minnesota winter being cold enough to kill out the thrips.

If in storing my gladiolus bulbs I keep the temperature near 40° F. from December 1 to March 1, will I be free of thrips? No, you will need to treat the bulbs in storage, or else dip them before planting, or both.

I am using naphthalene flakes on my gladiolus bulbs this winter to check thrips. Will you tell me when, how long, and how much to use? Use 5%DDT or 1% dieldrin dust on the corms for greater effectiveness and safety.

I lost almost 1000 glads this last season. My husband refuses to use naphthalene flakes, as he says they injure the bulbs. How about this? See above statement.

I have to store my gladioli, tigridia and zephyranthes, side by side in the fruit closet. Should they all be treated? (Michigan.) The gladiolus thrips does infest tigridia, its near relative. So far as I know the galdiolus thrips has not been reported on zephyranthes.

Is Semesan good for treating glad bulbs in spring before planting? It is used to control scab, a bacterial disease, and sometimes thrips. Soak for 7 hours in a 1 per cent solution.

I have heard that soaking bulbs for thrips will delay blooming for 2 weeks. Is it true? (Wisconsin.) Disinfectants frequently have a slight retarding effect on growth and bloom; the length of delay varies with circumstances.

If glad bulbs are put in DDT dust this fall, do they need treating before planting in spring to kill thrips? Dipping before planting as well as dusting is a double precaution and will take care of scab as well as thrips.

Are there any cultural practices which aid in the control of thrips? Digging early in the fall, before the corms are quite mature, and cutting off and burning the tops before the thrips can work down into the corms will help.

When bulbs are taken from ground there appears a brown scale or spot. Is this a disease, and what steps may be taken? (Virginia.) This is probably scab, a bacterial disease which shows as circular black depressions with a raised margin. Clean off husks before planting in the spring. Discard corms where the scab has gone through to the corm itself and treat the rest in 1 to 1000 bichloride of mercury for 2 hours, or else for 5 minutes in calomel, 1 oz. to 1 gal. of water.

The tips of the leaves start turning brown, and this continues down the stem until the plant dies and bulbs rot. What will correct this? (Indiana.) This may be scab, although usually there are definite spots on the leaves. It may also be dry rot, a fungous disease which turns the leaves yellow and produces dark sunken lesions on the corms and root decay. Discard all spotted corms, treat before planting, and, if possible, practice a 4-year rotation, that is, do not replant gladioli in infested soil inside 4 years.

How do you treat gladiolus bulbs for fusarium yellows? (Indiana.) You can't entirely prevent yellows by corm treatment. The fungus lives in the soil and is widely distributed throughout the Middle West. Some varieties are more resistant than others. Wait at least 4 years before replanting gladioli on diseased soil. Use only corms that bear cormels; treat as for scab.

If space is limited and you must replant gladiolus bulbs in the same place, is there any way of inoculating the soil against disease and thrips? (Mississippi.) You can't inoculate it, but you can disinfect a small area with soil sterilizers. (See Soil Sterilization.)

GLOXINIA

What causes gloxinia buds to blast when nicely started? Sometimes a gray mold fungus, botrytis, of the same genus that causes peony buds to blast. Usually poor ventilation and excessive humidity are contributing causes. Remove all diseased parts as soon as noticed.

GOLDENGLOW

My goldenglow was eaten up this year by beetles, light green with black spots. What were they? (Kansas.) These were diabrotica, or spotted cucumber beetles. Try a DDT or methoxychlor dust.

GOURDS

How can I keep insects from ruining fancy gourds? (Georgia.) Gourds are afflicted by the same pests and diseases as cucumbers. A combination spray of methoxychlor, malathion and captan, should take care of wilt, borers, cucumber beetles, aphids, and white flies more or less successfully. Start spraying when the plants are small and repeat at 10-day to 2-week intervals. For chewing insects alone methoxychlor may be used as a spray or dust. Wipe the gourds with a disinfectant to prevent spotting after harvest.

GUM

Is there anything I can do to prevent the beetles from taking to the gum tree? (Maryland.) Do you mean Japanese beetles? Have your tree sprayed with DDT in early July and twice more at 2-week intervals.

HACKBERRY

How can leaf galls in hackberry trees be eradicated? (Colorado.) These galls are caused by plant lice. Spray with malathion when leaves are half out.

HAWTHORN

With what shall red hawthorns be sprayed when red cedars surround them? (New York.) Spray several times during May with wettable sulfur or ferbam.

What should I do about a sort of mildew which turns the leaves on my English hawthorn yellow and causes them to fall in midsummer? (Iowa.) The orange rust will cause defoliation, and so will a fungous leaf spot, to be controlled by spraying with ferbam or captan in May. If you have true mildew, a white coating on the leaves and buds, spray with 1 to 50 lime-sulfur before the buds open and after the petals have fallen.

What is the remedy for the lesser borer in the trunk of Paul's Scarlet Hawthorn? I am not sure which borer you mean. If it is one that brings sawdust to the mouth of holes, you can gas it with a few drops of Bore-Kill, sealing up the hole with putty or gum. If it is the flatheaded borer, keep your tree growing vigorously, paint pruning scars and other wounds, and perhaps try a repellent wash on the trunk—DDT or dieldrin.

HELENIUM

What shall I do for white grubs in roots of helenium? (Michigan.) There is not much you can do for plants where the roots are already eaten off. White grubs are usually worse in land recently taken over from sod. Perhaps you can transplant your heleniums to a bed that has been in cultivation for a long time. Spading a bed and leaving it rough over the winter will kill some grubs. You can work chlordane or dieldrin into the soil as a preventive measure.

What about the black "bugs" on helenium? (New Jersey.) The chief offenders are small black snout beetles, which start chewing the young shoots in early spring and often keep working until flowering.

Frequent spraying with methoxychlor or dieldrin keeps them fairly well in check. Later in the summer black aphids may appear. You can add malathion to the spray or use a separate application of malathion.

HEMLOCK

Hemlock branches turned brown and died until 4 or 5 had to be cut off. What can be the cause? (Tennessee.) It might be red-spider injury, or a fungous blight. You can dust with sulfur or spray with Ovex or other miticide for the former; for the latter you can only cut out and burn infected limbs.

HIBISCUS

What makes the leaves on Chinese hibiscus dry up and fall off? (Wyoming.) It is hard to say. There is a fungous blight, a stem rot, and a leaf spot which might have such symptoms, but your trouble is more likely one of water relations—either too dry soil or one waterlogged from overwatering.

The buds on my hibiscus formed but before blossoming turned brown and dropped off. Why? (Maine.) If you had a spell of rainy weather, it might have been botrytis blight, gray mold, which possibly might have been prevented by spraying with captan.

HICKORY

What spray will kill the grubs that get in hickory nuts? (Ohio.) These are the larvae of the hickory-nut weevil in all probability. Spraying has not been recommended for the control of this pest. The larvae leave the nuts in the late fall and pass the winter in the soil, and it has been suggested that harvesting early and fumigating with methyl bromide would kill the grubs and so prevent them from producing weevils for another year. However, this is probably not feasible for the homeowner with 1 or 2 hickory trees.

HOLLYHOCK

What is the cause of the rusting, yellowing, and dropping of foliage of hollyhocks? (Maine.) Rust is due to the rust fungus, which produces its spores in little reddish pustules on the under side of the leaves. Yellow areas appear on the upper surface, and with a bad case of rust the leaves turn yellow, wither, and may fall off. There are usually rust lesions on the stem as well as on the leaves.

Is there any way to prevent rust on hollyhocks? (Connecticut.) Remove and burn infected leaves as soon as noticed, and burn all old stalks and leaves in the fall. Dust with sulfur or ferbam starting in early spring, being careful to cover the under surface of the leaves.

I used dusting sulfur early on my hollyhocks but was unable to get more. What else could be used in place of it? (Maine.) Either

Ferbam or Sulfur will keep, so one can order it early, and keep a supply on hand.

I sprayed my hollyhocks from the beginning with Evergreen. Why didn't it stop the rust? (Maine.) There is no reason why it should, as Evergreen is a contact insecticide meant for the control of sucking insects. It might have some effect on red spiders, which turn hollyhock leaves yellow, but it would do nothing for the rust fungus.

Hollyhocks in different sections rot out. Why? I've put road ashes, lime, peatmoss in, as section is damp. (New Jersey.) Haven't you any well-drained place that has ordinary good garden soil? Any self-respecting plant might rot in such a mixture. Sand is the only thing you haven't tried, and that might work. Don't forget that hollyhocks are biennials. They die naturally after blooming.

HONEYSUCKLE

How can I exterminate aphids on honeysuckle? (Kentucky.) It is rather difficult, for the aphids congregate on the young shoots in great numbers and dwarf the leaves. Even the flower buds may be injured. Spray frequently with malathion; start when you see the first few aphids, and not the first few hundreds.

HOSTA

My hosta last fall looked lacelike, the leaves were so badly eaten. What is the cause and what shall I do? (Ohio.) Slugs will have this effect on hosta leaves. A metaldehyde bait is recommended (see Slugs).

HOUSE PLANTS

What are the white plant lice that look like cotton that come on house plants? These are mealy bugs, sucking insects like aphids. They are prevalent in greenhouses and on many house plants—coleus, croton, cactus, crassula, gardenia, poinsettia, rubber plant, and many others. A severe infestation is evidence of neglect.

What can be done to rid house plants of woolly aphis? These are mealy bugs. It is easier to prevent them than get rid of them. Keep your plants frequently syringed or washed, in a not-too-hot or dry atmosphere. Remove the first bit of white fluff you see with a tiny cotton swab wrapped around a toothpick and dipped in alcohol (omit the alcohol for cactus). Try house plant aerosol bomb.

How do you rid house plants of the white mealy bug that leaves a sticky substance on the leaves? The sticky substance is honeydew, secreted by various sucking insects. If mealy bugs get started despite picking them off, spray with malathion. Have the plants somewhat shaded from the sun and rinse with pure water several hours later.

Should house plants with mealy bugs be repotted after control? It is not necessary if you got control; if you did not, repotting would do no good. Of course repot your plants if their growth requires it.

Do you know a home remedy good for plant lice? Just ordinary soap and water will do, but malathion is much preferable. Aphids are not hard to kill if they are sprayed frequently.

My house plants show a brown scale and a sticky substance. Can the scale be avoided by treating the sticky substance? It's the other way around. You treat the scale and then it can no longer secrete the honeydew. Wash scales off in strong soap solution, scrubbing them off with a brush, and then spray with malathion spray, as given for aphids.

We are bothered with very small white bugs that suck the under side of leaves; when the plant is shaken, they fly off and settle back again. What are they? These are white flies. Spray the plants in the morning, before the flies get active, with malathion hitting the under side of the leaves.

What can you use to get rid of the little white maggots in the soil? These are fly maggots, often present in soil with much humus or plants fed with organic fertilizers. Water the plants with a solution of chlordane or dieldrin. Or the soil may be baked before using for potting.

What causes the small black flies on house plants, similar to fruit flies? These breed from the maggots or eggs that came in with the potting soil. Some recommend watering the soil with lime water as for earthworms, or working in tobacco dust, or watering in any contact insecticide.

Is there any way to keep red spiders off my indoor plants, other than constantly washing them off under running water? A frequent bath is the best way to keep red spiders in check. Any contact spray, or house plant aerosol bomb, will help fight spider mites.

How do you get rid of red spider in the greenhouse? Frequent syringing with pure water is helpful and this may be followed with a sulfur dust. However, too much syringing in a greenhouse is often accompanied by increased plant disease, in which case spraying with malathion or aramite or using a phosphate aerosol smoke bomb would be more satisfactory.

A small insect inhabiting greenhouse looks like a crab, spins web from leaf to leaf. Have tried dusting and force of plain water. What shall I use? Probably some species of spider, harmless to plants.

Can insects, scale, etc., be controlled in a small greenhouse by fumigating only? You will probably have to supplement with some spraying or aerosol smoke bombs. Nicotine fumigation is effective against aphids and does fairly well for thrips, but is not so good for white fly and scale.

Is there a way to destroy angleworms in a potted plant? Dust the surface of the soil with hydrated lime and water it in, or else water the plants with lime water. Earthworms do no damage in themselves, but they clog up the drainage hole.

Having trouble with soil nematodes in my house-plant soil. Can you recommend a procedure to be used on a small scale? Your potting soil may be fumigated with chloropicrin, tear gas, sold as Larvacide, and available in small quantities with complete directions for use, or methyl bromide. (See also Soil Sterilization.)

What is the yellowish-brown scale which forms on top of soil in pots? An indication that your soil needs cultivating and a little oxygen allowed to get into it. Scratch it up with the tines of an old fork.

My jade-plant, peperomia, and some others have a rust on the under side of the leaves. What is it? Probably not an organic disease so much as a reaction to environment, possibly too much water and not enough oxygen in the soil.

What causes powdery mildew to appear on house plants? This is a fungous growth that usually comes only when plants are kept in a too-moist atmosphere—something that seldom happens with house plants. Dusting sulfur will control it.

What will destroy or prevent wiggle-tails, or mosquitoes, in water garden or pots in the house without injuring the plants? Try spraying with pyrethrum, or rotenone.

HYDRANGEA

What shall I use on my hydrangeas to prevent brown spots on the leaves? (Texas.) To control leaf spot, spray with captan or dust with sulfur. Remove and burn infected leaves.

What solution should be used for mildew on hydrangeas, or should the soil be treated? (Texas.) Treating the soil won't do any good for mildew. Dust with fine dusting sulfur, or spray with Mildex or Karathane. Sometimes spraying with potassium sulfide has been recommended for the Southwest.

IMPATIENS

Why do my impatiens plants get a sticky substance on them? They have something like grains of sugar, especially variety sultani. These grains of sugar are honeydew secreted either by scale insects or aphids or else nymphs of white flies. (See House Plants.)

IRIS

Some of my iris rhizomes are rotting. Although the shell seems dry, the inside, if opened before destruction is complete, is wet and slimy.

What is this? (New York.) This is a perfect description of bacterial soft rot. You put your thumb on a supposedly firm shell only to have it sink into slimy, vile-smelling goo. The rot may start in the leaves, following punctures by young borers, and there is often a water-soaked appearance to the leaves.

What can I do to overcome soft rot in iris? (New York.) In the first place, take control measures against the borer (see below). Next, remove and destroy immediately any rotting rhizomes. Dig them out with surrounding soil and disinfect your trowel. If the rot gets very bad over a whole bed, plan on treating all the rhizomes at the time of division, right after flowering. Take up the clumps, separate the rhizomes, cut out all soft tissue, cut leaves back to 6-in. fans and immerse rhizome and fan for 30 minutes in 1 to 1000 solution of bichloride of mercury or for 1 hour in a Semesan solution, 1 oz. to 3 gals. of water. Work on newspapers so all debris can be gathered up and burned. Leave treated plants out in the sun for a day or two before replanting.

Is there any way I can clean up infested iris without relocating it? (New York.) After you have treated it in the disinfectant you can pour the solution into the iris bed and be fairly safe in replanting. There is less danger of rot if the upper surface of the rhizome is kept exposed to the sun rather than covered with soil.

Will applying hydrated lime to our soil prevent the dying out and disappearance of bearded iris? (Georgia.) No. Iris is said to like lime, but so do the bacteria that cause soft rot. If the soil is slightly acid, it will deter the bacteria responsible for the disappearance of your iris.

How do you destroy the borer which attacks iris, cosmos, calendula, etc.? (Illinois.) It is not the same borer. The iris borer, a fat, flesh-colored caterpillar with a dark head, specializes in iris. In cosmos it is probably the stalk borer. Sanitary measures are most important in getting rid of iris borers. If you are dividing the iris and treating for soft rot, do it early while the borer is still in the stalk and before it has eaten out the rhizome; in any case, before it has left the rhizome and pupated in the soil. The moth lays its eggs on old leaves and debris during the fall. Sometime in October or November, after a killing frost, clean up and burn all this old material, leaving only a clean fan of new leaves. In the spring start spraying new growth with DDT weekly for 3 to 4 applications.

Have you found an effective means of controlling the iris borer? An arsenic spray doesn't do much good. (Pennsylvania.) Sanitation is more important than spraying, but 3 to 4 applications of emulsifiable DDT are said to give good control. You have to start early in the spring, to get the borers before they actually enter the leaves.

What ate long holes or skletonized my vesper iris seedlings during

the summer? (New York.) My guess is that slugs were at work, but a zebra caterpillar also chews iris leaves. Spray or dust with DDT.

Does anyone but me know anything about the little round iris-wrecking beetle? Have fought it for years but never found it mentioned. (Connecticut.) A small, round, flat, dark weevil is said to eat iris pods and sometimes the petals. Try spraying with methoxychlor or dieldrin.

How can you lick thrips in iris? Does dark, rainy weather foster their growth? (Minnesota.) Thrips are especially disastrous to Japanese iris, but bearded iris may also be infested. DDT forcibly sprayed into the leaf bases will give about as good control as anything. You can also try dieldrin. Thrips are usually more numerous in hot, dry weather.

What is the meaning of brown spots on iris leaves? (Texas.) This is a fungous leaf-spot disease, usually fairly well controlled by cleaning up all old leaves in the fall, but occasionally requiring 2 or 3 applications of captan during the summer.

Why do iris leaves turn brown and dry during July and August? (Wyoming.) Crown or rhizome rot fungi may be the cause, or perhaps merely overcrowding and lack of water. If there are any signs of gray mold, or white fungous threads with seedlike bodies, remove and destroy infected rhizomes. Sterilize the area with Vapam.

Why do my iris blooms last only 1 or 2 days and die? (Oregon.) The life span of a single iris flower is only a day or two; that's the way it is made. But if you mean that after 1 or 2 flowers come out your whole stalk withers and dies, that may be some fungous disease working at the crown, or possibly a very serious infestation of thrips.

My beautiful iris garden is being ruined by root-knot nematodes. What can I do? (Arkansas.) The root-knot nematode is one of the worst Southern problems since it cannot be killed by winter cold nor readily starved because it attacks so many kinds of garden plants. If you have any land that has not been growing nematode-susceptible plants, you can start a new iris garden there. You'll have to start with new rhizomes also. If you must use the same location, you can take out the iris and disinfect the soil with Vapam, methyl bromide, or ethylene dibromide. (See Nematodes; Soil Sterilization.)

IVY

What can be done to keep red spider from killing house ivy? Give it a weekly bath. Water is the very best deterrent for spider mites, and if the foliage is washed frequently the creatures will never get started. If, however, the leaves are yellow and cobwebby, dip the vines in a malathion or chlorobenzilate solution.

My ivy gets a brown (looks like a flaxseed) sucking insect on it. I

have tried repeatedly to eliminate it. What is it? If it is brown and thin, it is evidently the soft brown scale, and not the white oleander scale which is equally common on ivy. Frequent spraying with malathion when the young are hatching and the scales are vulnerable is supposed to keep them under control.

How do I get rid of the tiny brown slugs on the leaves of an ivy plant? These are probably scale. (See previous question.) The best way to keep the plant free from them is to note the first one that appears and wipe it off with a soapy rag.

My English Ivy was infested with scale in September; picked off most of it and then noticed a sticky clear fluid oozing from the leaves. Is it from the scale? Yes, honeydew secreted by the insect. You will have to spray to clean it up.

My German Ivy is defoliated by a minute black insect. What is it and how can I make it feel very unwelcome? It is a black aphid, very common on ivy. Spraying with, or dipping in, a solution of malathion will make this plant louse unwelcome. So will the weekly bath that keeps red spider in check.

What makes ivy plants wilt and the leaves turn yellow? Red spider, usually encouraged by too dry an atmosphere, will cause leaves to turn yellow, but a bacterial disease, encouragd by too-high humidity and too-high temperatures, will also cause yellowing of leaves and sometimes their wilting if there are bacterial lesions on the petioles. This disease would be far more common in a greenhouse than in the dry air of the average home.

What causes new leaves on grapeivy to dry and drop? Grapeivy is susceptible to a fungous leaf spot and die back, which may kill the young leaves. Spraying with captan will control it. More probably your grapeivy does not like its soil conditions. The new leaves will dry if the soil is either too wet or too dry.

JAPANESE CHERRY

Why did my two Japanese cherries die after the fourth blooming year? (Illinois.) It sounds as if they might have had a harmful spray. An oil spray too strong, or applied when it is too cold, can kill ornamental trees.

JUNIPER

What spray shall I use for juniper scale? (Pennsylvania.) If your bushes are not too close to any painted surface, spray with 1 to 9 dilution of lime-sulfur before the new growth starts, about the first week in April in Pennsylvania. If your junipers are close to the house, this spray will discolor the paint and you should use a miscible oil or malathion during the summer. (See Dormant Spraying; also Evergreens.)

How can I keep bagworms off junipers? Does spraying do any good?

(New York.)   Yes. Spray with malathion or toxaphene when the young worms begin moving around with their bags and chewing, usually late May. Pick off bags and burn during fall and winter. (See Bagworms.)

How can I get rid of all the red spiders in my juniper? (Idaho.) Forceful spraying with malathion repeated several times or Ovex once or twice, may work. Or dust with fine dusting sulfur. Dormant spraying with a miscible oil may be necessary, but oil sprays sometimes injure junipers. (See Arborvitae).

What causes my pyramid juniper to be slowly dying; needles turn yellow-brown and drop off? Mate on other side of doorstep is just fine. (Wisconsin.)   It may be red spider, and a juniper near a wall, in a very hot position with little circulation of air, is far more susceptible to injury. The upright junipers very often get brown and unsightly in a few years, no matter what control measures are used.

LARKSPUR

What is good to kill little yellow lice on larkspur? (Arkansas.) Spray frequently with malathion.

Why does my larkspur turn yellow, soft at base, and rot? (South Carolina.)   This is probably crown rot, or Southern rot (due to *Sclerotium rolfsii*). Remove infected plants and soil. (See Delphinium.)

Why do my annual larkspur plants turn yellow and die just before or after first blooms appear? (Massachusetts.)   This may also be crown rot (due in Massachusetts to *Sclerotium delphini*). The fungus starts working in warm, humid weather which may coincide with blooming time of the larkspurs. (See Delphinium for control.)

LAUREL

What shall I do for laurel blight, when the leaves are spotted and burned followed by slow death? (New Jersey.)   You probably have two distinct troubles. The spotting is not often serious on mountain laurel, but when the shrubs are brought in from the woods and stay in shady places under the drip of trees, the leaf spot may become unsightly, in which case it may be controlled by spraying with ferbam. The burning is probably winter burn and sunscald, due to drying effect of winter wind and sun. Death may be due to neither the leaf spot nor the sunscald but to some unfavorable soil condition.

LAWN

How can I prevent neighbor's dogs from tearing up the grounds to get at moles aside from getting rid of the moles?   Why not attempt getting rid of the moles that attract the dogs? Dogs are a nuisance, but there is nothing except a fence and a gate tightly latched to keep them off a lawn. Even in suburbs, where dogs are kept on leash, their owners usually walk them on the lawn side of the sidewalk rather than curb them.

How can I get rid of moles in the lawn? We have tried traps, the pitchfork, castor beans, cyanide gas, Mol-o-gen, and we still have the moles. (Ohio.)   Traps have to be set with great care. A few chemicals you haven't tried are carbon disulfide, paradichlorbenzene, strychnine poison bait and Mo-Go. (See Moles.)

Can chinch bugs be controlled by applying tobacco dust around the edges of the lawn? (Massachusetts.)   No. You have to cover the entire area very thoroughly. Use chlordane or dieldrin dust. Make 1 application in June, and 1 in August for the second brood.

What caused white, slimy mildew spots on my lawn under red oak trees? (New Jersey.)   There are several fungous diseases of turf, most common being large brown patch, dollar spot, or small brown patch, and spot blight of pythium disease. The latter may be your particular trouble. It occurs in warm, humid weather and where the air is stagnant, as it might be under an oak tree, but thiram or captan will probably check its spread. Avoid overwatering. Avoid also, in humid weather, letting the clippings remain on the grass.

What causes the half-circle formation of toadstools, killing the grass, and what can we do to correct it? (Washington.)   This is a fairy ring of mushrooms rather common in lawns. The fungous mycelium starts in one spot and spreads in a circle, sending up the fruiting bodies at intervals. Various chemicals are recommended: 4 ozs. iron sulfate to 1 gal. water; 1 oz. potassium permanganate to 4 gals. of water; or 1 to 1000 bichloride of mercury dilution. Cut grass close for several feet around the rings and wet the ground thoroughly.

LILAC

What can be done to stop oyster-shell scale on a lilac hedge? (Massachusetts.)   If the hedge is away from any painted surface, spray with a dormant dinitro (Elgetol, Krenite, Dinitrosol, etc.) in the spring before new growth starts. In Massachusetts this would be the end of March. Miscible oil, 1 to 25 dilution, may also be used and is preferable if the bushes are close to a house.

I have a gray scale on lilacs; have used lime-sulfur. What spray do you suggest? (Ohio.)   Perhaps you have the round, scurfy scale. Use a miscible oil spray, such as Scale-O, or Scalecide, at a 1 to 16 dilution, before the buds break but on a clear day with the temperature above 45° F. or see above.

I sprayed my lilac bushes in early spring with Scalecide, but in spite of this I see a white scalelike lice on the branches. (New York.)   One dormant spraying does not always clean up an infestation of scale.

When the young hatch in the summer (your white scalelike lice), spray with DDT and malathion.

The bark of my lilac has cracked and breaks off, and I have found something like eggs on the ground. Do I have to cut out the infested shoot? (New York.)   Yes, cut it out and burn it. If the bark is breaking off, the shoot will not live and meanwhile you can burn up the borer. The eggs on the ground are frass, or excrement, which the borer has pushed out of the holes. If the bark is sound and the branches look healthy, you can gas the borer by injecting a few drops of Bore-Kill and plugging the hole with gum or putty. Or you can squeeze in some BHC paste, sold as Bortox, and need not plug up the hole.

What moth, beetle, or other insect is responsible for the borer in lilacs? (New Jersey.)   The adult of the lilac borer, an inch-long white grub, is a clear wing moth; the adult of another borer common in lilacs, a cream-colored larva with black spots, is the leopard moth, white with black markings. To control either borer, use a fumigant or a paste in the holes, or cut out and burn all infested branches. (See above).

How can I keep borers from getting into my lilacs? (Iowa.)   There are various repellent washes for the trunk and branches but there are none sure to be safe under all conditions. DDT and dieldrin are reported effective as preventives. Watch for the first sign of borer work, usually a hole with sawdust coming out, and treat immediately. (See answers to the two previous questions.)

How can I prevent lilac leaves from becoming mildewed during the summer? (Indiana.)   The mildew, or white powdery coating over the leaves, comes from a fungus which grows over the outside of the leaves and so can be readily killed by dusting with fine sulfur. Mildew usually appears in late summer. It is unsightly but has little permanent deleterious effect.

How do you rid lilacs of microsphaera? (Connecticut.)   *Microsphaera alni* is the scientific name of the powdery mildew fungus. Sulfur dust will eradicate it.

What shall I do for an insect that rolls up lilac leaves, leaving eggs and web? Eventually the leaf is eaten through in this spot and the leaves are scalloped, but I think this is done by another insect. (Washington.)   Probably 2 phases of the same insect, the lilac leaf roller, which is reported in the Puget Sound region. Spray with DDT or methoxychlor to kill the young larvae, before the leaves are rolled.

What causes the foliage to turn brown and die shortly after blooming?   Any one of several blight or leaf-spot fungi, a bacterial blight, a wilt from verticillium fungus in the soil, a graft blight due to grafting on privet stock, too much fertilizer, or not enough water.

Why did large lilac bushes develop black and brown spots on the

leaves and fall off?   Probably a fungous disease. Prune out blighted twigs and spray with captan or ferbam.

LILY

What causes lily buds to have brown spots on them? (Illinois.)   Presumably botrytis blight, a fungous disease, which produces oval, orange, or reddish-brown spots on the foliage, a bud blight, and sometimes stem lesions. The disease is more prevalent in rainy weather.

Can you spray the growing lilies with something to bring them through the blossoming period? (New York.)   Spraying with captan every 2 weeks, starting in early spring, should control botrytis blight sufficiently to obtain normal flowering. Pick off and burn each spotted leaf.

Just how does the lily-disease mosaic look on the foliage? (New York.)   The leaves of infected plants are patterned with light and dark-green mottled areas, varying with the species. Mottling is accompanied by stunting, and leaves may die, from the base upward, prematurely.

I have some formosanum giant white lilies grown from seed. After a few years the blooms twist and go completely bad. Is there anything I can do to correct this trouble?   Mosaic will distort the flowers. It is not seed-transmitted, but the melon (or cotton) aphid carries the virus from other diseased lilies to your healthy seedlings. There is no control except ruthlessly roguing out all diseased plants so the aphids cannot feed on them.

How do you tell the difference between mosaic and chlorosis in lilies? (California.)   Mosaic, the virus disease, shows up as a mottled green-and-yellow effect, while chlorosis, a physiological disease, often appearing in lilies grown with too much lime in heavy soil, is a yellowing of the entire leaf, except near the veins. Spraying with 0.5 per cent solution of ferrous sulfate, or applying iron chelates to the soil, will often bring back green color.

My lilies were a complete failure last year. Leaves on gold-banded and pink-spotted varieties became yellow and twisted and the bud died. Can you advise procedures for next year?   This may have been basal rot, due to a fungus, fusarium, which came to you in diseased bulbs. The lower leaves turn yellow and the plants seldom come to flowering. In buying new bulbs make sure they are healthy. It is said that some control is obtained by immersing diseased bulbs in formalin diluted 1 to 50.

Why do lily bulbs turn yellow and die after growing a few inches? Some never come through the ground. (Iowa.)   This may be bulb rot from diseased bulbs, or stump rot, caused by phytopthora living in the soil and attacking the new growth as it emerges from the soil. Spraying with captan will help in the latter case.

What would you suggest is wrong with our regal lilies which grow well, with firm stalks and buds, and then suddenly topple over with the stem withering halfway? (Minnesota.) There is a disease called limber neck, which seems to be due to unfavorable physiological conditions, but no one knows very much about it, or how to prevent it.

Why have my Madonna lilies grown smaller and poorer in quality? They have small white insects on bulbs when dug up. If these insects are very, very small, they are bulb mites, and doubtless responsible for your lilies getting poorer. Destroy infected bulbs; plant new ones in another place in a well-drained soil. If your insects are larger, they may be root aphids, and you may be able to kill them with a solution of malathion.

What can I use to keep bugs off the lily blossoms? (Illinois.) There are several species of aphids which infest lilies, one of which, the cotton aphid, carries the mosaic virus. In addition to aphids on the buds, the leaves, especially in late summer, are very often completely covered with these plant lice. Spray with malathion, repeating as needed.

How can one protect Madonna lilies from a worm that hollows out the stem? (Indiana.) This is the common stem or stalk borer that attacks many garden plants. Clean up the weeds round about and burn in the fall any plant tops suspected of harboring borers. It may be possible to save a lily in bloom by slitting the stem and killing the borer with a knife, or injecting some BHC paste.

How can I keep moles away from lilies? Plant bulbs in wire baskets, or use poison bait. (See Moles.)

LOCUST

I have noticed large bulges in the bark of our flowering locust. Is this a disease? What do you suggest as a remedy? (Connecticut.) The swellings are caused by the locust borer, a devasting pest not readily controlled. The larvae live in the wood, and the adult, black, yellow-marked beetles come out in September to feed on goldenrod and lay their eggs in crevices in the locust bark. If the tree is painted or sprayed with a DDT or dieldrin solution it will kill all the young larvae that come in contact with it.

LUPINE

What causes a large, healthy Russell lupine plant to die late in August? (Washington.) It may have been a fungous stem, crown or root rot, but it may also have been unfavorable soil conditions. Russell lupines have often been short-lived in this country. Some think a rather peaty soil, well supplied with organic matter and phosphorus, and testing pH 5.5 to 6.0, works best for lupines.

Can anything be done to Russell lupines to prevent aphids? I have

sprayed with everything. (Massachusetts.) You can't exactly prevent aphids, but you should be able to kill the first few before they multiply with a contact insecticide such as malathion.

MAGNOLIA

My beautiful small magnolia seems to have scale. Is this usual? Sprayed with lime-sulfur last spring. Correct? How strong? Large blackish magnolia scales are not unusual. A dormant lime-sulfur spray at 1 to 8 dilution should have gotten the scales, but it is an unpleasant spray to use. Try a miscible oil at a 1 to 25 dilution. (See Dormant Spraying.)

MAPLE

Last spring after getting its foliage in full my Norway maple began to die out in the small branches, finally getting so thin you could see through it. What caused this? (Virginia.) Verticillium wilt, a serious fungous disease of maples, works that way, with the sudden dying of a branch. There will be green streaks, later turning black, in the sapwood. Maples sometimes recover from mild cases of wilt if the infected branches are promptly pruned out. Often, however, the tree must be removed and destroyed as quickly as possible, getting out the roots also. Plant another kind of tree in that location.

My Silver Maple tree is all eaten up by worms. What can be done? (New York.) If it is the green-striped maple worm, a caterpillar 1½ ins. long with dark and yellow-green stripes alternating down the back, spray with DDT or methoxychlor when the caterpillars are young, probably in June. The forest tent caterpillar, blue-black with white diamonds, chews in May, and hence requires an earlier spray.

What insect works on the leaves of hard maple trees? (Illinois.) The green-striped maple worm and caterpillars of the tussock moth are reported feeding on foliage of hard maples in the Middle West.

Can you tell me how best to control maple aphids? (Massachusetts.) The Norway maple aphid, a large, greenish plant louse, not only wrinkles the leaves but drops its sticky honeydew on cars parked underneath. If you can afford it, have the tree sprayed with malathion. A tree expert with a power sprayer will be needed for large trees.

Our Japanese maple drops its leaves about the end of July; they seem to dry up. We give it plenty of water. What is the trouble? (Ohio.) It is possible to give it too much water. Aphids sometimes get so numerous the leaves curl and dry. This maple must be sprayed cautiously, for it is susceptible to spray injury which may cause the leaves to burn or fall. Malathion may be used on a not-too-hot day.

Why do the leaves of my Japanese maple get rust spots on them and roll up and fall off? (New York.) This may be sunscald, or perhaps spray injury. (See answer to previous question.)

Is the spray used for leaf curl on peach trees injurious to dwarf red maples? (Oregon.) It depends on what was in the peach spray. Ferbam should not be injurious.

I have a bug or a germ which splits the maple tree limbs. (Ohio.) There are several maple borers, the work of any one of which would so weaken the tree that branches might be split off. The callus borer is marked by swellings and abnormal growths.

What do you do for borers? (New York.) If they are in the branches of small limbs, cut out the infested parts and burn. Borers in larger limbs may sometimes be killed by inserting a wire, or gassed by injecting Bore-Kill or BHC paste.

Last season we had trouble with worms under the bark of young maples, causing excessive bleeding. Is there anything we can do to prevent their appearance this season? (Ohio.) In Ohio newly set maples are prey to the fly-headed borer. Trunks should be wrapped from ground to first branches with Kraft crepe paper, or a good grade of wrapping paper. It may not be too late to wrap for another year. Repellent washes with DDT or dieldrin may prevent further damage.

Do maple trees normally require a yearly spraying? (New Hampshire.) One treatment with DDT or methoxychlor after the leaves are well out will give protection against chewing insects such as the green-striped maple worm, but in some seasons of light infestation you may not absolutely require it. A *yearly* dormant spray is not necessary on maples, and oil sprays may even be injurious.

MARIGOLD

What insect, triangular in form, spotted brown or gray, stings top of marigolds before buds appear so they are flat and empty? (New York.) The tarnished plant bug works on marigolds. It is oval in shape, mottled brown in color, and stings the buds of many flowers. It is a sucking insect, subdued by malathion or DDT. Remove all near-by weeds.

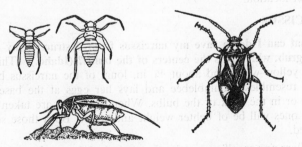

Tarnished Plant Bug: attacks marigolds and many other garden flowers. Triangular, spotted brown or gray.

Why do my dwarf marigolds turn brown and dry up after blossoming well for a month? It is not lack of water. (New York.) Perhaps you cultivate too close to them, perhaps it is a fungous stem or collar rot or wilt. If the latter, you must remove diseased plants and either sterilize soil or use another location for your next planting.

MATRIMONYVINE

What causes greenish warts on leaves of matrimonyvines? I cannot see the insects. (Illinois.) This is a leaf gall caused by an insect you can't see because it is inside the gall. It is a mite anyway, and almost too small to see. Try spraying with malathion when the leaves are half out.

MONKEYPUZZLE TREE

Do you know anything to do to a monkey tree whose branches are turning and dropping? (Virginia.) The lower branches of the monkeypuzzle tree may be attacked by a fungous blight. All you can do is remove and burn dying wood.

MOUNTAIN-ASH

How can I combat worms on my mountain-ash trees? They completely strip the foliage. (New York.) This is the worst of the wormlike larvae of the mountain-ash sawfly which works a couple of weeks ahead of the Japanese beetle. Spray with DDT in late May and get ahead of the worms. If they are already working, add malathion to your arsenate spray.

MYOSOTIS

Stems of Myosotis palustris turned black from soil toward tips. What caused this? (New York.) A wilt due to a fungus, probably sclerotinia, in the soil. All you can do is remove infected plants, digging out all surrounding soil and filling the hole with fresh soil from another location.

NARCISSUS

What can I do to save my narcissus from destruction by a large, short grub, which eats the centers of the bulbs? (Idaho.) This is the larva, yellow-white and about ¾ in. long, of the narcissus bulb fly, which resembles a bumblebee and lays her eggs at the base of the leaves or in the neck of the bulbs. When the bulbs are taken up, infested ones will be of lighter weight and softer. Burn those seriously infested.

Is there any specific spray for the control of the narcissus fly? Naphthalene flakes are not satisfactory. (Washington.) No, there is no spray nor any satisfactory treatment for the bulbs except immersion in 25% heptachlor (4 tbsp. per gal. of water) for 10 min. or 12% chlordane at same dosage for 30 min. It is easier to burn all infested bulbs and purchase more.

My daffodil bulbs, which have been in the ground for several years, are now being destroyed by maggots. Someone gave us a lot of tankage. Would that be the cause? (New York.) The maggots are probably the larvae of the lesser bulb fly—yellowish-gray, wrinkled, about ½ in. long. There are usually several to a bulb, as opposed to the narcissus bulb fly, where there is usually one. The life history and control are about the same. The tankage did not bring your maggots but might provide a favorable medium for them, since they are not confined to living tissue. (See previous question.)

If Von Sion Narcissi come up green and yellow, instead of their original beautiful yellow, is the soil, fertilizer, or what to blame? (Georgia.) This particular narcissus often loses its original character after growing out in gardens a year or two, but if the leaves were streaked with yellow along with the streaking of the flowers, you probably have mosaic, a virus disease, and the diseased individuals should be rogued out.

Why do my double white daffis, just before opening, turn brown and black? Have tried lime, shallow and deep planting, and moist places. (New York.) These late-flowering double narcissi frequently blast before flowering. Lack of continuous moisture and hot weather have been blamed. Be careful of too much lime.

When bulbs are started growing in the house, in darkness, what causes mold to occur on them? The mold may be one of the storage rots coming to you with the bulbs. Inspect bulbs before starting and discard any with mold. A piece of charcoal in the water will keep molds from the outside under control.

What causes buds to blast just before coming into bloom? Planted in water and pebbles. Some say the flower buds will blast if the water falls below the level of the shortest roots at any time during the growing period.

Why do Paperwhites and Soleil d'Or, planted indoors in sand, peatmoss, and gravel mixture, cease growing and wither without blooming? Did you start them too early in the fall? They need a dormant period to flower well. It is possible the bulbs had been treated for bulb flies or nematodes and somewhat injured. Why not try the simple pebble-and-water method for Paperwhites rather than your peatmoss mixture?

NASTURTIUM

How do you control black aphids on nasturtiums? (New York.) By using malathion or other contact spray frequently, faithfully, and usually frantically. These aphids are very hard to kill. Use an angle nozzle to reach the under side of the leaves; start spraying early and continue through the season. Sometimes it seems simpler either to ignore the aphids and yellowing leaves or omit nasturtiums.

What can I do to keep the plant lice formed by black ants off nasturtiums? (Michigan.) These black aphids (technically they are bean aphids) are not "formed" by the ants and they may appear quite independently of them, but often they are herded about by the ants, who feed on the honeydew secreted by the aphids. (For control see answer to the previous question.)

What do you use for cutworms? (Michigan.) Since paper collars are rather impractical for nasturtiums, you will probably have to resort to a poison bait or granulated chlordane or dieldrin. (See Cutworms.)

OAK

My large oak is infested with borers. All summer small branches were falling off the tree and each branch had a large brownish worm. What can I do? (Connecticut.) This worm, the grub stage of a beetle, is known as the oak-twig pruner because it cuts off the branches. Since the larvae winter in the fallen branches, your job is to clean up all these and burn them.

What can I do to put new life in an oak tree which was struck by lightning? (Maryland.) If possible have a tree expert go over it to note extent of damage, remove shattered limbs, and apply a wound dressing. Feed with a rapidly available fertilizer. Valuable trees may be equipped with lightning protectors—a very good form of insurance.

This fall there were loads of little white bugs clinging to the bark of our oak tree. Later they seemed to have disappeared. We are worried about the tree, which has not responded to treatment. (Kansas.) These could have been the young stage of scale insects, several of which infest oak; or, if they were fluffy white bits, some sort of woolly aphid or else woolly flata, rather common on many trees in late summer and causing no particular damage. The poor health of your tree may be due to borers, or to scale. Have it examined by a reputable tree expert.

OLEANDER

How can I keep my oleanders free from insects? Soap solution and nicotine seems to have little effect. Malathion will control the young, motile stage of the oleander, cottony cushion, hemispherical scales, and mealy bugs. (See House Plants.)

PALM

The soil of my potted palm seems to have many small insects like

soil lice, not worms or nematodes. Do they hurt the roots and how can I destroy them? They sound like root aphids. Out of doors root aphids can be killed by making a depression around the plants and pouring in malathion.

Little white spots form on the leaves of my palm. They can be washed off but reappear. What shall I do to prevent this? The spots are probably mealy bugs, possibly one of the many species of scale. Keep the leaves syringed frequently and keep bait around to control ants, for they often carry around young insects. Try malathion applications. (See House Plants.)

PANSY

What can be used to prevent rabbits from eating pansies? (Ohio.) Probably a wire fence around the pansy bed is the best method. If that is impossible, try moth balls or some other of the many repellents suggested under Rabbits.

How shall I get rid of cutworms? Have tried Snarol and moth balls without success. (Massachusetts.) Snarol should be fairly effective, but moth balls would be of little use. Use granulated chlordane or dieldrin around plants.

What is the white moth, similar to the cabbage moth, that lays its eggs on pansies? These hatch into small black hairless caterpillars that eat foliage and stems; during the day they lie on the the ground, climbing up the plants at night. Lead arsenate seems to help somewhat; rotenone and pyrethrum not at all. (Washington.) You have described the sluglike larva of the violet sawfly, the adult of which is a four-winged black fly; so the moth you mention must be something else. DDT or methoxychlor is by far the best control for dealing with false slugs or sawfly larvae.

What is it that eats leaves and flowers of pansies? Have found one mahogany-colored worm with short hairs. (North Carolina.) The woolly bear caterpillar comes close to your description. It has a brown body, black at each end, and clipped hairs. It eats all kinds of garden plants. Spray or dust with methoxychlor or other stomach poison.

How do you prevent pansy plants raised indoors from getting infested with lice? Keep them syringed frequently. Spray with a contact insecticide when necessary. Nicotine sulfate and soap used when the temperature is high may cause injury, the genus Viola being somewhat susceptible. Spray with an aerosol plant bomb.

What can I do for ants? (Iowa.) Find the nest and soak with chlordane or dieldrin solution. (See Ants.)

PECAN

What should I spray pecan trees with, and when? (Texas.) A suggested spray schedule lists a dormant oil spray for scale, and 4 applications of captan for scab, starting when the nuts set and repeating at 3-week intervals. Add malathion for aphids and DDT for caterpillars and leaf-case bearers. Clean up and burn old hulls and infested nuts to control shuckworm and nut weevils. Consult United States Department of Agriculture *Farmers' Bulletin 1654* and your State Experiment Station.

What caused my trees to shed the pecans before they matured? (Louisiana.) Pecan scab, a fungous disease, causes the nuts to dry up and fall. Control by spraying with captan. In buying new trees, choose resistant varieties such as Stuart, Frotcher, Moneymaker, and Success.

PENTSTEMON

Why didn't my Garnet Pentstemon bloom? Tips of branches blighted and turned black instead of forming buds. (Texas.) Crown rot, caused in Texas by *Sclerotium rolfsii,* is common on pentstemon and would blight the bugs; but generally the whole plant would wilt. (See Crown Rot.) Pentstemon likes a well-drained but not dry soil, and dies out in a year or two if kept in full sun.

Tips of buds are webbed together and a small worm bores down center of stalks. What shall I do to prevent this? (Indiana.) The tobacco bud worm reported on some garden plants is probably the pest you have. Spray thoroughly with DDT as the buds form. With the hydrangea leaf-tyer, also a bud worm, the leaves may be opened and the worm killed before it injures the flower buds.

PEONY

What causes peony buds to blight? (Michigan.) A disease called Botrytis blight, caused by *Botrytis paeoniae* and *B. cinerea,* and widely distributed across the United States. Young buds turn brown or black and fail to develop; irregular brown to black areas show on the leaves, and black pimples (sclerotia) form at the base of the stalks.

Why do stalks wilt and fall over? (Wisconsin.) Another symptom of Botrytis blight. If the old stalks are left in the ground, the sclerotia will produce spores in the spring to infect the young shoots coming up. In wet weather the shoots turn black and rot at the base, often being covered with a gray mold. If the weather is dry early in the season, the disease may not show up until the bud stage.

Why do peonies have brown spots on the petals? (Virginia.) Usually because of Botrytis blight. The rain splashes spores from infected buds to opening blossoms and everywhere a spore starts to germinate there is a brown spot on the petals. However, browning may also be due to thrips injury. (See Thrips.)

Is bud rot curable? (Wisconsin.) Not curable, but often preventable. In the fall cut down and burn all peony tops, so the sclerotia cannot overwinter. With a sharp knife cut each stalk just below soil level. Never use the tops for mulching. Spray several times in the spring with captan, starting when the reddish new shoots can first be seen poking through the ground.

Why does the foliage turn black after blooming period? (Tennessee.) It may, in a wet season, be due to Botrytis blight. Every infected bud or leaf should be cut off and every infected shoot carefully pulled up to prevent spread of the fungus. Blackening may also be due to stem rot, a fungous disease characterized by blighted foliage, white film areas (mycelium) on the stem, and large black sclerotia in the pith.

What can be done for stem rot? Remove the infected shoots very carefully so as not to drop out any of the sclerotia, which are formed loosely in the pith and fall out of the stalks. Burn.

What would cause roots to rot? (Montana.) Possibly Botrytis blight or stem rot; or sometimes a downy mildew which causes a wet rot of the crown. It may help to sprinkle a solution of PCNB (Terrachlor) over the soil. Peonies should not be planted in too-wet soil; if it is heavy clay, lighten it with coal ashes. Never leave manure on as a mulch so the shoots have to push up through it.

What insects or worms eat out the insides of roots? (New York.) Worms are probably millipedes feasting on tissue dying from some rot disease. They are not apt to be injurious to healthy roots. Eelworms, or root nematodes, may infest peonies and cause galls on the roots, but these worms are too small to be seen with the naked eye.

Is it natural for peonies to die during August? Should they be cut back at this time? (Wisconsin.) No, they should retain foliage all summer and not be cut back until late September or early October— just before frost. Your peonies may be afflicted with one of the diseases discussed above.

The foliage on my peonies turns a light color and looks blistered. What is wrong? What is the remedy? (Colorado.) Apparently a physiological disease called measles or edema and associated in some way with too much soil moisture or atmospheric humidity. There is no practical remedy known.

How can I control rose chafers on peonies? (Massachusetts.) There is no very satisfactory answer to this universal question. Pick off as many as you can and spray with DDT or methoxychlor. If it is any comfort to you, when the Japanese beetles get worse in Massachusetts, the rose chafers will diminish.

Should one discourage the big black ants that come on buds? (Pennsylvania.) They do no damage of themselves, merely feed on the sweet substance exuded from the peony buds. Some authorities think they carry botrytis spores around with them, so that it may be wise to spray the plants with DDT.

PETUNIA

We are bothered with slugs and sowbugs eating petunia stems. Used bran bait which killed birds, but didn't kill pests. Is there something safer to use? (Michigan.) If you use poison bait, put it out in the evening, and place under boards so birds cannot get at it. Spraying or dusting with DDT will deter slugs and not harm birds. (See Slugs; Sowbugs.)

Petunias in my flower boxes dry up and don't bloom well near the end of the season. What is the trouble? (Ohio.) It may be purely cultural difficulties—not enough water or poor soil conditions in the crowded box; but it may also be due to one or two fungi causing basal or root rots. Next time be sure to use fresh soil, and try treating the seed before planting. (See Seed Treatment.)

By the end of June insects start to eat petunia leaves in my window boxes. What kind of spray should I use, and how often? (Illinois.) Use a stomach poison as a spray either DDT or methoxychlor will do. If you have Tri-ogen on hand for roses, try that. Spray often enough to keep the new growth covered.

PHLOX

What is the cause of phlox foliage drying up from the roots to the bloom? (Colorado, Kansas, Illinois, Michigan, Minnesota, Missouri, Ohio, Pennsylvania, Washington, Wisconsin.) This question is almost as universal as the one about chrysanthemum foliage turning brown, and there is no real answer. It is evidently a physiological disease and not one caused by any specific organism. It may be due to a checking of the food and water movement at the point of union between current and old growth.

Is there any remedy for phlox blight? A liberal supply of water and cutting diseased stems back to sound wood may help. Fungous leaf spots may accompany the blight; these can be checked by spraying with captan or ferbam.

What is the best remedy for rust? (Maryland.) There is no rust common on phlox, gardeners all over the country notwithstanding. The reddish discoloration of the leaves termed "rust" is merely one phase of the leaf blight discussed in the two previous questions. (For a definition of the fungous disease see Rust.)

When our perennial phlox is in full bloom a stalk or two in a clump suddenly shows green wilted leaves, and in a day or two entire plant may be dead. What is the cause? (West Virginia.) This may be the leaf blight discussed above, or death may be due to the fungous crown rot or Southern blight. (See Crown Rot.)

How is mildew prevented? (New York, Texas.) Dust or spray the foliage with fine sulfur, Mildex or Karathane, being careful to cover the under surface. Except for phlox variety Miss Lingard, mildew on phlox in New York does not start much before July, so that treatment may be delayed until then. In Texas start when the foliage is well out. Phlox that is crowded or shaded is more subject to mildew.

Can phlox be sprayed with dusting sulfur when blooming? (Massachusetts.) You can't ever "spray" with a dust. Spraying is the application of chemicals in liquid form; dusting, the application of finely divided dry materials. If you are careful to dust the foliage from underneath, and not down onto the flowers from above, there will be little injury to the bloom. Sulfur, however, does fade bright colors.

What can be done to prevent phlox from turning yellow before blooming? (Virginia.) If the foliage is really yellow (and not brown, as in leaf blight), red spiders are probably to blame. These can be seen in mealy webs on the under side of the leaves. Malathion is the standard control measure. Frequent syringing with water, or spraying with other miticides will also give control. (See Red Spider.)

A small, soft-bodied insect, orange with black stripes, attacks my phlox. Nothing seems to control it, and I have never been able to find out what it is. What is it? (Indiana.) Probably the phlox bug, a sucking insect with reddish or orange margins on the wings and a black stripe on the back. Kill the nymphs by spraying with malathion.

What shall I do for a striped flying beetle? (Virginia.) Striped cucumber beetles attack flowers. Spray or dust with DDT or methoxychlor.

PHOTINIA

Please tell me what causes scale on photinia, and what to do for it? (Texas.) Scale is a sucking insect. Usually, when adult, it is covered with a shell and attached to the plant, although the young scales may move around. In Texas you can control scale by spraying with DDT and malathion when the young scales are crawling. Lace bugs are more common on photinia than scale, and can be controlled with the same combination. (See Scale Insects; Lace Bugs.)

PINE

Have white scale on mugho pine. What is the proper treatment? (Iowa.) Preferably lime-sulfur, 1 to 9 dilution, applied in spring before new growth starts. If the pine is near a house, substitute miscible oil at a 1 to 50 dilution with 1 teaspoon nicotine sulfate per gallon. Or spray with malathion when the young scales are in the crawling stage. Pines may be injured by oil sprays. (See Dormant Spraying.)

How can I save Scotch pines that have an insect or worm in the buds? (Michigan.) The worm is the grub of the European pine-shoot moth; it emerges as a reddish, white-marked adult sometime in June. The easiest method of control on small trees is to break off and burn the infested shoots (readily told by light color, or crooked bend, or mass of resin) before the moth comes out to lay her eggs. If the trees are too large, spray, about the middle of June and in early July, with DDT and malathion.

Is there any control for the worm that starts boring through the new growth of pines, killing the trees, if not found in time? (New York.) This may be the pine-shoot moth; but more likely is the white-pine weevil, the grub of which mines into and kills the leader of the tree. Cut out the infested shoot below the grub; remove some of the laterals, and tie up one to replace the leader. A DDT spray in early April may help prevent injury.

Why are the needles chewed off my pine twigs, leaving only a brush of new growth at the tip? (New Jersey.) This is the work of a sawfly which has become a very serious pest of pines in New Jersey. The larvae hatch from scalelike eggs on the needles in late April or the beginning of May. They work in groups and clean up one branch before moving to the next; but they feed only on the old growth, not the young needles. Spray with DDT or methoxychlor at the first sign of feeding. There are many sawfly species working on pines in the spring and summer. One type webs the needles together. Spray at the first sign of feeding.

What insect works on white pine, boring small holes in the trunk? What is the treatment to save the tree? (Minnesota.) There are several bark beetles which make such holes. Treatment is difficult, and a badly infested tree should be cut and burned to prevent beetles migrating to other pines. Newly transplanted trees should have the trunks wrapped. Keep the trees fed and watered properly. (See Borers.)

What can I do to save my trees from the pine beetle? (Louisiana.) The Southern pine beetle is distinguished by making pitch tubes at the base of the tree. It leaves no sawdust cast behind, as does the bark beetle, but produces a gummy exudation. Kill the beetles in the burrows, and spray the trunk with a strong solution of DDT or dieldrin. Treat all pines near by. Keep the trees well fed and watered, for this beetle works in weakened hosts.

How may pines be cleared of bagworms? (West Virginia.) Cut off all the "bags" you can reach. Spray with malathion or toxaphene when the young worms start feeding. (See Bagworms.)

What is best for red spider? (Ohio.) Ovex gives the best control of spruce mite, the common "red spider" on needled evergreens. (See Red Spider.)

What is the best way to get rid of white-pine rust? (Michigan.) Destroy all currants and gooseberries within 900 ft. of the pines, as these serve as alternate hosts for the white-pine blister rust, probably the most important disease of this tree.

PLUM, ORNAMENTAL

I have a Prunus pissardi which loses its leaves every summer. What causes this? How can it be corrected? (Pennsylvania.) Perhaps it was sprayed for the Japanese beetle, so prevalent on this host. *Prunus pissardi* objects strenuously to many spray materials, dropping its leaves at the first treatment. Rotenone dust or DDT will control the beetles without injuring the foliage. This tree often drops its leaves in unfavorable weather even when no spray has been used.

Plum Curculio: a small, gray, humpbacked snout beetle.

POINSETTIA

What can be done for mealy bugs on poinsettias? Remove them singly with a toothpick, spray with malathion or a house plant aerosol bomb, if the pest still persists. (See House Plants; Mealy Bugs.)

POPLAR

What control is possible for a bug or beetle that works on the leaves of our Lombardy poplars? (Indiana.) If it is a yellowish beetle with black stripes or spots, and the grubs skeletonize the leaves, it is the cottonwood or poplar-leaf beetle at work. Control by spraying with DDT in May.

A scale is forming on the trunk of our Lombardy poplar. Any cure? (Indiana.) The oyster-shell scale is common on poplar. Spray while dormant with a miscible oil, or with a dinitro compound. (See Dormant Spraying.)

PRIVET

What is the best spray for a brown scale our privet hedge gets every summer? (California.) Spray with malathion and DDT when the young are crawling. You may need to repeat spray once or twice during the summer.

PYRACANTHA

What causes the leaves of pyracantha to turn rusty brown and the

berries to fall? (Texas.)   Pyracantha is subject to fire blight, a bacterial disease which will suddenly kill back branches. Cut diseased branches out and spray with streptomycin when in bloom. (See Fire Blight.) If the leaves are merely discolored and not dead, lace bugs may be sucking underneath. If so, spray with any contact insecticide.

My pyracantha has a weblike substance, with twigs and leaves in meshes on the limbs. What shall I do? (Arkansas.)   Probably red spiders are at work. A strong spray from the hose every few days will keep them down. Spray with any of the recommended miticides.

RHODODENDRON

How can an amateur detect, and either prevent or destroy, rhododendron borers? (Pennsylvania.)   It is hard to prevent them, but you can detect them by the sawdust (insect frass) protruding from holes in the trunk or branches; and they can be killed by squirting in BHC paste, sold as Bortox or Borerkil. Keep bark coated with DDT or dieldrin during summer. (See Borers.)

What can be done for lace bugs? (New Jersey.)   Yellowed or speckled white leaves, with brownish bits of excreta on the under side, are sure signs of lace-bug injury. Spray with malathion or lindane or other contact insecticide when the young bugs hatch (usually late May or early June), and repeat in 2 weeks.

How can we get rid of red aphids on rhododendrons? (New York.) Are you sure you have aphids? They are most unusual on rhododendrons. The best rule for aphids on any shrub is to spray with malathion.

What is the cause of a black film on leaves? (New Jersey.)   It is a fungus, sooty mold growing in the honeydew dropped by scale insects or aphids working on some tree overhead or near by. There is little you can do for the rhododendrons, except scrubbing the film off. Having the trees sprayed for aphids or scales is usually expensive. Tulip trees are the worst offenders.

How do I get rid of the pest that eats the margins of the leaves? (Oregon.)   Any of several night feeders may do this, but the most important is the black vine weevil. Spray plants and soil under plants with chlordane or dieldrin in late June and 2 weeks later.

My rhododendrons have a dry curling blight on the leaves. They eventually drop off. I have sprayed with rotenone, without control. What shall I use? (Massachusetts.)   This may be a fungous blight or canker, but it is more likely the effect of winter wind and sun. Spraying will not help in either case. Watering the rhododendrons thoroughly in the fall and providing some sort of windbreak over the winter will be most helpful.

The leaves have dried up and turned brown. What can I do? (Cali-

fornia.) This can't be winter injury, as in Massachusetts, but it could be summer burning; or injury at the roots from the black vine weevil; or borer injury; or an attack of armillaria root rot. You'll have to call in some local expert for a real diagnosis, although it seems a little late to save your shrub.

What is the cause of large black spots on leaves? Adjacent plant that gets more sun is healthy. (California.) Sooty mold on the surface, or fungous leaf spots, which would be more likely to occur on a plant in the shade. It is probably not serious, and picking off infected leaves is sufficient control.

ROSE

The leaves of my roses have black spots. What is the cause? (New Jersey.) The causative agent is a fungus, *Diplocarpon rosae,* which grows into the leaf and forms the black spots by its dark mycelial threads just under the cuticle. In a few days little black pimples show up in the spots. These are the fungous fruiting bodies ready to discharge their spores, which are carried by rain or wind, by gardeners on hands, tools, or clothing, or even by beetles, to a healthy leaf. There they start another cycle if given 6 hours of continuous moisture for germination.

The leaves turn yellow and all drop off before the summer is over. Why? That's the way black spot works, first spotted leaves, then loss of color, and finally defoliation. There may also be lesions on the stems. Roses often put out a second set of leaves and lose these, too, thus weakening the plant so that it may not live through a hard winter.

What is an easy way to control black spot? (Nebraska.) There is none. A control program means applying a dormant spray in early spring and a summer spray or dust *weekly,* from the time the leaves come out until late frosts in the fall. It also means picking off and burning all infected leaves as soon as the spots appear.

What is an effective early spring treatment to kill the spots that may still be present on the canes? (New York.) A dormant spray of dinitro compound or lime-sulfur, 1 to 9 dilution, just as soon as the roses are uncovered and pruned in the spring.

Does sulfur really control black spot? If so, how should it be applied, on the foliage or on the ground around the bushes? (Michigan.) It works very well, if used faithfully. It will do no good on the ground. Get a good dust gun and cover the plant with a fine film of dust, working from underneath and making sure the lowest leaves are coated.

Is there a better remedy for prevention and cure of black spot than Massey dust (9 parts sulfur and 1 part arsenate of lead)? In spite of faithful use my roses develop spots by the end of the season. (Kansas.) Maneb, captan, or ferbam are all recommended for black spot with maneb giving the best control. Despite the best of care, black spot is apt to show up by the end of the season. For encouragement, compare your roses with those of your neighbor who has done no dusting or spraying.

Does Tri-ogen used as a spray give as good protection from black spot and mildew as Massey dust? (D.C.) It always has for me. I like it because it controls sucking and chewing insects also, in one operation, and leaves somewhat less noticeable residue on the foliage than sulfur. Also it is safer to use in hot weather, although in cold weather the sopper in the spray may spot certain varieties.

Is it harmful to pick off all leaves when all are infected? Yes, it probably is. Theoretically, you pick off every infected leaf, but this means starting early in the season and taking only an occasional one. If you wait until there is 100 per cent infection, the shock to the plant of sudden and total defoliation would be great. Pick off the worst leaves, remove all those fallen to the ground, and resolve to do better next year.

To control black spot, would it be wise to destroy all plants now in the garden, and plant new stock? (West Virginia.) No; you are more than likely to get black spot with your new plants from a nursery. Buy whatever new plants you like, but do not destroy the old for this reason. Merely start your spraying program with the dormant spray.

To destroy black spot, would it help to remove 2 or 3 ins. of topsoil, then sprinkle sulfur and put on new topsoil? This would remove some inoculum, old leaves rotting into the soil, but it might also injure some of the rose roots. Sulfur in the soil would not help much and might make the soil too acid. A mulch of peatmoss has been suggested as a barrier between spores in the soil and the developing new leaves.

Is there any way to sterilize the ground in a rose bed to prevent a recurrence of black spot? (Ohio.) No; and even if you could, the next new plant you bought could bring it back to your garden.

If rose leaves turn yellow and fall off with no sign of spot, is this black spot? (Pennsylvania.) Usually it is not. Leaves may turn yellow from too much moisture in the soil in early spring, or from drought in summer.

Can cow manure cause black spot? (Virginia.) No.

Where no winter protection is required, what can be done through the winter to guard against black spot? (Maryland.) You might put on the 1 to 9 lime-sulfur spray or the dinitro spray in December, after the plants are dormant, and repeat in early March before growth starts. Remove and burn infected leaves.

Black spot has been unusually bad this year in spite of constant

dusting with sulfur. Why? (Michigan.) The way the material is applied and the timing of the treatment before rains are important in control, but some seasons black spot flourishes in late summer despite the most careful control measures.

I am allergic to sulfur. Is there a substitute to take its place for black spot? What is the best all-around spray? (Texas.) Tri-ogen has been used successfully in Texas as an all-around spray, and it has a copper rather than a sulfur base. Maneb, captan or ferbam plus Karathane, malathion and methoxychlor make an excellent all-around spray. There are probably other combination sprays locally available to you which do not use sulfur.

Does cold weather freeze out black spot? (Indiana.) It kills the summer spores, but not the mycelium living in leaves fallen to the ground, or the special winter spores. In some states, probably including Indiana, the mycelium in lesions on the canes lives through the winter and produces summer spores again the next season.

Should roses be treated with any preparation before being covered with a mound of earth for the winter? (New York.) A late treatment of sulfur dust will have little effect; it would take lime-sulfur at dormant strength, and in New York roses are seldom sufficiently dormant when time comes to hill them up in November.

What causes mildew? (Utah.) The mildew fungus, which sends its white, felty, mycelial threads branching over the leaf or flower buds and gets its food by little rootlike suckers extending into the plant sap. The powdery effect comes from chains of summer spores growing upright from the mycelium. These spores are readily detached and carried by wind or rain to healthy leaves.

What was wrong with my Improved Lafayette polyanthas this summer? The calyx was swollen and white, leaves wrinkled, stems white, bloom scanty. Is there danger of this spreading to a bed of hybrid teas? (Ohio.) Mildew will deform the buds, curl the leaves, and cover everything with a white coating. Ordinarily mildew is severe on certain ramblers and polyanthas in May and June, and may affect hybrid teas in late summer. If your hybrid teas are regularly sprayed with a fungicide throughout the summer, you need not unduly fear infection from the polyanthas.

Why does one of my climbing roses always have mildew, even the shoots as they come through the ground? (Missouri.) Some varieties are more susceptible than others. Either change your roses for others more resistant to mildew in your locality, or make up your mind to keep them faithfully sprayed or dusted.

Can you tell me how to prevent blue mold from forming on my Dorothy Perkins rose arbor? I have cut back, every spring and fall, and sprayed, but it persists. (North Carolina.) Mildew is most per-

sistent on Dorothy Perkins. Cutting back shoots will do no good. The
spores will come on the wind from somewhere. Start treating as soon
as the leaves appear, and keep it up at least once a week through
flowering, and occasionally thereafter. If it is a large arbor, you can
probably get better coverage with a liquid spray than with a dust from
a small dust gun.

**What is the best treatment for white mold on climbers? (Massa-
chusetts.)**   Whatever is expedient. Sulfur, applied as a dust or a
spray, is the specific for controlling mildew. Karathane or Mildex is
very effective. If you have a dust gun large enough to give coverage
of your climbers, then dust with fine sulfur; otherwise spray with a
wettable sulfur, Karathane or Mildex, following manufacturer's directions. Tri-ogen will give excellent control on varieties that do not
object to the copper applied at May temperatures in your state. In
June you will have little injury.

**What causes mildew on Else Poulsen? I still have Tri-ogen. What
other spray could I use? To what extent does mildew injure plants?
(Iowa.)**   Else Poulsen is not subject to mildew in New Jersey gardens.
Try sulfur dust, Mildex or Karathane if Tri-ogen is unsatisfactory
for you. Mildew will cause curling and dropping of the leaves, imperfect flowers, and, in a bad infestation, injury to the stems.

What kind of spray is effective against mold on buds? (California.)
In California you have a very special problem with mildew, and although sulfur dust is often recommended, spraying with Mildex or
Karathane is sometimes more effective. Use a spreader and avoid
spraying when temperatures are above 85° F.

**How does one treat roses that build up big rust spots, like dust, on
the stems of bush and buds, which finally kill the plant? (Michigan.)**
These dusty pustules are made up of spores of the rust fungus; they are
orange early in the season, later turning dark brown. Clean up all
fallen leaves; treat with dormant lime-sulfur in the spring; and dust
weekly with sulfur or ferbam through the growing season.

**What can be used to rid bushes of yellow fungous growth? (Wis-
consin.)**   This also is rust, which attacks the canes as well as the
foliage. Prune out infected canes and follow directions given above.
Rust is prevalent in the Middle West, but is seldom seen in the East
except sometimes north of Albany and Boston.

**Foliage of rambler rose is spoiled during summer by brown spot on
leaves. Spray controls this on later leaves, but the early leaves are
infected while plant is blooming and spraying then spoils the appearance of the plants. What is the trouble? (Illinois.)**   There are several
fungous leaf spots, in addition to black spot, which may occur on
roses; but control would be the same. Tri-ogen is inconspicuous on
roses and may be used during blooming.

What is the best treatment for brown canker? (Ohio.)   The very best treatment is to refuse to plant in your garden any rose that comes to you with its canes covered with little white spots with reddish margins. Next best is to remove all cankered canes at spring pruning, following this with the dormant lime-sulfur spray. Any treatment for black spot will reduce canker infection during the summer.

Some of my bush roses and climbers have long canes which turn brown at the ends, and eventually the entire cane dies. Why? (Illinois.) Probably due to a canker which has girdled the base of the cane and cut off the water and food supply. Clean out infected canes at pruning. Use the dormant lime-sulfur spray.

What causes roses, when cut back, to start getting brown on the stems, and this brown to travel down until the whole stem is dead? (Florida.) Canker fungi often follow pruning cuts, unless these cuts are clean and sharp and made close to an eye, and on a slant, so water will not stand on the tissue. If you have much trouble, disinfect your pruning shears between cuts.

What is an effective control for peduncle necrosis, a disease quite prevalent here, chiefly in red varieties? (Illinois.) Peduncle necrosis, a drooping of the flower pedicle and a reddish lesion on the upper part, seems to be some physiological disease, for which no control is known. Possibly a feeding program can be developed to get these roses to hold their heads up. It is interesting that the disease has been reported on Radiance, ordinarily considered foolproof.

What causes the leaves to turn a pale yellowish-green, and what will prevent this? (Florida.) Red spiders will do this, but in Florida the trouble is probably too alkaline a soil, making iron unavailable. The soil can be treated with ferrous sulfate or iron chelates but it will be better to acidify the soil by adding sulfur. Send a soil sample to your State Experiment Station and ask for directions.

Why do my climbing roses turn black toward the stalk during the fall? (New York.) If roses are fed in late summer with an excess of nitrogen, so there is much succulent growth, this will turn black and soft at the first touch of frost.

I sprayed regularly with Black Leaf 40, but some of the leaves turned brown and dropped off. Used well-rotted cow manure and Vigoro as a fertilizer. (Illinois.) Defoliation could have been from black spot, Black Leaf 40 having no effect as a fungicide; but more probably the browning and leaf fall were due to too much attention in hot weather—a combination of spray and fertilizer injury. Apply commercial fertilizers only in small amounts, to a moist soil, and water in well afterward. Spray with nicotine only when the temperature is moderate.

Will lime-sulfur spray help roses? (New Jersey.) Very much when used as a 1 to 9 dormant spray, just after pruning in the spring. It controls scale and "burns out" overwintered cane lesions of black spot. It is not ordinarily used for a summer spray on roses.

What dormant spray is good for roses? (Washington.) Use the 1 to 9 lime-sulfur spray, if applied immediately after pruning— which will probably be sometime in midwinter in Washington. You may also use a dinitro spray.

What will kill scale on wood of climbing roses? (Pennsylvania.) If the bushes are not against the side of a garage or a house with light paint, give the dormant 1 to 9 lime-sulfur spray or a dinitro spray. If staining painted woodwork must be avoided, substitute a miscible oil. (See Dormant Spraying.) But, in my experience, this is a poor substitute for lime-sulfur on roses.

How do you kill the green licelike "beasties"? (Pennsylvania.) The "beasties" are plant lice, or aphids, sucking insects readily killed by thorough application of any contact insecticide; malathion solution is very effective.

What are the little green bugs that cover rose stems? (Pennsylvania.) More aphids. Both the pink and the green potato aphids are common on roses. They prefer new growth, either succulent new leaves, or stems and buds.

How early should one start spraying to get rid of aphids? (Michigan.) Fairly early in the spring. Since a contact insecticide is required, wait until the first few start working. Ordinarily cool, rainy weather in the spring and the cooler weather toward fall encourage aphids, and they are not so numerous in midsummer. One cannot predict insect invasions accurately, but must be prepared to cope with them immediately.

How can roses (indoors) be freed of a small black insect pest? I have tried nicotine to no purpose. Malathion should take care of aphids. Try scrubbing them off with a soapy rag and then spraying the entire plant. It may be black fly. (See House Plants.)

My rose garden is located near 2 old apple trees. Spraying with Tri-ogen twice weekly proved ineffective against a plague of white flies in September and October. What should I use? (Connecticut.) These white flies are apple leaf hoppers, whose late summer brood is often difficult to control. It would be better not to use Tri-ogen more than once a week. Try an alternate spray of malathion or DDT, directing your spray underneath the leaves. The stippled white leaves are unsightly, but there is no lasting injury from this late brood of leaf hoppers. The early brood comes in May and is more readily controlled with weekly sprays of Tri-ogen.

What is the best control of red spider on leaves? (California.) Probably an Aramite or chlorobenzilate spray on California roses. In the East, the contact insecticide included in a combination spray— plus an occasional washing with the hose—will keep red spiders in check. They are most serious in enclosed gardens or on roses under overhangs where there is little air circulation.

When buds open you can see numerous very minute white insects running along at the bottom of the petals. What kind of disease is this? (New Jersey.) It is not a disease. The insects are thrips, usually the flower thrips, but sometimes onion or greenhouse thrips. They are rasping-sucking insects and injure the flowers rather than the foliage.

⁕ What makes my roses turn brown? Just before they open the outside leaf is brown and dry, but if I take off the leaf the bud will open. (Wisconsin.) Thrips very often cause roses to "ball" in this way. Sometimes the bud will open normally, and sometimes all the petals turn brown.

How are thrips on roses controlled? (New York.) Frequent spraying with dieldrin gives control. (See Gladiolus.) Thrips injury is usually worse in a dry season. After a wet spring there is seldom a serious infestation of thrips in June.

I dug up some bushes this fall which had not thrived and found small white particles on the roots. What caused this? (New York.) If the particles were alive, you could have soaked the roots in a malathion solution, then poured the solution into the soil and re-planted, for they may have been root aphids. If the particles were a fungous growth, it would be too late to save the plants.

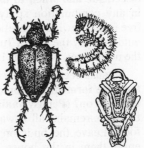

Rose Chafer or Rose Bug: brown beetle attacking many garden flowers.

How may one eliminate the rose chafer? (Rhode Island.) It is not easy; hand-picking is really the best control. A DDT spray will control the beetles. Tri-ogen used as a general rose spray gives fair control of rose chafers.

What is the trouble when the new shoots die on the end and the buds dry and fall off when the size of small peas? (Pennsylvania.) The rose midge is to blame. The adult is a yellow-brown minute fly which lays her eggs in the leaf and flower buds; these hatch and the maggots burrow into the new growth, causing the result you describe. When each maggot reaches maturity (indicated by the orange color), it drops to the ground, where it pupates just beneath the surface, and produces another midge. In warm weather the whole life cycle takes only 10 to 12 days, so there are many generations in a season.

What is the control for rose midge? (Indiana.) DDT sprays will control them.

How can I get rid of big insects on Paul's Scarlet? They eat up every plant. These bugs work in pairs by the hundred. They fly. (New York.) You describe the rose chafer, sometimes called rose bug, which is a long-bodied, long-legged tan or grayish, rather soft beetle. They are often found in pairs, mating. They feed on the flowers and are a destructive pest for about 6 weeks in late May and June. Their numbers diminish with the advent of Japanese beetles.

Japanese Beetle (left) and Asiatic Beetle.

What is the best way to save roses from the Jap beetle? How much insecticide and when to use it? (New York.) DDT or methoxychlor in any combination spray or dust will keep rose foliage reasonably free from chewing by beetles. Pick them off the flowers. Beetles become numerous by the end of June, and continue into September. To protect the new leaves, which the beetles prefer, a weekly treatment is required.

Japanse beetles destroy buds. Should the buds be cut off shortly after they are formed, or would it be more beneficial to the stalk to leave the buds on? (Pennsylvania.) The plant does not care whether or not the buds remain; all it wants is plenty of green leaves to make more food. Leave the buds on until they show color, then cut them and enjoy them in the house. Cut in the morning, or the beetle will get them before you do. Cut off fading, full-blown flowers, which attract beetles. When cutting, make a clean slanting cut just above an eye—as if you were spring pruning; it saves lots of canker trouble.

What is the Asiatic beetle? What color, how can it be recognized and found? (Illinois.) It resembles the Japanese beetle in size and shape, but is duller in color, which varies—either light-brown, purplish-black, or mottled. The Asiatic garden beetle (another species) is copper-brown and feeds only at night. Both beetles are most dangerous in the grub stage, feeding on grass roots, and both are chiefly pests of the Atlantic seaboard.

Is the Asiatic beetle the same as Fuller's rose beetle? (Oregon.) No, Fuller's rose weevil is a small gray snout beetle with grayish patches. It is also a pest of citrus trees on the West coast. Spray with methoxychlor, and pick off by hand.

What can I do about the Asiatic beetle which chews up my rose? (Michigan.) Are you sure you have the Asiatic beetle? This one and its cousin the Asiatic garden beetle are chiefly distributed along the Atlantic seaboard and are not primarily pests of roses. Perhaps you have rose chafers, or the rose curculio.

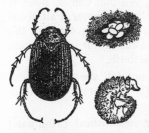

Asiatic Beetle: feeds at night; attacks asters, zinnias, carrots, beets, peppers, and other plants. Grubs injure grass roots and vegetables.

How do I get rid of green beetles with black spots on them? They get inside roses and ruin all blooms. (Texas.) These are the Diabrotica or 12-spotted cucumber beetles. They are controlled by the DDT or methoxychlor in your regular schedule.

Last year a little green worm (coiled) ate all the leaves off my roses. I used Black Leaf 40. (Minnesota.) This is the coiled rose worm, controlled by spraying with DDT or methoxychlor and by cleaning up all decayed wood and pithy stems in which the insect can hibernate over winter.

Why do the leaves turn brown early in summer? Find green worms on under side; spraying does not seem to help. (Michigan.) These are rose slugs, not true slugs but sawfly larvae, which skeletonize the leaves, eating out everything but the veins, and so cause the browning. Slugs work in the early spring, starting almost as soon as the leaves come out, occasionally in midsummer, and often have a late summer brood.

I used Black Leaf 40 for green worms but they weren't all killed. (Minnesota.) Rose slugs are chewing insects to be controlled with a stomach poison. Black Leaf 40 is a contact spray which would kill only those slugs it happened to hit. The DDT in the combination spray or Tri-ogen, gives almost perfect control if treatment is started early in the season and the *under side* of the leaves get covered.

What kind of a pest eats holes in the leaves and buds? (Missouri.) Perhaps the rose curculio, a red beetle with a black snout. Eggs are laid and larvae develop in the buds and young fruits, so pick off and burn all dried buds. Spray with methoxychlor.

I have observed wasps chewing the edges of my rose leaves. Should I try to poison them? (Wisconsin.) This is the leaf-cutter bee taking circles from the leaf to roll into a cylinder for a nest and then coming back to cut a larger circle which fits the top exactly. I am always so

intrigued by the seeming intelligence of this insect—which really does
little harm—I never want to poison it; but it will probably succumb
to DDT or methoxychlor on the leaf.

**In pruning my roses I found branches dry and dead inside, and a
small black beetle. What will exterminate this insect? (Oklahoma.)**
This is the rose cane borer or stem girdler. All that can be done is
remove and burn infested shoots, cutting below the borer. Fall pruning sometimes encourages the insect. If you leave long canes in the
fall and the borer works near the top, you can cut out the injured wood
in the spring without any real damage to the bush.

**What will kill ants around bushes and not kill the rose plants?
(Missouri.)** Soak soil around bushes with chlordane or dieldrin
solution. (See Ants for more suggestions.)

How can I keep moles from eating our rosebushes? (Montana.)
The eating is probably done by mice in the mole runs, but the tunnels
may disturb the roots. (See Moles; Mice.)

**How can I prevent rabbits from destroying my rosebushes? (Penn-
sylvania.)** If you don't like the looks of a fence, or cannot get the
materials, there are various chemicals which have an evanescent effect.
Moth balls work for me, but I think they are helped along by the
neighbors' cats. (See Rabbits.)

**What is the best all-purpose spray for hybrid tea roses? I am not
adept at diagnosing pests and diseases. How frequently should it be
used? (New York.)** Tri-ogen is probably the most widely used all-
purpose spray. It has some faults but fewer than some other combinations. Use it according to directions for single strength, *never double
strength*. Start about the first of May, continue to mid-October, every
7 to 9 days.

**What is the most practical, inexpensive, all-around spray or dust
for my rose garden of 500 bushes grown for commercial purposes?
(Mississippi.)** Captan, sulfur, malathion and methoxychlor make
an excellent all-around spray. See also above.

RUBBER PLANT

What is the cause of rust eating leaves of rubber plants? There is
a fungous disease, anthracnose, which appears as a scorching and
tip burn of the leaves, and has little rose-colored spore pustules;
there is a true scorching from dry air in a too-hot hothouse; and there
is a red scale. Pick off spotted leaves; do not let drops of water stand
on the leaves; keep the house cool, atmosphere humid. Spray for
scale with a contact insecticide.

SEDUM

What makes sedum rot off on top of the ground? (New York.)

Sedum is subject to both crown rot and stem rot, two fungous diseases. Remove diseased plant and surrounding soil and fill in the hole with fresh gritty soil before replanting; give perfect drainage.

SNAPDRAGON

Small brown dots appear on the under side of leaves of my snapdragons. Is this rust? (Louisiana.)   Yes, the rust pustules are chocolate brown and show on the under side of the leaves.

How can I control and kill snapdragon rust? (West Virginia.)   It can't be killed, but dusting with sulfur or ferbam will help prevent new infections. By far the easiest way to control this disease is to purchase rust-resistant varieties.

What causes snapdragon to wilt and die? (Texas.)   In Texas, Southern blight, cotton root rot, verticillium wilt, stem rot, and some others. Remove and burn diseased plants and try to replant in a new location.

SPRUCE

What is an effective remedy against spruce gall? (New York.) Spruce galls are caused by aphids. The one that causes the elongation and swelling of the tips of blue spruce has fir as an alternate host. When new growth starts, the aphids work at the base of the leaves, causing each cell to become enlarged and the whole gall to look something like a small pineapple. The best control is to remove and burn the galls before they open and free the new aphids in midsummer.

What kind of spray shall I use for spruce gall, and when is the proper time to spray? (New York.)   For Norway Spruce, where the galls are located at the base of the twigs, rather than at the tips where they are easily cut out, spray with nicotine sulfate and soap or malathion in the summer after galls open to expose the aphids; spray in the spring, just before new growth starts, with a malathion solution. With the blue spruce, if it was impossible to cut off all the galls while they were closed, give this tree the dormant spray on a warm day.

Why do needles of a Black Hills Spruce turn brown and fall off? (Illinois.)   All spruces are subject to infestation by spider mites (like red spiders), which suck the sap from the needles, turning them grayish, and later brown, and often causing defoliation. A dormant spray of 1 to 30 miscible oil or a summer spray of Ovex have been recommended. (See Mites; Red Spider.)

What causes the needles of our Norway Spruces to turn brown and fall next to the trunk? Have found a small moth hidden in the branches. (Illinois.)   There are several small moths the larvae of which mine in the leaves of spruces, feeding on them and webbing them together. Ordinarily they are not serious and the browning of the inner needles may be natural ripening. Spray with DDT or malathion if necessary to control the larvae.

What diseases get on Koster Blue Spruce? Should they be sprayed? The most serious disease is a canker or die back of the lower limbs, which is not amenable to sprays. Cut out and burn the diseased branches. Rust may sometimes attack spruce but is not important in ornamental plantings. In general you do not need to spray spruce for disease control, but occasionally for gall aphids and spider mites. (See above questions.)

A blue spruce suddenly drops all its needles with no apparent cause. Would you suggest a spray? (New York.) No, never spray unless you have "apparent cause." A tree in that condition might be made sicker with a spray. It sounds like a drouth reaction, but it could be too heavy, wet soil, or escaping gas, or too strong a spray or some other environmental cause.

Borers in my spruce trees cause white encrustations on the trunks. What spray should I use, and when? (Illinois.) If these are bark beetles, there is no spray that will help, and seriously infested trees should be cut and burned before the beetles escape to other spruces. Ask a tree expert to diagnose the trouble.

STOCK

Why can't I raise good-looking stocks? Mine are always spindly and buggy. Even when I spray them they are small and sickly. (California.) Stocks in California suffer from several diseases. Young seedlings get a bacterial wilt, controlled by immersing seed in hot water held at 127° F. for 10 minutes, and planting in a new location. A fungous crown rot appears on overwatered, poorly drained soil; mosaic stunts the plants. Remove infected plants and spray to control aphids with malathion.

What can be done to control stem rot? (Arizona.) Stem and root rot are caused by a soil fungus which yellows the lower leaves, girdles the stem, causing wilting, and rots the roots. Since the fungus spreads for several feet through the soil away from the plant, it is not removed by taking up diseased plants and surrounding soil. Sterilize the soil (see Soil Sterilization) or plant in a new location.

SWEETPEA

How do you control mildew on sweetpea? (Washington.) Dust frequently with fine dusting sulfur, starting before mildew usually appears or spray with Karathane or Mildex. This may be combined with malathion to control aphids.

Will treating soil prevent green lice on sweetpeas? (Wisconsin.) No. You must spray for aphids during the growing season, using malathion up to blooming time.

Will treating soil prevent blighting of sweetpeas? (Wisconsin.) It will help in the control of various root rot diseases which cause wilting or blighting of the plants. (See Soil Sterilization.) Treating seed is a further precaution—1 minute in 95 per cent alcohol and 20 minutes in 1 to 1000 bichloride of mercury.

What causes sweetpeas to wilt just below the flower buds, then the whole plant turns greenish white and dies? (Connecticut.) A fungous disease called anthracnose and common on outdoor sweetpeas has this effect. The fungus also causes a disease of apples and lives over winter in cankered limbs and mummied apples as well as on sweetpea pods and seed and soil debris. Burn all plant refuse in the fall. Plant only those seeds which appear sound and plump. If you save your own seed, use only those from healthy seed pods.

Why do my sweetpeas develop a curled and puckered appearance? I plant on new ground each year, treat seed with Nitragin, give plenty of moisture. (Idaho.) This is probably mosaic, carried from plant to plant by aphids. Virus diseases are common in the Northwest and there is nothing you can do except try to control aphids by sprays and to remove infected plants promptly.

SWEETWILLIAM

What causes sweetwilliams to rot and turn yellow? I do not over-water them. (California.) A stem rot caused by a soil fungus, usually most destructive during warm, rainy periods, which you don't often have in California. Change the location if you can or sterilize the soil; use a light soil; avoid wounding the stems in cultivating.

SYCAMORE

What causes sycamore leaves to turn yellow and drop all summer long? (Missouri.) The most common cause is the fungous disease known as anthracnose, scorch, or leaf-and-twig blight, but this usually appears as brown areas on the leaves and is serious chiefly following a wet spring. It is controlled by spraying 2 or 3 times with ferbam or captan in the spring, and by cleaning up all infested leaves in summer. Yellowing and leaf fall may be due to hot, dry weather rather than disease.

TIGRIDIA

What treatment should be given tigridia bulbs which, when lifted from the border, are found to be covered with aphids? (New Jersey.) This is probably the tulip-bulb aphid, which commonly infests gladioli, a relative of tigridia. For gladioli the 1% lindane treatment for thrips works for the aphids; also a 2-hour soaking in malathion solution. You will have to experiment to see if either treatment injures tigridia.

TULIPS

What causes tulip blossoms to blister? Is it a disease? Botrytis blight causes brown or water-soaked spots on the petals, which might be called blisters. This is a fungous disease, very contagious, often known as gray mold or tulip fire. The spores are carried by the wind and rain from infected leaves or blossoms to healthy ones. Small black sclerotia are formed on leaves and petals rotting into the soil, and on the bulbs, and serve to carry the fungus over the winter. Spray with ferbam or captan from early spring weekly until bloom is finished.

Can the bulbs of diseased tulips be dug up and treated and used again? (Maine.) If the blighted blossoms are picked off immediately, and if all blossoms are cut off as they start to fade; if diseased leaves are removed when seen, and all leaves are cut off at ground level as soon as they ripen, the fungus may never get down to the bulb, and it is safe to leave it in the ground. If the bulbs are dug, it is better to discard any showing sclerotia than to treat them. If healthy new bulbs are to be planted in old infested soil, then the soil should be treated. (See Soil Sterilization.) If tulips are seriously diseased early in the season, the bulb is also infected, and should be taken up and destroyed immediately without waiting for normal digging time.

Why did my last year's tulips grow headless stalks? (New York.) Botrytis blight often causes blind buds. These usually come when the bulb itself was diseased in the ground, and not as the result of secondary infection from plants near by.

Last spring most of my bulbs failed to grow; those that did were sickly looking. Was this due to not covering the bulbs, or disease? I planted large, healthy bulbs. (Minnesota.) It probably was disease. If you planted deep enough, there was no need to cover. You either had botrytis blight from sclerotia in soil, or on the bulbs under the husk so you did not see them, or else they had gray bulb rot. The latter also is a sclerotial disease; it is more often characterized by large numbers of tulips failing to come up than is the botrytis disease, which is characterized by a weak growth above the ground. Plant new bulbs in another location, and make sure there are no black bodies either on the surface of the bulb or under its outer covering.

Why do white or yellow varieties seem not to be affected by the virus disease which causes "breaking" of the colors? (New York.) The breaking is a depigmentation, and if there is no color pigment in the flower, or very little, it cannot "break." However, there is now known to be another virus which adds color to light-colored varieties.

How can I prevent my bulbs from being eaten by very small insects? (Missouri.) These are probably bulb mites, very small, yellowish-white spiders. A heavy infestation will pulverize the inside of a bulb. Discard all such bulbs; dip the rest in malathion 1 tbsp. per gallon, for 10 minutes, and replant in another location, or in sterilized soil.

What are the thin white worms, ½ in. long, that eat bulbs in the ground? (Illinois.)   These are probably scavenger worms, feeding on bulbs rotting from some other cause. Seek for the original culprit.

What treatment do you recommend for the earth of beds where ground aphids are present? (New Jersey.)   Soak it with malathion solution or apply chlordane or dieldrin to control ants.

How do you keep lice off tulips when starting an indoor garden?   Soak infested bulbs in malathion solution for an hour or two. If aphids appear on foliage, spray with nicotine or malathion.

Do moles eat tulip bulbs? (Washington.)   Moles are supposed to be carnivorous, living on grubs and other animal life. Usually the mole makes the run to the tulip bed and mice follow along to do the actual eating. (See Moles; Mice.)

TULIP TREE

How can I save a tulip tree that shows signs of fungous growth on the south side? (New Jersey.)   Consult a tree expert. If fungi are growing out from the trunk, it is a sign of internal decay.

Each year a blight on leaves of young tulips is temporarily stopped by a Bordeaux mixture. Why does it reappear after 2 weeks? (Illinois.)   Leaves of young tulip trees often turn yellow and fall due to hot, dry weather, but there are a few fungous leaf spots which may cause blotches in the leaves. Ordinarily, spraying is not necessary, and the best control is to clean up all infected leaves.

Can anything be done for a tulip tree, about 10 years old, badly infested with oyster-shell scale? (New Jersey.)   This may not be oyster-shell scale. There is a special tulip scale, oval, brown, ⅓ in. across, that is far more common and injurious on this tree. A miscible oil, 1 to 25 dilution, applied in early spring, should control it. (See Dormant Spraying.)

TRUMPET VINE

What do you use for green lice on trumpet plant? (Pennsylvania.)   Spray with malathion, starting early, before the leaves curl.

What can be done about leaves curling up on the trumpet vine, caused, I think, by red spider? (Pennsylvania.)   If the leaves are curled, it is more likely that aphids are at work. Red spiders are more apt to turn the leaves yellow and mealy. Spray with malathion or any other contact insecticide.

VIBURNUM

What treatment should be used on common viburnum to discourage pests which cause the leaves to curl? (Illinois.)   This is the snowball aphid, and it starts curling the leaves almost as soon as they unfold.

Spraying with malathion when the buds first break, will contol this pest. Better yet apply a dormant dinitro spray before the buds open. Usually after you fight the aphid for a few years you either ignore it or plant another variety of viburnum.

When a snowball tree, or any other shrub, is diseased, can one get it back to a normal, healthy condition, or must it be replaced? (Minnesota.) That all depends on the disease, or the pest. The common snowball will curl up with aphids every season. You would have to select a different variety.

Bush of Viburnum carlesi has a deposit of rough white along the stems. Is it mealy bug? What can I do to save the bush? (New Hampshire.) Probably not. Many woody shrubs in late summer are attacked by lightning leaf hoppers, whose young leave flocculent white masses over the twigs. There seems to be no permanent injury. Spray with malathion and don't worry.

Each summer black spot comes on the leaves of my Viburnum carlesi and they drop off. What preventive? (Kentucky.) There is a bacterial leaf spot listed for viburnum, but this may not be your trouble in Kentucky. Spraying with streptomycin may work. Try picking off and burning infected leaves and cleaning up fallen leaves.

VIOLET

What can be done to protect violets against caterpillars? (Louisiana.) Pick the caterpillars off by hand so far as possible. Dust with methoxychlor.

WALNUT

I have an English Walnut that makes a new growth every spring and then the leaves drop off, and it is bare the rest of the summer. What causes this? (Pennsylvania.) It may be a leaf-spot disease, but more likely uncongenial surroundings. The English Walnut is exceedingly particular as to soil requirements, being intolerant of wet soils but requiring very deep, fertile soil with no excess of alkali.

WILLOW

The beautiful willow on my lawn, which has reached gigantic proportions, keeps losing its leaves as a result of bugs. It seems a shame to cut down the tree. Is there something I could spray on the bark and branches within my reach? (Long Island.) It would not help to cut the tree down. These are doubtless willow beetles. Have your tree sprayed once a year, in late May or early June, with malathion and DDT. There are plenty of commercial treemen with adequate apparatus on Long Island; it will cost far less for spraying than to have the tree cut down.

What can I do about the millions of dark red lice that get on our

large weeping willow—midsummer to frost? It is impossible to use the yard for laundry. (Ohio.)   Have your tree sprayed with malathion or other contact insecticide by a tree expert with power apparatus.

Will whitewashing a willow keep tree borers from attacking it? (Illinois.)   It probably would have little effect. Wrapping the trunk with wrapping paper or Kraft crepe paper will keep borers out, but is usually done only the first 2 years after transplanting. Some repellent washes are effective such as DDT or dieldrin solutions. (See Borers.) Better get the advice of a reliable treeman in your vicinity.

Is there any relation between scale insects and borers on pussy willow? What is the prevention? (Pennsylvania.)   No relation. Spray for scale with a miscible oil. (See Dormant Spraying.) Borer repellents may work. Inject BHC paste into borer holes if you see fresh sawdust. Cut down seriously infested trees and start over. Pussy willows grow fast.

YEW

Are all insects injurious to yews controlled by applying arsenic to the surrounding ground? (Pennsylvania.)   No. Chlordane or dieldrin is used to kill the grubs and adults of the black vine weevil, which is probably its most injurious insect pest. Yew is also subject to attacks by scale insects and mealy bugs, which are controlled by spraying foliage with malathion.

YUCCA

What are the soft-bodied insects which infest yucca? What spray for control? (North Carolina.)   Aphids are soft-bodied insects infesting yucca, but mealy bugs—soft white creatures—are more likely to be the trouble. Spray forcefully with malathion. Repeat as necessary.

ZINNIA

What is the cause of the white, powderlike discoloration on zinnias? (New Jersey.)   This is powdery mildew, a fungous disease, which usually appears toward the end of the season and is chiefly of importance because of the unsightly foliage. Dust with fine dusting sulfur or spray with Mildex or Karathane.

What makes the leaves of zinnias curl up from the sides? (Vermont.)   Mildew sometimes has this effect. Or it may be a water relation.

Have been troubled by rust. What will stop it? Could it start from narrow strip of brush and small trees adjoining garden? (Massachusetts.)   There is no rust common on zinnias, but there is a bacterial, and also a fungous, leaf spot which may cause reddish discoloration of the leaves in late summer. It is not usually serious, and it might be prevented by spraying with captan. You need not fear the strip of brush as far as "rust" is concerned, but if the weeds flourish, too, it would be a source of insect pests.

The roots of zinnias planted in open ground are covered with aphids; the plants withered after they had grown a few inches. How can we get rid of them? (Rhode Island.) You can try making a shallow depression around each plant and pouring in a solution of malathion; but if your soil is so badly infested, it would be better to plant more zinnias in another location. (See also Soil Sterilization.)

What should be used to get rid of tarnished plant bugs? Have tried many sprays without success. (New York.) Frequent applications of DDT or malathion spray might help. The first and most important step is getting rid of the weeds that harbor this plant bug.

This year zinnias have been badly infested with stem borers, but there were no marks or sawdust visible on outside. Cannot find material telling life cycle or control. Can you supply? (California.) These probably are the common stalk borers, although they are listed as general only east of the Rockies. They winter as eggs on weeds and old stalks, so that the chief control measure is getting rid of these. (See also Borers.)

VEGETABLES

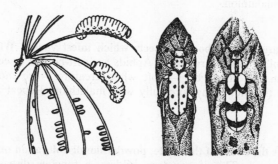

Asparagus Beetles: attack asparagus shoots; grubs eat foliage; center, Twelve-spotted Asparagus Beetle.

ASPARAGUS

Will rust-resistant asparagus always escape the disease? Not entirely. The Mary and Martha Washington varieties are reasonably rust resistant, but in some seasons in certain areas the red-and-black pustules show up on the leaves and stems, with yellowing of the tops. In that case dust with ferbam or sulfur 3 times at 2-week intervals after cutting season. Burn old tops.

Is there a spray or remedy of any kind for asparagus beetle? (Oregon.) This red, blue, and yellow beetle is chiefly controlled by clean cutting during the harvest season, although an occasional dusting with rotenone may be needed. After the cutting season dust with DDT or methoxychlor.

What about the Japanese beetle on asparagus? (New Jersey.) The Japanese beetle may appear in swarms on asparagus foliage in midsummer, but the injury is rarely sufficient to call for treatment.

BEAN

What is the chewing insect, colored yellow with black spots, shaped a little like the ladybug but longer? (Texas.) Either the Mexican bean beetle or the bean leaf beetle. The former looks more like a ladybug with its 16 small black spots, but it is larger, more convex, and coppery-yellow in color. Its yellow larvae are also found on the leaves. The bean leaf beetle is prevalent in Southern states. It is about the size of a ladybug, red to yellow in color, with 6 black spots and a black band around the wing covers. Its larva is a white grub which feeds on the stem and roots *below* the soil line. Both beetles are controlled by the same treatment. The yellow-green spotted cucumber beetle also feeds on bean foliage in Texas, and this, too, looks like a ladybug.

Mexican Bean Beetle: coppery yellow, sixteen black spots; both adults and spiny, dirty yellow larvae feed on under sides of leaves.

All known insecticides failed to destroy a ½-in. long yellow creeper on beans—looks like a caterpillar. What is it? (Massachusetts.) Probably larvae of Mexican bean beetles, which are fat, soft, covered with black-tipped spines, and something under ½ in. long. They succumb to rotenone dust in this stage. The larvae are easier to kill than the adult beetles.

Are little pests that look like a yellow bur on green beans the bean

beetle? (Ohio.) Yes. That is a very good description of the larvae of Mexican bean beetle.

What are the time-cycles of the Mexican bean beetle? With a succession of string beans I notice some plantings suffer more than others. (New York.) You are right. Beans planted in June in New York will mature in July between the two broods of beetles. The first beetles appear in May, when the early beans come up, feed for a week, lay their eggs in orange-yellow clusters on the under side of the leaves. The larvae hatch in another week, feed for 2 to 5 weeks, pupate on the leaves, and in 1 more week produce the adults which feed and lay eggs for the second generation. This is usually much more destructive than the first, untreated bean foliage being completely riddled during August and September.

How long a season has the bean beetle? (Virginia.) About as long as the beans are growing. In Virginia the Mexican bean beetle will probably have 3 broods a season.

What is the cheapest and most effective way to destroy bean beetles without harming the plants? (New York.) Apply rotenone, preferably in dust form for ease of application and coverage or malathion as a spray.

Will rotenone powder, used as a spray, control the Mexican bean beetle if applied frequently, starting a week after beans have come up? (New York.) Derris powder, analyzing 4 to 5 per cent rotenone, could be used as a spray. There are, however, proprietary rotenone sprays available. By watching the life cycle, described above, and treating only when larvae or beetles are present, much time and material may be saved. It is important to begin early, to get the overwintered beetles as they lay their eggs and the first larvae before they can produce more beetles.

Will turpentine in water sprayed on the soil where beans are to be planted keep away the bean beetle? No. You must spray or dust the foliage.

Is daily picking of the bean beetles and eggs the easiest way to control them? (Virginia.) An occasional dusting will be a lot easier than daily picking off, unless there are very, very few beans. Combine the two methods, picking off as many as you can whenever you have time. Each female removed before egg laying, or each cluster of eggs burned up, means fewer beetles for the next brood.

Is there anything other than spraying, dusting, and hand-picking to control the Mexican bean beetle? (New York.) Yes, sanitary measures at the end of the season are very important. Clean up and burn all plant debris, or else spade or plow it under deeply, and clean up all weeds and trash around garden so there will be no hiding place for the overwintering females.

Is there anything to be done about such pests as bean beetles and

cutworms during the winter? (Indiana.) Fall plowing or spading and keeping the garden clean during the winter will certainly help to discourage both of these pests.

What can I do for the little bugs that come on lima beans? (Maryland.) The Mexican bean beetle is as destructive to lima beans as it is to string beans. Use the same control measures.

What will destroy the Japanese beetle on string beans? (Massachusetts.) Rotenone dust or spray, as recommended for Mexican bean beetle, will also take care of Japanese beetles.

How can I kill or prevent small green bugs with black dots on back which eat bean foliage? Was afraid to spray on account of poisoning the vegetable. (California.) These are diabrotica, or 12-spotted cucumber beetles. You may safely spray with either rotenone or malathion.

My string beans had little greenish bugs all over the plants all season. What are these? How can I get rid of them? (New York.) The regular bean aphid is black; the pea aphid is green and sometimes attacks other legumes. A greenish leaf hopper sometimes infests beans. Malathion spray should keep any of these under control and may be applied almost to picking time. Or rely on the rotenone used for beetle control.

What shall I use, and when, for very tiny white flies that rise in a cloud from string beans? (California.) It is doubtful that white flies on beans are injurious enough to warrant control measures. They may be sprayed with malathion up to within 5 days of picking.

How does the bug called a weevil get into beans? (Massachusetts.) Eggs are laid on the pods while the beans are in the garden; these hatch into grubs which burrow through the pod into the bean. There they change into the small, dull gray adult weevils with reddish legs. Several broods may be produced in storage, ruining the beans for either seed or food.

The beans I raised last summer have little holes from which have come little beetles. What treatment should the vines have to prevent them? (Maine.) These are the bean weevils (weevil being merely the name given to a beetle with a little snout). There is no treatment for the vines except to clean them up and burn them. The beans have to be treated after harvest. (See next question.)

How can I protect the beans from weevils during storage? There are several methods: (1) Fumigate with methyl bromide. Place seeds in a box or container, such as a garbage can, that can be closed tightly; pour into saucer, ½ oz. per cu. ft., and keep closed 24 to 36 hours. (2) Spread out in pans and heat dry in the oven at 130° to 140° F. for 1 hour (some say 30 minutes). (3) Suspend seeds in cloth bag in kettle of cold water and heat to 140° F. Dry quickly. (4) Shake beans thoroughly in a container, with 1 pt. of lime to each qt. of beans.

Does treatment injure the beans for food or seed?   It should not, if directions are followed. The excess lime can be shaken off in a strainer and then the beans washed.

Last year my pole beans did poorly and when I pulled them up there were a lot of very small bugs on the roots. What were they? (Massachusetts.)   Root aphids, in all probability. Push the soil away slightly from around each stem and pour in a cupful of malathion solution, 1 tbsp. to 1 gal. of water.

I had some fine Kentucky Wonder beans, but after a while the leaves turned brown and the beans stopped growing. What caused this? (Massachusetts.)   This might have been the root aphids just mentioned; or perhaps dry root rot, caused by a fungus which lives several years in the soil, necessitating a long rotation; or rust. (See below.) It could have been heavy, wet soil without the fungus. In our town, in an "experience meeting" at the end of this past season, we learned that pole beans did extremely well in the plots that were almost pure ashes, and hence well drained, and very poorly at the other end of town, where the soil was heavy clay.

Last summer I was bothered with "rust spots" on my green beans, varying from skin deep to the center of the pod. What was the trouble? (North Carolina.)   Not true rust but a fungous disease called anthracnose or pod spot, which shows as round sunken spots with dark borders and pinkish spore pustules in the center. Anthracnose cannot be "cured" but it may be prevented by planting seed from healthy pods, or else seed grown in the West where the disease is not a problem. Avoid working with beans when they are wet, as this spreads the spores from diseased to healthy plants. Resistant varieties are chiefly of the shell-bean type. Ferbam sprays will prevent its spread.

What causes blight on leaf of green beans? (Ohio.)   If there are small angular lesions and black veins, this blight is anthracnose; your State Experiment Station lists Livingston's Pencil Pod Wax, Keeney's Rustless Golden Wax, Longfellow, Black Valentine, or Hopkins' Earliest Red Valentine as worth trying for resistance to anthracnose. If the blighting shows up as irregular light-green wilting patches on leaves and irregular blotches on pods, it is bacterial blight.

How is bacterial blight controlled? (Ohio.)   Use disease-free seed, either from healthy pods or Western grown. Do not work with wet plants. Varieties Refugee 1000 to 1, Refugee Wax, or Late Stringless Green Refugee are more or less resistant snap beans. For dry beans choose Michigan Robust Pea, Perry Marrow, Yellow Eye, or Scotia. Try streptomycin sprays.

What is the treatment for rust which comes about mid-season on pole beans? (Massachusetts.)   True rust is a fungous disease which shows as reddish powdery pustules on the leaves. In Massachusetts it is generally serious only on polebeans, where it causes early death of the vines. The rust winters over on dead plants and on stakes. Destroy vines after harvest, and next year use new poles or soak the old in formaldehyde (1 to 100 dilution), and keep them wet overnight by covering. Kentucky Wonder, U.S. No. 3, and U.S. No. 4 are resistant to some forms of rust.

How can rust spots be eliminated on green and yellow beans? (Illinois.) If you have true rust, and not anthracnose (see above) varieties like Hodson Long Pod, Wisconsin Refugee, Improved Rust-proof Golden Wax, and Black Valentine may be rust resistant in your section of the country. You cannot eliminate rust once it shows up in the planting.

What is the treatment for mosaic on green snap beans? (Washington.) There is no treatment. The virus usually comes in with the seed. Rogue out plants with mottled light and dark green leaves. Choose resistant varieties like Refugee, U.S. No. 5, Idaho Refugee, and Wisconsin Refugee. In Washington, curly-top, another virus disease, may affect beans. Rogue out dwarfed plants with puckered leaves.

Why do my string beans mildew? (California.) Powdery mildew is a fungous disease very prevalent in California. It usually attacks beans in cloudy weather or toward autumn. Dust with sulfur. The Refugee beans listed above as resistant to mosaic are also resistant to mildew.

Does mildew come on string beans because of soil or atmospheric conditions? (California.) This is not a soil fungus; the spores are carried by the wind. For some reason the California atmosphere is peculiarly conducive to mildew, not only on beans but many other vegetables and ornamentals.

BEET

How are leaf miners kept out of beet tops? (New York.) There is no spray that will prevent maggots from working inside the beet leaves, turning the tissues brown. Pick off infested leaves and destroy the wild host, lambsquarters. Incidentally, lambsquarters when young is a perfectly delicious vegetable, preferred by many to spinach, so a good way to destroy it is to cook it for dinner.

What about beet webworms? There are several species of caterpillars which eat the leaves and web them together. Dust with 5% methoxychlor dust and remove weeds like lambsquarters.

Should beet seed be treated before planting to prevent damping off? Definitely. The rough beet seed may carry spores of several disease organisms. Thiram (Arasan) or captan is very effective for beets. (See Seed Treatment.)

What causes spots that resemble warts on beets? The same organism that produces potato scab. Do not grow beets on land that has grown scabby potatoes. If the soil is alkaline, make it slightly acid with sulfur, and avoid any alkaline agents such as lime and manure. Use a cover crop of rye in place of the manure.

How can I keep beets and spinach from blighting? Our soil is slightly alkaline. (Washington.) In Washington blight probably means curly-top, a virus disease that used to be called Western yellow blight, characterized by yellowing, stunting, and death. The virus is transmitted by the beet leaf hopper, so that insect control with contact insecticides is important. There is little else you can do except rogue out diseased plants immediately and keep down weed hosts. Soil acidity is *not* a factor, as it is in scab.

Is leaf spot on beets prevented by spraying? Spraying with Bordeaux mixture may prevent the round, red-bordered spots from getting numerous, but in the small garden picking off spotted leaves is ordinarily sufficient control.

BROCCOLI

How can I keep aphids off Italian Broccoli? (Oregon.) Spray or dust with malathion until the heads form, then treat with pyrethrum if necessary. Often the aphids cluster on a single head or leaf which may be removed and burned. If aphids are numerous on a head cut for eating, separate into flowerettes and soak in strong salt water. The aphids will float out and can be poured off. Then rinse the broccoli well in pure water before cooking.

How are root maggots and worms controlled? See Cabbage. Broccoli is a member of the cabbage family, and while it is free from many cabbage diseases, it has its share of aphids, root maggots, and worms eating the foliage and flower heads. Use malathion, rotenone or pyrethrum for worms, chlordane or dieldrin for maggots.

BRUSSELS SPROUTS

What is the best control for worms and aphids on Brussels sprouts? Rotenone dust is allowed for worms on Brussels sprouts and will keep the aphids down to some extent. Or they may be sprayed or dusted with malathion. (See also Broccoli.)

CABBAGE

Is there any way to prevent white maggots from attacking the roots of cabbage plants? (Wisconsin.) When a young cabbage wilts and, upon being pulled up, discloses white maggots working on the underground stem and roots, it is too late for control. There are several ways of preventing maggot injury. Apply chlordane or dieldrin granules to plant bases when plants are set out.

How are tar-paper disks, for control of root maggots, applied? Cut a 4-in. square, or circle; make a hole in the center with a spike, and make a cut from the outer edge to the hole, so you can get the paper around the stem. (Or ready-made disks can be bought.) Work gently, so as not to bruise the young seedling. The disk should stay flat on the ground and fit snugly around the stem.

Cabbage Root Maggot. Eggs of this pest are laid on stems, near ground level, in early spring.

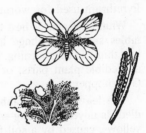

Cabbage Worm: adult white or yellow butterfly; worms, green.

What is the calomel treatment for seedlings? This treatment has been replaced by the cheaper and more effective 5% chlordane or 1% dieldrin granule treatment to plant bases.

How do you treat seedlings set out in the garden with bichloride of mercury? Dissolve 2 tablets in 1 qt. of water (1 to 1000 solution) and pour ½ cupful around stem of each plant. *Caution:* this is a virulent poison, and also corrosive; mix in a glass jar; keep away from children and pets.

What is the best way to control the black flea beetle on small cabbage plants? (Virginia.) These small but very active beetles do considerable damage to young plants, often riddling the leaves with tiny shot holes. Before the cabbage heads form it is safe to dust with 5% DDT or to spray with DDT wettable powder.

What can be used to keep worms from eating cabbages? Until the heads are the size of baseballs it is safe to dust or spray with DDT, as recommended for flea beetles above. After that spray or dust with rotenone or pyrethrum; or resort to hand-picking.

Is there more than one type of cabbage worm? There are 3. The true cabbage worm, green caterpillar of the common white or yellow butterfly; the cabbage looper, a striped pale-green worm that moves like an inchworm and changes into a brownish-gray moth; and a small, greenish caterpillar that is the larva of the diamondback moth. All these are controlled in the same way.

Will sulfur keep the worms from eating young cabbage plants? (California.) In certain experiments sulfur dust has prevented chewing by the tent caterpillar. It would be worth trying on cabbages, but do not expect too much from it. It seems to work chiefly on young larvae.

Is lump lime good to destroy cabbage worms, and those little dark worms which hold themselves in ring shape? (Maine.) Lime is used to control cabbage clubroot, if your soil is acid, but would have no effect on cabbage worms. The little dark worms are millipedes (which see) and not very injurious.

How can I control blue aphids on cabbage? (California.) By a malathion spray, or dust, which may be used almost to harvesttime. Pyrethrum used for worms will also control aphids.

What treatment is best to kill grasshoppers that attack garden vegetables such as cabbage and broccoli? (California.) Scatter poison bait thinly in the morning, being very sure that none of the bait touches any edible plant parts, or spray vegetables with methoxychlor. (See Grasshoppers.)

The leaves of my cabbage plants turned yellow and the cabbage died. Is anything wrong with the soil? (Wisconsin.) This is cabbage yellows, caused by a soil fungus—a species of Fusarium—very common in your state. Either plant in a new location or grow resistant varieties such as Jersey Queen, Marion Market, All Head Select or Improved Globe, Wisconsin All-Seasons, Wisconsin Ballhead, Wisconsin Hollander No. 8, or Red Hollander.

In order to grow cabbage, do I have to buy yellows-resistant seed? (New York.) Advisable, but it may not be necessary in New York. The disease is not so prevalent as in the Middle West, and if you have no previous record of cabbages dying or yellows on your soil, you need not worry much.

For years I have had trouble with cabbage plants. Just before ready to head up the leaves turn yellow and drop off. The plant dies. There is no evidence of insect pests. (Delaware.) Your soil is apparently well inoculated with the "yellows" or fusarium wilt fungus. Plant resistant varieties.

What causes cabbages to rot off the stalk? (Iowa.) Black rot or blight, a bacterial disease, is one cause. The plants are stunted, leaves turn yellow to brown, shrivel and drop off, or the head may decay and fall off in a slimy mass. The vascular ring in the stem and the leaf veins are black. Use clean seed, or disinfect with hot water (see Seed Treatment); plant in disease-free soil; remove and burn diseased plants; clean up all cabbage refuse.

What causes the tops of the cabbage leaves to turn black, sometimes running through entire head? (Wisconsin.) Either the black rot just discussed or a fungous disease called blackleg. There are dark areas with black dots on stems and leaves. If the stem is girdled near the ground line, the plants wilt and die. Use cabbage seed grown near Puget Sound, where disease is rare, or treat with hot water. Practice sanitary measures given above and a 4-year rotation.

What is the best remedy for preventing clubroot in cabbage and cauliflower? (Michigan.) Clubroot is the name of a disease which causes grossly enlarged and malformed roots and stunted, sickly plants. If the disease has been present previously, treat the soil with fresh hydrated lime, 10 lbs. to 100 sq. ft., and rake it in shortly before planting; or try soil treatment with PCNB (Terrachlor) when planting.

What is the cure for cabbage wilt—curled tips of leaves, whitish color? (California.) This may be powdery mildew, with the fungus growing over the leaves and causing the white color. If so, you can dust with sulfur. If it is a chlorosis (an actual loss of color in the leaf tissue), then perhaps some chemical is lacking for good nutrition, or your soil is too alkaline.

CARROT

We have trouble with maggots in the carrots. Can you give any help in controlling this pest? (Washington.) Your Experiment Station suggests that in western Washington early carrots be planted so they can be harvested by July 15, and in small blocks, so they can be screened and the rust fly prevented from laying her eggs. Do not plant late carrots before June 1. Heptachlor as used for grub-proofing will check the rust fly.

Please advise me about the small worms which make burrows in carrots. Are they wireworms? (Oregon.) Probably these are the maggots of the carrot rust fly discussed in the previous question. Control measures for Washington should also apply for Oregon.

What grub or bug eats tunnels through the sides of carrots? (Iowa.) In Iowa the carrot grub, which looks like the common white grub and eats pieces out of the carrots, and the rust-fly maggots, which make rust-colored tunnels, are the chief insect pests. Control both pests by dusting the ground along the row, as soon as the seed is planted, with heptachlor. Rotating is helpful.

Can carrot worms be avoided by harvesting early or by adding lime to the soil? (Michigan.) By planting in June the first brood of the rust fly can be avoided, and harvesting can be done before the second brood. Lime is sometimes recommended to drive away the carrot beetle but should not be used unless your soil requires it. Heptachlor will do a better job for the maggots. (See above.)

What are the insects which look like blue lice and infest my carrot roots? How can I get rid of them? (New York.) These are root aphids (plant lice); they look bluish because of a powdery coating. If the infestation is bad enough to require control, pour malathion 1 tbsp. per gal. of water, around the stems after loosening the soil.

How do I keep ants from putting plant lice on carrot roots? (New York.) Find the nest if you can and treat with 5% chlordane dust. (See Ants.)

How can I keep my carrot crop from rotting in the garden? (Arizona.) Your carrots either have Southern blight (see Crown Rot) or else bacterial soft rot, a bacterial disease that more often appears in storage, but occasionally in the garden. The fungi and bacteria are in the soil, so you must plant in a new location or treat the soil. (See Soil Sterilization.)

Is there a foliage disease of carrots? (New Jersey.) There is a leaf blight which produces spots on the leaves, after which they turn brown and die, but it is not ordinarily serious enough in the home garden to require more than cleaning up old tops. If necessary, spray with captan.

CAULIFLOWER

How are cauliflower troubles controlled? Treat seed and practice same sanitary measures as recommended for cabbage. Never use DDT or related compounds on cauliflower when flower heads have formed, but rely on rotenone or pyrethrum. Occasionally there is a bacterial or fungous spot on the heads; for this there is no practical control.

CELERY

Is blight on celery in seed or soil? (Indiana.) Both. There are 3 blights, early and late blight caused by fungi, and a bacterial blight. The organisms are carried over in celery refuse in the garden and on the seed. Practice a 3-year rotation and either use seed that is 2 years old or treat it with formaldehyde (1 part to 240 parts water) for 15 minutes, after pre-soaking for 30 minutes in lukewarm water.

How can celery blight be prevented? (Pennsylvania.) Spray with captan at weekly intervals in the seedbed; and at 7- to 10-day intervals after setting out in the garden. Blight is worse in a wet season and is spread by working with plants when they are wet.

Our celery is injured by slugs; is there any remedy? (Pennsylvania.) Clean up hiding places such as loose boards and old plant debris; sprinkle lime on the ground, or use a poison bait. (See Slugs.)

How can I get rid of beetlelike bugs in celery plants? (Pennsylvania.) These are tarnished plant bugs and very difficult to get rid of. Clean up weeds and try pyrethrum or malathion dusts or sprays.

COLLARDS

How may one overcome insects on collards? (Alabama.) Rotenone or pyrethrum sprays or dusts will take care of cabbage worms and aphids, or malathion sprays may be used for the latter if the greens are thoroughly washed. Pick off harlequin bugs—the brilliant red or yellow, black-and-blue sucking insects.

CORN

How can one tell when corn has been stung by the corn-borer moth? (New York.) The yellow-brown moth of the European corn borer lays its eggs in groups of 20 or more on the *under* side of the leaves, and the larvae, tiny, flesh-colored borers, tunnel their way into the stalk, leaf stems, and ears. Their presence is shown by tassels bending over or broken; fine sawdustlike castings on the leaves; small holes in the stalks, often with protruding borings.

When should table corn be planted to avoid the borer? (Michigan.) There are 2 broods of the European corn borer. Extra early corn will be injured by the first, and very late corn will be attacked by the second brood. Corn planted between the middle of May and the first of June will mature chiefly between the broods and thus escape much injury.

What is the latest on the control of corn borer? (Vermont.) That the treatments for the borer must be related to growth stages of the corn. Give the first dusting when tassels can be seen on half the plants by looking down into the tops. Dust into the tassel whorl, and give two more treatments at 5-day intervals. Five per cent DDT dust or granules has proved most satisfactory in borer control. Ryania dust is also used, but it is more expensive.

How else can one fight the borer? The corn borer feeds on more than 200 kinds of plants and winters, in the larval stage, in old herbaceous stems. It is extremely important to clean up in the fall not only old cornstalks and stubble, but to burn dahlia and gladiolus tops, and to clean up weeds, especially pigweed and smartweed.

Is the common stalk borer injurious to corn? Yes, especially at the edge of the corn patch near weeds, or where wasteland has been recently turned into garden. The young caterpillars are brown, white-striped, turning grayish as they increase in size. The moths lay their eggs in September on giant ragweed and many other weeds. Cleaning up is the only known control measure.

Can worms in sweet corn be avoided? (Washington.) The corn earworm is more widely distributed than the corn borer, and the caterpillars are large, brown to green in color, and striped. The moths lay their eggs chiefly on the corn silk, and the young larvae feed on that and the tip of the ear. Standard control is to dust the silks as soon as they appear with 5% DDT dust. Repeat 3 to 4 times at 2-day intervals.

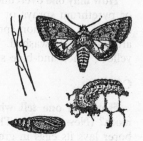

Corn Earworm: large brown to green worm, with distinct striping. (See Corn Borer, page 1121.)

I have read of a dust to sprinkle on the corn silk to keep out borers. What is it? (Ohio.)   Use 5% DDT as above.

Can anything be done about Japanese beetles on sweet corn? (New Jersey.)   They congregate on the silk, so the earworm applications will also control them.

How can squirrels be kept from eating corn? (Indiana.)   Squirrels, and occasionally raccoons, are very destructive pests of corn, and there is little to be done except shoot them, which is not permitted in many localities. In my garden the corn was planted in a square block this past season. The squirrels started to eat on the outside row, and when this was left to them they ignored the rest of the corn patch.

How eliminate smut from sweet corn? (New York.)   The only control measure is to cut off and burn the large smut boil—from ear, tassel or stalk—before it opens to discharge the black spores which will infect other corn. Avoid the use of manure likely to be infested, and burn up stalks after harvest. Spraying is not helpful and there are no resistant varieties.

Is there any other important corn disease? (New Jersey.)   Bacterial, or Stewart's, wilt may be serious after a mild winter. There are discolored streaks in the leaves, and young plants wilt and die. The bacteria are spread by corn flea beetles. Many of the new hybrid varieties are resistant to this disease.

CUCUMBER

What measures can be taken against striped cucumber beetles? They seem almost impossible to destroy. (Illinois.)   They are hard to control, but there are many ways to fight these green, black-striped beetles: 1. Remove weed hosts, especially Chinese-lantern plants. 2. Protect young seedlings with hotkaps or cheesecloth tents. 3. Plant extra seeds in the hills, and discard the most injured seedlings. 4. As soon as the ground cracks over the seedlings, start dusting with rotenone, lindane, methoxychlor or dieldrin. Repeat treatments as often as needed to keep plants covered with dust.

What causes bugs in the roots of cucumber plants? (Pennsylvania.) The larvae of the spotted cucumber beetle works on the roots of many plants and is known as the Southern corn rootworm. The beetle, green with 12 black spots, is controlled like the striped cucumber beetle. The spotted beetle also attacks many ornamental plants, where it is known as diabrotica beetle. "Bugs" may also be root aphids (see page 1054.)

A worm eats our pickle cucumbers. Is there a remedy? (Illinois.) The white or green pickle worm is especially destructive in Southern states but is occasionally found as far north as Illinois. It bores into the ripening fruits. The dusts listed for the striped cucumber beetle should be helpful. Destroy all old vines.

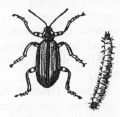

Striped Cucumber Beetle attacks cucumbers, melons, and squash; green with black stripes; larvae attack roots.

What is the control for the large, flat, gray beetle which attacks cucumber, pumpkin, squash, and melon vines? I have used moth balls in the hills with the seed and it seemed to work. Was it by accident? (Arkansas.) Probably, although the moth balls might have some repellent effect on the squash bug. (See Squash for more details.)

How rid cucumber vines of lice? (Texas.) The melon aphid is very destructive to all cucurbits, causing leaves to curl, wilt, and brown; it attacks many other plants, including lilies, to which it carries mosaic. Spray or dust with malathion, being careful to get underneath the leaves.

How are white flies on cucumbers killed? (New York.) The treatments for aphids (see previous question) should subdue them. They are often abundant on cucurbits, but of minor importance.

What pest or disease causes cucumber to wither, runner by runner, until the plant dies and semi-mature fruit shrivels up? (New York.) It is either the squash vine borer (see Squash) or wilt. The latter is a bacterial disease, very prevalent, disseminated by spotted and striped cucumber beetles, which carry the bacteria in their digestive tracts over the winter and deposit them in droppings on the leaves as they feed. The young vines may be sprayed or dusted to control the cucumber beetles.

My pickles show mosaic. What can I do about that? (Michigan.) Control the weeds, such as burweed, milkweed, catnip, pokeberry, and groundcherry, which harbor the virus; control the melon aphids and cucumber beetles, which carry the virus from the weeds to the cucumbers. Try resistant varieties such as Chicago Pickling.

My cucumber leaves look rusty and yellow. What causes this? (Massachusetts.) Bacteria produce angular leaf spots and fungus brownish circles. Treat seed with 1 to 1000 solution of bichloride of mercury for 5 minutes, rinse, and dry. Spray foliage with captan or maneb, especially latter part of season. Clean up and burn all old vines.

EGGPLANT

How can one get an eggplant that does not die of wilt? (Alabama.) You have to set healthy plants grown from clean seed in soil that has not grown eggplant for 4 years. Eggplant wilt—also called foot rot, blight, leaf spot, and wilt from its various symptoms—is so severe in the South that clean seed is rarely found. So soak in hot water, 122° F. for 5 minutes; then rinse in running water and dry thoroughly. Tie seed in cheesecloth bag before immersion. After drying, treat seed with Arasan or captan. (See Seed Treatment.)

What makes eggplants wilt? (New Jersey.) In New Jersey it is probably verticillium, which stunts the plants and turns the leaves yellow. The plant wilts in the heat of the day and the vessels are dark if the stem is cut. Use a long rotation which does not include tomatoes, potatoes, or raspberries. The fungus can live in the soil a long time. Or try soil sterilization.

LETTUCE

Why did my head lettuce rot after it was transplanted from the greenhouse? It was covered with a grayish fuzz. (New York.) This was botrytis blight, or gray mold disease, which infects seedlings if they are kept too wet in the greenhouse, and shows up as bottom rot. Remove plants carefully with surrounding soil, and soak the soil with captan solution. Sterilize the soil used for flats in greenhouse or cold frame. A similar rot, but starting from the top down, is called "drop," and is controlled in the same way.

MELON

How do you exterminate the small yellow chewing insect with black stripes known as the cantaloupe bug? (Texas.) The striped cucumber beetle frequently congregates on melon fruit. (See Cucumber for control.)

What insect kills my cantaloupes almost overnight? It is same color as leaves, small, egg-shaped, and the leaves scald and brown. (Missouri.) The melon aphid almost fits your description. (See Cucumber for control.)

Can root rot on melon vines be prevented? (Vermont.) Fusarium wilt, a soil fungus, causes the plants to become stunted and yellowed. Long rotations reduce the amount of wilt.

My muskmelons did well up to ripening, then wilted and died. Why? (Michigan.)   Perhaps the fusarium wilt just discussed; or cucumber wilt (see Cucumber); or the squash vine borer. (See Squash.)

ONION

Is there a practical method (for small garden) for keeping onions raised from seed free from the onion maggot? (New York.)   Treat the seed with calomel before planting (2 parts calomel to 1 part seed); or dust soil at base of plants with heptachlor or dieldrin. Use shallow planting.

What causes onions to rot? Seemingly a worm or bug bores through stalk. (Wisconsin.)   This is the onion maggot discussed above. When damaged onions are put in storage, they decay and cause surrounding bulbs to rot.

I pulled and stored my onions and found that majority are going bad. Why? (Pennsylvania.)   Fungi following after maggot injury are responsible. Onions should be stored only where there is free air circulation, either in a string bag, or else with the tops left on and braided into chains to hang up on the wall. The latter method is easy and very successful, and you can always cut off just the size onion you want without rummaging through a bag.

What is the best means of control for onion thrip? (Connecticut.)   It is very difficult to control this small sucking insect which rasps the leaves and turns them whitish. Early planting is said to be helpful, for most thrips are present after July 1. Spray or dust weekly with DDT, dieldrin or heptachlor.

Can cutworms be prevented from injuring young growing onions? (New York.)   Paper collars are impractical; so use poison bait if cutworms are too numerous to destroy by hand-picking. Take care in spreading the bait that it does not come in contact with the onions. (See Cutworms.) The maggot treatments will also take care of cutworms.

What is the black powdery mass on leaves and bulbs?   Onion smut, a fungous disease. The easiest way to avoid it is to grow onions from sets, because they can be infected only in the young seedling stage. In growing from seed, start in a clean, new seedbed and transplant; or else, treat seed with Arasan before planting.

PEA

How are damping off and root rots on peas prevented? (Connecticut.)   Early planting helps get peas started before the root-rot fungi can get in their work; but treating with Spergon or Arasan (which see) helps prevent root rot as well as damping off. Avoid heavy, low, and poorly drained soils. Use a 3- to 5-year rotation.

How can I control the pale-green plant lice that suck the sap from the vines? The pea aphis is very difficult to control, but malathion spray or dust is helpful.

How can moles be prevented from destroying green peas? I have read that moles eat only worms. If so, what becomes of the pea seed? (Washington.) Gardeners are frequently skeptical about the biologist's statement that moles live on animal life. If the mole tunnel disturbs the pea roots, various root-rot fungi might destroy the pea seed. (See Moles for control, if any.)

PEPPER

What should be used to kill lice on pepper plants? (Nebraska.) Malathion should be safe if the fruits are carefully washed; but pyrethrum or rotenone may be substituted as non-poisonous materials. In general, peppers have the same pests as potatoes, and control measures are the same.

Why do my peppers turn brown and fall off as soon as they are formed? (Connecticut.) This is probably due to unfavorable weather, which sometimes cause not only blossom and fruit drop of many plants, but a blossom-end rot of the fruits after they were formed. (See Squash; Tomato.)

POTATO

How prevent potato leaves from curling and turning brown, and the vine dying before the tubers are full grown? (New York.) This is late blight, the most destructive disease of potatoes. Plant only "certified" tubers, of a blight resistant variety such as Kennebeck and start spraying with Bordeaux mixture or maneb when the plants are 6 ins. high; repeat every 10 to 14 days until the plants stop growing.

How can the home gardener, with no power-spray equipment, prevent late potato blight? (Massachusetts.) Spraying is preferable, and may be done with a 3-gal. compressed-air sprayer, but dusting may be substituted, using a 20 to 80 copper-lime dust, or maneb dust.

When should blighted potatoes be dug? (Massachusetts.) If the vines are severely infected, dig as early as possible before the fungus gets down to rot the tubers.

Is there any treatment of the soil to prevent potato rot? (Connecticut.) No, it would not pay or help much to chemically treat soil for potatoes, and the best seed treatment is to make sure they are sound when cut for planting. The practice of hilling potatoes is in a sense a helpful soil treatment because it interposes more of a barrier between the fungous spores developing on the leaves and the tubers below.

What is the cause of scab on potatoes? (Vermont.) A common soil organism closely related to bacteria, *Actinomyces scabies* by name. It is unable to grow in an acid soil, but as the soil becomes increasingly alkaline scab injury increases, varying from slight russeting to greatly roughened scabby areas on the tubers.

What can be done for potatoes that get rough, scabby hides? We put plenty of cow manure on. Do we use it too green, or too much, or too often; or is it the weather? We used to have lovely potatoes. (Kansas.) You use it too much and too often for soil infested with scab organism. Manure has an alkaline effect, like lime and wood ashes, and the more alkaline the soil the better *Actinomyces* likes it. Resistant varieties are available.

What can be done with soil that produces scabby potatoes? (New York.) Get your pH (soil acidity) down to around 5.4. Adding flowers of sulfur will increase acidity. The amount needed varies with the original pH, but might run around 10 lbs. per 1000 sq. ft., or 300 to 400 lbs. per acre.

The Government puts out some kind of solution for potato seed. What is it? (New York.) State Experiment Stations or county agents may arrange co-operative seed treatments for farmers but I doubt if the Government gives out any such material. To control scab and rhizoctonia, uncut potatoes may be dipped in nabam solution (1 pint in 30 gals. water) just before planting; or in yellow oxide of mercury for 1 minute. The back-yard gardener would do better to make sure he is using clean, sound potatoes for seed and omit the treatment.

Potato Bug. Both the orange-and-black-striped adults and the fat, copper-colored larvae destroy foliage.

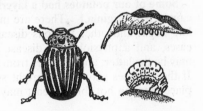

How are potato bugs controlled? (New York.) Spray or dust foliage with dieldrin or heptachlor, to take care of these large orange-yellow, black-striped beetles and their enormous humpbacked, reddish larvae. This is the famous Colorado potato beetle, which has become resistant to DDT in many areas.

How do you control the old-fashioned black potato bug? (Ohio.) Blister beetles are hard to kill. Hand-picking is excellent. The potato beetle treatments should work.

How shall I exterminate long-bodied gray or brown beetles that clean out potato patch in one night? (Nebraska.) These, too, are blister beetles. They may be plain black, or striped, or margined, or brown or gray, but, in any color, they have voracious appetites. (See previous question; also Blister Beetles.)

We were warned that if we planted potatoes in soil where nothing had recently been grown they would be wormy. Why? (Ohio.) White grubs and wireworms are usually prevalent in sod land, and when this land is prepared for a garden the worms remain until their life cycle is completed. Potatoes planted in newly broken sod land are very apt to have brown tunnels going through the tubers. If new land must be used, treat soil with heptachlor. (See Wireworms.)

Last year my potatoes were scabby from wireworms. How can I raise clean potatoes in the same ground another season? (Ohio.) After one year of cultivation you may have fewer wireworms, but it would be safer to treat soil with heptachlor before planting potatoes again.

Why do the edges of potato leaves get brown before the late blight season? (New Jersey.) This is a condition called hopperburn, due to the sucking of many leaf hoppers. DDT or malathion will control them; it will also take care of pink and green potato aphids. Bordeaux mixture itself has some repellent effect on leaf hoppers and also on flea beetles.

What about virus diseases of potato? (New Jersey.) There are a great many, and the names describe the symptoms. Some of these are "yellow dwarf," "leaf roll," "mosaic," and "spindle tuber." Plant certified seed, or resistant varieties, and rogue out any plant that seems to be infected.

Some of our potatoes had a layerlike black moss inside them. What caused it? (Virginia.) There are many causes of tuber discoloration: late blight and other fungous diseases, some bacterial and virus diseases, and a physiological disease called black heart. Your trouble may be the latter, and it comes from too great heat and lack of oxygen. If the potatoes stay out in bright sun after digging, or if the storage place gets too hot, black heart may develop.

PUMPKIN

How can cucumber beetles on pumpkins be controlled successfully? (Illinois.) Any of the treatments discussed under cucumber should be satisfactory on pumpkin.

How can the pumpkin vine borer be kept from entering vines as they are beginning to set fruit? (West Virginia.) For the control of the squash vine borer, and also squash bugs on pumpkin, see Squash.

RADISH

What control is there for the light-green worm, like a caterpillar,

that eats leaves of radish? (New Jersey.) This is probably the larva of the diamondback moth. (See Cabbage for control.)

Is it safe to eat radishes grown in soil treated with dieldrin or heptachlor corrosive to eliminate wormy root crops? (Pennsylvania.) As long as the radishes are scrubbed well, there should be no danger.

Why are my radishes small with a black spot up the middle? There is a disease called black root of radish, caused by a fungus, but there is not much known in the line of control. Try a different location, and the Red Globe type.

RHUBARB

Why does rhubarb rot? (Virginia.) Phytopthora foot, or crown rot, causes sunken spots at the base of the leaf stalks and a rot and wilting which progress from stalk to stalk until the whole plant dies. Dig out and burn diseased plants, being careful not to scatter infected soil. Disinfect the location with 1 to 50 formaldehyde. Plant only healthy roots.

What are the insects that bore holes in rhubarb stalks? (Pennsylvania.) Rhubarb curculios. Pick them off, because sprays do not seem to control. They are yellow-snout beetles which puncture stems and cause black spots. Destroy dockweed near rhubarb.

SQUASH

Is there any treatment for Hubbard squash, for worms that burrow inside stem? The squash vine borer is a white grub or caterpillar that works inside the vine, causing wilting beyond the point of attack, which is indicated by yellow excrement outside. Spray or dust plant bases and stems with methoxychlor in late June and weekly in July.

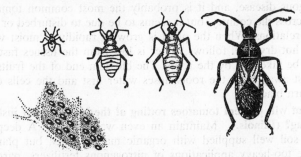

Squash Bug: large, rusty black, lively beetle, destructive at all stages, hatching from orange-colored eggs on under sides of leaves; attacks squash and pumpkins.

Is there any way of exterminating the rather hard-shelled sucking insect, with repugnant odor, which attacks squash plants first, then others? (Texas.) This is the squash bug, sometimes called stink bug, which is distributed all over the United States. The adults are brownish black, ⅔ in. long; they hide under the leaves and suck the sap, causing the vines to wilt. They attack all vine crops, but prefer squash. They may be killed with malathion sprays or dusts. Hand-pick the adults, or trap them under boards. Destroy all old vines in fall.

What causes summer squash buds to drop off? (Connecticut.) Chiefly unfavorable weather conditions. However, the male and female flowers are separate on squash plants, and the male flowers of course drop off without setting fruit.

Why can't I raise crookneck squash? Something attacks the roots and prevents fruits from maturing. (Michigan.) It may be a water relation rather than an organism at the roots. Blossom-end rot is common in squash, causing the small squash to wither at the blossom, which is followed by secondary rot fungi. This disease is thought due to an insufficient or uneven water supply.

What caused about 8 out of 10 straight-necked squash to rot shortly after setting? (Connecticut.) The weather, and resultant dry soil, caused this blossom-end rot. (See previous question.)

Is DDT effective as a control for squash vine borer? Yes, but only the "vine-safe" or aerosol grade should be used since the normal grade of DDT will stunt vine crops including squash. Methoxychlor is preferable. Apply spray or dust in late June and weekly during July to plant bases and stems.

TOMATO

What is the cause of blossom-end rot, which looks more like a fungous disease than a rot? It covers from ¼ to ½ of the fruit, is gray-black and quite firm. (Oregon.) Blossom-end rot does look like a fungous disease, and it is probably the most common tomato disease across the country, but it seems to be due to disturbed or uneven water relations. When the plant is growing rapidly in moist weather, and a hot dry spell follows, water is lost from the tissues faster than it can be taken up by the roots. The blossom end of the fruits, being farthest away from the roots, loses water first and the cells collapse and turn black.

What will prevent tomatoes rotting at the blossom end just before ripening? (Illinois.) Maintain an even water supply. A deeply prepared soil well supplied with organic matter helps; but plants that receive too-heavy applications of nitrogenous fertilizers, particularly manure, are more subject to this rot. A balanced fertilizer high in superphosphate and available calcium decreases susceptibility. Calcium nitrate is good to use as the source of nitrogen. Although blossom-end rot usually shows up in periods of drought, it may appear when the soil has received so much rainfall that the small roots are killed for lack of aeration. Spraying with calcium chloride (1 tbsp. in a gal. of water) will help prevent blossom-end rot. Pritchard and Marglobe are resistant, while Rutgers and Valient are susceptible.

What causes rot inside perfectly good-looking tomatoes? (Connecticut.) Probably the same type of weather and soil conditions that cause the blossom-end rot discussed above.

Is tomato wilt carried on the seed, or does it remain in the soil? (Mississippi.) Both. Primarily a soil organism, the wilt fungus may be carried on the seed. If doubtful seed is to be planted in clean soil, it should be treated before planting, but it is much wiser to use seed from healthy plants.

What is the cause of blight on tomatoes that begins at bottom of plant and works up? Leaves curl, fruit develops but does not come to completion, plant dies slowly. (Pennsylvania.) This is probably fusarium wilt, caused by a fungus that lives in the soil. At first the leaves roll up and wilt in the middle of the day, later there is a permanent wilting, yellow leaves, and death.

If tomato plants all succumbed to the wilt in damp season last year, will they do so again this year when planted on the same ground? (Connecticut.) If you plant susceptible varieties, they are very likely to, for the fungus lives several years in the soil. Rotation or soil sterilization is necessary; also cleaning up all tomato refuse.

My tomatoes wither and stop bearing about the first of August. What are wilt-resistant varieties? (Tennessee.) Marglobe, Pritchard, Rutgers, Pan American, Roma, Louisiana Gulf State, Minalucie and Prairiana are reasonably resistant to fusarium wilt.

What are the causes and cure for the mosaic disease of tomatoes? (Pennsylvania.) The cause of mottled dark and light-green misshapen leaves is a virus. The only cure is prevention: destroying diseased plants as soon as noticed and also weed hosts, and controlling insect carriers.

What are the weed hosts of mosaic? Groundcherry, horsenettle, jimsonweed, and nightshade are the most important. Tomatoes should also be grown as far away as possible from tobacco, petunias, and potatoes, for the same virus may be present in these plants.

Can tobacco dust or nicotine spray be used safely on tomato plants? I think I read somewhere that a virus disease results. (New Jersey.) The tomato mosaic virus is carried in ground tobacco, so that one should not smoke while working with tomatoes, nor use tobacco dust. However, nicotine sulfate used as a spray apparently does not carry the infective principle, and nicotine dust made from nicotine sulfate mixed with lime would also be safe. The gardener can carry the virus from plant to plant on his hands, which should be washed frequently with soapy water while working with tomatoes.

What can we do to overcome brown specks on our tomatoes? Will

lime overcome this? (New Hampshire.) Brown spots on the leaves and sunken black spots on stems and fruit may be due to early blight caused by a fungus (Alternaria). It is better to use sprays without lime, because this causes blossoms to drop off (lime in the soil is a perfectly good recommendation). Spray weekly or biweekly with ziram, zineb, maneb or captan. Use clean seed and practice crop rotation.

What causes anthracnose on tomatoes? What is remedy? (Indiana.) Anthracnose is a fruit spot rather common in the central states. The spots are dark, sunken, with concentric markings and pinkish spore pustules in the center. The fungus lives in the soil, so that a 4-year rotation should be practiced,. Avoid poorly drained soil, and fertilize properly. Pick all ripe fruit frequently. Spraying with ziram or maneb is effective.

My tomatoes had an earthy flavor and were mushy. Was it the variety, or soil conditions? August was a wet month. (New York.) The rainy weather may have caused growth cracks in which one of the mold fungi grew to produce the mushiness and the flavor, which should not be charged against the variety. Staked tomatoes suffer less in a wet season. Keep tomatoes picked frequently, and remove and burn all soft and rotting fruit.

What is the best formula to prevent rust on tomatoes in southern Florida? The "rust" is probably sunscald; there is no true rust common on tomatoes. Keep as much foliage as possible on the plants, so that the fruits are not exposed to the sun in hot, dry weather. Verticillium and other wilts that cause loss of lower foliage increase sunscald. A very light covering of straw over fruit clusters may reduce this disease.

Are there many diseases that attack tomatoes? United States Department of Agriculture *Farmers' Bulletin 1934,* published in 1943, lists 38 diseases (exclusive of insect pests) which may be important in one part of the country or another. There are many leaf and fruit spots, wilts, and blights; Southern states have to contend with nematode root knot and Southern blight, while virus diseases, curly-top, and spotted wilt are prevalent in the Northwest. Consult your State Experiment Station if you need help. Despite diseases, tomatoes are an easy and prolific crop for the home gardener.

What is the easiest way to circumvent cutworms on tomatoes? A paper collar put around each seedling as it is being transplanted. (See Cutworms.)

What causes little holes in the leaves of tomato seedlings? (New Jersey.) Flea beetles. They may riddle the foliage if not controlled and seriously injure the young plants. Dust with rotenone dust or spray or dust with dieldrin or heptachlor. (See Flea Beetles.)

How can I get rid of the huge green caterpillars on tomatoes? (New

York.) The large tomato hornworm is best controlled by picking off by hand. Or dust or spray with DDD (Rhothane). If the caterpillar is in the fruits, it is the corn earworm, also called tomato fruitworm. Destroy infested fruits as soon as discovered. The same treatment as for the hornworm will do; or use methoxychlor.

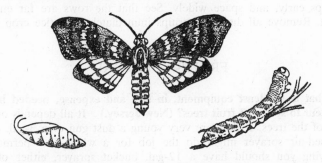

Tomato Hornworm: a rather fierce-looking, very large and nervous green worm; attacks tomatoes, and sometimes eggplants, peppers, and potatoes.

What is the pest on tomato leaves in August that looks like salt on the leaves and later turns into tiny flies? (Wyoming.) Your grains of salt are the nymphs of white flies, common on tomatoes in late summer, but not particularly injurious. Malathion sprays or pyrethrum or rotenone dusts may control them. (See White Flies.)

How get rid of the yellow bug on tomato plants that looks like a ladybug? (New York.) The Mexican bean beetle occasionally wanders over to tomato plants but ordinarily does not require treatment there. (See Beans.)

A green bug, with shield-shape marking, stings and ruins our tomatoes. Is there a remedy? (Texas.) This is the green stink bug, a close relative to the squash bug. The nymphs are greenish with black markings and the adults green or brown; they suck the sap of tomatoes, peas, beans, and other plants. Dust or spray with malathion when the young bugs first appear, and repeat as needed. Also hand-pick.

Is there a way to get rid of the worm that enters the stalks of tomatoes in bloom so that the plant dies or breaks over? (Missouri.) Getting rid of the weeds round about is the best and practically only way of getting rid of the common stalk borer. You may be able to kill the borer with BHC paste before the plant dies. (See Borers.)

TURNIP

What can be done about maggots in turnips? See Cabbage for directions.

Is it safe to eat turnips grown in soil treated with dieldrin or hep-

tachlor for wormy root crops? This apparently is not dangerous: no poisonous residue is taken in by the turnip root.

Why do yellow turnips rot in the ground? (New York.) Sometimes bacterial soft rot follows along with the maggots, especially in a wet season, and if the plants are crowded together in the row. Thin your turnips early, and space widely. See that the rows are far enough apart. Remove all diseased turnips immediately. Practice crop rotation.

FRUITS—GENERAL

What is the least equipment, in size and expense, needed by an amateur to spray 12 fruit trees? (New Jersey.) It all depends on the size of the trees. If they are very young a dust gun or a 3-gal. compressed-air sprayer might do the job for a while. For permanent spraying you should have a 12-gal. bucket sprayer, either of the Paragon type or one that has an agitator. It will come with a small truck for wheeling around and should cost around $50.00. Extra extension rods are available so you can get a spray up into a moderate-sized fruit tree. For a very large tree it may be necessary to hire someone with power equipment.

Three-gallon compressed-air sprayer, knapsack type, is convenient for spraying small fruit trees.

For back-yard fruit trees, what sprayings are really necessary? (Mississippi.) That depends on the back yard, but ordinarily several sprays including a calyx spray, when most of the petals have fallen, and a foliage spray 10 days to 2 weeks later are most indispensable. (See also discussions under the different fruit hosts.)

When should fruit trees be sprayed, just before or after the bloom opens? (Mississippi.) It depends on the fruit and the pests you want to control. In general, sprays are not applied when fruits are in full bloom for fear of preventing pollination. The farmer usually applies what is called a "pink" spray on apples, just before blooms open; but the amateur can often wait until the calyx spray, when most of the petals have fallen.

What is the best simple spray for fruit trees? (Michigan.) There is no one single spray that will take care of all fruit trees. Ask for help from your Experiment Station in revising a farmer's spray schedule to fit your needs. (See Spraying Calendar, Michigan State College, *Extension Bulletin 154*.)

What is the best spray material for fruit trees and when is the proper time to spray trees in Oklahoma? Your best help is "Orchard Spray Calendar," *Circular 168,* from the Oklahoma A. and M. College Extension Service. Dormant spraying in Oklahoma may be with either 1 to 8 lime-sulfur or a miscible oil applied before leaves come out when temperature is above 60° F. Wettable sulfur and ferbam are favored as summer fungicides. (See also discussion under individual fruits below.)

What is advisable to use as a general spray for apple, cherry, and plum trees, also grapes? (Illinois.) Methoxychlor, malathion and ferbam freshly mixed in the spray tank make an excellent general purpose spray on practically all fruits. For treatment see below under the separate hosts. Also send to the Illinois Agricultural Experiment Station, at Urbana, and ask for *Circular 492*, "Directions for Spraying Fruits in Illinois." There you will see that not only the kind of fruit may make a difference but also where you live in Illinois. Ask also for *Circular 524*, "Growing Fruits for Home Use."

When is the best time for dormant spray of fruit trees? What spray to use? Can this spray be the same for apples, peaches, plums, and cherries? (New York.) The dormant spray is best applied after the buds have begun to swell but before they show green at the tip. Probably you could safely use a 1 to 9 dilution of lime-sulfur on all these fruits, or even an oil spray, but you will get much better results if the spray is directed at specific pests for each kind of fruit and timed for these. Send for Cornell *Extension Bulletin 812*, "Spray Schedules for Tree Fruits." (See also discussion below under different hosts.)

How and when should fruit trees too small to have fruit or blossoms be sprayed? Bulletins tell about pre-blossom sprays, etc., but with no older trees around how are you to know when to spray? (New York.) Having no fruit, you do not have to use all the different sprays, for they are chiefly intended to provide sound fruit. *If* scale is present, put on a dormant spray; later you can spray foliage to control cankerworms, Japanese beetles, aphids, etc., if these insects appear and are injurious.

Do you know what will kill rose chafers without killing fruit trees and bushes, which they attack so furiously in June we get no fruit? (Michigan.) Your Experiment Station (*Extension Bulletin 154*) says that rose chafers attack in the vicinity of sandy quackgrass sod. They are not difficult to control, but you must be on the alert to spray immediately they appear. DDT sprays will keep them in check.

What is the best method to deal with Japanese beetles in a young orchard? (D.C.) If the trees have not come into bearing, foliage may be protected with DDT sprays. On trees where a poisonous residue on fruit must be avoided, spray weekly with rotenone or methoxychlor.

How can I get rid of lice on my fruit trees? (Minnesota.) Add 2 tbsp. malathion to a gallon of spray mixed up for other purposes. Malathion should be especially added to a delayed dormant spray to control aphids.

Mice or rabbits gnaw the bark of my young fruit trees. What shall I do? (New York.) Mechanical protectors such as wood veneer, tarpaper, cloth, or ¼-in. galvanized wire are most satisfactory in protecting young trees from injury. The wire is best. Keep it away from the trunk except at the top of the wrap. For repellents see Rabbits.

Is there any repellent I can put around young fruit trees to keep the deer and rabbits from eating the new leaves next spring? Various repellents have been tried with success in some cases and no success in others. The most successful has been Goodrite Z.I.P. sprayed on the foliage.

Cylinders of woven wire protect young fruit trees from winter injury by rabbits and other rodents.

APPLE

How can I get 1 or 2 large apple trees effectively sprayed without spending more money than the fruit is worth? Local sprayers charge me $5.00 per spraying and decline to use anything except lead arsenate. (Massachusetts.) You cannot expect to get 1 or 2 fruit trees sprayed without its costing you much more than the fruit itself is worth. You have to balance the account by considering apples also as ornamentals and think of the fun you have picking your own fruit. The charge of $5.00 is moderate when it must cover time of 2 men, cost of materials, transportation of a special trip for only 1 or 2 trees, and the seasonal nature of the work. To save money you must do the spraying yourself, which would not have much effect on a large tree, or else resign yourself to wormy apples. A surprising amount of pies and applesauce come from unsprayed apples. My own unsprayed tree provided 7 families this summer with all the applesauce they could can for winter. If trees are not sprayed, it is very important to clean up all dropped apples every week.

How many sprayings of apple trees are indispensable for reasonably satisfactory fruit in the home garden? When we have our trees sprayed 5 times it is much cheaper to buy apples. (Ohio.) Five sprays are supposed to be the minimum for sound fruit: dormant, cluster bud, calyx, and first and second codling-moth sprays, but often the dormant spray may be omitted if there are no scale insects, and possibly one or two others. The calyx spray, when 90 per cent of the petals have fallen, and the first codling-moth spray, 17 days after calyx, are probably most useful in providing reasonably clean fruits. Use a general purpose spray.

About how many gallons of spray should be used to cover a 5-year apple tree and a 10-year full growth—for dormant and full-leaf sprays? (New York.) A foliage spray for a 5-year-old apple requires 1 to 2 gals.; 10-year-old, 4 to 5 gals.; 25-year-old, 12 to 15 gals. A dormant spray might take about half as much.

Can old apple trees which bear many infected apples ever grow sound fruit? (New York.) Yes, with a definite spraying program combined with rigid sanitary measures.

What is the easiest and best way to spray a few apple trees infested with codling moth? (Massachusetts.) There is no easy way, but in Massachusetts the calyx and second cover sprays are most important.

Codling Moth: the worst apple pest; also attacks other fruits. The larvae, pinkish-white caterpillars ¾ in. long, tunnel through fruits.

What is a practical control of curculio on apples in the small garden? (Massachusetts.) Calyx and first cover sprays are most important in controlling curculio. (See schedule below.) Gather and destroy dropped fruit every week.

My McIntosh apples this year were covered with black spots ⅛ to ¼ in. in diameter. Trees were sprayed. Can you identify it and suggest a remedy? Seems to be a local infection. (Massachusetts.) McIntosh apples are very susceptible to scab, a fungous disease more prevalent following a wet spring. It is controlled by ferbam, captan or wettable sulfur sprays which must be carefully timed. (See spray schedule below.)

A spray schedule for Massachusetts is as follows:
Delayed Dormant—Desirable spray if red mite or San Jose scale is present. Miscible oil or oil emulsion according to manufacturer's recommendations.

Pre-Pink—Desirable on McIntosh and other susceptible varieties to control scab. Five level tablespoons wettable sulfur or 2 tablespoons ferbam and 3 tablespoons DDT to 1 gal. water.

Pink Spray—*Important* for scab-susceptible varieties. Same mixture as pre-pink but add 1 tablespoon malathion for aphids.

Calyx Spray—*Important* to control scab, codling moth, curculio. When 90 per cent petals have fallen, apply 5 tablespoons wettable sulfur or 2 tablespoons ferbam and 3 tablespoons methoxychlor to 1 gal. water.

First Cover Spray after Calyx—*Important* to control curculio, leaf hoppers, and scab. Apply when temperature reaches 75° F. 5 or more days after calyx spray, using 5 tablespoons wettable sulfur, 3 tablespoons methoxychlor, with 1 tablespoon malathion per gallon water.

Second Cover Spray—*Important* to control codling moth, scab, and sometimes curculio. Apply 7 to 10 days after first cover spray, using same materials as first cover.

Third Cover—*Important* for apple maggot and scab. About July 10, when maggot flies appear, apply 5 tablespoons wettable sulfur and 3 tablespoons methoxychlor to 1 gal. water.

Fourth Cover—*Important* for apple maggot and codling moth. Apply about July 25 to prevent maggot (railroad worm) tunnels. Same as for third cover.

What sprays should be used on an uncared-for apple orchard in New Jersey? About same sprays as above, but send for New Jersey Extension Bul. Apple Spray Schedule.

What causes brown spots through the interior of apples and what will prevent this? (New Jersey.) Probably the apple maggot, a slender white worm which feeds within the pulp and carries with it germs of a soft rot. The adult is a small black-and-white fly. The maggot winters in the soil as a small seedlike pupa; the flies come out in summer, usually in July. The 2 sprays listed as third and fourth cover in the Massachusetts spray schedule above should work in New Jersey but check with the New Jersey Agricultural College concerning the proper time to apply them. Cleaning up every rotten, dropped apple is very important in preventing more maggot trouble for another year.

How can I reclaim apple trees whose fruit is always badly infested with railroad worms, or I suppose codling moth? (Vermont.) Railroad worms are apple maggots (see preceding question) and quite different from codling-moth larvae, which are larger, ¾ in. long, pinkish white with brown heads. The larvae winter in cocoons in the crotches and under bark of trees. The moths emerge to lay their eggs in warm, dry weather about a week after the petals have fallen. The newly hatched caterpillars enter through the calyx cup of the fruit, unless a poison spray is in place. Later-hatched caterpillars enter the fruit through the side. After 3 to 4 weeks inside the apple the larva burrows through a mass of excrement from the surface and crawls down the branches for a suitable place for a cocoon. In addition to spraying, scraping the bark on the trunk up to 10 ft. during the winter will be very helpful in reducing codling-moth infestation. Chemically treated bands on scraped trees will collect larvae and prevent damage.

Apple Maggot. Small black-and-white fly is the parent of this well-known pest.

I have heard that dinitro-cresolate (sodium salt) is used for the control of codling moth on apple trees. Can you tell me how and when this is used? (New Jersey.) Oil- or water-soluble dinitro compounds are added to oil dormant sprays to control aphids, bud moths, and scale insects. I do not know of their use for codling moth. A sodium salt of dinitro-cresol is sold as Elgetol, Krenite, and Dinitrosol and should be used according to manufacturer's directions. It is water soluble and may be used as a dormant spray by itself or added to a 2 percent lubricating oil emulsion.

I spray my 1 apple tree 4 times as prescribed in all manuals, but recently the apples have brown spots throughout and are sort of knotty and misshapen. Why? (New York.) Probably the result of apple maggot. You need a summer spray in addition, about June 25 to July 1, which is a combined codling-moth cover spray and first apple-maggot spray. A second spray for maggots should go on about July 10 to 15. The misshapen, knotty apples are also occasionally the result of redbug punctures. Add malathion to the calyx spray if redbugs appear.

What is the proper formula and ingredients for spraying apple trees and how often should it be done? (New York.) Cornell *Extension Bulletin 812* gives a detailed schedule and formulae with modifications according to the pests you have in New York.

How do you prevent the apples from falling off the tree and getting wormy? (Illinois.) The 3 codling-moth sprays listed as minimum for Illinois are calyx, 17 days after calyx for first brood, and 9 weeks after calyx for the second brood. Amounts of methoxychlor to use are given in spray schedule for Massachusetts. (See also University of Illinois *Circular 524,* "Growing Fruits for Home Use.")

When and how often should I spray old Baldwin apple tree which bore very wormy apples this year? (New Hampshire.) Ask for University of New Hampshire *Extension Circular 252* for a complete spray schedule. For codling moth and railroad worms the calyx, first cover, and third cover (about July 7) are most important. (See Massachusetts schedule above for formulae.) Pick up all dropped apples.

My apple trees are young but will soon need a spray. What can I use that will not be injurious to the bees? (Iowa.) Any insecticide may be injurious to bees; that is why spraying schedules call for treatment before the blossoms open or after almost all the petals have fallen.

My apple trees have scaly bark and faulty apples. What should they be sprayed with and when? (Tennessee.) Consult University of Tennessee *Extension Publication* on Apple Spray Schedules.

I've had scale on an apple tree for more than a year. Will a dormant spray used next spring be effective to save this tree? (Illinois.) It should be. Unless there is an extreme infestation, scale insects will not kill a tree very quickly. Use a 3 per cent oil emulsion, a 1 to 25 miscible oil or a dinitro spray.

How can I raise apple trees without having them destroyed by borers? (New York.) Wrap the young trees when they are set out in Kraft crepe paper, starting several inches below the ground and going up to the lowest branch. Remove in August and rewrap in a few weeks for a second year. Wire wraps later will keep out rabbits and mice and check borer infestation. Commercial repellent paints may be purchased that are partially satisfactory in borer control. (See Borers.)

What should be done to borers deep in an apple tree? (New York.) Poke in a flexible wire where you see sawdust protruding from the bark and try to kill them in place. Borers nearer the outside may be cut out with a knife. Use a commercial fumigant such as Bore-Kill.

What is the best method to remove fungus from an apple tree? This runs from ground for about 4 ft. up. (New York.) If you mean a greenish moss on the trunk, that is of no consequence, but if you mean a collection of shelf fungi, they are indications of a heart rot inside the tree, which may or may not be worth saving by cavity treatment.

How do cedar evergreens harm apple trees? (Minnesota.) Because they form the alternate host for the cedar-apple rust. Spores are carried from the cedar galls in spring to infect young apples and foliage, which will show rusty spots in midsummer. Sulfur or ferbam sprays for apple scab will control rust. (See also Cedar.)

Blight on apple trees. Cause and cure? (Illinois.) You doubtless refer to the bacterial disease known as fire blight, which kills back branches and blights blossoms so they appear burned by fire, and produces cankers on twigs or main trunk. Cutting out infected portions well below the visibly blighted area is most important, and so is breaking out blighted fruit spurs. If the disease is serious, apply a special full-bloom spray of streptomycin.

What causes apples to rot on the tree and dry up? Is it a fungous disease or insects? What kind of spray should I use? (Illinois.) It sounds like black rot, a fungous disease characterized by mummied fruits and by frog-eye spots on leaves as well as a bark canker. Either ferbam, captan, dichlone or wettable sulfur in the regular pre-blossom sprays for apple scab should take care of black rot, provided all mummied and rotting fruits are cleaned up and burned. In southern Illinois another fruit rot, called bitter rot, may be prevalent. The normal spray schedule will take care of this.

How can I get rid of woolly mildew on an apple tree? (Washington.) Cut out mildewed twigs at the time of pruning. Spray with 1 to 100 lime-sulfur or wettable sulfur in the cluster-bud and calyx stage and again 2 weeks after petal-fall stages. If a regular schedule for scab is being carried on, powdery mildew will be taken care of.

Is there anything that can be sprayed into ground while tree is in blossom to prevent Winesap apples from ripening with specks and rottenness at core? (Maryland.) Elgetol has been used to spray on the ground to eradicate the apple-scab fungus, but this would not be the cause of rottenness at the core. Rot and specks may be due to apple maggots, controllable by summer fruit spraying. Corky brown specks through the fruit sometimes come from lack of boron in the soil. In that case you can apply powdered borax, ¼ to 1 lb., depending on age of tree. The larger amount is not safe on tree under 25 years old. Apply it like fertilizer. One dose will last 3 years.

What is the cause and remedy of brown bitter spots in apples? (Wisconsin.) Either the bitter rot or boron deficiency previously discussed, or a disease called bitter pit, due to some disturbed water relation with no very definite remedy.

What causes peculiar greenish sections in the flesh of some apples? (Connecticut.) Climate, variety, water relations seem to have something to do with this physiological condition called water core; maintain an even supply of water; maintain proper balance between root and top by pruning; pick fruit at proper maturity.

My apples no sooner form in the spring when they become wormy and practically all drop off. (Long Island.) This sounds like the European apple sawfly, a relatively new pest present in Southeastern New York and Connecticut. This damage may be prevented by using lindane or a combination of malathion and dieldrin in the calyx or petal fall spray and in the first cover spray.

APRICOT

What can be done against wormy apricots? A tiny worm starts eating around the stone and destroys fruit. (Michigan.) This is the plum curculio, common also on apple, peach, and cherry. It is controlled by methoxychlor or dieldrin sprays and a stringent cleaning-up campaign. (See Plum.)

May lead arsenate be used on apricot trees without injury to foliage? If so, in what strength solution? (Virginia.) Lead arsenate is injurious to both peach and apricot even though lime is added. Use the newer recommended insecticides.

My apricot trees turn yellow and the fruit loses all its flavor. Is this a condition of the soil? (Utah.) Quite probably in Utah it is a chlorosis due to too-alkaline soil, corrected by applying barnyard manure and equal parts of iron and aluminum sulfate, using 1 lb. of mixture to each inch of diameter of the trunk. Apply beneath the branch spread, either in water solution or in holes 12 to 18 ins. deep. Yellowing may also be symptoms of a virus disease. Consult your Experiment Station.

BLACKBERRY

How do you get rid of red rust in Alfred blackberry? It acts like fungi but does not yield to sulfur; very contagious. (Missouri.) It is a fungus, officially named orange rust of blackberry. It lives all through the interior of the plant and cannot be controlled by fungicides as other rusts. Remove diseased plants, getting out all roots, before the contagion spreads further.

BLUEBERRY

Why do my blueberry bushes have little pieces of wood, which look like worms, on the ground near the roots? (Massachusetts.) It sounds like frass (excrement) from a borer working in the stem. If you can find the hole, inject some borer fumigant—Borer-Sol, Bore-Kill.

CHERRY

When is the proper time to spray ox-heart cherry to get better fruit and prevent insects? (New Jersey.) Write to the New Jersey Agricultural Experiment Station, New Brunswick, N.J. and request their extension bulletin on home fruit pest control.

After my cherry tree blossoms the leaves curl up with aphids. When and with what will I spray? (New York.) A dormant spray of Elgetol or other dinitro compound (see apple) helps to control cherry aphids. When the aphids first appear and before the young leaves curl, spray thoroughly with nicotine sulfate and soap or malathion repeating as necessary.

How can I prevent rot of cherries on trees? (Illinois.) A sulfur-ferbam mixture is best for holding brown rot in check. Use in spray schedule at rate of 3 tbsp.—1 tbsp. per gal. of water.

What causes cherry leaves to turn yellow in midsummer and drop off? What spray do you recommend? (Wisconsin.) This is a fungous leaf spot, controlled by the sulfur-ferbam mixture in the preceding spray schedule. Proprietary low-soluble copper compounds may be substituted, but you should apply to your Experiment Station for safe brands and specific directions.

What will kill worms which feed on the roots of cherry trees until trees are killed? Will it be safe to plant another tree in this ground the following spring? (Michigan.) I am not sure whether you mean the peach-tree borer which works on the trunk under the soil surface, or the larvae of white grubs. Keeping the ground plowed and cultivated before replanting or grub-proofing it will help get rid of the latter. The peach-tree borer stays under the bark rather than the soil; replanting in the same spot would probably be fairly safe. (See Peach.)

CURRANT AND GOOSEBERRY

Is gooseberry or any other berry harmful to pine trees? (New Jersey.) Gooseberries and currants are alternate hosts for the white-pine blister rust. Where this disease is prevalent they should be removed whenever they are found within 900 ft. of white pines. Black currants are particularly susceptible to blister rust and should not be grown at all in rust areas.

Is there a disease-resistant currant? (Connecticut.) Variety Viking is said to be resistant to white-pine blister rust.

What causes red blotches on Red Lake currant? (North Dakota.) Large reddish blotches on leaves of currants frequently indicate aphids working on the under side. If there are rusty patches on the under side of leaves, it may be white-pine blister rust.

How can I rid currant bushes of aphids? (Illinois.) Add 2 teaspoons nicotine sulfate or 1 tablespoon malathion per gallon of water to any spray applied as soon as the foliage is developed, or put on a separate spray of nicotine sulfate and soap or malathion. Direct spray toward under side of leaves.

What is the best insecticide for worms in gooseberries and currants? (Washington.) The currant fruit fly is a serious pest of currants and gooseberries in western Washington. White maggots feed inside the berry, causing the fruit to turn red and drop. Write to your Agricultural Experiment Station for the latest information on its control.

What is best to use on gooseberry bushes affected with leaf-chewing worms? (Indiana.) A combination spray of malathion and captan applied as soon as the foliage is well developed will take care of the currant worm (your "leaf-chewing" worm) as well as aphis and leaf spot.

What causes leaves to turn brown early part of summer? (New York.) If there are dark spots on leaves and later defoliation, it is a fungous leaf spot controlled by spraying with captan. If the whole shoot blights, it is caused by an internal fungus. There is nothing to do but cut infected canes at ground level.

GRAPE

What is the proper spray to use for black rot on grapes? (Ohio.) Black rot causes more loss than any other grape disease. The berries turn purple prematurely and change to hard, black, shriveled mummies. Spray with ferbam when new shoots are ½ in. long and again when they are 8 to 12 ins. long; spray after blossom fall and repeat at 2-week intervals if disease has been serious in other years.

What causes grapes to drop before ripe? (Pennsylvania.) Frequently the grape berry moth, which may destroy 60 to 90 per cent of the fruit on an unsprayed vine. Add 2 tablespoons DDT to the ferbam spray applied just after petal fall, and again 10 to 14 days later.

What do you do to keep Japanese beetle off grapevines? (Michigan.) Apply DDT when beetles appear in numbers, repeat as needed.

How do you control rose bugs on grapes? (Massachusetts.) Cultivate the soil around the vines thoroughly in May and early June. Spray with 2 tablespoons DDT to 1 gal. water as soon as the beetles appear; repeat if necessary.

My grapevine is troubled with a small insect or fly early and a small bug or hopper in midseason. What spray? (Wisconsin.) The early "fly" is probably a flea beetle, which will be controlled by the DDT used for berry moths. Leaf hoppers are sucking insects very injurious to grapes during the summer. Apply DDT in late June and early July.

How do you control mildew on grapes? (Michigan.) A weak Bordeaux mixture or fixed copper spray should be effective.

PEACH

What is this white worm I find in the bark of my young fruit trees at the earth line? He buries himself in a jellylike mass. How can I keep him outside looking in only? (New Jersey.) This is the peach-tree borer, responsible for the death of many peach trees. The white, brown-headed worms, larvae of black-and-yellow wasplike moths, live in the bark from 8 to 10 ins. above the soil to 3 to 4 ins. below the surface. Control depends on chemical trunk treatments. Apply 3 DDT or malathion sprays to the trunks—first in early July, others at 21-day intervals.

Is there anything we can do for the peach-tree borer besides spray-

ing? (Ohio.)   You can fumigate it in early fall after the young worms
have hatched and are under the bark. The standard material is paradichlorbenzene. The crystals are placed carefully in a ring around the
trunk, not closer than 1 in. nor further than 2 ins. from the crown.
The dosage must be very exact: 1 oz. for trees 6 or more years old,
¾ oz. for 5-year-old trees, and ½ oz. for 4-year-old trees. No treatment should be given peaches set out less than 3 years. Before placing
the crystals remove all grass, weeds, and debris from around the tree
and immediately afterward mound up with additional soil, being careful not to disturb the crystals. The time of treatment varies according
to the state, usually September for New York and up to November 1
for the South. The soil temperature should not be much lower than 60°
F. for effective results. After several weeks the mound of soil should
be leveled off.

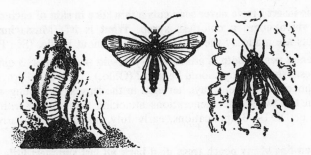

*Peach Borer: a fat white grub, burrowing into peach trees
at ground line.*

**How do you get rid of the worms that make gum at roots of peach
trees? (Indiana.)**   If trees are less than 3 years old, or there are only
1 or 2, you can go after worms with a knife or a wire, a process known
as worming. Another treatment, is ethylene dichloride emulsion, which
is not limited by soil temperature. In very small dosages it may also
be used on young trees. The emulsion has dosage directions which
must be followed exactly. Although it has given very favorable results
in many places, other localities have reported injury. Ask your own
State Experiment Station for advice.

**What other than a borer will cause peach trees to lose sap at the
trunk, and the tips of the branches to be coated with a gummy substance? (Pennsylvania.)**   The gum is one manifestation of brown rot,
controlled with sulfur, ziram or captan sprays or dusts and also by
cutting out diseased twigs and branches and destroying all infected
fruit or old mummies.

**Shortly before time for peaches to ripen they rot on tree and dry
up, still hanging in December. Is there danger of next season's crop**

being affected? Is so, what treatment? (Pennsylvania.) There is very much danger of brown-rot infection from these mummied fruits on the tree or others which have fallen to the ground. Pick them all and burn them. Follow a spray schedule. (See Plum.)

What is the spraying program for peach trees? (Massachusetts.) Write to the Experiment Station, Amherst, Mass., and request their latest spray program for peach trees.

Red blotches on peach leaves causing them to curl up. Why? (Massachusetts.) This is peach-leaf curl, a fungous disease. Its principal symptoms are much thickened distortions of the leaves, often followed by defoliation.

What is the best way to control peach-leaf curl? (Washington.) Spray any time during the dormant season with ferbam or a dormant dinitro spray.

Some insect I have never seen cuts a thin slice in skin of each peach, from which oozes a colorless syrup. What is it? (Massachusetts.) The cuts are made by the plum curculio, a snout beetle. (See Plum.)

Oriental peach moth is attacking 2-year-old peach trees; 3 different varieties. What remedy should be used? (Ohio.) This small gray moth with chocolate markings lays her eggs in the leaves; the young worms bore in the twigs, later generations attacking fruit. Spray with malathion or DDT—3 applications, early July, mid-July, and early August.

Green tips of my peach trees died back all last summer; little white worms inside shoots; told it was caused by tarnished plant bug; any control? (Indiana.) Tarnished plant bugs do sting peach twigs and turn them black. There is little control except to destroy weeds and sometimes dust with sulfur. I think, however, since there were worms in the twigs it was the Oriental fruit moth; this kills back the twigs also. (See previous question.)

What to do for yellows in young peach trees? (Alabama.) Yellows may be due to a virus or to an alkaline soil. Ask your county agent for diagnosis and help.

Why do our peach seeds split, causing the peach to rot? What remedy? (Washington.) There is a physiological disease called split pit which results in rotting embryos and a gummosis of the fruit. The cause and remedy are not exactly clear, but the symptoms are more pronounced on Phillip's Cling variety and in years of a light crop. It is suggested that thinning be delayed 5 weeks after pits start to harden.

What new spray is used to prevent dropping of premature fruits such as peaches? (Ohio.) Hormone sprays are used to prevent premature dropping of some fruits, usually apples. It is doubtful if they will work on peaches.

PEAR

What is the cause of fire blight in pear and apple trees? (Iowa.)
Bacteria cause the disease but there are contributing factors. The more vigorous a tree the more susceptible it is to fire blight because the bacteria prefer succulent tissue. Do not overfertilize (fall feeding is safer than spring), do not prune heavily, and do not cultivate around the trees. Some varieties, like Kieffer, are more or less immune.

Will spraying a pear tree while dormant check fire blight? There is no way to have all the diseased parts pruned out without ruining the tree. (New Mexico.) You will lose the tree anyway, if you do not have the diseased parts cut out, perhaps even if you do. The fire-blight bacteria are not on the outside, to be killed there by a spray, but are working down inside the twigs in the vascular system. Cut out *below* the infected portion of twigs and scrape away all dead wood from cankers on main trunks and large limbs. Paint these wounds with Bordeaux paint, made by stirring raw linseed oil into dry powder. In the spring the bacteria ooze out from dead twigs and cankers in little droplets which attract the bees. The bees, flying from blossom to blossom, carry around the bacteria and cause new infection. From blighted blossom clusters the bacteria work down inside the twigs into main branches. Spraying with streptomycin or 1–3–50 Bordeaux mixture when the blooms are open helps prevent this new infection. Break out all blighted blossom clusters.

Why did a few branches on my young pear tree die after fruit was hanging on? (Pennsylvania.) Probably fire blight. It may have been secondary infection from twigs or fruit blighted in primary early-spring infection.

Is there any practical remedy for curing fire blight on pear foliage? (Connecticut.) No. If you see blighted foliage, you must cut the whole branch out 6 ins. or more below the part that looks burned or blighted.

Is there anything that will cure pear blight? I had 4 dwarf trees; when the first one had it, I cut it down; the others all have it now. (Illinois.) You cannot "cure" fire blight by any method. All you can do is to clean up infected parts and spray to prevent reinfection through the blossoms. Were you very careful to disinfect your tools after cutting down the diseased tree before working on the others?

I planted some pear trees in 20-ft. square space of apple trees. Am told it will give the blight. Would you leave them, take them out, or use some spray to prevent it? (Indiana.) Pears are much more susceptible to fire blight than apples, and if blight is in your neighborhood, which is more than likely, they will probably acquire the disease first, after which bees may carry it to your apple trees; your pruning shears will carry it unless you disinfect them between cuts. Formalin at a 1 to 20 dilution makes a good disinfectant. If you leave your pears where they are, plan on a blossom spray as described above.

What may I spray on a pear tree to kill a snail-like insect that kills the foliage? (Ohio.) This is the pear slug, whose slimy dark green to orange larvae skeletonize the leaves before they turn into sawfly adults. If pears are getting the regular apple-spray schedule, slugs will be controlled, or a separate spray of DDT (2 tablespoons to 1 gal. water) may be applied as soon as young slugs are noticed.

How can I get rid of the pear and plum leaf slugs? (California.) The pear slug attacks pear, plum, and cherry. It may be killed by any kind of finely ground dust, but a 5% malathion dust is preferable. It may also be killed by regular malathion or DDT sprays.

How can I get rid of bugs on the pear tree—little worms eating the leaves? (New York.) See two previous questions for treatment of pear slug.

Will you please give me information about pear psylla? (Massachusetts.) The pear psylla is the most serious pest of pears, especially in the Northeast. The adult psyllids are only 1/10 in. long, reddish-brown with roof-like transparent wings. They live over winter under the bark and in orchard debris, emerging in early spring to lay eggs in cracks in the bark and on the buds; eggs hatch into yellow nymphs which suck sap from leaf and fruit stems and leaves. To control, spray with malathion or miscible oil or oil emulsion before growth starts, as for scale.

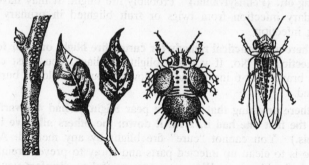

Pear Psylla. The adult (right) is a reddish-brown fly with transparent wings.

About the first of August the leaves of my young dwarf pear turned black and fell off. What caused this? (Maryland.) The pear psylla, whose sucking causes defoliation. The black discoloration was due to a sooty mold, growing in honeydew surrounding the psylla nymphs. A summer spray of malathion is helpful if the psylla were not cleaned up by a dormant spray.

Is it proper to spray in winter a pear tree which was covered with a sort of mildew during the summer, or wait until spring? (Maryland.) If you mean a true mildew, i.e., a white coating on the leaves, summer sulfur sprays or dust will control it, but more likely you refer to the blighted effect produced by pear psylla. (See above.)

PLUM

A fungus gathers on our plums each year and the fruit rots on the tree as soon as it starts to ripen. Why? (Michigan.) This is brown rot of stone fruits, a fungous disease very common on peaches, plums, and cherries and sometimes injurious to apples as well. In early spring spores are sent up from cup-shaped fruiting bodies growing out of old mummied fruits in the soil. The spores infect young fruits, producing a grayish mold. These are summer spores which are splashed by rain or carried by wind to infect other ripening fruits. Diseased fruits wrinkle and either hang on the trees or drop to the ground as "mummies."

Will you please tell me how to spray plum trees so that fruit will not rot and drop before ripening? (Illinois.) Sulfur, ziram or captan sprays or dusts are usually used to control brown rot. Write to your Experiment Station and ask for their latest spray schedule for plums.

What do you do for plum tree when the bark is dark and splitting and in a few places gum or a jelly is running out? (Virginia.) Gummosis is one of the symptoms of brown rot. (See above for advice.) Sanitation is even more important than spraying. Every mummied fruit fallen to the ground or left on the tree should be removed and burned.

How early do you spray plum trees? (Michigan.) If there is scale, especially San Jose scale, use a dormant spray, either a dinitro or oil, although this is needed only in occasional years. You can put on a pre-blossom or cluster-bud spray of wettable sulfur and methoxychlor, but for the home garden the shuck or husk-split stage may be early enough to start spraying.

What is the chemical that is put around plum trees to prevent curculio? (Florida.) The curculio, a small, gray, hump-backed snout beetle is the cause of wormy plums. I do not know of any chemical for the soil, but keeping it well cultivated to destroy pupae and larvae in their earth cells and picking up and burning all dropped fruits are very important in controlling this serious pest. The methoxychlor recommended above is for the curculio.

What is the best spray for plums that will not be injurious to small apiary in orchard? (Iowa.) The spray schedule is so adjusted that there will be no poison on the open flowers when the bees go after nectar.

QUINCE

When and with what material should quince trees be sprayed? (New York.) A spray schedule for New York State calls for a dormant oil spray if lecanium scale is present, a pink spray of ferbam, a calyx spray of ferbam with 2 tablespoons DDT, to gallon of water to control leaf blight, leaf spot, codling moth, and Oriental fruit moth. Repeat DDT or malathion spray at 3-week intervals until three weeks from harvest.

RASPBERRY

What are the various diseases that attack black raspberries? How can they be controlled? (Ohio.) Virus diseases—green mosaic, yellow mosaic, leaf curl, streak. Fungous diseases—verticillium wilt, orange rust, anthracnose, cane blight, spur blight, powdery mildew, leaf spot, bacterial crown gall. Most of these are controlled by sanitary measures: removing infected plants or plant parts. Many raspberry diseases are distributed in planting stock. A dormant spray of a dinitro and pre-blossom and after-blossom sprays of ferbam will help control anthracnose and cane blight.

During the bearing season we noticed overnight a bush or two stricken as if with heavy frost or a blowtorch, then turning black and drying up. We could find no insects. What caused this? (Michigan.) This is cane blight, caused by a fungus which frequently enters through insect wounds. Remove and burn blighted parts immediately, destroy fruiting canes after harvest; avoid sites with poor air and soil drainage; control weeds; spray with a dinitro, when buds show silver, for a dormant spray, and with ferbam 1 week before, again immediately after blossoming, and again after harvest.

How do I control orange rust on boysenberries? (New York.) Orange rust is a systemic disease, that is, the rust fungus is found throughout the whole plant, and not just on the leaves. Infected plants never recover; there is no control by spraying. Pull out diseased plants by the roots and burn before the rusty spores are shed to infect near-by brambles.

How can I rid my boysenberry vines of mildew? I used dry sulfur for 3 months but some of the runners died and the vines are all white. (Washington.) Try spraying with Mildex, Karathane or with wettable sulfur with a sticker. Consult your county agent for the best spray for your locality.

How can I get rid of crown gall without having to throw away all of my berry bushes? (Illinois.) You can't get rid of it. Even if you pull up these bushes, the bacteria will live in the soil for some years. Get healthy bushes and plant in a new location or sterilize soil. Never bring in diseased stock from a nursery; refuse plants showing any signs of enlargements or galls.

What about insects on raspberries? (Wyoming.) Raspberry pests in Wyoming includes aphids, false chinch bug, fruitworms, grasshoppers, leaf hoppers, leaf slugs, legume bugs, mites, scales, strawberry leaf roller, and root weevil. Your county agent will help you work out a schedule for control of pests most destructive in your garden.

Some insect cuts rings about ¼ in. apart on my red raspberry canes and deposits its eggs between. What is the insect and its control? (Ohio.) This is the raspberry cane borer. The adult is a black-and-yellow beetle who deposits her eggs in new growth after first encircling the stem with 2 rows of punctures. The girdled tips wilt, and unless they are cut out the young borers work down the canes. Cut and burn all infested portions; cut out old canes after harvest.

Do red raspberries have little worms in the caps? (Ohio.) Yes, these are the grubs of the raspberry fruitworm. The adult is a light-brown beetle that feeds and lays eggs on blossoms. Dust or spray with DDT or methoxychlor as the blossom clusters are forming, repeat in 10 days.

Is there anything that can be grown to attract Japanese beetles away from raspberry bushes? (New Jersey.) They exert such a potent attraction I doubt if even soybeans would entice them away. Pick your raspberries early in the morning and before beetles are active and keep bushes dusted with rotenone.

STRAWBERRY

How can you keep birds out of strawberry beds? (Illinois.) Cover the beds with tobacco cloth or cheesecloth.

What is the strawberry weevil? (New York.) The strawberry weevil is a dark, reddish-brown to black, small-snout beetle. It hibernates in rubbish in hedgerows and perhaps under the mulch in strawberry beds. It lays an egg in an unopened bud and causes it to fall by cutting the pedicel. The grub feeds on pollen and pupates inside the bud, going into hibernation in midsummer. Spray with DDT or methoxychlor when the blossom buds appear. Dust with pyrethrum or rotenone, after fruits start to form.

What causes strawberries to wilt and die just when in fruit? Roots turn yellow, brittle, and rot. (Wisconsin.) White grubs working on the roots will cause strawberries to wilt. These are most serious in land turned over from sod but may linger in soil in cultivation. They may be kept from injuring strawberries by grub-proofing the soil, which see. If no grubs are present, it may be a fungous root rot, in which case new plants should be set in fresh or sterilized soil.

How may I keep white grubs from destroying roots of new strawberry plants? (Missouri.) Set out in chlordane or dieldrin treated soil. (See previous question.)

What is the small black beetle that attacks our strawberries? (Illinois.) There are several beetle possibilities on strawberries. This one may be the adult of one of the strawberry root weevils. The grubs feed on the roots; later the weevils feed on the plants at night. Try a methoxychlor spray on the plants.

How do you deal with strawberry leaf roller? (Iowa.) This is a small greenish caterpillar which draws the leaflet together with a silken thread, feeds inside, and causes it to turn brown and die. Spray with DDD (TDE) in early spring just before first blossoms open. Rotenone dust may be used after fruits form. Burn leaves after crop is harvested.

Why do my strawberries turn white and the plants die? (Wyoming.) Chlorosis either from a virus disease or too-alkaline soil. Send a specimen and a soil sample to your Experiment Station.

SECTION IX

Regional Garden Problems

(*Arranged by States*)

INTRODUCTION

BY R. S. LEMMON

AMONG the thousands of questions which had to be sorted and organized in the preparation of this volume, there were many that dealt with problems quite local in character.

To the editors it has seemed best to retain this material, so far as possible, for the value to many readers of its local application; and the most practical way to do this has been to arrange the questions by states.

Climatic and soil conditions, of course, do not follow state lines. Even within state boundaries such conditions may vary to a very great degree. Altitude, the direction of prevailing winds, the proximity of large bodies of water—all these and many other factors enter into the picture.

However, a certain amount of generalization based on the broad factors of latitude, topography, and the prevailing movements of large bodies of air can properly be applied to the climate of any given state. The relation of this fact to the growing of plants in any particular section of the country is obvious.

The residents of different states will find in these pages much information that will be of use to them. But may we emphasize again, wherever some particular local problem is involved, the importance of consultation with some local authority, such as one's county agent, or State Agricultural College or Experiment Station. The locations of the latter are given on page 1318. Local seedmen or nurserymen are also convenient, and usually reliable, sources of information.

ALABAMA

What do you consider good group plantings of PERENNIALS and ANNUALS, separately and mixed? Daylilies and angelonia;

physostegia and shastadaisies; violets and zephyranthes; verbena and bouncing bet. For color combinations of annuals blended to taste try pink larkspur faced down with deep-blue petunias; lupines edged with pansies. The possibilities are limitless.

What FLOWERS can we grow to send to shut-ins during winter months? Pansies in little grape or strawberry boxes. Freesias, Paperwhite Narcissus bulbs in small bowls of pebbles, wanderingjew in attractive little pots, and many different kinds of easy-to-grow but much-appreciated succulents.

What APPLE can be raised in Alabama as a successful commercial venture? In extreme northern Alabama, Delicious, Black Twig, Jonathan, McIntosh, and several other varieties of apples should grow successfully.

When is the best time to set out AZALEAS and in what type of soil, for best results in this section? It is the custom, but not essential, to move azaleas when they are in full bloom. Balled plants should be moved carefully into beds that have been prepared with rotted hard wood leaves, rotted wood, and aluminum sulfate, and that are entirely free from lime. Be sure to set the plants at exactly the same level they grew in the nursery, and water well.

I am told that my AZALEAS and CAMELLIAS will do better if I pile oak leaves around them. Is this true? Yes. These plants succeed much better under a mulch than they do with clean cultivation. Oak leaves are excellent when applied about 4 ins. thick. As the leaves decompose and the mulch becomes more shallow, pile on more leaves to keep the blanket up to the original thickness. A mulch retains moisture, prevents extremes of temperature, and discourages weeds.

What are some of the best BULBS for fall planting on the Gulf Coast? Calla, cooperia, hemerocallis, hybrid amaryllis, iris species (native), leucojum, lilium, morea, narcissus, and zephyranthes.

Will AZALEAMUMS succeed in the Birmingham area? Yes, these popular garden perennials do well in this locality.

What can I do for the powdery mildew on my CRAPEMYRTLE? At first signs spray with Mildex or Karathane, new chemical fungicides and miticides. Use one ounce to 25 gallons of water. Do not apply when temperature is above 85° F. Grade sulfur will do as well, but it must be carefully applied after each rain until the mildew is under control.

Are any DAYLILIES evergreen in southern Alabama? Yes, many of the choice new hybrids are evergreen and are, therefore, of much value in the winter garden effect.

What sprays are recommended for various scales and insects com-

mon to FRUIT trees, and when should they be applied in middle Georgia? Combination or all-purpose sprays are now available for use on fruit trees in the home garden. One of these is duPont's Fruit Tree Spray, made up of the same materials as those used for control in commercial plantings. It is necessary, however, to spray a number of times each season to get satisfactory results. Spray as follows:

1. When leaves begin to bud out:—apple, peach, plum, apricot.
2. When bloom shows color:—apple, peach, plum, apricot, pear, quince, cherry.
3. When all petals have fallen:—apple, peach, plum, apricot, pear, quince, cherry.
4. When shucks fall:—cherry, peach, plum, apricot.
5. Every 2 weeks from petal fall to shuck fall:—apple, pear, quince, cherry, peach, plum, apricot.
6. Two weeks before harvest:—peach, plum, apricot.
7. After harvest:—cherry.

Can FUCHSIA plants be left in ground outdoors during winter in the South? In certain sections and in certain well-protected places fuchsias may be grown as garden perennials. If they are growing in the ground, they will be much hardier, of course, than if they are plunged in their pots. As potted plants they are quite likely to freeze.

When should GLADIOLUS be planted in Montgomery, Alabama? February or March, so that newly emerging flower scapes will miss the late frosts.

When should Bermuda GRASS seed be planted? Sow in early spring if it can be watered; during the summer rains; or in early autumn if winter rye grass is not going to be used. When the grass shows definitely green, make a light application of a nitrogenous fertilizer and water in well. These feedings may be repeated at 4- or 5-week intervals during growing weather.

If GRASS (Bermuda or Centipede) grows around the base of camellias or azaleas, does it hurt them? It is better to maintain circles free of grass around the bushes. A mulch of peatmoss, bugasse, or leafmold placed on ground surface is very beneficial.

How can I eradicate Nut GRASS? Nut Grass is very difficult to eradicate in the lower South, but trials have shown that it can be discouraged to a marked degree if it is possible to grow a heavy cover of cowpeas on the plot for several summers after the annuals or bulbs have been lifted. Use Brabham or some other variety resistant to root knot, and sow the seeds as early in summer as the garden is vacant. Fertilize the cowpeas well and turn them under in October. Weedazol is a new control (American Chemical Paint Company). It is effective against Nut Grass, Johnson Grass, Quack Grass and Bermuda Grass as well as poison ivy.

What HERBS are most suitable for southern Alabama? For fall:

anise, chives, Winter Savory, sage, and dill. For spring: sweet basil, Summer Savory, sweet fennel, coriander, thyme, and sweet marjoram.

Can we make Nada IRIS bloom in this locality?   As both parents like a moist, rich soil and a shady location, there should be no reason why Nada will not grow well if these conditions are furnished.

What are cultural requirements for Japanese IRISES in this state? Japanese irises prefer a moisture-retentive soil of slightly acid reaction. The roots may be planted after flowering, or during the autumn and winter. Applications of a plant food in March, May, and July should take care of nutritional needs; a mulch is highly desirable.

What is the best fertilizer for NANDINAS? I have strong, healthy plants, but the berries dry up and fall off before they turn red.   Any good commercial fertilizer mixture should suit nandinas. An application in January, hoed or spaded in, and another in June to mature the new growth, should be adequate under normal garden conditions. Nandina berries will color best in full sun; they may be destroyed by very low temperatures.

Can ORANGES be grown along the Gulf in Alabama and Mississippi?   Yes. Satsuma Oranges are dwarf citrus trees that belong to the kid-glove group. These are quite hardy, and when budded on hardy trifoliate stock will produce excellent early oranges along the upper Gulf coast.

What is the proper method for growing PANSIES from seed in the South?   Pansies are cool-weather annuals and the seeds will not germinate well in the warm weather of early autumn. Seeds sown after the weather turns cool in October or early November germinate well and give flowering plants in April and May. Sometimes germination in warm weather can be hastened by placing a small seed flat, properly prepared, in the refrigerator for a week or so.

Will PEONIES grow well in Alabama? Was told that they grow best near salt water. We are quite inland.   Peonies are temperate-zone plants and in many parts of the lower South will not succeed. It is not the proximity of salt water that assures success with peonies, but a combination of soil and a long, cold winter without warm breaks that will guarantee a complete dormancy in the peony crown.

Why are RHODODENDRONS practically failures in the lower South, where soil conditions appear to be ideal, as azaleas and the white dogwood grow and bloom luxuriously?   In the South there is not a sufficiently long or sufficiently severe winter season for rhododendrons. Soil conditions may be ideal but climatic conditions are definitely not right for these plants.

What ROCK GARDEN PLANTS will grow in partial shade in central Alabama?   Most rock gardens are exposed to full sun, and the usual list of plants for rock gardens include few shade-loving species.

There are many, however, which do excellently in partial shade. You could make a fine collection from the wildflowers of your locality. Deep pockets of earth may be prepared for hardy ferns, to be used as a dominant green note. Besides wild flowers you could add sweet violets, violas, Florists' Anemones and ranunculus, alliums, zephyranthes periwinkle, lily-of-the-valley, ladyslipper orchids.

What roses would you suggest for Alabama? In addition to the hybrid teas you can grow teas Duchesse de Brabant, Glorie de Dijon, Lady Hillington and Maman Cochet, which are too tender for northern gardens.

What about planting ROSES deeper than usual in the South? In this locality tests have showed that it is much better to set roses at exactly the same depth that they grew in the nursery.

When should bush ROSES be pruned in central Alabama? In February or in March, just before growth commences. Head the canes back to 4 or 5 good strong eyes if you wish to prune low to produce a few perfect flowers. If you prefer tall, luxuriant bushes covered with masses of smaller blooms, prune as high as you wish, but removing all half dead or diseased wood and cutting each healthy cane back somewhat. Pruning cuts should be made about ¼ in. above a strong eye that points away from the center of the plant.

I have been told I cannot grow TULIPS on account of the winter temperatures here. Is this true? Yes. Tulips cannot be successfully grown in the deep South. They require several months of cold weather and a cool spring to develop normally.

ARIZONA

What are the characteristics of the SOILS of Arizona, Colorado, and New Mexico? The whole Southwest region has, except for the mountain areas, but little forests or other vegetation to provide humus. Hence, in general, the soil, whether sand, silt, clay, or *Caliche,* requires the addition of much humus. The compost pile is very necessary here. Peatmoss, rotted strawy manure, any decayed vegetation is useful. One successful gardener in central New Mexico began with a half acre of *Caliche*—shale clay. She first put on a heavy layer of dairy manure, had a team plow and harrow this. Next came 20 bales of peatmoss. A surface mulch of peatmoss and manure each fall with constant additions from the compost pile keeps her garden growing and blooming with a lushness unbelievable when one sees the surrounding soil and vegetation. The lack of humidity in the air, as well as low rainfall, makes much watering necessary. Incorporation into the soil of generous amounts of humus helps it to retain moisture and so reduces labor of watering.

What are the best FLOWERING plants to stand Arizona desert heat? Perennials that flower early, followed by annuals that can stand heat and dry air. Native plants should be most satisfactory. Such early perennials as dwarf phlox; dianthus, iris, euphorbia, oenothera. Annuals: verbena, zinnia, marigold, mesembryanthemum, mirabilis, petunia, portulaca, salvia, *Xanthisma texanum* (Star of Texas), venidium, xeranthemum.

What kind of FLOWERS can be planted in the fall in high altitude (7000 ft.) where it is very cold? Fall planting of perennials is more successful in this climate if done early—even before the first killing frost. Plant shrubs and roses either fall or early spring. For fall planting: lilies, narcissus, peonies, pyrethrum, iris, campanulas, tulips, phlox, dianthus, dictamnus, heliopsis. Hybrid tea roses can be planted, if covered during the winter. Polyantha and floribunda roses should be quite satisfactory, and will give a long season's bloom and require little or no winter protection. Among the sturdiest are: Else Poulsen, Improved Lafayette, Kirsten Poulsen, Gloria Mundi, World's Fair, Spartan. Climbing roses are more difficult, since in your climate they require protection from winter sun. Some of the hardiest are: American Pillar, Silver Moon, Tausendschon, New Dawn, Blaze. Shrub roses include Rugosa and Rugosa Hybrids, *R. hugonis;* and the best of the Hybrid Perpetuals.

Can you advise me as to a good CLIMBER, either annual or perennial? I live in a hot, dry climate, and the season is long. Annual: madeira vine, coral vine, *Cobaea scandens,* gourds, thunbergia, cardinal vine, morningglory, moonflower. Perennial: passion flower, trumpetvine, kudzuvine, *Clematis texensis, Lonicera heckrotti,* silver lace vine.

When is the best time to plant CHRYSANTHEMUMS in Arizona? Spring. Even late-spring transplanting brings earlier and more profuse bloom than if the plants are left undisturbed.

Can wild "INDIAN PAINTBRUSH" be transplanted and if so, how and when? Indian Paintbrush (*Castilleja collina*) is partially a parasite. To transplant successfully its host must be transplanted with it. *Chrysothamnus* (rabbitbrush) is one host of *Castilleja collina.* Transplant any time when ground is sufficiently moist to make a ball. They move easily in full bloom if kept well watered. Dig a trench around the plant, then lift it with a ball or clump not less than 1 ft. in diameter, taking with it any other plants contained in the ball.

Can I grow LILIUM bakerianum in Arizona? *Lilium bakerianum* is listed among the difficult ones. Since it is a stem-rooting species, bulbs should be planted about 3 times their own depth. To prevent drying, as well as alternate freezing and thawing, a mulch is necessary. In its western China home it grows on steep, loamy slopes among shrubs and grasses.

When is the proper time to plant LILY bulbs in our Southern

country? Time to plant lily bulbs is determined by time of dormancy of the bulbs rather than by climate of their new home. *Lilium candidum* is planted in August and September. Top growth begins immediately. Plant lilies whose bulbs mature later, in September to November, such as: *Lilium regale, tenuifolium (pumilum), concolor, henryi, humboldti, tigrinum, croceum, umbellatum* and the new hybrid strains.

What climbing ROSE will do the best here? All the climbing forms of hybrid perpetuals and hybrid teas should do well. Some that are grown successfully in the Southwest are: Blaze, Cherokee, Max Graf, Silver Moon, Climbing Dainty Bess, Climbing Crimson Glory, Climbing Talisman, American Pillar, Gardenia, and Mme. Gregoire Staechelin. Protection from winter sun may be necessary on a southern exposure. Spruce branches or cornstalks may be woven into rose trellis, or roses, support and all, may be laid on ground and covered.

ARKANSAS

Will DELPHINIUM and Oriental poppies grow in this part of the country? Yes. *Delphinium belladonna* is more likely to prosper than some of the fancy hybrids.

What flowers can I plant in a COCO-GRASS-infested area? Few plants have the persistence of these stoloniferous grasses. Any that have, are little short of weeds themselves. Some that may fight their way are: Bishops goutweed (*Aegopodium variegatum*), Kenilworth Ivy, buttercup, Ageratum Little Gem, strawberry, and Moneywort (*Lysimachia nummularia*). Treat the infested area with Weedazol or other new chemical control for hard-to-kill grasses.

Can I put POINSETTIA plants outdoors in summer? They can be put out during warm weather, in a spot with sunshine, but sheltered from strong winds. Be sure to bring them in in the fall before night temperatures drop below 55° to 60° F.

What is a good yellow ROSE that will bloom monthly? Peace, Golden Masterpiece, Gold Cup, (Flor).

Are Marechal Niel ROSES out of style? In a way, yes. They are still grown in the South, but newer varieties of yellow climbers are often grown now, whereas Marechal Niel once had the field to itself. In the North it is not hardy. Golden Showers is a fine, new everblooming climber.

CALIFORNIA

SOIL AND FERTILIZER

What can I mix with adobe ground to make a garden? Two very good materials to mix with adobe soil are decomposed granite and bean straw. A 3-in. layer of granite, dug in deeply, followed by a deeper layer of bean straw, also dug in deeply, will help greatly. Decomposition of the straw should be permitted to advance well before planting is done. This treatment will not improve drainage, for adobe is generally too deep.

What kind of fertilizer is best for adobe soil? The best fertilizer for any soil is organic, either dairy, horse, or chicken manure. If not available, substitute dried cow manure. In addition use a complete commercial fertilizer. Acid phosphate will overcome the general lack of phosphate in California soil.

What is the treatment for hard, black soil, near Los Angeles? Soil conditioners and fertilizers have already been discussed. (See Section I.) The most important consideration of all is in respect to water. First, don't ever work adobe soil when it is wet, for it will cake and harden, and be put out of condition for a long time. Second, do not overirrigate, for it drains poorly. Check the soil to see how deeply it has dried, and aim to irrigate just enough to moisten the soil to that depth. Cultivate as soon as the soil surface is dry.

How can adobe soil be made to produce? See previous questions. Alkalinity must also be considered. If plants look yellow and stunted, there may be an alkaline condition. Soil sulfur or ferrous sulfate, at the rate of 2 lbs. per 100 sq. ft., will reduce the alkalinity. More or less may be used yearly, after the first application is made as a test. Normally, adobe soil produces heavily.

It is cold and often foggy here, and this seems to slow plant growth down. Would an extra amount of fertilizer give plants beneficial warmth? Commercial fertilizers will not supply any warmth to the soil. However, nitrogen fertilizer will stimulate growth if the soil is not too cold, and phosphorus and potash may be used to hasten maturity.

We had to import soil for our garden, but now it is worn out. Can it be improved? The lack of humus in most California soils is the cause. The imported soil may have had some, but the thin layer was stripped very soon. Soils wear out from lack of humus. Addition of bean straw, manures, or peatmoss would have helped maintain the purchased soil. Would suggest you follow a yearly program of planting the garden area to a cover crop of cow peas or other legumes, to be dug under when 6 ins. tall. This will provide a constantly increasing supply of humus. Fertilize with manure or dried manure mixed with peatmoss. During the growing season, feed little and often with a complete plant food or with liquid manure.

What can be done with soil spoiled by the oil from pods, leaves, and bark of eucalyptus trees? First clean off all debris, then turn the soil as deeply as possible. Permit rains and heavy waterings to leach out the toxic oils. After lying fallow over winter, the soil should be in fair condition. Constant raking must be practiced to keep off the debris.

My soil is light, has no clay subsoil, and requires too much water. How can I use less? The problem is not one of using less so much as of *losing* less. Add as much humus as possible, preferably with peatmoss. Cultivate as soon as the surface is dry. In irrigating, do not wet the soil too deeply for annuals, vegetables, or shallow-rooted plants, for the water will drain away. Trees and shrubs should be irrigated deeply and seldom, to encourage deep rooting.

What is a good book on soils and fertilizers for California? Some of the very best information on the subject is to be found in bulletiins of the State Agricultural College, at Berkeley, California.

PLANNING AND ENVIRONMENT

Can one make an attractive garden with perennials alone? It often seems like less work to grow perennials, but if results are desired, they involve about as much work as annuals. One should start off with a good shrub background, not too tall, to add to the appearance and break the wind. Then select perennials that are proven in your region. Select them for durability, successive blooming dates, and reasonably clean habit. Interplant with bulbs and corms like lilies, muscaris (grapehyacinths), watsonias, callas, narcissi, and others that grow in your area for several years without lifting.

What are the best flowers for winter, spring, summer, and fall? This could make a long list, but here are some good ones: Spring: freesias, callas, ixias, ismemnes, sparaxis, narcissi, minor bulbs, tulips; sweetpeas, snapdragons, columbine, mesembryanthemums. Summer: geraniums, heliotrope, lantanta, fuchsias; dahlia, gladiolus, montbretia, tigridia, haemanthus; gaillardia, marigold zinnia. Fall: hardy asters and chrysanthemums. Winter: sweetpeas, calendulas, snapdragons, stock and wallflowers.

What are some good border flowers or plants, not over 12 ins. high? Annuals which might answer the purpose are lobelia, portulaca, ageratum, *Tagetes pumila*, sweet alyssum, and *Phlox drummondi*. Perennials could be *Chrysanthemum mawi, Nierembergia hippomanica,* coralbells, aster frikarti and gazania.

What flowers will grow in pots in the sun all day? The reason most plants fail under these conditions is the rapid drying of the soil. Geraniums, nasturtiums, and petunias do the best, although portulaca is often used. They all need plenty of water under the circumstances.

What plants will hold adobe soil on hillsides? Nothing surpasses *Mesembryanthemum edule* for this purpose; but other good ones would be *M. floribunda,* honeysuckle, creeping lantana, Mermaid Rose, and St. Augustinegrass.

What are good plants for adobe soil, especially in the sun?   As a general rule, the same plants will grow in adobe as in any other soil, but the difficulty caused by poor drainage eliminates some. The doubtful type of plant would include choiseya, cistus, caesalpinia, helianthemum, leptospermum, and others known for their love of dry conditions.

What flowers or shrubs would do well on the west side of the house where the temperature sometimes reaches 140° F.?   In such hot, dry spots one must go in for heat-loving plants. Leptospermum, oleander, lantana, bougainvillea, cistus species, plumbago, *Cotoneaster parnayi,* diosma, felicia, helianthemum, leucophyllum, *Pittosporum tobira, Viburnum suspensum* and *V. tinus,* all should do well. For annuals, marigolds, petunias, portulacas, and tithonias will give summer color.

What low perennial may be planted in the shady strip between drive and house?   *Fragaria chiloensis* would be a happy choice. It is a creeper with bright-green foliage and bright-red fruits. *Campanula mayi* or *Saxifraga crassifolia* would give some color, but would grow 12 ins. to 15 ins. tall. *Ajuga repens* would also do very well.

What can be grown under eucalyptus trees?   The heavy demand for food and water by the eucalyptus and the toxic effect of its leaves and bark make trouble for most plants. Grass, heavily fed and watered, is satisfactory, for debris can be easily raked off. English Ivy is often used as a ground cover, but hand-picking of debris is necessary.

My house faces southwest, and the northeast corner gets little sun. What plants would do well there?   This is an ideal spot for some of the shrubs that do not like full sun, especially camellias, azaleas, gardenias, Star Jasmines, fuchias, *Daphne odora,* hydrangeas, eranthemums, ginger-lilies, English Holly, and nandina.

What flowers or vines will grow on the north side of our house, where it is shady all the time?   There are many plants that grow well in the shade, the degree of shade being a limiting factor. Camellias, fuchsias, begonias, violets, ferns, *Saxifraga crassifolia* all do well up to a certain amount of shade. If very dense, use ferns, aucuba, sarcococca, and aspidistra.

We live under oaks, and find violets, iris, ferns, coleus, and begonias growing fine. What would do well in sunny spots in such soil?   In sunny spots near oaks most plants should thrive. If coleus and begonias overwinter, it would indicate a frost-free area, so try primulas, cinerarias, calceolarias, and cyclamen for winter. In the shade, try azaleas and camellias, for they should do well. In summer, avoid rankgrowing annuals, but try the rest.

What climber would grow on the wall of a summerhouse facing

the ocean near Los Angeles? Few climbers compare with *Bignonia cherere* as a vine under such circumstances. If the large-leaved type is used, it has beautiful foliage every day of the year, and for most of the year it produces huge red trumpets of bloom. It does not object to the salt breezes. It will need a trellis till it has something to hold on to. An everblooming Climbing Rose like Blaze or Dr. Nicholas might survive if the plants themselves were placed on the side of the summerhouse farthest from the ocean, and protected from heavy storms coming in from the sea. Max Graf, a Hybrid Rugosa, would undoubtedly do well in such a location.

What vine similar to trumpetvine can I put on the north side of my house? The trumpetvine itself, *Bignonia cherere*, does very well on the north, as will also *Bignonia violacea*, *Thunbergia grandiflora*, and *Distictis lactiflora*, all of lavender and blue shades. *Tecomaria capensis*, even more vivid than the trumpetvine, does well too. None of these like heavy shade, but normal conditions on the north are satisfactory. All are equally hardy.

LAWN

How can I grow a beautiful dichondra lawn? The soil should be well enriched and perfectly graded. The plants are purchased in flats. They are divided with a knife into 2-in. or 3-in. squares. Planted about a foot apart, and well watered, these will soon spread. Frequent feedings with a balanced commercial fertilizer and plenty of water are needed to keep the lawn green. It should be cut 3 or 4 tiimes a year. The fussy care which it requires is fast stopping the fad for this type of lawn.

What time of year is the best for starting a lawn in southern California? A lawn may be started at any time, but the best time is fall—September or October. This will establish the plants well before heavy rains and give a good turf before the summer's heat.

What is the best lawn seed to use? There is much discussion about this, but most people like Merion Blue Grass, generally in a mixture of Meadow Fescue and redtop. Perennial Rye Grass must be renewed every few years. By all means buy the very best seed obtainable from a good seed house.

How much seed should be used? Oversowing of seed gives poor results, for the plants crowd themselves out. Use three lbs. of Merion Blue Grass per 1,000 sq. ft., and 8 lbs. of Perennial Rye Grass.

My lawn is shady, and very damp and soggy. Should I reseed bare spots? Some means should be used to drain the soil better, for the lawn will never do well under such conditions. Regrading may do the trick; or drain tile may have to be used. There are some good shady grass mixtures on the market.

How do you renovate an old lawn infested with "devilgrass"? It can hardly be eliminated, for a tiny piece of root starts a new plant. The customary procedure is to hire a nurseryman to run a renovator over the lawn several times and rake out the roots as well as possible. This gives the new sowing a chance to fight the "devilgrass" (Bermuda Grass), though it will succumb again sooner or later. Weedazol, a new selective weed killer, is the best chemical control to date.

How is a lawn of sagina moss made?   *Sagina subulata* is not a moss, but a flowering plant. It is used as a shady ground cover. It must have light soil and good drainage. It may be planted at any time of the year, but preferably in spring. Flats may be purchased at some nurseries, and the plants are divided and planted quite closely. It has a serious failing in that it turns yellow in spots and must be replanted, but it is fairly permanent.

How can I get rid of the worm that causes small piles of mud all over my lawn?   Chlordane, 20 lbs. of 5% dust per 1000 square feet will eliminate earthworms from your lawn.

HEDGES

What shrubs would make a good flowering hedge?   The list would be almost limitless in southern California, but some of the best would be abelias, white and red, *Cassia splendida, Plumbago capensis, Chalcis exotica, Choiseya ternata, Cotoneaster parnayi, Grewia caffra,* feijoa, pyracantha, *Solanum rantonetti, Viburnum suspensum* and *V. tinus,* and lantana. Properly cared for, a hedge of varicolored hibiscus may be beautiful. Oleanders, with pruning, work out well, especially the variety Mrs. Roeding.

How is a flowering hedge best planted?   Except for hibiscus, the plants mentioned could be planted from containers at any time. (Hibiscus should be well established before winter.) Allow plenty of room for each plant to develop into a good specimen. Drop a line, and stake out the center of each hole along it. Dig generous holes and add plenty of manure. In the rear, leave a good irrigation ditch. By all means carry on a program of pruning, so the hedge does not become an eyesore.

What are good plants for green hedges?   This would depend on the size required. For a very low hedge, nothing surpasses *Buxus japonica. Myrtus compacta* and *Ligustrum henryi* also make good low hedges. For a moderate-sized hedge, (up to 5 ft.) the Wax-Leaf Privet is excellent. Boxwood is fine anywhere up to this height. For the tall hedge, *Pittosporum undulatum* outdoes any other. In hot, dry areas, *Ligustrum japonicum* is a tough, tall hedge.

Our Dwarf Eucalyptus windbreak blew over in a storm. What could we use that would be sturdier?   *Eucalyptus globulus compacta* is so shallow-rooted that it blows over easily. One good substitute is *E. cornuta lehmanni.* Another would be *E. sideroxylon rosea,* if it were topped out at about 20 ft. *Pittosporum undulatum* also makes a good windbreak if it need not be high.

SHRUBS

What shrubs may be planted in southern California in January and February? Since most shrubs are grown in containers here, they may be planted at any time. Very tender plants, such as bougainvillea and hibiscus, are best planted later. Roses and other deciduous shrubs are best planted while dormant. These are sold as "bare-root" plants.

What are some shrubs that would make good foundation plants? Such a list should be made up of plants which will not cover the windows in a few years. Some good ones for sun are *Convolvulus cneorum, Correa speciosa, Juniperus tamariscifolia, Turraea obtusifolia* —all of which grow very low. *Choiseya ternata, Murraya exotica, Viburnum suspensum, Myrsine africana, Myrtus compacta, Ligustrum indicum, Abelia floribunda, Diosma reevesi,* Gardenia Mystery, *Pittosporum tobira*—all of which grow to moderate size, and can be kept down easily by pruning.

Will you name some shrubs that are quick to grow and easy to care for around a new home? This is really the worst thing to do in California, as quick-growing shrubs around the house in 3 or 4 years make a jungle and a mess. Be patient, and a permanent effect may be obtained by using slower-growing, more durable material.

My shrubs and trees grow too fast. How can this be prevented? Overwatering and overfeeding cause too rank a growth. Do not use fertilizer for several years, and water just enough to keep plants from wilting.

TREES

What are some good evergreen trees for a small home in the Los Angeles area? The evergreen elm, *Ulmus parvifolia sempervirens,* tops the list. *Pittosporum undulatum* and *P. rhombifolium* give beautiful fruits, as well as being good foliage trees. *Jacaranda acutifolia,* nearly evergreen, has a mass of blue flowers in the spring. *Calodendrum capense,* a mass of pink flowers in summer, is a good tree. *Magnolia grandiflora* is everyone's favorite. For certain types of homes, olive trees have a fine character.

What kind of tree do you suggest putting in a front yard only 40 ft. wide? One of the finest trees is the evergreen elm, *Ulmus parvifolia sempervirens.* Care must be used in its purchase, for seedling forms vary too much. The best nurseries grow only from cuttings taken from fine trees.

What fruits are most likely to do well on the Pacific coast? There is no fruit that does not do well somewhere on the coast, except very tropical types. In the North, all the deciduous fruits, like apple, cherry, and plum, do very well. Further south, the evergreen fruit area begins, and citrus, avocados, and other sub-tropicals do well.

How do you cure curly leaf on trees? First investigate for the presence of aphids. Most so-called curly leaf is the result of these plant lice. They are easily controlled by a spray of nicotine sulfate, 1 to 300: or by the newer chemical Malathion, 2 teaspoonsful 50% emulsion per gallon of water. If this is not the cause, it may be the curly-leaf virus and in such case one of the new antidotes should be used, such as Chloromycin (Parke Davis Co.) or Atriazolopyrimidine (Lederle Laboratory).

Where can one obtain information on tropical ornamentals? Not many truly tropical plants thrive in southern California, where subtropicals are the rule. Tropicals generally demand a moist climate, with never any frost. They like light, moisture-retentive soils. They desire at least partial shade. Obviously, lath houses and conservatories are the answers. If attempts are to be made to grow them, contact one of the large nurseries in southern California which specialize in exotic material, and the State Agricultural Experiment Station.

LATH HOUSE

Would you please make suggestions for growing plants in a lath house? On the whole, the plants that like shade prefer a light soil containing leafmold, which provides good drainage. This is often given by building raised beds and filling with prepared soil. Careful attention must be given to watering, but the results are worth while. Feeding should be done with cottonseed meal or an acid fertilizer. Do not grow heavy vines on the lath.

What plants are grown in lath houses? Camellias, fuchsias, and begonias are raised by every lath-house owner. Other desirable subjects are gloxinias, streptocarpus, achimenes, caladiums, anthuriums, cyclamen, stephanotis, *Hoya carnosa,* and sarcococca. Many orchids also do very well.

What evergreen vine may I use over my lath house that will not freeze easily? *Gelsemium sempervirens* is a good vine if the temperature does not drop below 15° F. It has a light growth that will not be too dense for the plants beneath, and in late winter, is a mass of yellow bloom. It is very clean, and has refreshingly green foliage all year.

INDIVIDUAL PLANTS

Why doesn't my ALMOND tree bear? A single tree never bears; 2 varieties must be planted together to get pollinization. Good combinations are Nonpareil and Ne Plus Ultra, or Ne Plus Ultra and I. X. L.

I have an ARBUTUS unedo which blooms but does not set fruit.

Why? Some arbutus do not bear well. It would be well to investigate its environment before deciding that it is a poor type. They like good drainage. They do not like to be exposed to hot, dry winds; nor do they like an alkaline soil. If conditions are favorable and the tree is healthy, then the seedling is evidently a poor type.

I have an AVOCADO tree 8 years old. Why do the blooms fall? There may be many factors. The tree may be still immature. Drainage may be poor. Overwatering or feeding before the fruits set may have forced off the bloom. Oil sprays are sometimes given at the wrong time, before the fruit is set.

My seedling AVOCADO has fruit. Will it be good? There is a chance that it will be good. All the good varieties were once seedlings. For new plantings, seedlings are not worth the gamble, when there are such fine varieties as Fuerte, Puebla, Nabal, Ryan, and others.

Should I destroy a seedling AVOCADO with black fruit, growing 8 ft. from another avocado? One tree or the other would be best removed, for the tops spread wide, and you would end up with 2 poor trees. The black fruit is typical of many fine kinds of avocados.

What time of the year should AVOCADOS be picked? Avocados are picked at any time of the year, depending on the varieties planted. For home use, they are best allowed to ripen on the trees. An avocado becomes somewhat soft when ripe.

Can AZALEAS be grown in southern California? Azaleas do beautifully with proper care. They should never be planted in full sun. A large amount of peatmoss should be mixed in the soil. Drainage must be perfect, and in heavy soils this means raising the plant above surrounding soil. During summer, water heavily, and feed generously with cottonseed meal or other acid fertilizer.

How may I encourage BANANAS to ripen in the Los Angeles area? First, types that fruit in this area should be purchased. Plant in a rich, well-drained spot that is protected from hot, dry winds. Keep the plant growing in healthy condition and fruit should ripen.

Is there any special care for BIRD-OF-PARADISE? Should it be pruned or divided? If you have it outdoors in your California garden, let it grow as it pleases. Remove only dead foliage, and don't divide before the foliage dies. Feed and water plentifully during summer.

How are BLACKBERRIES grown in California? Blackberries grow fairly well here, in heavy loam. Young plants are set out in early spring, about 3 ft. apart. The first growth is pinched when a few feet tall, to encourage branches which bear the fruit the next year. Each year canes that have fruited are cut out after harvesting. A mulch of manure in the spring and copious watering in the growing season are desirable.

Can BLUEBERRIES be grown in California? There are some places where they should grow well, but they seldom do. If you have a moist climate and cool winters, write to an Eastern nursery specializing in the new types, and try its recommendations.

What is the best care of BOXWOOD? Boxwood is a very easily grown plant. It likes a fertile soil, with plenty of organic fertilizer. It must never be allowed to become dry, or it will start to shed foliage. Frequent prunings or shearings will keep it dense. Be on the lookout for red spider, which mottles the foliage, and for scale. There are many sprays for red spider on the market, and scale is controlled by a 1½ per cent or 2 per cent oil spray or by malathion in June or July.

How are BOYSENBERRIES grown? Plant in early spring, at least 5 ft. apart. Allow the vines to grow on the ground. Be generous with water and manure. Early the next spring tie the vines on trellises. As the berries start ripening, cut out new growth. After harvesting, cut off the vines which bore the fruit, and allow new growths to grow on the ground. These should be tied up early the following spring. Plenty of manure in the spring and plenty of water in the summer will produce tremendous crops.

In the West, should ranunculus BULBS be lifted after flowering? Yes; when they are dormant, they resent the water given other plants. When the foliage is yellowed and dry, they are ready for digging. Seedling-grown ranunculus give far superior bloom, but are troublesome to start.

What is the proper care for CALLAS in California? Callas are almost weeds here, except in bad frost areas. They enjoy partial shade, but it is not necessary. They like a very rich soil and plenty of water and manure. They do not need a rest period. They may be divided at any time, but early fall is best.

Could you suggest a tree similar to the Deodar CEDAR? There are a number of fine coniferous trees for southern California. The Atlas Cedar and its blue variety the Canary Pine, the Aleppo Pine, the Stone Pine, the Monterey Pine, the Coast Redwood, and the California Incense Cedar, all do well in most sections.

When should CHRYSANTHEMUMS be planted, and how? New plants may be set out in the spring. They usually come in flats, and are planted about 12 ins. apart to the same depth they were growing. They enjoy a rich soil and reasonably generous watering. Pinch several times in summer to encourage branching and strong stems. Divide yearly, after blooming.

CITRUS FRUITS

We water our CITRUS trees by trenches and daily sprinkling. Is this too much? Citrus trees do not need much water when once established. Overwatering forces growth at the expense of fruit, and may kill the tree. A well established tree need not be watered more than once a month. This will encourage deep rooting.

How old must a seedling citrus tree be before it bears fruit? This would be extremely variable, but a guess would be between 4 and 8 years. Seedlings are seldom worth growing on.

Why does a young lemon tree produce hard lemons? The first fruit of citrus trees often has a very thick rind. If the tree is a seedling, there is a good chance that it is a hard type. Citrus is one fruit that responds to good care. The Sunkist standard is maintained by rigid adherence to best cultural methods. These methods may be obtained from your local county agent.

I have a lemon that is losing its leaves. Why? A very heavy crop of fruit often will strip a lemon of most of its foliage. Overwatering in poorly drained soil may cause the condition, but the poor health of the tree will be obvious. Less water and a feeding of commercial citrus food in the spring should bring it back. Lemon trees require very little water.

When should lemons be planted? Lemons and other citrus and evergreen fruits are best planted in a well-worked soil in spring when cold weather is over and before summer's heat. A stake should be provided immediately, and some kind of shade on the south side to prevent sunburn on the trunk. Watering should be liberal the first year.

How are Meyer Lemons and dwarf limes grown? There are no true dwarf limes, though the Rangpur is somewhat small. Lemons are quite hardy; limes definitely not. Where each can be grown, requirements are the same. Good drainage is essential. They want plenty of water when young, much less as they mature. Light feeding in spring is beneficial.

How can one tell the difference between young oranges and lemons? The best way is to note the foliage. The lemon has much paler foliage than the orange, if the orange has been growing well. It sometimes is very difficult, except for an expert.

How does one apply lime around orange trees? Lime is sprinkled on the soil rather heavily, as far out as the branches spread. It is cultivated in a few inches. Irrigation then carries it evenly through the soil. Ground limestone is the best form for amateurs.

What do you spray oranges with? Under normal conditions, oranges are sprayed in summer with a miscible oil, usually a 2 per cent solution of light medium. This will kill red spider, scale, aphids, etc. It should never be applied when the temperature is above 90° F. in the shade. A perfect coverage is essential.

How do you prune COTONEASTERS to get good berries? Cotoneasters fruit on 1-year-old wood. After the berries fall, the wood on which they were borne should be cut back about 6 ins. from the ground. New growths for the following year's berries will spring freely from the stubs. Never be afraid to cut the sprays for decoration, for this can become a part of the pruning, if the stems are cut back to about 6 ins.

My COTONEASTERS, though faithfully watered and fertilized for over a year, have had no berries. Could they be "duds"? Cotoneasters have perfect flowers, and are never "duds." Probably too much shade, too much water, too immature, or pruning off the flowering wood would be the difficulty. Since they are almost foolproof, patience will probably reward you with their showy berries. (See previous question.)

My CYPRESS tree yellows, then browns. It seems to be dying. Why? This is a disease called Coryneum canker and has no permanent cure. Cutting out the first cankers to appear will retard the disease; as will a spray of 5–5–50 Bordeaux. Monterey Cypress is the most frequent victim. Forbes' Cypress seems resistant.

What special culture is needed for TREEFERNS? The treefern, *Alsophila australis,* is not a temperamental plant, but it must be treated as a fern. It likes shade, leafmold, perfect drainage, and must never be allowed to dry out, even for an hour. During spring and summer it likes feedings of dried blood or liquid dairy manure.

How often should FIGS and PEACHES be watered? The texture of the soil decides this. Sandy soils need more water; heavy soils, less. During the growing season, deciduous fruits require a moist soil. Watering every 2 weeks in sandy soil might not be too much. On the other hand, 2 or 3 good soakings during the season might suffice in adobe soil.

What kind of soil and care do FUCHSIAS require? They like protection from hot sun; the north and east sides of the house are good. If possible, provide a light, well-drained soil. They must never suffer from lack of moisture. Regular monthly feedings of acid fertilizers are appreciated, the best being cottonseed meal. This feeding should be started in March and continued until September.

How should FUCHSIAS be pruned when in the ground? In February or March, cut back hard, leaving only a little of the previous season's growth. The best plants are obtained if the new growth is pinched when about 6 or 8 ins. long, thus making the plant bushy.

How are potted FUCHSIAS cared for? Fuchsias are generally grown in 6-in. pots as rapidly as growth permits, and then shifted into 8-in. pots. If feeding is carried out, every 2 years should be often enough to shift plants to larger pots. During the growing season they should be watered heavily and food applied monthly. Each February or March they should be pruned hard.

How often should GERBERAS be divided? Do they require ferti-

lizer? Gerberas are plants which really demand rich, well-drained soil. They particularly like organic fertilizer. Divide every 3 or 4 years in the early fall. They are subject to aphids, so spray with nicotine sulfate or malathion.

In California should GLADIOLUS bulbs be lifted? Yes. They multiply fast, and need separation, also to be kept dry when dormant. They can best be treated for thrips when out of the ground. After digging they should be kept in a sack for about 2 weeks with naphthalene flakes, to kill thrips, then removed, and the naphthalene screened off. DDT and Malathion also control thrips. Store in a cool, dry place.

When should we prune GRAPES set out last spring? There are 2 types of grapes in respect to pruning. Tokays, muscats, Ribier, and Zinfandel all require hard pruning. Pruning the first winter is to restrict the plant to 1 stem to form the trunk. It should be the most vigorous branch and should be cut back to 2 eyes. (See Grape.)

What is the difference between Strawberry and Pineapple GUAVAS? Though both belong to the myrtle family, they are different genera. The Strawberry Guava is *Psidium lucidum;* this and its variety The Yellow make 2 fine fruits and very attractive plants with light-green, glossy foliage. The Pineapple Guava (*Feijoa sellowiana*) has very pleasant fruit, excellent for jam, and is a beautiful large shrub with silvery foliage and bright-red flowers. Both are well worth growing for fruit and ornament.

I am interested in a small HERB garden. Can you suggest some herbs for it? Herbs do well in southern California, especially in light soils. They like poor soil and little water. Plant in early spring, and some yield will be had the same summer. The plants should be renewed every 3 or 4 years. A good list would include Sweet Basil, thyme, Sweet Marjoram, savory (both winter and summer types), tarragon, sage, rosemary, lavender, chives, mint and lemon balm.

Why is it some people have such bad luck with English HOLLY in California? English Holly is grown to perfection in California, but it will not thrive in the full blazing sun in summer. A slight shade must be provided.

What planting and care for IRIS in adobe soil? Irises are exceedingly easy to grow. The only precaution to take in adobe soil is not to plant too deeply. Barely cover the rhizomes, and do not water heavily. Every third year clumps should be dug, saving only the new, strong rhizomes. Except in interior hot areas, this is best done in June or July. In the hot areas, September is better. Feeding in spring and fairly generous watering until they flower will insure good bloom.

How shall I care for JASMINE vines? The two common jasmine vines in southern California are *Jasminum grandiflorum* and *J. Mesnyi* (*primulinum*). The former needs a sunny location, a rich soil, and plenty of irrigation, for it is most beautiful when the foliage is good at the time of flower, in summer. The latter needs sun, but too much water or fertility just adds to the rank growth which makes it disliked by many.

How should JASMINES be pruned?   True jasmines grow so abundantly that they should be severely pruned in winter. Old stems should be cut out at the ground each year, as the bloom is much finer on young growth. The bad reputation of the yellow jasmine is due to its excessive growth, but it can be kept in bounds and attractive by regular pruning.

What LILACS would bloom here in Los Angeles County?   Eastern lilacs are unsatisfactory, suffering either from excessive heat or mildew. The lilac that does very well is the Persian Lilac, *Syringa persica laciniata*. It has lavender flowers in the spring that are fine for cutting, and the plant is of graceful habit.

When should Regal LILIES be planted in California?   Regal Lilies should be planted as soon as they are on the market, in August or September. They like full sun and rich soil, but resent poor drainage, or fertilizer touching the bulbs.

Does LILY-OF-THE-VALLEY do well in the California coastal region?   There are a number of nice plantings here. They need shade and a light soil.

Can MANGOES be grown in southern California?   They can and are grown in frost-free areas. They need plenty of water, and the soil should be constantly mulched.

What would be a good covering under OAK TREES?   Three very good ground covers would be the evergreen ornamental strawberry (*Fragraria chiloensis*), bugle weed (*Ajuga reptens*), and English Ivy (*Hedera helix*).

How are OLEANDERS pruned to keep them vigorous and flowering freely?   After the plant is several years old, old stems, as soon as they are done flowering, are cut off almost to the ground. No plant suckers more freely, so do not be afraid of harsh cutting.

Can PAPAYAS be grown in California?   Only in a few sections, which never have frost. They are difficult to pollinize, and several trees must be planted. Though they are delicious, and have been fruited, they are a gamble.

How are flowering PEACHES pruned?   These plants have an unhappy life in the southern California area, because most people fail to cut them hard enough. They need the stimulus of hard pruning. They should be cut back each year after flowering, leaving only about 6 ins. of growth of the previous year. If pruned right after blooming, there will be plenty of time for the plant to send out and mature strong growth for next year's bloom.

Is the PEONY plant a shrub? Will it grow in southern California?
Though there is a shrubby type, most peonies are herbaceous, dying
to the ground in winter. In southern California they grow well in
only a few favored locations. The long, hot summer is too much for
them. They are not a good choice.

What should I do to have success with perennial PHLOX? Hardy
phlox grows well in southern California, but it takes clean, healthy
stock, planted in rich soil, with some little protection from the afternoon sun. They should be divided, in the fall, every few years. Flower
heads should be removed immediately after fading.

**What is the culture for NORFOLK-ISLAND-PINE in order to get
rapid development?** This plant is not a rapid grower even in California. If your section is not subject to hard frost, treat like any other
tree. It will not make more than 1 or 2 tiers a year.

How are dwarf POMEGRANATES grown? Dwarf pomegranates
are grown chiefly for their decorative bloom. They require little care.
Like most deciduous plants, they enjoy plenty of food and water during
the growing season. Thinning out occasionally in winter encourages
better bloom. Do not allow fruit to mature on the plant. There are
some new types which are really showy.

How should a Santa Rosa PLUM be pruned? Pruning fruit trees
is a long subject, well covered by bulletins obtainable from your county
agent. Training should be started the first year and practiced every
winter. (See Plums.)

How should PYRACANTHAS be pruned? Pyracanthas and cotoneasters have the same habits, and should be pruned much alike.
After the plant is several years old, each berry-producing branch
should be cut back to within about 6 ins. of the trunk; each year
thereafter the producing branches to within 6 ins. of their bases. They
should never be sheared, for it will result in a top-heavy plant. The
time for pruning is when the berries fall or dry.

ROSES

When should roses be planted? Roses are best planted in the
dormant season, from about December 15 to May 1. They are sold
without any soil then. A far more vigorous plant will result than from
one bought out of a container. For good results, buy only Grade 1.

How should roses be planted? Holes generous enough to receive
the roots without cramping should be dug. Depth depends on type of
soil, for in sandy soil the bud graft should be covered; in adobe, it
should be exposed. Mix a shovel of dairy manure in the bottom, then
hold the plant at the required depth and pull in a little soil, and work
it around the roots with the fingers. Gradually fill the hole, packing
the soil around the roots. Water thoroughly.

How should roses be fertilized? A liberal dressing of dairy manure in early spring and again in June, with light applications of commercial fertilizer, monthly, between April and August, will keep roses growing and blooming.

When should rosebushes be pruned? In southern California, roses try to be everblooming. This is not in the best interest of the plants. Water should be withheld after September, and the plants allowed to become dormant. Then, in December, a severe pruning is in order, every other year. Reserve only 3 or 4 stout canes, and reduce these to about ⅓ their length. Proper cutting of buds and dead blooms, leaving only about 3 eyes below the cut, will take care of most of the pruning in the intervening 2 years.

How should Climbing Etoile de Hollande be pruned? This and other climbing hybrid teas are not vigorous as a rule. If several year-old canes are cut back to a foot or so from the ground, new, strong breaks will result. In picking the blooms, cut long stems. They really appreciate a rest period, forced by withholding water after September.

How should a Belle of Portugal rose be pruned? Belle of Portugal is one of the most vigorous plants that grow. Pruning is mostly a matter of cutting it back to decent limits. Old heavy canes may be cut back hard, but the growth that is forced is so vigorous it is difficult to handle. One thing certain is that no matter how severe the pruning, little permanent harm can be done.

How should Large-flowered Climbers be pruned? Climbers of this type differ from the hybrid teas in that wood of the previous season is required for bloom. They are best pruned after blooming. Old canes should be cut down low. The new canes may be shortened, and lateral growths restricted to 2 or 3 eyes. At this time, tying and training are best done.

What is the method of, and time for, pruning roses? They are generally pruned by cutting off buds and dead blooms. If these are cut so that only 2 or 3 eyes are left on each cane, and all weak and crossing growths are removed, little more will be needed. Any heavier pruning that seems required should be done in December and January.

How should I care for roses in tubs on a patio? Roses may be well grown in large tubs, if feeding and watering are properly done. During winter, cease feeding, and hold down water. In the spring a top-dressing of manure will be appreciated. Thereafter, feed monthly with commercial fertilizer.

When are rose cuttings taken in California? Most roses are budded, for their own roots are weak. Understock roses are grown from hardwood cuttings inserted in the field in winter. Greenwood cuttings may be rooted at almost any time.

What are the best roses for southern California? With any rose list, people near the coast must check for mildew resistance, while those in the hot valleys must check for heat resistance. Some favorites are President Hoover, Dainty Bess, Etoile de Hollande, Mrs. E. P. Thom, Mrs. Sam McGredy, McGredy's Ivory, Los Angeles, Mojave, Charlotte Armstrong, Sutter's Gold, Capistrano. Grandifloras: Queen Elizabeth, Buccaneer and Roundelay.

How many years before SAPOTAS and CHERIMOYAS bear fruit? Are 2 trees necessary for cross-pollinization? Seedling sapotas take 7 to 8 years, budded stock takes 4 to 5 years. Seedling cherimoyas bear in 4 or 5 years; budded stock takes 2 or 3 years. Two trees are not necessary in either case, but some growers recommend hand pollinization of cherimoyas for greater yield.

What is the proper culture for SCHIZANTHUS and WALL-FLOWER? Neither plant is difficult to grow. Seed is sown from July to September. There may be difficulty with seed during the hot months, so the later date may be the more convenient. When a few inches high, the seedlings should be moved to the spot in the garden where they are to grow. Shade them for a few days, till they take hold. Neither seems too fussy about soil outdoors.

When are STRAWBERRIES planted, and what is their care? Strawberries in California may be set in the fall. They must have a well-worked soil with good drainage, and are planted on raised beds about 2 ft. wide, with a shallow irrigation trench. They need copious water during summer, for they are shallow rooting. They are generally left several years without replanting. A feeding of manure or a complete fertilizer in the spring is advisable.

What are TANGELOS? Tangelos are fruits resulting from crossing the grapefruit and tangerine. The old name of grapefruit was pomelo, hence the name "Tangelo." They grow the same as oranges, requiring identical care, and produce delicious, tangy fruits in winter. Several varieties are on the market which have fruiting periods from November till early summer.

Can THEA sinensis be safely planted outdoors in southern California? The true tea plant is frequently found in southern California, making a very attractive shrub. In adobe soil, plant it a little above the soil level. In sandy soils, plenty of water is necessary. Plant it in full sun. Acid fertilizer is most appreciated in spring.

What VEGETABLES may be planted in January and February? Among the many vegetables planted in southern California in winter are cabbage, broccoli, spinach, kohlrabi, beets, peas, turnips, carrots, and onions. Parsley also may be planted for flavoring. In some areas, more favored by good drainage and mild climate, squash (under hotkaps) may be planted at this time.

How are VIOLETS seeded or planted, and do they do well in south-

ern California? Violets do very well in California. They want a light soil and some shade. Though they must be divided every few years, they will become permanent if cared for. Try the huge type, "Royal Robe."

I have VIOLETS planted around an oak, growing and blossoming freely, but the whole plant heaves out. Why? Violets in California have this habit, and undoubtedly to a greater degree when leaves falling on them force them to grow upward for light. They should be divided every few years and replanted firmly, for they will lose vigor if growing too much on the surface.

How should WALNUTS be watered? Walnuts are irrigated more or less frequently, depending on the soil. Sandy soil may require monthly irrigation during the growing season, while adobe would need but 1 watering. Some experts claim an irrigation about 2 weeks before harvest makes shucking easier. If trees are grafted on black walnut stock, overwatering encourages black root rot.

COLORADO

Our springs are dry and late in Colorado. Can you give me a list of ANNUALS which can be planted in the fall? Larkspur, California Poppy, calendula, echium, bartonia; in short, all of the hardy annuals. Cover the seed bed with a winter mulch. Remove when seeds germinate in spring.

We live northeast of Colorado Springs, altitude 7500 ft.; I cannot get ANNUALS to grow more than 6 ins. high. Can it be the soil or cool weather? Cosmos and morningglories do well. Since these annuals thrive this high in other parts of your region, your trouble may be poor soil, alkali soil, or perhaps late planting.

How do you take care of BOYSENBERRY bushes over winter in Colorado? Remove the canes from supports; lay them flat and cover with straw, cornstalks, or spruce branches. It is advisable to spray first with lime sulfur, or aluminum sulfate, to make them less attractive to mice.

We irrigate our land in Colorado. I have a bare bank that I wish to cover with some drought-resistant GROUND COVER; it will have to depend on rain for moisture. What shall I use? *Sedum stoloniferum* can "take it," making a year-round cover. "Erosion Net" (sold by seed houses), or burlap, helps to hold the new surface if bank is steep.

What treatment should be given MONKSHOOD (aconitum)? In any except subalpine regions in Colorado aconitum would resent open sunshine and consequent dryness. Try changing to shade, or semi-shade, and deep, rich, peaty soil.

What can I do to raise PANSIES successfully in southern Colorado?
Sow seeds in prepared seedbed early in September. Keep moist and
mulch when ground begins to freeze. Next May transplant to permanent bed of good loam enriched with rotted manure and peatmoss,
in open sun. *Keep seed pods picked.*

**What are the best, showiest, and easiest grown PERENNIALS for
late summer blooming in this climate?** *Anemone japonica,* anthemis,
chrysanthemums, especially the "Cheyenne" strain, *Clematis davidiana,* eupatorium, helenium, *Heliopsis pitcheriana,* monarda, perennial
asters, *Phlox decussata, Physostegia virginiana, Plumbago larpentae*
(Ceratostigma), rudbeckia hybrids, *Salvia argentea, S. Pratensis.*

**What PERENNIAL, preferably a foliage plant, would make the
best low-growing border for my garden in eastern Colorado?** *Cerastium tomentosum* (kept within bounds), *Festuca glauca, Euphorbia
myrsinites*—all 3 have silver-gray foliage. *Teucrium chamaedrys,* kept
shorn, makes a neat green, miniature hedge, suggestive of boxwood
edging.

**Hybrid Tea ROSES bloom prolifically in this climate but are hard to
keep from freezing out during the winter months. How would you
advise to mulch and protect for winter?** Prune down to 6 or 8 ins.
in autumn, mound up soil or peatmoss around each plant. Cover
with a layer of any open material that will shade from sun and permit
air circulation, such as spruce or fir branches, or straw held down with
wire.

Will you suggest some hardy ROSES for high altitudes in Colorado?
Rosa hugonis, R. rugosa and its hybrids; Harison's Yellow; Frueh-
lings Gold; Hybrid Perpetuals Frau Karl Druschki, American Beauty,
General Jacquemot and Ulrich Brunner; Sub-zero Hybrid Teas.

**Can you give some information on spring versus fall planting of
ROSES, shrubs, and trees in Denver, a mile above sea level?** In such
regions of dry, sunny cold winters the difficulties of watering and protecting newly planted woody material make spring planting preferable.

How can I grow SWEETPEAS successfully in southern Colorado?
In autumn, dig a trench 12 ins. wide and 12 to 18 ins. deep. In the
bottom put a 6-in. layer of dairy manure. Fill with good, rich, friable
loam. Early the following March add a dash of bone meal and sow
seed.

FLORIDA

When is the best time to transplant AMARYLLIS? Root action
commences in late September or early October. The bulbs should be
lifted, divided, and reset, therefore, in the early autumn. Bone meal
or other alkaline plant food is good for these bulbs.

What is the best type of soil for BLACKBERRIES in Florida? A sandy loam soil that has a relatively high organic content is best suited for the bramble fruits. A heavy hammock type is ideal, particularly if there is a constant water table 2 or 3 ft. below the surface. A slightly acid soil is considered best.

How are CALADIUMS of the fancy-leaved varieties used to beautify the house and lawn? Plant the tubers in a partly shaded position that is sheltered from strong winds. The soil should contain an abundance of humus and should be reasonably moist at all times. Feeding with liquid fertilizer during season of active growth is very beneficial.

What is the correct culture for CALLAS in northern Florida? Callas are tropical bulbous plants easily injured by frost. The roots are usually received in November, and they can be planted at once in a rich, acid, mucky mixture in large pots or urns. These containers may be plunged under trees and taken indoors when frost is forecast. They may be held in a dormant state until danger of frost has passed in March, and then planted in a rich acid bed out of doors.

I am confused by descriptions in CITRUS catalogues. What are some of the best varieties for our garden near Orlando? Orange: Hamlin, Lue Gim Gong and Pineapple; grapefruit: Foster, Duncan, and Marsh; grapefruit hybrids: Eustis Limequat, Sampson Tangelo. Sour orange is the best understock, and many nurseries in your vicinity will be able to furnish first-class 2-year-old trees in these varieties budded on sour orange tree.

What is frenching and bronzing of CITRUS fruits, and how cured? Frenching is the result of a zinc deficiency, and is corrected by adding zinc sulfate to the sprays. Bronzing results when there is insufficient magnesium available to orange trees. Dolomite in judicious amounts will usually correct a bronzed condition. Epsom salts and a potassium-magnesium sulfate will also correct the deficiency.

What causes Pineapple ORANGES to split open before ripe, and how is this prevented? Usually thought to be caused by a deficiency of copper. Small amounts of copper sulfate (bluestone) will tend to ameliorate the condition.

What are the brown dots on the under sides of ORANGE leaves? Round brown dots with reddish centers are Florida red scale. This pest can be controlled with an oil emulsion spray, used according to the directions on the package.

What are some of the best CLIMBERS for central Florida? Bougainvilleas in their several attractive colors; the very colorful flame-vine; herald trumpet—a rampant tropical creeper; Queens wreath, with its gorgeous purple blossoms, Quisqualis; the luxuriant coralvine; the fast-growing skyflower; and the fragrant Confederate Jasmine, and several other climbing jasmines, are among the most popular of Florida's many vines.

What about COLUMBINES for central Florida?   Although columbines are native to extreme western Florida, they do not grow readily in the peninsula. They can be flowered, however, with good culture. Get plants from the North and set them in a partially shaded place in November, feeding them a balanced plant food every 2 or 3 weeks as they grow. They need an abundance of water and must not have too much root competition for water or nutrients.

When should DAHLIAS be planted in southern Florida?   For spring and summer bloom plant the roots in January or February; for autumn bloom arrange to have roots held in cold storage and delivered in late August or early September.

How may good DAHLIAS be grown in central Florida?   The roots are procured in February or March, and are planted about 5 ins. deep, in garden beds that have been enriched with compost and a commercial fertilizer. Drive a stout stake by the stem end of the root and tie the plant every 8 ins. or so as it grows. Feed liberally every 3 or 4 weeks. Dust with sulfur or malathion at the first signs of red spider.

How can I have autumn DAHLIAS in central Florida?   Arrange to have cold-storage roots delivered in August or early September. Set the roots in good soil about 5 ins. deep; water and feed liberally as the plants grow. These roots will be difficult to carry over in Florida, so it is suggested that you treat these as annuals starting over each autumn.

Will DIMORPHOTHECA ecklonis grow in northern Florida?   This perennial woody plant will probably grow during the spring as an annual. If you purchase the young plants in February and grow them for spring bloom, they will probably succeed. Certainly this species is very rare in Florida gardens at present.

Can I increase my very beautiful FLAME-OF-THE-WOODS?   Yes, use softwood tip cuttings in June or July and insert them in clean white sand in a new box. Place cheesecloth over the box; set in on the north side of the house, and daily sprinkle with a fine spray. The cuttings should root in 4 or 5 weeks.

Will FOXGLOVES grow in northern Florida?   Possibly in the extreme western end these perennials will succeed, but they are certain to be a disappointment in most parts of this state. Like many other perennials, they need a long, cold winter for inducing an unbroken dormancy.

What varieties of FRUIT—apples, peaches, and pears—will grow in Florida?   Apples are not satisfactory even in extreme western Florida, although some merit is claimed for the Helm apple there. The Chinese Sand or Pineapple Pear is the only one that withstands the ravages of pear blight well enough to warrant planting in Florida. Jewel, Waldos, Honey, and Angel peaches grow very well and fruit fairly well most years in northern Florida if they are properly sprayed and pruned.

How shall I fertilize, water, and care for lawn of Centipede GRASS? Centipede Grass is one of the best lawn materials for the light, sandy soils of Florida. An application of a balanced fertilizer, at the rate of 20 lbs. per 1000 sq. ft., in March, another in June or July, should suffice. Water the fertilizer in as soon as applied, and irrigate often enough to keep the grass leaves from curling and turning gray-green. Frequent mowing is necessary for a good Centipede turf. During the growing season, the mower must be used at least once each week.

Will HELIOPHILAS grow in northern Florida?   Yes, these South African annuals should do well if the seeds are sown in flats in January, the seedlings grown in a not-too-moist soil, and the plants set out in March.

What can I do to have IRISES from Kentucky bloom in Florida? Nothing! Excepting in extreme western Florida bearded irises are not successful. The light, sandy soils and lack of sustained low winter temperatures do not suit these favorites of temperate gardens. Why not use native Southern species that do succeed so beautifully?

When should I fertilize my LAWN?   Early in March apply a mixed plant food that is high in nitrogen; then again when the rains start in June make a second application. In all parts of Florida except the extreme North, additional small monthly feedings in January and February help to keep the grass green through the colder months and build it up for its spurt of spring growth.

At what rate should I apply a 5–7–5 mixed fertilizer to my LAWN? About 20 to 30 lbs. per 1000 sq. ft. constitutes an adequate feeding.

Can old-fashioned LILACS be raised as far south as Jacksonville? No, the light, sandy acid soils and lack of a real dormant season do not suit these popular temperate garden plants and they are certain to be disappointing.

When should a MULBERRY tree be pruned to be sure of a good crop in Florida?   Mulberry trees should be pruned directly after they have finished fruiting in the spring.

What is the best time to plant NASTURTIUMS in Florida?   Nasturtiums must be grown in autumn in order to mature blossoms before frost; or in spring, by sowing after last frost for blooming before hot weather sets in and kills the plants.

When should my OLEANDERS be cut back?   Just after flowering. If they are to be kept from getting very large, root prune them at this time by driving a spade deep in a circle about 2 or 3 ft. from the plant.

Is PEAT from local bogs good for us to use on our gardens?   Local peat is excellent if it comes from an inland bog. Be very certain that you do not buy muck from a tidal marsh, however, as this saline material will kill plants.

Can PEONIES be grown successfully in the central part of Florida?
Peonies are a complete failure in peninsular Florida. The light, sandy
soil and the lack of continuously cold winter to assure complete dormancy combine to defeat our best attempts to make Southerners out of
these temperate garden favorites.

What ROSES do best in Southern Florida? If you can give them
good loam, with enough humus in it to hold moisture, grow the old
Teas like Lady Hillington and Marechal Niel and the more enduring
of the Hybrid Teas such as Radiance, Red Radiance and Crimson
Glory. If the heat and sandy soil is too much for these, you may want
to purchase cheap plants from Texas yearly and grow them as annuals.

**I want to use old-fashioned ROSES. Which ones will do best with
least care?** The old French Rose grows well. Among our most dependable old roses are: Louis Philippe, Safrano, Duchesse de Brabant,
Marie van Houtte, Minnie Francis, Belle of Portugal and Mme. Lombard. Plants of these varieties will thrive in your Southern garden long
after plants of cutting varieties have succumbed. Several Texas nurseries are specializing in these old sorts.

When is the best time of year to set ROSE bushes? Roses planted
in December and early January will have time to make good root
growth before top growth is started by the warm days of early spring.
The earliest possible planting is considered best for Florida.

**How far back should ROSES be trimmed, and what time of the year
is best?** Bush roses should be pruned, in January or February, to
4 or 5 strong eyes on each of 4 or 5 canes. Make the pruning cuts
about ¼ in. above a strong eye that points away from the center of
plant. Ramblers may be pruned at same time, using a renewal system
to remove all of the canes more than 1 or 2 years old, as blossoms are
borne from spurs on 1-year canes. As Large-flowered Climbers bloom
on two-year old wood, with these merely prune out dead canes and
cut flowering stems back to 2 or 3 eyes. Train canes horizontally to
encourage many flowering shoots.

**Will Centaurea moschata (SWEETSULTAN) grow in northern
Florida?** Yes, very excellent sweetsultans have been grown and sold
in this section. Sow seeds in a flat in October or November. Transplant
seedlings to well-enriched beds in midwinter. Plants should blossom in
April and May. Red spiders must be forestalled with sulfur dust or
malathion during dry periods.

Will VIOLAS succeed here? Yes, these miniature pansies do very
well if plants are bought from a Northern specialist in November and
planted at once to grow through the cool winter.

What is culture for WATSONIAS in northern Florida? Watsonias,
like gladioli, may be planted in February in northern Florida. Set the
corms about 3 ins. deep in beds that have been enriched with compost
and a commercial plant food. The blossoms should be produced in
April and May.

Will the WILLOW OAK grow in Florida?   Yes, the Willow Oak (*Quercus phellos*) is native to northern Florida and will succeed as a fast-growing, desirable tree as far South as the central part of the peninsula.

Will the WEEPING WILLOW grow successfully in Florida?   It will grow in heavy soils close to watercourses in northern Florida, but it will not grow so well as it does farther North, nor can it be considered nearly so beautiful here as in the temperate states.

GEORGIA

What grows most satisfactorily in partial shade in this section, other than azaleas and camellias?   Oakleaf Hydrangea (*H. quercifolia*), St. Johnswort (*Hypericum*), heavenly-bamboo (*Nandina domestica*), stewartia, cydonia and illicium, are all excellent shrubs for the shady garden.

What is best position and soil for AMARYLLIS?   Amaryllis grown outdoors in the South does well in a sunny or lightly shaded position in a well-drained, fertile soil that is neutral or very slightly acid.

What are cultural needs of hybrid AMARYLLIS?   Apply balanced fertilizer immediately after blooming; water well through dry periods during growing season. In fall mulch with half-rotted leaves to which is added some bone meal and cow manure.

The tops of my AMARYLLIS are green the year around. Some of the outer leaves turn yellow and soft, but they do not yellow like other bulbs. When should they be dug?   They should be dug in late fall. If the foliage has not completely died down (and this does not happen with all amaryllis), it may be artificially ripened off by drying in a sunny, airy place.

About 20 months ago I planted some AMARYLLIS seeds, the plants from which have been green ever since, without blooming. What time of year should they be given a rest period? How?   The best results are obtained if seedling amaryllis are grown on without rest until after they produce their first blooms. This is usually in from 18 to 36 months from time of sowing.

My Fancy-leaved CALADIUMS die down in the fall. What shall I do with them?   In November lift them; cut off the few remaining leaves; pack in peat, dry sand, or sawdust, and store the container in a frost-free place until spring.

What causes the black scum on my CAPEJASMINE bush, and how can I prevent it?   This sooty mold on gardenia leaves follows the attacks of whitefly and can be corrected and prevented by occasional applications of an oil emulsion spray or malathion. One application in September, another 2 or 3 weeks later, and possibly a third during midwinter should prevent this condition. Your seed house will have oil sprays put up in small cans for your convenience.

I have read that DAFFODILS of the North have longer stems than those of the South. What can I add to the soil to make my daffodils have longer stems? In all probability the climate is responsible for the shorter daffodil stems, and even though your bulbs are adequately fed, there will be a tendency to shorter stems.

When do you plant DAHLIAS in Georgia? In March and April. If the emerging tips are nipped by the latest spring frosts, no great damage will be done; but it is best to plan your planting so that there will be no frost damage.

When is the best time to transplant DOGWOODS, redbuds, and other trees from the woods? December through February, while the trees are dormant and without leaves. Remember that transplanting is a surgical operation and that extreme care must be exercised to keep the roots covered and the trees protected from sun and wind during transport. Cut back moderately the lateral branches, plant at the same depth they formerly grew, and wrap the trunks with burlap or muslin as protection against sunscald and borers. Use trees under 8 ft. in height rather than larger ones.

What is the best method of protecting GERBERAS from cold? If gerbera plants are killed to the ground, you may cover the crowns with a light mulch of pine straw or oak leaves. If you are in the southern part of the state and wish to keep the plants from being killed on cold nights, cover with a heavy blanket of Spanish moss, uncovering after danger of severe cold has passed.

How are GERBERAS cared for? Gerberas are not particular as to soil type, provided it is well fortified with plant food and plants have enough water. They will be benefited by a good mulch of oak leaves, peat, or similar organic material.

Should I use fertilizer when I plant my GLADIOLUS? Balanced commercial fertilizer can be scattered in the bottom of the 4-in. deep planting furrow and lightly cultivated in. Then set out the corms.

How can I grow GOURDS in a hot, dry location? If it is too hot and dry for gourds to thrive in your part of Georgia, I think you would have to get an early start with them and allow them to mature in midsummer. However, gourds should thrive in most sections of Georgia.

How are HERBS grown in Georgia? Herbs may be grown exactly as you would grow garden vegetables, in the same soil and with the same fertilizer, care, and watering.

What HERBS are best for middle and south Georgia? For fall planting: anise, chives, Winter Savory, sage, and dill. For spring planting: Sweet Basil, Summer Savory, Sweet Fennel, coriander, thyme, and Sweet Marjoram.

What varieties of tall, preferably fragrant, IRISES are suitable for Southern climate? Which are the best red ones? Purissima, Frieda Mohr, Happy Days, Los Angeles, Golden Treasure, Destiny, Pale Moonlight, Shining Waters, and Sandalwood are all excellent tall varieties in the popular price range that have proved to be good in the Macon, Georgia, area. The best near reds are Ethel Peckham and the Red Douglas.

What is the IVY that is so effectively used around the huge oaks in the Tallahassee and Thomasville area? This is the Algerian Ivy (*Hedera canariensis*), a relative of the English Ivy. It is considered one of the very best ground covers for spots where grass will not grow.

Can I make a good LAWN in a wooded area? On the land spread a layer of cow manure, compost, rotted oak leaves, together with some balanced commercial fertilizer. Spade or plow this deeply; rake level; plant. In October or November sow Italian Rye Grass for a winter effect until warm weather, then plant sprigs of St. Augustine-grass in rows about 12 ins. apart. Always water well, as growing grass needs a great deal of moisture.

What is best grass for a wooded LAWN? Italian Rye in winter if there is partial protection from fallen pine needles. Charlestongrass is satisfactory in summer after it is well established. In southern Georgia, St. Augustinegrass is excellent for shady locations.

Why do NANDINA berries drop? They will not drop if there has been good pollination at flowering time. If there is rain when the blossoms open, the pollen will be washed away, and there will be either no set, or a poor one.

When is the proper time to plant NANDINA berries? How long does it take for them to come up? Nandina berries may be sown when they are red, or as they begin to fall from the plant. Germination is slow, and the plantlets will probably not appear until the following spring or summer.

What can I use in place of PANSIES during the heat of the summer? Torenia (wishbone-flower) is an excellent substitute for pansies that will grow during summer months. Sow seeds in flats in April or May, and transplant to garden when the pansies come out.

Will PEONIES do well in this climate? Would you advise early, midseason, or late varieties? None will succeed south of Atlanta. Use only tried early varieties in north Georgia.

How can we get PERENNIAL flower seed to come up in August and September, when, in this section, it is so hot and dry? Germination will be poor at this season. Hold the seeds until later in the autumn for best results.

Will perennial POPPIES grow year after year in this locality? Possibly they will succeeed in extreme north Georgia; from Macon southward they are a failure.

ROSES

Can roses be grown in the Far South in sandy soil? The sandy soils, and warm winters, and the prevalence of disease make rose growing difficult in the Far South. Large wholesale nurseries in eastern Texas have lowered the price of roses in recent years and many successful gardeners grow roses frankly as annuals. The plants are bought in the fall, planted well in very rich beds, and forced for blooms during the following spring. In summer they are usually discarded as worthless.

When should climbing roses be pruned? November to January in Georgia a renewal system is used, old canes are cut low down, leaving this year's and last year's shoots only. Climbing roses flower from spurs that are borne on last year's canes. Old wood is not floriferous.

What is the name of the hardy red rose that grows so freely here? There is also a light blush pink that seems to thrive without any care. The red rose is Louis Philippe, sometimes called the "cracker rose." The light, shell pink is probably Marie van Houtte. Safrano, Minnie Francis, and Duchesse de Brabant are also old-fashioned roses that will grow for many years in Southern gardens.

When is the best time to transplant the RED SPIDERLILY? This flower, *Nerine sarniensis* (often misnamed *Lycoris radiata*), is best transplanted in July or early August.

Will you give suggestions as to planting of SHRUBBERY around small residences in vicinity of Atlanta? Plants that are evergreen, slow growing, hardy, and resistant to drought would include azalea, camellia, podocarpus, box, Japanese Holly, Chinese Holly, boxthorn, cotoneaster, pyracantha, primrose, jasmine, Wax or Glossy Privet (*Ligustrum lucidum*), and abelia. These are all suitable for foundation planting.

When shall I prune SHRUBS that were injured by frost? It is more tidy to cut the shrubs back as soon as the injured parts turn brown, repeating later if inspection shows that the injury extends farther than your first pruning.

Can you suggest pink- and blue-flowering SHRUBS and flowers for my town garden, and yellow, orange, and white for my country place? For town garden: camellia, rose, azalea, deutzia, weigela—all pink; buddleia, plumbago, althea, vitex—all blue. For the country: yellow —hypericum, thryallis, tithonia, forsythia; orange—primrose, jasmine, *Alyssum saxatile, Rosa hugonis;* white—gardenia, philadelphus, camellia, rose, althea, ligustrum, azalea.

Can TULIP bulbs in South be grown and increased for a number of years, as are narcissi? They are not satisfactory for naturalizing. Certain varieties of tulips in sections of the upper South can be naturalized. In the lower South tulips of certain varieties must be placed in cold storage for 2 or 3 months and planted in December.

How can I grow large TULIPS in north Georgia? In extreme north Georgia use only varieties that are recommended; plant in well-enriched beds. (See Tulips.)

Will VERBENAS act as perennials in the lower South? Yes, they may be grown from seed or cuttings. Old plants may be lifted, divided and reset in winter, for spring bloom. Red spiders must be controlled in hot, dry weather with sulfur dust, or malathion.

IDAHO

What perennial DAISIES, other than white ones, would you suggest for Idaho, elevation about 3500? Any of the earlier Michaelmas daisies (hardy asters) should be suitable. Try Radar, N. A. Red Star. Harrington's Pink, Redrover, or Eventide. Aster Frikarti is more like a daisy, and very lovely. Hardy chrysanthemums are beautiful and are very satisfactory where the season is long enough. For northern gardens, Chippa Red, New Marjorie Mills (ruby) and Spellbinder (lemon-chrome) are September bloomers, as are the Granite Series introduced by the New Hampshire Experiment Station.

What are the names of some HEDGES which will stay green all year in this climate? Would a wild shrub (pachistima) do? Probably none except your native evergreens. Spruce and cedar make lovely hedges and can be kept clipped down. Pachistima might be suitable if it grows high enough. It is very difficult to transplant.

Can you give a list of low-growing (not to exceed 12 ins.) PERENNIAL flowers that will provide bloom from early spring to late fall? They would be in sun, no shade. *Anemone pulsatilla; Campanula carpatica, C. pusilla;* heuchera, various; *Phlox subulata; Gypsophila repens, Iberis semperflorens; Thymus serpyllum; Saponaria ocymoides; Penstemon crandalli, P. caespitosus, P. humulis;* alyssum, arabis; aubretia; lewisia; antennaria; helianthemum; dianthus, various; sempervivum; *Nepeta mussini, Veronica spuria; Melampodium cinereum; Malvastrum coccineum; Linum flavum* and *L. alpinum; Oenothera caespitosa, O. lavendulaefolia,* and *O. missouriensis; Ceratostigma plumbaginoides;* iris, dwarf varieties; *Abronia fragrans; Physaria didymocarpa; Teucrium chamaedrys.*

What causes red RASPBERRY blight in an irrigated country? If the blight referred to is the yellowing of the leaves, it is usually caused by too-wet subsoils, especially heavy or clay soils. Install underground drainage or plant in lighter, better-drained soils.

I live in an area having neutral to slightly alkaline soil, at an altitude of 4250 ft. It is irrigated country, so water does not have to be conserved. There are many plants that will not do well, either because of the short growing season, or because of water about the roots. Can you name some SHRUBS, besides lilacs, bridalwreath, and snowballs, that might thrive? The following shrubs are suggested for trial: Highbush Cranberry (*Viburnum opulus*); *Spiraea arguta*, or *S. thunbergi*; Austrian Copper Rose; River Birch (*Betula fontinalis*). Trees: Weeping Willow; Soft Maple or Silver Maple; birch; and possibly sycamore. Evergreens: Blue or Black-hill Spruce; and possibly *Juniperus scopulorum* and *J. pfitzeriana*.

Would gardenia, azalea, roses, and rhododendron SHRUBS do well in the mountains of Idaho, elevation about 3500 ft.? Gardenias and evergreen azaleas are usually grown in a greenhouse. Azaleas and rhododendrons require a very acid soil, and for this reason will not thrive in any of our Western soils. Roses should grow well in Idaho if protected in winter by a heavy mulch, or by mounding up with earth.

What hardy ROSES would you suggest for Idaho? In the Boise Valley and near Lewiston below 2500 feet, the species and species hybrids like *R. hugonis, R. setigera, R. rugosa* and hybrids, thrive without winter protection.

Can the TRUMPETVINE be grown where there are zero winters? Yes, it must have winter enough to cause it to lose its leaves and to give it several weeks' rest. Trumpetvine should grow in Idaho.

ILLINOIS

What are the best 4 or 5 APPLE trees for the Midwest, for the small home garden? A good list (which pleases the one making the list only, since tastes in apples differ) might include Melba for an early; Anoka or Joan or Beacon for fall; and Cortland, Jonathan, and Northwestern Greening for winter. Best way to pick apples is to try the fruit and see what you like.

Why don't I have any success with ASTERS? Is it the climate here in north Illinois? No, your difficulty (if by aster you mean the so-called annual aster grown from seed) is probably due to disease, either aster wilt or aster yellows. The answer to wilt is to use wilt-resistant varieties. For yellows, spray the plants with 4 tablespoons of 25% wettable DDT powder to a gallon of water. Malathion will kill the leaf hoppers which spread this disease.

What pruning is required on AZALEAS in the Middle West? Only enough to keep them shapely. Such pruning as is required should be done immediately after blooming. Careless use of the pruning shears can destroy bloom for 2 or 3 years.

How can I control orange rust in my BLACKBERRIES? Eliminate wild brambles from the locality; remove diseased plants in the patch, including roots, as soon as the disease appears in early spring; plant a resistant variety such as Eldorado.

Can BLUEBERRIES be raised successfully in northwestern Illinois? Yes, provided you acidify the soil properly. (See Blueberry.)

Can BLUEBERRIES be successfully raised in eastern central Illinois? Yes, provided good culture and soil acidification receive careful attention.

What is a sweet CHERRY for central Illinois? Black Tartarian is most universally successful, but it is necessary to have 2 or more trees, as they are self-sterile, and sour cherry pollen does not fertilize them.

Can large CHRYSANTHEMUMS be grown in garden in Chicago during usual season? Eugene A. Wander, Avalanche, and King Midas, all fairly large-flowered, do well. Suggest a visit to the hardy mum exhibits at the University of Chicago display grounds.

Can you suggest some small pompon MUMS that will bloom not later than October 1, and that are hardy in this climate? Try Early Bronze pompon or the more recent September Bronze; also the brilliant yellow, September Gold. The Granite Series of chrysanthemums are early bloomers.

Will CRAPEMYRTLE live through the winter in the latitude of Chicago? No, even the so-called hardy type will kill out.

In what localities is the new lawn plant, DICHONDRA REPENS, hardy? I have seen it in California and Texas. Is it hardy in Illinois? *Dichondra repens* (Ponyfoot) would not be hardy in Illinois. In the South it may have possibilities although it generally has been included among the lawn pests.

What is proper care for wintering perennial DIGITALIS? If possible, handle in cold frames, with the glass on, covered with mats to shut out winter sun. Lacking this, use umbrellalike coverings that allow the air to get in, but not water and sun. It is a tricky species to grow in Illinois.

What plants will provide the most cutting FLOWERS to be grown in a small yard in Chicago? Among the annuals, perhaps more blooms can be cut from marigolds and zinnias than from any others in this class. Petunias are excellent because they provide low edgings in the garden picture yet yield satisfactory flowers for cutting too.

For people who do not like the ever-present FOUNDATION PLANTINGS of evergreens, what do you consider the best substitute for my locality, near Chicago? It would have to be something that will do at least reasonably well in good deal of shade. A neat, healthy, clean shrub that will grow in shade is a problem, but *Euonymus alatus compactus* comes pretty close to filling the bill. With clean, dark-green foliage and striking autumn color, it is a highly desirable semi-formal shrub.

I have a home on Lake Michigan, and have plenty of sand in front down to the lake; what would you suggest for a GROUND COVER-ING of character? If in shade, and if you incorporate plenty of leafmold or peatmoss this sounds like a perfect spot for the bearberry (*Arctostaphylos uva-ursi*). There is no shrub, vine, or subshrub that will do well in sun on pure sand, at least to the point where it can be considered a ground cover.

Where can we secure information on extra-fine eating GRAPES that will grow in this locality? (Winnetka.) The New York Fruit Testing Association, Geneva, New York, or your local State Experiment Station, Urbana, Illinois, will give you the information you want, if your local seedsman cannot supply it.

Which are the varieties of HERBS most practical for growing in this latitude? How should the seedbed be prepared for best results in herb production? Perennials: sage, thyme, chives, mint. Annuals: Sweet Basil, Sweet Marjorum, and dill. These are the easiest to grow, but since taste is such a personal thing, the only criterion is, after all, what you like.

How far North will KERRIA JAPONICA grow? Into southern Wisconsin.

Have trouble in growing perennial LUPINE. Is there any special treatment? Yes. They are legumes and must have the special inoculating bacteria to form the nodules they require in order to extract nitrogen from the air. Also, while they require calcium, they need more iron than most legumes. The trick is to keep them at a pH of about 5.9 to 6.8, where by juggling iron and calcium you can give them what they want. A tricky species, and definitely not for the amateur, except where peculiar soil conditions prevail.

What MAGNOLIAS are suitable for Northern climes? Only two magnolias are commonly grown in Illinois, the Saucer Magnolia (*M. soulangeana*) and the Star Magnolia (*M. stellata*).

What pruning is required on MAGNOLIAS in the Middle West? In the Middle West, the problem is to get them to make adequate growth, not to cut out any excess wood. Throw away the pruning shears and you'll have better luck. Only if branches are badly placed or broken should they be touched.

How far North will NECTARINES bear? While they will bear in Illinois, they are so subject to curculio damage that they are seldom successful there.

Can I be sure of a crop if I plant Southern paper-shell PECANS in Illinois? Not as a general rule. Even in southern Illinois, the Stuart, one of the hardiest Southern varieties, seldom matures its kernels. The good Northern varieties succeed best south of central Illinois. Try Major, Posey, Indiana, and Green River. Plant more than one variety for cross-pollination.

How far North will PECAN nuts grow?   Southern Illinois is about the Northern limit of the pecan.

What is the best time to plant PEONIES in southern Illinois?   Specialists in this area try to plant as close to September 15 as possible.

Is it necessary to mulch such PERENNIALS as delphinium, phlox, or carnation in this latitude?   They are better for a mulch if it is not too dense and soggy. Think of a mulch for these plants as protecting the ground from winter sun, not as a blanket of insulation to shut out all cold. Make it airy but shady. Allow the breeze to blow through. Evergreen boughs are ideal.

Why can't we keep PERENNIALS over winter? We cover them for the winter months.   Probably killed with loving kindness: a dense covering of leaves or other compact material will smother rather than protect plants. Use light, airy mulches, but apply *after* the ground freezes, not before. Remove early in spring (say about March 15 in the Chicago area) to avoid damaging spring growth.

I have a RHODODENDRON in a 15-in. pot. Can this be planted in the garden and safely left outside all winter? I live in a suburb near Chicago.   Probably not. Most of the forcing types of rhododendrons are not winter hardy in Chicago.

Should ROSES be planted in full sunshine or in part shade?   Some of the delicate pinks and the types of red that "blue" in sunshine are better for light shade at midday. But should have at least five to six hours of full sun, preferably early in the day.

Can ROSES be hilled up 6 or 8 ins. with dirt before ground has frozen and before their leaves have fallen? I always wait for leaves to fall and wood ripen; then the ground freezes suddenly and I don't get them covered.   Choosing the right time to cover roses is one of those things that make gardening interesting (and confusing). The leaves must be off before they are covered, which means after a good sharp freeze, but usually we have a warm spell after such a freeze which allows for pulling the earth around the plant. If you have only a few plants, you might try the old trick of saving a few bushels of unfrozen earth in the cellar and applying this after the wood has ripened. For larger rose gardens place mounds of hilling soil or compost near the beds and cover with burlap or tarpaulins during the first cold night to prevent freezing. Then hill up the plants the following day.

What bush ROSES are best suited for Chicago region?   All hybrid perpetual roses are suited to Chicago; in fact, are much more so than the more favored hybrid teas. With hybrid perpetuals, choose any that strike your fancy: they're all hardy.

What climbing ROSES may be left on fence or trellis all winter with little protection? The old rambler types (which bloom on new wood) survive this sort of treatment, even though their condition horrifies the meticulous rosarian. The dead wood can be cut out after bloom. However, be prepared for the white mildew that attacks practically all roses of the rambler type.

How far North will SPICEBUSH grow? The spicebush (*Benzoin aestivale*) makes satisfactory growth as far North as southern Wisconsin.

Are there any STRAWBERRY varieties resistant to the red stele root-rot disease? Yes, the Aberdeen, Pathfinder, and Steelmaster varieties are resistant.

How can I succeed in growing everbearing STRAWBERRIES? It is not easy to grow these fruits well, especially during the heat of summer. They require very fertile soil of good texture and a continuous supply of water throughout the season. Ground should be mulched lightly to keep berries clean. A protective winter mulch is also necessary. Redrich is one of the best varieties. (See Strawberry.)

Is it possible to transplant the SWEETGUM TREE in central Illinois? I have been unable to do so successfully. Yes, but get a nursery-grown tree with fine, fibrous roots. And be sure you plant it in rich, deep land. It won't grow in dry soil.

Is the BIRCH family bothered with borers in central Illinois? The birch borer makes this beautiful tree all but impossible to grow in central Illinois. By the time the pest is discovered, the damage is done, and there is no preventive treatment.

Can ESPALIER FRUIT TREES be grown in Illinois? Yes, but do not expect too much from them. The training of fruit trees in special shapes was originated in Europe, so that they could be planted along stone walls where the heat would help ripen the fruit. In the Middle West, the problem is too much heat, not too little. Use espaliers for special ornamental effects, not where fruit in quantity is the object.

How late (in the fall) can FRUIT TREES be planted in central Illinois? Planting can go on all winter long provided good cultural practices are followed, but March or April should be equally satisfactory. It is a question of convenience and comfort, not of the thermometer, which ends the fall planting season.

What are the best FRUIT and NUT TREES for the average yard in this region? The best sure-fire fruit trees for Illinois are apples, crabapples, and sour cherries. Native walnuts are about the only nut trees that are really reliable, and these must have light, loamy soil and good drainage.

Are there any WILDFLOWERS which can be developed from seed, that can be grown in northern Illinois? Most wildflowers depend on seed for their continuation. Many are perennials and require as much care as other perennial seeds. Some possibilities are: *Aquilegia canadensis,* many violets, goldenrod, Allegheny Foamflower, butterflyweed, wild asters, Dutchman's-breeches, *Phlox divaricata.*

Will a tree WISTERIA grow in Chicago climate? Yes, provided its other requirements are met. Grows in almost any soil; thrives best in deep, rich loam that does not get too dry.

INDIANA

Can you tell me how to grow DELPHINIUM in Indiana? Delphiniums come from cold regions and resent hot summers. To coax them into good behavior give them a deeply prepared friable loam and under each plant put a 4-in. layer of peatmoss. Cut flower stems off before they begin to seed.

What are the most desirable FLOWERS to plant in a rock garden in northern Indiana? Arenaria, various; *Androsace carinata* and *A. sarmentosa; Antirrhinum glutinosum; Campanula pusilla* and *muralis;* dwarf iris in variety; *Thalictrum alpinum; Melampodium cinereum; Physaria didymocarpa; Phlox subulata, P. douglasi,* and *P. multiflora,* aubretia; arabis; alyssum, perennial; *Aquilegia alpina;* heuchera, various; lewisias; draba; primula, various; *Tiarella cordifolia; Hypericum reptans; Dianthus alpinus* and *D. neglectus;* Fern, *Woodsia scopulina; Iberis sempervirens;* dwarf penstemons; *Veronica rupestris; Gypsophila repens; Tunica saxifraga;* thymes, various; *Viola nuttalli; Saponaria ocymoides.*

Can Smyrna FIG plants winter in the back yard in this section of Indiana? Definitely not; but figs can be grown in tubs and carried over in a cool cellar (between freezing and 40° above) and set out again in early May. These will *not* be the Smyrna fig (which requires a special wasp for pollination) but the mission type which can be pollinated by American insects.

Is there an American HOLLY to use in climates such as Indiana in order to have enough berries to be attractive in winter? You can't grow holly such as you see on Christmas cards. The deciduous species *Ilex verticillata* (black-alder or winterberry) is deciduous but bears bright red holly berries on bare stems well into the winter.

Can PECANS, ENGLISH WALNUTS, and FILBERTS be successfully grown? What types are best? Only in the southern end of Indiana are pecans and English walnuts likely to succeed. Filberts can be grown over most of the state.

What kind of PEACH trees would be best for Indiana climates? Practically any varieties in commerce are successful in your state.

What is the best time to plant ROSES in southern and northern

Indiana? Should plants be 1, 2, or 3 years old? Either late fall or early-spring planting is satisfactory for roses of any age.

When is the best time to set out monthly blooming ROSES? Either late fall or early-spring planting should prove satisfactory. Which is the better depends upon what kind of a winter or summer follows planting—something no one can foretell.

Which are 2 of the best red hybrid tea ROSES particularly adapted for Indiana? Crimson Glory and Gruss an Teplitz have given wide satisfaction in your state. Newer ones are Chrysler Imperial, Nocturne, General Eisenhower and Mirandy.

What types of roses are preferable for this climate? Any but the tender noisette and tea roses. Hybrid teas, floribundas, grandifloras, climbers, pillars, and briars are better than hybrid perpetuals in Indiana.

What are the most desirable SHRUBS and EVERGREENS to plant in a rock garden? *Juniperus horizontalis, J. horizontalis douglasi,* and *J. horizontalis plumosa; Mahonia repens; Ceanothus fendleri; Arctostaphylos uva-ursi; Pachystima canbyi; Euonymus radicans kewensis; Daphne mezereum* and *D. cneorum; Yucca glauca; Cotoneaster horizontalis; Cotoneaster adpressa.*

What kinds of plants, shrubs or evergreens, shall I place on north and west side of house facing east and located on southwest side of 2 streets? Select enough of one variety on each side to give continuity. Large shrubs of coarse texture are suitable near a big old structure; while smaller, neater ones of fine texture are better for colonial or modern.

What summer- and fall-blooming SHRUBS, especially evergreens, are particularly suitable for this locality? Soil is sandy loam. There are practically no evergreen shrubs which would have good flowers during the summer and fall in this locality. Most evergreen shrubs like *Pieris japonica, Kalmia latifolia* and hardy evergreen azaleas bloom in the spring.

When is the best time to put out STRAWBERRY plants in this locality, and what variety do you recommend? Late March or early April if you can get them into the ground. Four varieties that give general satisfaction in Indiana are Dorsett, Fairfax, Catskill, and the everbearer Redrich.

IOWA

Has the Massachusetts BAYBERRY ever been grown in Midwestern gardens? Yes, but not successfully. It requires acid soil and a moist, cool atmosphere—conditions which cannot easily be supplied in Iowa.

Can BLUEBERRIES be grown successfully in central Iowa on our Tama loam? Yes, provided rules for cultivation and acidifying the soil are observed. (See Blueberry.)

What are some of the best hardy CHRYSANTHEMUMS for the central part of Iowa? Dean Kay, Dean Ladd, My Lady, Eugene A. Wander, September Bronze, September Gold.

What CHRYSANTHEMUMS will bloom before freezing in northeast Iowa? Most of them freeze here in September before blooming. Some seasons early varieties in full flower get caught while those in bud escape. Try varieties dated to flower in late September, such as September Bronze, September Gold, Chippewa and Algonquin. Avoid white and light pinks, as these are more susceptible to frost injury.

Are Flowering DOGWOODS hardy in south Iowa? Yes, although flower buds are usually killed in severe winters.

Is it possible to grow American HOLLY (Ilex opaca) in northern Iowa? No, it is not winter hardy in Iowa.

What could we plant on bare ground that would be LAWN enough for our 15-month-old son to play on by June? It needn't be a permanent lawn. This is a question to make a lawn man cringe, since the only answer is to recommend planting either of the 2 species he particularly hates: timothy or oats. Both will cover the ground with a rough, haylike coating which can be mowed, but neither is really satisfactory. The only other possibility, Perennial Ryegrass makes a very good temporary turf which lasts a couple of years.

Can I grow flowering MAGNOLIAS here in Iowa? *Magnolia soulangeana* and *M. stellata* do well on any rich, loamy soil well supplied with humus, but would probably need watering during summer droughts. Wrapping in burlap when small will protect buds from winter killing, but when the plant attains tree size, you will have to be reconciled to losing bloom about every third spring.

Will NECTARINE trees survive southeast Iowa winters? No.

What NUT TREES are hardy as far North as central Iowa? Butternut, black walnut, and hickory. Central Iowa is the Northern limit of all three.

Will the PASSION FLOWER (Passiflora) live out of doors in southeast Iowa? *Passiflora incarnata,* the Wild Passionflower, will survive in Iowa, but is not the exotic tropical beauty one might imagine from its name. The more showy species will not survive.

Are there varieties of PEACH and of APRICOT hardy in central Iowa? Specialists in Iowa have been working on the peach problem for years, but have not been able to offer a solution. In the case of apricots, however, the Hansen Manchurian hybrids, and those from the Dominion Experiment Station at Morden, Manitoba, can stand temperatures as low as 40° below zero.

What kinds of PEACH and PEAR trees are most adaptable to Iowa? No reliably hardy peaches can be recommended. Pear varieties that will withstand severe exposure are Parker, Bantam, Tait, Dropmore, Pioneer, Ming, and Patten (the latter originated in Iowa).

What is a good low-growing PERENNIAL for the north side of a house? If you mean the dense shade north of a house, where no sunshine ever falls, no showy perennial will grow. If the shade is only moderately dense, with sunshine sifting through the foliage of trees, you might try *Phlox divaricata canadensis, Vinca minor,* dwarf irises, *Dicentra eximia,* dwarf columbines, *Campanula carpatica,* or various primulas.

Is there a red RASPBERRY suited to this Middle West climate, for the home garden, that will bear the first year? Latham and Chief are two varieties that have been successful over a wide range of the Middle West, but neither should be allowed to bear the first year, nor should any other variety be allowed to do so.

My black RASPBERRIES dried up on the plants this summer. The canes are weak and all pitted with gray spots. What can I do about this condition? Your plants are infected with the common and serious disease known as anthracnose. Cut out the canes most badly infected; feed the plants with a straw-manure mulch or complete fertilizer in early spring; spray the canes carefully with either Bordeaux mixture or lime-sulfur at least twice a year, especially when the leaves are unfolding, and just before the blooms open. (See Section VIII.)

Can ROSES and SHRUBBERY be successfully planted in the fall in northern Iowa? Yes, provided the normal precautions are taken. Fall planting is much preferred to late-spring planting.

I understand the Large-flowered Climbers should not be pruned. How should they be grown in northern Iowa? Must one take them down each fall? This type needs pruning to keep them in bounds and to cut out old, unproductive wood. But remember that they bloom on 2-year-old wood, and if all the old growth is cut away, you get no bloom. Protect in winter by laying down and covering with earth. Old Queen of the Prairies should be hardy without protection.

When is the best time to transplant STRAWBERRIES in Iowa? I see some transplanted in fall and some in spring. As early in spring as the soil can be planted and worked is best. Only pot-grown plants have much chance to succeed if planted in late spring.

Should TRITOMA be stored for winter? Yes, dig the clump with dirt adhering to the roots and store in a cool (from 33° to 40° F.) cellar until late April.

Is VITEX hardy in this part of Iowa? Have tried to grow it and it winter kills. It is not hardy outdoors without very heavy protection;

or by means of cutting back, taking up the clumps of roots, and wintering in a cold frame.

Are Carpathian WALNUT trees hardy in Iowa?   No records are available, but they have survived severe weather in central Wisconsin. The Wisconsin State Horticultural Society, Madison, 6, Wisconsin, can probably give you the information you want.

Is the lovely low-growing YEW suitable to our Iowa climate? Practically all of the low-growing varieties of the Japanese Yew are fully winter hardy in your locality, provided drainage is good and suitable cultural practices are followed. Protect from harsh, drying winter winds.

KANSAS

I wish to plant a harvest APPLE tree (one that bears during our harvest in June) which will give me fruit in the shortest length of time. Is it possible to plant one to bear in a year or two, and what species would be best for this locality—a hot and usually dry section? One cannot usually expect an apple tree to bear much fruit until it is several years old. Write to your Department of Horticulture in the College of Agriculture at Manhattan, Kansas, for apple varieties recommended for your locality.

As a boy I spent many hours grubbing BUCKBRUSH. Recently I ordered some plants from a Minnesota nursery including one called Coralberry, and it turned out to be buckbrush. Did I get fleeced or do people really plant this bush? Coralberry (*Symphoricarpos vulgaris*) and buckbrush are the same thing, and it is an entirely respectable plant—away from its own home.

Should CHERRY trees be pruned each year to get larger fruit and better yield? If so, when? Cherry trees do not usually stand severe pruning. In early spring remove diseased wood and broken branches, and thin out crowding and crossing branches.

I have a good GRAPEVINE. How can I get more plants, just like it? Most native grapes are propagated easily by cuttings. In early spring cut several of the best 1-year-old canes into pieces about 15 ins. long with 2 or more buds on each piece. Plant these in good soil, with at least 1 good bud above ground. With good care many of these cuttings will root and grow. The best plants may be reset in a permanent location the following spring.

We seeded a new LAWN early this spring and have a good stand of grass. Should it be mowed, or left to grow this year? It can be mowed, but not shorter than 2 ins.

Should grass clippings be raked off the LAWN? Don't rake off the clippings unless they are very heavy and likely to smother the grass. If they are raked off, use them for the compost heap, and spread over the lawn after they are rotted.

We have been told that we should cut our GRASS high. How high is "high"? Leaving 2 to 3 ins. is a high cut.

How can we raise good LUPINES? Lupines are cool-season plants and consequently are not suited to your locality.

ROSES

Why do monthly ROSES grow tall instead of bushy? Shade will draw up the plants somewhat. If the canes are very long and don't produce blooms, they are probably coming from the understock on which the monthly rose was budded. Canes of this kind should be cut out.

I have hybrid tea ROSES I wish to transplant in the spring. When should this be done? Transplant as early as the soil can be worked. Prune the tops back, leaving only 3 or 4 ins. Take up a good ball of soil with each plant. (See Roses.)

A polyantha ROSE planted last spring did not have a bud on it all summer. What is the cause of its failing to bloom? Polyanthas normally bloom freely the first season. Possibly the polyantha top died and the understock on which it was budded came up, and did not bloom. If the plant is producing long, straggly canes, it would be better to replace it.

What is the best winter protection for ROSES in western Kansas? Hill soil up around the plants approximately 8 ins. Wait until the ground is frozen, and then add straw or similar material several inches deep, so that all of the soil mounds and the level soil between plants are mulched.

How heavily shall I prune ROSES in the fall that were put out in the spring? Don't prune your roses in the fall. Wait until spring, and then prune out the wood that has been winter killed. (See Roses.)

What everblooming ROSES will do well in this part of Kansas? Hybrid Teas, Betty Uprichard, Condesa de Sastago, Crimson Glory, Editor McFarland, Good News, Mme. Cochet-Cochet, Radiance, Red Radiance, Soeur Therese, New Yorker, Rubaiyat, Peace, Mirandy.

What climbing ROSE would be best for the arch over a garden gate? Blaze (scarlet); Mary Wallace (pink); Silver Moon (white). But they all need winter protection.

KENTUCKY

At what depth should FREESIA bulbs be planted? What month should they be planted? Freesias should be planted heavy end down, with the tips barely below soil level. A good test for depth is to be able to feel the bulb tops without being able to see them. September is the best planting month for freesias.

How can one get rid of BERMUDA GRASS in this section? If it gets a start on either lawn or farm land nothing else will grow. Where vegetables or flowers are planted Bermuda Grass must be constantly dug out until entirely eradicated. Several chemical preparations, such as Weedazol and Dupont Weed Killer, used according to directions, will eradicate this.

How may rural families raise their own HERBS? What type of soil is suitable? Practically all of the kitchen herbs may be grown in the open garden. Frequently home gardeners set off a special spot for these so that they may grow undisturbed year after year. They respond to extra fertilization and initial preparation. Most catalogues now list special collections of kitchen herbs, both in seeds and in established plants. See Herbs.

How can I get PANSIES started in winter? Pansies may be started in a cold frame or hotbed, or in flats in the house during winter. They cannot be successfully started from seeds outdoors after late summer or early fall. The plants themselves will be fairly hardy in your locality after becoming established, but winter-planted seeds outdoors would not germinate until the following spring.

Is it possible to have healthy perennial PHLOX plants in this vicinity, where we have very humid, hot summers? What soil conditions are suitable to them? Ohio Valley has the above summer conditions, and freezing and thawing for 5 months in winter. Perennial phlox may be grown in your section as successfully as anywhere else. They are entirely hardy and like good, rich soil. With established plantings, fertilizer may be put on top of the ground during winter. A mulch on the surface of the soil during the hot months of summer will keep the reflected heat from burning the lower foliage; watering should be done by laying the hose on the ground; soaking the soil but not sprinkling the leaves.

What is the proper culture for TRITOMA? Tritoma ("redhotpoker plant") should go through the winter safely, without extra protection. It is wise, however, to cut the foliage down after the first frost and cover the area with 6 or 8 ins. of leafmold or other mulch. Tritomas are not particular as to soil, but an occasional fertilization will produce larger blooms. Seeds may be planted in early spring or in a cold frame in fall. The usual method of propagation is from divisions of the old plants taken up in early fall and replanted promptly.

LOUISIANA

How can CHRYSANTHEMUMS be grown in northeastern Louisi-

ana? Garden chrysanthemums are started from tip cuttings rooted in sand in April and set into beds of fertilized soil when they have become well rooted. If divisions of the old clumps are used, the plants may have a great deal of leaf spot, and so cuttings are much to be preferred.

What is proper time to trim CRAPEMYRTLE in northern Louisiana? When the leaves fall in the autumn. Crapemyrtle flowers on the current year's wood, so pruning must be done *before* growth starts, never after.

What are the best flowering EVERGREENS to plant in vicinity of New Orleans? Among the choicest evergreens for this area are the many beautiful varieties of azaleas and camellias. The tea of commerce is a very beautiful flowering evergreen shrub, as are also illicium, bananashrub, the poinsettia, and (in sheltered locations) that queen of flowering shrubs, the hibiscus.

What care and culture do GERBERAS require? If you can get fresh seeds these will germinate well in about 2 weeks; if not, buy divisions of old plants, set them at the same depth at which they grew previously in beds that have been made rich by spading in compost. Use a mulch of oak leaves to cover the soil around the plants, and apply a balanced plant food in January and June—watering well, of course, during all dry periods.

Should one take up GLADIOLUS bulbs every year? Yes, it is by far the best practice to lift gladiolus corms every year, just after the foliage turns yellow. The tops are cut off, the mother corms are discarded, and the new corms are stored in shallow boxes in a cool, shaded place. See Gladiolus.

Is CENTIPEDE GRASS successful as a lawn grass in the deep South? It is being advertised quite a bit here. Yes, this is undoubtedly one of the finest grasses for this section, particularly for light, sandy soils and dry areas. The sprigs or runners are stuck into well-prepared soil after the rains have begun in early summer, and a good lawn should result before cold weather. Be sure to have the apical end *up* when you plant the runners.

Should CALLALILIES be left in ground all winter? Mine did not bloom, but leaves are still green. Planted them last February or March. In semi-tropical sections of Louisiana, callas may be left in the ground all the year round. The soil must be acid, mucky, retentive of moisture, and free from too much competition from the roots of large shrubs and trees.

When is the best time to move SPIDERLILIES? White Spiderlily (hymenocallis) in early spring. Red Spiderlily (lycoris), July or early August.

In Louisiana should PEONY roots be dug up in winter, stored, and

replanted in spring? The practice is sometimes followed in warm climates. The clumps are dug about the first of December and placed in *cold* storage where the temperature is held at about 35° F. In the early spring the clumps are replanted. Since the method is not entirely satisfactory, it is best to choose another type of plant which is better adapted to the warm climate.

Name several varieties of PEONIES (double) that grow and bloom well in the South. When is the time to plant them? Peonies are not happy in most parts of Louisiana. The winters are too mild to assure complete, long dormancy for the crowns of the peony clumps, and any attempt to grow these temperate perennials will only result in disappointment. See previous question.

Which ROSES thrive best in the Louisiana soil and climate? Many of the true tea roses, such as Safrano, Marie van Houtte, Minnie Francis, Duchess de Brabant, and Louis Philippe will survive for many years. It is best to grow the modern hybrid tea varieties as annuals, renewing a part of all of your rose bed each autumn.

How late can ROSE bushes be planted in central Louisiana? What is best fertilizer to use? Early planting is recommended, and December to February is considered the best period. However, the latest possible date would be about April 1. Cow manure is difficult to surpass as a plant food; commercial mixtures are excellent, either in conjunction with it, or, if manure cannot be obtained, alone.

What is proper care for ROSES and best time to plant in southern Louisiana? Roses should be set between December and February, the earlier the better, so that the root systems may become well established before the top starts to grow in the warm weather of spring. Have the beds fertilized in advance, plant at the same depth as they grew in the nursery, and water in well. Be sure that the plants never suffer from drought, and feed every 4 weeks during growing weather.

What is the best way to keep SNAPDRAGONS over winter in Louisiana? Young plants (less than 1 year old) should carry through the winter in the open ground without special preparation, if the drainage and other conditions are normally good.

MICHIGAN

Will CHRYSANTHEMUMS winter safely in northern Michigan, near Petoskey? Yes, with protection. A blanket of evergreen branches intermingled with leaves would be the best covering. Apply when soil is slightly frozen. Soil should be well drained.

How late is it safe to plant CROCUS, hyacinth bulbs, and other early spring-blooming bulbs in southern Michigan? Crocus, scilla, and hyacinth bulbs can be planted safely as late as sound unshriveled bulbs are available, although earlier planting is preferable. Tulips, on the other hand, should not go in until about the middle of October. While most experts condemn late planting of narcissi, I have planted these December 1 with good results by setting them 6 ins. deep—over the *top* of the bulb. They bloom late, but with perfect flowers.

Can you suggest EVERGREENS suitable for this climate? *Juniperus chinensis, J. pfitzeriana, J. monosperma, J. scopularum, J. horizontalis, J. sabina tamariscifolia; Picea canadensis albertiana* and *P. pungens; Pinus aristata, P. montana mughus, P. nigra, P. ponderosa, P. strobus,* and *P. sylvestris; Taxus canadensis; Thuyas; Tsugas; Abies lasicarpa* and *A. concolor; Pseudotsuga taxifolia; rhododendron* in variety.

Can you give me information on the raising of FOXGLOVE (Digitalis purpurea)? Plant seed in late May in shaded cold frame. When fall rains start, put on glass to protect from excess moisture. Cover plants with marsh hay or evergreen boughs after the first freeze, and replace the glass. Transplant into permanent situation (light shade and loose, loamy soil, with plenty of humus) toward the end of April or the first of May.

What varieties of FRUITS—strawberries, grapes, raspberries, blueberries, and peaches—are best suited to the highlands 40 miles south of Mackinaw Strait in Michigan (Otsego County)? Strawberries—Dunlap, Blakemore, Redrich (everbearing); grapes—Seneca, Fredonia, Seedless Concord, Golden Muscat; blueberries—Jersey, Harding; raspberry (red)—September and Sunrise; raspberry (black) —Major Blackcap and Cumberland Blackcap.

Can the GUM trees Liquidambar and Nyssa sylvatica be grown in central or northern Michigan? *Nyssa sylvatica* (Sourgum or Blackgum) is not considered hardy in central Michigan. It is difficult to transplant, unless nursery-grown stock is used. It likes low, damp soil with plenty of humus. Hardly worth trying in this region. Liquidambar (Sweetgum) is hardy over most of the lower peninsula of Michigan, provided conditions are right. This is the Northern limit of its range. Must have deep, rich, moist soil, and stand free from all shade. Neither species would attain full stature in Michigan.

Will you please give me, as nearly complete as possible, a list of HERBS which will thrive in this vicinity? Annual: basil, borage, parsley, Summer Savory, anise, burnet, caraway, coriander, dill, sweet marjoram. Perennial: balm, catnip, chives, fennel, camomile, horehound, lavender, mint, pennyroyal, rue, sage, thyme, and yarrow.

Can HIBISCUS (rosa-sinensis) be grown in Michigan? No, it is a tropical and will tolerate no frost whatever.

Will ILEX crenata nummularia be hardy in Grosse Pointe (Detroit), Michigan? The Japanese Holly is not considered reliably hardy north of the Ohio River, though it sometimes survives a hundred miles north of there in well-sheltered spots. Not a good bet for Michigan.

Can Virginia HOLLY (Ilex opaca) be grown in the Northern States? No; it is not hardy in the North. Grows in protected spots in Massachusetts, but Michigan winters would be too hard on it.

Is there any shrub HOLLY, 5 to 10 ft. high, that is reliably hardy in southern Michigan? The word "reliably" is the pinch. You probably mean an evergreen holly that is 100 per cent hardy and looks like the pictures on the Christmas cards. And the answer to that is "No." There are three deciduous hollies, all of which have attractive winter berries: *Ilex glabra* (Inkberry), *I. laevigata* (Smooth Winterberry), and *I. verticillata* (Black Alder).

Which are the best NUT trees to plant in Michigan? Black walnut, hickory, and butternut. If you are near any of the Great Lakes, toward the southern part of the state, the hazels or filberts may do well for you.

Can Alberta PEARS be raised successfully in lower Michigan? Do you mean the Elberta peach? The southwestern corner of Michigan is one of the world's great peach sections. On the other hand, if the newer Canadian hybrid pears (like Tait-Dropmore and Pioneer, or the Chinese Sand-pears grown in Canada) are meant, the answer is also "Yes." However, these pears are a compromise between hardiness and quality, and ought to be dropped from consideration for high-quality sorts that will do well in Michigan, such as the new Cayuga, or old favorites like Bartlett and Seckel.

Can perennial PHLOX be transplanted in the early spring in Michigan? Yes, this is the preferred time. Move as soon as ground can be worked.

What PLANTS are best for Michigan climate? Only the hardier types. Would suggest investigating the large number of species and varieties being grown in the Nichols Arboretum of the University of Michigan, Ann Arbor, Michigan.

What low-growing ROCK GARDEN perennials are hardy in northern Michigan—30° to 40° F. below zero in winter? *Actinella acaulis; Androsace sarmentosa; Anemone blanda* and *A. aephyra;* Aethionema, various; *Callirhoe involucrata; Gypsophila repens; Campanula muralis; Hypericum reptans; Iberis sempervirens; arenaria,* various; *Armeria laucheana;* aubretia; *Campanula pusilla; Dianthus alpinus; Heuchera sanguinea; Iris pumila; Linum alpinum; Aquilegia saximontana* and *A. alpina;* primula, various; *Phlox subulata, P. multiflora,* and *P. andicola; Penstemon caespitosus, P. crandalli* and *P. alpinus; Physaria didymocarpa; Saponaria ocymoides; Papaver alpinum; Veronica rupestris.*

Is it possible to grow RHODODENDRONS successfully in Detroit,

Michigan? Yes, but this is no tyro's job. Careful preparation of the soil is essential. Protection from *winter* sun and wind are particularly important. The best trick is to plant on the north side of a building or dense hedge, so that on June 21 the sun just touches the base of the stem. Then as the sun recedes to the south in winter the shade of the building will protect the plant from sun. In exposed locations, protection, such as burlap or wrapping in straw, will still be needed. Above all, don't neglect watering, even during the winter. And see that the soil remains acid.

When is the best time to set out hybrid tea ROSES in southeastern Michigan? There is no "best" time, since we cannot tell in advance what the weather will be. Plant as early as possible in spring, or as late as possible in fall. Many commercial growers and landscapers set out stocks during thaws in December and January. In fall planting, hilling up is necessary. Sometimes good pot-grown plants (7-in. to 8-in. pots) are available for late-spring and early-summer planting.

Is fall planting of hybrid tea ROSES considered safe in Michigan, in the area of Grand Rapids? If done *late* enough, fall planting is usually better than spring planting. Protection by hilling up is necessary.

Why can't ROSES in central Michigan be pruned in autumn? They can; but there is not much point in doing so, since the branches will have to be cut back to live buds in spring anyway, and the unpruned branches help hold snow in place, which forms a good mulch.

What are the hardiest varieties of climbing ROSES? Is CLEMATIS hardy in northern Michigan? No climbing roses are winter hardy in Michigan. All need protection afforded by laying them down and covering with earth. Most of the clematis species are hardy, with proper culture.

Will SAGE grow from seed in Michigan? Yes, but results are slower than from divisions, and variation can be expected. Better plant an improved variety, like Holt's Mammoth, from divisions.

What SHRUB or evergreen can you recommend for planting on north side of house where soil is dry? Your native *Cornus stolonifera,* the Red Osier Dogwood, is a highly desirable and hardy shrub for just such a situation. Pfitzer's Juniper is a desirable evergreen subject, but may need some watering to become established.

MINNESOTA

Will you please name several of the spring-flowering BULBS, other than tulips and narcissus, that we can grow here in southern Minnesota? Chionodoxa (glory-of-the-snow), crocus, galanthus (snowdrops), muscari (grapehyacinth), ornithogalum (Star-of-Bethlehem), scilla (squill).

How can I protect CANTERBURYBELLS for winter? They can be wintered satisfactorily in a cold frame. If this is not available, use a light straw mulch on the ground around plants and under leaves. Then place a thick layer of lightweight brush over the bed, and cover this with straw or marsh hay. The brush is necessary to keep straw from smothering the green leaves that remain all winter.

Will you give the name of a good CHERRY-PLUM tree which is suited to the climate in central Minnesota? The list of hardy varieties includes Oka, Sapa, and Zumbra. The Compass variety is an excellent pollinizer for the above.

I want to plant some CURRANTS. What is a good variety? There are several excellent varieties including the old Perfection and the newer Red Lake. These are hardy in your state. In some localities, however, planting is restricted because of danger from the spread of the white-pine blister rust. Consult your State Nursery Inspection Service at St. Paul.

We grow some DOGWOODS here, but not the beautiful large-flowering kind. Do you think that we could? The Flowering Dogwood of the South and East is not hardy in your section.

Our little EVERGREEN trees don't look quite right, and we have been told that they have red spiders. Is there a cure? See Spider Mites, Section VIII.

What is the best time to prune EVERGREENS like junipers and arborvitae? Prune lightly in the spring just as soon as the new growth begins to show. Evergreens make rapid growth right after that and will soon hide the cut ends or stubs.

We have extremely cold winters here. Last year the temperature went to 36° below before we had any snow. I have never seen a FORSYTHIA this far North. Would one survive our winters? Some of the hardier forsythias may survive, but the flower buds are winter killed when exposed to such low temperatures.

Can GLADIOLUS bulbs be left in the ground if heavily mulched and well drained? I recently read an article where it was claimed that they were being successfully wintered that way, even here in Minnesota. Yes. Cover with a 12-in. mulch of manure or straw after ground freezes. Usually considered better and easier to dig, store, and replant.

How can I raise Golden Muscat GRAPES in southern Minnesota? This variety is not recommended for general planting so far North. Possibly the plant could be protected from winter injury if entirely covered with straw; however, the growing season might not be sufficiently long for good crops to mature.

Is it necessary to give winter cover to GRAPEVINES here in southern Minnesota? Most of the standard grape varieties must be protected during winter. The varieties Alpha and Beta are usually winter hardy if the wood is well matured before cold weather.

My arborvitae HEDGE is almost 7 ft. tall, and I would like to have it just about 3 ft. Can it be cut back to that height? No. Evergreens like this should not be pruned back beyond the green, actively growing shoots. They do not renew themselves from old hardwood as deciduous shrubs do.

Even the hardiest privet HEDGES kill back here in the winter. What would you suggest for clipped hedge about 6 ft. tall? *Lonicera bella albida,* the White Belle Honeysuckle.

When and how is PANSY seed sown? Sow the seed about mid-July in a seedbed well loosened up with leafmold. When the seedlings are large enough, transplant to a coldframe, using a similar soil, where they are kept over winter.

When should PANSIES be planted out in the garden? Pansies if grown in a cold frame over winter will not be injured by the frosts and light freezing of early spring. Plant them in the garden as early as the soil can be worked.

Do you know the name of a good PEAR suited to the climate of central Minnesota? The Minnesota State Fruit Breeding Farm has originated several new and promising pear varieties. The Bantam and Patten Number 5 are now recommended. These 2 varieties planted together help, through cross-pollination, to insure heavier crops.

We have read about mixing PEATMOSS with soil to make it acid. There is a lot of peatmoss near here. Could we use it? Not all peatmoss is acid. The only way to be sure is to have it tested. It can be used as humus in your soil, however, whether acid or not. To acidify soil add aluminum sulfate.

How deep should PEONIES be set? Cover peonies with about 2 ins. of soil.

Will you give a list of hardy PERENNIALS for central Minnesota? Coreopsis, gaillardia, peonies, iris, delphinium, hosta, aquilegia, shasta-daisy, thalictrum, dictamnus, hardy asters, hemerocallis, hardy chrysanthemums, phlox, veronica.

What PERENNIALS would form a good backbone for a northern Minnesota garden where frost comes early and winter killing is a problem? Coreopsis, gaillardia, peony, iris, delphinium, aquilegia, shastadaisy, veronica.

Will black RASPBERRIES do well in this part of the country? Black raspberries are doubtfully hardy in the extreme North.

When is it best to plant ROSES, fall or spring? It is safer to plant roses in the early spring. If fall planted, they must be very well protected against severe winter temperatures.

What is the best way to protect a TREE ROSE during the winter in Minnesota? Dig up the plant carefully so as not to injure roots. Lay it in a long trench and carefully work soil around and over it.

Cover with at least 6 ins. of soil. After the ground freezes 1 or 2 ins., cover with several ins. of straw or evergreen boughs.

How much of hybrid tea ROSE tops should you prune off in the fall? Don't prune in the fall. After they are uncovered in the spring, cut back to good, sound, live wood.

We have sandy soil and 40° below zero in the winter. Can I raise climbing ROSES? Yes, if given good winter protection. Take the canes off their support in fall and tie them together to make one long bundle. Lay this bundle flat on the ground and completely cover with soil. Have 2 or 3 ins. of soil over all canes. Mulch over the soil with several ins. of straw. Climbers found hardy in Northern Minnesota, *if grown on the ground* include American Pillar, Max Graf, Baltimore Belle and Queen of the Prairies.

What ROSES are best for Northern Minnesota? Shrub Roses like *R. hugonis,* Persian Yellow, *R. rugosa* and hybrids and the creations of Dr. Hansen: Alika, Sioux Beauty, both red; and Lillian Gibson, pink. Also the Brownell sub-zeros.

What causes climbing ROSES, after being uncovered in spring, to die back to within 2 ft. of the ground? The buds are alive, yet the canes die back. The canes are wrapped with marsh hay and waterproof paper. If there is a section near the base where canes are exposed or poorly protected, canes will be killed from that point to their tips. Also canker, a fungous disease, may girdle the canes, producing similar results.

What fruit-bearing SHRUBS are hardy enough for our Northern climate? Korean Cherry, Juneberry, elderberry, American Highbush Cranberry, and some of the flowering quinces are hardy, especially in favorable situations.

Which of the cultivated varieties of WALNUT are hardy enough to be planted in central Minnesota? The named varieties are not always winter hardy in central Minnesota. Even in southern Minnesota the Thomas, Ohio, and Ten Eyck, standard varieties, are recommended only for trial.

MISSISSIPPI

When is the best time to set out new CHRYSANTHEMUM plants? Rooted cuttings of chrysanthemums should be set out in the garden in May or June. It is better to use cuttings than divisions from the old clumps, as in this way you will avoid carrying over infection of the leaf-spotting disease. Choose an overcast afternoon, water the plantlets in well, and shade them for a day or two.

How can RAINLILIES be made to bloom and thrive in the delta section of Mississippi? These little flowers (*Cooperia*) of the west will usually succeed quite well in this section. With sufficient moisture, fertilizer, and freedom from severe competition they should bloom profusely during the summer months.

How deep should GLADIOLUS corms be planted? In light, sandy soils of the lower South it is best to set gladiolus corms 3 to 4 ins. deep. Thus they will have better moisture and will not topple over when in bloom.

What GRASS is best suited for the Gulf coast? There are several excellent lawn grasses for this section. For shade, under trees—St. Augustine. Poor soil, not much shade—Centipede. Full sun, good soil—Bermuda. Good soil, lots of moisture—Carpet Grass or Meyer Zoysia which must have plenty of water until well established but is then drought resistant (grows in sun or shade).

Could I trim a GARDENIA bush to shape? Would it bloom? When should it be cut? If you have *Gardenia florida* (Capejasmine) prune, if necessary, just when growth begins in spring, by thinning out crowded shoots and cutting back straggly branches. (See Pruning *Gardenia veitchi*.)

Tell me why my white SPIDERLILIES (HYMENOCALLIS) will not bloom even though the foliage develops? They have been in the ground several years. Too much shade. Lack of plant food (they are gross feeders and respond well to fertilizing); or lack of moisture during growing season.

Will the LOQUAT or "Oriental plum" grow in the lower cotton belt? Yes, the loquat is a most ornamental evergreen tree, hardy in the Gulf coast region. Ordinarily it bears large annual crops of delicious yellow fruits that are esteemed as fresh fruit and for pies, tarts, and conserve.

Can NANDINA be grown from cuttings? Attempts to grow nandina from cuttings will be disappointing, in spite of the best possible care. Propagate these shrubs by sowing ripened seeds in a flat. Care for them until the following summer, when germination should be complete.

When is the best time to plant ROSES on the Gulf coast? Between December and February. Early planting is much to be preferred, as the root systems will then have time to become well established before top growth is forced out by the warm weather of spring.

What is the best soil for growing ROSES? A sandy loam or delta soil that is fairly high in organic matter, retentive of moisture, and well fortified with readily available nutrients.

Give me list of the best climbing ROSES, everblooming. Yellow Banksiae, Belle of Portugal, Silver Moon, Blaze, Cherokee, Parade, Golden Showers, and all the climbing hybrid teas.

Is the old-fashioned MOSS ROSE obtainable? Where? You will find the Moss Rose listed in many general catalogues, and by most specialists in roses.

MISSOURI

I would like to know when to plant bulbs of AMARYLLIS formosissima, also known as Jacobean Lily, in Missouri. Early spring, or should I wait until May? What kind of soil and fertilization? Plant after danger of hard frosts has passed. It will thrive on a variety of soils but prefers a medium loam. Soil should be highly fertile; very old manure and liberal supplies of bone meal are good.

What ANNUAL can I plant that will bloom all summer in a north bed that gets sun early morning and late afternoon? Annuals are notorious sun lovers. A few that will condescend to grow without full sunshine are: balsam, godetia, lobelia, nicotiana, *Centaurea imperialis* (Sweet Sultan), clarkia, California Poppy; *Cynoglossum amabile* (Chinese Forget-me-not). (These last two may be sown in fall.)

What care should I give perennial ASTERS set out in the fall? A light mulch of straw, hay, or dry leaves over winter is all they need. Remove mulch before growth starts early in spring.

What AZALEAS will grow well in Jackson, Missouri? *Azalea mollis* hybrids; *Azalea calendulacea; A. nudiflora, A. mucronata, A. obtusa,* var. *amoenum.*

What sweet CHERRIES are hardy and satisfactory in the Middle West? Sweet cherries are not a reliable crop in the Midwest. They lack hardiness, both as to heat and to cold. They are also troubled considerably by insects and diseases. Sour cherries and Duke hybrids are more adapted to this region. Varieties of sweet cherries which should do well are Napoleon, Black Tartarian, Bing, Windsor.

What would be the best type of living CHRISTMAS TREE for us? Colorado Blue Spruce or Red-cedar.

How can one grow large CHRYSANTHEMUMS outdoors in Missouri? Most large-flowering commercial or greenhouse mums do well outdoors in Missouri. Grow just 3 or 4 stems on each plant. Remove all side buds, letting only the top bud flower. *Plenty* of water, fertilizer and cultural care essential.

What shrubs and flowers would be good for a CITY GARDEN in this state? Shrubs: *Cotoneaster divaricata* and *C. acutifolia; Deutzia lemoinei; Kerria japonica;* Philadelphus, various; *Spiraea prunifolia; Virburnum carlesi.* Perennials: tulips; narcissi; ornithogalum; phlox, early varieties; Oriental poppy; dianthus; lupine; pyrethrum; linum; gaillardia; dictamnus; *Lilium croceum, L. tigrinum, L. superbum, L. umbellatum;* anchusa; chrysanthemum; aster (Michaelmas daisy). Annuals: calendula; marigold; petunia; verbena; *Phlox drummondi;* gypsophila; larkspur; dimorphotheca; zinnia; calliopsis; *Mirabilis jalapa* (Four-o'clock); *Bartonia aurea.*

I have a SHASTADAISY from Idaho. Its flowers there were very large, but mine are smaller. Does Missouri climate have something to do with it? Climate is not to blame. Shastadaisies need full sun, fertile loam soil, a good supply of water during the growing season, and a light mulch of straw or leaves over winter.

Can we raise DELPHINIUMS in the Midwest successfully? Set out strong plants in spring. A deep, fertile loam soil is required. Add a generous amount of ground limestone if the soil is acid. Full exposure to the sun and constant moisture at the roots during the growing season are essential. Cultivate frequently, and provide good drainage to prevent winter injury. A light mulch of straw or hay over winter may be beneficial.

What hardy FERNS will succeed in Missouri, and how are they grown? Ferns like a cool, shady exposure (north). Any soil that contains a good supply of leafmold or peat, and constant moisture, will be satisfactory. Plant ferns in fall before the ground freezes. Collect native species from your vicinity or purchase from a local grower.

What kind of HERBS can we raise here? Anise, caraway, chervil, chives, coriander, dill, fennel, tarragon, lavender, sage, Lemon Balm, rosemary, spearmint, Summer Savory, Sweet Basil, thyme, Sweet Marjoram.

Can LAVENDER be grown in Missouri? Where can a "start" be obtained? How is it cured (as used in sachet bags)? Yes, lavender can be grown in Missouri. Plants may be obtained from most nurseries. Hang small bunches of the flowers in a warm room or shed where they will dry quickly. They can be stripped from the flowering stems, put in sachet bags, etc., as soon as dry.

Is it possible to grow MAGNOLIA grandiflora in the vicinity of St. Louis, Missouri? What soil does it prefer? Yes; but St. Louis is about the Northern limit for this tree; consequently growth is slow and mature specimens relatively small. A southern exposure with a north to northwest windbreak is most favorable. Grows best in a fertile clay loam soil. Flowers appear in July.

What culture for hardy PHLOX in Missouri? Give full sun, fertile loam soil containing a good supply of organic matter, adequate drainage to prevent winter injury, frequent cultivation, and irrigation during a dry growing season. Transplanting or dividing may be necessary after the plants have grown in one spot for 3 or 4 years.

What is the proper winter protection for RHODODENDRONS and azaleas in Missouri? A 6- to 10-in. mulch of dry leaves, preferably oak leaves. Rhododendrons exposed to direct sun during winter should have a burlap or lath screen to prevent the leaves from "burning" or turning brown.

Can tree ROSES be grown in central Missouri?   Plant in spring in fertile clay loam soil well supplied with humus. Cut back the top growth or "head" to 3 or 4 eyes, and tie the main stem firmly to a strong stake. Full sun and a constant supply of moisture are necessary. For winter protection, loosen roots on one side, bend the plant over, cover top with soil and a heavy straw mulch, first wrapping main stem with burlap or paper. Uncover early in spring before growth starts.

What is the best time to plant ROSES and when is the best time to prune?   Set out roses in the fall, if the plants are dormant; otherwise wait until early spring. Prune hybrid teas in early spring. Climbing roses are pruned after they flower. See Roses.

Why do my ROSE bushes grow so tall, and have very few leaves?   Any of the following might be the cause: too much shade; suckers from seedling stock at base of grafted plant; black spot, defoliating plants; excess nitrogen in the soil.

How much should a Climbing PEACE ROSE be pruned each year (flowers 5 ins. in diameter—now 2 years old)? Also Blaze?   Depends on type of trellis and effect desired. For extensive coverage remove only the dead wood and a few of the oldest canes each year. Drastic pruning results in few flowers until the plant gets re-established. All large-flowered climbers bloom best on two-year-old canes.

What flowers would be best for a SHADY GARDEN, with some sun in afternoon?   Anchusa, balsam, bleedingheart, spring-flowering bulbs, campanula, columbine, ferns, forget-me-not, fuchsia, eupatorium, godetia, daylily, lobelia, mertensia, primula, lily-of-the-valley, plantainlily, tuberous-rooted begonia, thalictrum, tradescantia, vinca, violets.

Is it good or bad to cover STRAWBERRIES with straw or leaves during the winter, in Missouri?   A straw mulch is recommended, especially for young plants just getting established. Leaves are all right if they are not permitted to remain excessively wet, pack down, and thus smother out the plants.

How should URCEOLINA miniata be cared for in order to have it bloom?   This rare Andean bulb will probably not be hardy in Missouri. Suggest growing it in a pot of light but rich soil in a sunny greenhouse or window. Rest by keeping quite dry after leaves die away in winter. Repot in spring as growth begins.

Are there any large-flowered white or yellow VIOLETS which will grow well in Midwest climate?   *Viola blanda* (white), *Viola hastata* (yellow), *Viola rotundifolia* (yellow). Violets need light shade, friable soil containing lots of leafmold, and extra water during dry weather. Protect them with a light mulch of leaves or straw over winter.

MONTANA

What FLOWERS which grow here have attractive seed pods, or blooms, that may be used for winter bouquets? Echinops (Globe-thistle); eryngium (Sea-holly); asclepias (milkweed); yucca; *Martynia proboscidea* (Devilsclaws); *Clematis orientalis; Koelreuteria paniculata.*

What are some good shade-tolerant FLOWERS for north of house and under trees in this climate? *Anchusa myosotidiflora;* aconite; *Aster sub-coerulea;* lily-of-the-valley; bleedingheart; hosta; mertensia; myosotis; primula; *Phlox divaricata* and *P. carolina; Campanula carpatica* and *C. rotundifolia;* bloodroot; trollius; thalictrum; violet; *Epimedium niveum.*

Our GLADIOLUS bulbs seem to "run out." Is this because of the short season? Possibly the season is too short to mature the new corms. Rich, deeply prepared soil and sufficient moisture at roots to keep them growing vigorously in open sunny location, protected from wind, should help to produce better corms.

What HEDGE is best suited to this climate? To form a neat shorn hedge, Amur River Privet. For an informal taller hedge, Persian Lilac, *Rosa hugonis, Rosa rubrifolia,* and Chinese Elm.

Is the Moutan Tree PEONY adapted to the northern Rocky Mountain region? Peony Moutan may be grown in Montana if altitude is not more than about 4000 ft. above sea level. It grows with coaxing, in Denver, Colorado, at 5280 ft. altitude. Drying of the stems by winter wind and sun seems to be the difficulty.

Could you suggest PERENNIALS for cold climate and short growing season, at elevation of 5,700 ft.? Peony; iris; columbine; *Phlox subulata, P. divaricata, P. decussata; Trollius europaeus; Mertensia virginica;* campanula; pyrethrum; *Papaver orientale, P. nudicaule;* primula; delphinium; rudbeckia hybrids; *Centaurea macrocephala; Physostegia virginiana; Clematis integrifolia, C. recta, C. grandiflora;* Monarda Cambridge Scarlet.

Twenty-five years ago we had wonderful SWEETPEAS in Northwest Montana. Now rust or blight gets them. What can be done? See Section VIII. Where days are hot and nights cool, do all artificial watering as infrequently as practical, but always thoroughly, and always before noon. Try the new spring-flowering type.

NEBRASKA

Will you list some ANNUALS that bloom most of the summer and can endure the heat and drought of Nebraska? Zinnia, marigold, petunia, portulaca, annual gaillardia, *Vinca rosea, Anchusa capensis,* annual phlox, scabiosa, cosmos.

Is BOXWOOD out of the question in this locality? Boxwood is not hardy under your conditions.

Why did a hard November freeze kill CHINESE ELM and still not affect other trees in Nebraska? Most of the other shade trees used in your section go into a state of dormancy without the help of moderately cold weather in early fall. The Chinese Elm apparently requires some cold weather to harden it off before it becomes dormant and is able to stand a hard freeze.

We have some EVERGREENS planted against the front of the house. Do you advise mulching the ground there for winter? Yes, a loose mulch of peatmoss, leafmold, or some similar material helps to conserve soil moisture and prevents too-deep freezing.

What annual HERBS may be grown in Nebraska? Sweet Basil is easily propagated from seed and very easy to grow. It makes a dense, bushy growth about 24 ins. high. Sweet Marjoram, dill and Lemon Balm are propagated from seed and are also easily grown. (See Herbs.)

Will you name 3 perennial HERBS that may be grown in Nebraska, and give their uses? Chives are onionlike plants having small stems which are cut several times during the year and used as flavoring or as garnishing. Sage is the most commonly grown perennial herb. Its principal use is in the flavoring of sausage, in dressings for poultry or rabbit, and as sage tea. Lavender is a member of the mint family used as a natural perfume in silks and linens.

My tulips and narcissi do well, but my HYACINTHS always fail. Is there any special care they should have? Your experience appears to be typical. Hyacinths don't seem to be adapted to your section of the country.

I know that IRIS should be moved in summer, but if it is necessary, can they be transplanted in early fall? Yes; though it is beyond the recommended planting season.

What LILIES can we grow most easily here? The Tiger Lily, Regal Lily, and the Orangecup Lily (*Lilium elegans*) are the most adaptable. Try the new hybrids. (See Lilies.)

There are several gardens in town that have spotted orange LILIES. The flowers are close together and face upward. Can you tell me what they are? This is *Lilium elegans* (also sometimes listed as *Lilium umbellatum*). The common name is Orangecup Lily.

What PERENNIALS can we grow that will stand heat and drought? Iris, perennial sweetpea, veronica, lythrum, euphorbia, statice, gypsophila, hardy asters, liatris, physostegia.

When do you advise planting hybrid tea ROSES? Early spring is safer than fall planting in your section. If you plant early, just as soon as the ground can be worked in spring, the plants will come along as rapidly as fall-planted stock.

Must I hill up soil around hybrid tea ROSES for the winter? This makes good winter protection where temperatures drop low enough to freeze the ground deeply. After the ground freezes, add a mulch of some loose, light material.

On what date should I hill soil around my hybrid tea ROSES? About mid-October. It should be done just before the first hard freeze. If not done before the ground freezes, you will have trouble handling the soil.

What is the best kind of winter protection for ROSES in this section? Hill plants 10 to 12 ins. high. Fill holes so left with leaves or straw and cover plants completely. Climbers should be hilled and branches laid down and covered completely with soil and mulch.

Will you tell me what to do after I uncover my hybrid tea ROSES? Hybrid tea roses should be pruned after they are uncovered in the spring. Cut back to good, sound, live wood. Ordinarily that leaves canes of 6 ins. or less in length.

I know nothing about hybrid tea ROSES, but wish to have a rose garden. Will you advise me about a dozen good varieties to start with? Betty Uprichard, Condesa de Sastago, Crimson Glory, Sutter's Gold, yellow and orange; Chrysler Imperial, red; White Knight; Peace, yellow; Rubaiyat, rose-red; Mojave, orange.

When is the best time to plant TREES, spring or fall? Spring planting is safer than fall planting. Planting should be done *very* early to get the most good from spring moisture.

NEVADA

Are there any AZALEAS hardy enough for this climate? Last winter the coldest was 16° below zero but temperatures sometimes go to 37° below zero. Azaleas require very acid soils and refuse to grow in soils that contain lime. Most Western soils are filled with lime and for this reason azaleas will not thrive. It is doubtful if they would survive 37° below even if the soil is suitable.

When should one set out FRUIT trees? Plant in Nevada in early spring after severe cold is over but before the buds start to swell; latter part of March or first part of April, depending on the altitude.

Should ROSE bushes be trimmed back to 8 ins. in vicinity of Reno, Nevada? All roses except the shrub roses should be cut back to firm, healthy wood, in early spring. Flowers come on the new growth and too much old wood will produce small and inferior flowers.

NEW MEXICO

How long should DAHLIAS be kept out of the ground before planting again? Only until climatic conditons permit replanting.

What are the best bush FRUITS and when should they be planted?
Raspberry, loganberry, boysenberry, strawberry, and grape. Plant in spring in the North; fall or spring in central New Mexico and South.

What are the best tree FRUITS to plant in this climate? In the higher-altitude regions of northern New Mexico: apple, crab, pear, plum, and cherry. Toward the South, and in lower altitudes: peach, apricot, cherry, pear, fig, persimmon.

What is best lawn GRASS to plant in western New Mexico? In high-altitude regions of northern New Mexico, Kentucky Blue Grass. Central and southern: Bermuda Grass or Zoysia.

Is there any GRASS that will stay green the year around? In regions with sufficiently cool summers, yet not too extremely cold winters, Kentucky Blue Grass keeps green all winter if well watered.

When would you make a LAWN in New Mexico? March to June in the North; September to November in the South.

How can a LAWN be kept in good growing condition? First by providing a surface, at least 4 ins. deep, of good loam containing adequate humus on which to seed or plant the grass. In the dry air of the Southwest, lawns keep in better growing condition when given a mulch in November of 50 percent peatmoss and 50 per cent sheep manure pulverized and raked in, followed by watering as needed to keep roots moist. Meyer Zoysia is drought resistant when established.

How often should GRASS be mowed here? A little, secluded, intimate lawn should be kept shorn more frequently and closely than is necessary for a large expanse. In general, lawns in New Mexico are better mown not too frequently or too closely, since the slightly longer grass helps provide shade and so prevents surface drying.

What fertilizer should I use for a LAWN? Before seeding, apply a balanced fertilizer. If growth is not vigorous give an application of ammonium sulfate in June, substituting in alternate years a balanced commercial fertilizer. Fertilize monthly with a complete plant food during January, February and March to encourage growth.

How often should I water my LAWN? In New Mexico, lawns need watering as frequently and as thoroughly, both summer and winter, as is necessary to keep the grass roots moist at all times. This is true of even the higher-altitude regions, except where snow covers the ground most of the winter.

When is the best time to plant ROSES in New Mexico? Spring in the North; fall or early spring in the South.

What winter protection do ROSES need? In the North mound the plants up with soil, compost, or peatmoss; cover with spruce branches or cornstalks. In the center and South no winter protection is necessary. No protection is necessary for shrub roses or polyanthas anywhere below 7000 ft. altitude. Above that they are hardly worth the necessary coddling.

When is winter protection necessary for ROSES? Winter protection for hybrid teas and climbers may be put on after the surface inch or two of ground freezes.

What hybrid tea ROSES are continual bloomers here? Almost all hybrid teas thrive and bloom where the altitude does not exceed 6,500 ft. Some that are especially successful, non-fading in bright sunshine, are Better Times; Christopher Stone; Condesa de Sastago; Dainty Bess; Edith Nellie Perkins; Editor McFarland; Etoile de Hollande; Radiance; Joanna Hill. Hybrid perpetuals do well in alkaline soil.

Will you name some shrub ROSES for northern New Mexico? Persian Yellow, Fruehling's Gold, Harison's Yellow, *Rosa hugonis; R. setigera; R. rubrifolia; R. rugosas Agnes, Pink Grootendorst, Max Graf.* For central and southern New Mexico all of the above and Belle of Portugal, Cherokee Roses.

What climbing ROSES are suitable for New Mexico? Any and all climbers revel in the sun of southern New Mexico. Some that bloom most profusely are Gardenia; Silver Moon; Blaze, and all the climbing hybrid teas. In higher altitudes the choice is more limited and climbers require protection from winter sun.

What are the best STRAWBERRY plants to grow and when should they be planted? Everbearing Strawberry: Redrich, Rockhill (nonrunner). One-crop varieties: Senator Dunlap, Fairfax. They should be planted any time except midwinter. June transplants Redrich bear well the following September.

I IRRIGATE with water from a ditch, using trenches and rows for my garden. Will you give suggestion for arrangements of flowers in garden? Since ditching necessitates rows, regimentation of plants is difficult to avoid. Three possible combinations of plants suitable for your conditions might include:

Heliopsis, Lemoine's Star	Petunia, Salmon Supreme	Iris, Golden Hind
Aster, Robert Parker	Delphinium hybrids	Aster Harrington's Pink
Aster, Mt. Everest	Monarda, Salmon Rose	*Clematis recta grandiflora*
Aster, Beechwood Challenger	Chrysanthemum, Algonquin	Chrysanthemum, Algonquin
Phlox, R. P. Struthers	Phlox, Africa	Chrysanthemum, Early Bronze
Phlox, Africa	Zinnia, Old Rose	Monarda, Cambridge Scarlet
Phlox, Snowcap	Iris, Blue Triumph	Zinnia, Salmon Rose
Zinnia, Yellow	Phlox, Jules Sandeau	Lavatera, Loveliness
Chrysanthemum, Mars	*Helenium autumnale rubrum*	Scabiosa, Isaac House hybrids
Dictamnus rosea	*Salvia pratensis*	
Chrysanthemum, Santa Claus		
Echium, Blue Bedder		
Petunia, Elks Pride		

In lower altitudes and in southern New Mexico use fewer perennials and more annuals for continuity of summer bloom.

NORTH AND SOUTH CAROLINA

Will gardenias and CAMELLLIAS grow out of doors in this part of North Carolina? Camellias should do very well for you, blooming profusely in March. Gardenias would remain alive but it is doubtful whether you would ever have any blooms. The gardenia will stand temperatures as low as 20° to 24°, but anything lower than this kills the plant back to the roots. Both must have wood at least a year old on which to bloom. Your best chance would be to grow them as tub or box plants, keeping them indoors and well watered during the severer months of winter.

How often should CAMELLIAS planted in boxes be watered during the winter months in a greenhouse? What are the best plans for building a greenhouse 12 × 20 ft. especially for camellias? Often enough to keep soil always moist but never waterlogged. When water is applied, give enough to saturate whole body of soil. Build greenhouse where it receives full sunshine and with ample ventilation *both* at top and sides. Provide heating system to deep night temperature 50°.

What good varieties (double) of CAMELLIA japonica can be planted outside in South Carolina? *Alba plena, Candidissima,* Sarah Frost, *Chandleri elegans,* Comte de Gomer, Lady Marion, and Stiles Perfection.

Please give some hints on pruning or shearing EVERGREENS. Also, what is the proper time? I live in western North Carolina. Evergreens are not pruned in the general sense of that word. They may be clipped or sheared any time during the growing season, beginning in spring, just as new growth starts. This encourages bushier, more compact growth, but any late-fall or winter shearing would increase the danger of winter killing.

What is the best GRASS to sow in a yard where there is lots of shade? One of the shady mixtures, containing about 40% bluegrass, 35% Chewing's Fescue, 15% Redtop and 10% Domestic Ryegrass. After lawn is established, if tree roots compete with grass for nourishment and moisture, water in dry weather and feed with 10–6–4 or 8–6–4 complete fertilizer twice in early spring and twice in autumn, watering in thoroughly.

What is the proper fertilizer to use on NANDINA to produce maximum number of berries? Old rotted cow manure and bone meal. It needs a well-drained position and generous amounts of water in dry weather. (See next question.)

Why doesn't my NANDINA have berries after having bloomed? Rainfall influences production of berries. Cross-pollination from one plant to another is necessary. Plant in groups for this reason. There are chemical preparations sold under the names of Fruitone-B and Blossom-set which may be sprayed on the blossoms of nandinas, hollies, and many other plants. These usually produce heavier crops of fruits or berries. Try this on your nandinas next spring.

Do you trim NANDINA plants? If so, when? Pruning is usually unnecessary. If, however, they are too large for the space you want them to occupy, the entire plant may be trimmed back; or the older, heavier shoots may be cut clear back to the ground. During winter or very early spring new shoots will appear from the roots.

Will PANSY seeds planted December 1, bloom the following spring? If planted in a cold frame in October or in a hotbed the first of December the plants will be large enough to set out in the open in early spring and will start to bloom almost immediately. Planted in the open ground the first of December seeds will not germinate until spring, and would be several weeks coming into bloom.

Do PEONIES in South Carolina require partial shade or full sun to best stand our hot summers? Peonies will stand partial shade in temperate gardens, but do well only in the extreme northwestern corner of South Carolina. They require a long, cold winter to induce complete and unbroken dormancy, and are a disappointment in most parts of the cotton belt.

What hardy PERENNIALS can be depended upon for summer bloom in the mountain region of western North Carolina? You may almost take your choice from perennials listed in dealers' catalogues. The writer has seen practically all well-known and many unusual perennials flourishing in the western mountain section of your state. Pick the ones which appeal to you most, and plant them with full assurance that they will succeed for you there.

Will you please give information about the growing of all plants, especially ROSES, in this locality? Most articles are written for the states north of us or south of us, or the western part of the country. You live in a latitude where all annuals grow rapidly and where practically every variety of perennial plant will do well. Only the doubtfully hardy ones need any winter protection and your main handicap in growing hybrid tea roses would be the false springs and late freezes which occur almost every year. When roses go dormant in early winter, hill soil up around them to a depth of about 6 ins.; and do not give any other protection. Your section is ideal for growing climbing roses and floribundas. The same rules for fertilization and spraying apply there as in every other part of the country.

Are there any ROSES which will grow on a fairly windy shore (eastern exposure) in eastern North Carolina? The soil is well drained, good sand-humus mixture. You might not be able to succeed so well with hybrid tea roses as growers in other sections, but hardy climbers and floribundas adapt themselves perfectly to your locality, soil, and climatic conditions. *R. rugosa* and many of its hybrids like Max Graf and Pink Grootendorst are ideally suited to seashore conditions. A few of the more reliable hybrid tea roses are satisfactory if not given too much winter protection. This causes them to make premature growth in spring which frequently is killed back by late freezes.

Can you recommend quick-growing, medium-sized SHADE TREES for lawns in this area?   The fastest growing are Chinese Elm, Box Elder, and Weeping Willow, but they are not among the most desirable or longest lived. Tulip-poplar, sweetgum, and your native maple grow fast enough, and are among the best of the permanent shade trees for your locality. Native evergreens do well if moved when small.

What are the fruiting SHRUBS and TREES, semi-tropical and otherwise, which would grow and fruit in eastern North Carolina? All kinds of barberries, cotoneaster, dogwood (both tree and bush forms), euonymus, hollies, honeysuckles, privets, and viburnums will give a varied display in fall and winter. Many shrub roses also bear attractively colored hips. The callicarpas have lilac and violet fruits; snowberries and coralberries bear profusely, as do the various types of eleagnus which have orange and silvery fruits. Among the trees nothing is prettier than your native hawthorn, wild plum, magnolia, and mountain ash. Several North Carolina nurseries list most hardy trees and shrubs.

When should I plant SWEETPEAS in South Carolina?   Sow the early-flowering or later kinds in November. Protect with litter during severe spells. The early sorts should bloom in May, the late sorts 2 or 3 weeks later.

NORTH AND SOUTH DAKOTA

How deep should I plant DAFFODILS? Do they need any special winter protection?   Cover bulbs with 5 or 6 ins. of soil when planting. They can be protected with a loose mulch of straw or coarse hay. The mulch goes on after the ground is frozen.

When is the best time to sow KENTUCKY BLUE GRASS seed? In early spring or in late summer.

How can one grow and winter Regal LILIES in North Dakota? Plant in fall or early spring, in well-drained soil. The top of the bulb should have about 8 ins. of soil above it when planted. Mulch with 2 to 4 ins. of straw after the ground freezes in the fall.

Where can hybrid NUT seed or trees be obtained for trial in this locality (northern Great Plains)?   Contact the United States Department of Agriculture at Beltsville, Maryland; your State Experiment

Station at Fargo, North Dakota; the Experiment Station at Morden, Manitoba, and the secretary of the Northern Nut Growers' Association at Geneva, New York.

Can PEONIES be planted this spring or must we wait until fall? Fall is the better time to plant peonies, and you will be just as far ahead if planting is done then.

When is the best time to plant PERENNIALS in our cold country? Early spring. Good-sized clumps of the hardier sorts may be planted about the first of September, and if properly mulched will winter well.

Are there any climbing ROSES that will winter here without protection? Old hardy climbers like American Pillar, Max Graf, Baltimore Belle, Seven Sisters and Queen of the Prairies survive if grown on the ground but even these must be laid down and covered if grown on a trellis or arbor.

Will hybrid tea ROSES winter kill in South Dakota? No tea or hybrid tea rose will winter successfully in South Dakota without covering with a heavy mulch of earth. Some shrub roses like Persian Yellow, Austrian Copper, *R. hugonis, R. spinosissima, R. rugosa* and hybrids should winter without protection as will George F. Will, Isa Murdock, Alika and Zitkala, all bred for northern winters.

What is the best time to dig TULIP bulbs in North Dakota? Two or 3 weeks after foliage matures, dig the bulbs and leave stems and foliage attached. Spread them out in shallow trays and store in a dry, cool place. The tops can be removed and bulbs cleaned up in late summer.

How soon should TULIPS be replanted? They were dug in early summer and have been stored under the back porch. Replant these bulbs soon after mid-September.

OHIO

What is the best type of soil for growing APPLES in central Ohio? What cover crop would you recommend while the trees are small? Central Ohio is largely a silty clay loam. Make sure the soil is well drained. Sow soybeans in early June and plow under in September. Then sow Rye Grass as cover crop if soil is not to be kept cultivated.

Can GERBERAS be wintered over in Sandusky, Ohio? How are the roots stored? If by "wintering over" outdoor culture is meant, this is theoretically possible, except that a mulch heavy enough to protect the plant will probably smother it. Gerberas can be lifted after a sharp frost has killed leaves, with dirt adhering to the roots, and stored in a cool place (above freezing, but must not go above 40° F.) covered with damp sand or peat to retain moisture. Examine during winter and sprinkle if needed. Plant out again in spring when apples bloom.

Have you any suggestions for growing HERBS for condiments in Ohio? All of the annual and most of the perennial herbs can be grown in Ohio. In general a rather poor sandy soil in full sunshine is their preference. (See Herbs.) For fuller detail, with their uses, see *Gardening with Herbs* and *Gardening for Good Eating* by Helen M. Fox.

Will you please give me a list of some HERBS that will grow here? Annuals: basil, chervil, coriander, caraway, dill, fennel, Summer Savory. Perennials: burnet, chives, hyssop, Pot Marjoram, mint, sage, sorrel, tarragon, Winter Savory.

What are the best climbing ROSES for northern Ohio (especially yellow)? Two good yellow climbers are King Midas and the newer Golden Showers. Both will need protection. (See Roses.)

What is the best ROSE collection to plant in this part of the country? Plant the collection offered by your favorite seed house or rose specialist. They select varieties that are reasonably sure to satisfy anyone who grows them. All the hybrid teas may be grown in Ohio.

What is the proper time to plant hardy SHRUBS and PERENNIALS in northern Ohio in the spring? Crapemyrtle, catalogues state, is hardy north of Virginia, with protection. What kind of protection is meant? Plant any time before the leaf buds begin to open. "Protection" means some kind of burlap wrapping or screen, as of pine boughs, to protect it from winter winds.

How and when should I plant everbearing STRAWBERRIES in central Ohio? Plant as early in spring as plants are available and soil can be prepared. Avoid newly turned sod because of danger of grub damage. Any good loam will grow strawberries; even light sandy soils if fertilized. (See Strawberries.)

OKLAHOMA

Can you give me pointers on how to grow the garlandflower (DAPHNE)? Daphne is propagated by cuttings and layers. *Daphne cneorum* seems to need a green finger. It will tolerate much sunshine, also partial shade; resents acid soil, likes a little lime; a friable soil, and a rock at its back.

How can I succeed with DELPHINIUM in Oklahoma? Delphiniums are cool-climate plants and dislike heat. Deeply prepared, friable, sandy loam will help content them. A layer of peatmoss under their roots may even make them smile.

What FLOWERS, if any, can be grown as borders to shrubbery in a shady lawn? Chiefly early flowers that do their growing before trees are in leaf: *Anchusa myosotidiflora;* bleedingheart; columbine; daylily; Himalayan daisy; lily (*croceum,* Regal, Madonna, Tiger); narcissus; Oriental poppy; Phlox *divaricata; Plumbago (ceratostigma)* *larpentae;* primulas; *Trollius europaeus;* tulips, Tuberous Begonias.

What FLOWERS that are good honey producers will grow in an Oklahoma garden?   Willow, linden, apple, plum and pear trees. Crocus, nepeta, clover, Michaelmas daisy, and monarda (beebalm).

Can you give a list of FRUIT trees, berries and small fruits that do the best in this climate?   Strawberry; boysenberry; dewberry; plums: Japanese varieties and Greengage; cherry, early varieties; peach; apricot; apple; crab, and pear.

When shall I plant GLADIOLUS in Oklahoma?   First planting between March 1 and 15. Successive plantings every fortnight till mid-May.

Will you tell me how to get rid of BERMUDA GRASS?   Grasses are difficult to eradicate, since their narrow leaves do not succumb to poison sprays. An airtight covering of heavy building paper or old linoleum is effective, also persistent hoeing of grass blades as they appear. No plant survives long when smothered or sheared above ground in its growing season. Weedzol is a new chemical control.

What would be the best grass for a LAWN that will grow under trees and will stand dry weather?   Shady lawn mixture if it is to be sprinkled or irrigated; otherwise, Buffalo Grass or Carpet Grass; or if too shady for this, a ground cover such as *Vinca minor.*

Our LAWN is barren of Bermuda Grass in shade of trees and where their tiny roots come to the surface. Will you recommend a grass or ground vine that will overcome this and withstand the hot winds of Oklahoma?   *Vinca minor* is a presentable ground cover, tolerant of shade, heat, and dryness.

How shall we care for PEONIES in the South?   Peonies do not like a hot climate. Give them deeply prepared rich soil with a layer of peatmoss below their roots. Plant with the eyes 2½ ins. below the surface of the ground. For larger blooms remove all side flower buds. They must have a long dormancy induced by cold weather.

What varieties of PEONIES shall we plant?   Some of the older varieties stand Southern climate best: Karl Rosenfield, Auguste Dessert, Claire Dubois, Festiva Maxima, Duchess Denemours, Couronne d'Or.

What PERENNIALS will do well in partial shade, and in full shade?   If shade is caused by trees, enrich the soil and add leafmold or peatmoss. Aconitum; anemones, several varieties; *Anchusa myosotidiflora*;* columbine; bleedingheart; hosta*; ladyslipper; *Lilium concolor, L. philadelphicum, L. croceum;* lily-of-the-valley; *Mertensia virginica*; Phlox divaricata; Plumbago (ceratostigma) larpentiae*;* primula*; pulsatilla; bloodroot*; *Vinca minor*;* violets*; *Uvularia bellidifolia.*

*These will grow in full shade.

What PERENNIALS will give color from spring to frost? Continuous bloom spring till frost is possible from a succession of different varieties such as spring-flowering bulbs; mertensia; *Clematis davidiana;* peonies; irises; dictamnus; *Phlox divaricata, P. subulata, P. carolina ovata,* and *P. decussata; Campanula carpatica, C. persificifolia; Nepeta mussini;* eupatorium; monarda; chrysanthemums; michaelmas daisies.

Will you please give suggestion for HARDY FLOWERING PLANTS for central Oklahoma climate? Perennials: *Anthemis tinctoria;* chrysanthemums; dictamnus; heleniums; *Heliopsis pitcheriana; hemerocallis* (daylilies); *Iris pumila* varieties, *I. tectorum,* I. tallbearded; monardas: Cambridge, Scarlet, and Salmon-pink; *Phlox divaricata, P. subulata,* and the sturdier varieties of *decussata;* scabiosa.

What PERENNIALS grow best on north side of house in Oklahoma? Ferns, columbine, *Phlox divaricata, P. carolina ovata, Trollius europaeus, Anchusa myosotidiflora,* primulas, campanula, bleedingheart, *Uvularia bellidifolia.*

Will you give some information on ROSE culture and protection in the Southwest? Roses in the Southwest need a deep, rich soil—a 6-in. layer of rotted manure, or manure and peatmoss to keep their roots cool—and an open, sunny place with good air circulation. For winter protection, hill soil up around them, and cover with spruce branches, straw, or any light covering which will protect them from winter sun.

When should ROSES be pruned back in the summer? How much pruning should they receive? As soon as the rush of summer bloom is over. Prune back polyanthas to where individual rose stems leave main stem; hybrid teas more severely. A mulch of peatmoss in midsummer encourages fall bloom. As soon as first fall buds form, feed a balanced fertilizer. Climbing roses and hybrid perpetuals bloom on 2-year-old wood. Leave all vigorous canes of last season's growth. Cut out at the ground all wood older than this.

Our lot is entirely without shade. What TREES are the fastest growing and make good shade? Siberian and Chinese Elm will grow rapidly and provide shade. *Acer dasycarpum* (Soft Maple) is also a fast grower and a more permanent tree.

OREGON

Can I grow CAMELLIAS? Yes. See Tender Shrubs—Section III.

When should DAFFODIL bulbs be planted in Portland? Throughout the fall months; the earlier the better.

Should DAFFODILS be lifted annually and the soil fertilized before planting? Lift only when bulbs become overcrowded and flowers begin to deteriorate—usually after being in the ground for 3 or 4 years. The bulbs are rich feeders and should be fertilized annually.

Will you give a good list of hardy EVERGREENS for 20° below zero; and the soil they require? Blue Spruce, Norway Spruce, Douglasfirs, Concolor Firs, Scotch Pine, Ponderosa Pine, Austrian Pine, Mugho Pine, Juniper, both upright and spreading, any of the American Arborvitae, Alaska Cypress, California Nutmeg. Deciduous: *Betula nana* (Birch), Western Larch. They will grow in any good garden soil.

Will you name some FLOWERS that will bloom from spring to fall? *Early:* narcissus, tulips, primulas, mertensia, *Anemone pulsatilla,* lily-of-the-valley. *Midseason:* aquilegia, *Aster subcoeruleus,* dicentra, anchusa, *Delphinium chinense, Campanula glomerata, C. carpatica,* digitalis, geum, hemerocallis, *Sidalcea rosea, Lilium candidum* (Madonna), *L. regale* (Regal), *L. tigrinum, L. umbellatum,* and the new hybrids created in Oregon; Iceland Poppy, peonies. *Late:* aconitum, *Anemone japonica, Clematis davidiana, Plumbago larpentiae,* gentians, early chrysanthemums.

What annual HERBS are grown in Oregon? What perennial herbs? Annuals: Summer Savory, Sweet Marjoram, dill, chervil, Pot Marigold, coriander, Sweet Basil. Perennials: chives, tarragon, Sweet Woodruff, Lemon Balm, Curly Mint, Sweet Cicely, Wild Marjoram, rosemary, Winter Savory, Garden Thyme.

Do perennial HERBS require winter protection? In colder sections some of them do. (See Herbs.)

Was presented with a double red HIBISCUS plant sent from southern California. Local nurseryman advises it is hardy in this climate. On his advice planted on west side of house to protect from east winds. Looks sick. What do you advise? Herbaceous perennial species of hibiscus and the hardy shrub species (such as Rose-of-Sharon) will grow outside in the Northwest, but not tropical shrub species. We cannot tell from your description which kind yours is.

What is the best variety of Easter LILY to raise on Pacific coast, and how can I propagate and care for bulbs so they will flower at Eastertime? How are bulbs cared for after flowering? Formosum (tall) and giganteum (low-growing) have long been favorites but are not now obtainable; growers are using an excellent one known as Croft variety or L. F. Pricei. Start bulbs early in November; place single bulbs in 5-in. pots which have been provided with good drainage; use friable clay soil to which has been added a little old sifted manure; place an inch of soil in bottom; set bulbs and cover with soil; as foliage develops, add additional soil. Give a temperature of 65° to 75° F. and provide full light. Do not permit bulbs to dry out, but water sparingly. Grow only one stem. Spray with water or a weak nicotine solution for green fly. After blooming, plant bulbs outside; they usually require 2 years to recover from having been forced.

Where, and how, shall I plant LILIES-OF-THE-VALLEY for good blooms? My plants thrive but have no blooms.   On north side where they get plenty of light and filtered sunshine part of the day. Lily-of-the-valley, once established, becomes quite rampant. Plants must be confined by enclosing bed with cedar boards or in some similar way, otherwise they will not bloom freely. They like a rich, woodsy soil containing a little well-rotted manure.

Will MAGNOLIAS live in northern Oregon?   Deciduous magnolia can be grown. Some evergreen varieties succeed in milder parts, but are not recommended for colder areas.

Shall I plant NANDINA and Mexican orange in sun or shade? One nurseryman says in sun and another says in shade. I am perplexed.   Full sun in Pacific Northwest. Neither plant is given a high rating for hardiness, so both should be placed in a protected situation.

How shall I care for OLEANDER that is 6 years old, buds each year but never blooms? Is it too cold here? Have it outdoors all the year around.   If plant and buds do not suffer definite injury from frost, it is not too cold. Lack of sufficient light may cause lack of bloom. Prune previous year's shoots well back in spring.

Shall I plant PERNETTYA in sun or shade?   In the Pacific Northwest the plants do much better when planted in full sun.

How can I make PERNETTYA have more berries?   Three or more plants must be grown together; plants should be pruned annually, removing some of the old wood. Sometimes root pruning is necessary to prevent them from spreading and making too much sucker growth at the expense of fruiting.

When should ROSES be planted?   Plant in fall or spring (former preferably) in holes sufficiently wide and deep to accommodate roots without crowding. Set budded plants with bud about 2 ins. below surface of soil. Prune roots at time of planting. Shorten canes of fall-planted bushes; prune in spring. Prune spring-planted ones at time of planting. If soil is dry, water well. Surface dress with fertilizer after plants have become established.

Should ROSE bushes be planted in full sun, or where they have some shade?   A situation fully exposed to sun is best.

What makes SAGINA-MOSS (Lazyman's-lawn) turn brown in spots?   Air pockets which form under the "moss." Remove brown part and substitute a healthy piece of moss, first placing a little fresh soil and fertilizer in the hole. Sagina must be kept well pressed to the ground to avoid brown spots.

Will you suggest a few SHRUBS that will grow well at the coast in

the briny atmosphere? *Hypericum moserianum,* hydrangea, kerria, azalea, rhododendron, cydonia, deutzia, weigela, symphoricarpus, *Ilex aquifolium, Jasminum nudiflorum,* kalmia, *Viburnum tinus.*

Can you suggest locations for planting of SHRUBS—deutzia, Cydonia japonica, and pomegranate? In your state, growing conditions are so good that most shrubs are easy. Deutzias like well-drained soil with generous supply of humus; sun or part shade. *Cydonia japonica* (Japanese Quince) does well in any good soil in full sun. *Punica granatum* (pomegranate) needs deep, heavy soil, sun, and elbow room. Fertilize, if necessary, when planting by incorporating rotted dairy manure in soil below roots.

How shall I treat my VIOLETS to make them bloom? They do best in good loamy soil containing a little old manure and leafmold. To encourage plenty of blooms, runners must be removed. After plants of good size have flowered they should be lifted, divided, and replanted.

SOUTH CAROLINA (See page 1284)

SOUTH DAKOTA (See page 1286)

TENNESSEE

Will the pink AMARYLLIS grow outdoors in the climate of southern Tennessee? There are many so-called bulbous plants which belong to the amaryllis family. Those which are so frequently grown in pots are not reliable outdoor subjects. The best for your purpose is the one called "hardy amaryllis," frequently listed as *Amaryllis halli* but correctly known as *Lycoris squamigera.* The bulbs increase year after year in the open ground.

When should BOXWOOD be pruned in Tennessee? It is not customary to prune established boxwoods. Sometimes the smaller ones will send out precocious shoots which are cut off to retain the symmetry of the bush. Where pruning is necessary, this should be done during the growing season. Fall or winter pruning increases the danger of winter killing.

In Chattanooga BUDDLEIAS hold their green leaves all year. As they bloom on 1-year wood, where should they be cut back, to make the most flowers and the largest? The old, heavy canes should be cut back *to the ground,* in late fall or early winter. The strong younger shoots will bear larger blooms. If the entire plant is left undisturbed, you will have more blooms, but smaller ones.

If CANTERBURYBELL seeds are planted in a seedbed the latter part of winter, will they bloom that same summer? The canterburybell is a biennial plant and is best sown in late summer. Young plants may be transferred to the beds in early fall and given a light covering of leaves. These will bloom the following year. Seeds planted in late winter may be transplanted the following spring or fall for bloom the second year.

Will CAPEJASMINE stand the winters of this section (Johnson City) Tennessee? The capejasmine is a true gardenia, and so far there is no variety which is reliably hardy. It will stand 20° to 24° F. without damage. It blooms only on old wood, and if this is frozen back there will be no blooms the next year, even though the roots remain alive and the plant continues to send out new growth. In your section it would be far better to grow gardenias as tub plants: outdoors in spring, summer, and fall, and indoors during the cold winter months.

If DAHLIAS are left in ground over winter, will the new shoots bloom and do as well as if the bulbs had been taken up? Dahlias may be given extra covering and left in the open ground in your section. The clumps should be taken up in spring, however, divided, and replanted; such divisions will bloom just as well as those taken up and stored. The only danger is an occasional extremely severe winter during which they might be frozen.

What winter protection should be given ROSE trees planted in the upper South, where temperature goes to zero? Only the grafted head of a tree rose is likely to be damaged by zero weather. Dig up one side of the root, bend the plant down until the head touches the soil, and cover with mixed soil and leaves, pinning the mound down with a burlap sack. In spring this covering is taken off, the head pruned, and the soil packed around the roots to hold the tree upright again. In Tennessee packing the standing tree in straw bound in by burlap would probably be sufficient protection.

TEXAS

Will Japanese ANEMONE grow here? What location is best? Kind of soil? A partially shaded situation, sheltered from strong, drying winds, is best. They require a rich, moist soil, and a generous supply of water during dry periods.

Do I leave ANEMONE bulbs in the ground after they bloom? Are they supposed to come up year after year? It is better to lift the bulbs and store them in peatmoss or in dry sand until inspection shows that they are beginning to push for another season of growth.

Will you please give me some practical suggestions as to means of winter storage of tender tubers and BULBS, when basement or root-cellar facilities are not available? Tender bulbs can be lifted when the foliage turns brown or is frosted, and stored in containers of *slightly* moist peat, sand, bagasse, or rice hulls. The containers should be placed in a cool, shaded place. If they can be put in cold storage at about 50° F., they will keep very well.

How should I plant my CAMELLIAS? See Tender Shrubs.

When is the proper time to graft CITRUS fruit trees on trifoliate? When the bark will "slip" or separate easily from the wood; ordinarily after a good rain during May, June, or July.

Do you think COLUMBINE and BLEEDINGHEART can be grown in central Texas? With good care columbine will succeed; and bleedingheart also if the soil is slightly acid and a sheltered position is given.

Will you give care for DAHLIAS? Is late planting best for here? Set out tubers about 10 days before average date of latest spring frost. This will vary for different sections of the state, but March should be right for the warmer sections, April planting for sections farther North. Set roots about 5 ins. deep in beds enriched with compost; tie plants to a stout stake as they grow; feed every 3 or 4 weeks with a balanced fertilizer. Dahlias must have plenty of water if you wish to cut an abundance of fine blooms.

Is it O.K. to leave DAHLIA bulbs in the ground until ready to plant in the spring, or should they be taken up in fall after stalks die? Both systems work. If you have been successful in leaving them in the ground, well and good. But if too many clumps have been disappearing, lift and carefully store in peat, sand, or similar material in a cool, shady place.

Can SHASTADAISIES be dug up in spring to permit the soil's being turned over and sweetened? They can be lifted, divided, and reset in spring, but autumn is much to be preferred, so the plants will have many well-established roots before warm weather.

Will DOGWOOD grow in this section? Yes, with proper preparation. A neutral or slightly acid soil, a high amount of organic matter, and good drainage are essential. Water freely in periods of drought and wrap the trunks with burlap for the first season or two.

When is the best time to set out DOGWOOD? During early winter, when they are without leaves. Dig as much of the roots as you can, protect from sun and wind, and set at the same level as they formerly grew. Wrap the trunks with cloth as a protection against sunscald and the entry of borers.

Will you list some of the best annual and perennial FLOWERS for this section of the Gulf Coast? Annuals, for winter: alyssum, blanket flower, California Poppy, calliopsis, carnation, delphinium, larkspur, lupine, Moroccan toadflax, pansy, petunia, phlox, poppy, statice, sweetpea. Annuals, for summer: cosmos, flossflower, marigold, morningglory, nasturtium, portulaca, verbena, zinnia. Perennials: hemerocallis, Louisiana Iris, Blue Sage, Stokes'-aster, violet, canna, chrysanthemum, four-o'clock, morea, shastadaisy, Transvaal Daisy, golden glow.

Are there any new or unusual FLOWERS easily grown in the extreme South? (Gulf coastal area.) Practically all of the new annuals may be grown in the Gulf coastal area if fitted into the season that suits their needs. Hardy annuals during the autumn and winter; heat lovers, like marigolds, cosmos, and zinnias, during the hot, humid summers. See seed catalogue for new varieties.

What is the best time to plant FLOWERS this far South? Hardy annuals: alyssum, calendula, calliopsis, carnation, pansy, petunia, statice, sweetpea in the fall in warmer sections. Tender annuals for the summer: cosmos, flossflower, torenia, portulaca, nasturtium, and zinnia after danger of frost has passed. Perennials should be divided in the winter or when through blooming rather than in the spring.

What is the correct time to plant seeds of annual FLOWERS in Austin? To set out perennials? For the cool-weather group—such as calendula, snapdragon, and pansy—October through December. For the heat-tolerant group—such as marigold and zinnia—March to April. Perennials should be divided in winter, December through February, or immediately after blooming.

Should LEAVES be left on the flower beds in our climate? Yes, but do not let them pack down heavily over crowns of plants. New leaves should be added as the mulch decomposes.

What are the best FRUITS for this climate? Oranges, grapefruit, peaches, pears, plums, bramble fruits, and figs.

What is a sure-fire remedy or preventive of borers in FRUIT TREES? (In the Southwest.) It is generally agreed that there is no preventive. A remedy can be effected by using paradychlorbenzene. Your county agent, seedsman, or nurseryman can give the details of the treatment.

How can I grow GARDENIAS in Dallas? A slightly acid soil, rich in organic matter; a mulch of oak leaves; and facilities for watering during dry times are essential. An occasional watering with a solution of copperas will supply iron, and periodic spraying with an oil emulsion will control whitefly and sooty mold.

What is the best location for GLADIOLUS? Part shade or all sun? When is best time to plant for this part of the country? Gladiolus are sun-demanding; corms should always be set in full sun. The planting time should be gauged by the time of the latest killing frost for your section. Then plant about 2 or 3 weeks *ahead* of this date. Late February and early March for southern sections; 2 or 3 weeks later farther north in the state.

Is there a practical way to get rid of "Nut" or Coco GRASS? It is very difficult to eradicate once it gets beyond the hand-picking stage. Trials have shown that it is severely discouraged by growing a heavy cover of cowpeas on the plot for one or more summers. As soon as possible in early summer sow cowpeas thickly, fertilize well, and allow them to become thickly matted to shade the soil. The vines should be plowed or dug into the soil in October. Weedazol is a new chemical control.

How can I kill Bermuda GRASS in beds where yard has been filled in? Digging the roots by hand is the only practical way to eradicate Bermuda Grass. Naturally this is a tiresome job; it must be repeated several times. See previous question.

When is the time to plant California Privet HEDGE in central Texas? December to February. Cut the plants back heavily at planting time; set at the same level that the plants grew; water well at once.

What HERBS would you suggest for Gulf coast country, for growing on a commercial scale? Sage (*Salvia officinalis*) promises to be the best prospect for commercial production, following trials at experiment station in this section.

When should HIBISCUS be moved? December to February. If plant is frosted in early winter, cut it back severely, and move it to the selected site.

What variety of HOLLY that will bear berries can best be grown here? What soil and treatment are required? The Chinese Holly (*Ilex cornuta*), the Dahoon Holly (*Ilex cassine*), American Holly, (*Ilex opaca*), varieties of all of which species succeed in this locality.

My HYDRANGEAS do not grow and bloom as they should. What kind of soil and fertilizer are best for them in southeast Texas? I used well-rotted leaves and barnyard fertilizer. Are they too rich for them? Your soil sounds all right, provided it is not strongly alkaline. Sulfur and alum will acidify soil; rotting leaves will help. Be sure not to prune after the wood is mature, as flower buds would be removed. Pinch or prune no later than July.

How can I make HYDRANGEAS, planted outdoors in Texas, bloom? A soil not too alkaline, an abundance of organic matter, and water are essential. Severe competition from tree roots, winter killing, or late pruning can cause failure to bloom. The flower buds are formed before the plants go dormant in the fall.

How can I protect Dutch IRIS from cold? When low temperatures are forecast, cover plants with excelsior, evergreen boughs, or some other light mulch until the danger from that particular cold snap has passed. Generally the plants should be uncovered after 2 or 3 days. Newspapers or a single thickness of cloth is of no value.

Why do tall-bearded IRISES refuse to bloom along the Gulf coast?

Our light, sandy soils and lack of a real and prolonged dormant season combine to rule out this popular perennial for the Gulf coast. In some sections 1 or 2 varieties seem to be pretty much at home, but not like the semi-tropical perennials that really succeed here. Try some of the Louisiana Irises instead.

My yellow JASMINE is a beautiful shrub, three years old, and has had only 1 small bloom on it. Can you tell me why?   Jasmine requires plenty of sunshine. Possibly too much shade is the cause of your trouble.

Are LILACS and rhododendrons suitable for moist coastal areas? These temperate shrubs are sure to be disappointing to you here. They must have a complete dormant period (induced by long, unbroken cold) and a heavy, rich soil. Better stick to the beautiful semi-tropical flowering shrubs that succeed in your section.

What LILIES will do well in semi-alkaline soil?   Easter Lilies, Madonna Lilies, (*L. candidum*), *L. chalcedonicum*, *L. croceum*, *L. martagon*, *L. testaceum* and other European types should all succeed if your soil is not too basic (alkaline). Of course the incorporating of acid organic materials will help in the culture of all of these and other lilylike plants.

Please advise if LYCORIS is adapted to this climate. What will make it bloom?   *Lycoris squamigera* should flower in the northern section of Texas if the bulbs are properly fed and watered and do not suffer too much root competition. *Lycoris radiata* will probably succeed in the southern sections under conditions of good culture and freedom from too many roots.

Rice hulls make very light soil, but are they too rich for PANSIES? If so, what besides sand should be used?   Mixed with sandy soil, rice hulls make a good compost for pansies.

How many species of PASSION-FLOWER are there? Will any of these grow in Texas?   A nineteenth-century botanist listed 184 species, and many more have been discovered since then. The fruits and flowers are of many kinds; some few of the fruits are edible, most are not. *Passiflora caerulea* and *P. manicata* should do well in gardens in southern Texas.

What is the best understock for PEACHES in the South, where root rot is prevalent in sections with high alkaline soil?   Tennessee wild peaches are the most widely used understocks in all parts of Texas, but are not resistant to root rot.

Will PEONIES do well in central Texas in a black, waxy soil? If so, what varieties do best?   No, peonies will not succeed in this climate. (See question on Peonies in South Carolina.)

What is the best time to divide and reset PERENNIALS in Austin? Autumn or winter; or immediately after flowering. In this way the roots will be widespread and well established before spring growth commences.

What is the best time for planting PERENNIALS? Fall. Practically all herbaceous perennials can be lifted in late fall, or very early winter, and reset.

Should RANUNCULUS bulbs remain in ground year after year? It is better to lift them each year after the foliage has died down and store in dry place.

Will you list some good ROCK GARDEN plants for use in this section? Probably the best groups are the true cacti and semi-tropical succulents that succeed out of doors in the South. The usual alpine rock garden plants used in the North will be a disappointment to you in Texas.

What ROSES are best for Southern gardens? The teas do well if they have good care. Some old-fashioned roses, like Louis Philippe, Mme. Lombard, Minnie Francis, Duchesse de Brabant, and Safrano will thrive long years after many choice cutting roses have succumbed to this climate. Several Texas nurseries are specializing in these varieties for Southern gardens.

What makes ROSES die so quickly here? Black spot, dieback, crown gall, an excessively alkaline soil, lack of a distinct rest period—all contribute toward a short life for modern roses. In many Southern gardens hybrid teas are being grown as annuals.

Could I grow ROSES in a dry clay soil? To do so successfully it will be necessary to improve the soil by the addition of compost, rotted leaves, sand, and other materials. An abundance of water is essential, and frequent feeding, during growing weather, with a balanced commercial fertilizer.

Will you tell me the proper time to set out new ROSEBUSHES in southern Texas? Early planting is strongly recommended for the South, December to February being best by all odds.

Is fall or spring best time to plant ROSES in west Texas? Fall planting is better by far. If the plants are set in December to February, roots can become established before top growth starts in the spring.

What is the cause of ROSES planted in either fall or spring, growing and blooming all summer, apparently strong and healthy, then suddenly dying in the fall? The trouble starts with black patches on the stems, while 25 per cent of bushes are not affected. (Galveston.) Patches on the canes are caused by the so-called dieback disease, for which no dependable control is known. Prune away diseased parts and mop the cuts with Bordeaux or sulfur paste. Black spots followed by yellow areas on the leaves are manifestation of black spot, which see.

Will you please give some information as to the enemies of ROSES

in South and Southwest? Also what kinds are hardy for this section?
The greatest trouble is black spot, a fungous disease that can be controlled by the frequent use of captan or maneb. In the deep South so-
called dieback is a serious trouble for which no dependable control
is yet known. Old-fashioned varieties in the tea group are most dependable.

**What SHRUBS shall I plant in southwestern Texas, where there is
a dry climate, wind, and alkaline soil?**   It is best to use natives, and
some of the best of these are *Leucophyllum frutescens; Tecoma stans;
Diospyros texana; Rhus virens* and other species of sumacs; several
species of *acacia; Chilopsis linearis; Sophora secundiflora;* several species of salvia; *Clematis drummondi;* several species of *juniperus;*
several species of yucca and agave.

May I have a list of flowering trees or SHRUBS for Houston?
Trees: live oak, ash, hackberry, magnolia, mimosa, huisache, and
junipers. Shrubs: crapemyrtle, pittosporum, photinia, privet, oleander,
jasmine, forsythia, spirea, weigela, pyracantha, camellia, azalea, and
gardenia.

What are some of the best SHRUBS for foundation plantings?
Azalea, camellia, podocarpus, euonymus, cotoneaster, pyracantha,
Japanese Box, Japanese Holly, jasmine, abelia, feijoa, and hibiscus.

UTAH

Are AZALEAS difficult to raise in the garden?   If the soil is
slightly acid, moisture plentiful, and the location not too exposed to
sun or high winds, the culture of hardy varieties is not difficult.

Can I have a list of ROCK GARDEN PLANTS hardy in Utah?
The following should be hardy in Utah, at altitudes below 6,000 ft.:
any of the sedums, pinks (*dianthus*), dwarf phlox (*P. subulata*),
bellflower (*Campanula carpatica*), basket-of-gold (alyssum), saponaria, globeflowers (trollius), coralbells (heuchera), and violas. The
last 3 should have part shade.

**Is there any fairly good climbing ROSE that will go through the
winter without covering in a climate where temperature occasionally
goes from 10° to 15° F.?**   Try Blaze and Dr. Nicholas; south or east
exposure is preferable. Queen of the Prairies, with large clusters of
blush to rose, cupped, globular flowers, blooms late and only once
each season but is very hardy. Ramblers would also probably survive
without protection.

**Have you a list of flowering SHRUBS and TREES that would grow
in an altitude of 6,000 ft. to make an attractive outdoor living room?**
Try French hybrid lilacs; they should do well at this altitude. Recommended varieties are: Congo, Edith Cavell, Leon Gambetta, Miss

Ellen Willmott, Mme. Francisque, Morel, Paul Thirion, Captaine Ballet, Marechal Foch, Mme. Antoine Buchner, and President Fallieres. Other good shrubs would be mockorange (Virginalis or Norma); Highbush Cranberry; Wayfaring-tree, (*Viburnum lantana*). Small trees: Colorado Pink Locust; hawthorn; or Hopa Flowering Crab.

WASHINGTON

When and in what kind of soil and location should ALSTRO-MERIA be planted?   Plant tubers 5 to 6 in. deep in September or early October in a rich, well-drained soil, and in full sun or partial shade; place the little eyes up and the tubers down.

Do ALSTROMERIAS require winter protection in the Pacific Northwest?   Alstromerias make growth during the winter, and if the weather is cold should be mulched so that frosts do not freeze them down to the tubers, which are tender and will perish if once frozen.

What time should one take up DAHLIA tubers?   Lift as soon as early frosts have cut down the tops, usually in late October or early November.

Is there any secret to growing Cutleaf Weeping BIRCH trees? Every season I notice a few die off here in Yakima. It's heartbreaking to grow one for 6 or 7 years and then see it wither and die.   The tree calls for no special culture. It likes a sandy loam soil. Being a shallow rooter, it must have plenty of moisture, particularly during dry periods. Leaf diseases and a birch borer are among its enemies. The borer is known to be somewhat prevalent in your section and may be responsible for the death of the trees.

When is the proper time to plant FRUIT trees in the Seattle, Washington, area?   December is the ideal time. Planting, however, may be carried on through January and February.

How do I trim BOYSENBERRY, LOGANBERRY, and GRAPES in Seattle?   Grapes—in February, cut back previous year's growth to 2 or 3 eyes. Remove weak canes. Loganberry and boysenberry—cut back all old wood to the ground as early as possible after fruit has been picked. This gives new shoots, which produce the next crop, a better chance to develop. Thin these, leaving only the strong ones, and nip off ends or tips.

What is the best lawn GRASS that needs no cutting?   All lawn grasses require cutting if lawn is to look well and do well; some call for less cutting than others. White Dutch Clover seldom grows more than 2 or 3 ins. high; Chewing's Fescue is a low-grower; Annual Blue Grass stays within 2 ins. but is short-lived. Sagina-moss—"Lazyman's lawn" is sometimes used for lawns but must be rolled 2 or 3 times to prevent patches of it from turning brown.

What is LAZYMAN'S lawn, Moss-grass or Pearlwort? This is *Sagina subulata*, a creeping perennial, evergreen, hardy, bearing little white flowers, and in habit of growth similar to moss; but it is *not* a moss. It is used as a ground cover, also for planting between steppingstones, and sometimes for making lawns. It's much inclined to get humpy and must be kept flat by rolling or tamping. If this is neglected, the humps turn brown. Grass makes a much superior lawn and requires but little more care.

Are MONTBRETIAS hardy in Pacific Northwest? I lost mine last winter—the first time in 20 years. Montbretias are not always hardy, although in the milder parts of Washington they go through the average winter outside without being harmed. To be on the safe side, either mulch, or lift and store them in frost-free quarters for the winter.

What are some NUT trees that will grow in Spokane? The Black walnut and hardy filbert. Others, such as butternut and English Walnut, have been planted but do not long survive.

Would a RHODODENDRON be hardy in eastern Washington? Many fine rhododendrons may be grown in eastern Washington, provided they are given an acid soil, good drainage, some shade, and protection from cold winds. The soil in this area is alkaline and must be replaced with one that is on the acid side and which is kept so by an occasional application of aluminum sulfate or sulfur. Select only varieties of known hardiness.

What are a dozen or more good ROSES for a beginner in Washington? All the hybrid teas and floribundas do superbly well in your climate. Select varieties from the catalog of one of the famous West Coast rose breeders and growers. A few outstanding varieties are Hybrid Teas: Mojave, orange; Helen Traubel, apricot-pink; Chief Seattle, buff-gold; Charlotte Armstrong, rose; Chrysler Imperial, red. Grandifloras: Buccaneer, yellow; Montezuma, scarlet-orange; Queen Elizabeth, rose-pink; and Roundelay, red. Floribundas: Circus, multicolored; Spartan, orange-red; Fanfare, salmon-pink to orange; Frencham, red.

In the Pacific Northwest can ROSES be transplanted any time during the winter? Yes, but November and December are the preferred months.

Will a TAMARIX hedge grow well in a rainy climate? Yes. It grows very rapidly in the Pacific Northwest. It should be pruned annually.

What are some SHRUBS that will do well on a dry, hot hillside exposed to the south? Tolerance of widely varying conditions makes the following shrubs grow almost anywhere in the Temperate Zone: *Berberis thunbergi* and *B. mentorensis; Cotoneaster acutifolia, C. divaricata,* and *C. salicifolia; Amorpha fruticosa,* and *A. canescens;*

Holodiscus dumosus; Mahonia repens; Caragana arborescens, and *C. aurantiaca; Colutea arborescens; Hypericum prolificum; Ceanothus fendleri;* lonicera; *Pontentilla fruticosa; Prunus besseyi* and *P. Tomentosa;* rhus; *Rosa spinosissima,* and *R. woodsi; Shepherdia argentea; Symphoricarpos orbiculatus; Philadelphus microphyllus; Jamesia americana; Prunus tenella.*

Will you suggest SHRUBS that will do well in moist shade? *Mahonia aquifolium* and *M. repens; Euonymus radicans;* cornus; hydrangea; *Rhodotypos scandens; Ribes; Rubus deliciosus; Symphoricarpos albus,* and *S. orbiculatus; Viburnum lentago, V. carlesi,* and *V. burkwoodi; Arctostaphylos uva-ursi; Physocarpus opulifolius; Ptelea trifoliata; Lonicera involucrata; Genista tinctoria;* amelanchier; *Cotoneaster divaricata, C. horizontalis, C. acutifolia,* and *C. francheti.*

WISCONSIN

How and when should AZALEAMUMS be given winter protection in Kenosha County, Wisconsin? Apply a light covering of dry leaves, and top with evergreen branches, when soil is slightly frozen.

Are any varieties of AZALEAS or rhododendrons hardy as far North as Wisconsin? About the only plant in this group which is available in commerce and is hardy in the area mentioned is *Azalea mollis,* the Chinese Azalea. Some of the natives, like *A. viscosa,* which can be had from collectors, are winter hardy but don't like the hot summers of the Midwest.

Will BENT GRASS thrive in north central Wisconsin? Yes, provided you are willing to fuss with it. But for the home gardener, the less touchy, hardier grasses, such as blue grass, are far more satisfactory.

Is the Blue BEECH hardy in this Midwest climate? Yes. *Carpinus caroliniana* (Blue Beech or Hornbeam) is native from Minnesota to Florida, and is fully hardy if planted in rich, moist soil.

In this climate what is the best time to plant seeds of CANTERBURYBELLS? Plant in late May, to allow a full season's growth before the plants go through the winter. Carry over in the cold frame. Canterburybells all belong to the species *Campanula medium,* and all varieties are equally hardy, but none is easy to grow.

Can I grow the large-flowered CHRYSANTHEMUMS in the garden? These chrysanthemums are neither hardy nor early enough for Wisconsin. Consult your nearest Park Department concerning varieties for your section.

What is the proper method of planting and caring for DAPHNE cneorum in southeastern Wisconsin? *Daphne cneorum* likes a situation open to the sun, but sheltered from winter winds. An opening in a planting of evergreens which faces south is ideal. Plant slightly deeper than the plant stood in the nursery, and fill up to ground level with a mixture of half sand and half leafmold. A pH reaction of between 5.9 and 6.8 is satisfactory. Use balled and burlaped stock, and plant in spring.

What, if any, are the names of hardy APRICOTS for this section in Wisconsin? The only reliably hardy apricots for your region are the Manchurian sorts, and the hybrids of these developed by Prof. Hansen and the Manitoba Experiment Station. Some of these are Scout, Manchu, Mandarin, Golden Glow, Orange Sansin, Ninguta, and the straight Manchurian species. Don't expect too much in flavor from these; in some the flavor is quite strong and harsh, while in others it is green and sour. They are better canned and as sauce than when eaten raw.

What FRUITS (cherries, plums, pears, grapes) are hardy in Wisconsin? All sour cherries are reasonably hardy, but where high winds prevail, better stick to the sand-cherry and plum hybrids which, while not so high in quality, do make good jams and pies. Of the true plums, a whole new series from the University of Minnesota look promising. Superior, Redcoat, Ember, and Pipestone are all good. Add some of the Hansen hybrids, Kaga and Sapa, for variety. The Beta Grape (a Concord-wild-grape hybrid) is reliably hardy but should be used only if Concord does not do well near you. Parker, Patten, and Bantam are three good pears that can take it. Check with local nurserymen to see if older, tested sorts are hardy in your neighborhood, since most of those mentioned above are recommended largely because they will not winter kill, not for highest quality.

Is there a PEACH that will stand our winters? Yes, and no. The peach Hardee, has gone through some tough weather but has not yet been subjected to the lowest experienced in the Milwaukee area. It might be the answer. Stronger in flavor than peaches, but fully winter hardy, the Manchurian apricots, such as Manchurian and Mandarin, are somewhat peachlike in quality.

What dwarf FRUIT trees will grow well in southeastern Wisconsin? Whatever standard varieties are hardy in your area. Dwarfness does not affect hardiness. Pears and apples, the two species most commonly dwarfed by grafting, should be 100 per cent hardy. However, don't overlook the possibility of growing full-sized varieties as semidwarfs, keeping them cut down to shrub forms. This is often more satisfactory for regions where apples do not do too well. Most apples in England are grown in bush form, by the way.

Can white, or green, GRAPES be raised in central Wisconsin? Minnesota 66 is a green grape that has gone through 40° below zero. Worth trying, but not too sure, are the old green Niagara, yellowish Seneca, and early green Ontario.

Can you tell me what GRAPES and NUTS I can grow? The only grape that produces fair fruit and will survive your severe winter is the Concord-wild-grape hybrid, Beta. You are about on the northern limit of black walnut, hickory, and butternut.

Will the shrub LANTANA thrive in Wisconsin climate? What is meant by the shrub lantana is probably *Viburnum lantana,* the Wayfaringtree, which is hardy at Lake Geneva and possibly north of that point; *Viburnum carlesi* is about the same for hardiness, and is far superior in bloom and fragrance. *V. lantana* makes a splendid dense hedge. *Lantana Camara,* the true lantana, is a tender shrub grown in the north under glass or as a bedding plant like heliotrope.

Are PANSIES hardy in Wisconsin? Not in the sense that they can be left outdoors without protection and survive. In Wisconsin, they can be started in cold frames, wintered with the glass on, and set out in spring.

When and how should PANSIES be started from seed? Pansy seed does not germinate satisfactorily at temperatures above 65° F. This means late seeding (about August 20) in your area. Plant in a cold frame in well-drained soil, not too heavy, and not too rich in nitrogen. Potash (which promotes tougher growth) helps the plants to winter over. Wait until snow flies and cover lightly with pine or spruce boughs, or with marsh hay, and apply the sash to the frames. Remove glass about April 1, and set plants in permanent position about May 1.

I have my ROSE bushes hilled up about 8 ins. Where and when should the tops be cut off? Might as well wait until spring. The tops will have to be cut back to live wood anyway, and 1 cut is easier to make than 2. Also, the tops help catch and hold snow—the natural cover for roses.

Should a climbing ROSE be taken down from its trellis each year and covered with leaves over winter? In Wisconsin, climbing roses should be laid down (a trellis hinged at the bottom so it can be dropped over without removing the canes is best) and covered. But do not cover with leaves; damp soil is much better. It keeps the canes moist and does not allow wind to blow off the covering.

Will you name the 12 best all-around varieties of hybrid tea ROSES for this territory? As with horses, so no 2 people can agree on "best bets" in roses. The reliable rose specialists and large American seed houses usually offer collections which are made up of roses satisfactory over a wide range of territory, beautiful in flower, and reasonable in price. You can do far worse than to trust to their expert judgment in this matter of variety.

What kinds of SHRUBS with red berries are hardy for northern Wisconsin? *Berberis thunbergi,* Crataegus (various); *Euonymus* *europaeus; Lonicera tatarica* (Bush Honeysuckle); *Malus hopa* (Hopa Crab); *Prunus tomentosa; Rosa palustris; Sambucus microbotrys* (Bunchberry Elder); *Symphoricarpus orbiculatus.*

What PERENNIALS should I plant for continuous bloom in Wisconsin for spring and summer? Achillea Perry's White, *A. filipendula;* aconitum; delphinium; aquilegia; *Artemisia lactiflora.* Asters: Alaska, white; Ambrosia, pink; Aquilla, pale blue; Erma, orchid; Paloma, deep blue. *Dicentra spectabilis; Centaurea macrocephala;* chrysanthemum, earliest varieties; iris; dictamnus; peony; erigeron; hemerocallis; linum; lupine; *Papaver orientale* and *P. nudicaule;* Physostegia Vivid; *Phlox subulata, P. divaricata,* and *P. decussata; Trollius europaeus;* thalictrum.

When is TREE planting most successful, spring or fall? Unless one has the gift of long-range forecasting, this cannot be answered categorically. For most trees, the best time to plant is as soon as possible, since waiting merely means delay in getting the tree established. But certainly fall planting (any time after the leaves fall) is much to be preferred to the usual practice of waiting until trees are in leaf in May before setting out. Exceptions are the thin-barked trees like sycamore and birches, and those with fleshy roots like magnolias, which do best when planted as early as practicable in spring.

Can you suggest some reliable SHRUBS (flowering) for Wisconsin? Amelanchier; *Berberis thunbergi,* and *B. mentorensis; Buddleia alternifolia;* desmodium; *Euonymus europaeus; Exochorda racemosa; Hypericum prolificum,* syringa (lilac), various; lonicera; *Physocarpus opulifolius; Prunus tomentosa* and *P. cistena; Rubus deliciosus,* sambucus; spirea; viburnum; and species of Brier Roses.

WYOMING

Should I mulch my BLEEDINGHEART or in any way give it extra protection this winter? A mound of leafmold or peatmoss over its crown would be helpful, but not absolutely necessary.

Will you be sure to tell us some good PERENNIALS to grow in the different climates of the state of Wyoming? Variation in climate seems less a difficulty in Wyoming than quality and condition of soil. The following grow successfully where some protection from wind is possible: alyssum; *Centaurea macrocephala; Saponaria ocymoides; Pyrethrum hybridum;* peony; iris; oenothera; nepeta; lupine; linum; hemerocallis; *Heliopsis pitcheriana;* gypsophila; euphorbia; *Phlox subulata* and *P. decussata;* chrysanthemum; delphinium; Michaelmasdaisy; hollyhock; *Clematis integrifolia* and *C. recta;* anchusa.

What climbing ROSES would you recommend for Wyoming? Blaze, Dr. Nicholas, and New Dawn are extra hardy varieties which rebloom. Try also the new continuous bloomer Golden Showers. American Pillar and Chevy Chase are ramblers which can take it. Queen of the Prairies, a hybrid *setigera,* is another toughie.

What hybrid perpetual ROSES do well in Wyoming? Hybrid perpetuals in regions of high altitude and short summer are of less value than in other regions. They incline strongly to mildew. Paul Neyron, Soleil d'Or, Mrs. John Laing, Frau Karl Druschki, are among the best. Floribunda roses do excellently in Wyoming and require little or no winter care. Among the best of these are Frencham, red; Circus, multicolored; Spartan, orange-red and Fashion, coral-salmon.

Are there hybrid tea ROSES that will stand Wyoming winters? Select those not too double, and colors that do not fade in altitude sunshine. A few such are Edith Nellie Perkins, Etoile de Hollande, Joanna Hill, Editor McFarland, Caledonia, the McGredy introductions (any or all), Poinsettia, Mrs. E. P. Thom, Condesa de Sastago, Dame Edith Helen, E. G. Hill, Fandango, Sutter's Gold and Mirandy.

SECTION X

Miscellaneous: Sources for Further Information

BIBLIOGRAPHY

FOR THE convenience of readers who would like to obtain more detailed information on special phases of gardening, we present the following list of books, compiled by Miss Dorothy S. Manks, Librarian of the Massachusetts Horticultural Society.

AFRICAN VIOLETS

African Violet Handbook for Judges and Exhibitors. R. G. Carey. R. G. Carey, Knoxville, Tenn.

African Violets, Gloxinias and Their Relatives. H. E. Moore, Jr. Macmillan.

All About African Violets. Montague Free. American Garden Guild—Doubleday.

How to Grow Better African Violets. Esther C. Grayson. Hydroponic Chemical Co.

The Complete Book of African Violets. Helen Van Pelt Wilson. Barrows.

AMARYLLIS

Amaryllis—And How to Grow Them. Peggie Schulz. Barrows.

ANNUALS

Annuals for Every Garden. Dorothy H. Jenkins. Barrows.

Annuals for Your Garden. Daniel J. Foley. Macmillan.

The Book of Annuals. Alfred C. Hottes. DeLaMare.

The Complete Book of Annuals. F. F. Rockwell and E. C. Grayson. American Garden Guild—Doubleday.

BEGONIAS

Begonias for American Homes and Gardens. H. K. Krauss. Macmillan.

Tuberous Begonias, a Complete Guide for Amateur and Specialist. W. A. Brown. Barrows.

BIRDS

Audubon Guide to Attracting Birds. J. H. Baker, editor. Blue Ribbon Books.

Beginner's Guide to Attracting Birds. L. A. Hausman. Putnam.

Birds in the Garden and How to Attract Them. Margaret McKenny. Reynal & Hitchcock.

Handbook of Attracting Birds. T. P. McElroy, Jr. Knopf.

BOTANY

Botany for Gardeners. H. W. Rickett. Macmillan.

Manual of Cultivated Plants. L. H. Bailey. Macmillan.

Manual of Cultivated Trees and Shrubs Hardy in North America. A. Rehder. Macmillan.

The Living Garden. E. J. Salisbury. Macmillan.

This Green World. Richard Platt. Dodd, Mead.

BULBS

Bulbs for Beauty. C. H. Mueller. Barrows.

Garden Bulbs in Color. J. H. McFarland. Macmillan.

The American Gardener's Book of Bulbs. T. H. Everett. Random House.

The Complete Book of Bulbs. F. F. Rockwell and E. C. Grayson. American Garden Guild—Doubleday.

CACTI AND SUCCULENTS

Cacti. J. Borg. Macmillan.

Cacti for the Amateur. S. E. Haselton. Abbey Garden Press.

Succulents for the Amateur. J. R. Brown. Abbey Garden Press.

Succulent Plants of New and Old World Gardens. E. J. Alexander. New York Botanical Garden.

The Book of Cacti and Other Succulents. Claude Chidamian. American Garden Guild—Doubleday.

CHRYSANTHEMUMS

Chrysanthemums for Pleasure. E. L. and A. H. Scott. The Scotts, Bogota, N.J.

Greenhouse and Garden Chrysanthemums. D. C. Kiplinger. De LaMare.

Hardy Chrysanthemums. Alex. Cumming. American Garden Guild —Doubleday.

The Complete Book of Chrysanthemums. Cornelius Ackerson. American Garden Guild—Doubleday.

CITY GARDENING

Window Box Gardening. H. Teuscher. Macmillan.
Your City Garden. M. McKenny and E. L. D. Seymour. Appleton—Century.
Your Garden in the City. Natalie Gomez. Oxford University Press.

DAFFODILS

(See Bulbs)

DAHLIAS

Dahlias for Every Garden. M. C. Walker. Barrows.
Modern Dahlias. J. L. Roberts. Doubleday.

DELPHINIUMS

The Garden of Larkspurs. L. H. Bailey. Macmillan.

EVERGREENS

Cultivated Conifers in North America. L. H. Bailey. Macmillan.
Evergreens for the Small Place. F. F. Rockwell. Macmillan.

FLOWER GARDENING

Favorite Flowers in Color. E. L. D. Seymour. Wise.
Flower Garden for the Amateur. Alfred C. Hottes. Midland Pub.
Garden Flowers in Color. Daniel J. Foley. Macmillan.
The Concise Encyclopedia of Garden Flowers. M. P. Johnson and Montague Free. American Garden Guild—Doubleday.

FRUITS

Better Fruits for Your Home Garden. J. H. Melady. Grosset.
Small Fruits. R. E. Barker. Rinehart.

GARDEN CLUB PROGRAMS AND FLOWER SHOW MANAGEMENT

Exhibiting and Judging Fruits, Vegetables, Nuts and Gardens. H. C. Pettit. Mrs. H. C. Pettit, Oscaloosa, Iowa.
Flower Show Guide. A. W. Wood. Barrows.
Flower Show Know-How. A. W. Wood. Stephens Press, Asheville, N.C.
Flower Show Themes and Classes for Developing Them. Dorothy Biddle. Hearthside Press.
Junior Flower Arranging. K. N. Cutler. Barrows.
The Complete Book of Flower Arrangement. F. F. Rockwell and E. C. Grayson. American Garden Guild—Doubleday.
The Garden Club Handbook. F. Huttenlocher. Better Homes and Gardens.

GENERAL GARDENING

America's Garden Book. L. and J. Bush—Brown, Scribner's.
Around the Year in the Garden. F. F. Rockwell. Macmillan.
Encyclopedia of Gardening. Norman Taylor, editor. Garden City Pub. Co.
Gardening: a Complete Guide to Garden Making. Montague Free. Harcourt, Brace.
The Complete Book of Gardening and Lawn Care. W. Peigelbeck. Random House.
The Secret of the Green Thumb. H. T. and R. T. Northen. Ronald Press.
The How and Why of Better Gardening. L. Manning. Van Nostrand.
The Standard Cyclopedia of Horticulture. L. H. Bailey, editor. 3 volumes. Macmillan.

GARDEN FURNITURE AND ACCESSORIES

Garden Pools, Large and Small. L. W. Ramsey. Macmillan.
How to Build Garden Structures. H. B. Aul. Sheridan House.
How to Make Garden Pools. W. Longyear. Doubleday.
Planning and Building Your Patio. S. Stewart. Crown.
The Complete Book of Garden and Outdoor Lighting. B. Gladstone. Heartside Press.
Walks and Paths. R. R. Hawkins and C. H. Abbe. Van Nostrand.

GERANIUMS

Geraniums for Home and Garden. H. K. Krauss. Macmillan.
Geraniums—Pelargoniums for Windows and Gardens. Helen Van Pelt Wilson. Barrows.

GLADIOLUS

Gladiolus. F. F. Rockwell. Macmillan.
The Complete Book of the Gladiolus. L. M. Fairchild. Farrar, Straus and Young.

GLOXINIAS

African Violets, Gloxinias and Their Relatives. H. E. Moore Jr. Macmillan.
Gloxinias and How to Grow Them. Peggie Schulz. Barrows.

GREENHOUSES

Florist Crop Production and Marketing. K. Post. Orange Judd.
Gardening in a Small Greenhouse. M. Noble and J. L. Merkel. Van Nostrand.
Gardening Indoors under Lights. F. H. and L. Kranz. Viking.

Growing Plants under Artificial Light. Peggie Schulz. Barrows.
How to Grow Rare Greenhouse Plants. Ernest Chabot. Barrows.
The New Greenhouse Gardening for Everyone. Ernest Chabot. Barrows.
The Complete Book of Greenhouse Gardening. H. T. and R. T. Northen. Ronald Press.
Winter Flowers in the Sun-heated Pit. K. S. Taylor and E. W. Gregg. Scribner's.

GROUND COVERS

Climbers and Ground Covers. Alfred C. Hottes. DeLaMare.
Ground Cover Plants. Donald Wyman. Macmillan.

GROWTH REGULATORS

Handbook on Plant Hormones. Brooklyn Botanic Garden, Brooklyn, N.Y.
Plant Growth Substances. F. Skoog, editor. Univ. of Wisconsin Press.

HERBS

Gardening with Herbs for Flavor and Fragrance. Helen M. Fox. Macmillan.
Herbs from the Garden to the Table. D. C. Hogner. Oxford Univ. Press.
Herbs, Their Culture and Uses. R. E. Clarkson. Macmillan.
The Home Garden Book of Herbs and Spices. M. Miloradovich. Doubleday.
The Years in My Herb Garden. Helen M. Fox. Macmillan.

HOUSE PLANTS

All About House Plants. Montague Free. Doubleday.
Decorating with House Plants. R. Gannon. Studio—Crowell.
Enjoy Your House Plants. Helen Van Pelt Wilson and Dorothy Jenkins. Barrows.
House Plants, Everyday Questions and Answers. F. F. Rockwell and Montague Free. Garden City Books.
House Plants for Every Window. Dorothy Jenkins. Barrows.
How to Grow Better House Plants. Esther C. Grayson. Hydroponic Chemical Co.
Plants in Pots. W. H. Clark. Little, Brown.

IRIS

Iris for Every Garden. S. B. Mitchell. Barrows.
The Iris, an Ideal Hardy Perennial. American Iris Society, Nashville, Tenn.

LANDSCAPING AND DESIGN

Complete Home Landscaping and Garden Guide. R. P. Korbobo. Wise.

Gardens Are for People. T. D. Church. Reinhold.

Garden Design Illustrated. J. A. and C. L. Grant. Univ. of Washington Press.

How to Beautify and Improve Your Home Ground. H. B. Aul. Sheridan House.

Landscaping Plans for Small Homes. Ralph Bailey. American Garden Guild.

Small Home Landscaping. P. J. and A. B. McKenna. Sterling Pub. Co.

The Art of Home Landscaping. Garrett Eckbo. F. W. Dodge.

LAWNS

How to Grow and Keep a Better Lawn. J. F. Flynn. Simon and Schuster.

Lawns and Landscaping Handbook. T. H. Everett. Arco.

The Complete Book of Lawns. F. F. Rockwell and E. C. Grayson. American Garden Guild—Doubleday.

Your Guide to a Greener Lawn. G. S. Cornish. Massachusetts Horticultural Society, Boston.

LILIES

Garden Lilies. A. and E. MacNeil. Oxford Univ. Press.

Lilies for American Gardens. G. L. Slate. Scribner's.

Success with Lilies. R. B. Ware. Canby, Oregon.

The New Book of Lilies. Jan de Graaff. Barrows.

ORCHIDS

Home Orchid Growing. R. T. Northen. Van Nostrand.

Orchids Are Easy to Grow. H. B. Logan and L. C. Cosper. Ziff—Davis.

Orchids as House Plants. R. T. Northen. Van Nostrand.

Orchids for Home and Garden. T. A. Fennell, Jr. Rinehart.

The A B C of Orchid Growing. J. V. Watkins. Ziff—Davis.

You Can Grow Orchids. M. Noble. Mary Noble, Jacksonville, Fla.

ORGANIC GARDENING

Compost for Garden Plot or Thousand-acre Farm. F. H. Billington. Branford, Newton, Mass.

Farming with Nature. J. A. Cocannouer. Univ. of Oklahoma Press.

Gardening with Nature. L. Wickenden. Devin—Adair.

How to Have a Green Thumb Without an Aching Back. R. Stout. Exposition Press.

Organic Gardening. J. I. Rodale. Hanover House.
Weeds, Guardians of the Soil. J. A. Cocannouer. Devin—Adair.

PERENNIALS

All About the Perennial Garden. Montague Free. American Garden
Guild—Doubleday.
Perennials. Marjorie Johnson. Rinehart.
Perennials for Every Garden. Helen Van Pelt Wilson. Barrows.
The Book of Perennials. Alfred C. Hottes. DeLaMare.

PESTS AND DISEASES

Animal Control in Field, Farm and Forest. W. R. Eadie. Macmillan.
Diseases and Pests of Ornamental Plants. B. O. Dodge and H. W.
Rickett. Ronald Press.
Garden Enemies. Cynthia Westcott. Van Nostrand.
Modern Gardening. P. P. Pirone. Simon & Schuster.
Plant Disease Handbook. Cynthia Westcott. Van Nostrand.
The Gardener's A B C of Pest and Disease. A. W. Dimock. Barrows.
The Gardener's Bug Book. Cynthia Westcott. American Garden
Guild—Doubleday.
What's New in Gardening. P. P. Pirone. Hanover House.

PLANT BREEDING

Plant Breeding for Everyone. J. Y. Beaty. Branford, Newton, Mass.
Plant Magic. J. P. Haworth. Binfords and Mort, Portland, Oregon.
Understanding Heredity. R. B. Goldschmidt. Wiley.

PROPAGATION

How to Increase Plants; with a Supplement of Latest Developments.
E. L. D. Seymour and Alfred C. Hottes. Dodd, Mead.
Plant Propagation. J. P. Mahlstede and E. S. Haber. Wiley.
Plant Propagation in Pictures. Montague Free. American Garden
Guild—Doubleday.
Plant Propagation Practice. J. S. Wells. Macmillan.

PRUNING

Pruning is Simple. J. A. and C. L. Grant. McCaffrey, Seattle, Wash.
The Pruning Book, Fruit Trees and Ornamentals. G. L. Wittrock.
Rodale Press, Emmaus, Pa.
The Pruning Manual; based on Bailey's Pruning Manual. E. P.
Christopher. Macmillan.

RHODODENDRONS AND AZALEAS

Rhododendrons. American Rhododendron Society, Portland, Oregon.

Winter-hardy Azaleas and Rhododendrons. C. G. Bowers. Massachusetts Horticultural Society, Boston.

ROSES

Anyone Can Grow Roses. Cynthia Westcott. Van Nostrand.
Modern Roses IV. J. H. McFarland. The McFarland Co., Harrisburg, Pa.
Roses for Every Garden. R. C. Allen. Barrows.
Roses for Pleasure. R. Thomson and Helen Van Pelt Wilson. Van Nostrand.
The Guide to Roses. Bertram Park. Van Nostrand.
What Every Rose Grower Should Know. American Rose Society. Columbus, Ohio.

SHADED GARDENS

Gardening in the Shade. H. K. Morse. Scribner's.
Shady Gardens. E. S. Parcher. Prentice-Hall.

SHRUBS

Gardening with Shrubs and Flowering Trees. M. D. Lamson. Barrows.
Ground Cover Plants. Donald Wyman. Macmillan.
Ornamental American Shrubs. W. Van Dersal. Oxford.
Shrubs and Trees for the Small Place. P. J. Van Melle. American Garden Guild—Doubleday.
Shrubs and Vines for American Gardens. Donald Wyman. Macmillan.
The Book of Shrubs. Alfred C. Hottes. DeLaMare.

SOILLESS GARDENING

Soilless Culture Simplified. Alex Laurie. American Garden Guild.
Soilless Growth of Plants. C. Ellis. Reinhold.

SOILS AND FERTILIZERS

Improving Your Garden Through Soil Management. E. F. Downey. Crown.
Our Garden Soils. C. E. Kellogg. Macmillan.
Soils and Fertilizers for Greenhouse and Garden. A. Laurie and D. C. Kiplinger. DeLaMare.
The Care and Feeding of Garden Plants. American Society for Horticultural Science, Washington, D.C.

TREES

Gardening with Shrubs and Flowering Trees. M. D. Lamson. Barrows.

Shrubs and Trees for the Small Place. P. J. Van Melle. American Garden Guild—Doubleday.
The Book of Trees. Alfred C. Hottes. DeLaMare.
The Complete Modern Tree Expert's Manual. R. H. Fenska. Dodd Mead.
Trees and Shrubs for Landscape Effects. M. C. Coffin. Scribner's.
Tree Care. J. M. Haller. Macmillan.

TULIPS

(See Bulbs)

VEGETABLES

A Manual of Home Vegetable Gardening. F. C. Coulter. Blue Ribbon Books.
  Burrage on Vegetables. A. C. Burrage. Van Nostrand.
  Gardening for Good Eating. Helen M. Fox. Macmillan.
  How to Grow Vegetables. L. C. Cosper and H. B. Logan. Duell, Sloan and Pearce.
  Pocket Book of Vegetable Gardening. C. H. Nissley. Pocket Books.
  The Kitchen Garden Book. S. Barr and S. Standard. Viking.

VINES

Climbers and Ground Covers. Alfred C. Hottes. DeLaMare.
  Ground Cover Plants. Donald Wyman. Macmillan.
  Handbook on Vines. Brooklyn Botanic Garden, Brooklyn, N.Y.
  Shrubs and Vines for American Gardens. Donald Wyman. Macmillan.

WEEDS

Just Weeds. E. R. Spencer. Scribner's.
  New Ways to Kill Weeds in Your Lawn and Garden. R. M. Carleton. Fawcett.
  Weeds. W. C. Muenscher. Macmillan.
  Weeds of Lawn and Garden. J. M. Fogg, Jr. Univ. of Penna. Press, Phila.

WILD FLOWER GARDENING

American Plants for American Gardens. A. E. Roberts and E. Rehmann. Macmillan.
  Growing Woodland Plants. C. and E. Birdseye. Oxford Univ. Press.
  My Wild Flower Garden. H. Durand. Putnam.
  Pioneering with Wild Flowers. G. D. Aiken. Daye.
  The Wild Garden. Margaret McKenny. Doubleday.
  Wild Flower Gardening. Norman Taylor. Van Nostrand.
  Wild Flowers and How to Grow Them. E. F. Steffek. Crown.
  Wild Flowers for Your Garden. Helen S. Hull. Barrows.

AGRICULTURAL EXPERIMENT STATIONS

IN EACH state the Agricultural College, the Agricultural Experiment Station and the Extension Service publish many bulletins on gardening. Many of them are written for home gardeners, and are available free to residents of the state. Lists of available bulletins will be sent to anyone who asks for them.

Through the County Agricultural Agent located at the county seat, advice on gardening problems is available.

The following list gives the address of the Experiment Station (or Stations) in each state.

Alabama: *Auburn*
Alaska: *Palmer*
Arizona: *Tucson*
Arkansas: *Fayetteville*
California: *Berkeley, Davis, Los Angeles, Riverside* (*Horticulture station*)
Colorado: *Fort Collins*
Connecticut: *Storrs* (*Plant science station*), *New Haven*
Delaware: *Newark*
Florida: *Gainesville*
Georgia: *Athens, Tifton* (*Coastal plain station*), *Griffin*
Hawaii: *Honolulu*
Idaho: *Moscow*
Illinois: *Urbana*
Indiana: *Lafayette*
Iowa: *Ames*
Kansas: *Manhattan*
Kentucky: *Lexington*
Louisiana: *Baton Rouge*
Maine: *Orono*
Maryland: *College Park*
Massachusetts: *Amherst*
Michigan: *East Lansing*
Minnesota: *St. Paul*
Mississippi: *State College*
Missouri: *College Station, Columbia*

Montana: *Bozeman*
Nebraska: *Lincoln*
Nevada: *Reno*
New Hampshire: *Durham*
New Jersey: *New Brunswick*
New Mexico: *State College*
New York: *State Station, Geneva; Cornell Station, Ithaca*
North Carolina: *Raleigh*
North Dakota: *Fargo*
Ohio: *Wooster*
Oklahoma: *Stillwater*
Oregon: *Corvallis*
Pennsylvania: *University Park*
Puerto Rico: *Rìo Piedras*
Rhode Island: *Kingston*
South Carolina: *Clemson*
South Dakota: *College Station*
Tennessee: *Knoxville*
Texas: *College Station*
Utah: *Logan*
Vermont: *Burlington*
Virginia: *College Station, Blacksburg; Truck Station, Norfolk*
Washington: *Pullman*
West Virginia: *Morgantown*
Wisconsin: *Madison*
Wyoming: *Laramie*

HORTICULTURAL AND SPECIAL PLANT SOCIETIES
(*Including Names and Addresses of Secretaries*)

THE SOCIETIES listed here include in their programs activities for home gardeners and amateur hobbyists. In some parts of the country the state horticultural societies are trade organizations, affiliated with the state Department of Agriculture. Information about them may be obtained from the respective departments at the state capitals.

African Violet Society of America. Joseph D. Schulz. 3605 No. Audubon Rd., Indianapolis, Ind.

American Amaryllis Society (affiliate of the American Plant Life Society).

American Begonia Society. Mrs. Arline Stoddard. 768 Avenue B, Redondo Beach, Calif.

American Camellia Society. Arthur C. Brown. Box 2398, University Station, Gainesville, Fla.

American Daffodil Society. Willis H. Wheeler. 3171 No. Quincy St., Arlington 7, Va.

American Dahlia Society. Edward B. Lloyd. 10 Crestmont Rd., Montclair, N.J.

American Fuchsia Society. C. T. LeHew. California Academy of Sciences, Golden Gate Park, San Francisco 18, Calif.

American Gesneria Society. Mrs. Lois B. Hammond. 109 Copeland Lane, Irvington, Calif.

American Gloxinia Society. Kenneth W. Fielder. 4139 So. Rockford Pl., Tulsa, Okla.

American Hemerocallis Society. Mrs. Daisy L. Ferrick. 416 Arter Ave., Topeka, Kan.

American Iris Society. Clifford Benson. 2237 Tower Grove Blvd., St. Louis 10, Mo.

American Nature Association. James A. O'Hearn. Sea Girt, N.J.

American Orchid Society. Gordon W. Dillon. Botanical Museum, Harvard University, Cambridge 38, Mass.

American Peony Society. George W. Peyton. Box 1, Rapidan, Va.

American Plant Life Society. Dr. Thomas W. Whitaker. Box 150, La Jolla, Calif.

American Primrose Society. Mrs. P. B. Charles. 875 84th N.E., Bellevue, Wash.

American Rhododendron Society. Mrs. Ruth M. Hansen. 3514 No. Russet St., Portland 17, Ore.

American Rock Garden Society. Edgar L. Totten. 238 Sheridan Ave., Ho-Ho-Kus, N.J.

American Rose Society. James P. Gurney. 4048 Roselea Place, Columbus, Ohio.

Arbor Day Association. Harold Palmer Piser, Managing Dir. P.O. Box 187, Flushing 52, N.Y.

Bromeliad Society. Dr. Thomas W. Whitaker. Box 105, La Jolla, Calif.

Cactus and Succulent Society of America. Mary Glade. 132 W. Union St., Pasadena, Calif.

California Horticultural Society. Elizabeth McClintock. California Academy of Sciences, Golden Gate Park, San Francisco 18, Calif.

Chicago Horticultural Society. Mrs. C. Blair Coursen. 116 So. Michigan Blvd., Chicago, Ill.

Colorado Forestry and Horticultural Association. Mrs. Stanley H. Johnson. 1355 Bannock St., Denver 4, Colo.

Cymbidium Society. Alvin G. Embree. 214 W. Carter Ave., Sierra Madre, Calif.

Epiphyllum Society of America. Martha F. Maxwell. 500 Grove Pl., Glendale, Calif.

Garden Club Federations
There are three federations of garden clubs, the Garden Club of America, the National Council of State Garden Clubs, and the Men's Garden Clubs of America. Each is listed, and names of member clubs may be obtained through their offices.

Garden Club of America. Mrs. Edward Emerson, Corr. Sec. 15 East 58th St., New York 22, N.Y.

Gourd Society of America. Mrs. Raymond Wheeler. 300 Massachusetts Ave., Boston 15, Mass.

Herb Society of America. Miss Marguerite Dumbauld. 300 Massachusetts Ave., Boston 15, Mass.

Holly Society of America. Charles A. Young Jr. Bergner Mansion, Gwynn Falls Park, Baltimore 16, Md.

Horticultural Society of New York. Richard B. Farnham. 157 West 58th St., New York 19, N.Y.

International Pelargonium Society. Mrs. Jean H. Case. 1460 Tunnel Road, Santa Barbara, Calif.

Massachusetts Horticultural Society. Arno H. Nehrling. 300 Massachusetts Ave., Boston 15, Mass.

Men's Garden Clubs of America. George A. Spader. Morrisville, N.Y.

National Capital Garden Club League. Margaret C. Lancaster. 6615 Harlan Place N.W., Washington 12, D.C.

National Chrysanthemum Society. Dorothy P. Tuthill. 345 Milton Rd., Rye, N.Y.

National Council of State Garden Clubs, Inc. Mrs. G. Taylor Buchanan. 160 Central Park South, New York, N.Y.

National Snapdragon Society. H. C. Yoder. R.D. 3, Wooster, Ohio.

National Tulip Society. F. R. Tyroler. 55 West 42d St., New York 36, N.Y.

New England Gladiolus Society. Marian P. Ayer. 12 Newbury Park, Needham, Mass.

North American Lily Society. Mrs. Walter A. Rowell. 5537 15th Ave. S., Minneapolis 17, Minn.

Pennsylvania Horticultural Society. Mrs. E. Page Allinson. 1617 Pennsylvania Blvd., Philadelphia 3, Penna.

Potomac Rose Society. Mrs. Charlotte C. Hansbarger. 713 Poplar Drive, Falls Church, Va.

Queens Botanical Garden Society, Elizabeth Fedden. 215 Borough Hall, Kew Gardens, N.Y.

Rhode Island Horticultural Society. Ernest K. Thomas. 17 Exchange St., Providence, R.I.

San Diego Floral Association. Mrs. Robert Little. Park Administration Building, Balboa Park, San Diego 1, Calif.

Southern California Camellia Society. C. M. Gale. 40 South San Rafael Ave., Pasadena 2, Calif.

Southern California Horticultural Institute. George H. Spalding, Supt. P.O. Box 688, Arcadia, Calif.

Wild Flower Preservation Society. Clara M. Cheatham. 3740 Oliver St. N.W., Washington 15, D.C.

GARDEN CENTERS

IN MANY states there are one or more Garden Centers which function as headquarters for local garden groups and activities. These centers vary widely in size, in personnel, and in the kinds of programs they are prepared to carry on, but all have a common purpose to fill local needs and stimulate gardening activities. This list is probably not complete, but information about newly formed Centers, as well as advice on starting one, may be obtained from the National Council of State Garden Clubs, Inc., 160 Central Park South, New York, N.Y.

Arizona. Valley Garden Center, 1809 N. 15th Ave., Phoenix.
California. Bernard Garden Center, Cutler.
  Civic Garden Center, Griffith Park, Los Angeles
  Sacramento Garden Center, McKinley Park, Sacramento
  San Mateo Garden Center, 2501 Pacific Ave., San Mateo
  Garden Center and Memorial Garden, 20391 Newport Blvd., Santa Ana
  Luther Burbank Memorial Art and Garden Center, 4875 Montecito Ave., Santa Rosa
Colorado. Garden Center of Denver, 309 S. Kalmath St., Denver
Connecticut. Ni Wot Garden Center, Ni Wot
  Wilton Garden Center, Ridgefield Road, Wilton
Florida. Clearwater Federation of Garden Clubs, Clearwater
  Garden Center of the Halifax District, 1120 Volusia Ave., Daytona Beach

Belle Glade Garden Center, 30 S. West Ave., East Belle Glade
Glenn F. Bates Memorial Garden Center, Hugh Taylor Birch State
    Park, Fort Lauderdale
St. Lucie Garden Center, 911 Parkway, Fort Pierce
Manatee River Garden Club, 3120 First Ave. W., Manatee
New Smyrna Beach Garden Center, Washington and Faulkner St.,
    New Smyrna
Pioneer Garden Club, Ocala
Pensacola Garden Center, Wayside Park, Pensacola
Garden Center of the Sanford Garden Club, East First St. and
    Melonville Rd., Sanford
Garden Club of Sebring Garden Center, Municipal Pier, Sebring
St. Petersburg Garden Club Center, Municipal Bldg., 175 No. Fifth
    St., St. Petersburg
West Palm Beach Garden Club Garden Center, 1108 Locust St.,
    West Palm Beach
Garden Center of Winter Haven, 228 East Central Ave., Winter
    Haven
Zephyrhills Garden Center, 5th Ave., Zephyrhills
Georgia. Atlanta Garden Center, Rich's Department Store, Atlanta
Savannah Garden Center, c/o Sears, Roebuck & Co., Savannah
Garden Center, Inc., 904 Patterson St., Valdosta
Illinois. Winnetka Garden Center, Public Library, Oak St., Winnetka
Indiana. Lotus Garden Center, Bedford
Crown Point Garden Center, Community Building, Crown Point
Darlington Garden Center, Darlington
Dunkirk Garden Center, Public Library, No. Main St., Dunkirk
Evansville Garden Center, Central Library, No. 5th St., Evansville
Fort Wayne Garden Center, 1202 W. Wayne St., Fort Wayne
Limberlost Garden Center, Geneva
Huntington Garden Center, Library Park Dr., Huntington
Louisiana. Fifth Federal District Garden Club, Garden Center. Sears,
    Roebuck Farm Store, Monroe
New Orleans Garden Society's Garden Center, 3914 Prytania St.
    New Orleans
Werner Park Garden Center, 2903½ Corbitt St., Shreveport
Massachusetts. Berkshire Garden Center, Stockbridge
Michigan. Wayside Garden Center, Coopersville
Detroit Garden Center, Belle Isle, Detroit
Garden Center of Grand Rapids, 429 Fulton St., Grand Rapids
Grosse Pointe Garden Center, 32 Lake Shore Blvd., Grosse Pointe
Kalamazoo Garden Center, 616 Locust St., Kalamazoo
Scott Park Art and Garden Center, 915 Townsend St., Lansing
Monroe Garden Center, Dorsch Memorial Library, 18 E. First St.,
    Monroe

Missouri. Aurora Garden Center, 601 W. Pleasant St., Aurora
    Clayton Garden Center, Forsythe Bldg., Clayton
    Monnett Garden Center, Monnett
    North East Center, Shelbina
    Sorosis Garden Center, 910 E. Central Ave., Springfield
    University City Garden Center, 630 Trinity Ave., University City
    Webster Groves Garden Center, Public Library, Webster Groves
Mississippi. Jackson Garden Center, Sears, Roebuck & Co., 300 N.
    State St., Jackson
Nebraska. Ashland Garden Center. Ashland
New Jersey. Garden Center of Women's Club, 359 Union St., Hacken-
    sack
    Garden Center of Garden Clubs of Montclair, 60 Fullerton Ave.,
    Montclair
New York. Garden Center Institute of Buffalo, 1500 Elmwood Ave.,
    Buffalo 7
    Rochester Garden Center, Pine Tree Rd., Highland Park, Rochester
North Carolina. The Garden Center of Asheville, 40 Coxe Ave.,
    Asheville
    Charlotte Garden Center, 700 N. Tryon St., Charlotte
    Durham Garden Center, 416 E. Main St., Durham
    Fayetteville Garden Center, 420 Hay St., Fayetteville
    Greensboro Garden Center, 201 N. Eugene St., Greensboro
    Lenoir Garden Center, 115 N. Main St., Lenoir
    Ramseur Garden Center, Public Library, Ramseur
    Wadesboro Garden Center, 206 E. Morgan St., Wadesboro
    Garden Center of Wilmington, 307 N. Front St., Wilmington
    Garden Center of Winston-Salem, 801 W. 4th St., Winston-Salem
Ohio. Akron Garden Center, The M. O'Neil Co., Akron
    Canton Garden Center, 933 Market Ave., Canton
    Garden Center of Greater Cincinnati, 2715 Reading Rd., Cincinnati
    Garden Center of Greater Cleveland, 11190 East Blvd., Cleveland 6
    Fremont Garden Center, Birchard Library, Groghan St., Fremont
    Kingwood Center, 900 Park Ave. W., Mansfield
    Garden Center Committee of the Marion Garden Club, Public
    Library, Marion
    Toledo Garden Center, Zoological Park, Toledo
Oklahoma. Tulsa Garden Center, 3516 S. Peoria St., Tulsa
Pennsylvania. Pittsburgh Garden Center, 1059 Shadyside Ave.,
    Pittsburgh
South Carolina. Garden Center of the Council of Garden Clubs of
    Greater Charleston, 94 Rutledge Ave., Charleston
    Garden Center of Columbia, 1400 Sumter St., Columbia
    Greenville Garden Center, Ivey's Department Store, Greenville
    Orangeburg Garden Center, County Library, Orangeburg

Easley Garden Center, Pickens County Library, Easley
Walhalla Garden Center, Walhalla
Tennessee. Garden Club Center of the Knox County Council, Sears,
Roebuck Co., 1000 No. Central Ave., Knoxville
Garden Center of the Memphis and Shelby County Council, 448 N.
Watkins Ave., Memphis
Garden Center, 2020 West End Ave., Nashville
Texas. Park and Recreation Garden Center, 2801 Park St., Beaumont
Fort Worth Garden Center, Department of Parks, Fort Worth
West Virginia. Wheeling Garden Center, Oglebay Park, Wheeling

Frost Maps

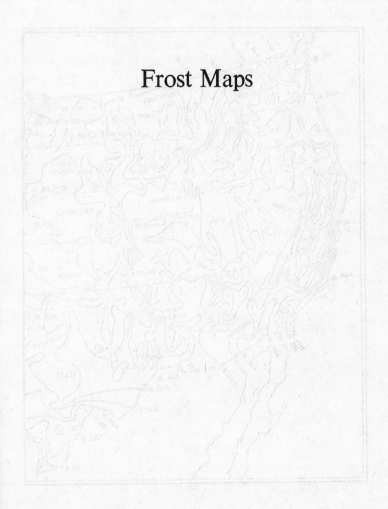

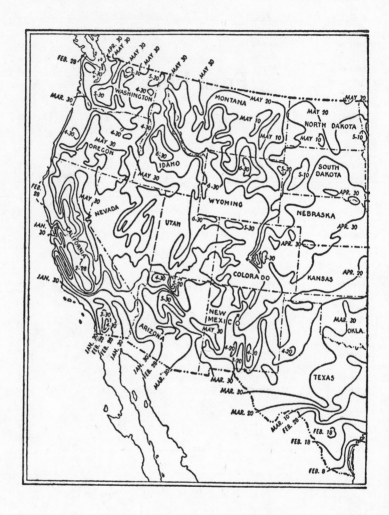

AVERAGE DATE OF LAST

"Tender" vegetables and flowers—those likely to be injured or killed by a light frost—should not be planted out until after danger of a late frost is past. *Seeds* of tender subjects (such as beans or corn) may be planted a few days earlier, as it will take them a week or ten days to germinate.

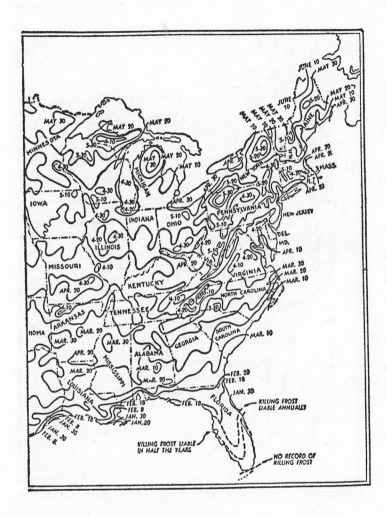

KILLING FROST IN SPRING

Local conditions—such as elevation above sea level, exposure to or protection from prevailing winds, and proximity to large bodies of water—may advance or delay the dates indicated on maps by a few days to a week or more. (Figures on the map—such as 4-20, 5-10—indicate dates, April 20, May 10, etc.)

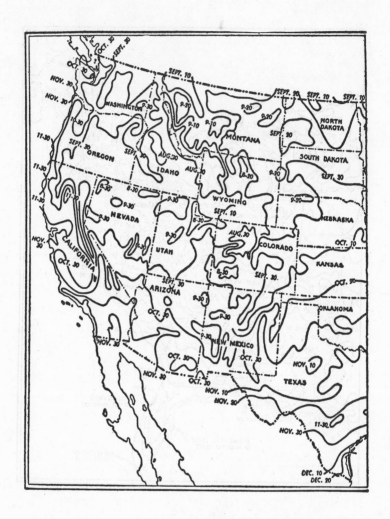

AVERAGE DATE OF FIRST

Hardy shrubs, roses, perennials, bulbs, and many fruits are usually planted in autumn about the time of, or just after, the first killing or "hard" frosts have checked growth. Many of these can be planted up until the time the ground begins to freeze, but in most instances earlier planting is advisable.

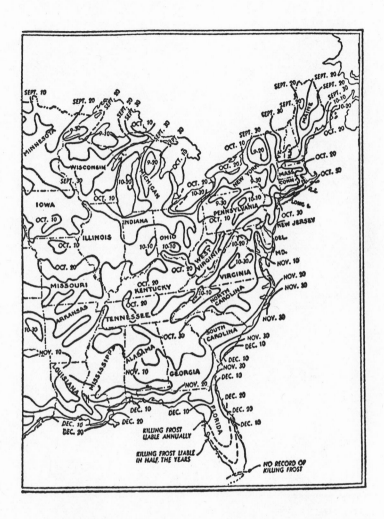

KILLING FROST IN FALL

If there is a period of a few weeks between planting and the time the ground begins to freeze, the newly set out plants or bulbs have an opportunity to make some root growth, and thus become established in their new positions. As in the case of spring frosts, local conditions will advance or delay the average dates (indicated on map) by a considerable period.

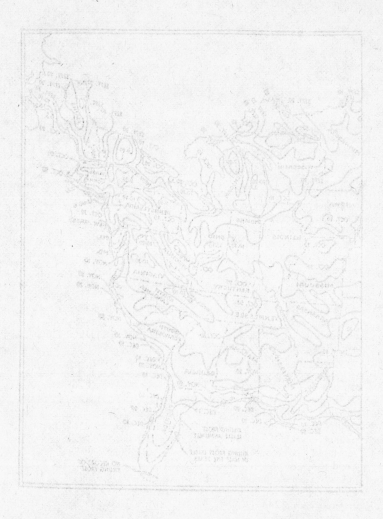

Index

Abelia, 321
Abies (*see* Fir)
Abutilon (Flowering Maple), 268,
958
Acacia, 268–69, 387
Acalypha, greenhouse, 262
Acanthopanax, 321
Accessories, garden, 115–33
(*see also* Equipment)
Acer, *negundo* (Box elder), 295
(*see also* Maples)
Achimenes, 447
Acidanthera, 447
Acids
gibberellic, 82
limestone with, 74
phosphoric
in bone, 66
in crab meal, 70
in sludge, 69
in tankage, 69
Acid soil, 9–10, 31–42
evergreens for, 221 ff.
shrubs for, 368
testing, 41–42
vegetable garden and, 725
wood ashes on, 69
(*see also* specific plants)
Aconites, 573
in Colorado, 1244
troubles, 1100–1
Winter-, 425
Acroclinium, for winter bouquet,
610
Actinidia, Bower, as screen, 111
Adco, 61, 63
Adders-tongue, moist soil, 175
Adiantum (*see* Maidenhair Fern)
Adlumia, 402–3
Adobe soil, 1228–29, 1229–30
Aeration, soil, 2–3
Aerosols, 1052–53

Aethionema, uses, 104, 165, 526
African-daisy
Arctotis, 606
Dimorphotheca, 610, 1247
(*see also* Gerbera)
Africanlily, 447
African-violet (Saintpaulia), 958–
63
culture, 958–61
pests and diseases, 961–62, 1101
propagation, 962–63
types, 963
Agapanthus
Africanlily, 447
indoors, 1028–29
Ageratum, 605–6
hardy (Eupatorium), 562
pinching, 597
troubles, 1107
Aglaonema modestum, 985
Agrico, 76–77
Agricultural lime (*see* Limestone)
Ailanthus, 290
Air (*see* Aeration; Ventilation)
Air-layering, 247, 251
Air-plant (Bryophyllum), 1023
Ajuga (Bugle-weed), 223 ff., 523 ff.
Akebia, 404–5
Alabama
crown rot in, 1116–17
plants in, 1221–25
petunias, 613
Albizzia (Mimosa), 338
Alders, killing, 289
Aldrin, 1053
Alfalfa, 57, 60
Algae
in bird bath, 116
in soil, 24, 25
Algerian Ivy, 1252
Alkaline soil, 9, 10, 18, 36–37
bone meal for, 67

Alkaline soil (*cont.*)
liming, fertilizing, 34
plants for, 32–33
wood ashes, cinders on, 70
Alkaline water
on evergreens, 352
in Kansas, 37
Alleghenyvine (Adlumia), 402–3
Allium (Onions), 797–800, 1193
Flowering, 415
Allspice tree, in greenhouse, 269
Almond, 922
California problems, 1234
Flowering, 321
Aloe, keep dry, 952
Alorco cryolite, 1063
Alpines, 160–61
moraine garden, 165
Alsophila australis, 1238
Alstroemaria, 447, 1301
Althea (Rose-of-Sharon), 317, 341
Aluminum, 10
Aluminum sulfate, 10, 34, 36–37
on hydrangeas, 333
on rhododendrons, 54, 376
Alyssum
annual (Sweet), 597, 606
indoors, 981
saxatile, 163, 536–37, 1101
shearing back, 597
Amaranthus, foliage, 595
Amarcrinum, thrips, 1102
Amaryllis, 448
formosissima, 474–75, 1276
indoors, 1029–31
in Florida, 1245
in Georgia, 1250
in greenhouse, 269
troubles, 1102
(*see also* Lycoris; *Vallota;*
Crinum)
Amazonlily (Eucharis), 273, 464
Amelanchier canadensis, 311, 917
Ammonia, 4, 51, 53
Ammonium nitrate, 34
Ammonium sulfate, 10, 34
caking of, 77
nitrogen source, 43, 73, 237
weed killer, 195, 197 ff.
Amorpha (Indigobush), 321
Ampelopsis (Porcelainvine), 405

Analysis, soil, 41–42
Anchusa, 537
Andromeda (Pieris), 383
Androsace, uses, 159 ff.
Anemone, 177–78, 415–16
in greenhouse, 269
in Texas, 1294
troubles, 1102
Angelica, 143
Angleworms (*see* Earthworms)
Animal manure (*see* Horse manure; Chicken manure; etc.)
Animals, and pesticides, 1085–86
(*see also* individual animals)
Anise, 143–44
Annuals, 593–623
flowers, 593–623
border, 100
in bulb beds, 224
child's garden, 184
city, 216
in cold frame, 257
culture, 596–98
cuttings, 605
fragrant, 185
propagation, 599–603, 603–5
regional
Alabama, 1221–22
Colorado, 1244
Idaho, 1254
Missouri, 1276
Nebraska, 1279
roof, 187
sandy soil, 225–26
seashore, 226
shade, 230
transplanting, 595–96
watering, 236–37 ff.
herbs, 137, 141, 148 ff.
house plants, 980–82
vines, 402–4
for fence, 121
(*see also* specific plants)
Anthemis, 101, 106, 226
Antholyza, 475
Anthracnose, on various plants, 1103 ff.
(*see* individual plants for treatment)

Anthuriums, 269, 963
Antibiotics, 1095
Antirrhinum (Snapdragon), 617–19, 1171
  greenhouse, 269
  indoors, 982
  Louisiana, 1268
Ants, 756, 1053–54
Aphids (Plant lice), 1054, 1101 ff.
  in compost heap, 65
  in greenhouse, 268
Apple pomace, 62
Apples, storing, 849–850
Apple trees, 854–64
  cross-pollination, 847
  culture, 857–61
  harvesting, 849
  multiple-variety, 861
  pests and diseases, 360, 861–63, 1204–9
  planting, 854–55
  propagation, 850–52
  pruning, 855–57
  regional
    Alabama, 1222
    Illinois, 1255
    Kansas, 1264
    Ohio, 1287
  varieties, 863
  (*see also* Crab Apples)
Apricot, 864
  in Iowa, 1262
  pests and diseases, 1210
  in Wisconsin, 1303–4
Aquilegia (*see* Columbines)
Aralia
  Fatsia japonica, 983
  Five-leaved, 321
Arasan, 1090
Araucaria (Norfolk-Island-Pine), 987
  in California, 1241
Arboretum, 279
Arbors, 115
Arborvitae, 356–57, 395
  cuttings, 356
  troubles, 352–53, 1102–3
  windbreak, 399, 400
Arbutus
  California problems, 1234–35
  Trailing, 178

Arctostaphylos (Bearberry), 323
Arctotis (African-daisy), 606
Arenaria, uses, 156 ff., 223 ff.
Aristolochia elegans, 269–70
Arizona problems, 1225–27
Arkansas problems, 1227
  iris nematodes, 1141
Armadillos, controlling, 1054
Armeria, uses, 158 ff.
Armillaria root rot, 1055
Army worm, 1054–55
Arsenate of lead, 20, 1075
Arsenite of soda, 172
Artichokes, 756–57
  Jerusalem, 756–57
Arum palaestinum (Black Calla), 416, 1031
Asarum canadense, 146
Asclepia tuberosa (Butterflyweed), 179
Ashes
  on clay soil, 14 ff.
  coal, 30–31
  of leaves, grass, 64
  wood, 69–70
Asiatic beetle, 1055–56, 1168–69
Asiatic garden beetle, 1168, 1169
Asparagus, 757–60
  eradicating, 194
  pests and diseases, 1178
Asparagusfern, 983–84
Asparagus knife, 752
Asperula, for rock garden, 158 ff.
Asphaltum paint, 239
Aspidistra, 984
  troubles, 1103
Astermums, 552–53
Asters
  annual, 606–8
  hardy, 537
  in Illinois, 1255
  in Missouri, 1276
  troubles, 1103–4
Astilbe (Spirea), greenhouse, 270
Atomic energy by-products, 202
Attic, vegetable growth, 754
Aubrieta, 156 ff., 163
Australian-silkoak (Grevillea), 984
Austrian Briar Rose, 514
Austrian peas, 60
Autumn (*see* Fall)

Avens (Geums), uses, 101 ff.
Avocado
  California growth, 1235
  indoors, 984
Azaleamums, 542 ff.
  in Alabama, 1222
  in Wisconsin, 1303
Azaleas, 376–82
  in foundation, 220, 221
  greenhouse, 263, 270
  indoors, 992–93
  regional
    Alabama, 1223
    California, 1235
    Illinois, 1255
    Missouri, 1276
    Nevada, 1281
    Utah, 1300
    Wisconsin, 1303
  troubles, 1104–6
  uses, 160 ff., 220 ff.

B₁, 78, 82, 348
Babiana, 448
Baby ramblers (*see* Polyantha roses)
Babysbreath (Gypsophila), 537–38
Baby Tears (Helxine soleiroli), 984
Bachelor-buttons (Cornflower), 609 –10
Backgrounds, garden, 102–3
Bacteria, soil, 4, 46, 75
Bacterial soft rot, on various plants, 1118 ff.
  (*see* individual plants for treatment)
Bacterized peat, 46
Badminton court, 123
Bagasse, 48
Bagworms, 1056
Baking powder, 83
Balloonflower, 221 ff.
Balm (Mellisa), 144
Balsam, 608
Bamboo, Mexican, 198
Bananas
  in California, 1235
  peels of, as compost, 62
Banks (*see* Slopes and Banks)
Barberries, 321–22
  hedges, 395–96

  other uses, 218 ff.
  Truehedge Columnberry, 322, 396
Bark
  peatmoss substitutes, 48
  repairing girdled tree, 291
Bark beetles, 1131
Bark-bound trees, 287
Bark grafting, 255, 851
Barnyard manure, 6–8, 49, 50
  (*see also* Horse Manure; Cow Manure; etc.)
Barrels
  strawberry-growing, 884–85
  vegetable storage, 746, 749
Basal rot in bulbs, 423
  (*see also* individual plants)
Basements (*see* Cellars)
Basic slag, 45
Basil, 144
Basket-of-Gold (*see Alyssum saxatile*)
Baskets
  hanging, 190
  to protect roses, 497
Bat manure (Guano), 55
Bayberries (Myrica), 322–23
  in Iowa, 1261
Bay trees, 387, 984–85
  Loblolly-, 306
  Sweet (Laurel), 397
  Sweet (Magnolia), 308, 309
Beans
  pests and diseases, 1179–83
  Scarlet Runner, 403
  seeds
    saving, 728
    sowing, 735
  storage, 749, 750
  supports, 743
  types
    Broad, 767
    bush, 735, 760–61
    lima, 743, 764–66
    Mung, 767–68
    pole, 743, 762
    shell, 762
    snap, 760–64
    soy, edible, 766–67
    string, 760–61
    yellow wax, 761

Bean sprouts, 767–68
Bearberry (Arctostaphylos), 323
Beautybush (Kolkwitzia), 323
Bedding plants, 103
Beebalm, uses, 137, 138, 230, 232
Beeches, Blue (Hornbeam), 294, 1303
Beetles, 1056, 1132
    Asiatic, 1055–56
    blister, 1058
    diabrotica, 1065
    flea, 1068
    ground, 1070
    Japanese, 1072–75
    June, 1099
    (*see* individual plants for other references)
Beets, 768–69
    pests and diseases, 1183–84
    in wet soil, 23
Beggarweed, alkaline soil, 33
Begonias, 963–67
    culture, 964–66
    greenhouse, 270
    potting, 964–66
    propagation, 966–67
    soil and fertilizer, 963–64
    Strawberry-, 991
    troubles, 968, 1106–7
    tuberous-rooted, 448–50
    varieties, 968
    Vigoro on, 940
Belamcanda chinensis, 416
Belgian blocks, 116
Bellflowers (*see Campanula*)
Bells of Ireland (Molucella), 594, 608
Beloperone guttata, 1000
Bent grasses, 656–61
    in Wisconsin, 1303
Benzene hexachloride (BHC), 1057
Benzoin (Spicebush), 323–24
    in Illinois, 1259
Berberis (Barberries), 321–22
    hedges, 395–96
    other uses, 218 ff.
Bergamot, uses, 137 ff.
Bermuda grass
    in Alabama, 1223
    eradicating
        in California, 1231–32

    in Kentucky, 1266
    in Oklahoma, 1289
    in Tennessee, 195
    in Texas, 1297
Bermuda onions, 799
Berries
    evergreens with, 348, 361
    shrubs with, 313–14, 315
        in Wisconsin, 1305
    (*see also* Raspberries; Strawberries; etc.)
BHC, 1057
Bichloride of mercury, 286, 1057
Biennials, 623–29
    (*see also* specific plants)
Bignonia (Trumpetvine), 1231
    eradicating, 200
    in Idaho, 1255
    pests in, 1175
Bindweed
    eradicating, 194–95
Biological pest control, 1057–58
Birch trees
    flowers under, 177
    in Illinois, 1259
    troubles, 1107
    types, 290–91
    in Washington, 1301
Bird baths, 115–16
Bird-of-Paradise flower, 980
    in California, 1235
    in greenhouse, 276
Birds
    gourds for houses, 191
    as pests, 604, 621, 1058
    plants to attract, 104
        shrubs, 314
        trees, 281
Bittersweet, 405–6
    evergreen, 408–9
    scale on, 1107
Blackalders (Winterberry), 346
Blackberries, 900–2
    in California, 1235
    eliminating, 26, 195
    in Florida, 1246
    pruning, 904
    rust on, 1210, 1255–56
Blackberry Lily, 416
Black Calla (Arum), 416, 1031
Blackeyedsusans, uses, 173 ff.

Blackgum (Nyssa sylvatica), 300
  in Michigan, 1269
Blackhaw, 173
Black Leaf 40, 1082–83
Black Rose, 514
Black snout beetles, 1136
Black Spot, on roses, 1161, 1162–63
Blackvine weevil, 388, 1106
Black walnut, 841, 925
Bleeding, tree wounds, 239, 285
Bleedingheart (Dicentra), 538
  in greenhouse, 273
  in Texas, 1295
  in Wyoming, 1306
Blister Beetles, 1058
Blocking plants in flats, 824
Blood, dried, 67
  rabbit repellent, 1087
  on vegetables, 719
Bloodlilies (Haemanthus), 472
  indoors, 1037
Bloodroot (Sanguinaria), 178–79
Blueberries, 324, 907–12
  borers in, 1210
  in California, 1236
  culture, 909–12
  in Illinois, 1256
  in Iowa, 1262
  soil and fertilizers, 907–9
Blue flags (see Iris)
Blue grasses, 633, 645
  in North, South Dakota, 1286
Bluets (Houstonia), 178
Bog
  gardens, 174–75
  material, use, 46
  (see also Wet Soil)
Boltonia, uses, 220, 232
Bone meal, 5, 66–67
  with coal ashes, 31
  for root crops, 77
Boneset (see Eupatorium)
Borage, 144
Borax, use, 45
Bordeaux mixture, 1058–59
  (see individual plants for use)
Borders, 99–100, 104–5
  fertilizer, 78
  greenhouse plants, 262
  herbaceous, 138

perennial, 526–27
  culture, 531
  labels, 135
  mulching, 234–35
  remaking, 530–31
  soil, 528–29
  spray schedule, 1095
  shady, 230
  shrubs for, 314
  terrace border, 132–33
  for vegetable garden, 392
  vegetables in flower border, 709
Borers, 1059
  (see individual plants for treatment)
Boron, 45
Bostonfern, 1008–9
Boston-ivy (Parthenocissus), 1011
Botrytis blight, 434, 444, 1134 ff.
  (see individual plants for treatment)
Bottom heat
  in greenhouse, 264
  for vegetable seedlings, 730
Bougainvillea
  cuttings, 950
  greenhouse, 270
Bouvardia, 270
Bovung, 45, 50, 54
Bowiea (Schizobasopsis), 1022
Bowling green, 123
Box-elder bug, 1059–60
Box elders, 295
  grass under, 653
  leaves, use, 319
Boxes (see Window boxes; Flats; Roof Garden)
Boxwood, 368–69
  in California, 1236
  hedge, 396
  in Nebraska, 1280
  in Tennessee, 1293
  troubles, 369, 1107–8
Boxwood leaf miner, 369
Boysenberries, 902
  in California, 1236
  in Colorado, 1244
  mildew on, 1218
Bramble fruits, 897–907
  (see also specific fruits)
Breadfruit, Mexican, 274

Bricks
for edging, 116
for paths, 127–28
Bridalwreath (Spirea), 342
Bridge grafting, 255
Briquette ashes, 31
Broad beans, 767
(*see also* Beans)
Broadiaeas, 416
Broad-leaved evergreens, 367–75
Broccoli, 769–70
pests, 1184
Bromeliads, 1022–23
Broom
Cytisus, 324
Genista, 273, 996
Brooms, witches'-, 1098–99
Browallia, 608
indoors, 981
smut on, 1108
Brown rot, 1213
Brunsvigia, 1031
Brush, eradicating, 201–2
Brussels sprouts, 770–71
freezing, 755
pests, 1184
Bryophyllum (Air-plant), 1023
(*see also* Kalanchoe)
Buckeye (Horsechestnut), 294
Buckthorn, uses, 314, 392
Buckwheat, 57, 58
Budding, 851, 852
(*see also* specific plants)
Buddleia (Butterflybush), 324–25
in greenhouse, 270
in Tennessee, 1293
Bug, defined, 1060
Bugbane, uses, 221, 230
Bugle-weed (Ajuga), 223 ff., 523 ff.
Bulb flies, treatment, 423
Bulbs, Corms, Tubers, 411–475
city garden, 217–18
cold frame, 257–58
fragrant, 185
greenhouse, 270–71, 263
ground covers for, 223–24
hardy, 411–46, 1025–28
culture, 413–14
pests, 415
planting, 412-13
soil and fertilizer, 412
winter protection, 415
house plants, 1025–41
hardy, 1025–28
tender, 1028–41
manure on single, 50–51
propagation, 243–44
regional
Alabama, 1222
Michigan, 1268–69
Minnesota, 1271
Texas, 1294
rock garden, 161–62
soil conditioning, 18
tender, 446–74, 1028–41
troubles, 415, 1108
(*see also* individual plants)
Bunchberry (Cornus canadensis), 176
Burlap, on new trees, 284
Burned lime, 38
Burned trees, saving, 363
Burning
garden in fall, 27
lawn, 665
tomato vines, 17
weeds, 27, 193
(*see also* various plants as disease preventive)
Burning Bush
Euonymus, 340, 343–44
Kochia, 611
Burning out of manure, 49, 55
Bushes (*see* Shrubs; Hedges)
Bush fruits (*see* specific fruits)
Buttercup (*see Ranunculus*)
Butterflybush (Buddleia), 324–25
in greenhouse, 270
in Tennessee, 1293
Butterflyweed (Asclepias), 179
Butternut, 922
Buttonball (Plane tree), 300–1
fungus disease, 1173
killing, 287, 288–89
Buttonbush, wet soil, 282
Buttonwood (*see* Plane Tree)
Buxus (*see* Boxwood)

Cabbage, 771–73
pests and diseases, 771–72, 1184–87
storage, 746, 748

Cabbage Rose, 514–15
Cabins, planting around, 111
Cacti
  indoors, 1016–25
    culture, 1017–18
    pests and diseases, 1108–9
    potting, 1017
    soil and fertilizer, 1016
    specific, 1018–25
  outdoors, 190–91
Caladiums, 450
  in Florida, 1246
  in Georgia, 1250
  indoors, 1031–32, 1109
Calceolarias, 608, 969
  in greenhouse, 271
Calcium, 6, 10, 19
  (*see also* Lime)
Calcium carbonate (*see* Limestone)
Calcium cyanamide, 64
Calcium nitrate, 34
Calcium oxide, 38
Calcium sulfate (Gypsum), 10, 24, 39
Calendar of lawn operations, 639–40
Calendula
  bugs on, 1109
  in greenhouse, 271
  officinalis, 149
California, 1227–44
  Asiatic beetle, 1056
  lath house, 1234–44
  mildew in, 1120
  pest information, 1071
  planning and environment, 1229–31
  plants, 1234–44
    annuals, 598
    apricot, 864
    azalea, 380, 1235
    cabbage, 771
    celery, 777–78
    crapemyrtle, 327
    hedges, 1232–33
    lawns, 1231–32
    peaches, 868
    potatoes, 809, 810
    rhododendrons, 1160–61
    rhubarb, 815
    roses, 1164, 1165

    shrubs, 1233
    stocks, 1172
    sweetwilliams, 1173
    trees, 1233–34
  soil and fertilizer, 1227–29
  12-spotted beetle, 1065
Calla
  Black, 416, 1031
  California problems, 1236
  Callalily, 1032–33, 1110
    in Louisiana, 1267
  troubles, 1110
Calliopsis (*see Coreopsis*)
Calluna, 382
Calochortus, 416
Caltha (Marshmarigold), 181
Calycanthus (Sweetshrub), 343
Camassia, 416–17
Camellias, 387–90
  indoors, 1000–1
  in North, South Carolina, 1284
  pests and diseases, 388–89, 389–90, 1110
Camomile for lawn, 646
Campanulas
  Canterburybells, 609, 625
    in Minnesota, 1272
    in Tennessee, 1293
    in Wisconsin, 1303
    troubles, 1110–11
  isophylla, 969
  for rock garden, 157 ff., 161
Camphor tree (Cinnamomum), 985
Canada, nut trees in, 923
Canada thistle, 196
Candytuft (Iberis), 538, 1110
  annual, 609
Cane fruits, 897–907
  (*see also* specific fruits)
Canker, 1107–8, 1164–65
Cankerworms, Fall, 1068
Canna, 450–51
Canned goods, storage, 750
Canned plants, 134–35
Cannel-coal ashes, 31
Cantaloupes (Muskmelons), 795–97
  pests and diseases, 796, 1192, 1193
Canterbury Bells, 609, 625, 1110–11
  in Minnesota, 1272

Canterbury bells (*cont.*)
  in Tennessee, 1293
  in Wisconsin, 1303
Cape bulbs, 475
Cape Cod house, plantings, 109
Capecowslips, 473
Capejasmine (Gardenia florida),
    390, 1003–5
  sooty mold, 1250–51
  in Tennessee, 1294
Captan, 1060
Caragana (Peashrub), 397
Caraway, 144–45
Carbon dioxide, and decomposition,
    2
Cardinal-climber, shade, 402
Cardinalflower (Lobelia), 176, 179
Carnations (Clove Pinks), 538–40
  greenhouse, 271–72
  troubles, 1111
Carrots, 773–75
  pests and diseases, 774–75, 1187
    –88
  seed sowing, 735
  weeds in, 193
  wild, 200
Cars
  driveways, parking spaces, 118–
    20
  exhaust gas damage by, 353
Caryopteris, 325
Castilleja Collina, 1226
Cast-iron plant (Aspidistra), 984,
    1103
Castor Bean, 609
  and Asiatic beetle, 1056
  saps soil, 83
Castor oil on plants, 83
Catalpa, 291–92
Catch basin, 114–15
Caterpillars
  Florida fern, 1130
  tent-, 1097
  woolly bear, 1153
Cats, 1060
  manure, 51
Cattails, eradicating, 196
Cattle manure (*see* Cow manure)
Cauliflower, 775–76
  pests and diseases, 1188
Ceanothus, bloom-time, 314

Cedar
  Cedar-of-Lebanon, 357
  Japanese Temple-cedar, 357–58
  plants with hedge, 525, 529
  Red-, (*see* Redcedar)
  troubles, 1111
Celeriac, 779–80
Celery, 776–79
  pests and diseases, 778–79, 1188
  storage of, 747
Cellars
  storage,
    bulbs, 446
    fruit, 849, 850
    vegetables, 747
  vegetable-growing, 754
  winter, flowers in, 941
Celosia, uses, 103 ff.
Cemeteries, flowers for, 525
Centaurea
  Cornflower, 609–10
  Sweetsultan, 1249
Centipede grass, 1248, 1267
Centipedes, 1060–61
Cephalanthus, wet soil, 232, 233
Cerastium, uses, 156 ff., 226, 228
Ceratostigma
  plumbaginoides, 586
  with azaleas, 377
Cercis (Redbud), 310–11
Cereus, Night-blooming, 1016, 1018
    –19
Ceriman (Monstera deliciosa), 274,
    987
Chaenomeles (Flowering Quince),
    340, 920
Chafers, Rose, 1167, 1168
Chamaecereus, 1018
Chamaecyparis, 347
Charcoal, 70
Chastetree (Vitex), 325
  in Iowa, 1263–64
Chayotes, 780
Cheiranthus (Wallflowers), 629
  in California, 1243
Chemical fertilizer, 72
  (*see also* Fertilizer)
Chemical gardening, 84–85
Chemicals
  and flower color, 202
  root stimulants, 247–48

Chemicals (*cont.*)
  for seeds, 733
  soil sterilization, 80–81
  (*see also* Pesticides)
Chemotherapy, 1052, 1096–97
Cherimoyas, 1243
Cherry trees, 864–67
  Cornelian- (Dogwood), 328
  flowering, 302
  Japanese, 1142
  pests and diseases, 867, 1210–11
  pruning, 865–67
  regional
    Illinois, 1256
    Kansas, 1264
    Missouri, 1276
  soils, 864–65
  wild, 288
Cherry-Plum Tree, in Minnesota, 1272
Chervil, 145
Chestnut trees, 921–23
  horsechestnut, 294
Chicken litter, use, 48
Chicken manure, 49, 51–53, 237
  on compost heap, 64
  in sand, 12
  for vegetables, 25
  with wood ashes, 69
Chicken yard, screening, 111
Chickweed, 197
Chicory (Witloof; French Endive), 749, 780–81
Children
  garden for, 184
  play equipment, 123
Chimaphilas, 183
Chimney, vines for, 400
Chinch bugs, 1061
Chinese cabbage, 781–82
Chinese Elm, 292–93
  for hedge, 396
Chinese-evergreen, 985
Chinese Jujube (Chinese Date), 917
Chineselantern, troubles, 1112
Chinese Sacred Lily, 1039
Chinese Scholar-tree, 300
Chionanthus (Fringetree), 279, 306
Chionodoxa (Glory-of-the-snow), 417
  for rock garden, 161

Chipmunks, 1096
Chives, 145, 782
  indoors, 957
Chlordane
  in soil, 1053
  for wireworms, 13
Chloride, potassium, 6, 51
Chlorine, 4, 45
Chlorophyll, 4
Chlorophytum (Spider-plant), 991
Chloropicrin, 80–81, 1061
Chlorotic (yellow) plants, 37, 38, 43
Chokeberries, uses, 220 ff., 313, 314
Christmas
  holly, 371–72
  trees, 348, 358–59
    poison from, 366
Christmas cactus (Zygocactus), 1019 –21
Christmasrose (Hellebore), 540–41
  in cold frame, 257
Chrysothamnus (Rabbitbrush), 226
Chrysanthemums, 541–53
  culture, 545–48
  fertilizer, 542–43
  indoors, 993–94
  in greenhouse, 272–73
  planting, 543
  problems, 548–49
  propagation, 549–51
  regional
    Arizona, 1226
    California, 1236
    Illinois, 1256
    Iowa, 1262
    Louisiana, 1266–67
    Michigan, 1268
    Mississippi, 1274
    Missouri, 1276
    Wisconsin, 1303
  soil preparation, 542
  transplanting, 543–44
  troubles, 551, 1112–15
  varieties, 551–53
  winter, 544–45
Cimicifuga, uses, 112, 527
Cinders
  cinder soil, 21
  in cold frame, 256–57
  hard-coal, 30

Cinders (*cont.*)
soil improvement, 25, 26, 29, 55
weeds in cinder drive, 194
Cineraria, 969–70
greenhouse, 273
Cinnamomum camphora, 985
Cinnamon for potpourri, 152
Cinquefoils (Potentilla), 163
Cissus antarctica, 1013
Cissus rhombifolia, 1013, 1142
Citrus fruits
in California, 1236–37
in Florida, 1246
indoors, 1001–2
in Texas, 1295
troubles, 1115
City conditions, 184–85, 216–19
cane fruits for, 898
compost heap, 65
hotbed heating, 260
house plants, 952
lawn for, 655–56
in Missouri, 1276–77
organics, nitrogen for, 59
town-house garden, 99
vegetables for, 709
on roof, 754–55
storage, 749
vines, 400
Cladrastis lutea, 312
Clary, 145
Clay soil, 2, 3, 11, 14–17
grass for, 646
improving, 19, 35, 39
vegetables for, 703, 704, 715–16
Clay tennis court, 123–24
Claytonia, 183
Cleaning fluid on weeds, 194
Cleaning tools, 134
Cleft grafting, 255, 851
Clematis, 94–95, 406–8
in Michigan, 1270
troubles, 1115–16
Cleome, 609
Clethra (Sweetpepperbush)
with azalea, 377
uses, 218 ff.
Click beetle, 1099–1100
Climbers (*see* Vines)
Climbingfern, 180
Climbing roses, 515–16

age of, to buy, 478
in greenhouse, 275
problems, 490–91, 1163–64 ff.
pruning, 504–6
ramblers, 505–6
regional
Arizona, 1227
Georgia, 1253
Michigan, 1271
Minnesota, 1274
North, South Dakota, 1287
Utah, 1300
Wyoming, 1306
soil, 481
supports, 492–93
winter protection, 500–1
Clinkers, 30
Clivia, 451
indoors, 1033
Clove Pinks (Carnations) 538–40
greenhouse, 271–72
troubles, 1111
Clover
green manure, 57 ff., 726
lawn, 647–48
weed, 200
Cloves, in potpourri, 152
Club mosses, 176, 181
Clubroot, 1187
Coal ashes, 30–31
on clay, 14 ff.
manure with, 55
for mites, 1124
Coal gas
in greenhouse, 266
and houseplants, 945–46
Coal oil, seeds in, 735
Cobaea scandens, 403
Cockspurthorn, 307
Coco-grass, 1227
eradicating, 1296–97
Codiaeum (Croton), 985
Codling moth, 1057–58
Cod-liver oil, 83–84
Coffee grounds, 62, 71, 235
Coke ashes, 31, 70
Colchicine, 82
Colchicums, 417
Cold frame, 256–58
hardening off plants, 216
herbs in, 141

Cold frame (*cont.*)
  vegetables in, 754
  wildflowers in, 173
Coleus, 985
  cuttings, 605
  troubles, 1116
Collards
  freezing, 755
  pests, 1189
Colocasia, 451
Colonial style
  doorways, 117
  house, 109
  patio with, 129
Color
  drainage and plants, 37
  of flowers,
    changing, 202, 495–96
    rock garden, 157–58
    producing new, 536, 550
  and furniture-painting, 122
  and garden plan, 105–6, 107
  nitrogen deficiency and plants, 43
  overliming and plants, 38
  phosphorous, potash and, 44
  of shrubs, 93, 313–14, 315
  in soil, 23–24, 45
  of trees, 280, 283
Colorado, 1244–55
  soil, 1225
Columbines (Aquilegia), 553, 1116–
  17
  in Florida, 1247
  in Texas, 1295
Commercial fertilizers, 8–10, 75–80
Commercial herb-growing, 142–43,
  146
Complete Commercial Fertilizer, 75
  –80
Compost, 7–8, 60–66
  with chicken manure, 52
  garbage, 62
  grass clippings, 62–63
  heaps, 55, 61–62
  hickory hulls, 63
  on lawns, 664, 676
  leaves, 63–64
  manure, 64
  mushroom compost, 64
  pests in, 65–66, 1061
  problems, 64–65

Concrete
  driveway material, 118
  lawn edging, 672
  pool, 130
  terrace, 132
  window boxes, 189
Coneflower, bloom-time, 527
Conifers, defined, 347
Connecticut, plants in
  acacias, 387
  benzoin, 323–24
  corn, 785
  delphinium, 559
  fruit trees, 854
  gardenias, 1004
  grass, 651
Constant mist, 246
Contact insecticides, 1062
Convallaria, 417–18
  in California, 1240
  indoors, 1026
  in Oregon, 1292
Cooking
  herbs for, 138, 143 ff.
  Jerusalem artichokes, 757
  kale, 791
  salsify, 815
  soybeans, 767
Cooperia (Rainlilies), 1274–75
Cooperas (*see* Iron sulfate)
Copper sprays, 1059
Copper sulfate
  on decayed tree, 286
  kills tree root, 287
Coralberry, in Kansas, 1264
Coreopsis, uses, 101 ff., 216 ff.
Coriander, 145
Cork tree (Phellodendron), 293
Corms (*see* Bulbs, Corms, Tubers)
Corn, 782–85
  crop rotation, 705
  fodder as mulch, 54
  harvesting, 746
  pests and diseases, 784, 1189–90
  with pumpkins, 813
  stalks, use, 61, 260
Cornelian-cherry, 328
Cornflower (Centaurea), 609–10
Cornus
  canadensis, 176

Cornus (*cont.*)
  mas, 328
  (*see also* Dogwood)
Corrosive sublimate (mercuric chloride), 286, 1057
Corsages, flowers for, 262
Corydalis, uses, 158, 159, 173
Corylus (Hazelnut), 923
  in Indiana, 1260
  ornamental, 329
Cosmos, 610
  pinching, 597
  troubles, 1117
Costmary, 145
Cotinus, 311–12
Cotoneaster, 326
  in California, 1237–38
  fall color, 315
Cottonseed meal, 67, 77
  on hotbed, 260
  on shrubs, 376
  on vegetables, 720
Cover crops, 16, 57
  for lawns, 673
  for orchards, 844
  (*see also* Green manures)
Cow manure, 49, 53–54
  dried, 45, 50, 54–55
  and sheep manure, 56
  substitutes, 57
Cowpeas, 57
Cows, on lawn, 668
Cowslips, 587
  Capecowslip, 473
Crabapples, 279, 302–3
  pruning, 857
  troubles, 1117–18
Crabgrass, 35, 638–39
Crab meal, 70
Cranberries, 912–13
Cranberry bush, 344
Crankcase drainings, use, 194
Crapemyrtle, 326–27, 1117
  indoors, 1003
  in Illinois, 1256
  in Louisiana, 1267
  mildew on, 1222
Crassulas (Jade-plants), 1023–24
Crataegus (Hawthorn), 306–7
  for city, 218
  Cockspurthorn, 307

  and hogs, 281
  killing, 202
  Maytree, 307
  troubles, 1135
  Washington thorn, 307
Crawfish, eradicating, 1062
Creeping Bluet, 178
Creeping Fig, 402, 1011–12
Creeping Jenny, 179
  eradicating, 196
Creeping-nettle (Helxine), 984
Creosote-treated posts, 754
Cress, 152
Crickets, 796
Crimson clover, 57, 60
Crinum, 451–52
  indoors, 1034
Crocosmia, 475
Crocus, 418
  in Michigan, 1268–69
  rock garden types, 161
  squirrels and, 1118
Croquet lawn, 123
Crossing flowers, 513, 536
Crotalaria, 57
Croton (Codiaeum), 985
Crown gall, 1062
Crown imperial, 426
Crown-of-thorns, 1024
Crown rot, 1062
  (*see also* individual plants)
Crow repellent, 1058
Cryolite, 1063
Cryptanthus, 986
Cryptomeria, 357–58
Cucumber beetles, 1065, 1112
Cucumbers, 785–87
  pests and diseases, 1190–92
Cucumbertree, 308
Cultivation, 27–29, 233–34
  benefits, 211–12
  of evergreens, 352
  ornamentals, 233–34
  trees, 285–86
  vegetables, 739–41
  for weeds, 193 ff., 212
Cultivators, 28–29
Culture
  annuals, 596–98
  bulbs
    hardy, 413–15

Culture (*cont.*)
  tender, 446–47
  evergreens, 349–56
  gourds, 191–92
  greenhouse, 264–66
  herbs, 141
  ornamentals, 233–42
  perennials, 531–32
  rock garden, 156–57
  shrubs, 315–21, 376
  soilless, 84–85
  trees, 282–89, 349–56
  (*see also* Lawns; various gardens;
    individual plants; etc.)
Cup-and-saucer, 625
Cup-and-saucer vine, 403
Curbings (*see* Edgings)
Curing
  gourds, 191
  herbs, 141–42
Curly top, 1184
Currants, 913–16
  in Minnesota, 1272
  pests and diseases, 916, 1211–12
Cutting flowers, 106–7
  in border, 104–5
  roses, 493–94
Cuttings, 209–10, 244–50
  annuals, 605
  in cold frame, 257
  evergreens, 356
  hormones on, 83
  house plants, 949, 950–51
  leaf, 250
  perennials, 535
  root, 249–50
  shrubs, 289, 319–20
Cutworms, 1062–63
  and coal ashes, 31
Cycas revoluta, 990–91
Cyclamen, 994–96
  pests and diseases, 995, 1118–19
Cydonia (Quince), 340, 920
  spraying, 1218
Cymbalaria (Kenilworth-Ivy), 1013
Cyperus alternifolius, 992
Cypress
  in California, 1238
  False-, 347
  for hedge, 393, 396
Cypripediums, 181–82

Cytisus (Broom), 324
  racemosus, 273, 996

Daffodils (Narcissi), 418–25
  culture, 421–23
  indoors, 1026–27, 1028, 1038–39
  planting, 420–21
  propagation, 423
  regional
    Georgia, 1251
    Michigan, 1269
    North, South Dakota, 1286
    Oregon, 1290–91
  soil and fertilizer, 419–20
  troubles, 423, 1150–51
  varieties, 424–25
Dahlias, 452–64, 610
  culture, 455–56
  planting, 453–55
  problems, 457–59, 462–63, 1119–
    22
  propagation, 459–62
  regional
    Florida, 1247
    Georgia, 1251
    Tennessee, 1294
    Texas, 1295
    Washington, 1301
  storage, 456–57
  varieties, 463–64
Daisies
  African,
    Arctotis, 606
    Dimorphotheca, 610, 1247
  in Idaho, 1254
  Michaelmas-, 537
  Northland-, 544, 547, 553
  Shasta-, 588
    in Missouri, 1277
    in Texas, 1295
Damask Rose, 516
Damping off, 264, 1063–64
Dampness, in walls from plantings,
  221
  (*see also* Moisture; Wet Soil)
Dandelions, 787
  eradicating, 196–97, 637–38
  seed sowing, 735
Daphne, 327, 370
  chlorosis, 1122
  for doorway, 368

Daphne (*cont.*)
  in Oklahoma, 1288
  in Wisconsin, 1303
Dasheens, 787–88
Dauben Nymphaea, 171–72
Daylily (Hemerocallis), 553–55
  in Alabama, 1222
  perennials with, 524
DDD (TDE), 1097
DDT, 1064
  pets' resistance to, 1075–76
Decay, treating tree for, 287
Deciduous plants, 202
  shrubs, 312–47
  trees, 279–312
  (*see also* individual trees, shrubs)
Deer repellent, 1204
Delaware, plants
  Creeping Fig, 402
  gerberia, 563
Delphinium, 555–61
  culture, 557–58
  pests and diseases, 560–61, 1122–
    25
  planting, 557
  propagation, 559–60
  regional
    Arkansas, 1227
    Indiana, 1260
    Missouri, 1277
    Oklahoma, 1288
  soil and fertilizer, 556–57
  types and varieties, 561
Dendrobium nobile, 275
Depleted soil, 18, 75
Derris, 1065
Deutzia, 327
Devilgrass (*see* Bermuda grass)
Dewberries, 902–3
  trellis for, 899
Dewdrop grass (Dichondra), 646,
    1231
  in Illinois, 1256
Diabrotica (Cucumber) beetles,
    1065, 1112
Diammonium phosphate, 34
Dianthus (Pinks), 538–40
  annual, 610
  barbatus, 628–29, 1173
  Carnations, 271–72, 538–40,
    1111

rock garden types, 156 ff., 163
Dibber, 134
Dicentra
  Bleedingheart, 538
  in greenhouse, 273
  in Texas, 1295
  in Wyoming, 1306
  Dutchman's-breeches, 179–80
Dichondra repens, 646, 1231
  in Illinois, 1256
Dieffenbachia, 986
Dieldrin, 1053, 1085
Digging, 25–27
Digitalis (Foxglove), 146, 626
  in Florida, 1247
  in Illinois, 1256
  in Michigan, 1269
Dill, 145–46
Dimet, on chickweed, 197
Dimorphotheca, 610
  in Florida, 1247
Dinitro compounds, 1065
Diospyros virginiana, 919–20
Disbudding, 239–40
  chrysanthemums, 546, 547
  peonies, 577–78
  roses, 493
Diseases
  and compost heap, 65–66
  and pests, 1043–1220
  pruning for, 239
  (*see also* diseases by name; in-
    dividual plants)
Dish gardens, 955
Disking, 714
Dithiocarbamic acid derivatives,
    1065
Dittany of Crete, 146
Division
  perennials, 535–56
  shrubs, 321
  (*see also* specific plants)
Dock, 197
Dockmackie, 344
Doctrine of Signatures, 142
Dodder, 197
Dodecatheon (Shootingstar), 183,
    412
Dogs
  manure, 51

Dogs (*cont.*)
  as pests, 219, 361, 1065
  repellents, 1127, 28
Dogtooth-violets, 425
Dogwood (Cornus), 303–5, 327–28
  in Iowa, 1262
  lime on, 40
  in Minnesota, 1272
  redbud with, 310
  shrubs, 327–28
  in Texas, 1295
  trees, 303–5
  troubles, 1125–26
Dolichos, 403
Dolomite, 45
Doorways, 117–18
  evergreens by, 348, 368
  plantings, 107–8
  vines for, 402
Dormancy
  dormant sprays, 1065–66, 1084–
    85, 1203
  gibberellic acid and, 82
  killing weeds in, 201–2
  and pruning, 214, 238, 318
  resting plants
    bulbs, 446
    greenhouse, 268
    house, 937
  transplanting during, 210
Doronicum, uses, 105 ff.
Douglasfir, 357, 358
Douglasia, uses, 156, 161
Downspouts (*see* Rainspouts)
Drabas, in rock garden, 158, 159
Dracaena, uses, 944, 952
Drainage, 29–30
  house plants, 934, 939
  lawns, 634, 644
    grading for, 126
  mossy soil, 23–24
  rock garden, 154
  sour soil, 35
  surface, 114–15
  vegetable garden, 693
  wet soil, 22–23
  window boxes, 89
Drains
  elms near, 292
  weeds in, 194
Dried blood, 67

rabbit repellent, 1087
  on vegetables, 719
Drill, defined, 734
Driveway, 118–20
  drainage, 114–15
  edging, 116
  gate, 125
  killing weeds in, 194
Droppings (*see* Manure)
Drying herbs, 141–42
Drying yard, 120
Dry wall, 136
  wall garden in, 167–68
Dry well, 114
Dumb cane, 986
Dust
  leather, 71
  as mulch, 234, 744
  stone, 72–73
  tobacco, 268
Duster, 1066
Dusting, 1066–67
Dutch elm disease, 91, 115, 1127
Dutch hoe (*see* Scuffle hoe)
Dutchman's Pipe, 408
Dutchman's-breeches (Dicentra),
    179–80
Dwarf plants
  evergreens, 348–49, 350
  flowers, 106
  fruit trees, 876
  gibberellic acid and, 82
  grafting to, 254
  house plants, 953
  how to make, 241
  shrubs, 313

Earthworms, 20, 65, 1067
  in pots, 1067, 1139
Earwigs, 1067
Echeverias, 1024
Echinops, uses, 226, 525
Edelweiss, 164
Edema of peonies, 1155
Edgings
  curbings, 116–17, 212
  plants, 526
    for flower bed, 103–4, 104–5,
      107
    for lawns, 672

Edgings, plants (*cont.*)
for sandy soil, 226
for sun, 231
Eel worms, 423, 1083
Eggplants, 788–89
wilt, 1192
Eggshells, 71
Eichornia, 170
Elaeagnus (Russian olive), 342
Elderberries, 916–17
eradicating, 288
Elder, Box, 295
grass under, 653
leaves, use, 319
Electric heating, 259, 260
Elecric light bulbs, 259, 260
for house plants, 216, 946
Elements, minor, 6, 45
Elephantsear (Colocasia), 451
Elevation and fruit, 837
Elm-leaf beetle, 1126
Elm trees
American, 293
Chinese, 280, 292–93
hedge, 396
close to house, 279
ground covers under, 224–25
killing roots, 287–88
leaves as compost, 63
regional
California, 1233
Nebraska, 1280
Siberian, 399
substitutes for, 115
Emseco, 77
Endive, 789
French, 749, 780–81
English Ivy (Hedra helix)
from cuttings, 225
ground covers, 223
indoors, 1012–13
troubles, 1142
uses, 224 ff.
English style
garden, 185
house, 110
English walnuts, 926–27
diseases, 1176
Enkianthus, 328
Environment of plants, 207–9

Epigaea repens (Trailing Arbutus), 178
Epimediums, uses, 158, 159, 228
Epiphyllum (Orchid cactus), 1021
Epsom salts, 55
Equipment
children's game, 123
game, storage, 124
gardening, 133–35
greenhouse, 261
vegetable gardening, 751–54
(*see also* Tools; Accessories)
Eranthis (Winter-Aconites), 425
Eremurus Foxtail-Lilies), 425, 561–62
Erica, greenhouse, 262, 263
Ericaceous shrubs, 375–87
Erosion prevention, 17–18
drain for, 114
in driveway, 118
grass for, 650
planting for, 227–28
in pool, 166
in rock garden, 156
terraces for, 18, 19
Eryngium, uses, 104, 226
Erythronium (Dogtooth-violet), 425
Espaliered plants
shrubs, 318
trees, 342, 875–76
in Illinois, 1259
Eucalyptus trees, California
hedges, 1232–33
soil, plants under, 1228–29, 1230
Eucharis (Amazon-Lily), 464
greenhouse, 273
Euonymus, 293, 328
americanus, 340, 343–44
coloratus, 223
fortunei, 408–9
Japanese, 370–71
troubles, 1129
Eupatorium (Hardy Ageratum), 562
Euphorbia (Spurge), 224, 588, 1024
European pine-shoot moth, 1157–58
Evaporation (*see* Moisture)
Evergreens
with abelias, 321
for birds, 104

Evergreens (*cont.*)
boughs as mulch, 147 ff., 157 ff.
broadleaved, 367–75
city, 217
foundation material, 219–20, 223, 221–22
hedges, 102, 391 ff.
and landscape plan, 92–93
regional
California, 1233, 1236
Indiana, 1261
Louisiana, 1267
Nebraska, 1280
North Carolina, 1284
Oregon, 1291
rock garden, 162
for seashore, 227
for shade, 221–22
shrubs under, 231
trees, 347–67, 399–400
care, 352–54
culture, 349–56
fertilizer, 350
low-growing, 348–49
pruning, 354
soil, 349–50
transplanting, 350–52
winter, 354–55
troubles, 1127–29 ff.
by water garden, 169
windbreaks, 399–400
window box, 190
Everlasting annuals, 610
Everlasting peas, 583
Exhibition
chrysanthemums for, 545
fruit for, 850
irises for, 568
roses for, 494
vegetables for, 750–51
Eyesight, and Vitamin A and vegetables, 756

Fairy (Miniature) Rose, 519
indoors, 999, 1000
in greenhouse, 276
Fall
annuals, planting, 604
bulb planting, 412, 413
color

shrubs, 93, 122, 315
trees, 280
evergreens, transplanting, 351
fertilizing, 50 ff., 78–79
herb planting, 143 ff.
house plants, care, 936, 943–44
lawn care, 640, 649
rock garden planting, 156
shrubs
color, 93, 122, 315
planting, 316–17
pruning, 317 ff.
trees
color, 280
planting, 283, 284–85
vegetable garden care, 723
work, 26 ff.
Fall Cankerworm, 1068
Fallowing, 29, 34
Fall Webworm, 1068
False-Cypress, 347
Farfugium (Leopard-plant), 986
in greenhouse, 274
Farmhouses, 110
foundation plantings, 220, 349
house plants in, 942
Farm manures (*see* Horse manure; Cow manure; Chicken manure; etc.)
Fatsia japonica (Aralia), 983
Feeding stations, 1096
Fences, 120–22
field-stone walls as, 136
gates in, 124
plants on, 525, 704
for vegetable garden, 693–94
vegetables on, 704
vines on, 218, 402, 704
weeds by, 193
Fennel, 146, 789
Ferbam, 1068
Ferns, 180
greenhouse, 273
house plants, 1006–9
culture, 1007–8
planting, 1006–7
propagation, 1010
soil and fertilizer, 1006
in Missouri, 1277
troubles, 1010, 1129–30
under trees, 176–177

Ferrous sulfate (*see* Iron sulfate)
Fertilizer, 1–86
  clay soil, 14–17
  commercial, 8–10, 75–80
  compost, 60–66
  on evergreens, 350
  on gourds, 191
  herbs and, 141
  on house plants, 933, 939–40
  inorganic, 72–74
  on lawns, 664–65, 674–76
  manure, 6–8, 48–60
    green, 57–60
  organic, 66–72
  radioactive, 203
  sandy soil, 12–13
  on shrubs, 315–16
    ericaceous, 375
  on trees, 285
    fruit trees, 841
  on vegetables, 718–24
Fescue grass, 228, 633, 646
Ficus (Fig), 917–18, 1238
  elastica, 950–51, 990
  in Indiana, 1260
  lyrata, 990
  pumila, 1011–12
Field-stone, 131, 136
Figs, 917–18, 1238
  Creeping, 1011–12
  in Indiana, 1260
Filberts (Hazelnuts), 923
  in Indiana, 1260
  ornamental, 329
Filings, iron, steel, 45
Fill, over tree roots, 286
Finocchio (Fennel), 146, 789
Fire blight (*see* Botrytis blight)
Firecracker plant (Brodiaea), 416
Firethorn (Pyracantha), 374–75
  hedge, 393
  pruning, 1241
  troubles, 1159–60
Fir trees, 357–58
  shaded soil, use, 25
  troubles, 1130–31
  as windbreaks, 399
Fish
  pond for, 169
  in pool in winter, 131

  trimmings, use, 71
Fixative, 153
Flags (*see* Iris)
Flagstone
  paths, 127, 128
  plantings with, 165–66, 166–67,
    526
  terrace, 132
Flame-of-the-woods, 1247
Flats, 599
  in cold frame, 258
  labels for, 135
  sour soil, counteracting, 35
  starting seeds in, 219, 728–32
  sterilizing, 81
  where to get, 753
Flax, seashore, 226
Flea bettles, 1068
Flies
  black, 1138, 1153
  white, 1101, 1117 ff.
  in greenhouse, 268
Floribunda Rose, 516
  pruning, 506
Floriculture, defined, 202
Florida
  flea beetles, 1068
  plants, 1245–50
    blueberries, 912
    delphiniums, 559
    peonies, 579, 1249
    roses, 1165, 1249
Flowering Maple (Abutilon), 268,
    958
Flowering plants
  foundation plantings, 112, 222
  ground covers, 223–24
  hedges, 391–92
  shrubs
    indoors, 1003–6
    for pool, 169
  regional
    California, 1232
    Georgia, 1253–54
    Indiana, 1261
    Texas, 1300
    Wisconsin, 1306
  (*see also* House plants; Ever-
    greens; etc.; specific plants)
Flowering Spurge, 588

Flowering Tobacco (Nicotiana), 612
annual, 603
Flower pots, 134
Flowers
backgrounds for, 102–3
beds, 103–4
for birds, 104
borders, 104–5
for city, 216–18
in cold frame, 257–58
color, 105–6
changing, 202
for cutting, 106–7
for edging, 107
foundation material, 220, 221
functions, 207
in greenhouse, 261 ff.
in hotbed, 259
landscape plan, 99–102
regional: (*see* individual states)
pinching, disbudding, 239–40
seashore, 226
shade, 112–13, 228–29, 229–30
soil, 19–20
clay, 16
sandy, 13, 225–26
soilless culture, 84
sun, 231
terrace, 132–33
troubles, 1100–1178
watering, 236
wet soil, 232, 233
(*see also* types of gardens; Perennials; Annuals; etc.; specific plants)
Fluoalminate, sodium, 1063
Fluorescent lights, 216
Foamflower, uses, 173, 175
Fog box, 246
Foliage
annual foliage plants, 595
in color scheme, 105
deficiencies and, 43, 44
distinctive trees, 280
house plants, 982–92, 1001–2
living plant arrangements, 956
pruning to stimulate, 214
shrubs for color, fragrance, 315
spraying in greenhouse, 264

Forget-me-nots (Myosotis)
greenhouse, 273
ground cover, 223
indoors, 981
in tulip bed, 224
wilt, 1150
Fork, spading, 752
Formaldehyde (Formalin), 81, 1068–69
Formal gardens, 97–98, 103
herb garden, 138
sunken garden, 188–89
topiary work, 135
Forsythia, 328–29
in Minnesota, 1272
produces stolons, 252
Fothergilla, fall color, 315
Foundation plantings, 107–15, 219–23
in California, 1233
crumbling plaster and, 40
evergreens, 349
in Illinois, 1256–57
in Texas, 1300
Fountains, 122
Four-o'clock, 611
Foxglove (Digitalis), 146, 626
in Florida, 1247
in Illinois, 1256
in Michigan, 1269
Foxtail-lilies, 425, 561–62
Fragaria chiloensis, 1230
Fragrance
annuals for, 594
garden, 185
geraniums for, 139
herbs for, 137, 138
potpourri, 152
shrubs for, 314, 315
Frames, propagating, 245, 248
(*see also* Cold Frame)
Franklinia, 306
Freesia, 464
indoors, 1034–35
in Kentucky, 1265–66
French Endive, 749, 780–81
French Roses, 516
French-style house, 110
Fringed Gentians, 37
Fringetree (Chionanthus), 279, 306

Fritillaries, 425–26
Frits, 6, 83
Froghoppers (Spittle bugs), 1093
Fruit, 833–927
  hormones on, 83
  orchard fruit, 840–75
    fertilizer and manure, 841–42
    fruiting, 847–49
    harvesting, 849
    mulch, 843–44
    planting, 842–43
    pollination, 847
    propagation, 850–52
    protection, 846
    pruning, 845–46
    soil, 840
    spraying, 843, 1202–4
    storing fruit, 849–50
    what to grow, 852–53
  pests and diseases, 837–38, 1202–20
  planting, 837
  rainfall, 835–36
  regional
    Florida, 1247–48
    Illinois, 1259
    Michigan, 1269
    Nevada, 1281
    New Mexico, 1282
    Oklahoma, 1289
    Texas, 1296
    Washington, 1301
    Wisconsin, 1304
  small, 835, 876–917
    cane, 897–907
  site, 837
  soil, 836–37
  temperature, 836
  transplanting to promote, 211
  trees, 840–75, 917–27
  weeds, 201
Fuchsias, 970–71
  in California, 1238
  hardy, 562–63
  in South, 1223
  troubles, 1131
Fuller's rose weevil, 1132, 1168
Fumigants, greenhouse, 268
Fungi, defined, 1069
Fungicides, 1051, 1069

(*see also* specific types)
Furniture
  garden, 122–23
  lawn, 89
  roof garden, 188
Furrow, defined, 734
Fusarium wilt (*see* specific plants for treatment)

Gaillardia
  annual, germinating temperature, 603
  grubs in, 1131
Galanthus, 426
Galax in rock garden, 160
Galinsoga, 197–98
Gall midge, 1113, 1115
Galls
  crown, 1062
  leaf, 1135
  rust, 1128
Galium aristatum, 538
Galtonia, 426
Game areas, 123–24
Garage as tool-house, 133
Garbage, use, 62, 71
Garden cress (Peppergrass), 152
Garden Features and Accessories, 115–133
Gardenia, 390
  florida, 390, 1003–5
  sooty mold, 1250–51
  in Tennessee, 1294
  in North Carolina, 1284
  In Texas, 1296
  troubles, 1005, 1131–32, 1250–51
Gardens
  design, 95–97
  formal, 97–98
  fragrant, 185
  herb, 137–43, 956–58
  informal, 97–98
  knot, 185–86
  and landscape plan, 88
  moraine, 165
  rock, 19, 153–69
  roof, 187–88
  sunken, 188–89
  and tree roots, 287

Gardens (*cont.*)
　wall, 167–69
　water, 169–72
　wildflower, 172–84
　window box, 189–90, 951–53
　(*see also* Flowers; Vegetables)
Garlic, 789–90
　wild, 200–1
Gas
　car exhaust, on evergreens, 353
　and house plants, 78, 933, 945–46
Gasterias, in dish garden, 955
Gates, 124–25
Gaultheria (Wintergreen), 183–84
Gelsemium sempervirens, 1234
Genista
　in greenhouse, 273
　indoors, 996
Gentians, 180
　andrewsi, 163
　fringed, 37
Georgia
　bagworms, 1056
　plants, 1249–54
　boxwood, 369–70
　cannas, 451
　fruit trees, 1222–23
　pecans, 924
　roses, 483, 1253
　snapdragons, 618
Geraniums (Pelargoniums), 971–77
　culture, 971–74
　fragrant, 139, 185
　in greenhouse, 274
　propagation, 605, 974–76
　Strawberry-, 991
　troubles, 976, 1074, 1132
　varieties, 185, 977
Gerberas, 563, 977
　in California, 1238–39
　in Georgia, 1251
　in greenhouse, 274
　in Louisiana, 1267
　in Ohio, 1287
Germander, uses, 138
German-ivy, 1013
Geums (Avens), uses, 101 ff.
Gibberellic acid, 82
Gift plants, 992–1001
Gilia, uses, 224, 604
Ginger, 146

Gingerlily, 472
Ginkgo, 293–94
Gladiolus, 464–72
　culture, 467–69
　pests and diseases, 471–72, 1132–
　　34
　planting, 466–67
　problems, 469–70
　propagation, 244, 470–71
　regional
　　Alabama, 1223
　　California, 1239
　　Georgia, 1251
　　Louisiana, 1267
　　Minnesota, 1272
　　Mississippi, 1275
　　Montana, 1279
　　Oklahoma, 1289
　　Texas, 1296
　soil and fertilizer, 465
Glass
　frits, 6, 83
　gardening under, 256–77
　　cold frame, 256–58
　　greenhouses, 261–77
　　hotbeds, 258–61
Globe artichoke, 756
Globeflower (*see* Trollius)
Gloriosa, 472
Glory-of-the-snow (Chionodoxa),
　417
　for rock garden, 161
Glory-of-the-sun, 473
Gloryvine, 402
Gloxinia, 1035–37, 1134
Goat manure, 55
Godetia, 611
Goldenbells (Forsythia), 328–29
　in Minnesota, 1272
　stolons of, 252
Goldenchain, 307
Goldrain tree, 306
Goldenrod, uses, 173 ff., 227
Golden tree, 307
Goldentuft (*see* Alyssum saxatile)
Goldfish in winter, 131
Gooseberries, 913–16
　pests and diseases, 916, 1211–12
Gophers, pocket, 1069–70
Gordonia, 306

Gourds, 191–92
  in Georgia, 1251
  troubles, 1134–35
Grading lawns to street, 126, 640–42
Grafting, 252–56
  chrysanthemum colors, 550
  fruit trees, 851, 852
Grandiflora Rose, 516
Granite
  paving blocks, 116, 118
  meal, fertilizer, 72
  soil, 19
Grapeferns, 173
Grapefruit tree, 1001–2, 1115
Grapehyacinth, 435
Grape-ivy, 1013
  leaf spot, 1142
Grapes, 886–97
  pests and diseases, 895–96, 1212
  problems, 894–95
  propagation, 1264
  pruning, 890–94
  regional
    California, 1239
    Illinois, 1257
    Kansas, 1264
    Minnesota, 1272
    Wisconsin, 1304
  varieties, 896–97
  wild, 201
  vine for terrace-roof, 401
Grass
  ashes of, 64
  cuttings, use, 62–63
  paths, 127
  regional
    Mississippi, 1275
    New Mexico, 1282
    North, South Carolina, 1284
  steps, 132
  under oak, 224
  (*see also* Lawns; specific grasses)
Grasshoppers, 1070
Gravel
  culture, 84
  paths, 128
  soil improvement, 12
Gray mold (*see* Botrytis blight)
Grease, soil-clogging, 83

Green beans (*see* Beans)
Greenhouses, 261–77
  general care, 264–66
  hardening off, 261
  labels, 135
  Polythene film on, 89
  repotting, 266–67
  rest, 268
  soilless culture, 84
  soil sterilization, 80
  temperatures, 263–64
  vegetables, 729
  ventilation, 267–68
  what to grow, 261–63
Green manures, 8, 57–60
  in city, 219
  on clay soil, 15, 16
  with dried manure, 55
    on poor soil, 22
  on vegetable garden, 725–27
  (*see also* Cover Crops)
Green Rose, 516–17
Grevillea robusta (Australian-silkoak), 984
Ground beetles, 1070
Ground covers, 223–25, 228–30
  berry-plant, 902
  in city, 217
  for clay soil, 19
  in Colorado, 1244
  evergreen, 92
  In Illinois, 1257
  sunny lawns, 646
  under trees, 109, 113
Ground rats (Pocket Gophers), 1069–70
Groundselbush, seashore, 227
Grubs, 1070
  lawn, 634–35, 1070, 1085
Grubworms, 1099
Guano, 55
Guava, 1239
Guineahen flower, 425–26
Gumbo soil, 18
Gum Storax in potpourri, 153
Gum Trees
  beetles in, 1135
  Sourgum (Blackgum, Tupelo, Pepperidge), 300, 1269
  Sweetgum, 295, 1259
Gynura aurantiaca, 992

Gypsophila (Babysbreath), 537–38
Gypsum, 10, 24, 39
Gypsy moth, 1082

Haberlea in shade, 167
Hackberries
  leaf galls, 1135
  witches'-brooms, 1098–99
Hackmatack (*see* Larch)
Haemanthus (Bloodlilies), 472
  indoors, 1037
Halesia (Silverbell), 311
Hamamelis (Witchhazel), 346–47
Hand cultivators, 28–29
Handling Soil, 25–31
Hardening off
  in greenhouse, 261
  vegetable plants, 737
Hardpan soil, 27
Hardy Bulbs, Corms, Tubers, 411–46, 1025–28
Hardy plants (*see* Perennials)
Harebells, under beeches, 177
Harlequin bug, 1070–71
Harrowing, 26, 27
Harvesting
  fruit, 849
  herbs, 141–42
  vegetables, 745–46
Hawkweed, for sun, 176
Hawthorns (Crataegus), 306–7
  for city, 218
  Cockspurthorn, 307
  and hogs, 281
  Maytree, 307
  troubles, 1135
  Wahington Thorn, 307
Hay
  alfalfa, 57
  with pig manure, 56
  salt, 157, 258, 319
Hazelnut, 923
  in Indiana, 1260
  ornamental, 329
Health and pesticides, 1083–86
Heartnut, 927
Heat
  bottom heat, 264, 730
  plants for
    California, 1230

  house plants, 944
Heather (Calluna), 382
Heating hotbed, 259, 260
Hedera (*see* Ivy)
Hedera helix (*see* English Ivy)
Hedges, 87, 92, 391–99
  background, types for, 102–3
  gate with clipped, 124–25
  herbs for low, 138
  for pool, 169
  pruning, 318
  regional
    California, 1232–33
    Idaho, 1254
    Minnesota, 1273
    Montana, 1279
  shade, plants for, 222–23
  shrubs, types, 94, 395–99
Hedychium, 472
Heeling in, 285
Helenium, troubles, 1135–36
Helianthemum, 165
Helianthus, for cutting, 107
Helichrysum, for winter bouquet, 610
Heliophilas, 1248
Heliopsis, 563
Heliotrope, 977
Hellebore (Christmasrose), 257, 540–41
Helxine soleiroli (Baby Tears), 984
Hemerocallis (Daylily), 553–55
  in Alabama, 1222
  perennials with, 524
Hemlock, 359–60
  fast growth, 348, 393
  flowers under, 177, 347
  hedge, 396
  troubles, 1136
Hen manure (*see* Chicken manure)
Hepatica, 180
Heptachlor in soil, 1053
Herbs, 137–52, 956–58
  Commercial growing, 142–43
  culture, 141
  harvesting, 141–42
  knot garden, 186
  planting, 140–41
  in potpourris, 152–53
  regional

Herbs, regional (*cont.*)
  Alabama, 1223–24
  California, 1239
  Georgia, 1251–52
  Illinois, 1257
  Kentucky, 1266
  Michigan, 1269
  Missouri, 1277
  Nebraska, 1280
  Ohio, 1288
  Oregon, 1291
  Texas, 1297
  soil, 140
Hibiscus (Rose-mallow), 588
  indoors, 1005
  in Michigan, 1269
  in Oregon, 1291
  syriacus (Rose-of-Sharon), 317,
    341
  in Texas, 1297
  troubles, 1136
Hickory, 923–24
  grubs, 1136
  hulls, compost, 63
  killing, 288
Highway, fence near, 122
Hill, defined, 734
Hilling
  roses, 498–500
  vegetables, 741
Hillsides
  planting, 111
  (*see also* Slopes and Banks; Ter-
    races; Rock gardens)
Hindu lotus, 170
Hippeastrums (Amaryllis), 448
  indoors, 1029–31
  in Florida, 1245
  in Georgia, 1250
  in greenhouse, 269
  troubles, 1102
Hippophae rhamnoides, used, 226,
  227
Hoeing (*see* Cultivation)
Hoes
  Dutch, scuffle, 28, 134, 739–40
  onion, 133
Hog bugs, 1093
Hogs and hawthorn, 281
Holly (Ilex), 371–73
  city, 367

color, 346
indoors, 986
regional
  California, 1239
  Indiana, 1260
  Iowa, 1262
  Michigan, 1269–70
  Texas, 1297
Hollyfern, 1009
Hollyhocks, 563
  troubles, 1136–37
Honesty (Lunaria), uses, 610, 624
Honey, flowers for, 1289
Honey Locust (Gleditsia), 294
  new form, 213
Honeysuckle, 330, 409–10
  aphids on, 1137
  uses, 218 ff.
Hops, spent, 260
Horehound, perennial, 137
Hormones, 82, 83, 249
Hornbeam (Blue Beech), 294, 1303
Hornpoppy, bloom-time, 624
Horsechestnut, 294
Horse manure, 49, 55
  and cow manure, 53
  in hotbed, 259–60
  with wood ashes, 69
Horse-radish, 790
Horseshoe-pitching area, 123
Horticulture, defined, 202
Hoses
  and lawn-watering, 671
  plastic, 134
  porous for vegetables, 753
Hosta (Plantainlily), 1137
Hotbeds, 258–61
  vegetables in, 731–32
  yew cuttings, in, 367
Hotkaps, 738–39, 754
Hot water
  soil sterilization, 80, 81
  tank as window box, 189
  treatment for bulbs, 423
House plants, 929–1041
  annual and biennial, 979–82
  and artificial light, 216, 946
  autumn lifting, 936, 943–44
  bulbs, 1025–41
  cacti, 1016–25

House plants (*cont.*)
citrus fruits, 1001–2
environment, 945–47
exposure, 930, 944–45
ferns, 1006–9
fertilizer, 933, 939–40
flowering,   958–81,   992–1001,
1025–41
foliage, 958–92, 1001–2
gift, 992–1001
herbs, 138
humidity, 930–31, 945 ff.
light, 930, 944–45
miniature, 953–58
propagation, 949–51
repotting, 934, 938–39
resting, 937
sanitation, 948–49
shrubs, 1003–6
soil, potting, 934–35, 937–38
soilless culture, 84
summer care, 935–36, 942–43
temperature, 930, 941–42
troubles, 947–48, 1077, 1137–39
ventilation, 932–33
vines, 1010–16
watering, 931–32, 940–41
window garden, 951–53
winter fertilizing, 78
Houses
foundation plantings, 88, 107–15
garden-, 123
tool-, 133
trees and, 279–80, 292
vines on, 94, 400, 401
Houstonia (Bluets), 178
Hoya carnosa, 1015–16
Huckleberries, 912
Hugonis (Roses), pruning, 506–7
Humidity
in greenhouse, 264–65
and house plants, 930–31, 945 ff.
Hummingbirds, flowers for, 104
Humus, 2, 45–47
angleworms and, 20
on lawn, 674
on mossy soil, 24
(*see also* Green manure; manure;
etc.)
Hyacinth-bean, 403
Hyacinths, 426

Grape-, 435
indoors, 1037
in Michigan, 1268–69
in Nebraska, 1280
Summer-, 426
Water-, 170
Hybridizing
perennials, 536
roses, 513
Hybrid Perpetual Rose, 517
pruning, 507
in Wyoming, 1306–7
Hybrid Sweetbriars, 521
Hybrid Tea Roses, 517–18
in greenhouse, 496
problems, 491
pruning, 507–8
regional
Michigan, 1271
Nebraska, 1280–81
South Dakota, 1287
Wyoming, 1307
winter, 499, 500
Hydrangeas, 330–33
climbing, 410
color-changing, 202, 332–33
in greenhouse, 274
indoors, 996–97
troubles, 1139
Hydrated (Slaked) **Lime**, 34, 37
on compost heap, 61
to correct hyperacidity, 41
when to use, 39
Hydrocleis, in pool, 169
Hydrocyanic gas, on whitefly, 268
Hydrogen, 4
Hydrosme, 473, 1037–38
Hydroxyquinoline sulfate, 1071
Hymenocallis, 1030, 1275
Hypericum, uses, 109, 226
Hypoxis by pool, 175
Hyssop, 146

Iberis (Candytuft), 538, 1110
annual, 609
Idaho
plants, 1254–55
blueberries, 908
chrysanthemums, 552
snapdragons, 617
pocket gophers, 445

Ilex
glabra, 371, 373
holly (*see* Holly)
verticillata, 346
Illinois
cedar-apple rust, 1118
dormant spraying, 1066
plants, 1255–60
asters, 607, 1255
clematis, 407
fruit trees, 853, 1255
lawn, 649
potatoes, 812, 820
rhododendrons, 384, 1258
rosemary, 149
roses, 500, 501, 1258–59
sweet potatoes, 820
Impatiens, 978
honeydew on, 1139
Indiana, plants, 1260–61
lawns, 649
petunias, 615
radishes, 814
roses, 500, 1260–61
Indian Paintbrush, 1226
Indigobush (Amorpha), 321
Indolebutyric acid, 248
Informal gardens, 97–98
(*see also* kinds by name)
Injury, plant, 1045–46
Inkberry (Ilex glabra), 371, 373
Innocence, 178
Inoculant powders, for legumes, 60
Inorganic fertilizer, 72–74
complete, 75–80
Insecticides, 1050–51, 1071–72
resistance to, 1088–89
systemic agents, 1052, 1096–97
(*see also* specific insecticides; individual plants, troubles)
Insects, 1053 ff.
beneficial, 1057
in compost heap, 65
in fruit, 837–38
in greenhouse, 268
in house plants, 947–48
in lawns, 639
(*see also* specific insects, plants)
Intercropping, 706
Iowa

Asiatic beetle, 1056
moles, 1081
plants, 1261–64
carrots, 775
pansies, 626–27
Ipomoea, for fence, 121
Iresine, uses, 186, 240
Iris, 564–72
culture, 566–68
fertilizer, 564–65
indoors, 1025–26
pests and diseases, 571, 1139–41
planting, 565–66
problems, 568–69
regional
Alabama, 1224
California, 1239
Florida, 1248
Georgia, 1252
Nebraska, 1280
Texas, 1297
rock garden, 163, 180–81
soil, 564
varieties, 571–72
Iron, and flower colors, 45, 496
Iron sulfate, 34, 197
Ironweed, 139–40
Irrigation, treating alkali water for, 37
Ismene, 473
Itea virginica, uses, 232, 315
Ivy, 410
ground cover, 223
indoors, 1012–13
troubles, 1141–42
(*see also* specific types)
Ixias, 473
indoors, 1038

Jack-in-the-Pulpit, 181
Jacobeanlily (Sprekelia), 474–75
in Missouri, 1269
Jadeplant (Crassula), 1023–24
Japanese beetle, 1072–75, 1168
Japanese cherry, 1142
Japanese hop, for fence, 402
Japanese Pagoda-tree, 300
Japanese Rubber Plant (Crassula), 1023–24
Japanese Temple-cedar, 357–58

Japanese walnut, 927
Jars, potpourri, 152–53
Jasione, for edging, 104
Jasmine, 390–91
  in California, 1239–40
  in Texas, 1298
Jellies, storage of, 750
Jerusalem artichokes, 756–57
Jerusalem-cherry, 997–98
Jetbead, uses, 219, 228, 231
Jewelweed, uses, 174, 232
Joepyeweed, uses, 175, 176
Johnsongrass (Quackgrass), 198, 199
  –200
Jonquils, 419, 423, 424
  (*see also* Narcissi)
June beetles, 1099
Juneberries (Shadblow), 311, 917
Junipers, 360–62
  Redcedar, 360–62
    and rust, 1111
    dry soil, 173
    for seashore, 227
  rock garden, 162
  troubles, 1111, 1142–43
  uses, 162, 320

Kafirlily, 474
Kalanchoe, 1023, 1024
Kale, 790–91
Kalmia (Mountain Laurel), 382–83
  blight, 1143
  soil, 376
Kangaroo-vine, 1013
Kansas
  alkali water, 37
  plants, 1264–65
    eggplant, 787
    hydrangea, 331
    poppies, 616
    potatoes, 810
    roses, 480, 516, 1265
    sweetpeas, 622
Karathane, 1075
Katsura tree, foliage, 280
Kelp, 71–72
Kenilworth-ivy, 1013
Kentucky, plants in, 1265–66
  African-daisies, 606
  chrysanthemums, 552

  crapemyrtle, 326
  snapdragons, 617, 618
Kentucky Blue Grass, 633, 645
  in North, South Dakota, 1286
Kerria, 334
  in Illinois, 1257
Kitchen gardens, 137, 138–39
  watering, 237
  in window, 956–58
Kitchen waste (*see* Garbage)
Knives, asparagus, 752
Knot garden, 185–86
Kochia, 611
Koelreuteria, 306
Kohlrabi, 791
Kolkwitzia (Beautybush), 323
Krilium, 282, 717
Kryocide, 1063
Kudzu-bean, 401–2

Labels, 135, 730
Labor saving, 212–13
Laburnum, 307–8
Lace bugs, 1075
Lachenalia (Capecowslip), 473
Lady beetles, for scale, 1090
Ladyslippers (Cypripediums), 181–
  82
Lagerstroemia (*see* Crapemyrtle)
Lake-shore soil, 20
Lambsquarters, 198, 1183
  use, 1183
Lamium, uses, 158 ff., 526
Landscaping, 87–203
Lantanas, 1005–6
  cuttings, 605
Lapeirousia, 475
Larches, 294–95
Larkspur, 611
  fertilizer, 529
  troubles, 1143
Larvacide (Chloropicrin), 80–81,
  1061
Lath house, 1234
Lathyrus
  Everlasting pea, 583
  Sweetpea (*see* Sweetpea)
Laurel
  hedge, 397
  Mountain-, 382–83

Laurel, Mountain- (*cont.*)
  blight, 1143
  soil, 376
Laurelcherry hedge, 392
Lavender, 147
  in Missouri, 1277
  uses, 137, 138
Lawn-moss (Sagina subulate), 663
  in California, 1232
  in Oregon, 1292
  in Washington, 1301–2
Lawn mowers, 670–71
  power, 212
Lawns, 125–26, 631–86
  bent, 656–60
    stolons, 660–61
  calendar, 639–40
  care, 636–37, 665–69
    mowing, 669–71
    rolling, 672–73
    watering, 671–72
  city, 217, 655–56
  cover crops, 673
  croquet, 123
  edging, 672
  fertilizer, 674–76
    composts, 676
    manure, 676–78
  grading, 640–42
  humus and peatmoss, 674
  liming, 678
  moss, 663–64
  play areas, 654–55
  regional
    California, 1231–32
    Florida, 1248
    Georgia, 1252
    Iowa, 1262
    New Mexico, 1282
    Oklahoma, 1289
    Washington, 1301–2
  rehabilitation, 664–65
  rock garden in, 155
  sandy soil, 12
  seed, 635–36, 645–48
    quantities, 649–50
    sowing, 642–45, 649, 650–51
  service areas, 655
  shaded, 653–54
  sodding, 636, 651–53
  soil, 633–35, 642–44
    terraces, 635, 651
    trees, specimen, 281, 347
    troubles, 639, 662–63, 678–79, 680–81, 1143–44
    turf types, 632–33
    vegetable garden on old, 715, 716
    weeds, 637–39, 661–62, 681–86
Layering, 250–52
  air-, 247, 251
  (*see also* specific plants)
Lazymans-Lawn (Sagina Subulata), 663
  in California, 1232
  in Oregon, 1292
  in Washington, 1301–2
Leaching, 33, 45
Lead arsenate, 20, 1075
  vegetables and, 28
Leadwort (Ceratostigma), 377, 586
Leaf-cutter bee, 1169–70
Leafgalls, 1135
Leaf hoppers
  on apples, 1166
  on dahlias, 463
Leaf miners
  on arborvitae, 1103
  on birches, 1107
  on boxwood, 369, 1108
  on delphinium, 1125
Leafmold, 46, 63, 67–68
Leaf nematodes, 1112–13
Leaf rollers
  on lilacs, 1145
  on strawberries, 1220
Leaf spots, 1046
Leather dust, 71
Leaves
  ashes, use, 69
  with chicken manure, 52
  colors of, as deficiencies, 44
  on compost heap, 63–64
  cuttings, 210, 249, 250
  functions, 207
  mulch
    shrubs, 319
    vegetables, 727
    wildflowers, 176–77
  in potpourri, 152
  rainfall and shedding, 286

Leeks, 791
 as offsets, 243
Legumes, 59–60
 (*see also* specific plants)
Lemon balm (Mellisa officinalis),
 144
Lemonlily, 553–54
Lemon oil, 1076
Lemon Trees, 1002
 in California, 1237
 troubles, 1115
Lemonverbena, 147–48
 indoors, 957
Leontopodiums (Edelweiss), 164
Leopard-plant, 986
 in greenhouse, 274
Lespedeza, 57
Lettuce, 791–94
 blight, 1192
 seed sowing, 735
Leucocoryne, 473
Leucocrinum, 426
Leucojum, 426–27
Leucothoe, 383
Liatris, by pool, 169
Lice, plant (*see* Aphids)
Lichens, and whitewash, 287
Light, houseplants and, 930, 944–45
 artificial, 216, 946
Light bulbs
 in hotbed, 259, 260
 for house plants, 216, 946
Lightning, and trees, 1152
Ligularia (Leopard-plant), 986
 in greenhouse, 274
Ligustrum (*see* Privet)
Lilacs, 334–37
  culture, 334–36
 ground cover under, 225
 hedge, 397
 killing, 288
 propagation, 337–38
 pruning, 336–37
 regional
  California, 1240
  Florida, 1248
  Texas, 1298
 troubles, 338, 1144–46
Lilies, 427–34

 culture, 430–32
 indoors, 1026
 pests and diseases, 433–34, 1146
  –47
 planting, 428
 problems, 429–30
 propagation, 423–33
 regional
  Arizona, 1226–27
  California, 1240
  Nebraska, 1280
  North Dakota, 1286
  Oregon, 1291–92
  Texas, 1298
 soil and fertilizer, 427–28
 types
  African-, 447
  Amazon-, 273, 464
  Blackberry, 416
  Blood-, 472, 1037
  Chinese sacred-, 1039
  Crinum-, 451–52, 1034
  Foxtail-, 425, 561–62
  Ginger-, 472
  Jacobean-, 474–75
  Kafir-, 474
  Rain-, 1274–75
  Scarborough-, 1040
  Star-, 426
  Trout-, 425
  Water-, 170–72
Lily-of-India (*see* Hydrosme)
Lily-of-the-Valley, 417–18
 in California, 1240
 indoors, 1026
 in Oregon, 1292
Lily-turf, 646
Lima beans, 764–66
 supports, 743
 (*see also* Beans)
Limber neck, 1147
Lime, 10, 37–41
 with cow manure, 54
 on lawns, 678
 on vegetables, 714–15
Limestone (Agricultural lime), 33–
  34, 38
 and acid phosphate, 74
 acid soil in limestone country, 36
 ground-, 35, 61

Limestone (*cont.*)
and hyperacidity, 41
when to use, 39
Lime-sulfur, 1076
Lime Trees, 1237
Limonium suworowi, 274
Linaria, uses, 158, 168, 262
Lindane, 1076
Lindera benzoin (Spicebush), 323–24
in Illinois, 1259
Linum, in rock garden, 158
Lippia canescens, 646
Liquidambar (Sweetgum), 295
in Illinois, 1259
Liquid manure, 55
on house plants, 939–40
on roof garden, 187
Liriodendron tulipfera, 301
pests and diseases, 1175
Liriope muscari, 646
Lithops, 1025
Litmus-paper, 34
Litter
hen coop, 48
sheep, 57
wood shavings, 52
Little-Pickles, 1025
Living plant arrangements, 955–56
Living Rocks (Lithops), 1025
Loam, 2, 11
Lobelia
annual, 611–12
cardinalis, 176, 179
indoors, 981
Loblolly Bay, 306
Lobularia (Sweet Alyssum), 597, 606
Locust Trees
borer in, 1147
for erosion, 19
Honey- (Gleditsia), 173, 294
soil for, 173
Loma, 77
Lonicera (Honeysuckle), 330, 409–10
aphids on, 1137
uses, 218 ff.
Loosestrife, wet soil, 169, 175
Loquat (Oriental Plum), 1275
Lotus, Hindu, 170

Louisiana
blister beetle, 1115–16
garden spray, 1095
plants, 1266–68
Lovage, 148
Lungwort, 142
Lupine, 572–73
in Illinois, 1257
in Kansas, 1265
troubles, 1147–48
Lychnis
Raggedrobin, 611
Rosecampion, 628
Lycopodiums (Club mosses), 176, 181
Lycoris (Amaryllis)
radiata, 473–74
squamigera, 434–35, 1293
in Tennessee, 1293
in Texas, 1298
Lygodium palmatum, 180
Lysimachia, 179, 196
Lythrum, wet soil, 169, 226, 232

Macadamia (Queensland) Nut, 924
Mace, in potpourri, 152
Maggots, 1076
Magnesium, 4, 6
and leaching, 33, 45
Magnesium sulfate, in liquid fertilizer, 55
Magnolia, 308–10
Cucumbertree, 308
ornamentals with, 279
regional
Illinois, 1257
Iowa, 1262
Missouri, 1277
Oregon, 1292
scale on, 1148
Mahonia, 374
Maidenhair (Ginkgo), 293–94
Maidenhair fern (Adiantum), 273, 1009
Maine, plants
alfalfa, 60
chayotes, 780
fruit, 899
berries, 900
blueberries, 910

Maine, plants (*cont.*)
  fuchsias, hardy, 563
  holly, 371–72
  landscaping material, 110
  Mountain-Ash, 297
  nut trees, 921
  roses, 497
Malathion, 1076
Malling rootstocks, 850
Mallows, 588
Malus (Crabapples), 279, 302–3
  pruning, 857
  troubles, 1117–18
Maneb, 1077
Manganese, 4, 6, 45
Mango, 987
  in California, 1240
Manures, 6–8, 48–60
  on clay soil, 14–17
  compost heap, 64
  on depleted soil, 18
  on eroded soil, 18, 19
  for first garden, 17
  on hotbed, 259–60
  humus source, 46
  on lake-shore soil, 20
  on lawns, 676–78
  on mossy soil, 24
  on poor soil, 21, 22
  on sandy soil, 12–13
  sterilization of, in soil, 81
  on vegetables, 720
  wood ashes and, 69
  (*see also* Horse manure; Cow
    manure; etc.; individual
    plants)
Maple Trees, 295–97
  evergreens near, 221
  Flowering, 268, 958
  leaves, use, 63, 68
  new type, 213
  plants under, 113, 225, 231
  seed storage, 289
  troubles, 1148–49
Maranta, 987
Marguerites, 978
Marica, 978–79
Marigold, 612
  in bulb bed, 224
  Marsh–, 181
  pests and diseases, 1149–50

  Pot–, 149
  on roof, 187
Mariposa tulip, 416
Marjoram, 147
Marl, 38
Marshmallow, wet soil, 175
Marshmarigold (Caltha), 181
Maryland, plants
  annuals, 604
  bulbs, 412–13
  crapemyrtle, 326
  fig tree, 917
  hawthorn-holly hedge, 392
  peas, 803
  poppies, 586
  vegetables, 735–56
Mascarene Grass, 645
Massachusetts
  anchusa, 537
  balsam fir, 358
  evergreens, 227
  flowering vines, 400
  fruit
    apricot, 864
    blackberry, 900
    currants, 915
    gooseberries, 915
    raspberries, 904–5
    watermelon, 832
  holly, 371
  hydrangea, 331
  laburnum, 307
  vegetables, 703
    bean rust, 1182–83
    corn, 785
    limas, 764–65
Matrimonyvine, leaf gall, 1150
Matthiola (Stock), 619
  greenhouse, 276
  troubles, 1172
Mayflower (Trailing Arbutus), 178
May-tree, 307
Mazus, uses, 128, 160, 168
Meadow garden, 173–74, 175–76
Meadowrue, shade, 221
Mealy bugs, 1077–78
  (*see also* individual plants for
    treatment)
Measles, in peonies, 1155

Medicinal herbs, 142
  for shade, 139
Mellisa officinalis, 144
Melons
  testing ripeness, 745
  troubles, 1192–93
  (*see also* Watermelons; Musk-
    melons)
Mercury, bichloride of, 286, 1057
Mertensia, 181
Mesembryanthemum edule, 1229–
    30
Metal
  edgers, 212
  furniture, 122, 188
  labels, 135
Metaldehyde, 213
Metallica, edging, 526
Methoxychlor, 1078
Methyl bromide, 80
Mexican bamboo, 198
Mexican bean beetle, 1179–81
Mexican breadfruit, 274
Mice, 1078–79
  and fruit trees, 846
Michaelmas daisies, 537
Michigan
  flowers, 1268–71
    dogwood, 304
    foxglove, 626, 1269
    lemonverbena, 957
    magnolia, 309–10
    mimosa, 338
  grapes, 897
  holly, 372, 1270
  peanuts, 802
  rose chafers, 1203
  vegetables, 755
    onions, 798–99
    squash, 819
Midges
  on roses, 1167
  on waterlilies, 171
Mignonette, fragrant, 152, 185
Mildew, 1079
  compost heap, 65
Mildex, 1075
Milk, on plants, 972, 983
Milk-and-wine Lily, 451–52
  indoors, 1034

Milk cows (*see* Aphids)
Milk disease, 1072–73
Milkweed, uses, 13, 173, 174
Millipedes, 1079
Mimosa, 338
  pudica, 991
Minerals, 6, 45
Miniature gardens, 953–58
Miniature (Fairy) Rose, 519
  indoors, 999, 1000
  in greenhouse, 276
Minnesota, plants, 1271–74
  azalea, 379
  chrysanthemum, 544
  gladiolus, 1133, 1272
  grapes, 897, 1272
  pansies, 626, 1273
  roses, 501, 1273–74
  tomatoes, 829–30
  tulips, 441
Minor elements, 6, 45
Mint, 148–49
  uses, 137 ff.
Mirabilis, 611
Mississippi, plants, 1274–76
  snapdragons, 617
Missouri, plants, 1276–78
  acacia, 387
  birches, 290
  Brussels sprouts, 771
  cabbage, 772
  four-o'clock, 611
  lettuce, 792
  onions, 800
  peas, 803
  petunias, 613
  sweetwilliam, 628
  tomatoes, 830
  tulips, 442
  walnuts, 926
Mistflower, color, 105
Mistletoe and fir trees, 1131
Mitchella in rock garden, 159, 160
Mites, 1079–80
Miticides, 1051, 1079–80
Moccasin plant (Ladyslipper), 181–
    82
Mockoranges, 338–39
Modern-style house, 111

Moisture, in soil, 3
cultivating and, 28
houseplants and, 952
mulch and, 234–35
peatmoss and, 48
in rock garden, 154
(*see also* Humidity; Wet Soil; Drainage)
Molds
gray (Botrytis blight), 434, 444, 1134 ff.
on house plants, soil, 949
sooty, 1092–93
Mole cricket, 1080
Moles, 1079, 1080–82
in lawn, 1143–44
Molucella (Bells of Ireland), 594, 608
Molybdenum, 4, 6, 45
Monarda, uses, 104, 185, 229
Mondo grass, 646
Moneywort (Lysimachia), 179, 196
Monkeyflower, uses, 175, 230, 232
Monkypuzzle tree, 1150
Monkshood (Aconite), 573
in Colorado, 1244
troubles, 1100–1
Monoammonium phosphate, 34
Monstera deliciosa, 274, 987
Montana, plants, 1279
fruit trees, 853
Montbretias, 474
in Washington, 1302
Moon and gardens, 203, 736
Moonvine, 403
eradicating, 198
open indoors, 404
(*see also* Morningglory)
Moraine garden, 165
Morningglory, 403–4
indoors, 982
wild, 196, 198, 201
Mosaic disease
dahlia, 462, 1120
hosts, 1199
lilies, 433, 434, 1146
tulips, 444
Mosquitoes, 1139
Moss
lawns, 663–64

on soil, 23–24
with steppingstones, 128
(*see also* Peatmoss)
Moss Rose, 519
pruning, 508
Mother-of-thyme, 152
Moths, 1082
codling, 1057–58
Crambid, 1082
European pine-shoot, 1157–58
gypsy, 1082
Mounding roses, 498–500
Mountain-Ash (Sorbus), 297–98
city growth, 218
sawfly worms in, 1150
Mountainfringe (Adlumia), 402–3
Mountain Laurel, 382–83
blight, 1143
soil, 376
Mourning-cloak butterfly, 1126
Mowing, 637, 669–71
Muck
fertilizer for, 80
humus for, 46
Muehlenbeckia, in rock garden, 159, 160
Mulberries, 918–19
in Florida, 1248
planting under, 229–30
Mulch, 3, 212–13, 234–36
on cold frame, 258
dust-, 234
evergreens, 352
on herbs, 147
on fruit trees, 843–44
on perennials, 532–33
pests in, 1078–79
on shrubs, 319
on vegetables, 744–45
(*see also* specific materials; individual plants; Winter)
Mullein Pink, 628
Mums (*see* Chrysanthemums)
Mung beans, 767–68
Muriate of potash, 44, 74
Muscari (Grapehyacinths), 435
Mushrooms, 794–95
compost, 64
manure, 50
ring, 1144

Muskmelons (Cantaloupes), 795–97
  pests and diseases, 796, 1192, 1193
Mustard greens, 735
Myosotis (Forget-me-not)
  greenhouse, 273
  ground cover, 223
  indoors, 981
  in tulip bed, 224
  wilt, 1150
Myrica (Bayberries), 322–23
  in Iowa, 1261
Myrtle
  indoors, 1013–14
  in window box, 190

Nails, rusty, and hydrangeas, 333
Nandinas
  in Alabama, 1224
  in Georgia, 1252
  in Mississippi, 1275
  in North, South Carolina, 1284–85
  in Oregon, 1292
Narcissi (Daffodils), 418–25
  culture, 421–23
  indoors, 1026–27, 1028, 1038–39
  planting, 420–21
  propagation, 423
  regional
    Georgia, 1251
    Michigan, 1269
    North, South Dakota, 1286
    Oregon, 1290–91
  soil and fertilizer, 419–20
  troubles, 423, 1150–51
  varieties, 424–25
Nasturtiums, 403, 602
  indoors, 982
  in Florida, 1248
  troubles, 1151–52
Nebraska, plants, 1279–81
  roses, 499, 1280–81
Nectarine Tree, 870
  in Illinois, 1257
  in Iowa, 1262
Neglected soil, 20–21, 26
  ridding of weeds, 193
Neillia sinensis, foliage, 315
Nematodes, 1083–84

  leaf, 1112–13
Nemesia, 594–95
  pinching, 597
Nepeta, uses, 104, 168, 226
Nephrolepsis, in greenhouse, 273
Nephthytis, 987
Nerine sarniensis, 1253
Nettle, eradicating, 198
Nevada, plants in, 1281
New England, plants
  andromeda, 383
  evergreens, 347
  foundation plantings, 222
  rhododendrons, 383–84
  trees, 280, 281
    fruit, 864
    Goldrain Tree, 306
  vegetables, 704
  (*see also* individual states)
New Hampshire, plants
  annuals, 603
  fir tree, 358
  foundation plantings, 220
New Jersey
  cacti, 191
  cedar-apple rust, 1118
  eggplant wilt, 1192
  flowers
    agapanthus, 447
    azaleas, 382
    begonias, 965
    chrysanthemums, 514
    gardenias, 1004
    house plants, 942, 943
    Kafirlily, 474
    roses, 1164
    scabiosa, 617
  fruit
    apples, 864
    blueberries, 911
    grapes, 896–97
    muskmelons, 796
    trees, 853, 864
    watermelons, 831–32
  nut trees, 921
  shrubs
    bayberry, 322
    privet, 397
  trees
    balsam fir, 358

New Jersey, trees (*cont.*)
    fruit, 853, 864
    Mountain-Ash, 297
    nut, 921
    peach, 310
   vegetables
    cabbage, 771, 772
    peas, 804
    turnips, 830
   whitepine sawfly, 1158
New Mexico, plants, 1281–84
   rock garden, 156
   soil, 1225
Newspaper, on roses, 497
New York City
   crapemyrtle in, 326
   evergreens in, 217, 367
   soil, 19
   sweetpeas in, 216–17
   window boxes, 190
New York State
   flowers
    alstroemeria, 447
    anemone, 415–16
    annuals, 603 ff.
    aster, 607
    Canterbury bells, 625
    chrysanthemums, 994
    dahlia, 460
    gerberia, 563
    helianthemum, 165
    ornithogalum, 435
    pansy, 627
    perennials, 533, 563
    petunias, 613
    roses, 480, 500, 1163
    salpiglossis, 616
    snapdragons, 618
    sweetpeas, 620
    waterlilies, 171
   fruit, small, 899
    muskmelon, 796–97
    raspberry, 904
   fruit trees, 840, 853
    apple, 864
    pear, 873
   herbs, 139, 151
   lawns, 649, 655
   pests
    gladiolus thrips, 1133

    Mexican bean beetle, 1180
    moles, 1081–82
    moths, 1082
   shrubs
    andromeda, 383
    azalea, 376–77, 379, 381
    foundation plantings, 222
    gardenia, 390
    hydrangea, 330, 331, 332
    Scotchheather, 382
   trees
    apple, 864
    birch, 290
    dogwood, 304
    evergreens, 350, 351, 355
    fig, 917–18
    hemlock, 359
    Japanese maple, 296
    magnolia, 308
    nut, 922, 925–26, 927
    pear, 873
    pine, 362–63
    quince, 1218
   vegetables, 704, 736
    potatoes, 809, 810, 812
   vines, 400–1
New Zealand spinach, 745–46, 817
Nicotiana, 612
   annual, 603
Nicotine sulfate (Black Leaf 40),
   1082–83
   to discourage dogs, 219
Nierembergia, 595, 612
Nigella, uses, 224, 263
Night-blooming Cereus, 1018–19
   soil, 1016
Night crawlers, 1067
Night fragrance, flowers for, 185
Nitrate of ammonia, 34
Nitrate of calcium, 34
Nitrate of potash (Saltpeter), 34, 55,
   289
Nitrates, 34
Nitrate of soda, 34, 43, 73
   with cow manure, 54
   on vegetables, 76, 719–20
Nitrogen, 3, 42–44
   in bone meal, 66
   for city garden, 59
   in commercial fertilizer, 8

Nitrogen (*cont.*)
  in cottonseed meal, 67
  in dried blood, 67
  legumes and, 57, 59–60
  manures and, 7, 24, 52 ff.
  mulch and, 212–13, 237
  plastic frits, 83
  on vegetables, 719
Norfolk-Island-Pine, 987
  in California, 1241
North Carolina, plants, 1284–86
  cacti, 191
  crinum, 452
  dogwood, 304
  hedges, 392
  pansies, 190
  snapdragons, 617
  sweetpeas, 620–21
North Dakota, plants, 721, 1286–87
Northland daisies, 544, 547, 553
Nurse grass, 645
Nutgrass, 198–99, 1223, 1296–97
Nut trees, 921–27
  regional
    Illinois, 1259
    Indiana, 1260
    Iowa, 1262
    Michigan, 1270
    North, South Dakota, 1286–87
    Washington, 1302
    Wisconsin, 1304
Nyssa sylvatica (Sourgum), 300
  in Michigan, 1269

Oaks, 298–99
  in Florida, 1250
  by house, 279–80
  leafmold, 36, 63
  leaves, use, 53–54, 68
  plants under, 177, 229, 231
    evergreens, 221
    ground covers, 224, 1240
    rock plants, 160
  seed storage, 289
  wood ashes, 70
Oats, 16, 57, 58
Ocean, plants near, 226–27
  evergreens, 355
  shrubs, 1292–93
  vegetables, 703, 712, 717

Oenothera, uses, 106, 525, 526
Offsets, 243
Ohio, plants, 1287–88
  flowers
    amaryllis, 1029
    annuals, 604
    petunias, 613
    tulips, 438
  fruit and vegetables, 708, 716–17
    blueberries, 908, 911
    kale, 790
    onions, 799
    squash, 819
  lawns, 649
  shrubs
    azalea, 378–79
    holly, 371, 372
    indigobush, 321
    jasmine, 391
    Mountain Laurel, 382
    rhododendrons, 378–79
  trees
    elm, 1127
    fig, 918
    larch, 295
Oil burner
  fumes, 946
  soot, 72
Oil spray, 353, 1084–85
Oklahoma, plants, 1288–90
  cacti, 191
  fruit trees, 1203
  gladiolus, 1133, 1289
  Mung beans, 768
  sweetpeas, 621
  vegetables, 703, 768
Okra, 797
  seeds, 727
Oleanders, 391
  in California, 1240
  indoors, 1006
  in Florida, 1248
  in Oregon, 1292
  insects, 1152
Olive oil, on plants, 983
Olives
  Russian, 342
  Sweet-, 980
Oncocyclus irises, 567

Onion hoe, 133
Onions (Allium), 797–800
  Flowering, 415
  troubles, 1193
Ophiopogon jaburan, with cedar, 525
Opuntia, 190–91
Orange peels, compost, 62
Orange trees, 1002, 1237
  in Alabama, 1224
  in Florida, 1115
  in Mississippi, 1224
  troubles, 1115, 1246
Orchard fruit, 840–75
  fertilizer and manure, 841–42
  mulch, 843–44
  planting, 842–44
  pollination and fruiting, 847–49
  propagation, 850–52
  pruning and trimming, 845–46
  regional
    Florida, 1247–48
    Illinois, 1259
    Nevada, 1281
    New Mexico, 1282
    Washington, 1301
  soil, 840
  space limits, 834
  specific, 854–75
  spraying, 843, 1202–4
  storage, 849–50
Orchid cactus (Epiphyllum), 1021
Orchids
  in greenhouse, 274, 275
  in terrarium, 954
  wild, 181–82
Orchis, 182
Oregon, 1290–93
  mole control, 1081
Organic fertilizer, 64–65, 66–72
  (*see also* specific types)
Organic gardening, 755
Origanum dictamnus, 146
Ornamental plants, 205–475
  troubles, 1100–78
  (*see also* Trees; Shrubs; Flowers; etc.)
Ornithogalum, 435
  indoors, 1039–40
Orrisroot, in potpourri, 152, 153

Osmanthus
  fragrans, 980
  holly and, 371
Osmunda fiber, for orchids, 275
Ostrich fern, 1010
Othonna crassifolia, 1025
Outdoor living room, 186–87
  shrubs for wall, 312–13
  trees to screen, 392
Oxalis, 436
  indoors, 1040
  tender, 474
Oxygen, 4
Oyster-plant (Salsify), 815–16
  storage, 749

Pachysandra, ground cover, 225, 229–30
Pagoda-tree, Japanese, 300
Painting
  flower pots, 939
  garden furniture, 122
  pool, 130
  trees, 239, 287, 846
Paling fence, 120
Palms
  indoors, 988, 990–91
  in greenhouse, 275
  troubles, 1152–53
Pandanus (Screwpine), 988
Pansies, 626–28
  in greenhouse, 275
  as ground cover, 223–24
  indoors, 979
  regional
    Alabama, 1224
    Colorado, 1245
    Kentucky, 1266
    Minnesota 1273
    North, South Carolina, 1285
    Wisconsin, 1305
  troubles, 1153
  in window box, 190
Papayas, 1240
Paper mulch, 212, 235, 745
Parking space, with driveway, 118–19
Parlor Palm (Aspidistra), 984, 1103
Parnassia, by pool, 175

Parsley, 800–1
  housegrown, 957
  weeding, 193
  winter, 749
Parsnips, 801–2
  seeds, 727
  storage, 749
Parthenocissus
  Boston-ivy, 1011
  St. Paul Virginiacreeper, 405
Partridge-berries, 182
Pass court, 119
Passion-flower, 1014
  in Iowa, 1262
  in Texas, 1298
Paths (Walks), 127
  edging, 116
  pavement planting, 165–66
  perennials along, 526
  roses along, 480
  thymes along, 152
Patience-plant (Impatiens), 978, 1139
Patios, 129
Pavement planting, 165–66
Paving blocks, 116, 118
PCNB, 1098
Peaches, 867–71
  Flowering, 310
  in California, 1240–41
  pests and diseases, 870, 1212–17
  pruning, 869–70
  regional
    California, 1238
    Indiana, 1260
    Iowa, 1262–63
    Michigan, 1270,
    Texas, 1298
    Wisconsin, 1304
Peanut cactus, 1018
Peanuts, 802
Pear trees, 871–73
  in Iowa, 1263
  in Michigan, 1270
  mildew, 1217
  in Minnesota, 1273
  pests and diseases, 873
Peas, 802–5
  Austrian, 60
  pests and diseases, 804–5, 1193–94

  storage, 750
Peas, everlasting, 583
  (*see also* Sweetpeas)
Peashrub (Caragana), 397
Peat, 46, 47, 48
  soil, 79
Peatmoss, 11, 47–48
  in clay soil, 15–17
  on compost heap, 63
  on foundation plantings, 220
  for humus, 46
  on lawns, 674
  with manure, 56
  in sandy soil, 12
  (*see also* specific plants for use)
Pecans, 924–25
  in Illinois, 1257–58
  troubles, 1153–54
Peduncle necrosis, 1165
Pelargoniums (*see* Geraniums)
Pellionias in terrarium, 954
Pennsylvania, plants
  abelia, 321
  abutilon, 958
  butterflybush, 325
  camellia, 388
  crapemyrtle, 321
  flowers, 603
    chrysanthemum, 548
    crinum, 451–52
    dahlias, 453
    lilies, 430
    narcissi, 1039
    tulips, 439
  grapes, 897
  trees
    birch, 290–91
    cedar, 357
    Christmas, 348
    juniper, 1142
    magnolia, 308, 309
    nut, 921–22
    Sweetgum, 295
  vegetables, 736
    artichokes, 756
    cauliflower, 776
    lettuce, 793
Pennyroyal, in moist soil, 140
Pentstemon, 573–74
  rock garden, 164
  troubles, 1154

Peonies, 574–82
culture, 577–79
fertilizer, 575
planting, 575–76
problems, 579–80
propagation, 580
regional
Alabama, 1224
California, 1241
Florida, 1249
Georgia, 1252
Illinois, 1258
Louisiana, 1267–68
Minnesota, 1273
Montana, 1279
North, South Dakota, 1287
Oklahoma, 1289
South Carolina, 1285
Texas, 1298
soil, 574–75
Tree-, 582
varieties, 581–82
Peperomia, 988–89
Peppergrass (Garden Cress), 152
Pepperidge (Nyssa sylvatic), 300
in Michigan, 1269
Peppermint, 148
Peppers, ornamental, 998
pests and diseases, 1194
Perennial pea, 583
Perennial Rye Grass, 57
Perennials, 523–91
borders, 526–27
labels, 135
mulching, 234–35
spray schedule, 1095
culture, 531–32
fertilizer, 529–30
herbs, 137, 141
planting, 530–31
propagation, 534–36
cuttings, 535
division, 535–36
hybridizing, 536
seed, 534–35
regional
Alabama, 1221–22
California, 1229
Colorado, 1245
Illinois, 1258
Minnesota, 1273

Montana, 1279
Nebraska, 1280
North Carolina, 1285
Oklahoma, 1289–90
Texas, 1298
Wisconsin, 1305–6
Wyoming, 1306
soil, 528–29
winter protection, 532–34
(*see also* individual plants)
Pergola, 129
Periwinkle (Vinca), 612–13
uses, 216 ff.
Pernettya, 1292
Persian stonecress, edging, 104
Persian (English) walnuts, 926–27
Persimmon, 919–20
Peruvian-daffodil, 473
Pests and Pesticides, 1043–1220
formulations, 1085
and public health, 1085–86
(*see also* specific pests; Weeds;
Insects; individual plants:
troubles)
Petals, for potpourri, 152–53
Pets and insecticides, 1075–76,
1085–86
Petunias, 613–15
eradicating, 199
ground cover, 224
indoors, 982
troubles, 1156
pH, 9, 32–33
Phellodendron (Corktree), 293
Philadelphus, 338–39
Philodendron, 1014–15
Monstera deliciosa, 274, 987
Phlox, 164, 583–85
divaricata, 182–83
with peonies, roses, 101
regional
California, 1241
Kentucky, 1266
Michigan, 1270
Missouri, 1277
subulata, for erosion, 19
troubles, 1156–57
Phosphoric acid
in bone meal, 66
in dried blood, 67

Phosphoric acid (*cont.*)
lime with, 74
in sludge, 69
in tankage, 69
Phosphorous, 4–5, 42–45, 73–74
activated, 203
and aluminum sulfate, 10
in basic slag, 45
in bone meal, 66, 67
in commercial fertilizer, 8
in cottenseed meal, 67
in manure, 53, 56
on vegetables, 719
(*see also* Superphosphate)
Photinia, scale, 1157
Physocarpus, in foundation, 219 ff.
Physostegia, uses, 104, 106
Picea (Spruce), 364–66
hedge, 393, 398
troubles, 1171–72
windbreak, 399
Pick-a-back plant, 951, 989
Picket fence, 121
gates with, 124
Pickles, 787
Pickle worm, 1191
Picture windows, 88
Pie-plant (Rhubarb), 814–15
Pieris (Andromedas), 383
Pigeon manure, 56
Pig manure, 56
Pigweed, 200
Pilea, uses, 953 ff.
Pillar Rose, 519–20
Pill bugs, 1093
Pimenta officinalis, 269
Pinching, 215, 239–40
annuals, 597
(*see also* specific plants)
Pineapple plant, 989
Pines, 348, 362–64
in city, 217
hedge, 397
needles, 40, 68, 235
as peatmoss substitute, 48
plants under, 225
roses, 25
wildflowers, 176
shavings with manure, 49
troubles, 1157–59
windbreaks, 399

Pinks (Dianthus), 538–40
annual, 610
Clove Pinks (*see* Carnations)
Mullein-, 628
rock garden types, 156 ff., 163
Pipe
plastic, 134
tree roots in, 287
vine to mask, 404
Pipe clay, 15
Pipsissewa (Chimaphila), 183, 184
under pines, 176
Pistachio, 925
Pitcherplant, 183
Pits, storage
manure, 49
vegetables, 746, 749
Plane Tree (Sycamore), 300–1
fungus disease, 1173
killing, 287, 288–89
Planning
for color, 105
rock garden, 153–54
rose garden, 479–81
vegetable garden, 696–99, 699–704, 707–9
wildflower garden, 172–73
Plantain, eradicating, 195, 199
Plantainlily (Hosta), 1137
Plant bands, 134
Planting
bulbs, 412–13
fruit, 837
trees, 842–43
green manure, 57
hedges, 394
herbs, 140–41
and landscape design, 95
perennials, 530–31
chrysanthemums, 543
iris, 565–66
peonies, 575–76
rhododendrons, 385
rock garden, 156
roses, 486–89
shrubs, 316–17
vegetables, 699
rotation, 704–5
succession, 705–7
wall garden, 167–68

Planting (*cont.*)
  woodland flowers, 177 ff.
  (*see also* Lawns; Trees; Trans-
    planting; specific plants)
Plant lice (see Aphids)
Plants
  nutrients for, 42–48
  stimulants for, 82–83
  structure, 206–7
  (*see also* Flowers; Trees; Shrubs;
    Foundation plantings; etc.)
Plant tablets, 77–78
Plant troubles, 1043–1220
  advances in control, 1050–52
  specific plants
    fruits, 1202–20
    ornamental, 1100–78
    vegetables, 1178–1202
  specific troubles, controls, 1052–
    1100
  types of control, 1046–50
Plaster
foundation plants and, 40
  in soil, 38
Plastics
  hose, pipe, 134
  hotkaps, 739
  nitrogen frits, 83
  Polythene, 89, 235
    in propagation, 244–45, 245–
    46
  pool, 130
Platycodon, 585–86
Playground areas, 123–24, 654–55
Plowing, 3, 25–27
  vegetable garden, 712–14
Plumbago (Ceratostigma, 586
Plums, 873–75
  Flowering, 310
    spraying, 1159
  Oriental, 1275
  pests and diseases, 1217
Pocket gophers, 1069–70
Poinsettia, 615, 998–99
  in Arkansas, 1227
  bugs on, 1159
  in greenhouse, 268
Poison
  in castor beans, 609
  from Christmas trees, 366

  in foxglove, 626
  (*see also* Pesticides)
Poison ivy, 26, 199, 201
Poison oak, 199
Poke for birds, 104
Polemonium, uses, 104, 105
Polianthes, 474
Pollination, fruit trees, 847
Pollination, fruit trees, 847
Polyantha roses, 519–20
  pruning, 506, 508
  troubles, 1163
Polygala, Fringed, 184
Polygonum cuspidatum, 198
Polypody, for shade, 176, 177
Polythene (Polyethylene), 89, 235
  in propagation, 244–45, 245–46
Pomegranate, 391
  in California, 1241
  indoors, 989–90
Ponds (*see* Pools)
Ponyfoot (*see* Dichondra repens)
Pools, 129–31
  plantings around, 233
  rock garden, 155, 166
  water garden, 169–72
  weeping evergreens by, 347
  wildflowers by, 175
Poor soil, 21–22
Poplars, 299–300
  flowers under, 68, 229
  killing, 201
  roots, combating, 288
  troubles, 1159
Poppies
  annual, 211, 616
  in Arkansas, 1227
  in Georgia, 1253
  hardy, 586–87
Porcelainvine (Ampelopsis), 405
Porches
  box for vegetables, 707
  house plants on, 942, 944
Portulaca, 616
Potassium (Potash), 4, 5–6, 42–45,
  74
  bone meal, none, 66
  in charcoal, 70
  in commercial fertilizer, 8
  in cottonseed meal, 67

Potassium, potash (*cont.*)
  in dried blood, 67
  glass frits, 83
  in kelp, 71–72
  manure and, 7, 53, 56
  in sludge, 69
  from stone dust, 72
  on vegetables, 719
Potassium alum, 333
Potassium nitrate, 34, 55, 289
Potassium, sulfate (muriate) of, 74
Potatoes, 806–13
  pests and diseases, 811–12, 1194–96
  planting, 807–10
  soil and fertilizer, 806–7
  storage, 749, 811
  Sweet-, 819–21
  varieties, 812–13
Potentilla (Cinquefoils), 163
Potentiometer, 9
Pothos, 990, 1015
Potmarigold (Calendula officinalis), 149
Pot marjoram, 147
Potpourris, 152–53
Pots, disintegrating, 134
Potted plants
  angleworms in, 1067
  azaleas in winter, 380
  bone meal for, 67
  city, 216
  in cold frame, 257, 258
  greenhouse
    repotting, 266–67
    watering, 264
  hardening off, 261
  on patio, 129
  resting bulbs, 446
  roses, 496
  soil, 48
    sterilization, 81
  on terrace, 229
  by tree roots, 113
  vegetables, 737–38
  watering, 214, 264
  (*see also* House plants)
Potting shed, 133
Poultry manure (*see* Chicken manure)
Powders, inoculant, 60

Prayer plant (Maranta), 987
Praying mantis, 1086
Prickly poppy, uses, 594, 595
Primroses (Primula), 163–64, 587
  in cold frame, 257
  indoors, 979–80
  in greenhouse, 275
  uses, 156 ff.
Princesspine, transplanting, 181
Privets (Ligustrum), 339
  hedge, 397–98
  scale, 1159
  in Texas, 1297
  trimming, 395
Propagation, 209–10, 243–55
  annuals, 599–605
    cuttings, 605
    indoor, 599–603, 605
    outdoor, 603–5
  bulbs, corms, tubers, 243–44
  cuttings, 244–50
    root and leaf, 249–50
  evergreens, 355–56
  fruit trees, 850–52
  grafting, 252–56
  house plants, 949–51
  layering, 250–52
  perennials, 534–35
    chrysanthemums, 549–51
    iris, 569–71
    peonies, 580
  rhododendrons, 386–87
  roses, 509–13
  seeds, 243
  shrubs, 319–21
  suckers, stolons, runners, 52
  wildflowers, 173–74
  (*see also* Greenhouse; Cold frame; Hotbed; individual plants)
Proteins, 4, 6
Protex, 284
Pruning, 214–15, 237–39
  disbudding and pinching, 239–40
  evergreens, 354
  fruit trees, 845
  hedges, 394–95
  house plants, 933
  new trees, 284–85
  root-, 240–41
  roses, 501–9
  shrubs, 317–19

Pruning (*cont.*)
topiary work, 135
(*see also* individual plants)
Prunus (*see* Plums; Peaches; Almonds)
Pseudotsuga taxifolia, 357, 358
Pteretis struthiopteris, 1010
Pteris, 1009
Public health and pesticides, 1085–86
Pulmonaria, uses, 113, 159, 228
Pulsatillas, rock garden, 156
Pulverized manure (*see* Bovung)
Pumpkins, 813–14
pests, 1196
storage, 748
Punica (Pomegranate), 391
in California, 1241
indoors, 989–90
Purslane, killing, 194–99
Puschkinia, 436
Pussy willow, 345–46
Pyracantha, 374–75
hedge, 393
pruning, 1241
troubles, 1159–60
Pyrethrum (insecticide), 1086–87
Pyrethrum (plant), 587
Pyrolos, 183–84
Pythium, on begonia, 1106

Quackgrass (Johnsongrass), 198, 199–200
Quakerlady, 178
Queensland (Macadamia) nut, 924
Quercus (*see* Oaks)
Quicklime (Calcium oxide), 38
Quince, 920
flowering, 340
spraying, 1218

Rabbitbrush (Chrysothamnus), 1226
Rabbitfootfern, 1009–10
Rabbits, 1087–88
manure, 56
Raccoons, 1096
Radio-active fertilizer, 203
Radishes, 814
pests and diseases, 1196–97
Raggedrobin, 611
Railroad worms, 1206–7

Rain
cultivation after, 212, 233, 234
drainage, 114–15
erosion, 114
and fruit, 835–36
and leaf-shedding, 286
Rainlilies (Cooperia), 1274–75
Rainspouts, vines for, 94
Rambler Roses
pruning, 505–6
supports, 492
Ranunculus, 474
in California, 1236
indoors, 275
in greenhouse, 275
starting, 446
in Texas, 1299
Raspberries, 903–7
in Idaho, 1254
in Iowa, 1263
in Minnesota, 1273
pests and diseases, 905–6, 1218–19
varieties, 906–7
Rats, 1078
ground rats, 1069–70
Redbud (Cercis), 310–11
Redcedar (Juniper), 360–62
and cedar-apple rust, 1111
in dry stony soil, 173
for seashore, 227
Redhotpokerplant (Tritoma), 589
in Iowa, 1263
in Kentucky, 1266
Redroot, 200
Red soil, 45
Red spider, 1079–80
(*see* individual plants for treatment)
Redwood
bark, 48
burl, indoors, 990
Refuse (*see* Garbage)
Regional Garden Problems, 1221–1307
Repotting
geraniums, 972
in greenhouse, 266–67
house plants, 934, 938–39
Resting plants
bulbs, 446

Resting plants (*cont.*)
greenhouse, 268
house, 937
Retaining wall, 136
Retinosporas, 347
Rhododendrons, 383–87
culture, 385
propagation, 386–87
regional
Alabama, 1224
Illinois, 1258
Michigan, 1270–71
Texas, 1298
Washington, 1302
soil and fertilizer, 376, 384
troubles, 387, 1160–61
winter, 385–86
Rhodotypos (Jetbead), 218, 222
Rhubarb, 814–15
pests and diseases, 1197
Rhus, uses, 315
Rice hulls, 1298
Ringing fruit trees, 845–46
Robinia
hispida (Rose-acacia), 341
pseudoacacia, 173
Rockcress, uses, 104, 154
Rock gardens, 19, 153–69
city, 217–18
conifers, 349
herbs, 139
labels, 135
regional
Alabama, 1224–25
Indiana, 1260
Michigan, 1270
Texas, 1299
Utah, 1300
roses, 480
Rocks
Creeping Fig on, 402
Living, 1025
planting by, 111
(*see also* Stones)
Rodents
and bulbs, 415
and compost heap, 62
(*see also* Rats; Mice; Squirrels; etc.)
Rolling lawns, 672–73

Roof gardens, 187–88
vegetables, 754–55
Roofs, vines over terrace, 401
Root crops, 17, 26
for exhibition, 750
fertilizer, 722, 724
soil preparation, 714
storage, 746–47
Rooting, 247–48
hormones, 83
Root nematodes, 1083–84
Roots
in clay, 14–15
cuttings, 249–50
functions, 206
killing, 200, 287–89
legumes, and nitrogen, 59–60
plants near large, 102–3, 113, 287
pruning, 240–41
soil needs, 11
tree, grade around, 286
greedy, 279
watering, 742, 743
Rose-acacia, 341
Rosecampion, 628
Rose chafers, 1167, 1168
Rose jars, 152–53
Rose-mallow (Hibiscus), 588
indoors, 1005
in Michigan, 1269
in Oregon, 1291
Rose-of-Sharon, 317, 341
in Texas, 1297
troubles, 1136
Rosemary, 149
outdoors, 957
uses, 137
Rose-of-Sharon (Althea), 317, 341
Roses, 477–521
Austrian briar, 514
black, 514
cabbage, 514–15
city, 218
climbing, 500–1, 504–5, 515–16
color change, 495–96
culture, 489–501
cultivating, 491
cutting, 493–94
disbudding, 493
problems, 489–91

Roses (*cont.*)
summer mulch, 492
supports, 492–93
water, 491–92
damask, 516
fertilizer, 484–86
floribunda, 506, 516
French, 516
grandiflora, 516
green, 516–17
greenhouse, 275–76, 496
hilling, 498–500
house plants, 999–1000
hugonis, 506–7
hybrid perpetual, 507, 517
hybrid tea, 507–8, 517–18
labels, 135
miniature, 519, 999–1000
moss, 519
mulch, 492, 500
old-fashioned, 508
pillar, 519
planning, 186–87, 479–81
planting, 486–89
    transplanting, 488–89
polyantha, 508, 519–20
propagation, 509–13
    budding, 509–10
    cuttings, 510–12
    grafting, 512
    hybridizing, 513
    layering, 512
    seeds, 513
    understock, 513
pruning, 501–9
    climbing, 504–5
    floribunda, 506
    hugonis, 506–7
    hybrid perpetuals, 507
    hybrid teas, 507–8
    old-fashioned, 508
    polyantha, 508
    ramblers, 505
    shrub, 508–9
    tree, 509
    rambler, 505–6
regional
    Alabama, 1225
    Arizona, 1227
    Arkansas, 1227
    California, 1241–43
    Colorado, 1245
    Florida, 1249
    Georgia, 1253
    Idaho, 1255
    Illinois, 1258–59
    Indiana, 1260–61
    Iowa, 1263
    Kansas, 1265
    Louisiana, 1268
    Michigan, 1271
    Minnesota, 1273–74
    Mississippi, 1275–76
    Missouri, 1278
    Nebraska, 1280–81
    Nevada, 1281
    New Mexico, 1282–83
    North, South Carolina, 1285–86
    North, South Dakota, 1287
    Ohio, 1288
    Oklahoma, 1290
    Oregon, 1292
    Tennessee, 1294
    Texas, 1299
    Utah, 1300
    Washington, 1302
    Wisconsin, 1305
    Wyoming, 1306–7
reversion, 495
rugosa, 520
Scotch, 520
selecting, 478–80
shrub, 508–9, 520
soil, 481–83
species, 520
suckers, 495
sweetbriar hybrids, 521
tea, 521
tree, 500, 509, 521
troubles, 489–91, 513–14, 1161–70
winter injury, 497–98
winter protection, 497
    climbing roses, 500–1
    hilling, 498–500
    mulch, 500
    tree rose, 500
Rotating cultivators, 28–29
Rotation, vegetables, 704–5

Rotenone, 1089
Rototiller, 752
Rots (*see* Brown Rot; Crown Rot; etc.)
Roundworms, 1083–84
Rowan-tree, 297
Rubber plant
    anthracnose on, 1170
    Japanese (Crassula), 1023–24
Rubbertree (Ficus elastica), 950–51, 990
Rudbeckia, uses, 103, 104, 226
Rue, 149
Rugosa rose, 520
    pruning, 508–9
Runners, 252
Runningpine, uses, 176, 181
Rushes, eradicating, 196
Russian olive, 342
Russian statice, 274
Rustic cabin, 111
Rusts, 1089
    (*see* specific plants for treatment)
Rye, 59
    green manure, 16, 57, 58, 725
    on poor soil, 22
Rye grass, 20, 633, 725
    on slope, 228

Sacco, 77
Sachets, 152
Sacred-lily, Chinese, 1039
Sacred Lily-of-India, (Hydrosme), 473, 1037–38
Sacred (Hindu) Lotus, 170
Sage, 150
    in Michigan, 1270
    uses, 137 ff.
    (*see also* Salvia)
Sagina subulata, 663
    in California, 1232
    in Oregon, 1292
    in Washington, 1301–2
Sago-palm, 990–91
Saint Johnswort, use, 109
Saintpaulias (*see* African-violet)
Saint Paul Virginiacreeper, 405
Salpiglossis, 616
    greenhouse, 276
Salsify, 815–16
    storage, 749

Salt, 45
    to kill lilac bush, 288
Salt air, plants for, 226–27
    vegetables, 712
Salt hay, 319
    in cold frame, 258
    in rock garden, 157
    winter mulch, 157
Saltpeter (Potassium nitrate), 34, 55, 289
Salts, Epsom, 55
Salvia
    annual, 616
    officinalis, 150
    perennial, 588
Sand, 2, 3
    culture, 84
    in gumbo, 18
    sterilization, 81
    (*see also* Sandy soil)
Sandburs, eradicating, 200
Sandlilies, 426
Sand-washing plant, 23
Sandy soil, 11–13
    evergreens, 221
    grass for, 647
    herbs, 140
    plants, 225–26
    rock plants, 160
    vegetables, 703, 712
Sanguinaria (Bloodroot), 178–79
Sanitation, house plants, 948–49
Sansevieria, 991
Santolina, uses, 152, 158, 226
Saplings, wattle fence of, 120–21
Saponaria, uses, 106, 156, 158
Sapotas, 1243
Sarracenia purpurea, 183
Sassafras, 300
Satin flower, 611
Savory, 150
Sawdust, 71, 235–36
    on evergreens, 352
    on gumbo, 18
    peatmoss substitute, 48
Sawflies
    on Mountain-ash, 1150
    on pansy, 1153
    on white pine, 1158
Saxifragas, 164

Saxifragas (*cont.*)
    sarmentosa, 991
    uses, 156 ff.
Scab (*see* individual plants for treatment)
Scabiosa, 617
    dividing, 588
Scale insects, 1089–90
    pruning for, 239
Scarborough-lily, 1040
Scarlet Runner Bean, 403
Schizanthus
    in California, 1243
    pinching, 597
Schizobasopsis (Bowiea), 1022
Schizostylis, 474
Scholar-tree, Chinese, 300
Scillas (Squills)
    in ground year-round, 412
    in Michigan, 1268–69
    uses, 158 ff.
Scindapsus (Pothos), 990, 1015
Scion, 252–53
Scotch Heather, 382
Scotch Rose, 520
Scree, 164
Screens, 111
    fences as, 120–21
    hedges, 392, 394
    shrubs, 312–13
    vines for, 401
    wet-soil plants for, 232
Screwpine, 988
Scuffle hoe, 28, 134, 739–40
Scum, green, 24
Seafowl manure, 55
Sea kelp, 71–72
Seal manure, 55
Seashore
    evergreens for, 355
    plants for, 226–27
    shrubs (Oregon), 1292–93
    vegetables, 703, 712, 717
        peas, 804
Seaweed, 71–72
    kelp, 71–72
    mulch, 235
Sedge peat, 47, 48
Sedums, 164–65
    indoors, 1025

troubles, 1170–71
uses, 154 ff., 523 ff.
Seedlings
    in greenhouse, 262 ff.
    labels for flats, 135
    transplanting, 211
    watering, 260
    winter care, 354
Seeds, 243, 289
    annuals, 598–603
    in cold frame, 257, 258
    evergreens, 355–56
    fertilizer, 79
    flats, sour soil in, 35
    fruit tree, 852
    greenhouse, 261 ff.
    herbs, 142
    in house, 219
    lawns, 635–36, 645–48, 649–50
    perennials, 534–35
    roses, 512–13
    treatment, 80, 1064, 1090
    vegetable, 727–36
    wildflowers, 173–74
    X ray on, 202
Selaginellas, terrarium, 954
Selfheal, for shade, 139
Semesan, 1090, 1133
Sempervivums, uses, 156, 168, 217
Senecio (German-ivy), 1013
Sensitive-plant, 991
Septic tanks
    sludge use, 68
    vegetable gardens over, 755
Serviceberries, 311, 917
Sewage sludge, 40, 68–69
Sewers, 23
    tree roots in, 287, 301–2
Sex, of trees, 281–82
Shadblow (Amelanchier), 311, 917
Shade, 24–25, 112–13, 228–31
    annuals, 594
    city plants, 216, 217
        shrubs, 218, 282–83
    foundation material, 221–23
    grass for, 647, 653–54
    ground covers, 224–25
    herbs for, 139
    house plants, 944–45
    lawns, 653–54
    maple, plants for, 159–60

Shade, regional plants (*cont.*)
  perennials, 525, 526
  regional plants
    California, 1230
    Missouri, 1278
    Montana, 1279
    Oklahoma, 1289
    Washington, 1303
  rock garden, 159–60
  shrubs, 218, 282–83, 314
  and vegetables, 710–12
  vines, 400, 401–2, 409
  wall gardens, 167
  window boxes, 190
  woodland gardens, 176
Shade trees, 90–91, 281–82
  fast-growing, 280–81
Shallots, 799
Shastadaisy, 588
  in Missouri, 1277
  in Texas, 1295
Shavings, wood, 55
Shearing, 237
Shears
  edging, 672
  hedge, 239, 395
Sheep manure, 49, 56–57
  dried, 54
Sheepsorrel, eradicating, 200
Shellac on tree-wounds, 239
Shellstone, 42
Shieldfern under pines, 176
Shinleaf (Pyrola), 183
  under pines, 176
Shootingstar, 183, 412
Shortia, uses, 160, 177
Shrimp plant, 1000
Shrub-Althea (Rose-of-Sharon), 317, 341
Shrub Rose, 520
  pruning, 508–9
Shrubs
  berried, 313–14
  for birds, 104, 314
  city, 218
  culture, 315–21
  deciduous, 312–47
  in dry stony soil, 173
  ericaceous, 375–81
  espaliered, 242

  evergreen, 347–67
    broadleaved, 367–75
  fertilizer, 75, 78
  flowering, 314–15
    foundation material, 222
    for pool, 169
  for foliage, 315
  foundation material, 107–8 ff., 219–23
  fragrant, 185
  hedges, 391–99
  indoors, 1003–6
  new types, 213
  planting, 316–17
  Polythene mulch, 235
  propagation, 319–21
    cuttings, 257, 289
    layering, 250–51, 251–52
  pruning, 214–15, 317–19
    root-, 240–41
  rabbits and, 1087–88
  regional
    California, 1232–33
    Georgia, 1253–54
    Idaho, 1255
    Indiana, 1261
    Iowa, 1263
    Minnesota, 1274
    North Carolina, 1286
    Oregon, 1292–93
    Texas, 1300
    Utah, 1300
    Washington, 1302–3
    Wisconsin, 1305, 1306
  rock garden, 162–63
  roots, combating, 288
  sandy soil, 230, 231
  seashore, 226–27
  soil and fertilizer, 315–16
  sun, 231
  tender, 387–91
  wet soil, 232, 233, 282
  windbreaks, 399–400
Side dressing, 718–19
Sideritis, foliage, 595
Silene, uses, 158, 165, 226
Silt, 2, 3
Silverbell, 311
Simples, 142
Skullcap, use, 104
Slag, basic, 45

Slaked (Hydrated) lime, 34, 37
on compost, 41
and hyperacidity, 41
when to use, 39
Slaughterhouses, 69
Slime flux, 239, 1127
Slips (*see* Cuttings)
Slopes and Banks, 113–14
driveway, 118
ground covers, 223, 224
protective, 227–28, 410
lawn-grading, 126
sowing grass, 650–51
vegetable garden on, 700
watering grass, 671
(*see also* Terraces)
Sludge, 68–69
Slugs, 1090–92
mulches increase, 212–13
Smoke, and trees, 287
Smoke-tree, 311–12
Smut
Browallia, 1108
corn, 1190
Snails and slugs, 1090–92
Snakegrass, 589
Snake-palm (Hydrosme), 473, 1037
–38
Snake-plant (Sansevieria), 991
Snakeroot, eradicating, 200
Snap beans, 760–64
Snapdragons (Antirrhinums), 617–
19, 1171
greenhouse, 269
indoors, 982
in Louisiana, 1268
Sneezeweed, bloom-time, 527
Snow, and trees, 279, 353–54
Snowballs (*see* Viburnums)
Snowberries, 342
Snowdrops (Galanthus), 426
Snowflakes (Leucojum), 426–27
Soapy water, 71, 83
for house plants, 948–49
Soda, nitrate of (*see* Nitrate of
soda)
Sodar, on chickweed, 197
Sodium, 4, 45
Sodium arsenite, 172
Sodium chlorate, 196 ff.

Sodium fluoalminate, 1063
Sodium sulfamate, 199 ff.
Sod webworms, 1082
Soft rot, bacterial, 1118 ff.
Soil, 1–85
acidity, 9–10, 31–41
detriments, 83–84
fertility, 10–11
in greenhouse, 262, 264, 267
handling, 25–31
potting, 934–35, 937–38
problems, 17–25
regional
Arizona, Colorado, New Mexico, 1225
sterilization, 80–81, 1092
types, 1–2, 11–17
(*see also* Sandy soil; Wet soil;
etc.)
Soilless culture, 84–85
Soil-tex test, 34
Solomonseal, 142
Soot, 72
on vegetables, 723
Sooty mold, 1092–93
Sophora, 300
Sorbus (Mountain-Ash), 297–98
city growth, 218
sawfly worms in, 1150
Sourgum (Nyssa sylvatica), 300
in Michigan, 1269
Sour soil, 35
Sourwood, foliage, 280
South African bulbs, 475
South Carolina, plants, 1284–86
Brussels sprouts, 771
shrubs, 318
peatmoss substitutes, 48
South Dakota, plants, 1286–87
poppies, 587
salvia, 616
Southern corn rootworm, 1191
Southernwood, uses, 104, 138, 152
Sovosol, on weeds, 194
Sowbugs, 1093
Sowers, seed, 753
Sowing
annuals
indoors, 600–1
outdoors, 603–5
lawns, 642–45, 649–50

Sowing (*cont.*)
 slopes and terraces, 650–51
 vegetables, 727–36
  indoors, 728–32
Soybeans, 16, 57, 58, 60, 726–27
 in city, 59
 with corn, 1067
 edible, 746
  and rabbits, 1087
 on poor soil, 22
Spade, 752
Spading, 3, 27
 vegetable garden, 713
Spading fork, 752
Sparaxis, 473
Sparrow, eradicating, 1058
Species Roses, 520–21
Speedwell (*see* Veronica)
Spergon, 1090
Sphagnum peat, 47
Spice bush (Lindera benzoin), 323–24
 in Illinois, 1259
Spices, in potpourri, 152
Spiderflower, 609
Spiderlily
 Hymenocallis, 1030, 1275
 Nerine, 1253
Spider mites, 1079–80
Spiderwort, 589
Spiking lawns, 668
Spinach, 815–17
 New Zealand, 745–46, 817
Spirea, 342
 in greenhouse, 270
 hedge, 398
 by vegetable garden, 391
Spittle bugs, 1093
Spleenwort, for shade, 176, 177
Split pit, 1214
Sprayers, 1093–94, 1202
 Aerosol, 1052–53
Spraying
 dormant, 1084–85
  evergreens, 353
  fruit trees, 843, 1202–4 ff.
 materials, 1094–95
 (*see also* Pesticides)
Sprekelia (Jacobeanlily), 474–75
 in Missouri, 1269
Spring

rock garden effects, 153
trees with tinted leaves, 280
(*see also* Planting; Transplanting; Plowing; etc.)
Springbeauty (Claytonia), 183
Spring snowflake, 427
Sprinklers
 on lawn, 671
 on vegetables, 753
Spruce, 364–66
 hedge, 393, 398
 troubles, 1171–72
 windbreak, 399
Spurge (Euphorbia)
 Crown-of-thorns, 1024
 Flowering, 588
 Japanese, 224
Squash, 817–19
 forcing large, 813
 pests and diseases, 818, 1197–98
 storage, 748
 summer-, 817, 746
Squills (Scilla)
 in ground year-round 412
 in Michigan, 1268–69
 uses, 158 ff.
Squirrels, 1096
 and corn, 1190
 and crocus bulbs, 1118
 and tulips, 445
Stable manure (*see* Horse manure; Cow manure)
Staghorn, for shade, 176
Stakes (*see* Supports)
Standard Rose, 521
 watering, 492
 winter, 500
Stapelia, 1025
Starlilies, 426
Star-of-Bethlehem, 969
Starter solution, 718
Statice, Russian, 274
Statuary, 131
Steam
 heating hotbed, 260
 sterilization, 80, 81
Steel filings, 45
Steeple-bellflower, uses, 624, 625
Stephanandra, 343
Stepping stones, 89, 128

Steps, 131–32
creeping thymes for, 152
planting, 166–67
Sterilization
seed, 733
soil, 80–81
Sternbergia, 436
Stevia, greenhouse, 276
Stimulants, 82–83, 247–48
Stink bug (Squash bug), 1197–98
Stock, 619
greenhouse, 276
troubles, 1172
Stokesia, 103 ff.
Stolons, 252
grass from, 660–61
Stonecress, for edging, 104
Stonecrop, bloom-time, 527
Stones, 89
dust, 72–73
edging, 117
path, 128
in soil, 22
steps, 131
by terrace, 113
in vegetable garden, 715
walls, 136
Storage
bulbs, 412–13, 446
fertilizer, 49, 77
fruit, 849–50
game equipment, 124
herbs, 141–42
seeds, 243, 289, 728
tools, 133, 134
vegetables, 746–50
Stratification, of seeds, 243
Straw, 54, 57
mulch roses, 500
Strawberries, 876–86
culture, 880–82
everbearing, 883–85
mulching, 882–83
ornamental, 1240
pests and diseases, 885, 1219–20
regional
California, 1243
Illinois, 1259
Indiana, 1261
Iowa, 1263
Missouri, 1278

New Mexico, 1283
Ohio, 1288
transplanting, 886
Strawberry-begonia, 991
Strawberry root weevil, 366
Strawberry-shrub, 340, 343–44
Streams, ground covers, 223, 232
Strelitzia (Bird-of-Paradise), 980
in California, 1235
in greenhouse, 276
Streptomycin, 1095
String beans, 760–61
Striped cucumber beetle, 1112
Stripped land, 22
Stripping (*see* Edging)
Stucco, vines on, 401, 402
Stumps, killing, 289
Subsoil, conversion, 21
Succession planting, 706–7
Succulents, 1022–25
Suckers, 252
on roses, 495
on transplanted trees, 284
Sudangrass, 57
Sugar cane, 48, 52
Sugars, 4
Sulfate, aluminum (*see* Aluminum sulfate)
Sulfate, calcium (Gypsum), 10, 24, 39
Sulfate, iron, 34, 197
Sulfate, magnesium, 55
Sulfate of potash, 44
Sulfur, 1095–96
acidifier, 10, 36, 34
on alkaline soil, 36–37
for overliming, 39
on lilacs, 338
and roses, 496
Sulfuric acid, 197, 289
Sumac
eradicating, 200
Fragrant, 343
and soil, 84
Summer-hyacinth, 426
Summer savory, 150
Summer snowflake, 427
Summersweet (Clethra)
with azaleas, 377
uses, 218 ff.

Sundials, 132
Sunflowers, uses, 104, 174
Sunken gardens, 188–89
  annuals for, 594
  hedge for, 393
Sunlight, 25
  and fruit, 837
  grass, 647
  ground covers, 223, 646
  house plants and, 944
  perennials for, 524–25, 526, 1254
  plants for, 231
    flowering, 202
  shrubs for, 219–20
  vegetables and, 710
    seeds, 728
  watering in, 236
  wildflowers for, 175–76
Sunroses, 165
Superphosphate, 5, 73–74
  on alkaline soil, 36
  with chicken manure, 51
  on depleted soil, 18
  for flowers, 27
  with hen coop litter, 48
  with lime, 39
  for liquid fertilizer, 55
  on neglected soil, 20
  for sewage sludge, 40
  with stored manure, 49
  on vegetables, 719
Supports, 215, 241–42
  chrysanthemums, 547–58
  delphiniums, 557
  peonies, 578
  roses, 492–93
  trees, 284
  vegetables, 743–44
  vines, 94, 187
Surface drainage, 114–15
Swamp, fertilizer for drained, 80
  (*see also* Bogs; Wet soil)
Swamp Magnolia, 308, 309
Sweet Alyssum, 597, 606
Sweet Balm, 144
Sweet Bay
  Laurel, 397
  Magnolia, 308, 309
Sweetbriar Hybrids, 521
Sweetcicely, 150
  uses, 137 ff.

Sweetflag, 150–51
Sweetgum (Liquidambar), 295
  in Illinois, 1259
Sweet Marjoram, 147
Sweet-olive, 980
Sweetpea, 583, 619–22
  in Colorado, 1245
  in greenhouse, 276–77, 621–22
  in New York City, 216–17
  in South Carolina, 1286
  troubles, 1172–73
Sweetpepper bush (Clethra)
  with azalea, 377
  uses, 218 ff.
Sweet Potatoes, 819–21
  harvesting, 746
  storage, 748
  vine, 1015
Sweetshrub (Calycanthus), 343
Sweetsultan, 1249
Sweetwilliam 628–29
  stem rot, 1173
Sweet Woodruff, 151
Sweet Wormwood, fragrant, 137
Swiss Chard, 821–22
  sowing, 735
Sycamore (Buttonball; Plane), 300–1
  fungus disease, 1173
  killing, 287, 288–89
Symphoricarpos
  coralberry, 1264
  snowberry, 342
Symplocos, fruit, 313
Synthetic manure (*see* Compost)
Syringa (*see* Lilac)
Systemic insecticides, 1052, 1096–97

Table salt, 45
  to kill lilac, 288
Tablets, plant, 77–78
Tagates, pinching, 597
Tamarack (*see* Larch)
Tamarisk (Tamarix), 344
  hedge, 398–99
  in Washington, 1302
Tamper, 600
Tanbark
  in hotbed, 260
  paths, 128–29
  steps, 132

Tangelos, 1243
Tankage, 69
  on shrubs, 376
  on vegetables, 720
Tank farming, 84–85
Tarnished plant bug (*see* specific plants for treatment)
Taro, in pool, 169
Tar paper
  on roses, 497
  for spreading roots, 287
Tarragon, 151
  indoors, 957–58
  uses, 137 ff.
Taxus (*see* Yew)
TDE (DDD), 1097
Tea, 71
  on ferns, 940
  herbs for, 137–38, 391
  leaf compost, 62
Tea plant, 1243
Tear gas (Chloropicrin), 80–81, 1061
Tea Roses, 521
  (*see also* Hybrid Tea Roses)
Tea scale, 390
Temperature
  and fruit-growing, 836
  greenhouse, 263–64
  house plants, 930, 941–42
    foliage plants, 982
  starting vegetable seed, 729
  vegetable storage, 747
Tender shrubs, 387–91
Tennessee, plants in, 1293–94
  fruit trees, 848
  tulips, 440
Tennis courts, 123–24
Tent caterpillars, 1097
Termites, 1097–98
Terraces, 132–33
  for erosion, 18, 19
  evergreens edging, 348, 393
  ground covers, 223, 224
  lawns, 635, 651
    mowing, 669
    watering, 671
  plants for, 113–14
    shade, 229, 230
  vines to roof, 401
Terrachlor, 1098

Terrariums, 953–55
  orchids in, 954–55
Testing, soil, 34, 41–42
Teucrium, uses, 104, 114, 231
Texas, plants, 1294–1300
  pansies, 627, 1298
  roses, 481, 1163, 1299
  sweetpeas, 621–22
Texas root rot, 1098
Thalictrum, 535
Thea sinensis, 1243
Thermopsis, 535
Thinning
  annuals, 595
  vegetables, 729, 736–37
Thistles, Canada, 196
Thorns (*see* Hawthorns)
Thrift, for edging, 104
Thrips, 472, 1132–34
Thuja (Arborvitae), 356–57, 395
  cuttings, 356
  troubles, 352–53, 1102–3
  windbreak, 399, 400
Thymus, 151–52
  uses, 137 ff., 156 ff.
  winter care, 147
Tigridia, 475
  aphids, 1173
  thrips, 1133
Tile
  catch basin, 114–15
  soil drainage, 23, 29–30
Tillage, 3
Timothy, 645
Tithonia, 622
Toadstools (*see* Mushrooms)
Tobacco
  annual, 603
  Flowering, 612
Tobacco bud worm, 1154
Tobacco dust on aphids, 268
Tolmiea menziesi (Pick-a-back), 951, 989
Tomatoes, 822–30
  culture, 826–28
  in hotbed, 259
  pests and diseases, 1198–1201
  pruning, 825–26
  rotation of, 705
  staking, 824–25

Tomatoes (*cont.*)
  starting, 823–24
  supports, 743–44
  test for gas leaks, 945
  varieties, 828–30
Tool house, 133
Tools, 133–35
  cultivators, 28–29
  hoes
    onion, 133
    scuffle, 28, 134, 739–40
  pruning, 239
Topiary work, 135
Topsoil, 11, 21, 22
Torenia, 622
  in Georgia, 1252
Tortoise beetle, 1112
Toxaphene, 1098
Toxicodendrons, 26, 199, 201
Trace elements, 6, 45
Tradescantia
  fluminensis, 1015
  virginiana, 589
Trailing Arbutus (Epigaea repens), 178
Transplanting, 210–11
  annuals, 595–96
  bulbs, 413
  evergreens, 350–52
  perennials, 530–31
  shrubs, 316–17
  trees, 283–85
  vegetables, 724, 737–39
  (*see also* specific plants)
Tray gardens, 955
Treeferns, in California, 1238
Tree-of-Heaven (Ailanthus), 290
Tree peonies, 582
Tree Roses, 521
  pruning, 509
  watering, 492
  winter, 500
Trees (Deciduous), 279–312
  for birds, 104, 281
  care, 285–87
  espaliered, 242
  fast-growing, 280–81
  flowering, 281
  foliage, distinctive, 280
  grading lawn by, 641–42
  grafting, 252

ground covers under, 224–25
killing, 201, 202, 287–89
lawns under, 653–54, 675–76
new types, 213
plants under, 229–30, 231
propagation, 289
pruning, 214–15, 238–39
  root-, 240–41
rabbits and, 1088
regional
  California, 1233–34
  Georgia, 1251
  North Carolina, 1286
  Utah, 1300
roots, plants near, 113
seashore, 227
shade, 281–82
soil, 282–83
  sandy, 226
  stony, 173
  wet, 232–33
transplanting, 210–11, 283–85
vegetables under, 711–12
(*see also* Fruit Trees; Evergreens)
Trench
  defined, 734
  to kill tree roots, 287–88
Tricalcium phosphate, 5
Trillium
  types, 183
  uses, 173 ff.
Trimming (*see* Pruning)
Tri-ogen, 1162
Tritoma, 589
  Iowa, 1263
  Kentucky, 1266
Tritonia, 475
Trollius, 535
Troutlilies, 425
Trowels, 29, 162
Truehedge Columnberry (Barberry), 322, 396
Trumpet creeper, uses, 176, 400
Trumpetvines (Bignonia), 1231
  eradicating, 200
  in Idaho, 1255
  as pests, 1175
Tuberose, 474
Tuberous-rooted Begonia, 448–50
Tubers (*see* Bulbs, Corms, Tubers)

Tubs
canned plants, 134
Christmas trees in, 358–59
roses in, 496
(*see also* Potted plants)
Tufa rock, 155
Tulips, 436–46
culture, 440–43
ground covers with, 223–24
indoors, 1027, 1028
Mariposa-, 416
pests and diseases, 444–45, 1174–75
planting, 438–40
propagation, 443–44
regional
Alabama, 1225
Georgia, 1254
Michigan, 1269
North Dakota, 1287
soil and fertilizer, 437–38
Tuliptree, 301
pests and diseases, 1175
Tunica, with steppingstones, 128, 166
Tupelo (Sourgum), 300
in Michigan, 1269
Turf (*see* Lawns)
Turfing-daisy, 646
Turn-around, 119–20
Turn court, 119
Turnips, 830–31
pests and diseases, 1201–2
Turquoise-berry, for screen, 401
Turtlehead, by stream, 175
Turtle manure, 55
Twelve Apostles, 978–79
Twelve-spotted cucumber beetles, 1065
Twigs for staking, 242
Twining vines (*see* Vines)
2,4-D; 2,4,5-T
how to use, 194
on waterlilies, 172
on weeds, 195 ff.

Umbrella-plant, 992
Umbrella tree (Catalpa), 291–92
Understock, 252–53
Urceolina miniata, in Missouri, 1278

Urea, 73
acidifying power, 34
Ureaform, 83
Urginea, thrips on, 1102
Utah, plants, 1300
apricots, 1210
chrysanthemums, 1113
dogwood, 304

Vaccinium, color, 315
Valerian, uses, 104, 112, 140
Valotta purpurea (Scarborough-lily), 1040
Vapam, 80
Vegetables, 691–832
and arsenate of lead, 28
in California, 1243
care, 736–45
cultivation, 28, 739–41
mulch, 744–45
supports, 743–44
thinning, 736–37
transplanting, 737–39
watering, 742–43
weeds, 741–42
for child's garden, 184
coal ashes on, 30, 31
in cold frame, 257
equipment, 751–54
exhibition, 750–51
garden border, 392
harvesting, 745–46
hedge for garden, 391
hotbed, 259
location, 692, 710–12
pests and diseases, 1178–1202
planning, 696–98, 699–704, 707–9
planting, 704–7
rotation, 704–5
succession, 706–7
roof garden, 187
seed sowing, 727–36
indoor, 728–32
outdoor, 732–36
soil
acidity, 725
fertilizer, 718–24
green manure on, 725–27
liming, 714–15

Vegetables, soil (*cont.*)
  neglected, 20
  plowing, 712–14
  preparation, 712–27
  problems, 715–17
  types, 32–33
  wet, 23
  woodland, 24, 25
  soilless culture, 84–85
Veltheimia viridifolia, 1040–41
Velvet plant, 992
Ventilation
  flowering plants, 202
  greenhouse, 267–68
  house plants, 932–33, 942
Verbenas, 147–48, 622, 957
  in Georgia, 1254
Vermont, plants
  flowers, 594
    chrysanthemums, 544
    foxgloves, 626
    roses, 49, 515
  ground covers, 225
  hotbed, 259
  lettuce, 792
  raspberries, 899
  shrubs, 314, 317
    azalea, 993
  woodland garden, 176
Vernonia (Ironweed), 139–40
Veronicas, 589
Verticillium wilt (*see* individual
    plants for treatment)
Vetch, 57, 727
Viburnums, 344–45
  evergreen, 375
  pests and diseases, 1175–76
  in Wisconsin, 1304–5
Views, 135–36
Vigoro, 77
  on house plants, 940
  with lime, 39–40
Vinca (Periwinkle), 612–13
  uses, 216 ff.
Vinegar, on cuttings, 248
Vines, 94–95, 400–10
  annual, 402–4
  for birds, 104
  in city, 218
  foundation planting, 111
  indoors, 1010–16

  perennial, 404–10
  regional
    Arizona, 1226
    California, 1230–31, 1234
    Florida, 1246
    Iowa, 1263
  on roof, 187, 188
  supports, 242
  (*see also* Ground Covers; Weeds;
    Vegetables; individual plants)
Violas, 589–90
  in Florida, 1249
Violets, 183, 590
  African-, 958–63, 1101
  caterpillars on, 1176
  dogtooth-, 425
  regional
    California, 1243–44
    Missouri, 1278
    Oregon, 1293
Virginia
  flowers
    chrysanthemums, 552
    larkspur, 611
    primroses, 587
    snapdragons, 617
    sweetpeas, 621
  Mexican bean beetle, 1180
  peas, 804
  pecans, 924
  window boxes, 190
Virginiacreeper, 405
Virginsbower (Clematis), 406
Vista, defined, 97
Vitamin A, 756
Vitamin B$_1$, 78, 82, 248
Vitex (Chastetree), 325
  in Iowa, 1263–64
Vitis coignetiae, 402

Wahoo (Euonymus), 340, 343–44
Walkingfern, 180
Walks (*see* Paths)
Wallflowers, 629
  in California, 1243
Walls, 136
  gardens on, 167–69
  roses for, 480
  shade-loving plants by, 113
  shrubs on, 242, 313

Walls (*cont.*)
trees on, 242
vegetables on, 709
vines for, 400 ff.
Walnuts, 925–27
black, 925–26
toxic roots, 841
diseases and pests, 1176
English, 926–27, 1176
Japanese, 927
regional
California, 1244
Iowa, 1264
Minnesota, 1274
Wanderingjew, 1015
Washing
herbs, 141
house plants, 948–49, 982–83
vines 1011
Washington, 1301–3
beet disease, 1185
boysenberries, 902, 1301
fir disease, 1131
flowers
chrysanthemums, 544
dimorphotheca, 610
narcissi, 1039
window box, 190
peanuts, 802
walnuts, 927
Washington, D.C., tuberose in, 474
Washington thorn, 307
Waste (*see* Garbage)
Water
acidification, 37
alkaline, on evergreens, 352
boiling, for sterilization, 80, 81
culture, 84–85
soapy, 71, 83, 948–49
vines in, 401, 1011
(*see also* Wet Soil; Moisture;
Drainage; Watering; individual plants)
Watercress, 152, 831
Water culture, 84–85
Water gardens, 169–72
Waterhyacinth, 170
Watering, 213–14, 236–37
after fertilization, 80
annual seedlings, 602
in greenhouse, 264–65

herbs, 141
house plants, 931–32, 940–41
lawns, 637, 671–72
city, 656
perennial, 532
plastic pipe for, 134
rock garden, 157
trees, 286
vegetables, 738, 742–43
seedlings, 731
seeds, 735
with porous hose, 753
wall garden, 168–69
window boxes, 189
Waterlilies, 170–72
Waterlogged soil, 22
Watermelons, 831–32
Watsonias, in Florida, 1249
Wattle fence, 120–21
Waxplant, 1015–16
Weather vanes, 136
Webworms, 1068
Weed killers, 193–94
(*see also* specific methods)
Weeds, 193–202
on compost heap, 61
edible, 787
fallowing for, 29
in lawns, 637–39, 661–62, 681–
86
mulch for, 212–13
on neglected soil, 20, 21
in perennial border, 531
in vegetable garden, 741–42
vines, 26
wildflowers, 174
Weevils
bean, 1181
black vine, 388, 1106
hickory-nut, 1136
on iris, 1141
strawberry-root, 366
white pine, 1158
Weigelas, 345
Well, dry, 114
West Virginia
cacti, 12
leeks, 791
Wet soil, 22–23, 25–26
bog garden, 174–75

Wet soil (*cont.*)
drainage, 29–30
grass for, 645
herbs for, 140
humus and, 46
plants for, 230, 232–33, 282
testing, 28, 29
and vegetables, 710
(*see also* Moisture; Drainage)
Wheelbarrow, 752–53
Wheel hoe, 740
Wheels, herb, 143
Whip grafting, 255
White clover
eradicating, 200
lawn, 647–48
White flies, 1101, 1117 ff.
in greenhouse, 268
White grubs, 1099
Whitewash, on trees, 287, 846
Widow's tears, 588
Wildflowers, 172–84
bone meal on, 67
evergreens with, 347
in Illinois, 1259–60
in oak-tree shade, 112–13
Wildginger, 146
Wild honeysuckle, eliminating, 26
Wild plants
living plant arrangements, 956
terrariums, 954
Willows, 301–2
in Florida, 1250
golden, 399
pests and diseases, 1176–77
pussy-, 345–46
Wilts, 1046
Wind
and evergreens, 93, 163, 355
flowers for, 132
perennials for, 226
Polythene film protection from, 89
trees for, 281
Windbreaks, 399–400
in California, 1232–33
for vegetable garden, 701
Windflower (Anemone), 177–78, 415–16
in greenhouse, 269
in Texas, 1294

troubles, 1102
Window boxes, 189–90, 951–53
Windows
evergreens by, 368
gardens in, 951–53, 955–58
Wine grapes, 897
Winter, 215
azaleas, 379–80
bulbs, 414–15, 446–47
cold frame, 257, 258
herbs in, 141
vegetables in, 754
evergreens, 354–55
pruning, 354
for rock garden, 162, 163
transplanting, 351
fruit trees, 846
goldfish in pool, 131
greenhouse plants for, 262 ff.
green manure crops, 57, 58, 727
herbs, 137, 141
hotbeds, 260
house plants, 942 ff.
lawn, 639, 665
perennials, 532–34
chrysanthemums, 544–45
delphiniums, 558
Polythene film, use, 89
rhododendrons, 385–86
rock gardens, 157, 161
roses, 497–501
seed storage, 289
shrubs, 93, 312
protection, 319
soil improvement, 17
tree-planting, 283
vegetables, 695–98
in cold frame, 754
in garden, 755
storage, 746–50
wall garden, 168
water plants, 170–72
window box, 190
Winter-aconites, 425
Winterberry (Blackalder), 346
Wintercreeper, 408–9
Wintergreens, 183–84
Winter savory, 150
Wire
gates, 125

Wire (*cont.*)
labels, 135
netting for bulbs, 414, 434
Wiregrass, eradicating, 201
Wires, trees near, 91
Wireworms, 13, 1099–1100
Wisconsin, plants, 1303–6
Canterbury bells, 625, 1303
fruit trees, 858–59, 1304
pines, 362
shrubs, 319, 1305, 1306
snapdragons, 617
tomatoes, 828
Wishboneflower, 622
in Georgia, 1252
Wisteria, in Illinois, 1260
Witches'-brooms, 1098–99
Witchhazel (Hamamelis), 346–47
Witloof chicory (French endive), 749, 780–81
Wood
garden furniture, 122
labels, 135
window boxes, 189
Wood ashes, 17, 69–70
on clay, 14
with chicken manure, 52
Woodchucks, 1100
Woodfern, with mertensia, 173
Woodland soil, 24–25, 176–77
evergreens with wildflowers, 347
vegetables on, 722
Wood shavings
with horse manure, 55
as litter, 52
Wood soil
humus, 46
woods dirt, 77
Woolly speedwell, for edging, 104
Worms, in various plants, 1054 ff.
and nematodes, 1083–84
(*see also* Centipedes; Caterpillars; specific worms)

Wormwood, Sweet, fragrant, 137
Worn-out soil, 18, 75
Wyoming, plants, 1306–7
foxtaillilies, 561
pansies, 628

Xeranthemum for winter bouquet, 610
X ray on seeds, 202

Yards
drying, 120
screens for, 111
(*see also* Lawns)
Yarrow, for sun, 176
Yellow (Chlorotic) plants, 37, 38, 43
Yellowroot, uses, 224 ff., 315
Yellows
on aster, 1104
on delphinium, 1124
on gladioli, 1134
Yellowwood (Cladrastis), 312
Yew, 366–67
hedge, 399
in Iowa, 1264
pests, 1177
shade, 353
Yucca, 590–91
pests, 1177

Zebrina pendula, 1015
Zephyranthes, thrips, 1133
Zinc, 4, 6, 45
Zingiber officinale, 146
Zinnias, 623
for bulb bed, 224
pests and diseases, 1177–78
Zodiac, and planting, 203
Zoysia, 645
Zygocactus truncatus, 1019–21